Proceedings: Conservation, Restoration, and Management of Tortoises and Turtles—An International Conference

11–16 July 1993
State University of New York
Purchase, New York, USA

Jim Van Abbema	**Peter C. H. Pritchard**	**Suzanne Dohm**	**Michael W. Klemens**
Editor	*Consulting Editor*	*Production*	*Conference Chair*

Kristin H. Berry, Michael W. Klemens, Peter C. H Pritchard
Editorial Advisiory Board

A Joint Publication of the
New York Turtle and Tortoise Society
and the
WCS Turtle Recovery Program
1997

CONTRIBUTORS

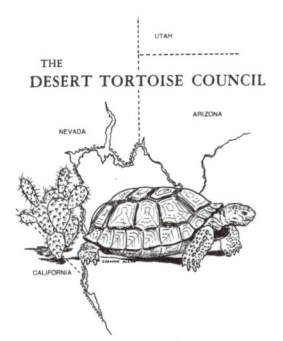

© 1997 by the New York Turtle and Tortoise Society
163 Amsterdam Avenue, Suite 365
New York, New York 10023, USA

Portions of this publication may be reproduced or republished for educational or non-commercial purposes only with the written permission of the publishers. Permission to quote from this volume is granted provided that proper acknowlegment is made of the source.

Cover Art: Carolyn Sgandurra
Conference Photographer: Anita Baskin-Salzberg; additional photographs by Rita Divine
Assistant Editor and Copy Editor: Barbara Daddario
Proofreaders: William Cermack, Douglas Daly, Allen Foust, Norberto Muller, Phil Puccio
Design and Layout: Jim Van Abbema
Printing and Binding: Hatco Printing Corp., Hauppauge, New York
Production and Distribution: Suzanne Dohm, Allen Foust, Allen Salzberg, Dorothy Windsor

All photographs in presented papers are by senior author unless otherwise noted. Color printing of photographs by Wil Luiijf, TRAFFIC Europe, are courtesy of a private donor; color printing of all other photographs were funded by the authors or authors' institutions.

The following organizations provided original funding and organizational support for the conference: American Museum of Natural History, U.S. Bureau of Land Management (Department of the Interior), Desert Tortoise Council, IUCN-World Conservation/Species Survival Commission, National Science Foundation, New York Turtle and Tortoise Society, State University of New York at Purchase, U.S. Department of Defense.

Library of Congress Cataloging-in-Publication Data
Proceedings: conservation, restoration, and management of tortoises and turtles: an international conference: 11–16 July 1993, State University of New York, Purchase, New York, USA / Jim Van Abbema, editor.
    p.   cm.
  "A joint publication of the New York Turtle and Tortoise Society and the WCS Turtle Recovery Program."
  Includes bibliographical references and index.
  ISBN 0-9659050-0-4 (alk. paper)
  1. Turtles—Congresses. 2. Wildlife conservation—Congresses. 3. Wildlife management—Congresses. I. Van Abbema, Jim. II. New York Turtle and Tortoise Society. III. WCS Turtle Recovery Program.
QL666.C5P86   1997
333.95'792—dc21   97-44399
                                                                            CIP

The paper used in this publication meets the minimum requirements of the American National Standard for Permanence of Paper for Printed Library Materials Z39.48-1984.

Printed in the United States of America

Contents

Conference Photography	ix
Acknowledgments	xiii
A New Paradigm for Conservation — MICHAEL W. KLEMENS	xv
Troubled Times for Turtles — JOHN L. BEHLER	xviii

PRESENTED PAPERS

DIRECT AND INDIRECT THREATS TO HABITAT

CHANGES TO VEGETATION

Land Use and Grazing in Relation to the Genus *Geochelone* in Argentina
TOMÁS WALLER AND PATRICIO A. MICUCCI — 2

Invasions of Exotic Plants: Implications for the Desert Tortoise, *Gopherus agassizii*, and Its Habitat in the Western Mojave Desert
W. BRYAN JENNINGS — 10

Effects of Cattle Grazing on the Desert Tortoise, *Gopherus agassizii*: Nutritional and Behavioral Interactions
HAROLD W. AVERY AND ALEXANDER NEIBERGS — 13

Agricultural Development and Grazing as the Major Causes of Population Declines in Horsefield's Tortoise in the Turkmen Republic (Abstract)
VIKTORIJ M. MAKEYEV, SAHAT SHAMMAKOV, ANATOLIJ T. BOZHANSKII, RONALD W. MARLOW, AND KAREN VON SECKENDORFF HOFF — 20

ANTHROPOGENIC IMPACTS AND HABITAT ALTERATION

The Impact of Commercial Crab Traps on Northern Diamondback Terrapins, *Malaclemys terrapin terrapin*
ROGER CONANT WOOD — 21

Potential Threats to Tortoise Populations in Parc National de "W," Niger, West Africa
JAMES E. MOORE — 28

Biophysical Analysis of the Impact of Shifting Land Use on Ornate Box Turtles, Wisconsin, USA
CHARLES G. CURTIN — 31

Effects of Habitat Alteration on River Turtles of Tropical Asia with Emphasis on Sand Mining and Dams
EDWARD O. MOLL — 37

Habitat Utilization of the Desert Tortoise, *Gopherus agassizii*, in the Western Mojave Desert and Impacts of Off-Road Vehicles
W. BRYAN JENNINGS — 42

Turtles and Tires: The Impact of Roadkills on Northern Diamondback Terrapin, *Malaclemys terrapin terrapin*, Populations on the Cape May Peninsula, Southern New Jersey, USA
ROGER CONANT WOOD AND ROSALIND HERLANDS — 46

The Effect of Roads, Barrier Fences, and Culverts on Desert Tortoise Populations in California, USA
WILLIAM I. BOARMAN, MARC SAZAKI, AND W. BRYAN JENNINGS — 54

IMPACTS OF MILITARY ACTIVITIES

Blanding's Turtles at Fort Devens, Massachusetts, USA: A Case of "Mutualism" between Turtles and Tanks
BRIAN O. BUTLER — 59

Desert Tortoise Populations in the Mojave Desert and a Half-Century of Military Training Activities
ANTHONY J. KRZYSIK — 61

Effects of Military Activities on Tortoises in Israel (Abstract)
ELI GEFFEN AND HEINRICH MENDELSSOHN — 73

DIRECT LOSSES TO POPULATIONS—
DISEASE, PREDATION, AND HUMAN EXPLOITATION

DISEASE

**Laboratory Health Profiles of Desert Tortoises in the Mojave Desert:
A Model for Health Status Evaluation of Chelonian Populations** (Plenary Lecture)
MARY M. CHRISTOPHER, KEN A. NAGY,
IAN WALLIS, JAMES K. KLAASSEN, AND KRISTIN H. BERRY 76

**Baseline Health Parameters of Free-Ranging
Pancake Tortoises, *Malacochersus tornieri*, in Tanzania** (Summary Report)
MICHAEL W. KLEMENS, BONNIE L. RAPHAEL,
WILLIAM B. KARESH, PATRICIA D. MOEHLMAN, AND REGINALD T. MWAYA 83

Field Techniques for Collection of Biological Samples in Turtles and Tortoises (Summary Report)
BONNIE L. RAPHAEL AND ELLIOTT R. JACOBSON 84

**A Serologic Test to Monitor Desert Tortoises, *Gopherus agassizii*,
for Exposure to a Pathogenic Mycoplasma** (Summary Report)
ISABELLA M. SCHUMACHER, MARY B. BROWN,
ELLIOTT R. JACOBSON, BOBBY R. COLLINS, AND PAUL A. KLEIN 86

**Diseases in Wild Populations of Turtles and Tortoises:
The Chelonian Charisma vs. Coincidence Conundrum**
ELLIOTT R. JACOBSON 87

Demographic Consequences of Disease in Two Desert Tortoise Populations in California, USA
KRISTIN H. BERRY 91

PREDATION

Survivorship of Hatchling Gopher Tortoises in North-Central Florida
LORA L. SMITH 100

Predation on Turtles and Tortoises by a "Subsidized Predator" (Summary Report)
WILLIAM I. BOARMAN 103

Avian Predation on Tortoises in Israel (Summary Report)
ELI GEFFEN AND HEINRICH MENDELSSOHN 105

TURTLES AS A FOOD RESOURCE

Turtle Rearing in Village Ponds
ROMULUS WHITAKER 106

Biology and Conservation of Aquatic Turtles in the Cinaruco-Capanaparo National Park, Venezuela
JOHN B. THORBJARNARSON, NAYIBE PÉREZ, AND TIBISAY ESCALONA 109

**Patterns of Exploitation, Decline, and Extinction of
Erymnochelys madagascariensis: Implications for Conservation**
GERALD KUCHLING 113

WILDLIFE TRADE

Exploitation and Trade of *Geochelone chilensis*
TOMÁS WALLER 118

CITES and the Tortoise and Turtle Trade
WIL LUIIJF 125

Ecology and Exploitation of the Pancake Tortoise in Tanzania
DON MOLL AND MICHAEL W. KLEMENS 135

BREEDING, REPATRIATION, AND RELOCATION

Survival of Relocated Tortoises: Feasibility of Relocating Tortoises as a Successful Mitigation Tool 140
  EDWARD B. MULLEN AND PATRICK ROSS

Evaluating the Effectiveness of Headstarting Redbelly Turtles in Massachusetts (Abstract) 146
  ALISON HASKELL, TERRY E. GRAHAM, CURTICE R. GRIFFIN, AND JAY B. HESTBECK

Predator-Proof Field Enclosures for Enhancing Hatching Success and Survivorship of Juvenile Tortoises: A Critical Evaluation 147
  DAVID J. MORAFKA, KRISTIN H. BERRY, AND E. KAREN SPANGENBERG

Captive Breeding of Indian Turtles and Tortoises at the Centre for Herpetology/Madras Crocodile Bank 166
  ROMULUS WHITAKER AND HARRY V. ANDREWS

Management Plan for the Giant Amazonian Turtle, *Podocnemis expansa*, in De La Tortuga Arrau Wildlife Refuge, Orinoco River, Venezuela 171
  LINA LICATA AND XABIER ELGUEZABAL

Large-Scale Breeding of Turtles at São Paulo Zoo: Implications for Turtle Conservation in Brazil 174
  FLAVIO DE BARROS MOLINA

Rearing and Repatriation of Galápagos Tortoises: *Geochelone nigra hoodensis*, a Case Study 178
  LINDA J. CAYOT AND GERMÁN E. MORILLO

APPLICATION OF DEMOGRAPHY, ECOLOGY, AND GENETICS TO CONSERVATION

Can Management Intervention Achieve Sustainable Exploitation of Turtles? 186
  DAVID A. GALBRAITH, RONALD J. BROOKS, AND GREGORY P. BROWN

Effects of Geographic Origin and Incubation Temperature on Hatchling Snapping Turtles, *Chelydra serpentina*: Implications for Turtle Conservation Practices across the Species' Range 195
  HEATHER L. PASSMORE AND RONALD J. BROOKS

A Proposal to Standardize Data Collection and Implications for Management of the Wood Turtle, *Clemmys insculpta*, and other Freshwater Turtles in Ontario, Canada 203
  DINA A. FOSCARINI AND RONALD J. BROOKS

Species Abundance and Biomass Distributions in Freshwater Turtles 210
  RICHARD C. VOGT AND JOSÉ-LUIS VILLARREAL BENITEZ

Nesting Ecology of the Yellow-Spotted River Turtle in the Colombian Amazon 219
  VIVIAN P. PÁEZ AND BRIAN C. BOCK

On the Ecology of Some Freshwater Turtles in Bangladesh 225
  SHEIK M. A. RASHID AND IAN R. SWINGLAND

Measuring Declines and Natural Variation in Turtle Populations: Spatial Lessons from Long-Term Studies (Plenary Lecture) 243
  J. WHITFIELD GIBBONS

Development of Predictive Models for Wetland-Dependent Turtles in New England 247
  ALISON L. WHITLOCK AND JOSEPH S. LARSON

Patterns of Gopher Tortoise Demography in Florida 252
  HENRY R. MUSHINSKY, EARL D. MCCOY, AND DAWN S. WILSON

Genetic Methodologies as a Technique for Captive Management (Abstract) 258
  WALTER SACHSSE

Molecular Variation in the Bog Turtle, *Clemmys muhlenbergii* 259
  GEORGE D. AMATO, JOHN L. BEHLER, BERN W. TRYON, AND DENNIS W. HERMAN

STATUS REPORTS

Turtle Conservation in Myanmar: Past, Present, and Future
PETER PAUL VAN DIJK ... 265

The Turtles of Western Thailand—Pushed to the Edge by Progress
KUMTHORN THIRAKHUPT AND PETER PAUL VAN DIJK ... 272

Status, Biology, Conservation, and Management of Tortoises and Turtles in the Himalayan Foothills of Nepal
TEJ KUMAR SHRESTHA ... 278

The Bostami or Black Softshell Turtle, *Aspideretes nigricans*: Problems and Proposed Conservation Measures
M. FARID AHSAN ... 287

Population and Habitat Status of Freshwater Turtles and Tortoises of Bangladesh and Their Conservation Aspects
MD. SOHRAB UDDIN SARKER AND MD. LOKMAN HOSSAIN ... 290

Conservation Problems of Tropical Asia's Most-Threatened Turtles
INDRANEIL DAS ... 295

Conservation and Management of Freshwater Turtles and Land Tortoises in India (Executive Summary)
B. C. CHOUDHURY, S. BHUPATHY, AND EDWARD O. MOLL ... 301

Status of the Tortoises and Freshwater Turtles of Colombia
OLGA VICTORIA CASTAÑO-MORA ... 302

Land Tortoises in Spain: Their Status and Conservation
RAMON MASCORT ... 307

An Overview of a Threatened Population of the European Pond Turtle, *Emys orbicularis* (Summary Report)
RAMON MASCORT ... 312

The Distribution and Status of Pancake Tortoises, *Malacochersus tornieri*, in Kenya
ROGER C. WOOD AND ALEC MACKAY ... 314

Specific Threats to Tortoises in Israel (Abstract)
ELI GEFFEN AND HEINRICH MENDELSSOHN ... 321

SPECIES RECOVERY AND MANAGEMENT STRATEGIES

A Conservation Strategy for the Geometric Tortoise, *Psammobates geometricus*
ERNST H. W. BAARD ... 324

Species Recovery Programme for Hermann's Tortoise in Southern France
BERNARD DEVAUX AND DAVID STUBBS ... 330

Conservation Strategies for the Bolson Tortoise, *Gopherus flavomarginatus*, in the Chihuahuan Desert
GUSTAVO AGUIRRE, DAVID J. MORAFKA, AND GARY A. ADEST ... 333

Managing the Last Survivors: Integration of *in situ* and *ex situ* Conservation of *Pseudemydura umbrina*
GERALD KUCHLING ... 339

The Conservation Biology of the Angonoka, *Geochelone yniphora*, in Northwestern Madagascar: Progress Report
JAMES O. JUVIK, A. ROSS KIESTER, DON REID, BRUCE COBLENTZ, AND JEFFREY HOFFMAN ... 345

RESERVES AND PROGRAMS

BUFFER ZONES

Use of Terrestrial Habitat by Western Pond Turtles, *Clemmys marmorata*: Implications for Management ... 352
DEVIN A. REESE AND HARTWELL H. WELSH

Evaluating Wetland Conservation Policies with GIS Models of Habitat Use by Aquatic Turtles (Abstract) ... 358
VINCENT J. BURKE AND J. WHITFIELD GIBBONS

LANDSCAPE PRESERVATION

New Approaches for the Conservation of Bog Turtles, *Clemmys muhlenbergii*, in Virginia ... 359
KURT A. BUHLMANN, JOSEPH C. MITCHELL, AND MEGAN G. ROLLINS

Land Use, Development, and Natural Succession and Their Effects on Bog Turtle Habitat in the Southeastern United States ... 364
DENNIS W. HERMAN AND BERN W. TRYON

Life on the Edge: Managing Peripheral Populations in a Changing Landscape ... 372
THOMAS B. HERMAN

Blanding's Turtle Habitat Requirements and Implications for Conservation in Dutchess County, New York ... 377
ERIK KIVIAT

Identification of Wood Turtle Nesting Areas for Protection and Management ... 383
RICHARD R. BUECH, LYNELLE G. HANSON, AND MARK D. NELSON

Transportation Corridor Impact Assessment: A Regulatory Process and An Associated Analytical Tool ... 392
ROBERT S. DE SANTO

CONSERVATION PROGRAMS

The Amazon Turtles—Conservation and Management in Brazil ... 407
VITOR HUGO CANTARELLI

An Action Plan for Nonprofit Organizations in Turtle and Tortoise Conservation ... 411
ROGER DALE AND JUN LEE

RESERVE PLANNING

Identifying Areas of High Herpetological Diversity in the Western Ghats, Southwestern India ... 414
INDRANEIL DAS

A Second Reserve for the Bolson Tortoise, *Gopherus flavomarginatus*, at Rancho Sombreretillo, Chihuahua, Mexico ... 417
EDDIE TREVIÑO, DAVID J. MORAFKA, AND GUSTAVO AGUIRRE

INTEGRATED MANAGEMENT STRATEGIES AND PUBLIC POLICY

Turtle Conservation and Halfway Technology: What Is the Problem? (Plenary Lecture) ... 422
NAT B. FRAZER

Conservation of Covert Species: Protecting Species We Don't Even Know ... 426
JEFFERY E. LOVICH AND J. WHITFIELD GIBBONS

The Desert Tortoise Recovery Plan: An Ambitious Effort to Conserve Biodiversity in the Mojave and Colorado Deserts of the United States ... 430
KRISTIN H. BERRY

Effects of Exploitation on *Dermatemys mawii* Populations in Northern Belize and Conservation Strategies for Rural Riverside Villages ... 441
JOHN POLISAR

Turtles as a Resource: Avoiding the "Tragedy of the Commons" (Summary Report)
  PETER C. H. PRITCHARD 444

Management of Tropical Chelonians: Dream or Nightmare? — Part 2
  JOHN G. FRAZIER 446

Global Conservation and the Sciences: People, Policy, and Pennies (Plenary Lecture)
  IAN R. SWINGLAND 453

International Conservation Partnerships (Text of Presentation)
  MOLLY H. OLSON 465

The Role of Policy Makers in the Development of Conservation Strategies (Summary)
  SENATOR SUZI OPPENHEIMER 466

Conservation Strategies—An Overview: Implications for Policy
  PETER C. H. PRITCHARD 467

POSTER SESSION: ECOLOGY, CONSERVATION, AND HUSBANDRY
ABSTRACTS OF PRESENTED POSTERS 473

Challenges to a Changing Plant Community: Food Selectivity and Digestive Performance of Desert Tortoises Fed Native vs. Exotic Forage Plants
  HAROLD W. AVERY 474

The Dynamics of Two Sympatric Tortoise Communities in a Stressful Environment
  ERNST H. W. BAARD 475

Wood Turtle Habitat Research
  RICHARD R. BUECH, MARK D. NELSON, LYNELLE G. HANSON, AND BRUCE BRECKE 475

Wetland Functions and Values: Documentation Methods and Tools that Give Landscape Perspectives
  ROBERT S. DE SANTO 476

The Importance of Biological Research in the Habitat Conservation Planning Process
  TODD C. ESQUE AND R. A. FRIDELL 477

A Twenty-Year Study Documenting the Relationship between Turtle Decline and Human Recreation
  STEVEN D. GARBER AND JOANNA BURGER 477

Eggs and Clutch Production of Captive *Graptemys*
  MIKE GOODE 478

Reproduction in Captive *Heosemys grandis*
  MIKE GOODE 478

A Methodology for Determining Tortoise Food Habits in Arid Regions
  W. BRYAN JENNINGS 479

Management of Wild Tortoise Populations is Complicated by Escape or Release of Captives
  RONALD W. MARLOW, KARIN VON SECKENDORFF HOFF, AND PETER BRUSSARD 479

Spotted Turtle Population Ecology and Habitat Use in Central Massachusetts
  JOAN C. MILAM AND S. MELVIN 480

Establishment of the Chelonian Research Foundation, a Private Nonprofit Organization for Support and Publication of Turtle and Tortoise Research
  ANDERS G. J. RHODIN 480

Turtle Conservation in Nepal: Maintaining Ecological Integrity of the Wetlands Habitat
  TEJ KUMAR SHRESTHA 482

Highways and Roads are Population Sinks for Desert Tortoises
  KARIN VON SECKENDORFF HOFF AND RONALD W. MARLOW 482

AZA Chelonian Advisory Group Hispaniolan Slider, *Trachemys decorata*, Conservation Program
  RICO WALDER 483

Index to Contributing Authors 484

Conference Directory 485

U.S./Metric Conversion Tables 494

PRE-CONFERENCE FIELD TRIP

Conference delegates enter the Wildlife Conservation Park (Bronx Zoo) led by Fred Caporaso (Chapman University, Orange, California) *foreground right*, and Walter Allen (Casa de Tortuga, Fountain Valley, California) *center right*.

At the Bronx Zoo Reptile House: *Left to right* — Cassandra Costley (Baltimore, Maryland), Brett Stearns (Institute for Herpetological Research, Menlo Park, California), Edward Moll (Eastern Illinois University, Charleston), and John Behler (Curator of Herpetology, Wildlife Conservation Society, New York).

Behind the scenes at the Reptile House: David Galbraith (Royal Botanical Gardens, Hamilton, Ontario), Walter Sachsse (Johannes Gutenberg Universität, Mainz, Germany), John Behler (Curator of Herpetology, Wildlife Conservation Society), Cassandra Costley (Baltimore, Maryland), Hal Avery and Bill Boarman (U.S. Geological Survey, Biological Resources Division, Riverside, California), and Md. Sohrab Sarker (Dhaka University, Bangladesh).

Photos by Anita-Baskin Salzberg (unless otherwise noted).

Names in photo captions are listed from left to right throughout this volume.

CONFERENCE STAFF

Conference Organizing Committee: Suzanne Dohm (President, New York Turtle and Tortoise Society) and Michael Klemens (Conference Chairman; Wildlife Conservation Society).

Conference Coordinating Staff: *Standing* — Rita Devine, Danny Novo, and Al Gubar. *Seated* — Conference Coordinator Craig Vitamanti and Julie Bank.

THE OPENING PLENARY SESSION

J. Whitfield Gibbons

"Measuring Declines and Natural Variation in Turtle Populations:
Spatial Lessons from Long-Term Studies"

(page 243)

Mary Christopher

"Laboratory Health Profiles of Desert Tortoises in the Mojave Desert:
A Model for Health Status Evaluation of Chelonian Populations"

(page 76)

Ian R. Swingland

"Global Conservation and the Sciences: People, Policy, and Pennies"

(page 453)

Nat B. Frazer

"Turtle Conservation and Halfway Technology: What is the Problem?"

(page 422)

Michael W. Klemens (Conference Chairman, Wildlife Conservation Society, New York), Suzanne Dohm (President, New York Turtle and Tortoise Society), Mary Christopher (University of California—Davis), Ian R. Swingland (Durrell Institute of Conservation and Ecology, University of Kent, Canterbury, UK), Kristin H. Berry (Program Committee Co-Chair, U.S. Geological Survey, Biological Resources Division, Riverside, California), and J. Whitfield Gibbons and Nat Frazer (Savannah River Ecology Laboratory, Aiken, South Carolina).

Closing Banquet

Alex Ypsilanti (New York Turtle and Tortoise Society), Celestine Ravaoarinoromanga (Antananarivo, Madagascar), and David Galbraith (Royal Botanical Gardens, Hamilton, Ontario). (Photo by Rita Devine.)

Featured banquet speaker Robert F. Kennedy, Jr.

The New York Turtle and Tortoise Society presents awards to Craig Vitamanti (Conference Coordinator), Kristin Berry (Program Committee Co-Chair), Michael Klemens (Conference Chairman), and Jim Van Abbema (Conference Technical Director) for their extraordinary effort in helping to make the Conference a success.

Acknowledgments

A remarkable group of ecologists, conservationists, land managers, governmental officials, and policy makers, representing 25 nations gathered in July 1993 at Purchase, and the 77 papers and summary reports (as well as abstracts of presented posters) included here represent the combined efforts of more than 130 authors and 35 reviewers. This extraordinary endeavor offers us just a glimpse of the troubled conservation status of the world's 270-plus species of tortoises and turtles. It is only a snapshot of the condition of chelonians in this decade, but it speaks loudly and clearly of their plight. And it challenges us. Only many decades (or centuries) in the future will anyone know whether we have met that challenge. It is evident that far more than the conservation of turtles is at stake; our endeavor cannot be isolated, unrelated to the preservation of entire ecosystems. It is our sincere hope—not only for those who share an appreciation for these magnificent creatures, but for the sake of all—that we will have, at least in part, succeeded.

In the four years since the gathering of the 230 delegates and attendees at Purchase, this proceedings volume has become more than simply documentation of that event. Nearly all of the 82 papers presented at the conference were submitted for inclusion in the proceedings (papers not submitted are represented here by their abstracts). Most of the submitted manuscripts have been subsequently updated by the authors to reflect current field data wherever possible. All papers have been peer reviewed and, in response to an understandably broad variety of writing styles, a primary thrust of the editorial effort was to ensure accessibility of language for a diverse readership.

The material in the present volume is organized by the major subject areas (which, in general, correspond to the daily sessions) of the 1993 conference. The plenary lectures from the opening-day session have been placed in their respective subject areas. Abstracts of the presented posters are included in a separate final section.

Reviewers

The reviewers are gratefully acknowledged for their invaluable contribution to this volume.

George D. Amato, Science Resource Center, Wildlife Conservation Society, New York

John L. Behler, Department of Herpetology, Wildlife Conservation Society, New York

Joan E. Berish, Florida Game and Fresh Water Fish Commission, Gainesville, Florida

Kristin H. Berry, U.S. Geological Survey, Biological Resources Division, Riverside, California

James R. Buskirk, Oakland, California

Fred Caporaso, Chapman University, Orange, California

Dave E. Collins, Tennessee Aquarium, Chattanooga, Tennessee

Robert A. Cook, Wildlife Health Center, Wildlife Conservation Society, New York

Robert P. Cook, Gateway National Recreation Area, Brooklyn, New York

Douglas Daly, New York Botanical Garden, New York

Scott K. Davis, Department of Animal Science, Texas A&M University, College Station, Texas

C. Kenneth Dodd, Jr., National Biological Service, Gainesville, Florida

David A. Galbraith, Royal Botanical Gardens, Hamilton, Ontario, Canada

Marc D. Graff, Northridge, California

Thomas B. Herman, Biology Department, Acadia University, Wolfville, Canada

William F. Holmstrom, Department of Herpetology, Wildlife Conservation Society, New York

John B. Iverson, Department of Biology, Earlham College, Richmond, Indiana

Elliott R. Jacobson, College of Veterinary Medicine, University of Florida, Gainesville, Florida

Erik Kiviat, Hudsonia, Ltd., Bard College Field Station, Annandale, New York

Michael W. Klemens, International Conservation, Wildlife Conservation Society, New York

Jeffrey E. Lovich, U.S. Geological Survey, Biological Resources Division, North Palm Springs, California

Joseph C. Mitchell, Department of Biology, University of Richmond, Richmond, Virginia

Don Moll, Department of Zoology, Eastern Illinois University, Charleston, Illinois

Edward O. Moll, Biology Department, Southwest Missouri State University, Springfield, Missouri

Henry R. Mushinsky, Department of Biology, University of South Florida, Tampa, Florida

John Payne, Department of Zoology, University of Washington, Seattle, Washington

Peter C. H. Pritchard, Florida Audubon Society, Winter Park, Florida

Christopher J. Raithel, Rhode Island Department of Environmental Management, West Kingston, Rhode Island

John G. Robinson, International Conservation, Wildlife Conservation Society, New York

Lora L. Smith, Department of Wildlife Ecology and Conservation, University of Florida, Gainesville, Florida

John B. Thorbjarnarson, International Conservation, Wildlife Conservation Society, New York

Peter Walsh, International Conservation, Wildlife Conservation Society, New York

Michael Weinstein, El Morro Institute for Ecological Research, Solvang, California

Kristin H. Berry, **Michael W. Klemens**, and **Peter C. H. Pritchard** served on the Editorial Advisory Board.

Many individuals, whose support and encouragement have been critical to this project, deserve special recognition.

Michael W. Klemens, Director, Turtle Recovery Program (whose design and organization of the 1993 conference are reflected in the organization of the subject material in this volume) was responsible for securing initial funding and office facilities at the American Museum of Natural History for the acquisition of manuscripts and preliminary editing, as well as for additional funding support during the review process. As primary reviewer and advisor for this project, his guidance and focus are gratefully acknowledged.

Peter C. H. Pritchard must be given special recognition for his role as Editorial Consultant throughout the editorial and review process; his extraordinary knowledge, skill, and diplomacy were responsible for bringing together the final pieces of this volume. His endorsements for financial support from the Chelonia Institute made completion of the work possible.

Kristin H. Berry, Editorial Advisory Board, provided invaluable editorial advice; her contributions to the work of a number of authors and her assistance and support in the securing of additional funding were also critical to the completion of this work.

Suzanne Dohm, President, New York Turtle and Tortoise Society, provided constant support throughout this undertaking. From the onset her vision and enthusiasm for the proceedings project were a primary source of inspiration and are deeply appreciated.

Charles W. Myers, Chair, Department of Ichthyology and Herpetology, American Museum of Natural History, and the Herpetology Department staff provided office and library facilities and are thanked for their support and encouragement during the editorial and review process.

John L. Behler, Curator, Department of Herpetology, Wildlife Conservation Society, generously provided additional office services, advice, and encouragement.

David J. Morafka provided additional funding for the editorial phase, acting on behalf of the Department of Public Works, National Training Center, United States Army at Fort Irwin, California.

Fred W. Koontz, Director, Science Resource Center, Wildlife Conservation Society, is thanked for providing the services of the Center's facilities during the layout process.

Barbara Daddario, Assistant Editor and Copy Editor, was largely responsible for the successful completion of this volume. Her precision and painstaking thoroughness during the final proofreading were invaluable.

Douglas Daly, Curator of Amazonian Botany, New York Botanical Garden, is thanked for the proofreading of botanical names.

Gail Bonsignore, Department of Herpetology, Wildlife Conservation Society; **U.S. Senator Alfonse D'Amato** and his staff; **Marydele Donnelly**, Center for Marine Conservation and IUCN; **Timothy Meyer**, G. P. Putnam & Sons; **Anders G. J. Rhodin**, Chelonian Research Foundation; and **Joe Ventura**, U.S. Fish and Wildlife Service, are all thanked for providing valuable information and/or assistance.

Finally, many colleagues and friends must be recognized for their encouragement, assistance, and patience throughout the entire assembly of this work: Robert Anderson, Anthony Boya, Bill Cermack, Lorri Cramer, Dean Dinnebeil, Rita Devine, Allen Foust, Joan Frumkies, Jack Gambino, Daniel Greenberger, Vittorio Maestro, Norberto Muller, Gerald Otte, Alex Padagas, Phil Puccio, Allen Salzberg, Anita Baskin-Salzberg, Craig Vitamanti, and Alex Ypsilanti.

— Jim Van Abbema

"Conservation, Restoration, and Management of Tortoises and Turtles—An International Conference" was largely an outgrowth of the New York Turtle and Tortoise Society's Annual Seminars, held since 1985, and the California Turtle & Tortoise Club's "First International Symposium on Turtles & Tortoises: Conservation and Captive Husbandry," held in August 1990. These meetings had made clear the enormous value of bringing together the amateur and professional turtle communities.

The Purchase conference was coordinated and co-sponsored by the New York Turtle and Tortoise Society and the American Museum of Natural History Turtle Recovery Program.* The meeting brought together a wide variety of people concerned with conservation, including the academic, government, and private sectors, making a profound impact upon all who attended.

In recognition of the conservation imperative that has become clear to us all, other groups have continued the sponsorship of these critically important meetings. Bernard Devaux and David Stubbs, Village des Tortues, Gonfaron, France, organized the "International Congress of Chelonian Conservation," held in Gonfaron in July 1995, and another meeting, to be sponsored by the California Turtle & Tortoise Club and the National Turtle and Tortoise Society, has recently been announced for summer 1998.

*Present address: Turtle Recovery Program, Wildlife Conservation Society, 185th St. and Southern Blvd., Bronx, NY 10460

A New Paradigm for Conservation

MICHAEL W. KLEMENS, CONFERENCE CHAIR
DIRECTOR, WCS TURTLE RECOVERY PROGRAM
DIRECTOR FOR PROGRAM DEVELOPMENT, WILDLIFE CONSERVATION SOCIETY

Wildlife Conservation Society, 185th and Southern Blvd., Bronx, NY 10460, USA

In July 1993 an international conference, devoted to the current state of knowledge of the world's turtles and tortoises and future efforts to conserve them, was held at the State University of New York at Purchase. More than 200 conservation biologists, ecologists, land managers, zoo and museum professionals, and concerned individuals representing 25 nations gathered for this event. Although the news reported at the conference was alarming—over 100 of the world's 260+ species of tortoises and turtles were in need of some form of conservation attention, there was optimism. This optimism was fueled in part by an expectation that the United States was prepared to assume a conservation leadership role in both domestic and international arenas.

By the beginning of 1994 the realities of American politics began to erode that optimism. High-level administrative shifts, a gridlocked Congress, and a bitter battle over the reauthorization of the Endangered Species Act dashed the hopes of those who looked to Washington for environmental leadership. It became apparent that a new paradigm for conservation was needed—one that places less reliance on "top-down" conservation and is more dependent upon grassroots support from the local communities that have the most to gain—or to lose—from conservation activities.

Threats

Over 100 species of turtles are threatened with extinction unless exploitation and habitat loss are halted. Certain groups have been hit especially hard and include our most vulnerable turtle species. Both marine and river turtles are exploited; adults and eggs are harvested for food. Sea turtles are threatened by loss in shrimp trawls, ocean pollution, "subsistence" take for meat and eggs, harvest for tortoiseshell and leather, and by loss of their nesting beaches to development and beachfront replenishment and armoring. River turtle nesting sites are also being lost as riverine habitat is degraded by dams, sand mining, and channelization. Because marine and river turtles are the most economically important species, more attention has been focused on them, and such interventionist techniques as headstarting, ranching, and limited-harvest programs have been undertaken.

The Testudinidae, or true tortoises, number over 40 species, typically characterized by a long reproductive life span,

Robert F. Kennedy, Jr., featured banquet speaker, and Conference Chair Michael W. Klemens.

low egg production, and low juvenile survivorship. Because their long reproductive life span is predicated on relative freedom from predation upon adults, tortoises are biologically ill-equipped to cope with the accelerated loss of adults caused by human activities. Some of the most destructive of these include habitat conversion, development, or fragmentation; elevated predation levels from species commensal with humans; and overcollection for the wildlife trade, for which tortoises are among the most popular chelonian species.

Many semi-aquatic turtles share the life history traits of tortoises (i.e., long reproductive life span, low egg output, and low juvenile survivorship) and also suffer from habitat degradation and loss and overcollection. The wetland and riparian habitats of many species are inadequately protected. Examples include wood, spotted, and bog turtles (*Clemmys*), Blanding's turtle (*Emydoidea*), and many of the tropical American and Asian batagurids (e.g., *Rhinoclemmys, Pyxidea, Geoemyda,* and *Cuora*).

Causes of Decline

Loss and alteration of habitat is the major cause of turtle decline around the world. Because many turtle species have complex habitat requirements and use a variety of different habitats, habitat fragmentation is particularly significant. Blanding's turtles often use a series of small wetlands over a season. After hibernating in a marsh, they move early in the spring to vernal pools, which are warmer and contain abundant food in the form of tadpoles and salamander larvae. As the vernal pools dry up, they shift to wooded swamps, and as the weather cools, they move back into more open, warm habitats before returning to the marsh to hibernate. Spotted turtles may move onto land and burrow into leaves for several days or even weeks. These complex patterns require the protection of habitat blocks, a mosaic of different wetland types with intact upland habitat adjoining them—a landscape complex that is not factored into most development plans. Instead, when wetlands *are* afforded protection, they are protected individually, which fails to maintain the ecological continuity needed for many wetland-dependent species, including turtles. Developed habitat is further compromised by the introduction of pet and feral animals such as dogs, cats, and rats; introduced plant species (such as purple loosestrife into bog and swamp habitat); and even by native species that flourish and increase in disturbed habitats ("subsidized species"), which include raccoons, crows, skunks, and the giant reed (*Phragmites*).

Turtles and tortoises have been overharvested for food by local inhabitants, and increasingly by commercial hunters who transport them to urban centers. The bulk of this harvest occurs in developing countries, but there are also active freshwater turtle "fisheries" in the southeastern United States. Although the concept of sustainable management of species has been highly promoted, there are many, including myself, who question whether such long-lived animals as turtles and tortoises can be managed on a sustained-yield basis. The wildlife trade is clearly a contributing factor in the decline of tortoises and many freshwater turtle species, but threats to turtles usually work in tandem: Habitat alteration or destruction is often followed by increased human pressures, which result in further destruction of the ecosystem. Introduced species, subsidized predators, and commercial exploitation for food and the wildlife trade then follow.

As epidemic outbreaks in wild populations have increased, disease has become a major issue in the management of turtles and tortoises. The desert tortoise in southern California has already been decimated. Many of these outbreaks are attributed to captives (that have contracted various diseases while in confinement) released into the wild where they rapidly infect free-ranging tortoises. Pollution of marine habitats by chemicals and heavy metals may be responsible for depressed immune systems in sea turtles, resulting in increased outbreaks of fibropapilloma tumors.

Solutions

Conservation programs must be firmly rooted in "good science," but good science alone is not sufficient to conserve turtles and tortoises. Science and conservation must interact, and wildlife managers must access the appropriate scientific information necessary to develop sound recovery and management strategies.

Unfortunately, interventionist management (including captive breeding, translocations, and headstarting) has been overemphasized—often to the exclusion of appropriate protection of both populations and habitat. Headstarting is useful *only* when used in tandem with a strategy that will reduce the loss of adults. Clearly, if turtles have become scarce because of overharvesting, throwing more hatchlings into the rivers and seas without curbing the exploitation of adults cannot be a successful strategy. Yet, it is precisely these measures that have been and are still being used to "conserve" turtles. Such measures have an intrinsic appeal to many institutional bureaucrats because they require a visible infrastructure (e.g., hatcheries), which serves as tangible "proof" that they are "doing conservation." Hatcheries produce fairly predictable and consistent results: Eggs are gathered and incubated, and hatchlings are released, often as part of a well-publicized media opportunity. And wildlife managers are gratified by the perception they have gained a hands-on control over nature.

Addressing the loss of adult turtles, however, requires making hard, often politically unpopular choices, which have the potential to pit turtles against the perceived economic interests of the local community. Such choices may include mitigating the impacts of proposed projects (such as developments, roads, and dams) or regulating turtle harvest. While the conservation of turtles may require society to make hard decisions to protect wilderness and biodiversity, it need not result in controversy. Substantial grassroots conservation can be accomplished at the local level. Upper levels of government can provide the framework (e.g., designation of "Endangered" or "Threatened" species and technical assistance) to enable local communities to participate in conservation. Some of the most effective conservation programs are now being created at the local level.

I have increasingly chosen to work at the local level because the complex landscape-scale habitat demands of turtle conservation cannot be accommodated by legislation alone. In New York, for example, many wetlands are protected by a 100-foot upland buffer, but this mandate focuses upon water quality, not biological diversity. Species, such as Blanding's turtle, which use wetlands on a rotational basis require habitat protection that extends beyond the regulatory scope. Such protection can only be secured when landowners are convinced that it is in their own best interests to develop the land in a manner that will maintain the upland habitat that links small wetlands. It is vital that these choices are seen as voluntary decisions, decisions that not only conserve wildlife, but benefit the local community's economic well-being and quality of life. The major difference between these "bottom-up" conservation strategies and the more traditional "top-down" approaches is that they are originated and supported locally, not imposed by federal, provincial, state, or even county governments. For chelonians to benefit from such community-based conservation enterprises, it will require:

- Building conservation partnerships by integrating turtle and tortoise conservation into larger, multi-disciplinary efforts.

- Linking conservation initiatives to public policy issues—especially in the spheres of regional land-use planning, watershed management, landscape preservation, and the sponsorship of legislation to enhance sound land-use planning at local, regional, national, and international levels.

- Developing educational programs, including programs designed to foster national and regional pride in natural resources and to develop conservation awareness in both developed and developing countries.

- Developing ecotourism and other economically driven systems that will value wildlife resources *in situ* and that will accurately portray in financial terms the long-term costs of depleting natural resources. Too often resource exploitation is viewed *only* as the value of what is harvested, not the value of what is lost to future generations.

- Recognizing the inclusive nature of conservation, which requires the formation of coalitions to maximize human capital, linking scientists, conservationists, zoos, museums, educational institutions, turtle fanciers, and other concerned individuals and institutions with the local communities that share their land with these animals.

Although turtle conservation has proceeded along a pathway different from what many who attended the Purchase conference may have anticipated, the gathering sparked a renewed interest in conserving these fascinating creatures. It brought together a wide range of people concerned with chelonian conservation from many nations, creating a diverse coalition of interest groups and professions. And from this diverse assemblage came the clear message that unlike "pure" research, the "applied research" needed to effect better conservation management requires an interdisciplinary approach.

Finally, the conference would not have been possible without the efforts of many individuals and organizations, which are acknowledged elsewhere in this volume. Furthermore, I would be remiss if I did not single out three individuals, who were the heart and soul of the conference —Kristin Berry, who encouraged me to pursue my vision of an interdisciplinary turtle summit with her contacts at the Bureau of Land Management, which led to the organization of the conference; Jim Van Abbema, whose dedication to the conference and to the subsequent production of the proceedings must be recognized by all of us—when promises of financial support to produce the proceedings evaporated, Jim forged ahead, determined to produce a volume worthy of the conference; and Suzanne Dohm, President of the New York Turtle and Tortoise Society, who recognized the importance of bringing together the "professional" and "non-professional" turtle conservation constituencies. If we are to save the world's turtles from the destructive impulses of our own species, we'd best begin to focus upon our shared concerns and values, rather than accentuating our points of difference.

Troubled Times for Turtles

JOHN L. BEHLER
CHAIRMAN, IUCN/SSC TORTOISE AND FRESHWATER TURTLE SPECIALIST GROUP
CURATOR OF HERPETOLOGY, WILDLIFE CONSERVATION SOCIETY

Wildlife Conservation Society, 185th St. and Southern Blvd., Bronx, NY 10460, USA

It has been 1,500 days since "Purchase." That we can compress the International Conference on Conservation, Restoration, and Management of Tortoises and Turtles into a one-word moniker is clear evidence that the event was an extraordinary happening for the 200-plus chelonian specialists and aficionados in attendance. Some 25 countries were represented. Herpetologists, conservation biologists, veterinarians, infectious disease specialists, ecologists, land managers, law enforcers, politicians, geneticists, zoo workers, museum curators, taxonomists, wildlife agency representatives, lawyers, humane society representatives, captive breeders, and turtle society members from New York to California came together for common cause at the Purchase, New York, conference. It was an amalgam of "turtle people" of the first order. And it was a benchmark for chelonian conservation. Kudos must go to Michael Klemens, Director of the Turtle Recovery Program, for the conception and execution of this event, and we are indeed fortunate that it is chronicled so magnificently in these proceedings.

What we carry away from special conferences and symposia is unique to each of us. Early in my career I learned that there are far more important reasons for attending them than the formal paper presentations. One of my colleagues, who prided himself in *never* listening to a paper ("You can read the abstracts on the plane...and if the papers are any good they'll be published"), told me that the essence of the meeting is the people themselves and what is important is getting to know them and what they really think. Well, I confess I missed a few of the 80+ Purchase papers to collegial chatter and attendance to business, but I didn't miss many. Frankly, most conferees were so passionate about the turtle conservation matters at hand that they jammed the lecture hall, leaving few attendees with whom to talk in the great room beyond it. Now, thankfully, we can rejoice in having the very polished, better than original, papers (thank you, again, Jim Van Abbema, Peter Pritchard, and others who pitched in to iron out wrinkles) as well as the many good memories beyond the formalities. For me, the take-home message of the Purchase conference remains much the same today as it did in July 1993. It came from a distillation of the papers, posters, focused formal discussion groups, one-on-one discussions at breaks, and exchanges made during evening gatherings. Boiled down to simplest terms, it reaffirmed my contention that our 270 chelonians, as a consequence of burgeoning human numbers and their insidious activities, are facing the greatest challenge of their evolutionary history. And that there were people out there who were fighting like hell to save them.

Purchase verified that there are altruistic individuals in our ranks who, to me, are the true turtle conservation heroes. They passionately sound the alarm, work quietly year after year as indefatigable spirits gathering hard data, or dare to venture into the new age of conservation biology. They may passionately fight for all turtles or champion their special research species. And many continue onward despite detractors who spend so much time attacking the real workers that whatever validity their caustic comments hold about methodology or interpretation of data falls victim to their hostile style. I believe, however, that Purchase served to defuse many of the well-worn, old turtle politics and helped to heal old wounds. If nothing else, we were reminded that there are so few of us to do the battle of legions that the necessities of common cause and sense had to prevail if we are to save the resources we cherish. New alliances and marriages of talents were forged among the aforementioned conferee elements. And these interactions have been evident in both the papers herein and the turtle conferences that have been held in the years that have followed.

Unfortunately, the four years that have elapsed since the Purchase conference have not been so kind to turtles. Wildlife resource destruction and misguided human activity have grown at an ever-increasing pace. In the interval between Purchase and today, more than 25 million turtles (mostly hatchling *Trachemys scripta*) from the United States have been exported to foreign markets, with the highest numbers going to Asian ports, then Mediterranean countries. With them went assorted *Salmonella* serotypes and other pathogenic enterics, potential health threats to their keepers and to native chelonians in wetlands where the foreign turtles are liberated. Sliders are now commonly seen in the wild alongside local aquatic turtles in southern Europe, Africa, Asia, and the United States far beyond their natural range (Branch, 1988; Ernst et al., 1994; Jenkins, 1995). Along with the slider exports, tens of thousands of eastern and western box turtles (*Terrapene carolina* and *T. ornata*) and smaller numbers of pond turtles (*Clemmys* spp.) were exported. While state, federal, and international laws now offer these taxa a greater measure of protection, attention has turned to alligator snappers (*Macroclemys temminckii*), Florida softshells (*Apalone ferox*), and map turtles (*Graptemys* spp.). Exported snappers and softshells help fill food bowls in Asia as local stocks of large batagurids and trionychids vanish.

The great turtle drain in Asia kicked into high gear about the same time as the Purchase conference. While tortoises and freshwater turtles have been subjected to human predation for centuries, recent changes in Asian economics, spawned when Chinese currency became convertible, have opened direct access to foreign markets. A highly organized turtle trade system has replaced relatively modest subsistence hunting for family consumption and sale in local markets. Many of Asia's 50 tortoises and freshwater turtle species are now at risk of unbridled commercial exploitation. Peter Paul van Dijk advised us that "what had been a barter trade has become a cash-fueled import to a vast and increasingly wealthy market." Le Dien Duc and Steven Broad (1995) reported that in Vietnam all but four of 21 species of that country's freshwater turtles and tortoises are seen in the trade. Further, these chelonians are systematically collected and routed to Ho Chi Minh City and Hanoi. With unregulated turtle imports from Cambodia and Lao PDR, they are sent on to China where they are used for food, in the preparation of Oriental medicines and tonics, or as religious objects released in temple pools or into questionable or unsuitable habitat in the wild. Turtle exports from Vietnam alone are estimated (very conservatively) to be 450–750 kg/day (Le Dien Duc and Broad, 1995), which translates to 200,000 ("conceivably several times this") living turtles and tortoises annually. And the (Martin D. Jenkins, 1995) TRAFFIC International report "Tortoises and Freshwater Turtles: The trade in Southeast Asia" offers a very similar but holistic view of the resurgent trade between Southeast Asian countries and China. He also points to the lack of basic natural history information and survey data on the species being harvested. Management and recovery plans cannot be crafted without them. For the majority of the species involved, we currently know so little about their status in the wild that it is impossible to quantify the effects of the turtle trade in Asia. Yet the anecdotal information from the aforementioned reports, as well as that received from turtle specialists working in the region, turtle hunters, and those who collect rare forms for the exotic turtle trade, paint a picture of dramatic chelonian decline. W. P. McCord advises me that the recently described golden-headed box turtle, *Cuora aurocapitata*, has vanished in nature and cannot be purchased at any price. He also notes that Zhou's, Pan's, and McCord's box turtles (*C. zhoui*, *C. pani*, and *C. mccordi*) are commercially extinct. Further, the Chinese three-striped box turtle, *C. trifasciata*, formerly a common pet shop turtle, now sells for $500–$1,000 U.S. in Asian markets because of its rarity and perceived cancer-curing properties. It is almost incomprehensible that Reeves' turtle, *Chinemys reevesii*, has disappeared; market hunters claim it is so. The great Asian river turtles (*Batagur baska*, *Callagur borneoensis*, and *Orlitia borneensis*) and the giant softshells (*Chitra* spp. and *Pelochelys bibroni*) are seriously depressed and will not long survive without heroic intervention.

Today, there is no more serious turtle crisis than that which is taking place in Southeast Asia and southern China. Some species are very likely being lost in nature before they can be described. And the tentacles of this trade have reached around the globe to New York, Florida, Seattle, and southern California. Transplanted Asians have brought their Old World food customs with them to North America. With the disappearance of imported Asian turtle species, New World species have been substituted: adult sliders (*Trachemys. scripta*), diamondback terrapins (*Malaclemys terrapin*), snappers (*Chelydra serpentina*), softshells (*Apalone* sp.) and gopher and desert tortoises (*Gopherus* spp.). Some of you sounded the alarm at Purchase. It is unlikely that any of these species can long tolerate accelerated exploitation at a level sufficient to satisfy Chinese markets of the Old and New Worlds. Significant numbers of adult sliders and snappers are exported to the food markets of China. In some, McCord reports that they make up the bulk of the trade.

The living chelonians of the world are in perilous decline. Causes include elevated subsistence hunting, commercial collection for food and the exotic pet market, debilitating diseases, increased pressure from growing predator populations, alien plant introductions that diminish graze quality or accelerate plant succession, dramatic mortality as a consequence of highway construction, human-set fires, habitat fragmentation, protracted droughts, and poor wildlife management and land use practices.

These stories are carried in this document. Of the 42 extant tortoise species, four are considered "Endangered," another is "Critically Endangered," and 18 species are listed as "Vulnerable" in the *1996 IUCN Red List of Threatened Animals*. The leatherback and six other marine turtles are "Critically Endangered" (2) and "Endangered" (3) or "Vulnerable" (1). Among freshwater turtles, 51 are considered "Threatened," with five listed "Critically Endangered," 17 "Endangered," and 29 "Vulnerable." These are desperate times for those who minister to vanishing chelonians and their habitats.

The exotic pet trade is especially worrisome, for it preys heavily on wild populations where habitat remains intact. Turtle harvesting usually continues at a given location until supplies are exhausted or until it is no longer profitable. Results of long-term studies (Congdon et al., 1993; Congdon et al., 1994; Garber and Burger, 1995) indicate that the removal of modest numbers of adults and older juvenile turtles had very deleterious effects on their populations, which cannot easily be offset, and strongly suggest that long-lived chelonians cannot tolerate commercial collection. *"The concept of sustainable harvest of already-reduced populations of long-lived organisms appears to be an oxymoron"* (Congdon et al., 1993).

Despite CITES and the wildlife laws of treaty signatories, the world's exotic pet markets are poorly regulated. Millions of chelonians are marketed each year without quarantine or adequate health assessment by the recipient nations.

The impact to local species is unknown. Added to the long list of legally exported and imported turtles are those that move clandestinely across borders or are shipped in waves to distant destinations with the hope that officials will not seize them for wildlife law or humane standards violations. Apparently, no species is safe from exploitation. Not even the world's rarest tortoise species is sacred. In May 1996 villains broke into the Eaux et Forêts compound at the Ampijoroa Forest Reserve and made off with 75 (73 juveniles, 2 adult females) angonoka, or plowshare, tortoises, *Geochelone yniphora*, which had been carefully bred and nurtured by Jersey Wildlife Preservation Trust for ten years. An international alarm was sounded. A lackluster investigation by Malagasy officials followed, and the trail ran cold in Prague—the site where the Third World Congress of Herpetology is scheduled for summer 1997. Senior CITES and TRAFFIC officials were frustrated by this episode. Indeed, weaknesses in the wildlife laws and actions of signatories were exposed. This was further demonstrated by the illegal export of thousands of star tortoises, *G. elegans*, from India smuggled to the United Arab Emirates. There they were "laundered" and sent on to America and Europe as "captive-bred" beauties with born-in-UAE CITES documentation. The alleged breeding compound was a storefront address.

Whether or not turtles move legally across a border, they are very rarely placed in quarantine, even though they may have serious maladies. They move quickly to food or pet markets without veterinary health assessment or, in the case of animals seized by authorities, to individuals or institutions where protocols for strict isolation and health screens are rarely in place. Since the Purchase conference, very large numbers of tortoises listed on CITES Appendix I or II, including African pancake (*Malacochersus tornieri*) and leopard tortoises (*Geochelone pardalis*), Madagascan radiated (*G. radiata*) and spider tortoises (*Pyxis arachnoides*), Indian star tortoises (*G. elegans*), and "Russian" (*Testudo horsfieldii*), spur-thighed (*T. graeca*), Hermann's (*T. hermanni*), and Egyptian tortoises (*T. kleinmanni*) have been seized. Chelonian specialists and humane organizations were marshaled into action. In some cases, seized tortoises were placed with zoological institutions, and breeding programs were initiated. Sadly, many of the animals died or had to be euthanized because of serious diseases, injury as a consequence of grossly inhumane shipping practices (see Luiijf, this volume), or it was impossible to quickly find a suitable home in a long-term care facility. In perhaps the worst-case scenarios, tortoises were returned to the country of origin and repatriated without adequate health screens and against the advice of recognized chelonian health care specialists.

I confess to being especially chagrined by an ill-considered act (Boullay, 1995) that involved repatriation of 169 illegally imported radiated tortoises seized by customs officials in Réunion between 1989 and 1993. A plan was hatched by France's Ministère de l'Environnement, WWF, and Madagascar's Direction des Eaux et Forêts to return the tortoises to Madagascar and repatriate them to the Lemur Reserve of Berenty in the southeastern region of the country. Ignoring TFTSG veterinary and resource management counsel, the parties arranged for the tortoises to be released into the compounds at Berenty. Counter to the published claim, the site is *not* well supervised, other tortoises (i.e., spider tortoises, *Pyxis arachnoides*) *are* present on the reserve, locals *do* exploit remnant tortoise stocks (and openly offer them for sale), and one of the two enclosures is not escape-proof (chicken wire fence <20 cm in height). Further, the Berenty compound is largely barren compacted earth and provides little opportunity for captive propagation. And the illegal exports of radiated and spider tortoises to Europe, North America, and Asia (and almost certainly Réunion) have *not* declined in recent years despite the claims of customs officer vigilance. A review of TRAFFIC-reported seizures indicates the converse is most likely true. The bottom line is that *G. radiata* was not helped by this ill-conceived and poorly executed mission. Rather, it carried the potential to introduce herpes viruses, assorted *Mycoplasma* sp., "internuclear coccidia," and other viral, bacterial, and fungal pathogens and parasites to which they may have been exposed during their expatriate travels. We've moved beyond the days of veterinary alchemy and gaze-in-their-eyes health check technology. But that knowledge appears to have been lost here and in most other chelonian return-to-nature "simple fixes."

If we consider the magnitude of the open trade in turtles and the propensity for governments to exercise single-solution or quick fixes without recognition of the potential to compound conservation problems around the world, it is very easy to conjure up doomsday scenarios for wild chelonian stocks. Indeed, the international trade and the lack of quarantine and health screens on chelonian exports and imports make it possible for the diseases of practically any tortoise or freshwater turtle to be shared with the desert tortoises, *Gopherus agassizii*, in the backyard of a southern California chelonian enthusiast or with Hermann's tortoises in a similar situation in Italy. Thus, disease transfer from these captive stocks to their wild counterparts seems almost inevitable.

I believe that chelonians evoke a significantly higher degree of compassion in herpetologists than do taxa in other reptilian orders. At Purchase I saw hardened scientific collectors with wobbly knees after Wil Luiijf's graphic presentation of turtle trade horrors. Others of us were left speechless and we remained reflective for quite some time. What can we do? What can we save? We are floundering. Zoos have developed Species Survival Plan programs, but their ark is small and spaces are at a premium and mostly reserved for the charismatic megavertebrates. The Madagascar radiated tortoise qualifies. It is endangered, is perhaps the world's most beautiful tortoise, is sought-after for living herpetological collections, and has prospered in captivity. Some 700 specimens, most hatched in captivity, are in the

Species Survival Plan studbook for North America. Unfortunately, it is the only SSP for the entire order. While it is highly unlikely that any of these tortoises will or should be returned to Madagascar, the zoo herds are extremely useful for developing health assessment and screening protocols, nutrition studies, and reintroduction models.

Other institutions have created turtle and tortoise breeding stations, conservation undertakings, and headstarting programs in response to the dramatic decline of wild stocks, the huge numbers of displaced animals, unwanted pets, and confiscations. Significant programs have developed for tortoises and/or freshwater turtles at centers in southern Europe, Africa, northwestern Madagascar, India, Galápagos, and western North America. Others, for marine turtles, are scattered circumtropically. Often these centers operate with meager funding. Nevertheless, they typically have impressive educational programs and serve local communities well in that capacity. Unfortunately, shortcuts are often the rule for the captive management and repatriation elements of the centers' conservation programs—too often they lack the required herpetological and veterinary expertise, and they can ill afford to contract out for it. Health screens and genetic assessments are cut short, quarantine facilities are inadequate or absent, and repatriation protocols are developed without counsel from wildlife and veterinary science experts. When a recovery center includes relocation, repatriation, or translocation exercises among its programs, the motives for advocating these strategies must be carefully examined through peer review before the mission (Burke, 1991; Dodd and Seigel, 1991; Reinert, 1991). It is imperative that projects be carefully monitored so that accurate results, either positive or negative, can be published.

Despite problems, there appear to be success stories: the Galápagos tortoise (*Geochelone elephantopus*) captive breeding program at the Charles Darwin Research Station (see Cayot and Morillo, this volume), the western swamp tortoise (*Pseudemydura umbrina*) at the Western Australian Wildlife Research Centre (Kuchling, this volume), and, just maybe, Kemp's ridley (*Lepidochelys kempii*) at South Padre Island, Texas (Pritchard, 1997). These have been long, arduous affairs. And for the most part, they have been the work of extraordinarily dedicated individuals, not legions of bureaucrats. I suspect that the turtle wars will be fought and won and lost by individual "turtle men" and "turtle women" who are on divine missions from their chelonian gods to save *their* species. What compels Gerald Kuchling to save the western swamp tortoise, or Lora Smith to invest two years of her life studying the last populations of plowshare tortoises in one of the most inhospitable areas on Earth? Peter Pritchard's name has become synonymous with the giant chelonians—Galápagos tortoise and leatherback; Kristin Berry with the desert tortoise; Roger Wood, the diamondback terrapin; and Ed Moll with giant batagurids. And Whit Gibbons has become the dean of long-term chelonian ecological studies and Elliott Jacobson his counterpart in disease and health assessment. All came to the Purchase conference to share their special expertise and to stir us to action. There are no clear-cut, by-the-book conservation strategies, and battles won will all be case studies in unconventional politics and resource management. They will be played out in a context where there is too little time for exhaustive field studies and data collection. We'll be winging it and extrapolating from long-term study models of North American species: *Chrysemys picta*, *Trachemys scripta*, *Emydoidea blandingii*, and *Chelydra serpentina*. And there will still be those (perhaps even among us) who will quibble endlessly about the degree of correctness of the angle of decline in the vortex to e.

Purchase, however measured, was extraordinarily successful. And it set a high standard for the chelonian specialist gatherings that followed. It stimulated new friendships, unconventional marriages of interests and talents, and collaboration on conservation issues of common concern. Before the Purchase conference concluded, a plan for "Gonfaron II" (International Congress of Chelonian Conservation, Gonfaron, France, July 1995) was conceived and the need for a specialized meeting to address chelonian disease and health assessment protocols was articulated and subsequently held (Conference on Health Profiles, Health Reference Ranges, and Diseases in Desert Tortoises, Soda Springs, California, November 1996). The New York Turtle and Tortoise Society, which played such a commanding role at the Purchase meeting, has continued the Purchase spirit through its annual seminars.

Purchase also was the birthplace of *Chelonian Conservation and Biology*, the Journal of the IUCN/SSC Tortoise and Freshwater Turtle Specialist Group and International Bulletin of Chelonian Research. The need for improved synergy and communication among the specialist group and the communities it serves and with which it collaborates was clear. Anders Rhodin stepped forward and offered a plan and a commitment to drive the communication project. He has given generously of his time and financial resources, and with the help of his co-editor Peter Pritchard and his editorial board, he has carefully and very masterfully guided *CC&B* throughout its first two volumes. The journal serves to communicate the state of our knowledge and conservation status of tortoises and freshwater turtles as well as marine turtles to a thousand subscribers who share a common interest and concern. The eclectic initiatives that were born at Purchase and grew during the years that followed have been and will continue to be chronicled here. *CC&B* is for you. I urge you to participate however best you can.

The journal will report that chelonians are at the biggest crossroads of their 200-million-year history. Humans are their adversaries, but we are also their champions. Let us continue the good work of Purchase and pull *together*, be inventive, be creative, be daring, and do whatever we can as individuals and institutions to save our turtles and tortoises for more benevolent generations.

LITERATURE CITED

Boullay, S. 1995. Repatriation of radiated tortoises, *Geochelone radiata*, from Réunion Island to Madagascar. Chelon. Conserv. Biol. 1(4):319–320.

Branch, W. R. 1988. Field Guide to the Snakes and other Reptiles of Southern Africa. Strick Publishers, Cape Town. 326 pp.

Burke, R. L. 1991. Relocations, repatriations, and translocations of amphibians and reptiles: Taking a broader view. Herpetologica 47:350–357.

Congdon, J. D., A. E. Durham, and R. C. Van Loben Sels. 1993. Delayed sexual maturity and demographics of Blanding's turtles (*Emydoidea blandingii*): Implications for conservation and management of long-lived organisms. Conserv. Biol. 7(4):826–833.

Congdon, J. D., A. E. Durham, and R. C. Van Loben Sels. 1994. Demographics of common snapping turtles (*Chelydra serpentina*): Implications for conservation and management of long-lived organisms. American Zoologist 34:397–408.

Dodd, C. K. and R. A. Seigel. 1991. Relocation, repatriation, and translocation of amphibians and reptiles: Are they conservation strategies that work? Herpetologica 47:336–350.

Ernst, C. H., J. E. Lovich, and R. W. Barbour. 1994. Turtles of the United States and Canada. Smithsonian Institution Press, Washington, D.C. 578 pp.

Garber, S. D. and J. Burger. 1995. A 20-yr study documenting the relationship between turtle decline and human recreation. Ecol. Appl. 5(4):1151–1162.

Jenkins, M. D. 1995. Tortoises and Freshwater Turtles: The Trade in Southeast Asia. TRAFFIC International, United Kingdom. 48 pp.

Le Dien Duc and S. Broad. 1995. Investigations into Tortoise and Freshwater Turtle Trade in Vietnam. IUCN Species Survival Commission, IUCN, Gland, Switzerland and Cambridge, UK. 34 pp.

Pritchard, P. C. H. 1997. A new interpretation of Mexican ridley population trends. Marine Turtle Newsletter 76:14–17.

Reinert, H. K. 1991. Translocation as a conservation strategy for amphibians and reptiles: Some comments, concerns, and observations. Herpetologica 47:357–363.

PRESENTED PAPERS

CONSERVATION, RESTORATION, AND MANAGEMENT OF TORTOISES AND TURTLES — AN INTERNATIONAL CONFERENCE

Direct and Indirect Threats to Habitat

CHANGES TO VEGETATION, ANTHROPOGENIC IMPACTS AND HABITAT ALTERATION, IMPACTS OF MILITARY ACTIVITIES

Ronald Marlow (University of Nevada, Reno, Nevada), Brian Butler (Waltham, Massachusetts), Tomás Waller (Buenos Aires, Argentina), James Moore (The Nature Conservancy, Las Vegas, Nevada), Anthony Krzysik (U.S. Army, Champaign, Illinois), Eli Geffen (Tel Aviv University, Israel), Bryan Jennings (University of Texas, Arlington, Texas), and Harold Avery (U.S. Geological Survey, Biological Resources Division, Riverside, California).

Tomás Waller (Buenos Aires, Argentina).

Land Use and Grazing in Relation to the Genus *Geochelone* in Argentina

TOMÁS WALLER AND PATRICIO A. MICUCCI

Zavalia 2090 - 3.B., 1428 Buenos Aires, Argentina [e-mail: curiyu@interserver.com.ar]

ABSTRACT: *Geochelone chilensis* is similar in its ecology to *Gopherus agassizii*. It dwells throughout semi-xerophytic forests (Chaco) and desert scrublands (Monte) subjected to varying levels of human disturbance. Agriculture in these ecosystems is marginal, but it has a drastic impact on *Geochelone* habitat. For several decades forests and deserts throughout the tortoises' range have been affected by free-ranging livestock, mainly goats but also cattle and sheep. Field studies conducted in desert habitats show that tortoises there depend on annual ephemeral plants and the summer fruits of various shrubs. The low densities and biased population structures related to the presence of livestock and the clear evidence of habitat disturbance suggest that free-ranging domestic mammals are threatening tortoise populations. Here, we hypothesize that livestock impacts *Geochelone* in the following ways: (1) domestic animals consume spring ephemerals and summer fruits more efficiently than do tortoises; (2) shrubs are sometimes seriously denuded by foraging and whatever vegetation survives falls prey to local burning practices, thus diminishing the overall diversity of perennials (which rarely recover because of the damage to emerging shoots); (3) fire injures or kills tortoises; and (4) livestock trampling destroys tortoise burrows and results in compacted soil, which also could affect plant regeneration. The end result of these processes is a uniform landscape of low floral diversity and an overall reduction in the quality of primary tortoise habitat. Populations are consequently marginalized to places such as road edges, sand hills, edges of salt lakes, and rugged landscapes where livestock seem to have low impact.

The Patagonian tortoise, *Geochelone donosobarrosi*, was described by Freiberg (1973). Waller et al. (1989) included it together with *G. chilensis* in the "chilensis complex" because of affinities between the two forms. It was synonymized with *G. chilensis* by Buskirk (1993).

Available information on the southern tortoise population is limited to the original description of *G. donosobarrosi* (Freiberg, 1973) and general notes on biology (Ormeño, 1983). It is also included in several taxonomic or distributional lists (King and Burke, 1989; Richard, 1990; Richard et al., 1990). There are practically no data based on field studies. The first studies on the natural history of the tortoises inhabiting the Monte, in a volcanic area in Mendoza province, were published by Richard (1987, 1988) and in Río Negro province, Argentina, by Buskirk (1993).

During field studies conducted between 1987 and 1988 on the ecology of a *G. chilensis* population in Río Negro, serious effects of livestock on the species were evident. Although the initial objective of our research was to study the age structure and sex ratio of the population as well as provide data on relative population density and habitat use, signs of degradation, both in the population and in the habitat, have led us to examine the livestock impact more critically. The purpose of this paper is to describe the ecology of the species in relation to the effects of livestock rearing activities in the area.

METHODS

Research was conducted in Río Negro province, 15 km NNW of San Antonio Oeste (Figure 1), during the months of January (summer), April (autumn), and November (spring) of the years 1987 and 1988. Field studies concentrated upon a sector of approximately 20 hectares in which livestock were not permanently present; however, the area was bordered by areas under intensive grazing by cattle and sheep. Complementary observations were made in a saline environment (Salina del Gualicho, Río Negro—perimeter of a dry salt lake bed) and in a mountainous area in northern Neuquén province west of Catriel. Habitat observations consisted of extensive sampling of dominant plant species and characterizations of soil types and topography.

Preliminary estimates of population density were obtained from a general survey, during which two or three persons searched randomly for tortoises. Tortoises were identified by painting a number on the shell with indelible ink; special or peculiar features were recorded on an individual file card. The following data were recorded on each card: date, time, temperature, relative position within the area, sex, number of growth annuli (rings), carapace length (CL), width, height, head width, weight, presence of malformations, mutilations, external parasites (ticks), and activity. If the tortoise was found in a burrow, burrow width and height were noted to determine correlations between body size and size of burrow. Scats were collected for diet analysis.

Body length was measured using calipers and individuals were weighed. Tortoises were classified as adults or juveniles, and sex was determined on the basis of secondary sexual characteristics, primarily by the presence of a plastral concavity in males (Graham, 1979; Meek, 1985; Stubbs et al., 1985). Age was estimated by counting the number of growth annuli on the third and fourth vertebral scutes. This method has been applied with good results in various chelonian species inhabiting seasonal environments but assumes that each distinguishable annulus is generated by cessation of growth of the laminae of the shell in correspondence with the winter cycles (Graham, 1979; Meek, 1985). Some individuals did not have conspicuous annuli. In these cases, age was estimated using a regression curve (number of rings vs. length) constructed on the basis of the remainder of the specimens that had rings.

Diet was determined by analysis of scats found in each sampling locality. The scats were classified by season and pulverized. The composition was analyzed using two methods: (1) the percentage of scats containing a given diet item, and (2) percentage of each diet item expressed in dry weight. In this way, a species list of plants composing the diet was determined, and the value of each item was related to season. Retreats used by tortoises were analyzed (Chi square test) in relation to topography, soil, and vegetation types. Activity patterns were analyzed (Chi square test) on the basis of the proportion of tortoises found in burrows or above the ground at various times of day or seasons, assuming that tortoises were inactive in burrows.

Morphometric data were analyzed using a one-way ANOVA, Mann-Whitney test, and regression curves to detect secondary sexual dimorphic characters and other aspects related to individual growth. Malformations were recorded following Zangerl and Johnson (1957); the presence of sex-associated malformations was analyzed using Chi square. To increase the size of the sample, some animals from neighbouring areas were included in the analysis.

RESULTS AND DISCUSSION

Habitat

The sector of approximately 20 hectares is bordered on the east by a paved road and on the north and west by a fence that keeps livestock out. It is situated on a somewhat rolling plain, almost at sea level, in the southern portion of the Monte Phytogeographic and Biogeographic Province (Cabrera, 1971; Cabrera and Willink, 1980). According to the *Mapa de la vegetación de América del Sur* (UNESCO Vegetation Map for South America, 1981), the vegetation community is dry or temperate-deciduous scrub, representing an ecotone between the Patagonian steppe and the scrubland of the Monte region. The area of study was characterized by a sparse vegetation cover with a predominance of shrubs and isolated tufts of Poaceae [= Gramineae]; the most frequent shrub was jarilla, *Larrea divaricata*. Dominant plant species are listed in Table 1. The area is traversed in a S–N direction by a wash almost devoid of soil cover and by a series of small, parallel berms which constitute micro-topographical land features. The soil is sandy with a low percentage of clay and with abundant rounded pebbles. Mean annual temperature for San Antonio Oeste is 15.3°C with an absolute minimum of -7.5°C and a recorded high of 41.7°C. Annual mean rainfall is 245 mm with minor peaks in the spring and fall. Average relative

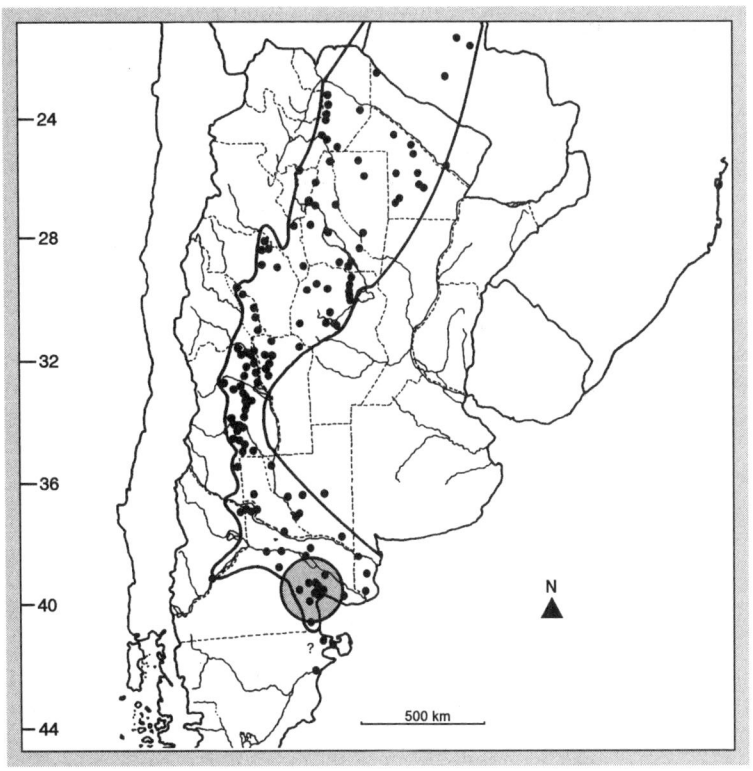

Figure 1. Distribution of *G. chilensis* complex. Field study site lies within shaded area. The southernmost locality records for the species (province of Chubut, "?") represent probable human introductions.

humidity is 58% (data for 1961–70 provided by the National Meteorological Service). The conservation status of this small sector is exceptionally good given the almost continuous absence of livestock. There is a marked difference in the landscape between this livestock-free sector and that on the other side of the fence now under intensive livestock rearing. This difference is reflected in three main features: (1) the lower diversity of shrubs and perennial plants in the area with livestock, (2) the scarce vegetation

TABLE 1
Main plant species in study site.

Shrubs	Other
Fabaceae (= Leguminosae)	Cactaceae
Cassia aphylla	*Cereus aethiops*
Geoffroea decorticans	*Echinopsis* sp.
Prosopis alpataco	Poaceae (= Gramineae)
Zigophyllaceae	*Bromus brevis*
Larrea cuneifolia	*Hordeum euclaston*
Larrea divaricata	*Poa lanuginosa*
Solanaceae	*Schismus barbatus*
Lycium chilensis	*Stipa speciosa*
Lycium gillesianum	*Stipa tenuis*
Lycium tenuispinosum	Malvaceae
Scrophulariaceae	*Sphaeralcea mendocina*
Monttea aphylla	Plantaginaceae
Anacardaceae	*Plantago patagonica*
Schinus polygamus	Asteraceae (= Compositae)
Nyctaginaceae	*Senecio subulatum*
Bougainvillea spinosa	*Senecio filaginoides*
Asteraceae (= Compositae)	*Senecio goldsacki*
Chuquiraga hystrix	*Hyalis argentea*
Gutierrezia spatulata	Fabaceae (= Leguminoseae)
Capparaceae	*Hoffmanseggia trifoliata*
Atamisquea emarginata	*Goldmania paraguensis*
Rhamnaceae	Apiaceae (= Umbelliferae)
Condalia microphylla	*Daucus pucillus*

cover of certain spring ephemeral species such as plantain, *Plantago patagonica*, in the area with livestock, and (3) a high degree of soil trampling in the disrupted area.

Population Structure

The carapace length and the number of growth annuli were positively and significantly correlated (F = 302.0, $P < 0.01$, $r^2 = 0.91$, n = 33) so that age could be estimated based on non-distinguishable annuli. Thus, it was possible to assess population structure (Figure 2). Most specimens (86.4%) were presumably more than 20 years of age (length more than 170 mm; N = 59). The adult/subadult ratio was 7.4:1 (n = 59) and the sex ratio was 1.1:1 (n = 52) favouring males. Taking into account that reproductive animals would be more than 20 cm in length, the low percentage of hatchlings, subadults, and young adults is noteworthy. The low capture rate of hatchlings may be attributed to difficulties in locating very small animals, but this bias seems insufficient to account for the scarcity of young adults and subadults. The observed age structure, biased toward adult animals, suggests that the juvenile age classes are not replacing adult classes, thus indicating a declining trend in the population. A similar age class distribution was observed previously in this species in Mendoza province (Richard, 1987, 1988) as well as in other tortoise species such as *Testudo hermanni* in Yugoslavia and Greece and *T. graeca* in northern Africa (Meek, 1985). The North American *Gopherus agassizii*, a species very similar to *G. chilensis*, reportedly includes populations with 40–90% adults. The highest figure corresponds to a population that had been severely depleted because of human intervention, yet populations of this species have decreased over its entire range (Luckenbach, 1982).

Relative Density

Preliminarily estimated relative density, by means of counting and marking tortoises, is 3–4 individuals/hectare (60–80 specimens in the 20 ha area). This represents a base value as it has no statistical significance because of the methodology used in the survey (the smaller age classes are underestimated and variation caused by occasional movement of individuals is not accounted for). However, this preliminary density estimate is high compared to that of *G. agassizii*, which has a current density of <1 individual/hectare (Luckenbach, 1982). It is somewhat low compared with preliminary census in Mendoza province (1–11 individuals/ha, Richard, 1987). Nevertheless, the area was relatively protected from livestock, and this sector probably plays an important role as a refuge for tortoises from the margins of the studied area, especially taking into account its floristic richness compared with neighbouring areas. Efforts to find tortoises in the adjacent areas in which livestock was kept were completely unsuccessful. The density in adjacent areas affected by the presence of livestock must be extremely low. The potential for error when extrapolating observed densities to other areas is clearly evident, especially as prevailing conditions in the study area are apparently exceptional.

Burrows

Subadults and adult tortoises dig burrows that they use as a refuge during the night or during periods of peak solar radiation. Burrows usually have a depth of 50–60 cm, but we found dens several meters deep.* No significant relationship was found between the dimensions of the entrance of the burrow and the size of the individual inhabiting it (tortoise height vs. burrow height, $r^2 = 0.024$, F = 0.55, $P = 0.47$, n = 24; tortoise width vs. burrow width, $r^2 = 0.11$, F = 2.7, $P = 0.11$, n = 25). This suggests that tortoises shift from one burrow to another, using several burrows per season (an activity we actually observed).

Sixty-two percent of active burrows (those in which tortoises were found) were constructed against small earthen

---

*Burrows are usually short (<0.8 m deep) and constructed in sandy soil at the beginning of each spring; dens are deeper (usually >2 m), constructed in hard soil (limestone), are more durable, and are used over several seasons, apparently also communally as winter refuges.

mounds or berms, 22.1% on flat ground, and 13.8% against limestone banks (usually dens); differences between these habitats were significant (Chi square = 38.8, $P < 0.01$). Of the active burrows, 62.2% were found under or close to jarilla shrubs (*Larrea* spp.), 31% with no associated vegetation, and the remaining 6.9% under molle shrubs, *Schinus polygamus*. These differences were also significant (Chi square = 45.9, $P < 0.01$).

Tortoises showed a clear preference for constructing burrows under jarilla scrub, possibly as a means of obtaining protection from solar radiation or achieving the additional firmness of burrow walls provided by the root system of the shrub. Tortoises also seemed to prefer berms or earth mounds, abundant in the study area, for digging burrows and avoided adjacent zones for this purpose. This topographical feature, in addition to floral diversity, favours tortoise concentration within the sector studied (Figure 3).

Active burrows were not detected in areas close to those with livestock. The few burrows identified in such sectors had been abandoned. The entire area with livestock showed signs of extensive trampling. The presence of livestock seems to be a factor adversely affecting burrows, as is reportedly the case for *G. agassizii* (Berry, 1978; Avery, this volume) and as suggested for Patagonian tortoises in Mendoza province by Richard (1987).

Activity Pattern

Considering activity records for all sampling stations jointly, activity was significantly greater in the hours before midday: 72.9% of active tortoises were recorded before 1200 hrs whereas only 16.3% were active after 1200 hrs

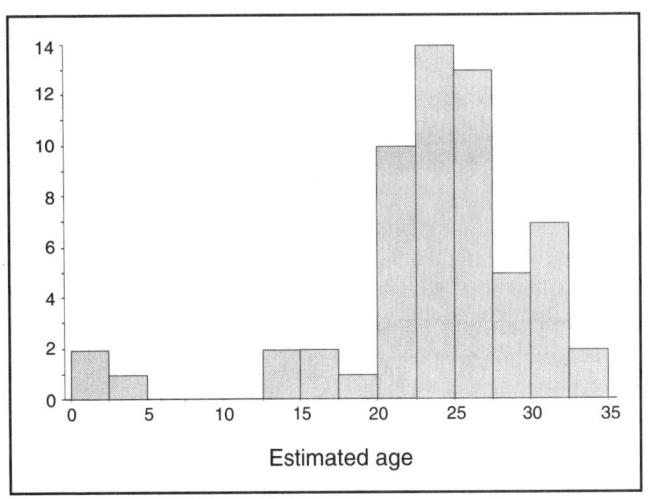

Figure 2. Population structure (estimated age, n = 59).

(Chi square corr. = 27, $P < 0.01$, n = 91). Activity was greater during the spring (64.6%) compared with summer (25.6%) (Chi square corr. = 12.4, $P < 0.01$, n = 48).

Differences between daily and seasonal activity (greatest in the morning hours and particularly high during the spring) indicate a tendency to avoid the noon heat and high summer temperatures. No activity was recorded in the early fall, a fact that can be attributed to low temperatures. On the other hand, investment in foraging activities is maximised during the spring because of higher availability of forage (which provides additional water and larger amounts of usable material), whereas it tends to decrease in the summer when available forage consists only of dry grasses (hemicryptophytes) and some fruits.

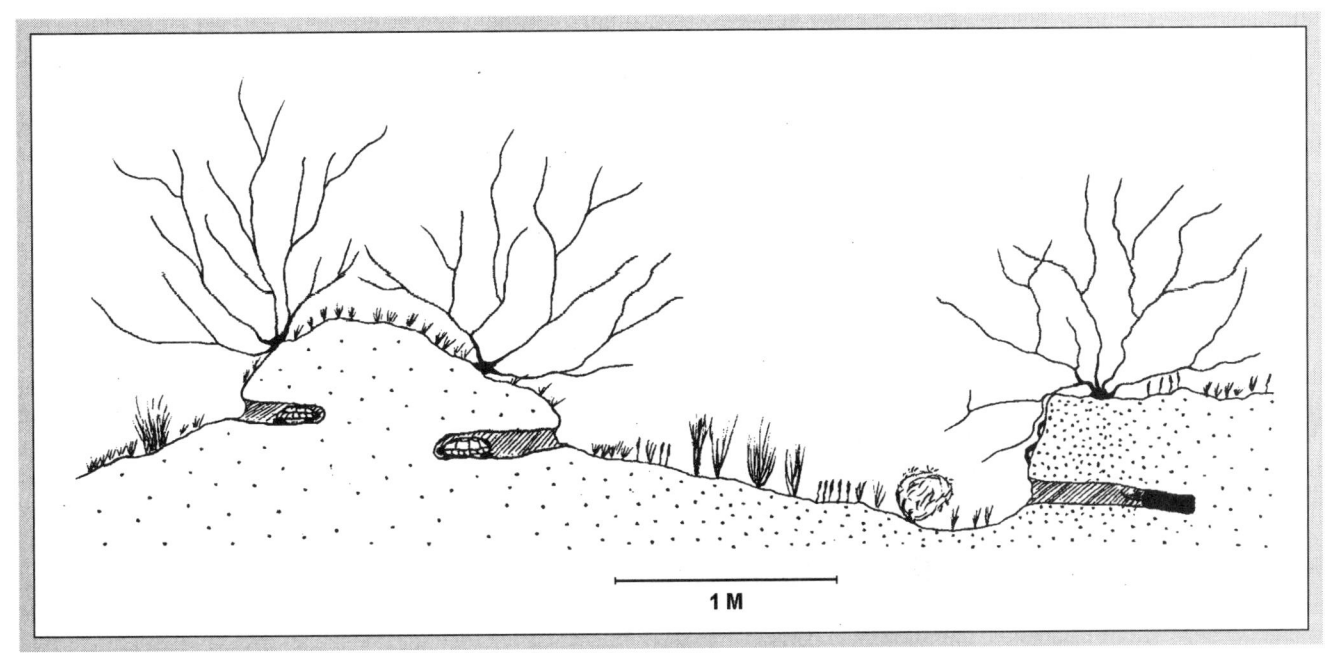

Figure 3. Schematic representation of tortoise microhabitat in Río Negro, Argentina.

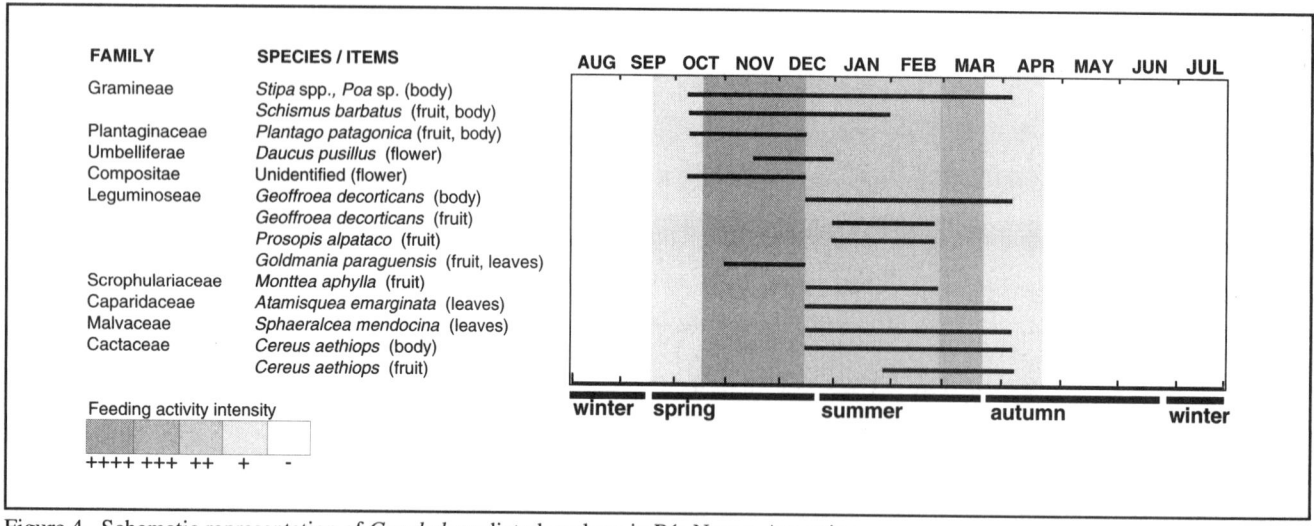

Figure 4. Schematic representation of *Geochelone* diet phenology in Río Negro, Argentina.

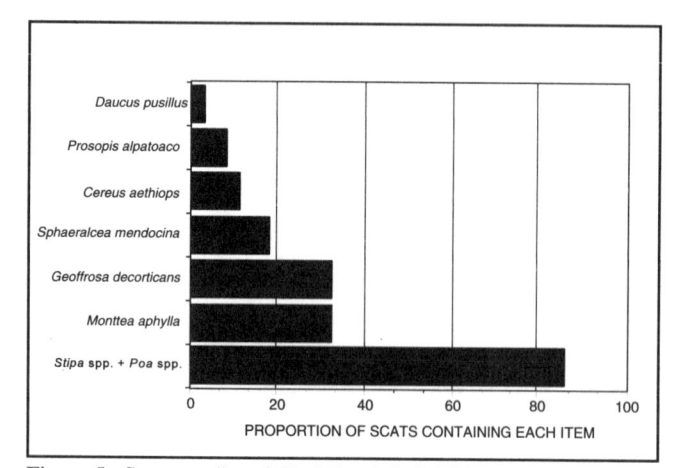

Figure 5. Summer diet of *G. chilensis* in Río Negro, Argentina.

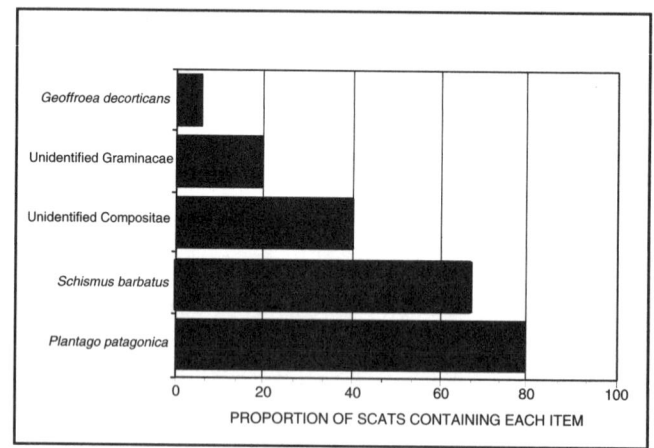

Figure 6. Spring diet of *G. chilensis* in Río Negro, Argentina.

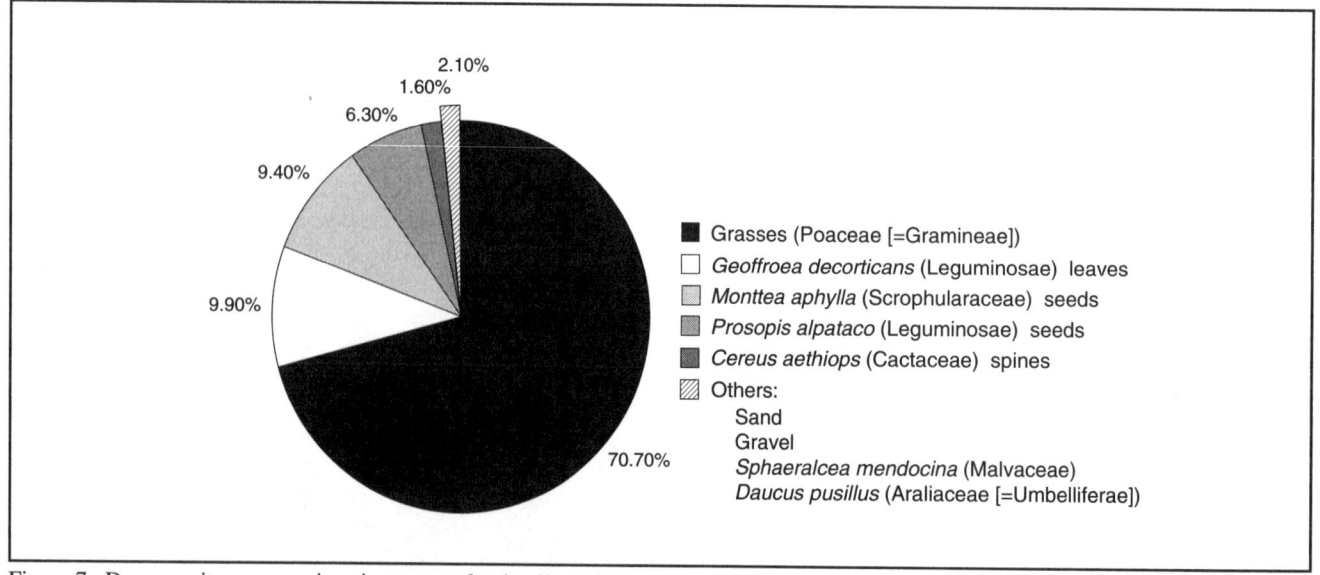

Figure 7. Dry mass item proportions in summer fecal pellets of *G. chilensis* in Río Negro, Argentina.

Diet

Diet composition was assessed on the basis of frequency of the different items found in scats (n = 77) collected during spring and summer; differences in specific composition between seasons were found to occur (Figures 4, 5, and 6). Figure 7 shows the incidence of certain items by weight for the summer months. Results show the amount of Poaceae (= Gramineae) in both seasons, although different species were involved: In spring, Poaceae are represented by the ephemeral *Schismus barbatus*, whereas in the summer the preferred items are the dry stems of *Stipa* and *Poa*. During this season, the latter two are in a vegetative stage and while readily consumed, are of less nutritional value.

In the spring, tortoises feed mainly on the ephemeral plantain, *Plantago patagonica*. This herb also is preferred by livestock as forage and is almost absent from overgrazed areas. Río Negro tortoises seem to depend on the abundance of plantain during the spring. A great degree of dietary overlap in the spring has also been reported in Arizona, where both *G. agassizii* and cattle ate plantain as well as other ephemerals (Hohman and Ohmart, unpubl. report, *in* Oldemeyer, 1994). A decrease in food availability could result in a lower fitness (lower growth rate and reduced breeding activity) as has also been reported for *G. agassizii* in California (Luckenbach, 1982). Should the relationship between seasonal ephemerals of Río Negro and *G. chilensis* be confirmed, grazing by livestock (which has competitive advantages for grazing on *P. patagonica*) could be one of the causes for apparently declining population trends in this tortoise.

In the summer the tortoises' diet is composed of Poaceae and fruits of bushes such as *Monttea aphylla* and *Prosopis alpataco*. However, analyses based on dry weight tend to underestimate ingested volumes of certain fruits and succulents because only seeds and non-digestible fibers are assessed while the soft portions are lost during digestion. The large proportion of seeds of *Monttea aphylla*, a fleshy fruit, would indicate a high incidence of this species in the summer diet. In the area subjected to livestock grazing, no fruits were found lying on the ground. Fruits were absent even from the lower portions of plants because they are consumed by livestock in large amounts.

A common practice in the region associated with grazing practices is the burning of fields to favour the growth of new shoots and to eliminate shrubs. Species such as *Geoffroea decorticans* and *Monttea aphylla*, whose fruits are part of the diet of *G. chilensis* in the summer, were practically absent from neighbouring areas with livestock. Their absence could be attributed to the historical sequence of fires followed by intense grazing. Most of the shrubs, once established, are not likely to be destroyed by grazing; however, livestock may inhibit regeneration by consuming sprouts. Burning practices bring about extensive destruction of shrubs, which fail to regenerate because of livestock grazing on new shoots. Finally, a homogeneous landscape of low diversity ensues, composed mainly of non-palatable species such as *Larrea divaricata* and annuals that invade the zone from neighbouring areas. A similar pattern of habitat degradation has been described in Mendoza province by Richard (1987).

Morphometry, Mutilations, and Malformations

Female mean adult carapace length (236.3 mm, range 210–275) was significantly greater than that of males (201.3 mm, range 184–239) (ANOVA, F = 107.8, $P < 0.01$, n = 69), whereas the latter had proportionately larger heads. The carapace length/head width relationship was significantly lower in males (5.4) than in females (6.2) (Mann-Whitney test, Z = –4.49, $P < 0.01$, n = 34). Thirty-five percent of the specimens (n = 59) had slight malformations of the scutes of the carapace, with a predominance of supernumerary marginal scutes (type IV in Zangerl and Johnson, 1957). No correlations between these malformations and sex was observed (Chi square corr. = 0.04, $P = 0.85$, n = 53). The frequency of benign teratogenies could indicate the existence of potentially lethal ones, which could adversely affect the individual during its embryonic development. According to Lynn and Ulrich (1959), such malformations seemingly are related to variations in humidity or water stress during ontogeny. However, Richard and de Richard (1986) have stressed the importance of malformations as indicators of possible soil structure disruption derived from livestock trampling. Fifteen percent of the specimens showed some sort of mutilation, mostly of a mechanical nature because of predation (loss of limbs), physiological or unknown reasons (perforations of the carapace, peeling of epidermal scutes), or burning (2.1%) (n = 93) (Figure 8). Fires deliberately set in the area seem to affect mainly juveniles. Individuals from this age class frequently seek refuge under small tufts of grass or shrubs, thus becoming more vulnerable to fire.

Figure 8. Adult female Patagonian tortoise with burn injuries.

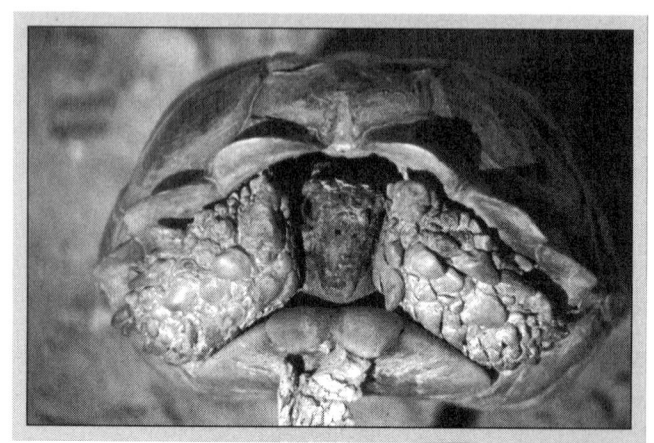

Figure 9. Forelimbs of an adult male tortoise showing hypertrophied scales.

Figure 10. Adult female tortoise showing normal forelimbs.

Figure 11. Adult female Patagonian tortoise in its sandy habitat.

Adult males (89.2%) had a characteristic and almost universal scarring of the front scales of the forelimbs as a result of aggressive encounters with other males (Figure 9). On the other hand, only 2.4% of females had such injuries. The hypothesis that these abnormalities, not reported for Chaco populations of *G. chilensis*, could be a result of increased competition in an impoverished environment has been suggested (K. Berry, pers. comm.). From a practical point of view, these deformities typically found in males, the proportionately larger head in males, and males' smaller size are secondary sexual characters that facilitate determination of sex. In contrast with populations of similar species inhabiting central and northern Argentina (Richard, 1988), no infestation by ticks was found in Patagonian populations. The only commensal repeatedly encountered in burrows with tortoises was the spider *Sicarius rupestris*.

Conclusions

Although restricted to specific areas (so-called "cultivation oases"), the impact of land cultivation is often dramatic because the natural native community becomes artificial as a result of this activity. On the other hand, the entire southern range of *G. chilensis* is subjected to grazing by goats, sheep, cattle, or horses, depending on the degree of aridity and topographic conditions. Livestock may therefore have a wide variety of effects depending on the type of animal, number of animals per hectare, and the characteristics of each environment that may mitigate or intensify disruptions.

During the period of study, three possible impacts of livestock on a southern *G. chilensis* population were identified: (1) direct competition for ephemerals in spring and for fruits in summer, (2) physical-mechanical soil alterations affecting plant regeneration and the construction of burrows, and (3) successional changes in plant communities induced by livestock rearing and associated management practices (fires). We believe that current levels and methods of livestock rearing are a major conservation problem for *G. chilensis*. Because it is a common practice over the entire southern geographic range of the species and because most of these scrublands have been classified by land management offices as suffering from the effects of "severe" or "destructive" overgrazing, the conservation impacts of livestock rearing deserve further investigation. Results of studies on the North American desert tortoise, *Gopherus agassizii*, inhabiting a remarkably similar environment and with strikingly analogous habits, whose populations have been severely depleted, underscore the importance of assessing and quantifying the effects of livestock rearing activities on southern *G. chilensis* populations before it is too late.

ACKNOWLEDGEMENTS

This work was made possible by the financial support of the Kantonaler Zürcher Tierschutzverein (Switzerland) and the continuous encouragement of Mr. René Honegger (Curator of Herpetology, Zürich Zoo), to whom we are greatly indebted. Prof. Zumilda Aurora Manuel, from the Vegetation and Soils Agency of Río Negro province, aided in the taxonomic identification of plant species. We also wish to express our gratitude to Michael W. Klemens for sponsoring the presentation of our paper during Conservation, Restoration, and Management of Tortoises and Turtles—An International Conference, held in Purchase, New York in July 1993; to the editor of this volume, Jim Van Abbema, for his patience and helpful suggestions; to Victoria Lichtschein for reviewing and translating the manuscript; and to the anonymous reviewers for their valuable comments.

LITERATURE CITED

Avery, H. W. and A. G. Neibergs. 1997. Effects of cattle grazing on the desert tortoise, *Gopherus agassizii*: Nutritional and behavioral interactions. *In* J. Van Abbema (ed.), Proceedings: Conservation, Restoration, and Management of Tortoises and Turtles—An International Conference, pp. 13–20. July 1993, State University of New York, Purchase. New York Turtle and Tortoise Society, New York.

Berry, K. H. 1978. Livestock grazing and the desert tortoise. Transactions of the 43rd North American Wildlife and Natural Resources Conference. Wildlife Management Institute, Washington, D.C.

Bury, R. B. (ed.) 1982. North American tortoises: Conservation and ecology. Wildlife Research Report 12, U.S. Department of the Interior, U.S. Fish and Wildlife Service, Washington, D.C. 126 pp.

Buskirk, J. R. 1993. Distribution, status and biology of the tortoise, *Geochelone chilensis*, in Río Negro province, Argentina. Studies on Neotropical Fauna and Environment 28(4):233–249. Lisse.

Cabrera, A. L. 1971. Fitogeografía de la República Argentina. Bol. Soc. Arg. Botánica 14(1–2):1–42. Buenos Aires.

Cabrera, A. L. and A. Willink. 1980. Biogeografía de América Latina. OEA, Washington, D.C. 122 pp.

Davis, E. D. and R. L. Winstead. 1980. Estimación de tamaños de poblaciones de vida silvestre. *In* R. Rodríguez Tarres (ed.), Manual de Técnicas de Gestión de Vida Silvestre, pp. 233–258. WWF, Washington, D.C.

Freiberg, M. A. 1973. Dos nuevas tortugas terrestres de Argentina. Bol. Soc. Biol. Concepción 46:81–93. Chile.

Graham, T. E. 1979. Life history techniques. *In* M. Harless and H. Morlock (eds.), Turtles: Perspectives and Research, pp. 73–95. John Wiley & Sons, Inc., New York.

Harless, M. and H. Morlock (eds.). 1979. Turtles: Perspectives and Research. John Wiley & Sons, Inc., New York. 693 pp.

King, F. W. and R. L. Burke (eds.). 1989. Crocodilian, Tuatara and Turtle Species of the World. A taxonomic and geographic reference. Association of Systematics Collections, Washington, D.C. 216 pp.

Luckenbach, R. A. 1982. Ecology and management of the desert tortoise (*Gopherus agassizii*) in California. *In* R. B. Bury (ed.), North American Tortoises: Conservation and Ecology, pp. 1–37. Wildlife Research Report 12, USDI-USFWS, Washington, D.C.

Lynn, W. G. and M. C. Ullrich. 1950. Experimental production of shell abnormalities in turtles. Copeia 1950(4):253–262.

Meek, R. 1985. Aspects of the ecology of *Testudo hermanni* in southern Yugoslavia. Brit. J. Herpetol. 6:437–445.

Morafka, D. J. and C. J. McCoy. 1988. The ecogeography of the Mexican Bolson tortoise (*Gopherus flavomarginatus*): Derivation of its endangered status and recommendations for its conservation. Ann. Carnegie Mus. 57(1):1–72.

Oldemeyer, J. L. 1994. Livestock grazing and the desert tortoise in the Mojave Desert. *In* R. B. Bury and D. J. Germano (eds.), Biology of North American Tortoises, pp. 95–103. Fish and Wildlife Research 13, Technical Report Series, U.S. Department of the Interior, National Biological Survey, Washington, D.C.

Ormeño, E. A. 1983. Distribución de la tortuga terrestre *Geochelone chilensis* (Gray) en la provincia de Mendoza. Deserta 7:179–182. Mendoza, Argentina.

Richard, E. 1987. Notas ecológicas sobre *Chelonoidis donosobarrosi* (Freiberg, 1973) (Chelonii: Testudinidae) en el sur de la provincia de Mendoza (República Argentina). Acta Zool. Lilloana 41:349–356. Tucumán.

Richard, E. 1988. Las "Yatache" (*Chelonoidis donosobarrosi*: Chelonii, Testudinidae) de la región del Nevado (Mendoza, Argentina). Apuntes sobre su historia natural. FVSA-Amp. y Rept. (cons.) 1(4):79–92. Buenos Aires.

Richard, E. 1990. Elementos descriptivos para la identificación de las tortugas argentinas. Fac. Cs. Nats. e Inst. Miguel Lillo, Serie Monográfica y Didáctica 7:31–43.

Richard, E. and P. B. de Richard. 1986. Análisis causal de la ocurrencia de anormalidades en la caparazón de tortugas argentinas. Res. III Jorn. Cientif. Soc. Biol. Tucumán 34. Tucumán.

Richard, E., P. E. Belmonte, and J. C. Chebez. 1990. Nombres vernáculos y distribución geográfica de las tortugas argentinas. Fac. Cs. Nats. e Inst. Miguel Lillo, Serie Monográfica y Didáctica 7:1–30.

Ricker, W. E. 1975. Computation and Interpretation of Biological Statistics of Fish Populations. Fish. Res. Bd. Canada Bul. 191. 382 pp.

Servicio Meteorológico Nacional. 1985. Estadística Climatológica 1961–70. Buenos Aires. 188 pp.

Stubbs, D., A. Hailey, E. Pulford, and W. Tyler. 1984. Population ecology of European tortoises: Review of field techniques. Amphibia-Reptilia 5:57–68. Leiden.

UNESCO. 1981. Mapa de la vegetación de América del Sur. Investigaciones sobre los recursos naturales 17. Paris. 189 pp.

Waller, T., P. A. Micucci, and E. Richard. 1989. Preliminary results of the research on the biology, ecology, and conservation of the *Chelonoidis chilensis* (sensu lato) (Gray, 1870) tortoise in Argentina (Testudines: Testudinidae). KZT-TRAFFIC Sudamérica—Secretaría CITES, Buenos Aires. 22 pp. Unpubl. report.

Zangerl, R. and R. G. Johnson. 1957. The nature of shield abnormalities in the turtle shell. Fieldiana Geology, Chicago Nat. Hist. Mus. 10(29):341–362.

Invasions of Exotic Plants: Implications for the Desert Tortoise, *Gopherus agassizii*, and Its Habitat in the Western Mojave Desert

W. BRYAN JENNINGS

Department of Biology, University of Texas, Arlington, TX 76019, USA
Current address: Department of Zoology, University of Texas at Austin, Austin, TX 78712, USA
[e-mail: jennings@mail.utexas.edu]

ABSTRACT: Populations of the desert tortoise, *Gopherus agassizii*, in the western Mojave Desert of California have declined precipitously over the past few decades. Many factors may be associated with the ongoing decline, including the anthropogenically induced proliferation of exotic plants. Exotic plant invasions may negatively affect tortoises by reducing or eliminating important food plants through competition, by altering tortoise nutrition, and by altering the landscape through fire.

The desert tortoise, *Gopherus agassizii*, is a "Threatened" species throughout approximately 30% of its geographic range (U.S. Fish and Wildlife Service [USFWS], 1994; Berry, this volume). In some portions of its range, such as the western Mojave Desert, populations have declined precipitously due to a myriad of causes, including the invasion of exotic plants.

Exotic plant species appear to have arrived in the western Mojave Desert with the early settlers in the late 1880s and early 1900s. The exotic plants came from Europe and Asia and include the annual grasses *Schismus arabicus*, *S. barbatus*, *Bromus madritensis* ssp. *rubens* and *B. tectorum*, and the forb *Erodium cicutarium* (USFWS, 1994). The exotic plants most likely spread through urban and agricultural development of desert lands as well as by roads, utility lines, livestock grazing, and other anthropogenic disturbances (e.g., see U.S. Bureau of Land Management, 1980). Since the 1960s, recreational off-road vehicle (ORV) use has been another source of land disturbances (Busack and Bury, 1974; Bury et al., 1977; Campbell, 1981, 1982; Luckenbach, 1982), and sheep grazing has continually disturbed soils and vegetation, which has contributed to the spread of exotics (Busack and Bury, 1974; Nicholson and Humphreys, 1981). Exotic species of annuals now comprise a significant portion of the ephemeral vegetation (Webb and Stielstra, 1979; Nicholson and Humphreys, 1981; Rowlands, 1990; Jennings, 1993; Brooks, 1995).

Invasions of exotic plants may pose threats to desert tortoises by competitively reducing or excluding important native forage species, compromising nutrition and health, and by contributing to the frequency and severity of fires in a region where fire was previously rare (USFWS, 1994). D'Antonio and Vitousek (1992) noted that second to changes in land use, "biological invasions have caused more extinctions than have resulted from human-caused climatic change or the changing composition of the atmosphere."

Effects of Sheep and Off-Road Vehicles on Desert Tortoise Habitat

Sheep grazing and ORVs probably have had the most pervasive impact on the western Mojave Desert since the 1960s. Both types of activities affect large areas and result in loss of vegetation and altered soil characteristics (Woodbury and Hardy, 1948; Bury et al., 1977; Berry, 1978; Webb and Stielstra, 1979; Nicholson and Humphreys, 1981; Rowlands, 1990). These disturbances further enhance invasions of exotic plants by (1) removing native vegetation, which reduces competition for water and nutrients (Bock et al., 1986; Medina, 1988); and (2) creating soil disturbances that favor exotic plants (Davidson and Fox, 1974; Webb and Stielstra, 1979; Holland and Kiel, 1989). Livestock grazing has been implicated in the alteration of vegetation and proliferation of exotic plants elsewhere in the West (e.g., Young and Evans, 1971; Mack, 1981; West, 1988; Billings, 1990; D'Antonio and Vitousek, 1992).

Exotic plant invasions can alter the frequency and intensity of fires (Van Wilgen and Richardson, 1985; MacDonald and Frame, 1988; Smith and Tunison, 1992). Not only have grass-dominated systems greatly increased risk of fire, they can also set in motion a grass/fire cycle—a phenomenon in which both grasses and fire are increased synergistically (D'Antonio and Vitousek, 1992). Overall, the disturbances and exotic plants contribute to deterioration and degradation of the desert tortoise habitat (USFWS, 1994).

Foraging Ecology of Desert Tortoises in the Western Mojave

Tortoises in the western Mojave Desert are dietary specialists and feed primarily upon succulent ephemeral vegetation (Berry, 1978; Jennings and Fontenot, 1993; Jennings, 1993; Spangenberg, 1994). Most of the preferred foods—*Astragalus didymocarpus*, *A. layneae*, *Euphorbia albomar-*

ginata, Lotus humistratus, Lygodesmia exigua, and *Mirabilis bigelovii*—are locally uncommon (Jennings, 1993). However, tortoises systematically locate these plants, which grow in characteristic areas. For example, *Astragalus layneae* and *Euphorbia albomarginata* are restricted to the margins of small washes (approx. 1 m wide), and tortoises locate them by traveling up or down the washes. Similarly, tortoises locate *Lotus humistratus, A. didymocarpus, Lygodesmia exigua*, and *Mirabilis bigelovii* by searching low gravelly/rocky hills.

Legumes and herbaceous perennials are important dietary constituents (43% and 30% of adult tortoise diets respectively, Jennings, 1993) in this region. The leguminous species (e.g., *Lotus* and *Astragalus* spp.) are probably important because of their high nutritional values, and the herbaceous perennials (e.g., *Astragalus layneae, Mirabilis bigelovii*, and *Euphorbia albomarginata*) may play an important role during drought years.

The temporal and spatial variation in distribution of food plants influences diet, seasonal movements, and locations and types of cover sites of the tortoises (Jennings, 1993). For example, early in spring tortoises almost exclusively use shrubs as cover sites, whereas later in spring they show strong fidelity to permanent burrows located next to "patches" (approx. 100–600 m²) of preferred food plants such as *Lotus humistratus* or *Lygodesmia exigua*.

Loss of preferred foods can have deleterious effects. Most preferred plant species are distributed in patches within the habitat, which may serve as focal points for tortoise activities (e.g., foraging and social interactions). Extirpation of these patchy resources may not only result in deprivation of preferred foods but may also disrupt or preclude social activities.

Tortoises may congregate at patches of high-value native forage plants, which also affords the opportunity for courtship and mating. In spring 1992 I observed the interactions of three tortoises at the Desert Tortoise Research Natural Area. In mid-May a large male tortoise (269 mm carapace length, 4.04 kg) was observed using an old burrow at the edge of a *Lotus* patch for the two-week period when the *Lotus* was flowering. Each day the tortoise visited the patch and fed exclusively upon *Lotus* before returning to the same burrow. Concurrently an adult female was also observed using an old burrow on the edge of the same *Lotus* patch. A week later, a subadult male (195 mm carapace length, 1.4 kg) appeared at the patch and began to feed upon *Lotus*. The larger male attacked the smaller male, which subsequently left the area. A few days later the large male mated with the female at the patch. It is possible that the large male tortoise may have used the old burrow previously and may have also previously defended the *Lotus* patch. In any case, the *Lotus* served as a setting for the observed social interactions.

Potential Effects of Exotic Annual Plants on Desert Tortoises and Their Habitats

The invasion of exotic plants in the western Mojave Desert has several adverse implications for desert tortoise populations. Recent research has revealed that desert tortoises are highly selective feeders and that they have evolved behaviors that allow them to locate rare food plants. Therefore, reduction or extirpation of the native plant species through competition with exotic plants could be detrimental to their well-being. Such an occurrence would not be unprecedented. The exotic grass *Eragrostis lehmanniana* has replaced many native Sonoran Desert plants, which has caused local declines in native bird and insect species (Bock et al., 1986; Medina, 1988). Similarly, the alien beach grass *Ammophila arenaria* has replaced several native dune plants, causing precipitous declines and extinction in some native insect species (Slobodchikoff and Doyen, 1977).

Tortoises occasionally consume exotic plants, and some have argued that tortoises could subsist on an exotic plant diet in the event their preferred native foods became unavailable. However, the negative correlation between exotic grass cover and native plant diversity or growth is well established (D'Antonio and Vitousek, 1992). If tortoises depend on a complex association of plant species for a nutritionally balanced diet, the elimination of even those food species that are consumed infrequently may negatively affect tortoises. Recent research has shown that the annual exotic grasses, *Schismus* sp., may be relatively deficient in key nutrients and may contain higher levels of metals than native plants (H. Avery, pers. comm.). High quantities of exotic plants in the habitat may compromise the health of the tortoises, thus rendering them susceptible to disease. The potential links between habitat quality, nutrition, and upper respiratory tract disease in desert tortoises have been described by Jacobson et al. (1991).

Perhaps the most significant consequence of invasions of exotic grasses in the western Mojave Desert is the increased frequency and severity of fires (USFWS, 1994). Fire was formerly a rare event in the Mojave Desert, even as recently as 30 years ago, and the native flora is not adapted to fire regimes. Thus habitat damage is often severe.

CONCLUSION

Exotic plants are now a significant component of the ephemeral vegetation in the western Mojave Desert, which has numerous implications for desert tortoises. These include competitive exclusion of food plants, altered nutrition, disturbance of social behavior, and a new-found fire hazard. Although these studies were conducted in the western Mojave Desert, they may be applicable to other desert tortoise populations as well as other tortoise species living in arid regions. Because disturbances to the habitat largely contribute to these exotic plant invasions, it is possible that if such disturbances are halted, habitats may stabilize or improve (Brooks, 1995).

ACKNOWLEDGMENTS

I would like to thank Dr. Michael Klemens and Dr. Kristin Berry for inviting me to participate in this conference and Jim Van Abbema for his invaluable assistance. The U.S. Bureau of Land Management supported research on the foraging ecology and habitat utilization of the desert tortoise under Contract No. B950-C2-0014.

LITERATURE CITED

Berry, K. H. 1978. Livestock grazing and the desert tortoise. Transactions of the 43rd North American Wildlife and Natural Resources Conference, 1978, Wildlife Management Institute, Washington D.C.

Berry, K. H. 1997. The desert tortoise recovery plan: An ambitious effort to conserve biodiversity in the Mojave and Colorado deserts of the United States. *In* J. Van Abbema (ed.), Proceedings: Conservation, Restoration, and Management of Tortoises and Turtles —An International Conference, pp. 430–440. July 1993, Purchase, New York. New York Turtle and Tortoise Society, New York.

Billings, W. D. 1990. *Bromus tectorum*, a biotic cause of ecosystem impoverishment in the Great Basin. *In* G. M. Woodell (ed.), The Earth in Transition: Patterns and Processes of Biotic Impoverishment, pp. 301–322. Cambridge Univ. Press, Cambridge and New York.

Bock, C. E., J. H. Bock, K. L. Jepson, and J. C. Ortega. 1986. Ecological effects of planting African lovegrasses in Arizona. Nat. Geogr. Res. 2(4):456–463.

Brooks, M. L. 1995. Benefits of protective fencing to plant and rodent communities of the western Mojave Desert, California. Environ. Manage. 19(1):65–74.

Bury, R. B., R. A. Luckenbach, and S. D. Busack. 1977. Effects of off-road vehicles on vertebrates in the California desert. U.S.D.I. Fish and Wildlife Service, Wildlife Research Report 8, Washington D.C.

Busack, S. D. and R. B. Bury. 1974. Some effects of off-road vehicles and sheep grazing on lizard populations in the Mojave Desert. Biol. Conserv. 6(3):179–183.

Campbell, T. 1981. Some effects of recreational activities at the Desert Tortoise Natural Area. Proc. Desert Tortoise Council Symp. 1981:121–127.

Campbell, T. 1982. Hunting and other activities on and near the Desert Tortoise Natural Area, eastern Kern County, California. Proc. Desert Tortoise Council Symp. 1982:90–98.

D'Antonio, C. M. and P. M. Vitousek. 1992. Biological invasions by exotic grasses, the grass/fire cycle, and global change. Annu. Rev. Ecol. Syst. 23:63–87.

Davidson, E. and M. Fox. 1974. Effects of off-road motorcycle activity on Mojave Desert vegetation and soil. Madroño 22(8):381–412.

Jacobson, E. R., J. M. Gaskin, M. B. Brown, R. K. Harris, C. H. Gardiner, J. L. LaPointe, H. P. Adams, and C. Reggiardo. 1991. Chronic upper respiratory tract disease of free-ranging desert tortoises (*Xerobates agassizii*). J. Wildl. Dis. 27(2):296–316.

Jennings, W. B. 1993. Foraging ecology and habitat utilization of the desert tortoise (*Gopherus agassizii*) at the Desert Tortoise Research Natural Area, eastern Kern County, California. Report prepared for the U.S. Bureau of Land Management, Riverside, California, Contract B950-C2-0014. 110 pp.

Jennings, W. B. and C. L. Fontenot. 1993. Observations on the feeding behavior of desert tortoises (*Gopherus agassizii*) at the Desert Tortoise Research Natural Area, Kern County, California. Proc. Desert Tortoise Council Symp. 1992:69–81.

Luckenbach, R. A. 1982. Ecology and management of the desert tortoise (*Gopherus agassizii*) in California. *In* R. B. Bury (ed.), North American Tortoises: Conservation and Ecology, pp. 1–37. Wildlife Research Report 12, U.S. Fish and Wildlife Service, Washington, D.C.

MacDonald, I. A. W. and G. W. Frame. 1988. The invasion of introduced species into nature reserves in tropical savannas and dry woodlands. Biol. Conserv. 44:67–93.

Mack, R. N. 1981. Invasion of *Bromus tectorum* L. into western North America: An ecological chronicle. Agroecosystems 7:145–165.

Medina, A. L. 1988. Diets of scaled quail in southern Arizona. J. Wildl. Manage. 52:753–757.

Nicholson, L. and K. Humphreys. 1981. Sheep grazing at the Kramer Study Plot, San Bernardino County, California. Proc. Desert Tortoise Council Symp. 1981:163–193.

Rowlands, P. G. 1990. Assessment of production of annual plant species in the western Mojave Desert, California. Proc. Desert Tortoise Council Symp. 1986:141–150.

Slobodchikoff, C. F. and J. T. Doyen. 1977. Effects of *Ammophila arenaria* on sand dune arthropod communities. Ecology 58:1171–1175.

Smith, C. W. and T. Tunison. 1992. Fire and alien plants in Hawaii: Research and management implications for native ecosystems. *In* C. P. Stone, C. W. Smith, and J. T. Tunison (eds.), Alien Plant Invasion in Hawaii: Management and Research in Native Ecosystems, pp. 394–408. Univ. Hawaii Press, Honolulu.

Spangenberg, K. E. 1994. Spring foraging behavior, movements, and general activities of two adult female and two immature desert tortoises near Kramer Junction, San Bernardino County, California. Progress report (No. 1) prepared for the California Energy Commission, Sacramento, California.

U.S. Bureau of Land Management. 1980. Final environmental impact statement and proposed plan, Appendix XIII, Vol. F. Part 1, A short history of grazing in the California Desert Conservation Area. U.S.D.I. Bureau of Land Management, Riverside, California.

U.S. Fish and Wildlife Service. 1994. The desert tortoise (Mojave population) recovery plan. U.S. Fish and Wildlife Service, Region 1- Lead Region, Portland, Oregon. 73 pp.+ appendices.

Van Wilgen, B. W. and D. M. Richardson. 1985. The effects of alien shrub invasions on vegetation structure and fire behavior in South African fynbos shrublands: A simulation study. J. Appl. Ecol. 22: 955–966.

Webb, R. H. and S. S. Stielstra. 1979. Sheep grazing effects on Mojave Desert vegetation and soils. Environ. Manage. 3(6):517–529.

West, N. E. 1988. Intermountain deserts, shrub steppes, and woodlands. *In* M. G. Barbour and W. D. Billings (eds.), North American Terrestrial Vegetation, pp. 209–230. Cambridge Univ. Press, Cambridge and New York.

Woodbury, A. M. and R. Hardy. 1948. Studies of the desert tortoise (*Gopherus agassizii*). Ecol. Monogr. 18(2):145–200.

Young, J. A. and R. A. Evans. 1971. Invasion of medusahead into the Great Basin. Weed Science 18:89–97.

Effects of Cattle Grazing on the Desert Tortoise, *Gopherus agassizii*: Nutritional and Behavioral Interactions

HAROLD W. AVERY[1] AND ALEXANDER G. NEIBERGS[2]

[1]*U.S. Geological Survey, Biological Resources Division,
6221 Box Springs Blvd., Riverside, CA 92507, USA [e-mail: hal_avery@usgs.gov]*
[2]*USDI Bureau of Land Management, Ridgecrest Resource Area, 300 South Richmond Road, Ridgecrest, CA 93555-4436, USA*

ABSTRACT: As in most species of tortoises, the desert tortoise, *Gopherus agassizii*, relies inextricably on vegetation and soil for its survival. In addition to meeting energy and nutrient needs, the desert tortoise uses vegetation as cover for thermal protection, predator avoidance, and intraspecific behavioral interactions. Soil condition affects the ability to construct burrows and affects tortoise nutrition. Tortoises acquire minerals and nutrients by consuming soil (geophagy), and they consume plants whose abundance and nutrient content are directly related to soil quality. Studies on vegetation and soil changes are therefore of paramount importance to the conservation and management of wild tortoise populations.

For over a century, range cattle and sheep have grazed the arid regions of the southwestern United States. Because of the relatively slow recovery times of vegetation in desert ecosystems, the United States Bureau of Land Management is interested in determining long-term impacts of grazing on desert habitat and on populations of threatened and endangered wildlife. We have been conducting research to determine the effects of cattle grazing on desert tortoise habitat and desert tortoise populations since 1991. Vegetation and soil parameters were compared inside and outside a cattle exclosure, which has been in existence since 1980. We also followed individual cattle and tortoises to document feeding behavior and to observe direct and indirect behavioral interactions of free-ranging cattle and wild desert tortoises.

When comparing habitat in grazed and ungrazed areas, we found no significant difference in annual plant cover, biomass, or density between areas outside (grazed area) versus inside the cattle exclosure. Individual volumes of two predominant shrub species, *Larrea tridentata* and *Ambrosia dumosa*, were greater outside the exclosure than inside the exclosure. These shrubs were rarely or never consumed by range cattle or tortoises and are considered unpalatable. In contrast, the densities and individual volumes of palatable perennial grass, *Hilaria rigida*, were greater in the grazed area versus the ungrazed area. No significant difference was found in total cover of perennial plants between the grazed and ungrazed areas.

Bulk density and penetration resistance of soils were greater in the grazed area versus the ungrazed area, indicating that soils are more compacted in the grazed area. There was no measurable difference in hydraulic conductivity between the grazed and ungrazed areas, indicating that soil compaction was not sufficient to reduce the rate of water transit into the soil.

Direct and indirect interactions were observed between cattle and tortoises. Direct interactions included cattle making physical contact with tortoises (e.g., nudging and rubbing). Indirect interactions included trampling of actively used burrows, attempts of tortoises to enter destroyed burrows, and the destruction of vegetation shading actively used burrows. Cow dung was an insignificant component of tortoise diets (<0.5%).

We evaluate how changes in vegetation and soils caused by cattle grazing affect the conservation biology of the desert tortoise within the framework of behavioral, thermal, and nutritional ecology.

Livestock have grazed on public and private lands of the arid southwestern United States for more than a century (U.S. Bureau of Land Management, 1980). Changes in vegetation and soils are among the most observable effects of livestock grazing on desert ecosystems. Some observed and hypothesized effects of livestock grazing on desert tortoises, *Gopherus agassizii*, and desert tortoise habitat include dietary overlap and food competition (Webb and Stielstra, 1979; Berry, 1989), destruction of cover and biomass of perennial shrubs used as shade (Berry, 1989), trampling of tortoises and tortoise burrows (Nicholson and Humphreys, 1981), alteration of species composition of plants by the invasion of non-native plants (Berry, 1989), and compaction of soil (Webb and Stielstra, 1979), which may inhibit the construction of tortoise burrows.

The abundances of annual and perennial vegetation influence the densities of tortoises (Weinstein, 1989). An hypothesized effect of cattle grazing is the reduction of annual plant and palatable grass biomass by consumption and trampling. Such reductions in forage availability could alter the diet of tortoises by increasing the relative numbers of less-palatable plants. Changes in the distribution and abundance of plants that tortoises eat may reduce the viability of tortoise populations by causing nutritional deficiencies, starvation, or reduced fecundity.

Competition for forage may be an important effect of livestock grazing on desert tortoise populations. Hansen et al. (1976) and Coombs (1979) documented dietary overlap between livestock and desert tortoises by comparing feces from both species during the same time periods. Hohman and Omart (1980) found that forbs comprised the largest percentage of the diet for range cattle and desert tortoises in early spring and that the percentages of diets that are identical for cattle and tortoises were approximately 40% in a relatively dry year and approximately 61% in a wet year. Dietary overlaps were lower in late spring because cattle switched to perennial shrubs and grasses (Hohman and Omart, 1980).

Dietary overlap of forage species does not necessarily imply food competition. Food competition requires substantial dietary overlap and limiting food resources (Pianka, 1986). In their study, Hohman and Omart (1980) could not quantify the degree of competition between tortoises and range cattle because they did not relate the extent of dietary overlap to food availability.

In 1980 the U.S. Bureau of Land Management constructed a 0.4 km² cattle exclosure in Ivanpah Valley, California to facilitate long-term research on the effects of cattle grazing upon desert tortoise populations and habitat. The exclosure is fenced with three strands of barbed wire, which allow other native vertebrates (including tortoises) to move into and out of the exclosure.

In 1980 and 1981 Medica et al. (1981) compared the vegetation and attributes of tortoise populations on the inside and outside of the exclosure to determine whether plots were similar in plant species composition, density, and individual plant size. Turner et al. (1980) found no differences in the home range, estimated clutch frequency and clutch size, and other parameters of tortoise populations between the inside and the outside of the cattle exclosure (Medica, Lyons, and Turner, 1982). The only major difference between study plots at the time of exclosure construction was a significantly greater frequency of perennial grass, *Hilaria rigida*, inside the exclosed area compared to outside the exclosure. The Ivanpah Valley exclosure has been maintained since 1980. Few incidences of cattle trespassing inside the exclosure have been reported, and cattle have continued to graze outside the exclosure at densities of approximately 0.4 head/km². The exclosure offers a unique opportunity to study the effects of cattle grazing on tortoise populations and habitat under a typical year-round rotational grazing regime in the Mojave Desert of the southwestern United States.

Our objectives were to (1) determine which annual and perennial plant species are consumed by desert tortoises and range cattle in a location of the Mojave Desert, (2) quantify the selectivity of desert tortoises and range cattle for consuming desert vegetation, (3) determine the availability of annual and perennial plants to desert tortoises and range cattle, (4) determine the nutrient content of forage plants that desert tortoises and range cattle consume, (5) quantify the existence of competition for forage between desert tortoises and range cattle, (6) determine the effects of rainfall on annual plant productivity, and (7) quantify the incidence of trampling of tortoise burrows by grazing range cattle. Here we discuss the preliminary results of this study.

MATERIALS AND METHODS

Foraging Behavior of Tortoises

Sixteen adult desert tortoises, *Gopherus agassizii*, were observed in summer of 1991 and in spring of 1992 and 1993. Nine were males. Of these, two had home ranges outside the cattle exclosure, three had home ranges that extended outside and inside the cattle exclosure, and four had home ranges completely inside the exclosure. Of seven female tortoises followed, two had home ranges outside the exclosure, two had home ranges both inside and outside the cattle exclosure, and three had home ranges inside the exclosure.

Radio transmitters were mounted on the carapace of each of the 16 tortoises by researchers from the University of California Los Angeles (UCLA). Tortoises were not handled thereafter by us because the same animals were used for determining health profiles and field energetics. Individual tortoises were located each morning with radio receivers (Sony Pro-80) and Telonics antennas designed to receive frequencies of 150–152 MHz. They were observed throughout the day with binoculars. Field-workers positioned themselves behind shrubs and watched for the initiation of activity by each tortoise. Tortoises were followed throughout daytime activity by field-workers on hands and knees. A distance of approximately 10 m was sufficient to minimize disturbance to tortoises.

Using a hand-held microcassette recorder, field-workers recorded the number of bites a tortoise took of various plant species. Plant species, plant parts consumed, number of different plants of the same species, locations of consumed plants, time of day, and duration of foraging were recorded for all observed tortoises. Duration of other behaviors (e.g., mating, digging, basking) were also recorded.

Foraging paths of desert tortoises were marked with forester's flagging tape. Trails were marked while tortoises were foraging so that distance traveled, locations of feeding, and distance between forage patches could be determined. Flagging was removed within two days.

Availability of Forage to Tortoises

Annual plant quadrats were used to determine food availability along the foraging paths of tortoises. Plant quadrats were rectangular (10 × 50 cm) and placed at 0%, 25%, 50%, and 75% of the total distance along morning and afternoon foraging paths. At each location, annual quadrats were placed in the open, under the dripline of the nearest creosote bush, and under its canopy. This allowed comprehensive determination of food availability in different microhabitats along each foraging path. In addition, annual plants were quantified at each food patch used by tortoises.

Density, total cover, and biomass were measured for each annual plant species within each quadrat. From these data species composition and forage availability of annuals were determined.

Cattle Foraging

Twenty cows were followed from late October 1992 to late April 1993. Field-workers arrived at cattle watering tanks before sunrise to determine locations of cattle. If no cattle were seen, other watering tanks were checked until a herd was found. When a herd was found it was followed as it moved from the watering tank and corral area to feeding areas. Cattle were followed on horseback and observed with binoculars. When foraging began a cow that tolerated the presence of the field-worker was chosen. The plant species, number of bites of plants consumed, and duration of feeding were recorded for each cow observed. Trails made by foraging cattle were marked with flagging tape, which was tied to large fender washers so that it would not blow away. Field-workers maintained a 10–15 m distance from foraging cows. Breed, ear tag identification number, brand type, and other discriminating physical characteristics were recorded for each monitored cow. Two or more observations were completed for some of the cows.

Determination of Forage Availability to Cattle

When cattle stopped foraging for the day (or when darkness came), cattle tracking was ended. Distance traveled by the foraging cow was determined with a meter wheel. The exact distance and direction of travel was determined by following the foraging path previously marked with flagging. Annual plant quadrats were completed at 0%, 25%, 50%, and 75% along the total distance of the foraging paths made by cattle. Morning and afternoon foraging paths were analyzed separately. In addition, annual plants were quantified at each food patch used by cattle. Food availability was measured with similar methods to those used with tortoises.

Species of consumed plants and number of individual plants consumed were recorded for each cow. Diet composition was determined and consumption rates were estimated for each cow from the number of observed bites. Bites of food were quantified only when vegetation was actually ingested. Chewing associated with rumination was not counted as bites. Frequency, density, and total cover of perennial grasses and shrubs were measured along foraging paths of cattle using 100 m line transects. Volumes and canopy areas of individual plants that intersected each line transect were measured. The total linear cover provided by all perennial shrubs and grasses was also determined for each 100 m transect. Use of watering areas and the provision and use of mineral licks and supplemental feed were recorded in field notes.

Nutritional Content of Forage Plants Consumed by Tortoises and Cattle

Plant species that comprised tortoise and cattle diets were collected for nutrient analyses during spring 1993. Only plant parts that were consumed by tortoises and cattle were collected and analyzed for nutrient and energy content. Water, crude protein, cell wall components (cellulose, hemicellulose, and lignin), fat, and energy were determined. All analyses were completed using standard methods approved by the Association of Official Analytical Chemists (Helrich, 1990).

Thirteen samples of plants that desert tortoises consumed were sent for nutrient analysis to the Hazleton Wisconsin Nutrition Laboratory, Madison, Wisconsin. Separate samples of plant parts (e.g., flowers, stems) were analyzed for *Malacothrix glabrata* and *Opuntia basilaris* because they represented temporally distinct sources of food for tortoises. In addition, a sample of sphinx moth larvae, *Hyles lineata*, was analyzed, when it was determined in summer 1991 that desert tortoises preferentially consumed these caterpillars when available.

Precipitation

Thirty-four rain gauges were used to determine the mean precipitation rates inside and outside the cattle exclosure. Precipitation can affect primary productivity, which may influence tortoise and cattle foraging ecology. Variation in precipitation can help explain variation in feeding rates and other aspects of foraging ecology. Rain gauges were checked monthly from October 1992 to October 1994.

RESULTS

Foraging by Tortoises

Tortoises were rarely disturbed by being followed and observed. Those that did respond to the presence of field-workers soon resumed feeding. Food items that desert tortoises consumed are presented as "Major Spring Forage Species" and "Minor Spring Forage Species" (Table 1). (Other food items included cattle feces and soil.)

TABLE 1
Major and minor plants desert tortoises, *Gopherus agassizii*, consumed in spring 1992 and 1993. Taxonomy based on Hickman (1993).

Plant species	Family	Part(s) consumed
Major Spring Forage Species		
Camissonia boothii	Onagraceae	entire plant
Cryptantha angustifolia	Boraginaceae	entire plant
Malacothrix glabrata	Asteraceae	flower heads, stems, and leaves
Opuntia basilaris	Cactaceae	pads and flower buds
Rafinesquia neomexicana	Asteraceae	flowers
Schismus barbata	Poaceae	entire plant
Stephanomeria exigua	Asteraceae	stem and flower
Minor Spring Forage Species		
Camissonia dentata	Onagraceae	entire plant
Descurainia pinnata	Brassicaceae	stem and leaves
Eriophyllum pringlii	Asteraceae	entire plant
Erodium cicutarium	Geranaceae	entire plant
Hilaria rigida	Poaceae	stem
Langloisia schottii	Polemoniaceae	entire plant
Lepidium lasiocarpum	Brassicaceae	entire plant
Linanthus aureus	Polemoniaceae	flowers and stem
Opuntia echinocarpa	Cactaceae	stem and dry flowers
Pectocarya platycarpa	Boraginaceae	stem and nutlets
Pectocarya recurvata	Boraginaceae	stem and nutlets
Stylocline micropoides	Asteraceae	entire plant

(Other foods: cattle feces and soil)

Cattle Foraging

Twenty different cattle were observed consuming annual and perennial forage from late October 1992 through April 1993. Field-workers on horseback were successful in observing foraging cattle, although individual cattle varied in their tolerance to being observed. More than 30,000 bites were recorded by field-workers during this time period. Food plants that range cattle consumed are divided into "Major Spring Forage Species" and "Minor Spring Forage Species" (Table 2).

Use of Supplemental Feed at Water Tank Areas in Ivanpah Valley

During the fall and winter of 1992 and early spring of 1993 we observed the use of supplemental feed at Ivanpah Valley, California. Two types of feeds were provided by ranchers. Crystalyx®, a dark brown, hardened block of material that smells of molasses, was supplied in metal barrels. Several barrels of Crystalyx® were provided at each water tank from October 1992 to February 1993. IFA 36% Range Blocks® were supplied from December 1992 to late February 1993. Twenty or more of these supplemental feed blocks were provided monthly on the ground at each monitored water tank. In addition to the supplemental feed, at least one mineral lick was provided for cattle by the rancher at each water tank throughout 1992 and 1993.

Nutritional Content of Forage Plants

Nutrient content of forage plants from Ivanpah Valley, California was determined (Table 3). Annual grasses (family Poaceae) were significantly higher in total cell wall content (Neutral Detergent Fiber, or NDF) and ligno-cellulose (Acid Detergent Fiber, or ADF) than other plant types sampled (Table 3). Tortoises ate immature native *Bouteloua* at Ivanpah Valley, California in the summer of 1991. Immature grasses had greater crude protein concentrations than mature grasses analyzed. Energy values of all plant species were similar (Table 3).

In summer 1991 desert tortoises selectively ate sphinx moth larvae, *Hyles lineata*. These moths were much greater in water, crude protein, fat, and energy content but lower in cell wall content and ligno-cellulose than summer annual plants (Table 3).

TABLE 2
Major and minor plants that range cattle consumed foraging in spring 1992 and 1993. Taxonomy based on Hickman (1993).

Plant species	Family	Part(s) consumed
Major Spring Forage Species		
Bromus rubens	Poaceae	entire plant
Ephedra californica	Ephedraceae	stems and leaves
Erodium cicutarium	Geranaceae	entire plant
Camissonia boothii	Onagraceae	entire plant
Cryptantha sp.	Boraginaceae	entire plant
Hilaria rigida	Poaceae	entire plant
Malacothrix glabrata	Asteraceae	flower heads, stems, and leaves
Pectocarya sp.	Boraginaceae	entire plant
Plagiobothrys arizonicus	Boraginaceae	entire plant
Rafinesquia neomexicana	Asteraceae	flowers and stems
Schismus barbata	Poaceae	entire plant
Stephanomeria exigua	Asteraceae	stem and flower
Minor Spring Forage Species		
Ambrosia dumosa	Asteraceae	leaves and flowers
Amsinckia tessellata	Boraginaceae	leaves
Camissonia dentata	Onagraceae	entire plant
Camissonia kernensis	Onagraceae	entire plant
Eriogonum trichopes	Polygonaceae	entire plant
Erodium cicutarium	Boraginaceae	entire plant
Pectocarya platycarpa	Boraginaceae	entire plant
Pectocarya recurvata	Boraginaceae	entire plant

TABLE 3
Nutritional values of some plants consumed by desert tortoises in Ivanpah Valley, California, and the Desert Tortoise Natural Area near California City, Califonia. H_2O = moisture content; CP = crude protein; NDF = Neutral Detergent Fiber; ADF = Acid Detergent Fiber; Fat = total fat content. Energy = gross energy content, expressed as Kjoul/gram dry wt. Moisture content is expressed as percent wet weight; all other data are expressed as percent of dry weight. * = summer forage species.

Forage species	H_2O	CP	NDF	ADF	Fat	Energy
*Bouteloua barbata**	51.9	10.8	49.1	31.2	1.0	16.4
*Bouteloua aristidoides**	51.1	8.3	57.3	36.8	1.8	17.1
Bouteloua sp. (immature)*	51.3	12.9	—	—	1.5	—
Camissonia kernensis	72.2	6.5	30.6	25.9	0.7	16.2
Chaenactis fremontii	70.6	6.8	35.0	27.2	1.0	17.8
Cryptantha pterocarya nutlet	67.7	9.6	23.8	9.6	2.7	15.7
Hilaria rigida	57.1	8.6	64.6	37.1	0.8	17.9
Malacothrix glabrata flowers	78.1	12.3	14.2	12.8	1.3	18.7
Malacothrix glabrata stem	80.2	5.6	41.4	34.3	0.6	16.0
Mentzelia albicaulis	76.6	10.7	31.6	13.2	0.9	17.2
Opuntia basilaris flowers	89.3	8.4	10.3	8.4	0.2	15.4
Opuntia basilaris pads	89.2	6.5	13.0	11.1	0.2	14.6
Pectocarya platycarpa	67.1	11.6	38.6	37.4	1.5	17.3
Hyles lineata, sphinx moth (larvae)*	85.2	52.7	—	8.1	2.0	21.3

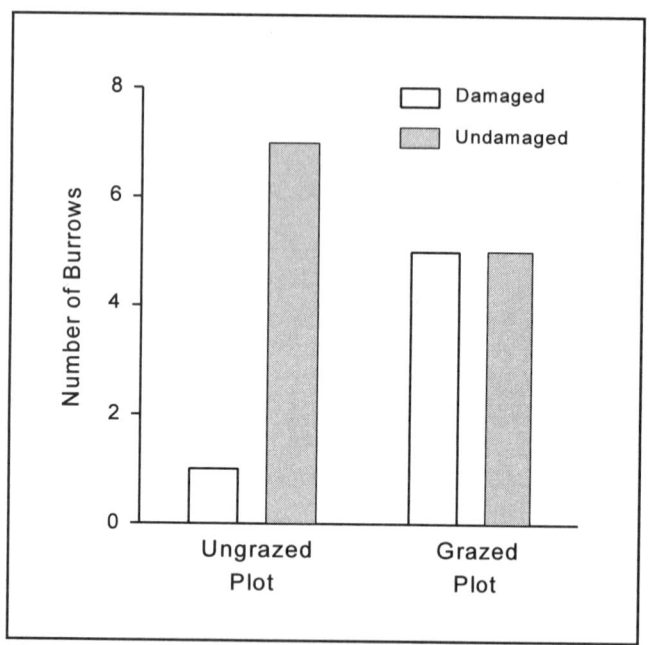

Figure 1. Frequency of damaged tortoise burrows on ungrazed plot (inside the cattle exclosure) and on grazed plot (outside the cattle exclosure) at Ivanpah Valley, California. Shaded bars represent the frequency of undamaged burrows; hollow bars represent the frequency of damaged burrows. Data are preliminary findings from spring 1993.

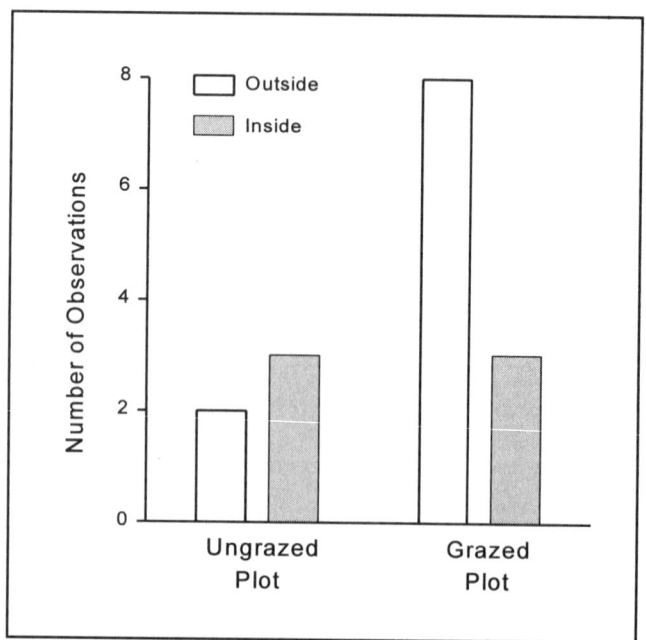

Figure 2. Incidence of desert tortoises remaining overnight outside and inside of burrows on ungrazed plot (inside of cattle exclosure) compared to grazed plot (outside of cattle exclosure) at Ivanpah Valley, California. Shaded bars represent the frequency of tortoises observed to remain overnight inside of burrows; hollow bars represent frequency of tortoises observed to remain overnight outside of burrows. Data are preliminary findings from spring 1993.

Determination of Feeding Selectivity and Dietary Overlap of Range Cattle and Desert Tortoises

Range cattle and free-living desert tortoises preferred green annual vegetation over other available plants. Cattle and tortoises consumed some exotic annuals (i.e., *Schismus barbata* and *Erodium cicutarium*) but did not prefer them. In late spring desert tortoises consumed increasing amounts of *Opuntia basilaris* and dry annuals. During this same time, range cattle consumed large quantities of *Hilaria rigida* and *Ephedra californica* and had greatly reduced their consumption of annual plants. *Bromus rubens* and *Schismus barbata* were still consumed by range cattle during this time. Tortoises still active in early- to mid-summer consumed stems and dry flowers of *Opuntia echinocarpa* that had fallen on the ground. Very few dry annuals and perennial grasses were eaten by tortoises. During this same time, range cattle predominantly consumed perennial grass, *Hilaria rigida*.

Incidence of Tortoise Burrow Trampling

In spring 1993 some tortoise burrows were partially or completely destroyed by cattle trampling (Figure 1). The number of partially or completely destroyed burrows was greater outside (i.e., where grazing persists) than inside the cattle exclosure (Figure 1). Tortoises tried unsuccessfully to enter completely destroyed burrows. Tortoises entered and used partially destroyed burrows.

In addition, preliminary results indicate that desert tortoises located outside the cattle exclosure remained outside of their burrows all night significantly more often than tortoises located inside the exclosure (Figure 2). This is consistent with the occurrence of having more damaged burrows outside the cattle exclosure than inside the exclosure (Figure 1).

Precipitation

Similar amounts of rainfall occurred inside and outside the exclosure from October 1992 through September 1993 (Table 4). Greatest differences in monthly rainfall were found in January, May, and August of 1993. During these months this area received thundershowers, which resulted in unevenly distributed precipitation.

Interactions of Cattle and Tortoises

On one occasion three calves rubbed their heads and necks on an adult tortoise that was consuming soil near a watering area. Calves also nudged the tortoise with their heads, but never stepped on the tortoise. Out of hundreds of hours of observation time, this was the only observed occasion that an active desert tortoise came into contact with range cattle.

TABLE 4
Amounts of monthly precipitation inside vs. outside the Ivanpah Valley cattle exclosure. Precipitation data are mean values in millimeters (±SE). Plot 1 = inside exclosure; Plot 2 = outside exclosure.

Month	Plot 1	Plot 2
October 1992	17.9 (±0.3)	20.7 (±0.50)
November	0	0
December	37.4 (±1.5)	32.5 (±3.1)
January 1993	53.4 (±3.7)	44.1 (±5.4)
February	37.4 (±0.4)	40.8 (±1.9)
March	11.6 (±0.1)	10.0 (0)
April	0	0
May	2.1 (±1.1)	10.1 (±1.5)
June	8.3 (±0.1)	7.0 (±0.4)
July	0	0
August	18.2 (±1.1)	12.0 (±2.6)
September	0	0
Total	186.4 (±8.3)	177.2 (±15.4)

DISCUSSION AND CONCLUSIONS

Dietary Overlap

Data on the foraging behavior and food preference of range cattle and desert tortoises indicate that dietary overlap exists between range cattle and desert tortoises in one region of the eastern Mojave Desert in California. The potential for spatial and temporal overlap of cattle and tortoises exists and is greatest in the spring, when the biomass of fresh annuals are at their peak biomass and densities. During these times (approx. 1 April–31 May) dietary overlaps of cattle and tortoises appear greatest. These preliminary findings are consistent with those reported from the Beaver Dam Slope of Utah (Hohman and Omart, 1980). Food competition between desert tortoises and range cattle is expected to be greatest when annual plants start to dry in the spring, before cattle and tortoises switch to other forage plants. Further analyses are being completed to determine whether food competition existed between tortoises and range cattle during this study.

Supplemental Feed

Supplemental feed may enhance the impacts of grazing on perennial grasses. By supplying additional carbohydrates and protein to range cattle, cattle may graze longer in already heavily grazed areas. We have documented areas greater than 1 km from watering areas where utilization of perennial grass, *Hilaria rigida*, exceeds 100% during winter months. Further research is necessary to determine whether overgrazing causes significantly higher mortality to overutilized plants and whether supplemental feed influences the incidence of overgrazing.

Incidence of Trampling

In the early spring tortoises recently emerging from winter hibernation search within their home ranges for burrows that were used in the fall of the previous year. Our preliminary findings from spring 1993 suggest that cattle grazing during winter may destroy large percentages of active tortoise burrows. We found evidence that range cattle avoid trampling tortoise burrows, but it is apparent that a significant percentage of burrows are still trampled by cattle. Increased risk of mortality, increased energetic costs, and changes in activity time budgets (caused by additional time required to build new burrows) may occur for tortoises whose home ranges (burrows) are located in areas of heavy cattle grazing.

Further studies must be completed to determine the interactions of livestock and tortoises. It is particularly important to determine how cattle stocking rates affect desert tortoise populations and to determine what stocking rates are permissible in areas where tortoise populations exhibit population decline.

ACKNOWLEDGMENTS

Dr. J. E. Lovich, Larry Morgan, Dr. Kristin H. Berry, and W. Bryan Jennings provided ideas and suggestions regarding methods and experimental design. Kevin Madsen, Terrie Willow Yumiko, and Alan Pfister of the U.S. Bureau of Land Management Needles Resource Area, California, provided invaluable field and logistical assistance. Previous drafts of this manuscript were reviewed by Drs. W. I. Boarman and J. E. Lovich, Kevin Madsen, and an anonymous reviewer. Funds for the project were provided by the U.S. Department of the Interior, Bureau of Land Management and National Biological Survey.

LITERATURE CITED

Berry, K. H. 1989. A brief summary of the effects of sheep grazing on desert tortoises in the western Mojave Desert. Unpublished report. 13 pp.

Coombs, E. M. 1979. Food habits and livestock competition with the desert tortoise on the Beaver Dam Slope, Utah. Proc. Desert Tortoise Council Symp. 1979:132–147.

Hansen, R. M., M. K. Johnson, and T. R. VanDevender. 1976. Foods of the desert tortoise, *Gopherus agassizii*, in Arizona and Utah. Herpetologica 32:247–251.

Helrich, K. 1990. Official Methods of Analysis of the Association of Official Analytical Chemists. 15th Edition, AOAC Inc., Arlington, Virginia. 1298 pp.

Hickman, J. C. 1993. The Jepson Manual: Higher Plants of California. University of California Press, Los Angeles, California. 1400 pp.

Hohman, J. P. and R. D. Omart. 1978. Historical range use of the Beaver Dam Slope, Arizona, and its possible effects on a desert tortoise population. Proc. Desert Tortoise Council Symp. 1978: 116–125.

Medica, P. A., C. L. Lyons, and F. B. Turner. 1981. A comparison of populations of the desert tortoise (*Gopherus agassizii*) in grazed and ungrazed areas in Ivanpah Valley, California. Report on Contract No. SS00012/UCLA, CA 950-1A1-1211 to the U.S. Department of the Interior, Bureau of Land Management.

Medica, P. A., C. L. Lyons, and F. B. Turner. 1982. A comparison of 1981 populations of desert tortoises (*Gopherus agassizii*) in grazed and ungrazed areas in Ivanpah Valley, California. Proc. Desert Tortoise Council Symp. 1982: 99–124.

Nicholson, L. and K. Humphreys. 1981. Sheep grazing at the Kramer study plot, San Bernardino County, California. Proc. Desert Tortoise Council Symp. 1981:163–194.

Pianka, E. R. 1986. Ecology and Natural History of Desert Lizards. Princeton University Press, Princeton, New Jersey. 208 pp.

Turner, F. B. 1980. A comparison of populations of the desert tortoise (*Gopherus agassizii*) in grazed and ungrazed areas in Ivanpah Valley, California. Report on Contract No. SS00012/UCLA, CA 950-1A1-1211 to the U.S. Department of the Interior, Bureau of Land Management. 66 pp.

U.S. Bureau of Land Management. 1980. The California desert conservation area plan. U.S. Dept. of the Interior, Bureau of Land Management, California Desert District, Riverside, California. 173 pp.

Webb, R. H. and S. S. Stielstra. 1979. Sheep grazing effects on Mojave Desert vegetation and soils. Environ. Manage. 3:517–529.

Weinstein, M. N. 1989. Modeling desert tortoise habitat: Can a useful management tool be developed from existing transect data? Ph.D. dissertation, University of California Los Angeles. 121 pp.

Agricultural Development and Grazing as the Major Causes of Population Declines in Horsfield's Tortoise in the Turkmen Republic

— ABSTRACT —

VIKTORIJ M. MAKEYEV,[1] SAHAT SHAMMAKOV,[2] ANATOLIJ T. BOZHANSKII,[1] RONALD W. MARLOW,[3] AND KAREN VON SECKENDORFF HOFF[3]

[1]*All-Union Institute of Nature Conservation and Reserves, District P.B. Villar, Znamenskoe-Sadki, 142790, Moscow, Russia*
[2]*Institute of Zoology, Turkmenian Academy of Sciences, Ashkabad 744000, Turkmen Republic*
[3]*Biology Department, University of Nevada, Reno, NV 89557, USA*

Horsfield's tortoise, *Testudo (Agrionemys) horsfieldi*, is widespread and locally abundant throughout Central Asia and in the Turkmen Republic. These tortoises are found in the Kara Kum Desert in semi-stabilized dune communities dominated by saxaul where they reach densities of >20/ha. Recent water development projects on the Amu Darya River have brought irrigation to desert lands and have resulted in conversion of thousands of km² of tortoise habitat into farms. In addition, the water projects have altered traditional nomadic and semi-nomadic lifestyles for many Turkmenis. Now, with readily available water, Turkmenis have established permanent habitations. Camel and sheep grazing are destroying the saxaul and destabilizing the sand dunes, and tortoise populations are declining.

The Impact of Commercial Crab Traps on Northern Diamondback Terrapins, *Malaclemys terrapin terrapin*

ROGER CONANT WOOD

Faculty of Science and Mathematics, Richard Stockton College of New Jersey, Pomona, NJ 08240, USA;
The Wetlands Institute, 1075 Stone Harbor Blvd., Stone Harbor, NJ 08247, USA

ABSTRACT: Commercial crab traps are widely used throughout the range of diamondback terrapins (i.e., salt marshes along the Atlantic and Gulf coasts of the United States). Experiments on the Cape May Peninsula in southernmost New Jersey and elsewhere show that crab traps catch significant numbers of terrapins of both sexes, including both juveniles and adults. Unfortunately, a substantial proportion of these terrapins drown before the traps are pulled for the daily crab harvest. Conservative estimates project that tens of thousands are inadvertently killed in this manner annually along the New Jersey coast alone. It is likely that considerably larger numbers of terrapins are killed throughout this species' range every year.

During summer 1992 a rectangular wire excluder device was fitted into the inner (narrow) end of entrance funnels in typical commercial crab traps. This device, known as the "Bycatch Reduction Apparatus" (or BRA), was designed to prohibit the entry of most terrapins, yet not impair the number or size of crabs caught. Preliminary results of this pilot study and of subsequent large-scale experiments have been encouraging. Not only have the excluder rectangles greatly reduced the number of terrapins caught in modified traps, but they have also actually increased the crab catch over unmodified traps of standard design. Results of this research make prospects for the widespread adoption of terrapin excluder devices seem highly favorable.

The high mortality of nesting northern diamondback terrapins, *Malaclemys terrapin terrapin*, on roads adjacent to salt marshes in southern New Jersey is clear evidence that these turtles are affected by human activities (Wood and Herlands, this volume). However, anecdotal information from commercial and recreational crabbers suggests that crab traps are a greater source of mortality than is vehicular traffic.

Bishop's (1983) data (from South Carolina) demonstrates that commercial crab traps catch and drown significant numbers of terrapins. Data collected by the New Jersey Bureau of Marine Fisheries (P. Scarlett, pers. comm., 1991), indicates a recent dramatic increase in the number of crab traps deployed statewide and suggests that lethal bycatch of terrapins is increasing.

In New Jersey, diamondback terrapins are designated "game animals" and may be legally taken from 1 November through 30 March, a season that approximately coincides with their hibernation period. During the remainder of the year terrapins and their eggs are fully protected by New Jersey game regulations.

Commercial crabbers apparently do not sell the terrapins they find as bycatch in their traps, but because possession of terrapins during the closed season is illegal, they are generally reluctant to provide information on incidental captures.

In this paper I assess the impact of crabbing upon terrapin populations in New Jersey and describe measures developed to mitigate this impact.

Figure 1. Northern diamondback terrapin in commercial crab trap.

I investigated the following: (1) the extent of terrapin bycatch in commercial crab traps, (2) the mortality levels of terrapins caught in commercial crab traps, (3) trap designs to enable terrapin survival within the traps, and (4) trap designs to exclude terrapins and their effect on the crab catch.

METHODS

Most of our fieldwork was conducted in the vicinity of the Wetlands Institute, a research facility located on the eastern side of the Cape May Peninsula in southern New Jersey (Figure 2). Salt marshes here are situated between a barrier island (Seven Mile Beach) and the mainland, approximately 5 km (≈3 mi) to the west. Although bounded by developed areas on both their western and eastern margins, the marshes are relatively pristine and represent typical diamondback terrapin habitat—a mixture of sinuous creeks and open shallow sounds with thousands of acres of intertidal marsh vegetation (dominated by *Spartina* spp.). Fieldwork concentrated in three areas near the Wetlands Institute: Holmes Cove at the southwestern side of Great Sound, Mulford Creek, and Stone Harbor Creek, which represent, respectively, the marshes' landward, central, and oceanside areas.

A second study area was near the Nacote Creek Research Station (New Jersey Bureau of Marine Fisheries), approximately 65 km (35 mi) north of the Wetlands Institute. Fieldwork here was conducted upstream from the mouth of the Mullica River and along the southwestern edge of Great Bay below the mouth of the Mullica during the summers of 1993 and 1994.

Fieldwork was also conducted in summer 1994 on the Delaware Bay side of the Cape May Peninsula near the mouth of Dias Creek, within the Cape May National Wildlife Refuge. Fieldwork began in summer 1989 and is ongoing.

In summer 1989 we used four Maryland-style crab traps* constructed of rectangular-mesh galvanized wire. The traps measured 24 × 24 in (61 × 61 cm) and were 21 in (53 cm) deep. Four entrance funnels, one at the base of each side, permitted entry from any direction (see Warner, 1976, for detailed description). After 1989 we used more durable traps of vinyl-coated hexagonal mesh wire, but the size and basic design of the trap remained unchanged. The new traps were weighted with bricks or rebar. Elastic cords or wire were used to keep the bait holder closed on the bottom of the trap. Styrofoam floats, painted fluorescent orange and labeled with our scientific collecting permit number, were attached to each trap by a 12–15 ft line.

We attempted to mimic the equipment and the techniques used by commercial crabbers to ensure that our results would be comparable to those of a typical crabbing operation. Traps were checked at least daily, and for our early experiments (before the development of an effective terrapin excluder) we endeavored to check every trap twice daily to minimize drowning of terrapins. When traps were checked, all blue crabs, *Callinectes sapidus*, and other bycatch (spider crabs, conchs, various species of fish, and terrapins) were removed, and the traps were re-baited. A variety of baits were used in early experiments, including bunker (menhaden) as well as heads and filleted carcasses of various market fish (primarily flounder and salmon). Since 1993 we have used only bunker, which is used by virtually all commercial crabbers in southern New Jersey. In some study sites, strong tidal currents and storms occasionally shifted the positions of traps, altering the trap sequence and resulting in the loss of a few traps. Inadvertent and deliberate human activities may also have been responsible for some trap losses. Lost traps were promptly replaced unless the experiment was nearly concluded.

All captured terrapins were removed from the traps and were sexed and measured. With some exceptions (in which only plastron length was recorded), measurements of terrapin shells are straight-line carapace length (SLCL). In-

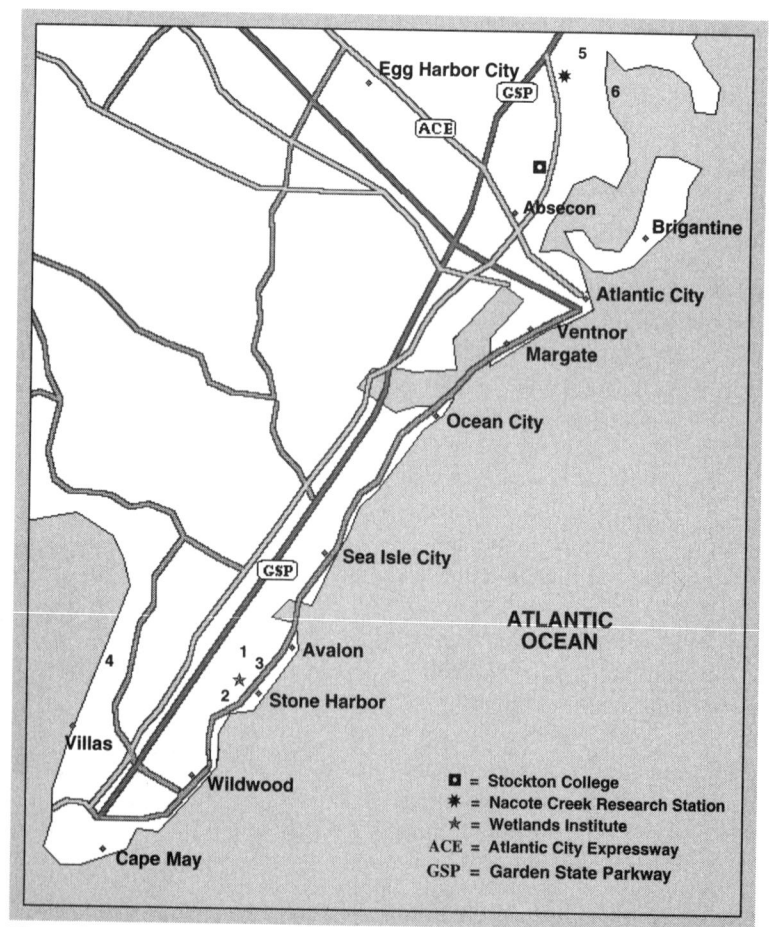

Figure 2. Map of southern New Jersey shore and Cape May Peninsula. Study areas: 1 = Holmes Cove, Great Sound; 2 = Mulford Creek; 3 = Stone Harbor Creek; 4 = Dias Creek; 5 = upstream from mouth of Mullica River; 6 = southwestern edge of Great Bay.

---

* All traps were purchased from the Maryland Crab Trap Company, Berlin, New Jersey.

complete processing of some terrapins was due to miscommunication among field personal, and certain adverse field conditions (rain, strong winds, approaching thunderstorms, or nightfall). However, these inconsistencies did not compromise the results of our experiments.

RESULTS

Tests of Unmodified Commercial Traps

A pilot project with commercial crab traps was conducted from 29 May to 29 June 1989 to determine extent of terrapin catch. Four traps were deployed alternately at two small creeks adjacent to the Wetlands Institute, resulting in 124 trap-days of effort. Because commercial crabbers typically move their traps over the course of the summer, shifting our traps between two sites simulated the practice of commercial operations. Traps were checked twice daily to minimize drowning of terrapins.

Nineteen terrapins (8 males, 11 females) were caught, a capture rate of 15 animals per 100 trap-days. Females ranged in size from 7.3 to 13.1 cm. In comparison, the carapace lengths of 16 adult females that nested in close proximity to the sites where the traps were set ranged from 15.5 to 20.0 cm (Figure 3). Males were clustered within a much smaller size range of 10.2–12.6 cm, representing the typical adult size for this sexually dimorphic species. Thus, it appeared that subadult females were being selectively trapped and adult males were routinely caught.

Four terrapins (3 females, 1 male) were drowned, a slightly greater than 20% mortality rate. Under actual operating conditions, commercial crabbers check traps no more than once a day, and New Jersey state regulations require that traps be pulled no less frequently than once every three days. Our terrapin mortality would have increased substantially had we checked our traps only once daily and may have approached 100% had we checked them less than once daily.

Test of Floating Traps

From 27 June through 14 July 1991 we conducted an experiment in Holmes Cove intended to improve terrapin survivorship in crab traps. Nine traps were set in the conventional manner, submerged and resting on the bottom of the cove, and eight traps were equipped with a pair of rectangular Styrofoam floats to keep the trap's upper portion approximately 10–15 cm above water, allowing any captured terrapins access to the surface to avoid drowning. Traps were checked daily. Traps set on the bottom caught 85 terrapins, of which 20 (24%) drowned. Only one terrapin was caught in a floating trap and it was not drowned. The floating traps were also largely ineffective in catching crabs.* In addition, the floating crab traps were considerably more unwieldy than unmodified traps and were subsequently rejected as a mitigation strategy.

In all, bottom traps were deployed for a total of 175 working days, during which 85 terrapins were caught, a rate of 49 terrapins/100 trap-days. The sex of captured terrapins was recorded in all but two instances. The sex ratio of roughly 1:3 (21 males, 54 females) is similar to that previously calculated for this population (Yearicks et al., 1981, based on winter capture of hibernating terrapins).

Additional information on terrapin bycatch in commercial crab traps was gathered during 1991. Six commercial traps checked near our experimental area in July contained three drowned females, a capture rate similar to that in the experiment with bottom traps just described. Two additional unmarked traps adjacent to our experimental area were also checked on 13 and 14 July. One was located close to the banks of the salt marsh, while the other was farther offshore. In four trap-days (minimum), a total of 25 terrapins were captured, of which 17 (nearly 75%) had drowned. Such catches underscore the devastating effect that commercial crab traps can have upon terrapin populations.

Test of the First Excluder Design

In 1992 we attempted to design a simple, inexpensive device that would prevent terrapins from entering traps. Our goal was to reduce the aperture size to prevent access by most terrapins without compromising the crab catch. Two designs of excluder devices were tested in trapping trials from late May to early September at three sites near the

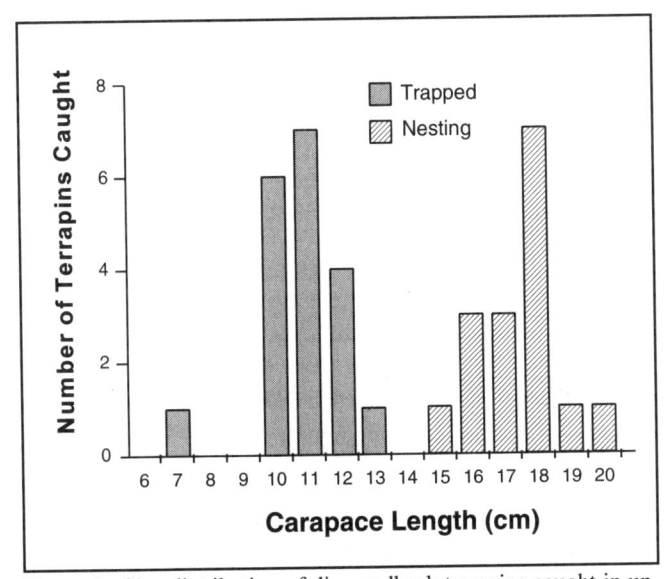

Figure 3. Size distribution of diamondback terrapins caught in unmodified commercial crab traps (dark shading) and terrapins observed nesting nearby (diagonal stripes) during summer of 1989.

*This observation is a qualitative impression; the numbers, sexes, and sizes of the individual crabs caught were not recorded, so quantitative crab catch data are unfortunately lacking.

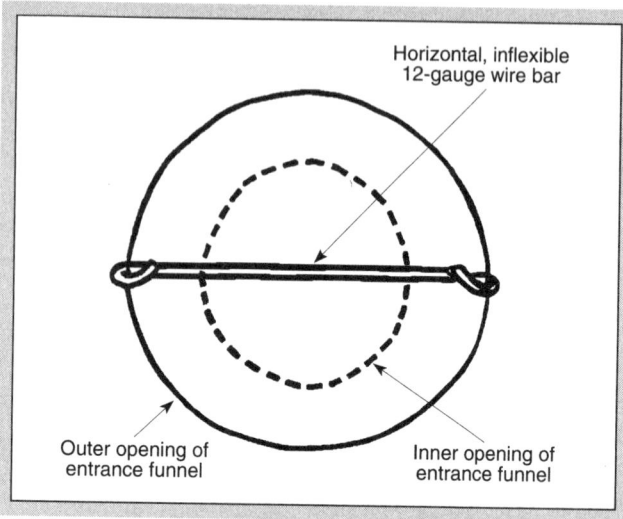

Figure 4. Sketch of the first terrapin excluder design tested (8–17 July 1992). A wire bar (approx. 10 gauge AWG, 2.6 mm) was fastened horizontally across the outer opening of each of the four funnels leading into the trap. This design proved ineffective.

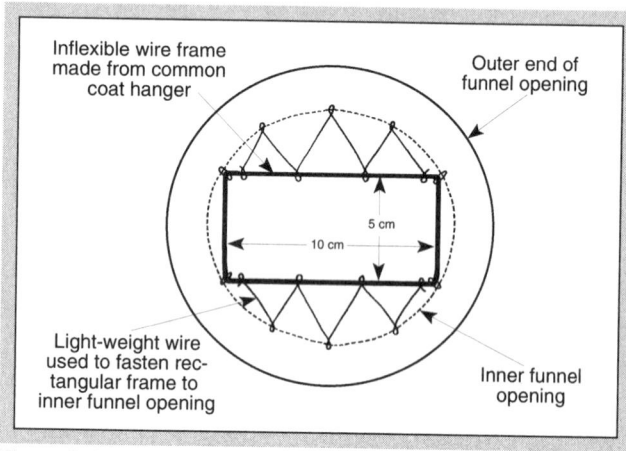

Figure 5. Second terrapin excluder design tested in summer 1992 (14 August–5 September). This was a 5 × 10 cm rectangular wire frame fastened to the inner (narrower) end of each of the four funnels opening into the trap. This device proved to be highly effective in preventing terrapins from entering commercial crab traps.

Wetlands Institute. These were checked at least once and often twice daily during these experiments.

The first excluder device tested was a stiff wire cut from a metal coat hanger (approx. 10 gauge AWG, 2.6 mm) and fastened horizontally across the mouth of each entrance funnel (Figure 4).

To control trap bias associated with subtle differences in location, substrate, etc., traps with modified openings were paired with unmodified traps by wiring them together side by side. Exchange of terrapins between paired traps was prevented by blocking facing entrance funnels with heavy screening. Eight sets of coupled traps were set in Holmes Cove, an area known to support a robust terrapin population.

The traps were checked daily over a ten-day period (8–17 July), a total of 160 trap-days of effort.

The results were disappointing. A total of 12 terrapins were caught during this experiment, six in modified traps and six in unmodified traps. Eleven were females ranging in midline plastron length (MPL) from 8.8 to 17.1 cm ($\bar{x}$ = 12.6); one was an adult male with plastron length of 10.6 cm. The six terrapins captured in modified traps were all females ranging from 8.8 to 12.4 cm MPL ($\bar{x}$ = 10.8). Though the six animals (both sexes) in the unmodified traps were on average larger ($\bar{x}$ = 14.0 cm MPL), both juveniles and adults were captured in the modified traps, and it was apparent that this device was ineffective.

First Tests of Second Excluder Design

The second excluder device tested during 1992 was a stiff rectangular frame, again made from coat hanger wire. One of these frames was attached to the inner end of each of the four entrance funnels. Each frame was held in position with light-weight copper or steel wire laced between the rectangular frame and the inner funnel opening, or by hog rings. Both crabs and terrapins would thereby be prevented from entering the trap except through the excluder (Figures 5 and 7). The dimensions of the rectangular wire excluder were 5 × 10 cm (approx. 2 × 4 in). The aperture size was based on shell measurements (maximum height and maximum width) of 68 terrapins caught in crab traps in 1992. Our data showed that 90% of this sample of terrapins would not fit through an opening less than 4 × 8 cm. However, slightly larger dimensions (5 × 10 cm) to accommodate the largest crabs were chosen for our tests. We set out a line of 16 traps, half of which were modified with 5 × 10 cm rectangular excluders. Modified traps were alternated with unmodified ones along the length of the trap line. Traps were checked almost daily (2 days missed) over a period of 23 days (14 August–5 September 1992), a total of 368 trap-days of effort.

The results of this experiment were considerably more encouraging. A total of 15 terrapins were caught, 13 in unmodified traps and only two in traps fitted with excluders. The two terrapins caught in the excluder-modified traps were an adult male (10.4 cm MPL) and a juvenile female (10.5 cm MPL). Moreover, traps modified with 5 × 10 cm rectangular excluders did not adversely affect the crab catch; the catch was actually increased.

Tests of Various Excluder Sizes

In 1993 additional trials of the rectangular terrapin excluder device were conducted to broaden the scope and sample of both terrapins and crabs and to investigate the effects of various excluder sizes.

The first experiment was designed to test the effectiveness of an excluder rectangle smaller than the 5 × 10 cm size originally used in 1992 and to determine how small an opening could be used without adversely affecting the crab catch. For 11 days from late June through early July, 20 traps were placed in Mulford Creek. Ten traps were fitted with 4 × 8 cm rectangular excluders and were alternated with ten identical, unmodified crab traps. This array resulted in 210 trap-days of effort.

Approximately two dozen terrapins were caught in the unmodified traps, whereas only one individual was caught in a trap modified with an excluder device. This single capture occurred because of equipment failure; one of the wire excluders had disassembled, allowing the turtle to enter the trap. However, the crab catch was significantly reduced in the traps equipped with 4 × 8 cm excluders, and the experiment was discontinued.

In a second experiment (conducted 7–28 July), the dimensions of the excluder were increased. Sixteen traps were set in Stone Harbor Creek, of which ten were fitted with 4.5 × 10 cm excluder rectangles (nearly identical in size to the 5 × 10 cm excluders tested in 1992). Again, modified traps were set in the water interspersed with unmodified traps. Traps were checked twice daily, and the experiment comprised 336 trap-days of effort. Twenty-two terrapins were caught, all in unmodified traps. Carapace lengths of these terrapins ranged from 11.1 to 19.8 cm. Seven were caught in one trap on a single day (9 July).

Based on these results, it is apparent that a 4.5 × 10 cm rectangular excluder is effective in preventing terrapins from entering commercial crab traps. In this experiment, modified traps caught approximately eight crabs per day (with the average size of legally harvestable* crabs being 12.5 cm), while unmodified traps caught approximately ten crabs per day (with the average size being 12.8 cm). This suggests that the size of crabs caught in traps with 4.5 × 10 cm excluders is not significantly reduced by these devices, although for reasons not immediately obvious the average numbers of crabs caught by the two types of traps differed slightly.

Subsequently, 20 traps were set (near the Nacote Creek Research Station of the New Jersey Division of Fish, Game and Wildlife) in an alternating pattern, ten modified with 4.5 × 10 cm excluders. Personnel from the Research Station and Stockton College research interns monitored the traps once a day over a 55-day period (7 July–31 August), an effort of 1,110 trap-days. Two additional areas were trapped, one

---

*Through 1993 the minimum legal body width (point-to-point) size for blue crabs in New Jersey, whether caught for commercial or recreational purposes, was 4 in (10.2 cm). In 1994 the minimum legal marketable crab size was increased to 4¾ in (12.06 cm). Recreational crabbers (permitted a maximum of two traps, catch restricted to personal consumption) are permitted to keep crabs of 4½ in (11.4 cm) from point to point.

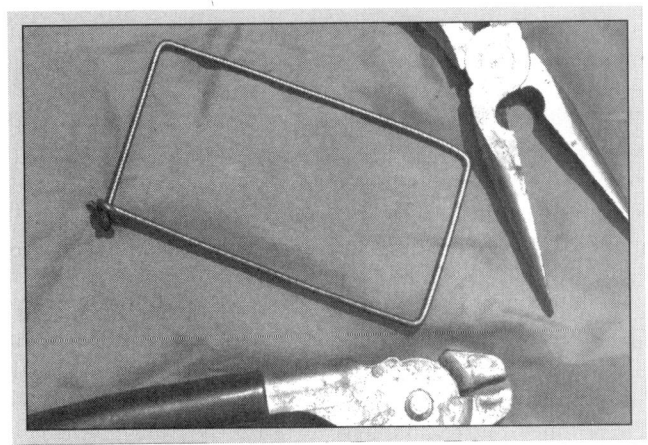

Figure 6. An effective excluder device for commercial crab traps is constructed from 12 gauge wire bent into a stiff rectangular frame.

Figure 7. Wire excluder frame is fastened to inner funnel opening with lightweight copper or steel wire, or hog rings as in this photograph.

located between the mouths of Motts and Oyster creeks on the southern fringe of Great Bay and the other in the Mullica River, just downstream from the mouth of Nacote Creek. As before, efforts were made to replicate the activities of the commercial crab fishery. Traps were rigged the same, the typical bait fish (bunker) was used, and traps were set in locations concurrently used by commercial crabbers.

All data above were pooled for analysis. Only three terrapins were caught, all juveniles and all in unmodified traps. The weekly total crab catch declined, with some intervening fluctuations, from 1,786 in the first week to 1,021 in the final week of trapping. Over the course of this experiment modified traps caught more crabs (6,145 vs. 5,274) of essentially the same average size (13.2 vs. 13.3 cm, not counting sub-legal specimens) than did conventional, unmodified traps. (One of the unmodified traps was lost early in this experiment and not replaced; the total of 5,274 is therefore not directly comparable. The adjusted unmodified trap total would be approximately 5,500 crabs or 9% fewer crabs than in traps fitted with excluders.)

There are two notable results from this experiment: (1) traps fitted with excluders actually increased the crab catch, and (2) few terrapins were caught despite exhaustive trapping efforts. The low terrapin catch may have been due to the severe depletion of the local population by sustained, heavy commercial trapping in the experimental area that has long been favored by commercial crabbers. Seasonal movement of terrapins within the estuary may also account for their absence from the trapping area.

By the end of 1993 we had established that rectangular excluders with dimensions of 4.5 × 10 cm were effective (nearly 100%) in excluding terrapins. However, we also had evidence indicating that excluders of this size may sometimes (as in our 1993 Stone Harbor Creek experiment) slightly decrease the number of marketable crabs caught in comparison to conventional traps.

1994 Tests

We therefore returned to a further test of 5 × 10 cm excluders in 1994. We set 16 traps in Stone Harbor Creek, again alternating modified and unmodified traps. Traps were deployed for a 34-day period (8 July–10 August, which generated 544 trap-days of effort.

Twenty-nine terrapins were caught. Only four terrapins (2 males and 2 subadult females) were caught in excluder-equipped traps, whereas 25 were removed from unmodified traps. This represents a capture rate of only 1.5 terrapins/100 trap-days for excluder-equipped traps versus a capture rate of 9.2 terrapins/100 trap-days for unmodified traps—a six-fold increase. The size distribution of the trapped terrapins is shown in Figure 8. Specimens ranged in carapace length from 10.0 to 20.0 cm and showed a bimodal distribution, with one peak in the 13 cm range (fully adult males and subadult females) and another at the 18 cm increment (adult females only for this sexually dimorphic species). The four terrapins caught in excluder-equipped traps were all small, ranging from 11 to 13 cm SLCL. Therefore, no large (reproductive) females were caught in traps with 5 × 10 cm excluders.

Additional testing of excluders was conducted for 61 days (1 May–20 June 1994) by the Nacote Creek Research Station. Twenty traps, half of them fitted with 5 × 10 cm rectangular excluders, were deployed in much the same areas as in 1993 (Mazzarella, 1995). Thirty-six terrapins were caught —three in excluder-equipped traps and 33 in unmodified traps. These results are consistent with those obtained from our experiment in Stone Harbor Creek. The capture rate of terrapins/100 trap-days for excluder-equipped traps (0.5) is substantially lower than for unmodified traps (5.4).

Combining the crab catch data for the Mullica River estuary experiments of 1993 and 1994 is of considerable interest and potential economic benefit to commercial crabbers. Only marketable crabs (12.0 cm and larger) are taken into consideration. Gravid females, which may not be legally taken or sold, have been factored out of these statistics. The resultant data are unambiguous and striking. Over the two-year period, excluder-modified traps caught 9,675 marketable crabs while the same number of unmodified traps caught 8,706. The difference of 969 marketable crabs represents an 11% greater catch for the excluder-modified traps.

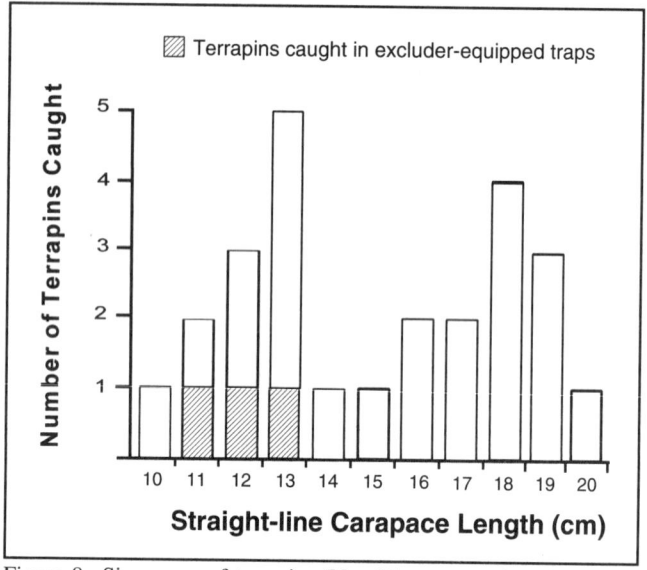

Figure 8. Size range of terrapins (N = 25; carapace lengths of four additional specimens not recorded) caught in 16 commercial crab traps set in Stone Harbor Creek 8 July–10 August 1994. Half the traps were equipped with 5 × 10 cm rectangular excluders; half were unmodified. Each carapace length represents a 1 cm interval, i.e., 10 = 10.0–10.9, etc.

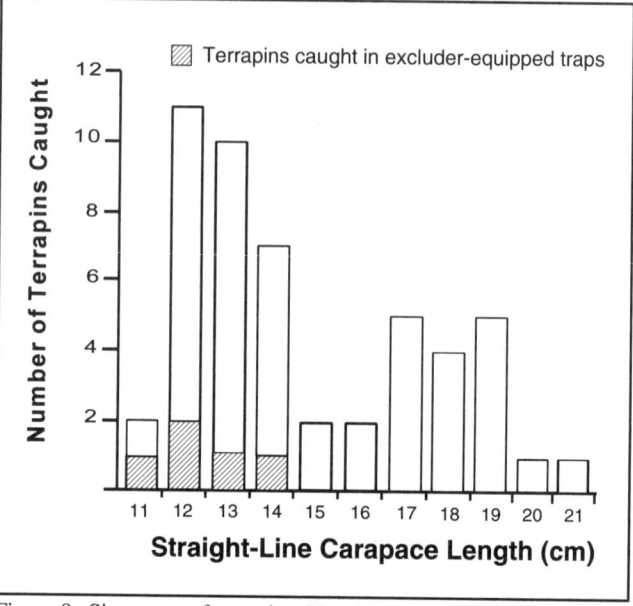

Figure 9. Size range of terrapins (N = 51) caught in commercial crab traps, both conventional and modified, during summer 1995. Each carapace length represents a 1 cm interval, i.e., 11 = 11.0–11.9, etc.

1995 Testing

In 1995 we trapped a single site, Stone Harbor Creek, to continue to build a large data base for an area where commercial crabbing regularly occurs. Twenty traps were set for a period of 61 days (14 June–13 August), a total effort of 1,220 trap-days. As before, traps were deployed linearly, alternating excluder-modified and unmodified traps.

A total of 51 terrapins were caught. Ten were males, 38 were females, and three were of unrecorded sex. Five of the terrapins (ranging from 11.9 cm to 14.9 cm SLCL) were caught in traps equipped with excluders, whereas 46 (ranging from 11.6 cm to 21.6 cm) were caught in conventional commercial crab traps. This disparate capture rate between excluder-equipped traps (0.8 terrapins caught/100 trap-days) and unmodified commercial crab traps (7.5 terrapins/100 trap-days) is comparable to previous results. Nineteen of the 46 terrapins (41%) caught in unmodified traps were larger in size than the largest terrapin caught in a modified trap. Thus, conventional traps not only caught considerably more terrapins but also a substantial proportion of larger ones.

Figure 9 shows the size range of terrapins caught during summer 1995. All terrapins ≥15 cm SLCL were females. Of the seven terrapins measuring between 14.0 and 14.9 cm SLCL, only one was a male at 14.0 cm. Nineteen terrapins (37% of all those trapped) drowned. Neither sex appeared to be disproportionately susceptible to drowning.

The 1995 trapping yielded 5,404 marketable (≥12.1 cm) crabs (366 males and 2,743 females). Gravid females of legal size are excluded from these statistics as it is illegal to catch, sell, or consume them. Of the total, 3,237 were taken from excluder-equipped traps, whereas only 2,167 were caught in conventional traps. The difference of 1,070 represents a 49% increase in the marketable crab catch. A daily average of 53.1 marketable crabs was caught by the ten modified traps, whereas a daily average of only 35.5 crabs was caught by the ten unmodified traps.

SUMMARY

• Commercial crab traps kill subadult and adult diamondback terrapins of both sexes. From the most conservative estimates, it is clear that large numbers are drowned annually in New Jersey's coastal waters, during the time of year when terrapins are officially protected by state laws.

• Trap-induced mortality is also common throughout much or all of the rest of the range of diamondback terrapins; the cumulative annual drownings are having a drastic impact upon the species as a whole (Seigel and Gibbons, 1995; Mann, 1995; G. S. Grant, pers. comm.).

• The widespread use of a rectangular wire excluder device (termed the Bycatch Reduction Apparatus, or BRA) can greatly reduce overall terrapin mortality and eliminate mortality of large females almost entirely.

• Installation of excluders in commercial crab traps also seems to increase the numbers of marketable crabs caught. The use of excluders will therefore not only save thousands of terrapins annually but should also increase the profits of the commercial crabbers who use them.

ACKNOWLEDGMENTS

Many people and organizations have contributed to the work described here. In particular, I am especially grateful to the many college, university, and high school students who have served with great dedication as summer research interns under the auspices of the Wetlands institute and Stockton College. I also wish to thank Dave Jenkins from the New Jersey Division of Fish, Game and Wildlife, as well as Pete Himchak, Paul Scarlett, and Tony Mazzarella, all from the New Jersey Bureau of Marine Fisheries, for information and cooperation. Thanks are also extended to Gilbert Grant, University of North Carolina at Wilmington, for sharing the results of his BRA experiments during the summers of 1995 and 1996. For financial support over the years, I am indebted to the Wetlands Institute, Richard Stockton College of New Jersey, the New Jersey Division of Fish, Game and Wildlife, and the Cape May Zoological Society. Finally, I thank the New Jersey Division of Fish, Game and Wildlife for scientific research permits.

LITERATURE CITED

Bishop. J. H. 1983. Incidental capture of diamondback terrapin by crab pots. Estuaries 6(4):426–430.

Mann, T. M. 1995. Population surveys for diamondback terrapins (*Malaclemys terrapin*) and Gulf salt marsh snakes (*Nerodia clarkii clarkii*) in Mississippi. Museum Technical Report No. 37, Miss. Mus. Nat. Sci., Jackson, Mississippi. 75 pp.

Mazzarella, A. D. 1995. Test of turtle excluder device in commercial crab pots. Unpubl. report prepared for the New Jersey Division of Fish, Game and Wildlife, Bureau of Marine Fisheries, Trenton, New Jersey. 9 pp.

Seigel, R. A. and J. W. Gibbons. 1995. Workshop on the ecology, status and management of the diamondback terrapin (*Malaclemys terrapin*), Savannah River Ecology Laboratory, 3 August 1994, final results and recommendations. Chelon. Conserv. Biol. 1(3):240–243.

Warner, W. W. 1996. Beautiful Swimmers. Little, Brown and Co., Boston. 304 pp.

Wood, R. C., and R. Herlands. 1997. Turtles and tires: The impact of roadkills on northern diamondback terrapin, *Malaclemys terrapin terrapin*, populations on the Cape May Peninsula, southern New Jersey, USA. *In* J. Van Abbema (ed.), Proceedings: Conservation, Restoration, and Management of Tortoises and Turtles—An International Conference, pp. 46–53. July 1993, Purchase, New York. New York Turtle and Tortoise Society, New York.

Yearicks, E. F., R. C. Wood, and W. S. Johnson. 1981. Hibernation of the northern diamondback terrapin, *Malaclemys terrapin terrapin*. Estuaries 4(1):78–80.

Potential Threats to Tortoise Populations in Parc National de "W," Niger, West Africa

JAMES E. MOORE

The Nature Conservancy of Nevada, 1771 East Flamingo Road, Suite 111B, Las Vegas, NV 89119, USA [e-mail: nvfo@aol.com]

ABSTRACT: In 1984–1985, during regular inventories of large mammals in Parc National de "W" in Niger, West Africa, observations were made of the African spurred tortoise, *Geochelone sulcata*. A species of hinge-backed tortoise (*Kinixys belliana*) is also found in unknown densities throughout the park. Both species were regularly captured when encountered on the roads by park guards, guides, and unsupervised tourists. The fates of these animals after capture and whether this practice continues today, is unknown.

The management objectives of the national park during this period were geared towards increasing and improving the tourist experience. Controlled early dry-season burning of this arid grass and scrub ecosystem was implemented to improve visibility of large mammals, to provide a fresh forage for the many ungulate species, and to stem the sweeping, uncontrolled fires typically started by trespassing pastoralists. The effects these burns may be having on the tortoise population, as well as on a host of other less visible or less tourist-important species, have raised serious concerns.

From June 1984 to June 1985 the author was posted at Parc National de "W" in Niger, West Africa, as the Park Biologist representing the U.S. Peace Corps. As part of regular anti-poaching patrols, vegetation mapping, and large mammal surveys, a plan for controlled early dry-season burns was developed to ameliorate habitat for the dual purpose of improving tourist visibility of the key large mammals (African elephant, cape buffalo, warthog, lion, baboon, topi antelope, hartebeest, roan antelope, and waterbuck) and to provide a series of fire breaks to stem large-scale uncontrolled fires later in the dry season. These wildfires are typically started by trespassing pastoralists to promote new grass growth for their livestock.

During the course of performing wildlife management duties and assisting tourists, several sightings of the African spurred tortoise (*Geochelone sulcata*) and the hinge-back tortoise (*Kinixys belliana*) were made. This raised concerns that habitat alterations from the regular, controlled burns may have been selecting against the less fire resistant species in this unique Sahelian reserve.

Site Description and History

Following Niger's independence from France, Park National de "W" was created in the early 1960s as the concept of natural reserves began to gain in popularity throughout the continent. Although it was initially established to provide a hunting area for wealthy expatriate hunters, as tourism increased in East African countries (e.g., Kenya and Tanzania), the focus of Park W shifted to more passive recreational activity such as wildlife viewing. By the mid-

Figure 1. *Geochelone sulcata* in Park W.

1970s hunting had been officially outlawed within the park boundaries and in the adjacent Tamou Faunal Reserve.

The park is named after the W-shaped bend in the Niger River that forms part of the northern border of the park (Figure 3). The southeastern boundary is created by the Mekrou River and the northwestern boundary by the Tapoa River. The total area encompassed by this "green triangle" is approximately 1250 km² and represents one of the few consistently vegetated regions of this Sahel country, which suffers from the increasing effects of desertification.

During the devastating drought of 1984–1986, word spread through the nomadic pastoralist communities that abundant green vegetation persisted in this minimally protected area, and Park W began to suffer from increasing trespass problems. Cattle, sheep, and goat herds were regularly brought across the borders by Peul and Fulani tribesmen from neighboring Burkina Faso and Benin as well as from other regions of Niger. Fires, intentionally set by the herdsmen to produce fresh forage, spread rapidly and often consumed large areas of the park. Attempts to control trespass were futile, given the meager and poorly motivated guard staff, who had infrequent access to vehicles, fuel, or equipment. Along with livestock trespass came an increase in poaching of baboons, antelope, and elephants for pelts, meat, and ivory.

Observations of Tortoises

On several occasions large burrow openings (>45 cm in width) were discovered in the sandier soil regions of the park. Recent tortoise tracks were frequently seen, although the tortoises responsible for them were not encountered. Juvenile tortoises (<30 cm) were occasionally found during the dry season (November–March) on the unpaved roads that serve as wildlife viewing trails for tourists. This may have been the result of the decrease in vegetation as the dry season progressed, making these age classes more visible.

It appeared that movement of tortoises occurred during the early morning hours or late afternoon towards dusk, since they were rarely seen from the hours of 8:00 A.M. to 5:00 P.M. when most of our work was done. Tourist vehicles would enter the park in the early morning (6:00 A.M.) and would usually be out by 3:00 or 4:00 P.M. when temperatures became uncomfortably high.

Figure 2. Map of Niger. Parc National de "W" is shown in black. Courtesy CIA Publications.

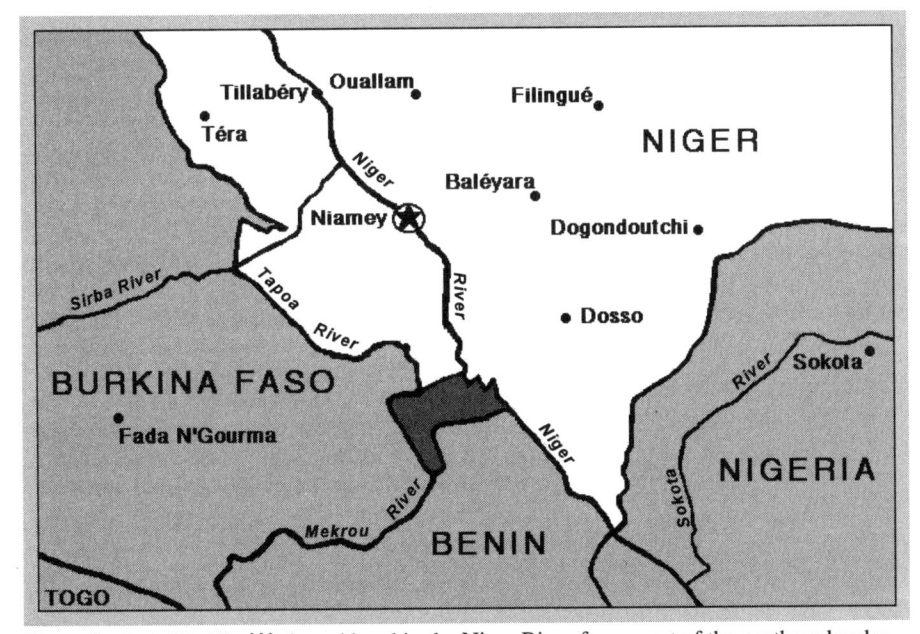

Figure 3. Park W. The W-shaped bend in the Niger River forms part of the northern border.

The largest burrow entrance encountered during controlled burning activities in November 1984 was more than 60 cm in width, and the accompanying tracks of hind feet were 8–10 cm wide at their widest point. A sharp turn about a meter into the tunnel prevented observation of the deepest parts. Despite numerous return visits to this site, the individual tortoise was never spotted, although the park guards indicated they were familiar with this large-sized animal. This particular burrow was found in thorn-scrub grassland interfaced with sandy-loam soil.

Kinixys were regularly spotted in the open, forested zones bordering the rivers that form the boundary of Park W. They were easily tracked in the sandy topsoil and were typically found wedged under bushes and in thorn-scrub brush. Park guards reported that hyenas fed on them, indicating that they were the only predator with jaws strong enough to crack the shell.

Management Considerations

The early dry season controlled-burning program began in 1984, and it would be important to review records of sightings of these two tortoise species and other reptiles and amphibians that may be encountered in the park. Of particular interest would be evidence of fire-burned shells of tortoises—living or dead.

The controlled burning program itself should be re-evaluated from an ecosystem perspective to insure that this lush grassland and riparian forested park is not being adversely impacted by the annual burning. It should be noted that fires are probably an annual occurrence anyway, especially with the increasing encroachment of human populations, both from Niger itself and two bordering countries (Burkina Faso and Benin). Rotational burning was envisioned in the preliminary plan to allow some regeneration between burns. It is not known if this burning prescription was followed in subsequent years.

While tourism is certainly responsible for the continued protection of this large green reserve of biodiversity in an otherwise arid country, it is imperative that steps taken to improve the tourist experience not adversely affect the capability of that ecosystem to function under natural processes. Above all, these tourist-friendly management decisions must not have the undesired effect of selecting against individual species or groups of associated species that may not be of high priority to the tourists.

Direct take of tortoises was apparently not so common as to seriously deplete the population. Occasionally the guides accompanying the tourist vehicles would pick up tortoises and bring them back to the park headquarters area to display in the small museum of park wildlife. It was also rumored that some visitors paid their guides to allow them to cache tortoises in their vehicle to take back to their houses in the capital city Niamey. However, the numbers of tortoises taken were unknown, and without knowledge of the status of the population in the park, no conclusion can be drawn about the effect these removals had on the resident population.

During their anti-poaching patrols, guards would occasionally bring back to the headquarters a particularly large or attractive specimen they encountered on the trails. This was done despite the park rule that all wildlife be left *in situ*. Enforcement of this rule is varied because it largely depends on consistent education of the guards and guides and to some extent on the commitment of the Park Conservator to the overall goal of biodiversity preservation.

Recommendations

Determining the current status of the tortoise populations should be a high priority in Park W as well as throughout the country of Niger. Occurrences of *G. sulcata* as far north as Agadez have been reported (J. Newby, pers. comm.). After a baseline status report is produced, these populations should be monitored on at least an annual basis, and management actions currently undertaken in the park should be examined in the light of population trends. If negative effects are determined, areas protected from any of the suspected adverse management actions should be set aside in the park for the populations to recover. It is not realistic to advocate abolishment of the management practices that enhance tourism. Tourism is the primary source of funding for enforcement and monitoring within the park boundary. These continuing revenues also offer the Niger government further justification for setting aside this fertile sector of an increasingly arid country, thereby protecting it from the growing agricultural and human population pressures.

Biophysical Analysis of the Impact of Shifting Land Use on Ornate Box Turtles, Wisconsin, USA

CHARLES G. CURTIN

Department of Zoology, University of Wisconsin, 1117 W. Johnson St., Madison, WI 53706, USA
Current address: Department of Biology, 167 Castetter Hall, Albuquerque, NM 87131-1091, USA
[e-mail: ccurtin@unm.edu]

ABSTRACT: Field studies using telemetry and microclimate analysis were used to examine the impact of habitat alteration on the ornate box turtle, *Terrapene ornata*, in southwestern Wisconsin. This work determined the biophysical characteristics that make sand prairies and savanna critical box turtle habitats, how changes in vegetation affect potential daily and seasonal activity periods of box turtles, and how these changes in activity period relate to physiological costs. Initial results from studies of box turtles in relatively contiguous habitat contrasted with those in severely fragmented areas indicate that the reduction in savanna and prairie habitats by habitat fragmentation has severe impacts on box turtle populations. Turtles in disturbed habitats appear to have shorter activity seasons, larger home ranges, and longer incubation periods. This appears to lead to lower recruitment and higher adult mortality. Because they exhibit a strong site fidelity, this suggests that habitat protection and restoration are key to protecting ornate box turtles, which are listed as "Endangered" in Wisconsin.

In Wisconsin the ornate box turtle, *Terrapene ornata*, a small terrestrial turtle, is at the northeastern edge of its broad geographical range. Wisconsin box turtles are dry prairie and savanna specialists (Vogt, 1981). The predominant plant communities in southern Wisconsin prior to European settlement (prairie and savanna) have been reduced and fragmented over the past century to a fraction (approx. 10%) of their original area (Curtis, 1959; Dunn and Stearns, 1993). While land area, soils, and topography have remained relatively constant over the past 40 years, plant community structure has shifted significantly, altering the microclimate (Curtin, 1995). Ornate box turtles are now reduced to a few isolated populations in the remaining disjunct patches of prairie and savanna. They have been listed as "Endangered" in Wisconsin since 1972 (Vogt, 1981). The examination of populations at the northern edge of their range, where they are subject to climatic constraints, provides a model system for predicting patterns and processes that may be acting upon box turtle populations throughout their range. My studies of box turtles in Wisconsin present an alternative biophysical framework to traditional population study methods.

In this study I focus on population response to shifts in landscape structure. While studies of habitat fragmentation per se are numerous (Ambuel and Temple, 1983; Bolger et al., 1991; Robinson et al., 1992; Wilcox, 1980; Soulé et al., 1988; Temple, 1987; Tinkle et al., 1981), few address the costs and consequences of habitat modification. Because reptile behavior and physiology are tightly coupled with climatic constraints, they are well suited for study of the climatological effects of habitat modification.

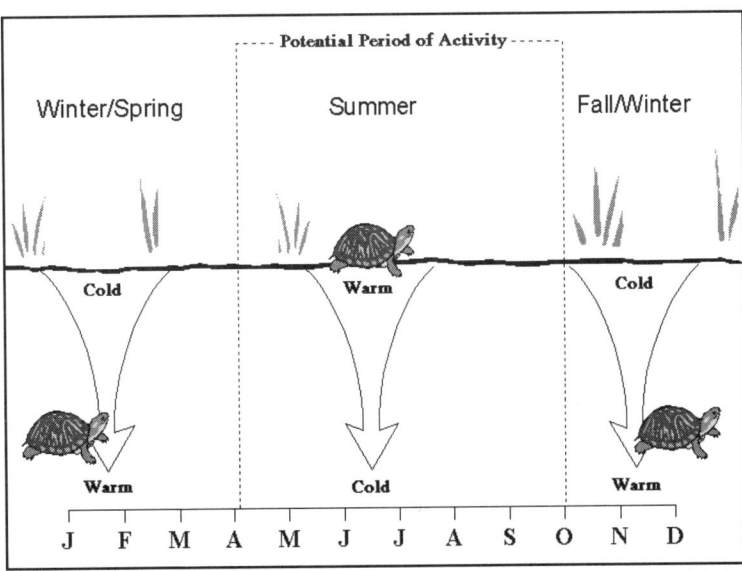

Figure 1. Daily and seasonal turtle activity periods are tightly coupled with the thermal environment. My measurements with data loggers and thermocouples set in soil probes indicate that spring emergence is correlated with an inversion in soil temperature that persists for longer than 48 hrs. Work by Grobman (1990) on box turtle populations in Missouri recorded a similar pattern with animals emerging from the ground when subsoil temperatures were consistently above 7°C.

EXPERIMENTAL DESIGN AND METHODS

I hypothesized that the altered physical structure of degraded plant communities leads to cooler microclimate than native plant communities with preserved disturbance patterns (Curtin, 1995). I used clay models of box turtles to determine whether changes in vegetation caused thermal alterations of habitats. Using a Beckman DK-2A Spectroreflectometer, the solar reflectivity of live ornate box turtle carapaces was determined to be between 0.808 and 0.816 (Curtin, 1995; Ellner and Karasov, 1993). Hollow clay replicas of turtles were painted to match this reflectivity (Bakken, 1992). I compared my models with body temperatures of turtles in the same location in the field and consistently found the models to be within 2°C of that of the live animals (n = 20). A digital thermometer (Omega Engineering, Inc., Stamford, Connecticut) attached to box turtle models in shade, part shade (60% shade/40% sun), part sun (60% sun/40% shade), and full sun at ambient temperatures of 13–16°, 17–19°, 20–23°, 24–26°, and 27–29°C (n = 50 measurements at each temperature range) was used to measure environmental temperatures.

A cooling in the environment resulting from shifting plant community structure (Curtin, 1995) was hypothesized to result in reduced box turtle growth rates. In the laboratory, nine juvenile box turtles (hatched in September 1993 from two clutches from the same population of Wisconsin box turtles) were placed in a 2 × 1 × .25 m box divided into eight identical sections. Five turtles where kept at one end with a Sylvania heat lamp producing an ambient daytime air temperature similar to that experienced by populations in dry prairie and savanna habitats (28–30°C). The other half of the enclosure was kept at a daytime temperature similar to that of degraded (old-field or woodlot plant associations) habitats (21–22°C). A divider maintained the thermal difference between the sections. The animals were fed ad lib identical amounts of food. The turtles were kept in the different microclimates for four months (the equivalent of one growing season) and after the first month were weighed every two weeks.

Microclimate cooling was predicted to result in shorter activity periods and lower recruitment. During the active season body temperature (T_b) and air temperature (T_a) were measured in the field using cloacal (Miller & Weber, Inc., Queens, New York) and digital (Omega Engineering, Inc., Stamford, Connecticut) thermometers. In summer 1992 during studies at the Mazomanie Wildlife Area in south-central Wisconsin, I monitored a population of 14 box turtles (eight with Wildlife Materials 2160 LD transmitters, attached by snap swivel to a hole drilled in the rear of the carapace, and dragged behind the animal) on a site with minimal habitat modification (40%) and microclimate alteration. In the summer of 1993 radiotelemetry studies monitored 36 turtles at four different sites. Again, Wildlife Materials transmitters were used with transmitters attached either via snap swivels in a hole in the carapace as in 1992 or glued flush to the rear of the carapace. (Gluing reduced the chance of a transmitter becoming entangled in vegetation and the likelihood of its loss.) Studies monitored two turtle populations at The Nature Conservancy's Spring Green Preserve, one in contiguous high quality prairie (90% open) and one in old-field habitat (70% open); the Mazomanie Wildlife Area population studied in 1992 (60% open); and the American Players Theater population (10% open). These studies were contrasted with studies by Doroff and Keith (1990), Ellner and Karasov (1993), and Temple (1987) on a severely fragmented site (>10% open) in Dunlap Hollow, Wisconsin. Data on population structure, home range size, microhabitat selection, and thermal preference were collected to determine how box turtles respond to changes in microclimate caused by habitat alteration. Tanglefoot™ trap and net surveys conducted at the Mazomanie site in 1992 and 1993 showed no difference in insect abundance between degraded and prairie/savanna plant association (Curtin, unpubl.), indicating it is microclimate and not food that limits activity in degraded habitats.

RESULTS AND DISCUSSION

The effect of microclimate on species activity, growth, and reproduction is well established (Adolph and Porter, 1993; Congdon, 1989; Grant and Porter, 1992; Spotila et al., 1989; Porter, 1989; Porter and Tracy, 1983). Studies in the field and in the laboratory have consistently demonstrated that box turtles and many other reptiles have narrow, well-defined thermal preferences (Ellner and Karasov, 1993; Gatten, 1974; Legler, 1960). In Wisconsin and elsewhere box turtles respond to both daily and seasonal temperature fluctuations (Figure 1).

The cooler, more homogeneous plant assemblages limit box turtle activity periods, particularly during the cool season. Environmental temperatures recorded using model box turtles were compared to data on box turtle thermal constraints from lab experiments (Ellner and Karasov, 1993; Curtin, 1995) to illustrate how altered communities severely limit turtle activity (Figure 2). This prediction is corroborated by telemetry data showing that box turtles differentially select warmer sites, particularly during the cool season (Figure 3). Similar results exist for studies from Dunlap Hollow (Doroff and Keith, 1990). Contrasts of seasonal activity periods from Doroff and Keith's (1990) studies in the severely degraded Dunlap Hollow (155 days) and my study at Mazomanie (177 days) suggest a three-week difference in yearly activity between the two populations. In contrast, studies by Legler (1960) indicate that populations at the heart of the species range in Kansas had yearly activity periods of 186 days. Thus, the total yearly

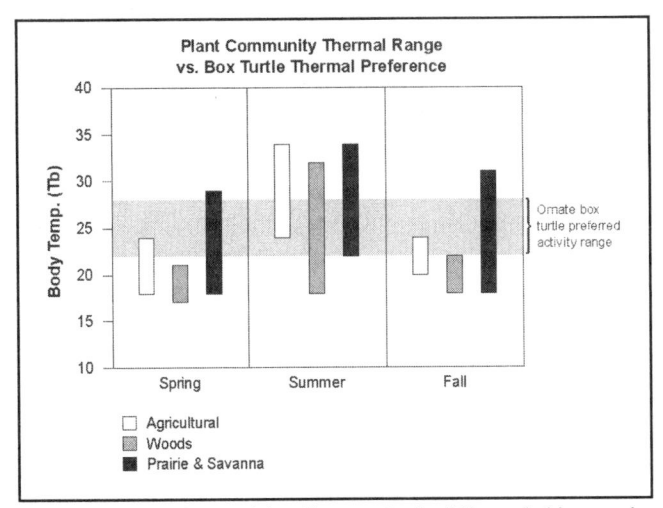

Figure 2. Using clay models of box turtles in different habitats under average daily spring (19–22°C), summer (25–28°C), and fall (16–23°C) temperatures, potential box turtle body temperatures in different plant communities were estimated. This graph demonstrates how cooler, more homogeneous habitats restrict box turtle activity during the cool season, while conferring no advantage during the warm season.

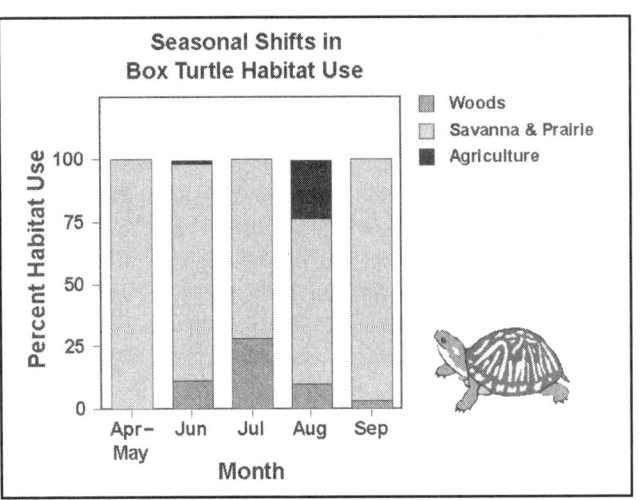

Figure 3. Results from the 1992 telemetry studies at the Mazomanie site corroborate predictions made in Figure 2 by showing that turtles disproportionately selected habitats in native plant communities (even though they represented less that 25% of available habitat), particularly during cool seasons. The disproportionate use of warmer habitats was also evident in other studies of Wisconsin box turtles (Doroff and Keith, 1990).

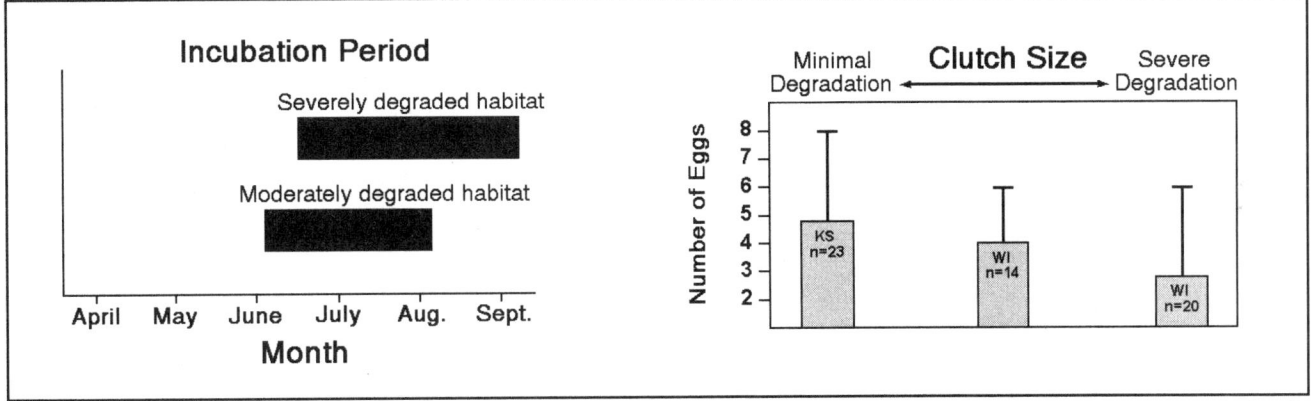

Figure 4. Populations at the severely degraded Dunlap Hollow typically emerged from overwintering several weeks later than populations in other habitats (even though studies carried out at Dunlap Hollow were done during some of the warmest seasons on record, and my studies were completed during several of the coolest seasons on record). This late emergence, combined with later egg laying and longer incubation periods, appears to lead to reduced hatching success. The lower clutch sizes at Dunlap Hollow (Doroff and Keith, 1990) in contrast with studies from Kansas (Legler, 1960) suggested that habitat degradation might lead to smaller clutches. X rays of gravid females from four moderately disturbed Wisconsin sites contrasted with work by Legler (1960) on relatively contiguous habitats in Kansas, and Doroff and Keith in severely degraded sites at Dunlap hollow, indicate that, while there is a trend toward smaller clutches, it is not significant.

activity period available to turtles at Mazomanie has more in common with populations in Kansas (500 km to the south) than in Dunlap Hollow (5 km to the east). This reduction in activity has profound implications for the life history of the species. A delay of spring emergence appears to affect the timing of oviposition but not clutch size (Figure 4). Populations in degraded habitats in Wisconsin typically emerged in late April or early May (Curtin, 1995; Doroff and Keith, 1990), whereas in the relatively undegraded populations I have studied, first emergence typically occurs in the first week of April. A delay in nesting can compromise reproduction by not allowing developing animals to hatch before fall. Populations in the severely disturbed sites in Dunlap Hollow, even in warm years, did not hatch before fall and often suffered winter kill (Doroff and Keith, 1990). This, combined with increased nest predation in these fragmented sites (Temple, 1987), appears to lead to highly skewed age structure, indicative of low levels of recruitment (Figure 5).

Laboratory comparison of hatchlings subjected to temperatures equivalent to a degraded habitat (21–22°C) versus temperatures available to animals in good quality habitats

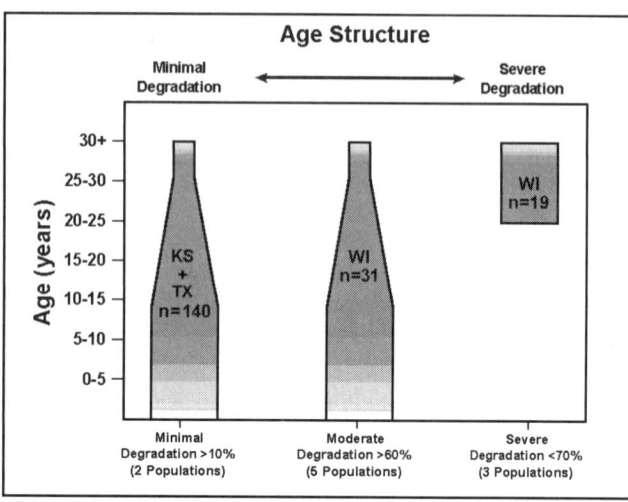

Figure 5. While shell ring counts offer only an approximate estimate of population age structure, the diagram of the approximate age structure of populations experiencing differing degrees of habitat alteration illustrates the highly skewed population structures indicative of populations experiencing little or no recruitment.

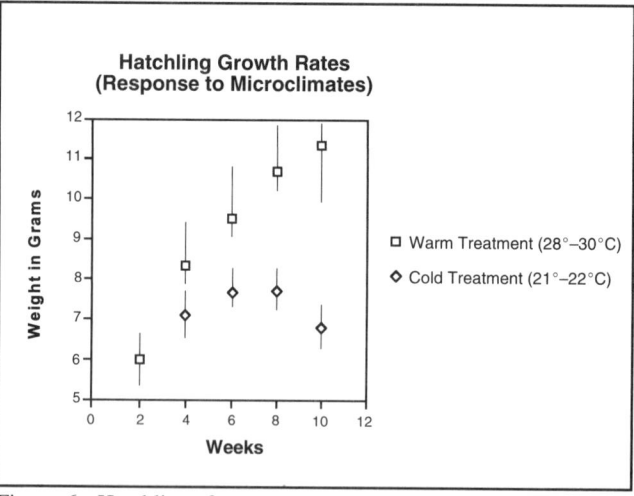

Figure 6. Hatchlings from two clutches in a Wisconsin population show significantly different growth ($P < .05$) in temperatures indicative of degraded habitats, contrasted with those held in a microclimate typical of warmer habitats. This demonstrates how degraded habitats can reduce population growth potential.

(28–30°C) (Curtin, 1995) showed that hatchlings in warmer environments have significantly higher growth rates (Figure 6), while growth of hatchlings in degraded habitats is greatly reduced. This is expected to lead to delayed reproduction and increased mortality.

The invasion of exotic plant species (non-prairie-savanna species of European/Asian origin) also works on a macro scale, altering the spatial relationships of the landscape. Adults appear to shuttle between habitat remnants, leading to increases in home range size. Typical home range sizes at Dunlap Hollow (Doroff and Keith, 1990) were almost four times those at my study sites: 8.7 ha vs. 2.5 ha (Figure 7). The larger home range sizes, created by deteriorated habitat, increase the likelihood of adult turtles encountering people. Encounters with humans (roadkills, collecting, etc.) are the major cause of adult mortality for adult ornate box turtles (Blair, 1976; Doroff and Keith, 1990; Legler, 1960). Long-lived, K-selected organisms like ornate box turtles have a life history strategy predicated on low adult mortality. Studies indicate that a survival rate of lower than 91% per annum will lead to population declines (Doroff and Keith, 1990; Congdon et al., 1993). While too short to determine long-term trends, short-term mortality rates recorded in my studies suggest that most populations are in steep decline. Telemetry data in the severely degraded Dunlap Hollow indicated an adult survival rate of 81% (Doroff and Keith, 1990), indicating that these populations were not viable and would be extirpated in the near future if mortality rates continued at that level. These predictions have come to pass. Populations (over 50 individuals), studied by Doroff and Keith (1990) at Dunlap Hollow in the mid-1980s, are nearly gone (Keith, pers. comm.). The Mazomanie site with intermediate disturbance was the only site appearing to be viable, with adult survival of 91%. This population also had the most stable age structure with the largest cohort of young turtles. The Spring Green sites had a lower adult survival rate of 87% in 1993 and a skewed age structure, indicating that these populations, previously assumed to be viable, are in decline. Intensive land use surrounding the preserve and high predator densities apparently associated with river corridor habitats (Curtin, unpubl. obs.) may be responsible for these trends. The populations studied are not isolated examples. Surveys suggest that virtually all Wisconsin box turtle populations are in steep decline (Curtin, 1995; Hay and

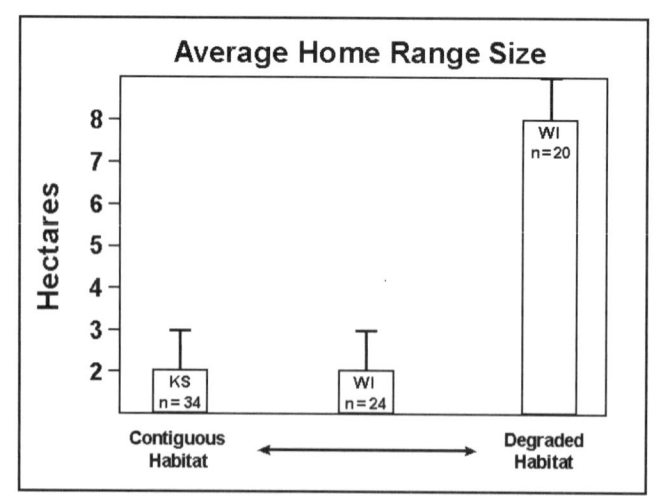

Figure 7. As adults shuttle increasing distances between remaining habitat patches, home range sizes increase dramatically. Typical home range sizes at Dunlap Hollow (Doroff and Keith, 1990) were almost four times larger than at the Mazomanie sites (5 km away) or at other relatively undegraded habitats. The enlarged home ranges are expected to raise adult mortality by increasing the likelihood of encounters with people and other predators.

Moore, unpubl.). At current rates, without habitat restoration or management, box turtle populations are likely to disappear from the region in the near future.

Conservation of Ornate Box Turtles

The decline of box turtles appears to be widespread and of increasing concern (Anderson, 1965; Doroff and Keith, 1990; Schwartz and Schwartz, 1974; Yahner, 1974; Stickel, 1978; Williams and Parker, 1987). Yet, because turtles are long lived and successful reproduction is not consistent, traditional demographic approaches to determining population viability through long-term population studies are logistically difficult and not feasible for most populations (Congdon et al., 1993). While collecting and roadkills are significant problems throughout the ornate box turtle's range (various authors, this volume), I believe habitat deterioration is an important factor in increasing mortality and decreasing reproduction. My studies indicate that box turtle populations, because of their small, well-defined home ranges, can persist in relatively small areas of non-degraded habitat (2–3 ha), suggesting it is not exclusively habitat fragmentation, but habitat degradation that is leading to box turtle declines. Rather than outside influences affecting populations, it is microscale, within-patch degradation of habitats that increases movement and home range sizes. Adults consequently encounter increasing pressures from the outside. This, coupled with decreased recruitment resulting from cooler microclimates, indicate that box turtle declines in Wisconsin are often the result of environmental rather than structural modification of the landscape, and suggests that habitat restoration is a critical component of box turtle habitat preservation.

Habitat Restoration

Studies of microclimates in burned and unburned grassland habitats in Wisconsin indicate that burned areas were several degrees C warmer and more thermally diverse than unburned grasslands with denser plant concentrations (Curtin, 1995). Burning and clearing of old-field portions of the Mazomanie research site by the Wisconsin Department of Natural Resources provided an opportunity to test whether burning and clearing would expand available box turtle habitat (Figure 8). In the summer of 1992 box turtles spent less than 5% of the time in the old-field areas, which covered almost 40% of the site. After burning in 1993, activity in the burned, old-field habitats was almost 50%, suggesting that the cool, dense plant associations were limiting activity and that increases in habitat area could be attained with relatively modest management efforts.

CONCLUSIONS

Box turtles in remnant sand prairies and savanna represent a model system for studying the costs and consequences of habitat degradation and the factors limiting species range. My studies demonstrate how relatively subtle shifts in plant community structure, resulting in shifts in microclimate and altering life history, can lead to steep population declines. Relatively modest habitat restoration is shown to lead to increases in the amount of available habitat for endangered

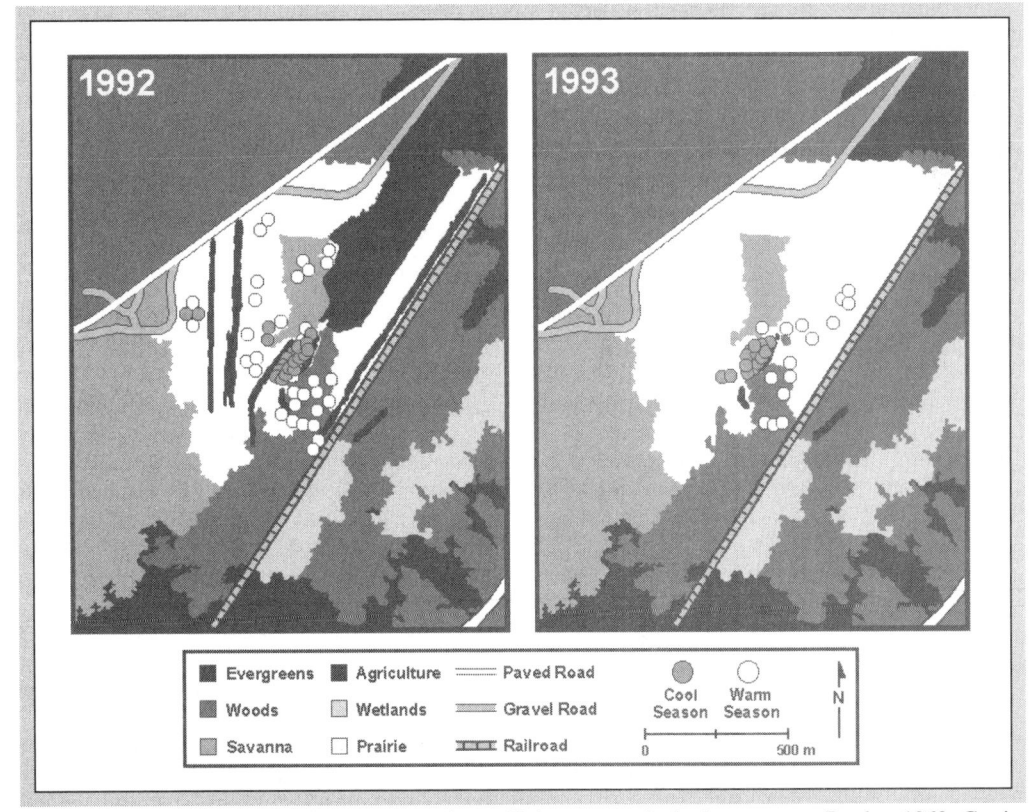

Figure 8. Because of box turtles' apparent close affinity to a particular home range (Legler, 1960; Curtin, unpubl.), it was questionable whether turtle populations would respond to habitat restoration, even if the restoration resulted in warmer, more heterogeneous microclimates. Telemetry data from representative ten-day periods in spring and summer illustrate how habitat clearing and burning by the Wisconsin Department of Natural Resources in early spring 1993 greatly increased the amount of warm season habitat available to the animals.

box turtle populations, greatly increasing a population's potential for recruitment and survival.

Acknowledgments

This work was supported by funding from the U.S. Department of Energy (DOE.ER/60633), The Nature Conservancy's graduate student conservation biology grant program, The Zoological Society of Milwaukee County, The Wisconsin Academy of Arts, Letters, and Sciences, Wisconsin Power & Light, and the Wisconsin Department of Natural Resources. I wish to express my thanks to the following individuals who provided major advice or assistance during the project: S. C. Adolph, B. W. Grant, R. Hay, T. Hunt, L. B. Keith, N. B. O'Connor, W. P. Porter, S. A. Temple, and C. R. Tracy.

Literature Cited

Adolph, S. C. and W. P. Porter. 1993. Temperature, activity, and lizard life histories. Am. Nat. 142(2):273–295.

Anderson, D. 1965. Reptiles of Missouri. University of Missouri Press, Columbia.

Ambuel, B. and S. A. Temple. 1983. Area-dependent changes in the bird communities and vegetation of southern Wisconsin forests. Ecology 64:1057–1068.

Bakken, G. W. 1992. Measurement and application of the operative and standard operative temperatures in ecology. Amer. Zool. 32: 194–216.

Blair, W. F. 1976. Some aspects of the biology of the ornate box turtle, *Terrapene ornata*. The Southwest Naturalist 21(1):89–104.

Bolger, D. T., A. C. Alberts, and M. E. Soulé. 1991. Bird species occurrence patterns in habitat fragments: Sampling, extinction, and nested subsets. Am. Nat. 137:155–166.

Congdon, J. D. 1989. Proximate and evolutionary constraints on energy relations in reptiles. Physiological Zoology 62(2):356–373.

Congdon, J. D., A. E. Dunham, and R. C. van Loben Sels. 1993. Delayed sexual maturity and demographics of Blanding's turtle (*Emydoidea blandingii*): Implications for conservation and management of long-lived animals. Conserv. Biol. 7(4):826–833.

Curtin, C. G. 1995. Latitudinal compensation in ornate box turtle: Implications for species response to shifting land-use and climate. Ph.D. thesis, University of Wisconsin, Madison.

Curtis, J. T. 1959. The Vegetation of Wisconsin. University of Wisconsin Press, Madison.

Doroff, A. M. and L. B. Keith. 1990. Demography and ecology of an ornate box turtle (*Terrapene ornata*) population in south-central Wisconsin. Copeia 2:387–399.

Dunn, C. P. and F. Stearns. 1993. Landscape ecology in Wisconsin: 1830–1990. *In* J. S. Fralish, R. P. McIntosh, and O. L. Loucks, (eds.), John T. Curtis: Fifty Years of Wisconsin Plant Ecology, pp. 197–216. The Wisconsin Academy of Arts, Letters, and Sciences, Madison.

Ellner, L. R. and W. H. Karasov. 1993. Latitudinal variation in the thermal biology of ornate box turtles. Copeia 1993(2):447–455.

Gatten, R. E. 1974. Effect of nutritional status on the preferred body temperature of the turtles *Pseudemys scripta* and *Terrapene ornata*. Copeia 1974:912–917.

Grant, B. W. and W. P. Porter. 1992. Modeling global macroclimate constraints on ectotherm energy budgets. Amer. Zool. 32:154–178.

Grobman, A. B. 1990. The effect of soil temperatures on emergence from hibernation of *Terrapene carolina* and *Terrapene ornata*. Am. Mid. Nat. 124:366–371.

Legler, J. M. 1960. Natural history of the ornate box turtle, *Terrapene ornata ornata* Agassiz. Univ. of Kan. Publ. Mus. Nat. Hist. 11 (10):527–669.

Porter, W. P. 1989. New animal models and experiments for calculating growth potential at different elevations. Physiol. Zool. 62(2): 286–313.

Porter, W. P. and C. R. Tracy. 1983. Biophysical analysis of energetics, time-space utilizations, and distributional limits. *In* R. B. Huey, E. Pianka, and T. Schoener (eds.), Lizard Ecology: Studies of a Model Organism, pp. 55–81. Harvard University Press, Cambridge, Massachusetts.

Robinson, G. R., R. D. Holt, M. S. Gaines, S. P. Hamburg, M. L. Johnson, H. S. Fitch, and E. A. Martinko. 1992. Diverse and contrasting effects of habitat fragmentation. Science 257:524–526.

Soulé, M. E., B. A. Bolger, A. C. Alberts, J. Wright, S. Sorice, and S. Hill. 1988. Reconstructing dynamics of the rapid extinctions of chaparral-requiring birds in urban habitat islands. Biol. Conserv. 2:75–96.

Schwartz, C. W. and E. R. Schwartz. 1974. The three-toed box turtle in Missouri: Its populations, home range, and movements. Pub. Miss. Dept. Cons. Terr. Series 5:1–28.

Stickel, L. F. 1978. Changes in box turtle population during three decades. Copeia 78:221–225.

Spotila, J. R., E. A. Standora, D. P. Easton, and P. S. Rutledge. 1989. Bioenergetics, behavior, and resource partitioning in stressed habitats: Biophysical and molecular approaches. Physiol. Zool. 62(2): 253–285.

Temple, S. A. 1987. Predation on turtle nests increases near ecological edges. Copeia 1987:250–252.

Tinkle, D. W., J. D. Congdon, and P. C. Rosen. 1981. Nesting frequency and success: Implications for the demography of painted turtles. Ecology 62:1426–1432.

Vogt, R. C. 1981. Natural History of Amphibians and Reptiles of Wisconsin. Milwaukee Public Museum, Milwaukee.

Wilcox, B. A. 1980. Insular ecology and conservation. *In* M. E. Soulé and B. A. Wilcox (eds.), Conservation Biology: An Evolutionary-Ecological Perspective, pp. 95–118. Sinuar Press, Sunderland, Massachusetts.

Williams, E. C. and W. S. Parker. 1987. A long-term study of a box turtle (*Terrapene carolina*) population at Allen Memorial Woods, Indiana, with emphasis on survivorship. Herpetologica 1987:328–335.

Yahner, R. H. 1974. Weight change, survival rate, and the home range of the box turtle. Copeia 1974:546–548.

Effects of Habitat Alteration on River Turtles of Tropical Asia with Emphasis on Sand Mining and Dams

EDWARD O. MOLL

Department of Zoology, Eastern Illinois University, Charleston, IL 61920-3099, USA [e-mail: cfeom@eiu.edu]

ABSTRACT: By destroying nesting beaches, sand mining has become one of the most serious factors threatening the survival of tropical Asian turtles. Removal of sand from beaches along Asian rivers to supply construction projects, involving the use of large earth moving equipment, has accelerated over the past two decades. Many rivers are becoming devoid of nesting sites for such sand-nesting chelonians as *Batagur baska*, *Callagur borneoensis*, *Kachuga* spp., *Chitra indica*, and *Pelochelys cantorii*. Upriver dams exacerbate the problem by preventing replacement sand from coming downriver while increasing erosion by periodic and unseasonable elevation of water levels. The Kedah River in Malaysia is cited as a case history, exemplifying how the combined effects of sand mining and dams can destroy riverine chelonian populations. Establishment of refuges and zoning of sand mining activities are recommended actions.

With few exceptions, populations of large river turtles in tropical Asia have experienced serious declines in recent decades. The IUCN/SSC Tortoise and Freshwater Turtle Specialist Group (1991) lists four of the 11 large river turtles in the region as APR 1 (badly threatened/heavily exploited) and six others as APR 2 or 3 (species requiring conservation action). Two quite different sets of factors are responsible for these declines. First and most obvious are direct factors that include overexploitation for food or products. The second group, although less publicized, is equally or perhaps even more serious and involves indirect factors, particularly habitat alteration and destruction.

I have previously reviewed the effects and problems of the direct factors associated with tropical Asian river turtles elsewhere (Moll, 1976, 1978, 1984a, 1984b, 1985, 1989, and 1990a). This paper concentrates on indirect factors, particularly sand mining, which has received little attention to date.

Habitat Alteration

In areas of human habitation, some form of habitat alteration is always occurring. It is not always immediately obvious how these alterations may affect the turtles of the region. Typically, human changes affect the majority of species negatively; however, some generalists may benefit and even thrive as a result.

The Neotropical slider turtle is a case in point. Pleistocene climatic changes along with human expansion opened up the Neotropical forest, providing nesting areas for this opportunistic species of Nearctic origin and presumably fostered its expansion through tropical America (Moll and Legler, 1971; Pritchard and Trebbeau, 1984; Moll and Moll, 1990). Also, by increasing the amount of water in arid areas, dams in western Mexico may have augmented slider habitat.

In tropical Asia, other generalists such as *Cuora amboinensis* and *Siebenrockiella crassicollis* are today more abundant in human-disturbed areas than in relatively unaltered forest habitat (Moll and Mohd. Khan, 1990). Typically, large river turtles are much less adaptable and respond negatively to a majority of habitat changes.

Even alterations well outside of the habitat may have negative consequences. For example, forest clearing may seem to have little impact on the largely aquatic denizens of a river. However, in the absence of trees to hold the soil and water, rivers become deluged with runoff and silt, which leads to problems for river turtles. One harmful effect results when the silt is deposited over riverside sand banks during flooding, thus forming an organic base on which tropical grasses can grow. River turtles typically utilize open sand banks for nesting and either can not or will not utilize heavily vegetated banks.

On Malaysia's Perak River, where tin mines and deforestation have greatly increased the silt load, virtually all of the upstream sand banks are covered with lalang grass, *Imperata cylindrica*. The river terrapin, *Batagur baska*, presently nests only on those banks that are cleared each year by egg collectors. The Perak *Batagur* has thus become completely dependent upon man to provide it with nesting sites. After clearing the grass to attract gravid females to nest, the egg collectors harvest all the eggs they can find. Sources for recruitment are therefore limited: A few nests escape detection during mass laying, and the Department of Wildlife buys some of the eggs from the collectors to hatch.

Another effect is that the silt tends to clog the stream channel and this, along with the greater runoff from the

Figure 1. Sand removal the old fashioned way—Malaysians returning to their village with a dug-out-load of sand, ca. 1975. Sand mining of this type was the norm on tropical Asian rivers until recently. As long as there are no dams that prevent new sand from being carried downstream, damage by this practice is negligible.

deforested watershed, leads to both increased and unseasonable floods. When these floods occur just after the peak of the nesting season, most of the annual reproductive output of a river turtle population can be destroyed.

Figure 2. Sand mining using modern machinery greatly speeds the destruction of riverine sand banks —a serious problem for sand-nesting turtles and crocodiles in tropical Asia. Sand mining on the Chambal River of India consists of human labor for digging and trucks and tractors to haul the sand away. Bulldozers and backhoes used for digging at other sites further accelerate the destruction.

Sand Mining

Perhaps the most insidious and potentially one of the greatest dangers for tropical Asian river turtles today is sand removal from river banks. Sand is in demand throughout the region for construction purposes and river banks are a very accessible source. Earlier in the century sand removal was relatively slow. It had to be hand loaded into small boats (Figure 1), and it took a long time to do any appreciable damage to a large bank. Over the last two to three decades modern technology has taken over. With bulldozers and backhoes to dig and trucks and tractors to haul the sand away, an extensive sand bank can be eliminated in a matter of days (Figures 2 and 3).

Many large river turtles and crocodiles require sand for nesting. Populations of the following sand-nesting chelonians in tropical Asia are being adversely effected: *Batagur baska*, *Callagur borneoensis*, *Kachuga dhongoka*, *K. kachuga*, *Chitra indica*, and *Pelochelys cantorii*. An extensive survey of *Batagur* populations in five countries (Moll, 1990b) failed to find any river inhabited by the turtle that was not suffering some degree of sand removal (Table 1). At the extreme, exemplified by the Kelantan and Kedah Rivers of Malaysia, virtually every sandbank suitable for nesting has now been removed.

The Chambal River in India is a stronghold for a number of large river turtles, *Kachuga dhongoka*, *K. kachuga*, *Aspideretes gangeticus*, and *Chitra indica*, which have been heavily exploited. It also provides optimum habitat for the endangered gharial and is the site of the largest Indian sanctuary for that species. Unfortunately, many of the best nesting banks for these species occur near the highway bridge between Rajasthan and Madhya Pradesh and thus are easily accessible. When the Chambal River Gharial Sanctuary was established here in 1978, the Government of India granted construction concerns the right to mine sand in a three-kilometer stretch from the bridge. However, funds for enforcement of this edict have dwindled, and now sand is being mined well outside of the set limits. Turtle nests are being destroyed at an ever-accelerating rate.

Dams

Dams have exacerbated the problems caused by sand mining. Those built upstream of nesting areas prevent the downstream flow of sand from replacing mined or eroded nesting beaches, which never recover. Further, many of these dams periodically release water in massive amounts, creating excessive erosion and unseasonable flooding of sand banks. On the Terengganu River, an island known as Pasir Lubok Kawah has long been an important nesting beach for *Batagur*, with an average of 60 females nesting each year—at least since the Department of Conservation began a hatchery program there in 1976. Less than a decade after the completion of the massive Kenyir Dam on the river, the island has eroded away to the point that only a half dozen females now utilize the site.

Figure 3. The daily line up of trucks and tractors removing sand from a Chambal River beach.

Dams downstream from nesting areas can interfere with the nesting migrations of turtles. Tidal barrages built on small tributaries prevent river turtles from moving upstream at high tide to utilize the productivity of the stream. *Batagur* and *Callagur* exemplify riverine species that make extensive nesting migrations. Both feed in tidal portions of

TABLE 1
Levels of sand mining on potential or known nesting beaches of river turtles on tropical Asian rivers visited in the course of a 1989–1990 status survey sponsored by the World Wide Fund for Nature. Asterisks indicate level of sand removal: * some local use, ** moderate commercial usage, *** heavy commercial exploitation, **** near total destruction of sand banks. Affected species are abbreviated: *Batagur baska* (*Bb*), *Callagur borneoensis* (*Cb*), *Kachuga dhongoka* (*Kd*), *K. kachuga* (*Kk*), *K. smithi* (*Ks*), *K. tentoria* (*Kt*), *Orlitia borneensis* (*Ob*), *Amyda cartilaginea* (*Ac*), *Aspideretes hurum* (*Ah*), *Chitra indica* (*Ci*), *Pelochelys cantorii* (*Pc*).

River	Country	District	Damage	Species
Kali Ganga	Bangladesh	Dhaka	***	*Kd, Kk, Ks, Kt, Ah*
Padma	Bangladesh	Dhaka	***	*Kd, Kk, Ks, Kt, Ah*
Chambal	India	Rajasthan/MP	***	*Kd, Kk, Kt, Ci*
Khrasrota	India	Orissa	***	*Kt, Ah, Pc*
Tulangbawang	Indonesia	Lampung-Sumatra	*	*Bb, Cb, Ob*
Kelantan	Malaysia	Kelantan	****	*Bb, Cb, Ac*
Dungun	Malaysia	Terengganu	**	*Bb, Cb, Ac, Pc*
Terennganu	Malaysia	Terengganu	**	*Bb, Cb, Ac, Pc*
Pahang	Malaysia	Pahang	**	*Bb, Cb, Ac, Pc*
Kedah	Malaysia	Kedah	****	*Bb, Cb, Ac*
Mudah	Malaysia	Kedah	****	*Bb, Cb, Ac*
Perak	Malaysia	Perak	***	*Bb, Cb, Ac, Pc*
Muar	Malaysia	Johor	***	*Cb, Ob, Ac*
La-ngu	Thailand	Satun	**	*Bb, Cb, Ac*
Pakpara	Thailand	Satun	**	*Bb, Cb, Ac*

Figure 4. A female painted terrapin, *Callagur borneoensis*, in a nesting enclosure on the Kedah River of Malaysia. As all nesting beaches on this river have been destroyed by sand mining, female river turtles seeking nest sites are captured by local egg collectors (note pitfall trenches at upper left) and placed in these sand-filled enclosures until they lay their eggs.

the river that are rich in food but often lack the sand banks needed for nesting. Depending upon the river, females of both species will travel as far as 100 km, either upriver or downriver to the coast, to find suitable beaches.

The Kedah River—A Case History

This river in northwestern Malaysia exemplifies the problems that can result from dams and sand mining. The following brief history of turtle egg collecting on the Kedah River was assembled from interviews with Kedah Game Department personnel and long-time egg collectors.

Prior to 1960 the river supported large populations of *Batagur* and *Callagur*. The river terrapin population annually laid in excess of 20,000 eggs on Pantai Raja, a nesting bank controlled by the Sultan of Kedah. The eggs are highly prized by Malaysians for their reputed aphrodisiac properties, and it was traditional for Sultans to have the prerogative of collecting eggs at the best sites.

Long-time residents report that the Sultan's staff once recorded over 700 turtles nesting in a single night at Pantai Rajah. At nesting time, the Sultan declared a holiday. He and his guests would travel to Pantai Rajah, staying overnight in a small guest house near the beach. At dawn they dug up terrapin eggs until the sand became too hot to continue. The excavated eggs were placed on a 6 × 10 ft rattan mat, and it would not be unusual for the pile to exceed four feet in height.

The demise of this population occurred quickly as the result of two actions—sand mining and dam building. Beginning in the early 1960s, extensive construction in the capital city of Alor Setar created a demand for sand, and much of the demand was met by mining the banks of the Kedah River. By the late sixties two dams were completed on the river. One, above the nesting area, prevented any sand from upstream replenishing the nesting banks. The other, constructed between the tidal area of the river and the nesting sites, prevented turtles from moving between their traditional feeding areas and ancestral nest sites. Within a decade the sand banks between the dams had disappeared and natural reproduction of *Batagur* and *Callagur* ceased on the Kedah River.

Each nesting season, some surviving females still arrive

at the former sand banks and emerge to wander aimlessly over the mud searching for the once-plentiful sand. Local egg collectors take advantage of this behavior. They dig trenches parallel to the river, which serve as pitfall traps for the emerging females. Captured females are then placed into artificially constructed sand pits within bamboo enclosures and kept there until they lay their eggs (Figure 4). After nesting they are released. The Kedah Game Department purchases some of the collectors' eggs each year for a hatchery in an attempt to keep the turtles from disappearing from the river.

The plight of the Kedah terrapins could well become the norm rather than the exception in tropical Asian rivers unless sand mining is controlled.

Action

The methods required to address this problem will differ in each country depending upon its laws, mores, and the priorities. However, the following recommendations seem generally applicable:

1. Licenses should be required before any sand mining is allowed on a river. Departments of Wildlife and Fisheries should be among the agencies that review license applications. These agencies can best assess the impact that sand mining will have on the local fish and wildlife, and each should have the authority to reject applications when the impact is too great.

2. Quotas should be established to control the amount of sand mining allowable on any river. For example, a quota may limit the mining to no more than a quarter of the sand banks in any area of the river. Or, as on the Chambal River Gharial Sanctuary, sand removal can be restricted to a certain stretch of the river (e.g., 3 km from the highway bridge). These quotas would have to be strictly enforced.

Dams greatly complicate the problem. Once a dam is in place, downstream sand banks are ultimately doomed. No matter how much protection is provided, these banks will gradually erode away, and there will be no annual replacement of sand from upstream. Unless major rivers are kept free flowing or unless new sand is brought in to replace that being carried out to sea, the majority of tropical Asian river turtles will suffer the fate of those on the Kedah River.

LITERATURE CITED

IUCN/SSC Tortoise and Freshwater Turtle Specialist Group. 1991. Tortoises and freshwater turtles: An action plan for their conservation, 2d ed. (D. Stubbs, comp.). IUCN/SSC Tortoise and Freshwater Turtle Specialist Group, Gland, Switzerland. i–iv + 47 pp.

Moll, D. L. and E. O. Moll. 1990. The slider turtle in the Neotropics: Adaptation of a temperate species to a tropical environment. In J. W. Gibbons (ed.), Life History and Ecology of the Slider Turtle, pp. 152–161. Smithsonian Inst. Press, Washington D.C. i–xiv + 368 pp.

Moll, E. O. 1976. West Malaysian turtles: Utilization and conservation. Herpetol. Rev. 7:163–166.

Moll, E. O. 1978. Drumming along the Perak. Natur. Hist. 77(5): 36–43.

Moll, E. O. 1984a. Freshwater turtles in India: Their status, conservation, and management. Hamadryad 9(3):9–17.

Moll, E. O. 1984b. River terrapin recovery plan for Malaysia. J. Wildlife and Parks 3:37–47.

Moll, E. O. 1985. Estuarine turtles of tropical Asia: Status and management. Proc. Symp. Endangered Marine Mammals and Marine Parks 1:214–226.

Moll, E. O. 1989. Malaysia's efforts in the conservation of the river terrapin. In Proceedings of the International Conference on National Parks and Protected Areas, pp. 152–161. Department of Wildlife and National Parks, Peninsular Malaysia.

Moll, E. O. 1990a. India's freshwater turtle resource with recommendations for management. In J. C. Daniel and J. S. Serrao (eds.), Conservation in Developing Countries: Problems and Prospects, pp. 501–515. Oxford University Press, Oxford.

Moll, E. O. 1990b. Final report: WWF 3901/Asia—Status and management of the river terrapin (*Batagur baska*) in tropical Asia. Unpubl. report to World Wide Fund for Nature, Gland, Switzerland. 36 pp. + 8 figs.

Moll, E. O. and J. M. Legler. 1971. The life history of a Neotropical slider turtle, *Pseudemys scripta* (Schoepff), in Panama. Bull. Los Angeles Co. Mus. Natur. Hist. Sci. (11):1–102.

Moll, E. O. and Mohd. Khan bin Momin Khan. 1990. Turtles of Taman Negara. J. Wildlife and Parks 10:135–138.

Pritchard, P. C. H. and P. Trebbeau. 1984. Turtles of Venezuela. Soc. Stud. Amph. Rept., Contrib. Herpetol. 403 pp.

Habitat Use and Food Preferences of the Desert Tortoise, *Gopherus agassizii*, in the Western Mojave Desert and Impacts of Off-Road Vehicles

W. BRYAN JENNINGS

Department of Biology, University of Texas, Arlington, TX 76019, USA
Current address: Department of Zoology, University of Texas at Austin, Austin, TX 78712, USA [e-mail: jennings@mail.utexas.edu]

ABSTRACT: The desert tortoise, *Gopherus agassizii*, and its habitats in the western Mojave Desert and elsewhere are negatively affected by off-road vehicles (ORVs). Data from a study conducted at the Desert Tortoise Research Natural Area during 1992 provide insights into why ORVs are likely to affect tortoises. To determine habitat use and food preferences, 18 large immature and adult tortoises were observed. The study site contained four subhabitats or strata: washes (comprising 7.9% of the area), washlets (2.4%), hills (42.3%), and flats (47.4%). The tortoises used the four habitat strata differentially, spending significantly more time (92%) in washes, washlets, and hills throughout spring than in the flats (8%). They were observed to take bites from 2,423 individual plants of at least 43 plant species (37 annual, 6 perennial). They showed preferences for native plants (95.3% of bites) compared to non-native plants. Some of the ten most-preferred food plants were uncommon to rare in the environment. Three of the ten most-preferred food plants occurred largely in the wash strata, and an additional four species were found only in hill strata. Users of recreational vehicles also prefer washes and hills in this region, where they are more likely to encounter tortoises, increasing the possibility of direct mortality, and where they are more likely to have a greater impact upon preferred forage and habitats.

Recreational use of off-road vehicles (ORVs), popular since the late 1960s in the southwestern deserts of the United States, poses significant threats to desert tortoises in some parts of their geographic range (U. S. Fish and Wildlife Service [USFWS], 1994). The threats are both direct and indirect: direct encounters, damage to and loss of habitat, damage to or loss of burrows, and loss or changes in both the composition of the forage and the quality of shrub cover. In this paper, I report findings from research conducted in the western Mojave Desert in and adjacent to the Desert Tortoise Research Natural Area (Jennings, 1993), specifically, desert tortoise use of different habitat types, their preferred forage plants, and the possible impacts of ORVs on these two critical aspects of desert tortoise ecology.

METHODS

The study area was typical of the western Mojave Desert, a topographic and vegetational mosaic of subhabitats or strata that includes washes, sandy flats, low hills, and rocky slopes where the most common vegetation types are saltbush (*Atriplex* spp.) scrub and creosote bush (*Larrea tridentata*) (U. S. Bureau of Land Management and California Dept. of Fish and Game, 1988; USFWS, 1994). Specifically, the 2.6 km² study area was composed of four strata or subhabitats, each with its unique composition of perennial and ephemeral plants (Jennings, 1993). The four strata were flats (comprising 47.4% of the study area), hills (42.3%), washes (7.9%), and washlets (2.4%). Wash and washlet strata were lumped for a portion of the analyses. In the flats, the dominant species were three shrubs: goldenhead (*Acamptopappus sphaerocephalus*), burro bush (*Ambrosia dumosa*), and creosote bush. In the hills the most diverse of the strata with 11 species, five species of shrubs were dominant: burrobush, California buckwheat (*Eriogonum fasiculatum*), goldenhead, Mojave aster (*Xylorhiza tortifolia*), and creosote bush. Shrubs in wash and washlet strata were burrobush, cheesebush (*Hymenoclea salsola*), goldenhead, bladdersage (*Salazaria mexicana*), creosote bush, and Anderson thornbush (*Lycium andersonii*). Data on absolute and relative densities of plant species were collected once for the perennial shrubs using linear transects and 2×5 m quadrats. Similar data were collected using the same method for herbaceous perennial and ephemeral plant species on 17–20 April, 12–15 May, and 12–13 June. Details of methodology are in Jennings (1993). Scientific names of plants are taken from Hickman (1993).

To determine how the tortoises used the four habitat strata, I observed 18 large immature and adult tortoises (8 females and 10 males), which ranged from 179 to approximately 380 mm in carapace length at the midline (Jennings, 1993). Most tortoises had been fitted with radio transmitters as part of other research programs. The tortoises were tracked from the time they emerged from hibernation through the spring (1 March–30 June), and their activities, use of habitat, and forage items were recorded. Because the ephemeral and herbaceous perennial plants on which tortoises feed have different growth, flowering, and fruiting periods during the year, I grouped the species into three phenological periods for analysis: 1 March to 30 April, 1 to 31 May, and 1 to 30 June. The use of phenological periods for data analysis also provided a better understanding of when and where tortoises were foraging, how they were using the habitats, and when the different forage plants were consumed.

RESULTS

The tortoises made differential use of the four habitat strata (Jennings, 1993). Between 1 March and 30 April, they spent a disproportionately longer time within the hill and washlet strata (84%; $\chi^2 = 1353.01$, d.f. = 2, $P = 0.0001$) and foraged on preferred food plants located exclusively in hill areas (*Mirabilis bigelovii*, *Astragalus didymocarpus*) and washlet margins (*A. layneae*, *Camissonia boothii*). During the second phenological period, the use of hill, wash, and washlet areas continued to be important (100%; $\chi^2 = 1405.8$, d.f. = 2, $P = 0.0001$). Tortoises foraged on *A. layneae* and *C. boothii* and then moved into the hills to eat the preferred *Lotus humistratus* and *Prenanthella exigua*. (Both *Lotus* and *Prenanthella* were restricted to the hills.) During the third phenological period, tortoise activity declined markedly because of heat and dry weather, and the few tortoises that remained above ground used primarily washes and washlets (68%; $\chi^2 = 753.83$, d.f. = 2, $P = 0.0001$), drawing on plants confined to those areas (*Euphorbia albomarginata* and *C. boothii*). Overall, tortoises made little use of the more common flat stratum.

The tortoises' diet and preferred foods were determined from observations of a total of 34,657 bites taken from 2,423 individual plants between 24 March and 21 June of 1992 (Jennings, 1993). Tortoises foraged from at least 43 species of plants (37 species of winter-spring annuals and 6 perennial species) as well as a dead leopard lizard (*Gambelia wislizenii*) and tortoise scat. Some important patterns emerged. These tortoises were highly selective foragers and preferred to consume native plants (33,712 bites or 95.3%) over non-native species (1,644 bites, 4.1%). The non-native species were filaree (*Erodium cicutarium*), Mediterranean grass (*Schismus arabicus*, *S. barbatus*), and foxtail chess (*Bromus madritensis* ssp. *rubens*), and were readily available. The tortoises also took more bites from annuals (69.2%) than from perennial plants (30.8%); with the exception of four bites from cheesebush, all bites of perennial plants were from herbaceous or suffrutescent perennial plant species. Tortoises took more bites from legumes (44%) than from any other plant family.

Some of the ten most-preferred food plants consumed during 1992 were uncommon to rare in the environment (Jennings, 1993). For example, during the first phenological period, plants of the suffrutescent perennial *M. bigelovii* constituted 29.7% of the bites taken by tortoises, yet *M. bigelovii* constituted <1% of the perennial plants in the environment and far less of the total biomass of both ephemeral and perennial plants. *A. layneae* was also an important forage plant (3.9% of bites) but was not found on plant transects. During the second phenological period the annual *L. humistratus* constituted 63.9% of bites taken, yet was not found in annual plant samples. During the third phenological period, the herbaceous perennial *Euphorbia albomarginata* constituted 57.4% of bites but did not appear on any plant transects. Overall, >25% of all the plants on which tortoises fed were in the washes and washlets, about twice the number as might be expected considering that washes and washlets comprised only 10.3% of the study area habitats. Three of the ten most-preferred plants, *E. albomarginata*, *A. layneae*, and *C. boothii*, were largely confined to washes.

DISCUSSION

Desert vertebrates and their habitats are vulnerable to and negatively affected by ORVs (Busack and Bury, 1974; Bury et al. 1977; Luckenbach, 1982; Webb and Wilshire 1983). The desert tortoise is not exempt from these effects (Berry et al., 1986). In the western Mojave Desert where the use of ORVs is prevalent, tortoise populations have undergone steep declines, compared to relatively undisturbed desert tortoise populations and in habitat in the eastern parts of their geographic range (USFWS, 1994).

Hills and washes are favored in the western Mojave Desert for use by ORV recreationists (U.S. Bureau of Land Management, 1980). Four major ORV recreation areas with hills, washes, and canyons are adjacent to the Desert Tortoise Research Natural Area (Rand Mountains) or are within 50 km (Jawbone Canyon, Dove Springs, and Spangler Hills). The users of motorcycles, trail bikes, all-terrain vehicles, and other four-wheel vehicles prefer the washes, washlets, canyon bottoms, and hilly country for riding (see Goodlett and Goodlett, 1993 for an example of trail densities in flats, hills, and wash habitats). They gradually widen trails and create more individual tracks and trails, which damages or destroys increasing amounts of habitat. The flats are used primarily for camping, as staging areas for competitive events, and as play areas.

Desert tortoises are vulnerable to negative effects from ORVs because of their habitat preferences. The tortoises in this study spent significantly more time traveling and foraging in hills, washes, and washlets than on the flats, the same areas preferred by ORV users. In other parts of the species' geographic range (the southern, eastern, and northeastern Mojave and the Sonoran deserts), washes are also important in the ecology and behavior (Woodbury and Hardy, 1948; Burge, 1978; Baxter, 1988). The tortoises use the washes for travel, excavation of burrows or dens, and for feeding. Because tortoises spend so much more time in washes and hills, they are also more likely to suffer direct mortality from vehicles than if they used the habitat randomly.

The food preferences and forage locations of the tortoises provide additional insights. A substantial portion of the food bites taken by tortoises were from plants that were infrequent to rare in the environment and occurred in the hill, wash, and washlet strata. Four of the ten most-preferred food plants were found exclusively in the hills, and an additional three were confined largely to washes. At least 25% of the forage plants were in or on the margins of washes or washlets. Vehicles disturb the soil and terrain in washes and other areas, which results in deterioration or denudation of vegetation (Burge, 1983; Woodman, 1983; Goodlett and Goodlett, 1993). They destroy the natural margins of washes and small washlets as the trails are widened over time (Berry et al., 1986). If the preferred forage plants are damaged or destroyed, tortoises will be forced to select other less-preferred and possibly less-nutritious species.

The 18 desert tortoises preferred native to non-native or alien plant species. The Desert Tortoise Reserve Natural Area has been protected from disturbance for almost two decades, and it has a relatively lower biomass of the alien plants than do the adjacent areas outside its protective fence (Brooks, 1995), where sheep grazing and uncontrolled ORV use occur. Most native desert plant species thrive in undisturbed habitats, in contrast to the alien species, which are common in disturbed lands. Some alien species, particularly the grasses, have invaded arid habitats, are fire prone, and have increased fire regimes globally (D'Antonio and Vitousek, 1992). The alien plant/fire cycle is prevalent throughout parts of the Mojave and Great Basin deserts, and wildfires burn thousands of hectares of desert annually (D'Antonio and Vitousek, 1992; USFWS, 1994). In areas disturbed by ORVs, these alien species are likely to constitute increasingly greater portions of the floral biomass, thus increasing the threat of fires.

Recommendations to Protect Desert Tortoises and Their Habitats

1. Reduce or prohibit vehicle travel off existing roads. Disturbance to desert soils increases the potential for alien plants to invade and become established, causing significant and deleterious alterations to the flora. And, although washes and washlets constitute only a small portion of desert habitats, they have a disproportionate share of the forage plants favored by tortoises and are frequented by tortoises a significantly greater amount of the time. Therefore, vehicle travel off existing highways and established roads—particularly in desert washes and washlets—in desert tortoise Critical Habitat should be minimized and, where possible, prohibited (see USFWS, 1994).

2. Investigate food habits of neonates and juveniles. The tortoises observed in this study were large immature and adult animals. Neonates and juveniles are likely to have different forage requirements and patterns of use because of their small body sizes, limited activity areas, and inability to travel great distances. The food habits of neonate and juvenile tortoises should therefore be determined also by desert region and habitat strata.

Acknowledgments

Thanks are due to Dr. Michael Klemens and Dr. Kristin Berry for inviting me to participate in this conference and to Dr. Berry and Jim Van Abbema for valuable assistance on the manuscript. The U. S. Bureau of Land Management supported research on the foraging ecology and habitat utilization of the desert tortoise under Contract No. B950-C2-0014.

Literature Cited

Baxter, R. J. 1988. Spatial distribution of desert tortoises (*Gopherus agassizii*) at Twentynine Palms, California: Implications of relocations. *In* Proc. Symposium Management of Amphibians, Reptiles, and Small Mammals in North America, pp. 180–189. 19–21 July 1988, Flagstaff, Arizona.

Berry, K. H., T. Shields, A. P. Woodman, T. Campbell, J. Roberson, K. Bohuski, and A. Karl. 1986. Changes in desert tortoise populations at the Desert Tortoise Research Natural Area between 1979 and 1985. Proc. Desert Tortoise Council Symp. 1986:100–123.

Brooks, M. 1995. Benefits of protective fencing to plant and rodent communities of the western Mojave Desert, California. Environ. Manage. 19(1):65–74.

Burge, B. L. 1978. Physical characteristics and patterns of utilization of cover sites used by *Gopherus agassizii* in southern Nevada. Proc. Desert Tortoise Council Symp. 1978:132–140.

Burge, B. L. 1983. Impact of Frontier 500 off-road vehicle race on desert tortoise habitat. Proc. Desert Tortoise Council Symp. 1983:27–38.

Bury, R. B., R. A. Luckenbach, and S. D. Busack. 1977. Effects of off-road vehicles on vertebrates in the California desert. Wildlife Research Report 8, U.S.D.I. Fish and Wildlife Service, Washington, D.C.

Busack, S. D. and R. B. Bury. 1974. Some effects of off-road vehicles and sheep grazing on lizard populations in the Mojave Desert. Biol. Conserv. 6(3):179–183.

D'Antonio, C. M. and P. M. Vitousek. 1992. Biological invasions by exotic grasses, the grass/fire cycle, and global change. Ann. Rev. Ecol. Syst. 23:63–87.

Goodlett, G. O. and G. C. Goodlett. 1993. Studies of unauthorized off-highway vehicle activity in the Rand Mountains and Fremont Valley, Kern County. Proc. Desert Tortoise Council Symp. 1993:163–187.

Hickman, J. C. (ed.). 1993. The Jepson Manual. Higher Plants of California. University of California Press, Berkeley and Los Angeles, California. 1400 pp.

Jennings, W. B. 1993. Foraging ecology and habitat utilization of the desert tortoise (*Gopherus agassizii*) at the Desert Tortoise Research Natural Area, eastern Kern County, California. Report for the U. S. Bureau of Land Management, Contract No. B950-C2-0014, Riverside, California. 101 pp.

Luckenbach, R. A. 1982. Ecology and management of the desert tortoise (*Gopherus agassizii*) in California. *In* R. B. Bury (ed.), North American Tortoises: Conservation and Ecology, pp. 1–37. Wildlife Research Report 12, U.S.D.I. Fish and Wildlife Service, Washington, D.C.

U.S. Bureau of Land Management. 1980. The California Desert Conservation Area Plan. U.S. Bureau of Land Management, Riverside, California. 173 pp.

U.S. Bureau of Land Management and California Department of Fish and Game. 1988. A Sikes Act Management Plan for the Desert Tortoise Research Natural Area and Area of Critical Environmental Concern. U.S. Bureau of Land Management, Ridgecrest, California. 43 pp. + unpaginated appendices.

U.S. Fish and Wildlife Service. 1994. The desert tortoise (Mojave population) recovery plan. U. S. Fish and Wildlife Service, Region 1, Lead Region, Portland, Oregon. 73 pp. + appendices.

Webb, R. H. and H. G. Wilshire (eds.). 1983. Environmental Effects of Off-Road Vehicles. Impacts and Management in Arid Regions. Springer-Verlag New York, Inc. 534 pp.

Woodbury, A.M. and R. Hardy. 1948. Studies of the desert tortoise, *Gopherus agassizi*. Ecol. Monogr. 18:146–200.

Woodman, A. P. 1983. Effects of Parker 400 off-road race on desert tortoise habitat in the Chemehuevi Valley, California. Proc. Desert Tortoise Council Symp. 1983:69-79.

Turtles and Tires: The Impact of Roadkills on Northern Diamondback Terrapin, *Malaclemys terrapin terrapin*, Populations on the Cape May Peninsula, Southern New Jersey, USA

ROGER CONANT WOOD [1,2] AND ROSALIND HERLANDS [1]

[1] Faculty of Science and Mathematics, Richard Stockton College of New Jersey, Pomona, NJ 08240, USA
[2] The Wetlands Institute, 1075 Stone Harbor Boulevard, Stone Harbor, NJ 08247, USA

ABSTRACT: A century ago overhunting of the northern diamondback terrapin, *Malaclemys terrapin terrapin*, nearly extirpated populations in many parts of its range. More recently, coastal development has led to considerable habitat destruction, especially of traditional nesting sites on barrier beach islands. Along the Atlantic coast of New Jersey, the search for alternative nesting sites on highway embankments has resulted in large numbers of roadkills every nesting season.

We have documented the annual mortality of nesting diamondback terrapins on the Cape May Peninsula of southern New Jersey from 1989 through 1995. A total of 4,020 roadkills were recorded on roads crossing or adjacent to our study area. Potentially viable eggs were recovered from carcasses and 32% were successfully incubated. Since 1991 hatchlings have been headstarted for ten months and 782 (an 81% hatchling survivorship) have been released into the salt marshes of the parents' origin. Roadkill mortality of adult females remains considerably higher than their rate of replacement, and we have noted a substantial decrease in numbers of mature female terrapins in our study area.

Diamondback terrapins, *Malaclemys terrapin*, include several subspecies within a unique genus and species of emydid turtles. The terrapin is the only one of more than 270 extant species of turtles whose habitat is confined to coastal brackish (as opposed to fresh or truly oceanic) waters. The species' range is several thousand miles long but never more than a few miles wide, extending from the north-temperate zone into the subtropics, from Cape Cod, Massachusetts, through the Florida peninsula and Keys, to the Gulf Coast of the United States. The western terminus of its range has not been precisely determined, but probably lies near Corpus Christi, Texas. *Malaclemys terrapin terrapin* (the focus of this report) is the northernmost of the seven described subspecies. It ranges from Cape Cod, Massachusetts, to Cape Hatteras, North Carolina.

Because their geographic distribution coincides with densely settled coastal areas, terrapins have long been exploited by humans. In the late 1800s and early 1900s diamondback terrapins were considered a gourmet delicacy and a valuable commodity, and by 1920 they sold for as much as $90 per dozen (Carr, 1952). As a result of this extraordinary bounty, terrapins were so heavily hunted that the mid-Atlantic population from Long Island Sound to Virginia was nearly wiped out.

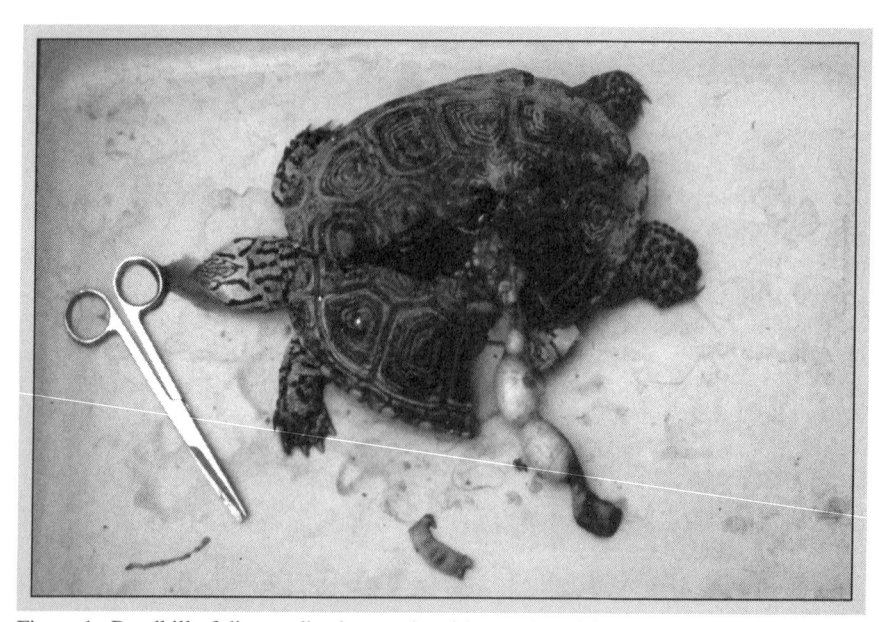

Figure 1. Roadkill of diamondback terrapin with eggs in oviduct exposed.

Eventually, the combined effects of Prohibition (sherry was an essential ingredient of terrapin stew recipes) and the economic stresses of the Great Depression in the 1930s signaled the end of significant commercial demand for terrapins (Conant, 1955, 1964). But not until nearly a half-century later (approximately the late 1960s) did terrapin populations recover to a level approaching their former "pre-gourmet" abundance. Unfortunately, terrapins are again becoming popular as a food item in urban areas (Garber, 1988, 1990). If the current gastronomic interest in terrapins persists, populations of these beleaguered turtles may once more be severely depleted.

The unsustainable exploitation of terrapins at the turn of this century raised such concern for their well-being that protective legislation was enacted by most of the states where terrapins are found (Donnelly and Owens, 1988). These regulations vary widely from state to state, and while penalties for violating these laws may be imposing, they appear to be largely unenforceable and do not address issues of habitat degradation. At the federal level, several subspecies of terrapins (including the northern diamondback terrapin) were, until recently, listed as a "Category-2 candidates," i.e., ones that are being considered for addition to the national list of "Endangered" and "Threatened" Wildlife and Plants (Lovich, 1995), but this category was recently eliminated by the U.S. Fish and Wildlife Service (USFWS, 1996). Consequently, neither the species as a whole nor any of its component subspecies is currently afforded any special federal protection.

While terrapin populations struggled to recover through the middle decades of this century, a considerable portion of their habitat was degraded or destroyed by industrial activities and real estate development, especially in urbanized areas along the mid-Atlantic coast. Diamondback terrapins' preferred nesting sites (sand dunes) were largely obliterated when the coastal barrier beach islands became densely settled summer resorts. Because shoulders of heavily trafficked roads crossing or adjacent to the salt marshes often provide the only available nesting substrate, large numbers of nesting terrapins are killed each season by motor vehicles. Despite growing awareness of this new source of mortality, no systematic attempt had been made to quantify its impact. In early summer 1989, the Wetlands Institute initiated a long-term terrapin research and conservation project to assess the impact of roadkills and to take steps to mitigate them.

The Study Area

Fieldwork was centered around the Wetlands Institute, a coastal research and environmental education facility located on a salt marsh of the Cape May Peninsula, adjacent to Stone Harbor, New Jersey (Figure 2). This expanse of marsh extends continuously along a NE–SW axis and parallels the Atlantic Ocean coastline from Cape May north to Ocean City, a distance of approximately 35 km. The width of this salt marsh never exceeds 4–5 km. Tidal amplitude within the marsh is about 4.5 feet (1.5 m). Salinity is similar to that of nearby ocean waters (usually 30–32 ppt) as there are few freshwater streams emptying into this marsh and several large inlets connect directly to the ocean.

The salt marsh is bounded on the ocean side by barrier beach island resort communities, which are densely populated during the summer terrapin nesting season. Causeways and bridges across the marsh provide access to the resorts from the mainland and also connect neighboring islands along the coastline.

During the late 1960s much of this marshland was

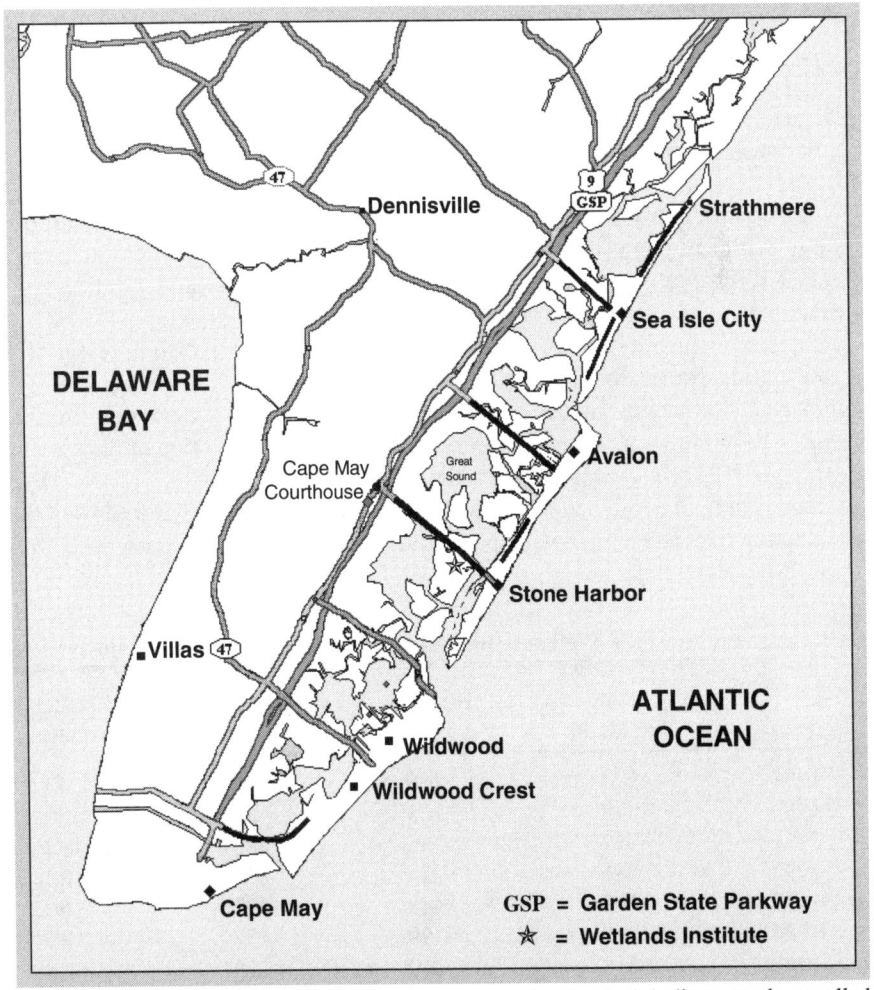

Figure 2. Map of Cape May Peninsula. Stretches marked in black indicate roads patrolled during summers of 1990–1995 (see also Appendix I, p. 53).

preserved from the drastic alteration that characterized many other parts of the New Jersey coast. The World Wildlife Fund, through the auspices of its then U.S. president, the late Herbert Mills, purchased approximately 6,000 acres (2,400 ha) of privately owned salt marsh extending from the vicinity of Wildwood northward to Sea Isle City. After passage of New Jersey's Coastal Wetlands Protection Act in 1971, the state acquired most of this acreage from the World Wildlife Fund, with the exception of 30 acres (approx. 12 ha) set aside near the center of the area for the Wetlands Institute, which was established at that time.

While this marshland is no longer subject to development, the waterways coursing through it are subject to heavy use, particularly during the warmer months of the year. These activities include commercial and recreational crabbing, clamming, recreational fishing, jet skiing, water skiing, pleasure boating, and swimming. Few tributaries (all only small creeks) drain into this marsh, and the only major industrial installation is a large clam cannery at the southern edge of our study area. There is also a large, ocean-going commercial fishing fleet that docks in the vicinity of the cannery.

While this salt marsh was largely spared from toxic industrial pollutants, the island resort communities' antiquated sewage treatment facilities have been regularly overwhelmed by the mushrooming human populations, especially in the decades following World War II. Consequently, untreated sewage was routinely pumped into the marshes. Regional sewage treatment plants constructed in the mid-1980s have eliminated this problem, and the marsh waters may now be cleaner than at any time since very early in this century.

The establishment of resort communities on the barrier beach islands drastically altered the eastern borders of the salt marsh. The islands' landward side was filled in, the adjacent waterways were extensively dredged, and the construction of bulkheads created a sharp demarcation between land and water. In combination, these alterations eliminated prime terrapin habitat and, more importantly, blocked access for the turtles to the islands' sand dunes, their traditional nesting sites. The dunes themselves were almost entirely eliminated by development activities. Notwithstanding these circumstances, in some southern New Jersey island communities, terrapins still find access to former dune areas and attempt to nest in residential yards and gardens.

Considerable alteration of the mainland side of the marsh in our study area also occurred in the 1950s as the result of construction of the Garden State Parkway. This high-speed, limited-access highway borders the marsh and frequently crosses branches of it that extend westward towards the higher ground of the Cape May Peninsula. Thus, while much of the marsh proper has been preserved in a relatively pristine state, both its eastern and western edges have undergone considerable alteration, which has substantially restricted terrapin access to natural nesting sites. Terrapins are therefore left with little alternative than to nest on the shoulders of the roads crossing and adjacent to the marshes.

METHODS

Road Patrols

In June 1989, the Wetlands Institute conducted a pilot project to assess the extent of terrapin mortality from motor vehicle traffic during the nesting season. Two heavily used roads that cross salt marshes in the vicinity of the Wetlands Institute (totaling approx. 7 mi or 11.5 km in length) were regularly patrolled day and night throughout the entire nesting season (early June to mid-July) to tabulate both numbers and locations of terrapin roadkills. Because terrapins are known to nest both by day and night, nocturnal patrols were also necessary (Figure 3).

Since 1989 we have also retrieved outwardly undamaged eggs from fresh terrapin carcasses, and subsequent incubation of the eggs has produced a significant number of hatchlings (Table 1). Each dead terrapin found during a patrol is removed from the road to prevent overcounting. Data such as date, time, weather conditions, tide, location, and number

TABLE 1
Data summary from the Wetlands Institute's diamondback terrapin conservation project (1989–1995). NR = not recorded.

Year	No. roadkills	No. eggs salvaged	Resultant hatchlings	% hatching success	No. juveniles released	% surviving headstarting
1989	273	180	77	43	NR	NR
1990	1,077	933	85	9	NR	NR
1991	712	746	286	38	80	80
1992	586	734	235	32	230	61
1993	535	448	222	50	143	94
1994	419	399	157	39	210	76
1995	418	250	113	45	119	78
Totals	4,020	3,690	1,175	32	782	81

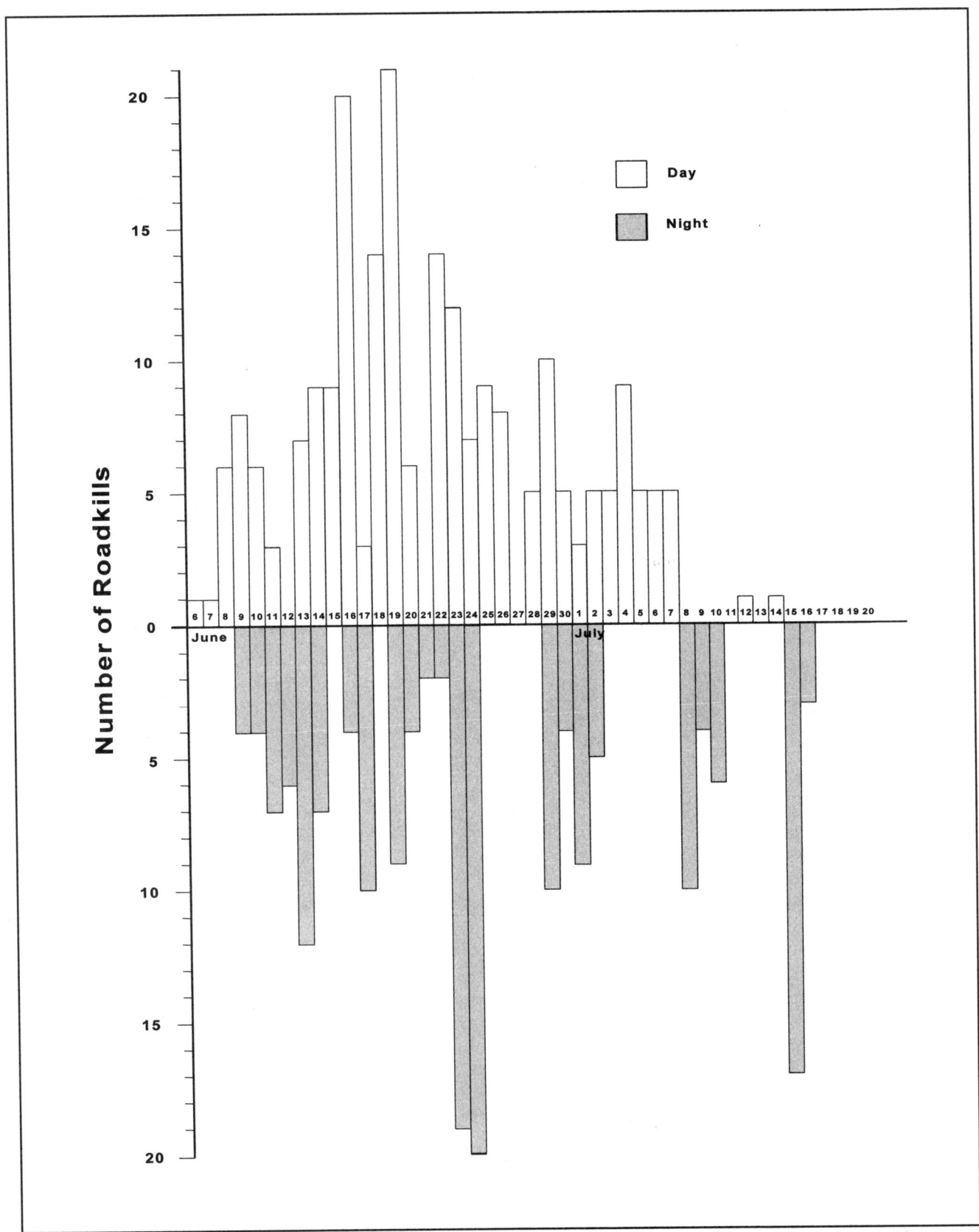

Figure 3. Diamondback terrapin roadkills during day and night hours in June and July 1994. Each shaded bar represents the period from sunset to dawn of the next day (e.g., the four nocturnal roadkills recorded under 9 June occurred between nightfall on 9 June and dawn on 10 June).

of potentially viable eggs retrieved are recorded on standardized forms.

Encouraged by our successful efforts to quantify terrapin roadkills as well as to recover and hatch eggs during our 1989 pilot study, we expanded the project in 1990. Since the 1990 nesting season, at least a half-dozen student interns and community volunteers have annually participated in the monitoring of terrapin roadkills. The survey was considerably enlarged in 1990 with the addition of approximately 10.5 mi (16 km) of roads and has remained essentially unchanged since that time.

Retrieval and Incubation of Eggs

Because adult females were being selectively killed on roads during the nesting season, we wanted to return a high proportion of female hatchlings to the salt marshes. In many turtle species sex determination is temperature dependent (Bull et al., 1982). Typically, only females are produced at higher incubation temperatures while eggs developing at lower temperatures generally yield only males. We have confirmed experimentally that this is the case for diamondback terrapins. Eggs retrieved during the 1989 nesting season were therefore incubated at relatively high temperatures (approx. 30–31°C).

Eggs retrieved from roadkills are placed on a bed of coarse, slightly moistened vermiculite inside plastic containers that each hold approximately 25 eggs. The containers are covered to retain moisture, and condensation generated inside the containers makes it necessary to remove the covers periodically to check the condition of the eggs. Freshly laid eggs are a pale, pinkish color. Viable eggs will turn chalky white within approximately one week; eggs that retain their original color are inviable.

In 1989 and 1990 our makeshift incubators were placed in the attic of a garage, which was chosen to provide an appropriate high temperature environment. Unfortunately, a prolonged heat wave in summer 1990 overheated most of the eggs, which resulted in a very low percentage of hatchlings. In subsequent years, all retrieved eggs have been incubated under temperature-controlled laboratory conditions, resulting in markedly higher hatching success (Table 1).

Headstarting

Freshly hatched terrapins, with soft, largely unossified shells approximately 25 mm (1 in) in length, are preyed upon by a variety of birds, mammals, fish, and crabs. The natural survival rate of hatchlings is undoubtedly very low. Once a terrapin has grown to a shell length of 75–100 mm (3–4 in), or approximately half adult female size, its shell has fully ossified and provides effective protection against most predators.

To maximize the chances of survival for our roadkill hatchlings, we undertook a headstart program modeled on procedures originally developed for marine turtle hatchlings. In 1991 we constructed a rearing facility at Stockton College, equipped with saltwater tanks and heat lamps that maintain room temperature at or near 27°C (80°F). The warm temperature inhibits normal winter hibernation, and hatchlings are fed constantly to promote rapid growth. After ten months of this husbandry, the hatchlings reach approximately half their expected adult size and are ready for release. This facility can comfortably house 200 hatchlings. Some of our hatchlings have been headstarted at the Cape May County Zoo Reptile House, thus dividing the work load and reducing the risk of accidental loss or disease.

In view of the possibility that hatchling terrapins imprint on their release point and subsequently return as adults to nest at the same site, the headstarted juvenile terrapins have been released at nine different localities throughout our study area. This may prevent an unnatural future clustering of nesting adults at a single former release point.

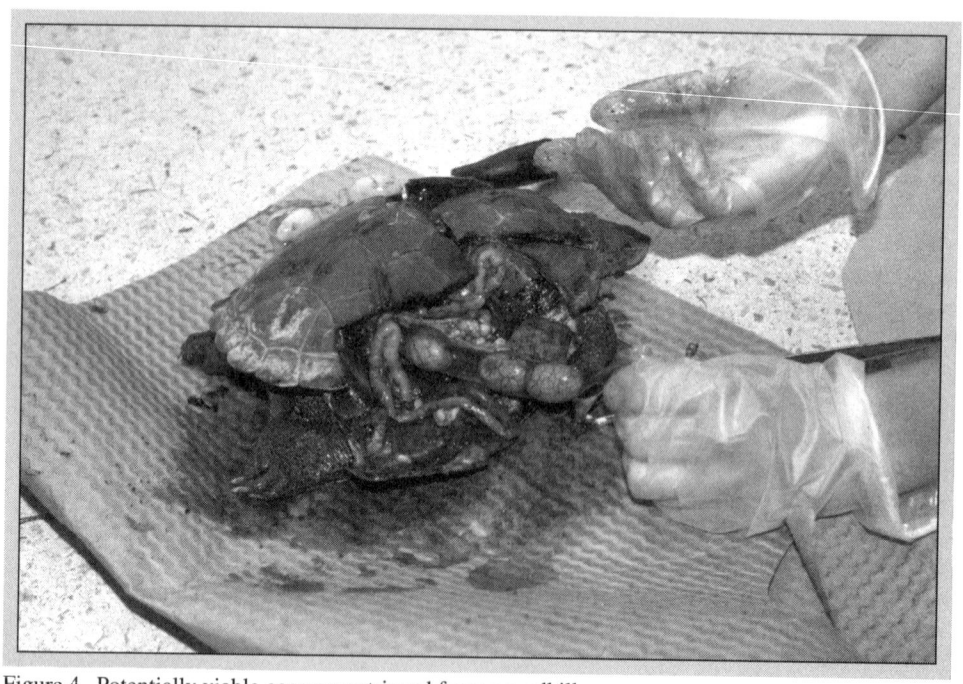

Figure 4. Potentially viable eggs are retrieved from a roadkill carcass.

RESULTS

Roadkill Mortality

Data for the first seven years (1989–1995) of this project are summarized in Table 1. Over this period of time 4,020 roadkills have been recorded within our study area. From these dead terrapins, 3,690 eggs have been salvaged and incubated, nearly a third of which (1,175) produced hatchlings, resulting in a cumulative overall hatching success of 32%. With improved incubation techniques, hatching success now approaches 39%.

Only two roads were patrolled in 1989, while six roads of our study area were patrolled in subsequent years. Thus, only the annual data since 1990 are directly comparable.

The total number of roadkills recorded for 1991 (712) is less than expected for two reasons: (1) one of the routinely patrolled roads in our study area was repaved during the nesting season and was blocked to traffic, and (2) the 1991 nesting season started unusually early (in late May rather than early June) before road patrols had been organized, and the first big surge of nesting activity (and therefore terrapin roadkills) was missed.

Figure 3 shows the pattern of terrapin roadkills (which also reflects relative levels of nesting activity) in our study area during summer 1994. The pattern depicted is typical of every nesting season we have so far monitored. Nesting started in early June and continued almost without interruption for 41 days through mid-July.

After nightfall terrapins on a road are almost impossible to detect and cannot be avoided, even by conscientious motorists. Thus, despite the fact that the hours of darkness during the nesting season are from roughly 9:30 P.M. to 5:00 A.M., or only about one third of a 24-hour day, nearly half (43%) of all roadkills (180 of 419) occurred at night in 1994.

As indicated in Figure 3, the number of roadkills varied greatly throughout the nesting season. Daily fluctuations in mortality are not correlated with increased weekend traffic, variations in weather conditions, tidal cycles, or any other perceivable factor. Peak numbers of roadkills were recorded on 16 June (24), 19 June (30), 23 June (31), and 24 June (27). Occasionally, other days in the midst of the nesting season featured little or no nesting activity and hence few, if any, roadkills (only 2, for example, on 21 June and none on 27 June). After 10 July nesting activity was desultory except for a major spike on 15 July, which we suspect may represent terrapins emerging to lay their second clutches of the nesting season.

There is more nesting activity in the earlier part of the nesting season than in its latter part. In 1994, for example, there were 264 roadkills (156 during the day, 108 at night) over the course of the first 20 days, while during the remaining 21 days of the nesting season there were 136 roadkills almost evenly distributed between daylight (67) and darkness (69). Thus, almost twice as many terrapins were killed by motor vehicles in the first half of the 1994 nesting season compared to the last half.

Eggs and Hatchlings

As many as 14 potentially viable eggs have been recovered from a single roadkill, but such is exceptional, the usual number of salvageable eggs being from one to five.

Figure 5. Hatchling terrapins produced by eggs retrieved from roadkills.

Undisturbed nesting terrapins in our study area typically lay 8–12 eggs per clutch.

Temperature-dependent sex determination (TSD) in terrapins was experimentally verified. Eggs maintained at relatively high temperatures (30–31°C) hatch in the least time (usually 6–8 weeks) and produce only females. These hatchlings have a relatively high proportion of scute anomalies (particularly on the carapace), which is consistent with our observations of female scute abnormalities in natural populations. Eggs incubated at lower temperatures (25–28°C) take 2–3 weeks longer to hatch and usually produce males. At even lower temperatures (<25°C), a mixture of males and females results, with males more numerous. These latter eggs may incubate for as long as 12–15 weeks before hatching. Eggs never hatch below 23°C, although embryos may develop to an advanced stage.

Post-natal mortality among hatchlings from the retrieved eggs varies unpredictably from year to year. From 6 to 39% of the hatchlings die while being headstarted (Table 1) for unknown reasons. Most of these deaths occur relatively soon after hatching.

After seven seasons of rescue efforts, as of June 1995 we have repatriated 782 headstarted juvenile terrapins (Table 1).

DISCUSSION

Over a period of four years, we maintained reasonably accurate records of the total number of miles driven each year on road patrols. From 1990 through 1992, the total annual road patrol mileage increased substantially from approximately 9,000 to more than 12,000 mi. During this same period of time, the number of terrapin roadkills fell to almost half (from 1,077 to 586).

We suspected that some of this decreased mortality was attributable to the removal of a higher proportion of terrapins from harm's way as a result of more frequent road patrols. If this were the case, the number of roadkills during the 1993 nesting season should have noticeably increased, when road patrol mileage decreased by approximately 25%. However, roadkills continued to decline in 1993 (by approx. 10%). An even greater decrease in roadkills between the 1993 and 1994 nesting seasons were recorded (from 535 to 419, a drop of approx. 22%).

Thus, increased vigilance in the form of more frequent road patrols during a given nesting season does not account for the steadily decreasing numbers of roadkills over the course of the last six years of our study. During this period of time, roadkill mortality has dropped from 1,077 to 418, a nearly 62% reduction. Superficially, this appears encouraging, suggesting that our conservation efforts are increasingly successful at saving nesting terrapins. However, roadkills account for only a fraction of the overall annual terrapin mortality in our study area (see Wood, this volume, on the drowning of terrapins in commercial crab traps). We fear that our local terrapin population is, in fact, undergoing a severe collapse not unlike the dramatic decline in terrapin populations associated with the terrapin stew fad of the late 1800s. We intend to continue monitoring terrapin nesting activities in coming years to determine whether roadkill numbers continue to decrease.

We have established the feasibility of large-scale incubation of eggs retrieved from roadkills. We can now hatch 40–50% of the eggs removed from fresh terrapin carcasses. Because newly hatched terrapins are easy targets for a host of predators, we have also developed a headstart program that promotes the rapid growth of hatchlings in captivity for the first nine to ten months. By the time we release our headstarted juvenile terrapins (in June following their late summer or early fall hatching of the preceding year), they have attained a size sufficient to substantially increase their probability of reaching adulthood.

Our experiments with incubation of eggs retrieved from roadkills show that diamondback terrapins, like most other turtle species so far investigated, are characterized by temperature-dependent sex determination. Our observations have shown that hatching size is not correlated with incubation temperature (Herlands and Wood, in prep.). Hatchling size is, however, (and not surprisingly) correlated with egg size. Our data confirm a similar study of a terrapin population in the Chesapeake Bay (Jeyasuria et al., 1994).

Our results clearly show that our terrapin conservation efforts, however well-intentioned and well-publicized, are the equivalent of waging a losing battle. We simply lack the capacity to replace adult road-killed terrapins with headstarted juveniles as fast as the adults are killed by vehicles. After seven years of extremely labor-intensive efforts, we will have released nearly 800 headstarted terrapins. Unfortunately, during these same seven years, 4,020 adult female roadkills have been documented. Thus, even in the unlikely event that every headstarted juvenile we released actually survived to reproductive age, we would at best be replacing one adult for every five killed by motor traffic. Under current circumstances, therefore, we can neither reverse nor even stabilize the precipitous population decline now taking place. At best, we are merely slowing the rate of the local terrapin population crash.

Finally, we are continuing to strongly publicize the current plight of terrapins. While it is unknown whether these activities have actually benefited the terrapins in our study area by reducing roadkill mortality during the nesting season, public awareness and concern has substantially increased since we started our project seven years ago. We have created both temporary and permanent public exhibits about terrapins for the New Jersey State Aquarium, Sesame Place Amusement Park in Langhorne, Pennsylvania, and the Diller Coastal Education Building at the Wetlands Institute. We also routinely set up short-term terrapin displays for public events, such as the annual New Jersey Wings 'n Water Festival, the Avalon Seafood Festival, and Sea Isle City's annual Terrapin Day. Our conservation efforts have been featured in the Emmy Award-winning TV documentary *Terrapin*, produced by New Jersey Network (a PBS affiliate), and terrapins were also featured in the award-winning film *Secrets of the Salt Marsh*, produced by the Wetlands Institute. Numerous newspaper and magazine articles (some with national distribution) have been published, and stories about our terrapin project have also been carried on local, regional, and national TV.

The public has also participated in our conservation efforts. School and scouting groups (most notably the Avalon/Stone Harbor kindergarten) have raised money in a variety of creative ways to help support the costs of our program, and hundreds of people have taken part in the Wetlands Institute "Adopt An Egg" program, which has provided funding for some of the expenses associated with our project.

ACKNOWLEDGMENTS

The data presented in this report, accumulated over seven years (1989–1995), were made possible only by the dedicated efforts of large numbers of volunteers. Especially deserving of recognition are the nearly 30 college and university students, two high school students, and one high school teacher, who have served as summer-long participants in the diamondback terrapin research and conservation project since its inception at the Wetlands Institute. Others who have contributed significantly to the success of the project include Lisa Roselli, Joe Grottola, Tom McFarland, Townsend Dickinson, and last but by no means least, Gary and Nat Wood. To all of these associates we are enormously indebted.

Meriting special thanks are John Rokita and his several student assistants who, over the years, have nurtured our terrapin hatchlings with outstanding success at the Stockton College science laboratory complex. We are also most grateful to the staff of the Reptile House at the Cape May County Zoo for providing care for some of our terrapin hatchlings.

Financial support has come from a wide and, in some cases, improbable variety of donors. Sustained and substantial sources of long-term support have been the Wetlands Institute and Stockton State College. Much-appreciated contributions have also been provided by the teachers and children of the Avalon/Stone Harbor combined kindergarten as well as the fourth and fifth grade Science Club of the Port Republic Elementary School, the Cape May County Zoological Society, the Lehigh Valley Herpetological Society, Sturdy Savings Bank, and the hundreds of visitors and contributors to the Wetlands Institute whose $10 donations for the "adopted" or "orphaned" terrapin eggs have supported our headstarting operations.

Considerable thanks are also due to New Jersey Network, and especially to producer Leandra Little, for the production and broadcasting of the television documentary *Terrapin*. This has been a wonderful and continuing source of information about our project for the general public.

We wish to express our appreciation to the New Jersey Division of Fish, Game, and Wildlife for issuing us annual scientific research permits.

LITERATURE CITED

Bull, J. J., R. C. Vogt, and C. J. McCoy. 1982. Sex determining temperatures in turtles: A geographic comparison. Evolution 36:326–332.

Carr, A. F. 1952. Handbook of Turtles. Cornell University Press, Ithica, New York. 542 pp.

Conant, R. 1955. Correspondence. Brit. J. Herpetol. 1(12):252–253.

Conant, R. 1964. Turtle Soup. America's First Zoo 16:28–30.

Donnelly, M. and K. Owens. 1988. An informal survey of diamondback terrapin populations from Massachusetts to Texas. Center for Environmental Education, Washington, D.C. 9 pp.

Garber, S. 1988. Diamondback terrapin exploitation. Plastron Papers 17(6):18–22.

Garber, S. 1990. The ups and downs of the diamondback terrapin. The Conservationist, New York State Department of Environmental Conservation, May–June 1990:44–47.

Jeyasuria, P., W. M. Roosenburg, and A. R. Place. 1994. Role of P-450 aromatase in sex determination of the diamondback terrapin, *Malaclemys terrapin*. J. of Exp. Zool. 170:95–111.

Lovich, J. E. 1995. Turtles. *In* E. T. Laroe, C. E. Puckett, P. D. Doran, and M. J. Mac (eds.), Our Living Resources: A Report to the Nation on the Distribution, Abundance and Health of U.S. Plants, Animals and Ecosystems, pp. 118–121. National Biological Service, Washington, D.C.

U.S. Fish and Wildlife Service. 1996. Endangered and threatened wildlife and plants; Notice of final decision on identification of candidates for listing as endangered or threatened. Federal Register 61(235):64481–64485 (5 December 1996).

Wood, R. C. 1997. The impact of commercial crab traps on diamondback terrapins. *In* J. Van Abbema (ed.), Proceedings: Conservation, Restoration, and Management of Tortoises and Turtles—An International Conference, 21–27. 1993, State University of New York, Purchase. New York Turtle and Tortoise Society, New York.

Appendix I. Stretches of roads patrolled in Cape May County, New Jersey during summers of 1990–1995.

- Ocean Drive between 29th Street in Sea Isle City and Strathmore, and Ocean Drive between 74th and 53rd streets in Avalon (Cape May County Highway 619).
- Central Avenue between 82nd and 49th streets on the bay side of Sea Isle City.
- Sea Isle Boulevard (Cape May County Highway 625).
- Avalon Boulevard (Cape May County Highway 601).
- Stone Harbor Boulevard (Cape May County Highway 657).
- East Railroad Avenue in Wildwood Crest.
- Ocean Drive (Cape May County Highway 621) between Cold Spring Harbor and Wildwood Crest.

The Effect of Roads, Barrier Fences, and Culverts on Desert Tortoise Populations in California, USA

WILLIAM I. BOARMAN,[1] MARC SAZAKI,[2] AND W. BRYAN JENNINGS[3]

[1]U.S. Geological Survey, Biological Resources Division, 6221 Box Springs Blvd., Riverside, CA 92507, USA [e-mail: william_boarman@usgs.gov] [2]California Energy Commission, 1516 Ninth St., Sacramento, CA 95814, USA [3]Department of Zoology, University of Texas, Austin, TX 70712, USA

ABSTRACT: Roads and highways pose several direct and indirect threats to turtle and tortoise populations. As barriers they inhibit dispersal and subsequent gene flow between subpopulations and metapopulations. In providing access to turtle and tortoise populations, they foster such threats as development, vandalism, and collecting. Increased diversity and productivity of vegetation, resulting from enhanced hydrological conditions beside roads, attracts tortoises, which place them at greater risk of direct mortality from both predators and motorized vehicles.

Roadkills are a substantial source of mortality in desert tortoises, *Gopherus agassizii*, in California (USA) as evidenced by data on roadkills from two highways. Desert tortoise populations are depauperate along highways and this depression may extend for at least 0.8 km or more from the road. Our study of the movements of desert tortoises equipped with radio transmitters suggests that tortoises living near highways move considerable distances over short periods of time and that these movements may place the tortoises at great risk of traffic-related mortality. Other studies show that common ravens, *Corvus corax*, predators on juvenile desert tortoises, are more common along heavily-traveled roads than away from them.

A 24 km long tortoise-proof fence was erected along one highway in California. The barrier fence is made of 60 cm wide, 1 cm mesh hardware cloth, sunk 15 cm into the ground. The fence is supported by a 1.5 m high, six-strand wire fence. Several storm drain culverts span the highway. We report on a project that is now underway to monitor the effectiveness of the fence in preventing roadkills and facilitating the recovery of the local tortoise population. We are also measuring use of the culverts by tortoises to determine whether storm drain culverts are an effective mitigation for the fragmenting effects of the fence and highway.

Causes of increased mortality and reduced natality must be investigated when a population of animals is declining to the point of being threatened with extirpation. When the causes are known, actions to reverse the population declines must be developed and implemented. However, before broad application, the action should be tested in a realistic setting, particularly when the action may be costly in terms of resources (financial, material, or human) or public relations.

Desert tortoise, *Gopherus agassizii*, populations in the Mojave and Colorado deserts of the southwestern United States of America are listed as "Threatened" by the United States Fish and Wildlife Service (USFWS, 1990). Several of these populations are suffering rapid declines from many causes including disease, predation by ravens, on- and off-road vehicle traffic, livestock grazing, and loss of habitat (USFWS, 1994). Many various and complex human uses of the desert have cumulative, harmful effects on the tortoises. We report here on the harm highway traffic has on desert tortoise populations and on the progress of research to determine the effectiveness of barrier fences to decrease the harm.

Effects of Highways on Desert Tortoise and Other Animal Populations

Desert tortoise populations are depleted within at least 0.8 km of highway edges (Nicholson, 1978; Boarman, 1992; Boarman et al., in prep.) and may be affected as far away as 3.5 km from the highways (von Seckendorff Hoff and Marlow, this volume). A preliminary study (Nicholson, 1978) revealed that the distance and intensity of the population depletion may increase with level of traffic and age of the road. The causes for the population declines are not well documented.

Highways are direct sources of mortality when animals are struck by motor vehicles while moving within their home ranges or while dispersing. Large numbers of animals are often killed along roads (Lalo, 1987; Bennett, 1991). Many collisions are accidental, but D. Sheppard (pers. comm.) demonstrated that people will often turn their vehicles towards turtles to hit them intentionally. On three surveys conducted during a 2.5-year period, we found the remains of 39 dead tortoises along a 24 km section of highway in the western Mojave Desert of California (Boarman et al., 1993; Boarman, 1994). This was probably an underrepresentation of actual tortoise deaths because some carcasses may have been removed by scavengers (e.g., common ravens, *Corvus corax*, and coyotes, *Canis latrans*) before our survey and because some animals probably do not die instantly and may have moved well away from the highway edge (LaRue, 1993).

One indirect impact of linear corridors such as roads on surrounding animal populations is the fragmentation of the populations by the reduction or prevention of movement of individuals across the corridor. Population fragmentation can elevate the risk of localized extinctions from stochastic or catastrophic events or from inbreeding depression (Gilpin, 1987).

A second profound indirect impact of linear corridors such as highways or other roads is their promotion of dispersal of other sources of detriment. Frenkel (1970) and Johnson et al. (1975) found that the proportion of exotic species of plants, which may be of lower desirability or nutritional value than endemic forage to tortoises (Jennings, 1993; Avery, this volume), increased closer to roads in California. Common ravens, predators of juvenile desert tortoises (Berry, 1985; Boarman, 1993), are significantly more common along highways than in power line corridors and in the open desert (Knight and Kawashima, 1993). Highways also provide access by humans to otherwise inaccessible habitat, which in turn allows more commercial development and such activities as livestock grazing and recreation.

Vegetation along roads—particularly in arid regions—can be more productive and diverse, in part because of favorable hydrological conditions beside roads (Johnson et. al., 1975). Indeed, Johnson et. al. (1975) found that annual and perennial diversity and productivity (density, cover, and biomass) were considerably higher (as much as 17.85 times greater) along paved roads than in control areas in the western Mojave Desert. Moreover, several plant species that desert tortoises prefer, such as *Astragalus lentiginosus* (Luckenbach, 1982), *Euphorbia albomarginata* (Burge and Bradley, 1976; Jennings, 1993), and *Sphaeralcea ambigua* (Burge and Bradley, 1976; Hansen et. al., 1976) exist along roadsides in the western Mojave Desert (Jennings, 1992). Thus, the availability of appropriate forage along roadsides may attract desert tortoises, which could put them at greater risk of mortality from motor vehicles (Coombs, 1977; Jennings, 1992).

Highways also provide access for tortoise collectors, which may explain a significant proportion of the loss of tortoises along highway edges. Desert tortoises have long been sources of food for people in the southwestern deserts of the United States (Schneider and Everson, 1989) and are frequently taken as pets (Berry and Nicholson, 1984).

Chaco tortoises, *Geochelone chilensis*, are found along road edges in Argentina for an entirely different reason. Cattle grazing has denuded major portions of Chaco tortoise habitat. Because cattle are often killed by vehicles on roads, many roads in Argentina are fenced. The result is habitat along the road edge undisturbed by grazing cattle, which serves as a refuge for tortoises (T. Waller, pers. comm.).

Design of Barrier Fences as Mitigation of Impacts from Highway

Traffic-related mortality of desert tortoises may be reduced by erecting barrier fences along the edges of roads and highways. Several features must be considered for a specific fence design: height, burying depth, opacity, mesh size, durability, and maintenance. Optimal design depends on function, duration, animal behavior, and environment. The height of the barrier depends on the size of the animals that are to be excluded and their ability to climb or jump over a barrier. Depth depends on the ability of the animals to dig under the fence to surface on the other side and the depth to which the animals can burrow. If other species may create an opening beneath the fence, the sizes and behavior of these animals must be considered in the fence design.

Opacity should be determined by the animal's response to different mesh sizes and to solid barriers, and by the function of the barrier. Ruby et al. (1994) demonstrated that desert tortoises attempted to push through wide-mesh fence materials but left the edge of opaque ones after a short time. In response to intermediate-sized mesh (1 cm), tortoises did not attempt to get through but continued to walk along the fence for longer periods of time. Thus, to keep animals out of a specific area (e.g., a construction or building site), an opaque barrier may be most useful. However, if the intent is to direct animals to a passageway (e.g., a culvert or bridge), a non-opaque, intermediate-mesh fence is useful because it permits visibility of the other side and maintains the animal's interest in getting to the other side of the barrier (the animal would probably leave the edge of a solid barrier rather than search for an opening). The mesh size must not be so large that it captures and traps or injures the animals, nor so small that it either appears opaque to the animal or catches too much debris or other smaller animal species (Engelke et al., 1993).

Durability and maintenance of fences depend on biotic and abiotic factors and the time span the barrier must be in place: humans, vehicles, or large wild or domestic animals that may contact the fence; the presence of flowing water or blowing sand; the intensity of sunlight; and excessive acidity or alkalinity of the soil. Durability also varies with differential degeneration of the fence material in various environments (e.g., Ruby et al., 1994).

Barrier Fence Project

In 1991 the California Department of Transportation erected a tortoise-barrier fence along a 24 km section of State Highway 58, San Bernardino County, California, USA. The fence consists of six strands of 10 gauge galvanized steel wire and 60 cm wide, 1.3 cm mesh hardware cloth, which is buried to a depth of 15 cm beneath ground level and extends 45 cm above the ground (Figure 1). The top three wire strands are barbed to prevent access by humans and livestock; the three bottom strands are not barbed to facilitate installation of the hardware cloth and to allow medium-sized mammals to climb over without being injured. The hardware cloth is attached by steel rings to the bottom two strands for structural support. The fence is supported by 2 m metal posts spaced approximately 3 m apart.

Gates, which are required to allow access to private property along the highway edge, were also designed as barriers to tortoises. The same hardware cloth used on the fence is attached to the lower part of the gate (Figure 1). To prevent tortoises from escaping beneath the gates, they are hung close to the ground and flush to 20 × 20 cm wood beams that are buried in the ground from gatepost to gatepost.

To facilitate movement by tortoises under the highway, culverts designed for rainwater runoff were adapted for use by tortoises. The barrier fence was installed to form funnels into the storm drain culverts (Figure 2). The 48–63 m long culverts range approximately 1–3.6 m in diameter and are constructed from corrugated steel pipe or reinforced concrete. The fence and culverts connected in this manner provide an unobstructed pathway between the opposite sides of the fenced highway.

In 1991 we implemented a cooperative study by several state and federal agencies. The four primary goals of the study are to determine (1) whether the barrier fence reduces road kills, (2) whether tortoise populations recover along the highway edge, (3) whether tortoises use culverts to cross beneath the highway, and (4) how individual tortoises interact with the fence and culverts. Fieldwork began in 1991 and will continue through 1997 or longer (Boarman et al., 1993; Boarman and Sazaki, 1994).

To determine whether the barrier fence reduces direct mortality, in 1993 we began to compare the number of road-killed tortoises along a fenced highway with those along an unfenced highway. Once per year we survey on foot both sides of two highways: 24 km of the fenced Highway 58 and 24 km of the unfenced Highway 395, which are approximately 8–38 km apart. In 1993 we found five carcasses (1/4.8 km of highway) along the unfenced Highway 395 and none along the fenced section of Highway 58. All carcasses were from animals that had been dead for less than one year (Berry and Woodman, 1984). The numbers of roadkills found may have been less than the actual number of animals killed because some carcasses may have been removed by scavenging common ravens, coyotes, and kit foxes (*Vulpes macrotis*); by highway maintenance; by vehicles driving and parking on the shoulder; and by weather. Furthermore, some animals may have died after moving too far off the highway to be seen by field-workers (LaRue, 1993).

To determine whether tortoises use more of the habitat closer to the highway, we established a permanent study site in 1991 in a 1.6 km² area contiguous with the fence along Highway 58. With standardized procedures (Berry, 1984;

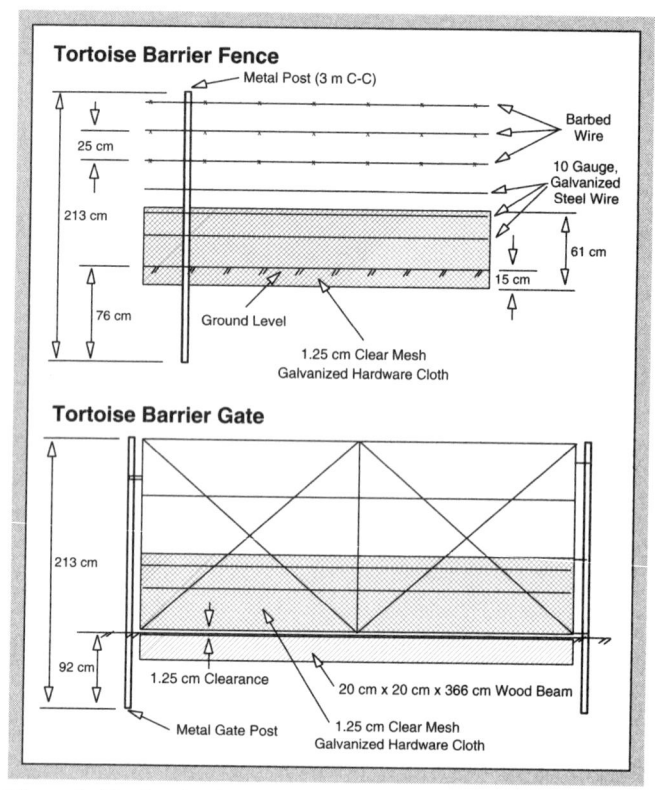

Figure 1. The barrier fence and gates constructed along State Highway 58, San Bernardino County, California, USA. The fence and gates are designed to prevent desert tortoises from wandering onto the highway.

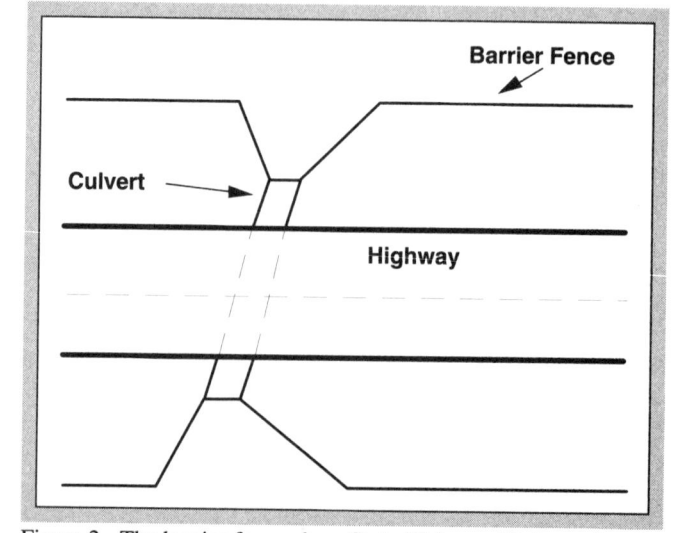

Figure 2. The barrier fence along State Highway 58 shown in relationship to culverts and highway. The fence is attached to the edges of culverts to funnel moving tortoises into the culvert so they can safely cross beneath the highway.

Boarman et al., 1993) we sampled the population to determine its density. All tortoises found were permanently marked, and their locations were mapped. We again sampled the population in 1995 and will do so every four years to detect changes in population density.

Between 1991 and 1993 radio transmitters were attached to 52 tortoises, and in 1992 and 1993 we mapped the location of 28 radio-marked tortoises every 2–3 days throughout spring, when surface activity is greatest. These locations will be compared with future data to determine whether tortoises are increasing their use of the area near the highway. By radio tracking tortoises, we learned that many animals make long-distance, one-way movements. In 1992 and 1993, 15 of the 52 radio-marked tortoises moved between 0.8 and 7.0 linear km over periods of 2–47 days (Boarman, 1994). Only one of these animals returned to its previously known seasonal home range. (Two animals moved 13.3 and 15.5 km but are removed from the analysis because one was assisted across the road and another across the barrier fence by field-workers.) The reasons for the long-distance moves are uncertain, but the risk is clear: one of the 15 animals was killed on the road, three of the 15 attempted to cross heavily traveled highways and would certainly have been killed if they had not been carried across by people (two by field-workers, one by a well-intentioned citizen), and the fates of six are unknown despite of our intensive efforts to track the animals.

Culverts are monitored in two ways: Passive Integrated Transponder (PIT) tags were attached to 94 tortoises on or near the study site. PIT tags are electronic microchips with coiled antennas all enclosed in a 1 × 14–18 mm glass tube. They are programmed to transmit a unique code when they pass through a magnetic field emitted by an electronic reading coil (Camper and Dixon, 1988). In cooperation with M. Beigel, American Veterinary Identification Devices (AVID, Inc.), we are developing an automated reading system (ARS) that records and stores the PIT tag identity, time, and date each time a tagged tortoise passes over the coil. An ARS has been placed at both ends of four culverts in the study site to indicate when a tortoise enters and passes through the culverts. In addition, we are periodically checking for tracks in previously swept soil at the entrances to four culverts and beneath one bridge. No tortoise tracks were found in 1993, but the tracks of several other animal species (kit fox; coyote; jackrabbit (*Lepus californicus*); and unidentified species of snakes, lizards, and rodents) were found; many had crossed through to the other side.

Finally, to determine how individual tortoises respond to the fence and culverts, we periodically survey a 3.2 km section of barrier fence, which includes four culverts. When an animal is found near the fence, we attach a radio transmitter (if one is not already attached) and observe the animal more regularly. In 1992 and 1993, 10 animals were observed at or near the fence. Some moved away from the fence, and others moved along the fence for various distances (up to 6.5 km). Animals at the fence tried to climb, bite, walk along the edge of, and rest at the fence. One tortoise, which had probably walked beneath a poorly adjusted gate approximately 50 m away, was observed along the fence on the highway side. None of the tortoises we observed was injured by the fence. We found five other species of reptiles, leopard lizard (*Gambelia wislizenii*), zebra-tailed lizard (*Callisaurus draconoides*), Mojave rattlesnake (*Crotalus scutulatus*), coachwhip snake (*Masticophis flagellum*), and western whiptail lizard (*Cnemidophorus tigris*), climbing over, running through, or getting caught in the fence. Dead individuals of the former three species were also found on the highway (Boarman, 1994).

CONCLUSIONS

Roads can harm animal populations in many ways, by direct mortality, population fragmentation, and alteration of habitat. The detrimental effects of new and existing roads must be considered in the design of animal preserves and in other management actions. Preliminary data suggest that barrier fences can reduce mortality of desert tortoises and other species of animals, but may only increase population fragmentation by the road if animals cannot or do not use a safe means of crossing corridors such as culverts.

ACKNOWLEDGMENTS

Harold W. Avery, Sherry Barrett, Dr. Kristin Berry, Ray Bransfield, Stan Ford, Dr. Whit Gibbons, Frank Hoover, Jack Kawashima (deceased), Dr. Jeffery E. Lovich, Dr. Jim Spotila, Dr. Sam Sweet, and Dr. Mike Weinstein provided ideas and suggestions for all aspects of the project. William Clark, Paul Frank, Gilbert Goodlett, Glenn Goodlett, Tracy Okamoto, and Ray Romero performed most of the fieldwork and provided data and reports that were used to prepare portions of this paper. Harold W. Avery, Dr. Jeffrey Lovich, Dr. Elizabeth D. Rockwell, and Jim Van Abbema provided useful comments on earlier drafts. The fence and culvert construction was funded by Caltrans. Funds for the monitoring project were provided by the California Energy Commission (Contract Nos. 700-89-007 and 700-90-015 to USBLM), Federal Highways Administration, Nevada Department of Transportation, U.S. Bureau of Land Management, and National Biological Service. California Department of Fish and Game conducted aerial surveys for radio-tagged tortoises. Mike Beigel, Glenn Goodlett, and AVID have contributed substantially to the development of the culvert monitoring system. (Mention of collaboration with AVID does not constitute an endorsement of their products.)

LITERATURE CITED

Avery, H. W. 1997. Challenges to a Changing Plant Community: Food Selectivity and Digestive Performance of Desert Tortoises Fed Native vs. Exotic Forage Plants (poster abstract). In J. Van Abbema (ed.), Proceedings: Conservation, Restoration, and Management of Tortoises and Turtles—An International Conference, p. 474. July 1993, State University of New York, Purchase. New York Turtle and Tortoise Society, New York.

Bennett, A. F. 1991. Roads, roadsides and wildlife conservation: A review. In D. A. Saunders and R. J. Hobbs (eds.), Nature Conservation 2: The Role of Corridors, pp. 99–118. Surrey Beatty & Sons, NSW, Australia.

Berry, K. H. 1984. Appendix 2. A description and comparison of field methods used in studying and censusing desert tortoises. In K. H. Berry (ed.), The status of the desert tortoise (*Gopherus agassizii*) in the United States. Report to U.S. Fish Wildlife Service from Desert Tortoise Council, Order No. 11310-0083-81.

Berry, K. H. 1985. Avian predation on the desert tortoise (*Gopherus agassizii*) in California. Report to Southern Calif. Edison Co., Bureau of Land management, Riverside, California.

Berry, K. H. 1986. Desert tortoise (*Gopherus agassizii*) relocation: Implications of social behavior and movements. Herpetologica 42: 113–125.

Berry, K. H. and L. L. Nicholson. 1984. A summary of human activities and their impacts on desert tortoise populations and habitat in California. In K. H. Berry (ed.), The status of the desert tortoise (*Gopherus agassizii*) in the United States, Ch. 3, pp. 1–58. Report to U.S. Fish Wildlife Service from Desert Tortoise Council, Order No. 11310-0083-81.

Berry, K. H. and P. Woodman. 1984. Appendix 7. Methods used in analyzing mortality data for most tortoise populations in California, Nevada, Arizona, and Utah. In K. H. Berry (ed.), The status of the desert tortoise (*Gopherus agassizii*) in the United States. Report to U.S. Fish and Wildlife Service from Desert Tortoise Council, Order No. 11310-0083-81.

Boarman, W. I. 1992. Effectiveness of fences and culverts for protecting desert tortoises along California State Highway 58: Summary of initial field season. Report to California Energy Commission, Contract No. 700-89-007. U.S. Bureau of Land Management, Riverside, California.

Boarman, W. I. 1993. When a native predator becomes a pest: A case study. In S. K. Majumdar, E. W. Miller, D. E. Baker, E. K. Brown, J. R. Pratt, and R. F. Schmalz (eds.), Conservation and Resource Management, pp. 186–201. Pennsylvania Academy of Science, Philadelphia.

Boarman, W. I. 1994. Effectiveness of fences and culverts for protecting desert tortoises along California State Highway 58: Summary of 1993 field season. Report to California Energy Commission, Contract No. 700-90-015. National Biological Survey, Riverside, California.

Boarman, W. I. and M. Sazaki. 1994. Methods for measuring the effectiveness of tortoise-proof fences and culverts along Hwy 58, California. Proc. Desert Tortoise Council Symp. 1987–1991:284–291.

Boarman, W. I., M. Sazaki, K. H. Berry, G. O. Goodlett, W. B. Jennings, and A. P. Woodman. 1993. Measuring the effectiveness of a tortoise-proof fence and culverts: Status report from the first field season. Proc. Desert Tortoise Council Symp. 1992:126–142.

Boarman, W. I., M. Sazaki, G. C. Goodlett, and T. Goodlett. In prep. Effect of highways on vertebrate and desert tortoise populations and a method to reduce highway mortality.

Burge, B. L. and W. G. Bradley. 1976. Population density, structure and feeding habits of the desert tortoise, *Gopherus agassizii*, in a low desert study area in southern Nevada. Proc. Desert Tortoise Council Symp. 1976:50–74.

Camper, J. D. and J. R. Dixon. 1988. Evaluation of a microchip marking system for amphibians and reptiles. Texas Parks and Wildlife Dept., Research Publ. 7100-159, Austin, Texas.

Coombs, E. M. 1977. Status of the desert tortoise, *Gopherus agassizii*, in the state of Utah. Proc. Desert Tortoise Council Symp. 1977: 95–101.

Engelke, E. M. 1993. Effects of tortoise fencing on indigenous desert species (abstract). Proc. Desert Tortoise Council Symp. 1992:159.

Frenkel, R. E. 1970. Ruderal Vegetation along Some California Roadsides. Univ. Calif. Press, Berkeley, California.

Gilin, M. E. 1987. Spatial structure and population vulnerability. In M. E. Soulé (ed.), Viable Populations for Conservation, pp. 125–139. Cambridge Univ. Press., Cambridge.

Hansen, R. M., M. K. Johnson, and T. R. Van Devender. 1976. Foods of the desert tortoise (*Gopherus agassizii*) in Arizona and Utah. Herpetologica 32:247–251.

Jahn, L. R. 1959. Highway mortality as an index of deer population change. J. Wildl. Manage. 23:187–197.

Jennings, W. B. 1992. Desert tortoise carcass surveys along State Highways 58 and 395 San Bernardino County, California. Unpublished report, U.S. Bureau of Land Management, Riverside, California.

Jennings, W. B. 1993. Foraging ecology of the desert tortoise (*Gopherus agassizii*) in the western Mojave Desert. M.S. thesis, University of Texas at Arlington.

Johnson, H. B., F. C. Vasek, and T. Yonkers. 1975. Productivity, diversity and stability relationships in Mojave Desert roadside vegetation. Bull. Torrey Botan. Club 102:106–115.

Knight, R. L. and J. Y. Kawashima. 1993. Responses of raven and red-tailed hawk populations to linear right-of-ways. J. Wildl. Manage. 57:266–271.

Lalo, J. 1987. The problem of road kill. Amer. Forests (Sept.-Oct.): 50–52, 72.

LaRue, E. L., Jr. 1993. Distribution of desert tortoise sign adjacent to Highway 395, San Bernardino County, California. Proc. Desert Tortoise Council Symp. 1992:190–204.

Luckenbach, R. A. 1982. Ecology and management of the desert tortoise (*Gopherus agassizii*) in California. In R. B. Bury (ed.), North American Tortoises: Conservation and Ecology, pp. 1–37. U.S. Department of the Interior Fish and Wildlife Service Wildlife Research Report 12, Washington D.C.

McClure, H. E. 1951. An analysis of animal victims on Nebraska highways. J. Wildl. Manage. 15:410–420.

Nicholson, L. 1978. The effects of roads on desert tortoise populations. Proc. Desert Tortoise Council Symp. 1978:127–129.

Ruby, D. E., J. R. Spotila, S. K. Martin, and S. J. Kemp. 1994. Behavioral responses to barriers by desert tortoises: Implications for wildlife management. Herpetol. Monogr. 8:144–160.

Schneider, J. S. and G. D. Everson. 1989. The desert tortoise (*Xerobates agassizii*) in the prehistory of the southwestern Great Basin and adjacent areas. J. Calif. and Great Basin Anthrop. 11:175–202.

Schwartz, E. R., C. W. Schwartz, and A. R. Kiester. 1984. The three-toed box turtle in central Missouri. Part II: A nineteen-year study of home range, movements and population. Terrestrial Series #12, Missouri Dept. of Conservation, Jefferson City, Missouri.

U.S. Fish and Wildlife Service. 1990. Endangered and threatened wildlife and plants; determination of threatened status for the Mojave population of the desert tortoise. Federal Register 55:12178–12191.

U.S. Fish and Wildlife Service. 1994. Desert tortoise (Mojave population) recovery plan. U.S. Fish and Wildlife Service, Portland, Oregon.

Blanding's Turtles at Fort Devens, Massachusetts, USA: A Case of "Mutualism" between Turtles and Tanks

BRIAN O. BUTLER

Oxbow Wetlands Associates, P. O. Box 533, Lunenburg, MA 01462, USA [e-mail: bbutler@bicnet.net]

ABSTRACT: The largest known northeastern metapopulation of the Blanding's turtle, *Emydoidea blandingii*, occurs in the Nashua River Valley on lands now or formerly part of the Fort Devens Tactical Training Area ("Range"), Massachusetts, USA. Ongoing study in the region continues to demonstrate newly discovered adult, newly matured, and subadult animals from wetlands that range from large emergent marshland to floodplain ponds, kettleholes, and human-created wetlands. The current *adult* population estimate for a single, partially surveyed 300 ha former training area is 224–316 animals, of which 147 are marked. Overall, more than 200 individuals have been marked in the 2,200 ha complex. Documentation of this metapopulation is far from complete, and much of the habitat remains to be evaluated. The Nashua River Valley area of Massachusetts is believed, based on available unsurveyed habitat, to support more than 400 individuals.

Military training activity over the last 50 years and more recent wildlife management practices have generated wetland and upland habitat encompassing a range of seral stages of regrowth or habitat succession within the fort. One limiting habitat parameter for *E. blandingii* is the presence of well-drained, sparsely vegetated, open soil for nesting. Blanding's turtles have been found to nest in at least four distinct current or former military training areas where sandy glacial meltwater soils have been exposed and maintained by training activity. Radio-tagged or marked females have been found to cross the Nashua River from expansive emergent marshlands to nest in disturbed upland training areas, a distance frequently exceeding 1 km. Radio-tracking has shown that females may wander overland for up to five days in association with nesting, during which time they may visit secondary wetlands and exceed straight-line terrestrial distances of 1 km.

Abundant disturbed habitat coupled with overall low-intensity land use and lack of development are considered to be responsible for the substantial extant metapopulation of *E. blandingii* in the Fort Devens area. Management strategies are being developed in cooperation with Fort Devens to maintain nesting habitat in a manner compatible with military training requirements and to enhance or restore wetland habitats where *E. blandingii* is currently found in low numbers.

The distribution of Blanding's turtles in the northeastern United States is discontinuous both with the species' primary midwestern range and within the region (McCoy, 1973). *E. blandingii* is known from a limited area of three New England states (northeastern Massachusetts, southeastern New Hampshire, and southern Maine), generally in association with the Merrimack River and its major tributaries. In addition, disjunct populations are known from New York (Dutchess County) and Nova Scotia. Population densities are assumed to be typically low in New England, and the greatest currently known concentration of *E. blandingii* is found in the Nashua River drainages of east-central Massachusetts.

In the early 1940s Fort Devens was expanded southward along the Nashua River, acquiring the largely agricultural 2,200 ha area that would become its training range. The range complex is small compared to most military installations. However, in the contemporary Massachusetts landscape, undeveloped properties of this dimension are uncommon. Although Fort Devens was closed in 1996, the range will remain a U.S. Army Reserve training facility for the indefinite future. Because of the uncertain ultimate fate of the properties that are now part of the fort, the current ongoing evaluation of habitat use and population status of Blanding's turtles was initiated by the Fort Devens Natural Resources Office.

Few historic data exist on the status of *E. blandingii* in the Nashua River Valley, and it is only within the last decade that population centers and nesting areas have been discovered. A review of sequential aerial photographs (1940s to present) of parts of the Fort Devens Range and adjacent areas where Blanding's turtles are currently found shows a net increase in suitable Blanding's turtle wetlands habitat, which is due to modifications brought about by military training. Similarly, substantial increases in disturbed, well-drained sandy soils, preferred as nesting substrate by the species in the region, are seen following military acquisition of the property. These disturbed sandy areas have now become firing ranges, bivouac areas, and equipment testing sites and lie adjacent to and up to more than a kilometer from Blanding's turtle aquatic habitat. Several currently known nesting areas have been maintained in a disturbed state throughout the fifty-year history of the range.

The exceptional abundance of suitable nesting substrate in proximity to wetland habitat (due to 50 years of military activities) appears to have contributed significantly to the overall suitability of the Nashua Valley for Blanding's turtles and, unintentionally, to the species' conservation in New England. Lacking historical data on the turtles' population status, this supposition is admittedly circumstantial.

However, evidence of recent recruitment within current and former training areas lends support to this conjecture. Eleven to 45 percent of individuals captured by hoop traps in various Blanding's turtle habitats are subadults (6–15 years old). Blanding's turtle hatchlings (Butler and Graham, 1995) and juveniles (Pappas and Brecke, 1992) tend to be cryptic and prefer different habitat from that of adults. Hatchlings, juveniles, and subadults may therefore comprise a much greater component of the population than is reflected by trap data.

Blanding's turtles in the Nashua River Valley are found at greatest density in emergent marshland. Thirty-nine individuals were trapped in one open pool in an emergent vegetation mat measuring <100 m². In the Fort Devens area, Blanding's turtles have also been frequently observed to use small, isolated natural and man-made ponds. These include floodplain buttonbush (*Cephalanthus occidentalis*) ponds, kettleholes, borrow pits, and impoundments. Deeper isolated ponds (≥ 1 m) have been used as hibernation sites for one to four individuals that summered elsewhere (Graham and Butler, 1993) in at least six locations, and adults are frequently trapped or observed in isolated ponds and vernal pools in April and May.

The use of novel or alternative nest sites by *E. blandingii* has been observed (A. Breisch, J. Haskins, pers. comm.). In five instances (4 females), animals were found to construct nests >2 km from nesting sites used in previous years. Overland movements by individuals exceeding 1 km are commonly demonstrated with radiotelemetry. These movements are frequently associated with nesting or occur between wetland systems. The Massachusetts Wetlands Protection Act provides conservation commissions with jurisdiction only within 100 ft (32 m) of a wetland edge and is therefore grossly inadequate for the protection of this species.

Fort Devens is a large contiguous land area (approx. 4,200 ha in total) containing diverse wetland and upland habitats. Adjacency to the Nashua River and other protected lands in the valley probably adds substantially to the value of the Fort Devens Range as a Blanding's turtle resource. In addition, upland and wetland habitat modifications on the base are now conducted with consideration for Blanding's turtles. To minimize potential adverse effects on nesting and recruitment by Blanding's turtles, berm reconstruction, training, and maintenance within the range are being scheduled in consultation with the Natural Resources Officer. The installation of drift fencing in nesting areas and other cooperative measures by the military have also contributed to ongoing research. However, the greatest single asset to the conservation of Blanding's turtles in this area is this range's continued protection from commercial development. This and the considerations made for behavior and habitat needs have created conditions conducive to successful conservation of *E. blandingii* in the area.

Acknowledgments

Thanks are due to Natural Resources Officer Thomas Poole, the Range Control Staff, and the Installation Commander, Fort Devens. Funding was provided by the Department of Defense's Legacy Fund. Research contracts (MA HP 92SR-05, MAHER, 93SMM3) and funds were administered by the Massachusetts Natural Heritage and Endangered Species Program and The Nature Conservancy. Work was conducted under Massachusetts Division of Fish and Wildlife Permits 032.92SCRA and 040.93SCRA and U.S. Fish and Wildlife Permit 41705.

Literature Cited

Butler, B. O. and T. E. Graham. 1995. Early post-emergent behavior and habitat selection in hatchling Blanding's turtles, *Emydoidea blandingii*, in Massachusetts. Chelon. Conserv. Biol. 1(3):187–196.

Graham, T. E. and B. O. Butler. 1993. Metabolic rates of wintering Blanding's turtles, *Emydoidea blandingii*. Comp. Biochem. Physiol. 106A:663–665.

McCoy, C. J. 1973. *Emydoidea, E. blandingii*. Catalogue of American Amphibians and Reptiles 136.1–136.4. SSAR.

Pappas, M. J. and B. J. Brecke. 1992. Habitat selection of juvenile Blanding's turtles, *Emydoidea blandingii*. J. Herpetol. 26:233–234.

Desert Tortoise Populations in the Mojave Desert and a Half-Century of Military Training Activities

ANTHONY J. KRZYSIK

U.S. Army-CERL, P.O. Box 9005, Champaign, IL 61826-9005, USA
[e-mail: krzysik@gis.uiuc.edu]

ABSTRACT: The history of the United States military in the Mojave Desert is summarized, and a detailed case study of the effects of landscape-scale military training activities on the desert tortoise in the central Mojave is presented.

Thirty-five years of Army training activities (occurring between 1940 and 1983) have fragmented tortoise populations at Fort Irwin, the Army's National Training Center (NTC). Recent data have demonstrated that tortoise population densities in areas that are not used or lightly used by tactical vehicles are stable, even after six years of intensive war games at the NTC. These areas of the fort include installation boundaries, high rugged bajadas along mountain ranges, Goldstone (off-limits to training), a multi-purpose range complex (a live-fire range off-limits to maneuvering vehicles), and areas between the cantonment area (housing and associated infrastructure) and the actual training ranges. Tortoise densities have declined significantly in those portions of Fort Irwin used as training ranges for tactical vehicle maneuvers.

Two novel approaches are demonstrated to analyze, interpret, and visualize desert tortoise distribution and density patterns on a landscape scale. A statistical analysis and inference strategy was developed that is independent of the usual statistical assumptions. Desert tortoise distribution and density data were spatially modeled on a landscape scale with an analytical interpolation and smoothing technique refined in our laboratory—"Smoothing Thin-Plate Splines with Tension." This technique may have promising applications in ecology and conservation biology for modeling distribution and density patterns of populations or genetic structure and species-habitat relationships on landscape scales, and further research is being conducted.

The Mojave Desert

The Mojave Desert is located in southeastern California and extends into southern Nevada, northwest Arizona, and extreme southwestern Utah. The diversity of geomorphic landscapes in the Mojave is as rich as anywhere in the world (Mabbutt, 1977). It lies in the Basin and Range Physiographic Province and is characterized by rugged block-faulted mountain ranges separated by alluvium-filled basins. The basins consist of broad valley plains, gentle sloping bajadas (ancient coalesced alluvial fans), and low rolling hills. The lowest basins form playas or dry lake beds of silty-clay soils. The eroding mountains produce talus slopes, boulder fields, and rocky or gravelly alluvial fans, which merge into the sandy soils and fine gravels of bajadas and plains. A dominant visual feature of the landscape, especially impressive from an aerial view, is the extensive and complex dendritic network of washes, arroyos, and canyons. Washes often form extensive networks of braided channels on the bajadas. Although washes provide only an ephemeral source of water following adequate rain showers, ground water in these channels remains closer to the surface than in the surrounding uplands. Other common features of the landscape include rolling hills with gravelly or rocky substrates, highly fractured boulder ridges, rugged boulder/rock outcrops of granite or volcanic basalt, sand dunes, lava flows, and desert pavement (a gravelly tiled surface possessing structural integrity and resistant to water or wind erosion). Springs and seeps are rare in the Mojave Desert but where present represent critical ecological elements for landscape biodiversity.

The Mojave Desert is known as the "high desert" as three-quarters of its elevation lies from 600 to 1,200 m (2,000–3,900 ft) (MacMahon and Wagner, 1985). The lower elevations (150 m, 500 ft) are found along the Colorado River, and the highest point is Charleston Peak at 3,633 m (11,920 ft) approximately 50 km northwest of Las Vegas. The Mojave Desert is characterized by dramatic contrasts in elevation—the extreme example being Badwater in Death Valley at -86 m (-282 ft), the lowest point in the western hemisphere, and adjacent Telescope Peak at 3,368 m (11,050 ft) in the Panamint Mountains.

Typically, the desert's hot summers have highs of 35–46°C (95–115°F) and cool winters with lows of -7 to +5°C (20–41°F). The record high for the western hemisphere is 56.7°C (134°F) at Death Valley. The Mojave Desert receives primarily winter precipitation and is the driest of the four North American Deserts. Rainfall is patchy and unpredictable both spatially and temporally. Summer rains are the most unpredictable, occurring as brief thunderstorm squalls. In a given region of the Mojave in a given year, precipitation may vary from 0 to 20 cm (0–8 in); more typically it is 2–13 cm (0.75–5 in). High winds of 45–100 kmph (28–63 mph) are a common feature, especially in the spring, with gusts up to 150 kmph (94 mph).

The dominant vegetation in the Mojave Desert is creosote-bursage scrub (*Larrea tridentata* and *Ambrosia dumosa*). This community exists in either its pure form or with a variety of subdominant shrubs in complex combinations. The Mojave is characterized by spring blooms of winter annuals, and 80% of Mojave annuals are endemics (MacMahon, 1988). The blooms can be very extensive but are directly related to winter precipitation. Saltbush scrub (*Atriplex* sp.) typically occurs around playas, springs or seeps, and some washes. Cacti are not characteristic of the Mojave and are poorly represented in abundance, size, and species richness. Typically, no more than four to six species are found in an area. Visually, the most notable plant is the Joshua tree (*Yucca brevifolia*). It occurs only rarely in dense stands and is typically found scattered over the landscape. Uncommon in the central portion of the desert, the Joshua tree is more abundant along its periphery at elevations of 900–500 m but can also be found as low as 600 m. At elevations above 1,200–1,500 m (depending on slope aspect and other local factors) creosote-bursage is replaced with other plant communities, e.g., blackbrush (*Coleogyne ramosissima*) and piñon-juniper (*Pinus monophylla* and *Juniperus californica*).

The Mojave Desert (140,000 km²) comprises 11% of the landscape of North American deserts (MacMahon, 1988). U.S. Department of Defense (DoD) military installations utilize approximately one-tenth of the Mojave, with four major facilities representing 10,663 km², or 7.6% of the Mojave.

History of Military Training in the Mojave Desert

The U.S. Army was among the first to arrive and develop settlements in the harsh Mojave climate when it established several forts in the mid-19th century along the Mojave Trail from Cajon Pass in the San Bernardino Mountains (Interstate Highway 15) to Fort Mojave, Arizona on the Colorado River (Casebier, 1986). Fort Mojave was established in 1859 across the river 15 km north of the present Needles, California (at the extreme southern tip of Nevada). Before the establishment of Fort Mojave, Congress authorized funds in 1853 for the U.S. Army Corps of Engineers to conduct surveys for railroad routes through the Southwest, and in 1855 Colonel Henry Washington arrived at the oasis at Twentynine Palms, California, and provided the first official report of the region (Ludwig, 1989). Despite their early presence in the Mojave Desert, the military's impact on the landscape was insignificant for almost 90 years, until the beginning of World War II.

U.S. Army Desert Training Center (DTC). General George S. Patton, Jr. established the DTC in April 1942. It was the site of armor training maneuvers with tanks and armored personnel carriers (APCs) until May 1944 (Meller, 1946, in Prose, 1985; Ludwig, 1989). Patton trained his command extensively at the DTC from its establishment until early fall when he departed to land on 8 November 1942 in North Africa (Ludwig, 1989). The DTC reached a size of 47,105 km² (18,400 mi²) including all of the eastern Mojave Desert and a large portion of the Sonoran Desert in southern California and southwestern Arizona (Prose, 1986a).* Tracked vehicle impressions are still visible and studies have been conducted to evaluate any lasting effects on soil and vegetation (Prose, 1985, 1986b; Prose and Metzger, 1985; Prose and Wilshire, 1986) and on secondary plant succession (Lathrop, 1983; Prose et al., 1987). The effects of military training on vertebrate populations in the DTC are unknown.

Fort Irwin. Located in the central Mojave Desert approximately 50 km northeast of Barstow, California, Fort Irwin is 2,600 km² (approx. the size of the state Rhode Island) and consists of three management units (Figure 1): the National Training Center (2,096 km²), Goldstone Deep Space Communications Complex (135 km²), and Leach Lake Bombing Range (369 km²). Goldstone is leased by National Aeronautics and Space Administration (NASA) and Jet Propulsion Laboratory (JPL) for communications with satellites and deep space probes and is off-limits to both the public and military maneuvers. The Leach Lake Range is an off-limits, live-fire impact zone leased by the Air Force for bombing and missile practice. Figure 1 also shows the four former live-fire impact zones (Langford, Lucky Fuse, Nelson, and Gary Owen), which were cleared of hazardous ordinance (unexploded munitions) in 1984–1985.

In 1940, the War Department withdrew public lands and established the Mojave Army Anti-Aircraft Range, which was renamed Camp Irwin in 1942. The post was placed on surplus status in 1947 but was reactivated in 1951 for training troops during the Korean War. Between 1972 and 1980 it was used as a training area for the California Army National Guard. Fort Irwin was selected as the Army's National Training Center (NTC) in August of 1979. Although the first NTC training exercise took place 13 April 1981,

---

*The DTC extended eastward from Twentynine Palms across the Colorado River to approximately 50 km (31 mi) west of Phoenix and Prescott, Arizona; southward across I-10 to the Mexican border and Yuma, Arizona; and northward across I-40 into the southern tip of Nevada.

NTC's massive force-on-force training maneuvers did not begin until 17 January 1982. Therefore, before the NTC became established, the Fort Irwin landscape was subjected to 35 years of cumulative military training exercises.

Typical training at the NTC consists of landscape-scale engagements of tanks and APCs. Figure 2 shows the cumulative tracked vehicle-days (tanks + APCs) since the establishment of the NTC. The ratio of wheeled-to-tracked vehicles is approximately 3:1. Details of the Army training mission at the NTC can be found in Krzysik (1994a) and are summarized in Krzysik and Woodman (1991). Actual war games and rotational training exercises at the NTC are described in Bolger (1986) and Halberstadt (1989).

Marine Corps Air Ground Combat Center (MCAGCC). The MCAGCC is located in the southern Mojave Desert approximately 5 km north of Twentynine Palms, California, and Joshua Tree National Monument. The entire installation (2,413 km^2) is used for landscape-scale training maneuvers with tanks and APCs similar to but on a smaller scale than at the NTC. However, unlike the NTC, the training mission at MCAGCC includes live-fire battle scenarios, both air to ground and ground to ground, throughout the installation. MCAGCC also conducts Combined Arms Exercises (CAX), which includes training maneuvers with all four services (Army, Navy, Marine Corps, and Air Force).

The early history of the MCAGCC is summarized from Ludwig (1989). To take advantage of the thermal updrafts in the desert, the U.S. Army established a glider school on the dry lake beds near Twentynine Palms in November 1941. General Patton trained his command extensively in this area in 1942. On 20 August 1952, the Marine Corps Training Center was established at its current location. Throughout the 1970s the Marine base expanded its mission and an airfield was officially opened on 29 June 1976. On 16 February 1979 the base was redesignated as MCAGCC.

Naval Air Weapons Station, China Lake (NAWS). NAWS is located in the western and northwestern portions of the Mojave Desert. The 4,432 km^2 installation consists of two units separated by Searles Valley: China Lake Complex (2,460 km^2) in the northwest and Mojave B Ranges/Randsburg Wash Complex (1,972 km^2) to the southeast and adjacent to the western boundary of Fort Irwin.

NAWS was withdrawn from public lands in 1943 and established as an aerial gunnery range to support World War II training as well as a post-war Naval weapons research and development laboratory/test range (NAWS, 1982). Only approximately 1.8% of NAWS has been developed; the remainder is relatively pristine (USFWS, 1988a). Other than specific target test pads, the installation is not used for extensive live-fire or bombing exercises. It is significant that NAWS is not used for tactical vehicle maneuvers or extensively for off-road vehicles (ORVs). However, the NTC (Fort Irwin) has been negotiating with

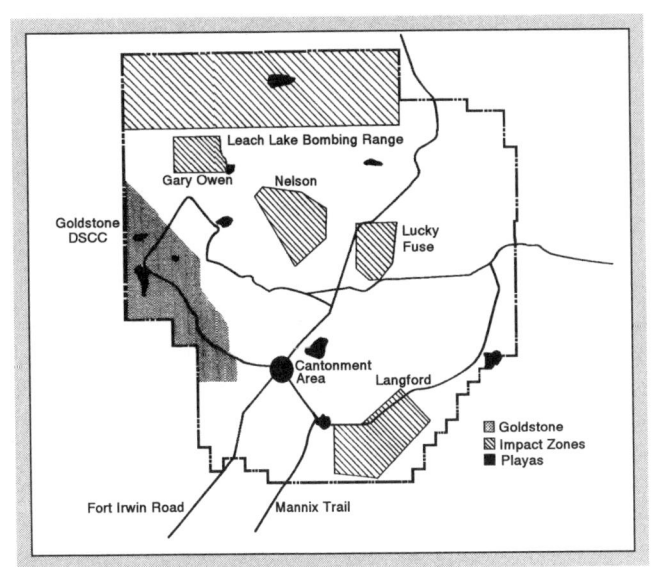

Figure 1. Map of Fort Irwin illustrating its three management units: Goldstone Deep Space Communications Complex, Leach Lake Bombing Range, National Training Center NTC (rest of installation); four live-fire impact zones, playas, cantonment area (housing and infrastructure), and major roads.

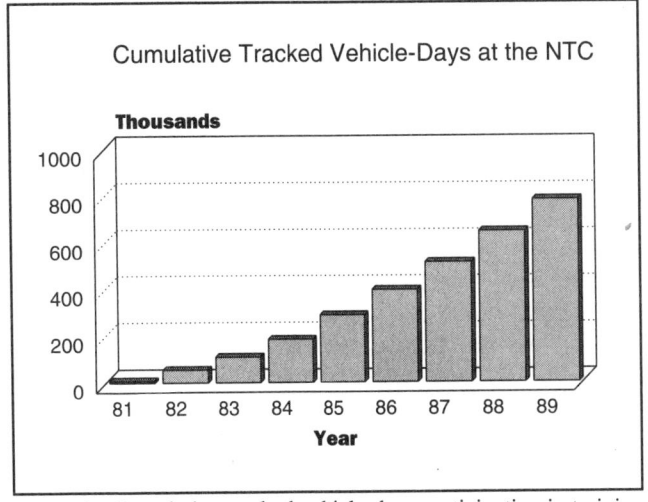

Figure 2. Cumulative tracked vehicle-days participating in training exercise maneuvers at Fort Irwin's National Training Center. The NTC began its first training exercise 13 April 1981. Note the geometrical increase in training, especially since 1985.

NAWS to use the Mojave B South Ranges for tactical vehicle maneuvers.

Edwards Air Force Base (EAFB). EAFB (1,218 km^2) is in the western Mojave approximately 30 km northeast of Lancaster, California, south of State Highway 58, just west of Boron. Used primarily as a flight testing and research facility for new aircraft and avionic systems and controls, EAFB also conducts static rocket testing and is a landing site for NASA space shuttle missions. Approximately one third of the base is zoned for target practice using inert ordinance (non-explosive shells). Actual target areas are relatively small and most of the terrain serves as buffer zones; only occasionally is it subjected to troop deployment.

METHODS

Tortoise surveys were conducted at Fort Irwin in 1983 and 1989 using the 10 yd (9.1 m) wide × 1.5 mi (2.4 km) long triangular strip transect method adopted by the Bureau of Land Management (BLM) (Berry and Nicholson, 1984). Independent tortoise burrow and scat counts were recorded within each strip transect. Because several scats are frequently found together and a tortoise burrow may be associated with a large clump of scats, the recording of "independent" events refers to counting a clump of scats of similar age and size as a single sign, and scats associated with a burrow are not counted. To estimate tortoise density, calibration coefficients were derived by conducting identical surveys by each surveyor in three calibration plots (1 mi² BLM population monitoring plots) where accurate tortoise densities have been calculated from an extensive mark-recapture program. The calibration plots yielded a calibration coefficient for each surveyor. The calibration coefficient of an experienced tortoise surveyor typically ranges from 12 to 13 (less observant surveyors generate higher coefficients). Hence, the presence of a single tortoise burrow or scat along the 1.5 mile strip transect translates to an estimated tortoise density of 12–13/mi², and ten tortoise burrows and scats would estimate 120/mi². On the basis of tortoise densities interpreted from the calibration plots, each 1.5 mile triangular transect surveyed at Fort Irwin represented a survey plot of 0.64 km² (0.25 mi²). More specific details concerning study design and survey methods can be found in Krzysik and Woodman (1991) or in Krzysik (1994b).

The 1983 Fort Irwin tortoise survey consisted of 255 transects, and consequently, some of the surveyed areas of the installation possessed small sample sizes. The 1989 survey consisted of 406 transects and represented a sampling average of 0.81 mi²/transect at the eight tortoise sites, 2.25 mi²/transect at impacted military training ranges, and 3.65 mi²/transect in the rest of the installation. A large portion of this latter category consisted of landscapes unsuitable for the desert tortoise and therefore not surveyed: mountainous terrain, developed areas, and playas. This accounted for the sparse sampling in this category.

A Nontraditional Statistical Approach

The reliability of statistical inference is increased if exact P-values are calculated with tight Confidence Intervals, and no assumptions are made of statistic distributions (e.g., normal, chi-square, etc.). This is particularly critical when sample sizes are very small and the data are highly skewed or unbalanced (e.g., sparse or heavily tied contingency tables). P-values are more commonly known as "statistical significance," and generally a value of 0.05 (5%) is used in biological research. However, there are no *a priori* rules, logic, or magic concerning the 5% level of significance. In social research, where data sets typically possess high variance, a value of 0.1 is often used for P, while in the physical sciences or engineering P-values of 0.01 or smaller may be used. P represents the probability of making a Type I (or α) error—the rejection of a true null hypothesis (we conclude that two populations possess significantly different means when in fact they do not; the difference we observe occurred by chance alone). We cannot make P unreasonably small and therefore minimize Type I error because when we do we increase Type II error (1-α or β)—the failure to reject a false null hypothesis (we conclude that the variation between two population means is due to chance alone, and the two means come from identical distributions when in fact they do not, e. g., we find no significant difference in populations means). Type II errors in conservation biology are particularly critical as we must be conservative and err on the side that there *may be* potential impacts, degradation, or population trends rather than "miss early warning signals" in monitoring data.

This study compares tortoise densities between 1983 and 1989. Sample sizes in the 1983 data are small, and the data for both years contain many "0" counts on transects, typical of tortoise sign count data. Data of this nature are skewed and possess heterogeneous variances and sparse contingency tables, increasing the probability of α error in paired comparisons. A statistical approach is needed that is independent of the usual statistical assumptions, and emphasis is placed on minimizing α error. In ecological field studies and conservation biology, exact statistical methods may be a more desirable alternative to traditional methods that are based on asymptotic assumptions.

Calculating exact P-values belongs in the domain of resampling and randomization tests and Monte Carlo sampling (Efron, 1982; Noreen, 1989; Manly, 1991), including multiple comparisons (Westfall and Young, 1993). Nonparametric tests are desirable because they make no assumptions on the distribution of test statistics (Siegel, 1956; Hollander and Wolfe, 1973). However, like parametric tests they still rely on asymptotic behavior that requires reasonable sample sizes and balanced data. Asymptotic theory is not valid for data sets that are small, highly skewed, sparse, or unbalanced (Bishop et al., 1975). These limitations have been recognized for quite some time, and Fisher (1935) suggested the use of permutational P-values for randomized experiments. However, the routine use of permutation methods directly depends upon the availability of inexpensive high-powered computers. Indeed, it is now possible to conduct resampling and Monte Carlo sampling tests and compute exact permutated *P*-values for parametric and nonparametric tests and thus avoid asymptotic assumptions (Mehta et al., 1988; Agresti et al., 1990; Good, 1994; Weerahandi, 1995).

In this study the 1983 and 1989 tortoise data were compared by the nonparametric Kruskal-Wallis test treating the data as 2 × n contingency tables, where the two rows represent survey years and n represents independent tortoise burrow and scat count data (columns = sample size). Kruskal-Wallis tests the null hypothesis that the rows of the contingency table (1983 vs. 1989 samples) came from the same underlying distribution. For each 1983 and 1989 comparison, 50,000 Monte Carlo 2 × n contingency tables were generated, and the exact *P*-value and its 99% Confidence Interval were calculated.

To visually illustrate the 1983 and 1989 comparisons, an independent computer-intensive procedure was implemented. For each 1983 and 1989 comparison the data pairs were bootstrapped* 10,000 times, and the difference between means for each pair was plotted. The median and associated first and third quartiles of the resulting distribution were plotted as rectangular boxes. The resulting graphical displays are interpreted as follows: When the box lies in the positive plane above the abscissa, densities have increased in 1989, and when the box lies in the negative plane, density has decreased. Boxes crossing the abscissa axis (or close to the axis) suggest similar densities in the two survey periods. Each paired comparison (rectangular box) was associated with the exact *P*-value calculated from the Monte Carlo Kruskal-Wallis analysis.

Military Installations and the Desert Tortoise

Edwards Air Force Base. The eastern and southeastern portions of EAFB, consisting of 243 km² and representing 20% of the installation, is being managed as Critical Habitat for the desert tortoise (Mark Hagan, EAFB biologist, pers. comm.). This has been undertaken in cooperation with the U.S. Fish and Wildlife Service and the Desert Tortoise Recovery Plan under the Endangered Species Act. Some of this area serves as buffer zones for inert ordinance target sites. By August 1994 tortoise surveys were completed on 854 km² of the base. Fieldwork was also conducted in the summer of 1994 to compare the effectiveness of three different survey methods for estimating desert tortoise burrow and scat densities. The work also included an evaluation of the Zippin method (Zippin, 1958) for estimating tortoise densities (Krzysik et al., 1995). A long-term desert tortoise monitoring program is in the planning stages at EAFB.

Naval Air Weapons Station, China Lake. Desert tortoises are not abundant at NAWS. Surveys in 1987 determined that populations were patchy and, when present, occurred at densities of 0–20/mi² (USFWS, 1988a). Studies are underway to further assess and monitor desert tortoises at NAWS.

Marine Corps Air Ground Combat Center. Sand Hill training Area is located in the southwest corner of MCAGCC, and the central portion of this range has been declared a desert tortoise conservation area, off-limits to military training exercises. Tortoise densities at two study plots at Sand Hill have been estimated at 80–100/mi² (MCAGCC, 1993). At least some portions of training ranges just north and east of Sand Hill may possess comparable densities, and other small populations have been reported throughout the installation. However, tortoise distribution is highly patchy at the installation, and with some notable exceptions (e. g., Sand Hill), population densities are probably low (Krzysik, pers. obs.). Research is currently being conducted at this installation and Joshua Tree National Park to develop methods to assess and monitor distribution and density patterns of tortoise populations on landscape scales (Krzysik, current research).

Fort Irwin (Army National Training Center). Desert tortoise monitoring research at Fort Irwin has provided us an opportunity to assess the distribution and density patterns of tortoises experiencing landscape-scale military training activities. The first desert tortoise survey on Fort Irwin was conducted in the summer of 1983 (Woodman et al., 1986). The live-fire impact zones (Figure 1) were not surveyed. Although the large scale war games at the NTC were initiated only the previous year (Figure 2), 35 years of military training activities had occurred since 1940 (training activities did not occur in some years). Valley and bajada shrub cover in 1983 at the NTC (southern training corridor) and Goldstone are compared in Figure 3. Goldstone was used as a control as it is off-limits to off-road vehicles (ORVs) and its habitats remain undisturbed. As illustrated, NTC habitats were already severely disturbed in 1983, and Woodman et al. (1986) found that the Fort Irwin tortoises were highly fragmented and population densities were low. Only two areas had relatively high tortoise densities (50–100+/mi²): the southern boundary of the installation and the high bajada in the vicinity of Granite Pass between Lucky Fuse and Nelson impact zones (see Figure 1).

With the exception of Leach Lake Bombing Range, the other four impact zones were cleared of ordinance (unexploded munitions) in 1984–1985. An impact zone consists of an extensive buffer zone, while the actual target area is relatively small. Target areas are highly impacted, but the buffer areas receive little habitat damage. Because the potential hazards of unexploded ordinance makes these areas off-limits to tactical or civilian vehicles, military impact

---

*Resampled with replacement (Efron, 1982).

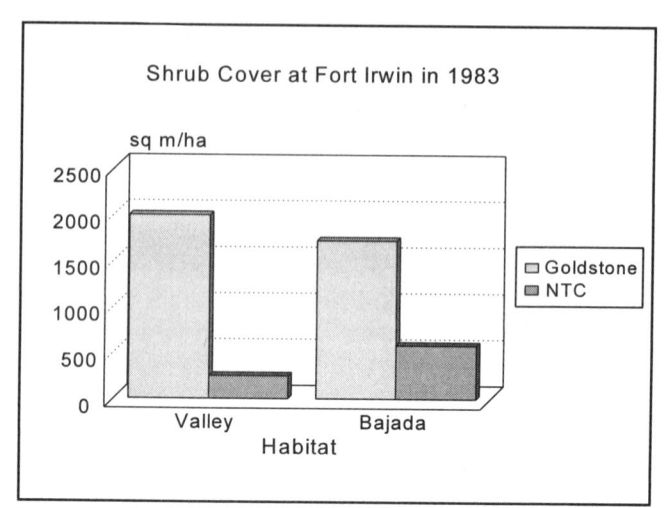

Figure 3. Cover of woody perennial vegetation at Fort Irwin and Goldstone (control) in 1983. Shrub cover at the NTC was assessed in the southern training corridor. The vegetation survey was conducted before the tortoise survey.

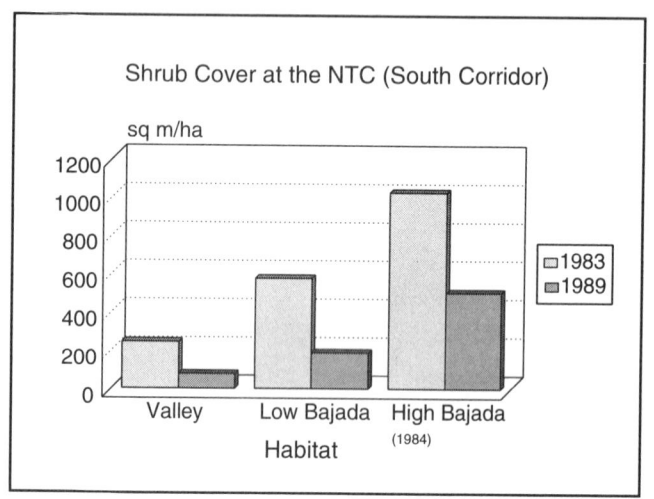

Figure 4. Cover of woody perennial vegetation at Fort Irwin's NTC southern corridor in 1983 and 1989. The initial data for the high bajada was collected in 1984.

zones typically represent undisturbed habitats. However, the clearing of these impact zones not only increased the land area for training but also permitted the opportunity for broader sweeps of the entire landscape by maneuvering convoys of tactical vehicles. The southern corridor was extended southward, but of particular importance, the removal of Lucky Fuse and Nelson impact zones as obstacles projecting into the central corridor dramatically increased the scale of east-to-west tactical maneuvers. Concurrent with the clearing of impact areas the NTC expanded its training mission in 1985 by increasing the number of annual training rotations to 14 (there were 9 in 1982, 11 in 1983, and 12 in 1984), increased the size of each rotation, and initiated longer-range battle scenarios to simulate longer-range weapon systems. Thus, three factors were responsible for accelerated habitat degradation on the NTC since 1985: (1) an increase in training intensity; (2) the use of once off-limits impact zones; and (3) the exposure of portions of the landscape that although physically accessible to training vehicles pre-1985, were tactically undesirable because the presence of impact zones isolated (trapped) engaging forces, limited the terrain for maneuvers, or prevented rapid cross-country movement or access to other areas of engagement.

Desert Tortoise Monitoring and Military Training

A desert tortoise survey at Fort Irwin was repeated during the summer and fall of 1989 (Krzysik and Woodman, 1991). The objectives of the survey were to (1) establish the current distribution and density patterns of the desert tortoise after six years of NTC training activities, (2) compare the 1983 and 1989 surveys to determine the effects of the NTC mission on desert tortoise populations, and (3) determine the status of tortoises in the previously unsurveyed impact zones. Eighty-four landscape-scale training exercises were conducted at the NTC between the 1983 and 1989 tortoise surveys. This training effort consisted of 1,265 training days, 7,595,313 soldier days, 2,080,997 wheeled-vehicle days, and 681,798 tracked-vehicle days. This effort represented 87% of all NTC training exercises conducted from the first rotation in 1981 through 1989.

Figure 4 shows the decrease in shrub cover between 1983 and 1989 in the NTC southern corridor in valley, low bajada, and high bajada habitats. The already-low cover of woody perennial vegetation in the southern corridor (see Figure 3) decreased an additional 69% in the valley, 67% on the low bajada, and 51% on the high bajada. Sampling design and field methods for monitoring woody perennials can be found in Krzysik (1984 or 1985).

Krzysik and Woodman (1991) used traditional parametric inference to compare 1983 estimated tortoise population densities to those of 1989. Analysis of variance (ANOVA) was used with appropriate transformations applied to the raw data. The validity of parametric statistics requires assumptions about the properties of the collected data, particularly with respect to normal distribution, homogeneity of sample variances, and adequate sample sizes. However, ANOVA is considered robust with respect to parametric assumptions, particularly with properly transformed data and reasonable sample sizes (Zar, 1984; Sokal and Rohlf, 1994). Even data sets that are not normally distributed possess sample means that are normally distributed when sample sizes are large because of the central limit theorem. Krzysik and Woodman (1991) discussed in detail the difficulties in statistical inference when estimating tortoise densities from field data of tortoise sign (burrow and scat) counts. Tortoise sign counts are characterized by small sample sizes, strongly skewed count data, an abundance of "0" cells in the data set, and extreme spatial patchiness in sign counts.

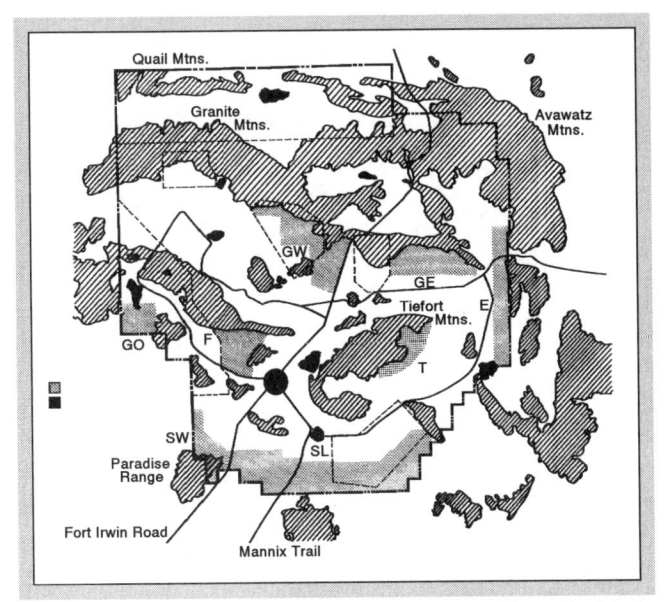

Figure 5. Map of Fort Irwin. This map is similar to Figure 1 with the addition of mountain ranges and the eight desert tortoise populations (sites) identified in the 1989 survey.

In this study, the 1983 and 1989 data were reanalyzed using a radical departure from traditional statistical methodology. This approach is summarized in the Methods section and avoids all assumptions of data distribution, skewness, variance heterogeneity, unbalanced contingency tables, and small sample sizes.

Desert Tortoise Populations at Fort Irwin

Desert tortoises at Fort Irwin in 1989 could be delineated into eight populations or tortoise sites (Krzysik and Woodman, 1991; Krzysik, 1994b). Figure 5 illustrates these sites in relation to mountain ranges, playas, and major roads. Refer to Figure 1 for the location of the cantonment area (housing facilities and associated infrastructure), Goldstone, Leach Lake Bombing Range, and the former live-fire impact zones. These populations were isolated from each other by mountain ranges, the cantonment area, playas, major roads, and severely disturbed training ranges. The major roads are typically 50–100 m wide as they are used extensively by convoys of tactical vehicles traveling to training ranges.

Four additional areas contained low tortoise densities in 1983 and 1989. Two of these areas are adjacent to the cantonment area just to the north (NS) and south (C), and although large numbers of tactical vehicles traverse these areas, they primarily use roads because the areas are too close to the cantonment for training maneuvers. The other two areas are NTC training ranges that are characterized by extensive tactical vehicle maneuvers. Site V represents the southeastern valleys of the installation, south of the Granite Mountains and east of Fort Irwin Road (see Figure 5). These valleys comprise the NTC's entire southern, and the eastern half of the central, training corridors. Site NN is located in the northwestern portion of the installation south of the Granites and north of Goldstone and includes the western half of the central corridor (see Figure 5). The northern portion of Goldstone was withdrawn in 1985 by the NTC for training maneuvers.

Figure 6 ranks the 12 sites on the basis of 1989 estimated tortoise densities. These 12 sites have been classified into five categories:

1. Sites along installation boundaries: South (SL), Southwest (SW), East (E), Figure 7;
2. Sites located on high bajadas along mountain ranges: Tiefort (T), Granite East (GE), Granite West (GW), Figure 8;
3. Sites closed to ORVs: Goldstone (GO), Multi-Purpose Range Complex (F), Figure 9;
4. Sites with limited ORV use: Cantonment area (C), Nelson South (NS), Figure 10;
5. Sites present in NTC training ranges: Southern and Central Training Corridors-Valleys (V) and Nelson North (NN), Figure 11.

Despite six years of intense training activities at the NTC (Figure 2), desert tortoise populations have not changed significantly from 1983 to 1989 at:

1. Installation boundaries: SW ($P = 0.89$), E ($P = 0.79$), Figure 7;
2. High bajadas: T ($P = 0.43$), GE ($P = 0.88$), GW ($P = 0.27$), Figure 8;
3. Habitats with no ORVs: F ($P = 0.12$), GO ($P = 0.77$), Figure 9;
4. Habitats with limited use of ORVs: C ($P = 0.22$), NS ($P = 0.55$), Figure 10.

The major tortoise population at Fort Irwin, located along the south boundary (SL), increased in density between 1983 to 1989 ($P = 0.002$, Figure 7). Sample size at SL was increased by 50% in 1989, and therefore, it is possible that more thorough sampling provided a better estimate of tortoise densities, accounting for the "perceived" increase. The SL tortoise population is found in prime tortoise habitat. The topography is gently rolling bajadas with deep sandy-loam soils. Vegetation is diverse and perennial shrubs, forbs, and grasses, and annual forbs are well represented. Galleta grass, *Pleuraphis (=Hilaria) rigida*, is particularly dense in some areas and is important summer forage for the desert tortoise. Because this site lies along the NTC southern boundary, habitat disturbance up to 1989 was light. However, tactical vehicle damage has increased along this southern boundary since 1984 when live munitions were cleared from the Langford impact zone. It is notable that adjacent BLM lands south of Fort Irwin contain high tortoise densities (USFWS, 1988b). Similarly, the southwestern and eastern boundaries of Fort Irwin receive less ORV traffic

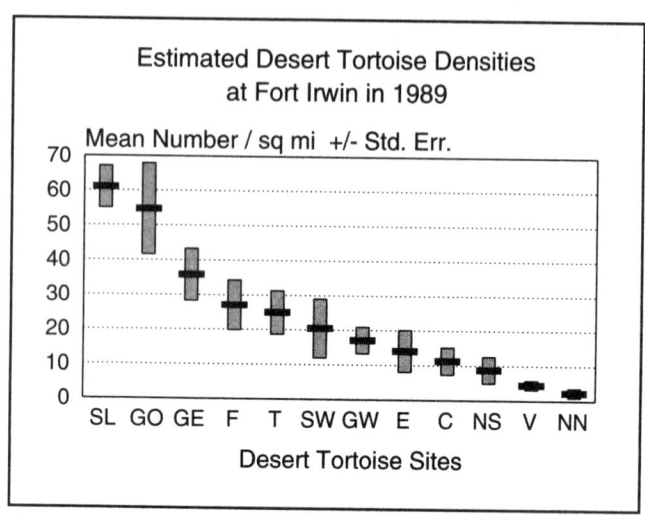

Figure 6. Estimated densities and their standard errors of all 12 tortoise sites surveyed on Fort Irwin in 1989 and discussed in this paper. The sites are ranked by their abundance.

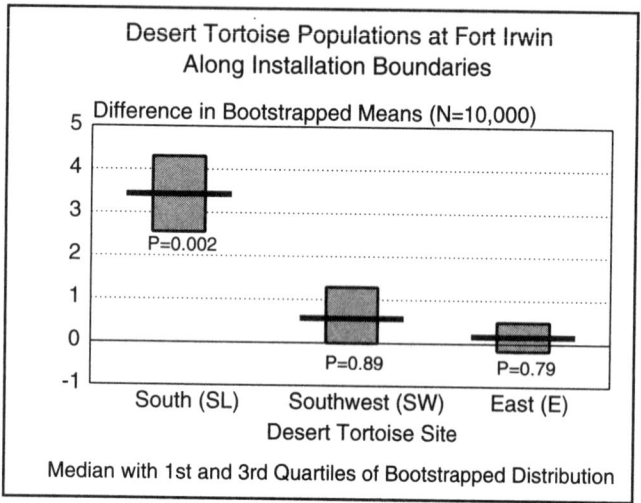

Figure 7. Statistical inference with exact *P*-values (see METHODS) for Fort Irwin desert tortoise populations located along installation boundaries.

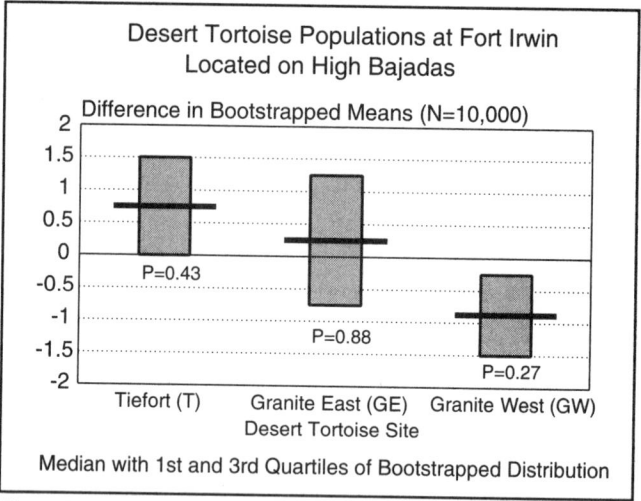

Figure 8. Statistical inference with exact *P*-values (see METHODS) for Fort Irwin desert tortoise populations located on high bajadas.

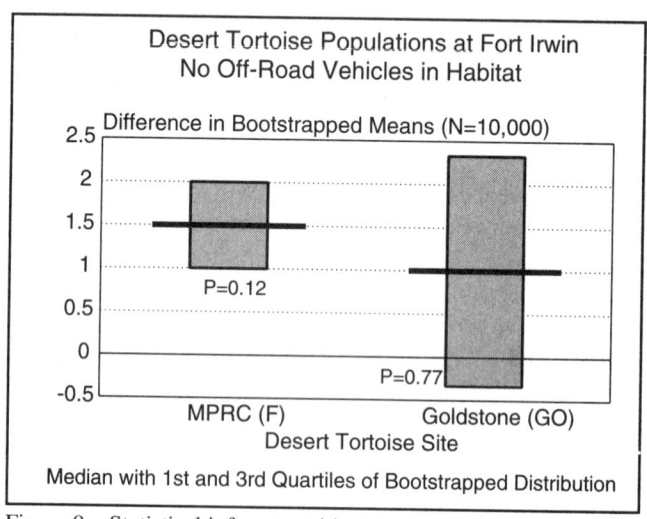

Figure 9. Statistical inference with exact *P*-values (see METHODS) for Fort Irwin desert tortoise populations present in habitats that are off-limits to off-road vehicles.

than interior training ranges, and they are also adjacent to relatively undisturbed habitats containing tortoises on BLM lands.

Tactical vehicle impacts at the NTC are most severe in valleys where force-on-force engagements are staged. These impacts steadily decrease as high bajadas, talus slopes, and rugged mountain ranges are approached (Krzysik, 1985). However, since 1985 the simulation of longer-range weapon systems has significantly affected higher bajada habitats (Krzysik, 1994a). Although washes are extensively used for travel in desert regions, high bajada washes form deep, steep-walled arroyos, making off-road travel slow and treacherous when following topographic contours. Vehicles are forced to cut across these arroyos along existing roads and trails. Therefore, habitat degradation by tactical vehicles on Fort Irwin's high bajadas is more patchy than in the valleys. Tortoise populations have remained secure but isolated in the high bajadas of Fort Irwin (T, GE, GW). The Granite West population decreased between 1983 and 1989, but on the basis of the statistical inference used in the present analysis, it was not a significant decline. Additional monitoring is warranted.

Tortoises on Goldstone (GO) are not subjected to habitat damage by tactical vehicles or human harassment because it is closed to military training, and the public and resident personnel are limited to the main road or secondary maintenance roads. Tactical vehicles do not maneuver in NTC's multi-purpose range complex (F), and maintenance vehicles are restricted to target pads and their associated roads. The "perceived" increase in tortoise density at the MPRC (F) is

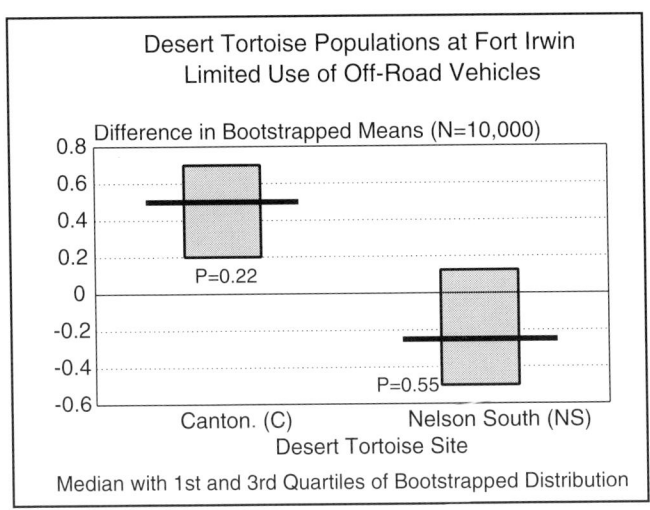

Figure 10. Statistical inference with exact *P*-values (see METHODS) for Fort Irwin desert tortoise populations that present in habitats that receive limited use of off-road vehicles.

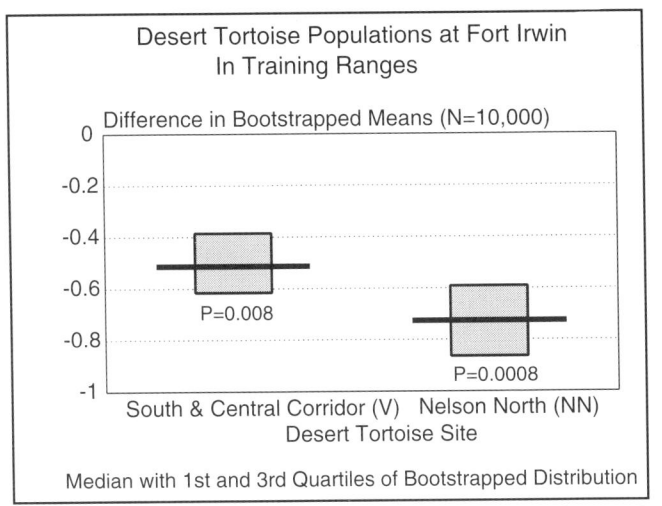

Figure 11. Statistical inference with exact *P*-values (see METHODS) for Fort Irwin desert tortoise populations present in NTC military training ranges subjected to extensive off-road tactical vehicle maneuvers.

probably attributable to inadequate sampling in 1983.

Tortoise populations in habitats subjected to limited ORV use have not shown significant declines between 1983 and 1989 (sites C and NS). Tortoises at site C are contiguous with the high-density SL population to the south. The cantonment area and its associated infrastructure and construction activities have more than doubled in land area between 1983 and 1989, and disturbed tortoises have possibly moved southward into C or even SL.

Figure 11 clearly demonstrates that tortoises in the southern and central corridors (V, *P* = 0.008) and in the northwest (NN, *P* = 0.0008) NTC training ranges have declined significantly between 1983 and 1989. The NN population declined by 81%, which parallels increases in training activities and the development of staging areas at this site since 1985 (Krzysik, 1994a). The population in the southern and central corridors (V) declined by 62%, which parallels shrub losses of 69% in the southern corridor valley and 67% on the low bajada (Figure 4). An important component of desert tortoise habitat is adequate shrub cover for burrow and pallet construction, predator avoidance (especially important for juveniles), thermoregulation, nest shading (which may affect sex ratios), and production of annual forbs (reviewed in Krzysik, 1994b).

Modeling Desert Tortoise Populations on Landscape Scales

Three federal agencies, USBLM, DoD, and National Park Service, are charged with the responsibilities of both land management and environmental compliance in the Mojave Desert. These include the protection of "Threatened," "Endangered," and "Sensitive" species. Because the desert tortoise is a federally listed "Threatened" species, population assessment and monitoring are an integral component of these management responsibilities. The patchiness of tortoise populations on landscape scales presents a major problem for land managers responsible for the acquisition and interpretation of tortoise distribution and density data. In addition, the management of desert tortoises requires a regional approach. The need for ecoregional approaches in ecologically responsible natural resources management is admirably presented in Noss and Cooperrider (1994). Field ecology on landscape and regional scales requires new approaches.

A robust description of ecological elements (e.g., plot estimates of desert tortoise densities) on a landscape can be defined by a three-dimensional surface. The x and y axes represent easting and northing respectively in a UTM coordinate grid,* while the z axis represents estimated tortoise densities in 0.64 km² plots. A number of methods are available to interpolate and smooth the field data to produce a "fitted" surface, analogous in principle at least, to the well-known two-dimensional linear least squares fit.

Least squares fit (linear regression) of data points is used for simplifying and visualizing two-dimensional parameter relationships. In actuality, least squares fit to data does not have to be linear (a nonlinear polynomial fit) and can be conducted on any number of dimensions. A two-dimension fit results in a line segment. In three dimensions an interpolated and smoothed fit to data points results in a surface. However, this surface cannot typically be defined by a single

---

*UTM (Universal Transverse Mercator Projection) is a commonly used standard cartographic projection for geographical coordinates and can be routinely converted to other systems such as latitude and longitude.

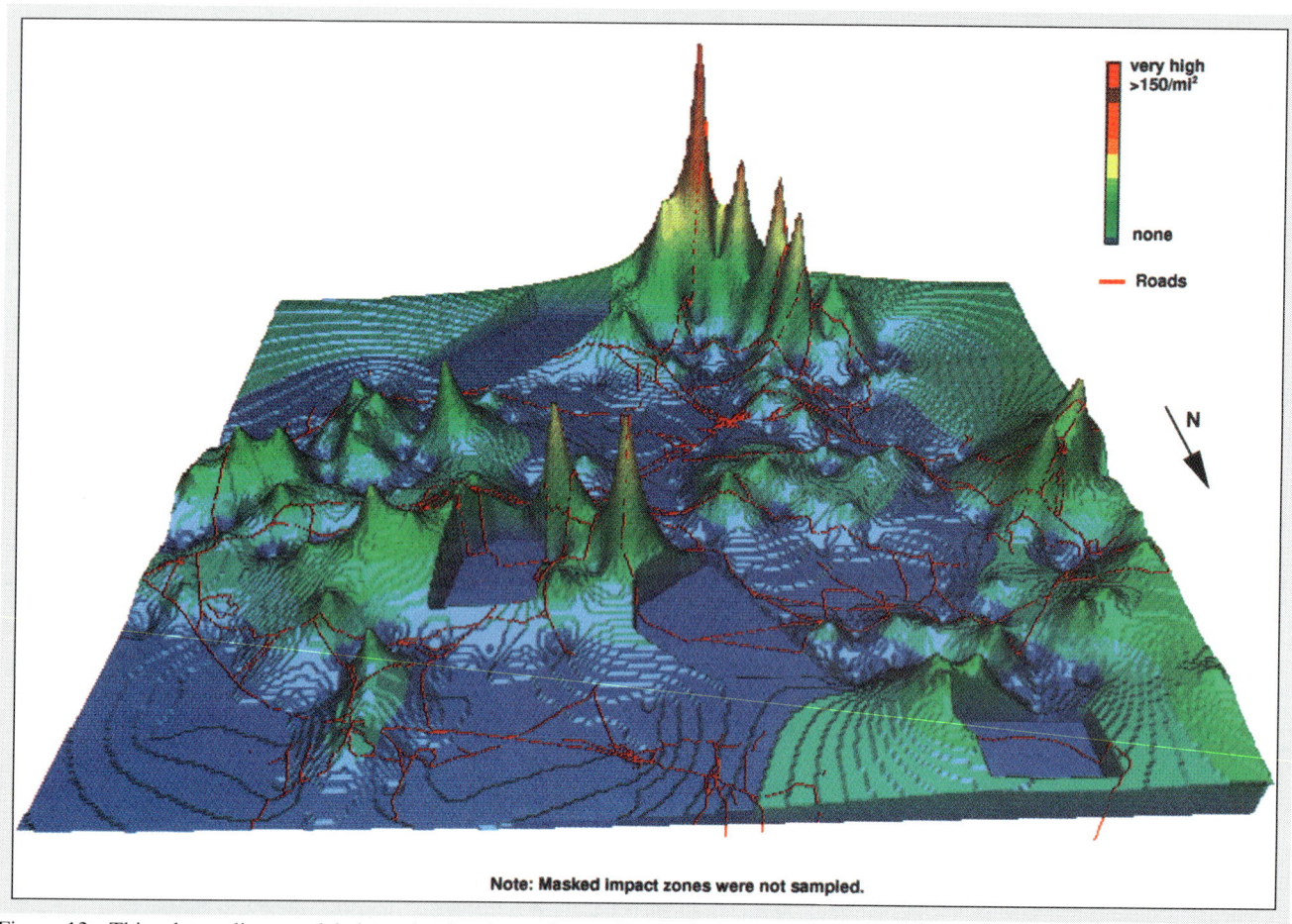

Figure 12. Thin-plate splines modeled tortoise density surface at Fort Irwin in 1983. The orientation is toward the south. Compare with Figures 1 and 5 for pertinent landscape features. Peak amplitudes are proportional to estimated tortoise densities. Note that the impact zones are masked out, since these were not cleared of hazardous ordinance until 1984–1985.

analytic function but can be represented as a mosaic of surface patches (plates) constructed from "spline curve segments." Spline methods are a technique based on fitting a polynomial (curve) in each interval between the actual data points and extracting equation parameters to give continuity to a selected number of derivatives at each data point (Ripley, 1981; Cressie, 1991). Spline methods are very computer intensive, and their widespread use was closely related to the availability of "inexpensive" high-speed workstations and even more recently to current high-powered microcomputers.

We have been researching a novel technology to interpolate, smooth, and model geographical spatial data. The technique is Smoothing Thin-Plate Splines with Tension (TPS). Preliminary modeling results in our laboratory and at Purdue University have shown advantages of TPS over other methods, including kriging. TPS possesses a number of robust properties: It is independent of the spatial distribution of input data, uses a standard GIS grid structure for topographic analysis, maintains the quality of contours, and has consistently demonstrated flexibility and accuracy in model development. TPS is based on minimization of interpolation-smoothing functions that possess global derivatives of all orders and include a tension parameter for controlling (smoothing) function fit to the geometric scatter of data points. Thin-Plate Splines are related to kriging (Wahba, 1990), a common tool in spatial analysis and originally used by mining geologists to optimize ore extraction (Krige, 1966). TPS algorithms have been developed for hydrological modeling (Mitášová and Mitáš, 1993; Mitášová and Hofierka, 1993), but I believe that TPS may have promising applications in ecology and conservation biology for modeling distribution and density patterns of populations or genetic structure and species-habitat relationships on landscape scales, and further research is being conducted. TPS was therefore used on the Fort Irwin tortoise data as a demonstrating example.

Figure 12 represents the TPS surface model of the 1983 Fort Irwin tortoise landscape, with the amplitude of the peaks representing tortoise density. Note that the orienta-

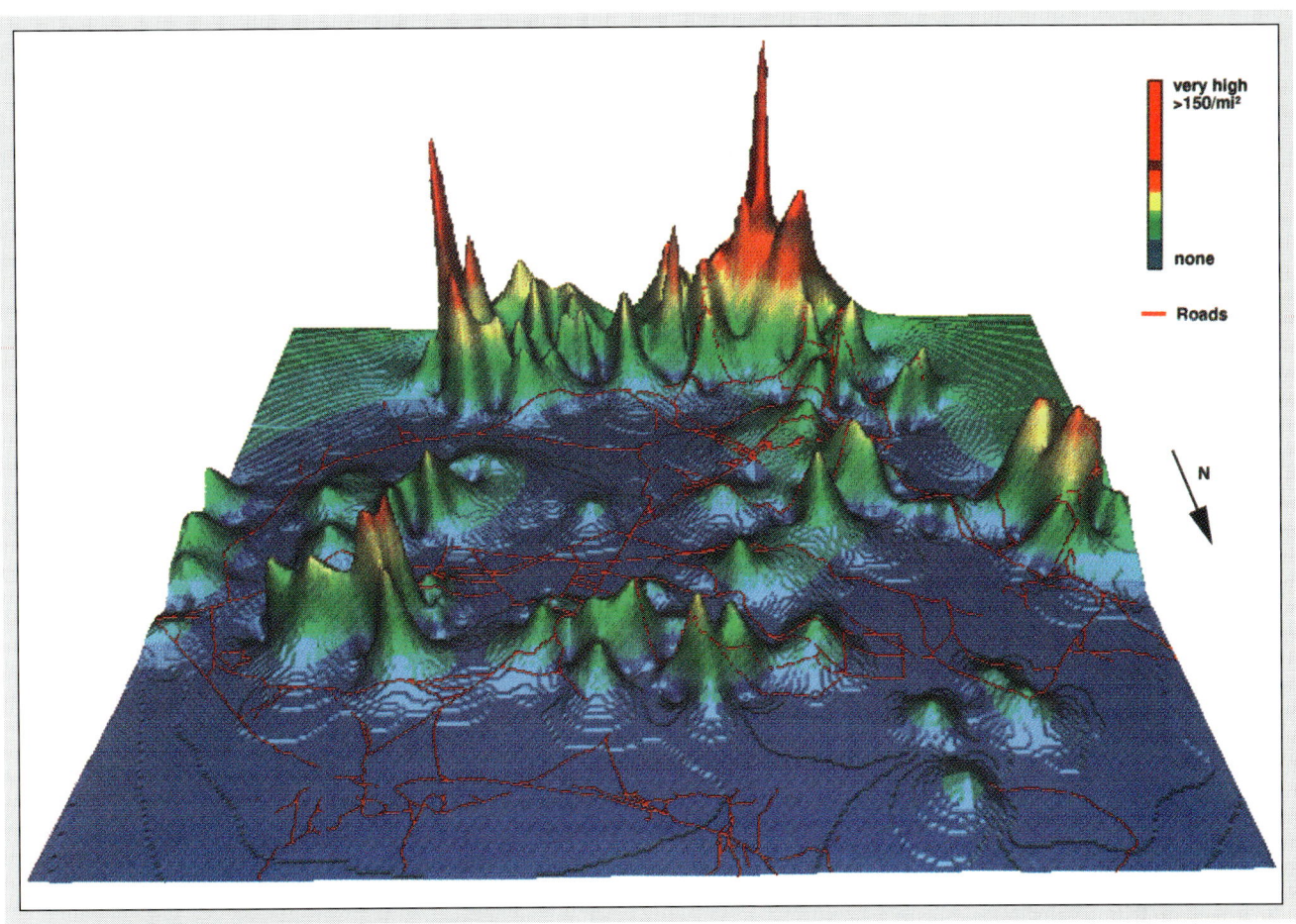

Figure 13. Thin-plate splines modeled tortoise density surface at Fort Irwin in 1989. See Figure 12 legend for interpretation. Note the presence of tortoises in the Langford and Nelson impact zones.

tion is southward (looking from the northern portion of the installation). This is necessary because of the high tortoise population along the southern boundary. Note that the locations of Lucky Fuse, Nelson, and Langford impact zones are masked (compare with Figure 1). The TSP model clearly shows the high tortoise population densities along the installation's southern boundary and in Granite Pass between Lucky Fuse and Nelson. The Goldstone (GO) population is also visible in the right center of the figure.

Figure 13 represents the TPS of the 1989 Fort Irwin tortoise landscape. Note that the southern boundary population has remained viable and extends into the former unsurveyed Langford impact zone, clearly showing a strong population density peak in the extreme southeastern corner of the installation. This portion of the installation has been relatively immune to tactical vehicles and represents very high-quality habitat. Note that the former population in Granite Pass is no longer present, and the once-continuous population along the southern bajada of the Granites has been fragmented into two segments GE and GW, which have retreated higher into the bajada. The population at Goldstone was still viable in 1989, and the increased sampling effort in 1989 "exposed" the tortoise population in the multipurpose range complex (F). A comparison of figures 12 and 13 demonstrates the population losses in the northwestern portion of the installation (NN) and in the junction of the southern and central corridors (a portion of site V). TPS tortoise density modeling visually demonstrates the statistical treatment presented above.

Acknowledgments

This paper is dedicated to Jack McCoy, who passed away just before this symposium and who was Curator of Amphibians and Reptiles at the Carnegie Museum of Natural History. Jack was an encouraging member of my Ph.D. dissertation committee, and his considerable enthusiasm for herpetology was a source of inspiration. This research and its presentation would not have been possible without the assistance, support, and constructive criticism of a large number of colleagues and DoD installation natural resources managers. Although space prevents an extensive listing, the following must be especially acknowledged: Pete Woodman, John Wright, Jocelyn Aycrigg, Helena Mitášová, Jeff Duda, Richard Stevens, Kevin Seel, Scott Tweddale, Tom and Debbie Clark, Jerry Freilich, Ray Bransfield, Dave Morafka, Roy Madden, Sharon Jones, Ken Kreklau, and Mark Hagan. Jim Van Abbema, editor, and four reviewers helped a great deal to clarify the material in this article.

LITERATURE CITED

Agresti, A., C. R. Mehta, and N. R. Patel. 1990. Exact inference for contingency tables with ordered categories. Journal of the American Statistical Association 85:453–458.

Berry, K. H., and L. L. Nicholson. 1984. The distribution and density of desert tortoise populations in California in the 1970's. In K. H. Berry (ed.), The Status of Desert Tortoise (*Gopherus agassizii*) in the United States, pp. 22–60. Desert Tortoise Council Report to U.S. Fish and Wildlife Service on Purchase Order No. 11310-0083-81.

Bishop, Y. M. M., S. E. Fienberg, and P. W. Holland. 1975. Discrete Multivariate Analysis: Theory and Practice. MIT Press, Cambridge, Massachusetts.

Bolger, D. P. 1986. Dragons at War: 2-34th Infantry in the Mojave. Presidio Press, Novato, California.

Casebier, D. G. 1986. Mojave Road Guide. Tales of the Mojave Road Publishing Co., Norco, California.

Cressie, N. 1991. Statistics for Spatial Data. John Wiley & Sons, New York.

Efron, B. 1982. The Jackknife, the Bootstrap and Other Resampling Plans. Society for Industrial and Applied Mathematics, Philadelphia, Pennsylvania.

Fisher, R. A. 1935. The Design of Experiments. Oliver and Boyde, Edinburgh.

Good, P. 1994. Permutation Tests—A Practical Guide to Resampling Methods for Testing Hypotheses. Springer-Verlag, New York.

Halberstadt, H. 1989. NTC: A Primer of Modern Land Combat. Presidio Press, Novato, California.

Hollander, M. and D. A. Wolfe. 1973. Nonparametric Statistical Methods. John Wiley & Sons, New York.

Krige, D. G. 1966. Two dimensional weighted moving average trend surfaces for ore observation. Journal of the South African Institute of Mining and Metallurgy 66:13–38.

Krzysik, A. J. 1984. Habitat relationships and the effects of environmental impacts on the bird and small mammal communities of the central Mojave Desert. In W. C. McComb (ed.), Proceedings—Workshop on Management of Nongame Species and Ecological Communities, pp. 358–394. University of Kentucky, Lexington.

Krzysik, A. J. 1985. Ecological Assessment of the effects of Army training activities on a desert ecosystem: National Training Center, Fort Irwin, California. USACERL Technical Report N-85/13, Champaign, Illinois. 139 pp.

Krzysik, A. J. 1994a. Biodiversity and threatened/endangered/sensitive species of Fort Irwin, California: The National Training Center mission, training effects, and options for natural resources management and mitigation. USACERL Technical Report EN-94/07, Champaign, Illinois. 114 pp.

Krzysik, A. J. 1994b. The desert tortoise at Fort Irwin, California: A federal threatened species. USACERL Technical Report EN-94/10, Champaign, Illinois. 99 pp.

Krzysik, A. J. and A. P. Woodman. 1991. Six years of Army training activities and the desert tortoise. Proc. Desert Tortoise Council Symp. 1987–1991:337–368.

Krzysik, A. J., A. P. Woodman, and M. Hagan. 1995. A field evaluation of four methods for estimating desert tortoise densities. Presentation given at the Desert Tortoise Council Symp., Las Vegas, Nevada.

Lathrop, E. W. 1983. Recovery of perennial vegetation in military maneuver areas. In R. H. Webb and H. G. Wilshire (eds.), Environmental Effects of Off-Road Vehicles: Impacts and Management in Arid Regions, pp. 265–277. Springer-Verlag, New York.

Ludwig, V. E. 1989. U.S. Marines at Twentynine Palms, California. History and Museums Division Headquarters, U.S. Marine Corps., Washington, D.C.

Mabbutt, J. A. 1977. Desert Landforms. MIT Press, Cambridge, Massachusetts.

MacMahon, J. A. 1988. Warm deserts. In M. G. Barbour and W. D. Billings (eds.), North American Terrestrial Vegetation, pp. 231–264. Cambridge University Press, New York.

MacMahon, J. A. and F. H. Wagner. 1985. The Mojave, Sonoran and Chihuahuan Deserts of North America. In M. Evenari, I. Noy-Meir, and D. W. Goodall (eds.), Ecosystems of the World 12A: Hot Deserts and Arid Shrublands, pp. 105–202. Elsevier, New York.

Manly, B. F. J. 1991. Randomization and Monte Carlo Methods in Biology. Chapman and Hall, New York.

MCAGCC. 1993. Natural Resources Management Plan: Marine Corps Air-Ground Combat Center, Twentynine Palms, California.

Mehta, C. R., N. R. Patel, and L. J. Wei. 1988. Computing exact significance tests with restricted randomization rules. Biometrika 75:295–302.

Mitášová, H. and J. Hofierka. 1993. Interpolation by regularized spline with tension: II. Application to terrain modeling and surface geometry analysis. Mathematical Geology 25:657–669.

Mitášová, H., and L. Mitáš. 1993. Interpolation by regularized spline with tension: I. Theory and implementation. Mathematical Geology 25:641–655.

NAWS. 1982. Naval Weapons Center Resource Management Programs and Implementation Plans for the Mojave B Ranges. NWC ADPUB 283. 46 pp.

Noreen, E. W. 1989. Computer Intensive Methods for Testing Hypotheses. John Wiley & Sons, New York.

Noss, R. F. and A. Y. Cooperrider. 1994. Saving Nature's Legacy: Protecting and Restoring Biodiversity. Island Press, Washington, D.C.

Prose, D. V. 1985. Persisting effects of armored military maneuvers on some soils of the Mojave Desert. Environmental Geology and Water Sciences Journal 7:163–170.

Prose, D. V. 1986a. Map showing areas of visible land disturbances caused by two military training operations in the Mojave Desert, California. U.S. Geological Survey Miscellaneous Field Studies Map MF-1855.

Prose, D. V. 1986b. Differences in soil compaction persisting in military vehicle tracks after 21 and 41 years. Proc. Pacific Division, American Association for the Advancement of Science 5:43.

Prose, D. V. and S. K. Metzger. 1985. Recovery of soils and vegetation in World War II military base camps, Mojave Desert. U.S. Geological Survey Openfile Report 85–234. 37 pp.

Prose, D. V. and H. G. Wilshire. 1986. Long-term effects of military training exercises on soils and vegetation in the arid southwestern United States. Transactions of the Congress of the International Society of Soil Science 2:136.

Prose, D. V., S. K. Metzger, and H. G. Wilshire. 1987. Effects of substrate disturbance on secondary plant succession; Mojave Desert, California. J. Appl. Ecol. 24:305–313.

Ripley, B. D. 1981. Spatial Statistics. John Wiley & Sons, New York.

Siegel, S. 1956. Nonparametric Statistics for the Behavioral Sciences. McGraw-Hill, New York.

Sokal, R. R. and F. J. Rohlf. 1994. Biometry, 3rd ed. W. H. Freeman & Co., New York.

USFWS. 1988a. Biological resource inventory: Mohave B—Range South. Report to U.S. Army Corps of Engineers, U.S. Fish and Wildlife Service. 63 pp.

USFWS. 1988b. Biological resource inventory: Expansion of Fort Irwin National Training Center, San Bernardino County, California. Report to U.S. Army Corps of Engineers, U.S. Fish and Wildlife Service. 112pp.

Wahba, G. 1990. Spline Models for Observational Data. Society for Industrial and Applied Mathematics. Philadelphia, Pennsylvania.

Weerahandi, S. 1995. Exact Statistical Methods for Data Analysis. Springer-Verlag, New York.

Westfall, P. H. and S. S. Young. 1993. Resampling-Based Multiple Testing. John Wiley & Sons, New York.

Woodman, A. P., S. M. Juarez, E. D. Humphreys, K. Kirtland, and L. F. LaPre. 1986. Estimated density and distribution of the desert tortoise at Fort Irwin, National Training Center and Goldstone Space Communications Complex. Proc. Desert Tortoise Council Symp. 1986:81–99.

Zar, J. H. 1984. Biostatistical Analysis, 2nd ed. Prentice-Hall, Englewood Cliffs, New Jersey.

Zippin, C. 1958. The removal method of population estimation. J. Wildl. Manage. 22:82–90.

Effects of Military Activities on Tortoises in Israel

— ABSTRACT OF PRESENTATION —

ELI GEFFEN AND HEINRICH MENDELSSOHN

Department of Zoology, Tel Aviv University, Ramat Aviv, Tel Aviv 69978, Israel [e-mail: geffene@post.tau.ac.il]

Because of the generally good cooperation between the army and the Nature Reserves Authority (the government conservation agency), excessive damage to tortoise habitat has been prevented in most areas. Habitats in which tank maneuvers are conducted are, of course, completely destroyed, but when supervised, other military activities cause little damage. In recent years grazers and their herds have not been permitted to enter military areas, and habitats in these areas are in much better condition than the badly overgrazed areas. Such is the case with the proposed Holot Agur Nature Reserve, which is a military zone. Holot Agur has little human disturbance and the flora and fauna are in excellent condition. In contrast, just across the border in Egypt, similar habitat is badly overgrazed, and the vegetation cover is close to nil (Mendelssohn, 1982; Zohary, 1980). Little information is available on the situation in countries neighboring Israel.

LITERATURE CITED

Mendelssohn, H. 1982. Egyptian tortoise. *In* The IUCN Amphibia-Reptilia Red Data Book. Part 1. Testudinidae, Crocodylia, Rhynchocephalia, B. Groombridge (comp.), pp. 133–136. IUCN, Gland, Switzerland. xiii + 426 pp.

Zohary, M. 1980. Vegetal Landscapes in Israel. Am Oved Publishing Limited, Tel Aviv, Israel.

Direct Losses to Populations

DISEASE, PREDATION, TURTLES AS A FOOD RESOURCE, WILDLIFE TRADE

John Behler (Curator of Herpetology, Wildlife Conservation Society) chairs the Workshop on Wildlife Trade.

Wil Luiijf (TRAFFIC Europe) and New York State Senator Suzi Oppenheimer examine softshell turtle purchased from New York Chinatown market.

Kristin Berry (U.S. Geological Survey, Biological Resources Division, Riverside, California), Lora Smith (University of Florida, Gainesville), Gerald Kuchling (University of Western Australia, Nedlands), Isabella Schumacher (University of Florida, Gainesville), William Boarman (U.S. Geological Survey, Biological Resources Division, Riverside, California), M. Farid Ahsan (University of Chittagong, Bangladesh), Romulus Whitaker (Centre for Herpetology/Madras Crocodile Bank, Mamallapuram, Tamil Nadu, India), Bonnie Raphael and Michael Klemens (Wildlife Conservation Society, New York), and Eli Geffen (Tel Aviv University, Israel).

Don Moll (Southwest Missouri State University, Springfield, Missouri).

Laboratory Health Profiles of Desert Tortoises in the Mojave Desert: A Model for Health Status Evaluation of Chelonian Populations

— PLENARY LECTURE —

MARY M. CHRISTOPHER,[1] KEN A. NAGY,[2] IAN WALLIS,[3] JAMES K. KLAASSEN,[2] AND KRISTIN H. BERRY[4]

[1]*University of California—Davis, Davis, CA 95616 USA [e-mail: mmchristopher@ucdavis.edu]*
[2]*University of California, Los Angeles, CA 90024, USA* [3]*APL Laboratories, Las Vegas, NV 89119, USA*
[4]*U.S. Geological Survey, Biological Resources Division, Riverside, CA 92507-0714, USA*

ABSTRACT: Survival of the desert tortoise, *Gopherus agassizii*, in today's world depends upon its ability to adapt to drought, habitat loss, competition for forage, and our ability to detect and eradicate diseases such as mycoplasmosis. In 1989, the Bureau of Land Management instituted a Laboratory and Health Profile Research Program designed to analyze and interpret laboratory and health data from free-ranging desert tortoises over a 3–5 year period. The goals of this program were to establish reference ranges under a variety of environmental and physiological conditions, to differentiate physiologic and pathologic changes, and to assess the utility of specific laboratory tests for evaluating desert tortoise health. Between 1989 and 1992 blood samples were obtained for hematological and biochemical profiles from tortoises at three sites in the Mojave Desert of California. Physical examinations, nasal cultures, and serology for *Mycoplasma agassizii* were also performed and interpreted in conjunction with changes in laboratory data.

The first year of the program was a trial during which sampling protocols, test parameters, methodology, and data formats were optimized. Consistent data that permitted year-to-year comparisons were obtained between 1990 and 1992. Significant differences were observed in several parameters between male and female tortoises. Marked seasonal differences were observed in association with hibernation, rainfall, and dietary intake. Urea nitrogen was the best overall indicator of hydration status. Marked elevations in blood urea nitrogen occurred during a drought year and were associated with significant mortality in tortoises at one study site. Plasma iron, glucose, and total protein values were good longitudinal indicators of nutritional status, and values were often lower in tortoises serologically positive for *M. agassizii*. Individual tortoises showed laboratory and physical evidence for anemia, renal failure, and inflammatory disease. These results support the need for baseline laboratory and health data to assess the effects of environmental degradation, physiological changes, and disease exposure, as well as to monitor both immediate and long-term changes in population health.

Normal reference values for hematological, biochemical, and microbiological parameters in wild desert tortoises are essential for studying stress and disease in tortoise populations, and for differentiating natural physiological changes due to sex, diet, age, stress, and environment from latent and overt disease conditions (Nagy and Medica, 1986; Dickinson and Reggiardo, 1992). Laboratory values also reflect analytical variation due to specimen handling, precision, methods, and level of quality control (Martin et al., 1975). Deviations from expected values may provide diagnostic and prognostic information and may help in assessing impacts of environmental degradation, habitat loss, and competition for forage on the physical health of desert tortoises.

In 1989, in response to several developing problems in desert tortoise populations, Dr. Kristin Berry, U.S. Bureau of Land Management (USBLM), initiated a research program on health profiles of desert tortoises in California. An outbreak and subsequent epidemic of URTD* or mycoplasmosis occurred in tortoises at the Desert Tortoise Research Natural Area (DTNA) in eastern Kern County, California. Abnormalities in some biochemical parameters were noted, and *Mycoplasma agassizii* and *Pasteurella testudinis* organisms were isolated from the upper respiratory tract (Jacobson et al., 1991). In addition, evidence was growing to suggest a link between shell disease and tortoise mortality at the Chuckwalla Bench, and laboratory findings suggested possible systemic health problems (Jacobson et al., 1994). Scientists conducting research on desert tortoises recognized

---

* The term *upper respiratory tract disease (URTD)* is used synonymously with the term *mycoplasmosis*, because a mycoplasma organism, *Mycoplasma agassizii*, is the causative agent of URTD in desert tortoises (Brown et al., 1994a). Upper respiratory infections in general, however, may be caused by a number of other infectious agents, including other bacteria, viruses, and fungi. Signs of upper respiratory infection may also be associated with non-infectious causes, such as allergy or the presence of a foreign body. In this report, the term *URTD* is used only when mycoplasmosis has been confirmed by a positive serologic test for *M. agassizii*.

that reference ranges from blood and other analytes could provide information on the effects of various uses of public lands on the overall well-being of populations.

A five-year program was designed to gather baseline data on health as well as water balance, energy flow, and nutritional requirements. In this paper, we present the analysis and interpretation of laboratory data obtained during the first 3½ years of this study (May 1989–October 1992) from free-ranging desert tortoises at three sites in the Mojave Desert of California. This study design can be used as a model for other chelonian populations to develop a core of accurate laboratory and clinical information that can be used to identify pathologic processes and predict impending illness or mortality.

MATERIALS AND METHODS

Blood and other tissue samples were obtained from tortoises at three sites in the deserts of California: the DTNA in the western Mojave Desert, Goffs in the Fenner Valley of the eastern Mojave Desert and northern Colorado Desert, and Ivanpah Valley in the eastern Mojave Desert. In 1989 ten adult males and ten adult females at each site were captured, marked, and fitted with radio transmitters (Wallis et al., 1992). Tortoises that died or disappeared were replaced to keep the totals at ten adult males and ten adult females for each of the three sites.

Samples were collected during March (early spring, post-hibernation), May (late spring/early summer, peak resource quality and availability), July/August (summer, food and water generally unavailable depending on site), and October (fall, pre-hibernation). Rainfall data were obtained for each site at each season. Body weight and carapace length at the midline (MCL) were measured at each sampling time.

Health profile forms, completed for each tortoise at each sampling, included location, weather conditions, and tortoise identification and physical measurements. Tortoises were examined for nasal discharges and other signs of URTD by evaluation of beak, nares, forelegs, and breathing. In addition, eyes/eyelids, integument, oral cavity, and posture/behavior were carefully examined. Blood and tissue sampling sites, and field packed cell volume (PCV) were recorded. Tortoises were examined for shell disease, markings, and trauma.

The period from May 1989 through March 1990 was considered a trial period, during which time various laboratory and sampling protocols were tested and optimized. Subsequent to March 1990, all data were obtained using strict protocols and quality control measures as described below. Cystocentesis samples (bladder taps) taken from tortoises beginning in May 1989 were discontinued after summer 1991 due to the development of bladder peritonitis in one tortoise.

Sterile technique was used to obtain blood and bacteriological specimens. Aliquots of blood (4.0–4.7 ml) obtained by jugular venipuncture (Jacobson et al., 1992) were placed into Microtainer™ tubes containing lithium heparin gel (Becton Dickinson, Rutherford, New Jersey) for whole blood analysis, and Vacutainer™ tubes containing lithium heparin (Becton Dickinson, Rutherford, New Jersey) for separation of plasma. Plasma was separated immediately from centrifuged heparinized samples, transferred to separate tubes, and placed on ice. Heparinized microhematocrit tubes were used for determination of PCV, and air-dried blood smears were fixed in methanol for hematology. Nasal swabs were obtained for bacterial culture, and nasal flushes were performed using 1.0 ml tryptic soy broth for mycoplasma culture. Whole blood and plasma samples were transported on ice to the laboratory (APL Laboratories, Las Vegas, Nevada) and analyzed within 24 hours. Plasma and culture samples were stored in liquid nitrogen for up to ten days prior to analysis. A plasma sample was also sent to the University of Florida for *Mycoplasma agassizii* serology (Schumacher et al., 1993).

Packed cell volume was determined by microhematocrit centrifugation, red blood cell (RBC) and white blood cell (WBC) counts were conducted using a hemacytometer and Nate & Herrick's solution, and hemoglobin (Hb) was determined by a cyanmethemoglobin method. Mean cell volume (MCV), mean cell hemoglobin (MCH), and mean cell hemoglobin concentration (MCHC) were calculated (Duncan and Prasse, 1986). Blood smears stained with modified Wright's stain were microscopically examined for differential leukocyte counts (heterophils, lymphocytes, monocytes, azurophils, eosinophils, and basophils) and evaluation of thrombocyte, leukocyte, and RBC morphology (Alleman et al., 1992). Plasma chemistries were done on an Olympus AU5000 automated chemistry analyzer (Olympus, Inc., Chicago, Illinois). Bacterial cultures were incubated on 5% sheep blood agar for isolation of *Pasteurella testudinis* and on SP4 mycoplasma media (Jacobson et al., 1991), which detects all mycoplasma organisms. Serology for antibodies to *M. agassizii* was performed using an ELISA test (Schumacher et al., 1993).

Data sets were summarized by calculation of means ($\bar{x}$) and standard deviations (SD). Tests for normality were performed on ten data sets (one sex within one site for one season), and tests for homoscedasticity were conducted on all data sets. Data sets satisfied the criteria for normality, and all data were subsequently analyzed using parametric statistical tests. Data were considered significant when $P < 0.05$.

Significant differences between sexes were analyzed by two-tailed Student's *t*-tests. Repeated measures analysis of variance was used to test for significant differences due to the effects of season, site, and interactions of sex, season, and site. Duncan's multiple range test was used to identify specific differences between means. Correlations were made using linear regression analysis.

Annual reference ranges were calculated as the mean ±2 SD of all values for all tortoises, after deletion of outliers. In the case of range limits that fell outside of the measured range, the minimum or maximum value for that data set was used. To evaluate individual animals, values 2–3 SD outside of the reference range were considered possibly abnormal (5% of normal animals also lie outside of the range), and values greater than ±3 SD of the mean were considered probably abnormal. Tortoises with abnormal test results were evaluated for additional evidence of disease, and a likely disease process was suggested. Because pooled data from all seasons were included in the final reference ranges, values provided an accurate representation of the range of values that occur in healthy tortoises throughout the year at a variety of locations.

Results and Discussion

Significant differences were noted between male and female desert tortoises for body weight, MCL, PCV, Hb, iron, cholesterol, calcium, phosphorus, and aspartate aminotransferase (AST) values (Table 1). Two female tortoises at Goffs had anemia consistent with iron deficiency, with persistently low PCV, MCH, MCHC, and Hb values. It should be noted that PCVs obtained in the field were consistently higher than laboratory PCVs ($P < 0.0001$) at all times and sites, probably due to RBC shrinkage or slight hemolysis during transport to the laboratory.

Cholesterol and phosphorus values in both males and females were lower during hibernation and highest in late spring and summer. Calcium values varied seasonally in females but remained relatively constant in males. Higher calcium, phosphorus, and cholesterol values in the spring in female tortoises were attributed to vitellogenesis (Turner and Berry, 1986). The linear relationship ($r = 0.54$; $P < 0.03$) between calcium and total protein (TP) values suggested that a portion of calcium was protein-bound, possibly to a vitellogenic plasma protein (Dessauer, 1974).

Rainfall strongly affected regional differences in food type and availability, and was the most crucial determinant of changes in those parameters showing significant seasonal alterations. In 1989 severe drought was present at all sites, particularly DTNA (Figure 1). Conditions in 1990–1991 were still dryer than normal (Wallis et al., 1992), but considerable rain fell in March 1992.

Most mortality occurred prior to or during October 1990, reflecting the severe effect of drought. Mycoplasmosis was also an important factor at the DTNA, and the cystocenteses contributed to at least two deaths (DTNA, Ivanpah Valley). Of 59 tortoises sampled between May 1989 and October 1991, overall mortality was 36% over the 30 month period (32% at DTNA, 25% at Goffs, and 53% at Ivanpah). Of 55 tortoises entering the study in 1992, when rainfall had increased, only 2 (3.6%) are now dead.

Laboratory test results that reflected dehydration associated with lack of rainfall were increased PCV, RBC, Hb, blood urea nitrogen (BUN), TP, osmolality, Na^+, K^+, Cl^-, and decreased body weight. BUN was the most sensitive indicator of changes in hydration, whereas uric acid was less reliable. BUN values were highest during the 1989–1990 drought and may have contributed to high tortoise mortality prior to 1991, particularly at Ivanpah. BUN values remained quite low during the 1991–1992 season (Figure 2). A marked physiological response to dehydration occurred in Goffs tortoises during two dry seasons (July/August 1991 and October 1992), in which most BUN values rose to between 40 and 75 mg/dl.

Hibernation was also characterized by increased BUN, which contributed to increased plasma osmolality. Posthibernation elevations in BUN correlated with decreases in TP values (Figures 2 and 3), suggesting that protein catabolism was a source of energy during hibernation (Christopher et al., 1994).

Rosskopf (1982) suggested that a BUN >40 mg/dl was indicative of compromised renal function in captive tortoises, yet values of this degree were reached with regularity due to dehydration and/or hibernation in apparently healthy, free-ranging tortoises. Renal failure secondary to dehydration and/or urine retention due to lack of food and/or water intake did occur occasionally. These tortoises, including one tortoise with peritonitis, had BUN values in excess of 100 mg/dl and subsequently died or were reported missing. Guidelines for interpretation of BUN are indicated in Table 2.

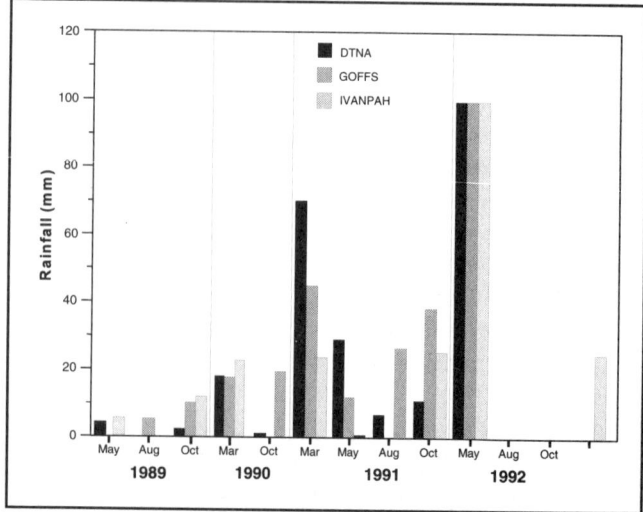

Figure 1. Mean seasonal rainfall at three sites in the Mojave Desert, California, USA (1989–1992).

TABLE 1
Laboratory values for adult desert tortoises in the Mojave Desert of California. Values represent data from 1992, a year of relatively normal rainfall, and represent annual means for all tortoises. See text for seasonal and site variations.

Parameter		Mean ± SD (n)	Range
Body weight (g)	Males	3309.2 ± 749.0 (106)	1811–4807
	Females	1982.5 ± 442.9 (97)	1097–2868
MCL (mm)	Males	263.7 ± 17.8 (104)	228–299
	Females	219.6 ± 14.7 (97)	190–248
PCV (Field; %)	Males	28.9 ± 3.8 (106)	21.3–36.5
	Females	24.2 ± 3.9 (97)	16.4–32.0
PCV (Lab; %)	Males	27.5 ± 4.0 (100)	19.5–35.5
	Females	23.9 ± 4.4 (84)	15.1–32.7
Hb (g/dl)	Males	7.4 ± 1.1 (100)	5.2–9.6
	Females	6.3 ± 1.3 (84)	3.7–8.9
Iron (μg/dl)	Males	459.5 ± 181.1 (106)	97–822
	Females	604.1 ± 287.5 (97)	32–1114
Cholesterol (mg/dl)	Males	90.6 ± 46.2 (103)	14–183
	Females	201.5 ± 72.0 (95)	69–346
Calcium (mg/dl)	Males	10.8 ± 1.2 (105)	8.4–13.2
	Females	16.3 ± 4.0 (96)	9.3–24.3
Phosphorus (mg/dl)	Males	1.9 ± 0.8 (105)	0.5–3.5
	Females	2.9 ± 1.8 (95)	0.4–6.5
AST (IU/L)	Males	68.2 ± 43.4 (103)	18–155
	Females	44.9 ± 29.3 (94)	9–104
RBC ($\times 10^6/\mu$l)		0.59 ± 0.14 (183)	0.33–0.87
MCV (fl)		451.5 ± 94.5 (183)	262.5–640.5
MCH (pg)		120.2 ± 26.5 (183)	67.2–173.2
MCHC (g/dl)		26.9 ± 3.7 (183)	19.5–34.3
WBC (/μl)		4876 ± 2535 (181)	820–9946
Heterophils (/μl)		2917 ± 1565 (182)	570–6047
Lymphocytes (/μl)		838 ± 793 (181)	20–2424
Monocytes (/μl)		75 ± 131 (182)	0–336
Eosinophils (/μl)		111 ± 174 (179)	0–459
Basophils (/μl)		804 ± 686 (180)	0–2176
Azurophils (/μl)		21 ± 45 (179)	0–111
Glucose (mg/dl)		103.4 ± 33.8 (200)	43–171
BUN (mg/dl)		13.2 ± 12.4 (199)	1–38
Uric Acid (mg/dl)		5.5 ± 2.3 (194)	1.3–10.1
Total Protein (g/dl)		3.9 ± 0.9 (201)	2.1–5.7
Albumin (g/dl)		1.2 ± 0.2 (210)	0.8–1.6
Globulins (g/dl)		2.7 ± 0.6 (199)	1.5–3.9
A/G Ratio		0.46 ± 0.07 (200)	0.32–0.60
Total Bilirubin (mg/dl)		0.13 ± 0.05 (197)	0–0.3
Alkaline phosphatase (IU/L)		40.1 ± 20.9 (197)	4–82
Alanine aminotransferase (IU/L)		5.5 ± 2.1 (198)	5–10
Osmolality (mOsm/kg)		293.7 ± 25.9 (199)	245–346
Na$^+$ (mmol/L)		147.3 ± 12.4 (200)	124–172
K$^+$ (mmol/L)		5.1 ± 1.0 (198)	3.2–7.1
Cl$^-$ (mmol/L)		114.7 ± 13.7 (201)	89–142
Total CO$_2$ (mmol/L)		27.8 ± 5.0 (198)	18–38
Anion Gap (mmol/L)		9.9 ± 6.2 (198)	−3–22

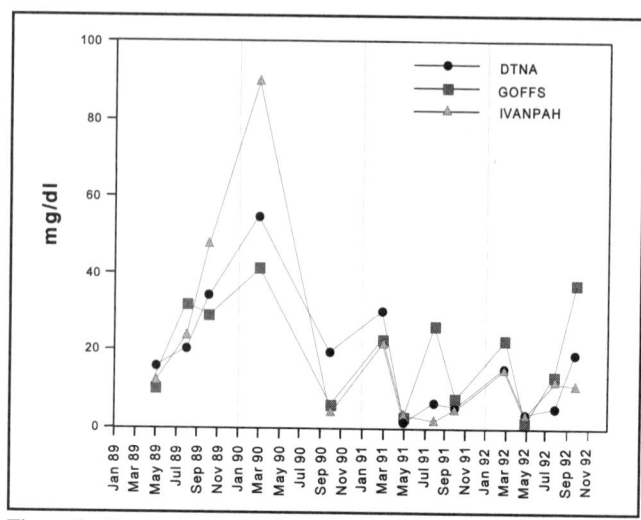

Figure 2. Seasonal changes in blood urea nitrogen (BUN).

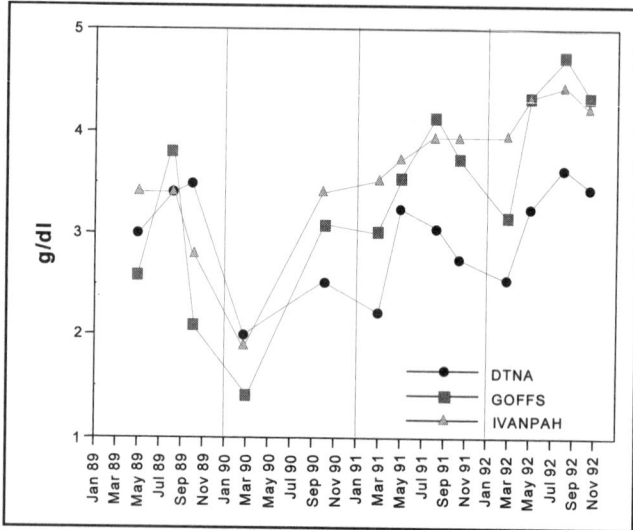

Figure 3. Seasonal changes in plasma total protein.

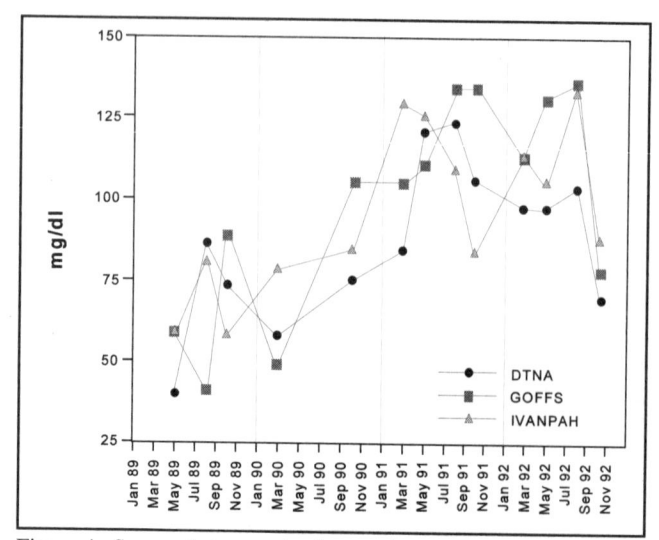

Figure 4. Seasonal changes in plasma glucose.

TABLE 2
Recommended guidelines for interpretation of BUN values in free-ranging desert tortoises.

1–35 mg/dl	Normal, well-hydrated
35–60 mg/dl	Physiological dehydration or hibernation; tolerated response
>60 mg/dl	Severe (pathologic) dehydration, urine retention, and/or renal failure

Glucose, TP, and iron values usually increased in May, with greater nutrient availability and intake, and remained high throughout the summer, such that plasma levels reflected nutrient status and food intake (Figures 3 and 4). At all sites, body weights were also greater in May. Plasma glucose and TP values were lowest in the 1989–1990 season and progressively increased during 1991 and 1992, suggesting increased available food during the past two years (Figures 3 and 4). Low TP in March 1989 indicated use of body protein stores for energy. DTNA tortoises consistently had lower TP (and PCV) values than tortoises at other sites throughout the year, suggesting debilitation in association with high URTD morbidity.

Changes in total WBC counts were usually the result of changes in the number of heterophils. Azurophilia occurred in Goffs tortoises in March, perhaps due to renewed exposure to antigens following emergence from hibernation. A decreased number of lymphocytes was noted at the time of emergence from hibernation. Hibernational lymphopenia has been observed in other species of tortoises (Lawrence and Hawkey, 1986) and may reflect decreased immune function secondary to low ambient temperatures and elevated plasma cortisol level (Saad, 1988). Ivanpah tortoises consistently had higher basophil counts than tortoises at other sites.

Several tortoises at Ivanpah had evidence of inflammation characterized by markedly increased WBC, heterophil, and/or basophil counts. High heterophil counts in Ivanpah tortoises were sometimes associated with heavy growth of *Pasteurella testudinis* in nasal cultures, and Ivanpah tortoises also had a higher incidence of ocular and/or nasal discharge. There was no relation however between respiratory inflammation and positive mycoplasma culture or serology in Ivanpah tortoises. Signs of upper respiratory infections and heavy growth of nasal *P. testudinis* were most common in March and May.

Between October 1990 and October 1992 ten positive mycoplasma cultures (of 425 total) were observed in seven tortoises (six at Goffs and one at Ivanpah), none of which had clinical signs or abnormal laboratory data. Also, none of the tortoises with positive nasal cultures for mycoplasma had positive antibody titers for *M. agassizii* by ELISA (Schumacher et al., 1993). Although most positive mycoplasma cultures occurred at Goffs, Goffs tortoises had the lowest overall mortality rate, the fewest missing tortoises, and the lowest incidence of serological evidence for mycoplasmosis. Mycoplasma cultures were not, therefore, a reliable indicator of URTD. It is possible that the species of mycoplasma cultured was not *M. agassizii*; alternatively, Goffs tortoises may have been resistant to clinical infection. Definitive diagnosis of URTD is based on histopathologic lesions in the nasal cavity; definitive previous exposure to *M. agassizii* can be determined by the ELISA test (Jacobson et al., 1991; Schumacher et al., 1993; Brown et al., 1994a).

Four of 13 tortoises with ocular or nasal abnormalities (swollen or encrusted eyes/eyelids) were seropositive for *M. agassizii*. Serologically positive tortoises had significantly lower TP values (3.5 ±0.7 g/dl vs. 4.0 ±0.9 g/dl) and globulins (2.4 ±0.5 g/dl vs. 2.8 ±0.7 g/dl) as well as lower glucose, iron, PCV, and increased AST values (Table 3). None of the hematologic or biochemical tests, however, was a reliable indicator or predictor of mycoplasmosis.

TABLE 3
Laboratory abnormalities in tortoises with positive titers for *Mycoplasma agassizii*.

- Decreased total protein, albumin, and globulins
- Decreased plasma glucose and iron values
- Decreased PCV at emergence from hibernation
- Increased AST (probably due to more males being affected)

DTNA tortoises accounted for 58% of serologically positive samples for *M. agassizii*, and many had positive titers for multiple seasons. DTNA tortoises had lower PCV, iron, glucose, uric acid, TP, albumin, globulins, and phosphorus than tortoises at other sites, suggesting decreased dietary intake secondary to infection with *M. agassizii*. Lower globulins may also represent an inability to mount an adequate immune response. Low PCV and TP values persisted despite dehydration, indicating anemia and debilitation. Given the high incidence of *M. agassizii* seropositivity, it is likely that abnormal laboratory values in tortoises at DTNA reflected the debilitating effect of chronic URTD (Brown et al., 1994b).

CONCLUSIONS

Quality control and sample management were of utmost importance in laboratory test profiles—specifically, appropriate sampling technique, timely sample handling and analysis, and use of a quality laboratory and laboratory professionals. Reference ranges must acknowledge seasonal, site, age, and sex differences for interpretation of individual tortoise values. Ill tortoises were best identified by a combination of laboratory tests, microbiology, and physical findings. Abnormal tests in tortoises seropositive for *M. agassizii* were neither specific nor dramatic, but suggested debilitation and lower nutritional status. Goffs tortoises appeared to be the healthiest, with strong physiologic responses. Severe drought probably contributed to high tortoise mortality and possibly to bacterial infections in tortoises at Ivanpah.

Laboratory health research programs require development of population reference ranges as well as attention to individual tortoise values to identify ill and diseased animals. The laboratory used for analysis must be accessible, be expert in evaluating reptile samples, and employ a certifiable quality control program. Professional supervision and consultation by a board-certified veterinary clinical pathologist is highly desirable. Ample preparation and planning time must precede initiation of field sampling.

Recommendations for Management and Future Research

1. Conduct research on all size/age classes. Adult tortoises were used in the health profile research program, in large part because they could carry the weight of radio transmitters and more easily tolerate the loss of blood from the sampling. In the future, juvenile and immature tortoises (≤ 180 mm MCL) should be included in sampling programs to determine whether, and if so, how their laboratory parameters differ from those of adults.

2. Invest in long-term, longitudinal data. It is apparent that subtle, gradual changes occur in some laboratory parameters in desert tortoises, which point to the need for long-term, longitudinal data to assess chronic disease conditions and effects of nutrition and disease on populations.

3. Investigate additional disease processes and agents in desert tortoise illness. The observation of respiratory signs and inflammation in tortoises without serologic evidence of URTD suggests, not unexpectedly, that other agents may contribute to upper respiratory illness. Also, lack of correlation between mycoplasma culture results and serologic evidence of exposure to *M. agassizii* suggests a greater complexity to tortoise mycoplasmal infections. All disease conditions should be fully investigated.

4. Perform necropsies on debilitating and/or dying tortoises. The value of relating organ and tissue pathology to abnormal laboratory data is immeasurable. It is strongly recommended that, whenever possible, a complete necropsy be performed on any tortoise appearing to be suffering from disease when the etiology or severity is such that the case is determined to be hopeless and euthanasia is appropriate, or on a tortoise that has just died. Complete laboratory data should also be obtained at the time of necropsy. Euthanasia and necropsy should be performed by a board-certified veterinary pathologist experienced in reptile pathology.

5. Conduct basic research. Additional research is needed to address (a) tortoise nutrition and nutritional requirements, (b) genetic and environmental variables affecting susceptibility to disease, (c) immunology and microbiology, and (d) age-dependent laboratory parameters.

Acknowledgments

This work was made possible by the U.S. Bureau of Land Management (USBLM), which provided funding via Contract No. YA-651-CT0-340079 (Dr. Kenneth Nagy), Contract No. CA950-CT0-47 (Dr. James Klaassen), Contract No. B950-C1-0060 (Dr. Mary Christopher), and Contract No. B950-C2-0046 (Dr. Mary Brown).

Literature Cited

Alleman, A. R., E. R. Jacobson, and R. E. Raskin. 1992. Morphologic and cytochemical characteristics of blood cells from the desert tortoise (*Gopherus agassizii*). Am. J. Vet. Res. 53:1645–1651.

Brown, M. B., I. M. Schumacher, P. A. Klein, K. Harris, T. Correl, and E. R. Jacobson. 1994a. *Mycoplasma agassizii* causes upper respiratory tract disease in the desert tortoise. Infection and Immunity 62(10):4580–4586.

Brown, M. B., P. A. Klein, I. M. Schumacher, and K. H. Berry. 1994b. Health profiles of free-ranging desert tortoises in California: Results of a two-year study of serological testing for antibody to *Mycoplasma agassizii*. Final Report. U.S. Bureau of Land Management, Contract No. B950-C2-0046, Riverside, California.

Christopher, M. M., R. Brigmon, and E. R. Jacobson. 1994. Seasonal alterations in plasma β-hydroxybutyrate and related biochemical parameters in the desert tortoise (*Gopherus agassizii*). Comp. Biochem. Physiol. 108A:303–310.

Dessauer, H. C. 1974. Plasma proteins of reptilia. *In* M. Florkin and B. T. Scheer (eds.), Chemical Zoology, Volume IX, pp. 187–216. Academic Press, New York.

Dickinson, V. M. and C. Reggiardo. 1992. Health studies of Mojave Desert tortoises. 1991 Annual Report, Arizona Game and Fish Department, Phoenix, Arizona.

Duncan, J. R. and K. W. Prasse. 1986. Veterinary Laboratory Medicine. Iowa State University Press, Ames, Iowa.

Jacobson, E. R., J. M. Gaskin, M. B. Brown, R. K. Harris, C. H. Gardiner, J. L. LaPointe, H. P. Adams, and C. Reggiardo. 1991. Chronic upper respiratory tract disease of free-ranging desert tortoises (*Xerobates agassizii*). J. Wild. Dis. 27:296–316.

Jacobson, E. R., J. Schumacher, and M. E. Green. 1992. Field and clinical techniques for sampling and handling blood for hematologic and selected biochemical determinations in the desert tortoise, *Xerobates agassizii*. Copeia 1992:237-241.

Jacobson, E. R., T. J. Wronski, J. Schumacher, C. Reggiardo, and K. H. Berry. 1994. Shell disease in free-ranging desert tortoises (*Gopherus agassizii*) in the Colorado Desert. J. Zoo. Wild. Med. 25:68–81.

Lawrence, K. and C. M. Hawkey. 1986. Seasonal variations in haematological data from Mediterranean tortoises (*Testudo graeca* and *Testudo hermanni*) in captivity. Res. Vet. Sci. 40:225–230.

Martin, H. F., B. J. Gudzinowicz, and H. Fanger. 1975. Normal Values in Clinical Chemistry: A Guide to Statistical Analysis of Laboratory Data. Marcel Dekker, Inc., New York.

Nagy, K. A. and P. A. Medica. 1986. Physiological ecology of desert tortoises in southern Nevada. Herpetologica 42:73–92.

Rosskopf, W. J. 1982. Normal hemogram and blood chemistry values for California desert tortoises. Vet. Med./Sm. Anim. Clin. 77:85–87.

Saad, A. H. 1988. Corticosteroids and immune systems of non-mammalian vertebrates: A review. Devel. Comp. Immunol. 12:281–494.

Schumacher, I. M., M. B. Brown, E. R. Jacobson, B. R. Collins, and P. A. Klein. 1993. Detection of antibodies to a pathogenic mycoplasma in desert tortoises (*Gopherus agassizii*) with upper respiratory tract disease. J. Clin. Micro. 31:1454–1460.

Turner, F. B. and K. H. Berry. 1986. Population ecology of the desert tortoise at Goffs, California in 1985. University of California at Los Angeles Publication #12-1544. 48 pp.

Wallis, I. R., K. A. Nagy, B. S. Wilson, B. T. Helen, C. C. Peterson, C. Meienberger, and I. A. Girard. 1992. Mortality and upper respiratory tract disease (URTD) in wild desert tortoises: Hematological, biochemical, and physiological correlates during two drought years in the Mojave Desert of California. Report to United States Dept. of the Interior/Bureau of Land Management, Contract YA651-CTO-340079.

Baseline Health Parameters of Free-Ranging Pancake Tortoises, *Malacochersus tornieri*, in Tanzania

— SUMMARY REPORT —

MICHAEL W. KLEMENS,[1] BONNIE L. RAPHAEL,[2] WILLIAM B. KARESH,[2]
PATRICIA D. MOEHLMAN,[2] AND REGINALD T. MWAYA[3]

[1]*International Conservation;* [2]*International Field Veterinary Program;
Wildlife Conservation Society, 185th St. and Southern Blvd., Bronx, NY 10460, USA*
[3]*College of African Wildlife Management—Mweka, P. O. Box 3031, Moshi, Tanzania*

In March 1991 a shipment of several hundred pancake tortoises, *Malacochersus tornieri*, en route from Tanzania to the United States, was seized by customs authorities in the Netherlands. This was one of many tortoise shipments in what had grown to be a flourishing trade. The attendant publicity that surrounded this seizure, including the cruel and illegal method of shipment which resulted in heavy mortality, set in motion a chain of events in which political and public relations considerations took precedence over sound wildlife management practices. These tortoises were eventually shipped back to Tanzania to be released into the wild. The IUCN/SSC Tortoise and Freshwater Turtle Specialist Group had been consulted throughout this process by various international agencies concerning the disposition of the tortoises and unequivocally advised *against* releasing them back into the wild. The reasoning was quite clear: Captive tortoises frequently harbor pathogens acquired from a variety of sources, both chelonian and non-chelonian. Such pathogens may persist with only minor clinical symptoms if the tortoises are well fed and amply watered (as captives usually are). However, if these pathogens are introduced into wild populations, the results may be devastating. As these tortoises had been exported from Tanzania and subsequently rehabilitated at various animal holding facilities and zoos in western Europe, they posed a significant health threat if released into the wild.

Once the tortoises were returned, the Tanzanian wildlife authorities determined that they should be held in captivity until the various wildlife management issues and controversies surrounding repatriation had been adequately investigated and resolved. In February 1993 Klemens conducted health evaluations of free-ranging pancake tortoises at two widely separated sites in Tanzania—Tarangire National Park (with Mwaya) and Ruaha National Park (with Moehlman) as well as a portion of the captive herd that was being housed at the College of African Wildlife Management (with Moehlman and Mwaya).

The wild populations were sampled to create a baseline of data upon which to evaluate the health of the captive herd. Each tortoise in the study received a complete physical exam, a fecal sample was collected, a nasal flush was conducted if the nares of the tortoise were large enough, and a blood sample of 1–2 cc (dependent upon the size of the tortoise) was drawn. The nasal flush was flash-frozen in liquid nitrogen, the fecal sample was preserved and stored at room temperature, and the blood sample was refrigerated and processed within several hours after collection.

Blood work consisted of several phases. Three blood smear slides were prepared for each animal. A small sample (2 microhematocrit tubules) of blood were spun in a battery-powered centrifuge for five minutes. Packed blood cell volume and total blood solids were determined from this sample. The remaining blood was spun for ten minutes, the plasma pipetted off and flash-frozen in liquid nitrogen, and a small amount of the red blood cells was fixed in buffer for subsequent genetic analysis.

Analyses of blood values of the free-ranging pancake tortoises conducted both in the field and in the veterinary laboratory of the Wildlife Conservation Society are reported by Raphael et al. (1994). Noteworthy aspects of the ecology of this species are reported by Klemens and Moll (1995), Moll and Klemens (1996), and by Moll and Klemens (this volume). This research was conducted with the endorsement of and/or permits issued by the Tanzanian Commission for Science and Technology (COSTECH), Tanzanian National Parks (TANAPA), and the CITES office of the Tanzanian Division of Wildlife.

LITERATURE CITED

Klemens, M. W. and D. Moll. 1995. An assessment of the effects of commercial exploitation on the pancake tortoise, *Malacochersus tornieri*, in Tanzania. Chelon. Conserv. Biol. 1(3):197–206.

Moll, D. and M. W. Klemens. 1996. Ecological characteristics of the pancake tortoise, *Malacochersus tornieri* (Siebenrock), in Tanzania. Chelon. Conserv. Biol. (2)1:26–35.

Raphael, B., M. W. Klemens, P. Moehlman, E. Dierenfeld, and W. B. Karesh. 1994. Blood values in free-ranging pancake tortoises (*Malacochersus tornieri*). J. Zoo and Wildl. Med. 25(1):63–67.

Field Techniques for Collection of Biological Samples in Turtles and Tortoises

— SUMMARY REPORT —

BONNIE L. RAPHAEL[1] AND ELLIOTT R. JACOBSON[2]

[1]*Wildlife Health Center, Wildlife Conservation Society, 185th St. and Southern Blvd., Bronx, NY 10460, USA*
[2]*P.O. Box 100126, HSC, College of Veterinary Medicine, University of Florida, Gainesville, FL 32610, USA*

Health surveys of free-ranging turtles and tortoises are important for establishing baseline information on populations. Samples that can be collected in the field with minimal stress to the turtle or tortoise include nasal flushes, blood, feces, and cutaneous and dermal biopsies. These samples can be used for complete blood counts, biochemical analysis, microbacterial culture, serology, parasitology surveys, and nutritional analysis. Some of the methods for proper collection of samples in the field are summarized below.

It is important that field workers are trained in consistent collection techniques so that valid comparisons between studies can be made. Further, collecting bad samples will yield poor results and possibly lead to spurious findings.

Field Equipment

Appropriate supplies for field collection of biomaterials range from equipment as elaborate (and costly) as a centrifuge for spinning down blood samples to as simple as alcohol. A sample list may include:

- Syringes
- Needles
- Butterfly catheters
- Serum tubes
- Glass slides
- Gauze squares
- Cooler with ice
- Test tube racks
- Latex gloves
- Liquid heparin
- Heparin-containing blood tubes
- Appropriate media in which to place microbiological specimens.
- "Dry shipper" for freezing specimens in the field. The container's lining is charged with liquid nitrogen and remains cold for approx. two weeks before recharging is required. (It is particularly important for blood and microbial samples that processing take place within a maximum of 12 hours, and interim storage in dry shippers until processing is especially useful.)
- Centrifuge. If working in remote places where electricity is not available, the centrifuge may be operated from a battery recharged with solar panels, or from a vehicle battery.

Note: *Do not* use Styrofoam "popcorn" for packing material in the field; it is quickly lost in a gust of wind and produces environmental litter.

Cleanliness and Sterility

Cleanliness in the collection of field samples is critical. It is of particular importance in the performance of nasal flushes (e.g., for determination of the presence of *Mycoplasma* in tortoises). Nares are first thoroughly cleaned with sterile saline to remove any external debris. A syringe containing media or saline fluid is placed against the nares, which are then flushed by expressing and withdrawing the fluid. Care must be taken not to contaminate the syringe before transferring the sample into a sterile tube.

Care of Samples

Proper handling of samples subsequent to collection is critically important. A portable cooler with ice for storage will prevent heat degradation. Samples must be processed in a timely fashion. In blood samples, red cells must be separated from plasma as soon as is reasonable (the longer red blood cells remain in contact with plasma, the more the electrolytes will change and certain enzymes may be lost from red cells, which can give misleading results). It should also be remembered that red blood cells are fragile (e.g., mixing heparin with red cells must be done by gentle rotation of the tube, not by shaking).

Sampling Techniques

Cloacal or Fecal Samples. Examination of cloacal swabs or feces can indicate of the status of gut flora. Microbiological samples are somewhat more difficult to handle in the field and should be brought to the laboratory within a day or two for analysis; because of the great number of different organisms present in the GI tract, one organism may overtake or dominate its competitors, rendering the sample no longer representative.

Preserving Fecal Samples. Feces may be preserved in formalin or polyvinyl acetate for later examination for parasites. Kits containing vials of PVA and formalin are available, and samples may be preserved for prolonged periods of time (up to 2 years).

Dermal Bone Biopsies. More specialized field techniques (developed by Jacobson et al.) include dermal bone biopsies. The surface of the shell is prepped using a

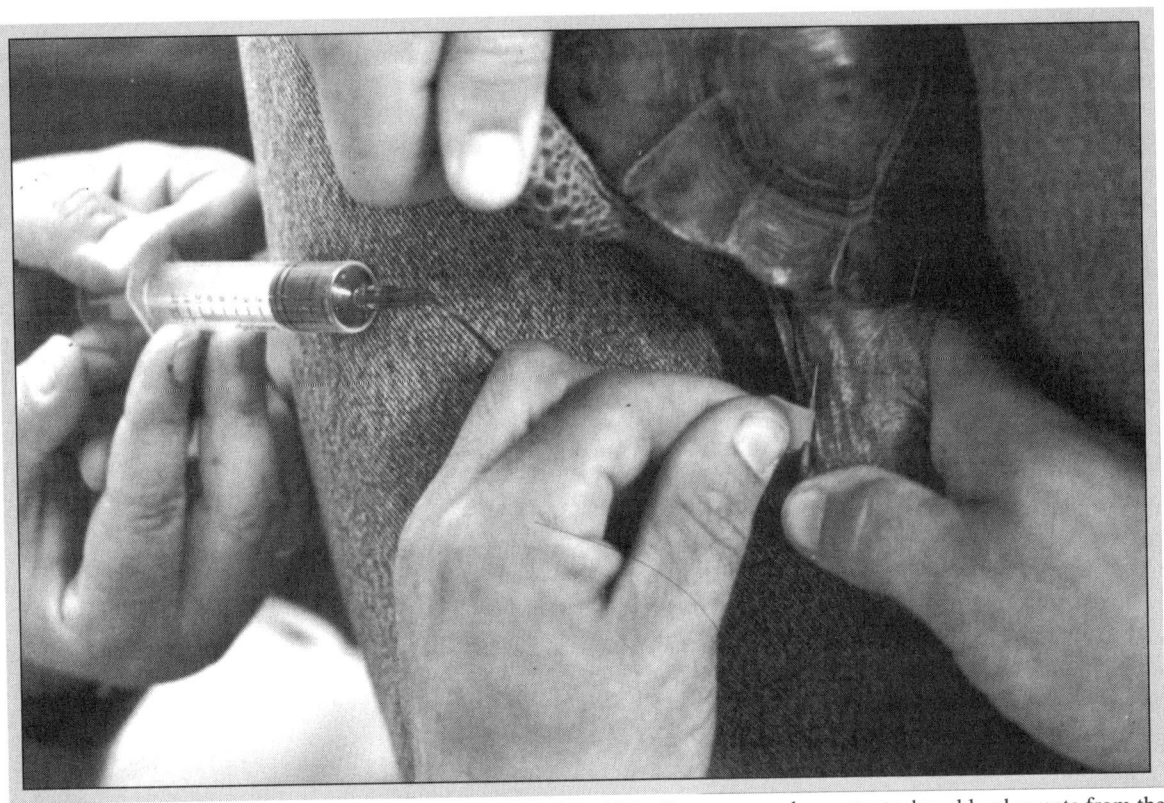

Figure 1. A butterfly catheter is inserted into the jugular vein, which allows a second operator to draw blood remote from the animal, thus avoiding pressure on the vessel should any movement by the animal occur.

Betadine-saline solution or alcohol, or with only saline if the specimen is to be examined for fungal or microbial organisms. A trephine bone drill is used to extract a sample 2–3 mm deep. The area is then covered to prevent contamination from debris while the animal produces its own fibrous covering, which normally occurs quite rapidly. The sample is placed in media for microbiology, or formalin for histopathology.

Blood Collection Techniques. Three practical blood collection sites include (1) brachial or ulnar veins or arteries of the forelimb—a good site if the head is impossible to extract, or if one needs the sample only for blood smears or genetic analysis; (2) occipital area—a plexus of blood vessels behind the occipital bone yields a substantial amount of blood, but there is a likelihood of contamination from the lymphatics at this site (as well as at the brachial/ulnar sites); and (3) the jugular vein.

Significant differences in packed cell volume as well as plasma chemistry can be found between samples taken from jugular and occipital sites. The lymphatics associated with both the occipital and brachial regions in reptiles are complex, and sampling from these sites can, without the knowledge of the technician, result in significant dilution of the sample. The site of sampling may have profound effects on the values generated, and one must be consistent in the techniques used.

The preferred site is the jugular but may require more than one operator (Figure 1). A butterfly catheter is inserted into the jugular by one operator while the animal's neck is held in an extended position. A second operator, remote from the animal, draws blood into a syringe. Pressure on the vessel is thereby avoided if the animal should move or if the syringe is changed.

The sample is drawn into a heparinized syringe (one that has a minimal coating so as not to dilute the sample), or the sample is placed immediately into a heparin-containing tube. For packed cell volume and total solids determinations, the sample of whole blood is placed in a microhematocrit tube and spun down in a centrifuge; a refractometer is used to determine total solids. Plasma is placed in the liquid nitrogen container for later analysis. Blood smears are prepared and may be fixed in the field. A more complete discussion of this blood collection technique may be found in Jacobson et al. (1992).

LITERATURE CITED

Jacobson, E. R., J. Schumacher, and M. Green. 1992. Field and clinical techniques for sampling and handling blood for hematologic and selected biochemical determinations in the desert tortoise, *Xerobates agassizii*. Copeia 1992 (1):237–241.

A Serologic Test to Monitor the Desert Tortoise, *Gopherus agassizii*, for Exposure to a Pathogenic Mycoplasma

— SUMMARY REPORT —

ISABELLA M. SCHUMACHER,[1] MARY B. BROWN,[2] ELLIOTT R. JACOBSON,[3] BOBBY R. COLLINS,[3] AND PAUL A. KLEIN[1]

[1]*BEECS Immunological Analysis Core;*
[2]*Interdisciplinary Center for Biotechnology Research, Department of Infectious Diseases;*
[3]*Department of Small Animal Clinical Sciences, College of Veterinary Medicine;*
University of Florida, Gainesville, FL 32610, USA

Worldwide experience has pointed to the central role of the immunological defense systems of all animal species in resistance to and recovery from infectious diseases. Future improvements in the diagnosis and control of infectious diseases in wildlife populations will require an increased understanding of the immunology of threatened animal species, their associated pathogens, and the environmental factors that may undermine the immune system's ability to cope effectively with pathogens.

Over the past two decades an upper respiratory tract disease (URTD) in the desert tortoise, *Gopherus agassizii*, has contributed significantly to the decline of this species. Tortoises with URTD characteristically show clinical signs of rhinitis with clear-to-purulent nasal discharge, palpebral edema, dehydration and cachexia in the late stages, and a high mortality rate. In April 1990 desert tortoises in areas north and west of the Colorado River in the USA were listed as "Threatened" by the U.S. federal government.

During the course of recent studies on the pathology of URTD, a new *Mycoplasma* strain was isolated from clinically sick tortoises. This strain, designated *Mycoplasma agassizii* (proposed species novum) was shown to be the principal etiologic agent of URTD by fulfillment of Koch's postulates in experimental transmission studies.

A serologic test, enzyme-linked immunosorbent assay (ELISA) to detect antibodies to *M. agassizii* in desert tortoises, *G. agassizii*, has been developed by us. In a transmission study, the ELISA detected seroconversion as early as one month following infection with *M. agassizii*. Although the ELISA does not detect the pathogen itself, the direct correlation between the presence of clinical signs of URTD and of histologic lesions of the nasal mucosa and *M. agassizii*-specific antibodies proved that this test can reliably diagnose past exposure to *M. agassizii* in desert tortoises.

The ELISA has been applied to detect antibodies to *Mycoplasma agassizii* in 61 desert tortoises from three different study sites in California—Desert Tortoise Natural Area (DTNA) (n = 19), Goffs (n = 21), and Ivanpah (n = 21)—in order to determine the distribution of exposed individuals within the different populations. Antibody levels were determined for plasma samples from March, May, July–August, and October 1992 and March 1993 to study seasonal effects, the dynamics of the immune response of the individual tortoises, and the dynamics of the spread of the infection through the populations. Antibody levels were also correlated with field and laboratory data on health and body condition.

When antibody levels for a given location were compared based on sex and time of sampling, no statistically significant differences ($P \geq 0.2$) were seen for any location at any time. However, significant differences by geographic population and by month were observed. The highest percentage of seropositive tortoises (32%, 6 of 19) was found in DTNA. Ivanpah and Goffs each had 4.8% (1 of 21) positive animals. Mean levels of specific antibody were higher at each time point in sera from tortoises in the DTNA than from tortoises at either Ivanpah or Goffs ($P \leq 0.001$), with Goffs having the lowest overall levels. None of the tortoises showed clinical signs of URTD. In all three populations antibody levels increased in summer and decreased in fall. Because both weight and packed cell volume (PCV) have been suggested as indicators of health status, we attempted to correlate the levels of specific antibody to *M. agassizii* with these variables. No consistent relationships emerged.

It was concluded that the three populations represent different stages in the development of URTD. It is hypothesized that DTNA may be representative of a population that has seen severe, epidemic disease. The population remaining in DTNA may be a convalescent population. Some tortoises may potentially be less susceptible to disease; others may still carry this pathogenic mycoplasma. Ivanpah may represent a population in transition from naive to infected status. Goffs represents an essentially naive population, which would be at greatest risk if exposed to this pathogenic mycoplasma. Further monitoring of the populations is necessary to confirm these hypotheses.

Diseases in Wild Populations of Turtles and Tortoises: The Chelonian Charisma vs. Coincidence Conundrum

ELLIOTT R. JACOBSON

P.O. Box 100126, HSC, College of Veterinary Medicine, University of Florida, Gainesville, FL 32610, USA
[e-mail: ERJ@vetmed1.vetmed.ufl.edu]

ABSTRACT: Within the class Reptilia, while relatively few diseases have been reported in wild populations of squamates and crocodilians, over the last ten years a variety of diseases have been seen in wild chelonians. Starting in the early 1980s there was a worldwide increased prevalence of fibropapillomas in populations of the green turtle, *Chelonia mydas*, with more than 50% of juvenile green turtles in certain populations affected. The causative agent of this disease and reasons for the worldwide epizootic remain unknown. In the mid-1980s moribund flattened musk turtles, *Sternotherus depressus*, with ulcerative lesions of the integument and pneumonia were identified in the Sipsey Fork in north-central Alabama, and several species of emydine turtles with proliferative shell lesions were seen in Lake Blackshear in southwest Georgia. A major decline in populations of the desert tortoise, *Gopherus agassizii*, in the western Mojave Desert was associated with an upper respiratory tract disease, and gopher tortoises, *Gopherus polyphemus*, with a similar disease have been seen at multiple sites in Florida. Declines of desert tortoises on the Chuckwalla Bench Area of Critical Concern, Riverside County, California, have been associated with an unusual shell disease. Is the sudden increase in the number of disease problems recognized in wild populations of chelonians merely coincidence, or are problems just being seen in a charismatic group of vertebrates? Because of their size and popularity as a research animal for studies in the field, chelonians may represent an excellent indicator species for fluxes in the quality of the environment in which they live.

Of the four orders comprising the class Reptilia, more disease problems have been seen in free-ranging chelonians than in the other groups. Various diseases have been seen in marine turtles, freshwater aquatics, and terrestrial chelonians. Whether this is truly an indication of a greater prevalence of disease in this order compared to other reptiles, or simply a reflection of the intensity in which these animals are being studied, remains to be determined. Clearly, when chelonians die the shell is left behind as a monument to the loss of the individual from the population. This certainly favors the discovery of epizootics in this group. Additionally, because of their benign image, chelonians are often observed in the field by the lay public, which also favors the reporting of disease problems in ill populations.

In this paper I will review the most significant infectious disease problems seen in free-ranging chelonians, beginning with viral infections. More than likely, this just represents the tip of the iceberg existing in the wild.

Viral Diseases

Herpetoviridae. While herpesviruses are well documented as causes of mortality in captive chelonians (Rebell et al., 1975; Frye et al., 1977; Jacobson et al., 1982, 1986), including captive *Testudo hermanni* and *T. graeca* in a conservation program in France (Jacobson, unpubl. findings), it is only recently that members of this family of viruses have been found to infect free-ranging turtles. Histologic evaluation of two green turtles, *Chelonia mydas*, from the vicinity of Key West, Florida, with multiple fibropapillomas indicated the presence of intranuclear inclusions within ballooning epidermal cells (Jacobson et al., 1991). By electron microscopy, inclusions consisted of virus-like particles measuring 77–90 nm. Envelopment of these particles was observed at the nuclear membrane. Based upon morphology, size, and location, the particles were compatible with those of the family Herpetoviridae. A causal relationship could not be demonstrated, and it is quite possible that this virus may only represent a secondary infection, merely present in a growing tumor. In another case, herpesvirus-like particles were observed in skin lesions and pharyngeal lesions in a loggerhead sea turtle, *Caretta caretta*, from the east coast of central Florida (R. Homer, pers. comm.). The significance of herpesvirus infections in wild populations of turtles is unknown.

Bacterial Diseases

Mycoplasmosis. In 1988 desert tortoises with signs of upper respiratory tract disease (URTD) were seen in the Desert Tortoise Natural Area (DTNA), Kern County,

California (Jacobson et al., 1991). In 1989 a detailed survey of the DTNA and nearby areas in the Rand Mountains and Freemont Valley indicated that 43% of 468 live desert tortoises encountered on the sections surveyed showed signs of this disease (Knowles, 1989). Additionally, carcasses of 627 tortoises were recovered from the sampled areas. Since first being seen in desert tortoises in the DTNA, desert tortoises with URTD have been seen in multiple locations throughout the Mojave Desert of southern California. Desert tortoises with URTD have also been seen in the Las Vegas Valley, Nevada; the Beaver Dam Slope, Utah/Arizona; and the Sonoran Desert, Arizona.

Pathologic studies of 17 ill desert tortoises from the DTNA and one ill desert tortoise from Utah indicated that major microscopic lesions were confined to the upper respiratory tract (URT) of ill tortoises (Jacobson et al., 1991). Electron microscopic studies revealed small (350–900 nm), pleomorphic organisms resembling mycoplasma in close association with the surface epithelium of the URT of ill tortoises. *Pasteurella testudinis* was cultured from the nasal cavity of all ill tortoises and one of four healthy tortoises. A mycoplasma-like organism was cultured from the nasal passageways of four ill tortoises and was ultrastructurally similar to the pleomorphic organism present on the mucosa in tissue sections. This is only the second report of isolation of a mycoplasma from a reptile. *Mycoplasma testudinis* was isolated from the cloaca of a spur-thighed tortoise, *Testudo graeca* (Hill, 1985). Because the strains isolated from the desert tortoise did not cross-react serologically with other known species of *Mycoplasma*, it was concluded that these strains represent a new species of pathogenic *Mycoplasma* as defined by the Subcommittee on the Taxonomy of *Mollicutes* of the International Committee on Systematic Bacteriology. The species name proposed was *Mycoplasma agassizii*; PS6 is the type strain (Schumacher et al., 1993). In a recent transmission study, this organism was demonstrated as the cause of URTD in the desert tortoise (Brown et al., 1994).

Because many captive desert tortoises ill with respiratory tract disease exist in private collections throughout southern California, possibly an extremely pathogenic organism has been introduced into wild populations at multiple sites by released pet tortoises. Other predisposing factors such as habitat degradation and drought may also be contributing to the severity and spread of this disease.

Middle-ear infections and pulmonary disease of box turtles, *Terrapene* spp. Middle and inner ear infections are well documented for American box turtles (Jackson et al., 1972), and the author has on occasion seen this problem in freshwater and marine chelonians. Box turtles are usually presented with unilateral or bilateral swellings below the tympanic scale that consist of caseous laminar material surrounded by a mixed inflammatory reaction. *Citrobacter*, *Enterobacter*, *Proteus morgani*, *P. rettgeri*, and *Pseudomonas* have been cultured from these lesions. The pathogenesis of this disease is poorly understood.

Wild-caught box turtles with stomatitis and rhinitis have been presented to the author for evaluation. Chronic bacterial pneumonia was diagnosed in two wild box turtles, *T. carolina carolina*, from Illinois (Evans, 1983). Both turtles were found half buried in a dry creek bed and were found to be severely emaciated and physically depressed. Histologically, chronic inflammation was identified in the nasal sinuses and lungs. A mixture of gram-negative bacteria including *Morganella morgani*, *Acinetobacter calcoaceticus*, *Serratia marcescens*, and *Pseudomonas* sp. were isolated from both turtles. No other pathogens were identified. The bacteria collectively were considered the causative agents of the pneumonia.

Parasitic Diseases

Spirochidiasis. Adult members of the family Spirorchidae inhabit the circulatory system of susceptible reptiles. Turtles appear to be the most commonly infected reptilian host. Adult parasites are generally found within the great vessels leaving the heart or within the heart chambers, where focal endothelial hyperplasia has been seen. A variety of species have been identified in freshwater turtles, with *Spirorchis* the most significant genus (Yamaguti, 1958). In marine turtles, the most significant genera include *Amphiorchis*, *Carettacola*, *Haemoxenicon*, *Hapalotrema*, *Laeredius*, *Monticellius*, *Neospirorchis*, and *Squaroacetabulum* (Lauckner, 1985). Pathological findings associated with eggs of these parasites have been described for the loggerhead sea turtle (Wolke et al., 1982), and in both farmed (Greiner et al., 1980; Glazebrook and Campbell, 1990a) and wild (Glazebrook and Campbell, 1990b) green turtles. Eggs can elicit a severe inflammatory response at any site in which they become lodged. The author has examined sections of brain from loggerhead sea turtles with signs of central nervous system disease and has found inflammation in the meninges in response to spirorchid eggs. Spirorchid trematode eggs have also been seen in dermal capillaries within green turtle fibropapillomas (see below).

Dipteran infections. Larval stages of the dipteran fly (*Cistudinomyia cistudinis*) frequently parasitize box turtles (*Terrapene carolina*) and gopher tortoises (*Gopherus polyphemus*) in the southeastern United States. This parasite was first described as *Sarcophaga cistudinis* (Aldrich, 1916) and was subsequently renamed *Cistudinomyia* (Townsend, 1917). Investigation of the life cycle demonstrated that adult flies lay larvae directly on the host (Knipling, 1937). However, larvae are unable to penetrate intact skin, requiring breaks in the integument to gain access to subcutaneous sites. The larvae can cause significant tissue damage and death.

Diseases of Unknown Cause

Fibropapillomatosis of marine turtles. While relatively few types of tumors have been reported in chelonians (Jacobson, 1981), fibropapillomas are commonly encountered in free-ranging green turtles, *Chelonia mydas* (Jacobson et al., 1989). Green turtle fibropapilloma (GTF) was first described in green turtles from the Florida Keys (USA) in 1938 (Lucke, 1938; Smith and Coates, 1938) and almost 50 years later from green turtles in Hawaii (Balazs, 1986). Based upon anecdotal reports of fishermen, GTF was seen around 1900 in Florida (L. Ehrhart, pers. comm.) and in 1958 in Hawaii (G. Balazs, pers. comm.). GTF has been seen in near shore sites in Puerto Rico, Cayman Islands, Virgin Islands, Barbados, Venezuela, Colombia, Panama, Belize, and Australia. Over the last ten years there has been an increased incidence of GTF in the Indian River Lagoon System of east central Florida (Jacobson et al., 1989) and Hawaii (G. Balazs, pers. comm.).

The light and electron microscopic characteristics of GTF have recently been described (Jacobson et al., 1989). The earliest lesions exhibited ballooning degeneration of basal epidermal cells, with intracytoplasmic vacuoles occasionally containing particles with electron dense centers; the nature of these particles could not be determined. Molecular studies using cloned mammalian papillomavirus probes failed to identify members of this group of viruses in GTF. While spirorchid trematode eggs are commonly observed within dermal capillaries (Smith and Coates, 1939), tumors without eggs have also been observed, and the role of these parasites in the development of GTF has been questioned (Jacobson et al., 1989). The etiology of GTF remains unknown.

Dyskeratosis of desert tortoises. High mortality rates and a shell disease originally described as shell necrosis were observed in the population of desert tortoises, *Gopherus agassizii*, in the Colorado Desert, on the Chuckwalla Bench Area of Critical Environmental Concern, Riverside County, California, USA (Jacobson et al., 1994). In a retrospective review of photographic slides of desert tortoises from the Chuckwalla Bench, the disease was evident in 1979 when tortoises on a permanent study site were first photographed. Lesions were in both sexes and all size classes of tortoises in all years in which tortoises were photographed. In those tortoises where sequential photographs were taken, the most severe lesions were seen in 1988. While the disease was present on the carapace, plastron, and thickened forelimb scutes, the plastron was more severely affected than other areas of the integument. The affected portions of the shell were gray-white or orange and had a roughened flaky appearance. The lesion commenced at seams between scutes and spread toward the middle of each scute in an irregular pattern. Shell biopsies of nine affected tortoises were evaluated by light microscopy. No inflammatory infiltrates were in the lesions and while bacterial organisms were identified in tissue sections, they were superficially located and were considered to be secondary invaders. Special staining by the Giemsa method indicated a loss of the normal integrity of the horny material covering affected scutes. For the most part, the epithelial cells that formed a pseudostratified layer under affected portions of each scute remained intact. The location and histological appearance of the lesions were compatible with a dyskeratosis and suggestive of either a deficiency disease or toxicosis. However, the exact cause of the disease could not be determined.

Osteomyelitis of emydine turtles. The author has seen a variety of emydine pond turtles (*Pseudemys*, *Trachemys*, and *Deirochelys reticularia*) in Florida with ulcerative shell lesions. The author has also received photographs of painted turtles, *Chrysemys picta*, from Westchester County, New York (J. Behler, pers. comm.) and *Pseudemys* from the Rappahannock River of northern Virginia (R. Mills, pers. comm.) with ulcerative shell lesions. Shell disease, representing proliferative osteomyelitis, has been seen in river cooters (*Pseudemys concinna*) and yellow-bellied turtles (*Trachemys scripta*) from Lake Blackshear, Georgia, since 1984 (Garner et al., 1997). Necropsies on affected turtles indicated segmental necrosis of the epidermis, followed by necrosis of the underlying dermis, and proliferative remodeling of bone. The absence of a consistent microbial isolate from the lesions suggested a toxic etiology. However, the exact cause of this disease is yet to be determined.

Disease in the flattened musk turtle, *Sternotherus depressus*. Ill flattened musk turtles were seen during surveys of the Sipsey Fork in north central Alabama beginning in July 1985 (Dodd, 1988). The following clinical observations were made: emaciation, lesions on the plastron which caused the overlying scutes to peel away, discolored carapace, eroded marginals, eyelids that were kept closed and appeared swollen, pale appearance of the face, the lack of leeches in ill turtles compared to healthy turtles, and more frequent basking by ill turtles compared to healthy turtles. Several affected turtles were euthanized and submitted for pathologic evaluations. The most significant findings included multifocal areas of epidermal necrosis, areas of coagulation necrosis in the liver, edema fluid in the submucosa of the intestinal tract, and inflammatory cells in air passageways of the lung, with edema fluid in the interstitium. A variety of gram-negative microorganisms were isolated from multiple organs, with *Arizona hinshawii* as the dominant organism. In a subsequent survey conducted in 1986, severely affected turtles were not found. More than likely, predisposing factors are responsible for initiating the bacterial septicemia. One possibility is that a toxic substance in the Sipsey Fork is adversely affecting the immune systems of these turtles.

LITERATURE CITED

Aldrich, J. M. 1916. *Sarcophaga* and Allies in North America. Lafayette, Indiana. 301 pp.

Balazs, G. H. 1986. Fibropapillomas in Hawaiian green turtles. Mar. Turt. Newsl. 39:1–3.

Brown, M. B., I. M. Schumacher, P. A. Klein, R. K. Harris, T. Correll, and E. R. Jacobson. 1994. *Mycoplasma agassizii* causes upper respiratory tract disease in the desert tortoise. Inf. Immun. 62: 4580–4586.

Dodd, C. K. 1988. Disease and population declines in the flattened musk turtle *Sternotherus depressus*. Amer. Midl. Natur. 119:394–401.

Evans, R. H. 1983. Chronic bacterial pneumonia in free-ranging eastern box turtles (*Terrapene carolina carolina*). J. Wildl. Dis. 19: 349–352.

Frye, F. L., L. S. Oshiro, F. R. Dutra, et al. 1977. Herpesvirus-like infection in two Pacific pond turtles. J. Amer. Vet. Med. Assoc. 171:882–884.

Garner, M. M., R. Herrington, E. W. Howerth, B. L. Homer, V. F. Nettles, R. Isaza, E. B. Shots, and E. R. Jacobson. 1997. Shell disease in river cooters (*Pseudemys concinna*) and yellow-bellied turtles (*Trachemys scripta*) in a Georgia lake. J. Wildl. Dis. 33: 76–86.

Glazebrook, J. S., and R. S. F. Campbell. 1990a. A survey of the diseases of marine turtles in northern Australia. I. Farmed turtles. Dis. Aquat. Org. 9:83–95.

Glazebrook, J. S., and R. S. F. Campbell. 1990b. A survey of the diseases of marine turtles in northern Australia. II. Oceanarium-reared and wild turtles. Dis. aquat. Org. 9:97–104.

Greiner, E. C., D. J. Forrester, and E. R. Jacobson. 1980. Helminths of mariculture-reared green turtles (*Chelonia mydas mydas*) from Grand Cayman, British West Indies. Proc. Helminth. Soc. Wash. 47:142–144.

Hill, A. C. 1985. *Mycoplasma testudinis*, a new species isolated from a tortoise. Inter. J. Syst. Bact. 35:489–492.

Jackson, C. G., M. Fulton, and M. M. Jackson. 1972. Cranial asymmetry with massive infection in a box turtle. J. Wildl. Dis. 8:275–277.

Jacobson, E. R. 1981. Neoplastic diseases. *In* J. E. Cooper and O. F. Jackson (eds.), Diseases of the Reptilia. Vol.2, pp. 429–468. Academic Press, London.

Jacobson, E. R., J. M. Gaskin, and H. Wahlquist. 1982. Herpes-like virus infection in map turtles. J.A.V.M.A. 181:1322–1324.

Jacobson, E. R., J. M. Gaskin, M. Roelke, et al. 1986. Conjunctivitis, tracheitis, and pneumonia associated with herpesvirus infection in green sea turtles. J. Amer. Vet. Med. Assoc. 189:1020–1023.

Jacobson, E. R., J. L. Mansell, J. P. Sundberg, et al. 1989. Cutaneous fibropapillomas of green turtles (*Chelonia mydas*). J. Comp. Path. 101:39–52.

Jacobson, E. R., C. Buergelt, B. Williams, and R. K. Harris. 1991a. Herpesvirus in cutaneous fibropapillomas of the green turtle, *Chelonia mydas*. Dis. Aq. Org. 12:1–6.

Jacobson, E. R., J. M. Gaskin, M. B. Brown, R. K. Harris, C. H. Gardiner, J. L. LaPointe, H. P. Adams, and C. Reggiardo. 1991b. Chronic upper respiratory tract disease of free-ranging desert tortoises, *Xerobates agassizii*. J. Wildl. Dis. 27:296–316.

Jacobson, E. R., T. J. Wronski, J. Schumacher, C. Reggiardo, and K. H. Berry. 1994. Cutaneous dyskeratosis in free-ranging desert tortoises, *Gopherus agassizii*, in the Colorado Desert of southern California. J. Zoo Wildl. Med. 25:68—81.

Knipling, E. F. 1937. The biology of *Sarcophaga cistudinis* Aldrich (Diptera), a species of Sarcophagidae parasitic on turtles and tortoises. Proc. Entomol. Soc. of Washington 39:91–101.

Knowles, C. 1989. A survey for diseased desert tortoises in and near the Desert Tortoise Natural Area, Spring 1989. Report prepared for the Bureau of Land Management, Riverside, California, Contract No CA 950-(T9-23), June.

Lauckner, G. 1985. Diseases of reptilia. *In* O. Kinne (ed.), Diseases of Marine Animals, pp. 443–626. Biologische Anstalt Helgoland, Hamburg, Germany.

Lucké, B. 1938. Studies on tumors in cold-blooded vertebrates. Ann. Rep. Tortugas Lab., Carnegie Inst. Washington 38:92–94.

Rebell, H., A. Rywlin, and H. Haines. 1975. A herpesvirus-type agent associated with skin lesions of green turtles in aquaculture. Amer. J. Vet. Res. 36:1221–1224.

Schumacher, I. M., M. Brown, E. R. Jacobson, B. R. Collins, and P. A. Klein. 1993. Detection of antibodies to a pathogenic *Mycoplasma* in the desert tortoise (*Gopherus agassizii*). J. Clin. Microbiol. 31: 1454–1460.

Smith, G. M. and C. W. Coates. 1938. Fibro-epithelial growths of the skin in large marine turtles, *Chelonia mydas* (Linnaeus). Zoologica, N.Y. 23:93–98.

Smith, G. M., and C. W. Coates. 1939. The occurrence of trematode ova (*Hapalotrema constrictum*) (Leared) in fibroepithelial tumours of the marine turtle *Chelonia mydas* (Linnaeus). Zoologica, N.Y. 24:379–382.

Townsend, C. H. 1917. New genera and species of American muscoid diptera. Proc. Biol. Soc. Washington, D.C. 30:43–50.

Wolke, R. E., D. R. Brooks, and A. George. 1982. Spirorchidiasis in loggerhead sea turtles (*Caretta caretta*): Pathology. J. Wildl. Dis. 18:175–185.

Yamaguti, Y. 1958. The digenetic trematodes of vertebrates. *In* Systema Helminthum. Vol. I. 2 Parts. Interscience, New York. 1575 pp.

Demographic Consequences of Disease in Two Desert Tortoise Populations in California, USA

KRISTIN H. BERRY

U.S. Bureau of Land Management, 6221 Box Springs Boulevard, Riverside, CA 92507-0714, USA
Current Agency: U.S. Geological Survey, Biological Resources Division (same address) [e-mail: kristin_berry@nbs.gov]

ABSTRACT: Disease is a causal factor in declines of desert tortoise, *Gopherus agassizii*, populations at two locations in California. In the interior of the Desert Tortoise Research Natural Area (DTNA), population densities of all sizes of tortoises declined 76% from 75/km^2 in 1979 to 18/km^2 in 1992. Densities of adults followed the same pattern and declined 90% from 61/km^2 in 1979 to 6/km^2 in 1992. Declines of adult tortoises are attributed primarily to an upper respiratory tract disease (URTD) caused by the pathogen *Mycoplasma agassizii*. Additional disease-related mortalities are expected to occur, because 25–38% of four samples of adult tortoises from an adjacent site within the DTNA tested positive for antibodies to *M. agassizii* in 1992. This disease may have been introduced to the DTNA through release of ill captive tortoises.

A second disease, cutaneous dyskeratosis, is present at another reserve, the Chuckwalla Bench Area of Critical Environmental Concern, and is linked to population declines. Between 1982 and 1988 the incidence of cutaneous dyskeratosis increased and lesions became more severe. Between 1982 and 1992 the total tortoise population (all size classes) declined 54% from 153 tortoises/km^2 to 70 tortoises/km^2. The adult population declined 61% from 87 tortoises/km^2 to 34 tortoises/km^2. The cause(s) of cutaneous dyskeratosis remain uncertain, but possibilities include deficiency diseases or environmental toxicosis.

Diseases, especially if introduced to a native population or if environmentally caused, can have serious consequences for threatened chelonians and will complicate conservation and recovery efforts. Of the two diseases, URTD is of the greatest immediate concern because of its potential to harm tortoise populations on a global scale.

Desert tortoise, *Gopherus agassizii*, populations have declined substantially in the past two decades due to a wide variety of causes, including collecting, vandalism, predation, and habitat loss and deterioration (U.S. Fish and Wildlife Service [USFWS], 1994). Declines became so precipitous that in August 1989, the USFWS listed the species as "Endangered" under the emergency provisions of the Endangered Species Act of 1973, as amended. Disease was a factor in the emergency listing. Subsequently, in April 1990 the USFWS permanently listed the desert tortoise as "Threatened."

Disease was first implicated as having a significant role in mortality of wild desert tortoises in the 1980s, when remains of tortoises from the Beaver Dam Slope of Arizona and Utah were found to have osteopenia, indicative of malnutrition (Jacobson, 1994). Disease was documented as the major cause of mortality in a wild desert tortoise population in 1988, when ill tortoises with upper respiratory disease were observed by field-workers at a long-term permanent study plot in the interior of the Desert Tortoise Research Natural Area (DTNA) in the western Mojave Desert of California (Berry, 1990; Jacobson et al., 1991). Further research in 1989 and 1990 (e.g., Knowles, 1989; Berry, 1990) confirmed that many tortoises at the DTNA were ill, dying, or had recently died. The signs of disease (nasal discharge, lassitude, cachexia) were similar to signs observed in an often fatal upper respiratory disease of captive desert tortoises throughout southern California (W. Rosskopf, DVM, pers. comm.). Prior to 1988 upper respiratory disease had not been observed in wild, free-living tortoises at the DTNA (Berry and Nicholson, 1984; Berry et al., 1986).

Upper respiratory disease was considered a threat to wild populations of the desert tortoise in the 1970s, long before the disease appeared. When the DTNA was established in 1972, the author and the U.S. Bureau of Land Management (USBLM) expressed concerns about the potentially infectious nature of the disease. We suspected wild populations may become infected through release of ill captive tortoises, which were numerous throughout southern and central California (St. Amant, 1977; Berry and Nicholson, 1984). Because of the potential threat, the USBLM provided funds to Dr. Murray Fowler and his students to conduct research on the disease (Fowler, 1977; Snipes and Biberstein, 1982). No specific bacterial organism was identified as causing respiratory disease. Fowler (1977) concluded that the disease was not caused by a single organism and was not infectious. Stress, especially from malnutrition, was considered the prime predisposing factor.

By the mid-1970s the USBLM, the California Department of Fish and Game (CDFG), the Desert Tortoise Preserve Committee, Inc., and the California Turtle & Tortoise Club distributed literature and issued public statements warning that captive tortoises should not be released to wild lands because of the potential for spreading disease, contaminating genetic stock, and adversely affecting the behavior of wild resident populations (e.g., St. Amant, 1979, 1980; Berry and Nicholson, 1984).

When several wild tortoises with respiratory disease were discovered at a long-term permanent study plot in the DTNA interior in 1988, the CDFG and USBLM provided financial support to initiate research on the pathogenesis of the disease. Within two years research scientists at the University of Florida described the disease as an upper respiratory tract disease (URTD) associated with a new and undescribed mycoplasma (Jacobson et al., 1991). Shortly thereafter a transmission study demonstrated that a new mycoplasma, *M. agassizii*, is a highly infectious pathogen and causes URTD (Brown et al., 1994). An enzyme-linked immunosorbent assay (ELISA) test for *M. agassizii* was developed (Schumacher et al., 1993) and was used to determine whether wild desert tortoises carried antibodies to the pathogen (Brown et al., 1994b; Jacobson et al., 1995).

Within weeks of the time that ill tortoises were discovered at the DTNA in 1988, tortoises at another long-term study site in the Chuckwalla Bench Area of Critical Environmental Concern (ACEC), in the eastern Colorado Desert of Riverside County, were discovered to have shell lesions. An abnormally high number of tortoises, many of which were previously marked, were discovered dead (Berry, 1990). Research on the pathogenesis of shell lesions was initiated by Jacobson et al. (1994).

In this paper, I describe the demographic consequences of disease on desert tortoises at the long-term permanent study sites in the interior of the DTNA and on the Chuckwalla Bench, and the evidence linking disease to deaths. I also review the status of the populations as of 1992, discuss the implications of the two diseases for chelonian populations, and outline actions taken to cope with diseases within the two preserves and elsewhere.

METHODS

Description of the Two Long-Term Permanent Study Sites for Desert Tortoise Populations

Desert Tortoise Research Natural Area (DTNA). The DTNA is a 100 km² reserve established in 1972 in the western Mojave Desert to protect high-density tortoise populations and their habitats (Figure 1) (USBLM and CDFG, 1988). Formally designated as a Research Natural Area and Area of Critical Environmental Concern in 1980, the DTNA is protected from recreational vehicle use and sheep grazing

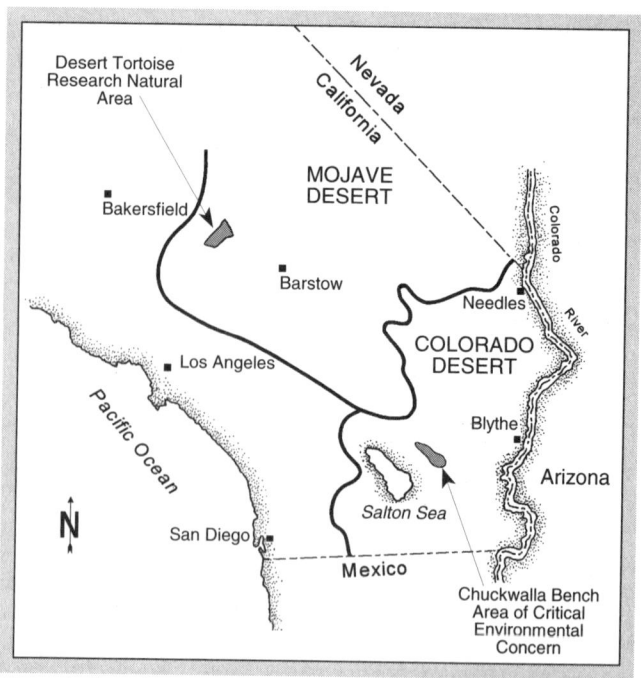

Figure 1. Locations of two protected areas for the desert tortoise: the Desert Tortoise Research Natural Area in the western Mojave Desert, eastern Kern County, California, and the Chuckwalla Bench Area of Critical Environmental Concern in the eastern Colorado Desert, Riverside County, California.

by a hog wire fence of which the lower edge is approximately 25 cm above the ground (USBLM, 1980; USBLM and CDFG, 1988). The raised fence permits wild animals to move into and out of the DTNA unimpeded. Since 1972 federal and state governments and the Desert Tortoise Preserve Committee, Inc. have invested considerable effort in establishing and securing habitat in the DTNA to create a viable reserve. To date, more than 8,000 km² of private inholdings have been acquired. The USBLM took action to eliminate all livestock grazing and hardrock mineral mining and also established long-term stewardship and education programs.

Two research study sites on the DTNA were sources of information: (1) a long-term study plot (2.8 km²), established in 1973 in the central interior to monitor changes in populations and habitat (Berry, 1984, 1990); and (2) a short-term, adjacent study plot, established in 1988 for research on health profiles (Christopher et al., 1993, this volume), physiology (water balance and energy flow), and epidemiology of diseases (Brown, 1994b). Habitats within the study plots are typical of diverse creosote bush (*Larrea tridentata*) scrub plant communities in the western Mojave Desert. Joshua trees (*Yucca brevifolia*) are widely scattered; creosote bushes are the predominant shrub; and more than three dozen perennial species of shrubs and grasses are present in the understory, e.g., burrobush (*Ambrosia dumosa*), goldenhead (*Acamptopappus sphaerocephalus*), cheesebush (*Hymenoclea salsola*), Anderson thornbush (*Lycium andersonii*), Nevada joint fir (*Ephedra nevadensis*), desert needle grass (*Achnatherum speciosum*), Indian rice grass (*A. hymenoides*), and one-sided blue grass (*Poa secunda* ssp. *secunda*). Elevations range from 853 to 914 m.

Chuckwalla Bench ACEC. In 1980 the USBLM established the Chuckwalla Bench ACEC in the eastern Colorado Desert in recognition of unique wildlife and vegetation values, including high densities of desert tortoises (Figure 1) (USBLM, 1980, 1986). The 371 km² protected area is long (approx. 60 km) and narrow (2.4–12 km) and is a raised bench between the Orocopia, Chocolate, and the Chuckwalla mountains. The bench drains into Milpitas Wash, which has the largest known populations of ironwood, *Olneya tesota*. In 1980, 35% of the ACEC was in numerous scattered privately owned parcels. Since that time, the USBLM has acquired most of these inholdings (S. Eubanks, pers. comm.) through land acquisition and mitigation programs.

The 2.8 km² long-term study plot (elev. 640 m) contains areas of desert pavement cut by rocky gullies and microphyll woodland washes. The predominant vegetation on the pavements and flat areas is diverse creosote bush scrub typical of the eastern Colorado Desert. It contains burrobush, white rhatany (*Krameria grayi*), California joint fir (*Ephedra californica*), cheesebush, ocotillo (*Fouquieria splendens* ssp. *splendens*), silver cholla (*Opuntia echinocarpa*), and Mojave yucca (*Yucca schidigera*). Washes are dominated by blue palo verde (*Cercidium floridum*), smoke tree (*Psorothamnus spinosus*), desert willow (*Chilopsis linearis* ssp. *arcuata*), ironwood, and catclaw (*Acacia greggii*).

Collecting Data on Population Densities of Desert Tortoises

Data for estimates of densities were collected during 60 day spring surveys conducted in 1979, 1982, 1988, and 1992 (Berry, 1984, 1990), according to the following procedure established for these ongoing studies: Each study site was divided into a grid of quadrats, each of which was 0.0259 km², and was permanently marked by rebar (iron reinforcing rods). Between late March and early June, one or two field-workers walked transects on each quadrat in search of tortoises. The plot was thoroughly and evenly covered twice, with each coverage requiring about 30 person days of effort. Each coverage constituted a census, with a total of two censuses conducted in each survey year. Surveys were conducted over a minimum of 45 and a maximum of 90 calendar days to minimize the effects of immigration and emigration of tortoises. For each tortoise located, the following data were collected for density estimates: date, unique identification number assigned to each tortoise, size (carapace length at the midline or MCL), sex, capture type (i.e., first capture of a previously unmarked tortoise, first capture in a given year of a previously marked tortoise, second or subsequent capture of a previously marked tortoise in a given year), location, and survey type (first or second census).

Analyzing Data on Population Densities of Desert Tortoises

The Stratified Lincoln Index (Overton, 1971) was selected as the density estimator because it satisfies two critical criteria for estimating densities of long-lived species such as the tortoise: (1) the population data can be stratified into size classes based on capturability, and (2) the equations allow for growth of individual tortoises and their shift from a smaller to a larger size-age class between the first and second censuses (Berry, 1990). The stratification is of particular importance, because larger tortoises are much easier to find than smaller tortoises.

Samples were sorted for analysis by study site, year, and census period (Berry, 1990). For each census within a year, each tortoise was assigned to one of five strata based on MCL: juveniles 1 and 2 (<100 mm MCL), immature 1 (100–139 mm MCL), immature 2 (140–179 mm MCL), small or young adults (180–208 mm MCL), and adult (>208 mm MCL). Tortoises were placed in three groups based on time of capture: (1) tortoises captured during the first census, (2) tortoises captured during the second census, and (3) tortoises captured during both the first and second censuses. Capture-recapture data were arranged in matrices to allow for growth of individual tortoises from one size group to another between censuses. The 95% Confidence Interval (CI) was used to establish level of significance for changes in population densities. An additional source of data was the number of individual tortoises encountered and marked during the 60-day survey for each sample year. If CIs did not overlap from one survey year to the next, the changes in the density estimates were considered statistically significant.

Evaluating Effects of Diseases on the Populations

Data on health status was gathered in detail on the two plots in 1992, including information on presence or absence and type of nasal discharge, patency of the nares, appearance of eyelids and eyes, condition of chin glands, presence or absence of ocular discharge, presence of active or healed injuries, presence and extent of lesions on the shell and limbs, and other signs of disease. In all survey years, 35 mm slide transparencies were taken of the plastron and carapace of most tortoises (Berry, 1984, 1990). These slides document the presence and extent of shell lesions.

Data were also available from necropsies of ill and dying tortoises salvaged from or adjacent to the plots (Jacobson et al., 1991, 1994; J. Klaassen, pers. comm.) from the

ELISA tests of tortoises in the research program on epidemiology of URTD at the DTNA (Brown et al., 1994b) and from mortality rates of tortoises in the health profile research program at the DTNA (Christopher et al., 1993). The latter program began in May 1989 with ten adult males and ten adult female tortoises, each fitted with radio transmitters. The tortoises were monitored four times annually (Christopher et al., 1993). Over the next 35 months—through March 1992—as tortoises died, new individuals were added to the program.

RESULTS

The DTNA

In the 13 years between 1979 and 1992, both the total population and the adult component of the tortoise population experienced statistically significant declines in densities (Figure 2). The total population density, which included all sizes of tortoises, steadily decreased 76%, from a high of 149 tortoises/km² (95% CI = 115–195) in 1979 to a low of 18 tortoises/km² (95% CI = 8–44) in 1992. The pattern of decline of adults differed. First, the adult population component rose in density from 59 tortoises/km² (95% CI = 43–78) in 1979 to 92 tortoises/km² (95% CI = 71–119) in 1982 as a result of recruitment of immature tortoises into the adult size class (Berry, 1990). However, the adult component then steadily declined to 61 tortoises/km² (95% CI = 47–79) in 1988 and thence to 6 adults/km² (95% CI = 2–15) in 1992. The 13-year decline resulted in a 90% loss of adults, during which the total of number of tortoises registered per survey year declined from 189 to 25 individuals.

The deaths of tortoises and the population declines are attributable to several causes (Berry, 1990), including predation by common ravens on the juvenile and small immature size classes. However, between 1988 and 1992 the declines of adults are clearly attributable to URTD caused by *M. agassizii*. The evidence is from several sources. Prior to 1988 wild, free-ranging tortoises at the DTNA and other long-term tortoise study plots in California were not observed with signs of URTD, and very few were observed with signs of illness or in a dying state (Berry and Nicholson, 1984; Berry et al., 1986). In contrast, many ill, dying, and dead tortoises (remains of animals dead <2 years), most of which were previously marked during censuses, were found on the DTNA plot in 1988, 1989, and 1990, and many dead animals were discovered in 1992 (Berry, unpubl. data). Ill tortoises showed classic signs of URTD (Jacobson et al., 1991; Brown et al., 1994a). In May 1989, 12 tortoises (11 males and 1 female), all of which showed signs of advanced and chronic URTD, were removed from the DTNA for observation and necropsies during the initial research on URTD (Jacobson et al., 1991). The tortoises had chronic inflammatory changes in the upper respiratory tract. A mycoplasma-like organism was seen on the surfaces of the macroepithelial cells (Jacobson et al., 1991). Subsequently, a transmission research program demonstrated that *M. agassizii* was the causative pathogen (Brown et al., 1994a).

Tortoises with signs of URTD were not confined to a single part of the DTNA but were present throughout the DTNA and in adjacent areas of the Fremont Valley and Rand Mountains (Knowles, 1989; Berry, unpubl. data). In spring 1989, 13 sample plots (1.3–2.6 km² each) were established in the 100 km² DTNA and in adjacent lands within the Fremont Valley and Rand Mountains to determine distribution and frequency of ill tortoises (Knowles, 1989). The sample plots totaled 31.2 km². Four hundred sixty-eight live tortoises were found, of which 202 (43%) showed signs of URTD. From 9.4% to 66.7% of tortoises on 12 of the 13 sample plots showed signs of URTD.

The DTNA experienced a catastrophic epidemic that is not yet over. In 1992 from 12 to 14 adult tortoises in the research program for epidemiology of URTD were tested for antibodies to *M. agassizii* (Brown et al., 1994b) using the ELISA test (Schumacher et al., 1993). The tortoises were tested during late winter, spring, summer, and fall and were in a study area immediately adjacent to the long-term plot. From 25 to 38 percent of the tortoises in the four seasonal samples tested positive for *M. agassizii*, indicating that the tortoises had been exposed to the pathogen, or were currently ill, or had been ill and were recovered. Between 1993 and 1995, from 7 to 62% of the tortoises in the four samples taken each year have produced positive ELISA

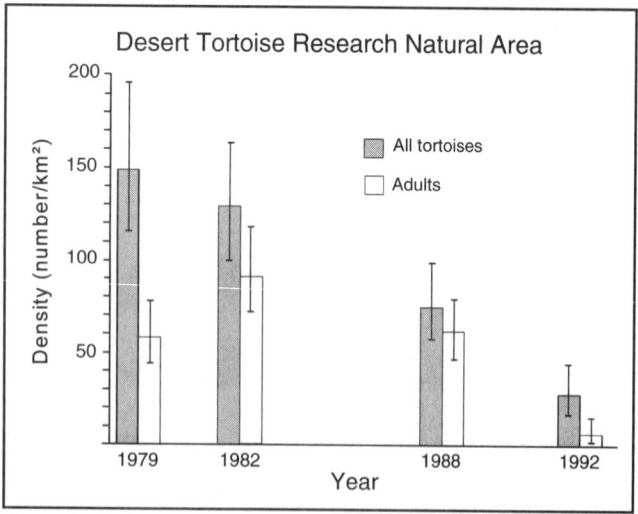

Figure 2. Estimates of population densities of desert tortoises at the Desert Tortoise Research Natural Area in Kern County, California in 1979, 1982, 1988, and 1992. Density estimates are presented for all sizes of tortoises and for the adult tortoises (≥180 mm carapace length at midline). The histogram shows the midpoint of the density estimates, and the brackets enclose the 95% Confidence Intervals for the population estimates.

tests, indicating that the population is in a chronic disease state (M. B. Brown et al., pers. comm.).

Of the 27 tortoises in the health profile research program between May 1989 and March 1992, six died between late 1989 and mid-1991. An additional 11 tortoises disappeared and have not been found as of October 1995. The death rate for adults is abnormally high, compared to approximately 2% per year in stable populations (Turner et al., 1987). The disappearance rate is also high and unusual for tortoises fitted with radio transmitters. Many of the missing animals should be considered dead.

Chuckwalla Bench ACEC

Between 1979 and 1992 both the total population and the adult component of the tortoise population exhibited statistically significant declines (Figure 3). The total population density, which included all sizes of tortoises, steadily decreased from a high of 223 tortoises/km² (95% CI = 177–283) in 1979 to a low of 64 tortoises/km² (95% CI = 46–92) in 1988 (Berry, 1990). The 1992 census figures were slightly higher but not significantly different from the figures recorded for 1988: 70 tortoises/km² (95% CI = 48–102). The pattern of decline of adults was similar. There were no statistically significant differences in the adult population component in the 1979 and 1982 censuses; in 1979 density estimates were 75 tortoises/km² (95% CI = 56–98), whereas in 1982 estimates were 87 tortoises/km² (95% CI = 68–112). By 1988 census figures showed statistically significant declines with 42 tortoises/km² (95% CI = 29–62). The 1992 estimates were lower still, 33 adults/km² (95% CI = 22–49), but not significantly different from the 1988 figures.

During the 13-year time frame, the total number of tortoises registered per survey year on the study site also declined, from 265 individuals in 1979 and 262 in 1982 (Berry, 1990) to 107 individuals in 1992 (Berry, unpubl. data). Of considerable concern is the differential loss of adult females. In 1979, 74 adult females and 79 adult males were registered. The numbers of registered tortoises increased to 98 adult females and 80 adult males in 1982 and then declined to 42 adult females and 44 adult males in 1988. By 1992 female numbers had further declined to 26 individuals, while male numbers remained similar at 42. As of mid-1992 (the end of the 1992 field survey season), deaths of adults continued to occur at a rate higher than the 2% annualized death rate estimated for stable populations in the Mojave Desert (Turner et al., 1987). The remains of 20 adults, all of which had been captured in previous years, were found during the 1992 survey. Of the 20, eight had died within the last year and ten had died within the last one to two years. Of the 20 adults, 15 were females.

The population decline appears to be linked to the appearance of shell lesions on the tortoises. In a retrospective analysis of the 35 mm slides taken during surveys conducted between 1979 and 1990, the disease was evident in 1979 but affected only 56% of the tortoises and was generally of limited extent (mild) on the shell (Jacobson et al., 1994). Between 1982 and 1988 the percentage of tortoises affected increased to 90%, and the severity of the lesions on the shells likewise increased. The lesions, which were on the scutes of the plastron and carapace and on the scales of the forelimbs, consisted of white-gray or sometimes orange flaky areas. They appeared at the seams, spreading outward in irregular patterns onto the scutes. In severe cases, bone was exposed. The lesions were described as cutaneous dyskeratosis, but the exact cause could not be determined. The locations on the shell and body and histology of the lesions were suggestive of either a deficiency disease or toxicosis. Both deficiency diseases and environmental toxicants are known to affect keratin in other vertebrates. A wide variety of toxicants are responsible for lesions in the epidermal hard parts of domestic hoofstock, for example (Blood et al., 1989).

Subsequent to the study of the shell and limb lesions in tortoises at the Chuckwalla Bench, 32 ill or damaged tortoises (including some with similar shell lesions) were salvaged for necropsy from the Mojave and Colorado deserts of California and the Sonoran Desert of Arizona (Homer et al., 1994, 1996a, 1996b). The salvaged tortoises with cutaneous dyskeratosis had elevated concentrations of toxicants in the liver, kidney, or plasma (e.g., barium, calcium, cadmium, chromium, magnesium, molybdenum, nickel, phthalates, and selenium in plasma), and/or nutritional deficiencies (e.g., low copper, zinc, selenium, plasma vitamin

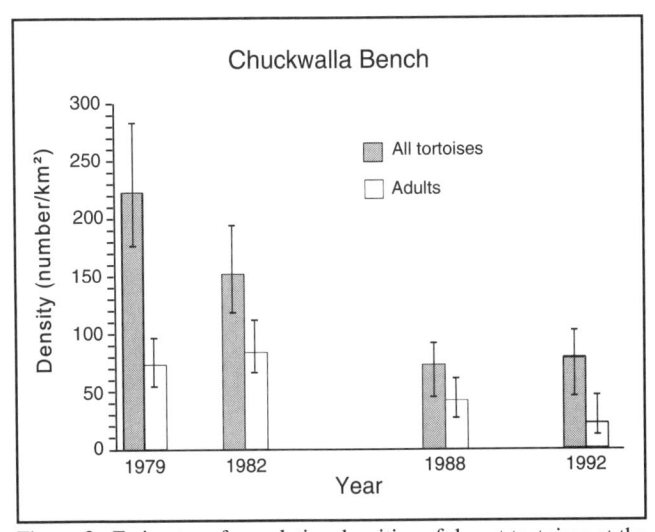

Figure 3. Estimates of population densities of desert tortoises at the Chuckwalla Bench Area of Critical Environmental Concern in Riverside County, California in 1979, 1982, 1988, and 1992. Density estimates are presented for all sizes of tortoises and for the adult tortoises (≥180 mm carapace length at midline). The histogram shows the midpoint of the density estimates, and the brackets enclose the 95% Confidence Intervals for the population estimates.

A). The toxicants and/or nutritional deficiencies may be the cause of the shell disease. Tortoises with cutaneous dyskeratosis may be more vulnerable to bacterial and fungal infections, other diseases, and predation because of the thin scutes and loss of laminae.

DISCUSSION

Desert tortoises are slow-maturing animals that require 15–20 years to reach reproductive maturity (Woodbury and Hardy, 1948). Once reproductive maturity is reached, wild females generally produce relatively small and few clutches of eggs (Turner et al., 1986, 1987; Henen, 1994). During a six-year study of egg production in the eastern Mojave Desert, females produced from 0 to 3 clutches per year. Mean clutch sizes ranged from 3.53 ±0.26 to 5.15 ±0.34 eggs and clutch frequency from 1.06 ±0.06 to 1.89 ±0.11 per year. Eggs and hatchlings are vulnerable to many predators and pre-adult mortality is generally high (Turner et al., 1987). However, under normal conditions, adult survivorship is about 98% per year. Populations cannot rapidly recover from catastrophic losses of adults, such as the 90% decline experienced at the DTNA or the 50–60% losses at the Chuckwalla Bench because recruitment of young adults requires so many years. These populations face serious threat of extinction (USFWS, 1994). According to analyses prepared by the Desert Tortoise Recovery Team, desert tortoise populations that have declined to 4 adults/km² would require three doublings, or 210 years, to reach a density of 31 adults/km²—if the population is able to grow at an average rate of 1% per year (USFWS, 1994). Using these projections, the adult population at the DTNA would require 280 years to reach the 1979 level of 61 adults/km². One of the more serious aspects of the population declines for the DTNA and the Chuckwalla Bench is that the declines may not have reached the lowest point and recovery may not be underway. Furthermore, the long-term effects of the two diseases on reproduction, viability of eggs, and general health of young are not yet known.

One of the diseases, URTD, is highly infectious (Brown et al., 1994a) and has demonstrated its potential for producing catastrophic impacts on populations at the DTNA. Captive tortoises are implicated in the spread of this disease to wild populations of both desert and gopher tortoises, *G. polyphemus* (Jacobson, 1993a; Jacobson et al., 1995). In the last five years the number of desert tortoise populations with clinical signs of URTD has increased and the disease appears to be spreading. Wild tortoises that have positive ELISA tests and show clinical signs of disease have been identified throughout the Mojave Desert in California (Brown et al., 1994b; Homer et al., 1994), Nevada (Jacobson et al., 1995), northern Arizona (Dickinson et al., 1995), and Utah (Dickinson et al, 1995; Jacobson et al., 1991).

In California, government agencies have taken measures to prevent release of captive turtles and tortoises since the late 1970s (e.g., St. Amant, 1979, 1980). In 1993 more than 7,500 copies of a booklet with information about wild and captive desert tortoises, URTD, and adoption programs for captives (Berry, 1993) were distributed to people perceived to be authorities on management of wild and captive tortoises (government agencies, librarians, humane societies, police departments and county sheriffs, and veterinarians). The booklet focuses on why captive tortoises should not be released, what one should do when encountering desert tortoises in wild settings, and whom to contact when a tortoise is found in a city or town. A four-page brochure that addresses scientific and medical aspects of URTD, including treatment and guidelines for care and husbandry of tortoises, (Jacobson, 1993b) was also distributed with the booklet. These materials were prepared and distributed not only to educate the public but also to protect the considerable investment by both government and the Desert Tortoise Preserve Committee in existing reserves and legally designated Critical Habitat (USFWS, 1994) for the desert tortoise.

Will education reduce the threat of captive releases and better protect the tortoise? Education is likely to reduce but not entirely eliminate the threat. Data are available on behavior of the general public from the monitoring reports of naturalists at the DTNA (Howland, 1989; Ginn, 1990; Jennings, 1992; Ogg and Gallant, 1992; Kidd, 1993; Boland, 1994, 1995). Since spring 1989 the Desert Tortoise Preserve Committee and the USBLM have sponsored naturalists at the DTNA. Naturalists, who are generally present five to seven days per week for three months in spring at the Interpretive Center, a single site on the 57.5 km fenced boundary of the reserve, have reported that visitors arrive from throughout the state with the intention of releasing captives for various reasons. These reasons include the belief that the DTNA is the appropriate place to release tortoises or that public officials have told them to do so. Some of these captives showed signs of URTD. The naturalists also reported that visitors bring wild tortoises from nearby areas to the DTNA, believing it to be a place that is safe from the hazards of vehicles and other land uses. The 31 illegal incidents summarized in Table 1 occurred at a rate of 2.4 incidents/1000 visitors over a seven-year period. The documented incidents are a minimum number; they represent only incidents of which the naturalists were aware and only at a single point along the DTNA boundary. Certainly, such illegal activities occur more widely in the Southwest (USFWS, 1994).

The second disease, cutaneous dyskeratosis, is also widespread in desert tortoise populations (Berry, unpubl. data; Homer et al., 1994, 1996a, 1996b), with some populations more affected than others. Cutaneous dyskeratosis may have multiple causes and be associated with the presence of environmental toxicants and/or nutritional deficiencies.

TABLE 1
Number of attempts to release captive and illegally translocated desert tortoises at or adjacent to the Desert Tortoise Research Natural Area, eastern Kern County, California, between 1989 and 1995.

Year	Number of incidents regarding tortoises: Captive releases	Translocations	Number of illegal incidents per 1000 visitors	Reference
1989	5	0	2	Howland, 1989
1990	1	4	5	Ginn, 1990
1991	2	2	2	Jennings, 1992
1992	3	4	4	Ogg and Gallant, 1992
1993	0	3	1	Kidd, 1993
1994	2	2	2	Boland, 1994
1995	1	2	1	Boland, 1995
Totals	14	17		

Field-workers and research scientists need to be taught to identify and describe the lesions. The sources of the environmental toxicants need to be identified, and the link of toxicants to cutaneous dyskeratosis and to the high mortality rates needs to be established. Ultimately, the cause(s) of the disease must be identified and actions taken to reduce the deaths in wild populations.

Recommendations

1. Because our knowledge of infectious diseases in tortoises is limited (Jacobson, 1993a), research scientists and government biologists should take precautions to prevent transmission of known and unidentified diseases from one tortoise to another in the laboratory and field. The field-worker should use a separate pair of disposable gloves for each tortoise; sterilize equipment (e.g., calipers, scales) after use with each animal; sterilize probes used to measure or view burrows after use at each burrow; and ensure that the tortoise does not touch or contaminate the field worker's clothing, day pack, or other equipment. Equipment should be sterilized or properly disinfected between uses at different sites. If the field-worker is visiting more than one study site, consideration should be given to sterilizing clothing and shoes before traveling to the second site. Where an infectious disease is known to occur in a population, protocols must be established to prevent spread to unexposed populations (including cleaning field vehicles and camping equipment). Sites where infectious diseases are known to occur should be visited last on field trips.

2. Field-workers should keep detailed records on the health of each wild tortoise in research programs, including 35 mm slides of both healthy and ill individuals.

3. Ill, dying, and recently dead (but not autolyzed) wild tortoises should be salvaged for necropsies (especially if the tortoise is ill or is a victim of trauma from a vehicle or predator). Where possible, necropsies should be performed by a licensed veterinary pathologist, or a professional pathologist with expertise in reptile pathology. A complete necropsy can provide invaluable information on diseases of tortoises.

4. Legally designated "Natural Areas" and reserves can appear as attractive, natural, and safe places for release of unwanted captive or illegally collected tortoises. Government employees, research scientists, and the general public must be educated about the hazards of releasing captive tortoises or translocating wild tortoises to a reserve. As a minimum precautionary measure, Natural Areas and reserves should be posted with signs to reduce the likelihood of release. Costs for patrols by recreation specialists and law enforcement personnel should be included in management plans.

5. Persons with unwanted captive tortoises must have ready access to facilities (e.g., adoption centers) or groups that will accept and properly care for the unwanted animals. Such facilities and organizations serve as deterrents to illegal releases.

Acknowledgments

C. Knowles, P. Knowles, and P. Gould contributed to the fieldwork at the DTNA study site, and A. P. Woodman, J. Howland, and T. Shields made significant contributions at the Chuckwalla Bench study site. The following people provided constructive comments on the manuscript: B. Homer, M. Brown, V. Dickinson, E. R. Jacobson, and J. Oldemeyer. The USBLM at Riverside, California supported all long-term research efforts on desert tortoise study plots. Research on pathogenesis and epidemiology of URTD was supported by USBLM contracts to E. R. Jacobson at the University of

Florida (Contract No. CA-950-CT9-28) and M. B. Brown (Contract No. B950-C2-0046), respectively. Research on cutaneous dyskeratosis was supported through USBLM contracts to E. R. Jacobson and T. J. Wronski (No. CA951-CT0-046) and to B. Homer and E. R. Jacobson (No. CA 950-C1-0062), as well as a National Biological Service Research Work Order to B. Homer and E. R. Jacobson.

LITERATURE CITED

Berry, K. H. 1984. A description and comparison of field methods used in studying and censusing desert tortoises. Appendix 2. *In* K. H. Berry (ed.), The Status of the Desert Tortoise (*Gopherus agassizii*) in the United States. Desert Tortoise Council report to U.S. Fish and Wildlife Service, Order No. 11310-0083-81, Sacramento, California.

Berry, K. H. 1990. The status of the desert tortoise (*Gopherus agassizii*) in California in 1989. Draft report to the U. S. Fish and Wildlife Service, Portland, Oregon.

Berry, K. H. 1993. Answering questions about desert tortoises: A guide for people who work with the public in California. Report No. BLM-CA-PT-93-003-6840, U.S. Bureau of Land Management and California Department of Parks and Recreation. 43 pp.

Berry, K. H. and L. L. Nicholson. 1984. A summary of human activities and their impacts on desert tortoise populations and habitat in California. Chapter 3. *In* K. H. Berry (ed.), The Status of the Desert Tortoise (*Gopherus agassizii*) in the United States. Desert Tortoise Council report to U.S. Fish and Wildlife Service, Order No. 11310-0083-81, Sacramento, California.

Berry, K. H., T. Shields, A. P. Woodman, T. Campbell, J. Roberson, K. Bohuski, and A. Karl. 1986. Changes in desert tortoise populations at the Desert Tortoise Research Natural Area between 1979 and 1985. Proc. Desert Tortoise Council Symp. 1986:100–123.

Blood, D. C., O. M. Radostits, J. H. Arundel, and C. C. Gay. 1989. Veterinary Medicine. A Textbook of the Diseases of Cattle, Sheep, Pigs, Goats, and Horses. 7th ed. Bailliere Tindall, London. 1502 pp.

Boland, C. 1994. Observations and activities of the naturalists at the Desert Tortoise Research Natural Area, Kern County, California: 1 March through 31 May 1994. Prepared for the Desert Tortoise Preserve Committee, Inc., in cooperation with the U.S. Bureau of Land Management, Riverside, California. 39 pp.

Boland, C. 1995. Observations and activities of the naturalists at the Desert Tortoise Research Natural Area, Kern County, California: 1 March through 31 May 1995. Prepared for the Desert Tortoise Preserve Committee, Inc., in cooperation with the U.S. Bureau of Land Management, Riverside, California. 45 pp.

Brown, M. B., I. M. Schumacher, P. A. Klein, K. Harris, T. Correll, and E. R. Jacobson. 1994a. *Mycoplasma agassizii* causes upper respiratory tract disease in the desert tortoise. Infection and Immunity 62(10):4580–4586.

Brown, M. B., P. A. Klein, I. M. Schumacher, and K. H. Berry. 1994b. Health profiles of free-ranging desert tortoises in California: Results of a two-year study of serological testing for antibody to *Mycoplasma agassizii*. Final Report. U. S. Bureau of Land Management, Contract. No. B950-C3-0046, Riverside, California. 54 pp.

Christopher, M. M., I. Wallis, K. A. Nagy, B. T. Henen, C. C. Peterson, B. Wilson, C. Meienberger, and I. Girard. 1993. Laboratory health profiles of free-ranging desert tortoises in California: Interpretation of physiologic and pathologic alterations (March 1992–October 1992). Report to the U.S. Dept. of the Interior, Bureau of Land Management, Contract No. B950-C1-0060, Riverside, California.

Christopher, M., K. A. Nagy, I. Wallis, and K. H. Berry. 1997. Laboratory health profiles of desert tortoises in the Mojave Desert: A model for health status evaluation of chelonian populations. *In* J. Van Abbema (ed.), Proceedings: Conservation, Restoration, and Management of Tortoises and Turtles—An International Conference, pp. 76-82. July 1993, State University of New York, Purchase. New York Turtle and Tortoise Society, New York.

Dickinson, V. M., T. Duck, C. R. Schwalbe, and J. L. Jarchow. 1995. Health status of free-ranging Mojave desert tortoises in Utah and Arizona. Arizona Game and Fish Department Tech. Rept. 21, Phoenix. 70 pp.

Fowler, M. E. 1977. Respiratory disease in desert tortoises. *In* Annual Proceedings of the American Association of Zoo Veterinarians, pp. 79–99.

Ginn, S. 1990. Observations and activities of the naturalist for the Desert Tortoise Natural Area, Kern County, California: March 18–June 2, 1990. Report. to the Desert Tortoise Preserve Committee, Ridgecrest, California and the U. S. Bureau of Land Management, Riverside, California. 37 pp.

Henen, B. T. 1994. Seasonal and annual energy and water budgets of female desert tortoises (*Xerobates agassizii*) at Goffs, California. Ph.D. dissertation, University of California, Los Angeles.

Homer, B. L., K. H. Berry, M. M. Christopher, M. B. Brown, and E. R. Jacobson. 1994. Necropsies of desert tortoises from the Mojave and Colorado deserts of California and the Sonoran Desert of Arizona. Final report to U.S. Dept. of the Interior, Bureau of Land Management, Contract No. B950-C1-0062, Riverside, California.

Homer, B. L., K. H. Berry, and E. R. Jacobson. 1996a. Necropsies of eighteen desert tortoises from the Mojave and Colorado deserts of California: 1994–1995. Final Report for U.S. Dept. of Interior, National Biological Service Work Order No. 131. 120 pp.

Homer, B. L., K. H. Berry, F. Ross, C. Reggiardo, and E. R. Jacobson. 1996b. Potentially toxic metals and minerals in liver and kidney of desert tortoises in California. *In* Abstracts from the Twenty-first Annual Meeting and Symposium of the Desert Tortoise Council, pp 19–20. Held 29 March–1 April 1996, Las Vegas, Nevada.

Howland, J. 1989. Observations and activities of the naturalist for the Desert Tortoise Natural Area, Kern County, California: March 12–July 12, 1989. Report from the Desert Tortoise Preserve Committee, Inc., Ridgecrest, California to U.S. Bureau of Land Management, Contract No. CA950-CT9-44, Riverside, California. 59 pp.

Jacobson, E. R. 1993a. Implications of infectious diseases for captive propagation and introduction programs of threatened/endangered reptiles. J. Zoo Wildl. Med. 24(3):245–255.

Jacobson, E. R. 1993b. The desert tortoise and upper respiratory tract disease. Prepared for the Desert Tortoise Preserve Committee, Inc., and U.S. Bureau of Land Management, Report No. BLM-CA-PT-93-004-6840, Riverside, California. 4 pp.

Jacobson, E. R. 1994. Causes of mortality and disease in tortoises: A review. J. Zoo Wildl. Med. 25(1):2–17.

Jacobson, E. R., J. M. Gaskin, M. B. Brown, R. K. Harris, C. H. Gardiner, J. L. LaPointe, H. P. Adams, and C. Reggiardo. 1991. Chronic upper respiratory tract disease of free-ranging desert tortoises (*Xerobates agassizii*). J. Wildl. Dis. 27(2):296–316.

Jacobson, E. R., T. J. Wronski, J. Schumacher, C. Reggiardo, and K. H. Berry. 1994. Cutaneous dyskeratosis in free-ranging desert tortoises, *Gopherus agassizii*, in the Colorado Desert of Southern California. J. Zoo Wildl. Med. 25(1):68–81.

Jacobson, E. R., M. B. Brown, I. M. Schumacher, B. R. Collins, R. K. Harris, and P. A. Klein. 1995. Mycoplasmosis and the desert tortoise (*Gopherus agassizii*) in Las Vegas Valley, Nevada. Chelon. Conserv. Biol. 1(4):279–284.

Jennings, W. B. 1992. Observations and activities of the naturalists for the Desert Tortoise Natural Area, Kern County, California: March 2–May 27, 1991. Report to the Desert Tortoise Preserve Committee, Inc., Ridgecrest, California, in cooperation with the U.S. Bureau of Land Management, Grant No. B950-A1-0034, Riverside, California. 40 pp.

Kidd, J. 1993. Observations and activities of the naturalists at the Desert Tortoise Research Natural Area, Kern County, California: 1 March through 31 May 1993. Prepared for the Desert Tortoise Preserve Committee, Inc., San Bernardino, California, in cooperation with the U.S. Bureau of Land Management, Riverside, California.

Knowles, C. 1989. A survey for diseased desert tortoises in and near the Desert Tortoise Natural Area. Spring 1989. Report for the U.S. Bureau of Land Management, Contract No. CA950-CT9-23, Riverside, California. 26 pp.

Ogg, S. and R. Gallant. 1992. Observations and activities of the naturalists for the Desert Tortoise Natural Area, Kern County, California: 3 March–31 May, 1992. Report to the Desert Tortoise Preserve Committee, Inc., San Bernardino County, California, in cooperation with the U.S. Bureau of Land Management, Grant No. B950-A1-0034, Riverside, California. 53 pp.

Overton, W. C. 1971. Estimating the numbers of animals in wildlife populations. *In* R. G. Giles (ed.), Wildlife Management Techniques, pp. 403–456. The Wildlife Society, Washington, D.C.

Schumacher, I. M., M. B. Brown, E. R. Jacobson, B. R. Collins, and P. A. Klein. 1993. Detection of antibodies to a pathogenic mycoplasma in desert tortoises (*Gopherus agassizii*) with upper respiratory tract disease. J. Clin. Microbiol. 31:1454–1460.

Snipes, K. P. and E. L. Biberstein. 1982. *Pasteurella testudinis* sp. nov.: A parasite of desert tortoises (*Gopherus agassizi*). International Journal of Systematic Bacteriology 32(2):201–210.

St. Amant, J. 1977. State Report—California. *In* M. Trotter (ed.), Proc. 1977 Symposium of the Desert Tortoise Council, pp. 21–22. Desert Tortoise Council, San Diego, California.

St. Amant, J. 1979. State Report—California. *In* E. St. Amant (ed.), Proc. 1979 Symposium of the Desert Tortoise Council, pp. 75–77. Desert Tortoise Council, Long Beach, California.

St. Amant, J. 1980. State Report—California. *In* K. A. Hashagen (ed.), Proc. 1980 Symposium of the Desert Tortoise Council, pp. 68–69. Desert Tortoise Council, Long Beach, California.

Swingland, I. R. and M. W. Klemens (eds.). 1989. The Conservation Biology of Tortoises. Occasional Papers of the IUCN Species Survival Commission (SSC) No. 5. IUCN, Gland, Switzerland. iv + 202 pp.

Turner, F. B., K. H. Berry, D. C. Randall, and G. C. White. 1987. Population ecology of the desert tortoise at Goffs, California, 1983–1986. Report to Southern California Edison Co., Rosemead, California. 101 pp.

Turner, F. B., P. Hayden, B. L. Burge, and J. B. Roberson. 1986. Egg production by the desert tortoise (*Gopherus agassizii*) in California. Herpetologica 42:93–104.

U.S. Bureau of Land Management. 1980. The California Desert Conservation Area Plan. U.S. Dept. of the Interior, Bureau of Land Management, Desert District, Riverside, California. 173 pp.

U.S. Bureau of Land Management. 1986. Chuckwalla Bench Area of Critical Environmental Concern: Management Plan and Environmental Assessment. U.S. Dept. of the Interior, Bureau of Land Management, California Desert District, Indio Resource Area, California. 40 pp. + appendices.

U.S. Bureau of Land Management and California Dept. of Fish and Game. 1988. A Sikes Act management plan for the Desert Tortoise Research Natural Area and Area of Critical Environmental Concern. U. S. Dept. of the Interior, Bureau of Land Management, California Desert District, Ridgecrest Resource Area, California. 43 pp. + unpaginated appendices.

U.S. Fish and Wildlife Service. 1994. Desert Tortoise (Mojave Population) Recovery Plan. U.S. Dept. of the Interior, Fish and Wildlife Service, Portland, Oregon. 73 pp. + appendices.

Woodbury, A. M. and R. Hardy. 1948. Studies of the desert tortoise, *Gopherus agassizi*. Ecol. Monogr. 81:146–200.

Survivorship of Hatchling Gopher Tortoises in North-Central Florida

LORA L. SMITH

Department of Wildlife Ecology and Conservation, University of Florida, Gainesville, FL 32611, USA
[e-mail: angonoka@grove.ufl.edu]

ABSTRACT: Gopher tortoises, *Gopherus polyphemus*, are declining in number throughout their range as a result of habitat degradation and urbanization. Under natural conditions, the low reproductive potential and low hatchling survival of the gopher tortoise is compensated by a long life span, low adult mortality, and the persistence of extensive, unchanging habitat. Human activities have altered habitat and predator-prey relationships. Although raccoons, *Procyon lotor*, historically probably had little effect on gopher tortoise populations, raccoon predation may presently play a significant role in limiting gopher tortoise numbers.

Hatchling survivorship in a north-central Florida gopher tortoise population was studied using a technique that employed lightweight metal tags and a metal detector to locate hatchlings. Survivorship of hatchlings within protective enclosures was compared to that of unprotected nests. Within the protective enclosures, 43% of the hatchlings released were alive after 280 days, compared to less than 20% from unprotected nests. Seven of the nine recovered dead hatchlings had been killed by a mammalian predator. Predation occurred even at protected nests, indicating that it is a very significant factor in hatchling gopher tortoise mortality.

Gopher tortoise, *Gopherus polyphemus*, numbers are estimated to have declined by 80% in the past 100 years (Auffenberg and Franz, 1982), largely as a result of habitat alteration (Means, 1986; Diemer, 1986). Gopher tortoises (like most testudinids) are long-lived and slow to mature, and produce a single, small clutch of eggs annually. These life history constraints limit the ability of tortoise populations to recover from human and other impacts.

Many gopher tortoise populations are assumed to have a low natural rate of recruitment because of high mortality of eggs and juveniles (Alford, 1980; Landers et al., 1980; Marshall, 1987). A high rate of predation on juvenile tortoises (1–4 years old) was documented in a west-central Florida population (Wilson, 1991). However, estimates of hatchling mortality have usually been based on circumstantial evidence, such as a scarcity of small burrows (Alford, 1980) or predator disturbance to burrows (Wright, 1982). In a 1990 telemetry study in north-central Florida, only one of six hatchlings was confirmed to be alive 38 days after hatching (Smith, 1992). Predators of hatchling and juvenile gopher tortoises include eastern coachwhip (*Masticophis flagellum*), eastern diamondback rattlesnake (*Crotalus adamanteus*), eastern indigo snake (*Drymarchon corais couperi*), raccoon (*Procyon lotor*), gray fox (*Urocyon cinereoargenteus*), opossum (*Didelphis virginiana*), striped skunk (*Mephitis mephitis*) (Douglass and Winegarner, 1977), and red-tailed hawk (*Buteo jamaicensis*) (Fitzpatrick and Woolfenden, 1978).

In this study, a technique was developed to locate hatchling gopher tortoises using lightweight metal tags and a metal detector. The technique was used in a field experiment designed to compare hatchling survivorship at nests protected from predators to that at unprotected nests.

TABLE 1

Status of 36 gopher tortoise hatchlings at protected and unprotected nests after 280 days at the Ordway Preserve, Putnam County, Florida. Treatment 1 = low enclosures that retained hatchlings and did not exclude predators; Treatment 2 = enclosures that retained hatchlings and excluded predators. Percent of total is indicated in parentheses.

No. of hatchlings	Treatment 1	Treatment 2	Control
Released	16	7	13
Confirmed dead	4 (25.0)	3 (42.8)	2 (15.4)
Unaccounted for	9 (56.2)	1 (14.3)	10 (79.9)
Confirmed alive at completion	3 (18.8)	3 (42.8)	1 (7.7)

METHODS

The study was conducted on the Katharine Ordway Preserve-Carl S. Swisher Memorial Sanctuary (hereafter referred to as the Ordway Preserve) in Putnam County, Florida (29°41′ N, 82°00′ W). The dominant plant community on the upland ridges is sandhill with an overstory of longleaf pine (*Pinus palustris*) and turkey oak (*Quercus laevis*), and an herbaceous cover of wiregrass (*Aristida stricta*), pineywoods dropseed (*Sporobolus junceus*), and a variety of legumes (Fabaceae). Portions of the ridges are in various "old field" successional stages as a result of past farming practices.

Hatchlings were followed using metal tags and a Garrett Master Hunter 7X metal detector (KELLYCO Metal Detector Distributors, Winter Springs, Florida). Tags were made from 12 × 12 cm sheets of aluminum foil folded into 2 × 3 cm tags that weighed approximately 1 g (less than 5% of the hatchling's body weight). The tags could be detected up to 30 cm below the soil. Tags were painted green to blend with ground cover vegetation and attached to vertebral scutes 1–3 with epoxy gel. Enamel paint was used to mark individual hatchlings.

To assess hatchling survivorship, 36 hatchlings from nine nests received one of three experimental treatments (Table 1). Three nests were enclosed in low fences that retained the hatchlings and did not exclude predators (Treatment 1), three nests were enclosed in fences designed to retain hatchlings and exclude predators (Treatment 2), and the remaining three nests were not fenced (control).

The low enclosures (Treatment 1) were 30 m square with the nest located at the center. The enclosures were constructed from 25 cm high × 2.5 m long strips of Masonite®, which were buried 10 cm below ground and installed end-to-end to form the 30 m square enclosure.

Predator exclusion fences (Treatment 2) were also 30 m square with the nest at the center. Chicken wire fences were constructed 30 cm high with wooden posts at the four corners and metal support posts placed every 10 m. Lawn edging (strips of plastic 15 cm high × 60 cm long) was buried 10 cm deep along the fence line to prevent hatchlings from digging under the fence. Wire, strung along the top of the fence at 45 cm above the ground and outside the fence at 15 cm above the ground, was electrified with an electric fence controller (Electro Line Products, Rochester, Minnesota) and a 6 volt battery.

Immediately upon emergence, the hatchlings were tagged and released above the nest. Each animal was located with the metal detector at least twice a day (morning and evening) for two weeks after release and three days a week thereafter. Hatchlings were followed for periods of 1–280 days.

RESULTS AND DISCUSSION

Hatchling survivorship after 280 days was 42.8% at Treatment 2 nests compared to 18.8% at Treatment 1 nests and 7.7% at control nests (Figure 1). Survivorship was lower than expected at protected nests (Treatment 2) because the fences failed to exclude all predators, and three of the seven hatchlings from these nests were killed (Table 1). The first hatchling was killed by fire ants, *Solenopsis geminata*, eight days after its release. The second hatchling was apparently killed and consumed by a raccoon. Raccoon tracks were observed along the outside of the fence, and the electrical unit had been knocked over and disconnected. The aluminum tag was recovered within 1 m of the hatchling's burrow, and it had impressions of teeth indicating that the predator was a mammal. The third hatchling was found outside the enclosure on day 272. The carapace was intact but the head and flesh on all four limbs had been removed. This tortoise was probably carried outside the pen by a bird. Another hatchling could not be located at a predator exclusion enclosure and may also have been taken by an avian predator. Fish crows, *Corvus ossifragus*, are common on the Ordway Preserve and may prey on hatchling and juvenile gopher tortoises. A closely related species, the common raven, *C. corax*, preys on young desert tortoises in the western United States (Berry, 1985; Berry et al., 1986; Woodman and Juarez, 1988). Other diurnal avian predators that occur on the Ordway Preserve are red-tailed hawk (*Buteo jamaicensis*), red-shouldered hawk (*B. lineatus*), American kestrel (*Falco sparverius*), northern harrier (*Circus cyaneus*), and American crow (*Corvus brachyrhynchos*) (Franz, 1989).

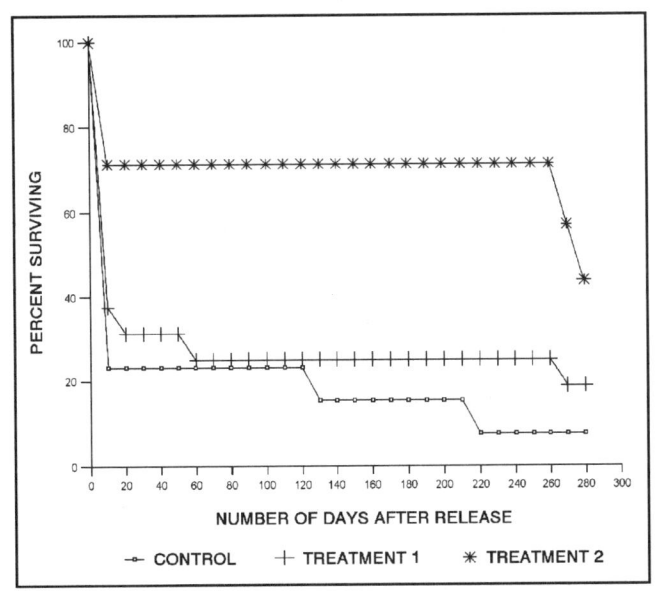

Figure 1. Survivorship of hatchling gopher tortoises at control, Treatment 1, and Treatment 2 nests on the Ordway Preserve, Putnam County, Florida. Control nests were not fenced, Treatment 1 nests were enclosed in low fences, and Treatment 2 nests were enclosed in predator exclusion fences. Percent survivorship was calculated using only individuals known to be alive at a given time.

Fifteen percent of hatchlings at control nests and 25% at Treatment 1 nests were killed by predators. Tags retrieved from dead hatchlings had tooth impressions of mammals. Predation probably was greater at Treatment 1 nests than at control nests because the hatchlings were concentrated within the 30 m square fenced area. Four hatchlings at Treatment 1 nests excavated burrows along the fence line, suggesting that they might have dispersed further if their movement had not been restricted by the fence.

At control and Treatment 1 nests, more than 50% of all hatchlings could not be located (Table 1). Although the fate of missing hatchlings was not confirmed, hatchling movement was restricted by the fences at Treatment 1, suggesting that predation rather than dispersal accounted for most of the lost animals. However, at least some of the missing hatchlings at the control nests may have dispersed beyond the search area. In previous studies of hatchling dispersal, the mean distance from the nest to a hatchling's first burrow ranged from 8.3 m (McRae et al., 1981) to 14.5 m (Smith, 1992). In this study, the area within a 60 m radius of the nest was carefully searched for hatchlings. However, the metal detector's vertical and horizontal range was limited; because the search coil had to be directly above the animal to detect the tag, the presence of thick ground cover vegetation may have resulted in failure to locate some hatchlings.

All of the missing hatchlings were lost in the first week after release. Hatchlings are probably particularly susceptible to predation in the first few days after they emerge from the nest, before they establish some form of shelter. In contrast, juvenile gopher tortoises (1–4 years old) at a central Florida site were found to be most vulnerable to predation during cool months, when more time is spent above ground basking (Wilson, 1991).

Conclusions

Despite the limitations imposed by the technique used to locate hatchlings in this study, it appears that survivorship of hatchling gopher tortoises on the Ordway Preserve is low. Hatchling predators included raccoons, unidentified avian predators, and fire ants. Of the nine hatchlings that were confirmed dead (all treatments combined), seven were killed by mammalian predators. Carnivorous mammals found on the Ordway Preserve are raccoon, opossum, gray fox, red fox, striped skunk, and feral cats and dogs. Raccoons have been observed to prey on juvenile and adult aquatic turtles on the Ordway Preserve (Walker, 1993) and probably are important predators of young gopher tortoises.

Human activities may favor an opportunistic predator such as the raccoon (Means, 1988). Overabundance of native species that have benefited from human-caused habitat alteration is increasingly recognized as a serious concern in habitat and species management (Garrott et al., 1993). Raccoons were historically hunted on the Ordway Preserve (R. Franz and T. Perry, pers. comm.) but are no longer removed. With the eradication of large carnivores in the southeastern United States, small predators such as raccoon and opossum probably have had an increased impact on the eggs and young of the gopher tortoise (Landers, 1980). Monitoring and control (through hunting and trapping) of mammals that prey on tortoise eggs and hatchlings may be necessary. Raccoon removal enhanced hatchling yield among turtles (*Chelydra serpentina*, *Chrysemys picta*, *Graptemys* spp., *Kinosternon flavescens*, and *Trionyx* spp.) in a study in Iowa; however, raccoons returned to the area within two years (Christiansen and Gallaway, 1984). A program to control raccoon numbers by trapping and removal would have to be continuous to be effective. In gopher tortoise populations, where recruitment is low, it may be necessary to monitor and control raccoons, protect nests from predators, and to headstart hatchlings in on-site enclosures.

Literature Cited

Alford, R. A. 1980. Population structure of *Gopherus polyphemus* in northern Florida. J. Herpetol. 14(2):177–82.

Auffenberg, W. and R. Franz. 1982. The status and distribution of the gopher tortoise (*Gopherus polyphemus*). *In* R. B. Bury (ed.), North American Tortoises: Conservation and Ecology, pp. 95–126. Wildl. Res. Rep. 12, U.S. Fish and Wildlife Service, Washington, D.C.

Berry, K. H. 1985. Avian predation on the desert tortoise (*Gopherus agassizii*) in California. Report from the U.S. Bureau of Land Management to Southern California Edison Company, Rosemead, California. 20 pp.

Berry, K. H., T. Shields, A. P. Woodman, T. Campbell, J. Roberson, K. Bohuski, and A. Karl. 1986. Changes in desert tortoise populations at the Desert Tortoise Research Natural Area between 1975 and 1985. U.S. Bureau of Land Management, Riverside, California. 46 pp.

Christiansen, J. L. and B. J. Gallaway. 1984. Raccoon removal, nesting success, and hatchling emergence in Iowa turtles with special reference to *Kinosternon flavescens* (Kinosternidae). The Southwestern Naturalist 29:343–348.

Diemer, J. E. 1986. The ecology and management of the gopher tortoise in the southeastern United States. Herpetologica 42(1):125–133.

Douglass, J. and C. E. Winegarner. 1977. Predators of eggs and young of the gopher tortoise, *Gopherus polyphemus*, in southern Florida. J. Herpetol. 11(2):236–238.

Fitzpatrick, J. W. and G. E. Woolfenden. 1978. Red-tailed hawk preys on juvenile gopher tortoise. Florida Field Natur. 6:49.

Franz, R. 1989. Annotated list of the vertebrates of the Katharine Ordway Preserve-Carl Swisher Memorial Sanctuary, Putnam County, Florida (1983–1989). Ordway Preserve Research Series, Report No. 2., Florida Museum of Natural History, Gainesville, Florida. 89 pp.

Garrott, R. A., P. J. White, and C. A. Vanderbilt White. 1993. Overabundance: An issue for conservation biologists? Conserv. Biol. 7:946–949.

Landers, J. L. 1980. Recent research on the gopher tortoise and its implications. *In* R. Franz and R. J. Bryant (eds.), The Dilemma of the Gopher Tortoise—Is There a Solution?, pp. 8–14. Proc. First Ann. Mtg., Gopher Tortoise Council, Florida State Museum.

Landers, J. L., J. A. Garner, and W. A. McRae. 1980. Reproduction of gopher tortoises (*Gopherus polyphemus*) in southwestern Georgia. Herpetologica 36(4):353–361.

Marshall, J. E. 1987. The effects of nest predation on hatchling gopher tortoises (*Gopherus polyphemus*). M.S. thesis, Univ. of Southern Alabama, Mobile, Alabama.

McRae, W. A., J. L. Landers, and J. A. Garner. 1981. Movement patterns and home range of the gopher tortoise. Amer. Midl. Natur. 106(1):165–179.

Means, D. B. 1986. John Muir's walk through the southeast—One hundred seventeen years later. *In* D. R. Jackson and R. J. Bryant (eds.), The Gopher Tortoise and its Community, pp. 1–3. Proc. Fifth Ann. Mtg., Gopher Tortoise Council, Florida State Museum.

Means, D. B. 1988. Management recommendations for the gopher tortoise in longleaf pine ecosystems. *In* C. K. Dodd, Jr. (ed.), Gopher Tortoise Habitat Management—Strategies and Options, pp. 41–56. Proc. Sixth Ann. Mtg., Gopher Tortoise Council, Florida Museum of Natural History.

Smith, L. L. 1992. Nesting ecology, female home range and activity patterns, and hatchling survivorship in the gopher tortoise (*Gopherus polyphemus*). M.S. thesis, Univ. of Florida, Gainesville, Florida.

Walker, R. S. 1993. Habitat use, movement, and density of the raccoon (*Procyon lotor*) in a wetland/sandhill mosaic of north-central Florida. M.S. thesis, Univ. of Florida, Gainesville, Florida.

Wilson, D. S. 1991. Estimates of survival for juvenile gopher tortoises, *Gopherus polyphemus*. J. Herpetol. 25(3):376–379.

Woodman, A. P. and S. M. Juarez. 1988. Juvenile desert tortoises utilized as primary prey of nesting common ravens near Kramer, California. Proc. Desert Tortoise Council Symp. 1988:53–62.

Wright, S. 1982. The distribution and population biology of the gopher tortoise (*Gopherus polyphemus*) in South Carolina. M.S. thesis, Clemson Univ., Clemson, South Carolina.

Proceedings: Conservation, Restoration, and Management of Tortoises and Turtles—An International Conference, pp. 103–104
© 1997 by the New York Turtle and Tortoise Society

Predation on Turtles and Tortoises by a "Subsidized Predator"

— SUMMARY REPORT —

WILLIAM I. BOARMAN

U.S. Geological Survey, Biological Resources Division, 6221 Box Springs Blvd., Riverside, CA 92507, USA
[e-mail: william_boarman@usgs.gov]

While predation is a natural source of mortality for turtles and tortoises, it can become an important factor affecting the survival of populations that are in decline. Predators can be assigned to two categories: those that cause natural levels of mortality and those that elevate mortality to unnaturally high levels. "Subsidized predators" are those animals, native or introduced, whose populations flourish as a result of close association with humans and human-altered habitats. The "subsidies" provided to these predators by humans include ready access to food, water, and shelter, which increase their chances of (1) survival during times when resources are limited, (2) greater reproductive success, and/or (3) expanding their geographic range.

In the Mojave and Colorado deserts of the southwestern United States, populations of the common raven, *Corvus corax*, have undergone tremendous increases in recent years (over 1000% from 1968 to 1992, Boarman and Berry, 1995). These increases are attributable to increased food and water from landfills, urban expansion, agriculture, and other human activities, as well as to additional nesting sites provided by high-tension electric line towers, telephone poles, bridges, other artificial structures, and cultivated trees. Ravens, in addition to coyotes (*Canis latrans*), kit foxes (*Vulpes macrotis*), and other native predators, prey on hatchling and juvenile (up to seven years old) desert tortoises (*Gopherus agassizii*), a species designated as "Threatened" under the U.S. Endangered Species Act. Two hundred fifty tortoise shells were found beneath one active raven nest in the Western Mojave Desert of California over a two-year period. Shells showing evidence of raven predation have been found beneath raven nests, electric transmission towers, telephone poles, signs, fence posts, and trees, as well as on the desert floor away from elevated perches. Evidence of predation includes holes pecked into the soft or thin portions of the carapace or plastron and head or limbs removed.

A plan, under development by the United States Bureau of Land Management (USBLM), to reduce raven predation on desert tortoises focuses primarily on reducing the food subsidies responsible for maintaining high raven densities. The plan also calls for elimination of specific ravens, monitoring the interactions between raven and juvenile tortoise populations, study of raven ecology, and cooperation with other government agencies to ensure a coordinated strategy. The long-term plan seeks to reduce the availability of anthropogenic subsidies, thereby decreasing the number of ravens. The USBLM is working with landfill managers and sponsors of proposed large-scale landfill projects to ensure that garbage will remain covered day and night. Methods are also being developed to modify sewage containment practices and to limit other sources of water. Experiments are planned to test chemical repellents (e.g., methylanthranilate) that may deter ravens from eating garbage or drinking water at specific locations.

Removal of ravens will be limited those individuals known to prey on juvenile tortoises and all ravens hunting within specific, limited areas where the tortoise populations are declining rapidly and raven predation is known to occur. More aggressive elimination will be implemented only when scientific evidence shows that broader, non-specific removal is necessary to effect the recovery of tortoise populations. Rifles, shotguns, and trapping will be used to kill or remove the targeted ravens.

Knowledge of the ecology and behavior of the predator is essential to design an effective program. Research now being conducted by the U.S. Geological Survey will focus on the dynamics of raven territoriality, dispersal, and daily movements among natural and anthropogenic resources to better understand the contributions that anthropogenic subsidies make to raven predation on tortoises. The relative effectiveness of reducing predation on tortoises by shooting, poisoning, live trapping, relocating, and disrupting the behavior of the birds is also under investigation.

Because the goal of the program is to improve survival of juvenile tortoises, its success will be measured by a significant increase in the numbers of juveniles in tortoise populations. Therefore, improved methods to monitor numbers of hard-to-find juvenile tortoises will also be developed and tested. Population trends must be measured with proper controls to ensure that any observed increases in juvenile numbers are not due to other negative factors.

Corvids and other subsidized predators are threats to certain turtle and tortoise species in other parts of the world. For example, brown-necked ravens (*Corvus ruficollis*) prey on juvenile Mediterranean spur-thighed tortoises (*Testudo graeca*) and Egyptian tortoises (*Testudo kleinmanni*) in Israel (Geffen and Mendelssohn, this volume). While the plan under development by the USBLM is specifically tailored to the biological, political, and economic circumstances in the United States, it may be adaptable to similar problems elsewhere (Boarman, 1993).

Factors to consider when evaluating a predator management program are whether (1) the predator in question is at least partially responsible for either causing the population to decline or preventing recovery, (2) the proposed solutions will solve the problems caused by predation, (3) reducing predation will alone effect the recovery of the threatened populations, or other measures may also be required, and (4) the predator itself is an endangered or threatened species (Boarman, 1993).

LITERATURE CITED

Boarman, W. I. 1993. When a native predator becomes a pest: A case study. *In* S. K. Majumdar, E. W. Miller, D. E. Baker, E. K. Brown, J. R. Pratt, and R. F. Schmalz (eds.), Conservation and Resource Management, pp. 186–201. Pennsylvania Academy of Science, Philadelphia.

Boarman, W. I. and K. H. Berry. 1995. Common ravens in the southwestern U.S. *In* Our living resouces: A report to the nation on the distribution, abundance, and health of U.S. plants, animals, and ecosystems, pp. 73–201. National Biological Service, Washington, D.C.

Geffen, E. and H. Mendelssohn. 1997. Avian predation on tortoises in Israel (abstract). *In* J. Van Abbema (ed.), Proceedings: Conservation, Restoration, and Management of Tortoises and Turtles—An International Conference, p. 105. July 1993, State University of New York, Purchase. New York Turtle and Tortoise Society, New York.

Avian Predation on Tortoises in Israel

— SUMMARY REPORT —

ELI GEFFEN AND HEINRICH MENDELSSOHN

Department of Zoology, Tel Aviv University, Ramat Aviv, Tel Aviv 69978, Israel [e-mail: geffene@post.tau.ac.il]

Formerly, the bird most commonly known to prey on chelonians in Israel was the Egyptian vulture, *Neophron peronopterus*. Its thin bill enables it to extract the contents of the tortoises' shells. However, the extent of this predation has always been insignificant, and since the 1950s when the population of the Egyptian vulture decreased considerably, predation has become even less significant. The serpent eagle, *Circaetus gallicus*, which feeds almost exclusively on reptiles, occasionally preys on small tortoises, but this predation is negligible.

Another, much more extensive predation was discovered in April 1982, when a pair of brown-necked ravens, *Corvus ruficollis*, was flushed from an isolated tree on a broad, open plain in the western Negev. Each raven dropped a young tortoise, one partly eaten but still alive, the other almost a completely empty shell. Under this same tree, almost 40 empty shells of young tortoises were found in all stages of predation—from freshly dismembered to completely dried out. Apparently, the pair of ravens regularly used this tree from which to feed upon young tortoises collected from the area. About one third of the shells were of *Testudo kleinmanni*; the remaining were of *Testudo graeca* (Mendelssohn, 1982).

During a survey of *Testudo kleinmanni*, it was found that adults of the species are also eaten. Tortoises were preyed upon from both front and rear openings, and in some cases, the two movable rear lobes of the plastron had been deflected or removed.

Predation by corvids is likely to increase considerably in the near future. Two species, the brown-necked raven (*Corvus ruficollis*) and the hooded crow (*Corvus corone sardonius*), are undergoing a population explosion as a result of increased numbers of open garbage dumps and other food sources created by human activities. *C. ruficollis* is a desert species, penetrating the range of *T. kleinmanni* from the east and south, whereas *C. corone sardonius* has a Mediterranean distribution and invades the area from the north and west. Both species seem able to coexist in the same area, and both feed on small tortoises. Formerly, no corvids existed within the range of *Testudo kleinmanni* and there was no problem with avian predation. Following agricultural and urban development, however, both species of corvids have expanded into the area and now exert considerable predation pressure. In addition, population densities of both *Corvus* species are now significantly higher. The hooded crows may presently number up to 17 breeding pairs per km^2, and breeding success is generally good (Erez, 1990). It is unknown if these high densities of crows affect the *Testudo graeca* populations. Adult tortoises seem to be immune to crow attacks, but small individuals are certainly vulnerable, although they are rarely seen as they inhabit dense vegetation.

LITERATURE CITED

Erez, A. 1990. On the breeding ecology of the hooded crow (*Corvus corone sardonius*) in Israel. M.S. thesis, Tel Aviv University, Ramat-Aviv, Israel.

Mendelssohn, H. 1982. Egyptian tortoise. *In* The IUCN Reptilia-Amphibia Red Data Book. Part 1. Testudinidae, Crocodylia, Rhynchocephalia (B. Groombridge, comp.), pp. 133–136. IUCN, Gland, Switzerland. xiii + 426 pp.

Turtle Rearing in Village Ponds

ROMULUS WHITAKER

Centre for Herpetology/Madras Crocodile Bank, Post Bag 4, Mamallapuram, Tamil Nadu 603 104, India

ABSTRACT: In India, the commercial turtle meat industry is largely concentrated in the state of West Bengal, where thousands of turtles of numerous species, caught mainly in neighboring states, are sent to be sold in markets. Though most species are protected under the Wildlife Act, the trade continues. In West Bengal alone, several traditionally exploited species, including the large *Batagur baska* and *Aspideretes* spp., are virtually extirpated.

Most of the turtles used for meat are hardy and omnivorous and can be reared in captivity. The flapshell turtle, *Lissemys punctata*, is particularly well suited to rearing in small impoundments of water. Fish are often reared for home consumption and sale in small ponds or "tanks" in villages in West Bengal. This paper proposes a pilot project to rear *Lissemys* in village ponds for human consumption, which, if successful, could help ease the present heavy pressure from human exploitation on wild turtle populations.

Turtles in India are used as food by 50 million tribal people, many of whom still partly subsist by hunting and gathering. However, only the state of West Bengal has well-developed urban and suburban turtle meat markets.

The Bengali people are consumers of fish, preferring freshwater species such as hilsa and the major carps. They also favor freshwater turtles, which are brought through the railway and bus stations in the same baskets as the fish, and which command some of the highest prices. Perhaps the most popular species in the market is *Lissemys punctata*, the flapshell, desired for its sweet, soft meat and chewy, cartilaginous shell. Usually weighing under a kilogram, they are a convenient size to carry home from work. Alternatively, the "kachin wallah" or "turtle sellers" at the market will carve off one or more kilos of meat and shell from a large living *Aspideretes gangeticus*, or (more rarely) a *Chitra indica* or *Aspideretes hurum*. Hard-shelled turtles that appear on the market include *Hardella* and various species of *Kachuga*.

This use of turtle meat as a dietary staple has resulted in the steady decline of most, if not all, of the ten or more species of turtles in West Bengal. The *Batagur* survives only in the Sunderbans Tiger Reserve (Bhupathy, 1994; Das, 1995). The larger softshells, such as *Aspideretes gangeticus* and *A. hurum*, are no longer seen (or caught) in the state.

The Turtle Trade

Statistical data on the turtle meat trade in West Bengal are lacking. Recently, Bhupathy et al. (1992) conducted brief market surveys in and around Calcutta and found numbers of flapshells and Ganges softshells for sale. While no formal assessment of the number of turtles traded in West Bengal has been made, a conservative estimate would range into the tens of thousands. Moll (1991) estimated that Calcutta's Howrah market alone received 50,000–75,000 *Lissemys*, 7,000–8,000 *Aspideretes*, and 1,000–1,500 hard-shelled turtles annually in the early 1980s. At that time turtles were more numerous, the rivers were less polluted, and direct pressure on habi-

Figure 1. Turtle market in Bangladesh, typical also of Indian markets.

tats from human activity was less severe. In addition, turtles are now nominally protected. As a result, most of the markets that formerly sold turtle meat have either closed or gone "underground," making turtles available only on certain days in a week. Protecting turtles appears to have contributed to the increase in price. We observed prices of Rs 10 to Rs 25 per kilogram ten years ago. However, turtle meat now commands an average price of Rs 20 to Rs 30 per kg (less expensive than chicken and mutton), and it climbs to a remarkable Rs 150 to Rs 200 per kg in northeastern India (Bhupathy et al., 1992). (U.S. $1 = approx. Rs 31 in 1992.)

Since most turtles, except *Lissemys*, are no longer found in commercially exploitable numbers in West Bengal, fish and turtle contractors go far afield to the states of Uttar Pradesh, Bihar, and Orissa to supply the demand. When the trade was legal, large basketfuls of up to six or more species arrived daily at the main railway stations around Calcutta. The turtles still arrive in baskets but always packed with fish to prevent detection by wildlife officials.

Over the decades this trade has continued; millions of turtles have been taken from north Indian rivers and ponds. The impact upon turtle populations of this level of exploitation has been aggravated by water pollution and the drastic alteration of aquatic habitats. Anecdotal evidence from fishermen and turtle hunters indicates a decline in the availability of most of the species that were once common.

Conservation and Management Options

Most turtles are protected under the Indian Wildlife Act of 1972. Some, like the flapshell (*Lissemys punctata*) and Ganges softshell (*Aspideretes gangeticus*), are listed on Schedule I, the highest order of protection, violation of which can lead to a mandatory jail term. However, the state wildlife departments are sparsely staffed and ill-equipped to deal with the problems of poaching, transport, and sale. Nevertheless, the authorities have been able to exert at least some pressure and have largely forced the markets underground, causing them to operate at a reduced level.

There are few convictions under the Wildlife Act, and it does not serve as a major deterrent to the trade. Only some of the conservation measures suggested by Moll (1987) have been undertaken. While surveys have been initiated, recommendations made to the Indian government on the listing and downlisting of some species have yet to be implemented. Regulation by closing seasons and limiting size and number of turtles taken from the areas where they are exploited has been considered (Moll, 1991). However, such regulation is difficult to enforce and monitor unless the Wildlife Department is provided with the necessary personnel and infrastructure.

The development of a sustained-yield program, as opposed to purely theoretical protection, is an option worthy of serious consideration.

Figure 2. *Lissemys punctata*.

Figure 3. *Batagur baska*.

A Pilot Project for Rearing Turtles in Village Ponds

Virtually every West Bengal village has one or more seasonal or permanent ponds, which are used for agriculture, bathing, and fish farming. The ponds average 20–30 m in diameter and are up to 3 m deep at high water. Flapshell turtles often inhabit these ponds, but are usually caught and eaten if found.

The flapshell is a favorite food turtle and is hardy, omnivorous, and grows rapidly. It preys on living organisms, scavenges organic detritus from the pond bottom, and can literally be fattened on household garbage as one would rear a pig in one's backyard.

A village near Calcutta will be chosen as the site for a pilot project to rear turtles. The project will initially emphasize home use, but with a view to rearing larger numbers later for the nearby urban commercial market. It has already been established at the Centre for Herpetology/Madras Crocodile Bank that *Lissemys* breed readily in captivity. However, more research is needed on feeding, growth rates, maturation time, and stocking densities, which may best be conducted at the actual pilot project site.*

A low wall will be required around the high-water edge of the pond, which can be constructed inexpensively out of locally available waste materials (earth, broken bricks, tiles, bamboo matting, etc.). The dumping of humus-producing litter (primarily yard sweepings) on the edges of the ponds is a common practice, and this will help fulfill a *Lissemys* habitat requirement by providing aestivation sites during the dry season when ponds can dry up.

Captive breeding groups may be maintained in the village ponds and the offspring reared for consumption (i.e., farming). In another scenario, central hatcheries operated by the Forest Department could breed *Lissemys* and/or collect wild eggs from flood-prone sites and distribute the hatchlings in the same manner the Fisheries Department distributes fingerling fish for rearing (i.e., ranching). The Forest Department may realize a small amount of revenue from the offspring supplied, and the system can be closely monitored by the Department.

Basic workshops for the participating villagers can answer questions on stocking densities, feeding, sexing, and prevention of predation. The villagers can be encouraged to permanently retain some adults in the ponds as breeding stock to supplement the supply of hatchlings from the Forest Department.

It is hoped that through the initial, limited program of rearing turtles for home consumption, the technology for rearing large numbers for the market can be developed. Similarly, other species of hardy common turtles (such as the herbivorous *Hardella* and the large *Aspideretes gangeticus*) should be considered for rearing.

Constraints

Both subspecies of *Lissemys punctata* are now protected under Schedule I of the Wildlife Act. However, it is without doubt India's most common and widely distributed turtle and should be downlisted to Schedule IV (see Moll, 1991; Das, 1995). This would make it available for sustained-yield use by villagers with a permit issued by the Forest Department, maintaining necessary regulatory mechanisms to ensure that wild populations are protected. If the formalities of downlisting *Lissemys* take too long a time, other species not on the higher schedules of protection will be used first.

The lengthy incubation period of *Lissemys punctata* and *Aspideretes gangeticus* eggs will necessitate professional training of egg collectors and hatchery staff (as well as villagers if captive breeding is to be widely encouraged). It is essential that we have a detailed understanding of the biology of the species that is to be bred, reared, and harvested before any large-scale scheme is formulated.

ACKNOWLEDGMENTS

The author thanks Harry Andrews and Purnima Govindarajulu for commenting on the draft of this paper. He is also grateful to Romaine Andrews for editing and typing this manuscript.

LITERATURE CITED

Bhupathy, S. 1995. Status and distribution of the river terrapin *Batagur baska* in the Sunderban of India. Final report, SACON Technical Report, Salim Ali Centre for Ornithology and Natural History. Coimbatore, India. 37 pp.

Bhupathy, S., B. C. Choudhury, and E. O. Moll. 1992. Conservation and management of freshwater turtles and land tortoises of India. Technical Report (May 1991–July 1992), Wildlife Institute of India, Dehra Dun. 22 pp.

Das, I. 1995. Turtles and Tortoises of India. WWF India, Oxford University Press, Bombay. 176 pp.

Moll, E. O. 1987. Survey of freshwater turtles of India Part I: The genus *Kachuga*. J. Bombay Nat. Hist. Soc. 84(1):7–25.

Moll, E. O. 1991. India's freshwater turtle resource with recommendations for management. *In* J. C. Daniel and J. S. Serrao (eds.), Conservation in Developing Countries: Problems and Prospects, pp. 501–515. Bombay Natural History Society and Oxford University Press, Bombay. a

---

*At Madras Crocodile Bank Trust, where nesting occurs from August to December, 12 clutches of *Lissemys* each contained 5–12 eggs. After rearing for approximately two years, the young turtles can reach 400–500 grams, the average harvestable size (J. Vijaya, 1983, unpubl. data from 23 animals at MCBT).

Biology and Conservation of Aquatic Turtles in the Cinaruco-Capanaparo National Park, Venezuela

JOHN B. THORBJARNARSON,[1] NAYIBE PÉREZ,[2] AND TIBISAY ESCALONA[3]

[1]*Wildlife Conservation Society, 185th St. and Southern Blvd., Bronx, NY 10460, USA [e-mail: jcaiman@aol.com]*
[2]*INPARQUES, San Fernando de Apure, Apure, Venezuela*
[3]*Pro Vita Animalium, Apdo. 47552, Caracas 1041-A, Venezuela*

ABSTRACT: As in many parts of South America, turtles in the llanos region of Venezuela are widely hunted for subsistence and commercial purposes. The Capanaparo River, much of which is situated within the recently declared Capanaparo-Cinaruco National Park, has populations of *Podocnemis expansa, P. unifilis, P. vogli,* and *Chelus fimbriatus*. During the annual dry season, eggs of all three of the *Podocnemis* are widely consumed. Yaruro Indians also hunt adults and subadults of these species, principally using drop lines baited with plantain. Some turtles are consumed by the Indians, but the majority are sold or bartered for other food or for alcohol. Anecdotal information suggests that populations have declined significantly during the lifetimes of the Yaruros who presently hunt them.

Local populations of *P. expansa* are apparently quite small. Isolated females nest on the riverbanks in March, coincidental with the lowest annual water levels, and the eggs hatch in May as the river rises. *P. vogli* is principally a savanna pond species, but occasionally individuals are found in the river. The most abundant turtle is *P. unifilis*, locally called "terecay." *P. unifilis* nests in the early dry season (late January–early February) as the river level is falling, and the eggs hatch in April. In 1991–1992 mean clutch size was 23.3 and average egg mass was 26.5 g. Incubation time averaged 62.8 days in simulated nests. Nest predation rates were quite high, with the principal predators being the Yaruro people, *Tupinambis* lizards, and crested caracaras (*Polyborus plancus*).

From a sample of 188 *P. unifilis* captured by the Yaruro, mean female maximum plastron length was 30.9 cm and mean male maximum plastron length was 22.9 cm. A conservation program is currently being designed in collaboration with the Venezuelan National Parks Department (INPARQUES) to restrict the commercialization of turtles. The program may also involve a trial headstarting project.

Early European explorers left colorful accounts of the abundance and human utilization of pelomedusine turtles in lowland South America. One of the earliest chroniclers of life in the Venezuelan llanos, Gumilla (1741), recorded the massive take of *Podocnemis expansa*, the largest of the Neotropical freshwater turtles, as eggs, hatchlings, and adults. Similar accounts were given later by von Humboldt (1860) for the Orinoco, and Bates (1989, originally from 1863) for the central Amazon. However, centuries of intensive exploitation have taken their toll on populations of *P. expansa*, and this species is now rare throughout most of its range (IUCN, 1982; IUCN/SSC, 1991).

With the decline of *P. expansa*, much of the human utilization of turtles has switched to the smaller pelomedusines (Mittermeier, 1975, 1978; Dixon and Soini, 1977; Smith, 1979; Johns, 1987). In Brazil, *P. unifilis* and *P. sextuberculata* are now the turtles most commonly consumed (Mittermeier, 1975; Smith, 1979), and in the Venezuelan llanos, it is *P. unifilis* and the savanna pond turtle, *P. vogli* (Pritchard and Trebbau, 1984). Although the terecay, *P. unifilis*, is still relatively abundant in some lowland riverine habitats in Venezuela, a significant dry-season turtle trade exists, and anecdotal information suggests that populations have declined. Some areas, particularly near urban centers (e.g., the lower Apure River), are now almost devoid of the larger pelomedusines. *P. expansa* is considered to be "Endangered" in the *IUCN Red Data Book* (IUCN, 1982) and is listed on Appendix II of CITES. *P. unifilis* is listed as "Vulnerable" by the IUCN and is on Appendix II of CITES. The conservation of this turtle has been given high priority (APR = 1) by the IUCN Tortoise and Freshwater Turtle Specialist Group (IUCN/SSC, 1991). Although *P. vogli* still remains locally abundant (Pritchard and Trebbau, 1984) in certain areas, particularly on private lands where turtle collecting is prohibited or controlled, overhunting has had noticeable impacts in other areas. This species, unlike others, is confined to the Orinoco llanos.

Cinaruco-Capanaparo National Park

This park encompasses more than half a million hectares of open, nutrient-poor savannas in southern Apure state. The region is dominated by large expanses of treeless savannas interspersed with sparse, mixed woodlands, *Maritia*, palm-lined streams, and deciduous gallery forest. The Cinaruco and Capanaparo rivers form the southern and northern boundaries of the park. Most of the area is sparsely settled due to its inaccessibility, its tendency to flood extensively during the annual wet season, and because the principal rivers are shallow and largely unnavigable with motor boats during the dry season. The Capanaparo region is the home of Guahibo and Yaruro Indians, who traditionally consumed pelomedusine turtles (Petrullo, 1969). The most abundant turtle observed in the Capanaparo River was *P. unifilis*. A small population of *P. expansa* still remains in the Capanaparo, and *P. vogli*, although principally a savanna pond-dwelling species, is occasionally observed in the river. The mata-mata, *Chelus fimbriatus*, is also known from the Capanaparo. Aside from turtles the aquatic fauna of the region is still quite diverse, including Orinoco crocodiles (*Crocodylus intermedius*), freshwater dolphins (*Inia geoffrensis*), giant river otters (*Pteroneura brasiliensis*), and a small population of manatees (*Trichechus manatus*). We studied aspects of the nesting ecology and utilization of pelomedusines in the vicinity of San José de Capanaparo (7°00′ N, 68°25′ W) in 1991 and 1992.

Nesting Biology

Aspects of the nesting ecology of *P. unifilis* in the Capanaparo were reported by Thorbjarnarson et al. (1993). Terecays nest during the annual dry season (late January–early February), when falling water levels expose nesting habitat. Eggs hatched in early April after a mean incubation period of 62.8 days (eggs incubated in simulated natural nests). Nests were shallow excavations made in the open, and two types of nesting areas were used: sand beaches (depositional features) and river banks (erosional features). Females nesting on beaches would regularly move long distances before ovipositing ($\bar{x}$ = 20.6 m from river's edge), occasionally traveling hundreds of meters along an irregular path. In contrast, bank nesting sites were close to the river ($\bar{x}$ = 5.4 m). Beach and bank nesting habitat was abundant and nests were widely scattered. Mean clutch size (n = 22) was 23.3, ranging from 14 to 31. Oviposition occurred at night and recently laid eggs were subject to predation by tegu lizards (*Tupinambis nigropunctatus*) and crested caracaras (*Polyborus plancus*). Nests in the process of hatching were also found preyed upon by caracaras.

Only a very small reproductive population of *P. expansa* remains in the Capanaparo. Nesting appears to peak about one month later than *P. unifilis*, and unlike the colonial nesting habits of this species in the main Orinoco River, nests in the Capanaparo are scattered among the many available beaches. In March 1992 one nest with 66 eggs was found in the process of being preyed upon by caracaras, and others were reported by residents who consumed the eggs. *P. vogli* does not appear to nest along the Capanaparo riverbanks, instead preferring to oviposit in hard-packed savanna soils with a high clay content (Ramo, 1982).

Human Utilization of Turtles

All turtles except *C. fimbriatus* were heavily exploited for food by Yaruro Indians and Venezuelan colonists. During the dry season turtles and their eggs became a significant component of the diet of the human communities along the Capanaparo River. Although both Indians and Venezuelan colonists (criollos) consumed turtles, the collection of turtles in the vicinity of San José was done almost entirely by Yaruro Indians, who used the turtles to barter with criollos for other foodstuffs or liquor. Turtles were not hunted to any significant degree during the wet season.

In the dry season Yaruro communities moved from permanent village sites to seasonal riverside camps. Camping on the exposed sandbars facilitated hunting and fishing activities, including searching for turtle nests. Eggs were also collected as the Yaruro moved up and down the river in small dugout canoes. Typically, as the canoe was paddled along the river, children were employed to search the riverbanks and follow the tracks of female turtles.

Subadult and adult turtles were captured using one of several different methods. One technique was hunting from a dugout at night using a bow and arrow with a detachable arrow tip tied to a string. Some turtles, principally *P. expansa*, were captured at night on nesting beaches when they emerged to oviposit. However, by far the most prevalent method of capturing turtles was with a trotline referred to locally as an "espiñel." The trotlines were typically 20–50 m long, with a series of small hooks that were baited with plantain. Small plastic bottles were used as buoys, and the trotlines were usually left overnight. Turtles were either consumed by the Yaruro themselves or traded to local criollos or to middlemen who in turn sold them in llanos urban centers, particularly the town of Achaguas. The activity of these traders appeared to be the most significant in terms of its impact on the turtle population. One individual was known to come weekly from Achaguas during the dry season to purchase cheese and trade liquor for turtles. Although the area is a national park and the trade of liquor and commercialization of wildlife is illegal, the remoteness of the area precluded any strict enforcement of laws. In some cases the Venezuelan National Guard, charged with protecting wildlife, was involved in the trade of turtles or would receive turtles as gifts when the turtle traders passed though checkpoints along access roads to the Capanaparo River.

In 1992 we measured the discarded shells of turtles at 28 Yaruro villages and seasonal hunting camps along the Capanaparo. Examination of plastrons allowed us to identify the species and the sex of the turtles. Plastrons were used because they were more likely to be found intact than carapaces, and the form of the anal notch allowed us to determine the sex of the turtle. Maximum plastron length was measured from the anterior end of the epiplastron to the posterior-most projecton of the xiphiplastron. Plastron length was converted into estimated straight-line carapace length using a conversion formula for 14 entire shells (Thorbjarnarson et al., 1993). Of 300 plastrons, 258 (86%) belonged to *P. unifilis*, 30 (10%) were *P. vogli*, and 12 (4%) were *P. expansa* (Table 1). The sample was heavily biased towards females, with 100% of the *P. expansa*, 63% of the *P. unifilis*, and 80% of the *P. vogli* being female. This may reflect a bias in the natural sex ratio of the turtles, sex-related differences in the likelihood of capture, or simply a bias in the sex of turtles retained for consumption versus those traded.

Management Considerations

In many parts of South America freshwater turtles are heavily exploited for food. Centuries of subsistence utilization by indigenous peoples and colonists of European and African descent has been replaced by widespread commercial utilization (Ojasti, 1967; Mittermeier, 1975; Smith, 1979; Johns, 1987). Although almost no information exists on the effect of subsistence utilization on wild turtle populations, it is apparent that commercialization of turtle meat and eggs has greatly broadened the turtle consuming constituency and increased the demand for a dwindling resource. Freshwater turtle populations may not be able to compensate for long-term reduction in neonate survivorship, and are especially vulnerable to increased mortality of adults (Congdon et al., 1993). Although the life history strategy of aquatic turtles makes them resilient to high mortality as eggs and juveniles, the widespread, unmanaged utilization of turtles at all life stages is likely to have devastating consequences on natural populations. This has already been seen with the largest and most economically important of the aquatic turtles, *P. expansa*, and is now happening with *P. unifilis*. Our sample of 300 turtles was not based on an exhaustive search of riverside communities and undoubtedly represents a significant underestimation of the level of subsistence harvest of turtles along approximately 30 km of river during one dry season. However, the majority of turtles are most likely traded and would not be represented as shells at villages or hunting camps. As judged by this sample, very few *P. expansa* remain in the Capanaparo, and the brunt of human utilization is now falling on the terecay. Anecdotal accounts by Indians and criollos suggest that the population of *P. expansa* has declined precipitously, and the population of *P. unifilis* has been significantly reduced. Most Yaruro we talked to were worried about this but felt there was little they could do about it.

In most areas the recovery of threatened freshwater turtle populations will require a reduction in the offtake and consumption of turtles. One potential solution is to permit subsistence utilization by riverside communities but eliminate commercial utilization. However, in many rural communities, especially where trade is based on barter, the distinction between subsistence and commercial utilization is blurred, and control will be difficult, particularly given the present realities of enforcement of wildlife trade in rural regions. Polisar (1994) proposed a turtle management program based on utilization but controlled through possession

TABLE 1
Straight-line carapace length (CL) in cm, estimated from plastron length, for turtles found in Yaruro Indian camps along the Capanaparo River in the vicinity of San José de Capanaparo. Data from 1992.

Species	Mean CL	SD	Minimum	Maximum	N
Males					
P. expansa	—	—	—	—	—
P. unifilis	25.7	3.2	18.2	33.0	79
P. vogli	23.8	3.9	20.0	27.7	2
Females					
P. expansa	54.9	0.6	54.3	55.5	2
P. unifilis	33.1	3.3	21.7	41.4	109
P. vogli	26.5	3.4	19.4	33.7	14

limits, a restricted hunting season, and the declaration of protected areas for *Dermatemys mawii* in Belize. In areas that are beyond the reach of effective law enforcement, the success of programs such as these will require the active involvement of local communities to protect their turtles and avoid the dilemma of the unmanaged commons (Hardin, 1968, 1994).

In the case of the Capanaparo River, it is clear that the offtake of turtles needs to be controlled by restricting commercial trade. Collection of eggs is principally done on a subsistence basis, whereas the capture of adults is both a subsistence and a commercial activity. The sale of turtles in urban markets needs to be curtailed. Current legislation limits the take of *P. unifilis* to two turtles per year per hunter, but is not enforced. The hunting of *P. expansa* has been completely prohibited since 1962 (Anon., 1988) and is likewise seldom enforced. Nevertheless, the restriction of commercial trade is feasible as the sale of turtles is a highly seasonal activity, and a control infrastructure exists through the Venezuelan National Guard, a branch of the military, which is posted throughout the region and regularly examines passing vehicles for contraband. However, lacking are political or community support for the enforcement of existing legislation, as well as training programs for the National Guard devoted to the control of the commercialization of wildlife. Working with local communities to develop a proprietary attitude towards their turtle populations may provide some impetus for effective enforcement. However, this will require that communities be given some control over the management of their turtle populations, necessitating certain changes in wildlife management procedures at the national level. Pilot programs of this sort are sorely needed to test the idea that the promotion of managed subsistence utilization can provide a mechanism to control widespread illegal commercialization, and such programs need to be carried out in conjunction with long-term studies of the effects of human utilization on wild turtle populations.

Acknowledgments

This study was supported with funds from the Wildlife Conservation Society, the National Geographic Society, the Venezuelan Fundación para la Defensa de la Naturaleza (FUDENA), and the Venezuelan National Parks Department (INPARQUES). Fieldwork was greatly assisted by M. Benitez, G. Hernández, M. Muñoz, A. Osto, C. Laya, and J. Rivas. Special thanks to T. and C. Blohm.

Literature Cited

Anonymous. 1988. Las tortugas de río. Proposiciones para la recuperación y el manejo de dos valiosas especies. Flora, Fauna y Areas Silvestres 3:23–29.

Bates, H. W. 1989. The Naturalist on the River Amazons. Penguin, New York.

Congdon, J. D., A. E. Dunham, and R. C. van Loben Sels. 1993. Delayed sexual maturity and demography of Blanding's turtles (*Emydoidea blandingi*): Implications for conservation and management of long-lived organisms. Conserv. Biol. 7:826–833.

Dixon, J. R. and P. Soini. 1977. The reptiles of the upper Amazon basin, Iquitos region. Peru. II. crocodilians, turtles and snakes. Contrib. Biol. Geol., Milwaukee Publ. Mus. 12:1–91.

Gumilla, J. S. J. 1741. El Orinoco Ilustrado. Historia Natural y Geografia de este Gran Río y sus Caudalosos Vertientes. Manuel Fernandez, Madrid.

Harding, G. 1968. The tragedy of the commons. Science 62:1242–1248.

Harding, G. 1994. The tragedy of the unmanaged commons. Trends in Ecol. and Evol. 9:19.

von Humboldt, A. B. 1860. Reise in die Aquinoctial-Gegenden des Neuen Continents. J. C. Cottascher Verlag, Stuttgart.

IUCN. 1982. The IUCN Amphibia-Reptilia Red Data Book, Part 1: Testudines, Crocodylia, Rhynchocephalia (B. Groombridge, comp.). IUCN, Gland, Switzerland.

Johns, A. D. 1987. Continuing problems for Amazon River turtles. Oryx 21:25–28.

Mittermeier, R. 1975. A turtle in every pot. Animal Kingdom, April–May, pp. 9–14.

Mittermeier, R. 1978. South America's river turtles: Saving them by use. Oryx 14:222–230.

Mondolfi, E. 1955. Anotaciones sobre la biología de tres quelonios de los llanos de Venezuela. Mem. Soc. Cienc. Nat. La Salle 15:177–183.

Ojasti, J. 1967. Consideraciones sobre la ecología y conservación de la tortuga *Podocnemis expansa* (Chelonia, Pelomedusidae). Atas do Simpósio sobre la a Biota Amazonica 7:201–206.

Petrullo, V. 1969. Los Yaruros del Río Capanaparo. Instituto de Antropologia e Historia. Universidad Central de Venezuela, Caracas.

Pritchard, P. C. H. and P. Trebbau. 1984. The Turtles of Venezuela. Soc. Stud. Amph. Rept., Contrib. Herpetol. 403 pp.

Ramo, C. 1982. Biología del galapago (*Podocnemis vogli* Muller, 1935) en el Hato El Frio. Doñana Acta Vertebrata 9:1–161.

Smith, N. J. H. 1979. Aquatic turtles of Amazonia: An endangered resource. Biol. Conserv. 16:165–176.

IUCN/SSC Tortoise and Freshwater Turtle Specialist Group. 1991. Tortoises and freshwater turtles: An action plan for their conservation, 2d ed. (D. Stubbs, comp.). IUCN/SSC Tortoise and Freshwater Turtle Specialist Group, Gland, Switzerland. i–iv + 47 pp.

Thorbjarnarson, J. B., N. Pérez, and T. Escalona. 1993. Nesting of *Podocnemis unifilis* in the Capanaparo River, Venezuela. J. Herpetol. 27:344–347.

Patterns of Exploitation, Decline, and Extinction of *Erymnochelys madagascariensis*: Implications for Conservation

GERALD KUCHLING

Department of Zoology, The University of Western Australia, Nedlands, WA 6907, Australia
[e-mail: kuchling@cyllene.uwa.edu.au]

ABSTRACT: A survey of populations of *Erymnochelys madagascariensis*, based on interviews with local fishermen at 46 localities, was conducted in Western Madagascar in 1991 and 1992. Eleven percent of the populations were considered to be "exploited but relatively good," 28% "exploited and declining," 28% "heavily exploited and depleted," 31% "possibly extirpated" or "extirpated," and at one locality *Erymnochelys* may have "never existed." Exploitation for human consumption at a local subsistence level is the main reason for the decline of populations. *Erymnochelys* and crocodiles are caught in the same habitats, but trade in the turtles is limited and illegal; market prices for *Erymnochelys* are much lower than for crocodiles and their products. Conservation action should include education campaigns for fishermen, a captive breeding or rearing program, and the establishment of a protected area.

Erymnochelys is a monotypic freshwater turtle genus endemic to Madagascar and is of great zoogeographic interest. It is the only living member of the subfamily Podocneminae (family Pelomedusidae) to inhabit the Old World. Its closest living relatives are the South American turtles of the genera *Podocnemis* and *Peltocephalus*. *Erymnochelys madagascariensis* is little known and is one of 15 chelonian species given an Action Plan Rating of 1 by the IUCN/SSC Tortoise and Freshwater Turtle Action Plan. APR 1 = "known threatened species in need of specific conservation measures" (IUCN/SSC, 1989).

A survey of some habitats of *Erymnochelys madagascariensis* in May and June 1991 revealed heavy exploitation of the species, serious depletion, and local extinction of populations (Kuchling, 1991; Kuchling and Mittermeier, 1993). It became obvious that populations should be surveyed over the whole known range of the species to assess the urgency for conservation action. Most of the *Erymnochelys* habitats not covered in the 1991 survey were visited during August and September 1992, and a rapid survey technique was used to gain an overview of the species' status (Kuchling, 1992). This paper is based on the results of the surveys in 1991 and 1992.

METHODS

To gain information on populations and exploitation of *Erymnochelys*, localities and habitats where the species was assumed or reported to occur were visited and local fishermen were interviewed. The areas and habitats were selected according to the distribution map of *E. madagascariensis* provided by Bour (1985) and according to anecdotal information collected during previous visits (Kuchling, 1988, 1991). Fishermen were routinely asked specific questions concerning methods and rates of capture and exploitation of freshwater turtles, the identity of which was confirmed by presenting photographs of the different local turtle species (*Erymnochelys madagascariensis*, *Pelomedusa subrufa*, *Pelusios castanoides*, sea turtles, and terrestrial tortoises). When available, empty carapaces of recently consumed turtles were examined. Questions to fishermen were structured in the following way:

1. Name of the lake/river; is the water permanent/semi-permanent/ephemeral? How do water levels change seasonally? Are there water courses between lakes and rivers; are they permanent or present only during high-water levels? What is the vegetation in the water and on the shores?
2. Name of the village; age class of the informant (young, middle-aged, old); for how many years does he/she know the waters and fish (e.g., born in the village or moved to this place)?
3. Which turtle/tortoise species live in the area (according to photos of the different species)? Which species are most common in the area/at the lake/in the swamps?
4. In cases where *Erymnochelys* are known, where do they live (aquatic, terrestrial, in the ocean, large lakes, small lakes/ponds, swamps, or in the river)?
5. The informant is asked to show the size of *Erymnochelys* (with the hands or as a sketch in the sand), then the size of other turtles (*Pelusios*, *Pelomedusa*), then the size of the largest *Erymnochelys* that he/she ever saw.
6. Are *Erymnochelys* or other turtles being captured and consumed by locals? How many *Erymnochelys* or other turtles are captured per day/week/month/year by the informant and by the whole fishing community? When was the last one caught?

7. How many fishermen live in the area? How many families altogether? How many nets exist? Are fish consumed only locally; freshly marketed in cities; or dried, smoked, or salted?
8. Are all sizes of *Erymnochelys* consumed or only larger ones? Are large *Erymnochelys* caught frequently; when was the last really large one caught (i.e., how many years ago)? Are medium size ranges common?
9. Are eggs collected and eaten? How many eggs are found per nest? During which months or season? Where does *Erymnochelys* nest? Are eggs preyed upon by wild pigs, dogs? Are wild boars hunted in the area; are they common?
10. What are the common methods to catch *Erymnochelys* (seine nets, baited hoop nets or traps, lance, line and hook, diving, etc.)? Are crocodiles common in the area; are they hunted? Do *Erymnochelys* (and crocodiles) occur throughout the whole area or only at certain localities?
11. In the opinion of the informant, is the *Erymnochelys* population stable, increasing, or declining? Was *Erymnochelys* more common in the past? Is the number of animals caught per year constant, increasing, or declining? In the case of a decreasing population, since when (a few years, several decades) has it been declining?
12. Over the last years or decades, were there long-term changes in the water level; in vegetation (e.g., since when was rice grown at the shores or in the area)? Since when were nets (seine nets) used in the lake(s)?
13. Is the number of fishermen in the area stable or increasing? Since when and at what rate is it increasing? Are most fishermen locals; do they fish as their sole occupation or only occasionally? Are fishermen coming into the area from outside (e.g., from the highlands); is their technology and approach to fishing different? Do outsiders have permits or do they fish illegally?
14. Are there traditional customs, taboos, prohibitions ("fady") concerning the lake, swamp, river; concerning fishing; or concerning turtles? Did taboos exist in the past?

The sequence of the questions was flexible and depended upon the progress of the conversation. Because confusion occurred, even with sea turtles, it was important to be particular about species identification and to inquire carefully about sizes, appearance, and habitats (terrestrial, aquatic, living in lakes or tidal zones). Furthermore, it was important to talk to people who really lived in and knew the area. Stories about "many-many" *Erymnochelys* at other distant places were seldom reliable (although often worthwhile following up).

Some questions touched aspects that most informants would not openly discuss in front of government officials.

For example, the number of nets admitted in an area may, in theory, be regulated by a permit system; areas may be closed for nets in certain seasons; outsiders whose fishing practises are often much more exploitative than those of locals may not pay permit fees and taxes; and last but not least, *Erymnochelys* is legally protected and must not therefore be captured, collected, killed, eaten, or sold at markets without authorisation of the Ministère de la Production Animale et des Eaux et Forêts. It took some experience to determine whether answers to these questions were truthful. To get a realistic picture it was often necessary to talk to various informants and to inquire in a discrete manner.

The survey method did not permit qualitative estimates of the size of particular populations. It was, however, possible to rank populations according to the following scale of status estimates:

1. Unexploited and healthy
2. Exploited but relatively good
3. Exploited and declining
4. Heavily exploited and depleted
5. Possibly extirpated
6. Extirpated
0. Possibly never existed.

Methods of Hunting and Capturing *Erymnochelys*

The main methods are baited hoop nets or traps (called "treko"), hooks and lines, spears or harpoons, diving after turtles, striking the water to provoke surfacing, collecting nesting females, and collecting eggs. Most methods are self-explanatory; only the method of striking the water surface is unusual: A wooden pestle (a short wood block on a pole) is used from a boat to strike the water's surface a single time. If an *Erymnochelys* happens to be close by, it will surface, and the turtle is then speared or dived after. A variation of this method is to simply strike the bow of a pirogue. It is not clear why the turtles come to the surface in response to the striking; fishermen explained they would come up only once and then dive and disappear. This method is widespread throughout the range of this species.

Exploitation of Populations

A total of 46 localities and populations of *Erymnochelys madagascariensis* were surveyed in Western Madagascar. It was beyond the means of the study to assess every possible habitat. But these localities represent most of the best habitats and the major populations.

None of the populations was considered "unexploited and healthy (Rank 1)." All major populations are therefore under some degree of pressure from exploitation. Only five populations out of 46 (11%) were considered to be "exploited but relatively good (Rank 2)." Thirteen populations (28%) were scored as "exploited and declining (Rank 3)," and the same number as "heavily exploited and depleted

(Rank 4)." Four populations (9%) were "possibly extirpated (Rank 5)," and eight populations (17%) "extirpated (Rank 6)". At two sites (4%) the former existence of *Erymnochelys* could not be confirmed through interviews, and whether the species was "extirpated (6)" or "possibly never existed (Rank 0)" could not be ascertained, although I am inclined to suspect the former. This leaves one locality, Lake Ihotry, where *Erymnochelys* "possibly never existed (0)," despite an old record (Bour, 1985). To summarise, from 45 populations surveyed, 31% were extirpated or possibly extirpated; 58% were declining or depleted; and only 11% were in relatively good condition.

When local fishermen were asked why *Erymnochelys* had declined or disappeared, a wide variety of reasons was given. These included the expansion of the human population (and the increased fishing pressure), the decrease in water levels and the temporary drying of lakes, the loss of too many eggs (collected by people and taken by wild pigs), and the conversion of reed fields and shores into rice fields. Some people thought floods carried turtles away.

Many informants, particularly at smaller lakes, were startled by the sudden disappearance of *Erymnochelys*: "Suddenly they were gone." People had the impression they were plentiful until the moment they were extirpated and only realised later what had happened.

Market Prices for *Erymnochelys* and Crocodiles

In many habitats in Madagascar, *Erymnochelys madagascariensis* and *Crocodylus niloticus* face similar problems—both species are overexploited. Experience in several tropical countries has shown that a regulated exploitation of wild crocodile populations on a sustainable basis (e.g., collection of eggs from wild nests for ranches and farms) is a more realistic conservation strategy than a total ban on the use of wild populations. Such programs for crocodiles are now being implemented in Madagascar. These programs are expected to finance themselves through the monetary return from crocodile products (which are often exported). To evaluate the economic viability of sustainable use and farming programs for *Erymnochelys* similar to the crocodile programs, it is necessary to assess market prices for the species.

Erymnochelys, because of its protected status, is sold only infrequently and surreptitiously at public markets. Nobody would admit in front of government officials that sales occur. The basic value of *Erymnochelys* is its meat, which is a delicacy. Empty carapaces are used as feeding dishes for domestic fowl, but have no commercial value. The eggs are also consumed and are frequently considered superior to poultry eggs, but they are generally not sold and it is difficult to determine prices.

The market prices (1992 figures) of *Erymnochelys* and crocodiles were assessed at Bevilany, 30 km NNE of Maevatanana, one of the few places where *Erymnochelys* is still clandestinely marketed. Only live turtles are sold; a large one (>35 cm CL) sells for about 2000 FMG (≈U.S. $1.50),

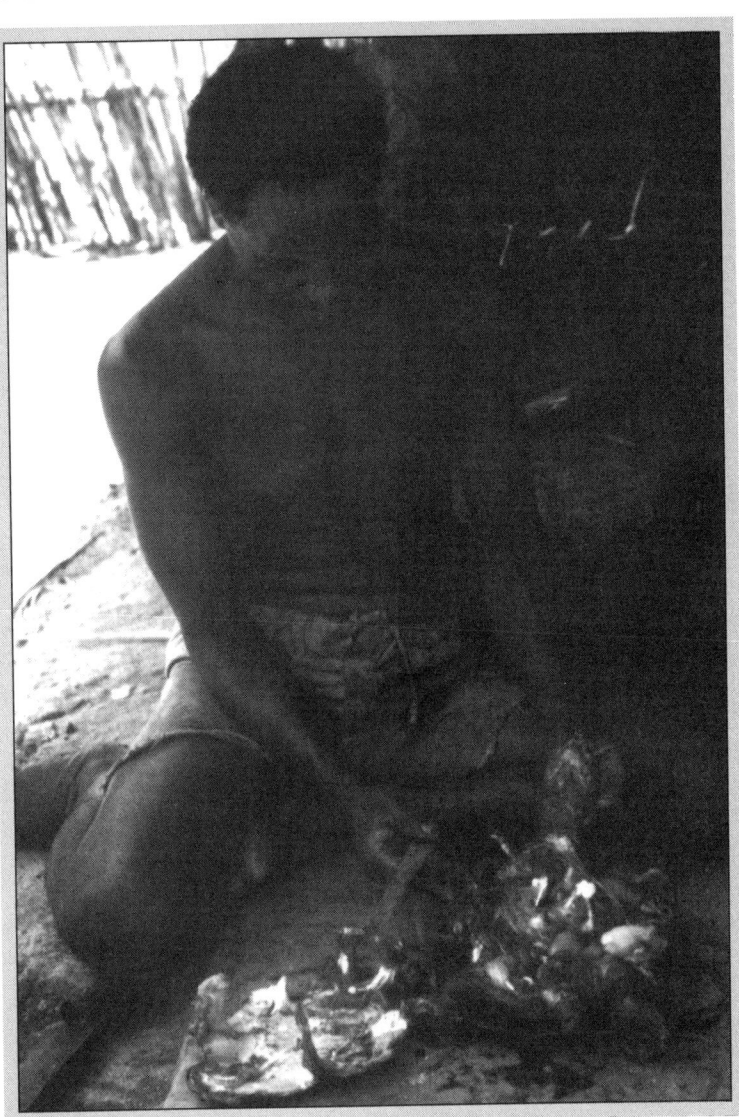

Figure 1. Slaughter of *Erymnochelys madagascariensis* by Malagasy fisherman.

medium-sized turtles (25–30 cm CL) for about 700 FMG (≈U.S. $0.50). This is in the lower range of prices for chickens at the same market.

The people who hunt *Erymnochelys* in the area of Bevilany also hunt crocodiles. Salted skins of crocodiles under 120 cm in length sell for 700 FMG/cm of skin-width, skins of larger crocodiles for 400 FMG/cm skin-width. Some people also eat crocodile meat. Crocodile oil (fat) is sought for pharmaceutical purposes in Madagascar and sells for 20,000 FMG/litre in Bevilany and for 40,000 FMG/litre in Antananarivo or Mahajanga (a large crocodile may provide up to 100 litres of oil). Another survey in Madagascar reported a price of U.S. $10/litre for crocodile oil for use in hospitals (Behra, 1992).

DISCUSSION

The rapid survey technique provided an overview of the exploitation of *Erymnochelys madagascariensis* over most of its range. The study was restricted to the species' best habitats, which would underestimate the number of extirpated populations. Many smaller lakes and marginal habitats, where the species may have disappeared long ago through overexploitation, were not surveyed. On the other hand, small habitat pockets in areas where access is difficult and the human population low may still harbour small but viable populations.

The survey technique was chosen to allow a large number of populations to be surveyed in a time- and cost-efficient way. Despite the methodological limitations, I believe the study offers an adequate picture of the status of the species. The habitats surveyed are of different sizes and reflect the whole range of wetland diversity inhabited by *Erymnochelys*: rivers, swamp areas with small lakes, and larger lakes. The overall status of the 45 sites where *Erymnochelys* populations occurred (31% extirpated or possibly extirpated, 58% declining or depleted, and 11% relatively good) changes slightly when only the 17 larger lakes (>400 ha) are considered: 18% extirpated, 64% declining or depleted, and 18% relatively good. The smaller percentage of extirpated populations (18% vs. 31%) and the larger component of declining or depleted populations (64% vs. 58%) in large lakes may indicate that in these habitats populations collapse more slowly and take longer to reach the point of extinction.

Five localities were considered to support *Erymnochelys* populations that are "exploited but relatively good." Two of them are relatively large lakes, two are groups of small lakes with extensive fields of *Phragmites mauritianus* and floating plants in flood areas of large rivers, and one is an isolated, cut-off branch of a river where the water flows only during floods. The five good populations are therefore more or less equally distributed over the whole range of habitat types used by *Erymnochelys*. Fishing is strongly limited in all of them. In the smaller lakes, difficult access and vegetation hinder fishing with seine nets; tree trunks as well as water depth hinder fishing in isolated river branches; and the large lakes, because of their remoteness, have a relatively low number of fishermen. Strong local traditions—"fadys" or taboos—still regulate fishing activities and prohibit the taking of turtles at one site.

The new data support the conclusions of Kuchling and Mittermeier (1993) regarding the decline of *Erymnochelys*: Exploitation pressure is the main reason for its decrease and physical characteristics of the habitat, especially size, water depth, and obstructions to net fishing may accelerate or retard the extinction process.

The present status of the various *Erymnochelys* populations should not be viewed as static. It is dynamic and changing. Unfortunately, all information collected points towards progressive reduction of populations. The continuing downward trend, as discussed by Kuchling and Mittermeier (1993), is more alarming than the current number of populations or absolute current population level (which was not assessed during this study). The human population of Madagascar is expected to double in the next 30 years. The need for food will further expand fishing activities, making the survival of *Erymnochelys* unlikely if conservation action is not taken.

The main threat to the survival of *Erymnochelys madagascariensis*—overexploitation for human consumption—has been recognised by Malagasy authorities, who have responded with protective legislation. Malagasy law fully protects the species, which may not be hunted, killed, captured, collected, or sold without the authorisation of the highest authority, and then only if required in the national interest or for scientific purposes. However, this is very difficult to enforce. One benefit of its protected status is the limitation of trade in the species; it is not openly sold at markets. The legislation, however, does not curb the taking and killing of *Erymnochelys* at a local subsistence level. Most turtles are slaughtered and consumed despite the illegality of this action. Law enforcement by confrontation seems impossible. The enlightenment of fishermen to the problems of *Erymnochelys* through an education campaign may be more helpful in the long term, although this alone may not be sufficient to ensure the survival of the species.

No major *Erymnochelys* populations of reasonable size occur in fully protected areas. Several small populations occur in rivers and small lakes in the Réserve Naturelle Intégrale 7 Ankarafantsika and the Forêt Classée Ampijoroa. Nicoll and Langrand (1989) list the species as possibly occurring in the Reserve Speciale d'Andranomena and in the private reserve of Analabe. But these reserves at best offer marginal habitat (Kuchling, 1991). The classification of the lakes Bemamba, Masama, Befotaka, and Kinkony as "Reserves de Chasses" unfortunately offers no protection for *Erymnochelys*.

All major populations occur in wetlands that are important for the inland fishery of Madagascar. Because of the present human population pressure and food shortages, it may be difficult to establish a number of protected areas for *Erymnochelys* where fishermen are excluded. At least one core habitat should be fully protected. In addition, it is imperative that any exploitation of small populations in existing protected areas (e.g., Ankarafantsika and Ampijoroa) be stopped. A further sound conservation initiative would support local traditions and customs that ensure the survival of turtle populations despite fishing. Unfortunately, local social structures and traditions are being undermined by progress and development in several areas of western Madagascar.

Erymnochelys madagascariensis has similar habitat requirements to *Crocodylus niloticus* and generally occupies the same waters and wetlands, although the recent distribution of *Erymnochelys* in Madagascar is more restricted than that of the crocodile. As previously mentioned, the major survival problem for both species is overexploitation; it is therefore interesting to compare them. All localities at which *Erymnochelys* populations were found were also occupied by crocodiles. Further, crocodiles were still found (sometimes at very low density) at all localities where the turtle populations were recently extirpated or possibly extirpated. Crocodile populations in Madagascar generally fare better than *Erymnochelys* populations (and much better than previously reported—Kuchling, 1989).

Exploitation of the two species differs in that larger crocodile (>≈120 cm) are taken only by specialised hunters and are not directly affected by normal fishing practices. Crocodile hunters hunt only in areas where crocodiles are common enough to make hunting efforts rewarding. Traditional hunting of crocodiles in Madagascar is directed mainly at animals <2 m in length and not as much at large, breeding adults (Kuchling, 1989). Turtles, apart from being taken by people specialised in their capture, are a regular bycatch of fishing operations, and every turtle caught is slaughtered and consumed by local people. A main difference in the exploitation of the two species is that the adult breeding stock of crocodiles is not directly affected by fishing pressure, whereas the adult breeding stock as well as the juvenile stock of *Erymnochelys* is decimated by normal fishing practices. Turtles of any size, but particularly large ones, are taken and eaten wherever they are found (except where they are "fady" or taboo). Larger crocodiles are not caught accidentally during fishing. If they were, it would be more dangerous for the fishermen than for the crocodiles.

A current strategy for crocodile conservation in Madagascar is farming (or ranching) from eggs collected in the wild. A proportion of the farm-raised crocodiles can be released to supplement the wild stock, and most can be marketed to support the operation. This ranching model is viable because of the high prices fetched by crocodile products for which a national and international demand exists.

Because *Erymnochelys* is consumed only locally and its market price may be one percent of that of a crocodile, farming or ranching operations for *Erymnochelys*, unlike those for crocodiles, may never be self-sufficient. Captive breeding, or the collection and artificial incubation of eggs, and the release of hatchlings or headstarted juveniles into the wild (similar to the release of fish from hatcheries to supplement wild stocks for sportfishing) could still be a sound strategy to increase wild populations despite local exploitation. This strategy, however, would raise the same conservation concerns as it does in the case of fish—that regional genetic differences and genetic variability of wild stocks may be lost. A prerequisite would therefore be to compare the genetic makeup of *Erymnochelys* populations in different areas of its distribution.

ACKNOWLEDGEMENTS

This study was funded by and conducted on behalf of Conservation International. I thank P. S. Daniels, R. Mast, R. A. Mittermeier, S. Rajaobelina, and the staff of Conservation International in Antananarivo for facilitating the work. The Ministère de la Production Animale et des Eaux et Forêts provided the necessary authorisations for the fieldwork. I acknowledge the help of A. Raselimanana of the University of Madagascar, who contributed substantially to the success of interviews and the help of A. Andriamamonjisoa with translations during interviews. The following representatives of the Direction des Eaux et Forêts assisted and contributed to the fieldwork: B. J. Derason, A. Hafany, M. Joanary, L. T. Rabearisoa, R. C. Rabelahy, M. Ralaivao, C. M. Ramanantsoa, and R. S. Veroni.

LITERATURE CITED

Behra, O. 1992. Crocodile oil medicine. Traffic Bulletin 13(2):50.

Bour, R. 1985. Les tortues terrestres et d'eau douce de Madagascar et des iles voisines. Bull. APARS-MAD. 18:54–80.

IUCN/SSC Tortoise and Freshwater Turtle Specialist Group. 1989. Tortoises and freshwater turtles: An action plan for their conservation (D. Stubbs, comp.). IUCN/SSC Tortoise and Freshwater Turtle Specialist Group, Gland, Switzerland. 47 pp.

Kuchling, G. 1988. Population structure, reproductive potential and increasing exploitation of the freshwater turtle *Erymnochelys madagascariensis*. Biol. Conserv. 43:107–113.

Kuchling, G. 1989. *Crocodylus niloticus* in Madagascar (letter to the editor). Biol. Conserv. 47:315–317.

Kuchling, G. 1991. Biology and status of *Erymnochelys madagascariensis*. Unpubl. report to Conservation International and Ministère de la Production Animale et des Eaux et Forêts. 27 pp.

Kuchling, G. 1992. Distribution and status of *Erymnochelys madagascariensis* (Grandidier, 1867). Unpubl. report to Conservation International and Ministère de la Production Animale et des Eaux et Forêts. 34 pp.

Kuchling, G. and R. A. Mittermeier. 1993. Field data on status and exploitation of *Erymnochelys madagascariensis*. Chelon. Conserv. Biol. 1:13–18.

Nicoll, M. E. and O. Langrand. 1989. Madagascar: Revue de la Conservation et Des Aires Protegees. World Wildlife Fund, Gland, Switzerland.

Exploitation and Trade of *Geochelone chilensis*

TOMÁS WALLER

Zavalia 2090 - 3.B., 1428 Buenos Aires, Argentina [e-mail: curiyu@interserver.com.ar]

ABSTRACT: *Geochelone chilensis* are collected for various purposes and to varying extents in certain parts of their range in Argentina. Although the practice is not widespread, local inhabitants hunt them for food in some areas. Since the 1950s hatchlings and young specimens of *G. chilensis* have been captured and sold as pets in major cities. They have been in demand in foreign countries since the 1980s as replacements for other species that were progressively banned in international trade (i.e., European species of *Testudo*). Despite protection by national and provincial laws, it has been estimated that from 20,000 to 50,000 tortoises, from only two provinces (Córdoba and Santiago del Estero), are taken annually within the domestic market, mainly in Buenos Aires. In the past, annual exports accounted for 5–10% of this figure and were allowed because of the establishment of two hatcheries. In 1989 the Convention on Trade in Endangered Species (CITES) Management Authority stopped authorizing these exports after taking into account the suspect nature of these breeding centers. In spite of restrictive administrative and legislative measures, conflicting interests with provincial states that allow hatcheries and the permanent establishment of a consumer market has lead to a continuous illegal domestic trade of thousands of specimens throughout Argentina. Various institutions now discourage this market by promoting the release of captive and confiscated animals. This practice could have negative consequences for wild populations (i.e., spread of disease, mixing gene pools, and the translocation of species). The local impact of collecting activities, consumption as food, and release practices should be assessed, and new releases should be discouraged.

The designation *Geochelone chilensis* (Gray, 1870) has previously comprised three South American species of tortoises: *G. chilensis* (Gray, 1870) (sensu strictu), *G. donosobarrosi* Freiberg (1973), and *G. petersi* Freiberg (1973). While recognizing the validity of *G. donosobarrosi*, King and Burke (1989) synonymized *G. petersi* with *G. chilensis*, and *G. donosobarrosi* has been further synonymized with *G. chilensis* by Buskirk (1993).

The Chaco tortoise, *G. chilensis*, ranges from southeastern Bolivia and Paraguay to northern Patagonia, Argentina. It inhabits plains and sub-montane habitats of desert and semidesert areas with scrub and arborescent vegetation. This species feeds on grasses and annual vegetation, cacti, succulents, and the fruits of a variety of trees and shrubs. Breeding is seasonal and nesting takes place up to three times a year during the summer, with clutch sizes varying from two to seven eggs (varying with location). Incubation lasts 12–16 months. Hatchlings measure approximately 4 cm. Growth is slow and sexual maturity is thought to occur after the age of 12 years (Waller et al., 1989b). Although high densities have been reported (approx. 30–40 individuals/ha for *G. chilensis*, Auffenberg, 1969), recent surveys indicate much lower densities for different populations (Waller et al., 1989a, 1989b).

G. chilensis (then comprising both *G. chilensis* and *G. donosobarrosi*) was initially classified as "Insufficiently Known" by the IUCN (1982). Today, with evidence of serious conservation problems, it is considered "Vulnerable" (Walker, 1989). The factors determining population decline, and the two main purposes for which it is exploited in Argentina, appear to be disruption of the habitat and direct take of specimens for local consumption as food or for the pet market. Although they are collected occasionally for other purposes (for sale as stuffed specimens or handicraft, in the manufacture of musical instruments, etc.), the volume is not significant.

Consumption of Tortoises as Food

Hunting tortoises for food was first reported by Freiberg (1974) and has since been documented by additional authors as one of the many threats affecting this species in Argentina (Richard, 1988a; Walker, 1989; Waller et al., 1989a, 1989b; Buskirk, 1993). Hudson (1917) mentioned this practice by the north Patagonian indigenous peoples. Little is known of its extent or significance with respect to population status, yet available information suggests that it is a traditional custom, scattered throughout the range of the species, locally intensive but showing a declining trend.

The use of tortoises for food dates from pre-Hispanic times (Richard, 1988). The criollo peoples inhabiting inland Argentina inherited this custom from their indigenous ancestors, and it has remained popular to the present day. During pre-Hispanic times the impact of tortoise collection was offset by the nomadic habits of the indigenous peoples.

However, these communities gradually became sedentary, and tortoise collection increased considerably in certain areas (Richard, 1988b). At present young people tend to migrate from rural areas to the cities in search of better opportunities, so that a decrease in hunting pressure on tortoises may be expected.

Current consumption levels are more related to the area and to the customs and traditions of human settlers than to the species. In this respect, Chaco tortoises are infrequently hunted in Córdoba province, the center of their geographical range (Auffenberg, 1969), and based on my own observations, it is not a common practice in southern provinces such as La Pampa or Río Negro. Although Buskirk (1993) reported occasional consumption in some Patagonian localities, he attributed the practice to Asian communities or itinerant workers.

Tortoise consumption is currently associated with less-developed areas where hunting plays a complementary role in food acquisition, or, as suggested by Richard (1988b), in communities with a well-established tradition inherited from the indigenous peoples. Such is apparently the case in Mendoza province in the western extreme of the species' range. In northern sections of this province as well as in the south, both tortoises and their eggs are consumed extensively (Richard, 1988b, 1988c; Waller et al., 1989b). In the provinces of Santiago del Estero, Salta, and Formosa in the northern extremity of the range of *G. chilensis* in Argentina where indigenous influences still survive, both the criollo and the indigenous local inhabitants consume adults and eggs, the latter collected from newly laid nests with the help of dogs (E. Richard, pers. comm.; E. Astort, pers. comm.). Some indigenous communities from northern Paraguay are assiduous consumers of the related species, *G. carbonaria* (Aquino-Shuster et al., 1991). In this area, the species co-exists with *G. chilensis*, according to the indigenous inhabitants. Although not mentioned in the report, the latter species may be also consumed occasionally. Based on my observations in the field, indigenous peoples of the Paraguayan Dry Chaco (Ayoreo groups) consume *G. chilensis* extensively and use the shells in making maracas (musical instruments), which they later sell in urban centers such as Filadelfia, Paraguay (Figure 1).

Because of the relatively small size of *G. chilensis*, the meal of an average family group includes several adult tortoises. Indeed, they are frequently cooked in substantial numbers with other food items in a stew (Richard, 1988c), although in many places tortoises are grilled on coals ("rescoldo") or boiled (Richard, 1988b). Richard (1988b, 1988c) also stated that in southern Mendoza province, dozens of carapaces and bones of consumed tortoises were scattered in areas surrounding the homes of local inhabitants, stressing the virtual extirpation of chelonians from these areas. In northern Mendoza province, as many as 12 live Chaco tortoises may be kept by a local family, a sufficient amount for the occasional consumption of an average family group

Figure 1. After using the tortoises for food, the Ayoreo Indians from the Paraguayan Chaco region (Filadelfia) make maracas from *G. chilensis* carapaces.

(Richard, 1988b). Eating tortoises is also a tradition among some inhabitants of Salta province where the same species occurs. The fact that consumption of tortoises occurs mostly in the summer, coinciding with the egg-laying season, and that the nests are actively sought, increases the impact on wild populations.

Collection of tortoises for food differs from collection for the pet trade in that the former is based primarily on adult specimens. Considering the biological and ecological characteristics of this species, a dramatic effect may be predicted on wild populations in those areas where there is intensive consumption. However, there are no quantitative data on these practices or on their effects on wild populations.

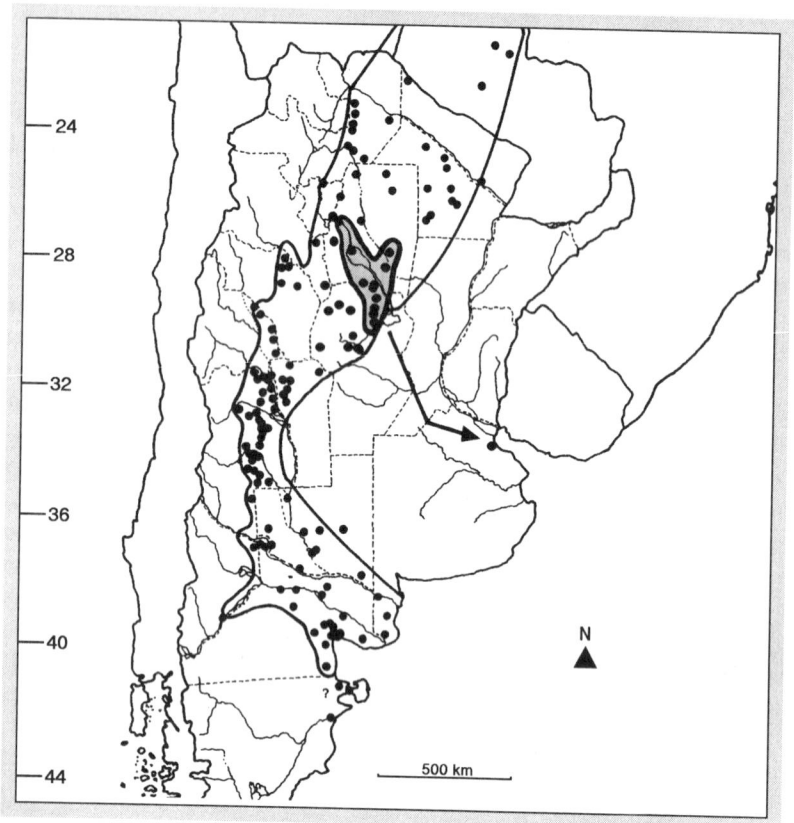

Figure 2. Distribution of *G. chilensis* complex and pet trade collection area (shaded). The southernmost locality records for the species (province of Chubut "?") represent probable human introductions.

Tortoises and the Pet Trade

In Argentina, trade for the pet market is based on the Chaco tortoise, *Geochelone chilensis*, because only this species occurs in the areas where tortoises are traditionally collected (Santiago del Estero and Córdoba provinces). The ultimate destination of captured tortoises is both the domestic trade and the international market, the latter notably less significant than the former (Waller et al., 1989). The Chaco tortoise has a long-standing tradition as a pet in Argentine homes. Because of its relatively small size and apparently minimal food and space requirements, it has become the ideal "domestic" reptile. It is widely available in a variety of shops in Argentina (veterinary shops, pet stores, bird stores, garden houses, and public fairs). Tortoises are often the first and most popular pets of Argentine children and are also frequently given as presents. According to a study by Gruss (1986), 63.5% of a group (n = 788) of people from Buenos Aires and suburbs (an area of approx. 10,000,000 inhabitants and a major center of distribution for the pet trade) acknowledged having had a at least one pet tortoise. This same study indicated a preference for hatchlings or juveniles.

Results of polls (Gruss, 1986) have indicated that at least 80% of tortoises bought as pets were kept in backyards, gardens, or balconies, and the remaining 20% indoors (in boxes or fish bowls). Subadult and adult mortality after three years in captivity was estimated at 80% and 65% respectively. Nevertheless, reliable data indicate that some specimens have lived over 30 years in captivity (Gruss, 1986). In this study, mortality in captivity was attributed to accidents and predation by domestic pets (23%), to escape of tortoises from gardens (35%), and to other unknown causes, presumably related to adaptation problems, nutritional deficiencies, etc. (30%). Many individuals were given away by their owners after a certain period in captivity, probably because the owners had lost interest and no longer desired to keep the animals, which illustrates the public's perception of tortoises as playthings (Gruss, 1986). Nevertheless, the low survival rate in captivity contributes to a sustained demand.

Trade in tortoises dates at least from the 1950s (Freiberg, 1954). Godoy (1963) estimated the number of tortoises traded annually in Argentina during the period 1956–1960 to be 5,000. Since then trade has remained at least at this level, and several authors (Auffenberg, 1969; Freiberg, 1970, 1974; Gnida and Viñas, 1985; Gruss and Waller, 1988) consider it to have even increased. In 1985 the number of animals involved in domestic trade was estimated at 20,000 (Gnida and Viñas, 1985); other authors have proposed a figure of 75,000 (Gruss, 1986; Waller et al., 1989a, 1989b). Currently the extent of domestic trade is probably between 20,000 and 50,000 individuals annually. The elevated trade estimate is based upon the increasing human urban population, leading to an increased demand for tortoises. As in the 1980s, the broadcast media has used tortoises for promotional purposes, either by including them in shows or by using them as gifts for participants, which has enhanced the popularity of these animals.

Collection of and trade in wild tortoises was prohibited by provincial laws in the 1960s. Since that time, the market was comprised of tortoises from two origins: those illegally removed from the wild (95% of historically traded tortoises within Argentina) and those declared by the provinces to have been produced in captive-breeding operations (tortoises exported during the 1980s, see Figure 3). In 1986 the federal government banned domestic trade (in those areas under federal jurisdiction) as well as exports of live animals, including tortoises (Resolución 62/86 issued by the Secretariat of Agriculture, Livestock, and Fisheries). Captive-bred animals originating in rearing facilities approved by both provincial and federal authorities are exempt from this ban. However, the federal government does not consider current methods and facilities viable for breeding tortoises, and there have been no significant numbers of exports of captive tortoises in recent years.

Wild tortoises are collected in a small sector of the range of *G. chilensis* in Argentina: northern Córdoba province and south-central Santiago del Estero province (Figure 2). Collection in this area is apparently related to the history of agricultural colonization, the layout of railroads (tortoises were mostly transported by railway in the past), and tortoise abundance in this zone. Tortoise collection is so strictly confined to this area that animals offered for sale in Paraguay originate from this distant Argentine region.

Tortoises are collected in the forest by rural inhabitants (generally the children of woodsmen or ranch employees), who later take them to general store owners or to rural shopkeepers who act as middlemen, or directly to wholesalers (usually "captive-breeding" facilities). These three levels of the trade are under provincial jurisdiction, whereas in major urban centers, such as Buenos Aires, trade is managed by large wholesalers. The wholesalers often buy tortoises in the provinces from where they are sent by the hundreds in boxes or bags, by railway or bus, to be distributed to small shops (pet stores, garden houses, veterinary shops, markets, and public fairs), or exported. Historically, the main importing countries of legally exported tortoises have been the United States, Germany, Japan, The Netherlands, Denmark, the United Kingdom, and Switzerland (Figure 4). Illegal exports to Chile, Uruguay, Paraguay, Spain, and the USA have also been reported.

Because legislation prohibited exports of wild-caught tortoises and the legal infrastructure was better able to control exports than domestic trade, the captive-breeding operations were initiated in the 1970s to supply the export market. Dealers were fully aware that the profitable domestic tortoise trade was practically impossible to control, and it had not been necessary for them to set up captive-breeding operations for the domestic trade, which could be conducted illegally at a lower cost.

However, when Argentina became a party to CITES in 1981, the international community focused more attention on exports originating from the captive-breeding operations, and it became clear that these centers were acting as façades for trade in wild specimens (Waller et al., 1989a, 1989b). *In situ* inspections of these sites revealed high annual mortality of adults (20–30%), massive tick (*Amblyomma* sp.) infestation, and tortoises that were seriously emaciated. The local inhabitants were also discovered constantly providing the breeding centers with hatchlings or yearlings. While considerable egg laying and hatching success has been observed within the breeding centers, the

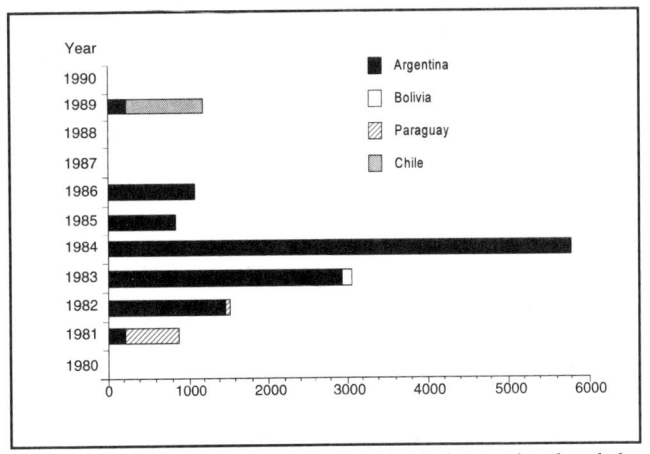

Figure 3. Live specimens of *G. chilensis* in the international trade by reported country of origin (CITES data).

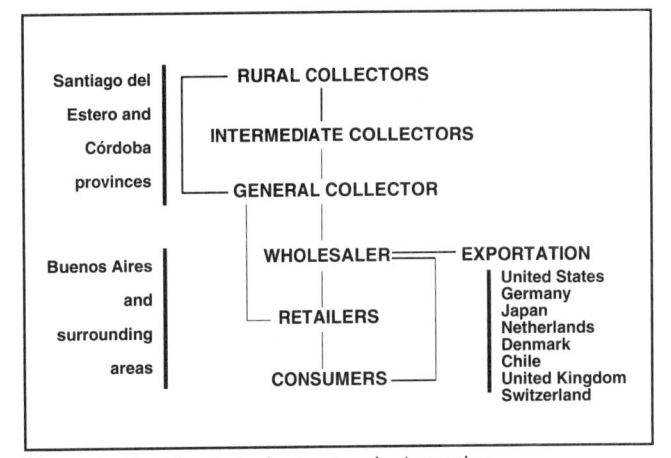

Figure 4. *G. chilensis* trade structure in Argentina.

high mortality and continuous replacement of adults taken from the wild make the centers biologically unreliable. There are no means of following the breeding centers' effectiveness because adults, eggs, and hatchlings are not individually marked. Extensive commercial breeding of tortoises in Argentina seems to be economically unfeasible. The low fertility rate, the lengthy incubation period (lasting over one year), the low feeding efficiency, and low prices on the international market (U.S. $30–$40 retail price in the United States) rendered these operations unprofitable.

Because the Argentine wildlife agency has not recognized any captive breeding operations as viable since 1990, the current domestic trade in tortoises is based on illegally obtained specimens. The federal government has recently intensified control of illegal trade, which has resulted in a partial curtailment of trade, although levels are still significant. On the other hand, there is constant pressure on the federal government from the two provinces that host the oldest breeding centers to be granted official recognition and thus regain access to the international market.

Figure 5. Facilities at one of the Chaco tortoise "hatcheries" in Sabastián Elcano, Córdoba province, Argentina.

Release of Tortoises to the Wild

The Fifth Conference of the Parties to the Convention on International Trade in Endangered Species (CITES), held in Buenos Aires in 1985, resulted in an increase in public awareness of wildlife trade and particularly in wild tortoises in Argentina. Since that date, field studies on the biology of the species as well as research on the structure and extent of trade have been undertaken. Consequently, both *G. chilensis* and wild birds became national symbols of illegal wildlife trade. Although this new focus upon tortoises was mostly positive (the urban population has become increasingly aware of the deleterious effects of uncontrolled trade), it also has had some negative effects.

Argentina has a federal government, but the provinces retain constitutional autonomy over the management of natural resources within their boundaries. Species of the genus *Geochelone* range into at least 15 provinces. Because of the extensive flow of illegally removed tortoises from collection sites (Santiago del Estero and Córdoba provinces) to different important cities in the country, the provincial authorities frequently seize large shipments which are then released. In some cases, animals are returned to those areas from which they have been presumably removed, but in many other cases, they are released hundreds of kilometers from their localities of origin. In some instances, provincial officials have released tortoises in national parks in which the species does not actually occur!

Nongovernmental conservation organizations have endorsed these activities in the belief that the release of tortoises represents a strongly positive element in campaigns against illegal wildlife trade. As a result of such campaigns, pet owners donate their pets to these nongovernmental organizations for release to the wild. Tortoises are sometimes classified according to their presumed geographical origin, taxonomic identification, and health conditions before release, but usually these aspects are not addressed.

This increasingly widespread practice has two seriously negative results: gene pool mixing and the risk of disease introduction. Release of tortoises from a given region into a different one carries a potential risk of genetic pollution; when conducted "for the sake of conservation," the policy appears to be contradictory. The taxonomy of the "*chilensis*" group is still a matter of controversy, and the situation is further complicated by the high degree of polymorphism within this group, which may lead to the description of nonvalid species as well as to the masking of as yet undescribed species.

The spread of disease resulting from the release of tortoises is a phenomenon that has been reported for another species of similar habits and habitat, *Gopherus agassizii* from the deserts of the western United States (Jacobson, 1992). The desert tortoise is endangered by human activities such as habitat disruption and collection, the effects of which have been partially mitigated with the creation of reserves. However, the occasional release of captive tortoises into such reserves has resulted in a dramatic decline of the populations "under strict protection." The disease known as URTD (upper respiratory tract disease), apparently caused by bacterial infection (*Mycoplasma* and other associated bacteria), is responsible for the decline (Jacobson et al., 1991; Jacobson, 1992, 1993, 1994).

The lack of data on similar cases in Argentine tortoises may reflect the absence of research on this issue rather than the absence of actual cases. Because *Mycoplasma* is commonly found in reptiles, the risk of infection in tortoises by this bacterium should not be overlooked. Captive *G. chilensis* specimens commonly present infections in the mouth and nasal cavities, which increases the risk in releasing captive specimens to the wild.

The practice of releasing captive specimens should be carefully considered. Generally speaking, releases are a response to two main concerns: Hundreds of tortoises are confiscated from dealers, so that release is considered a practical and popular solution. Secondly, because releasing is interpreted as exactly the opposite of collecting, it is expected to generate a public awareness of illegal trade. However, important questions from a conservation viewpoint are seldom put forth: What is needed to preserve the Chaco tortoise in its own environment? Does release of captive tortoises represent a contribution to wild populations? Unfortunately, the public is inclined to think more of the fate of captive specimens than of the conservation of wild populations, an indication of the current confusion between animal welfare and conservation.

From a numerical viewpoint, the introduction of captive specimens into wild populations is unnecessary because natural populations are not currently critically endangered and are therefore in no need of such augmentation. Indeed, this practice may prove to be even more deleterious than commercial collecting because individuals harbouring potentially hazardous pathogens are now being scattered in several subpopulations, whereas historically collection has been focused on one area. Governmental agencies and nongovernmental conservation organizations should recognize a clear distinction between conservation and animal welfare and give priority to those factors that guarantee the survival of the species in the wild. Confiscated animals could be distributed among zoos and research institutes as well as to the public through an adoption programme established clearly for educational purposes.

CONCLUSIONS

The use of tortoises as a food source is related, not to subsistence needs that could eventually be satisfied with other wild resources, but rather to cultural and practical aspects. It seems unlikely that consumption of these species, not widespread but locally significant, may be discouraged in the short term; however, a reduction in the total volume of collection can only be expected to occur as a result of a gradual decrease in human population densities in marginal rural areas. An impact assessment of this activity on wild populations would be advisable, both as a contribution to knowledge of the status of tortoise populations and because of the tortoise's social significance for the local inhabitants.

In Argentina, large-scale and virtually uncontrolled illegal trade is encouraged by a deep-rooted tradition of keeping tortoises as pets. The 20,000–50,000 specimens that annually reach large cities such as Buenos Aires are collected from one specific area. The impact on wild populations should be assessed in this area, especially considering that collection probably will never be completely stopped, de-

Figure 6. Starving specimen at the Sabastián Elcano hatchery, Córdoba.

spite improved enforcement by governmental agencies. The structure of trade in tortoises is similar to that of the trade in small birds: hundreds of rural collectors, a dozen rural wholesalers, middlemen, urban wholesalers who receive the largest share of the profit, and hundreds of retailers. In general terms, tortoises do not appear to represent an important subsistence item for marginal human communities of the Chaco ecosystem, although this deserves further analysis. The only commercial activity permitted in past years was export, based on the existence of two alleged captive-breeding facilities that acted as fronts for the delivery of wild specimens to the international market. These operations, however, involved relatively few tortoises.

Enforcement efforts and campaigns organized by nongovernmental organizations have brought about large-scale release of tortoises. Because the taxonomy of this group is yet to be clarified and because of the risk of disease transmission (as has been the case in other species with catastrophic results), this practice is a matter of serious concern. Releases should be discouraged as they may be detrimental to the conservation of the species. Health surveys should be conducted on wild populations in areas where tortoises have been released as well as on captive animals.

ACKNOWLEDGMENTS

Most of the observations upon which this paper is based were made possible by the financial support of the Kantonaler Zürcher Tierschutzverein (Switzerland) and the continuous encouragement of Mr. René Honegger (Curator of Herpetology, Zürich Zoo), to whom I am greatly indebted. I also wish to express my gratitude to Michael W. Klemens for sponsoring the presentation of our paper at Conservation, Restoration, and Management of Tortoises and Turtles —An International Conference; to the editor of this volume, Jim Van Abbema, for his patience and helpful suggestions; to Victoria Lichtschein for reviewing and translating the manuscript; and to the anonymous reviewers for their valuable comments on it.

LITERATURE CITED

Aquino-Shuster, A. L., M. Motte, and G. Sequera. 1991. Relación del indígena Chamacoco con la herpetofauna del Alto Paraguay. Bol. Mus. Nac. Hist. Nat. Paraguay (10):11–22. Asunción.

Auffenberg, W. 1969. Land of the Chaco tortoise *Geochelone chilensis*. Int. Turtle & Tortoise Soc. J. 3(3):16–19, 36–37.

Buskirk, J. R. 1993. Distribution, status and biology of the tortoise, *Geochelone chilensis*, in Río Negro Province, Argentina. Studies on Neotropical Fauna and Environment 28(4):233–249. Lisse.

Freiberg, M. A. 1954. Vida de Batracios y Reptiles Sudamericanos. Cesarini Hnos., Editores, Buenos Aires. 192 pp.

Freiberg, M. A. 1970. La tortuga argentina. Diario La Prensa, 1° de noviembre. Buenos Aires.

Freiberg, M. A. 1973. Dos nuevas tortugas terrestres de Argentina. Bol. Soc. Biol. de Concepción 46:81–93.

Freiberg, M. A. 1974. The Argentine land tortoise, *Geochelone chilensis*, an endangered species. Bull. Maryland Herpetol. Soc. 10(2):39–41.

Gnida, G. and M. Viñas. 1985. Sobre el comercio de anfibios y reptiles en la República Argentina. Bol. Asoc. Herpetológica Argentina, 2(4). Buenos Aires.

Godoy, J. C. 1963. Fauna Silvestre. Volumen 1. Serie: Evaluación de los Recursos Naturales de la Argentina (Primera etapa), tomo 8. Consejo Federal de Inversiones, Buenos Aires. 527 pp.

Gruss, J. X. 1986. *Geochelone chilensis* en cautividad, descripción. FVSA-Amph. & Rept. (cons.) 1(2):29–35. Buenos Aires.

Gruss, J. X. and T. Waller. 1988. Diagnóstico y recomendaciones sobre la administración de los recursos silvestres en la Argentina: la década reciente (un análisis sobre la administración de la fauna terrestre). WWF-TRAFFIC Sudamérica-Secretaría CITES, Buenos Aires. 114 pp.

Hudson, W. H. 1917. Idle Days in Patagonia. E. P. Dutton & Co., New York. 249 pp.

IUCN. 1982. The IUCN Amphibia-Reptilia Red Data Book, Part 1: Testudines, Crocodylia, Rhynchocephalia (B. Groombridge, comp.). IUCN, Gland, Switzerland.

Jacobson, E. R. 1992. The desert tortoise and upper respiratory tract disease. Desert Tortoise Preserve Committee, Inc. and U.S. Bureau of Land Management, special report (November, 1992):1–4. Gainesville.

Jacobson, E. R. 1993. Implications of infectious diseases for captive propagation and introduction programs of theatened/endangered reptiles. J. Zoo Wildl. Med. 24:245–255.

Jacobson, E. R. 1994. Causes of mortality and diseases in tortoises: A review. J. Zoo Wildl. Med. 25:2–17.

Jacobson, E. R., J. M. Gaskin, M. B. Brown, R. K. Harris, C. H. Gardiner, J. L. Lapoite, H. P. Adams, and C. Reggiardo. 1991. Chronic upper respiratory disease of free-ranging desert tortoises (*Xerobates agassizii*). J. Wildl. Dis. 27:296–316.

King, F. W. and R. L. Burke. 1989. Crocodilian, Tuatara, and Turtle Species of the World: A Taxonomic and Geographic Reference. Association of Systematics Collections, Washington, D.C. 216 pp.

Richard, E. 1988a. El aprovechamiento humano de tortugas en la provincia de Mendoza. I. Período pre-hispánico. Informativo Lilloano 1(7/8):10–12. Tucumán.

Richard, E. 1988b. El aprovechamiento humano de tortugas en la provincia de Mendoza. II. Períodos hispánico y actual. Informativo Lilloano 1(9/10):11–18. Tucumán.

Richard, E. 1988c. Las Yataché (*Chelonoidis donosobarrosi*: Chelonii, Testudinidae) de la región del Nevado (Mendoza, Argentina). Apuntes sobre su historia natural. FVSA-Amp. y Rept. (cons.) 1(4):79–92. Buenos Aires.

Walker, P. 1989. *Geochelone chilensis*: Chaco tortoise. In I. R. Swingland and M. W. Klemens (eds.), The Conservation Biology of Tortoises, pp. 20–21. Occasional Papers of the IUCN Species Survival Commission (SSC) No. 5. IUCN, Gland, Switzerland.

Waller, T., P. A. Micucci, and E. Richard. 1989a. Current status of the research on the bioecology and conservation of the *Chelonoidis chilensis* (sensu lato) tortoise in Argentina (Abstract). In First World Congress of Herpetology Abstracts, 11–19 September. Canterbury.

Waller, T., P. A. Micucci, and E. Richard. 1989b. Preliminary results of the research on the biology, ecology and conservation of the *Chelonoidis chilensis* (sensu lato) (Gray, 1870) tortoise in Argentina (Testudines: Testudinidae). Results report, FVSA-TRAFFIC Sudamérica-CITES Secretariat. Buenos Aires, Argentina. 22 pp.

CITES and the Tortoise and Turtle Trade

WIL LUIIJF

*TRAFFIC Europe Enforcement Project,
Barbaralaan 120, 4834 SM - P.O. Box 4625, 4803 EP Breda, The Netherlands [e-mail: traffeur@antenna.nl]*

ABSTRACT: The expanding international wildlife trade has contributed significantly to the decline of many tortoise and turtle populations in the wild. Regulations set forth by the Convention on Trade in Endangered Species (CITES) could be used as a tool to help stem these declines, but serious problems in enforcement have prevented their successful application. While serving as a CITES enforcement officer, the author made observations in the course of day-to-day inspections of wildlife shipments. These are reported here as a series of case studies that document many of these enforcement failures. These cases also reveal extensive failures in compliance with the International Air Transport Association (IATA) Live Animals Regulations for the proper air transport of chelonians. The consequent inhumane and often deplorable conditions frequently result in the death of high numbers of the transported animals.

Tortoises and turtles are exploited as a food resource in many parts of the world. The shell of some species is highly prized for its ornamental value and in some areas is utilized in the making of tools and musical instruments by tribal peoples. Adult tortoises and turtles are often kept in village pens for food and as a source of eggs and hatchlings, which are of increasing economic importance. Hatchlings of certain species fetch high prices in the pet trade and are easily smuggled worldwide. A serious adverse effect of this expanding international trade in both hatchlings and adults is a concomitant decline of tortoise and turtle populations in the wild.

The use of the Convention on Trade in Endangered Species (CITES) as a tool to defend species from extinction is mandated in its preamble. In it, the contracting parties recognize "that wild fauna and flora must be protected for this and generations to come . . ." and that "international cooperation is essential for the protection of certain species of wild fauna and flora against overexploitation through international trade . . ." Accordingly, CITES has established different requirements for trade in species listed on three species appendices (Table 1). The minimum requirement to engage in trade in the listed species is the issuance of a permit by the competent government authority indicating that such trade will not be detrimental to the survival of the wild population (IUCN/SSC, 1996).

Unfortunately, failures in enforcement of CITES requirements have prevented the successful application of CITES as a conservation tool. These, as well as failures in compliance with International Air Transport Association (IATA) regulations (see Figure 6), which have resulted in the inhumane treatment and the death of large numbers of tortoises, are illustrated in the following case studies and photos.

TABLE 1
Definition of CITES appendices, from Article II of the Convention (IUCN/SSC, 1996).

Article II of the Convention sets forth the following among its fundamental principles:

Appendix I shall include all species threatened with extinction which are or may be affected by trade. Trade in specimens of these species must be subject to particularly strict regulation in order not to endanger further their survival and must only be authorized in exceptional circumstances.

Appendix II shall include
(a) all species which, although not necessarily now threatened with extinction, may become so unless trade in specimens of such species is subject to strict regulation in order to avoid utilization incompatible with their survival; and
(b) other species which must be subject to regulation in order that trade in specimens of certain species referred to in the above sub-paragraph may be brought under effective control.

Appendix III shall include all species which any Party identifies as being subject to regulation within its jurisdiction for the purpose of preventing or restricting exploitation, and as needing the cooperation of other parties in the control of trade.

Documentation and Enforcement Failures of Local CITES Management Authorities

Case Study I

On 15 September 1990 authorities in the Netherlands inspected a KLM shipment from Togo in transit to Japan.[1] According to the Togolese-issued CITES permit[2] (see Table 2), it contained 20 African spurred tortoises (*Geochelone sulcata*) and 100 west African black forest turtles (*Pelusios* spp.). There were in fact, mixed with 52 *Pelusios niger* and *Pelusios subniger*, 46 helmeted turtles (*Pelomedusa subrufa*), which were not recorded on the export permit. The shipment also included 20 serrated hinge-back tortoises (*Kinixys erosa*) and 14 Home's hinge-back tortoises (*Kinixys homeana*). The Togolese CITES permit[3] declared that the *G. sulcata*, *K. homeana*, *K. erosa*, and *Pelusios* spp. had been wild caught in Togo. However, there is no evidence that wild populations of *G. sulcata*, *K. homeana*, and *K. erosa* occur in Togo (Swingland and Klemens, 1989). The documents issued by the Togolese CITES Management Authority (MA) were invalid with respect to shipment contents and origin, and the physical condition of the animals was extremely poor. KLM stopped the shipment to avoid prosecution.

Case Study II

On 29 January 1991 authorities in the Netherlands inspected another KLM shipment from Togo in transit to Japan.[4] According to the CITES documents,[5] this shipment contained 40 *Geochelone sulcata* and 40 *Pelomedusa subrufa*. Again, *Pelusios niger*—not recorded on the CITES export permit—were mixed with the *P. subrufa*.

The shipment also included Bell's hinge-back tortoises (*Kinixys belliana*), as well as *K. erosa* and *K. homeana*. Adult tortoises had been packed on top of juveniles, crushing them, and the *G. sulcata* were in exceedingly poor condition—two had broken carapaces, some were bleeding, and a number were missing legs. Even the oldest *G. sulcata*, estimated to be several decades old, was claimed to be captive bred in Togo.[5] The *G. sulcata* were seized, and the CITES Secretariat and the Togo MA were informed of the seizure.

During an official visit to Togo in July 1991, a staff member of the Secretariat discussed this case with Togo MA officials, who were not convinced that the Dutch seizure had been legal. Maintaining that the tortoises were captive bred and that the shipment had been prepared in accordance with IATA Live Animals Regulations, the Togo MA asked that the specimens be returned to the exporter.

However, there is no large-scale captive breeding of *G. sulcata* that could account for the number of tortoises exported from Togo to Europe and elsewhere. The Netherlands MA replied that there was sufficient evidence that the seized specimens were not captive bred and that their shipment had not complied with IATA regulations. On 22 August 1991 the CITES Secretariat, following a mission to Togo, concurred with the Netherlands MA[6]; the alleged "farms" for the breeding of African spurred tortoises in Togo had not met the criteria of CITES Resolution Conf. 2.12 for captive breeding (IUCN/SSC, 1996).

In March 1993 I spoke to the owner of a large reptile retail establishment in Fort Myers, Florida, USA. I knew that he regularly imported shipments of *G. sulcata* from Togo and that some of the animals destined for his company had been amongst those confiscated in the Netherlands during 1990–1993. He informed me that the Togolese exporter, a Frenchmen, had recently visited his business in the USA and had complained that many of his shipments to the USA and Japan had been confiscated in the Netherlands because the "captive-breeding story no longer worked." When asked where the French exporter obtained his *G. sulcata*, he stated that they originated from Mali, where he employed locals to collect them from the wild.* He also described how the newly caught tortoises were loaded onto trucks, covered with fuel wood and kindling, and then driven across the border to Togo. Then, with the help of the Togolese authorities (with whom the French dealer is known to have excellent relations), CITES export documentation, stating that the *G. sulcata* had been captive bred in Togo, was issued.

TABLE 2
CITES listings of species mentioned in this paper.

Species	Appendix	
Chelonians		
Aldabrachelys elephantina	II	
Geochelone pardalis	II	
Geochelone sulcata	II	
Kinixys belliana	II	
Kinixys erosa	II	
Kinixys homeana	II	
Malacochersus tornieri	II	
Pelusios niger	III	Ghana
Pelusios subniger	III	Ghana
Testudo horsfieldi	II	
Testudo kleinmanni	I	
Other Reptiles		
Chamaeleo chameleon	II	
Eryx colubrinus	II	
Eryx jaculus	II	
Euromastyx aegyptius	II	

---

*See also Lambert, 1993.

Figure 1. Case Study II. Shipment including *Geochelone sulcata, Kinixys* spp., *Pelomedusa subrufa*, and *Pelusios niger*. Documentation for even the largest *G. sulcata*, estimated to be several decades old, claimed it to have been captive bred in Togo.

Case Study III

On 28 February 1992 KLM informed the Dutch authorities that two more shipments from Togo destined for the USA and Japan[7] were arriving at Schiphol Airport, Amsterdam. These shipments were inspected on 29 February and, according to the CITES export documents,[8] 12 *Geochelone sulcata* were consigned to Japan and 50 *Kinixys homeana* to the USA. All had reportedly been wild caught in Togo, though these species are not found in Togo (Broadley, 1989). Again, the shipment was not packed in accordance with IATA requirements; adult and juvenile animals were found in the same crates and crawling on top of one another. KLM was ordered to repack the tortoises from one crate to five crates. Unfortunately, because the inspector lacked sufficient training, no legal action was taken against KLM, the shipment continued to its final destination, and the CITES Secretariat was not informed.[8]

Case Study IV

In March 1991 a KLM shipment from Tanzania,[9] comprised of 511 pancake tortoises (*Malacochersus tornieri*) and 307 leopard tortoises (*Geochelone pardalis*), was seized at Schiphol Airport while in transit to the USA. The shipment was opened because it appeared to be poorly packed. The CITES export documentation was subsequently found to be forged. More that 800 tortoises were packed in layers on top of one another in six crates (a total weight of 450 kg); 50 tortoises were dead, and it was feared that at least 400 others would not survive. The physical condition of the tortoises was extremely poor: Many had broken carapaces, some had pelvic bones protruding through their carapaces, many were bleeding, dozens had legs missing, and nearly all were seriously dehydrated. Approximately 50 female tortoises had broken eggs in their oviducts and had suffered severe tissue damage. This shipment was accompanied by an apparently proper CITES document issued by the United Republic of Tanzania.[10]

The Netherlands Management Authority informed both the Secretariat and the Tanzanian MA and suggested that the live specimens be returned to Tanzania. The Tanzanian MA informed the Secretariat that the CITES export permit accompanying the shipment had actually been issued for birds and not for tortoises, and that an investigation was to be undertaken with the intention of prosecuting those responsible. Tanzania also requested that the animals be returned and arranged for their rehabilitation and return to the wild. To date the results of the investigation have not been received by the Secretariat.

The Netherlands MA stated that, due to the lack of co-operation by the country of origin, by January 1992 it still had not been possible to return the tortoises to Tanzania. The costs for housing and care over this ten-month period had exceeded 150,000 Dutch guilders (U.S. $75,000) and had been paid by the Government of the Netherlands. As the airline responsible, KLM offered to pay 20,000 Dutch guilders, assuming that this would be sufficient for the care of the tortoises and their repatriation to Tanzania. The CITES Secretariat agreed that the lack of response from Tanzania had created an unnecessary administrative and financial burden on the Netherlands government. In the Netherlands, legal action was taken against KLM in connection with this case.

On 16 March 1988 the European Community CITES Committee, determining that the trade in *Malacochersus tornieri* was too great a burden on wild populations, banned further imports of this species into the EC. However, the Tanzanian pancake tortoise trade continued with other major import countries, such as the USA and Japan. In March 1988 Tanzania imposed a quota system. Initially, each of the 40 licensed dealers was allowed to capture and export five pancake tortoises per year, and thus a maximum of 200 would be exported annually (WCS of Tanzania, 1988). However, a greater number apparently leave the country each year. Some dealers based in Tanzania and several major importers in the European Union and USA are now working with illicit couriers who travel by air. The couriers use specially prepared suitcases in which they can transport as many as 100–200 tortoises (which fetch U.S. $75–$200 each on the European and U.S. markets). On 12 June 1992 the Dutch authorities, suspecting an illegal import, confiscated 359 live tortoises (juvenile *Aldabrachelys elephantina*, *Geochelone elegans*, *G. pardalis*, and *Malacochersus tornieri*) and 154 dead tortoises* (*G. pardalis* and *M. tornieri*) from a Dutch dealer. During the search of his shop they also found a used smuggler's suitcase. Legal action was taken against the dealer.[11]

---

*Freezing and storing deceased specimens is a common practice amongst Dutch animal dealers. If tax officials check their accounts, they can "prove" that they have had a very bad year financially, alleging that almost all their imported animals died of a "strange sickness," could not be sold, and no profit was made.

Figure 2. Case Study IV. Authorities confiscate illegally imported tortoises from a Dutch dealer's shop. The 154 dead tortoises (shown in this photo) included *Geochelone pardalis* and *Malacochersus tornieri*. Authorities seized 359 live tortoises, which also included *Aldabrachelys elephantina* and *Geochelone elegans*.

Figure 3a. Case Study IV. Leopard tortoises, *Geochelone pardalis*, packed in layers on top of one another inside crates in this shipment from Tanzania. The animals were in extremely poor condition; 50 were dead.

Figure 3b. Case Study IV. Pancake tortoises, *Malacochersus tornieri*, from the same shipment from Tanzania.

Problem shipments of *Testudo horsfieldii*

Horsfield's tortoise occurs east of the Caspian Sea; its range includes the former southern USSR, Afghanistan, eastern Iran, northwest Pakistan, and also possibly the western tip of China. Populations are thought to have declined markedly in all areas (Stubbs, 1989). In the former USSR the combined effect of heavy collecting for the pet trade and habitat destruction from cultivation following the irrigation of desert and semi-desert areas have been the principal causes of this decline. Collecting has supposedly been severely restricted since 1984 (Stubbs, 1989), but recent reports indicate that large numbers continue to appear in Western Europe and the USA.[12, 13] Other serious threats to these populations include increased livestock grazing and the killing of tortoises by farmers who claim that they consume significant amounts of vegetables and fruit tree seedlings. Stray dogs, pigs, and small mammals are also known to destroy tortoise nests.

Because of the serious threats to this species, the EC listed it in their CITES/EC database and imposed an import ban[14] on 10 March 1988. However, the illegal trade in *T. horsfieldii* continues on a large scale. The Polish journalist Janusz Mlynarski described the "tortoise train" from Kiev arriving at Przemysl, bringing "several thousand passengers who carry their homes on their backs. Every day the four Polish customs officers who inspect the train discover approximately 1,000 tortoises hidden in boxes, under clothes, in specially prepared train compartments, under seats, in cases marked 'soap,' and so on. Most of the time the persons involved are citizens of republics of the former USSR, such as Kazakhstan." (*Gazeta Wyborgza*, 10 July 1992). The fate of these animals was not indicated.

In Kazakhstan one can buy a tortoise for U.S. $5; a discount of up to 50% is possible if one buys in bulk. As recently as 1990 free-wandering tortoises could be found in the suburbs of Alma-Ata, the capital of Kazakhstan. This is no longer the case; the heavy collection has taken its toll. Large numbers of the *T. horsfieldi* imported into Poland have been found with significant levels of radioactivity, apparently attributable to the military nuclear testing program of the former USSR.

A number of recent investigations by the TRAFFIC Europe Enforcement Project[12] have found people from eastern European countries to be supplying pet shops in western Europe. It is easy to order as many as 1,000 or 2,000 *T. horsfieldii* delivered to your front door within a few days. A 1993 British Channel 4 documentary (*True Stories* series entitled "Dog Eat Dog") showed several Russian animal dealers on one of their *horsfieldii* collecting trips in the Azerbaijani deserts. The dealers complained that there were not as many tortoises as in previous years and that they "have to catch ten tortoises to buy one beer." A Polish animal dealer was shown buying Horsfield's tortoises in a Moscow market and hiding approximately 500 juvenile tortoises under a specially prepared, double-bottomed seat on the train to Poland.

Recent investigations of the EU market[13] have revealed that *T. horsfieldi* can be readily obtained in the Netherlands, Belgium, France, England, Germany and Spain. Because legislation is inadequate, these animals are sold openly in pet shops throughout the Netherlands and Belgium at prices of U.S. $50–$100 per animal. Dutch authorities regularly encounter large numbers of this species in shipments that usually originate from Poland and the former USSR and are destined for the USA, Hong Kong, and Japan.

Case Study V

On 23 July 1990 Dutch officials inspected a KLM shipment[15] that had originated from LOT Polish Airlines. According to the documents,[16] the four cartons contained a total of 500 *T. horsfieldii* from the USSR en route from Poland to Hong Kong. The estimated value of the shipment on the invoice was U.S. $3500. The cartons were opened because of the foul odor emanating from them. The 500 juvenile *T. horsfieldii*, ranging 5–7 cm, had been packed eight layers deep. The extended length of time the animals had been confined in these containers was evidenced by the presence of numerous maggots.

Three independent veterinary surgeons who examined the shipment verified that the tortoises were severely dehydrated. In addition to the crushed animals, numerous individuals had fractured carapaces, crushed skulls, and severed limbs. The shipment was immediately confiscated, and legal proceedings were initiated against KLM, the airline responsible for transport.

Case Study VI

On 28 October 1993 Dutch authorities intercepted a KLM shipment containing 1,000 *T. horsfieldii* from the former USSR on its way to a dealer in the USA. Again, the containers failed to comply with IATA requirements. After KLM staff had been ordered to repack the tortoises appropriately, the shipment was allowed to continue to its destination. Legal action was taken against KLM.[17]

Case Study VII

On 12 June 1994 Dutch officials in Amsterdam checked a Moscow–USA shipment on KLM that had originated from Kazakhstan.[18] Sixty ramshackle crates contained 3,000 *Testudo horsfieldii*, and as in previous shipments intercepted, these animals were in extremely poor condition. Their carapaces were broken or crushed; they were dehydrated, undernourished, and had not been packed in accordance with IATA requirements. One hundred twenty-seven animals were dead on arrival.

The Russian-issued CITES (re-export) document[19] stated

Figure 4a. Case Study V. A KLM shipment en route from Poland to Hong Kong was opened because of the foul odor emanating from the cartons. The 500 juvenile dead and dying *Testudo horsfieldii* had been packed eight layers deep.

Figure 4b. Case Study V. Inspector points to one of the maggots in the shipment of 500 *Testudo horsfieldii*.

Figure 5. Case Study VII. In a shipment from Kazakhstan destined for the USA (intercepted in Amsterdam), 3,000 *Testudo horsfieldii* had been packed in 60 crates without regard to IATA regulations; 127 were dead.

that the tortoises were wild caught in the former USSR and that the permit was valid only if the transport conditions conformed to IATA guidelines. This was clearly not the case and the shipment was immediately seized. Legal action was taken against KLM.

Problem Shipments of *Testudo kleinmanni*

In October 1990 the Egyptian Government issued a Ministerial Decree[20] banning the export of a number of species of reptiles, including *Testudo kleinmanni*, which originates from that country. However, only after several incidents in 1991 involving falsified export permits did the Egyptian MA inform the Secretariat of the Ministerial Decree, and the Parties were not advised of the Egyptian trade ban until 19 December 1991.[21] The cases outlined below concern incidents of invalid (altered or forged) permits used in the export and re-export of *T. kleinmanni*.

Case Study VIII

On 4 September 1992 the Netherlands MA intercepted a shipment that had arrived on a KLM flight from Cairo in transit to the United States. The shipment was accompanied by Sudanese permits and a KLM air waybill issued in Cairo indicated "transit ex Khartoum." The permits were for 200 each of common chameleons (*Chamaeleo chameleon*), Egyptian tortoises (*Testudo kleinmanni*),* sand boas (*Eryx*

*At that time *T. kleinmanni* was listed on Appendix II. The species was moved to Appendix I in November 1994.

jaculus), Kenyan sand boas (*Eryx colubrinus*), and 100 Egyptian spiny-tailed lizards (*Uromastyx aegyptius*). Except for *Eryx colubrinus*, none of these species is known to occur in Sudan. As the shipment was in transit, the Netherlands MA notified the U.S. MA that the shipment was on its way, and it was allowed to continue on to the U.S.

Meanwhile, the Sudanese MA confirmed that no consignment of reptiles had left Khartoum and that the permits were invalid because the export endorsement had not been co-signed by one of the designated Sudanese MA officials. The Secretariat concluded that the Sudanese documents were being used as a cover for specimens from Egypt that were banned from export and recommended that U.S. authorities confiscate the shipment.[22] However, no action was taken to stop this shipment in the U.S. The Sudanese MA subsequently prohibited the exporter, who had offices in both Cairo and Khartoum, from exporting any wildlife from Sudan. The Egyptian MA failed to take similar action.

Case Study IX

On 21 August 1992 a shipment from Egypt containing 12 *Testudo kleinmanni* was seized by the authorities in Frankfurt, Germany because the permit[23] was forged. Several other shipments were found with invalid permits.[24] In June 1993 the Director of TRAFFIC-USA expressed concern to the U.S. MA over the import of *Testudo kleinmanni* from Egypt and subsequently forwarded copies of a number of permits, presented in the U.S., believed to be either forged or falsified, to the CITES Secretariat.

CITES AND THE TORTOISE AND TURTLE TRADE

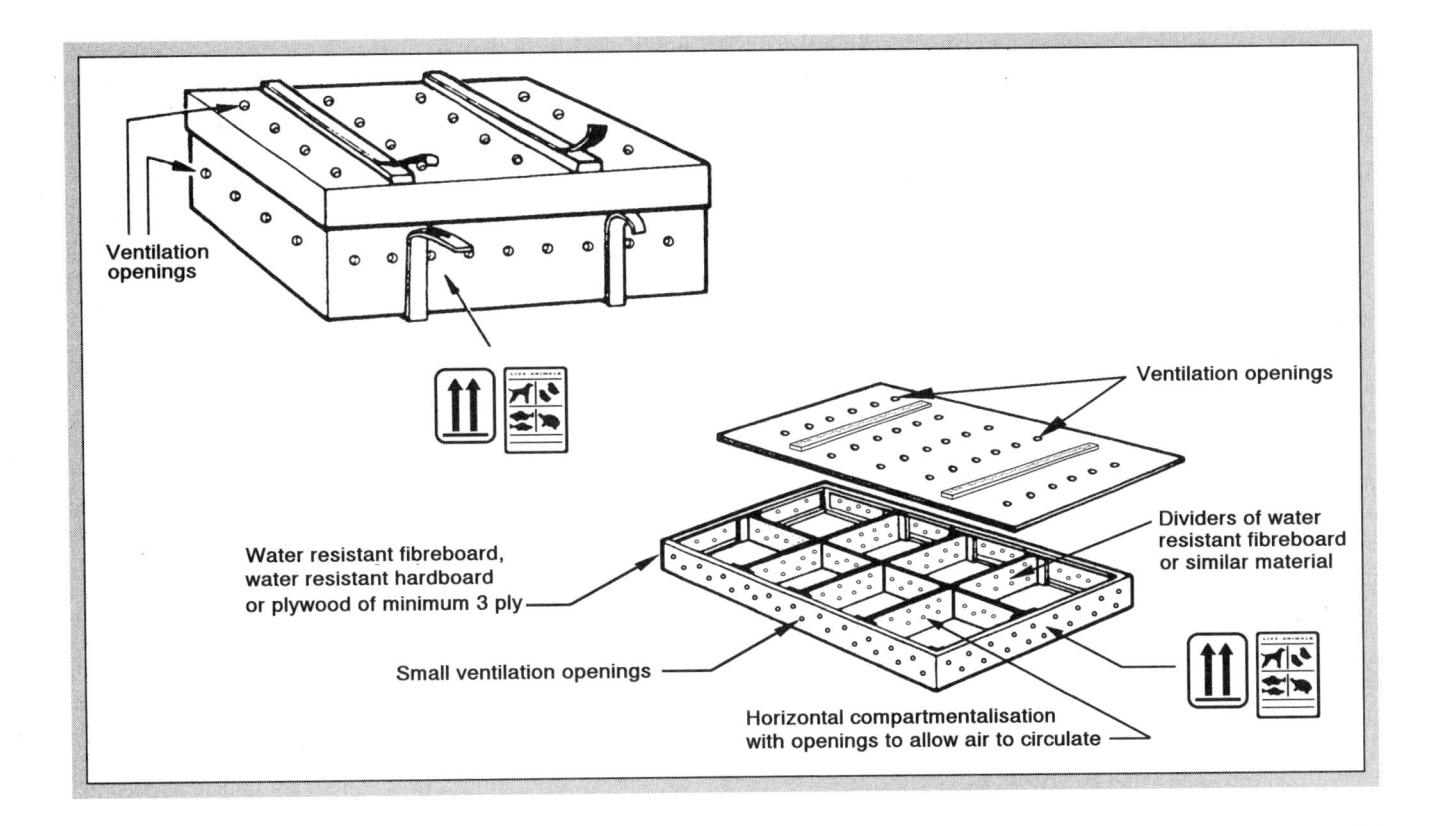

IATA Live Animal Regulations — Container Requirement 43
Applicable to sea turtle, terrapin, tortoise, and [freshwater] turtle species *(see USG Exceptions in Chapter 2).*

1. **Design and Construction** *(see Exception QF-01 in Chapter 3)*
   Materials. Medium density (or higher) water-resistant fibreboard, water-resistant hardboard, plywood of minimum 3 ply, fine nylon mesh, rigid plastics. *Note: Containers must not be constructed out of corrugated card board or corrugated board.*
   Principles of Design. The following principles of design must be met in addition to the General Container Requirements outlined at the beginning of this chapter.
   • Fibreboard, hardboard, plywood, or rigid plastic boxes provided with ventilation openings on the sides and top cover. Fine nylon mesh must be fixed inside the box to screen the ventilation openings which must be a minimum of 1 cm (½ in) in diameter.
   • The box must be shallow so that [the animals] are unable to clamber on top of one another and must be large enough to allow free movement. Most species travel better in small groups of similar size. Where a species is less than 10 cm (4 in) in carapace length, no more than ten (10) individuals must be permitted per compartment/container in order to prevent clambering.
   • For the large shipments, only 5 individuals must be placed in the compartment of a container or in a container. Most species travel better in small groups of similar size.
   • Certain species are aggressive, e.g., snapping turtles, big-headed turtles, and all aquatic soft-shelled turtles, must be packed individually.
   • If partitions are used within a container, they must be strong enough to withstand the weight of the animals and be fixed securely to the floor and sides of the container so that they do not collapse if the container is stacked on a pallet.

   • Only one layer of horizontal compartments is allowed per container.

2. **Preparations Before Dispatch** *(see Chapter 5)*
   Where necessary, moss or suitable brushwood material must be placed in the box. Terrapins and turtles must be packed in damp, *not* wet, soft non-toxic absorbent inorganic bedding to minimise injury.

3. **Feeding and Watering Guide**
   The need to feed or water any of these species during the journey must not arise.

4. **General Care and Loading**
   • In case of more than one type of specimen per shipment, [animals] must not be mixed or combined with other species of reptiles in a container. Only species of the same size must be loaded in the same container.
   • Special care must be taken to avoid exposure to extreme temperatures. Particularly during cold weather, these animals lie dormant for prolonged periods and therefore must not be presumed dead. On no account must unnatural hibernation be induced by loading the consignments in thermally controlled containers.

   Warning 1: Containers must not be placed in direct sunlight or in draughty areas.

   Warning 2: In extreme temperatures, the container must be placed inside a ventilated polystyrene [Styrofoam] container that permits air to circulate around the inner container.

Figure 6. Container Requirement 43, excerpted from *IATA Live Animal Regulations, 23rd Edition* (IATA, 1996).

Problem Shipments of *Aldabrachelys* and *Geochelone* spp.

Case Study X (numerous shipments)[25]

In August 1992 the Secretariat became aware of an increasing number of permits and re-export certificates authorizing commercial trade in large numbers of *Aldabrachelys elephantina*, *Geochelone elegans*, and *Geochelone pardalis*. These tortoises were declared to have been bred in captivity in Myanmar, the Seychelles, Tanzania, or the United Arab Emirates. Several re-export certificates for trade in these species indicated that they were "pre-Convention" but failed to note their date of acquisition, a violation of CITES Resolutions Conf. 5.1 1 and 8.5 (IUCN/SSC, 1996). The United Arab Emirates MA had authorized commercial trade in captive-bred *G. elegans*, which were reported as originating in Myanmar and UAE, where wild populations of this species do not exist. Several experts indicated that it was extremely unlikely that such large numbers of *G. elegans* had been bred in captivity; the tortoises were undoubtedly wild caught and illegally imported. Frequent requests by the Secretariat to the UAE MA to provide the location of the *G. elegans* captive-breeding operation received no response.

On 10 March 1994 the Secretariat issued an official Notification[26] that the parties refuse to accept export permits or re-export certificates for captive-bred or wild-caught *Aldabrachelys elephantina*, *Geochelone elegans*, and *G. pardalis* without prior verification of the certificates' validity with the Secretariat.

Conditions of Transport

Articles III, IV, and V of the Convention require that, before issuing a CITES permit, the "Management Authority of the state of export is satisfied that any living specimen will be so prepared and shipped as to minimize the risk of injury, damage to health, or cruel treatment" (IUCN/SSC, 1996). Clearly, many of the Parties have not followed this requirement, and shipments continue in a manner contrary to both CITES guidelines and IATA Live Animal Regulations.

LITERATURE CITED

Broadley, D. G. 1989. *Geochelone sulcata*: spurred tortoise (English): abu gatta, abu gefne (Arabic). In I. R. Swingland and M. W. Klemens (eds.), The Conservation Biology of Tortoises, pp. 47–48. Occasional Papers of the IUCN Species Survival Commission (SSC) No. 5. IUCN, Gland, Switzerland. i–iv + 202 pp.

International Air Transport Association (IATA). 1996. IATA Live Animal Regulations, 23d ed. International Air Transport Association, Montreal. 320 pp.

IUCN Species Survival Commission. 1996. CITES: A Conservation Tool. A Guide to Amending the Appendices to the Convention on International Trade in Endangered Species of Wild Fauna and Flora, (A. Rosser and M. Haywood, eds.). Prepared for the tenth meeting of the conference of the parties, 9–20 June 1996, Harare, Zimbabwe. IUCN Species Survival Commission, Cambridge, UK.

Lambert, M. R. K. 1993. On growth, sexual dimorphism, and the general ecology of the African spurrred tortoise, *Geochelone sulcata*, in Mali. Chelon. Conserv. Biol. 1(1):37–46.

Stubbs, D. 1989. *Testudo horsfieldi*: Horsfield's tortoise. In I. R. Swingland and M. W. Klemens (eds.), The Conservation Biology of Tortoises, pp. 37–38. Occasional Papers of the IUCN Species Survival Commission (SSC) No. 5. IUCN, Gland, Switzerland. i–iv + 202 pp.

Swingland, I. R. and M. W. Klemens (eds.). 1989. The Conservation Biology of Tortoises. Occasional Papers of the IUCN Species Survival Commission (SSC) No. 5. IUCN, Gland, Switzerland. i–iv + 202 pp.

U.S. Fish and Wildlife Service. 1992. CITES: Appendices I, II, and III to the Convention on International Trade in Endangered Species of Wild Fauna and Flora. Title 50—Wildlife and Fisheries, Part 23, §23.23. Publication Unit, U.S. Fish and Wildlife Service, Washington, D.C.

WCS of Tanzania. 1988. Eagle Eye: The commercial trade in pancake tortoises. Miombo, Newsletter of the Wildlife Conservation Society of Tanzania, May, 13–14.

TRAVEL AND LEGAL DOCUMENTS CITED

[1] Air waybill 074-9096-9502.
[2] CITES-405/90, Security stamp TG 9119996.
[3] CITES 405/90, Security Stamp TG 91199960.
[4] Air waybill 074-2638-2436.
[5] CITES-13/91, Security Stamp TG 9120199, *Geochelone sulcata*.
[6] CITES Infractions report No. 9, Kyoto case No. 91, Reference 50373 "Tortoises from Togo to Japan via the Netherlands."
[7] Air waybills 074-1375-0225 JAPAN and 074-2912-6252 USA.
[8] AID (General Inspection Service) internal report: 158592013 d.d. 29.02.1992.
[9] Air waybill 074-2635-9443. CITES No. 90; Reference 50310; Title: Pancake tortoises from the United Republic of Tanzania to the USA via the Netherlands.
[10] CITES No. 05437, Ssecurity stamp TZ 0123934 (issued 25 January 1991, valid until 25 April 1991).
[11] Proces-verbaal Veld en Milieupolitie Boxtel No. 62/1992 d.d. 31 June 1992.
[12] TRAFFIC Europe Enforcement Project, INTERPOL. Internal report (1991–1992) 1868/217.
[13] TRAFFIC Europe Enforcement Project, INTERPOL. Internal report (1992–1994) 1868/314.
[14] 16/03/88 COM Import Ban, Art. 10.1b, 3rd indent.
[15] Air waybill 080-5109 9786.
[16] Permit No. 608-4-05-1990.
[17] General Inspection Service, 1993.
[18] Air waybill 074-5264-5154.
[19] CITES No. 3952, Security stamp SU 9120223. Official export permit No. 1/15-10.05.94.
[20] Ministerial Decree No. 1403, Government of Egypt, October 1990.
[21] Egyptian trade ban, CITES Notification No. 662.
[22] CITES Secretariat Case No. 50803.
[23] CITES Permit, Reference 50799.
[24] CITES Permits, References 50667, 50803, 51073.
[25] CITES Secretariat Case No. 50584.
[26] Notification to the Parties No. 786 (10 March 1994).

Ecology and Exploitation the Pancake Tortoise in Tanzania

DON MOLL[1] AND MICHAEL W. KLEMENS[2]

[1]*Southwest Missouri State University, Springfield, MO 65804, USA [e-mail: dlm505f@wpgate.smsu.edu]*
[2]*Wildlife Conservation Society, 185th St. and Southern Blvd., Bronx, NY 10460, USA [e-mail: mklemens.wcs@mcimail.com]*

ABSTRACT: The pancake tortoise, *Malacochersus tornieri*, is an unusual crevice-dwelling species endemic to small, rocky outcrops scattered through the Somalia-Masai floristic region of Kenya and Tanzania. Its flattened morphology and lizard-like behavior heighten its appeal in the international pet trade, which, until a recent temporary ban stopped export, was solely supplied by Tanzania. Surveys were conducted in June and July 1992 to gather basic information concerning the ecology, status, and patterns and effects of exploitation of this tortoise in northern and central Tanzania. This paper focuses on this species' habitat requirements and the comparison of population characteristics and habitat utilization in both exploited and unexploited sites.

This paper summarizes the material presented in much greater detail in Klemens and Moll (1995) and Moll and Klemens (1996).

The pancake tortoise, *Malacochersus tornieri*, of East Africa is one of the world's most unusual chelonians. An extremely flattened flexible shell and almost lizard-like agility allow it to use rock crevices for shelter and protection from predators. While enabling it to successfully cope with the rigorous conditions of its arid rupicolous habitat, these unique characteristics have triggered the major threat to its survival—collection for export to fill demand in the international wildlife trade. Subsequent to Kenya discontinuing export of this species in 1981, Tanzania has been the only supplier for this trade. The magnitude of the trade, and the inhumane conditions under which tortoises are shipped, became cause for increasing concern by Tanzanian officials as well as national and international conservation organizations (Moll et al., 1991; WCMC and IUCN/SSC, 1991, 1992; Luiijf, this volume). This concern stimulated interest in assessing the status and effects of exploitation on this tortoise. In 1992 the CITES Animals Committee recommended a moratorium on export of this species, pending assessment of field survey results. This moratorium was subsequently instituted by Tanzanian authorities. We initiated field surveys in 1992 to provide basic information concerning the ecology, status, and effects of commercial collection of the species in Tanzania.

METHODS

The results, conclusions, and recommendations presented here are drawn primarily from field research conducted by the authors and Ayoub Njalale of the Wildlife Conservation Society of Tanzania. Field data were collected from 3 June to 9 July 1992.

Searches for pancake tortoises were conducted in suitable habitats in the Arusha and Dodoma Regions of north and central Tanzania. Locations of potentially suitable areas of habitat were identified by examination of topographic maps and through interviews with individuals knowledgeable of the terrain and its flora and fauna. We visited as many of these areas as possible, and with the aid of flashlights, deep crevices in rocks were carefully examined for the presence of tortoises. The physical characteristics of the habitats examined and the number of live and dead pancake tortoises found were recorded, and the number of man-hours of search (hours of search × number of searchers) were logged at most sites.

Recorded data (tortoises collected per man-hour of search, population structure, and ratios of juveniles to adults) from suitable habitats considered to be uncollected (due mainly to their location in protected or remote areas) were compared with the data from habitats in which collection was known to have occurred or was considered highly probable (i.e., proximate and accessible to collecting centers).

RESULTS AND DISCUSSION

Distribution and Habitat Requirement

The pancake tortoise is distributed in suitable habitats below 1800 m throughout northern and central Tanzania (Broadley, 1989). It is listed as a component of the Tanzanian fauna associated with White's (1983) Somalia-Masai floristic region (arid semi-desert and grassland) by Broadley and Howell (1991), although a few records also exist from White's slightly more moist Zambezian region.

As pancake tortoises' habitat requirements are extremely specific, their distribution tends to be discontinuous. We found tortoises only where crevices were of suitable dimensions, usually in outcrops of exfoliating granite in *Acacia-Commiphora*-baobab bushland and on *Brachystegia*-wooded hillsides (Figure 1). The tortoises spend much of their time

Figure 1. Typical pancake tortoise macrohabitat in *Acacia-Commiphora*-baobab bushland in Tarangire National Park.

Figure 2. Field assistant Ayoub Njalale near a horizontal crevice that contained ten pancake tortoises.

Suitable crevices allowed pancake tortoises to retreat a considerable distance into the fissure (usually several tortoise lengths) where the height of the crevice was approximately 5 cm or less. These areas with low ceilings enabled resident tortoises to wedge themselves tightly between the floor and ceiling, using their legs as braces. We observed that the unossified area of the plastron bulged outwards when the extremities were withdrawn, which serves to wedge the tortoise even more tightly within the crevice. This observation may have prompted earlier reports of active pulmonary inflation in this species, a phenomenon discounted by Ireland and Gans (1972).

Crevice Usage Patterns in Unexploited Habitats

Although we were not always able or permitted to extract the tortoises we observed within crevices, we were able to observe the way in which tortoises in six unexploited populations utilized the crevices. The pancake tortoises encountered in the field in June and July 1992 were always in crevices (although tortoises were seen outside in subsequent surveys) and most often they were alone. Pairs (sometimes confirmed to be adult males and females) were also common, and larger groups (up to ten individuals) were occasionally observed. Usually, adults and juveniles were not found in the same crevices. The latter were often discovered in crevices that were shallower than those used by adults. In unexploited habitats the average number of juveniles encountered per population was about 10% of the total individuals observed. The mean number of tortoises encountered per man-hour of search in these habitats was 2.42.

hiding within these crevices, which may be quite variable externally, but usually have certain internal characteristics in common (Figures 2 and 3). Probably the most important crevice characteristics that determine their suitability as pancake habitat are their relative depth and degree of progressive narrowing. The number of suitable crevices is limited even in favorable macrohabitats, and this may play an important role in population regulation of pancake tortoises.

Effects of Exploitation by Commercial Collectors

We surveyed five habitats that had been exploited by commercial tortoise collectors to compare with population characteristics in the six unexploited habitats discussed above. Typically, exploited habitats were characterized by several different features in their remnant tortoise populations and occasionally by physical evidence (Figure 4). Usually only one tortoise was encountered per crevice, and a far higher proportion of those encountered were juveniles ($\bar{x} = 60.1\%$). This may have resulted from a collectors' bias toward adults, as juveniles are seldom seen in export shipments. In addition, only a mean of 0.27 tortoises per man-hour of search were found, and many apparently suitable crevices were vacant in these habitats. Thus, these aspects collectively form the "signature" of exploited habitats and may be used to differentiate them from undisturbed locations.

Figure 3. This vertically oriented crevice contained a pair of pancake tortoises.

Threats to Tanzanian Pancake Tortoise Populations

We identified illegal commercial collecting for the international wildlife market as the only threat to the pancake tortoise in Tanzania at this time. With the exception of limited subsistence use as food by women of the Hadza tribe near Lake Eyasi (Klemens, 1992), we know of no other direct human use of the pancake tortoise. Also, we have no evidence that overgrazing, land use patterns, or feral animals seriously threaten pancake tortoises. Our impression is that if it were not for large-scale collecting activity, which is still occurring (for illegal export or in anticipation that the current ban will be lifted), the pancake tortoise's survival would be secure in Tanzania.

Figure 4. A large slab of rock is propped up by another smaller stone of a different type to allow freer access underneath—probably indicating that pancake tortoises had been collected here (Mawe Mbiti area of Tarangire National Park).

Acknowledgments

We wish to acknowledge the cooperation of the Tanzanian Commission for Science and Technology, the Ministry of Tourism, Environment, and Natural Resources, the Division of Wildlife, and the Department of National Parks, and Serengeti Wildlife Research Institute which not only permitted but facilitated this research effort. Financial support for this study was received from the Wildlife Conservation

Society, the American Museum of Natural History, the IUCN/SSC Trade Specialist Group, and the People's Trust for Endangered Species.

We are particularly indebted to Ayoub Njalale for his efforts and contributions in the field, to Bjørn Figenschou for providing a Land Rover and driver for our use during the study, and to Patricia Moehlman, Amie Bräutigam, Kim Howell, Nigel Leader-Williams, and Frank Lambert for advice and guidance concerning our investigations. The impetus for this project was the Tortoise and Freshwater Turtle Action Plan (IUCN/SSC Tortoise and Freshwater Turtle Specialist Group, 1989) and the IUCN/SSC Trade Specialist Group's efforts in support of the CITES Significant Trade Project.

LITERATURE CITED

Broadley, D. G. 1989. *Malacochersus tornieri*. In I. R. Swingland and M. W. Klemens (eds.), The Conservation Biology of Tortoises, pp. 62–64. Occasional Papers of the IUCN Species Survival Commission (SSC) No. 5. IUCN, Gland, Switzerland.

Broadley, D. G. and K. M. Howell. 1991. A checklist of the reptiles of Tanzania with synoptic keys. Syntarsus, Occasional Publ. of Natural History Museum of Zimbabwe, Bulawayo, No. 1.

Ireland, L. C. and C. Gans. 1972. The adaptive significance of the flexible shell of the tortoise, *Malacochersus tornieri*. Anim. Behav. 20:778–781.

IUCN/SSC Tortoise and Freshwater Turtle Specialist Group. 1989. Tortoises and freshwater turtles: An action plan for their conservation (D. Stubbs, comp.). IUCN/SSC Tortoise and Freshwater Turtle Specialist Group, Gland, Switzerland. i–iv + 47 pp.

Klemens, M. W. 1992. Letter from the field: Hunting and gathering among the Hadza. Rotunda 17(9):4–5.

Klemens, M. W. and D. Moll. 1995. An assessment of the effects of commercial exploitation on the pancake tortoise, *Malacochersus tornieri*, in Tanzania. Chelon. Conserv. Biol. 1(3):197–206.

Luiijf, W. 1997. CITES and the tortoise and turtle trade. In J. Van Abbema (ed.), Proceedings: Conservation, Restoration, and Management of Tortoises and Turtles—An International Conference, pp. 125–134. July 1993, State University of New York, Purchase. New York Turtle and Tortoise Society, New York.

Moll, D. and M. W. Klemens. 1996. Ecological characteristics of the pancake tortoise, *Malacochersus tornieri* (Seibenrock) in Tanzania. Chelon. Conserv. Biol. 2(1):26–35.

Moll, D., M. W. Klemens, K. M. Howell, and A. Bräutigam. 1991. Field assessment of the status and exploitation of the pancake tortoise (*Malacochersus tornieri*) in Tanzania. Grant Proposal to Wildlife Conservation International.

White, F. 1983. The vegetation of Africa. A descriptive memoir to accompany the UNESCO-AETFAT-UNSO Vegetation Map of Africa. UNESCO, Paris.

World Conservation Monitoring Centre and the IUCN/SSC Trade Specialist Group. 1991. A review of significant trade animals listed in Appendix II of CITES. Draft report to the CITES Animals Committee. World Conservation Monitoring Centre and the IUCN/SSC Trade Specialist Group, Cambridge, UK.

World Conservation Monitoring Centre and the IUCN/SSC Trade Specialist Group. 1992. A review of significant trade animal species including CITES appendix II. A report to the CITES Animals Committee (T. Inskipp and H. Corrigan, eds.). WCMC and the IUCN/SSC Trade Specialist Group, Cambridge, UK.

Breeding, Repatriation, and Relocation

Flavio de Barros Molina (São Paulo Zoo, Brazil), Peter Pritchard (Florida Audobon Society, Winter Park), Linda Cayot (Charles Darwin Research Station, Quito, Ecuador), David Morafka (California State University—Dominguez Hills, Carson, California), Walter Sachsse (Institut für Genetik, Arbeitsgruppe Cytogenetik, Mainz, Germany), Vivian Páez (Proyecto Terecay, Fundación Natura, Santa Fe de Bogotá, Colombia), Xavier Elguezabal (Servicio Autonomo de Fauna, Ministerio del Ambiente y de los Recursos, Naturales Renovables, Caracas, Venezuela), and Edward Mullen (Science Applications International Corporation, Santa Barbara, California).

David Morafka (California State University—Dominguez Hills, Carson, California).

Survival of Relocated Tortoises: Feasibility of Relocating Tortoises as a Successful Mitigation Tool

EDWARD B. MULLEN AND PATRICK ROSS

Science Applications International Corporation, 816 State St., Suite 500, Santa Barbara, CA 93101, USA
[e-mail: edward.b.mullen@cmpx.saic.com]

ABSTRACT: To evaluate the feasibility of desert tortoise relocation as a mitigation tool, and relocation as a viable component of habitat conservation plans for the species, a study was designed to assess the effects of relocation on tortoise health and survival.

In 1989, 72 desert tortoises, *Gopherus agassizii*, were removed from a section (one square mile, 2.59 km²) of habitat in Cantil, California, on the western edge of the Mojave Desert. Tortoises were relocated to a diagonally adjacent section of fenced habitat in the Desert Tortoise Natural Area. Supplemental irrigation was added to half the study site to assess whether the additional water would positively affect the survival and health of both the relocated tortoises and the original resident population of tortoises. Relocated and resident tortoises were studied for three years after the relocation.

Data from the study indicate that the relocated tortoises were less likely to survive than the resident tortoises. The negative impact on survival was most pronounced in the first year after the relocation. That year was the driest year of the study and was the last year of an extended drought throughout the area. The survival of tortoises improved in the irrigated half of the study site only in this first, driest year. Males had significantly higher survivorship than females, but it was again apparent only in the first year of the study. Results indicate that the survival of the resident population of tortoises was not negatively affected by the addition of new tortoises onto their range.

Project History

In 1988, American Honda Motor Company, Inc. purchased six township sections of land for the construction of a vehicle testing facility in Cantil, California, eastern Kern County, on the western edge of the Mojave Desert (Figure 1). The primary feature of the testing facility was an oval track that traversed all six sections. Five of the six sections had been used for irrigated agriculture, reportedly for approximately 40 years, and at the time of Honda's acquisition no longer offered viable desert tortoise habitat. The sixth section (Section 6), however, had remained undeveloped and was inhabited by desert tortoises.

On 31 May 1989, the California Department of Fish and Game (CDFG) and Honda executed an "Agreement for Habitat Mitigation/Acquisition and Wildlife Mitigation" relating to the desert tortoise. Under this agreement, Honda was given permission to remove desert tortoises from Section 6 in two phases under prescribed conditions and protocols.

During Phase 1 (from 1 June to 3 August 1989), Honda enclosed the strip of Section 6 where the test track would be constructed with tortoise-proof fencing. Nineteen tortoises were removed from the construction zone during the summer of 1989. Two of the 19 tortoises were symptomatic for upper respiratory tract disease (URTD) and were donated, under the direction of the CDFG, to a URTD study; another tortoise died of a chronic kidney malfunction, and a fourth of unknown causes. The remaining 15 tortoises were relocated to specially designed pens until the following spring. Pens were monitored and supplemented with food and water.

On 4 August 1989, the U.S. Fish and Wildlife Service (USFWS) announced an emergency listing for the desert tortoise, giving it protected status under the federal Endangered Species Act (presently, the tortoise is both federally and state listed as "Endangered"). Phase 2 tortoise relocations and the three-year research project were authorized by the USFWS.

During the spring of 1990 (under Phase 2) an additional 57 tortoises were removed from Section 6 and, with the original 15 tortoises, were relocated to Section 8, which is part of the Desert Tortoise Natural Area (DTNA) and is under the jurisdiction of the Bureau of Land Management. (The northwest corner of Section 8 abuts the southeast corner of Section 6.) The 72 relocated tortoises consisted of 23 males, 41 females, and 8 juvenile tortoises that were too small for sex to be determined (<180 mm MCL).

Section 8 is one square mile (2.59 km²) in area and was divided into four approximately one-quarter-square-mile test plots (Figure 2). Each of the four test plots of Section 8 was separately double-fenced to prevent tortoises from moving off site or having direct contact with tortoises outside their plot. The one-inch-mesh chicken wire fence was buried six inches underground and extended 1.5 feet above ground. In

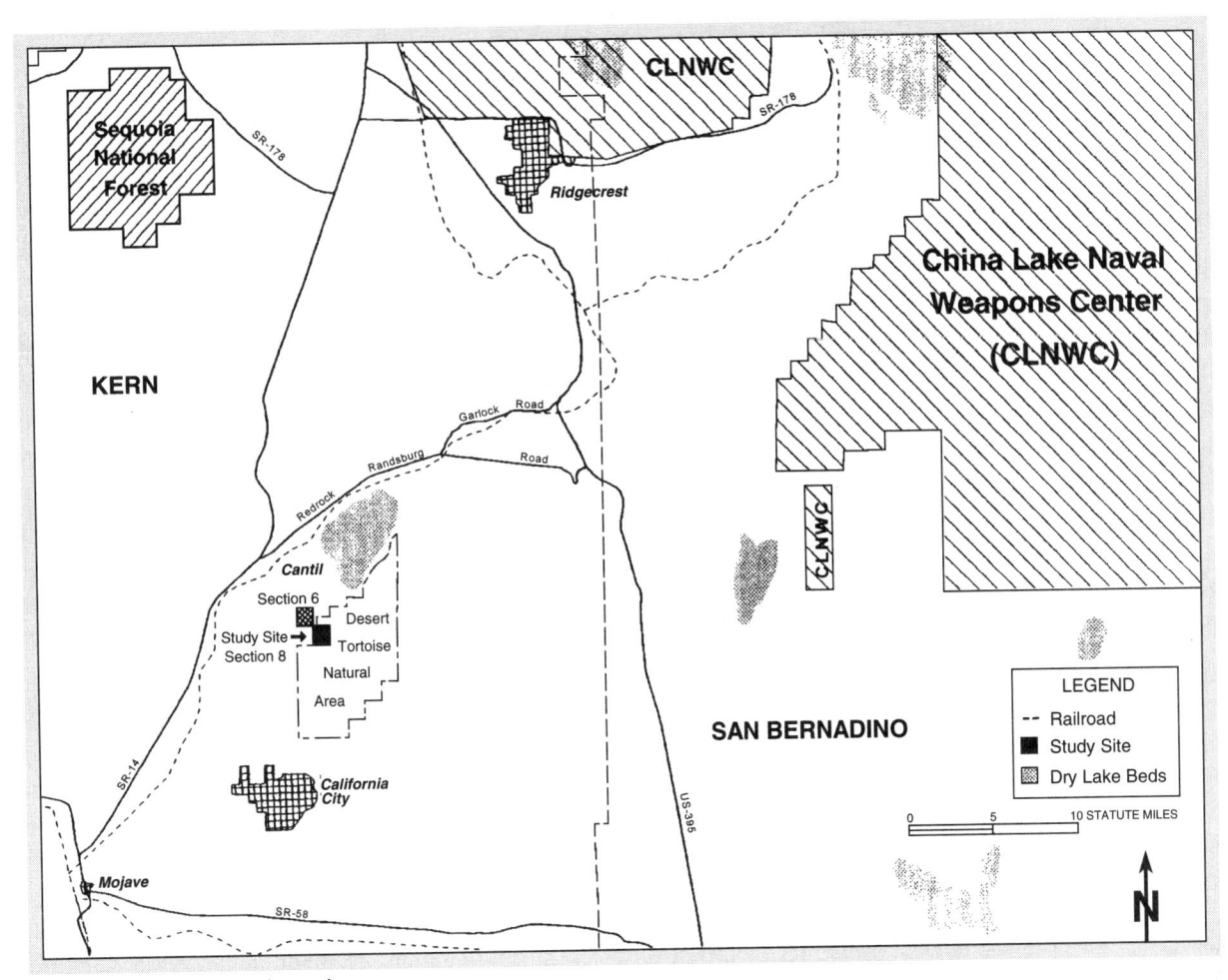

Figure 1. Map of study site region.

addition, the DTNA had previously erected a hog wire fence to restrict grazing animals from the study site.

The study site is topographically characterized by a gentle slope descending from the southeast to the northwest. The only exception to this broad plain is an area of greater relief to the northeast. This corner area was eliminated from the study site because it was not possible to continue the boundary fences through the steep, rocky terrain. This required the fencing to cut diagonally through the northeast plot (Plot 3), excluding approximately 30% of the plot from the study site.

An irrigation system was installed to supplement natural precipitation on the western half (plots 1 and 4) of Section 8. The irrigation sprinklers watered a circle approximately 200 ft in diameter and delivered approximately 4 in of precipitation each winter.

Telemeters were attached to all the adult tortoises relocated from Section 6 and most of the resident tortoises from Section 8. There was a high level of mortality during the first year of the project. To increase the sample size of the different cohorts and replace tortoises that had died the first year, additional tortoises were found on the study site,

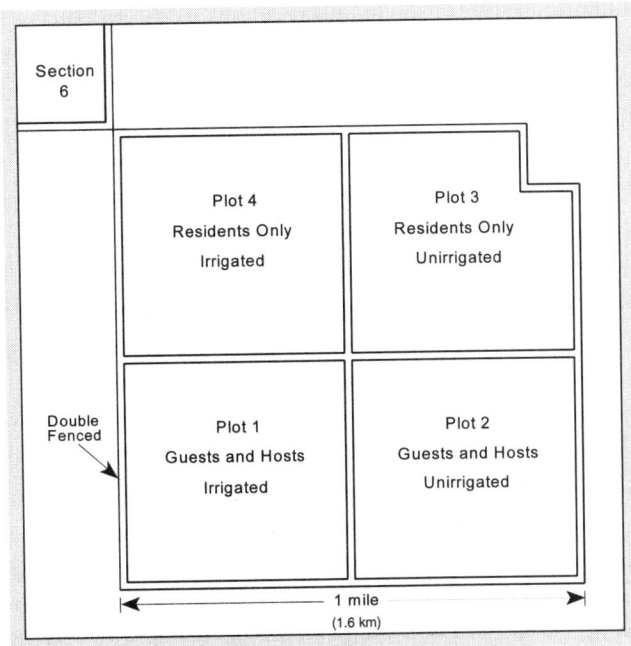

Figure 2. Study plot design diagram of Section 8, Desert Tortoise Natural Area. Not to scale.

TABLE 1
Number of tortoises in each cohort.

	1990 season			Added during 1991 season			
	Males	Females	Juveniles	Males	Females	Juveniles	Total
Residents							
Irrigated	6	6	0	3	4	1	20
Unirrigated	4	5	1	1	3	2	16
Hosts							
Irrigated	4	5	2	2	2	1	16
Unirrigated	4	3	2	1	4	2	16
Guests							
Irrigated	11	21	4	—	—	—	36
Unirrigated	12	20	4	—	—	—	36
Total	41	60	13	7	13	6	140

equipped with radio telemeters, and subsequently added to the resident and host populations during the 1991 field season. Survivorship values and analyses include these additional tortoises when appropriate.

Experimental Treatment Groups

Tortoises were grouped into one of six treatment groups or cohorts. Cohort grouping was dependent on (1) status, whether a tortoise was a resident, guest, or host, and (2) by the presence or absence of irrigation. The number of tortoises found in each of the four plots is listed by sex and age in Table 1 (including, but separating, the tortoises added to the cohorts in 1991).

The cohorts consisted of the following populations:

Cohort 1: "Residents" alone on an irrigated plot,
Cohort 2: "Residents" alone on an unirrigated plot,
Cohort 3: "Host" tortoises (resident tortoises) sharing an irrigated plot with relocated tortoises,
Cohort 4: "Host" tortoises (resident tortoises) sharing an unirrigated plot with relocated tortoises,
Cohort 5: "Guest" tortoises relocated into an irrigated plot, and
Cohort 6: "Guest" tortoises relocated into an unirrigated plot.

The study sought to determine:

- whether there were differences in survivorship between relocated and resident tortoises,
- the effect of habitat enhancement through irrigation upon the survivorship of both relocated and unrelocated tortoises,
- yearly variation in survivorship in relationship to both relocation and irrigation, and
- differences in the survivorship of male and female tortoises.

METHODS

Tortoise Revisit Procedure

During most full calendar months of tortoise activity (April through October) as many tortoises as possible were located (or revisited) using radiotelemetry. During most revisits each tortoise was measured in length (in millimeters along the mid-line of the carapace), was weighed (in grams), and was inspected for external symptoms of URTD. This monthly sampling produced a history of each tortoise's survivorship.

In spring 1993 a final survey of the study site was conducted in an attempt to locate all tortoises and determine their status. Transect surveys (the transect width was approx. 40 ft or 12.2 m) and radiotelemetry were used to assure a high probability of observing the remaining tortoises.

Survivorship Estimation

While all tortoise carcasses found were used in the mortality data, it was assumed that not all carcasses were found. Some tortoises die underground, especially during hibernation. The range of radio transmitters decreases when underground, making it difficult to find tortoises in burrows. Even when the signal can be located, the burrow is often too long to allow the biologist to inspect its full length. Under such circumstances, it is not possible to determine with certainty if the tortoise is alive or dead. In addition, predators (coyotes, eagles) may carry a tortoise, including its radio, from the study area into an area where its signal cannot be located. Counts of observed carcasses consequently underestimate mortality. Also, the small number of carcasses observed makes statistical analysis problematic.

Therefore, a tortoise was considered dead if it had not been seen alive during an entire season (March–October) of fieldwork. Because an attempt was made to locate tortoises every month, it was judged unlikely that a tortoise could go undetected during the entire field season. This procedure allowed an estimate of survivorship for the intervals 1990–1991 and 1991–1992. Only one tortoise remained undetected for an entire field season and was subsequently observed in a later field season.

A different procedure was used to estimate the 1992–1993 survivorship. Unlike the other intervals, the entire 1993 field season was not available to determine the survival of each tortoise. However, the intensive nature of the survey conducted in the spring of 1993 gave reasonable assurance that most of the surviving tortoises were revisited. Consequently, any tortoise that had not been observed in the 1993 survey was presumed to be dead. This procedure potentially overestimated mortality (if a living tortoise was not relocated it was considered dead) for the 1992–1993 interval, but it was the only estimate available for analysis.

Statistical Methods

The counts of surviving and dead tortoises were analyzed using loglinear procedures. This analysis determined the association between the percentage of surviving tortoises and other factors such as status, the presence or absence of irrigation, and sex.

A few of the tortoises did not have radios attached because they were too small; other small tortoises had solar-powered radios that did not always function properly. The survivorship of these individuals could not be reliably determined, and their inclusion in the analysis could therefore produce misleading results. Analyses were conducted with and without these tortoises. It was found that their inclusion did not affect the final results, so all analyses presented include these individuals.

RESULTS

Observed Survivorship Using Carcass Data

Thirteen tortoise carcasses were recovered during the study. Although a valid statistical analysis of the data from these animals was not possible because of the small number of observations, there are some clear patterns. An unusually high and disproportionate number of carcasses were of guest tortoises. This is true in terms of both absolute numbers and the percentages of relocated and unrelocated tortoises in the total population. Eleven of the 13 carcasses found were relocated tortoises. An unusually high number of female carcasses was also found; of the 13, ten were female, one was male, and two were juvenile.

It was usually not possible to precisely determine the cause of death, making it difficult to ascertain the relevance of the data. Teeth marks and other possible signs of predation that were found and recorded could actually be the result of scavenging after the death of the tortoise. This is also true for the presence of bullet holes, which were recorded once and may either have been the cause of death or may have occurred long after death.

Estimated Survivorship

The relationship of status, irrigation, and sex to estimated survivorship (which is based on carcass data and the inability to relocate individual tortoises) in each of the three yearly intervals was analyzed simultaneously using a loglinear model. Results of these analyses are presented in Table 2.

TABLE 2
Analysis of deviance results for survivorship. Boldface indicates significant results ($P < 0.05$).

	Deviance[a]	Degrees of freedom	P
1990–1991			
Status	**10.46**	**2**	**0.005**
Irrigation	1.17	1	0.279
Sex[b]	**8.76**	**2**	**0.013**
Status × Irrigation	3.06	2	0.217
Status × Sex	8.26	7	0.310
Irrigation × Sex	1.72	2	0.423
1991–1992			
Status	1.72	2	0.423
Irrigation	0.70	1	0.403
Sex	**15.98**	**2**	**<0.001**
Status × Irrigation	2.15	5	0.828
Status × Sex	3.94	8	0.862
Irrigation × Sex	5.28	8	0.727
1992–1993			
Status	0.93	2	0.628
Irrigation	0.17	1	0.680
Sex	0.50	2	0.779
Status × Irrigation	4.64	5	0.461
Status × Sex	7.51	10	0.677
Irrigation × Sex	0.10	2	0.951

[a] Deviance is derived from the G-statistic for goodness of fit, which has an approximate chi-squared distribution. [b] There are three categories within sex: adult males, adult females, and juveniles of unknown sex.

Relocation Effects

The percentage of surviving tortoises for each year, grouped by status and the presence of irrigation, is presented in Tables 3, 4, and 5. In the 1990–1991 interval (Table 3) survivorship was significantly related to status: Mortality in the guest tortoises was significantly higher than either the host or resident tortoises. The residents and hosts, on the other hand, had similar percentages of survival, which means the addition of guests did not negatively affect the survival of the hosts.

In the subsequent intervals of 1991–1992 (Table 4) and 1992–1993 (Table 5) there was no significant relationship between status and survival. During the 1991–1992 interval the guest survivorship had increased from 43% (in the first field season, 1990–1991) to 81% and was no longer significantly lower than the hosts (93%) and residents (87%). This trend is similar to results of the 1992–1993 field season. Host survivorship was not affected by the presence of guests in any of the following years.

Irrigation Effects

None of the intervals showed survivorship to be significantly related to the presence of irrigation. However, relocation occurred in late spring of 1990, and the guest tortoises were put on site after most of the benefits of irrigation were gone. Due to the timing of the relocation, the presence of supplemental irrigation on a plot would not have affected the relocated tortoises during the first year. Consequently, the relationship between irrigation and mortality in the 1990–1991 season could only be validly assessed by comparing host and resident populations. Thus, an additional loglinear analysis of the relationship between irrigation and survivorship in the 1990–1991 interval was conducted for only host and resident tortoises. The results of this analysis are presented in Table 6. The analysis of this modified data set showed a significant relationship between irrigation and survivorship: Resident and host tortoises on irrigated plots had higher survivorship than residents and hosts on unirrigated plots (87% vs. 58%).

Yearly Effects

The highest mortality was observed in the 1990–1991 interval. The percentages of surviving resident, host, and guest tortoises increased after the first field season. Resident survival increased from 73% in the first interval to 87 and 85% in the second and third intervals, respectively. Host survival increased from 75% to 93 and 92% during the next two intervals. Guest survival increased from 43% in the first interval to 81% and 84% during the second and third years, respectively.

TABLE 3
Percentage of tortoises surviving 1990–1991.

	Resident n = 22	Host n = 20	Guest n = 72	Total
Irrigated n = 59	83%	91%	44%	61%
Unirrigated n = 55	60%	56%	42%	47%
Total	73%	75%	43%	54%

TABLE 4
Percentage of tortoises surviving 1991–1992.

	Resident n = 30	Host n = 27	Guest n = 31	Total
Irrigated n = 49	83%	87%	81%	84%
Unirrigated n = 39	92%	100%	80%	90%
Total	87%	93%	81%	86%

TABLE 5
Percentage of tortoises surviving 1992–1993.

	Resident n = 26	Host n = 25	Guest n = 25	Total
Irrigated n = 41	80%	100%	77%	85%
Unirrigated n = 35	91%	83%	92%	89%
Total	85%	92%	84%	87%

TABLE 6
Analysis of deviance results for 1990–1991 survivorship of residents and hosts only. Boldface indicates significant results ($P < 0.05$).

	Deviance[a]	Degrees of freedom	P
Status	0.02	1	0.888
Irrigation	**4.62**	**1**	**0.032**
Sex[b]	**7.92**	**2**	**0.019**
Status × irrigation	0.31	1	0.578
Status × sex	4.48	6	0.612
Irrigation × sex	1.37	6	0.968

[a]Deviance is derived from the G-statistic for goodness of fit, which has an approximate chi-squared distribution. [b]There are three categories within sex: adult males, adult females, and juveniles of unknown sex.

Sex and Age Effects

The percentage of surviving tortoises for each year, grouped by sex, is presented in Table 7.

In the 1990–1991 interval, survivorship was significantly different between adult males, adult females, and juvenile tortoises. This effect was due primarily to a higher survivorship for adult males (71% surviving) than adult females (42% surviving). In the subsequent intervals (1991–1992 and 1992–1993) there were no significant differences between adult males and adult females.

TABLE 7
Percentage of tortoises surviving.

	1990–91	1991–92	1992–93
Male (n = 48)	71%	97%	86%
Female (n = 73)	42%	89%	92%
Juveniles (n = 19)	62%	50%	71%

In the 1991–1992 interval, survivorship was again significantly different between adult males, adult females, and juveniles. This was due primarily to a significantly lower survivorship of juvenile tortoises. However, the small number of juveniles in the sample allowed the death of a few individuals to cause a large change in the percent survival. Conclusions based on changes in survival in this age class are therefore speculative.

Health Effects

Health data recorded prior to relocation (Ross and Mullen, in prep.) indicated a significantly lower body weight relative to body length among the guest tortoises, suggesting that the guest population was already in poor health before the relocation.

DISCUSSION

The survival of the guest population was significantly lower than resident and host tortoises in the 1990–1991 field season. This first field season was obviously the most traumatic for the guest tortoises due to the direct short-term effects of relocation. Not only did relocation require considerable handling (which can often be stressful to tortoises), but these tortoises had to withstand the expected disorientation after relocation to a new and unfamiliar habitat, possibly making the establishment of proper burrows and location of adequate food difficult just prior to the summer's heat. They also had to withstand these pressures in an extremely dry year, when both food and water were in exceptionally short supply. This year was the driest of the study and concluded a long drought in the area. Although the resident tortoises also felt the pressures of this drought, the compounded effect of both the relocation and drought conditions could have caused the lower survivorship in the guest tortoises. Finally, the relocated tortoises' health was apparently compromised prior to location. We cannot be completely certain if the first-year high mortality of the relocated tortoises was the result of the stresses of relocation, the stresses from human disturbance to their natal sites, the pressures of an extended period of drought, or a combination of these factors.

The guests' survival increased to levels similar to those of the residents and hosts by the second field season. This similarity persisted into the third season. The two subsequent years of the study had greater precipitation and more food was available. The relocated tortoises were now more familiar with their surroundings, had presumably established burrows, and had located adequate forage. In addition, the stressful conditions of the first year had probably eliminated many of the weaker individuals among the relocated tortoises, leaving a more robust population in the following years. All these factors would have increased the survivorship of relocated tortoises in the subsequent two years of the study.

The addition of guests did not negatively affect the survivorship of the hosts in any of the years of the study. Host and resident tortoises had similar survival rates for all three years of the study. It is important to note for future projects that this tortoise relocation negatively affected only the survival of relocated tortoises.

During the driest year of the project, the 1990–1991 season, the survival of resident and host tortoises on plots with irrigation was higher than those without irrigation. If tortoises must be relocated during drought condition, a higher survivorship would be expected with the addition of on-site irrigation. However, it is important that relocation be timed to take advantage of the additional vegetation that would result from this irrigation. Tortoises should be moved early enough to gain the benefits of the spring growth.

There was no relationship detected between irrigation and survivorship in 1991 or 1992 when precipitation levels attained normal levels. This indicates that during years of normal rainfall, supplemental irrigation may not increase the survival or success of relocated tortoises.

Different levels of survival between males and females were evident only during the first year of the project. Males had a higher survivorship than females during that first harsh season. Expenditure of energy during egg production and relatively smaller size may have been contributing factors.

CONCLUSIONS

The tortoises relocated from Section 6 did not fare as well as the resident and host tortoises of Section 8. The survivorship of guest tortoises was significantly lower than the survivorship of residents and hosts in the first year of the project. This lower survivorship was not necessarily due exclusively to the relocation, but possibly the combined effect of poor health and harsh environmental conditions as well as relocation.

Differences in survival between the relocated and resident tortoises were much smaller during the second and third years of the study, which suggests that the major negative effects of the relocation were short-lived. The fact that the survival of host tortoises did not differ significantly from resident tortoises indicates that the addition of relocated tortoises did not adversely impact the health of populations into which they were relocated.

It is apparent that successfully relocating tortoises is affected by several factors, including the health of the tortoises prior to relocation and the timing of the relocation with respect to overall annual precipitation as well as to seasonal precipitation and food availability.

ACKNOWLEDGMENTS

Phase 2 and the three-year research project were authorized by the USFWS permit #PRT 746049. The project's design was advised by a Desert Tortoise Advisory Committee consisting of tortoise experts from federal and state agencies and the academic field. The committee included Dr. Kristin Berry (USBLM), Dr. Ken Nagy (UCLA), Dr. Elliot Jacobson (University of Florida), and Dr. Frank Vasek (Emeritus Professor, UCR).

Evaluating the Effectiveness of Headstarting Redbelly Turtles in Massachusetts

— ABSTRACT OF PRESENTATION AND PUBLISHED ARTICLE* —

ALISON HASKELL,[1,2] TERRY E. GRAHAM,[3] CURTICE R. GRIFFIN,[1] AND JAY B. HESTBECK[4]

[1]*Department of Forestry and Wildlife Management, University of Massachusetts, Amherst, MA 01003, USA*
[2]*Current address: U.S. Fish and Wildlife Service, 300 Westgate Center Drive, Hadley, MA 01035, USA [e-mail: Alison_Haskell@mail.fws.gov]*
[3]*Department of Biology, Worcester State College, Worcester, MA 01602, USA*
[4]*National Biological Service, University of Massachusetts, Amherst, MA 01003, USA*

As part of the federal recovery plan for the endangered redbelly turtle, *Pseudemys rubriventris*, in Massachusetts, a headstart project was initiated in 1984 to increase numbers of turtles. In this project, hatchlings are collected from a single donor population, raised in captivity (to increase their size) for about nine months, and subsequently released into one of several targeted ponds. We evaluate the effectiveness of headstarting redbelly turtles in Massachusetts by assessing survival of headstarted (HS) turtles and their effect on turtle numbers. The survival of headstarted turtles was assessed by determining (1) size-specific survival rates of HS turtles at one pond—Crooked (CR), and (2) average annual recapture rates of HS turtles at four ponds—Crooked (CR), Island (IS), Gunner's Exchange-Hoyts' (GH), and Federal (FE). The effect of HS turtles in increasing turtle numbers was examined by determining post-release changes in population size of four populations. Survival of HS turtles at CR Pond was lowest during the first year post-release, with substantial increases in following years. Lower survival rates of HS turtles at CR Pond was size-related (carapace length <65 mm). Higher survival rates, similar to rates observed for non-HS subadult and adult turtles, were observed for larger HS turtles (carapace length >95 mm). Average annual recapture rates of HS turtles at CR, IS, GH, and FE ponds were highest (0.70–0.84) for the three smaller ponds (CR, IS, GH) and lower (0.44) for the largest pond (FE). The observed difference in recapture rates was likely the result of variable trap effort, with more accurate rates observed for the smaller, more intensively trapped ponds. Sufficient numbers of HS turtles are surviving to increase turtle numbers at the three smaller ponds (CR, IS, GH) but not at FE Pond. Despite the increases in turtle numbers due to HS turtles, successful recovery requires the establishment of self-perpetuating populations. Because factors limiting population growth of the Massachusetts redbelly turtle probably still exist, headstarting should not be considered an appropriate longterm conservation strategy. Clearly, more research is needed to identify factors limiting natural recruitment if self-perpetuating populations are to be achieved.

*Haskell, A., T. E. Graham, C. R. Griffin, and J. B. Hestbeck. 1996. Size related survival of headstarted redbelly turtles (*Pseudemys rubriventris*) in Massachusetts. J. Herpetol. 30(4):524–527.

Predator-Proof Field Enclosures for Enhancing Hatching Success and Survivorship of Juvenile Tortoises: A Critical Evaluation

DAVID J. MORAFKA,[1] KRISTIN H. BERRY,[2] AND E. KAREN SPANGENBERG[1]

[1]*Department of Biology, California State University, Dominguez Hills, Carson, CA 90747-0005, USA [email: papaherp@aol.com]*
[2]*U.S. Geological Survey, Biological Resources Division, 6221 Box Springs Blvd., Riverside, CA 92507-0714, USA*

ABSTRACT: *In situ* predator-proof enclosures or pens can provide low-cost technology to conduct research on early life stages of tortoises and improve hatching success and juvenile survivorship of threatened and endangered species without the negative effects commonly experienced with captive-reared tortoises.

In situ experiments with two North American tortoise species, the Bolson tortoise (*Gopherus flavomarginatus*) and the desert tortoise (*G. agassizii*), provided valuable insights. The initial work (1983) with *G. flavomarginatus* at Mapimí, Durango, Mexico was characterized by extensive human manipulation and relatively low survivorship. Eggs were harvested from wild females using injections of oxytocin and were hatched in outdoor solar-powered incubators with a 65–67% success rate. Neonates were transferred to 20, 1 × 3 m wood and adobe pens constructed within an 11 × 13 × 2.5 m outdoor wire enclosure. Each pen held 1–2 neonates, which were provided with water and food. During the three-year trial, survivorship in the nursery was 76% (n = 86). Annual growth rates of juveniles declined from 184.7% (in weight) in the first year to nearly zero in the third year. For the 1983 cohort of neonates, three-year survivorship was 60%.

Building on the experience of the 1983 project, a second, but more passive, program was initiated in 1990 for *G. agassizii* at Fort Irwin in the Mojave Desert of California, USA. Wild females were temporarily relocated to a 60 × 60 × 2.6 m high fenced enclosure with natural, undisturbed desert vegetation. Females were permitted to range freely and nest, after which most were returned to their home sites. Hatching success was 90–94%. Some neonates constructed their own burrows, while others exploited pre-existing shelters or artificial burrows. No food or water was provided. Most individuals showed continuous growth into the third year. Drought conditions were probably responsible for declines in their growth and weights in the fourth year, and by the end of the fifth year, five (4.5%, n = 110) juveniles had died of starvation and dehydration. Excluding juveniles killed by predators (in a control area and in an exposed section of the enclosure), overall survivorship for the first three and one half years (between 1990 and 1994) was 88%. Despite the losses to drought during the fourth and fifth years, this passive treatment shows greater promise of success. The issue of carrying capacity within an enclosure, however, requires further investigation. Designs for two different field enclosures and alternate treatments are proposed, and recommendations are made for future *in situ* field programs.

Most hatchery and nursery operations undertaken to conserve chelonians have focused on sea turtles (Bjorndal, 1982) as well as some species of freshwater turtles. Because aquatic turtle nests are often aggregated, eggs and neonates can be located and protected more easily than those of terrestrial turtles and tortoises. Projects intended to protect eggs and neonates of aquatic chelonians subsequently developed into extended programs to raise juveniles to sizes that were less vulnerable to predation. Designed to counterbalance increasing losses to predators, habitat degradation, or habitat elimination, such intervention programs have been called "headstart efforts" (Carr, 1984).

Like the aquatic turtles, the majority of terrestrial chelonians are threatened by both direct human take and anthropogenic degradation of their ecosystems. In contrast to many species of aquatic turtles, however, testudinids and terrestrial emydids rarely have concentrated or communal nesting sites (Moll, 1979; Mrosovsky, 1983; Swingland and Klemens, 1989).

Yet after 30 years of intermittent sea turtle headstart programs, there is little evidence that progeny from hatchery and nursery programs survive to reach breeding age. Some authors (e.g., Mrosovsky, 1983; Frazer, 1992) have given negative reviews of these intervention programs. Frazer (1992, this volume) identified five areas of criticism. First, artificial propagation of young may be rendered ineffective unless the original causes of population declines are eliminated. In Frazer's classic example of sea turtles, habitat degradation from oil spills and global warming and loss of adults to shrimp nets could not be compensated by the "half-way technology" of simply producing more juvenile turtles for release into environments no longer able to sustain them. Second, headstart operations can perpetuate themselves as self-serving sociopolitical institutions that are attractive to a naive public. Such endeavors are often inaccurately equated to livestock husbandry. Third, evaluations of the efficacy of hatcheries and nurseries are often deferred for a generation, because only successful reproduction is a valid determinant of the survivorship to adulthood of the released juveniles. Fourth, the normal and appropriate roles of eggs and juveniles as prey in the context of food webs may be diminished by hatchery and nursery operations (Frazer, 1992). Erosion of gene pool diversity and heterozygosity may also result when a few females provide almost all progeny for the F_1 generation. Rarely do effective population numbers reach the hypothesized requisite of 500 reproducing adults (N_e) necessary to minimize inbreeding depression and drift-related losses in genetic diversity (Lande and Barrowclough, 1987). Fifth, hatchery efforts also direct conservation efforts to juveniles, which individually have the lowest probability of contributing to recruitment, rather than to reproductive adult females, which have the highest.

Mrosovsky (1983) provided three additional pragmatic considerations: Captive-reared juveniles released into natural surroundings may suffer spatial disorientation, lack wariness of predators, and be conditioned to inappropriate food items. In addition, the artificially elevated densities in captive chelonian colonies may result in malnutrition and epidemic disease.

It should be noted that the tactics and technology of headstart programs have evolved considerably over the last three decades: Nutrition has been improved, which promotes more normal growth; holding centers provide better hygiene and more space to accommodate growth and activity; longer rearing periods permit the release of larger turtles, which are less vulnerable to predators; the use of TEDs has reduced incidental take; in some marine habitats local pollution may have abated sufficiently to reduce environmental loss; and public education may also reduce losses to human activities. Given sea turtle generation intervals, however, it may be at least another 20 years before headstart programs receive a full and impartial evaluation.

During the past decade, headstart technologies developed for sea turtles have been modified for terrestrial chelonians. In this paper we evaluate field-based enclosures both as hatcheries and nurseries for restocking threatened and endangered tortoises and as research tools for obtaining more data on life history attributes.

Definition of Field Enclosures

At minimum, a field enclosure is a fenced area of suitable habitat on or within the historic range of the particular species and is capable of physically housing at least one clutch of eggs and sustaining the resulting neonate tortoises. (Neonate here refers to a juvenile <1 year of age and for which age is absolutely known, e.g., through mark-recapture data, Morafka, 1994.) The site need not sustain young tortoises for any particular time period beyond hatching and emergence. The individual tortoises need not be drawn from the local surrounding habitat. This core definition can include interventions as simple as a small cone or "tent" (sufficient to sustain the neonates from a single clutch for one season) or as complex as a field hatchery for hundreds of eggs with fenced pens extending over several hectares. We focus here on the larger and more complex structures used as hatcheries and nurseries. Most projects have been directed toward restocking or reintroduction.

Other Testudinid Hatchery and Nursery Programs that Utilize Enclosures

In the last three decades, at least a dozen hatchery and nursery operations have been proposed or implemented for 11 taxa of tortoises (Table 1) in 12 wild or semi-wild settings within or bordering on historic geographic ranges. The limited number is understandable, considering logistical difficulties, costs, and lack of critical life history data for many species. Purposes for the facilities vary considerably and range from raising highly endangered species for restocking, translocation, or repatriation into natural and historical habitats to providing holding facilities for captives. One important function in North America continues to be the gathering of scientific data on survivorship, behavior, physiology, and health of wild-raised tortoises, even when locally robust populations render restocking unnecessary. Education of local residents and visitors has also been incorporated into some programs, and one program for *Aldabrachelys elephantina* (formerly *Geochelone gigantea*) on Curieuse Island was established in part to provide a tourist attraction and deflect tourist pressure from the atoll of Aldabra (Stoddart et al., 1982; Hambler, 1994). At least one program (for *Geochelone sulcata*) in western Africa was designed to provide food for human consumption (IUCN/SSC, 1989). The best known, longest-term, largest, and most successful operation is for *G. nigra* in the Galápagos Islands (McFarland et al., 1974; Cayot et al., 1994; Cayot and Morillo, this volume). The program has single-handedly saved *G. n. hoodensis*, of which *all* wild specimens at present were headstarted and are now breeding. Other hatchery and nursery programs (e.g., for *Geochelone radiata*) have been established at zoological parks and reserves outside the historic geographic ranges of species.

Two Case Studies in North America

Two studies of field enclosures for the Bolson tortoise (*Gopherus flavomarginatus*) and the desert tortoise (*G. agassizii*) are presented below. The *G. flavomarginatus* program was actively managed, whereas the *G. agassizii* program, drawing upon the experiences of the former, used a passive strategy. The purposes of the two projects and ecological and societal contexts in which they existed also differed substantially.

The Mapimí Site

Purpose of the Project. The first long-term tortoise enclosure was established in North America in 1983 by Mexico's Instituto de Ecología at its Laboratorio del Desierto in the state of Durango to (1) provide baseline data on life history attributes, and (2) attempt to enhance recruitment in local populations of the Bolson tortoise, an endangered endemic species confined to the Bolsones (closed basins) de Mapimí of Mexico's central Chihuahuan Desert. Artificial enclosures were established because few young tortoises were observed during early studies (Legler and Webb, 1961), and 20 years later only captive juveniles were available to characterize juveniles and their growth (Morafka, 1982). A critical component of this project was the active involvement of local residents who were employed in the construction and maintenance of the physical enclosure and in care and maintenance of the juvenile tortoises. This was a labor-intensive endeavor in which a small space was managed and supplemented by human effort.

Location and Description of the Study Site. Situated in the endemically rich Mapimían Subprovince of the Chihuahuan Desert (Morafka, 1977), the vegetation is a patchy distribution of thorn scrub on a 2–3% grade (Martinez and Morello, 1977; Morafka et al., 1981). Dominant and important plant species are creosote bush (*Larrea tridentata*), prickly pear cactus (*Opuntia rostrata*), mesquite (*Prosopis glandulosa*), tar bush (*Flourensia cernua*), tobosa grass (*Hilaria mutica*), mallow (*Sphaeralcea angustifolia*), and grama grass (*Bouteloua* sp.).

The hatchery, nursery, and adjacent release site were in the Mapimí Reserve 26°29′–26°52′ N, 103°32′–103°58 W at 1,100 m approximately 1 km NE of the Laboratorio del Desierto field station in Durango, Mexico (Tom, 1994).

The Local Tortoise Population. Local populations tend to be dominated by adults and neonates with low percentages in intermediate age classes (Adest et al., 1989a). Aguirre et al. (1984) suggested that high density population clusters may reach 300 adults/km², whereas more widespread, low density areas would average approximately 10 adults/km².

Parental Stock and Handling of Eggs. Healthy, free-living adults served as parental stock (Morafka et al., 1986). Gravid females collected from a wild population 10 km NW of the Laboratorio were the source of eggs. Carotid and axillary blood samples were taken, and hematologic and serum biochemistries indicated no particular health problems, but fecal samples revealed high ascarid (nematode) egg counts. Such parasite loads are not necessarily detrimental to health as nematodes may serve as detritivores (shredders) in facilitating digestion (as suggested for iguanines by Iverson, 1982).

Presence of eggs was determined by inguinal palpation. Some females were induced to deposit their clutches by an intramuscular injection of oxytocin at a dosage of 1.0 USP unit/kg of body weight, whereas some laid eggs without artificial stimulation (Adest et al., 1989b).

Three incubation designs were utilized: (1) a constant temperature-controlled water-bath incubator (30°C), with eggs in cardboard trays; (2) eggs partially buried in sand in a wood box enclosure with ambient fluctuating temperatures (22–37°C); and (3) eggs incubated outdoors in nests naturally excavated in soil (protected only by the courtyard walls of the institute). Incubation required from 95 to 115 days, depending on the date of deposition, type of incubation, thermal regimes, and other factors (Adest et al., 1989b; G. Aguirre, pers. comm.).

Hatching Success. Hatching success, when completely infertile clutches were excluded from the calculations, averaged 65–77% (Adest et al., 1989b).

Raising Juvenile Tortoises. The enclosure, measuring 11 × 13 × 2.5 m high, was constructed of adobe and wood and was covered with 13 mm chicken wire mesh (Adest et al., 1989b). In its first year of operation, the enclosure was stocked with freshly hatched neonates and with one-year-old individuals previously maintained in terraria. Ten stalls, each 1 × 3 m and facing west, were divided by wood partitions and were backed by an equal and opposite set facing east. Each stall was entirely separated from adjacent stalls with 1 × 3 m wood partitions. Insulation cloth covered the back third of the enclosure to provide shade. Each stall was equipped with a pre-excavated burrow (approx. 30 cm long) and a shallow water dish (approx. 20 cm in diameter × 5 cm deep). Each pen held 1–2 tortoises. A single door with a lock provided access to the entire unit.

Growth Rates of Juveniles. All nursery-raised tortoises were provided with water and fed hand-cut and stored native grasses and forbs when available (*Hilaria mutica, Bouteloua barbata, Eragrostis intermedia, Solanum elaeagnifolium, Sphaeralcea angustifolia*), or dried baled alfalfa when native plants were unavailable between November and June (Adest et al., 1989b). The selection of native grasses and forbs was based on the known diet of adults.

Growth data are available for the first cohort (n = 23) of neonates from 1983 (Adest et al., 1989b). Carapace length (CL) and weight increased an average of 48.8% (SD ±5.7)

TABLE 1
A global survey of tortoise species for which breeding programs have been established in wild or semi-wild settings, or are proposed for restocking of native habitats.

Species	Location	Type of program	Reference
North America			
Gopherus agassizii	National Training Center at Ft. Irwin, California, USA	Two semi-wild, predator-proof enclosures for nesting females and raising of hatchlings and neonates. Minimal manipulation of eggs, neonates, and juveniles.	Joyner-Griffith, 1991; Morafka, 1994
G. flavomarginatus	Mapimi, Durango, Mexico	Incubators and predator-proof nurseries; considerable manipulation of females, eggs, neonates, and juveniles.	Morafka et al., 1986; Adest et al., 1989a, 1989b
South America			
Geochelone nigra hoodensis	Charles Darwin Research Station (CDRS), Galápagos Islands, Ecuador	A wide variety of actions, including nest protection in the wild; eggs removed to CDRS for hatching, raising of young, and restocking of wild populations. Approach by specific populations or races. *G. n. hoodensis* is the only ssp. captive bred, but several other species are headstarted.	MacFarland et al., 1974; Cayot et al., 1994; Cayot and Morillo, 1997
Europe			
Testudo h. hermanni	La Station D'Observation et de Protection des Tortues des Maures (SOPTUM), Gonfaron, France	A mix of captive breeding as well as management of wild tortoises; a large restocking effort. The last remaining Hermann's tortoise population in mainland France.	Stubbs, 1989b; Devaux and Stubbs, 1997
T. h. hermanni	Northeastern Spain	Captive breeding center.	Mascort, 1997
T. h. boettgeri	Port-Cros National Park and Porquerolle, France	Two rearing trials in enclosures; 150 tortoises released on island.	Cheylan, 1984
Testudo graeca	Elche, Alcante Province, Spain	A private facility, goal of reintroductions to the wild.	Stubbs, 1989a

Species	Location	Type of program	Reference
Sub-Saharan Africa			
Geochelone sulcata	Nazinga Ranch, Burkina Faso, Sudan	Small-scale captive breeding program to evaluate potential for meat production; potential pilot project for reintroduction of tortoises to Sudan using stock from Al-Ain Zoo, Abu Dhabi.	IUCN/SSC, 1989
Indian Ocean—Madagascar			
Geochelone yniphora	Ampijoroa Forestry Station, Madagascar	In 1985, the IUCN/SSC Tortoise Specialist Group in collaboration with the WWF-International Jersey Wildlife Preservation Trust initiated a recovery program for relocating and breeding tortoises.	Curl et al., 1985; Durrell et al., 1989c; IUCN/SSC, 1989
Geochelone radiata[a]	Ivolohina; Parc Tsimbazzaza; Réunion Island	Groups of tortoises at three sites; several groups introduced on Réunion, where breeding occurs naturally.	Durrell et al., 1989b
Acinixys (Pyxis) planicauda	Ampijoroa breeding facility, Madagascar	Identified need and proposal to expand breeding facility at the Ampijoroa Forestry Station for site captive rearing and protected breeding.	Durrell et al., 1989a; IUCN/SSC, 1989
Indian Ocean—Aldabra Island			
Aldabrachelys elephantina (formerly *Geochelone gigantea*)	Curieuse Island, Seychelles	Operation Curieuse: 299 Aldabran giant tortoises introduced to Curieuse Island to establish a second (reserve) population. Purposes: tourist attraction to deflect tourism from Aldabra, monitor growth and demography, re-establish tortoises recently lost to central Seychelles, use new population to supply zoos overseas, and meet local demand for domestic tortoises.	Stoddart et al., 1982; Swingland, 1989; IUCN/SSC, 1989

[a] Does not include the successful colonies of the Wildlife Conservation Society's breeding herd at St. Catherines Island, Georgia, USA (1981–). This program is outside the historic geographic range.

and an average of 184.7% (SD ±37.9), respectively, in the first year (n = 23). By the second year, 19 of the 23 first-year tortoises remained. For the 19, CL increased an average of 19.8 mm (SD ±4.5) or 29.5% (SD ±5.5), and weight increased an average of 77.0 g (SD ±29.4) or 108.4% (SD ±19.8) during the second year. By the third year, growth rates declined to an average of 0.2 mm (SD ±0.4) CL, and the average weight increment was only 1.8 g (SD ±3.7) for the eight tortoises for which data were available. Third-year values are effectively zero when SD and sampling error are considered.

Status of Health. Some juveniles in the enclosure showed signs of illness. Third-year juveniles failed to grow, and the majority of second-year and third-year tortoises developed pyramiding carapaces and knobby plastrons (Adest et al., 1989b). Knobby carapaces have been described in cases of severe nutritional osteodystrophy due to a calcium-deficient diet (Jackson and Cooper, 1981). Such conditions compromise shell hardness and probably reduce long-term viability. After nutrient deficiencies were suspected in 1985, the natural diet was analyzed by fresh plant parts rather than by species (Adest et al., 1989b). Human caretakers had provided the young tortoises with forage from dried bundles of whole native grasses and locally grown alfalfa. Analyses of these and similar dried whole mature grasses yielded only 3.5–8% protein whereas immature fresh green shoots, preferred by juvenile tortoises, averaged approximately 16% protein (Adest et al., 1989b). Studies of another chelonian, *Trachemys scripta,* have indicated that higher protein (≥16%) diets are critical to sustain normal growth in juveniles (Parmenter and Avery, 1990). After 1985 the protein and mineral content of the young tortoises' diet was enriched by feeding fresh-cut alfalfa, and in subsequent cohorts and year classes shell abnormalities were reduced and new growth was sustained.

Survivorship and Causes of Death. In 1985, 86 living neonate and juvenile tortoises remained from the three cohort years of 1983, 1984, and 1985. The combined survivorship for all three cohort years is 76% (Adest et al., 1989b). Survivorship was 60% for the 1983 cohort year, 55% for the 1984 cohort year, and 86% for the 1985 cohort year.

Tortoise deaths (n = 21) were attributed to six causes: 7 (33%) from decalcification and desiccation, (probably from malnutrition); 6 (28.6%) from either drowning in water dishes or prolonged insolation after being overturned while attempting to climb the wood dividers separating the stalls; 1 (4.8%) from exposure to cold; and 7 (33%) from undetermined causes.

Survivorship after Release. In 1986 ten neonate tortoises, hatched from the passive solar incubator and held ≤18 days, were released in August and September to the wild (Tom, 1994). Only four of the ten were still alive 11 months after release.

The Fort Irwin Study Site (FISS)

Purpose of the Project and Enclosure. In 1990 a field enclosure was constructed at the National Training Center (NTC), Fort Irwin, California, for a population of the threatened Mojave Desert tortoise (USFWS, 1994; Joyner-Griffith, 1991). This study population was robust both in absolute numbers and in age class representation. The objectives for the enclosure were twofold: to gather baseline data on life history attributes of juveniles and to determine survivorship of released juveniles. Restocking the general area was not an objective. The new enclosure was 60 times larger than the enclosure for the Bolson tortoise, it was remote from human populations, and it was serviced only twice a month. The enclosure was assumed to have a carrying capacity sufficient to sustain the confined and protected juveniles with minimal human intervention.

Location and Description of the Study Site. The Fort Irwin Study Site (FISS) is on the SE corner of the U.S. Army's NTC at Ft. Irwin, approximately 15 km NW of Afton Canyon, San Bernardino County, California (35°06′49″ N, 116°29′27″ W, 650 m elev.). Two enclosures, FISS I and FISS II, are situated on 2% slope of NE-facing sandy hillsides, which are cut by dry washes draining east to West Cronese Dry Lake. The soil surface is stabilized by a well-developed desert crust. Vegetation is Mojave Desert creosote bush scrub (Vasek and Barbour, 1988), specifically big galleta shrub steppe (USFWS, 1994) dominated by creosote bush and white bursage (*Ambrosia dumosa*), with other common shrubs including *Lycium pallidum* and *Ephedra nevadensis*. The native bunch grass galleta, *Pleuraphis rigida*, is common despite the intrusion of Mediterranean annual grasses such as *Bromus madritensis* ssp. *rubens* and *Schismus barbatus*. The study site, which has not been used for military training or comparable activities, is protected within the confines of the NTC and remains one of the most pristine landscapes in the region.

The Local Tortoise Population. The study population is part of the Superior-Cronese Desert Wildlife Management Area (USFWS, 1994), with densities of local tortoise populations estimated at an average 19 adults/km² (range 8–97 adults/km²).

Description of the Enclosure. The enclosure was constructed in a manner that would conserve the natural vegetation and limit disruption of the natural crust of desert soil. The 60 × 60 m area is enclosed by chicken wire fencing and roofing, supported by 2.6 m poles anchored in concrete. The perimeter of the enclosure is bounded by 1 cm mesh hardware cloth buried 0.76 m deep and continued 0.6 m above ground to exclude small vertebrate predators. The unit is divided into northern and southern sections by a 2 m high chicken wire fence. The frames of the two locking entrance doors have 10 cm raised sills to confine juvenile tortoises should the doors be left ajar.

When first constructed in May 1990, chicken wire roofing was installed over only the northern half of the enclosure. After an attack by avian predators (probably the common raven, *Corvus corax*) in May 1991, roofing was installed over the southern half by July 1991. Midway along the southern fence a bamboo blind (approx. 3 m wide × 2 m tall × 2 m deep) permits young tortoises to be observed without disturbance from human movements or shadows. A solar-powered Campbell Scientific Instrument weather station, located at the southwest corner of the site, records air and soil temperatures, wind velocity, and precipitation every 15 minutes and downloads the data to a remote computer at designated intervals by cellular phone.

Neonates were free to roam the 60 × 30 m subdivision in which they were hatched. Most (83%) constructed their own burrows within a few days of hatching, whereas others used abandoned rodent burrows or shared artificial burrows that had been constructed for adults (0.25 m wide × 1 m long beneath 0.5 m of soil) (M. Joyner, pers. comm.). Researchers and occasional visitors walked through the enclosure to collect data on tortoises, and created a network of small trails and trampled soils.

Source and Handling of Eggs. Each May from 1990 through 1993, 8–10 adult females were collected from the surrounding 5 km², and their field sites were recorded. Gravid females were identified by radiograph and placed in the enclosure to nest virtually undisturbed. Non-gravid females were immediately returned to their original field sites. After depositing their eggs, most of the remaining females were also returned to their original field sites. Typically, two females were retained in the enclosure to generate fresh feces for ingestion by fall neonates (Dezfulian et al., 1994). To avoid mechanical disturbances that might compromise hatching success, nests were not examined.

Hatching Success. Neonate tortoises emerged 85–110 days after egg deposition. The incubation period was estimated by starting with the week in which eggs were first absent from radiographs of previously gravid females. Radiography was conducted at the field site to minimize disturbance to nesting females. Females were moved no more than 50 m during the 15-minute examination procedure, which occurred no more often than once per week. The rate of hatching (based on radiographs of gravid females and fall 1990 capture records of neonates) was estimated at 90–94%, which is substantially higher than the 46% reported by Turner et al. (1986) for eggs relocated from natural deposition sites to predator-proof nests.

Sex Ratios. Twenty-nine tortoises hatched at FISS, ranging in age from three to five years, were sexed in 1995. Twenty-four males, five possible males, and ten females suggested a three-to-one sex ratio (Lance, 1995). This significantly skewed finding ($P < 0.05$) contrasted with the 1:1 ratio reported as typical for natural populations (Dodd, 1986). Populations with sex ratios highly skewed toward males have been considered to be in poor condition (Berry, 1976).

Growth Rates of Neonates and Juveniles. The length and weight increased an average of 8.7% (SD ±3.9) and 21.7% (SD ±16.5), respectively, for all age classes (first- to third-year tortoises) pooled during the 1993 growing season, a year which had above-average rainfall. However, in 1994 when annual precipitation was 70% below average, no increase in CL occurred, and weight decreased by an average of 25% (SD ±6.5). With above-average rainfall in spring 1995, weights of juveniles increased an average of 70% compared with the lowest values recorded in 1994.

Neonates and Juveniles Released from the Enclosure. In March of 1991, 12 neonates were fitted with radio transmitters and released from the enclosure to the surrounding area. Juvenile tortoises have been monitored since 1991 on a quarterly (seasonal) or triennial basis for external signs of disease, evidence of fecal parasites, and blood chemistries and peripheral blood cell counts obtained by axillary samples or cardiocentesis. Some individuals showed elevated values for blood urea nitrogen (BUN) and uric acid levels during the driest sampling periods. These elevated values are indicative of episodic dehydration (R. Yates, pers. comm.; Christopher et al., this volume). While abnormal blood cell counts were rarely observed, clinically normal animals occasionally displayed mild leukocytosis or mildly depressed packed-cell volumes (Morafka, 1993). No abnormal loads of parasites or bacteria were reported, though the potentially mutualistic fermenting anaerobe, *Clostridium bifermentans*, was isolated (Dezfulian et al., 1994).

Survivorship and Causes of Death. Sixty-eight percent (n = 162) of neonates and juveniles have survived 1–5 years. In May of the first year (1991) 18 of 24 juveniles occupying the unroofed southern enclosure were lost to avian predators, probably the common raven (Morafka, 1993). This first year survivorship does not differ significantly ($P > 0.05$) from that reported by Tom (1994). Eight of 12 free-ranging, control group juveniles, fitted with radio transmitters, were similarly preyed upon at this time. If these avian predation numbers are excluded, overall survivorship rises to 76%. In comparison, Turner et al. (1987) reported a similar but higher annual survivorship of 76.7% for juveniles <60 mm CL, 79.5% for juveniles 60–79 mm CL, and 80.4% for juveniles 80–99 mm CL (figures are for geometric annual means) in a wild population in the eastern Mojave Desert for periods spanning nine years. These high survivorship values suggest that interventions may not provide significant advantages except in unusual situations, e.g., when local ravens or other predators are increasing the rates of predation or where interventions significantly reduce nest predation by foxes.

Annual survivorship from fall 1993 to spring 1994 for all age classes (first through third years) pooled was 86%. In spring 1994 survivorship was greatest for the 1990 (age 3.5 years) and 1991 (age 2.5 years) cohorts at 88%. This three-year survivorship was significantly greater ($P < 0.05$) than 60% reported for the equivalent Mapimí cohort of enclosed tortoises. It decreased to 80% for the 1992 cohort and was only 50% for the 1993 cohort. In the 1994 drought growth rates and weights of juveniles declined. Five (4.5%) juveniles had died of starvation and dehydration by December 1994.

Population Density within the Enclosure. Juvenile tortoise densities increased annually with each newly hatched cohort. Densities inside the enclosure were the equivalent of 152/ha in 1990 and 344/ha in 1993 (Table 2). The numerical densities for juveniles within the enclosure are 300× to 900× the densities of wild juvenile and immature tortoises estimated by Berry (1990) using mark-recapture data for four nearby study sites in the western Mojave Desert (Table 3). Berry's density figures apply to a wider range of sizes and include immature tortoises up to 139 mm CL with estimated ages of 8–12 years. If Berry's density figures are adjusted for the younger and smaller tortoises found at FISS, the density of juveniles in the enclosure surpasses field estimates by factors of 50× to 100×.

Some behaviors exhibited by both juveniles and adults within the enclosure were aberrant, a possible indication of overcrowding. Thirty-five percent of FISS tortoises shared burrows with two or more tortoises, a pattern not observed in the wild for 1,403 juvenile and immature tortoises at 18 study sites in California (Berry and Turner, 1984, 1986). Juveniles that shared burrows frequently were observed to cluster in the entrances, preventing those inside from emerging and those outside from retreating into the burrow. Thus, the individuals outside the burrow were exposed to excessive temperatures. On one occasion, a small juvenile was observed to follow its larger burrow-mate through the shrub canopy to the burrow.

TABLE 2
Population density and survivorship of neonate and juvenile desert tortoises hatched and maintained in a semi-wild enclosure at the Fort Irwin National Training Center, San Bernardino, California.

Cohort by year	1990	1991	1992	1993	1994
1990 Cohort	55	31	23–26	26–28	22–25
1991 Cohort	—	88	73–76	74–79	67–73
1992 Cohort	—	—	13	10–11	8–9
1993 Cohort	—	—	—	6	3
Totals	55	119	115	124	110
Density/ha	152	329	319	344	305

TABLE 3
Population densities of juvenile and small immature (<140 mm carapace length at the midline) desert tortoises at four sites in the western Mojave Desert of California. This size range includes tortoises from emerging neonates to individuals estimated at 8–12 years of age. Data from Berry, 1990.

Site name	Year	No. juvenile and small immature tortoises/ha (95% Confidence Interval)
Fremont Valley	1981	0.43 (0.36–0.53)
Desert Tortoise Natural Area interior	1979	0.75 (0.58–0.98)
Desert Tortoise Natural Area interpretive center (inside fence)	1979	0.44 (0.37–0.51)
Kramer Hills	1982	0.69 (0.54–0.87)

Adults placed in the enclosure to lay eggs and produce scats were observed to usurp juvenile burrows and enlarge them into pallets or adult burrows. Adults also visibly reduced the limited supply of desert annual plants available as forage.

Survivorship after Release to the Wild. Nine 3-year and 4-year juveniles were fitted with radio transmitters and released outside the enclosure in May 1994. Nine months later 66.7% were still alive.

Status of Health. The local tortoise population is robust, and intermediate age-size cohorts are well represented. In 1994, 20+ tortoises of various ages within and outside the enclosure were screened for antibodies to *Mycoplasma agassizii*, the pathogen responsible for infectious upper respiratory tract disease (URTD), using an ELISA test (Schumacher et al., 1993; E. Jacobson, pers. comm.). Four (7.7%) of 52 tortoises sampled between 1993 and 1995 were seropositive, and an additional six (11.5%) were suspect for *M. agassizii* (Jacobson et al., 1996). Of the four seropositive tortoises, three were adult females and one was a juvenile in the FISS enclosure.

Comparison and Evaluation of the Two *Gopherus* Hatcheries, Nurseries, and Release Programs

Both active and passive management approaches have advantages and liabilities and must be viewed as hypothesis-testing experiments. Neither management approach provides guaranteed recipes for hatching, rearing, and restocking young tortoises to the wild. Ecological and socioeconomic contexts may determine which experimental approach is more appropriate. If it is cost-effective to utilize local resident caretakers and if the enclosure is small relative to the density of tortoises it is expected to maintain, an actively maintained enclosure may be justified. Active manipulation would also be favored at sites where weather conditions are too varied and production of forage is too uncertain for successful passive operation. An actively maintained (and closely monitored) enclosure may also be justified when poaching and/or vandalism would otherwise disable the effort. Conversely, a passive approach is justified if weather patterns, forage production, physical space, and soil provide consistently sufficient resources to support a high density of juvenile cohorts. At remote sites where humans are not resident and the risk of human interference low, the need for costly on-site caretakers is diminished, and a passive operation may be more appropriate.

Criteria for Defining and Developing Successful Tortoise Enclosures

Mrosovsky (1983, p. 25) stated the best criteria for judging success of headstarting in sea turtle programs:

"Perhaps the best—the ultimate—validation would be, after many years, a greater percentage of headstarted turtles among the breeding females than might be expected on the basis of the percentage of eggs taken for headstarting (Buitrago, 1981; Pritchard, 1981). For this it would be necessary to know not only how many eggs were taken for headstarting but also the percentage of the total laid that this take compromised."

His definition applies equally well to assessments of similar conservation efforts for tortoises. Determination of success could require 20 years of intensive monitoring, not only of specific cohorts but of the entire population. A very important milestone would be a demonstration of successful reproduction of a majority of the headstarted animals.

The Role of Enclosures in the Future

Tortoises may be better candidates for hatcheries and nurseries than many species of aquatic turtles because of their life history characteristics. Manipulation of tortoise eggs is often unnecessary, imprinting on ancestral nesting beaches is not an issue, conditioning to appropriate diets may be less critical for generally opportunistic herbivores (and for some omnivorous taxa such as *Kinixys*, Obst et al., 1988), and acquired skills at predator avoidance may be less critical for fossorial species that spend >95% of their lives in burrows. Furthermore, some tortoises live in terrestrial habitats that can be more easily managed, e.g., controlled burning to stimulate disclimax grassland in Florida forests for *Gopherus polyphemus* populations (Auffenberg, 1969; Diemer, 1986). We offer four applications of enclosures for tortoises in wild or semi-wild settings:

1. Augment recovery of "Threatened" and "Endangered" populations by adding annual cohorts of juveniles. Traditionally, biologists have assigned low values to neonates and juveniles because of their high assumed mortality rates (e.g., Auffenberg and Iverson, 1979). Despite the many difficulties inherent in hatchery and nursery operations, protected eggs and juveniles have the potential to accelerate recovery of threatened and endangered populations, especially if large cohorts can survive the early vulnerable years. From this perspective neonates and juveniles are the most important age classes for achieving rapid recovery. The 25-year program of successful hatching, nursery, rearing, and releases of Galápagos tortoises is a prime example of the benefits of such techniques (MacFarland et al., 1974; Cayot et al., 1994; Cayot and Morillo, this volume).

In some cases, while habitats have remained intact, tortoise populations have declined because of commercial uses, collection for pets or food, vandalism, disease, or subsidized native predators (Boarman, 1993). In the last case, native predators' numbers have increased to densities that exert abnormally high predation pressures on the tortoises. Predator populations often proliferate because their food sources are subsidized by urban and agricultural wastes and landfills. If specific threats can be eliminated, artificially enhanced hatching success and juvenile survivorship may prove to be an effective technology.

For species such as *Gopherus polyphemus*, evidence exists that recruitment in wild tortoise populations may be a highly stochastic process: A decade of reproductive effort may yield only one good year in which predation pressures on eggs and young are sufficiently abated, or production of forage elevated, to usher through a particular cohort of neonates (Landers et al., 1982). Accordingly, chelonian conservationists could employ *in situ* predator-proof enclosures to artificially suppress predation to create the equivalent of one or more good years to enhance or accelerate recruitment.

2. Collect data on life history attributes of difficult-to-find neonates and juveniles. Young tortoises in the wild are so elusive that if they were treated as a species separate from adults, they would be among the rarest and the least understood terrestrial vertebrates. Even for one of the most thoroughly studied species, *Gopherus polyphemus*, a review of the past 200 years of scientific literature revealed only five citations that addressed juvenile tortoise biology (Douglass, 1978). Similar but less extreme circumstances were noted by Berry and Turner (1984, 1986) and Morafka (1994) for the well-studied desert tortoise, *G. agassizii*, and by Adest et al. (1989a) for the Bolson tortoise, *G. flavomarginatus*.

Juvenile desert tortoises are relatively inaccessible in the field for a variety of reasons. The small and inconspicuous animals are often obscured from view by surrounding vegetation, they are sequestered in their burrows up to 98% of the time, and they are active very early in the spring and early in the day (Berry and Turner, 1986; Morafka, pers. obs.). In addition, neonates may disperse rapidly from scattered nest sites, or they may be rapidly depleted by intense predation. Juveniles of many taxa function ecologically as if they were different species from the adults (Polis, 1984). Predator-proof field sites provide opportunities to observe concentrations of juvenile tortoises for sustained periods in a largely natural setting. The resulting insights into the utilization of food, shelter, and water by juveniles are valuable scientifically and contribute to more effective management of critical habitats as well as to the improvement of techniques in population recruitment (Morafka, 1994).

3. Study life history attributes of poorly known species that do not thrive or survive in captivity. Some species of tortoises—e.g., *Homopus boulengeri* (Boycott, 1989; Baard, 1994), *H. femoralis* (Branch, 1989a; Baard, 1994), *Psammobates oculifer* (Boycott and Branch, 1989), *P. tentorius* (Branch, 1989b), and *Pyxis arachnoides* (Durrell et al., 1989a)—do not thrive in captivity. Durrell et al. (1989) noted that there were only five *P. arachnoides* in captivity in 1989, and none had reproduced. The reasons for failure in captivity of these species are unknown. Potential reasons include specialized diets and unusual thermal requirements. For example, Jackson's chameleon, *Chameleo jacksonii*, requires a diurnal temperature of 25°C and nocturnal temperatures of 10–15°C (Obst et al., 1988). Similar regimes have been recommended for the central Asian geckos of the genus *Teratoscincus* and many other arid-adapted and upland reptiles.

4. Provide domesticated stock to address human needs: food and pet trade. Occasionally, reptile hatcheries and nurseries are promoted as a means of satisfying local human dietary (and commercial) needs. In addition to the farming of crocodilians, captive-breeding projects for the green turtle, *Chelonia mydas* (Wood, 1982), and the African spurred tortoise, *Geochelone sulcata* (IUCN/SSC, 1989), have been developed to help serve human food needs. However, for tortoises, typically slow-growing compared to homeothermic livestock, these strategies generally prove impractical as they provide a very small and delayed (10–20 years) yield of tortoises (Congdon et al., 1993) in return for a substantial economic investment. No circumstances have been reported in which the production of enclosure- or captive-bred tortoises has significantly reduced the exploitation of wild tortoises for food.

Whether tortoise hatcheries and nurseries could help alleviate the demand for wild juvenile tortoises in the pet trade is a more problematic and controversial issue. Breeding and distribution of tortoises for the pet trade could stimulate demand beyond the capacity of the breeding facilities and thus fuel rather than suppress trade in poached animals. Furthermore, identification of contraband animals is made more difficult for law enforcement, placing a greater burden on inspectors to establish illegal origins. However, leopard geckos (*Eublepharis macularus*), veiled chameleons (*Chameleo calyptratus*), and a few species of boids and colubrids are now bred in such numbers that most of the profit incentive has been removed from smuggling wild-caught conspecifics to American and European markets. In southern California, captive breeding programs have probably alleviated the pressures of collecting on the wild rosy boa, *Lichanura trivergata*. The captive breeding of leopard tortoises, *Geochelone pardalis*, in the United States may be a more germane example (e.g., Street, 1996). Similar breeding programs (in either terraria or field enclosures) established in the exotic pet's country of origin would provide jobs for local communities. The sale of a small percentage of the enclosure-produced neonates could avoid the diminished and delayed financial reward of raising them to adulthood. Such tortoise farms have been advocated to supply the pet trade (e.g., *Testudo h. hermanni*, Kirsche, 1984). Sales of 1–10% of the annual harvest could be considered, especially when alternative funding is not available. However, no recommendation is made here, given the case-specific nature of the risks and benefits in such undertakings.

Recommendations for Future Field Enclosures

1. **Develop a plan**. Each project should have a well-developed and peer-reviewed plan of action, i.e., established objectives, defined phases, and periods of formal evaluations. Where appropriate, the advice of experts should be sought in the fields of captive breeding, chelonian biology, veterinary medical research and husbandry, and repatriation and reintroduction. The project should be reviewed by appropriate government agencies and community representatives.

2. **Utilize the natural setting**. The enclosure should include topographical features (with undisturbed substrates) common to the species' natural habitat, appropriate soils for shelter and egg deposition, native vegetation, small native animal species other than tortoise predators, and a sufficient thermal mosaic to allow thermoregulation. Stream channels, washes, and other sites susceptible to temporary flooding should be avoided. Temperature (including sun and shade temperatures at various depths of soil) and precipitation in each enclosure should be monitored frequently to provide data on burrow requirements, activity levels, and thermal preferences. A fully automated, solar-powered weather station can regularly transmit data to computerized logs.

3. **Evaluate carrying capacity**. One of the more difficult attributes to determine is the carrying capacity of the natural environment or of the enclosure. Data on densities of natural tortoise populations are so limited that scientists are often required to use estimates. Efforts should be made to gather data on densities of wild populations by size class so that appropriate stocking levels for enclosures and for future release programs can be determined. Behaviors of individual tortoises and their intraspecific interactions in the wild should be observed to determine normal patterns, especially territorial tolerances. Such behaviors can then be compared with similar behaviors observed within the enclosures. In the absence of such data, caretakers of the enclosure-maintained animals may miss critical cues of overcrowding.

4. **Select genetic stock and maintain genetic diversity**. The breeding stock should be carefully selected to maximize heterozygosity and allelic diversity. Because single males or a few dominant males are often responsible for fertilizing most females within a cluster of tortoises (Adest et al., 1984), the risk of inbreeding depression may be higher than total numbers indicate. Even wild North American tortoises have relatively low levels of protein (allozyme) differentiation both within and between species (Morafka et al., 1994). Breeding programs should preserve those regional genetic differences that correlate with adaptive phenotypic differences (MacFarland et al., 1974; Cayot et al., 1994).

Genetic diversity may be enhanced by replacing the breeding stock annually. Small sets of breeding females should not be reused as egg sources because of the potential for genetic bottlenecks and inbreeding depression. Genetic diversity is especially critical for large, highly fecund species such as *Geochelone pardalis*, *G. sulcata*, *G. nigra*, and *Aldabrachelys elephantina* (formerly *Geochelone gigantea*) where a few females could be responsible for large numbers of eggs and their surviving neonates. If the breeding protocol requires an annual turnover of new females as egg sources, this risk is reduced.

If females are locally available, they should be obtained from the wild population adjacent to the enclosure. The locations of their captures should be recorded so that they can be later returned to their home sites. The females should be radiographed, and the gravid females released into the enclosure to deposit eggs. Additional radiographs will confirm whether the eggs have been deposited. Should artificial nest sites and burrows be required, their construction should be undertaken in advance. Females should be returned to their home sites outside the enclosure as soon as possible to avoid overgrazing within the enclosure. If adult scats are to be introduced into the enclosure to benefit potentially coprophagous juveniles, the scats should be taken from clinically healthy animals.

5. **Maintain healthy breeding stock, neonates, and juveniles**. Health profiles such as blood counts, blood chemistry, and tests for diseases known or suspected to occur in the region should be completed on the proposed breeding stock prior to initiation of the project (Christopher et al., this volume). Once the project is initiated, all animals should be screened annually until released.

Diseases are a growing concern not only in captive but also in wild populations (Jacobson, 1993, 1994). One of the newest and potentially most serious diseases discovered in at least two species of North American tortoises is URTD, caused by the bacterium *Mycoplasma agassizii* (Brown et al., 1994a). The disease is infectious and appears to have been introduced to wild populations through release of captive tortoises (Jacobson, 1993). It is spreading rapidly in wild populations of desert tortoises (Brown et al., 1994b) and is a local problem with the gopher tortoise. In the case of the desert tortoise, some wild populations have suffered catastrophic declines (Berry, this volume). In captivity juvenile tortoises with URTD have been unable to thrive despite careful feeding and nurturing (Oftedal et al., 1995). Adults that survive exposure and illness may have compromised reproductive systems (Lance et al., 1995). All tortoises in hatchery, nursery, and rearing programs should be carefully screened for mycoplasmas (using an ELISA test, Schumacher et al., 1993) as well as other diseases. Protocols should be developed to determine when ill or potentially ill individuals should be removed from experimental programs.

6. **Monitor nesting and hatching.** Females should be permitted to select nest sites and nest without interference. Frequent (weekly) X-rays (or at least palpation) of adult females should be combined with nest monitoring to determine whether hatching rates are comparable to free-ranging

controls. In general, hatching success should be >80% if nests are undisturbed. Stancyk (1982) reported that hatching successes in hatcheries were lower (65%, range = 55–85%) than hatching successes in natural nests (approx. 80%, range = 50–95%) for several species of sea turtles.

Incubation temperatures play a critical role in chelonian hatcheries because sea turtles (Yntema and Mrosovsky, 1980), most freshwater turtle species (Ewert and Nelson, 1991; Pieau and Dorizzi, 1981), and tortoises are subject to temperature dependent sex determination (TSD). Before the role of TSD was known for sea turtles (Yntema, 1976), artificial incubation often produced skewed sex ratios that favored males (Mrosovsky and Yntema, 1980), because eggs were frequently incubated at inadvertently lower temperatures above ground in Styrofoam boxes. Our own enclosure data, previously cited, indicated a similarly skewed sex ratio for *G. agassizii*. The limited data for tortoises, e.g., *Gopherus agassizii* (Spotila et al., 1994) and *Testudo graeca* (Pieau, 1971), suggest that different species have different pivotal temperatures. While higher temperatures favor females in virtually all emydids and testudinids tested, research should be conducted to confirm that TSD affects sex ratios for the species of interest and to determine the pivotal temperature, which in some cases may be population specific (Spotila et al., 1994).

Another important research topic is the range of temperatures suitable for incubation. Incubation temperatures can affect hatching success and later growth of juveniles (Spotila et al., 1994). The fixed-value pivotal temperatures determined by laboratory experiments do not precisely parallel the variable temperatures recorded in nests. While we may expect that a range of suitable temperatures would be present within field enclosures, the enclosed habitat may offer only a small portion of the microenvironments available to free-ranging gravid females. Thus, data should be gathered on daily and seasonal temperature cycles, especially during the time of the sensitive second trimester of incubation (Yntema, 1979; Bull and Vogt, 1981).

7. Provide conditions for development of normal behaviors. Juvenile tortoises should have sufficient space to develop burrows, pallets, and home ranges without abnormal interference from siblings or older or younger tortoises. Naturally occurring vegetation should be sufficient to allow development of normal foraging patterns. Vegetation is also critical for providing an adequately diverse thermal mosaic for thermoregulation. Inadequate cover could expose tortoises to lethal temperatures (e.g., *Gopherus agassizii* and *G. berlandieri* in McGinnis and Voigt, 1971; Rose et al., 1988).

Space should be sufficient to promote normal daily activity and adequate exercise for skeletomuscular development. When tortoises are released from the enclosure, they must be able to navigate, disperse, forage, find or construct shelters, and ultimately locate mates with a capacity comparable to wild-hatched, free-ranging controls.

8. Provide natural diets essential for normal growth, health, and survivorship. Food items must supply an adequate and balanced diet in terms of vitamins, minerals, and especially protein (e.g., 15–17% of total by weight, Adest et al., 1989b). The carrying capacity of the enclosure must be sufficient (i.e., sufficient quantities and distribution of food) to support all the tortoises. In less ideal circumstances, supplemental food, water, and shelter must be provided. Site selection should never be based solely on plant growth and weather data from one season or calendar year. Subsequent years may produce drastic changes in carrying capacity.

General characterizations of ecosystem carrying capacity are likely to be of limited use when tortoises are confined to specific locales. Some tortoise species (e.g., *Gopherus agassizii* and *G. berlandieri*) are characterized as nomadic (Auffenberg, 1969). Some tortoises may qualify as fugitive species (Grimaldi and Jaenicke, 1984), which may simply use ephemeral disclimax or subclimax habitats, and they may shift from site to site to exploit resources. Frail desert grasslands are classic examples as are open habitats created by fire subclimax (Auffenberg, 1969). When normal nomadic movements are curtailed, carrying capacity is likely to be compromised.

Much remains to be learned about the dietary requirements of tortoises in the wild and in captivity (Jackson and Cooper, 1981; Frye, 1991). Numerous crippling and deforming diseases caused by nutritional imbalances and deficiencies have been identified and are likely to occur in tortoises that are raised in hatcheries, nurseries, and other rearing projects. Dietary content should be evaluated and analyses undertaken. Careful records should be kept on environmental conditions, quality and quantity of food items, and amounts of water available. Such data can be used in subsequent evaluations of growth, survivorship, and normal reproductive capacity.

A single adult may need to be present to generate fresh feces bearing the fermenting anaerobic bacterium, *Clostridium bifermentans*, which appears to be instrumental in cellulose digestion for some tortoises (Bjorndal, 1987). Conspecific coprophagy is common in tortoises and iguanas, *I. iguana* (Troyer, 1982; Morafka, 1994), and feces may provide the critical inoculum for the requisite bacteria. The subject of coprophagy requires additional research. Frye (1991) cautions against interspecific coprophagy, but Dezfulian et al. (1994) think consumption of parental feces by neonates may facilitate the inoculation of their large intestines with *Clostridium*, which is assumed to be mutualistic. If scats of adults are made available to the juveniles, the providers of the scats should be clinically healthy.

9. Gather population data for a life table. The demographic attributes (length, mass, sex ratios, density, natality and mortality rates of cohorts, causes of death) of the population should be recorded and analyzed seasonally (preferably) or annually to assess well-being. Annual survivorship records should be kept for each cohort. If survivorship within the enclosure equals or falls below estimates for free-ranging control animals, population and recruitment objectives will not have been met. Data must also be kept on the time required for juveniles to reach reproductive maturity and on the fertility and overall reproductive health of these animals as adults.

10. Conduct a financial analysis and determine cost-effectiveness. Individuals or organizations proposing field enclosure projects should determine how the operations will involve or possibly benefit local human residents. Will jobs for caretakers or monitors be created? Will ecotourism play a role? Are the costs of installation reasonable in light of available financial resources? Is the cost of monitoring and maintenance acceptable? Is the cost for producing each juvenile (and eventually each reproductive adult female) efficient when compared to alternative actions? For each proposed and completed project, a cost analysis should be performed. The cost should be estimated for the production of each emergent neonate, for each juvenile of appropriate size for release, and especially for each juvenile that survives to reproductive maturity.

11. Collect comparable data on wild, free-ranging tortoises. Data on the comparable attributes of free-ranging tortoises are vital to the evaluation of progress within enclosures. Locally-occurring, free-ranging tortoises may serve as valuable controls to their counterparts of the same age classes in the enclosure. Comparisons of the two groups would illustrate differences in growth, health, selection of food and shelter, and most dramatically, in behaviors that may be induced by confinement, higher densities, and artificial protection. Radiotelemetry and emissive tags (pit tags) have greatly increased the practicality of tracking free-ranging tortoises.

Designs for Future Enclosures

Two types of enclosures—permanent pens and mobile, "lift-off" pens—are proposed and varied treatments are reviewed below. The proposed enclosures employ primarily passive management. Female tortoises are temporarily held to deposit eggs, and neonates are raised to conduct life history studies, to restock diminishing wild populations, and/or to repatriate individuals into habitats from which tortoise populations have been extirpated.

Permanent Pens

The permanent pen, such as the design of FISS I at NTC Fort Irwin (Figure 1), offers the cost efficiency of a permanent and reusable structure. Built of durable materials on a stable foundation, it may be less subject to weathering, vandalism, and intrusions, especially by larger carnivores with fossorial proclivities. The permanent structure also lends itself to the installation of automated monitoring systems (such as a solar-powered remote reporting weather station), which are invaluable to the interpretation of life history observations.

The permanent structure also permits the installation of an irrigation system (e.g., sprinklers) for artificially increasing annual precipitation and thereby the available biomass of forage. Such an irrigation system was developed for a small part of the Desert Tortoise Research Natural Area in Kern County, California, for a relocation project encompassing approximately 1.25 km² (Science Applications International Corporation, 1993; Mullen and Ross, this volume). Irrigation or sprinkling systems are particularly suitable for desert environments where drought is a common occurrence and where sprinkling during appropriate seasons can enhance the production of food plants used by tortoises. With more forage, juveniles are likely to grow larger at earlier ages (Medica et al., 1975) and have higher rates of survivorship. Also, more juveniles could be maintained in the enclosures.

One previously described concern is the carrying capacity of small enclosures in arid environments. Carrying capacity, often defined as the ability of land to support populations of organisms on a long-term basis, has been determined for very few species and sites. Since carry capacities for juvenile tortoises are unknown for any given study site, densities (expressed as "standing crop" estimates) of juvenile age classes are the best available estimates of natural concentrations of young tortoises. For example, average densities of juvenile and young immature desert tortoises (<140 mm CL, <12 yrs) ranged from 0.43 to 0.75 individuals/ha (0.36–0.98, 95% Confidence Interval) at four long-term study sites in the western Mojave Desert (Berry, 1990; Table 3). These sites were within 50 km of FISS. In contrast, densities of juvenile tortoises at the FISS enclosure ranged from 152 to 305/ha (Table 2), >200× the densities recorded in similar habitats in the wild. If the figures reported for wild settings (Table 3) are used to stock an enclosure, very few individual desert tortoises could be placed in the enclosure without supplemental food and water on a long-term basis.

It is possible that the juveniles may become dependent on receiving adequate food supplies regularly throughout the year, and after release from the enclosure, when irrigation and regular forage are no longer available, they may be subject to rates of mortality higher than that of non-head-started juveniles.

Manipulated Release Program. Some species, such as the desert tortoise, require 5–10 years of growth and shell calcification before they are sufficiently resistant to predators.

Figure 1. The Fort Irwin study site, Enclosure 1, in the central Mojave Desert of California. This enclosure was established to study neonatal and juvenile tortoise biology in *Gopherus agassizii*.

The permanent facility allows the juveniles to achieve the appropriate size-age class—without frequent maintenance or intensive management—before release from the enclosure. At FISS I, when a cohort of juveniles had grown to a size appropriate for release, field workers hand carried them to preformed burrows at random sites 200–300 m from the enclosure. Releases at random sites also avoid local concentrations of prey, which could otherwise concentrate predator attacks or even establish a pattern of subsidized predation. The juveniles were released in the morning to anticipate a 0900–1200 peak of activity.

The principal disadvantage of this strategy is that the increasing concentrations of young tortoises within the enclosure (resulting from holding several cohorts until they are of sufficient size for release) are likely to exceed the carrying capacity. In addition, fixed long-term sites are vulnerable to local weather factors such as wind, flash flood, drought, and fire. Some difficulties may be ameliorated by the construction of up to five subpens to separate each cohort for five years (Morgan and Foreman, 1994). A single subpen is constructed for the first-year cohort, and in subsequent years additional subpens are constructed (one/year) until the first-year cohort reaches the age or size appropriate for release. Then the cycle begins again using the first subpen.

Unimpeded Dispersion Program. Another approach is conceptually similar to the Manipulated Release Program, but juveniles are accorded opportunities for unimpeded, or passive, dispersal from the permanent enclosure. This strategy was implemented by one of us (EKS) in spring 1995 at FISS II, a new enclosure constructed in late fall 1994. A cyclone-fenced enclosure was constructed south of FISS I for this purpose. FISS II has the same general dimensions as FISS I, but is not subdivided into two sections. One- to five-year juvenile tortoises were transferred from FISS I to FISS II and allowed to disperse and establish burrows in April 1995. A few weeks later, ten radio-equipped, 4–5-year tortoises were allowed to establish burrows in the southernmost 20% of FISS II. A barrier was constructed from 20 cm wide flexible, galvanized metal flashing (rising approx. 15 cm above ground, buried to a depth of 5 cm, and held erect by 30 cm metal stakes at approx. 50 cm intervals) to completely isolate the tortoises in the southern one-fifth of the enclosure. While tortoises north of the divider remained confined by the enclosure walls, modifications of the perimeter fencing south of the divider would make it possible for individuals to escape the enclosure entirely. In May, openings 10 cm high × 30 cm wide, flush with the ground, were cut in the fence. The openings converted FISS II into a true exclosure, which now excludes large, non-avian predators but allows juveniles to leave passively. The survivorship rates of passively-released juveniles will be compared with survivorship rates of juveniles released from FISS I.

A possible advantage of this "trickle-out" approach is that a slow, episodic release of individuals may be less likely to provoke interest and attacks by avian and canid predators. The approach also allows juveniles to time their movements to microclimates that are more favorable to their physiologies and to select routes and shelters that provide more protection than those selected by human monitors. Consequently, a more natural dispersion may result, and more natural behaviors may be observed for the released individuals.

The FISS II approach has two potential disadvantages not inherent in other models. First, if predators identify a point of dispersion for juveniles, they may lie in wait or repeatedly return to the site and destroy the stock of dispersing tortoises. A second disadvantage is that tortoises may fail to disperse from the enclosure to the unprotected environment outside.

Mobile Pens

The mobile pen alternative is radically different from the permanent pen: In this modality the enclosure is moved, but not the tortoises within it. In concept, a dome or roofed quadrilateral structure, much like an aviary (but one which excludes birds rather than confines them), could be mounted over a parcel of favorable habitat (good soils, shelters, and forage). The unit should inscribe at least 400 m² (as in a 20 × 20 m square) if it is to provide sufficient carrying capacity for the neonates generated by even a few clutches of eggs. Carrying capacity may be amplified by artificially enhancing precipitation and thereby the food supply. At the Desert Tortoise Research Natural Area, an irrigation system of sprinklers was constructed in a 1.25 km² area. Mobile pens could be placed throughout the area and frequently moved.

Mobile units may also require temporary peripheral foundations of hardware cloth buried 0.3–0.5 m deep and equipped with concrete-anchored posts for mounting the protective fencing. A modular, overhead unit could be assembled from small subunits, which would facilitate both transport to the field and transfer from site to site. The study site would be stocked with tortoises as described above. Given the particularly small size of these units, prompt removal of most females after oviposition would be essential. The time for lifting or moving of the enclosure would be contingent not only on needs of the protected species but also the carrying capacity of the landscape. For example, tortoises may be released during periods when predator populations are low and precipitation and food supplies are high. The modular unit could be relocated to a new site, perhaps with less impacted forage, or to one where natural nesting had already been observed. Tortoises at the previous site would be free to disperse without human intervention, though manipulated dispersion, as described above, could be employed.

This model has the advantages of both low cost and mobility for transfer to other suitable sites. It also can support the tortoises through drought years and may enhance carrying capacity of the site. Such a small enclosure is unlikely to permit normal growth of juveniles. However, as a temporary structure remaining operational for three to six months, this alternative may have fewer negative impacts on the ecosystem and on the behavior of the tortoises that are temporarily confined (especially if they are released within a year of hatching). Temporary structures are more vulnerable to penetration by predators or to destruction by the elements, and the small sizes may lead to overcrowding, depletion of forage, and limited shelter sites.

SUMMARY

For the purposes of this review, we defined predator-proof enclosures as fenced units housing reproducing tortoises and/or their eggs and neonates in natural settings within or peripheral to their historic distributions. Such endeavors were designed to serve two separate functions. First, they concentrated juvenile tortoises in natural but protected settings, making difficult-to-obtain data on life history characteristics accessible. Secondly, enclosures were developed to increase survivorship of eggs, neonates, and juveniles for potential restocking of depleted but contiguous natural populations or for translocation to other sites. Hatcheries, nurseries, and holding facilities also have been developed as tourist attractions and/or public education centers. In developing nations, field-based hatcheries give local residents opportunities to participate in husbandry and release programs that can support, rather than disrupt, local economies and societies. Endeavors addressing these objectives have been operating in North America, the Galápagos Islands, Europe, Africa, Madagascar, and adjacent Indian Ocean islands.

The contributions of enclosures to tortoise biology and conservation, both now and in the future, are more problematic. Certainly these facilities assemble and conserve statistically significant numbers of juveniles in a semi-natural setting. For short-term (single-season) observations, they provide a unique opportunity to study the ecology and behavior of juvenile tortoises when alternatives are prohibitively costly and time consuming. However, scientific accuracy may be compromised. Artificially maintained high-population densities affect behavior, potentially alter socialization, skew sex ratios, and threaten degradation of habitat both from foraging by the tortoises themselves and from foot traffic of human observers working in the pens. These units are most effective when used for the short term, when densities are kept low, and if human intrusion is reduced to a minimum.

The same conditions apply to pens used to enhance recruitment in conservation programs. In the short term, they are an effective technology to reduce nest predation and enhance neonate survival. Juvenile survivorship at fenced sites may be superior to that of equivalent cohorts ranging freely in adjacent field sites. However, we do not know whether these protected sites support growth and behavioral development that result in healthy reproductive adults. Modular enclosures may be relocated to reduce high density impacts on habitat, and permanent units that are equipped with supplemental precipitation systems may improve their carrying capacities and long-term effectiveness. Only when long-term (generational) studies compare tandem cohorts of juveniles raised in pens to their wild counterparts—in terms of survivorship, growth, health, and reproduction—will the success of these enclosures be determined. Our current assessment is that these enclosures are especially useful in filling gaps in tortoise life histories. However, still another decade may pass before we are able to critically judge these experimental projects as conservation tools.

Acknowledgments

The National Training Center at Fort Irwin, California, and Southern California Edison Company supported the research program at the Fort Irwin Study Site, and the World Wildlife Fund provided the grants that supported research at Mapimí. We thank L. Foreman, J. Behler, E. R. Jacobson, and J. Van Abbema for constructive criticisms that substantially improved the manuscript and M. Marolda for editorial assistance. The senior author also thanks S. Williams, Dean of the College of Arts and Sciences, California State University, Dominguez Hills, for providing him with a reduced teaching assignment, which made his participation in this work possible.

Literature Cited

Adest, G. A., G. Aguirre, D. J. Morafka, and J. V. Jarchow. 1989a. Bolson tortoise (*Gopherus flavomarginatus*) conservation: I. Life history. Vida Sylvestre Neotropical 2(1):7–13.

Adest, G. A., G. Aguirre, D. J. Morafka, and J. V. Jarchow. 1989b. Bolson tortoise (*Gopherus flavomarginatus*) conservation: II. Husbandry and reintroduction. Vida Sylvestre Neotropical 2(1):14–20.

Aguirre, G., G. A. Adest, and D. J. Morafka. 1984. Home range and movement patterns of the Bolson tortoise, *Gopherus flavomarginatus*. Acta Zoológica Mexicana Nueva Serie (1):1–28.

Auffenberg, W. 1969. Tortoise Behavior and Survival. Biological Science Curriculum Study. Patterns of Life Series. Rand McNally Co., Chicago. 38 pp.

Auffenberg, W. and J. B. Iverson. 1979. Demography of terrestrial turtles. In M. Harless and H. Morlock (eds.), Turtles: Perspectives and Research, pp. 541–569. John Wiley & Sons, New York.

Baard, E. H. W. 1994. Cape Tortoises. Their Identification and Care. Cape Nature Conservation, Western Cape Province, Cape Town, Republic of South Africa.

Berry, K. H. 1976. A comparison of size classes and sex ratios in four populations of the desert tortoise. In K. A. Hashagen (ed.), Proc. Symp. Desert Tortoise Council 1976:38–50. 23–24 March 1976. Desert Tortoise Council, Long Beach, California.

Berry, K. H. 1990. The status of the desert tortoise (*Gopherus agassizii*) in California. Draft report to the U.S. Fish and Wildlife Service, Portland, Oregon.

Berry, K. H. 1997. Demographic consequences of disease in two desert tortoise populations in California, USA. In J. Van Abbema (ed.), Proceedings: Conservation, Restoration, and Management of Tortoises and Turtles—An International Conference, pp. 91–99. July 1993, State University of New York, Purchase. New York Turtle and Tortoise Society, New York.

Berry, K. H. and F. B. Turner. 1984. Notes on the behavior and habitat preferences of juvenile desert tortoises (*Gopherus agassizii*) in California. Proc. Desert Tortoise Council Symp. 1984:111–130.

Berry, K. H. and F. B. Turner. 1986. Spring activities and habits of juvenile desert tortoises in California. Copeia 1986(4):1010–1012.

Bjorndal, K. A. (ed.). 1982. Biology and Conservation of the Sea Turtles. Proceedings of the World Conference on Sea Turtle Conservation, 26–30 November 1979, Washington, D.C. Smithsonian Institution Press, Washington, D.C. 583 pp.

Bjorndal, K. A. 1987. Digestive efficiency in a temperate herbivorous reptile, *Gopherus polyphemus*. Copeia 1987(3):714–720.

Boarman, W. I. 1993. When a native predator becomes a pest: A case study. In S. K. Majumdar, E. W. Miller, D. E. Baker, E. K. Brown, J. R. Pratt, and R. F. Schmalz (eds.), Conservation and Resource Management, pp. 190–206. The Pennsylvania Academy of Science, Philadelphia.

Boycott, R. C. 1989. *Homopus boulengeri*: Karoo padloper, Boulenger's padloper, red padloper, biltong tortoise (English); karoo skilpadjie, roosiskilpadjie, donderweerskilpad, biltongskilpad (Afrikaans). In I. R. Swingland and M. W. Klemens (eds.), The Conservation Biology of Tortoises, pp. 78–79. Occasional Papers of the IUCN Species Survival Commission (SSC) No. 5. IUCN, Gland, Switzerland.

Boycott, R. C. and W. Branch. 1989. *Psammobates oculifer*: Serrated tortoise, kalahari tent tortoise, kalahari geometric tortoise (English); skulprandiskilpad, kalahari skilpad (Afrikaans). In I. R. Swingland and M. W. Klemens (eds.), The Conservation Biology of Tortoises, pp. 88–90. Occasional Papers of the IUCN Species Survival Commission (SSC) No. 5. IUCN, Gland, Switzerland.

Branch, W. 1989a. *Homopus femoralis*: Greater padloper, karoo tortoise (English); vlakskilpad, bergskilpadjie, groter padloper (Afrikaans). In I. R. Swingland and M. W. Klemens (eds.), The Conservation Biology of Tortoises, pp. 80–81. Occasional Papers of the IUCN Species Survival Commission (SSC) No. 5. IUCN, Gland, Switzerland.

Branch, W. 1989b. *Psammobates tentorius*. Tent tortoise, starred tortoise, Union Jack tortoise (English); knoppiesdopskilpad, tent-skilpad, sterretjieskilpad, skuwedop, vlakskilpad, vledskilpad (Afrikaans). *In* I. R. Swingland and M. W. Klemens (eds.), The Conservation Biology of Tortoises, pp. 91–93. Occasional Papers of the IUCN Species Survival Commission (SSC) No. 5. IUCN, Gland, Switzerland.

Brown, M. B., I. M. Schumacher, P. A. Klein, K. Harris, T. Correll, and E. R. Jacobson. 1994a. *Mycoplasma agassizii* causes upper respiratory tract disease in the desert tortoise. Infection and Immunity 62(10):4580–4586.

Brown, M. B., P. A. Klein, I. M. Schumacher, and K. H. Berry. 1994b. Health profiles of free-ranging desert tortoises in California: Results of a two-year study of serological testing for antibody to *Mycoplasma agassizii*. Final Report. U. S. Bureau of Land Management, Contract No. B950-C2-0046, Riverside, California.

Buitrago, J. 1981. Percentage of head-started turtles in a population as a criterion. Marine Turtle Newsletter 19:3.

Bull, J. J. and R. C. Vogt. 1981. Temperature sensitive periods of sex determination in emydid turtles. J. Experimental Zool. 218:435–440.

Carr, A. 1984. Rips, FADS and little loggerheads. BioScience 36:92–100.

Cayot, L. and G. Morillo. 1997. Rearing and repatriation of Galápagos tortoises: *Geochelone nigra hoodensis*, a case study. *In* J. Van Abbema (ed.), Proceedings: Conservation, Restoration, and Management of Tortoises and Turtles–An International Conference, pp. 178-183. July 1993, State University of New York, Purchase. New York Turtle and Tortoise Society, New York.

Cayot, L. J., H. L. Snell, W. Llerena, and H. M. Snell. 1994. Conservation biology of Galapágos Reptiles: Twenty-five years of successful research and management. *In* J. B. Murphy, K. Adler, and J. T. Collins (eds.), Captive Management and Conservation of Amphibians and Reptiles, pp. 297–305. Contributions to Herpetology, Vol. 11. Society for the Study of Amphibians and Reptiles, Ithaca, New York.

Cheylan, M. 1984. The true status and future of Hermann's tortoise *Testudo hermanni robertmertensi* Wermuth 1952 in western Europe. Amphibia-Reptilia 5:17–26.

Christopher, M., K. A. Nagy, I. Wallis, J. K. Klaassen, and K. H. Berry. 1997. Laboratory health profiles of desert tortoises in the Mojave Desert: A model for health status evaluation of chelonian populations. *In* J. Van Abbema (ed.), Proceedings: Conservation, Restoration, and Management of Tortoises and Turtles—An International Conference, pp. 76–82. July 1993, State University of New York, Purchase. New York Turtle and Tortoise Society, New York.

Congdon, J. L., A. E. Dunham, and R. C. van Loben Sels. 1993. Delayed sexual maturity and demographics of Blanding's turtles (*Emydoidea blandingii*): Implications for conservation and management of long-lived organisms. Conserv. Biol. 7(4):826–833.

Curl, D. A., I. C. Scoones, M. K. Guy., and G. Rakotoarisoa. 1985. The Madagascar tortoise, *Geochelone yniphora*: Current status and distribution. Biol. Conserv. 34:35–54.

Devaux, B. and D. Stubbs. 1997. Species recovery program for Hermann's Tortoise in Southern France. *In* J. Van Abbema (ed.), Proceedings: Conservation, Restoration, and Management of Tortoises and Turtles—An International Conference, pp. 330–332. July 1993, State University of New York, Purchase. New York Turtle and Tortoise Society, New York.

Dezfulian, M., J. Quintana, D. Soleymani, and D. Morafka. 1994. Physiological characteristics of *Clostridium bifermentans* selectively isolated from California desert tortoises. Folia Microbiologia 39(6):496–500.

Diemer, J. 1986. The ecology and management of the gopher tortoise in the southeastern United States. Herpetologica 42(1):125–133.

Dodd, C. K., Jr. 1986. Desert and gopher tortoises: Perspectives on conservation approaches. *In* The Gopher Tortoise and Its Community. Proc. Fifth Ann. Mtg., Gopher Tortoise Council, Florida Museum of Natural History. 93 pp.

Douglass, J. F. 1978. Refugia of juvenile gopher tortoises, *Gopher polyphemus* (Reptilia, Testudines, Testudinidae). J. Herpetology 2:413–415.

Durrell, L., B. Groombridge, S. Tonge, and Q. Bloxam. 1989a. *Acinixys planicauda*: Madagascar flat-tailed tortoise, kapidolo. *In* I. R. Swingland and M. W. Klemens (eds.), The Conservation Biology of Tortoises, pp. 94–95. Occasional Papers of the IUCN Species Survival Commission (SSC) No. 5. IUCN, Gland, Switzerland.

Durrell, L., B. Groombridge, S. Tonge, and Q. Bloxam. 1989b. *Geochelone radiata*: radiated tortoise, sokake. *In* I. R. Swingland and M. W. Klemens (eds.), The Conservation Biology of Tortoises, pp. 96–98. Occasional Papers of the IUCN Species Survival Commission (SSC) No. 5. IUCN, Gland, Switzerland.

Durrell, L., B. Groombridge, S. Tonge, and Q. Bloxam. 1989c. *Geochelone yniphora*: ploughshare tortoise, plowshare tortoise, angulated tortoise, angonoka. *In* I. R. Swingland and M. W. Klemens (eds.), The Conservation Biology of Tortoises, pp. 99–102. Occasional Papers of the IUCN Species Survival Commission (SSC) No. 5. IUCN, Gland, Switzerland.

Ewert, M. A. and C. E. Nelson. 1991. Sex determination in turtle: Diverse patterns and some possible adaptive values. Copeia 1991 (1):50–69.

Frazer, N. B. 1992. Sea turtle conservation and halfway technology. Conserv. Biol. 6(2):179–184.

Frazer, N. B. 1997. Turtle conservation and halfway technology: What is the problem? *In* J. Van Abbema (ed.), Proceedings: Conservation, Restoration, and Management of Tortoises and Turtles—An International Conference, pp. 422–425. July 1993, State University of New York, Purchase. New York Turtle and Tortoise Society, New York.

Frye, F. L. 1991. Biomedical and Surgical Aspects of Captive Reptile Husbandry. Vol. 1, 2nd ed. Kreiger Publishing Co., Malabar, Florida.

Grimaldi, D. and J. Jaenicke. 1984. Competition in natural populations of mycophagous *Drosophila*. Ecology 65:1113–1120.

Hambler, C. 1994. Giant tortoise *Geochelone gigantea* translocation to Curieuse Island (Seychelles): Success or failure? Biol. Conserv. 69:293–299.

IUCN/SSC, Tortoise and Freshwater Turtle Specialist Group. 1989. Tortoises and freshwater turtles: An action plan for their conservation (D. Stubbs, comp.). IUCN/SSC Tortoise and Freshwater Turtle Specialist Group, Gland, Switzerland.

Iverson, J. B. 1982. Adaptations to herbivory in iguanine lizards. *In* G. M. Burghardt and A. S. Rand (eds.), Iguanas of the World, pp. 60–76. Noyes Publishers, Park Ridge, New Jersey.

Jackson, O. F. and J. E. Cooper. 1981. Nutritional diseases, Chapter 12. *In* J. E. Cooper and O. F. Jackson (eds.), Diseases of the Reptilia, Vol. 2, pp. 409–428. Academic Press, Inc. (London) Ltd., London.

Jacobson, E. R. 1993. Implications of infectious diseases for captive propagation and introduction programs of threatened/endangered reptiles. J. Zoo and Wildlife Medicine 24(3):245–255.

Jacobson, E. R. 1994. Causes of mortality and diseases in tortoises: A review. J. Zoo Wildl. Med. 25(1):2–17.

Jacobson, E. R., M. B. Brown, P. A. Klein, I. Schumacher, D. Morafka, and R. A. Yates. 1996. Serologic survey of desert tortoises, *Gopherus agassizii*, in and around the National Training Center, Fort Irwin, California, for exposure to *Mycoplasma agassizii*, the causative agent of upper respiratory tract disease. Abstract. Paper presented at the 21st Annual Meeting and Symposium of the Desert Tortoise Council, 29 March–1 April 1996, Las Vegas, Nevada.

Joyner-Griffith, M. A. 1991. Neonatal desert tortoise (*Gopherus agassizii*) biology: Analyses of morphology, evaporative water loss and natural egg production followed by neonatal emergence in the central Mojave Desert. M.A. thesis, Calif. State Univ., Dominguez Hills, Carson, California.

Kirsche, W. 1984. An F_2-generation of *Testudo hermanni hermanni* Gmelin bred in captivity with remarks on the breeding of Mediterranean Tortoises 1976–1981. Amphibia-Reptilia 5:31–35.

Lance, V. 1995. Sexual diagnosis and differentiation in Fort Irwin desert tortoises, National Training Center, Fort Irwin, California. Contract No. DACA09-93-D-0027, Delivery Order No. 0008, Project 96.8. Robert D. Neihous, Inc., Santa Barbara, California.

Lance, V., D. C. Rostal, J. S. Grumbles, and I. Schumacher. 1995. Effects of upper respiratory tract disease (URTD) on reproductive and steroid hormone levels in male and female desert tortoises. Paper presented at the 20th Ann. Mtg. and Symp. of the Desert Tortoise Council, 31 March–2 April 1995, Las Vegas, Nevada.

Lande, R. and G. Barrowclough. 1987. Effective population size, genetic variation, and their use in population management. *In* M. E. Soule (ed.), Viable Populations for Conservation, pp. 87–123. Cambridge University Press, New York.

Landers, J. L., W. A. McRae, and J. A. Garner. 1982. Growth and maturity of the gopher tortoise *Gopherus polyphemus* in southwestern Georgia, USA. Bull. Florida State Mus. Biol. Sci. 27(2): 81–110.

Legler, J. M. and R. G. Webb. 1961. Remarks on a collection of Bolson tortoise, *Gopherus flavomarginatus*. Herpetologica 17 (1):26–37.

MacFarland, C. G., J. Villa, and B. Toro. 1974. The Galápagos giant tortoise *Geochelone elephantopus* Part 2: Conservation methods. Biol. Conserv. 6(3):198–212.

Martinez, O. E. and J. Morello. 1977. El medio fisico y las unidades fisonomico-floristicas del Bolson de Mapimí. Publicaciones del Insituto de Ecología, Mexico 3. 63 pp.

Mascort, R. 1997. Land tortoises in Spain: Their status and conservation. *In* J. Van Abbema (ed.), Proceedings: Conservation, Restoration, and Management of Tortoises and Turtles—An International Conference, pp. 307-312. July 1993, State University of New York, Purchase. New York Turtle and Tortoise Society, New York.

McGinnis, S. M. and W. G. Voigt. 1971. Thermoregulation in the desert tortoise, *Gopherus agassizii*. Comp. Biochem. Physiol. 40A:639–643.

Medica, P. A., R. B. Bury, and F. B. Turner. 1975. Growth of the desert tortoise (*Gopherus agassizi*) in Nevada. Copeia 1975(4): 639–643.

Moll, E. O. 1979. Reproductive cycles and adaptations. *In* M. Harless and H. Morlock (eds.), Turtles: Perspectives and Research, pp. 305–332. John Wiley and Sons, New York.

Morafka, D. J. 1977. A biogeographical analysis of the Chihuahuan Desert through its herpetofauna. Dr. W. Junk, B.V., Publishers, The Hague, Netherlands.

Morafka, D. J. 1982. The status and distribution of the Bolson tortoise (*Gopherus flavomarginatus*). *In* R. B. Bury (ed.), North American Tortoises: Conservation and Ecology, pp. 71–94. Wildlife Research Report No. 12, U.S. Dept. of the Interior, U.S. Fish and Wildlife Service, Washington, D.C. 126 pp.

Morafka, D. J. 1993. Juvenile desert tortoise biology. Final 1993 report. Submitted to the Department of Public Works, Natl. Training Center, Ft. Irwin, California. 57 pp.

Morafka, D. J. 1994. Neonates: Missing links in the life histories of North American tortoises. *In* R. B. Bury and D. J. Germano (eds.), Biology of North American Tortoises, pp. 161–173. Fish and Wildlife Research 13, Technical Report Series, U.S. Department of the Interior, National Biological Survey, Washington, D.C.

Morafka, D. J., G. A. Adest, G. Aguirre, and M. Recht. 1981. The ecology of the Bolson tortoise *Gopherus flavomarginatus*. *In* R. Barbault and G. Halfter (eds.), Ecology of the Chihuahuan Desert, pp. 35–78. Instituto de Ecología, A.C., Mexico, D.F.

Morafka, D. J., G. Aguirre L., and R. W. Murphy. 1994. Allozyme differentiation among gopher tortoises (*Gopherus*): Conservation genetics and phylogenetic and taxonomic implications. Canadian J. Zoology 72:1665–1671.

Morafka, D. J., R. A. Yates, J. Jarchow, W. J. Rosskopf, G. A. Adest, and G. Aguirre. 1986. Preliminary results of microbial and physiological monitoring of the Bolson tortoise (*Gopherus flavomarginatus*). *In* Z. Rocek (ed.), Studies in Herpetology, pp. 657–662. 1985, Third Annual Symposium of the Societas Europaea Herpetologica, Prague.

Morgan, L. E. and L. D. Foreman. 1994. Proposal: Hatching and rearing program for desert tortoise. U.S. Bureau of Land Management, California Desert District, Riverside, California. 9 pp.

Mrosovsky, N. 1983. Conserving Sea Turtles. British Herpetological Society, London.

Mrosovsky, N. and C. L. Yntema. 1980. Temperature dependence of sexual differentiation in sea turtles: Implications for conservation practices. Biol. Conserv. 18:271–280.

Mullen, E. B. and P. Ross. 1997. Survival of relocated desert tortoises: Feasibility of relocating tortoises as a successful mitigation tool. *In* J. Van Abbema (ed.), Proceedings: Conservation, Restoration, and Management of Tortoises and Turtles—An International Conference, pp. 140–146. July 1993, State University of New York, Purchase. New York Turtle and Tortoise Society, New York.

Obst, F. J., K. Richter, and U. Jacob. 1988. Completely Illustrated Atlas of Reptiles and Amphibians for the Terrarium. Tropical Fish Hobbyists (TFH) Press, Neptune, New Jersey.

Oftedal, O. T., M. E. Allen, and T. Christopher. 1995. Dietary potassium affects food choice, nitrogen retention and growth of desert tortoises. Paper presented at the 20th Annual Meeting and Symposium of the Desert Tortoise Council, 31 March–2 April 1995, Las Vegas, Nevada.

Pieau, C. 1971. Sur la proportion sexuelle chez les embryons de deux cheloniens (*Testudo graeca* L. et *Emys orbicularis* L.) issus d'oeufs incubes artificiellement. C. R. Hebd. Seanc. Acad. Sci. Paris 272 D:3071–3074.

Pieau, C. and M. Dorizzi. 1981. Determination of temperature sensitive stages for sexual differentiation of the gonads in embryos of the turtle, *Emys orbicularis*. J. of Morphology 170:375–382.

Polis, G. A. 1984. Age structure component of niche width and intraspecific resource partitioning: Can age groups function as ecological species? American Naturalist 123:541–564.

Parmenter, R. R. and H. W. Avery. 1990. The feeding ecology of the slider turtle. *In* J. W. Gibbons (ed.), Life History and Ecology of the Slider Turtle, pp. 257–266. Smithsonian Inst. Press, Washington, D.C.

Pritchard, P. C. H. 1981. Criteria for scientific evaluation of headstarting. Marine Turtle Newsletter 19:3–4.

Rose, F. L., M. E. T. Scioli, and M. P. Moulton. 1988. Thermal preferentia of Berlandieri's tortoise (*Gopherus berlandieri*) and the ornate box turtle (*Terrapene ornata*). Southwest Nat. 33(3):357–361.

Schumacher, I. M., M. B. Brown, E. R. Jacobson, B. R. Collins, and P. A. Klein. 1993. Detection of antibodies to a pathogenic mycoplasma in desert tortoises (*Gopherus agassizii*) with upper respiratory tract disease. J. Clinical Microbiology 31(6):1454–1460.

Science Applications International Corporation. 1993. American Honda desert tortoise relocation project. Final Report. Science Applications International Corporation, Environmental Programs Division, Santa Barbara, California.

Spotila, J. R., L. C. Zimmerman, C. A. Binckley, J. S. Grumbles, D. C. Rostal, A. List Jr., E. C. Beyer, K. M. Phillips, and S. J. Kemp. 1994. Effects of incubation conditions on sex determination, hatching success, and growth of hatchling desert tortoises, *Gopherus agassizii*. Herp. Mon. 8 (1994):103116.

Stancyk, S. 1982. Non-human predators of sea turtles and their control. *In* K. A. Bjorndal (ed.), Biology and Conservation of the Sea Turtles, pp. 139–152. Proceedings of the World Conference on Sea Turtle Conservation, 26–30 November 1979, Washington, D.C. Smithsonian Institution Press, Washington, D.C. 583 pp.

Stoddart, D. R., D. Cowx, C. Peet, and J. R. Wilson. 1982. Tortoises and tourists in the western Indian Ocean: The Curieuse experiment. Biol. Conserv. 24:67–80.

Street, C. 1996. 1994 hatching-hatchling survey: The results. Tortuga Gazette 32(4):9.

Stubbs, D. 1989a. *Testudo graeca*, spur-thighed tortoise. *In* I. R. Swingland and M. W. Klemens (eds.), The Conservation Biology of Tortoises, pp. 31–33. IUCN/SSC Occasional Papers No. 5., IUCN, Gland, Switzerland.

Stubbs, D. 1989b. *Testudo hermanni*, Hermann's Tortoise. *In* I. R. Swingland and M. W. Klemens (eds.), The Conservation Biology of Tortoises, pp. 34–36. Occasional Papers of the IUCN Species Survival Commission (SSC) No. 5. IUCN, Gland, Switzerland.

Swingland, I. R. 1989. *Geochelone gigantea*, Aldabran Giant Tortoise. *In* I. R. Swingland and M. W. Klemens (eds.), The Conservation Biology of Tortoises, pp. 105–110. Occasional Papers of the IUCN Species Survival Commission (SSC) No. 5. IUCN, Gland, Switzerland.

Swingland, I. R. and M. W. Klemens (eds.). 1989. The Conservation Biology of Tortoises. Occasional Papers of the IUCN Species Survival Commission (SSC) No. 5. IUCN, Gland, Switzerland.

Tom, J. 1994. Microhabitats and use of burrows of Bolson tortoise hatchlings. *In* R. B. Bury and D. J. Germano (eds.), Biology of North American Tortoises, pp. 139–146. Fish and Wildlife Research 13, Technical Report Series, U.S. Department of the Interior, National Biological Survey, Washington, D.C.

Troyer, K. 1982. Transfer of fermentative microbes between generations in a herbivorous lizard. Science 216:540–542.

Turner, F. B., P. Hayden, B. L. Burge, and J. B. Roberson. 1986. Egg production by the desert tortoise (*Gopherus agassizii*) in California. Herpetologica 42:93–104.

Turner, F. B., K. H. Berry, D. C. Randall, and G. C. White. 1987. Population ecology of the desert tortoise at Goffs, California, 1983–1986. Report to Southern California Edison Company, Rosemead, California.

U.S. Fish and Wildlife Service. 1994. Desert Tortoise (Mojave Population) Recovery Plan. U. S. Fish and Wildlife Service, Portland, Oregon. 173 pp. + appendices.

Vasek, F. C. and M. G. Barbour. 1988. Mojave Desert scrub vegetation. *In* M. G. Barbour and J. Major (eds.), Terrestrial Vegetation of California, pp. 835–867. Wiley, New York.

Wood, J. R. 1982. Release of captive-bred green sea turtles by Cayman Turtle Farm Ltd. Marine Turtle Newsletter 20:6–7.

Yntema, C. L. 1976. Effects of incubation temperatures on sexual differentiation in the turtle *Chelydra serpentina*. J. Morphology 150:453–462.

Yntema, C. L. 1979. Temperature levels and period of sex determination during incubation of eggs of *Chelydra serpentina*. J. Morphology 159:17–28.

Yntema, C. L. and N. Mrosovsky. 1980. Sexual differentiation in hatchling loggerheads (*Caretta caretta*) incubated at different controlled temperatures. Herpetologica 36(1):33–36.

Captive Breeding of Indian Turtles and Tortoises at the Centre for Herpetology/Madras Crocodile Bank

ROMULUS WHITAKER AND HARRY V. ANDREWS

Centre for Herpetology/Madras Crocodile Bank, Post Bag 4, Mamallapuram, Tamil Nadu 603 104, India

Abstract: Since its inception in 1976 the Centre for Herpetology/Madras Crocodile Bank has maintained breeding groups of Indian turtles and tortoises. A total of 300 individuals of 20 species are kept as part of the Centre's ongoing research program. Several species have bred regularly, and we present data from the past several years.

India's population of nearly one billion people creates immense pressures on habitat, particularly in aquatic areas, and uncontrolled commercial exploitation of turtles poses significant threats to turtle populations. Captive breeding and restocking programs, combined with habitat protection and management, may prove crucial to the survival of several species. Captive breeding and/or rearing of turtles of commercial importance may also help curb the exploitation of wild turtles. Knowledge of the breeding biology of these animals is critical to the success of both captive breeding and habitat management programs.

While few intensive efforts have been made to breed Indian turtles and tortoises in captivity, several species (especially *Geochelone elegans* and *Melanochelys trijuga*) have bred sporadically in various zoos and private collections, and a large-scale egg collection, rearing, and release program for these species was launched by the Government of India as part of the Ganga Cleanup Project (Basu, 1985). Captive breeding and restocking of rare species may be used to aid in their conservation, provided adequate protection for habitats is also offered. Commercially valuable species and scavenging species such as those used in the Ganga Project may also be reared from field-collected eggs and from captive stock.

To this end, the Centre for Herpetology/Madras Crocodile Bank has conducted an ongoing study and breeding project for over ten years. While our work was previously sporadic because we lacked full-time personnel committed to this project, our breeding and display facilities have recently been enhanced. We have also been conducting a study of the large softshell, *Aspideretes gangeticus*, in the Chambal River, which is the last remaining optimal turtle habitat among the major north Indian rivers.

Breeding Biology

The existing knowledge of the breeding biology of Indian turtles and tortoises is summarized in Table 1. There are many gaps and much remains to be learned or verified. Unfortunately, the basic biological data, fundamental to good management, are just not in hand (Frazier, 1992). While some of this information may be learned in the field, facilitated by increased interest, support, and numbers of field-workers, a concentrated effort should also be made to establish breeding groups of all Indian turtles and tortoises

Figure 1. Hatchling *Melanochelys trijuga* from the nursery at Madras Crocodile Bank.

at institutions that have the requisite facilities and expertise. The development of the principal breeding centres (identified by Bhupathy and Choudhury, 1992) will not only advance our captive breeding efforts, but will also provide a practical means to supplement our knowledge and contribute significantly to management planning.

TABLE 1
Breeding biology of turtles and tortoises of India.[a]

Species	Nesting season	Clutch size	Incubation period (days)	Bred in captivity	Wild eggs hatched
Family Bataguridae					
Batagur baska, river terrapin	Feb.–Mar.	19–38	60–68	No	Yes[b]
Cuora amboinensis, Malayan box turtle	Jan.–Feb., Apr.	1 or 2	76–77	No	Yes
Cyclemys dentata, Asian leaf turtle	—	2–4	76–77	No	No[c]
Geoclemys hamiltonii, spotted pond turtle	May, Oct.	—	82	No	No
Geoemyda silvatica, forest cane turtle	Dec.	2	—	No	Yes
Hardella thurjii, crowned river turtle	Aug., Sept.	20	—	No	Yes
Kachuga dhongoka, three-striped roof turtle	Mar.–Apr.	28	—	No	Yes
Kachuga kachuga, red-crowned roof turtle	Mar.–Apr., Dec.	20–25	80–86	No	Yes
Kachuga smithii, brown roofed turtle	Aug.–Nov.	3–11	—	No	Yes
Kachuga sylhetensis, Assam roofed turtle	—	—	—	No	Yes
Kachuga tecta, Indian roofed turtle	Dec.	4–11	—	No	Yes
Kachuga tentoria, Indian tent turtle	Oct.–Dec.	3–12	125–144	No	Yes
Melanochelys tricarinata, tricarinate hill turtle	Dec.	1–3	—	No	Yes
Melanochelys trijuga, Indian black turtle	year round[d]	3–9	76–180	Yes	Yes
Morenia petersi, Indian eyed turtle	Apr.–May	2	—	No	Yes
Pyxidea mouhotii, keeled box turtle	—	1–3	—	No	No
Family Testudinidae					
Geochelone elegans, Indian star tortoise	Oct.–Jan.	6	112–170	Yes	Yes[c]
Indotestudo elongata, elongated tortoise	Jun., Oct.	1–5	104–165	Yes	No[c]
Indotestudo forstenii, Travancore tortoise	Oct., Jan.–Mar.	1–3	146–149	Yes	Yes
Manouria emys, Asian brown tortoise	Apr.–May, Sep.–Oct.	23–51	63–71	Yes	No
Family Trionychidae					
Aspideretes gangeticus, Indian softshell turtle	Jul.–Nov.	8–27	216–314	Yes	Yes[e]
Aspideretes hurum, Indian peacock softshell turtle	winter	—	—	No	Yes[e]
Aspideretes leithii, Leith's softshell turtle	Feb.–Apr.	—	—	No	No
Chitra indica, narrow headed softshell turtle	Jul.–Nov.	65–178	40–70	No	Yes
Pelochelys cantorii, Asian giant softshell turtle	Feb.–Mar.	20–28	—	No	No[f]
Lissemys punctata, Indian flapshell turtle	year round[g]	5–12	60–230[h]	No	Yes[i]

[a] Much of these data are subject to confirmation. [b] Sunderbans. [c] Has multiple clutches. [d] Breeds year round at Madras Crocodile Bank Trust. [e] Soaking induces hatching. [f] Nests on sea beaches. [g] Nests year round at Madras Crocodile Bank Trust; Sep.–Oct. in north India. [h] Incubation periods for eggs in north India can vary from 60 to 260 days depending on before- or after-winter nesting. [i] Thunder may elicit hatching.

Breeding Program at the Centre for Herpetology

A large 25 × 30 × 2.5 m deep pond was constructed, which houses over 200 turtles of 12 species. The mixture of species, sizes, and numbers, however, renders it unsuitable for breeding. Keeping this problem in mind, and to ensure optimum viewing of the smaller freshwater turtle species, a full-scale turtle exhibit (eight new glass-fronted 3 × 3 × 1 m aquaria) was constructed for breeding, rearing, and exhibit purposes. Each aquarium has a shaded, 2 m × 75 cm water area and a partially shaded, sloping, landscaped sand bank. Control of algae and clean water are ensured by continuous pumping through a pre-filter and an algae filter, recycling the water every 24 hours. Both the pond and the new aquaria were constructed with the financial support of the Wildlife Preservation Trust International.

Three species have laid eggs in the new aquaria: *Lissemys punctata punctata*, *Melanochelys trijuga trijuga*, and *M. t. thermalis*. Breeding results at the Centre are summarized in Table 2.

TABLE 2
Captive breeding of turtles and tortoises at the Centre for Herpetology/Madras Crocodile Bank.

Species	Years of breeding	Number of clutches
Geochelone elegans	1988–1989	5
Indotestudo forstenii	1988–1995	21
Aspideretes gangeticus	1986–1995	49
Lissemys punctata	1988–1995	65
Melanochelys t. trijuga	1986–1995	72
Melanochelys t. thermalis	1988–1995	25

One part-time researcher is helping with maintenance and data management, a full-time researcher is conducting field research, and we plan to soon hire a full-time turtle research and maintenance person. The long-term goal is to establish breeding groups of all of India's freshwater turtles and tortoises. Constraints have included lack of funds to pay salaries as well as the time-consuming and laborious process of obtaining permits for those species protected under the Wildlife Act.

Eggs and Incubation

Eggs are collected the morning after they are laid and are marked, measured, separated by clutch, and candled to determine their viability. Because *A. gangeticus* and *Lissemys p. punctata* eggs are sometimes difficult to candle, viability can be determined by incubation for 4–5 days, after which the tops of viable eggs turn white ("chalking"). Fertile eggs of *Melanochelys t. trijuga* and *M. t. thermalis* candled in the second week of incubation reveal well-defined embryos and eye spots. Eggs from the latter two subspecies have been successfully incubated at Madras Crocodile Bank.

Eggs are placed in small plastic boxes (10–15 cm in height) containing approximately 5 cm of slightly moist medium (sand or vermiculite) and are covered with another 5 cm layer of medium. The containers are periodically monitored to prevent dehydration, and the medium is moistened using a water sprayer when necessary. The egg boxes are held in a temperature-controlled room heated by four to six 60 watt bulbs, regulated by a thermostat. The system has been in use for the past seven years for incubating crocodilian, turtle, and water monitor eggs.

Eggs of north Indian species have proven more difficult to incubate in south India, where year-round temperatures are higher and lack cool extremes. *A. gangeticus* eggs require an initial chilling period followed by a gradual rise in temperature, which simulates the diapause period and triggers development of the embryo (Ewert, 1985). The following procedure (as suggested by M. Ewert, pers. comm.) was conducted at the Madras Crocodile Bank in 1986: Eggs were chilled by refrigeration from 30°C to 17°C for 30, 45, and 60 days. They were incubated thereafter at 30–32°C and monitored by candling. Eggs that had been chilled for 60 days developed in 20–30 days, and a horseshoe-shaped embryo could be seen on candling. Eggs that were not chilled and those chilled for the periods shorter than 60 days failed to develop.

When we judged that development was complete, the eggs were soaked in water, which usually resulted in immediate hatching. The response to soaking was also observed in the field in 1990 in eggs from *A. hurum* nests along the Chambal River. Due to hatch in July, eggs in these nests had not hatched, apparently because of the delay in the monsoon. Eggs removed from various nests and soaked in water started to hatch after soaking for 3–7 minutes, which suggests that rain induces hatching. While the experimental chilling led to only partial success with the north Indian species, we have had better results with the breeding of *Lissemys p. punctata*, a taxon that occurs in Madras, in south India.

Retention of viable sperm (Das, 1992) over an eight-year period was demonstrated by our breeding group of *A. gangeticus*, which continued to lay fertile clutches, despite the absence of a male from 1986 to 1994.

Captive Breeding as a Conservation Strategy

Captive breeding programs must be closely linked with habitat protection, management, and public awareness. The two south Indian forest chelonians, *Indotestudo forstenii* and *Geoemyda silvatica*, for example, are strongly impacted by tribal consumption for food, by forest fires, and by destruction of habitat from the conversion of forest land into plantations or wasteland. Deforestation, even on a small scale (through so-called "selection felling"), can increase forest floor temperatures and desiccation to intolerable levels. While *I. forstenii* has bred in captivity and its requirements are better known, *G. silvatica* remains poorly known and there is no captive group. Small but significant numbers of offspring of both species could be produced in a well-conceived breeding project, and surveys in the Western Ghats could pinpoint protected areas (such as the Nilgiri Biosphere Reserve), where tortoise and turtle numbers are low, for potential release sites.

Curbing or moderating indigenous peoples' traditional consumption of native tortoises poses significant difficulty. However, involving them in the rehabilitation of these species—a program that would require imaginative planning—is an important conservation strategy.

Herpetological Sanctuary

We have proposed a reptile and amphibian sanctuary in Chalakudi District in the state of Kerala to protect the area known to have the highest concentration of *G. silvatica* and a stable population of *I. forstenii*. We have worked with the Kadar people in this area on several occasions, and they are sensitive to the concerns of forest destruction and the depletion of the animals and plants they hunt, gather, and use. If accepted by the government, our proposal would establish a field research station in the forest for the use of herpetologists from India and abroad. Involvement of the Kadar people in this program is an essential component and will help ensure the maintenance of habitat conditions required by many of the native rainforest reptiles and amphibians.

Egg Collection, Rearing, and Release

The Ganga River is well-known for the problems caused by the accumulation of incompletely cremated human corpses. As part of the Government of India's Ganga River Cleanup Project, large-scale collection of eggs, and rearing and release of river turtles was proposed (Basu, 1985). Large softshell turtles in particular are efficient scavengers. Since the project began about 85,000 *Aspideretes gangeticus* eggs have been collected with a 44% hatching average achieved (Table 3). Approximately 25,000 hatchling turtles have already been released in the Varanasi Turtle Sanctuary on the Ganga, and considering the high mortality observed in natural nests, this artificial recruitment should enhance the rehabilitation of river turtles (D. Basu, pers. comm.). *Chitra indica* and *Batagur baska* are now receiving more attention, and it is hoped that future consideration will be given to the development of sustainable use programs for the more common species to help appease the West Bengal turtle demand.

TABLE 3
Aspideretes gangeticus eggs collected and hatched at two Government hatcheries for the Ganga Cleanup Project, 1987–1993 (data from subsequent years are unavailable).

Year	Eggs collected (September–October)			Eggs hatched (June–July)			Survival of hatchlings		
	Kukrail	Sarnath	Total	Kukrail	Sarnath	Total	Kukrail	Sarnath	Total
1987–88	2,831	5,290	8,121	404	3,126	3,530	1	2,904	2,905
1988–89	5,265	9,402	14,667	936	4,271	5,207	391	3,927	4,318
1989–90	5,553	12,006	17,559	3,741	6,928	10,669	3,371	6,773	10,144
1990–91	6,198	13,879	20,077	4,191	5,845	11,036	3,999	6,674	10,673
1991–92	4,696	9,997	14,693	1,100	5,386	6,486	1,095	5,297	6,392
1992–93	4,079	5,116	9,195						
	28,622	55,690	84,312	10,372	25,556	36,928 (43.8%)	8,857	25,575	34,432 (93.2%)

By 1993, 4,888 turtles up to two years of age from the Kukrail Centre and about 20,000 turtles from the Sarnath Centre had been released into the Ganga River in the Varanasi Turtle Sanctuary, which was established in 1989. (Source: D. Basu, June, 1993.)

TABLE 4
List of Indian turtles and tortoises at the Centre for Herpetology/Madras Crocodile Bank.

A. Bataguridae
1. *Batagur baska*
2. *Cuora amboinensis*
3. *Geoclemys hamiltonii*
4. *Hardella thurjii*
5. *Kachuga dhongoka*
6. *Kachuga kachuga*
7. *Kachuga smithii*
8. *Kachuga tecta*
9. *Kachuga tentoria circumdata*
10. *Kachuga tentoria flaviventer*
11. *Kachuga tentoria tentoria*
12. *Melanochelys tricarinata*
13. *Melanochelys trijuga coronata*
14. *Melanochelys trijuga indopeninsularis*
15. *Melanochelys trijuga thermalis*
16. *Melanochelys trijuga trijuga*

B. Trionychidae
1. *Aspideretes gangeticus*
2. *Aspideretes leithii*
3. *Lissemys punctata punctata*

C. Testudinidae
1. *Geochelone elegans*
2. *Indotestudo forstenii*

ACKNOWLEDGMENTS

The authors thank Dr. E. O. Moll and Purnima Govindarajulu for their input. They are also grateful to Romaine Andrews for editing and typing the manuscript.

LITERATURE CITED AND SELECTED BIBLIOGRAPHY

Ahsan, M. F. and M. A. Saeed. 1992. Some aspects of the breeding biology of the black softshell turtle, *Aspideretes nigricans*. Hamadryad 17:28–31.

Basu, D. 1985. Rehabilitation of freshwater scavenger turtles for control of pollution due to corpses. Uttar Pradesh Government Wildlife Department report. 17 pp.

Bhadauria, R. S., A. Pai, and D. Basu. 1990. Habitat, nesting and reproductive adaptations in the narrow-headed softshell turtle (*Chitra indica*). J. Bombay Nat. Hist. Soc. 87(3):364–367.

Bhaskar, S. 1990. Biology and conservation of *Batagur baska*. Report to World Wildlife Fund. 24 pp.

Biswas, S., L. M. Acharjyo, and S. Mohapatra. 1978. Notes on distribution, sexual dimorphism and growth in captivity of *Geochelone elongata* (Blyth). J. Bombay Nat. Hist. Soc. 75:928–930.

Bhupathy, S. and B. C. Choudhury. 1992. An inventory of freshwater turtles and land tortoises in captivity in Indian zoos: Results of a survey. Zoo's Print, December 1992, pp. 4–10.

Bhupathy, S. and V. S. Vijayan. 1993. Aspects of the feeding ecology of *Lissemys punctata* (Testudines: Trionnychidae) in Keoladeo National Park, Bharatpur, India. Hamadryad 18:13–16.

Bhupathy, S., B. C. Choudhury, and E. O. Moll. 1992. Conservation and management of freshwater turtles and land tortoises of India. Technical report (May 1991–July 1992), Wildlife Institute of India, Dehra Dun. 22 pp.

Caporaso, F. 1990. The Galapagos tortoise conservation program. *In* K. R. Beaman, F. Caporaso, S. McKeown, and M. Graff (eds.), Proceedings of the First International Symposium on Turtles & Tortoises: Conservation and Captive Husbandry, pp. 113–126. August 1990, Chapman University, Orange, California. California Turtle & Tortoise Club and Chapman University.

Das, I. 1991. Colour Guide to the Turtles of the Indian Subcontinent. R & A Publishing Ltd., Portishead, UK. 149 pp.

Das, I. 1992. Turtle conservation programme at the Madras Crocodile Bank. Tigerpaper 29(1):16–17 (January–March).

Das, I. 1995. Turtles and Tortoises of India. WWF India, Oxford University Press, Bombay. 176 pp.

Duda, P. L., A. K. Velma, and D. N. Sahi. 1993. Sex ratios in freshwater turtles from Jammu, India. Hamadryad 18:10–12.

Ewert, M. A. 1985. Embryology of turtles. *In* C. Gans (ed.), Biology of the Reptilia, Vol. 14, pp. 75–267. John Wiley & Sons, New York.

Frazier, J. 1992. Management of tropical chelonians: Dream or nightmare? *In* K. P. Singh and J. S. Singh (eds.), Tropical Ecosystems: Ecology and Management, pp. 125–135. Wiley Eastern Ltd., New Delhi, India.

Ghosh, A. and N. R. Mandal. 1990. Studies on nesting and artificial hatching of the endangered river terrapin, *Batagur baska* (Gray), in the Sundarbans Tiger Reserve, West Bengal. J. Bombay Nat. Hist. Soc. 87(1):50–52.

Moll, E. O. 1987. India's freshwater turtle resource with recommendations for management. *In* Bombay Natural History Society Centenary Seminar Proceedings, pp. 501–515. Bombay Nat. Hist. Soc., Bombay.

Rao, K. T. and M. V. S. Rao. 1990. Incubation and hatching of the Indian star tortoise, *Geochelone elegans*, in captivity. J. Bombay Nat. Hist. Soc. 87(3):461–462.

Rao, R. J. 1990. Ecological relationships among freshwater turtles in the National Chambal Sanctuary. Progress report, Wildlife Institute of India, Dehra Dun. 8 pp.

Smith, M. A. 1931. Fauna of British India. Vol. I. Taylor & Francis Ltd., London.

Vijaya, J. 1982. Breeding data on *M. trijuga trijuga* and *M. t. coronata*. Hamadryad 7(3):16.

Vijaya, J. 1982. *Kachuga tecta* hatching at the Snake Park. Hamadryad 8(3):14–15.

Vyas, R. and B. H. Patel. 1992. Studies on the reproduction of the Indian softshell turtle *Aspideretes gangeticus*. Hamadryad 17: 32–34.

Yadava, M. R. 1980. Hatching time for the eggs of softshell (*sic*) turtle, *Kachuga dhongoka* (Gray), at various temperatures. Indian Forester 106 (10):721–725.

Yadava, M. R. and B. Prasad. 1982. Observations on the breeding biology of Indian tropical pond turtle, *Lissemys punctata granosa* (Schoepff), Uttar Pradesh. Ind. J. of Zootomy 23(1):51–56.

Management Plan for the Giant Amazonian Turtle, *Podocnemis expansa*, in De La Tortuga Arrau Wildlife Refuge, Orinoco River, Venezuela

LINA LICATA AND XABIER ELGUEZABAL

Ministerio del Ambiente y de los Recursos, Naturales Renovables (MARNR), Servicio Autonómo de Fauna, Nivel Mezzanina, Entrada Oeste, Centro Simón Bolivar, Caracas, República de Venezuela [e-mail: profauna@conicit.ve]

ABSTRACT: The giant Amazonian turtle or arrau, *Podocnemis expansa*, is considered endangered by the IUCN and has been placed on Appendix II of CITES. Several factors have contributed to the species' decline, including poaching of females, collection of eggs and hatchlings, intentional and incidental capture of adult turtles by fisherman, urban and industrial development near nesting sites, and lack of conservation education.

Despite its present status, the species' high reproductive potential should enable it to recover rapidly in areas where human interference is limited and where a well-designed management program has been established. The Management Plan for the Arrau Turtle, *Podocnemis expansa*, at the Middle Orinoco River has included the protection of nesting beaches, a nursery program for the care and release of hatchlings, and an Environmental Education Program for the public. The Plan appears to have slowed the decline of nesting turtles, and a modest increase in their numbers has been recorded at the nesting beaches since 1992.

The Tortuga Arrau in Venezuela

The Venezuelan arrau turtle population is geographically isolated from the rest of its distribution by the Atures Falls on the Orinoco River, which prevents it from traveling upstream to the Río Negro basin through the Casiquiare River. The species is found in most of the tributaries of the Orinoco river.

In Venezuela, the arrau has shown rapid population declines in the past 150 years. Numbers dropped from 330,000 individuals reported by Humboldt in 1820, to 36,000 in 1950 (Ramirez, 1956), to 17,000 in 1965 (Ojasti and Rutkis, 1965), and to 1,576 in 1988 (MARNR, 1989). The Venezuelan arrau population is threatened by several factors: Nesting beaches are frequently flooded; hatchlings are preyed upon by mammals, birds, and fish; adults are preyed upon by mammals and suffer from poaching as well as incidental capture.

In the 18th and 19th centuries, eggs were collected for human consumption (Gumilla, 1714 and Humboldt, 1820, cited by Paolillo, 1982). By the mid-twentieth century, female adults were captured for meat with annual yields of 7,400–15,800 adults from 1950 to 1956 (Ramirez, 1956). Currently, despite legal protection and guards on the main nesting areas, commercial exploitation continues with certain intensity, with both eggs and adults taken.

In 1946 the collection of eggs and hatchlings was prohibited, but the capture of adults was still allowed. According to Ramirez (1956), up to 93% of the laying females were taken. As the numbers of turtles continued to decline, a ban on the taking of nesting females was established in 1962. In the late 1970s the Wildlife Protection Law was approved by

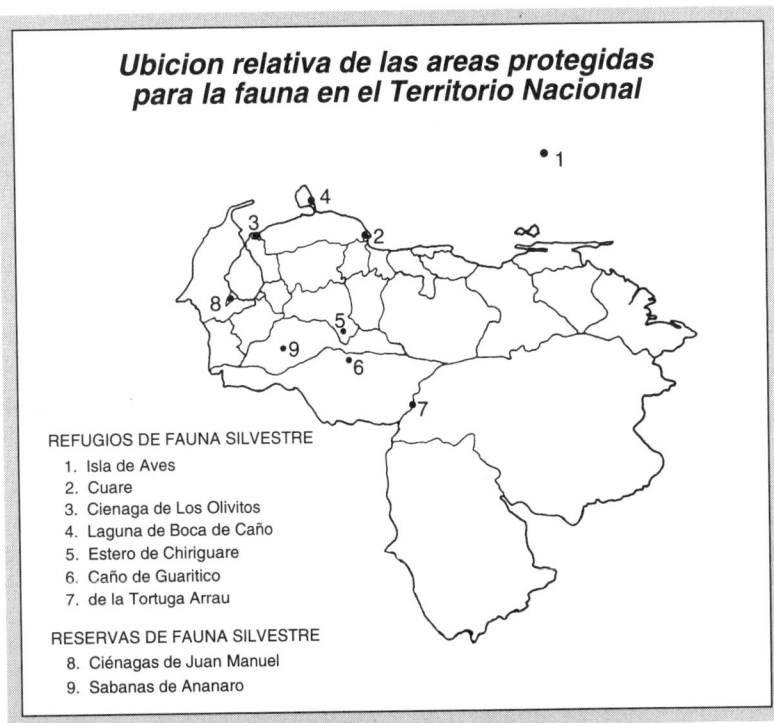

Figure 1. Animal refuges and reserves in Venezuela.

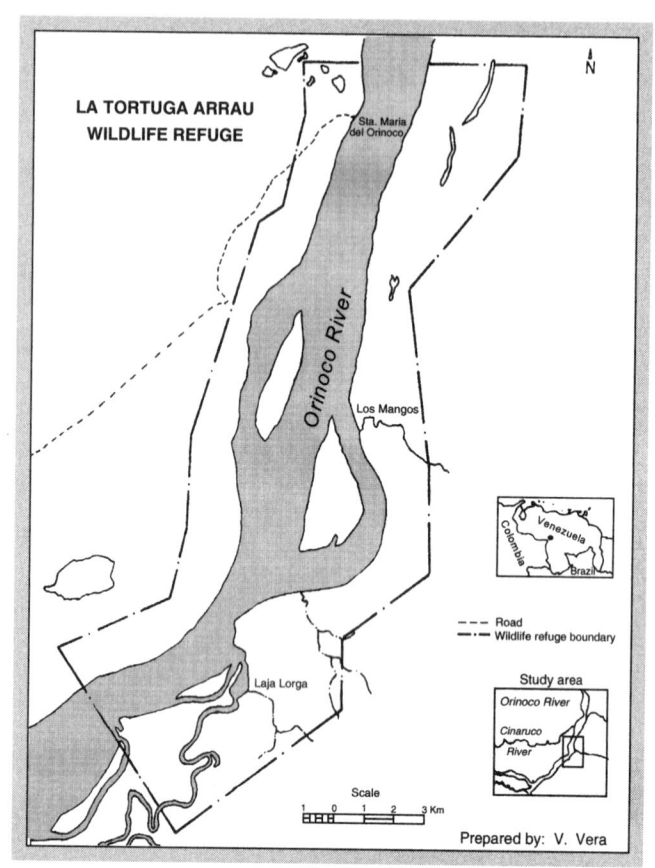

Figure 2. De La Tortuga Arrau Wildlife Refuge.

the Venezuelan Congress, and later the same year the arrau and 135 other wildlife species were placed in the Official Game List. Finally, in 1979 the capture and commerce of the arrau and 36 other species were permanently prohibited.

In 1988 the Santos Luzardo National Park, north of the main nesting beaches, was established. The following year De La Tortuga Arrau Wildlife Refuge was created to protect the most important nesting beaches in the middle course section of the Orinoco River.

The Management Plan

In 1989, PROFAUNA, the Venezuelan Fish and Wildlife Service of the Ministry of the Environment and Renewable Natural Resources (MARNR), created and implemented a Management Plan for the Arrau Turtle, *Podocnemis expansa*, at the Middle Orinoco River.

Geographically, the Plan covers a section of the Orinoco River from the mouth of the Parguaza River 90 km downstream to the mouth of the Capanaparo River, and includes the beaches of both the Santos Luzardo National Park and De La Tortuga Arrau Wildlife Refuge.

The objectives of the Plan were (1) protection of nesting beaches in the species' critical reproductive area (the middle Orinoco River), (2) recovery and conservation of viable population levels, and (3) raising environmental consciousness and generating changing attitudes among the inhabitants of the area.

The Plan comprises of three main activities: the Warden Program, the Management Program, and the Environmental Education Program. From October through June, researchers (members of PROFAUNA and the Ministry of Environment at Puerto Ayacucho) take two-week shifts at the Refuge base camp in the village of Santa Maria. Members of the Venezuelan National Guard are also quartered at the camp to help with patrolling and warden activities. The Plan is implemented in four stages:

Stage I. From 15 October to 15 February, the turtles concentrate at the nesting sites, and activities include inspection of boats, checking of fishing nets and other gear, and patrolling the river.

Stage II. From 16 February to 15 March, during oviposition, the nesting beaches are guarded overnight, in addition to the continuation of the Stage I activities. Nests are marked and any nest threatened by flooding is relocated (taking note of its depth, temperature, humidity, and time of relocation). The females' shells are marked to determine frequency of nesting, and the over-the-curve length and width of the shell and the weight of the animal are recorded.

Stage III. From 16 March to 15 May, the first hatchlings emerge. Stage II activities continue.

Stage IV. From 16 May to 15 June, hatchlings continue to emerge on the beaches and move into the nearby shallow waters. In addition to the above activities, hatchlings are captured for later release, nest relocation continues, and data are processed.

The environmental education activities (workshops, talks, and others) are conducted throughout all stages.

In 1992 a nursery was established at San Fernando de Apure (a five-hour drive from the nesting beaches). The main objective of the nursery was to increase the hatchlings' chances of reaching one year of age. The animals were kept in one artificial pond 56 × 22 × 2.2 m deep and fed with commercial dry dog food, in daily amounts that were 1.5–2% of their weight.

RESULTS

The results of the management program are shown in Tables 1, 2, and 3. The decline in the number of rescued hatchlings in 1993 (Table 1) is the result of our concentrating efforts in just two of the nesting beaches and because of the early onset of the rainy season, which caused flooding of the nesting sites.

Table 3 shows the mean physical measurements of the hatchlings at the time of capture and release in 1992–1993. A sample of 200 hatchlings was measured monthly. The survival rate was 81.7%. In 50% of the cases, death was related to birth deformities. Mean monthly growth increments were from 8 to 9 mm.

The Warden Program activities have resulted in a strong decrease in turtle-related legal proceedings from 1991 to 1994 (Table 4). Data for 1995 have yet to be evaluated. In late 1994 and early 1995 living conditions were upgraded at the base camp of the Refuge, and permanent personnel (two wildlife wardens and two National Guard members) were placed at those quarters, permitting warden activities to continue, even through the turtles' low activity season (July–September).

Prior to the 1991–1992 season, education was limited to the training of the National Guard and occasional public lectures on the species. The Environmental Education Program was implemented during that season, and in 1992–1993 two workshops were given, one for the National Guard, the other for local schools at Puerto Páez. Also, a research project on the socioeconomic status of the inhabitants of the area was started, as were radio and TV talks. In 1994 an agreement was made between the Service and the Fundación para el Desarrollo de las Ciencias Físicas, Matemáticas, y Naturales, to improve the Environmental Education Program, under the guidelines of the Service, throughout the Amazonas state capital and the small towns within range of the Refuge. Also in 1994 a booklet on the species, "La Tortuga Arrau y su Conservación" (Cuadernos Lagoven, March 1994), was published. In the second quarter of 1995 a serious review of the objectives and general design of the program was made to improve local private and government agencies' participation and to present alternatives to turtle capture to the local communities. However, no effective alternatives have yet been found that can be accepted by all parties.

Conclusion

The Plan, now in its sixth year, continues implementation of the Warden, Management, and Environmental Education programs, and appears to have stopped the decline of nesting turtles at the nesting beaches; furthermore, a modest increase in their number has been recorded since 1992. Total implementation of the Plan is restricted by the lack of sufficient trained personnel to work on a year-round basis (especially in the Environmental Education Program) as well as by the high cost of building and maintaining a permanent base camp at the Tortuga Arrau Wildlife Refuge. The nursery program, even with its excellent results (81.7% hatchling survival and 8 mm per month average growth rate), is in need of better tanks and research facilities.

Slowly, the Plan is taking effect, and it is hoped that results will be seen in five to ten years as new adult females return to their beaches of origin. More than a thousand basking turtles were sighted on the nesting beaches in 1993, which is a promising sign.

TABLE 1 — General statistics.

Year	No. of nests	Rescued hatchlings	Marked turtles	Released hatchlings
1989	—	22.300	—	—
1990	937	29,800	—	—
1991	873	33,754	—	—
1992	765	27,540	37	4,892
1993	1,300	6,000	53	4,032
1994	>812	>14,500	—	10,000
1995	>1300	>37,000	—	14,000

TABLE 2 — Physical measurements.

Year	No.	Mean carapace length	Mean carapace width	Mean plastral length	Mean weight
1992	39	66.4	54.9	51.3	26.1
1993	53	67.0	56.2	51.5	27.3

TABLE 3 — Physical measures of nursery-released hatchlings (1992–1993) from a sample of 200 hatchlings.

	Mean carapace length	Mean carapace width	Weight
Initial	57.82	49.22	24.91
Final	124.05	104.12	240.94
Max final	189.90	155.50	732.00

TABLE 4 — Warden activities.

Year	Total proceedings	Turtle-related proceedings
1990	8	2 (25%)
1991	26	8 (31%)
1992	30	2 (6.6%)
1993	11	1 (9.9%)
1994	17	0

Literature Cited

Humboldt, A. 1985 (1820). Viaje a las Regiones Equinocciales del Nuevo Continente. Tomo III. Monte Avila Editores, Caracas. 406 pp.

MARNR-ZONA 10. 1988. Informe técnico. Programa de protección y vigilancia a la tortuga arrau, en el año 1988. Mimeografiado.

Ojasti, J. and E. Rutkis. 1965. Operación tortuguillo: un planteamiento para la conservación de la Tortuga del Orinoco. El Agricultor Venezolano 228:32–37.

Paolillo, A. 1982. Algunos aspectos de la ecología reproductiva de la Tortuga Arrau (*Podocnemis expansa*) en las playas del Orinoco medio. Trabajo especial de grado U.C.V., Caracas. 132 pp.

Ramirez, M. 1956. Estudio biológico de la Tortuga Arrau del Orinoco, Venezuela. El Agricultor Venezolano (190):44–63.

Large-Scale Breeding of Turtles at São Paulo Zoo: Implications for Turtle Conservation in Brazil

FLAVIO DE BARROS MOLINA

Fundação Parque Zoológico de São Paulo, Av. Miguel Stefano, 4241, Cep 04301-905, São Paulo, SP, Brazil

ABSTRACT: In 1985 a captive breeding program for Geoffroy's side-necked turtle, *Phrynops geoffroanus*, and Orbigny's slider, *Trachemys dorbigni*, was initiated at São Paulo Zoo. The program has facilitated the study of turtle biology and behavior, and methods for large-scale breeding, necessary for future reintroduction programs, have been developed. The methods are applicable to the breeding of related endangered species and may be of use to other Brazilian zoos.

There are 27 species of terrestrial and freshwater chelonians in Brazil (Iverson, 1992; Vanzolini, 1995), and probably all are subjected to negative human impact—mainly deforestation, environmental pollution, and illegal trade.

A captive breeding program for Geoffroy's side-necked turtle, *Phrynops geoffroanus*, and Orbigny's slider, *Trachemys dorbigni*, was initiated at São Paulo Zoo in 1985. These species were selected because their ecology and natural history were poorly known, their populations were believed to be threatened by human activities, and Brazilian zoos had devoted no effort to their conservation. Prior to 1985 almost no reproduction in these species had occurred at São Paulo Zoo, in spite of the significant number of adults in the collection.

P. geoffroanus is found from the Colombian Amazon to Rio Grande do Sul (Brazil), northern Bolivia, Uruguay, and northern Argentina (Vanzolini et al., 1980); *T. dorbigni* is found in Rio Grande do Sul (Brazil), Uruguay, and Argentina (Pritchard and Trebbau, 1984; Iverson, 1992; Ernst and Barbour, 1989).

Objectives of the Breeding Program

1. Study the biology and behavior of these poorly known species, thus gaining information important to future *in situ* conservation efforts.

2. Initiate a large-scale breeding program to provide stock for future reintroductions to the wild. (The São Paulo Zoo staff was especially concerned for the future of *T. dorbigni*, which appears to be the second most frequently encountered reptile in the widespread illegal Brazilian pet trade.)

3. Develop management techniques that could be applied to the maintenance and breeding of related endangered species (e.g., Hoge's side-necked turtle, *Phrynops hogei*).

4. Develop management techniques that could also be used in other Brazilian zoos, thus expanding Brazilian conservation efforts.

The captive breeding program concentrated efforts in three basic areas: adult housing and diet, egg collection and incubation techniques, and the maintenance of neonates and juveniles.

Adult Housing and Diet

Adult *P. geoffroanus* and *T. dorbigni* have been maintained in two outdoor exhibits. The larger exhibit is 400 m² and houses approximately 25.35 *P. geoffroanus* and 40.70 *T. dorbigni* (Figure 1). Since the inception of the program these species have been housed without problem with caimans (*Caiman latirostris*, *C. crocodilus crocodilus*, and *C. crocodilus yacare*) and several other species of turtles (*Phrynops hilarii*, *P. raniceps*, *Hydromedusa tectifera*, *Geochelone carbonaria*, and *G. denticulata*) (Figure 2). A central

Figure 1. Outdoor exhibit for maintaining chelonians (including *Trachemys dorbigni* and *Phrynops geoffroanus*) and caimans at São Paulo Zoo. (Photo by Glória Jafet.)

pool divides the exhibit into two land areas—one fully exposed to the sun, the other shaded by trees. The original substrate was soil covered by a thin layer of sand with few plants, which resulted in a relatively arid exhibit. In 1984 alterations were made to simulate a more natural environment and to improve the conditions for the reptiles (Rocha et al., 1986). The area exposed to the sun was divided into a sand beach and a grassed area of compacted soil planted with *Paspalum notatum* and *Ophiopogon japonicus*. Other plants (*Cymbopogon* sp., *Dietes* sp., *Morus* sp., and *Triplaris* sp.) were planted in the open area, and aquatic plants (*Eichhornia crassipes* and *Pistia stratiotes*) were placed in the pool. In the shaded area, sand and soil were mixed, then covered with dead leaves and branches. Bromeliads and philodendrons were planted around the trees, and epiphytic plants typical of the Atlantic rainforest were arranged on the trees. *Triplaris* sp., *Hedychium* sp., and *Cyperus* sp. were planted in the shaded area (Figure 1).

An exhibit that simulates a natural environment is more attractive to the zoo's visitors and can provide a more meaningful educational experience. In discussing the shift toward naturalism in zoo exhibits, Markowitz (1982) stressed that the captive environment should contribute to improved behavioral performance. The alterations to this exhibit at São Paulo Zoo resulted in improved nesting and feeding behavior. The original substrate of soil covered by sand had been too compact for nesting and resulted in the breakage of many eggs (Rocha et al., 1986). After the changes were made, this problem was solved. *P. geoffroanus* preferred to nest in soil, especially in areas planted with *Ophiopogon japonicus* grass (Molina, 1989). *T. dorbigni* preferred to nest on the sand beach (Molina, 1995).

The second exhibit is 37 m² and has a central pool. Originally designed to house a group of nutrias (*Myocastor coypus*), the terrestrial aspect of the enclosure had been divided into an area of concrete and an area of soil. In 1985 it was adapted to house approximately ten *P. geoffroanus* and ten *T. dorbigni* as well. Part of the concrete area was covered with sand to give the turtles more space for nesting, and the soil area was planted with *Eragrostis curvula* (Rodrigues et al., 1986). The exhibit has since housed both turtle species and nutrias without problem (Rodrigues et al., 1986, 1991).

P. geoffroanus are primarily carnivorous (Molina, 1989, 1990a, 1990b). Their captive diet consists of beef and fish, but they will occasionally accept the vegetables and fruits offered to the Orbigny's sliders. *T. dorbigni* are omnivorous (Molina, 1995), and their captive diet is composed of beef, fish, banana, papaya, orange, tomato, carrot, and chicory or other greens. The diet of both species is supplemented with bone meal.

Egg Collection and Incubation Techniques

In 1985 the staff at São Paulo Zoo developed a protocol for egg collection and trained keepers in proper egg collection technique. A standardized data sheet was completed for each nesting event to record the identification and measurements of the female, nesting behavior, nest location, and nest and egg measurements. We attempted to collect the eggs within 48 hours of laying and started incubating them immediately.

The first incubator designed for reptile eggs at São Paulo Zoo (used for *P. geoffroanus* and *T. dorbigni* until 1986) was a 1,000 liter tank adapted from a home water reservoir commonly used in Brazil (Rocha and Molina, 1986; Molina, 1989). The incubation medium consisted of a 15 cm layer of small stones covered by a 35 cm layer of an equal mixture of sand and soil. Eggs were buried to a depth of approximately 5 cm. The medium was heated 11 hours a day by infrared lamps and was moistened at approximately four-day intervals. The monthly average incubation temperature varied from 22 to 28°C.

In 1987 small plastic containers (containing no stones but the same sand-soil medium at a depth of 35 cm) were substituted for the 1,000 liter tank (Molina and Rocha, 1988; Molina, 1989). For 1987 and 1988 clutches, the same heating and moistening procedures were followed, and monthly average incubation temperatures varied from 22 to 28.5°C. For 1989–1991 clutches, the medium was heated 24 hours a day and was moistened every 2–3 days. The monthly average incubation temperature varied from 27 to 31°C.

From 1990 to 1991, clutches of *T. dorbigni* were incubated in vermiculite as well in open plastic containers in a heated room, but without

Figure 2. Adults of *Trachemys dorbigni* and *Caiman crocodilus yacare* basking at São Paulo Zoo. (Photo by Glória Jafet.)

TABLE 1
Results of the captive breeding program for Geoffroy's side-necked turtle, *Phrynops geoffroanus*,
and Orbigny's slider, *Trachemys dorbigni*, conducted at São Paulo Zoo from 1985 to 1994.

	Total no. of eggs	Incubated eggs	Number of hatchlings	Surviving young as of April 1995
P. geoffroanus	2,893[a]	2,449	343 (14.0%)	61 (17.8%)
T. dorbigni	6,351[b]	5,475	1,054 (19.3%)	311 (29.5%)

[a] 444 eggs were unsuitable for incubation. [b] 795 eggs were unsuitable for incubation; 81 eggs were sent to another scientific institution.

a direct heating source. The vermiculite was moistened every two weeks, and the monthly average room temperature varied from 25 to 29°C.

Various problems encountered in the incubation of eggs included occasional low incubation temperatures, maintenance of substrate moisture levels, delays in the collection and/or incubation of some of the eggs, and difficulty in maintaining regular, weekly observations of the development of all eggs.

Since 1992 new incubators (adapted from Verdade et al., 1992) have allowed more precise control of incubation temperatures. Eggs of both species are now buried in vermiculite (Figure 3) in open plastic containers, which are placed inside Styrofoam or plastic boxes equipped with household lamps and thermostats, thus allowing better control of substrate moisture. They have been incubated at various fixed temperatures between 20 and 34°C (Molina, 1995). Results are summarized in Table 1. Monitoring of incubating eggs was improved in 1992 when a biologist was assigned to give this task high priority.

Maintenance of Neonates and Juveniles

Neonates were individually identified (through the use of photographs, line drawings, or photocopies of plastra) and measured. They were maintained individually in small plastic containers in a temperature-controlled room for approximately 1–2 months. They were then transferred to 1,000 liter tanks (1.38 m², adapted from Brazilian home water reservoirs), in which one third of the area is dry sand and two thirds is water 13 cm deep (Figure 4).

We investigated the effects of various captive densities on growth and survival rates of juveniles. Groups of 5, 10, and 30 juvenile *T. dorbigni* maintained in similar tanks showed different growth and survival rates. The fewer the number of individuals per tank, the better the development and survivorship (Molina, pers. obs.). Our results indicate that up to 30 neonates (approx. 3.5 cm carapace length) can be maintained without difficulty in a 1,000 liter tank. As they grow, it is necessary to decrease the number of juveniles per tank. Up to 20 one-year-old turtles (approx. 8 cm) or 10 two-year-old turtles (approx. 12 cm) can be adequately maintained in this size tank.

The effects of three different diets on the growth and survival rates of juvenile *P. geoffroanus* were investigated: (1) commercial dog food; (2) beef, sardine, and fruit sprinkled with bone meal; and (3) fish (sprinkled with bone meal) and invertebrates. The best growth and survival rates were observed in those fed on fish and invertebrates; the poorest growth rate was observed in those fed on commercial dog food (Molina, 1989, 1991).

Figure 3. Hatching neonate *Trachemys dorbigni* (note caruncle). The egg was incubated in vermiculite. (Photo by Fábio Colombini.)

Figure 4. *Phrynops geoffforanus* juveniles maintained in 1,000 liter tank adapted from Brazilian home water reservoir. (Photo by Glória Jafet.)

CONCLUSIONS

Our management program proved to be effective, and some of the problems related to egg incubation were corrected. Successful hatching of at least 60% of the eggs laid each year by both turtle species is the desired goal. The survival rate for neonates and juveniles of both species has not been satisfactory, especially for *Phrynops geoffroanus*. Control of air and water temperatures in the rearing tanks appears to be critical and has been a priority. We are investigating the occurrence and the effects of social hierarchy in the groups of neonates and juveniles, as well as the effects of new diets and captive densities.

São Paulo Zoo is now prepared to undertake a breeding program for endangered and/or less common species, such as *Phrynops hogei*. Information on turtle maintenance and breeding is currently being shared with colleagues at other Brazilian zoos, and we anticipate the establishment of additional breeding programs.

ACKNOWLEDGMENTS

I am grateful to Fundação Parque Zoológico de São Paulo for support given to the captive breeding program and to its director, Dr. Adayr Mafuz Saliba, for stimulus and encouragement. I thank the reptile curator of the zoo, Mário B. da Rocha, for allowing me to develop this program and the Reptile Department staff for assisting with animal care. I thank Dr. Norma Gomes for her guidance in the development of my M.S. thesis and Ph.D. dissertation, which are related to the captive breeding program. The M.S. thesis was partially sponsored by a grant from Conselho Nacional de Desenvolvimento Científico e Tecnológico (CNPq, Brazil).

I thank Dr. Michael W. Klemens and the Program Committee for inviting me to present this paper at the conference, and I am also indebted to those involved in its organization and to the sponsoring institutions. I would like to express my deepest gratitude to Dennis and Elizabeth Frank, Milwaukee County Zoo, for receiving me in their home prior to the conference, and to Elizabeth Frank, Richard and Linn Sajdak, and Robert Henderson for their assistance. I am especially grateful to Richard Sajdak for helping me in the preparation of my slide presentation and to Craig Berg for inviting me to present this lecture to a meeting of the Milwaukee County Zoo Chapter of the American Association of Zoo Keepers. The manuscript was greatly improved by the comments and suggestions of Ray Pawley, Elizabeth Frank, Richard Sajdak, Jim Van Abbema, Peter Pritchard, Norma Gomes, Adriana Malvasio, and the anonymous reviewers. Lastly, I would like to thank my family for their vital support, encouragement, and friendship.

LITERATURE CITED

Ernst, C. H. and R. W. Barbour. 1989. Turtles of the World. Smithsonian Inst. Press, Washington, D.C.

Iverson, J. B. 1992. A Revised Checklist with Distribution Maps of the Turtles of the World. Privately printed, Richmond, Indiana. 363 pp.

Markowitz, H. 1982. Behavioral Enrichment in the Zoo. Van Nostrand Reinhold Company, New York.

Molina, F. B. 1989. Observações sobre a biologia e o comportamento de *Phrynops geoffroanus* (Schweigger, 1812) em cativeiro (Reptilia, Testudines, Chelidae). M.S. thesis, Universidade de São Paulo, São Paulo.

Molina, F. B. 1990a. Reproductive biology of *Phrynops geoffroanus* (Testudines: Chelidae) in captivity. Tortoises & Turtles, Newsletter of the IUCN Tortoise and Freshwater Turtle Specialist Group 5:8.

Molina, F. B. 1990b. Observações sobre os hábitos e o comportamento alimentar de *Phrynops geoffroanus* (Schweigger, 1812) em cativeiro (Reptilia, Testudines, Chelidae). Revta Bras. Zool. 7(3): 319–326.

Molina, F. B. 1991. Some observations on the biology and behavior of *Phrynops geoffroanus* (Schweigger, 1812) in captivity (Reptilia, Testudines, Chelidae). Grupo Estud. Ecol. Ser. Doc. 3:35–37.

Molina, F. B. 1995. Observações sobre a biologia e o comportamento reprodutivo de *Trachemys dorbignyi* (Duméril e Bibron, 1835) em cativeiro (Reptilia, Testudines, Emydidae). Ph.D. thesis, Universidade de São Paulo, São Paulo.

Molina, F. B. and M. B. Rocha. 1988. Sobre uma nova chocadeira para incubação de ovos de quelônios. Arq. Inst. Biol. 55(Supl.):41.

Pritchard, P. C. H. and P. Trebbau. 1984. The Turtles of Venezuela. Soc. Stud. Amph. Rept., Contrib. Herpetol. 403 pp.

Rocha, M. B. and F. B. Molina. 1986. Uma chocadeira para a incubação de ovos de quelônios desenvolvida na Fundação Parque Zoológico de São Paulo. Cienc. Cult. Supl. 38(7):1016.

Rocha, M. B., F. B. Molina, and F. Simon. 1986. Reestruturação de recinto coletivo de répteis na exposição da Fundação Parque Zoológico de São Paulo. Arq. SZB (6):46–49.

Rodrigues, A. S. M., M. B. Rocha, F. B. Molina, and F. Simon. 1986. Observações preliminares a respeito de um recinto para mamíferos e répteis na Fundação Parque Zoológico de São Paulo. Arq. SZB (6):43–45.

Rodrigues, A. S. M., P. Martuscelli, F. B. Molina, and M. B. Rocha. 1991. Novas observações sobre um recinto para mamíferos e répteis no Zoo de São Paulo. Arq. SZB (10):15.

Vanzolini, P. E. 1995. A new species of turtle, genus *Trachemys*, from the state of Maranhão, Brazil (Testudines, Emydidae). Rev. Brasil. Biol. 55(1):111–125.

Vanzolini, P. E., A. M. M. Ramos-Costa, and L. J. Vitt. 1980. Répteis das Caatingas. Academia Brasileira de Ciências, Rio de Janeiro.

Verdade, L. M., F. Michelotti, M. C. Rangel, L. Cullen Jr., M. M. Ernandes, and A. Lavorenti. 1992. Manejo dos ovos de jacaré-de-papo-amarelo (*Caiman latirostris*) no CIZBAS/ESALQ/USP. *In* L. M. Verdade and A. Lavorenti (eds.), Anais do 2º Workshop Sobre Conservação e Manejo do Jacaré-de-papo-amarelo (*Caiman latirostris*), pp. 92–99. ESALQ/USP, Piracicaba, Brasil.

Rearing and Repatriation of Galápagos Tortoises: *Geochelone nigra hoodensis*, a Case Study

LINDA J. CAYOT AND GERMÁN E. MORILLO

Charles Darwin Research Station, Casilla 17-01-3891, Quito, Ecuador [e-mail: lcayot@fcdarwin.org.ec]

ABSTRACT: The rearing and repatriation program for Galápagos tortoises, *Geochelone nigra*, was established in 1965 to save endangered populations from extinction. The tortoise population of Española, *G. n. hoodensis*, was so close to extinction that, between 1963 and 1974, all tortoises found on the island (12 females and 2 males) were removed to the Breeding Center. The first successful hatching occurred in the 1970–1971 season. Both incubation and rearing procedures have been greatly improved in the last ten years, resulting in much higher hatching and survival rates. The first tortoises were repatriated to Española in 1975. As of December 1994, a total of 664 juvenile tortoises have been returned to their native island. In 1990 the first hatchlings (both dead) and attempted nests were found on the island. In 1991 the first live hatchling was found. The long-term goal of establishing self-sustaining populations that do not require intervention by humans is probable for the Española tortoise population. As we enter the new century, intensive management of this population may no longer be necessary.

The rearing and repatriation* program for Galápagos tortoises was established by the Charles Darwin Research Station (CDRS) in 1965 to save the race of tortoises on Pinzón Island, *G. n. duncanensis* (MacFarland and Reeder, 1975). Over the years other threatened populations were included, and since 1968 the program has been a cooperative effort between the CDRS and the Galápagos National Park Service (GNPS). In the last 25 years all of the tortoise populations in the program have been saved from immediate danger (Cayot and Izurieta, 1993; Cayot et al., 1994). The ultimate goal of any repatriation program is to establish self-sustaining populations that do not require further intervention (Dodd and Seigel, 1991). The tortoise population from the island of Española, an arid island in the southeast corner of the archipelago, is now approaching this goal. In 1959 at the time of the establishment of the Charles Darwin Foundation and the Galápagos National Park (GNP), the tortoise population of Española was on the brink of extinction, and now, after almost 30 years of management (1965–1994), it is close to being self-sustaining.

When the GNP was established, three of the named 14 races of Galápagos tortoises were extinct (MacFarland and Reeder, 1975) and by the 1970s the Pinta race, *G. n. abingdoni*, had only one individual (Reynolds and Marlow, 1983). Of the remaining ten races, several were severely threatened. Tortoises were the species most exploited by nearly all groups of people coming to the Islands and have been negatively affected by nearly all species of introduced mammals. Since the discovery of the Islands in 1535 tortoises were exploited for meat, first by the buccaneers in the 1600s and 1700s, then by whalers and fur sealers in the 1800s, and also by colonists after 1832 (Townsend, 1925; Slevin, 1959; deVries, 1984; Hickman, 1985). A conservative estimate of the number of tortoises removed by the American whaling fleet from 1830 to 1900 exceeds 100,000 (Townsend, 1925). In the late 1800s and early 1900s research expeditions removed many of the relatively few tortoises remaining on several islands (Slevin, 1959). Then, in the early part of the 20th century, tortoises were commercially exploited for their oil (Beck, 1903; Slevin *in* Fritts and Fritts, 1982). Currently a few tortoises are killed every year by humans, principally on Isabela Island. A recent increase in this slaughter may have a major impact on small subpopulations (Cayot and Lewis, 1994).

Although overexploitation of tortoises by humans caused the initial and most drastic decline, especially in the small island populations, mammals, introduced by the early visitors and later by colonists, eventually became the major threat and remain so today (Eckhardt, 1972; MacFarland et al., 1974a; MacFarland and Reeder, 1975; Hoeck, 1984). Introduced predators, primarily pigs (*Sus scrofa*), rats (*Rattus rattus*), and dogs (*Canis familiaris*), have wreaked havoc on some populations. Introduced competitors, principally goats (*Capra hircus*) but also burros (*Equus asinus*) and wild cattle (*Bos taurus*), destroy tortoise habitat. The combination of low population size resulting from exploita-

---

* The term *repatriation* as used in this paper is defined as the "intentional release of individuals of a species into an area formerly occupied by that species" (Reinert, 1991).

tion by humans and the impact of introduced mammals on these same populations caused the extinction of at least two races and pushed several others to the edge of extinction.

The tortoise rearing and repatriation program, begun in 1965 to save the population on Pinzón Island, quickly expanded to encompass other threatened populations, including that of Española. Other than the single tortoise from the Pinta population, the Española population was closest to extinction. Española is a small (58 km²), relatively low island (220 m, 722 ft, Figure 1), which made the tortoises easily accessible to whalers and other visitors. In addition, the Española tortoises, *G. n. hoodensis*, are the smaller, saddle-backed type and were more easily carried by a single man. A review of the logbooks of 79 whaling vessels visiting the Islands between 1831 and 1868 (a small portion of the whaling fleet), indicated that more than 1,700 tortoises had been removed from Española (Townsend, 1925). The largest number taken from any island was 350 during a five-day period in 1831 on Española. By 1905–1906 tortoises on Española were already considered very rare (Van Denburgh, 1914), and only three were found (Slevin *in* Fritts and Fritts, 1982).

Between 1963 and 1974 only 14 tortoises (2 males and 12 females) were found on Española. There was no evidence of reproduction, possibly because they were dispersed over much of the island, and the males and females did not encounter one another. Their habitat and food supply had been severely compromised by feral goats, the only introduced mammal on the island. To save this population, all 14 tortoises were transferred to large corrals at the headquarters of the CDRS and the GNPS on Santa Cruz Island, where a captive breeding program was initiated.

In 1977 an additional adult male from the San Diego Zoo was added to the breeding population (Bacon, 1978; Fritts, 1978). The first 20 young from the Española herd hatched in 1971, and in 1975 the 17 surviving young tortoises of this first cohort were repatriated to Española.

METHODS AND RESULTS

Two interdependent management strategies are involved in the recovery of the population of giant tortoises on Española. The first, ongoing strategy is the captive breeding of adult tortoises and the rearing of hatchlings, followed by their release on Española. The second strategy was a campaign to eradicate feral goats from Española to allow eventual recuperation of the island's vegetation. Eradication of goats was completed in 1978. Studies on other islands of the archipelago indicate substantial regeneration of the vegetation after the eradication of goats (Hamann, 1979), and it appears that the same has occurred on Española. However, there is concern that the once-abundant *Opuntia* cactus is not recovering (D. J. Anderson, pers. comm.).

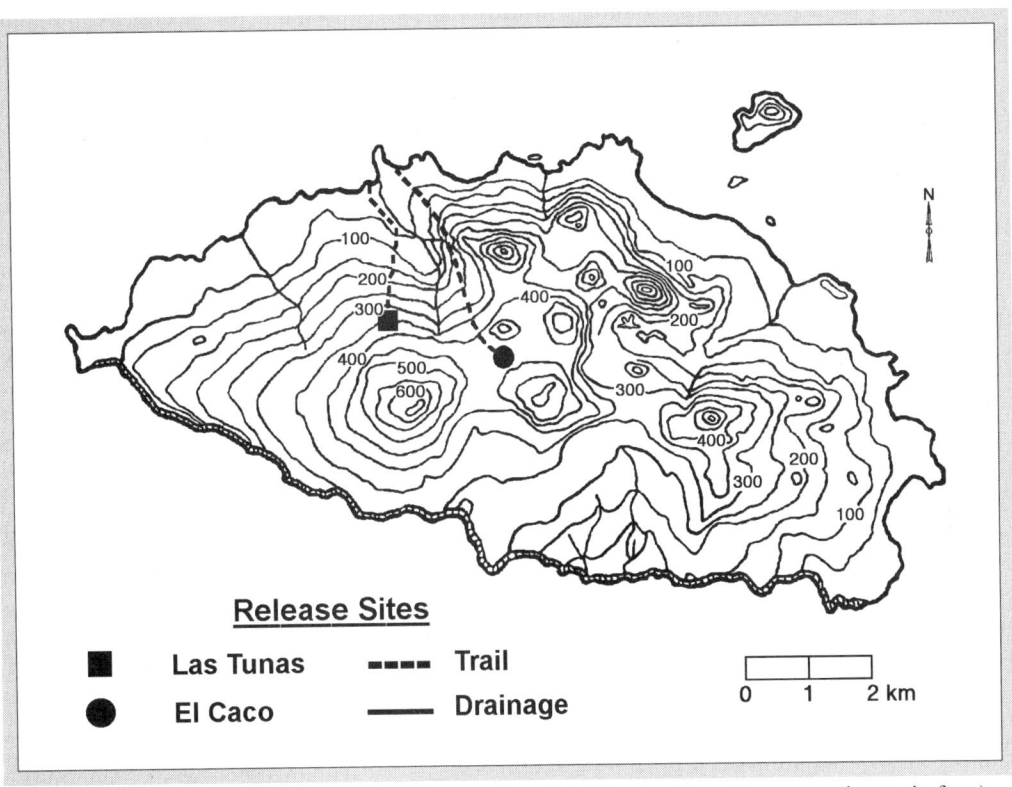

Figure 1. Release sites of repatriated tortoises on Española Island. (Elevation approximate, in feet.)

The breeding and rearing program developed during the early years used a system of trial and error in an effort to duplicate natural conditions (MacFarland et al., 1974b; MacFarland and Reeder, 1975). In the 1980s experiments to improve methods of incubation and rearing were conducted.

The Española tortoises are the only race bred in captivity on the Galápagos Islands. They are housed in two corrals (20 × 54 m); one male is housed with five females and the other two males with the remaining seven females. Various attempts to create appropriate nesting areas were made until the first successful nesting occurred in 1970 (MacFarland et al., 1974b; MacFarland and Reeder, 1975). Each corral now has six to eight small nesting zones available to the females.

Nesting

Copulation occurs primarily during the hot season, from February to June. During the nesting season (July to December), nesting areas are checked daily. The morning following each nesting event, the nest is opened and the eggs moved to the incubators.

Prior to the 1970–1971 reproductive season, nesting by the captive Española females was totally unsuccessful due to the lack of suitable nesting sites. In 1969–1970 the first adequate nesting sites were constructed, and the first successful nesting occurred in the 1970–1971 season (Table 1). Between 1971 and 1979 additional areas were constructed and methods developed to maintain the nesting areas. Until the 1978–1979 season the 12 Española females laid an average of 12.7 nests per year (range 8–17). Since 1979 they have averaged 28 nests per year (range 24–32).

Incubation

Initially, solar-heated incubators were used at the Center. In the 1980s a series of experiments was conducted to determine the optimum temperature and water potential (humidity) of the substrate for incubation (Snell, 1985). The more important results of these experiments include:

1. Galápagos tortoises have temperature-dependent sex determination, with lower temperatures producing males and higher temperatures producing females (Sancho, 1988).
2. Certain temperatures result in a higher hatching success (Snell, 1985).
3. Water potential (humidity) of the substrate is not critical for hard-shelled tortoise eggs (Snell, 1985).

The incubation system was changed as a result of these findings. Simple wooden incubators with thermostatic control and electric hair dryers as the heating elements are now used. From 1988 to 1991 tortoise eggs were incubated at a temperature of 28.5–29°C and a water potential of −1,100 kPa (kiloPascal). This produces the highest hatching success and a male-to-female ratio of approximately 1:2. Since 1992 the eggs have been incubated at two temperatures, two thirds of the eggs at 29.5°C (primarily females) and one third at 28°C (primarily males).

Advances in incubation methods in recent years have resulted in major improvements in hatching success (Table 1). In the early years (1970–1979), when few nests were laid, hatching success averaged 26.3%. With an increase in the number of nests, and thus eggs, and until the incubation experiments were begun (1980–1987), hatching success declined to an average of 19.5%. In the 1987–1988 and 1988–1989 seasons, while the experiments were still under way, percent hatching increased to 43.3%. From 1990 to 1992, with the use of one temperature producing two-thirds females and one-third males, hatching success averaged 54.4%. The first year using two temperatures (1992–1993), hatching success increased at the low temperature (59% at 28°C) and declined at the high temperature (40.2% at 30°C). In the 1993–1994 season the high temperature was lowered by half of a degree and hatching success increased to 67.2%, while that at the lower temperature increased to 70.7%.

In terms of overall tortoise production (a combination of the number of nests and eggs, and hatching success), an average of 24.3 tortoises hatched annually between 1971 and 1987 (range 10–52), while an average of 93 per year (range 82–121) hatched in the last seven years (Table 1).

Rearing of Young

Improvements in rearing procedures for tortoises have primarily involved changes in the physical conditions of the corrals. An experiment examining rearing conditions demonstrated that rearing tortoises outside on a natural substrate (soil with some lava) was best (Snell et al., 1985, 1988). Since December 1990, with the construction of the new corrals and visitor trail completed, all tortoises have been reared outdoors on a natural substrate where they have access to direct sunlight. Upon emerging from the egg, hatchling tortoises are kept in a dark box without food or water for a period of two to four weeks, simulating their time in

TABLE 1
Hatching success of Española tortoises at the Breeding and Rearing Center from 1971 to 1994.

Cohort	No. of nests	Number of eggs laid	Number of eggs hatched	Percent hatching
1970–71	8	46	20	43.5
1971–72	11	63	10	15.9
1972–73	21	113	22	19.5
1973–74	15	81	17	21.0
1974–75	15	81	24	29.6
1975–76	9	52	12	23.1
1976–77	9	47	24	51.1
1977–78	10	59	10	16.9
1978–79	17	104	17	16.3
1979–80	25	137	24	17.5
1980–81	27	149	14	9.4
1981–82	28	155	27	17.4
1982–83	25	138	32	23.2
1983–84	29	162	49	30.2
1984–85	32	199	52	26.1
1985–86	24	157	22	14.0
1986–87	32	204	37	18.1
1987–88	31	223	96	43.0
1988–89	28	188	82	43.6
1989–90	26	170	90	52.9
1990–91	28	161	84	52.2
1991–92	27	162	94	58.0
1992–93	30	186	85[a]	45.7
1993–94	29	183	121	66.1

[a] Twin tortoises hatched from one egg, producing a total of 86 hatchlings.

the nest under natural conditions (MacFarland et al., 1974a). They are then transferred to outdoor corrals, which are covered at night to prevent rat predation. Hatchlings are kept in confined corrals with a soil substrate for approximately two years and are then transferred to an adaptation corral, an enclosed natural area where they are free to move over the lava substrate. They remain in these areas until release.

Improvements in rearing conditions have resulted in lower mortality of juvenile tortoises (Table 2). Mortality averaged 14.0% annually (range 0–33%) between 1971 and 1988, while annual mortality averaged 1.6% between 1989 and 1994 (range 0.9–2.0%).

Repatriation

Repatriation of tortoises generally takes place during the hot or rainy season when feeding conditions are best. Prior to release the animals are measured and weighed, then permanently marked by shell notching. They are transferred by ship to Española in wooden boxes, then carried to the release site. On the other islands, tortoises have generally been released either in a nesting zone or in one of the major living areas of adults. On Española, however, the historic nesting and living areas were not known, so release sites were selected on the basis of vegetation and soil conditions known to be appropriate for tortoises.

Monitoring of Repatriated Tortoises

To determine the success of the repatriation program, the Española population is monitored semi-annually, with searches for tortoises concentrated in the areas around the two release sites. Tortoises encountered are measured, weighed, and their sex and identification number recorded. The Petersen Index (mark:recapture) is used in a defined quadrat at both release sites to estimate the number and density of tortoises in these areas.

The number of tortoises seen in the semi-annual visits is dependent upon the climate and vegetation. During wet years with thick vegetation the tortoises are difficult to find, while in dry years they are dispersed through a much larger area. Observations of tortoise scat throughout much of the island indicate substantial dispersal from the two release sites.

Between 1988 and 1991 a total of 202 different tortoises were observed on the island (average of 89 tortoises seen in each trip). Based on the total released by the end of 1991 (369), this gives a minimum survivorship of 55%. Due to heavy rains in 1992 and 1993 the regular monitoring methods were not used.

Since 1990 evidence of reproduction by the repatriated tortoises has been found in the El Caco area, but none in Las Tunas. In November 1990 the first hatchlings (both dead) and four nest attempts were found (Márquez et al., 1991). In June 1991 the first live hatchling was found and marked. In November of the same year 16 nests were located and the same hatchling recaptured. In 1993 two additional live hatchlings and 12 nests were observed.

DISCUSSION

Through the captive breeding, rearing, and repatriation program, the tortoise population of Española has been brought back from the brink of extinction. As a result of the combined management strategies of tortoise repatriation and goat eradication, the Española tortoise population will probably be the first in the program that may no longer require intervention by humans. However, due to the longevity of tortoises and the considerable age at first reproduction, evidence of a stable, self-sustaining, and (hopefully) increasing population will not be available for many years. Survival of the repatriated tortoises is not enough. Successful reproduction and recruitment into the population is required. Long-term monitoring of the Española population must be maintained in order to evaluate the eventual success of the project (Dodd and Seigel, 1991).

Determination of the optimal number of tortoises that

TABLE 2
Percent mortality of juvenile Española tortoises at the Rearing Center from 1971 to 1994.

Year	Total	Died-R [a]	Missing [a]	Percent mortality
1971	20	0	1	5.0
1972	29	4	0	13.8
1973	47	1	6	14.9
1974	57	7	0	12.3
1975	74	0	13	17.6
1976	56	2	1	5.4
1977 [b]	—	—	—	—
1978 [b]	—	—	—	—
1979	60	0	1	1.7
1980	74	5	2	9.5
1981	84	0	0	0
1982	75	19	0	25.3
1983	104	33	0	31.7
1984	97	31	1	33.0
1985	113	15	0	13.3
1986	120	9	1	8.3
1987	131	28	0	21.4
1988	160	18	0	11.3
1989	220	2	0	0.9
1990	234	4	0	1.7
1991	283	3	0	1.1
1992	350	6	1	2.0
1993	396	7	0	1.8
1994	332	6	0	1.8

[a] Dead tortoises include both known recorded deaths (Died-R) and presumed but unrecorded deaths (Missing) of tortoises. [b] There are no rearing records from 1977 and 1978.

should be repatriated to Española must be based upon both genetic considerations and the carrying capacity of the island. To determine this number, survivorship and reproduction of the repatriated tortoises must be evaluated. Minimum survivorship on Española is near 55% and successful reproduction has been observed. The only complete census of repatriated tortoises in Galápagos, carried out on Pinzón in 1989 and 1990, indicated a minimum survivorship (percentage of all tortoises repatriated between 1971 and 1989–1990) of 68.7% and an estimated survivorship of 77.2% (Cayot et al., 1994).

The working group on population genetics, minimum population sizes, and inbreeding at the international workshop "The Herpetology of the Galápagos Islands," held at the CDRS in 1988, recommended that repatriation continue until at least 50 individuals are established as reproductive adults (unpubl. report). Given an observed survivorship of greater than 50%, this goal will be reached around 1997, when the survivors of the first 103 repatriated tortoises will have reached a minimum of 20 years of age. (The percentage of observed survivorship may improve considerably now that the younger tortoises are no longer being released.) It is recommended that the breeding program continue until 1997 (three more cohorts), producing a total number of tortoises repatriated to Española that exceeds 1,200. This number will provide a good base of first-generation tortoises and should not approach the carrying capacity, given that several thousand tortoises were removed from the island during the last century.

Galápagos is an ideal site for repatriation programs. The longevity of tortoises was important in the survival of the populations until protection began. An important key to success in current management programs is the existence of habitats that are relatively free from adverse disturbances. In general, the quality of tortoise habitat for feeding, reproduction, thermoregulation, resting, etc. is high. In addition, the reptiles are reared in climatic conditions very similar to their natural conditions and are fed similar foods, both of which may help them survive after repatriation. Española is returning to a more pristine condition as a result of the research and management programs carried out by the CDRS and the GNPS. By the end of this century the Española tortoise population will be well on its way to complete recovery.

TABLE 3
Number and age of tortoises repatriated to Española between 1975 and 1994.

Date	Zone	Cohort	No. of tortoises	Age at repatriation (years)
May 1975	El Caco	1970–71	17	4
June 1976	El Caco	1971–72	5	4
June 1977	El Caco	1972–73	12	4
March 1978	El Caco	1973–74	23	4
July 1978	El Caco	1974–75	13	3
February 1979	Las Tunas	1975–76	9	3
November 1981	Las Tunas	1976–77	20	4.5
November 1982	Las Tunas	1977–78	13	3.5
November 1982	El Caco	1977–78	1	4.5
	El Caco	1978–79	15	3.5
February 1984	El Caco	1979–80	17	4
February 1985	El Caco	1980–81	6	4
March 1986	El Caco	1981–82	4	4
	Las Tunas	1981–82	4	4
	El Caco	1984–85	12	1
	Las Tunas	1984–85	13	1
March 1987	Las Tunas	1982–83	6	4
	Las Tunas	1983–84	16	3
February 1988	El Caco	1984–85	16	3
March 1989	Las Tunas	1984–85	1	4
	Las Tunas	1985–86	11	3
November 1989	Las Tunas	1986–87	15	2.5
	Las Tunas	1987–88	38	1.5
November 1990	El Caco	1988–89	40	1.5
	El Caco	Unknown	1	?
November 1991	Las Tunas	1987–88	39	3.5
	El Caco	Unknown	2	?
June 1992	El Caco	1988–89	38	3
February 1993	Las Tunas	1989–90	88	3
November 1993	El Caco	1990–91	80	2.5
November 1994	Las Tunas	1991–92	89	2.5

Acknowledgments

A long-term management program can only be maintained with the collaboration of many people. We thank the personnel and consultants of the Charles Darwin Research Station and the Galápagos National Park Service, who have worked together for many years for the conservation of the giant tortoises. In particular, we thank Fausto Llerena for his dedication both at the Center and in the field, Washington Llerena for his work on archiving the years of data on the computer, and Howard Snell for his review of the manuscript. This program has received major funding from the Government of Ecuador, the Zoological Society of San Diego, and the World Wide Fund for Nature (WWF); the Tinker Foundation, Inc., funded the International Workshop on Herpetology in 1988; donations of both equipment and funds have been received from many individuals and turtle and tortoise organizations; TAME provides continual logistical support.

Literature Cited

Bacon, J. P. 1978. A tortoise goes home. Zoonooz 51(2):4–7.

Beck, R. H. 1903. In the home of the giant tortoise. An. Rpt. N. Y. Zool. Soc. 7:160–174.

Cayot, L. J. and A. Izurieta. 1993. Manejo en cautiverio y conservación de reptiles en las Islas Galápagos. *In* P. A. Mena and L. Suárez (eds.), La Investigación para la Conservación de la Diversidad Biológica en el Ecuador, pp. 237–257. Ecociencia, Quito, Ecuador.

Cayot, L. J. and E. Lewis. 1994. Recent increase in killing of giant tortoises on Isabela Island. Not. Gal. 54:2–7.

Cayot, L. J., H. L. Snell, W. Llerena, and H. M. Snell. 1994. Conservation biology of Galápagos reptiles: Twenty-five years of successful research and management. *In* J. B. Murphy, K. Adler, and J. T. Collins (eds.), Captive Management and Conservation of Amphibians and Reptiles, pp. 297–305. Society for the Study of Amphibians and Reptiles, Athens, Ohio.

deVries, T. 1984. The giant tortoises: A natural history disturbed by man. *In* R. Perry (ed.), Key Environments: Galápagos, pp. 145–156. Pergamon Press, Oxford.

Dodd, C. K., Jr. and R. A. Seigel. 1991. Relocation, repatriation, and translocation of amphibians and reptiles: Are they conservation strategies that work? Herpetologica 47(3):336–350.

Eckhardt, R. C. 1972. Introduced plants and animals in the Galápagos Islands. BioScience 22:585–590.

Fritts, T. H. 1978. Española tortoise returns. Not. Gal. 28:17–18.

Fritts, T. H. and P. R. Fritts (eds.). 1982. Race with extinction: Herpetological notes of J. R. Slevin's journey to the Galápagos 1905–06. Herpetol. Monogr. 1:1–98.

Hamann, O. 1979. Regeneration of vegetation on Santa Fé and Pinta Islands, Galápagos, after the eradication of goats. Biol. Conserv. 15:215–236.

Hickman, J. 1985. The Enchanted Islands: The Galápagos Discovered. Tanager Books, Dover, New Hampshire.

Hoeck, H. N. 1984. Introduced fauna. *In* R. Perry (ed.), Key Environments: Galápagos, pp. 233–245. Pergamon Press, Oxford.

MacFarland, C. G. and W. G. Reeder. 1975. Breeding, raising and restocking of giant tortoises (*Geochelone elephantopus*) in the Galápagos Islands. *In* R. D. Martin (ed.), Breeding Endangered Species in Captivity, pp. 13–37. Academic Press, London.

MacFarland, C. G., J. Villa, and B. Toro. 1974a. The Galápagos giant tortoises (*Geochelone elephantopus*) part I: Status of the surviving populations. Biol. Conserv. 6:118–133.

MacFarland, C. G., J. Villa, and B. Toro. 1974b. The Galápagos giant tortoises (*Geochelone elephantopus*) part II: Conservation methods. Biol. Conserv. 6:198–212.

Márquez, C., G. Morillo, and L. J. Cayot. 1991. A 25-year management program pays off: Repatriated tortoises on Española reproduce. Not. Gal. 51:17–18.

Pinos O., F. 1987. Estudio de la supervivencia, el crecimiento, los movimientos y la alimentación de los galapaguitos repatriados a Española. Technical report submitted to the Charles Darwin Research Station, Galápagos, Ecuador.

Reinert, H. K. 1991. Translocation as a conservation strategy for amphibians and reptiles: Some comments, concerns, and observations. Herpetologica 47(3):357–363.

Reynolds, R. P. and R. W. Marlow. 1983. Lonesome George, the Pinta Island tortoise: A case of limited alternatives. Not. Gal. 37:14–17.

Sancho A., A. C. 1988. Influencia de la temperatura de incubación en el sexo y parámetros para el reconocimiento del sexo de la tortuga gigante de Galápagos (*Geochelone elephantopus*) e histología de la gónada juvenil de la iguana terrestre (*Conolophus subcristatus*). Thesis for the Licenciatura degree, Pontificia Universidad Católica del Ecuador, Quito.

Slevin, J. R. 1959. The Galápagos Islands: A history of their exploration. Occ. Pap. Cal. Acad. Sci. No. 25.

Snell, H. L. 1985. Investigation of optimal conditions for incubating eggs of Galápagos giant tortoises (*Geochelone elephantopus*) and land iguanas (*Conolophus subcristatus*). Technical report submitted to the Charles Darwin Research Station, Galápagos, Ecuador.

Snell, H. L., C. Márquez, and S. Rea. 1988. Informe final del experimento de crianza de galapaguitos. Technical report submitted to Charles Darwin Research Station, Galápagos, Ecuador.

Snell, H. L., C. Márquez, S. Rea, H. M. Snell, and F. Llerena. 1985. Un experimento sobre condiciones mejores para la crianza de los galapaguitos recién nacidos. Technical report submitted to the Charles Darwin Research Station, Galápagos, Ecuador.

Townsend, C. H. 1925. The Galápagos tortoises in their relation to the whaling industry: A study of old logbooks. Zoologica 4:55–135.

Van Denburgh, J. 1914. The gigantic land tortoises of the Galápagos Archipelago. Proc. Calif. Acad. Sci., 4th Series 2:203–374.

Applications of Demography, Ecology, and Genetics to Conservation

Brian Bock, *left* and Vivian Páez, *right* (Proyecto Terecay, Santa Fe de Bogotá, Colombia) and Vitor Hugo Cantarelli, *center* (CENAQUA/IBAMA, Goiânia, Brazil). (Photo by Rita Devine.)

David Galbraith (Royal Botannical Gardens, Hamilton, Ontario, Canada).

Jeffrey Lovich (Bureau of Land Management, Palm Springs, California), Richard Vogt (Estación de Biología Tropical Los Tuxtlas, Veracruz, Mexico), Sheik Rashid (Nature Conservation Movement, Dhaka, Bangladesh), Dina Foscarini and Heather Passmore (University of Guelph, Ontario, Canada), and George Amato (Wildlife Conservation Society, New York).

Can Management Intervention Achieve Sustainable Exploitation of Turtles?

DAVID A. GALBRAITH,[1] RONALD J. BROOKS,[2] AND GREGORY P. BROWN[2,3]

[1] Canadian Botanical Conservation Network, Royal Botanical Gardens,
P.O. Box 399, Hamilton, Ontario L8N 3H8, Canada [e-mail: turtle@earthling.net]
[2] Department of Zoology, University of Guelph, Guelph, Ontario N1G 2W1, Canada [e-mail: rjbrooks@uoguelph.ca]
[3] Current address: Department of Biology, Carleton University, Ottawa K1S 5B6, Ontario, Canada

ABSTRACT: We examined the feasibility of sustainable exploitation of adult snapping turtles, *Chelydra serpentina*, using data from a northern population. Three criteria were used to assess sustainable harvest: juvenile survivorship from life tables, density-dependent responses, and economic cost of hatchling supplementation to replace adults. Life table analyses suggest that turtle populations respond weakly to variation in survival or number of offspring relative to survival of adults. Furthermore, observed depletion of adult turtles within a population by natural predation events, which served as a natural removal experiment, indicated no density-dependent responses in size or number of eggs, rate of growth, age at maturity, or frequency of reproduction. Natural populations of these turtles do not therefore display a Maximum Sustainable Yield (MSY) inflection in growth rate. We analysed the economic sustainability of our study population under various modelled regimens, including harvesting of adults, supplementation by incubation of eggs, and protection of hatchlings. Our analysis indicated that removal of adults from supplemented populations can not be sustained economically, even assuming that survival and growth of the offspring compared favourably with that of incubated eggs. Mature turtles cannot therefore be harvested sustainably from northern populations. Without supplementation by artificially reared hatchlings or juveniles, produced at costs far exceeding any economic return, such populations will inevitably decline, even with low levels of exploitation. Northern populations must be afforded complete protection, and the public and wildlife biologists must be educated that even widespread and "common" turtle species have life histories that preclude sustainable exploitation under most circumstances.

Exploitation of natural resources for economic or recreational purposes should be based on two fundamental tenets, (1) the utilization should not reduce the capacity of the resource to withstand similar exploitation in the future (ecological sustainability), and (2) the utilization should generate revenue so that the community may ensure that the resource is managed competently (economic sustainability). Whether overtly consumptive or more passive, forms of utilization that violate either of these tenets should not be allowed by regulatory agencies.

When the capacity of a resource to withstand future utilization (the much-abused principle of sustainable use) declines, unchecked exploitation eventually destroys the resource. Where management costs exceed the revenues derived from the activity, subsidies will be necessary to maintain the resource. At best, actively supporting the destruction of a natural resource through public subsidization of the harvest can only be described as shortsighted.

Although these principles are widely recognized, they are rarely achieved. The consumption of freshwater turtles for food in North America presents a particularly important case of economic utilization. Although the standing crop biomass of freshwater turtles in some northern populations may be very large (exceeding 350 kg/ha in some unmanaged populations, Galbraith et al., 1988), they are generally long-lived and slow growing. Turtles are not generally recognized as charismatic species in need of protection, and thus little public attention has been drawn to consequences of trapping them for food or the pet trade. Because the economic return from turtle hunting is not large, hunting does not generate funds that could be reinvested in managing populations. Although there is some recognition that rare species need protection, there is little concern for widespread or "common" species.

We have examined the impact of turtle trapping in Ontario, Canada, to illustrate the various economic and life history issues in turtle consumption. Until the late 1980s, consumption of snapping turtles, *Chelydra serpentina*, was unregulated in Ontario. Trapping seasons, possession limits, and a ban on commercial turtle hunting were enacted in 1989. Prior to this act little research had been conducted on turtle hunting. An unpublished report commissioned by the

Ontario Ministry of Natural Resources (Lovisek, 1982) described the level of annual consumption at that time as between 5,000 and 10,000 adult snapping turtles per year.

The objectives of this paper are to assess whether a free-living population of snapping turtles can sustain exploitation of adults, and to assess the economic feasibility of active management intervention to supplement such populations. To determine whether the trapping of adults may be ecologically sustainable, we examined a life table for evidence of the relative importance of adults and juveniles on population growth. We also tested for posssible density-dependent responses in population growth to natural depletion of adult turtles by predation. Finally, we examined the effects of juvenile survivorship on four model scenarios for supplementation to predict whether artificial supplementation could stabilize the population during the commercial harvest of adults.

MATERIALS AND METHODS

Formulation of Horizontal Life Table

Demographic parameters of the population of snapping turtles in the Wildlife Research Area of Algonquin Provincial Park, Ontario, Canada, have been determined through long-term, mark-recapture studies (summarized by Brooks et al., 1991b). Although this population has been under study since 1972 (Loncke and Obbard, 1977), several important parameters can be only crudely estimated at this time, particularly the annual probability of survival for juvenile turtles, age classes 1–18 inclusive.

A previously published estimate of life table parameters for the Algonquin Park snapping turtle population (Brooks et al., 1988) relied heavily on estimates of recruitment based on observed numbers of females entering the population. However, recruitment in this population is highly stochastic. Although only approximately 6.35% of eggs hatch (Obbard, 1983), individual years vary greatly in the number of hatchlings produced, with most years showing zero success and occasional years showing high recruitment (Bobyn and Brooks, 1994).

We estimated mean annual probability of survival during the juvenile year classes (1–18) by the method of Congdon et al. (1993), in which we derived the solution to Euler's equation for r to allow for a net replacement rate of 1. Mark-recapture survival of adult females prior to the mortality event discussed below averaged 96.6% per year (Galbraith and Brooks, 1987). Estimates of the age at first reproduction vary from 17 to 25 years, depending on method (Galbraith et al., 1989). We have assumed that mean age of first reproduction is 19 years. Finally, annual reproduction was estimated to be 16.18 female-producing eggs per female per year (Brooks et al., 1988).

Observations on Natural Predation Serving as a Removal Experiment

Predation by river otters, *Lutra canadensis*, since 1987 has removed from the Algonquin population approximately 65% of the adult females known before 1987 (Brooks et al., 1991b). Known mortality of adults increased approximately 20-fold between 1987 and 1989. If the population could respond to this decrease in density, we predicted that it would either increase fecundity or increase individual survival. If the population is density dependent, an increase in reproductive output is predicted to follow the predation event.

Supplementation Scenarios

Two possible types of management intervention were postulated to supplement an exploited snapping turtle population: One could increase either the survival of eggs or the survival of the first year-class through headstarting. In all of our calculations we have assumed that artificial manipulation of the turtles does not change their ability to grow or survive relative to the other members of their cohorts.

Two effects were investigated for each management activity. One effect was the desired change to survivorship, estimated from laboratory experience with this population (Brooks et al., 1991a). The second effect was the financial cost of the activity, expressed as dollars per hatchling. The financial cost was estimated on the basis of laboratory experience, in which overhead costs were effectively subsidized, and wages were paid at student rates. All cost estimates were based on a gross wage (including benefits and taxes) of Can $20,500 per year.

The relative effectiveness of each management scenario was assessed by "appreciating" the financial cost of surviving adult females up to the mean age (34 years) (Galbraith and Brooks, 1989) of the wild population. Thus, the "cost" of a single female of age class x was calculated as the cost of producing sufficient hatchlings or yearlings to result in a single survivor in that age class. As the turtles are being considered for harvest, no adjustments have been made for effects of environmental sex determination.

Changes to Survival in Year Class 0

To effect a change in hatching rate of eggs or in survival during year class 0, we hypothesized two types of activity, (1) protection of nests from predation at the nesting site, and (2) incubation of eggs under laboratory conditions. In Algonquin Park, eggs in nests that were not destroyed by predators have an average annual rate of emergence of 6.35% (Obbard, 1983). Eggs incubated under artificial conditions have had a best survival rate to hatching of 94.6% (Brooks et al., 1991a).

The financial cost of protecting nests in the wild was

based on a field team of two persons locating and protecting 10 nests per day during the nesting season and excavating the same number per day during the hatching season. The financial cost of incubating eggs was assumed to be composed of the cost of protection and subsequent excavation plus the cost of handling and maintaining the eggs during the incubation period. Thus, all cost estimates have been deliberately made conservative by the omission of materials or infrastructure cost.

Changes to Survival in Year Class 1

Survival in year class 1 under natural conditions was conservatively estimated from the life table calculated above. Survival under 12 months of captive rearing, or "headstarting," was estimated from the observed survival of 170 of 186 hatchlings maintained for seven months in the laboratory (Brooks et al., 1991a). This is a conservative estimate, as rates of survival over one to two years in the laboratory are often much lower (Bobyn and Brooks, 1994).

The survival of hatchlings under natural conditions during year class 1 was assumed to present no financial cost. The cost of maintenance of a hatchling in the laboratory for one year was estimated on the basis of the cost of one full-time technician tending 3,250 hatchlings.

RESULTS

Results of Life Table Recalculation

The average annual survival during year classes 1–18 necessary to produce a replacement rate of 1 for the Algonquin Park population of snapping turtles is 82.8% per year (Tables 1 and 2), considerably higher than the estimated 75.4% rate of juvenile survival based on observed recruitment (Brooks et al., 1988).

Results of Removal Experiment

The reduction in the density of the Algonquin Park snapping turtle population in 1987–1988 by over 65% appears to be a permanent condition and has had no appreciable effect on most reproductive parameters. Early results have been previously summarized (Brooks et al., 1991b). Comparisons of clutch size from 1977 to 1992 show no increase even after the density of the population declined sharply in the late 1980s (Figure 1). No female has more than one clutch per year, and there has been no detectable increase in the proportion of females nesting each year. This proportion has remained consistently high at over 85% (R. J. Brooks, unpubl. data). In fact, reproduction in 1993 appeared to be at an all-time low because clutch size remained unchanged, whereas the total number of nesting females continued the decline begun in 1987. Egg size was the only measure of reproductive effort that changed significantly, by up to 25%, and it appeared to fluctuate according to annual variation in availability of resources (M. Bell, unpubl. MS). Therefore, females did not appear to respond to changes in density or resource availability by increases in survival, clutch size, or nesting frequency. Egg size appeared to correlate with annual variation in energy availability, but not with the changes in density.

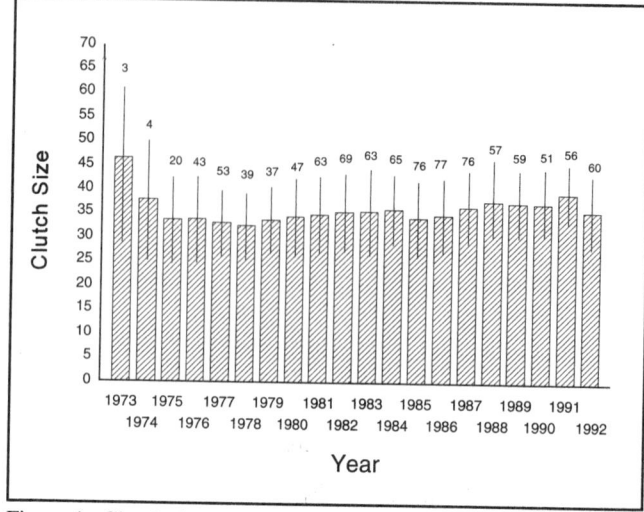

Figure 1. Clutch size of the snapping turtle, *Chelydra serpentina*, in Algonquin Provincial Park. Vertical lines represent standard error. Numbers above bars refer to sample size.

Models of Management Scenarios

The financial cost of protecting nests *in situ* was estimated (in Can$) as the cost of a crew of two persons locating and protecting 10 nests of mean size of 35 eggs (average before 1987) (Brooks et al., 1991b) per day during the nesting season. Thus, each egg was estimated to cost 2 × $78.85/day ÷ 350 eggs = $0.45 to protect. The same expenditure was assumed necessary in the fall to excavate the incubated eggs and release the hatchlings, resulting in a total per-hatchling cost of $0.90 for nest protection.

The financial cost of incubating eggs *ex situ* was estimated as the cost of one technician working full time for three months. It was estimated that one technician could provide care for 2,000 eggs (R. J. Brooks, unpubl.). The cost of laboratory incubation was therefore estimated to be $5,237.89 ÷ 2,000 = $2.62 per egg. As each laboratory-incubated egg also had to be located, excavated, transported, and the hatchling released to the wild following incubation, the estimated total cost of *ex situ* incubation was assumed to be the sum of the cost of incubation plus the cost of excavation, and release estimated above. Thus, the total cost of *ex situ* incubation was estimated to be $3.52 per released hatchling. Again, we have omitted overhead, infrastructure costs, and transportation and housing costs.

The financial cost of headstarting hatchlings for one

year was estimated as the cost of one technician working full time to provide care for hatchlings. Based on experience with 650 hatchling turtles requiring one day per week for care in a zoo setting following confiscation by customs agents (D. A. Galbraith, unpubl.), one full-time technician could provide care for 3,250 hatchlings. The cost per hatchling of one year of captivity would therefore be $20,500 ÷ 3,250 = $6.31. Four specific management scenarios were modelled. In Scenario One (EP + HR), eggs were protected *in situ* (EP) by placing predation exclusion devices over the nests. This scenario resulted in hatchling release (HR) in the fall and provided a survival in year class 0 of 6.35% at a per-hatchling cost of $0.90. When modelled for juvenile mortality in a life table, this scenario produced recruits of 19 years of age costing $26.93 each (Tables 3 and 4). The cost of producing a female of mean age 34 years was estimated to be $45.25 (Tables 3 and 4).

In Scenario Two (EP + HS), eggs were protected *in situ* (EP) and the resulting hatchlings were headstarted in captivity for 12 months prior to release (HS). This scenario resulted in the release of yearlings in the fall of the year after oviposition, with survival in year class 1 estimated to be 85.7%. The estimated cost of a single yearling in this scenario was $7.21. The estimated cost of a 34-year-old female produced by this method was $178.64, and the cost of protecting and headstarting sufficient yearlings to result in one adult female of average age was $300.13 (Tables 3 and 4).

In Scenario Three (EI + HR), eggs were collected from the field and incubated *ex situ* (EI), followed by release of hatchlings (HR). This scenario resulted in a 94.6% probability of hatching and a cost per hatchling of $3.52. The cost of producing a single female recruit (year class 19) by *ex-situ* incubation and release of hatchlings was estimated to be $105.34, and the cost of an average 34-year-old female survivor was estimated to be $176.98 (Tables 3 and 4).

In Scenario Four (EI+HS), eggs were incubated *ex situ* and then the hatchlings were headstarted for 12 months prior to release in the fall of the year after oviposition. Under this scenario it was assumed that eggs hatched at a rate of 94.6% and that survival during the year in captivity was 85.7% at a cost of $9.83 per released yearling. In this scenario, each recruit (year class 19) is the survivor of a cohort costing $243.55, and the estimated cost of producing a 34-year-old female is $409.20 (Tables 3 and 4).

DISCUSSION

The persistence of a population depends upon a balance of the factors that comprise its demographic environment. In this study we have investigated these factors in turtle populations close to the edge of their range, where either marginal habitat or marginal climatic conditions present challenges to population survival apart from human interference. This situation is particularly relevant in Canada where all native species of reptiles and amphibians reach the northern limits of their distribution, and where turtles are limited to one clutch per season, possibly have higher rates of failed clutches, and have longer delays to sexual maturity.

Life table studies indicate that the Algonquin Park population of snapping turtles is unstable. Prior to the sharp increase in adult mortality in 1987 (Brooks et al., 1991b), mark-recapture observations between 1973 and 1986 indicated an average adult survival rate of at least 96.6%

TABLE 1
Summary of the estimate of juvenile (age 1–18) survival rate for WRS snapping turtles necessary to produce stable population size, based solely on life-table.

Female-producing eggs per female per year:	16.18
Expected number of reproductive years:	29.126
Net lifetime egg production:	471.26
Mean rate of egg hatching per egg:	0.0635
Lifetime expected hatchling production per female:	29.925
$\ln(N_1/N_0)$	-3.398 kt
Age at first reproduction	19
$\ln(N_1/N_0)/t$	-0.188 k (t = alpha $-$ 1)
e^k	0.8279 per year
$SUM(m_x l_x)$	1

Where: N_1 is number alive at time 1; in this case, year class 19
N_0 is number alive at time 0
k is the logarithmic growth constant
l_x is probability of survival from year class 0 to year class x
m_x is net fecundity at year class x (female-destined embryos produced)

TABLE 2

Life-table for WRS snapping turtles calculated to produce net female replacement rate = 1. After age 30 every fifth year is presented. The table was truncated at age 152, when the probability of survival of adults became less than 1%. Legend: s_x = probability of survival from YC_x to YC_{x+1}; a_x = numbers of individuals; l_x = the probability of survival from YC_0 to YC_x; m_x = net fecundity at year class x (female-destined embryos produced).

YC	s_x^1	a_x^2	l_x^3	m_x^4	$m_x l_x$	SUM($m_x l_x$)
0	0.0635	471.264	1.0			
1	0.82793	29.9252	0.0635			
2	0.82793	24.7762	0.05257			
3	0.82793	20.5132	0.04352			
4	0.82793	16.9836	0.03603			
5	0.82793	14.0614	0.02983			
6	0.82793	11.6420	0.02470			
7	0.82793	9.63885	0.02045			
8	0.82793	7.98037	0.01693			
9	0.82793	6.60725	0.01402			
10	0.82793	5.47040	0.01160			
11	0.82793	4.52915	0.00961			
12	0.82793	3.74985	0.00795			
13	0.82793	3.10465	0.00658			
14	0.82793	2.57045	0.00545			
15	0.82793	2.12818	0.00451			
16	0.82793	1.76200	0.00373			
17	0.82793	1.45882	0.00309			
18	0.82793	1.20781	0.00256			
19	0.966	1.0	0.00212	16.18	0.03433	0.034333
20	0.966	0.966	0.00204	16.18	0.03316	0.067498
21	0.966	0.93315	0.00198	16.18	0.03203	0.099537
22	0.966	0.90142	0.00191	16.18	0.03094	0.130486
23	0.966	0.87078	0.00184	16.18	0.02989	0.160382
24	0.966	0.84117	0.00178	16.18	0.02888	0.189262
25	0.966	0.81257	0.00172	16.18	0.02789	0.217161
26	0.966	0.78494	0.00166	16.18	0.02694	0.244110
27	0.966	0.75825	0.00160	16.18	0.02603	0.270144
28	0.966	0.73247	0.00155	16.18	0.02514	0.295292
29	0.966	0.70757	0.00150	16.18	0.02429	0.319585
30	0.966	0.68351	0.00145	16.18	0.02346	0.343052
35	0.966	0.57495	0.00122	16.18	0.01974	0.448949
40	0.966	0.48363	0.00102	16.18	0.01660	0.538027
45	0.966	0.40682	0.00086	16.18	0.01396	0.612957
50	0.966	0.34220	0.00072	16.18	0.01174	0.675986
55	0.966	0.28785	0.00061	16.18	0.00988	0.729004
60	0.966	0.24213	0.00051	16.18	0.00831	0.773601
65	0.966	0.20367	0.00043	16.18	0.00699	0.811116
70	0.966	0.17133	0.00036	16.18	0.00588	0.842672
75	0.966	0.14411	0.00030	16.18	0.00494	0.869216
80	0.966	0.12122	0.00025	16.18	0.00416	0.891544
85	0.966	0.10197	0.00021	16.18	0.00350	0.910326
90	0.966	0.08577	0.00018	16.18	0.00294	0.926125
95	0.966	0.07215	0.00015	16.18	0.00247	0.939414
100	0.966	0.06069	0.00012	16.18	0.00208	0.950593
105	0.966	0.05105	0.00010	16.18	0.00175	0.959996
110	0.966	0.04294	0.00009	16.18	0.00147	0.967906
115	0.966	0.03612	0.00007	16.18	0.00124	0.974560
120	0.966	0.03038	0.00006	16.18	0.00104	0.980157
125	0.966	0.02556	0.00005	16.18	0.00087	0.984864
130	0.966	0.02150	0.00004	16.18	0.00073	0.988825
135	0.966	0.01808	0.00003	16.18	0.00062	0.992156
140	0.966	0.01521	0.00003	16.18	0.00052	0.994958
145	0.966	0.01279	0.00002	16.18	0.00043	0.997315
150	0.966	0.01076	0.00002	16.18	0.00036	0.999298

TABLE 3

Estimates of life-table components for a snapping turtle population under four management scenarios. Scenario One is the protection of eggs from predation in the field (EP), followed by release of hatchlings (HR). Scenario Two is the protection of eggs from predation in the field, followed by headstarting of hatchlings for one year (HS). Scenario Three is the artificial incubation of eggs (EI), followed by release of hatchlings. Scenario Four is the artificial incubation of eggs, followed by headstarting of hatchlings for one year. Year class (YC) 0 is defined as the egg incubation period, ending with the emergence of the hatchling from the egg. Key: s_x = survival during year x; l_x = proportion of cohort remaining at beginning of year x.

	\multicolumn{8}{c}{Management Scenarios}							
	One (EP+HR)		Two (EP+HS)		Three (EI+HR)		Four (EI+HS)	
YC	s_x^1	l_x^2	s_x	l_x	s_x	l_x	s_x	l_x
0	0.064	1.000	0.064	1.000	0.946	1.000	0.946	1.000
1	0.828	0.064	0.857	0.064	0.828	0.946	0.871	0.946
2	0.828	0.053	0.828	0.054	0.828	0.783	0.828	0.824
3	0.828	0.044	0.828	0.045	0.828	0.648	0.828	0.682
4	0.828	0.036	0.828	0.037	0.828	0.537	0.828	0.565
5	0.828	0.030	0.828	0.031	0.828	0.444	0.828	0.468
6	0.828	0.025	0.828	0.026	0.828	0.368	0.828	0.387
7	0.828	0.020	0.828	0.021	0.828	0.305	0.828	0.321
8	0.828	0.017	0.828	0.018	0.828	0.252	0.828	0.265
9	0.828	0.014	0.828	0.015	0.828	0.209	0.828	0.220
10	0.828	0.012	0.828	0.012	0.828	0.173	0.828	0.182
11	0.828	0.010	0.828	0.010	0.828	0.143	0.828	0.151
12	0.828	0.008	0.828	0.008	0.828	0.119	0.828	0.125
13	0.828	0.007	0.828	0.007	0.828	0.098	0.828	0.103
14	0.828	0.005	0.828	0.006	0.828	0.081	0.828	0.085
15	0.828	0.005	0.828	0.005	0.828	0.067	0.828	0.071
16	0.828	0.004	0.828	0.004	0.828	0.056	0.828	0.059
17	0.828	0.003	0.828	0.003	0.828	0.046	0.828	0.049
18	0.828	0.003	0.828	0.003	0.828	0.038	0.828	0.040
19	0.966	0.002	0.966	0.002	0.966	0.032	0.966	0.033
20	0.966	0.002	0.966	0.002	0.966	0.031	0.966	0.032
21	0.966	0.002	0.966	0.002	0.966	0.029	0.966	0.031
22	0.966	0.002	0.966	0.002	0.966	0.028	0.966	0.030
23	0.966	0.002	0.966	0.002	0.966	0.028	0.966	0.029
24	0.966	0.002	0.966	0.002	0.966	0.027	0.966	0.028
25	0.966	0.002	0.966	0.002	0.966	0.026	0.966	0.027
26	0.966	0.002	0.966	0.002	0.966	0.025	0.966	0.026
27	0.966	0.002	0.966	0.002	0.966	0.024	0.966	0.025
28	0.966	0.002	0.966	0.002	0.966	0.023	0.966	0.024
29	0.966	0.002	0.966	0.002	0.966	0.022	0.966	0.024
30	0.966	0.001	0.966	0.002	0.966	0.022	0.966	0.023
31	0.966	0.001	0.966	0.001	0.966	0.021	0.966	0.022
32	0.966	0.001	0.966	0.001	0.966	0.020	0.966	0.021
33	0.966	0.001	0.966	0.001	0.966	0.019	0.966	0.020
34	0.966	0.001	0.966	0.001	0.966	0.019	0.966	0.020
35	0.966	0.001	0.966	0.001	0.966	0.018	0.966	0.019

TABLE 4

Estimated appreciated costs of snapping turtles of various year classes (YC). Based on an estimated cost of protecting nests in the field of $0.90 per hatchling (Scenario One), headstarting hatchlings after *in situ* incubation of $7.21 per yearling (Scenario Two), incubating eggs *ex situ* and releasing the hatchlings of $3.52 per hatchling (Scenario Three), and *ex situ* incubation followed by head start of $9.83 per yearling (Scenario Four). Key: H_x = number of hatchlings or yearlings needed to be released to provide one surviving animal of year class x; C_x = total cost of hatchlings or yearlings represented by a single survivor in year class x.

YC	One (EP+HR) H_x^1	C_x^2	Two (EP+HS) H_x	C_x	Three (EI+HR) H_x	C_x	Four (EI+HS) H_x	C_x
1	1.00	$0.90			1.00	$3.52		
2	1.21	$1.09	1.00	$7.21	1.21	$4.25	1.00	$9.83
3	1.46	$1.31	1.21	$8.71	1.46	$5.14	1.21	$11.87
4	1.76	$1.59	1.46	$10.52	1.76	$6.20	1.46	$14.34
5	2.13	$1.92	1.76	$12.70	2.13	$7.49	1.76	$17.32
6	2.57	$2.31	2.13	$15.34	2.57	$9.05	2.13	$20.92
7	3.10	$2.79	2.57	$18.53	3.10	$10.93	2.57	$25.27
8	3.75	$3.37	3.10	$22.38	3.75	$13.20	3.10	$30.52
9	4.53	$4.08	3.75	$27.04	4.53	$15.94	3.75	$36.86
10	5.47	$4.92	4.53	$32.66	5.47	$19.26	4.53	$44.52
11	6.61	$5.95	5.47	$39.44	6.61	$23.26	5.47	$53.77
12	7.98	$7.18	6.61	$47.64	7.98	$28.09	6.61	$64.95
13	9.64	$8.67	7.98	$57.54	9.64	$33.93	7.98	$78.45
14	11.64	$10.48	9.64	$69.50	11.64	$40.98	9.64	$94.75
15	14.06	$12.66	11.64	$83.94	14.0	$49.50	11.64	$114.44
16	16.98	$15.29	14.06	$101.38	16.98	$59.78	14.06	$138.22
17	20.51	$18.46	16.98	$122.45	20.51	$72.21	16.98	$166.95
18	24.78	$22.30	20.51	$147.90	24.78	$87.21	20.51	$201.65
19	29.93	$26.93	24.78	$178.64	29.93	$105.34	24.78	$243.55
20	30.98	$27.88	25.65	$184.92	30.98	$109.04	25.65	$252.12
21	32.07	$28.86	26.55	$191.43	32.07	$112.88	26.55	$261.00
22	33.20	$29.88	27.49	$198.17	33.20	$116.86	27.49	$270.18
23	34.37	$30.93	28.45	$205.15	34.37	$120.97	28.45	$279.69
24	35.58	$32.02	29.45	$212.37	35.58	$125.23	29.45	$289.54
25	36.83	$33.15	30.49	$219.84	36.83	$129.63	30.49	$299.73
26	38.12	$34.31	31.56	$227.58	38.12	$134.20	31.56	$310.28
27	39.47	$35.52	32.68	$235.59	39.47	$138.92	32.68	$321.20
28	40.85	$36.77	33.83	$243.88	40.85	$143.81	33.83	$332.50
29	42.29	$38.06	35.02	$252.46	42.29	$148.87	35.02	$344.21
30	43.78	$39.40	36.25	$261.35	43.78	$154.11	36.25	$356.32
31	45.32	$40.79	37.52	$270.55	45.32	$159.53	37.52	$368.86
32	46.92	$42.23	38.84	$280.07	46.92	$165.15	38.84	$381.85
33	48.57	$43.71	40.21	$289.93	48.57	$170.96	40.21	$395.28
34	50.28	$45.25	41.63	$300.13	50.28	$176.98	41.63	$409.20
35	52.05	$46.84	43.09	$310.70	52.05	$183.21	43.09	$423.60

(Galbraith and Brooks, 1987), an average of 16.18 female-producing eggs per female per year (Brooks et al., 1988), and an age at first reproduction of between 17 and 19 years (Galbraith et al., 1989). Although a direct estimate of juvenile survivorship has not been possible, an average of approximately one new female recruited per year suggests that annual juvenile survivorship is no less than 75.4% per year.

In this population, net female reproduction is less than 60% of what is necessary to achieve a stable population (Brooks et al., 1988). In the present study, we have demonstrated that if this population is to remain stable in size, a mean juvenile survival rate of no less that 82.8% per year is necessary. In populations exhibiting great adult longevity, high juvenile survival, and highly stochastic egg survival, survival of adults outweighs survival of juveniles or hatchlings as the factor that most strongly affects population growth rate (Congdon et al., 1993).

There is a growing consensus (Congdon et al., 1994) that in most circumstances the life history constraints of turtles do not enable them to exhibit density-dependent population responses. This has rarely been tested directly. To test whether a population is capable of any density-dependent responses, it is necessary to either perform experiments in which density is manipulated or observe natural changes in density. In the Algonquin Park population, predation by river otters, *Lutra canadensis*, was observed. The life table can be used to predict the effects of various life history scenarios, such as predation or supplementation. For example, if the adult survivorship has been reduced to 90% per year from 96.6% per year by an increase in mortality, a 234% increase in egg production by females in all age classes is needed to bring the net replacement rate back to 1. In the Algonquin Park population, we have rejected the prediction that female snapping turtles would increase reproduction to compensate for decreased population density. Regardless of the location of the population, almost all conservation problems can be reduced to this crucial question: How does human interference at various stages of the life history affect subsequent persistence of the population? The discussion of appropriate technology regarding sea turtle conservation practices (Ehrenfeld, 1981; Frazer, 1991) can also be extended to the conservation of freshwater turtles. The intervention tactics chosen should be those that come closest to ameliorating the root cause of the problem.

The basic assumption underpinning the management of a renewable natural resource under commercial exploitation is that the resource is supplemented with an inexpensive seed source and that the growth process "adds value" to the seeded individuals. The value added can take two forms: the direct economic value of the product and the subsequent value to the resource for future reproduction should the individuals be allowed to reproduce.

To be economically sustainable, the value extracted from a resource under exploitation must exceed the cost of seeding, trapping, and other activities associated with the harvest. In addition, to be ecologically sustainable, the resource must be managed in such a way as to ensure the future survival of the resource in spite of exploitation.

We have demonstrated that free-living populations of snapping turtles in the northern areas of their range cannot respond to reduction in density and must have high adult and juvenile survivorship to persist. We have also demonstrated that programs to supplement free-living populations through egg incubation or headstarting are prohibitively expensive. These models have been made deliberately conservative by assuming no overhead costs, but by accounting only for a minimal cost of labor necessary to conduct the minimum of activities to manipulate survival rates in the first two age classes.

These models have also been made conservative by assuming that turtles produced through artificial manipulation are ecologically and demographically equivalent to hatchlings produced naturally *in situ*. This assumption may be false, as snapping turtles raised in the laboratory appear to have a high mortality rate once released into their parental habitat, even when headstarted to 10% of adult body size (R. J. Brooks, unpubl.).

If future exploitation of a population is premised on management intervention supported by the economic returns of present exploitation, then harvesting turtles under such circumstances is clearly not economically sustainable. Market values of snapping turtles in the early 1980s were $10 to $20 per turtle (Lovisek, 1982), equivalent to roughly $14 to $27 in 1990. Gross market prices fall far short of meeting our estimates of even the absolute minimum costs of intervention, which ranged from more than $45 per female to over $400 per female in this study.

One can envision other scenarios for management, such as the protection of females less than 30 cm carapace length, protection of females greater than 30 cm, augmentation of the population by relocation of individuals from other sources, or use of temperature-dependent sex determination to increase proportion of males and to harvest only males. It is unlikely, however, that any of these scenarios can be manipulated to produce a cost-effective population supplementation program.

These calculations demonstrate that turtle populations should be valued by wildlife managers, not by their market value but by their replacement value. These models also reinforce the need to consider the relative costs of habitat protection and population restoration in conservation programs. The total cost of a headstarting program, including infrastructure, equipment, and any necessary habitat restoration, will be much higher than the costs we have projected.

Therefore, planners of conservation programs for turtles must carefully weigh the costs of producing animals to replace depleted populations against the cost of protecting existing populations.

Population supplementation may be a useful conservation management tool under some circumstances. However, continuing exploitation of free-living turtle populations amounts to mining, not harvesting, and is neither financially nor biologically sustainable, particularly at the northern limits of a species' range. We urge wildlife biologists and management authorities to adopt the concept of valuing free-living natural resources by the cost of replacing consumptive human use rather than by attending only to short-term, unsustainable market value.

Literature Cited

Bobyn, M. L. and R. J. Brooks. In press. Incubation conditions as potential factors limiting the northern distribution of snapping turtles, *Chelydra serpentina*. Can. J. Zool.

Brooks, R. J., D. A. Galbraith, E. G. Nancekivell, and C. A. Bishop. 1988. Developing management guidelines for snapping turtles. *In* Management of Amphibians, Reptiles, and Small Mammals in North America (R. C. Szaro, K. E. Severson, and D. R. Patton, Tech. Coords.), pp. 174–179. USDA Forest Service, Gen. Tech. Rept. RM-166.

Brooks, R. J., M. L. Bobyn, D. A. Galbraith, J. A. Layfield, and E. G. Nancekivell. 1991a. Maternal and environmental influences on growth and survival of embryonic and hatchling snapping turtles (*Chelydra serpentina*). Can. J. Zool. 69:2667–2676.

Brooks, R. J., G. P. Brown, and D. A. Galbraith. 1991b. Effects of a sudden increase in natural mortality of adults on a population of the common snapping turtle (*Chelydra serpentina*). Can. J. Zool. 69:1314–1320.

Congdon, J. D., A. E. Dunham, and R. C. van Loben Sels. 1993. Delayed sexual maturity and demographics of Blanding's turtles (*Emydoidea blandingii*): Implications for conservation and management of long-lived organisms. Conserv. Biol. 7:826–833.

Congdon, J. D., A. E. Dunham, and R. C. van Loben Sels. 1994. Demographics of common snapping turtles (*Chelydra serpentina*): Implications for conservation and management of long-lived organisms. Amer. Zool. 34:397–408.

Ehrenfeld, D. 1981. Options and limitations in the conservation of sea turtles. *In* K. A. Bjorndal (ed.), Biology and Conservation of Sea Turtles, pp. 457–463. Smithsonian Inst. Press, Washington D.C.

Frazer, N. B. 1992. Sea turtle conservation and halfway technology. Conserv. Biol. 6:179–184.

Galbraith, D. A. and R. J. Brooks. 1987. Survivorship of adult females in a northern population of snapping turtles (*Chelydra serpentina*). Can. J. Zool. 65:1581–1586.

Galbraith, D. A. and R. J. Brooks. 1989. Age estimates for snapping turtles. J. Wildl. Manage. 53:502–508.

Galbraith, D. A., C. A. Bishop, R. J. Brooks, W. L. Simser, and K. Lampman. 1988. Factors affecting density of populations of common snapping turtles (*Chelydra serpentina serpentina*). Can. J. Zool. 66:1233–1240.

Galbraith, D. A., R. J. Brooks, and M. E. Obbard. 1989. The influence of growth on age and body size at maturity in female snapping turtles (*Chelydra serpentina*). Copeia 1989:896–904.

Loncke, D. J. and M. E. Obbard. 1977. Tag success, dimensions, clutch size and nesting site fidelity for the snapping turtle, *Chelydra serpentina* (Reptilia, Testudines, Chelydridae), in Algonquin Park, Ontario, Canada. J. Herpetol. 11:243–244.

Lovisek, J. 1982. An investigation of the harvesting of turtles in Ontario. Internal Report, Wildlife Branch, Ontario Ministry of Natural Resources.

Obbard, M. E. 1983. Population ecology of the common snapping turtle, *Chelydra serpentina*, in north-central Ontario. Ph.D. dissertation, Univ. Guelph, Guelph, Ontario.

Effects of Geographic Origin and Incubation Temperature on Hatchling Snapping Turtles, *Chelydra serpentina*: Implications for Turtle Conservation Practices across the Species' Range

HEATHER L. PASSMORE AND RONALD J. BROOKS

Department of Zoology, University of Guelph, Guelph, Ontario N1G 2W1, Canada

ABSTRACT: Snapping turtle eggs from four distinct populations across the species' North American range were artificially incubated at constant temperatures bordering the two pivotal, sex-determining temperatures. The hatchlings were then reared under constant laboratory conditions to investigate differences in survival in relation to incubation temperatures, geographic origin, and food availability. Both embryo and hatchling mortality were higher in eggs incubated under colder temperatures, particularly in the northernmost population. Embryo mortality was high in eggs from the two southern populations, but hatchlings from those populations had significantly lower mortality than hatchlings from the two northern populations. Variation in embryo viability and hatchling survival between populations indicates that each population responds differently to similar conditions in captivity, and each population should be considered unique with respect to criteria affecting population and individual survival and growth.

Our findings and those of others indicate that captive rearing of hatchlings of freshwater turtles may produce animals with poor rates of survival. The financial costs associated with this practice, the minimal potential for population recovery as evidenced by life table analysis, and many years of unsuccessful release experiments indicate that captive rearing and headstarting practices should be reconsidered in favor of other, more effective conservation programs.

Snapping turtles inhabit freshwater streams and marshes with soft mud bottoms and abundant aquatic vegetation (Ernst and Barbour, 1989) within a broad geographic range extending from their northern limit in Ontario and Quebec, west to southeastern Alberta, south to the Texas coast in the U.S., and from central Mexico and Central America to Ecuador (Ernst and Barbour, 1989). This range is exceptional for a reptile and affords an excellent opportunity to test hypotheses on adaptations to local conditions in long-lived ectotherms (Galbraith et al., 1987).

Ectothermy

In ectotherms, body temperature plays a key role in rates of physiological processes, growth, and maturation (Huey and Hertz, 1984; Knight et al., 1990) and may also play a role in ecologically important behavior patterns such as locomotion and feeding (Dawson, 1975; Huey and Stevenson, 1979; Huey and Hertz, 1984). The physiological attributes of an ectotherm are thus constrained by environmental challenges. Proximate constraints may take the form of resource availability, harvesting and processing rates, and predation pressures (Congdon, 1989). Turtles in far northern populations face additional constraints because of the gradient of decreasing temperatures with increasing latitude (Congdon, 1989; Galbraith et al., 1988). Constraints in incubation time may restrict the northern limit of the distribution of this species (Bobyn and Brooks, 1994a) and may affect the demography of such populations near the limits of their range (Congdon et al., 1993; Galbraith et al., this volume).

Comparisons of life history traits of turtles from diverse populations may reveal fundamental adaptations and aid in understanding the diversity between these biological systems. Interpretation of intraspecific adaptations within the environmental context will provide insight into the patterns of these adaptations (Dawson, 1987). Examination of these adaptive specializations may illuminate the limiting factors in the development and life history of turtles, and this knowledge will be valuable in constructing effective strategies for conservation of threatened populations, particularly near the limits of their distributions.

Incubation Conditions

The thermal environment is a critical component of successful incubation of turtle eggs because it may affect embryonic metabolism, length of incubation, hatchling size and post-hatching survival, growth and behavior (Packard et al., 1977; Yntema, 1978; Morris et al., 1983; Brooks et al., 1991; Burger, 1991; Bobyn, 1992; Van Damme et al., 1992; Packard et al., 1993; Bobyn and Brooks, 1994a, 1994b). Temperature during incubation may have important consequences for projects utilizing artificial incubation for headstarting programs (Mrosovsky and Yntema, 1980) not only because some turtles, such as *Chelydra serpentina*, exhibit environmental sex determination (Bull and Vogt, 1979; Vogt and Bull, 1982; Janzen and Paukstis, 1991) but also because temperature affects hatching success and the post-hatching survival of hatchlings (Brooks et al., 1991).

We report on the potential of incubation temperature to affect conservation programs. These effects of incubation temperatures have important implications for the recruitment rates and population dynamics of freshwater turtles and must be considered when formulating conservation strategies for these species.

Geographic Variation

We compared the effects of ambient temperature and food availability on survival of hatchling turtles from different populations and tested whether these differences represent phenotypically plastic responses to local differences in climate, or genetic differences that represent adaptations to specific conditions (Stearns, 1989; Bernardo, 1994). Specifically, we tested the hypothesis that snapping turtles show adaptive variation to local differences in climate and incubation conditions by testing for interpopulation differences in egg viability and hatchling survival under different temperature regimes.

If the observed variation between populations were actually phenotypic plasticity, with different phenotypes expressed under different conditions (Ferguson and Brockman, 1980; Stearns, 1989), we predicted that under uniform ambient conditions, zero predation pressure, and constant food availability these populations should show no differences in survival and growth rates.

The examination of the population parameters and their relationships with life history traits is useful in determining how conservation and management practices may be conducted most effectively within each population. Due to the extensive range of many species and the consequent diversity in their habitats, broad conservation techniques may not be sufficient for the effective management of such species. Each population may have to be regarded as unique, with distinct life history parameters and requirements for maximum persistence and growth.

MATERIALS AND METHODS

Egg Incubation and Hatchling Rearing

Snapping turtle eggs from Algonquin Park in north-central Ontario (45°38′ N, 78°22′ W), Cootes' Paradise in southwest Ontario (43°17′ N, 79°53′ W), Iowa (41° N, 93° W), and Alabama (30° N, 88° W) were obtained in June 1991 as representative samples from northern (Cook, 1984), central, and southern populations within the species' North American range. (Eggs from both Iowa and Alabama sources were obtained from commercial collectors.)

Incubation procedures followed those of Bobyn and Brooks (1994a, 1994b) and Brooks et al. (1991), except for the following changes: Viable eggs (those with an obvious white spot) from all populations were assigned equally and randomly to incubators (Koolatron Corp., Brantford, Ontario). A total of eight incubators were used; two were set at each of four temperatures: 21.5 ±0.46°C, 22.0 ±0.21°C, 26.5 ±0.29°C, and 27.5 ±0.33°C. Total numbers of apparently healthy eggs placed in incubators were 586 (Algonquin Park), 138 (Cootes' Paradise), 120 (Alabama), and 117 (Iowa). Eggs were assigned equally and positioned randomly within each of the three plastic boxes (22 × 23 cm) within each incubator to a maximum of 40 eggs per box. Vermiculite (medium grain Terra-Lite, horticultural grade, W. R. Grace Co., Ajax, Ontario) and distilled water (0.91 g /1 ml) (Morris et al., 1983; Packard et al., 1987; Bobyn, 1992) was used as a moisture-retaining, non-toxic substrate within each egg box.

When the first signs of pipping occurred in an incubator, all eggs at that temperature were removed. To facilitate individual identification on hatching, each egg was then placed in an individual 100 ml glass jar half filled with vermiculite of the same water potential as that in the incubator. The jars were loosely capped to provide air exchange. The eggs were left until the turtles had completed hatching.

On the day of hatching the turtles were washed of adhering vermiculite and membranes, patted dry with paper towels, weighed to the nearest 0.1 g (Mettle PJ3600 balance), and individually tagged with small wire loops on the posterior marginal scutes (Galbraith and Brooks, 1984; Layfield et al., 1988). Gross linear measurements were taken (carapace length, carapace width, carapace height, and plastron length) with callipers to the nearest 0.1 cm, and any deformities were noted. Turtles were then placed in small, plastic mouse cages to a maximum number of 15 hatchlings per cage. After all turtles had hatched, the turtles were assigned equally and randomly (by population and incubation temperature) to large plastic bins (107 cu lit Tupperware® containers) to a maximum of 25 hatchlings per bin. Water depth in the bins did not exceed 9 cm and the turtles were provided with rocks for basking. Bivalve shells and pieces of cuttlebone were added to the water to provide calcium for strengthening of the shell. Once all the turtles had hatched, the bins were moved to a photoperiod- and temperature-controlled room (12 h dark/12 h light at 24°C) (Murphy and Collins, 1982; Bobyn, 1992). Vita-Lite® fluorescent bulbs (Durotest Corp., Rexdale, Ontario) were used to as a source of simulated sunlight to provide the turtles with ultraviolet light (Murphy and Collins, 1982).

Hatchlings were allowed approximately one month to absorb their yolk sacs, after which they were fed a mixed diet, high in protein and calcium (Froom, 1976; Campbell and

Busack, 1979), primarily of chopped, whole freshwater fish, supplemented with mealworms and chicken livers, gizzards, and hearts. Occasionally, Trout Chow® pellets (starter and floating, Martin Feed Mills, Elmira, Ontario) were also offered. All meat was dusted with vitamin powder (Pervinal®, St. Aubroy, Brentwood, New York). Campbell and Busack (1979) recommended chicken liver as part of a high protein and calcium diet, particularly for captive hatchlings. It contains no exogenous and few endogenous hormones and may be considered safe as part of a turtle's diet (Department of Animal and Poultry Science, University of Guelph, pers. comm.). All food was provided *ad libitum* twice a week. This feeding schedule was continued for an additional two months to allow turtles to become accustomed to eating and to properly digest the provided diet. Turtles from each site and incubation temperature were randomly assigned to one of two feeding protocols. In one protocol, turtles were fed an excess diet (*ad libitum*) three times per week. In the second protocol, turtles were fed a restricted diet of food once per week (*ad libitum*). Each protocol was replicated five times for a total of ten bins. Each feeding protocol was conducted for a minimum of 104 weeks. The Tupperware holding bins were cleaned 24 hours after feeding. The bins were relocated in the room on the day of cleaning to eliminate any possible effects of positioning within the room. To reduce effects of crowding, the numbers of bins were increased and the numbers of turtles within each bin were reduced as the turtles grew.

Statistical Analysis

The response variables that we measured throughout these experiments were: embryo survival, stage at which embryo died, size at hatching, and hatchling survival. We used mass as the indicator of egg size (Packard et al., 1981; Congdon et al., 1983) and hatchling size (Packard et al., 1981; Sarnat et al., 1981; Ewert, 1985). The effects of geographic location on egg mass were analyzed with an ANOVA (SAS Institute, 1985).

Hatching success was analyzed after LOGIT transformation to normalize the data and stabilize the variability. The proportion of eggs successfully completing embryonic development was normalized using a LOGIT transformation (Snedecor and Cochran, 1989). This transformation uses a constant "C" to normalize proportion data and stabilize the variability (Snedecor and Cochran, 1989; Kuehl, 1994). The effects of location of origin and incubation protocols were analyzed with an ANOVA (SAS Institute, 1985).

The experimental unit in this experiment is the individual egg box within each incubator. There were two replications of each of the four incubation temperatures, and there were three experimental units nested within each incubator. Masses at hatching from the four populations and incubation temperatures were analyzed using SAS, taking into account the experimental units. The hatch weights were normalized with a log transformation before analysis.

Survival analysis (Lawless, 1982; Bobyn and Brooks, 1994a, 1994b) was used to determine the hazard or risk experienced by the hatchlings. We used the SAS procedure PROC LIFE Test, which calculates product-moment estimates of the survival distribution function for each treatment category and therefore provides a more realistic representation of the hatchlings' survival throughout the experimental period than do methods in which calculations are based on whether an animal was alive or dead by a certain period of time (Lawless, 1982; Bobyn, 1992). Hatchling survival was monitored from hatching in fall 1991 until December 1993.

RESULTS

Hatching Success

Population of origin had a significant effect on egg hatching success ($F = 34.224$, $df = 3$, $P < 0.0001$) (Table 1). Multiple *t*-tests (LSD) indicated significant differences in viability of eggs between all populations except Algonquin Park and Cootes' Paradise (Table 1). Overall, there were no significant temperature effects ($F = 0.113$, $df = 3$, $P = 0.94813$) or temperature-population interactions ($F = 1.277$, $df = 9$, $P = 0.33908$) on embryo survival. In a separate analysis, incubation temperature significantly affected egg hatching rate in the Algonquin Park population (H. Passmore, unpubl. data). Multiple *t*-tests (LSD) showed significant differences between, but not within, the high and low temperatures for Algonquin Park, indicating a higher hatching success at the higher incubation temperatures (H. Passmore, unpubl. data).

Survival Analysis

Survival analysis showed significant effects of population (Log-Rank Chi-square = 116.9307, $df = 3$, $P < 0.0001$) (Table 2) and incubation temperature (Log-Rank Chi-square = 35.2858, $df = 3$, $P < 0.0001$) on the survival of the hatchlings. There was a decrease in hatchling survival with an increase in latitude. Survival increased with an increase in incubation temperature, with the highest survival from incubation temperatures of 26.5°C (H. Passmore, unpubl. data). Feeding regime did not have a significant effect on the survival of the hatchlings (Log-Rank Chi-square = 0.0079, $df = 1$, $P = 0.9294$).

DISCUSSION

We investigated interpopulation differences in egg viability and survival in hatchling snapping turtles incubated at different temperatures. Geographic origin and incubation temperatures are major influences on differences in egg size

TABLE 1
Numbers of eggs that hatched and failed to hatch within each population.

Population	% Survival	Hatched	Failed	LSD
Algonquin Park	91.47	536	50	A
Cootes' Paradise	88.41	122	16	A
Iowa	70.69	82	34	B
Alabama	42.50	51	69	C

Percent survival was calculated using back transformation from logit transformation of egg hatchability.

TABLE 2
Survival from hatching (fall 1991) to end of experimental period (December 1993) within each population.

Population	Total hatched	Failed	Survived	% Survived
Algonquin Park	219	215	4	1.8
Cootes' Paradise	121	109	12	10
Iowa	83	60	23	27.7
Alabama	50	24	26	52

(Moll and Legler, 1971; Moll, 1979; Passmore, 1996), embryo viability (Bobyn and Brooks, 1994a, 1994b; this study), hatchling size (Passmore, 1996), and survival (Bobyn and Brooks, 1994a, 1994b; this study). This variation may reflect latitudinal gradients in environmental variables such as ambient temperature, productivity, and length of growing season, which may be producing genotypic differences among these populations that are manifested upon exposure to these environmental constraints. These variations between geographically distinct populations may be adaptations to environmental conditions experienced by natural populations (Galbraith et al., 1988; Bobyn and Brooks, 1994a, 1994b).

We found that an overall decrease in hatchling survival in laboratory conditions in populations from higher latitudes. Post-hatching survivorship was lowest in turtles from the northern limit of the range and from the site in central Ontario, which is heavily contaminated with organochlorine toxins (Bishop et al., 1991). Within the northern populations, survival increased with increased incubation temperatures. In fact, these hatchlings survived best after exposure to incubation temperatures higher than those they would usually experience in the natural environment. It would be expected that turtles from northern populations would have evolved with lower ambient temperatures (Brown and Brooks, 1991, 1993) and would therefore be adapted to these temperatures. However, the northern turtles in our study appeared to be especially susceptible to lower incubation temperatures, which had lasting negative effects on post-hatching survival (Brooks et al., 1991; Bobyn and Brooks, 1994b).

We have hypothesized that this occurs because exposure to low incubation temperatures at the species' northern limit is usually correlated with cooler, shorter summers and fewer heat units (Arnold, 1960; Obbard and Brooks, 1981a; Obbard and Brooks, 1981b; Bobyn and Brooks, 1994a). In these cool summers, most or all snapping turtle nests fail to complete incubation before winter and succumb to low temperatures during winter (Obbard and Brooks, 1981b). Therefore, only embryos exposed to warmer temperatures will survive, which would effectively prevent selection for adaptation to low temperatures.* Our data support this hypothesis, but a thorough test should examine this relationship in other species by comparing populations in areas in which incubation is usually completed despite the low incubation temperatures with those in areas in which low temperatures frequently prevent completion of incubation.

---

* Incubation temperatures of 21.5°C are considered low as embryological development does not proceed below or at 20°C (Yntema, 1976, 1978). The incubation temperatures of 21.5°C and 22.0°C fall within the lower range of ambient summer temperatures normally experienced by this northern population (23.4°C, Obbard and Brooks, 1979; 24.9°C, Brown et al., 1990; 16.8°C, Brown et al., 1994) and are also temperatures occurring within the nests (R. J. Brooks, unpubl. data). The poor post-hatching survival from eggs incubated at 21.5°C and 22.0°C (Brooks et al., 1991; Bobyn and Brooks, 1994b; this study) suggests a lack of adaptation to these cooler temperatures within this northern population.

The lower productivity (Galbraith et al., 1988) in these northern habitats may affect the resource harvesting rates by the turtles (Congdon, 1989). This constraint, coupled with lower environmental temperatures, in turn affects the processing rates of these resources (Congdon, 1989). Gibbons (1970) showed that turtles in warmer habitats had higher growth rates and attained larger body sizes than turtles in cooler habitats. This result coincides with the positive relationship between body temperature and gut clearance rate (Crawford et al., 1983). However, in sockeye salmon, *Oncorhynchus nerka*, the optimum temperature for growth was shunted from 15 to 5°C when food resources were limited (Hutchison and Maness, 1979). Such shifts probably also occur in some turtles (e.g., Brown and Brooks, 1991) and therefore, a positive correlation between ambient temperature and growth rates or body size would not always be expected, particularly as other factors could be more important in determining adult body size. Lowered metabolism (and consequent lowered energy requirements) during inactive periods or in habitats where productivity is low may be adaptive.

Our study suggests there are genetic differences adapting each population to the ambient temperature and environmental conditions, which is consistent with earlier findings (Galbraith et al., 1988; Brooks et al., 1991; Bobyn and Brooks, 1994b). Variation between populations in egg size, percent of eggs hatched, mass at hatching, growth, and survivorship of hatchlings indicates that each population of turtles should be considered unique with respect to population parameters and the criteria for maximum survival and growth of laboratory-reared eggs and hatchlings. Therefore, conservation strategies aimed at such widespread species as *Chelydra serpentina* should be specific to each individual population.

We found through this long-term captive rearing project that incubation temperature has profound effects on the subsequent survival of the hatchlings. In general, hatchlings (particularly those from Algonquin Park) did not survive well in our study, which was in contrast to an earlier study on the Algonquin population (Brooks et al., 1991). We suggest two possible reasons for our observed high mortality.

Confining our turtles in groups may have contributed to the high mortality we observed. Snapping turtles are not social animals, and placing them in groups may stress them. Few studies have been conducted on the social interactions of snapping turtles, but results indicate larger animals are more aggressive, intimidating, and successful in group feedings (Froese and Burghardt, 1974; Passmore, 1996). Rearing turtles in isolation does successfully produce larger turtles (McKnight and Gutzke, 1993), but the impracticality of such conditions in the context of headstarting programs outweighs economic and logistic benefits conferred by the elimination of social interaction.

Our rearing experiments were conducted under constant conditions. These conditions may be unsuitable for populations that normally experience hibernation and varying photoperiods. We found, as have others (Bobyn, 1992), that high numbers of hatchlings from northern populations died approximately four months after hatching. This mortality occurred when the animals, under natural conditions, would be in hibernation. The ambient temperatures in the laboratory did not provide the stimulus necessary for the turtles to go into dormancy. The high mortality of our northern turtles may be due to the fact they were not given the opportunity to hibernate. Although hatchlings were reared under conditions similar to those of natural populations during spring and summer (Brown et al., 1990), they still did not survive well in captivity, which suggests that optimal survival conditions are not provided by simply mimicking ambient temperatures and photoperiod of the natural growing season.

Interpopulation variation in rate of hatching and hatchling survival in relation to incubation temperature and geographic origin of population has important implications for headstarting programs and other conservation practices across the species' range. Headstarting involves the rearing of hatchlings in captivity until they are of sufficient size to circumvent predation by size-specific predators (Pritchard, 1980; Ehrenfeld, 1981; Frazer, 1992). Long-term headstarting projects must consider whether the animals that have been raised under conditions of reliable food, no predation, and lack of hibernation and sufficient exercise will actually be successful upon release, especially when they have been shown not to do well in captivity. The early environment of the snapping turtle has long-term influences (McKnight and Gutzke, 1993), even though this early period is relatively short for this long-lived reptile. Sarnat et al. (1981) found that an artificial diet was a limiting factor to growth in captive painted turtles. The captive-rearing studies imply that, even in captivity, these animals do not flourish, and overall long-term survival of these animals in the wild is doubtful.

There is no reliable evidence that any headstarted juvenile sea turtles have survived to reproductive age, and other problems have elicited considerable skepticism concerning the effectiveness of headstarting (Ehrenfeld, 1981; Frazer, 1992). From a conservation perspective this suggests that captive rearing of hatchlings is not beneficial to these animals in the long term. Also, it suggests that not all species may be amenable to headstarting, even the hardy snapper. Our results with headstarting *Chelydra serpentina* certainly do not raise confidence in the practice. Not only do turtles from some populations have poor post-hatching survival in captivity, even when fed *ad libitum*, but releases of more than 3,500 hatchlings and 1–2-year-old juveniles appear to have less than 1% survival after five years (R. J. Brooks, unpubl. data). Furthermore, life table analysis suggests that increasing the number of hatchlings or very young juveniles will have little impact on the population relative to the effects of maintaining high juvenile and adult survival (Congdon et al., 1993; Cunnington and Brooks, 1996).

Artificial incubation can skew sex ratios even if the incubation temperature is only one or two degrees from the pivotal value (Mrosovsky and Yntema, 1980; Pritchard, 1980). Skewed sex ratios may occur if population-specific pivotal temperatures are not taken into account (Passmore, 1996). Artificial incubation may also not correctly replicate temperatures experienced in natural environments. We have no evidence that pivotal temperatures vary systematically with latitude (Passmore, 1996), but there is significant variation between populations even within Ontario (Passmore, 1996). Artificial conditions are much different from the natural conditions (Froese and Burghardt, 1974) these animals would normally experience. Captive rearing projects, even when there are attempts to match all the pertinent factors, do not provide all the ecological variables that are necessary for the success of hatchlings (Ehrenfeld, 1981; Frazer, 1992).

The ecological environment to which the hatchling is exposed may be of vital importance to its development, survival, and well-being (Ehrenfeld, 1981), and there may be more interactions than we as researchers consider necessary for the hatchlings' survival. The ecological role of the hatchlings (Ehrenfeld, 1981; Frazer, 1992), as well as potential disadvantages of captive-reared hatchlings compared to wild (Frazer, 1992), are significant factors when implementing any captive rearing program. To be successful, conservation practices must be in accordance with the ecology of the animal in question. Without detailed understanding of the local circumstances or population variation, conservation practices will not work (Ehrenfeld, 1981). Each population should be considered as unique when applying conservation practices.

When dealing with the conservation of long-lived animals, any practices implemented now will often not have immediately noticeable consequences (Ehrenfeld, 1981). Good intentions through headstarting and artificial incubation may be inadvertently hazardous to the long-term survival of these animals. In populations where hatching success and hatchling survival are limiting factors, we think that incubation in natural conditions *in situ*, where predation is controlled and/or intercepted by nest protection with wire mesh, may be the most sensible practice (Pritchard, 1980; Ehrenfeld, 1981). This can be completed with a minimum of equipment and cost (Galbraith et al., this volume).

CONCLUSIONS

Incubation temperature and geographic origin of populations and the interaction of these variables had profound influences on survival and growth rates of embryonic and hatchling snapping turtles. These effects were expressed strongly even when hatchlings were reared in a common environment, suggesting that the differences were not phenotypic expression of adaptive norms, but rather were direct expression of interpopulational genetic differences. We interpreted these differences largely as expression of local adaptation, but of course they may not be adaptive to the specific test conditions. In any case, the important part of our findings in relation to conservation and management programs that involve artificial incubation or headstarting are obvious.

First, populations of the same species may differ markedly in their response to specific environmental variables. Therefore, using a single incubation temperature across populations may produce noticeably inferior hatchlings in terms of survival and growth. In species that exhibit environmental sex determination, sex ratios could be heavily skewed if pivotal temperatures vary across populations.

Second, our data suggest the possibility that mass rearing of hatchlings—even under conditions thought to be ideal with *ad libitum* food—may produce animals with poor rates of survival, even in captivity. Mass release of hatchlings in the Algonquin Park populations suggests poor survival. Whether poor survival of our turtles in laboratory conditions is due to crowding, nutritional deficiencies, undetected disease, or failure to allow the turtles to hibernate or experience their natural climatic variations is unknown. However the implications of our results are clear for conservation. If captive turtles do not survive well in a laboratory environment or after release from a laboratory environment, then headstarting programs cannot be justified and funds and efforts should be focused elsewhere in conservation strategies. Headstarting has also been deemed ineffective in aiding recovery of populations because of the life history of this reptile. The release of thousands of hatchlings in Algonquin Park over the years with no recaptures have clearly illustrated this. Conservation programs should concentrate on the more proximate causes of declining populations, such as loss of nesting sites and/or loss of breeding adults, which may be more effective than the production of additional young turtles before these issues have been properly addressed. If laboratory-released, headstarted animals are inferior to wild-born hatchlings or if the population is declining because of deteriorating habitat or loss of habitat, then the effectiveness of headstarting will be compromised even further.

ACKNOWLEDGMENTS

We would like to thank C. Bishop for Cootes' Paradise egg collection, L. Standing and E. G. Nancekivell for skilled field assistance, and W. Mathes-Sears for statistical advice. We thank the many volunteers who helped feed and maintain the hatchlings, particularly K. Halling and S. Solomon; L. Shirose for reviewing earlier drafts of this manuscript and offering helpful advice and recommendations; and fellow lab-mates M. Bobyn, G. Brown, D. Foscarini, and J. Litzgus for stimulating discussion during the project and preparation of this manuscript. Research for this paper was funded by NSERC grant A5990 to R. J. Brooks.

LITERATURE CITED

Arnold, C. Y. 1960. Maximum and minimum temperatures as a basis for computing heat units. Am. Soc. Hortic. Sci. 76:682–692.

Bernardo, J. 1994. Experimental analysis of allocation in two divergent, natural salamander populations. Amer. Nat. 143(1): 14–38.

Bishop, C. A., R. J. Brooks, J. H. Carey, P. O. Ng, R. J. Norstrom, and D. R. S. Lean. 1991. The case for a cause-effect linkage between environmental contamination and development in eggs of the common snapping turtle (*Chelydra s. serpentina*) from Ontario, Canada. J. of Toxicology and Env. Health 33:521–547.

Bobyn, M. L. 1992. Effects of incubation conditions on sex, survival and growth of hatchling snapping turtles (*Chelydra serpentina*) (Linné). M.S. thesis, Univ. of Guelph, Guelph, Ontario.

Bobyn, M. L. and R. J. Brooks. 1994a. Incubation conditions as potential factors limiting the northern distribution of the snapping turtle, *Chelydra serpentina*. Can. J. Zool. 72(1):28–37.

Bobyn, M. L. and R. J. Brooks. 1994b. Interclutch and interpopulation variation in the effects of incubation conditions on sex, survival and growth in hatchling turtles (*Chelydra serpentina*). J. Zool. (London) 233(2):233–257.

Brooks, R. J., M. L. Bobyn, D. A. Galbraith, J. A. Layfield, and E. G. Nancekivell. 1991. Maternal and environmental influences on growth and survival of embryonic and hatchling snapping turtles (*Chelydra serpentina*). Can. J. Zool. 69(10):2667–2676.

Brown, G. P. and R. J. Brooks. 1991. Thermal and behavioral responses to feeding in free-ranging turtles, *Chelydra serpentina*. J. Herpetol. 25(3):273–278.

Brown, G. P. and R. J. Brooks. 1993. Sexual and seasonal differences in activity in a northern population of snapping turtles, *Chelydra serpentina*. Herpetologica 49(3):311–318.

Bull, J. J. and R. C. Vogt. 1979. Temperature-dependent sex determination in turtles. Science 206:1186–1188.

Burger, J. 1991. Effects of incubation temperature on behaviour of hatchling pine snakes: Implications for reptilian distribution. Behavioral Ecology and Sociobiology 28:297–303.

Campbell, H. W. and S. D. Busack. 1979. Laboratory maintenance. *In* M. Harless and H. Morlock (eds.), Turtles: Perspectives and Research, pp. 109–125. John Wiley and Sons, New York.

Congdon, J. D. 1989. Proximate and evolutionary constraints on energy relations of reptiles. Physiol. Zool. 62(2):356–373.

Congdon, J. D., D. W. Tinkle, and P. C. Rosen. 1983. Egg components and utilization during development in aquatic turtles. Copeia 1983(1):264–268.

Congdon, J. D., A. E. Dunham, and R. C. van Loben Sels. 1993. Delayed sexual maturity and demographics of Blanding's turtles (*Emydoidea blandingii*): Implications for conservation and management of long-lived organisms. Conserv. Biol. 7(4):826–833.

Cook, F. R. 1984. Introduction to Canadian Amphibians and Reptiles. National Museum of Natural Sciences, Ottawa. 200 pp.

Crawford, K. M., J. R. Spotila, and E. A. Standora. 1983. Operative environmental temperatures and basking behavior of the turtle *Pseudemys scripta*. Ecology 64:989–999.

Cunnington, D. C. and R. J. Brooks. 1996. Bet-hedging theory and eigenelasticity: A comparison of the life histories of loggerhead sea turtles (*Caretta caretta*) and snapping turtles (*Chelydra serpentina*). Can. J. Zool. 74:291–296.

Dawson, W. R. 1975. On the physiological significance of the preferred body temperatures of reptiles. *In* D. M. Gates and R. B. Scherl (eds.), Perspectives of Biophysical Ecology (Ecological Studies, Vol. 12), pp. 443–473. Springer-Verlag, New York.

Dawson, W. R. 1987. Comparisons of species and populations: A discussion. *In* M. E. Feder, A. F. Bennett, W. W. Burggren, and R. B. Huey (eds.), New Directions in Ecological Physiology, pp. 135–144. Cambridge University Press, New York.

Ehrenfeld, D. 1981. Options and limitations in the conservation of sea turtles. *In* K. A. Bjorndal (ed.), Biology and Conservation of Sea Turtles, pp. 457–463. Smithsonian Inst. Press, Washington, D.C..

Ernst, C. H. and R. W. Barbour. 1989. Turtles of the World. Smithsonian Inst. Press, Washington, D.C.

Ewert, M. E. 1985. Embryology of turtles. *In* C. Gans, F. Billett, and P. F. A. Maderson (eds.), Biology of the Reptilia, Vol. 14, pp. 76–267. John Wiley and Sons, New York.

Ferguson, G. W. and T. Brockman. 1980. Geographic differences of growth rate of *Sceloporus* lizards (Sauria: Iguanidae). Copeia 1980(2):259–264.

Frazer, N. B. 1992. Sea turtle conservation and halfway technology. Conserv. Biol. 6(2):179–184.

Froese, A. D. and G. M. Burghardt. 1974. Food competition in captive juvenile snapping turtles, *Chelydra serpentina*. Anim. Behav. 22:735–740.

Froom, B. 1976. The Turtles of Canada. McClelland and Stewart, Toronto. 120 pp.

Galbraith, D. A. and R. J. Brooks. 1984. A tagging method for use in hatchling turtles. Herpetol. Rev. 15(3):73–75.

Galbraith, D. A., M. W. Chandler, and R. J. Brooks. 1987. The fine structure of home ranges of male *Chelydra serpentina*: Are snapping turtles territorial? Can. J. Zool. 65:262–2629.

Galbraith, D. A., C. A. Bishop, R. J. Brooks, W. L. Simser, and K. P. Lampman. 1988. Factors affecting the density of populations of common snapping turtles (*Chelydra serpentina serpentina*). Can. J. Zool. 66:1233–1240.

Galbraith, D. A., R. J. Brooks, and G. P. Brown. 1997. Can management intervention achieve sustainable exploitation of turtles? *In* J. Van Abbema (ed.), Proceedings: Conservation, Restoration, and Management of Tortoises and Turtles—An International Conference, pp. 186–194. July 1993, State University of New York, Purchase. New York Turtle and Tortoise Society, New York.

Gibbons, J. W. 1970. Sex ratios in turtles. Res. Popul. Ecol. 12:252–254.

Huey, R. B. and P. E. Hertz. 1984. Effects of body size and slope on acceleration of a lizard (*Stellio stellio*). J. Exp. Biol. 110:113–123.

Huey, R. B. and R. D. Stevenson. 1979. Integrating thermal physiology and ecology of ectotherms: A discussion of approaches. Am. Zool. 19:357–366.

Hutchison, V. H. and J. D. Maness. 1979. The role of behaviour in temperature acclimation and tolerance in ectotherms. Am. Zool. 19:367–384.

Janzen, F. J. and G. L. Paukstis. 1991. A preliminary test of the adaptive significance of environmental sex determination in reptiles. Evolution 45(2):435–440.

Knight, T. W., J. A. Layfield, and R. J. Brooks. 1990. Nutritional status and mean selected temperature of hatchling snapping turtles (*Chelydra serpentina*): Is there a thermophilic response to feeding? Copeia 1990(4):1067–1072.

Lawless, J. F. 1982. Statistical Models and Methods for Lifetime Data. John Wiley & Sons, New York.

Layfield, J. A., D. A. Galbraith, and R. J. Brooks. 1988. A simple method to mark hatchling turtles. Herpetol. Rev. 19(4):78–79.

McKnight, C. M. and W. H. N. Gutzke. 1993. Effects of the embryonic environment and of hatchling housing conditions on growth of young snapping turtles (*Chelydra serpentina*). Copeia 1993(2):475–482.

Moll, E. O. 1979. Reproductive cycles and adaptations. *In* M. Harless and H. Morlock (eds.), Turtles: Perspectives and Research, pp. 305–331. John Wiley & Sons, New York.

Moll, E. O. and J. M. Legler. 1971. The life history of a Neotropical slider turtle, *Pseudemys scripta* (Schoepff) in Panama. Bull. Los Angeles Co. Mus. Nat. Hist. (Sci.) 11:1–102.

Morris, K. A., G. C. Packard, T. J. Boardman, G. L. Paukstis, and M. J. Packard. 1983. Effect of the hydric environment on growth of embryonic snapping turtles (*Chelydra serpentina*). Herpetologica 39(3):272–285.

Mrosovsky, N. and C. L. Yntema. 1980. Temperature dependence of sexual differentiation in sea turtles: Implications for conservation practices. Biol. Conserv. 18:271–280.

Murphy, J. B. and J. T. Collins. 1982. A Review of the Diseases and Treatments of Captive Turtles. AMA Publications, Lawrence, Kansas. 56 pp.

Obbard, M. E. and R. J. Brooks. 1981a. A radio-telemetry and mark-recapture study of activity in the common snapping turtle, *Chelydra serpentina*. Copeia 1981(3):630–637.

Obbard, M. E. and R. J. Brooks. 1981b. Fate of overwintered clutches of the common snapping turtle (*Chelydra serpentina*) in Algonquin Park, Ontario. Can. Field. Nat. 95:350–352.

Packard, G. C., C. R. Tracy, and J. J. Roth. 1977. The physiological ecology of reptilian eggs and embryos, and the evolution of viviparity within the class reptilia. Biol. Rev. 52:71–105.

Packard, G. C., M. J. Packard, and T. J. Boardman. 1981. Patterns and possible significance of water exchange by flexible shelled eggs of painted turtles (*Chrysemys picta*). Physiol. Zool. 54(1):165–178.

Packard, G. C., M. J. Packard, K. Miller, and T. J. Boardman. 1987. Influence of moisture, temperature and substrate on snapping turtle eggs and embryos. Ecology 68(4):983–993.

Packard, G. C., K. Miller, and M. J. Packard. 1993. Environmentally induced variation in body size of turtles hatching in natural nests. Oecologia 93:445–448.

Passmore, H. L. 1996. Geographic variation in life-history traits in four populations of *Chelydra serpentina* (Linnaeus). M.S. thesis, Univ. of Guelph, Guelph, Ontario.

Pritchard, P. C. H. 1980. The conservation of sea turtles: Practices and problems. Amer. Zool. 20:609–617.

Sarnat, B. G., E. McNabb, and M. Glass. 1981. Growth of the turtle *Chrysemys scripta* under constant controlled laboratory conditions. Anat. Rec. 199:433–439.

SAS Institute, Inc. 1985. SAS User's Guide. Statistics Version 6. SAS Institute, Inc. Cary, North Carolina.

Snedecor, G. W. and W. G. Cochran. 1989. Statistical Methods, 8th ed. Iowa State University Press, Ames, Iowa. 503 pp.

Stearns, S. C. 1989. The evolutionary significance of phenotypic plasticity. BioScience 39(7):436–445.

Van Damme, R., D. Bauwens, F. Brana, and R. F. Verheyen. 1992. Incubation temperature differentially affects hatching time, egg survival, and hatchling performance in the lizard *Podarcis muralis*. Herpetologica 48(2):220–228.

Vogt, R. C. and J. J. Bull. 1982. Temperature controlled sex determination in turtles: Ecological and behavioral aspects. Herpetologica 38(1):156–164.

Yntema, C. L. 1976. Effect of incubation temperature on sexual differentiation in the turtle, *Chelydra serpentina*. J. Morphol. 150:453–462.

Yntema, C. L. 1978. Incubation times for eggs of the turtle *Chelydra serpentina* (Testudines: Chelydridae) at various temperatures. Herpetologica 34(3):274–277.

A Proposal to Standardize Data Collection and Implications for Management of the Wood Turtle, *Clemmys insculpta*, and other Freshwater Turtles in Ontario, Canada

DINA A. FOSCARINI AND RONALD J. BROOKS

Department of Zoology, University of Guelph, Guelph, Ontario, N1G 2W1 Canada

ABSTRACT: Long-term research is currently underway in Ontario to document the population and conservation biology of five species of freshwater turtles: the common snapping turtle (*Chelydra serpentina*), the painted turtle (*Chrysemys picta*), the spotted turtle (*Clemmys guttata*), the wood turtle (*Clemmys insculpta*), and the musk turtle (*Sternotherus odoratus*). Data on population density, demography, and reproductive success are being collected. Turtles were equipped with temperature-sensing radio transmitters and tracked to gain information on habitat selection, home range size and utilization, and characteristics of nesting and hibernating sites.

To build a valuable and accessible database for these and other declining species in Canada, we propose standardized measures of body size, population density, habitat use and characteristics, and reproductive output. Data are presented for one population of wood turtles in Ontario, and the implications that these data have for management of threatened populations of turtles are discussed.

The life history characteristics of many turtle species (long adult life expectancy; high stochastic egg, hatchling, and juvenile mortality; and delayed maturity) render them vulnerable to rapid decline, particularly when rates of adult mortality increase (Dunham et al., 1988; Wilbur and Morin, 1988; Brooks et al., 1988, 1991, 1992; Congdon et al. 1993). While investigating life history characteristics of turtles, with particular focus on the relationships between age at first reproduction, reproductive effort, body size, growth rates, and longevity, we have used a standardized method of data collection to build a database for five of the eight species of Ontario turtles. To date we have studied populations of *Chelydra serpentina*, *Chrysemys picta*, *Clemmys guttata*, *Clemmys insculpta*, and *Sternotherus odoratus* for 22, 16, 17, 8, and 3 years, respectively. Compared to their more southern conspecifics, northern populations of these five species display exceptionally delayed sexual maturity, larger size at maturity, slower growth rates, and lower annual reproductive output (Galbraith et al., 1989; Brooks et al., 1992; Brown et al., 1994; Edmonds and Brooks, 1996; Litzgus, 1996). These characteristics of northern populations appear to increase their vulnerability to extirpation from chronic disturbance. Life history data from different studies are often difficult or impossible to compare because of varying field techniques or data presentation. One population of wood turtles in Ontario is used as a case study to show the implications of these data for the preservation and management of turtle populations.

Site Description

Research on the southern Ontario wood turtles began in 1989 with a preliminary survey of the wood turtles at the study site. To prevent unauthorized collection of wood turtles, the precise location of the study site will be kept confidential; the entire study site will be referred to simply as the "Main River Valley," and the individual tributaries to the Main River will be designated by letters (i.e., stream A, B, etc.). The land at the study site is used primarily for cash crop agriculture (corn, beans, hay, and mixed grains). The vegetation of the Main River Valley is a mix of young deciduous forests, composed primarily of poplar (*Populus* sp.), maple (*Acer* sp.), basswood (*Tilia americana*), ash (*Fraxinus* sp.), and blue beech (*Carpinus caroliniana*). Some stands of white cedar (*Thuja occidentalis*) also occur. Within 50 m of the tributary margins are numerous thickets of mixed dogwood (*Cornus* sp.), hawthorn (*Crataegus* sp.), ninebark (*Physocarpus opulifolius*), willow (*Salix* sp.), and berry bushes (*Rubus* sp.). Cash crop agricultural fields occur within 50 m of each surveyed tributary, and in some cases farming occurs right up to the banks of the waterways.

Searches for wood turtles were conducted by one or two individuals six days of the week between 0800 and 1800 hours. When wood turtles were captured, straight-line measurements of carapace length, carapace width, and plastron length were taken to the nearest 0.1 mm with Mitutoyo™ calipers. Body mass was measured to the nearest gram with a calibrated 2.5 kg or 1,000 g Pesola™ field scale with a precision at maximum load of ±0.3%. Time of day, weather conditions, microhabitat, activity of the turtle, and any deformities or injuries were also noted. Each turtle was given an identification number by a unique combination of carapacial notches (Cagle, 1939). Weather changes were noted in a daily log, and an air temperature reading was taken daily from a maximum/minimum thermometer near stream B.

Wood turtles were captured in only three of nine tributaries of the Main River that were searched from 28 April 1991 to 17 June 1993. A population density estimate was calculated for each of these three tributaries (streams A, B, and C). To estimate density, we first estimated water surface area by multiplying the length of stream inhabited by turtles by the average stream width. The latter was obtained by averaging a set of width measurements taken at intervals along the stream length. Locations for width measurements were chosen at random by assigning a number to each grid coordinate along the length of the stream, and then using a random number table to choose grid coordinates at which to take measurements.

In June of 1991 ten adult wood turtles were equipped with temperature-sensitive radio transmitters (model SI-2T, Holohil Systems, RR#2 Woodlawn, Ontario). Radio transmitters (164.69-164.98 MHz) were encased in a 3.8 cm long brass cylinder with a 30 cm whip antenna. Each entire unit weighed approximately nine grams. A thermistor inside the brass transmitter housing monitored the ambient temperature at the turtle's location and varied the pulse rate of the transmitted signal.

Tracking of radio-tagged turtles was conducted on foot using a portable receiver and a four-element yagi antenna (Holohil Systems Ltd., RR#2 Woodlawn, Ontario). Ten transmitter pulse rates were timed using a wristwatch stopwatch, precise to 1/100 second. Transmitters had a battery life of 18 months and a range of up to 1 km depending on the climatic conditions and the turtle's location. Prior to mounting each transmitter, the transmitter pulse rate was used to construct a calibration graph which converted the pulse rate into temperature (°C). Turtles with transmitters were located daily from 11 June until 27 August 1991. Each time they were located a description of the habitat, temperature, and activity was recorded. From 27 August 1991 until 4 May 1992 recordings were made at three- to four-week intervals. Daily locations of each turtle were plotted on a range map. Transmitters were removed after nesting in 1992.

Using topographic maps, aerial photographs, and a foot survey, a map was drawn of stream sites A and B. A grid was superimposed on the map to give grid cells (10 × 10 m). We defined five main habitat types:

1. Water and water's edge (up to 5 m from the tributary),
2. Mixed woods ($\geq 75\%$ deciduous trees),
3. Mixed conifer ($\geq 75\%$ coniferous trees),
4. Open meadow or gravel pit ($\geq 75\%$ ground cover, below 1 m in height), and
5. Agricultural land (annually planted).

One of the five habitat types was assigned to each 100 m² grid cell overlaying the maps. These maps were used to calculate the availability of each of the five habitat types covered at stream sites A and B. Patterns of habitat use were determined only from radio-tracked turtles.

Sample Calculation

Stream B	inhabited length of stream (digitized distance) = 2,200 m
	average width of stream = 4.54 m
	population estimate = 90 wood turtles
Water surface area	(2,200 m × 4.54 m) = 10,005.6 m² = 1.0 ha
Density estimate	90 turtles / 1.0 ha = 90 turtles/ha

Stream Survey

Within the study site, six of the tributaries (three with resident turtles—streams A, B, and C; and three without turtles—streams D, E, and F) were surveyed, and quantitative measurements of each creek and its surrounding habitat were taken between 7 and 15 July 1992. We recorded depth (center of stream) and substrate composition of the creek, area of flood plain, and vegetation type (10, 50, and 100 m from the creek edge). Using the grid system for each of the six streams, each grid cell was assigned a number. Using a random numbers table, three grid cells were chosen to be surveyed on each of the streams. At each selected survey site, the stream width and depth were measured with a tape measure and meter stick, respectively. The substrate of the stream was categorized as either sand, mud, pebbles, rocks, or uniform rock beds of granite or slate. Using a compass bearing of 90° to the stream flow, width of the flood plain was measured to the nearest meter using the tape measure. Then at 10, 50, and 100 m from the stream edge, the major vegetation was noted (i.e., the closest tree in the north, south, east, and west directions, and the predominating ground cover and shrubs).

RESULTS AND DISCUSSION

Population Characteristics

Nearly all field-workers take standard measurements of turtles, but often they fail to report all the measurements, or worse, values are given without measures of variance. Whenever possible, means and variance of the important body and reproductive measurements, including age and size at sexual maturity, should be reported. A description of measurement protocols is also necessary. Morphological indicators of sexual maturity and functional maturity may differ within species, but if the criteria used to judge such characters are not specified, the data from different studies may not be directly comparable. Moreover, turtles are long-lived and generation times may be measured in decades. Most studies do not last this long, but comparisons may be made between successive short-term studies (e.g., Congdon et al., 1993). Such efforts will be much more valuable if the data are collected consistently and reported in a way that allows statistical comparisons.

A descriptive account of the habitat types that a turtle can potentially utilize should precede any detailed study or analysis. The description of habitat becomes increasingly important as habitats are lost or changed, or as we search for new populations of a species that is declining. Because descriptive biology has limited comparative value, it is beneficial to apply some quantitative measure to the availability of habitat zones. Further use of these measurements will be discussed below.

A total of 270 wood turtles were captured and marked throughout the 1991–1993 field study. Of the 250 wood turtles marked in 1991 and 1992, 112 (44.8%) were recaptured during the 1993 field season. Using the Jolly-Seber method, the size of the population was estimated at 412 turtles (95% Confidence Interval 379.8–458.8) in 1993. The Jolly-Seber method was chosen because it incorporates mark-recapture data for open populations, it estimates the probability of survival, and calculates standard error and confidence limits (Jolly, 1965; Seber 1965). According to the distribution of carapace lengths of wood turtles captured (Figure 1), over 80% were adults. This proportion was higher than reported in some other studies (Harding and Bloomer, 1979; Farrell and Graham, 1991) but similar to that reported by Ross et al. (1991). Presumably our population has low recruitment rates, or the hatchlings and juveniles are more difficult to find than in some other populations. As the habitats occupied by wood turtles are structurally similar between studies (Harding and Bloomer, 1979; Farrell and Graham, 1991; Kaufmann, 1992), and the methods of capture were the same, it is likely that the population in the Main River Valley has lower recruitment than those in the U.S. studies. Low recruitment may be caused by a low proportion of females nesting each year, poor nest success, low survival of hatchlings and juveniles, or a combination of these possibilities. In most studies of turtles, these factors are often identified, but the relative contribution of each to the populations' current status is only rarely tested rigorously. It is therefore often difficult to compare specific demographic components between studied populations.

The age distribution of individuals has important implications in the conservation or management of a population. Therefore, a thorough understanding of the basic life-history traits of the population is necessary to decide which age classes should be the focus of management intervention. For example, if it is impossible or uneconomical to prevent high rates of mortality among juveniles, management strategies should concentrate on prolonging the life of the adults, which may also increase reproductive output and reproductive success. Past turtle conservation efforts have tended to emphasize protection of eggs or headstarting hatchlings; this strategy needs to be combined with protection of adults (Harding, 1991; Frazer, 1992; Congdon et al., 1993; Cunnington and Brooks, 1996; Heppell et al., 1996).

Density

We estimated densities as 90.0 turtles/ha for stream B (2.2 km stream length), 66.9 turtles/ha for stream A (3.4 km stream length), and 5.6 turtles/ha for stream C (1.6 km stream length). Density estimates have been reported for several other wood turtle populations, but variable proportion of terrestrial habitat used in those calculations makes valid comparisons to our study impossible. Only the estimate from Algonquin Park in north-central Ontario (Brooks and Brown, 1992) provided enough information—population estimate 71 (57–103) turtles, stream length 2 km, average stream width 10.14 m—for us to calculate a density of 35 turtles/ha of stream (28/ha–51/ha). This estimate is less than the densities we found for streams A or B, but higher than for stream C. Again, measures of variance would allow a statistical test of differences. The difference in density may reflect differences of resource availability between areas and could indicate that the more southern site has higher productivity for wood turtles (e.g., Brown et al., 1994). Calculating population density per ha of stream surface area should simplify comparisons between sites for semi-aquatic species like the wood turtle.

Habitat Selection

Only a 2.2-km stretch of the creek at stream B and a 3.4 km stretch of the creek at stream A were used in the habitat analysis. These sections were chosen because they contained the highest densities of wood turtles. For stream A, the 3.4 km stretch had approximately 90% (140 of 155) of the wood turtles marked at that creek. For stream B, the 2.2 km length had approximately 80% (83 of 104) of the

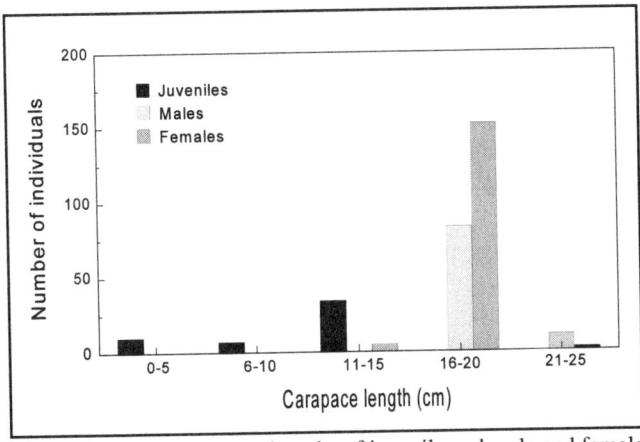

Figure 1. Midline carapace lengths of juvenile and male and female adult wood turtles captured in Main River Valley.

marked population. All turtles with radio transmitters were captured in these two sections of the stream valleys.

We used 585 radio locations from ten wood turtles, five (2 males and 3 females) on stream A and five (4 males and 1 female) on stream B, to analyze habitat use. We expected extensive use of aquatic habitats by wood turtles not only for hibernation but also to prevent desiccation in summer and freezing in early spring. In Pennsylvania, males spent significantly more time in the water, and females spent more time in open meadows. Kaufmann (1992) concluded that the wood turtles were selecting habitats as opposed to using them randomly. We also found that males stayed in the water more than did females. Throughout July and August, each female was observed returning to the stream on one or two occasions; most of their time was spent moving through large tracts of forest and agricultural fields. Because the stream represents a small part of the total habitat and females periodically return to it, we hypothesized that the likelihood of meeting and mating a female was increased by the males remaining in the water.

We predicted that agricultural fields, by acting as "dry zones," may limit the turtles' movement away from the creek. However, females spent lengthy periods in agricultural fields, even in the peak of summer heat, when desiccation and overheating were potential threats. It is possible that wood turtles derive water from metabolism of food as occurs in desert reptiles such as *Gopherus agassizii* (Cloudsley-Thompson, 1974; Strang, 1983). Strang (1983) compared *Clemmys insculpta* and *Terrapene carolina* and hypothesized that the presence of moisture (rain and humidity) is a significant factor in the diet and habitat selection of these two terrestrial turtles. *Clemmys insculpta* ingested a diet of 31% green leaves and had frequent contact with waterways by regularly traversing streams. Wood turtles on the Main River were observed consuming green vegetation, and they maintained home ranges close to a water source. It appears that multiple variables influence the types of habitats used by wood turtles. More research into the type of canopy and food availability, as well as a more thorough understanding of the cause of the long-distance movements seen by Quinn and Tate (1991) and in our study, may answer these questions. These questions cannot be addressed in wood turtles or other aquatic turtle species without using a tracking system, preferably radiotelemetry with temperature- sensing capability and automated data logging. Without such systems, studies of home range movements and activity will remain largely descriptive and relatively crude.

Seasonal Movements

Quinn and Tate (1991) described a wide variety of microhabitats used by wood turtles in the Algonquin area and noted a series of repeated seasonal movements. These repeated movements were remarkably similar for individuals from year to year. Harding and Bloomer (1979) found that most Michigan wood turtles remained within 150 meters of the waterways, and similar confinement to the stream area occurred in other populations in Pennsylvania (Strang, 1983) and in Wisconsin (Ross et al., 1991). However, the turtles in our population and Quinn and Tate's study (1991) were more mobile, with individuals ranging over 500 m from the streams.

The distance the wood turtles moved away from the tributaries differed between the sexes (Table 1). By late May to June the females had wandered farther afield, perhaps in search of a nest site. In May females with transmitters were found, on average, 5.1 m (±8.6 m) from the stream, which differed significantly from the average distance in June (63.1 m ±73.7 m; $t = 2.5$ df 51, $P < 0.025$). Males averaged 3.6 m (±4.7 m) and 5.7 m (±8.4 m) from the streams in May and June respectively, which were not significantly different. Males did move significantly further from the stream in May as compared to April (Table 1). Throughout June, July, and August, females remained significantly further away from the stream than did males (June $t = 4.9$ df 81, $P < 0.001$; July $t = 13.6$ df 236, $P < 0.0001$; and August $t = 12.8$ df 185, $P < 0.0001$; Table 1). The extensive use of open meadows by all the female wood turtles may represent niche separation in foraging between males and females, with males utilizing the stream and stream edge and the females foraging more on upland areas. We have not found reports of niche separation between the sexes elsewhere in the literature.

Stream Survey

Stream measurements were considered very important for this species because this methodology could be replicated at other field sites. The information provided by quantitative stream analysis may also facilitate finding additional wood turtle populations and aid in preserving habitat that wood turtles require. Surprisingly however, we found few significant quantitative differences between streams that maintained populations of wood turtles and those that did not. The streams that maintained a wood turtle population tended to show little variation in mean width (mean = 7.01 ±3.8 m), but having a width of seven meters was no assurance that wood turtles would be found on a stream. This mean width (7.01 m) of stream was however significantly wider than the mean width of streams that had no turtles ($t = 2.86$ df 16, $P < 0.025$). The mean depth of streams occupied by wood turtles (0.21 ±0.08 m) was significantly deeper than the streams without turtles (0.09 ±0.02 m) ($t = 4.6$ df 16, $P < 0.001$). Characteristics shared by the populated streams were free-flowing water year-round, variable depths in the stream ranging from 0.05 to 1.0+ m even when the water level was low, gravel/sandy base substrate, measurable current, and a mixture of surrounding habitats.

TABLE 1
Mean monthly distance (±SD) from a stream of radio locations
of six male and four female wood turtles from April to September 1991.

Months	Mean distance (m) from the stream Males	Females	Probability of differences between sexes
April	0.4 ±0.5 (11)	1.1 ±1.4 (4)	<0.2
May	a 3.6 ±4.7 (32)	5.1 ±8.6 (10)	<0.5
June	5.7 ±8.4 (40)	63.1 ±73.6 (43)	**<0.001***
July	b 17.1 ±20.4 (154)	d 112.1 ±82.2 (82)	**<0.0001***
August	11.6 ±25.1 (147)	95.7 ±63.1 (38)	**<0.0001***
September	c 0.5 ±2.1 (7)	e 2.5 ±1.2 (5)	<0.1

* Distances from the stream differ significantly between sexes. Distances are significantly different within sex between successive months as follows: **a:** $t = 2.3$ df 41, $P < 0.05$; **b:** $t = 3.5$ df 192, $P < 0.001$; **c:** $t = 2.1$ df 299, $P < 0.05$; **d:** $t = 2.5$ df 51, $P < 0.025$; **e:** $t = 3.3$ df 41, $P < 0.005$.

Conservation

This study demonstrated that the wood turtles of the Main River Valley utilize a variety of microhabitats and range up to 500 m from the waterways. Generally, the presence of rural residents and farming activities seemed to have little negative effect on the turtles. In fact, farm fields and other artificial openings may provide terrestrial basking, foraging, and nesting sites (Harding, 1990; Kaufmann, 1992; this study). Residents who are aware of and educated about wood turtles could prove to be of benefit to the turtles by alerting authorities to illegal collecting or by reporting any decline in the number of turtles. With their cooperation, waterways can be maintained, terrestrial habitats can be managed, and pesticides and other contaminants used cautiously in wood turtle areas. For example, if we further define the annual movements of turtles, the use of heavy machinery in the farm fields and the spraying of pesticides could be scheduled to minimize disturbance to and mortality of the wood turtles.

Garber and Burger (this volume) describe the rapid disappearance of a wood turtle population after public recreation was increased in their study area and felt that collection of adult turtles and general disturbance were responsible (see also Harding, 1991). At present, our study site is primarily on private land. The overall effect of sport fishing activities on wood turtle populations is largely unknown. Although this type of recreation may increase disturbance and result in some incidental take of individuals, wood turtle habitat as a whole derives protection from such legislation as the Fisheries Act, which is designed to maintain water quality for cold-water game fish.

A major concern is that 95% of the study population is restricted to two small sections of the tributaries, which makes the population highly susceptible to catastrophic decline. Our data for this population and for other species of turtles in Ontario, as well as data from other researchers (e.g., Harding, 1991; Congdon et al., 1993), show that protection of eggs and hatchlings would do little to compensate for chronic, increased loss of adults or older juveniles. Annual survivorship of juveniles would also have to be unrealistically high for nest protection to be an effective strategy for augmenting a declining population. Therefore, conservation efforts *must focus on protection of the adult population* (e.g., Cunnington and Brooks, 1996; Heppell et al., 1996).

Based on the information collected during this study, we are recommending that a conservation and monitoring program include a mark-recapture study, a nesting survey, and a project to enhance the awareness of local residents. It is particularly important to educate wildlife managers and others responsible for protection of long-lived species about the significance of adults to the persistence of the population. Most wildlife biologists deal with relatively short-lived species that have density-dependent population processes. Density-dependent responses are weak or non-existent in many turtle populations (Brooks et al., 1991; Congdon et al., 1993; Galbraith et al., this volume).

One of the major nesting sites for the Main River population is an active pit approximately 100 m north of stream A. This site is located in a less frequently used area of the gravel pit and could be purchased from the present owner and preserved as a nest site. This area could also serve as a research plot where various turtle species (*Clemmys insculpta*, *Chrysemys picta*, and *Chelydra serpentina* presently use this site) could be monitored and protected from predation. In addition, we believe that it is critical to continue the search for wood turtles in other areas of Ontario to achieve a province-wide population estimate, which would also refine our knowledge of the habitat requirements of this species. Habitat protection may be especially important for very long-lived species with large, complex home ranges because such species often have poor, if any, density-dependent responses and cannot recover quickly from rapid environmental disturbances.

Studies and models of turtle populations often draw comparisons between populations or species using data collected in different ways, by different investigators with varied experimental designs and with different methods of reporting the data. We recommend that those concerned with conservation of turtles and tortoises develop a set of guidelines for data collection that will allow quantitative comparisons between study populations in both space and time. Measurements and, just as important, the information reported on these measurements should be standardized. Population structure is especially important, and methods used to estimate age at maturity and age-class structure should be clarified. The use of annuli to age turtles is especially problematic; researchers often report casual counts of carapacial or plastral marks as confirmed ages. We also recommend use of telemetry to examine habitat selection, movements, and home range. Again, standardized methods of measuring home range size and of measuring turtles are sorely needed (Galbraith et al., 1987).

While many other areas of turtle ecology need standardization, one additional issue is noteworthy. Turtles may live a long time and studies of their populations require long-term studies. Even studies of 10–15 years do not cover one generation of many species. For example, a recent mark-recapture study of the spotted turtle in Ontario covered 17 years, but these data still did not allow the researchers to determine whether the population was stable or changing (J. Litzgus, pers. comm.). Although standard ecological methods can be applied to turtle populations, they require modification that takes the long-term requirements of the study into account. The long-term nature of the study site and the frequency of sampling necessary to obtain good estimates of abundance and key demographic factors are both important considerations.

Summary of Recommendations for Data Collection

• **Use a system of permanent marking.** Because of their longevity, the determination of turtles' critical demographic and life history data (e.g., age at maturity, life expectancy) requires long-term studies that employ the permanent marking (e.g., by PIT tags, permanent notches, etc.) of individual turtles. It is difficult to age turtles accurately after they reach sexual maturity. Neither size (Galbraith et al., 1989; Congdon and van Loben Sels, 1991) nor counts of annuli (Galbraith and Brooks, 1989) predict age accurately. At present, the only way to determine age-specific demographic measures in adult turtles is to follow marked individuals over time.

• **Establish standard measurement and analytic techniques and standard references.** Comparisons of the demography, life history, habitat requirements, and behavior within and among species are central to developing effective conservation strategies for turtles and tortoises. If these comparisons are to be made with valid quantitative methods, standard measurement and analytic techniques must be used to enhance our ability to test hypotheses. Finally, standard references should be established to direct methods of data collection and presentation. Although individual studies provide valuable information, deeper understanding can be gained only from testing key hypotheses that explain population and ecological phenomena. These hypotheses can be better addressed when data are comparable between studies.

CONCLUSIONS

Although our study population of wood turtles is dense, in most other respects it appears vulnerable to extirpation. The population has a low rate of recruitment (probably because of high egg, hatchling, and juvenile mortality), it is small in size and far from a stable age distribution (low proportion of younger age classes), and it is concentrated in a small area. Furthermore, these turtles are highly iteroparous with weak density-dependent responses. Hence, such populations are susceptible to sudden fluctuations, and the consequent probability of extirpation is high.

Finally, although wood turtles are protected in Ontario, enforcement is weak, and all of the species' current range (in southern Ontario) is privately owned, making protection of habitat quality difficult and uncertain. Most wood turtle populations—indeed, populations of many other species of Canadian freshwater turtles—have similar characteristics and problems. The future of the wood turtle in Canada and over most of its current range is not encouraging unless strong new preservation measures are enacted soon.

ACKNOWLEDGMENTS

We thank Krista Halling, Sherwyn Solomon, and the Environmental Youth Core students for their assistance in the field, and David Cunnington for reviewing a draft of this manuscript. We also thank local residents who allowed us passage on their land and added information to our initial search. This research was funded by grants from the Ontario Ministry of Natural Resources, the World Wildlife Fund

Canada, the Canadian Wildlife Service of Environment Canada, and the Natural Sciences and Engineering Research Council of Canada.

LITERATURE CITED

Brooks, R. J., D. A. Galbraith, E. G. Nancekivell, and C. A. Bishop. 1988. Developing management guidelines for snapping turtles. *In* R. C. Szaro, K. E. Severson, and D. R. Patton (Tech. Coords.), Management of Amphibians, Reptiles, and Small Mammals in North America, pp. 174–179. USDA Forest Service, Gen. Tech. Rept. RM-166, Flagstaff, Arizona.

Brooks, R. J., G. P. Brown, and D. A. Galbraith. 1991. Effects of a sudden increase in natural mortality of adults on a population of the common snapping turtle (*Chelydra serpentina*). Can. J. Zool. 69:1314–1320.

Brooks, R. J., C. M. Shilton, G. P. Brown, and N. W. S. Quinn. 1992. Body size, age distribution and reproduction in a northern population of wood turtles (*Clemmys insculpta*). Can. J. Zool. 70:462–469.

Brooks, R. J. and G. P. Brown. 1992. Population biology of the wood turtle, *Clemmys insculpta*, in the Madawaska River drainage. 1991 Progress Report and Proposal to the Ontario Ministry of Natural Resources, Algonquin District. 36 pp.

Brown, G. P., C. A. Bishop, and R. J. Brooks. 1994. Growth rate, reproductive output, and temperature selection of snapping turtles in habitats of different productivities. J. Herpetol. 28:405–410.

Cagle, F. R. 1939. A system of marking turtles for future identification. Copeia 1939:170–172.

Cloudsley-Thompson, J. L. 1974. Physiological thermoregulation in the spurred tortoise (*Testudo graeca* L.). J. Nat. Hist. 8:577–578.

Congdon, J. D., A. E. Dunham, and R. C. van Loben Sels. 1993. Delayed sexual maturity and demographics of Blanding's turtles (*Emydoidea blandingii*): Implications for conservation and management of long-lived organisms. Conserv. Biol. 7:826–833.

Congdon, J. D. and R. C. van Loben Sels. 1991. Growth and body size variation in Blanding's turtles (*Emydoidea blandingii*): Relationships to reproduction. Can. J. Zool. 69:239–245.

Cunnington, D. C. and R. J. Brooks. 1996. Bet-hedging theory and eigenelasticity: A comparison of the life histories of loggerhead sea turtles (*Caretta caretta*) and snapping turtles (*Chelydra serpentina*). Can. J. Zool. 74:291–296.

Dunham, A. E., D. M. Miles, and D. Resnick. 1988. Life history patterns in squamate reptiles. *In* C. Gans and R. Huey (eds.), Biology of the Reptilia 16b, pp. 443–511. Alan R. Liss, Inc., New York.

Edmonds, J. H. and R. J. Brooks. 1996. Demography, sex ratio, and sexual dimorphism in a northern population of common musk turtles (*Sternotherus odoratus*). Can. J. Zool. 74:918–925.

Farrell, R. F. and T. E. Graham. 1991. Ecological notes on the turtle *Clemmys insculpta* in northwestern New Jersey. J. Herpetol. 25: 1–9.

Frazer, N. B. 1992. Sea turtle conservation and halfway technology. Conserv. Biol. 6:179–184.

Galbraith, D. A. and R. J. Brooks. 1989. Age estimates for snapping turtles. J. Wildl. Manage. 53:502–508.

Galbraith, D. A., R. J. Brooks, and G. P. Brown. 1997. Can management intervention achieve sustainable exploitation of turtles? *In* J. Van Abbema (ed.), Proceedings: Conservation, Restoration, and Management of Tortoises and Turtles—An International Conference, pp. 186–194. July 1993, State University of New York, Purchase. New York Turtle and Tortoise Society, New York.

Galbraith, D. A., R. J. Brooks, and M. E. Obbard. 1989. The influence of growth rate on age and body size at maturity in female snapping turtles (*Chelydra serpentina*). Copeia 1989:896–904.

Galbraith, D. A., M. W. Chandler, and R. J. Brooks. 1987. The fine structure of home ranges of male *Chelydra serpentina*: Are snapping turtles territorial? Can. J. Zool. 65:2623–2629.

Garber, S. D. and J. Burger. 1997. A 20-year study documenting the relationship between turtle decline and human recreation (poster abstract). *In* J. Van Abbema (ed.), Proceedings: Conservation, Restoration, and Management of Tortoises and Turtles—An International Conference, p. 477. July 1993, State University of New York, Purchase. New York Turtle and Tortoise Society, New York.

Harding, J. H. 1990. A twenty year wood turtle study in Michigan: Implications for conservation. *In* K. R. Beaman, F. Caporaso, S. McKeown, and M. Graff (eds.), Proceedings of the First International Symposium on Turtles & Tortoises: Conservation and Captive Husbandry, pp. 31–35. August 1990, Chapman University, Orange, California. California Turtle & Tortoise Club and Chapman University.

Harding, J. H. 1991. Comments on herpetological collecting: The need for considering life history data in management and regulatory planning. Bull. Chicago Herpetol. Soc. 26:157–159.

Harding, J. H. and T. J. Bloomer. 1979. The wood turtle, *Clemmys insculpta*...a natural history. Bull. New York Herpetol. Soc. 15(1): 9–26.

Heppell, S. S., L. B. Crowder, and D. T. Crouse. 1996. Models to evaluate headstarting as a management tool for long-lived turtles. Ecol. Appl. 6:556–565.

Jolly, G. M. 1965. Explicit estimates from capture-recapture data with both death and immigration: Stochastic model. Biometrika 52:225–247.

Kaufmann, J. H. 1992. Habitat use by wood turtles in Central Pennsylvania. J. Herpetol. 26(3):315–321.

Litzgus, J. D. 1996. Life-history and demography of a northern population of spotted turtles (*Clemmys guttata*). M.S. thesis, University of Guelph, Guelph, Ontario. 145 pp.

Obbard, M. E. 1985. A status report for the wood turtle (*Clemmys insculpta*) in Ontario. Ontario Ministry of Natural Resources, Wildlife Branch, March 1985.

Quinn, N. W. S. and D. P. Tate. 1991. Seasonal movements and habitat of wood turtles (*Clemmys insculpta*) in Algonquin Park, Canada. J. Herpetol. 25:217–220.

Ross, D. A., K. N. Brewster, R. K. Anderson, N. Ratner, and C. M. Brewster. 1991. Aspects of the ecology of wood turtles, *Clemmys insculpta*, in Wisconsin. Can. Field-Nat. 105:363–367.

Seber, G. A. F. 1965. A note on the multiple-recapture census. Biometrika 52:249–259.

Strang, C. A. 1983. Spatial and temporal activity patterns in two terrestrial turtles. J. Herpetol. 17:43–47.

Tinkle, D. W. 1979. Long-term field studies. BioScience 29:717.

Wilbur, H. M. and P. J. Morin. 1988. Life history evolution in turtles. *In* C. Gans and R. Huey (eds.), Biology of the Reptilia 16b, pp. 396–447. Alan R. Liss, Inc., New York.

Species Abundance and Biomass Distributions in Freshwater Turtles

RICHARD C. VOGT[1] AND JOSÉ-LUIS VILLARREAL BENITEZ[2]

[1]*Estación de Biología Tropical "Los Tuxtlas," Instituto de Biología UNAM, A.P. 91, San Andres Tuxtla, Veracruz, C.P. 95700 México*
[2]*Matamoros No. 10, Catemaco, Veracruz, C.P. 95780 México*

ABSTRACT: Species abundance has been used to infer interspecific patterns in resource partitioning. However, these patterns can differ from those predicted by the distribution of species abundance, depending on the relationship within the communities between the abundance of a species and its body size. In many groups, the largest species in the community tend to have lower population densities than smaller ones. Many theories have tried to explain the patterns of species abundance in terms of resource use, by studying the ways that species partition the resources of the community. In this article we explore four patterns of turtle abundance and diversity with specific hypotheses; although the data are preliminary, they suggest many ideas useful for the conservation of chelonians. Our primary conclusion is that turtle species with relatively small body sizes have been more "successful"; however, the smallest turtles are not very "successful." Further research should be done to assess the significance of this pattern to the conservation of turtles throughout the world.

Before we can conserve turtles on a large spatial scale, we must understand turtle ecology on a large spatial scale.
—Vincent Burke, 1992

Many theories have been generated to explain the patterns of abundance of species in terms of resource use. They attempt to answer the question, what are the different ways in which the biological characteristics of a species vary as a result of partitioning the resources available in a community? Body size is possibly the most fundamental phenotypic trait in most animals (Naganuma and Roughgarden, 1990; Calder, 1984). For this reason, important factors in understanding community ecology are the ecological conditions that give rise to the relationship between species abundance and body size.

The diversity of species (the relative number of individuals belonging to each different species in a natural community) has been used to infer interspecific patterns in resource partitioning (Pagel et al., 1991). There is a simple inverse relationship between population density and body size, such that rare species should have large body size and common species should be small (Lawton, 1989). In addition, Damuth (1987) has speculated that the amount of energy flowing through each species in a community is independent of its body size; that is, species with different sizes still use the same energy per unit area. In contrast, other studies have suggested that per-capita resource use is lower in small individuals than in large ones, implying that a limited resource could support more individuals of a small species than a large one (Pagel et al., 1991). A precise understanding of the relationships between body size, abundance, species diversity, and energy use have been elusive, in part because of the paucity of samples of small and/or rare species, in part because of its sheer complexity.

Hypotheses and Predictions

First pattern: The distribution of species by their body sizes; local versus global patterns.

The frequency of species distributed by body size has been studied for mammals (Brown, 1981; Rusler, 1987), birds (Brown and Maurer, 1987; Maurer et al., 1991), insects (Gaston and Lawton, 1988; Morse et al., 1988), and amphibians and reptiles, inclusively (Peters, 1983). However, no such study of turtles exists, even though the list of the world's species is nearly complete (Iverson, 1992a), and our knowledge of their distributions is well advanced (Iverson, 1992b). Indeed, the ecological importance of turtles in their communities is so well recognized (e.g., Iverson, 1982), it is surprising that the literature has been neglected for so long.

Because all previously studied groups exhibit a lognormal distribution of number of species versus body size, we would expect the same global pattern for turtles. Once the global pattern is described, it can be compared to local patterns with the null hypothesis that species are assembled at random from appropriate larger-scale species pools. We have examined both the global and local patterns of turtle body size diversity with data from the USA, Mexico, and

Brazil to test the hypothesis that competitive exclusion tends to prevent local coexistence of similar-sized species with similar resource requirements.

Second pattern: The relationship between body size and population density, and the effects of diet and habitat.

The relationship between body size and population density has been studied in order to understand the processes that determine the number and variety of coexisting species, and to evaluate the ecological importance of the species in the relative utilization and transfer of energy. The general idea is that large individuals demand more from environmental resource pools than small ones, but also tend to occur at lower population densities. A more detailed analysis demands that constraints on the abilities of the populations to take or assimilate these resources be considered. Following Robinson and Redford (1986), we hypothesized that if the energy used by a population depends upon body size, then diet and body size could account for the variation in population densities. Specifically we predict:

1. Population densities among species should decline with an increase in mean species body mass.
2. Population densities of a species should depend upon diet. Because herbivores have more food available than omnivores, and omnivores more than carnivores, herbivores should have higher densities.
3. Within the same dietary category, population densities across species should decline with an increase in body mass.
4. Habitat should have a similar effect on the relationship between body mass and population density.

Third pattern: Are there more small species than large ones?

Small organisms are usually found to be more diverse than large ones, and this is purported to stem from an ability of small organisms to subdivide their environment more finely (May, 1978, 1988; Dial and Marzluff, 1988). However, some studies have shown that the smallest body-size category was not the most abundant, and it has been argued that these categories were insufficiently sampled (May, 1978, 1988; Dial and Marzluff, 1988). Because a virtually complete species list of turtles is available, it should offer a good test of this prediction.

Fourth pattern: What are the probable causes of the greater diversity of small species?

Many studies indicate that microevolutionary processes should select strongly for large body size because of the better ability of large organisms to tolerate short-term environmental variations, to acquire resources, and to avoid predators (Brown and Maurer, 1986, 1987). However, Gould (1988) has questioned these interpretations, suggesting that cladogenetic processes and the extinction of species within a lineage can explain a large part of the diversity of body size within a lineage, thus decoupling macroevolution from microevolution. Recently, Maurer et al. (1992) have concluded that although cladogenetic processes probably play a significant role in body size evolution, there must also be a significant anagenetic component and that macroevolution and microevolution have not been decoupled. We examined the effect of body size on speciation and extinction rates in the genus *Graptemys* and family Trionychidae. We then explored other biological characters that correlate with body size that may be related to speciation and extinction rates in turtles.

METHODS

Sources of Data

We used the taxonomic list of turtles of the world in Iverson (1992a). Body size data used in the analysis of size were taken from Ernst and Barbour (1989) if access to data in original research papers was lacking, or we did not have our own measurements. Density and biomass data were taken from Iverson (1982, 1992c) and Gibbons and Congdon (1989), supplemented by our own data.

Body size and density data were collected between 1972 and 1993 by one of us (RCV) in certain areas of the United States, Mexico, and Brazil: 1972–1977, principally in the Mississippi River and its tributaries in Wisconsin; 1978–1979, the Cahaba River in Alabama, and Chickasawhay and Pearl rivers in Mississippi; 1981–1988 and 1990–1993, Lagunas in the region of Los Tuxtlas, the Río Papaloapan Basin near Lerdo de Tejada, Veracruz, and the Río Lacantun and its tributaries in Chiapas, Mexico; 1989–1990, 1993, Rio Guaporé (Rondônia), Rio Negro and Ducke Reserve (Amazonas), and Rio Trombetas and Rio Tapajos (Pará), Brazil. RCV also trapped most major river courses from the Flint River in Georgia west through Florida, Alabama, Mississippi, and Louisiana; and west to the Pecos and Brazos rivers in Texas; and north through eastern Oklahoma and Arkansas to Reelfoot Lake, Tennessee. Much of the trapping throughout the southern USA was done with Jack McCoy, 1975–1979.

Since 1972 we have used the same trapping technique, unbaited fyke nets with leads (Vogt, 1980). This technique samples moving turtles regardless of their feeding preferences. A series of 20–28 nets, with 0.5–2.0 m diameter hoops, were placed in a variety of habitats for a minimum of five days per trapping session in the main study areas or for at least 24 hours in survey studies. If fewer than ten turtles per trap were being collected, traps were checked only once a day, unless data were being taken on activity patterns, in which case the traps were checked both at dawn and dusk. In areas with large crocodile, piranha, *Agkistrodon*, anaconda, or electric eel populations, traps were emptied and repaired at least twice a day. Turtles were measured, weighed, marked, and released at the site of capture at the next trap check. Since 1975 most turtles were also stomach flushed (Legler, 1975), and all gravid females were induced to oviposit through the injection of oxytocin. Even though trapping was done in a wide variety of habitats, the basic techniques were identical.

Statistical Treatments

1. The logarithmic frequency distribution of body size among turtle species globally was compared with that for assemblages of freshwater turtles in the north central and the southern USA, Mexico, and Brazil.
2. To explore the possibility that discrepancies between local diversity and global diversity can be determined by local factors, we analyzed the diversity at two levels in three habitats and three regions (southern USA, Mexico, and Brazil).
3. The relationship between body mass and population density was investigated using natural log-transformed data and standard linear regression techniques.
4. Within each dietary category (or habitat) we estimated the relationship between the population density and the average body mass across species with the simple linear regression model of natural log-transformed data. To determine whether population densities of species vary with diet (or habitat), we examined the extent to which membership of a species in one category affects its population density (see Robinson and Redford, 1986).
5. Following the method of Dial and Marzluff (1988), we used carapace length as a measure of body size because body mass is less frequently reported in the literature. When species were extremely sexually dimorphic in size (e.g., the genus *Graptemys*), the female's body size was used. We attempted to obtain the most representative size of each family by using measurement scales traditionally employed by researchers. The relative body size of the genus showing the greatest diversity within the family was calculated by dividing the number of species with a smaller-than-average body size (compared to the family average) by the total number of species in the genus. Multiplication by 100 produces a scale from 0 to 100%. A value of 0% indicates that the most diverse group is also the smallest in terms of body size, whereas a value of 100% indicates it is the largest.
6. To determine whether the smaller species had a greater success in the macroevolutionary sense, we related the number of living species per unit of time (millions of years) within a family (i.e., their persistence in the fossil record, data taken from Ernst and Barbour, 1989, as well as other sources) to their body size using natural log-transformed data and standard regression analysis.

RESULTS

Test of Pattern I.

The body size distribution of turtles of the world appears to be skewed toward smaller size classes (Figure 1). In contrast, comparable frequency distributions for assemblages of turtles in southern USA, Mexico, and Brazil were essentially uniform (Figure 2).

The continental turtle fauna is not simply the sum of species assemblages on smaller spatial scales, and the faunas of local habitats are not just random subsamples of the species pools on large spatial scales. Species near the modal size in the global pattern replace each other frequently across habitats (Table 1), whereas species of large size tend to have large geographic ranges and to occur in a greater number of different habitats. Comparison of the number of species in a geographic region to the number of species of turtles in any particular habitat may reveal radical differences. Diversity is typically greater in the tropics than in temperate regions. However, examination of individual habitats and individual rivers is necessary before making sweeping generalizations. Mexico may have 23 turtle species, Brazil 29 species, and the southern USA 28 species, but these are very different areas in terms of size and number of river basins, climate, etc. On a broad scale, these three areas seem to be similar in diversity, but under close scrutiny, the rivers in the southern USA have much more diverse turtle faunas than any river in Mexico or Brazil (Table 1).

Bury (1979) commented that turtle community studies were essentially nonexistent. Since then Vogt (1981) reported on an assemblage of three sympatric species of *Graptemys* and demonstrated how they partition available food. One species, *Graptemys geographica*, was a mollusk specialist, while *Graptemys ouachitensis* and *Graptemys pseudogeographica* were general omnivores.

Vogt and Guzman (1988) studied an assemblage of three sympatric species of turtles in southern Veracruz, Mexico. *Staurotypus triporcatus* was a mollusk specialist when mollusks were abundant, but also consumed hard seeds in areas where mollusk density was low. *Trachemys scripta*, a generalist, consumed 90% plant material and 10% fish and crustaceans. *Kinosternon leucostomum* varied its omnivorous diet depending on habitat and the presence of other species of turtles. Where *K. leucostomum* was the only species of turtle, only 33.5% of its diet was plant material; however, when it was found with *Staurotypus*, 89.4% of its diet was plant material.

Moll (1990) studied a community of Neotropical freshwater turtles in Belize, finding that adults of *Trachemys scripta* foraged throughout the stream and were omnivorous. More animal matter (primarily insects) was consumed by males (40% of diet) and juveniles (80%) than by females (31%). Juveniles were restricted primarily to vegetation

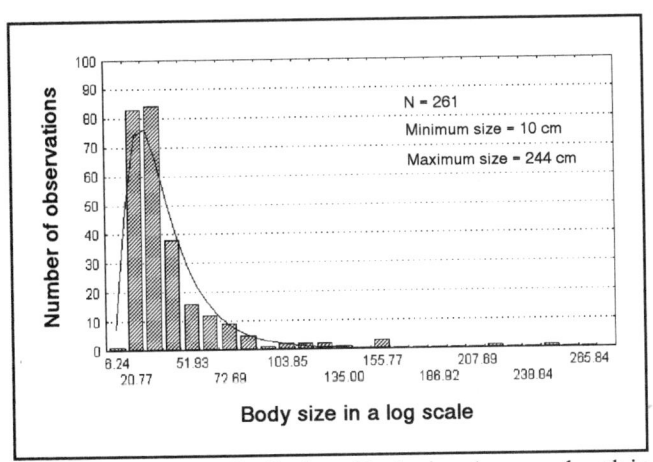

Figure 1. Log-normal distribution of body sizes (carapace length in cm) of all of the world's turtle species (Kolmogorov-Smirnov $P < 0.05$).

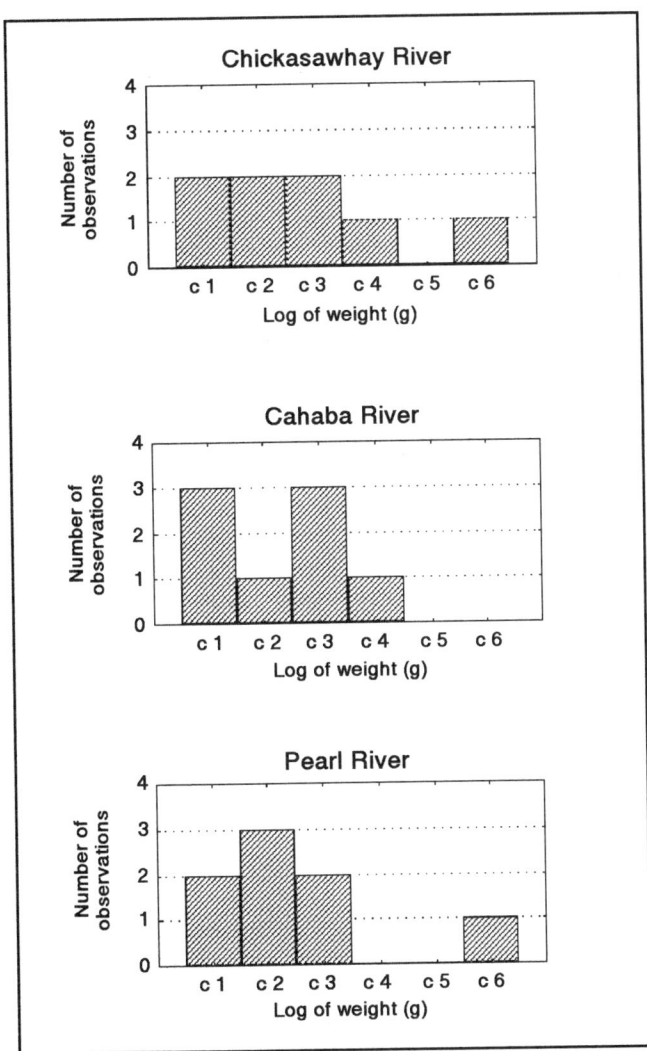

Figure 2. Distribution of turtle sizes in three different rivers in the southern USA, in order of smallest (c1, <1 kg) to largest (c6, >5 kg). Categories: c1 = <1 kg; c2 = 1–2 kg; c3 = 2–3 kg; c4 = 3–4 kg; c5 = 4–5 kg; c6 = >5 kg.

mats. *Kinosternon scorpioides* and *K. leucostomum* were omnivorous, feeding primarily on insects (50.25% and 62.8%, respectively) and vegetation (35% and 27.6%, respectively). *Staurotypus* was the only specialist in the community; snails made up 64% of the diet and small turtles an additional 29%.

Vogt (in prep.) in Chiapas Mexico studied a six-species assemblage of turtles. One large species, *Dermatemys mawii*, was completely herbivorous from hatchling to adult. Another large species, *Staurotypus triporcatus*, was a specialist on mollusks and large hard seeds. *Trachemys scripta* was omnivorous but consumed more plant than animal matter. The other three species were omnivorous but occurred in such small numbers that quantitative statements about their food preferences could not be made. We also studied an assemblage of five aquatic turtle species in the Rio Guapore in Brazil, and all five appear to be eating different food items. The population of *Podocnemis unifilis* is primarily herbivorous, as seeds, fruits, leaves, and stems comprised 89.5% of the total volume of the stomach contents examined, while animal material represented only 1.15%. *Podocnemis expansa* consumed primarily seeds and other plant material. *Phrynops geoffroanus* fed primarily on aquatic insects and crustaceans as well as some fruits. *Phrynops raniceps* ate predominately gastropods and *Chelus* only fish (Fachin-Teran et al., 1995).

Data from Brazil (Fachin-Teran et al., 1995), Mexico (Vogt and Guzman, 1988; Vogt and Flores, 1992; and Vogt, unpubl.) and large rivers in the USA (northern, Vogt 1981; southern, McCoy, Vogt, and Flores, in prep.) show the following niche equivalents (see also Table 1):

1. *Podocnemis expansa* (Brazil), *Dermatemys mawii* (Mexico), and *Pseudemys concinna* (southern USA) are all large, fast-moving species that feed exclusively on plants from hatchling to adulthood. They often swim and bask together in groups.

2. *Podocnemis unifilis* (Brazil), *Trachemys scripta* (both in Mexico and the southern USA), and possibly *Graptemys ouachitensis* (northern USA) are predominantly herbivorous species, but will take animal matter when present and more frequently so when young. They are dedicated baskers. Males are considerably smaller than females.

3. *Phrynops raniceps* (Brazil), *Staurotypus triporcatus* (Mexico), *Graptemys pulchra* (southern USA), and *Graptemys geographica* (northern USA) are all mollusk specialists with large heads and wide alveolar surfaces. They are usually found in lower densities than the other sympatric species, have smaller volumes of food in stomach contents, and have shorter intestines (Vogt, unpubl.).

TABLE 1
Composition of the turtle assemblages in three different regions. Turtles are listed in decreasing order of size. Changes in species composition is most often noted in the interchange of the smaller species.

REGION I, Southern USA (n = 15)		
HABITAT I Chickasawhay River	HABITAT II Cahaba River	HABITAT III Pearl River
Macroclemys temmincki *Chelydra serpentina* *Apalone spinifera* *Pseudemys concinna* *Graptemys gibbonsi* *Apalone mutica* *Trachemys scripta* *Graptemys flavimaculata* *Sternotherus carinatus* *Sternotherus odoratus* n = 10	*Macroclemys temmincki* *Chelydra serpentina* *Apalone spinifera* *Pseudemys concinna* *Apalone mutica* *Trachemys scripta* *Graptemys pulchra* *Graptemys nigrinoda* *Sternotherus minor* *Sternotherus odoratus* n = 10	*Macroclemys temmincki* *Chelydra serpentina* *Apalone spinifera* *Pseudemys concinna* *Graptemys gibbonsi* *Graptemys oculifera* *Apalone mutica* *Trachemys scripta* *Sternotherus carinatus* *Sternotherus odoratus* n = 10

REGION II, Chiapas, Mexico (n = 6)		
HABITAT I Laguna Oaxaca	HABITAT II Río Lacantun	HABITAT III Río Tzendales
Dermatemys mawii *Chelydra serpentina* *Staurotypus triporcatus* *Trachemys scripta* *Kinosternon leucostomum* n = 5	*Dermatemys mawii* *Chelydra serpentina* *Staurotypus triporcatus* *Trachemys scripta* *Kinosternon acutum* n = 5	*Dermatemys mawii* *Chelydra serpentina* *Staurotypus triporcatus* *Trachemys scripta* *Kinosternon acutum* n = 5

REGION III, Amazonia, Brazil (n = 8)		
HABITAT I Rio Guapore	HABITAT II Rio Trombetas	HABITAT III Rio Tapajos
Podocnemis expansa *Podocnemis unifilis* *Chelus fimbriatus* *Phrynops geoffroanus* *Phrynops raniceps* n = 5	*Podocnemis expansa* *Peltocephalus dumerilianus* *Podocnemis unifilis* *Podocnemis sextuberculata* n = 4	*Podocnemis expansa* *Podocnemis unifilis* *Podocnemis sextuberculata* *Podocnemis erythrocephala* n = 4

4. *Phrynops geoffroanus* (Brazil), *Graptemys nigrinoda*, *Graptemys oculifera*, *Graptemys flavimaculata* (southern USA), and *Graptemys pseudogeographica* (northern USA) are all fairly agile, fast-swimming species, often found in the river current. They feed predominately on insects and other invertebrates, but will take seeds and fruits (no ecological equivalent was present in Mexico).

5. There is not an exact trophic equivalent for *Chelus*; however, *Chelydra serpentina* in Mexico, southern USA, and northern USA, and *Macroclemys* in the southern USA are most similar in foraging activity. All are slow-moving, bottom-walking feeders that strike out rapidly, opening the well-developed hyoid apparatus to aid in sucking in fish and crayfish. *Chelydra* differs by being omnivorous in many localities, whereas *Chelus* and *Macroclemys* are strictly carnivorous.

Test of Pattern II.

The energy available for individuals of a particular species should depend upon diet, and their energy requirements should depend on their body size. As predicted, body size across all turtles increases as density decreases (Figure 3). However, this pattern is not evident within a local habitat (Figure 4), across diet categories (Figure 5), or between habitat categories (Figure 6).

Test of Pattern III.

As predicted, small species appear to be the most diverse within a taxonomic category (Figure 7); however, the sample size is too small to assess statistical significance. This pattern seems to follow the prediction of May (1978, 1986), although Dial and Marzluff (1988) found the highest diversity in average-sized taxa (see also Stanley, 1973). Our data analysis is compromised by the low diversity of living turtle families, because some families (e.g., the Dermatemydidae or Dermochelyidae) are considerably less diverse now than in the past.

Test of Pattern IV.

There is a distinct relationship between the paleontological age of a family and the average size of its extant species (Figure 8). Families with large species or those with small species have had less "success," whereas families with medium-size species (Chelidae, Bataguridae) have been the most "successful." There appear to be contrasting tendencies in two diverse turtle groups: the family Trionychidae and the genus *Graptemys*, the softshells becoming larger and the map turtles smaller. Recent trionychids are, for the most part, large turtles, with a few species approaching one meter in total carapace length. In other trionychoids, small size is common only in the Kinosternidae, with most species in the Dermatemydidae and Carettochelydae reaching 400–500 mm.

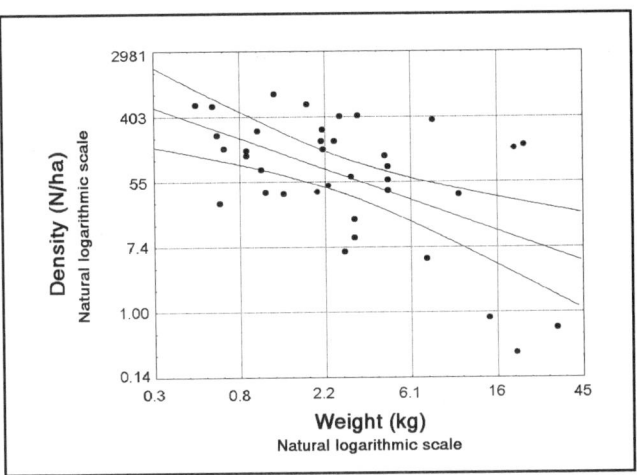

Figure 3. Relationship between density and body mass of turtles throughout the world (n = 37, r = 0.55, $P < 0.001$).

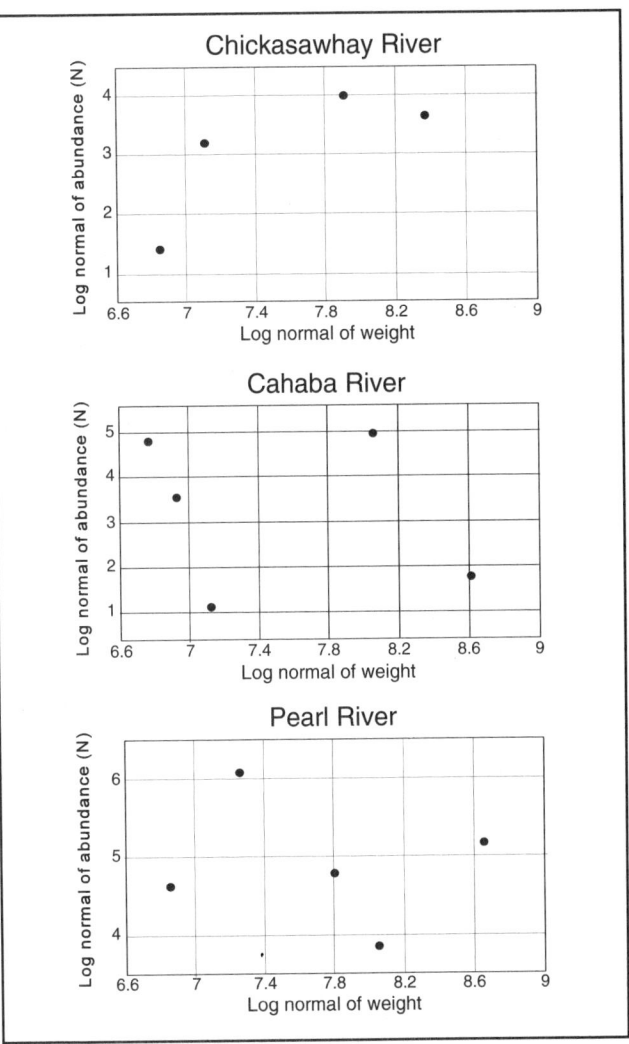

Figure 4. Relationship between abundance and body mass of turtles in three rivers in the USA. Abundances were estimated with Lincoln-Petersen method from capture-recapture data (R. C. Vogt, C. J. McCoy, and J.-L. Villarreal, unpubl. data).

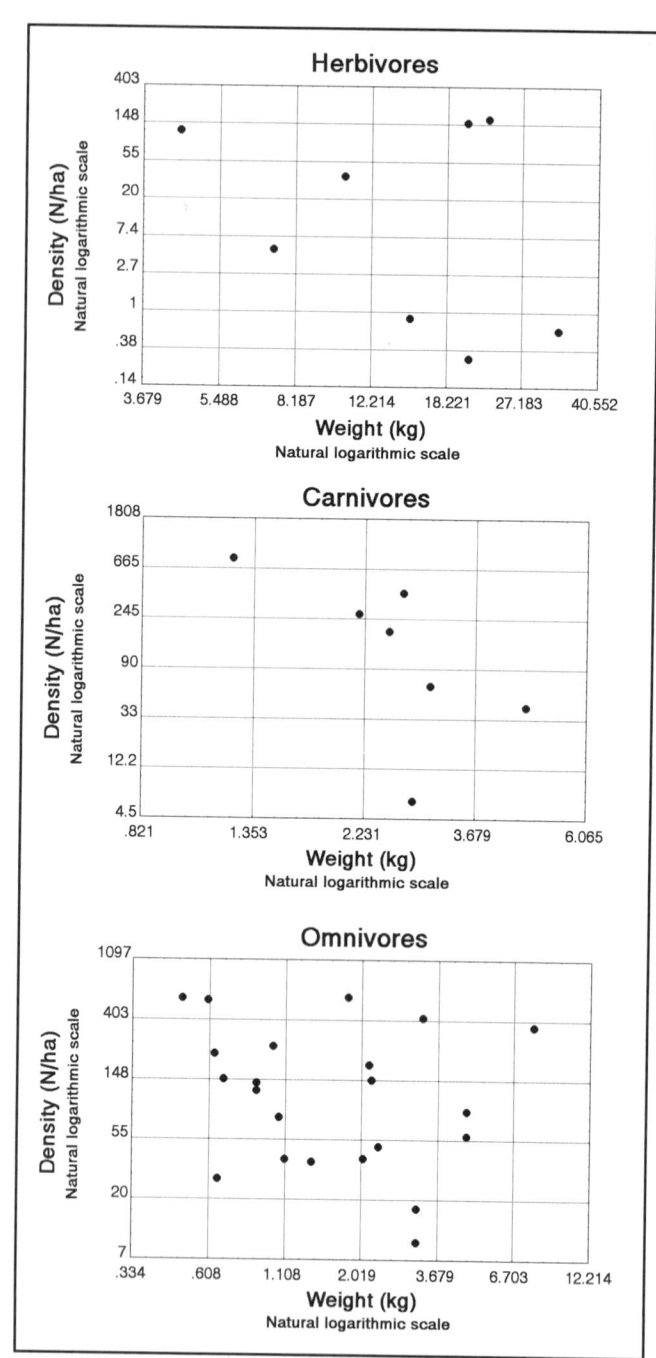

Figure 5. Relationship between density and body mass for different turtles with different diets: Herbivorous, n = 8, r = 0.35, P = 0.30; Carnivorous, n = 7, r = 0.63, P = 0.13; Omnivorous, n = 22, r = 0.22, P = 0.32.

Among the kinosternids, *Staurotypus* almost reaches the size of *Dermatemys*, whereas *Claudius*, *Kinosternon*, and *Sternotherus* are much smaller, usually less than 200 mm. It appears that the reduction in total size is a derived condition common to the Kinosternidae and that reduction in size occurs independently within some of the Trionychidae (Meylan, 1987).

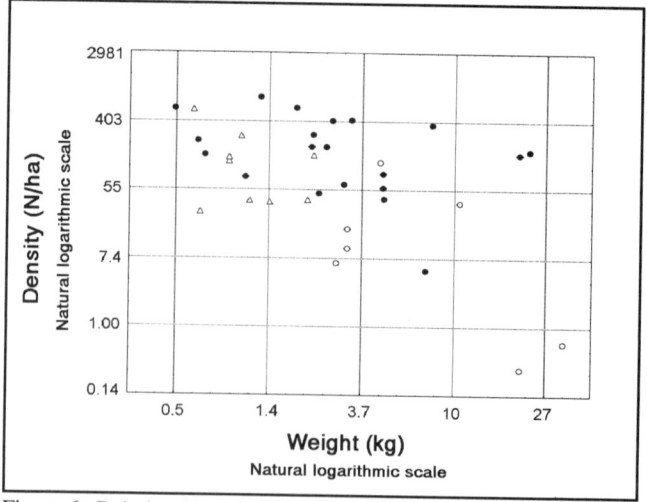

Figure 6. Relationship of body mass to density of turtles in different habitat types: aquatic (dark circles; n = 20, r = 0.33, NS), terrestrial (open circles; n = 7, r = 0.67, NS), semi-aquatic (open triangles; n = 9, r = 0.30, NS).

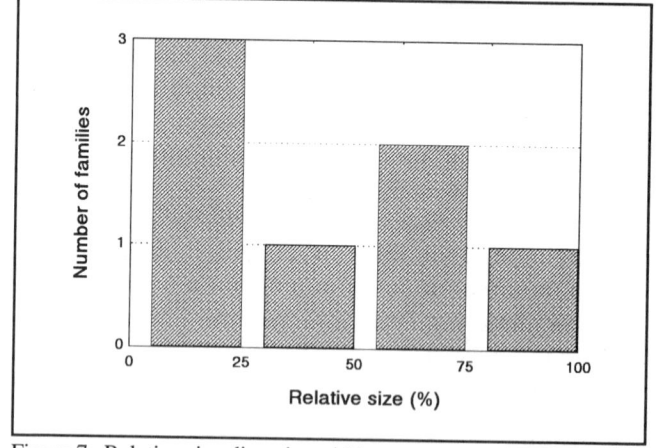

Figure 7. Relative size diversity within seven turtle families. A relative size of 0% indicates that the smallest turtle species in the family are the most diverse; 100%, that the largest sizes are the most diverse.

Following Brown and Maurer (1986), we can conclude that for turtles the ecological consequences of body size provide one mechanistic explanation for the pattern known as Cope's rule (i.e., where body size increases over time in a lineage). Increases in size are directed by sexual selection (in some cases) and by natural selection because of advantages in the monopolization of resources, increases in reproductive output, etc. However, small species appear to have a higher speciation rate (possibly due to higher birth rate), and large species have a higher extinction rate (e.g., the Kinosternidae versus the Dermatemydidae). Thus, Cope's rule as applied to turtles is the result of two evolutionary processes: one operating at the individual level and the other at the species level (Brown and Maurer, 1986).

Body size in turtles is correlated significantly with every life-history trait examined by Iverson (1992c). In general,

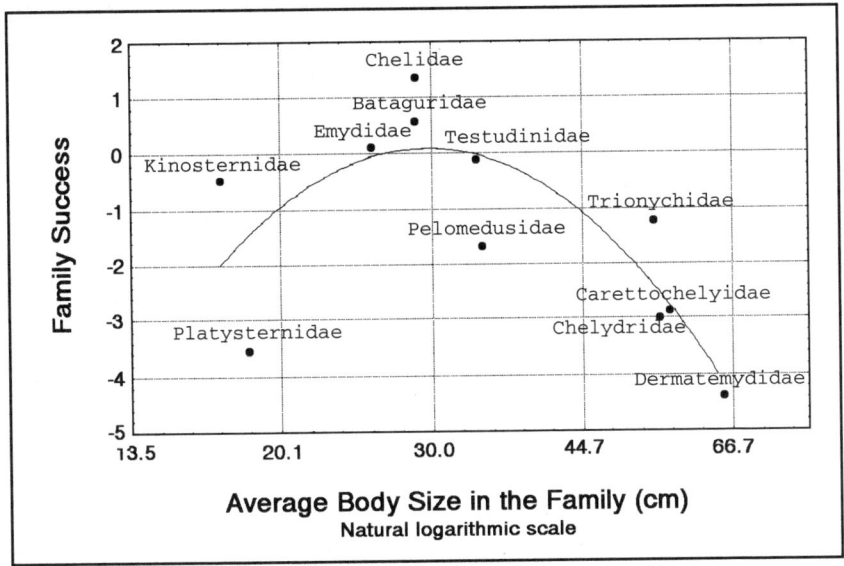

Figure 8. Relationship between body size (carapace length in cm) of turtles in a family and their success (natural logarithm of number of living species/age of the family in millions of years). The curve is a negative exponential regression (n = 11, r = 0.88, $P < 0.01$).

the largest species of turtles tend to be herbivorous, marine or terrestrial, and tend to produce heavier clutches and heavier total annual clutch mass. Age at maturity is correlated with size and early maturing species produce relatively higher clutch masses per year by having a higher clutch frequency. Small species have shorter generation times and higher densities. When the generation time is short and the birth rate is high, one would expect higher rates of speciation. Also, small species have lower individual energetic demands, so that the same resource base can support a larger population. The probability of extinction in smaller species should thus be lower.

CONCLUSIONS AND IMPLICATIONS FOR CONSERVATION

Although the available data are far from complete, turtles may help to clarify the patterns of species diversity in both aquatic and terrestrial communities. We have identified a few of these patterns, and they may help us better understand turtle community structure as well as aid us in making decisions about managing their populations for harvest or conservation.

Those processes that are operating at the local level (such as interspecific interactions) and those that are operating at the global level (such as speciation) interact to determine the composition of the biota at all levels (Cody, 1975; Orians, 1980; Ricklefs, 1987; Brown and Nicoletto, 1991). All of these processes are influenced by the body size of sympatric species because of the pervasive influence of size on physiology, ecology, and behavior. We need additional study at all levels: physiology, to understand energy requirements and energy transfer; population and community ecology, to understand resource use and the partitioning of it; and biogeography and macroevolution, to understand the processes of colonization, extinction, and speciation.

Turtle conservation must take into account (1) geographic distribution, and (2) vulnerability to extinction on the basis of body size and other variables. Together, these can point to spatial scales and habitat types that require protection. Reserves of different sizes and habitats will be differentially effective in prolonging the survival of different species, depending on their body size and other ecological parameters. Body sizes and their associated variables provide a way to assess the ecological roles of species. Understanding patterns of species replacement is important in order to direct our limited time and energy to protect those species most in need of protection and toward those that are savable. Some may already be below the level where populations can recover, and time and effort should not be wasted on them.

ACKNOWLEDGMENTS

Vogt is indebted to the late Jack McCoy for over 25 years of guidance and companionship. Without his enthusiasm, wit, incredible memory, knowledge, and sense of humor, we could not have begun to write this manuscript. The myriad of field assistants: Irish-Greek restaurateurs, zookeepers, airline stewardesses, Playboy bunnies, Wisconsin Department of Natural Resources personnel, USFWS service employees, undergraduate students, graduate students, ichthyologists, Mexican SEDUE employees, Brazilian IBAMA employees, collaborating herpetologists, and wives (one of them Vogt's own) are also all thanked for the help they gave us in generating these data. This paper was written while on sabbatical leave at INPA-CPEC. Paulo Vanzolini, Bill Magnusson, Vitor Hugo Cantarelli, CENAQUA-IBAMA, World Wildlife Fund–U.S. Conservation International, and CNPQ are thanked for their support in Brazil; the Instituto de Biología and DGAPA de UNAM, CONACYT, SEDUE, INIREB, Program for Tropical Studies, and Conservation International are thanked for their support in Mexico; and the University of Wisconsin, the Carnegie Museum of Natural History, and the USFWS are thanked for their support of Vogt's field work in the USA. John Iverson is appreciated for the many hours he devoted helping to whittle this manuscript into a more succinct size and trimming down our rambling prose.

LITERATURE CITED

Brown, J. H. and B. A. Maurer. 1986. Body size, ecological dominance and Cope's rule. Nature 324:248–250.

Brown, J. H. and B. A. Maurer. 1987. Evolution of species assemblages: Effects of energetic constraints and species dynamics on the diversification of the North American avifauna. Amer. Nat. 130:1–17.

Brown, J. H. and P. F. Nicoletto. 1991. Spatial scaling of species composition: Body masses of North American land mammals. Amer. Nat. 138:1478–1512.

Calder, W. A. III. 1984. Size, Function, and Life History. Harvard University Press, Cambridge, Massachusetts.

Cody, M. L. 1975. Towards a theory of continental species diversities: Birds' distribution over Mediterranean habitat gradients. *In* M. L. Cody and J. M. Diamond (eds.), Ecology and Evolution of Communities, pp. 214–257. Harvard University Press, Cambridge, Massachusetts.

Congdon, J. D. and J. W. Gibbons. 1989. Biomass productivity of turtles in freshwater wetlands: A geographic comparison. *In* R. R. Sharitz and J. W. Gibbons (eds.), Freshwater Wetlands and Wildlife, pp. 583–591. USDOE, Oakridge, Tennessee.

Congdon, J. D., J. L. Greene, and J. W. Gibbons. 1986. Biomass of freshwater turtles: A geographic comparison. Amer. Midl. Natur. 115:165–173.

Cotgreave, P. 1993. The relationship between body size and population abundance in animals. TREE 8:244–248.

Damuth, J. 1987. Interspecific allometry of population density in mammals and other animals: The independence of body mass and population energy-use. Biol. J. Linean Soc. 31:193–246.

Dial, K. P. and J. M. Marzluff. 1988. Are the smallest organisms the most diverse? Ecology 69:1620–1624.

Ernst, C. H. and R. Barbour. 1989. Turtles of the World. Smithsonian Inst. Press, Washington, DC. 313 pp. + i–xii.

Fachin-Teran, A., R. C. Vogt, and M. F. Soares Gomes. 1995. Food habits of an assemblage of five species of turtles in the Rio Guapore, Rondônia, Brazil. J. Herpetol. 29:(4)536–547.

Gaston, K. J. and J. H. Lawton. 1988. Patterns in the distribution and abundance of insect populations. Nature 332:709–712.

Gould, S. J. 1988. Trends as changes in variance: A new slant on progress and directionality in evolution. J. Paleo. 62:319–329.

Iverson, J. B. 1982. Biomass in turtle populations: A neglected subject. Oecologia 55:69–76.

Iverson, J. B. 1992a. A Revised Checklist with Distribution Maps of Turtles of the World. Privately printed, Richmond, Indiana. 363 pp.

Iverson, J. B. 1992b. Species richness maps of the freshwater and terrestrial turtles of the world. Smithson. Herpet. Info. Serv. No. 88.

Iverson, J. B. 1992c. Correlates of reproductive output in turtles (Order Testudines). Herpetol. Monogr. 6:25–42.

Lawton, J. H. 1989. What is the relationship between population density and body size in animals? Oikos 55: 429–434.

Maurer, B. A. and J. H. Brown. 1988. Distribution of energy use and biomass among species of North American terrestrial birds. Ecology 69:1923–1932.

Maurer, B. A., J. H. Brown, and R. D. Rusler. 1992. The micro and macro in body size evolution. Evolution 46:939–953.

Maurer, B. A., H. A. Ford, and E. H. Rapoport. 1991. Extinction rate, body size, and avifaunal diversity. Acta XX Cong. Int. Ornith. 2: 826–834.

May, R. M. 1978. The dynamics and diversity of insect faunas. *In* L. A. Mound and N. Waloff (eds.), Diversity of Insect Faunas, pp. 188–204. Blackwell Scientific, Oxford, England.

May, R. M. 1986. The search for patterns in the balance of nature: Advances and retreats. Ecology 67:1115–1126.

Meylan, P. A. 1987. The phylogenetic relationships of soft-shelled turtles (Family Trionychidae). Bull. Amer. Mus. Nat. Hist. 186(1): 1–101.

Morse, D. R., N. E. Stork, and J. H. Lawton. 1988. Species number, species abundance and body length relationships of arboreal beetles in Bornean lowland rain forest trees. Ecol. Entomol. 13:25–37.

Naganuma, K. H. and J. D. Roughgarden. 1990. Optimal body size in lesser Antillean *Anolis* lizards: A mechanistic approach. Ecol. Monogr. 60:239–256.

Nee, S., A. F. Read, J. J. D. Greenwood, and P. H. Harvey. 1991. The relationship between abundance and body size in British birds. Nature 351:312–313.

Orians, G. H. 1980. Micro and macro in ecological theory. BioScience 30:79.

Pagel, M. D., P. H. Harvey, and H. C. J. Godfray. 1991. Species-abundance, biomass, and resource-use distributions. Amer. Nat. 138:836–850.

Peters, R. H. 1983. The Ecological Implications of Body Size. Cambridge University Press, U.K.

Ricklefs, R. E. 1987. Community diversity: Relative roles of local and regional processes. Science 235:167–171.

Rusler, R. D. 1987. Frequency distribution of mammalian body size analyzed by continent. M.S. thesis, University of Arizona, Tucson, Arizona.

Stanley, S. M. 1973. An explanation for Cope's rule. Evolution 27: 1–26.

Vogt, R. C. 1980. New methods for trapping aquatic turtles. Copeia 1980:368–371.

Vogt, R. C. 1981. Food partitioning in three sympatric species of map turtle, genus *Graptemys* (Testudinata, Emydidae). Amer. Midl. Natur. 105:102–111.

Vogt, R. C. and S. G. Guzman. 1988. Food partitioning in a Neotropical freshwater turtle community. Copeia 1988:37–47.

Vrba, E. S. 1987. Ecology in relation to speciation rates: Some case histories of Miocene-Recent mammal clades. Evol. Ecol. 1:283–300.

Nesting Ecology of the Yellow-Spotted River Turtle in the Colombian Amazon

VIVIAN P. PÁEZ AND BRIAN C. BOCK

Proyecto Terecay, Fundación Natura, AA 55402, Santa Fe de Bogotá, Colombia
Present Address: Departmento de Biología, Universidad de Antioquía, Medellín, Colombia
[e-mail: vpaez@quimbaya.udea.edu.co]

ABSTRACT: *Podocnemis expansa* and *Podocnemis unifilis* occur in sympatry throughout much of the Amazon basin, and both are highly exploited for their meat and eggs. While *P. unifilis* has received much less research and conservation attention, it possesses a variety of life history traits that may ultimately make it easier to manage as a sustainable resource for local people. This paper presents preliminary data from the first year of a study of *P. unifilis* nesting ecology in the Río Caquetá of the Colombian Amazon. Results of artificial incubation and captive rearing studies also are presented.

The Department of Amazonas in Colombia is sparsely populated (approx. 0.5 persons/km^2), although the number of inhabitants has more than doubled in the past 12 years. As human population densities increase, traditional subsistence practices will cease to be sustainable, and alternative strategies for the management of natural resources will be needed. In the Amazon basin, aquatic species are often among the first to be impacted by increasing human densities, as settlements tend to be concentrated along the major rivers. For example, over 70% of the population of the Department of Amazonas resides along only 115 km of the Amazon River. In this area, residents complain that many traditional aquatic resources, including *Podocnemis* turtles, have become increasingly scarce in recent years.

In 1992 we began a project in the Colombian Amazon to obtain basic information on the ecology of the yellow-spotted river turtle, *Podocnemis unifilis*. We focused on *P. unifilis* rather than its larger congener, *P. expansa*, because *P. expansa* had already been studied extensively in Brazil (Vanzolini, 1967; Alho et al., 1979; Alho and Padua, 1982a, 1982b; Alho et al., 1984a, 1984b; Cantarelli and Herde, 1989), in Venezuela (Mosquiera Manso, 1945; Mondolfi, 1955; Ramirez, 1956; Roze, 1964; Ojasti, 1967, 1971; Flores, 1969), and in Colombia (Medem, 1960, 1969; von Hildebrand et al., 1988). Although *P. unifilis* is also of economic importance and highly over-exploited (IUCN, 1989), fewer studies of its ecology have been published (Mondolfi, 1955; Medem, 1964, 1969; Foote, 1978). In addition, *P. unifilis* exhibits characteristics that suggest it may be more feasible to manage than *P. expansa*. Unlike *P. expansa*, *P. unifilis* does not always nest in easily exploitable aggregations, and it may grow faster, mature earlier, reproduce more frequently, and tolerate captive conditions better. It also has the largest range of all species in the genus (Iverson, 1992), potentially making research findings more broadly applicable for management purposes. By investigating a variety of aspects of the life history of *P. unifilis* in the field and laboratory, we should be able to develop an effective local management program for this species. Here we report preliminary data from the first year of our project and summarize future research directions.

Study Site Selection

The project is based near the settlement of La Pedrera, located on the Río Caquetá near the Brazilian border (1°18′ S, 69°33′ W), in an area where *P. unifilis* is still abundant. Approximately 20 km upriver from La Pedrera are rapids navigable only by small boats. Past this point, a number of large beaches, seasonally exposed from October to April, are used as nesting sites by *P. unifilis*.

We began our field studies on a beach located adjacent to Isla Mirití, at the confluence of the Mirití-Paraná and Caquetá rivers. This site is within an indigenous "resguardo" (reserve), so we met with officials from nearby communities to explain our project and obtain their authorization to work on this beach. Even though the number of nesting females was relatively small, we documented unexpectedly high levels of human predation on turtles and nests during the first three weeks of nesting activity in December of 1993. Despite promises from the nearby communities that members would not visit this particular beach, every rainless night people came to the beach in search of turtles or eggs. On 50% of the nights, fishermen looked for tracks leading to fresh nests. On the remaining nights, people actually slept on the beach, making periodic rounds to capture nesting females. As we had no authority to prohibit these activities, we abandoned this site to search for one that was more isolated.

In January of 1994 we shifted our field studies to a nesting beach adjacent to the Isla Cahuinarí at the confluence of the Cahuinarí and Caquetá rivers within the Cahuinarí National Park, approximately 200 km upriver from La Pedrera. This area is much less densely populated, and fishing and river travel are also less common because of the scarcity of gasoline. In addition, a cabin for park guards is located within view of the beach. Human predation of turtle nests in much less frequent at this site. We encountered signs of people visiting this beach on only two nights during the second half of the nesting season and found no evidence that they had removed any nests. *P. unifilis* nesting activity at the beach was high.

Field Studies

On 12 January 1994 we encountered nine *P. unifilis* nests that had been constructed the preceding night. We implanted two Teflon-coated type T (Cu-constantan) thermocouples (Omega Engineering, Inc.) in each nest, a shallow probe at the level of the first egg and a deep probe at 10 cm into the egg mass. Nest temperatures were recorded several times daily during daylight hours with a digital thermometer (HH-25-TC, Omega Engineering, Inc.) to the nearest 0.1°C. It was our intention to monitor temperatures in these nests throughout the entire incubation period, but a rise in the river level after 61 days of incubation forced us to transfer all nine temperature-monitored nests, as well as seven other nests we had marked, to the highest part of the beach. Because the river level continued to rise, after eight more days we again transferred the seven temperature-monitored nests that had not yet hatched, as well as four additional nests, to an artificial incubation area we constructed near the park cabin. Despite these manipulations, 76% of the eggs from our temperature-monitored nests hatched successfully. Of the eggs that did not hatch, 14% were apparently infertile or otherwise failed to develop, and another 10% were infected with a parasitic fly larvae. The incubation periods we documented (Table 1) exceeded all other incubation periods reported for this species from natural nests (Soini, 1980; Cantarelli and Herde, 1989; Fachin, 1993; Thorbjarnarson et al., 1993), with the exception of those reported by Medem (1964, 1969) from the same river drainage.

The frequency of flooding during the turtle nesting season in this part of the Caquetá river is high (Medem, 1960; von Hildebrand et al., 1988; Duivenvoorden and Lips, 1993). As eggs tolerate transfer to higher beach sites, and even to artificial incubation areas, transferring nests may represent an important management technique for *P. unifilis* in this area. We are presently conducting additional studies to determine whether there is an optimal time during the incubation period to transfer *P. unifilis* nests, and whether nest transfer affects fly larvae infestation rates.

Because of the effect of incubation temperature on sex determination in many species, changes in incubation temperature resulting from the transfer of turtle nests must be taken into account (Morreale, et al., 1982; Janzen and Paukstis, 1991). Our temperature data indicated that moving the nests to the highest part of the beach did not significantly change nest temperatures (shallow or deep probes, ANOVA, $P > 0.05$), but transferring them off the beach to the artificial incubation area significantly lowered temperatures for the final days of incubation (shallow and deep probes, ANOVA, $P < 0.001$). Considering only the initial nest location temperature data, we documented consistent, significant differences between the nine temperature-monitored nests, with mean incubation temperatures ranging from 28.1 to 31.5°C

TABLE 1

Mean incubation temperatures recorded from the nine temperature nests at the Isla Cahuinarí beach (pre-transfer nest locations, n = 80 measurements per nest on 43 days during a total of 61 days of incubation), depths to the first egg, and total incubation periods for each nest.

Nest	Shallow probe temperature (°C) Mean	St. Dev.	Deep probe temperature (°C) Mean	St. Dev.	Depth of first egg (cm)	Incubation period (days)
1	31.5	4.0	30.6	3.5	12.4	69
2	31.1	3.9	29.4	2.6	7.4	69
3	30.7	3.9	29.2	2.3	10.2	73
4	30.4	3.5	29.5	2.6	14.3	78
5	30.3	3.4	29.1	2.2	8.1	71
6	30.3	3.4	29.7	3.1	13.7	76
7	30.3	3.6	29.0	1.9	9.9	78
8	30.0	3.4	28.8	2.2	10.4	78
9	29.5	3.2	28.1	1.7	10.1	83

(Table 1). The variation in mean incubation temperatures between the nests was not related to differences in nest depths (Spearman rank correlation for shallow probe data, r = 0.05, $P > 0.05$) or any other obvious environmental factor but was negatively correlated with incubation period (Spearman rank correlation for shallow probe data, r = −0.80, $P < 0.01$). Incubation periods from these nine nests (all laid on the same date) ranged from 69 to 83 days (Table 1).

We measured 15 morphological variables for each hatchling turtle obtained from the beach. Hatchlings from the two nests that exhibited the most extreme incubation temperatures were transferred to La Pedrera for part of our study of temperature effects on sex ratios (see below). Once the sexes of these individuals are determined, an analysis of the morphometric data may help confirm the statement by Medem (1969) that natives are able to distinguish male from female hatchlings in this population. If true, the morphometric data from the remaining turtles may be analyzed to approximate the overall sex ratio of the hatchlings produced on the beach this year.

Hatchlings from the remaining 24 nests were marked by notching marginal scutes (Cagle, 1939) and released after their yolk sacs had been fully absorbed. We released 50% of the turtles at the river's edge near the flooded beach site. Because local people had indicated that hatchling turtles disperse from the beaches into shallow lakes along the river margins or on the larger river islands, we released the remaining 50% in a lake on Isla Cahuinarí.

Laboratory Studies

Controlled artificial incubation studies were conducted during our first year at the project's laboratory facility in La Pedrera. Eggs from two nests were transferred to the laboratory and divided into three incubation treatments (Table 2). One third of the eggs were placed in an incubator that maintained relatively stable low temperatures throughout the incubation period. Another third were placed in an incubator set to maintain relatively stable high incubation temperatures. Finally, one third of the eggs were incubated in an outdoor area where the eggs were subject to natural daily fluctuations in soil temperatures. Hatching success rates were high for all three experimental conditions, although the differences in incubation temperatures between the treatments produced substantial differences in incubation periods (Table 2).

There were significant differences in mean initial hatchling sizes between the turtles from the two nests (carapace length, ANOVA, $P < 0.001$; mass, ANOVA, $P < 0.001$), which paralleled the significant differences we recorded in mean egg mass between the nests (ANOVA, $P < 0.001$). We also encountered significant initial size differences between hatchlings from the three incubation treatments, with the smallest hatchlings emerging earliest from the high incubation temperature treatment (carapace length, ANOVA, $P < 0.005$; mass, ANOVA, $P < 0.01$). There was no significant interaction between nest and incubation effects (carapace length and mass, two-way ANOVA, $P > 0.05$).

After emergence the turtles were isolated for a week until their yolk sacs were absorbed and then placed in individual feeding trials to assess their initial food preferences. Field data have shown that adult *P. unifilis* are primarily herbivorous (de Almeida et al., 1986), but data on natural juvenile diets are lacking. In captivity, juvenile *P. unifilis* accept a variety of food items, including meat (Belkin and Gans, 1968; Cole and Link, 1972). But in some turtle species, the initial food items presented to captive hatchlings influence their subsequent diet preferences (Burghardt and Hess, 1966; Burghardt, 1967). Because such food "imprinting" could have important implications for management projects that rear juveniles for later release, we offered small pieces of

TABLE 2
Mean incubation temperatures recorded from the three artificial incubation treatments in La Pedrera, with ranges of incubation periods of individual eggs in each treatment, by nest.

Incubation treatments	Mean incubation temperatures (°C) Mean	St. Dev.	Range in incubation period[a] (days) Nest 1	Nest 2
High temperature incubator	31.9	1.23	47–50	48–55
Artificial outdoor nest				
shallow probe	27.5	2.07	75	75–88
deep probe	27.1	1.43		
Low temperature incubator	27.1	0.75	82–86	81–94

[a]Nest 1 was transferred to the laboratory two days following oviposition; the age of Nest 2 at the time of transfer is not known. Thus, incubation period here refers to the number of days the eggs were incubated under the three laboratory treatments.

fresh meat, fruit, and leaves to each turtle daily, recording when they began to feed and their initial food preferences. Most turtles began feeding within two weeks following emergence and readily accepted all three types of food items presented. It was not possible to predict subsequent feeding preferences based upon what item an individual selected for its first feeding.

After completing the food preference trials, the majority of the hatchling turtles were incorporated into an ongoing study that is examining the effects of diet, density, and basking opportunities on captive juvenile growth rates. Our preliminary data showed that all turtles initially increased in body size but decreased in weight, presumably as they expended their internalized yolk reserves. Eventually, increases in both size and weight occurred. Although the turtles from the high incubation temperature treatment emerged at smaller sizes and weights, they had attained body sizes greater than (carapace length, ANOVA, $P < 0.001$) and weights equivalent to (mass, ANOVA, $P > 0.05$) the turtles in the other treatments when they finally hatched. Although eggs incubated at warmer temperatures produce smaller hatchlings, the reduced incubation period and earlier onset of feeding may result in warm nest neonates being larger, at a given time, than hatchlings from cool nests laid at the same time.

However, because incubation temperature determines sex in *P. unifilis* (Remor de Souza, 1992), and because juvenile growth rates often differ between sexes in turtles, we initiated studies of sex determination in these turtles. To determine the threshold temperature for this population, gonads were extracted from hatchlings from the high and low temperature treatments and from the extreme temperature nests in our field study. These are under examination for classification as either ovaries or testes. We hope that these results will allow us to infer the sexes of the turtles we are rearing in the captive juvenile growth study.

The theoretical literature on temperature-dependent sex determination in reptiles contends that this mechanism ultimately may be adaptive when (1) the kinds of environments offspring experience are unpredictable, and (2) certain environments favor one sex much more than the other (Charnov and Bull, 1977; Graham et al., 1987). In many turtle species, adult females are larger than males, presumably because larger size confers a greater advantage to females because of the relationship between female body size and fecundity (Gibbons, 1982). Recent reviews (Ewert and Nelson, 1991; Janzen and Paukstis, 1991) have shown that in those turtle species known to have both temperature-dependent sex determination and larger adult female sizes, most exhibit only one threshold temperature, with females being produced at higher incubation temperatures. Presumably, hatchlings from eggs that are incubated in warmer environments would be more likely to have a greater potential for growth. Eggs in cooler sites presumably produce hatchlings with less growth potential.

P. unifilis exhibits adult sexual dimorphism with females larger than males (Medem, 1964), and our preliminary data have shown that by the end of the emergence period, hatchlings from higher incubation temperatures do attain body sizes larger than those of the other treatments. It is difficult to imagine, however, that these small differences in initial sizes translate into adult size differences many years later. Yet studies with reptiles often demonstrate marked adult size variation that is not simply the result of age differences between individuals. Rather, in many species, adult size variation is determined largely by differences in juvenile growth rates and the sizes at which growth trajectories asymptote once breeding begins (Carr and Goodman, 1970; Halliday and Verrell, 1988). Our long-term captive rearing studies seek to document whether incubation treatment and/or initial size differences between hatchlings influence subsequent growth rates in *P. unifilis* maintained on controlled diets.

Our project is also investigating other potential effects of differing incubation temperatures on *P. unifilis* hatchlings. Perhaps the advantages of becoming females under warmer incubation temperatures and males under cooler incubation temperatures are more subtle and are related to developmental physiology or aspects of general physical condition. For example, in several reptile species (that do not exhibit temperature-dependent sex determination), it has been shown that incubation temperature influences subsequent behavioral attributes of the juveniles that may be correlated in the wild with survivorship abilities (Burger, 1989, 1990). We therefore have developed a series of tests to determine juvenile turtle physical condition (i.e., running speeds, swimming speeds, righting abilities), which are periodically administered to the individuals we are rearing.

We intend to expand our artificial incubation studies to include more temperature treatments, both to more precisely define the threshold temperature for this population and to more rigorously test predictions of sex determination theory concerning incubation effects on subsequent fitness. This research may also have relevance to future management programs intending to rear and release into a threatened population a given proportion of males and females that exhibit rapid growth and have good physical condition.

CONCLUSIONS

The conservation benefits of captive rearing turtles have been seriously questioned in the literature (Ehrenfeld, 1974; Dodd, 1982; Johns, 1987; Frazer, this volume). Opponents claim that commercial farming ventures merely expand the demand for products obtained from already overexploited species while providing little protein to needy people. Well-intentioned headstarting programs have also been criticized because eggs are often collected from natural nesting sites rather than produced via captive breeding and because data are often lacking to support claims that such programs actually benefit the populations into which captive-reared individuals are released.

Yet in many developing countries, less intrusive management practices, such as protecting turtle habitat or prohibiting turtle or egg consumption, are largely ineffective (Gomez, 1982) and often serve to alienate local people from conservation issues in general. Such methods may work in some cultures, but they do not work at all in others.

We believe that turtle hatchery, headstarting, and captive-breeding projects should be encouraged, but only if they explicitly include studies designed to evaluate the effectiveness of the techniques they employ and provide information on the basic biology of the species involved. Whatever the preferred management strategy, improvements in our knowledge of the species will lead to greater conservation success.

Acknowledgments

The Project Terecay has been funded by the Fondo Colombiano de Investigaciones Científicas y Proyectos Especiales "Francisco José de Caldas"—Colciencias, the Wildlife Conservation Society, the Turtle Recovery Program, and the IUCN Tortoise and Freshwater Turtle Specialist Group, the Chicago Zoological Society, the Sophie Danforth Conservation Fund of the Roger Williams Park Zoo and Rhode Island Zoological Society, and the Grupo Ecológico Gea.

We would like to thank INDERENA for permission to conduct our studies under the program "Universidad en los Parques." The project would not be feasible without the participation of our undergraduate thesis students, Oscar Almanza, Angela Ortega, and Néstor Pérez, or our indigenous field assistants, Dario Silva Cubeo and Crispin Miraña. We also would like to thank the following people for the special attention they have given to our project: Santiago Duque, Michael Klemens, Scott Moody, João Muñoz, Rosa Luz Nieto, Claudia Romero, Aureliano Sanint, Wilson Triviño, and Humberto Trujillo.

Literature Cited

Alho, C. J. R. and L. F. M. Padua. 1982a. Sincronia entre regime de vazante do rio e o comportamento de nidificação da tartaruga da Amazonia *Podocnemis expansa* (Testudinata: Pelomedusidae). Acta Amazon. 12:323–326.

Alho, C. J. R. and L. F. M. Padua. 1982b. Reproductive parameters and nesting behavior of the Amazon turtle *Podocnemis expansa* (Testudinata: Pelomedusidae) in Brasil. Can. J. Zool. 60:97–103.

Alho, C. J. R., A. G. Carvalho, and L. F. M. Padua. 1979. Ecologia da tartaruga da Amazônia e avaliação de seu manejo na Reserva Biólogica do Trombetas. Brasil Forestal 38:29–47.

Alho, C. J. R., T. M. S. Danni, and L. F. M. Padua. 1984a. Influencia da temperatura de incubação na determinação do sexo da tartaruga de Amazônia *Podocnemis expansa* (Testudinata, Pelomedusidae). Rev. Brasil. Biol. 44:305–311.

Alho, C. J. R., T. M. S. Danni, and L. F. M. Padua. 1984b. Temperature-dependent sex determination in *Podocnemis expansa* (Testudinata, Pelomedusidae). Biotropica 17:75–78.

Belkin, D. A. and C. Gans. 1968. An unusual chelonian feeding niche. Ecology 49:768–769.

Burger, J. 1989. Incubation temperature has long-term effects on behaviour of young pine snakes (*Pituophis melanoleucus*). Behav. Ecol. Sociobiol. 24:201–207.

Burger, J. 1990. Effects of incubation temperature on behavior of young black racers (*Coluber constrictor*) and kingsnakes (*Lampropeltus getulus*). J. Herpetol. 24:158–163.

Burghardt, G. M. 1967. The primacy effect of the first feeding experience in the snapping turtle. Psychonom. Sci. 7:383–384.

Burghardt, G. M. and E. H. Hess. 1966. Food imprinting in the snapping turtle, *Chelydra serpentina*. Science 151:108–109.

Cagle, F. R. 1939. A system for marking turtles for future identification. Copeia 1939:170–173.

Cantarelli, V. H. and L. C. Herde (eds.). 1989. Projeto Quelônios da Amazônia—10 Anos. Instituto Brasileiro do Meio Ambiente e dos Recursos Naturais Renováveis. Ministério do Interior, Brasília.

Carr, A. and D. Goodman. 1970. Ecological implications of size and growth in Chelonia. Copeia 1970:783–786.

Charnov, E. L. and J. J. Bull. 1977. When is sex environmentally determined? Nature 266:828–830.

Cole, M. and B. Link. 1972. *Podocnemis* in captivity. Int. Turtle Tortoise Soc. J. 6:12–14.

de Almeida, S. S., P. G. S. Sá, and A. Garcia. 1986. Vegetais utilizados como alimento por *Podocnemis* (Chelonia) na Região do Baixo Rio Xingu (Brasil-Pará). Bol. Mus. Para. Emilio Goeldi Bot. 2:199–211.

Dodd, C. K., Jr. 1982. Does sea turtle aquaculture benefit conservation? *In* K. A. Bjorndal (ed.), Biology and Conservation of Sea Turtles, pp. 473–480. Smithsonian Inst. Press, Washington, D.C.

Duivenvoorden, J. F. and J. M. Lips. 1993. Ecología del Paisaje del Medio Caquetá. Estudios en la Amazonía Colombiana. Vol. 3. Tropenbos, Bogotá.

Ehrenfeld, D. W. 1974. Conserving the edible sea turtle: Can mariculture help? Amer. Sci. 62:23–31.

Ewert, M. A. and C. E. Nelson. 1991. Sex determination in turtles: Diverse patterns and some possible adaptive values. Copeia 1991:50–69.

Fachin-T., A. 1993. Características de *Podocnemis unifilis* (Reptilia, Testudines) en el río Samaria, Loreto. Boletín de Lima 87:67–74.

Flores, C. 1969. Notas sobre reptiles acuáticos de Venezuela y su importancia económica. Lagena 21/22:1–19.

Foote, R. W. 1978. Nesting of *Podocnemis unifilis* (Testudines: Pelomedusidae) in the Colombian Amazon. Herpetologica 34:333–339.

Frazer, N. B. 1997. Turtle Conservation and Halfway Technology: What is the Problem? *In* J. Van Abbema (ed.), Proceedings: Conservation, Management, and Restoration of Tortoises and Turtles—An International Conference, pp. 422–425. July 1993, State University of New York, Purchase. New York Turtle and Tortoise Society, New York.

Gibbons, J. W. 1982. Reproductive patterns in freshwater turtles. Herpetologica 38:222–227.

Gomez, E. D. 1982. Problems of enforcing sea turtle conservation laws in developing countries. *In* K. A. Bjorndal (ed.), Biology and Conservation of Sea Turtles, pp. 537–539. Smithsonian Institution Press, Washington, D.C.

Graham, H., R. M. May, and L. Pendleton. 1987. Environmental determination of sex in reptiles. Nature 239:198–199.

Halliday, T. R. and P. A. Verrell. 1988. Body size and age in amphibians and reptiles. J. Herpetol. 22:253–265.

IUCN/SSC Tortoise and Freshwater Turtle Specialist Group. 1989. Tortoises and freshwater turtles: An action plan for their conservation (D. Stubbs, comp.). IUCN/SSC Tortoise and Freshwater Turtle Specialist Group, Gland, Switzerland.

Iverson, J. B. 1992. A Revised Checklist with Distribution Maps of the Turtles of the World. Privately printed, Richmond, Indiana.

Janzen, F. J. and G. L. Paukstis. 1991. Environmental sex determination in reptiles: Ecology, evolution, and experimental design. Quart. Rev. Biol. 66:149–179.

Johns, A. D. 1987. Continuing problems for Amazon river turtles. Oryx 21:25–28.

Medem, F. 1960. Datos zoogeográficos y ecológicos sobre los Crocodylia y Testudinata de los Rios Amazonas, Putumayo y Caquetá. Caldasia 8:341–351.

Medem, F. 1964. Morphologie, Ökologie, und Verbreitung der Schildkröte *Podocnemis unifilis* in Kolumbien (Testudinata, Pelomedusidae). Senckenb. Biol. 45:353–368.

Medem, F. 1969. Estudios adicionales sobre los Crocodylia y Testudinata del Alto Caquetá y Rio Caguan. Caldasia 10:329–353.

Mondolfi, E. 1955. Anotaciones sobre la biología de tres quelonios de los llanos de Venezuela. Mem. Soc. Cienc. Nat. La Salle (Caracas) 15:177–183.

Morreale, S. J., G. J. Ruiz, J. R. Spotila, and E. A. Standora. 1982. Temperature-dependent sex determination: Current practices threaten conservation of sea turtles. Science 216:1245–1247.

Mosquiera Manso, J. M. 1945. The tortoises of the Orinoco. Biological notes of *Podocnemis expansa*. 3d Interam. Conf. Agr. Caracas 29:5–43.

Ojasti, J. 1967. Consideraciones sobre la ecología y conservación de la tortuga *Podocnemis expansa* (Chelonia, Pelomedusidae). Atas Simpósio Biota Amazonica 7:201–206.

Ojasti, J. 1971. La tortuga arrua del Orinoco. Defensa de la Nat. 1:3–9.

Ramirez, E. M. V. 1956. Estudio biológico de la tortuga "Arrua" del Orinoco. Agr. Venez. 190:44–63.

Remor de Souza, R. 1992. Fatores que influenciam a determinação de sexo no tracajá (*Podocnemis unifilis*, Testudinata, Pelomedusidae). Masters thesis, Instituto Nacional de Pesquisas da Amazónia. Fundação Universidade do Amazonas, Manaus.

Roze, J. A. 1964. Pilgrim of the river. Nat. Hist. 73:34–41.

Soini, P. 1980. Reproducción, manejo, y conservación de los quelonios del genero *Podocnemis* (Charapa, Cupiso, y Taricaya). Informe de Pacaya No. 2. Estación Biológica de Cahuana, Reserva Nacional Pacaya-Samiria, Peru.

Thorbjarnarson, J. B., N. Perez, and T. Escalona. 1993. Nesting of *Podocnemis unifilis* in the Capanaparo River, Venezuela. J. Herpetol. 27:344–347.

Vanzolini, P. E. 1967. Notes on the nesting behavior of *Podocnemis expansa* in the Amazon valley (Testudines, Pelomedusidae). Pap. Avuls. Zool. Sao Paulo 20:191–215.

von Hildebrand, P., C. Sáenz, M. C. Peñuela, and C. Caro. 1988. Biología reproductiva y manejo de la tortuga Charapa (*Podocnemis expansa*) en el bajo Rio Caquetá. Colombia Amazónica 3:89–112.

On the Ecology of Some Freshwater Turtles in Bangladesh

SHEIK M. A. RASHID[1] AND IAN R. SWINGLAND[2]

[1]*Centre for Advanced Research in Natural Resources & Management (CARINAM), 70 Kakrail, Dhaka-1000, Bangladesh*
[e-mail: carinam@citecho.net]
[2]*Durrell Institute of Conservation & Ecology (DICE), University of Kent, Canterbury, Kent CT2 7NX, United Kingdom*
[e-mail: 106407.3135@compuserve.com]

ABSTRACT: The habitat, distribution, status, food and feeding habits, breeding, allometric relationships, and ecology of 11 freshwater and one estuarine turtle species inhabiting Bangladesh are reviewed in this paper. The species are *Geoclemys hamiltonii, Morenia petersi, Hardella thurjii, Kachuga smithii, Kachuga tecta, Kachuga tentoria, Batagur baska, Lissemys punctata, Chitra indica, Aspideretes nigricans*, *A. gangeticus*, and *A. hurum*. Four subspecies, *Kachuga tentoria tentoria* Gray 1834, *Kachuga tentoria flaviventer* Moll 1987, *Kachuga smithii smithii* Gray 1863, *Kachuga smithii pallidipes* Moll 1987, originally described from India are reported here for the first time from Bangladesh. Polymorphic forms of *Aspideretes hurum* are also reported.

The habitats of most of these species have degraded, and several species are now absent from parts of their former range. One species, *Kachuga tecta*, occupies brackish water habitats (Rashid, 1991a). The males of *Aspideretes nigricans*, *A. gangeticus*, and *A. hurum* were found to be larger than the females. A predominance of medium-size individuals suggests that most of the large adults have been exploited, and there is limited recruitment.

Of the species studied (except for *Hardella thurjii*), larger females have high fecundity, laying relatively large numbers of large, heavy eggs; and smaller females have lower fecundity, laying fewer, smaller, and lighter eggs. All members of the family Trionychidae lay multiple clutches of spherical eggs. Only some of the Bataguridae lay multiple clutches; all batagurid eggs are elongate. Trionychids are primarily carnivorous or omnivorous; batagurids are primarily herbivorous or omnivorous.

The conservation status of each species is discussed, and where appropriate, recommendations for management are made.

Ecology has long been of critical interest to biologists, naturalists, and conservationists. As human population has progressively increased, environmental problems have become of vital interest and importance to the public as well. It is now imperative that the ecological status and integrity of specific regions and their flora and fauna be understood by both lay and professional communities.

Among the reptiles, turtles are intriguing because of their longevity, survival in a variety of habitats, and relatively unchanged morphology throughout their 200-million-year history. Their box-like shell is in itself unique and distinguishes them from other vertebrates.

Turtles inhabit both the tropics and temperate regions, in diverse habitats. Tropical Bangladesh supports at least 10% of the world's living species of turtles. The country is rich in turtle species because its fauna comprises elements of both the Malayan and Indian subregions of the Oriental region. Much of Bangladesh comprises the vast Ganges-Brahmaputra-Meghna delta and associated floodplains, and these wetlands provide suitable habitats for a high diversity of freshwater turtle species.

Freshwater turtles in Bangladesh are represented by the families Bataguridae and Trionychidae. The Bataguridae, with its sister family the Emydidae, is the largest and most diverse assemblage of freshwater and semi-terrestrial turtles, with 33 genera and approximately 90 species worldwide. Emydids are found primarily in the Americas and batagurids in Europe, northern Africa, and Asia. Fossil evidence indicates that the family was formerly more widespread in Europe and Asia. The oldest known fossils are from Paleocene deposits in Saskatchewan (Russel, 1934) and Eocene deposits in Europe, North America, and Asia (Romer, 1956).

Most species inhabit fresh water but spend many hours basking everyday out of the water; a few species are found in brackish water, while some are largely terrestrial.

The softshell turtles of the family Trionychidae have scuteless, flexible carapaces, and only three claws on each foot. The distribution of the family includes temperate eastern North America, tropical south and southeast Asia, countries of the Mediterranean region, the Euphrates River drainage, and much of Africa.

Softshells are highly aquatic, generally wary in the wild, and capable of rapid locomotion both on land and in water. They have soft skin with scales that are reduced to a few sickle-shaped lamellae on the limbs. Peripheral bones are completely absent, except for rudiments (or neomorphs) in *Lissemys punctata*. They have long, highly mobile, flexible necks and frequently aggressive dispositions. The snout usually ends in a proboscis that may be long and thin or relatively short and stout. The genera of living softshells are separated into two sub-families, the Cyclanorbinae (represented in Bangladesh by *Lissemys punctata*) and the Trionychinae (represented in Bangladesh by *Aspideretes*, *Chitra*, and *Pelochelys*). The two groups are distinguished by the presence only in the former of fleshy femoral flaps which can be closed to conceal the hind limbs. Further details and descriptions for the classification of the turtles discussed here are given by Smith (1931), McDowell (1964), Meylan (1987), and Moll (1987).

The chelonians of Bangladesh are relatively undocumented; little work has been done on their ecology, life history, status, and distribution. An earlier work considered seminal in herpetological studies of the Indian subcontinent is Smith (1931), although very few specimens mentioned in this work were from localities under the jurisdiction of the present Bangladesh (formerly East Pakistan and East Bengal). Other earlier works that are noteworthy are Anderson (1879) and Boulenger (1890). Smith (1931) recognised 18 species of turtles in the subcontinent, of which 12 occurred in Bengal, whereas Ahamed (1958) listed nine species of edible freshwater turtles in East Pakistan. Daniel (1983) provided useful information on the chelonians of the Indian subcontinent. Shafi and Quddus (1977) describe chelonians from Bangladesh based on preserved museum specimens in the Department of Zoology, University of Dhaka. They added the Bangladesh marine species to the list but also erroneously included many turtle species belonging to the New World.

Husain (1979) reviewed the species found in Bangladesh and included an additional genus, *Indotestudo*. Later, Khan (1982a, 1987) reported 25 species of chelonians in Bangladesh, giving information on their status and distribution. He reported *Aspideretes* (= *Trionyx*) *nigricans* and *Morenia petersi* to be endemic and *Cuora amboinensis* for the first time in Bangladesh. Fugler (1984) enumerated 18 species of freshwater turtles in Bangladesh following Pritchard (1979).

Sarker and Sarker (1988) reported 31 chelonian species for Bangladesh. However, some of these—*Morenia ocellata*, *Aspideretes leithii*, *Pelochelys cantorii*, and *Kachuga lineata* (= *K. trivittata*)—are either restricted to the far eastern countries or to peninsular India, with no evidence of their occurrence within Bangladesh's borders (Pritchard, 1979; Ernst and Barbour, 1989; Das, 1991; Iverson, 1992), or may no longer be recognised by these names.

Uddin (1983) reported *Kachuga sylhetensis*, based on the examination of a shell, from the Sylhet district, and also the collection of a live specimen of *Cuora amboinensis* from Teknaf Peninsula. Unfortunately, neither the exact origin of the *K. sylhetensis* shell was known nor was the shell available for examination during a recent search (Rashid, 1991b). Uddin (1983) provided information on the distribution and status of *Morenia petersi*, *Kachuga tecta*, *Geoclemys hamiltonii*, *Aspideretes hurum*, and *A. gangeticus*.

Hossen (1989) studied the ecology and feeding habits, in the wild and in captivity, of *Geoclemys hamiltonii*, *Hardella thurjii*, *Morenia petersi*, *Kachuga tecta*, *K. dhongoka*, "*K. sylhetensis*," *Lissemys punctata*, *Chitra indica*, *Aspideretes hurum*, and *A. gangeticus*. The specimens of *K. sylhetensis* were subsequently re-identified as *K. tentoria flaviventer* (Günther, 1864).

Ecology and life history of 11 freshwater and one estuarine turtle species, *Geoclemys hamiltonii*, *Morenia petersi*, *Hardella thurjii*, *Kachuga smithii*, *K. tecta*, *K. tentoria*, *Batagur baska*, *Lissemys punctata*, *Chitra indica*, *Aspideretes nigricans*, *A. gangeticus*, and *A. hurum* are discussed in this paper. Each species is treated separately with discussions on their habitat, food, and nesting.

Commercial exploitation of the freshwater turtles is also examined, with information on the status and distribution of chelonian populations. Ten species of turtles are listed on Appendix I of the Convention on International Trade in Endangered Species of Wild Flora and Fauna (CITES). Moreover, the Bangladesh Wildlife Preservation Act, 1974 (BWPA) includes six chelonian species in Schedule III, which prohibits capture, killing, and trade in those species. But despite this theoretical protection, trade continues in these CITES I and BWPA III species. Indiscriminate exploitation of this resource, mostly for export, has been reported by Fugler (1984), Barua and Islam (1986), Das (1990), and Rashid and Swingland (1990). During the last decade trade in freshwater turtles has increased so drastically that many species have become either endangered or threatened with extinction. The late 1980s and early 1990s showed a decline in turtle exports (Source: EPB, 1992).

Materials and Methods

Allometric studies were conducted of various individuals of different species. Turtles collected from different parts of the country and brought to export centers were measured. The length and width of the carapace and plastron and height of the shell were measured using a measuring board. Small turtles were weighed using a 25 kg vertical hanging balance; a pan balance with a 100 kg capacity was used for larger individuals. Additional data such as locality of collection, mortality rate during transportation, and the sex ratio of the turtles exported were recorded.

Information on turtles' reproductive status was also gathered by dissection of individuals that had died during transport. We also collected turtles from their natural habitats for dissection. Local markets in various localities were visited to collect information on the species involved in trade. Examination of turtles butchered for sale in the local markets provided information on reproduction. Shelled eggs found in dead or dissected females were removed and measured with vernier callipers and weighed on a triple-beam balance.

The beginning of the nesting season was defined as the earliest date a female was found with mature eggs (from dissected or butchered animals at the export centres) or was observed nesting. Similarly, the end of the nesting season was defined as the last date mature eggs were found in dissected females or the last day females were observed to nest.

The first mature eggs examined or the earliest oviposition in nature was considered the first clutch for the season. If a second batch of mature eggs was found, or a female was observed laying after more than a month, those eggs were considered the second clutch of the season. Eggs found more than a month after second clutches were considered third clutches.

Data on food and feeding habits were gathered from direct observation and by identification of stomach contents.

Habitats of the species studied were observed by accompanying turtle collectors. This also facilitated our gathering of information on the methods of collection, including traps, hooks (baited and unbaited), nets, harpoons, spears, "muddling" (capture by hand in muddy areas), and diving. The field studies were conducted between May 1989 and April 1991.

Study Area

Bangladesh possesses enormous wetland areas, and at least one third of the country is inundated each year. The principal wetlands include rivers and streams, shallow freshwater lakes and marshes, water storage reservoirs, ponds, seasonally flooded cultivated plains, and estuarine systems with extensive mangrove swamps.

There are approximately 700 rivers in Bangladesh, with an estimated total length of 24,140 km, including small hill streams, meandering seasonal creeks, muddy channels ("khal"), and major rivers with their numerous tributaries. In some regions, such as Patuakhali and Barisal in the south, they form an intricate network across the land. All of the rivers, with the exception of those in the Chittagong region, belong to one of the three major river systems, the Ganges-Padma, the Brahmaputra-Jamuna, or the Surma-Meghna. Most of the effluent of these three systems joins together to form the Lower Meghna.

The numerous permanent and seasonal freshwater lakes and marshes of the flood plains are known as "haors," "baors," and "beels." A haor is a bowl-shaped depression between the natural levees of a river, or a succession of such depressions. Haors are flooded every year by the monsoon floods and usually retain some water throughout the dry season. Most are found in the greater districts of Mymensingh and Sylhet in the northeast region in an area known as Haor Basin. A baor is an oxbow lake or other wetland formed in a former bend of a river. Baors range in size from 50 ha to 1300 ha, and most retain water throughout the year. All are situated in the moribund delta of the Ganges in Kushtia, Jessore, and Faridpur in the southwest. Beels are usually saucer-like depressions that generally retain water throughout the year. Most become overgrown with marsh vegetation during the dry season, but a few dry out completely. There are several thousand beels in the country, the greatest concentrations being in the main delta region (Rajshahi, Pabna, Kushtia, Jessore, Faridpur, Comilla, and Noakhali) and in the Haor Basin (eastern Mymensingh and Sylhet). There are very few beels in the Chittagong region, and most of these contain water only in the rainy season. There are, however, extensive grass and reed marshes along many of the rivers in the Chittagong Hill Tracts, particularly along the lower course of the Sajjak River.

Vast areas of the low-lying alluvial plains between the rivers are flooded during the rainy season. The flood waters remain for two to five months. After the floods recede, the exposed land can again be cultivated for rice, jute, and other crops.

The coastal zone extends for approximately 700 km from the Indian border in the west to the Burmese border in the southeast. It includes the Sunderbans (numerous low-lying islands and vast mangrove swamps in the western part of the Ganges-Brahmaputra delta), the Chokoria Sunderbans and Naaf Estuary (similar but much smaller estuarine systems south of Chittagong), and St. Martins Islands (an archipelago of uplifted anticlines off the extreme southern tip of the country).

The total area of wetlands in Bangladesh has been estimated at between seven and eight million hectares, about 50% of the total land surface. This includes at least 480,000 ha of permanent rivers and streams; 610,000 ha of estuaries and mangrove swamps; between 120,000 and 290,000 ha of haors, baors, and beels; over 90,000 ha of large water storage reservoir; 150,000–180,000 ha of small tanks and fish ponds, 90,000–115,000 ha of shrimp ponds; and approximately 5,770,000 ha of land that is seasonally inundated to a depth of 30 cm or more (Akonda, 1989).

This abundance of wetlands supports a wide variety of wildlife, of which chelonians form an important component. Bangladesh supports at least 25 species of turtles and tortoises (Khan, 1982b), nearly 10% of the world's total species. Among these 25 species, 18 are freshwater turtles. The occurrence of four subspecies—*Kachuga tentoria tentoria* Gray 1834, *Kachuga tentoria flaviventer* Moll 1987, *Kachuga smithii smithii* Gray 1863, *Kachuga smithii pallidipes* Moll 1987—originally described from India are reported here for the first time from Bangladesh.

Results

Geoclemys hamiltonii (Gray 1831)
English Name: Spotted Pond Turtle
Local Names: Pura kaittha, Bhuna kaittha

Thirteen live male turtles measured 29.22 ±5.17 cm (SL) in carapace length (range 21.1–39.2 cm), 19.89 ±6.73 cm in carapace width (range 13.8–34 cm), 22.4 ±2.43 cm in plastral length (maximum) (range 18.4–25.2 cm), 13.16 ±3.97 cm in plastral width (range 10.2–21.5 cm), 11.89 ±2.87 in height (range 9.5–18.1 cm), and weighed 3 ±1.08 kg (range 1.5–5.2 kg).

Fourteen live females measured 30.14 ±5.09 cm in carapace length (range 20.7–40.5 cm), 21.2 ±6.69 cm in carapace width (range 13.8–35 cm), 23.91 ±3.38 cm in plastral length (range 18.4–30.3 cm), 14.65 ±4 cm in plastral width (range 10.2–21 cm), 12.71 ±3.22 cm in carapace height (range 9–18.2 cm), and weighed 3.5 ±1.4 kg (range 1.45–6 kg).

Status and Distribution

Geoclemys hamiltonii is rare in Bangladesh. Its population is rapidly declining, primarily due to commercial exploitation for meat and, to some extent, habitat loss. Formerly distributed throughout the country, this species is now confined primarily to the south-central and south, particularly the districts of Faridpur, Barisal, Patuakhali, Bakerhat, and Noakhali. Even in the recent past it inhabited the wetlands in Khulna district, but because of excessive exploitation it is no longer found there. It is widely distributed in the Haor Basin—Eastern Mymensingh and Sylhet, but the numbers are very low. However, no geographical variations have been noticed among the specimens.

Habitat

This turtle is found both on land and in still water but rarely in running water. During winter it remains under bushes, dry vegetation, water hyacinth, water weeds, and dry leaves. In summer it spends most of its time in ponds, tanks, ditches, lakes, and swampy areas. It may bask on banks or on floating objects, or it may remain submerged with its head above water, diving beneath the surface at the slightest disturbance. The turtle is easily captured; the collectors use nets, fences, and sometimes spears, and occasionally collect them manually.

Diet

Pritchard (1979) reports *G. hamiltonii* to be primarily carnivorous; Ernst and Barbour (1989) list it as entirely carnivorous. However, the stomach contents of seven individuals included grasses, cereals, and plant fibre; shells and legs of crabs, prawns, and other molluscs; fish bones; and undigested muscle tissue. Water skater, water bug, freshwater snail, prawn, freshwater mussel (*Unio bengalensis*), and *Oryza sativum* were identified. These observations conform with those of Hossen (1989).

Dietary shifts from young herbivores to adult carnivores and differences in food preferences between males and females have been established in some turtle species (e.g., *Chrysemys picta*, Hart, 1983). Detailed studies are required to determine dietary differences between young and adult individuals as well as between the sexes of this species.

Reproduction

Adult *G. hamiltonii* lay the first clutch between mid-December and mid-January, and a second clutch is laid between late February and early March. Nests are made in bushy areas in loamy soil. The nest is bowl shaped and approximately 6–10 cm deep.

A female with a carapace length of >27 cm and weight of >3 kg can be considered mature and may be expected to nest or will have nested during the nesting season. Females will usually lay 38–58 eggs per season in two clutches, the first clutch consisting of 20–30 eggs and the second 18–28 eggs. The eggs are oval and white in colour. Measurements of 40 eggs gave an average length of 51.28 ±0.65 mm, breadth 21.1 ±0.50 mm, and weight 11.5 ±0.13 g. The eggs hatch at the beginning of the rainy season in May–June.

Morenia petersi (Gray 1870)
English Names: Bengal Eyed Turtle
Local Names: Halud kaittha, Haldi kaittha/kacchup

Males are smaller than females and have longer tails; the vent usually lies beyond the carapacial rim. The anal notch in males is deeper than females, and the posterior end of females is more rounded than males.

Thirteen male specimens were observed. These were grouped in two size classes, medium and large.* The medium-size males measured 14.78 ±0.83 cm in carapace length (range 14–16 cm), 10.86 ±1.32 cm in carapace width (range 10.1–13.2 cm), 12.84 ±0.43 cm in plastral length (range 12–13 cm), 6.78 ±1.54 cm in plastral width (range 5.9–9.5 cm), 6.46 ±0.29 cm in height (range 6.0–6.9 cm), and weighed 522 ±75.3 g (range 450–600 g). The large males measured 17.88 ±1.27 cm in carapace length (range 16.3–19.4 cm), 14.75 ±2.76 cm in carapace width (range 13.4–17.8 cm), 14.52 ±1.49 cm in plastral length (range 12.2–16 cm), 10.83 ±3.21 cm in plastral width (range 6.4–13.9 cm), 6.96 ±0.24 cm in height (range 6.5–7.2 cm), and weighed 718.38 ±103.16 g (range 592–820 g).

---

*Because prominent differences in size and weight were observed that showed an apparently bimodal size distribution (roughly corresponding to adults and subadults), the turtles were classed in two size groups, medium and large.

Likewise, 12 females were measured and grouped. The medium-size females measured 16.96 ±1.17 cm in carapace length (range 15–18 cm), 11.6 ±0.69 cm in carapace width (range 10–12.2 cm), 14.94 ±2.03 cm in plastral length (range 14–17.2 cm), 10.04 ±1.40 cm in plastral width (range 8–12 cm), 7.62 ±0.94 cm in height (range 6.5–8.5 cm), and weighed 724 ±170.09 g (range 500–890 g). The larger specimens measured 19.56 ±1.39 cm in carapace length (range 18–22.2 cm), 14.56 ±2.57 cm in carapace width (range 12–18.2 cm), 17.67 ±0.71 cm in plastral length (range 17–19 cm), 10.86 ±2.30 cm in plastral width (range 7.9–14 cm), 8.93 ±0.42 cm in height (range 8.5–9.6 cm), and weighed 1010.71 ±76.18 g (range 950–1150 g).

Status and Distribution

Morenia petersi is uncommon in Bangladesh, distributed in the districts of Faridpur, Comilla, Noakhali, Brahmanbaria, Barisal, Bagherhat, Manikganj, Pabna, Jessore, Dhaka, Sylhet, Sunamganj, Netrokona, and Mymensingh. This species is exploited for food, being collected in considerable numbers, mostly with spears and fishing nets. Variation in pattern was observed between individuals; the bridge and undersides of marginals were totally yellow in some, whereas others had black blotches.

Habitat

M. petersi usually inhabits moderately shallow, standing water—large tanks, pools, puddles, ponds, baors, and slow-flowing canals and streams. Oxbow lakes are typical habitat. It spends most of its time at the water's edge and usually basks by resting its limbs and head on floating objects on sunny days. The turtle is shy and alert, diving and swimming away at the slightest disturbance.

Diet

M. petersi is herbivorous, feeding only upon floating and submerged vegetation. *Eichhornia crassipes* was the main plant species taken by this species, and *Hydrilla* sp. were among the submerged plants utilized. Stomach contents of seven wild-caught individuals consisted of only vegetable material.

Reproduction

This species nests in winter between the end of December and end of January. Multiple clutching has not been confirmed. Nests are dug in loamy soil with sparse vegetation, usually in undisturbed open areas with ample sunlight. The female becomes sexually mature at a weight of 650 g and a carapace length of 18 cm. Females usually nest at night, laying 6–10 longish oval white eggs slightly tapered at one end. Twenty eggs measured 49.51 ±0.22 mm in length, 20.15 ±0.20 mm in breadth, and weighed 10.33 ±0.03 g. The eggs were reported to hatch in April–May.

Hardella thurjii (Gray 1831)
English Names: Brahminy or Crowned River Turtle
Local Name: Kali kaittha

This species shows an extreme sexual size dimorphism (see dimensions below). The male tail is thick and long and the plastron shows signs of concavity.

Among the specimens observed, the males (n = 12) measured 18.27 ±1.69 cm in carapace length (range 15.8–20.5 cm), 16.2 ±1.40 cm in carapace width (range 14.6–19.2 cm), 16.01 ±1.11 cm in plastral length (range 14.8–17.3 cm), 13.03 ±1.35 cm in plastral width (range 11.2–15 cm), 6.44 ±0.78 cm in height (range 5.2–7.5 cm), and weighed 790.25 ±165.89 g (range 575–1,100 g).

The females (n = 13) measured 36.21 ±6.9 cm in carapace length (range 23–47.2 cm), 30.75 ±7.1 cm in carapace width (range 21–41.1 cm), 32.8 ±6.14 cm in plastral length (range 20.5–40.4 cm), 20.15 ±4.07 cm in plastral width (range 15.7–29.9 cm), 12.65 ±3.57 cm in height (range 6–16.2 cm), and weighed 6246.38 ±3356.61 g (range 1,200–10,500 g).

Status and Distribution

The Brahminy or crowned river turtle is common in Bangladesh. It is found in almost all the major rivers, their tributaries and distributaries, but principally in the River Brahmaputra; the Dholeswari (more common) in the greater district of Tangail; the Kushiyara and Surma in the greater district of Sylhet; the Dakatia River in Noakhali, the Gumti (more common), and Titas in the greater district of Comilla; the Dholeswari, Burigonga, and Sitalakkah in the greater district of Dhaka; and the Kirtankhola in Barisal district. This turtle is also occasionally found in other small rivers, canals, and oxbow lakes with little if any current, but it was not observed in stagnant, enclosed water bodies.

The plastron of the specimens was yellowish or cream coloured with a black blotch covering most of the posterior part of each scute.

Habitat

H. thurjii usually inhabits small rivers, canals, and oxbow lakes with slow current and with a moderate amount of submerged and floating vegetation. It was neither observed nor collected in stagnant, enclosed water bodies and was rarely seen to bask. Though timid, it should be handled carefully as larger individuals are inclined to bite.

Diet

It was found to be omnivorous though Ernst and Barbour (1979) indicate that it is normally a strict herbivore, feeding upon aquatic plants. Pritchard (1979) also reports it to be herbivorous, but Minton (1966) observed one small individual eat part of a frog.

Analysis of the stomach contents of seven wild-caught

individuals revealed that it is omnivorous. The stomach contents contained prawn carapace, fish bone, water hyacinth, water weeds, and other debris. Hossen (1989) reported that this species refused to take tadpoles, snails, or cabbage when offered in captivity. In the wild, this species feeds actively in the morning as well as in the evening but spends most of its time underwater during the day.

Reproduction

The nesting season for this species is November to January. Eggs are usually laid by the end of December, in a single clutch consisting of 12–16 eggs. Twenty-five eggs measured 57.9 ±1.05 mm in length, 34.1 ±0.78 mm in breadth, and weighed 45.2 ±1.36 g. It usually nests on the banks of the water body where it resides in comparatively dry, sandy to clayey soil, approximately 5–20 m from the water line. The incubation period for this species is not known.

Kachuga smithii (Gray 1863)
English Name: Brown Roofed Turtle
Local Name: Vaithal kaittha

Two subspecies, *Kachuga s. smithii* and *K. s. pallidipes*, have been recorded from India (Moll, 1987). However, this work reports the occurrence of both these subspecies for the first time in Bangladesh. *K. s. pallidipes* differs from the nominate form by the absence of a plastral pattern and a reduction of pigment on head, limbs, feet, and penis, whereas *K. s. smithii* has a plastral pattern of large black blotches on each scute, narrowly bordered with yellow; the sides of the head, anterior surface of limbs, feet, and penis are darkly pigmented (Moll, 1987).

The specimens observed measured, for males (n = 10), 8.87 ±0.6 cm in carapace length (range 7.8–9.7 cm), 6.28 ±0.42 cm in carapace width (range 5.6–7 cm), 8.19 ±1.02 cm in plastral length (range 6.3–9.6 cm), 4.58 ±0.75 cm in plastral width (range 3.5–5.5 cm), 3.65 ±0.48 cm in height (range 3.1–4.4 cm), and weighed 91.3 ±11.0 g (range 76–110 g).

For females (n = 18), medium-size adult females measured 15.72 ±1.77 cm in carapace length (range 13.5–19 cm), 11.51 ±1.11 cm in carapace width (range 10.3–13.5 cm), 15.53 ±1.59 cm in plastral length (range 13.6–18.1 cm), 9 ±1.47 cm in plastral width (range 6.7–11.2 cm), 6.21 ±0.64 cm in height (range 5.5–7.3 cm), and weighed 500.8 ±139.16 g (range 310–710 g). The large-size adult females measured 21.61 ±1.4 cm (range 19.5–24 cm) in carapace length, 14.51 ±1.18 cm (range 12.7–15.8 cm) in carapace width, 19.36 ±1.10 cm (range 17.9–20.6 cm) in plastral length, 11.06 ±0.61 cm (range 10.3–12.4 cm) in plastral width, 7.75 ±0.52 cm (range 7.3–8.6 cm) in height, and weighed 710 ±82.42 g (range 650–900 g). All these measurements were irrespective of the different subspecies.

Status and Distribution

Brown roofed turtles occur in the Indus, Ganges, and Brahmaputra drainages of Pakistan, Nepal, India, and Bangladesh (Moll, 1987). *K. smithii* is not a common species in Bangladesh, and it is apparently restricted to a particular type of riverine habitat, found mostly in central and northwestern Bangladesh along the old Brahmaputra and Padma rivers. It is also a poorly known species. Minton (1966) found the turtle to be common in the Indus drainage while Smith (1931) considered it to be much rarer in the Ganges drainage. Khan (1982a) reported it to be uncommon. Moll (1987) also mentions it to be rarer in the Ganges River system.

The occurrence of two subspecies, *K. s. smithii* and *K. s. pallidipes*, from Bangladesh is being reported for the first time.

Kachuga smithii smithii (Gray 1863)—a subspecies of *K. smithii* having a plastral pattern of large black blotches narrowly bordered with yellow on each scute; sides of head, anterior surface of limbs, feet, and penis are darkly pigmented. Carapace brownish olive with mid-dorsal dark brown stripe; plastron, bridge, and ventral side of marginal chiefly dark but narrowly bordered with light yellow; head and neck olive dorsally; a tawny blotch present behind the eye; vague striping evident on lateral portion of neck; iris pale blue-gray; mandibles deep buff yellow; skin on outer surface of limbs olive with band-like scales on forelegs that are appreciably lighter than ground colour; prominent striping present on hind legs and rump. It is distributed in the central, north-central, and northern areas of Bangladesh.

Kachuga smithii pallidipes (Moll 1987)—a subspecies of *K. smithii* differing from the nominate form by the absence of a plastral pattern and a reduction of pigment on head, limbs, feet, and penis. Carapace light grayish olive to brownish olive with pale yellow rim around the periphery; single mid-sagittal black stripe, broken in some specimens; plastron straw yellow, immaculate, having no dark pattern; dark blotches present on ventral side of marginals. Head brownish olive, lightly mottled with smoke gray dorsally; skin creamy white behind eyes; iris pale gray; throat immaculate, unmarked; mandibles bright spectrum yellow; neck smoke gray dorsally with faint stripes, unmarked ventrally and unstriped. Forelimbs smoke gray above elbow and lateral half of foreleg; large triangular scales on lateral border of foreleg; toes and webbing yellow; faint stripes on rump; posterior aspect of limbs and feet unmarked; penis unmarked. This subspecies is distributed in the south-central and southern areas of Bangladesh.

Habitat

This species was found only in slow-running rivers and canals, including dead rivers with shallow water and containing good aquatic vegetation, including algae.

Minton (1966) described them to be common in river channels and larger canals, also occasionally in lakes and ponds connected to rivers. It frequented muddy waters with some current where there are logs, bridge abutments, and other protruding objects. Khan (1982a) included marshes in its habitat. Moll (1987) mentions it to be typically associated with rivers and to occur in both fast-flowing and more lentic habitats.

It was observed to bask in aggregations along the banks of rivers but mostly on small islands within the rivers along with its sympatric congeners *Kachuga tentoria* and *K. tecta*, and was seen basking during the hottest period of the day in summer. Minton (1966) also found them to be a social basking species on the Indus, where they undergo a period of quiescence from early December to early March. They are very fast swimmers and drop into water at the slightest disturbance.

Diet

This species is totally herbivorous. Stomach contents of 20 individuals from the wild yielded only plant material, including some unidentified hard plant debris. No animal remains were found in the gut in contrast to the statements of Pritchard (1979), who reports *K. smithii* to be carnivorous, and of Ernst and Barbour (1989), who describe it as omnivorous. Others have reported it to be omnivorous with a carnivorous bias (Smith, 1931; Minton, 1966; Das, 1985). Moll (1987) found the gut contents of a subadult female to be entirely plant material.

Reproduction

The mating season for this species is from mid-July to September. Adult females usually start laying from the second week of August. Five females dissected on 8 August contained 5–6 hard-shelled eggs ready for laying. Minton (1966) found a female containing eggs in early October. Whether females lay multiple clutches is not known. The nests are dug in sandy places on the banks of rivers or other water bodies. Eighteen eggs measured 35.41 ±0.69 mm in length, 28.32 ±0.12 mm in breadth, and weighed 10.9 ±0.56 g. Seven eggs laid by a captive female measured 43–45 mm long and 22–24 mm wide (Minton, 1966). Chaudhuri (1912) reported that 5–8 eggs were buried in sand nests but gave no season. Incubation period is not known. Ewert (1979) reported the mean dimensions of four hatchlings to be 3.92 cm in carapace length and 3.67 cm in plastral length.

Kachuga tecta (Gray 1831)
English Names: Common Roof Terrapin
Local Names: Kori kaittha, Dora kaittha, Taposhi

No sexual dichromatism has been observed, but females are larger in size than males. In addition to size, males differ from females by having a longer, thicker tail in which the vent opens beyond the carapacial rim, as was also reported by Moll (1987).

The males observed (n = 7) measured 6.64 ±0.44 cm (range 5.8–7.1 cm) in carapace length, 5.36 ±0.58 cm in carapace width (range 4.2–6 cm), 6.06 ±0.44 cm in plastral length (range 5.1–6.2 cm), 4.06 ±0.05 cm in plastral width (range 4–4.1 cm), 3.71 ±0.18 cm in height (range 3.4–3.9 cm), and weighed 56.86 ±6.84 g (range 48–67 g).

Twenty-one female specimens were measured. Because of apparently bimodal size distribution that probably separated adults from subadults, the females were classed in two size groups, medium and large.

The medium-size individuals measured 16.97 ±1.13 cm in the carapace length (range 14.5–18.3 cm), 15.23 ±1.59 cm in carapace width (range 11.5–16.7 cm), 15.16 ±1.40 cm in plastral length (range 13.2–17.7 cm), 12.96 ±1.23 cm in plastral width (range 10.6–14.7 cm), 7.35 ±0.28 cm in height (range 6.8–7.9 cm), and weighed 673.62 ±162.77 g (range 350–980 g).

The large-size class measured 21.11 ±1.47 cm in carapace length (range 19.2–24 cm), 18.66 ±0.66 cm in carapace width (range 17.9–19.6 cm), 18.29 ±2.03 cm in plastral length (range 16.3–22.6 cm), 15.61 ±1.32 cm in plastral width (range 14.8–18.4 cm), 8.4 ±0.37 cm in height (range 7.9–9.1 cm), and weighed 990 ±100.96 g (range 830–1,120 g).

Status and Distribution

The roofed terrapin occurs in the Indus, Narmada, Ganges, and Brahmaputra river systems of Pakistan, India, Bangladesh, and possibly Nepal (Moll, 1987). In Bangladesh it is distributed almost everywhere (except the lower reaches of Teknaf Peninsula and possibly the Hill Tract districts in the southeast) including the Surma River system in the northeast. *K. tecta* is the most common turtle in Bangladesh and is captured in large numbers for consumption as food. Its brilliantly coloured hatchlings are exported for pet trade. Many are also smuggled into India where they are in great demand as food (Rashid and Swingland, 1990). Because of this excessive exploitation, the population is declining steadily, and the population change even in the last decade is obvious, particularly in the northern and north-central areas. This species is listed on Appendix I of CITES, although the initial reasons for this listing were either political or the result of ignorance, rather than based upon survey data (Moll, 1987).

Turtle populations in the northern areas are scarce, whereas they occur in much higher abundance in the southern areas. The females of the northern population are larger and heavier than those from the south. Moreover, the plastral pigmentation of the northern populations is much lighter and the reddish orange tinge is lacking.

Habitat

K. tecta inhabits freshwater bodies including ponds, lakes, canals, ditches, artificial impoundments, and stagnant or slow-flowing rivers. Small to moderate-size ponds with aquatic vegetation or algal bloom seemed to be the preferred habitat. Slow-moving or quiet vegetation-choked waters appear optimal (Moll, 1987). However, it has also been observed in weedy backwaters and in slow-moving canals with dense aquatic vegetation. Khan (1987) reported *K. tecta* in both flowing and still freshwater. Recently it has also been recorded in waterways (canals, creeks, and ditches) subject to daily influx of saline water from the Bay of Bengal in southern Bangladesh (Rashid, 1991a). In general, the turtle occurs in every type of inland water body.

K. tecta is commonly seen basking on floating or emergent objects including logs, banana tree stems, sunken boats, river banks, and sand bars. It has been observed basking in aggregations together with its sympatric congeners *K. smithii* and *K. tentoria*. It always extends its neck and raises its head when basking (unlike *Morenia petersi*), but its limbs are usually relaxed. One sometimes climbs on top of another while basking. There is no obvious social hierarchy although juveniles were sometimes observed to move out of the way of larger individuals. These turtles are good swimmers and drop into the water at the slightest disturbance. In some areas, they become habituated to human beings and can be approached to within 3–4 m. Very docile and timid in temperament, it never bites. Hatchlings are sometimes kept in home aquariums as pets.

Diet

K. tecta is primarily a herbivore but occasionally scavenges on animal matter. It was observed feeding on floating vegetation including water hyacinth (*Eichhornia crassipes*), water cabbage (*Pistia* sp.), and grasses (*Cynodon* sp.) on the banks of ponds. Dead fish, earthworms, or animal offal such as chicken or fish entrails were also taken. When the water level recedes in winter and summer (prior to the monsoon season), the water bodies become completely choked with vegetation. The turtles were then seen to feed on algal scum, dead crabs, and shrimp.

Stomach contents of 30 wild-caught individuals contained aquatic vegetation, mollusc shells, fruit seeds, cereals, grasses, shrimp carapaces, roots of grasses, and crab legs, but *K. tecta* was not observed to feed upon live animals. Although Smith (1931) reported this species to be herbivorous, Moll (1987) captured one individual in a hoop trap baited with chicken entrails. Khan (1987) observed *K. tecta* taking small live shrimp in captivity. Ernst and Barbour (1989) also mention it to be predominantly herbivorous.

Reproduction

K. tecta nests between December and March. Nesting sites are varied and include fallow lands, backyard gardens, banks of ponds, bushy areas with some hard soil, and loose, sandy areas. In most cases (n = 12), the nests were dug approximately 10–15 m from the water's edge; occasionally (n = 3) nests were found only 1–5 m from the water but about 1.8 m (elevation) above water level. All nests observed (n = 15) were 6–8 cm deep.

Clutch size is 8–14; clutch frequency was not determined. All nesting observations were in January and February, which argues against multiple clutching. However, Hossen (1989) reports multiple clutching, with females laying as early as 24 November. He also reports a female (780 g) laying eight eggs between 14 and 21 March. Moll (1987) reports a female laying a clutch of eight eggs on 13 January. The average of 100 eggs measured was 39.63 ±3.85 mm in length, 20.45 ±0.25 mm in breadth, and weighed 10.75 ±3.68 g. The actual incubation period is not known, but hatchlings are seen by the end of May or early June, perhaps liberated from their nests by the onset of the monsoon.

Kachuga tentoria (Gray 1834)
English Name: Indian Tent Terrapin
Local Name: Majhari kaittha

Significant sexual dimorphism has been observed in this species. Males are much smaller in size than females and have long, thick tails with the vent beyond the carapacial rim. Females have shorter tails with the vent under the carapace. The sexes are of similar colour, except that some males have a pale yellow ring at the junction of the marginals and costals.

The average measurements of 15 male specimens observed were 8.35 ±0.96 cm in carapace length (range 7–10.1 cm), 6.38 ±0.69 cm in carapace width (range 5.5–7.9 cm), 7.99 ±1.10 cm in plastral length (range 6.3–10.3cm), 4.79 ±0.72 cm in plastral width (range 3.5–6.4cm), 4.28 ±0.75 cm in carapace height (range 3.2–5.3 cm), and 86.3 ±12.13 g in weight (range 75–115 g).

Average measurements of 10 female specimens observed were 18.67 ±5.29 cm in carapace length (range 9.6–24 cm), 14.13 ±3.36 cm in carapace width (range 8.7–17.7 cm), 18.34 ±4.21 cm in plastral length (range 11.3–22.4 cm), 11.81 ±3.3 cm in plastral width (range 6.9–16.1 cm), 8.57 ±2.3 cm in height (range 4.9–11.2 cm), and 978.5 ±485.55g in weight (range 320–1585 g).

Status and Distribution

The Indian tent terrapin is restricted to river drainages in the Bay of Bengal in India, Nepal, and Bangladesh (Moll, 1987). Pritchard (1979) and McDowell (1964) have also reported it from Bangladesh.

In Bangladesh, this turtle is distributed in the north, central, and some parts of the south, and is associated with the Padma (Ganges), Brahmaputra. and the upper Meghna rivers and adjacent areas. A considerable number were observed near Rajshahi, Gaffargaon, and Raipur (Noakhali); nevertheless, it is uncommon in Bangladesh.

Two subspecies were reported by Pritchard (1979). Later Moll (1987) recognised three subspecies of *K. tentoria* (one resurrected): *K. t. tentoria* in the rivers of peninsular India, *K. t. circumdata* in the western and central drainages of the Ganges, and *K. t. flaviventer* in the Eastern Ganges and its northern tributaries. The latter is known from many museum specimens, but *tentoria* and *flaviventer* are now recorded for the first time in Bangladesh.

Kachuga tentoria tentoria **(Gray 1834)**—a race with a dark plastral pattern and no pleuro-marginal ring or reddish markings. Sexes alike in colour, carapace brown, unicolour except for the amber stripe along the mid-dorsal keel from vertebrals 1–3; the plastron is yellow with large dark blotches on each scute, bridge, axillary, inguinal, and underside of marginals; the head is olive-brown, a poorly defined clay band present behind eye; red markings include a small red post-ocular spot in the clayband, a smaller red mark located at dorsal posterior edge of eye, and a poorly defined thin red line in the occipital region; mandibles are straw-yellow; neck with dull straw-yellow stripes on lateral and ventral portions; limbs olive with edges of scales cream; rump marked with vertical black and cream stripes. Males are smaller than females but have longer tails. *K. t. tentoria* occurs in the Padma and Brahmaputra rivers in northern Bangladesh, extending to some areas in the central region.

Kachuga tentoria flaviventer **(Günther 1864)**—a small tent terrapin with reduced pigmentation, an unpatterned plastron, and little or no striping on neck and rump; it is also known as the plain-bellied tent terrapin. Sexes widely disparate in size; males average less than half the carapace length of females. There is no sexual dichromatism. Males have a brownish-olive carapace, light mid-dorsal stripe with a pale orange wash on vertebrals 1 and 2, cream on V 3 fading on V 4 and V 5; pleuro-marginal juncture and outer rim of marginals cream in colour; plastron, bridge, and underside of marginals unpatterned cream; head pale, mottled with brownish-olive, a nearly unmarked patch washed with pale salmon extending from behind eye back over rear crown of head contacting patch from other side; immediately posterior, a dark horizontal line marks juncture of head and neck; neck pale cream and unmarked, a small irregular splotch of cinnamon rufous occurs in the unmarked area immediately behind eye; iris light smoke-grey; limbs pale creamy white with dark pigment along leading surface, webbing and underside of feet cream coloured.

Females coloured as above except that carapace has a light buff ground colour, the central stripe is a darker, tawny colour; plastron unpatterned but dark blotches present on underside of marginals; head smoky grey dorsally, cream laterally and on mandibles, a light cinnamon brown spot behind eye and another at posterior dorsal edge of eye; webbing of feet pale yellow. *K. t. flaviventer* ranges from the old Brahmaputra in central Bangladesh down to the south in greater Noakhali and adjacent districts. One shell of a dead specimen was collected from Sindukbaria khal in the Sunderbans.

Apparent intergrade specimens of *K. tentoria x flaviventer* have also been collected from the old Brahmaputra River at Char Algi, Gaffargaon in central Bangladesh, but this locality needs confirmation.

Habitat

It is sympatric with *K. tecta* and *K. smithii*. Khan (1987) reported *K. tentoria* (no subspecies was mentioned) to inhabit the same pond with *K. tecta*. This species was found only in habitats associated with rivers, oxbow lakes, and other water bodies connected with the rivers. They prefer flowing rather than stagnant water with some vegetation. Although Khan (1987) reported them in stagnant, enclosed water bodies, we did not observe them in such locales.

They have been observed to bask on floating objects including logs and banana stems, and on river banks and sand bars in large aggregations, along with *K. smithii* and *K. tecta*. There seems to be no social hierarchy. Very accomplished swimmers, they drop into water at the slightest disturbance and dive and swim away immediately.

Diet

K. tentoria is herbivorous. The guts of 15 individuals of both sexes from southern and central Bangladesh contained only vegetable material. Differences in the diet of males and females have been reported; adult females appeared to be completely herbivorous, whereas males and juveniles were omnivorous (Moll, 1987). Further studies are needed.

Reproduction

K. tentoria breeds from December to February. A single clutch of 4–8 eggs was observed. Mean egg sizes of 10 eggs measured 39.32 ±2.67 mm in length and 28.31 ±1.38 mm in breadth, and weighed 11.48 ±2.73 g. While it has not been observed in Bangladesh, Rao and Singh (1987) reported multiple clutching in *K. t. circumdata* in India.

Three nests observed were made in river banks with clayey to sandy soil. Nests were unexpanded holes 14–20 cm deep and were 5–8 m from the water line. Vijaya (1982) found nests of this turtle in "soft, clayey river bank soil" on 6–8 December; they were 15–26 cm deep and were located 3–14 m from the water. Six nests contained 4–8 eggs each (mean = 6). Mean egg sizes ranged from 41 × 29 mm, 11.7 g to 45 × 27 mm, 18.5g. Incubation period in artificial nests ranged from 125 to 134 days at temperatures of 27–28°C.

Moll (1987) reported three clutches (6, 7, and 10 eggs) in nests made in sand banks on 5 December. Mean egg size was 42 × 45 mm, mean weight 15.3 g. Mean incubation time of 12 eggs was 95 days at 24–33°C. Two females collected in mid-February appeared post-reproductive, having few enlarged follicles and several small, old corpora lutea.

Batagur baska (Gray 1830)
English Name: Estuarine River Terrapin
Local Name: Baro kaitta

The four specimens collected were all males in breeding colours. The head, nape, and under surface of the neck were jet black, with areas around the nostrils steel blue. The base of the neck was rich crimson, and the forelimbs were entirely a brilliant rosy carmine. The hind parts were dull reddish purple. In addition to sexual dichromatism, males can be distinguished from females by their longer, thicker tails. Adult males are also somewhat smaller (to 50 cm) than adult females (to 60 cm) (Ernst and Barbour, 1989). The four specimens averaged 42.13 ±3.27 cm in carapace length, 21.38 ±13.90 cm in carapace width, 37.83 ±4.72 cm in plastral length, 16.13 ±1.75 cm in height, and 8.87 ±3.17 kg in weight.

Status and Distribution

Batagur baska has been recorded from the Sunderbans in India and Bangladesh, southeastward to the Ayeyarwady (Irrawaddy) River in Burma, and then southward through southern Thailand to southern Vietnam, and through Malaysia to Sumatra, but it is now extirpated in much of this range.

In Bangladesh, it inhabits the mangrove estuaries of the Sunderbans and eastwards, possibly to Borguna, where mangrove reforestation programmes are underway. Olivier (1979) and Gittins (1980) doubted the presence of *B. baska* in Bangladesh, but later Khan (1982b) confirmed its presence based on the identification of a shell from the Bangladesh Sunderbans. Rashid et al. (in prep.) discuss the current status in the wild based on a survey conducted from December 1989 to March 1990.

It is an endangered species, threatened with extirpation in Bangladesh. It is included in the *IUCN Red Data Book* (IUCN, 1982) and is listed on Appendix I of CITES. The main threat to this species is both local and international exploitation, mostly for its meat, which is highly prized and believed to have aphrodisiac properties.

Moll (1978) notes that *B. baska* from the east coast of Malaysia differ in colouration from those of the west coast. The only specimens observed were four males collected from the Sunderbans during a survey from December 1989 to March 1990. These individuals looked alike in colouration except that one of the males was more intensely black on the head and with more brilliant crimson red on the neck than the others (possibly nearer the peak of breeding colouration).

Habitat

This estuarine river terrapin is confined to large estuaries with mangrove forests, and to deep, slow-flowing rivers. Although they were not directly observed in the wild, the four males were trapped in nets from rivers in the Sunderbans mangrove forest in southwest Bangladesh. Maxwell (1911) mentioned that these turtles bask daily in the afternoon, irrespective of the state of the tide. They bask in aggregations and cannot be closely approached. In Malaysia these turtles have been reported to move up stream to freshwater habitats during the nesting season (Moll, 1978).

Diet

B. baska is predominantly herbivorous, feeding on the fruits and leaves of *Sonneratia apetala* and other mangrove species. They also browse on water hyacinth, carried downstream with the current. One of the captured males was kept in an artificial freshwater tank and provided with watercress, duckweed, and other freshwater aquatic plants but did not take any food for nine days, after which it was killed and preserved for the Bangladesh National Museum (Natural History). Hatchlings of this species are reported to be omnivorous in captivity (Davenport et al., 1992).

Reproduction

Virtually nothing is known about the breeding of *B. baska* in Bangladesh. It is reported to mate from December to March in Malaysia (Moll, 1978). Based on this information, a survey of nesting females and nest sites in Bangladesh (sponsored by WWF-Malaysia) was made in the Sunderbans from December 1989 to March 1990. Unfortunately, no nesting females were observed, but four males in breeding colours were trapped. We believe that they do nest on the beaches and islands adjacent to the sea but not along the mouths of the rivers Katka and Konga within the Sarankhola Range of the Sunderbans in Bangladesh, as was presumed by Whitaker (1982). Some nests were found in the Indian part of the Sunderbans, on islands adjacent to the sea (Moll, pers. comm. 1990). Elder fishermen at Nijhumdweep (an island in south-central Bangladesh) report that this species used to nest there (M. A. Khan, pers. comm. 1997).

Communal nesting occurs in sand bars and sand banks far upstream from the normal estuarine habitat, and some females may swim over 80 km to reach these sites (Moll, 1978). Information was gathered from the turtle traders and local consumers. It was reported that some females slaughtered in late March contained hard-shelled eggs, which suggests a likely time to search for nesting females and nests in the future. The nesting period may continue up to April in Bangladesh. There may be some relation between the nesting period of *Batagur* and the seasonal increase of salinity in the estuaries (Alam, 1988).

Lissemys punctata (Bonnaterre, 1789)
English Name: Spotted Flapshell Turtle
Local Names: Sundi kasim, Futi/Tila/Dhur kasim

Some of the specimens observed in southern Bangladesh, particularly the large females, were oblong in carapacial outline and highly domed whereas others from the same localities were less domed and oval in shape. They also varied in colouration: The highly domed individuals were brown, whereas the less-domed ones were olive green to dark green. The plastron was cream-yellow in most of the specimens, though some were reddish. One individual with a black plastron was also observed. Some specimens found (29 cm CL) exceeded those previously recorded (27.5 cm CL, Ernst and Barbour, 1989).

Three subspecies are recognised (following the taxonomy of Webb, 1980). In Bangladesh, *L. p. andersoni* is the one encountered in most of the cases, but we believe that *L. p. punctata* may also occur, as mentioned by Khan (1982b).

Twenty male turtles were measured and grouped in two size classes, medium and large. The medium-size group measured 16.83 ±1.06 cm (range 14.5–17.7 cm) in carapace length, 14.96 ±1.73 cm (range 12.2–16.8 cm) in carapace width, 14.84 ±0.54 cm (range 13.9–15.6 cm) in plastral length, 13.17 ±0.58 cm (range 12.1–13.7 cm) in plastral width, 4.98 ±0.17 cm (range 4.6–5.2 cm) in height, and weighed 625.92 ±33.57 g (range 550–670 g).

The large-size group of males measured 19.31 ±0.86 cm (range 18.3–21 cm) in carapace length, 17.03 ±1.16 cm (range 15.9–19 cm) in carapace width, 17.14 ±0.87 (range 15.8–18.1 cm) in plastral length, 14.26 ±0.65 cm (range 13.3–15 cm) in plastral width, 5.74 ±0.33 cm (range 5.3–6.3 cm) in height, and weighed 830.75 ±75.39 g (range 710–940g).

Twenty-two females were measured and also grouped into medium- and large-size groups. The medium-size group measured 19.08 ±3.37 cm (range 14.5–23.8 cm) in carapace length, 16.94 ±3.47 cm (range 12.2–21.5 cm) in carapace width, 16.28 ±2.09 cm (range 13.5–20 cm) in plastral length, 14.42 ±1.85 cm (range 12–17 cm) in plastral width, 5.95 ±0.88 cm (range 5.1–7.4 cm) in height, and weighed 845.55 ±255.73 g (range 550–1,350 g).

The large group of females measured 25.81 ±1.62 cm (range 24.4–29 cm) in carapace length, 21.42 ±2.28 cm (range 15.1–22.6 cm) in carapace width, 22.39 ±2.41 cm (range 19.5–26.5 cm) in plastral length, 18.12 ±1.65 cm (range 17–21.4 cm) in plastral width, 8.31 ±1.81 cm (range 6.9–12 cm) in height, and weighed 1,851.18 ±572.81 g (range 1,400–3,000 g).

Status and Distribution

L. punctata occurs in the Indus and Ganges drainages of Pakistan, northern India, Sikkim, Nepal, and Bangladesh, southward through peninsular India to Sri Lanka, and in the Ayeyarwady and Salween rivers of Burma (Ernst and Barbour, 1989; Iverson, 1992).

The spotted flapshell is common in Bangladesh and is found throughout the country, although it is most abundant in the southern districts. In the northern districts it is scarce, and its presence in the Hill Districts in the southeast still needs confirmation. It was recorded from the Teknaf Peninsula in the southeast bordering Burma (this study).

This species is included in the First Schedule of the Bangladesh Wildlife Preservation Act, 1974 (BWPA), which allows hunting and capture by permission from the relevant authorities. It is one of the main species involved in local trade, mostly for consumption as food. Large numbers are also smuggled into neighbouring India. It is also listed on Appendix I of CITES.

Habitat

L. punctata lives in the shallow, quiet, often stagnant waters of rivers, streams, marshes, ponds, lakes, and irrigation canals and tanks. Waters with mud or sand bottoms are preferred, but it is often forced to aestivate in the mud during dry periods. It often basks on sand bars, banks, and floating vegetation, or sometimes stays submerged with just the head above water. During the rainy season and at other times of the year, paddy fields with stagnant water are the most promising habitats. It seems to be nocturnal, as they were certainly more easily collected at night when they approached the shore (probably attracted by the search light). It has also been observed to migrate overland.

The species is collected in great numbers for local trade. During winter, when water levels are low, or when small bodies of water and paddy fields dry up during summer, it is hunted using spears. The hunters probe the shallow water and mud of ponds, ditches, and paddy fields with sticks, iron rods, or spears. When they hit a carapace (determined by listening to the sound), they extract the buried turtle by hand. Sometimes hunters also dig for them beneath the soil of dried bodies of water.

Diet

Lissemys punctata is totally carnivorous. It has been observed to feed on molluscs, shrimps, small fishes, and crabs. Stomach contents of 20 individuals included only animal remains. Molluscs seemed to form the major portion of their diet, but crab legs, carapaces and legs of prawns, fish bones, and undigested mussels were also found in stomachs. Freshwater snails were taken and crushed in the jaws; the muscular parts were consumed while discarding the shell.

Some of the food items observed taken in nature were

small fishes, freshwater snails, young apple snail (*Pila globosa*), freshwater mussel (*Unio bengalensis*), prawns (*Macrobrachium* sp.), and earthworm (*Perethima posthuma*).

Deraniyagala (1939) reported *L. punctata* to feed on frogs, fishes, crustaceans, aquatic snails, and earthworms in Sri Lanka, but Minton (1966) observed them eating aquatic vegetation in Pakistan. Ernst and Barbour (1989) describe them as omnivorous.

Reproduction

Courtship and mating were observed by Duda and Gupta (1981) during April in wild *Lissemys*, and from May to July in captives. Nesting occurs throughout most of the year, a female laying several clutches each year, 2–14 eggs each. The eggs are white and spherical (24–33 mm in diameter) with brittle shells. Hatching occurs from May to July, and hatchlings have carapaces 35–44 mm long.

Nesting activities were recorded from late August to mid-March and three clutches in a season were observed. The number of eggs varied from 7 to 28 in a clutch. The first clutch was laid between late August and mid-October, the second between mid-November and mid-January, and the third between mid-February and mid-March.

The earliest clutch of 28 eggs from a 22 cm female was recorded on 26 August at Char Jabbar, Noakhali. Hossen (1989) reported females laying 14 eggs on 26 December and 12 eggs on 11 March. The eggs were spherical, hard shelled, and white in colour. The mean diameter of 105 eggs measured 26 ±1.56 mm and weighed 14.75 ±2.32 g.

Nests (bowl-shaped, 15–18 cm deep) were made in damp, loose-to-hard soil, usually in backyard gardens, bamboo groves, pond banks and embankments, and even in the narrow aisles demarcating paddy fields from fallow land. Nests were found 10–30 m from the water. Nesting occurrence of *L. punctata* may vary at different locations, and it may nest year-round, but this needs confirmation.

Chitra indica (Gray 1844)
English Name: Narrow-headed Softshell Turtle
Local Names: Shim kasim, Thal kasim, Shuwa kasim, Chitra kasim

The turtles observed were allocated to two size groups. Among the 21 males observed, the large-size individuals (n = 8) measured 55.83 ±3.78 cm in carapace length (range 51–61.5 cm), 50.49 ±3.4 cm in carapace width (range 47–57 cm), 42.07 ±2.64 cm in plastral length (range 38–47 cm), 47.47 ±3.55 cm in plastral width (range 41–51 cm), and weighed 17,271.88 ±3,851.1 g (range 17,000–25,600 g). The medium-size males (n = 13) measured 42.26 ±5.18 cm in carapace length (range 32–49 cm), 38.16 ±5.92 cm in carapace width (range 28.5–46 cm), 33.03 ±5.58 cm in plastral length (range 23.5–39 cm), 35.05 ±6.46 cm in plastral width (range 25–44 cm), and weighed 8,478.46 ±3,750.58 g (range 3,000–14,250 g).

Among females (n = 21), large-size females measured 64.44 ±8.35 cm in carapace length (range 56–79.5 cm), 55.82 ±3.63 cm in carapace width (range 50–61.5 cm), 46.91 ±3.92 cm in plastral length (range 41–52.3 cm), 52.16 ±4.69 cm in plastral width (range 44.5–59.8 cm), and weighed 30,166.36 ±14,342.68 g (range 14,500–57,000 g). The medium-size females measured 41.32 ±6.71 cm in carapace length (range 30–51.2 cm), 41.42 ±6.55 cm in carapace width (range 26.2–47 cm), 36.19 ±6.19 cm in plastral length (range 21–41 cm), 38.45 ±7.89 cm in plastral width (range 20–45.4 cm), and weighed 10,875 ±4,114.27 g (range 2,800–13,200 g). Females are larger than males, but males have longer, thicker tails.

Status and Distribution

Chitra indica ranges from the Ganges, Godavari, Mahanadi, Sutlej, and Indus drainages of Pakistan, India, Nepal, and Bangladesh (Ernst and Barbour, 1989), and southward through Burma to western Thailand (Iverson, 1992).

In Bangladesh, it is distributed in all the major rivers, i.e., Padma, Jamuna, Meghna, Brahmaputra, Dholeswari rivers and their major tributaries. It is the largest freshwater turtle in Bangladesh and has recently become uncommon in the south and rarer in the northeast and central regions.

It is caught in quite large numbers for the local trade. Fugler (1984) and Barua and Islam (1986) reported it to be exported, although Rashid and Swingland (1990) did not confirm this. Its large size makes it difficult to transport, and local traders prefer to slaughter it to sell the fresh meat. The *Chitra* population is declining fast because of excessive exploitation to meet the demand for its meat in the local markets, and collectors now complain about its scarcity. *Chitra* individuals from the northern and central areas of Bangladesh are lighter in colour than those in the south.

Habitat

It mainly inhabits deep water, 5–20 m or more in depth, spending most of its time close to the river floor or buried in the substrate. Some young were observed in shallow, slow-flowing rivers with sandy bottoms. Its habits are nocturnal.

Pritchard (1979) suggested that it prefers large rivers with clear water and sandy bottoms. Ernst and Barbour (1989) also note that it prefers sandy sections of large rivers and is highly aquatic, seldom crawling on land except to nest. Its large, heavy body hinders terrestrial locomotion. Minton (1966) thought it to be capable of pharyngeal gas exchange while under water.

These turtles are very aggressive. Extending its long neck with extreme rapidity, it can inflict severe bite injuries. The turtle cannot rotate its head sideways but is able to extend the neck forwards to catch food and attack enemies. Smith (1931) commented on the severity of its bites, but Minton (1966) refers to a captive of mild disposition.

Diet

C. indica was found to be totally carnivorous. Stomach contents of seven wild-caught individuals consisted only of animal matter. These included fish bones and scales, mollusc shells, crab carapaces and legs, shrimp carapaces and legs, and unidentified vertebrate muscle tissue.

Because *Chitra* spends much of its time close to the silty river floor, it is frequently caught with thousands of unbaited hooks (hazari borshi), tied on a line and hanging vertically almost to the river bottom. The hooks catch the turtle's soft parts; the animal becomes entangled and is later collected by pulling the lines during periodic checks, or sometimes by diving. Occasionally, the turtles are trapped in dragnets used for deep-water fishing.

Reproduction

The nesting season extends from February to May, during which *C. indica* lays multiple clutches. The first clutch is laid between late February and mid-March, the second between late March and mid-April, and the third between late April and mid-May.

During the nesting season the female moves to shallow water and usually nests at night on the sandy riverbank. The nests are pear-shaped, 18–30 cm deep. As many as 170 eggs may be laid by a single female during a nesting season.

The eggs are spherical, with expandable, tough, white shells. The average dimensions of 150 eggs were 34.02 ±0.39 mm in diameter and 21.96 ±0.07 g in weight. Nutaphand (1979) reported that *C. chitra* lays 60–110 eggs and that a 110 cm female laid 107 eggs in captivity. The spherical eggs (34 mm) were white with tough, leathery shells. Hatchlings have a brightly marked olive carapace, about 35–40 mm long, and numerous dark-bordered yellow stripes on the head and neck.

A female *C. indica* weighing 34 kg contained 90 mature, spherical eggs on 26 March. The hatching season is probably June and July. Females reach sexual maturity at a carapace length of 45–55 cm and a body weight of 12–16 kg.

Aspideretes nigricans (Anderson 1875)
English Names: Black Softshell Turtle, Bostami Turtle
Local Names: Bostami kasim, Gazari, Mandari

The carapace is oval to round and olive-brown to black in colour. The sole existing population shows white patches on the carapace and also on the limbs and head. These are not actually the colouration but scars remaining from fungal infections. Several longitudinal rows of tubercles on the carapace and enlarged blunt tubercles occur on the anterior rim behind the neck. The plastron is almost black with well-developed callosities. Head, neck, and limbs are dark olive to black. Recently, Ahsan and Saeed (1989) conducted allometric studies showing that males are a little wider and heavier than females. Males have longer, thicker tails. Additional information regarding its breeding and nesting is reported by Ahsan et al. (1991). Ahsan and Saeed (1989) reported dimensions of 56 males and 44 females. The males measured 53.17 ±18.28 cm in carapace length, 54.01 ±16.96 cm in carapace width, and weighed 51.54 ±17.16 kg. The females measured 53.64 ±9.16 cm in carapace length, 51.28 ±9.78 cm in carapace width, and weighed 43.50 ±17.04 kg.

Status and Distribution

The only known population of this species is confined to the pond of the shrine of Hazrat Bayazid Bostami in Chittagong, Bangladesh and a few adjacent ponds (Khan, 1987; Ahsan and Saeed, 1989; Ahsan, this volume). The origin of this species is still a mystery, although many mythological accounts have been presented (Annandale and Shastri, 1914). Khan (1987) presumes it to have evolved from *A. gangeticus*, while others (F. Ahsan, pers. comm., 1990; Rashid, 1990) think it to be closer to *A. hurum*.

Habitat

The artificial tank at the shrine of Hazrat Bayazid Bostami (to which most of the turtles are confined) is lined with cement on all sides but has a muddy bottom. Stairs to the water level are used by pilgrims and visitors, who use the tank water for ablution, and who also feed the turtles. There is also a small hill with some large trees and cover behind the shrine, which is utilised by the turtles for nesting. The tank is surrounded by human habitations on all other sides.

Larger turtles are very docile and do not bite. They are considered sacred because the people think them to be related, in some way, to the saint. Visitors to the shrine touch and stroke their carapaces and collect mud and algae, which are considered to heal many diseases and to fulfil one's wishes!

Most of the larger turtles are heavily infected with a fungal disease. White areas visible on the carapace, limbs, neck, head, and jaws are scars from fungal infections.

Diet

These turtles are omnivorous and, because of semi-domestication, are habituated to take food from visitors who offer various items. These include banana, bread, chicken liver, meat, and fish liver, which are skewered on sticks and then offered to the turtles which accept them enthusiastically. Puffed rice and corn are also taken. The larger turtles come to the edge of the pond and gather at the platform to take food; some even climb the stairs to get food from the visitors.

Reproduction

These turtles mate from early February to early May. The usual clutch size is 16–24 (mean = 20.2) (one clutch of 38 was reported, F. Ahsan pers. comm. to P. C. H. Pritchard), and the incubation period is 99–104 days (mean = 100.9) (Ahsan et al., 1991). The females nest on the hill behind the shrine, usually at night. It is during this time they may get disoriented and sometimes end up in nearby ponds. They have also been found crossing the roads at night near the shrine.

Aspideretes gangeticus (Cuvier 1825)
English Names: Ganges Softshell Turtle
Local Names: Ganga kasim, Khalua kasim, kocha, nagashi

Adult males are larger than adult females and have longer, thicker tails. The individuals observed were grouped into large, medium, and small size categories, corresponding roughly to adult, subadult, and juvenile sizes. Among the 18 males observed, the larger individuals measured 68.69 ±5.12 cm in carapace length (range 61.5–77 cm), 54.26 ±5.11 cm in carapace width (range 46–61.5 cm), 49 ±2.59 cm in plastral length (range 46–53 cm), 47.11 ±8.76 cm in plastral width (range 28.8–56.5 cm), and weighed 29.36 ±7.58 kg (range 19–42 kg). The medium-size males measured 49.71 ±4.42 cm in carapace length (range 45.5–59 cm), 42.57 ±3.7 cm in carapace width (range 36.5–47 cm), 37.51 ±2.94 cm in plastral length (range 33.1–41.7 cm), 38.84 ±3.14 cm in plastral width (range 33.9–43.8 cm), and weighed 13.13 ±2.56 kg (range 10–15.63 kg). The small males measured 37.46 ±7.69 cm in carapace length (range 27.5–44 cm), 31.38 ±7.57 cm in carapace width (range 22–38 cm), 28.88 ±6.17 cm in plastral length (range 20.5–34 cm), 30.78 ±6.18 cm in plastral width (range 21.6–35 cm), and weighed 6.44 ±3.31 kg (range 2–9.7 kg).

Among the 20 females measured, the larger individuals measured 66.24 ±7.8 cm in carapace length (range 56–78 cm), 48.83 ±3.61 cm in carapace width (range 44–54 cm), 42.12 ±6.71 cm in plastral length (range 42.5–51 cm), 44.61 ±8.26 cm in plastral width (range 34.5–58 cm), and weighed 26.36 ±13.27 kg (range 15–54.7 kg). The medium-size females measured 47.75 ±3.51 cm in carapace length (range 42.5–52 cm), 44.25 ±5.04 cm in carapace width (range 36–51 cm), 37.64 ±2.94 cm in plastral length (range 33.1–41.5 cm), 38.15 ±3.21 cm in plastral width (range 33.9–42.8 cm), and weighed 14.47 ±3.73 kg (range 9.5–18.5 kg). The small females measured 34.82 ±5.55 cm in carapace length (range 25.5–39 cm), 30.21 ±5.99 cm in carapace width (range 20.8–35 cm), 26.8 ±4.5 cm in plastral length (range 19.8–31 cm), 27.5 ±4.82 cm in plastral width (range 20–31.8 cm).

Status and Distribution

Aspideretes gangeticus lives in the Ganges, Indus, and Mahanadi river systems in Pakistan, northern India, southern Nepal, and Bangladesh (Pritchard, 1979; Ernst and Barbour, 1989).

It was fairly common in Bangladesh a decade ago, but numbers have now been greatly reduced by the unregulated commercial exploitation, mainly for export to the Far Eastern countries. *A. gangeticus* formerly occurred in almost all the major rivers and their tributaries, but now it is confined mostly to the deeper areas of the large rivers, Padma, Brahmaputra, Jamuna, their tributaries, and the estuaries in the south, mainly in the districts of Barisal, Patuakhali, Noakhali, Chandpur, some areas of Rajshahi, Faridpur, Serajganj, and Pabna districts. The occurrence of this species in the Karnaphuli River system in Chittagong district is not confirmed.

Considerable variation has been observed between specimens from the northern and southern regions. In the north, individuals are bright olive-green to medium-green in colour with a complex network of reticulation on the carapace in the adults. The young and juveniles have four distinct, dark-centred ocelli on the carapace along with the reticulations. Furthermore, the average adult size of the northern individuals was smaller. Southern individuals are dark olive-green to olive-green in colour with, at best, only faint reticulations on the carapace at any age or size. Further investigation is needed to document the possibility of a distinct subspecies.

Habitat

The Ganges softshell turtle inhabits deep rivers with muddy bottoms, where the water current is slow to moderate; both clear and turbid waters are frequented. It is often seen in areas with plenty of loamy soil available for basking. It is frequently observed buried in the mud or resting in shallow waters with head exposed. Typical water depth is 5–20 m.

Ernst and Barbour (1989) reported this turtle to inhabit deep rivers, streams, and large canals with muddy or sandy bottoms. Minton (1966) and Pritchard (1979) indicate that it prefers turbid waters.

It is very aggressive, even ferocious, and can extend its long, flexible neck with great speed to bite and inflict severe injuries. It can also thrust its head sideways with similar speed. It produces a hissing sound when disturbed. Though a nocturnal feeder, it can often be seen basking on the sand bars and banks of large rivers.

Diet

This species is omnivorous. Stomachs of seven wild-caught individuals contained both plant and animal materials. These included mollusc shells, prawn carapaces, crab legs, fish bones, water hyacinth and other aquatic vegetation, fish scales, and mammalian muscle tissue.

Among the food items directly observed to be taken by this turtle were fishes, molluscs (such as the apple snail, *Pila globosus*), the freshwater mussel *Unio bengalensis*, crab, water hyacinth (*Eichhornia crassipes*), and water cabbage (*Pistia* sp).

Ernst and Barbour (1989) also describe it as omnivorous,

eating not only fish, amphibians, and carrion but aquatic plants as well. Pritchard (1979) describes it as more herbivorous than carnivorous.

Reproduction

Observations in Bangladesh show that *A. gangeticus* mates from August to January and lays multiple clutches. The first clutch of eggs is laid between mid-August and late September, the second between mid-October and late November, and the third between mid-December and January.

The turtle moves to shallow waters during the nesting season and usually nests in sandy, loamy soil. The nests are flask-shaped and usually 20–35 cm deep. Nest site selection and oviposition take place during the night. The eggs hatch between April and June at the onset of the monsoon.

The eggs are hard-shelled, white, and spherical. One hundred eggs had a mean diameter of 31.03 ±1.03 mm (range 29–34 mm). Mean weight of the eggs was 15.23 ±1.20 g (range 14–19 g).

Aspideretes hurum (Gray 1831)
English Name: Peacock Softshell Turtle
Local Names: Jat kasim, Dhum kasim, Bugum, Dairra kocchop

Differences were found between northern and southern specimens of *A. hurum*. The two could be differentiated by the presence of a larger number of yellowish spots on the carapace, mostly concentrated on the antero-lateral, lateral, and posterior edges of the margin, in southern individuals. These also had a black band across the hyoplastral region of the plastron, and the proboscis was shorter, thick-based, and more drooping than in the northern form.

Males were found to be larger than the females. The individuals observed were grouped into large, medium, and small size categories. Among the male specimens (n = 46), the large individuals measured 41.15 ±1.69 cm in carapace length (range 39–45.5 cm), 34.78 ±1.95 cm in carapace width (range 33–38 cm), 31.08 ±1.62 cm in plastral length (range 29–33.5 cm), 31.57 ±1.80 cm in plastral width (range 29.5–34.2 cm), and weighed 7.37 ±1.16 kg (range 6–9.1 kg). The medium-size males measured 33.99 ±1.86 cm in carapace length (range 31–38 cm), 28.75 ±1.68 cm in carapace width (range 26–31.2 cm), 25.93 ±1.51 cm in plastral length (range 23–29.2 cm), 26.55 ±1.36 cm in plastral width (range 24.3–28.7 cm), and weighed 4.24 ±0.84 kg (range 3.1–6.1 kg). The small males measured 28.52 ±1.44 cm in carapace length (range 25.5–30.5 cm), 24.19 ±1.23 cm in carapace width (range 21–26 cm), 22.39 ±1.11 in plastral length (range 21–24 cm), 23.02 ±1.14 cm in plastral width (range 20.8–24.5 cm), and weighed 2.6 ±0.56 kg (range 1.5–3.5kg).

Of the females (n = 106), the large individuals measured 34.20 ±2.97 cm in carapace length (range 24.5–41 cm), 30.74 ±3.52 cm in carapace width (range 23.5–43 cm), 27.23 ±3.17 cm in plastral length (range 23–37.5 cm), 27.44 ±2.32 cm in plastral width (range 24–32.5 cm), and weighed 4.89 ±1.38 kg (range 2.5–7.7 kg). The medium-size females measured 27.43 ±1.50 cm in carapace length (range 24.5–30 cm), 25.05 ±3.07 cm in carapace width (range 21.5–37 cm), 21.52 ±1.33 cm in plastral length (range 19.2–23.7 cm), 22.52 ±1.42 cm in plastral width (range 20.1–25.5 cm), and weighed 2.58 ±0.54 kg (range 1.7–4 kg). The small females measured 19.54 ±3.01 cm in carapace length (range 14.3–24 cm), 17.9 ±2.56 cm in carapace width (range 13.5–22.2 cm), 15.45 ±2.19 cm in plastral length (range 11.5–19 cm), 16.34 ±2.31 cm in plastral width (range 12.7–20.1 cm), and weighed 0.93 ±0.40 kg (range 0.5–1.6 kg).

Status and Distribution

A. hurum is one of the common species found throughout Bangladesh. It is found in almost all the river systems, including the Karnaphuli River system in Chittagong (Rashid, 1990). It is more abundant in the ponds, lakes, "dighees" (man-made reservoirs or large shallow lakes), beels, and estuaries of the southern region in the districts of Barisal, Patuakhali, Noakhali, Chandpur, and Borguna. It has also been recorded from ponds on the off-shore islands of Sandweep, Moheskhali, Hatiya, and Kutubdia.

It is one of the major species involved in the turtle trade, both internationally and locally. A large number of individuals are exported live to the Far East, mainly Hong Kong, Singapore, and Japan for consumption as food (Rashid and Swingland, 1990). *A. hurum* is listed on CITES Appendix I and BWPA-III, which prohibit capture, hunting, or trade in this species. Because of its abundance and wide distribution, a proposal for downlisting this species is under consideration by the CITES Secretariat (A. Brautigam, pers. comm. 1991), although this seems inadvisable in view of the intense level of exploitation—at least in Bangladesh.

Habitat

It is found in both deep and shallow rivers, streams, estuaries, and also in enclosed water bodies including ponds, lakes, and artificial impoundments. It is more common in rivers and streams but was also observed in vegetation-choked ponds and lakes.

It is often seen basking on river banks and sometimes floating on the surface with the back and head out of the water. It spends much of its time buried under the mud at the bottom, surfacing mainly at night. It has been observed to leave dried-up ponds in search of standing water.

Diet

A. hurum is carnivorous, feeding below the water surface and on the bottom. It catches its prey by rapidly extending its long neck, while simultaneously depressing the hyoid. Stomach contents of ten wild-caught individuals included mollusc shell, crustacean remains, fish bones and scales, and undigested mammalian muscle tissue. Annandale (1906) reported captive *A. hurum* taking rice and palm-sugar sweet meats.

The food items directly observed to be taken were freshwater snails; apple snail (*Pila globosa*); freshwater mussel (*Unio bengalensis*); fishes such as *Amblypharyngodon mola*, *Mystus tengra*, and *Nandus nandus*; crab; earthworm (*Pheretima posthuma*); and also carrion.

Reproduction

The nesting period is from August to December. Nesting usually takes place at night. Nests are excavated in clayey to sandy soil. The nests are unexpanded holes 15–25 cm deep, 10–30 m from the water.

Multiple clutching was observed in this species. The first clutch was laid between late August and late September, the second between mid-October and mid-November, and the third in December. The females with a carapace length of 30–40 cm and body weight of 4–5 kg were mature. The clutch size was 20–30 eggs, and an adult female weighing 7–8 kg usually laid 70–90 eggs in a season. The first clutch contained 30–38 eggs, the second 24–32 eggs, and the third 20–26 eggs. The eggs were white, hard shelled, and spherical. The mean diameter of 100 eggs was 27.97 ±2.05 mm and the mean weight was 15.04 ±2.74 g. The hatchlings usually emerge prior to the monsoon (May and June).

DISCUSSION

In general, species belonging to the family Bataguridae (*Morenia petersi*, *Kachuga tentoria*, *K. smithii*, and *K. tecta*) have low fecundity with smaller eggs. Exceptions to this rule are the large *Hardella thurjii*, which lays few eggs (although they are quite large) and *Geoclemys hamiltonii*, also a large species, which has a comparatively high fecundity but almost similar egg weight to the aforementioned small species. In general, species smaller in size have low fecundity and smaller eggs with less weight, whereas larger species have higher fecundity and larger eggs.

By contrast, the trionychids *Chitra indica*, *Aspideretes gangeticus*, and *A. hurum* are larger in size than the batagurids and have greater fecundity (except for *Lissemys punctata*, which has moderate clutch sizes). Eggs of trionychids are spherical and are larger and heavier than the average batagurid turtle eggs.

Female *Hardella thurjii* are the largest and heaviest batagurid turtles seen in Bangladesh. *Hardella* lays the largest and heaviest eggs but has a comparatively small clutch size, which may suggest the possibility of increased hatching success and hatchling survivability (Swingland, 1979). However, high hatchling survival rates are not proven; exploitation of adults and/or habitat degradation may also account for the turtle's rarity in the wild. *Geoclemys hamiltonii* has a comparatively higher fecundity, but its smaller eggs may result in lower hatchling survival. This is also exacerbated by predation and exploitation, as well as the extensive alteration, manipulation, or destruction of their restricted habitat niche.

The females of other batagurid species (*Kachuga smithii*, *K. tentoria*, *K. tecta*, and *Morenia petersi*) are similar in size and body mass and also have similar egg sizes and weights. *K. smithii* and *K. tentoria*, although less common, are widely distributed, whereas *K. tecta* and *M. petersi* are more common, especially the former. *K. smithii* and *K. tentoria* are more associated with riverine habitats.

Among the trionychids, *Chitra indica* is the heaviest, with fecundity data indicating that the heaviest females produce more and larger eggs. The egg size and weight of *C. indica* are greater than in the other Bangladesh trionychid species. Hatching success and hatchling survivability in nature is again debatable. Hatchlings of *indica* may encounter intense predation by large carnivorous fishes inhabiting the deeper waters. *A. gangeticus*, although often larger in size than *A. hurum*, has almost identical egg sizes and weights, but *gangeticus* has a higher fecundity. Ecologically, *hurum* adapts to varied habitats, whereas *gangeticus* is confined to rivers. *A. hurum* is the most common and widely distributed trionychid in the country. *L. punctata*, smallest of the trionychids studied, has moderate fecundity and size and relatively larger eggs (almost equal in size to those of *gangeticus*). Like *hurum*, it also inhabits diverse habitats, with extensive distribution throughout the country. The success of this species may again be its adaptability, aided by increased hatching success because of larger eggs and diffused predation pressure resulting from nesting in different habitats.

Conservation Efforts

Effective systems of management can ensure that biological resources not only survive but are not depleted, thus providing the foundation for sustainable development. Critical attention must be given to the management of renewable resources because they provide the basis for long-term sustainable production of goods and services essential for human welfare. Experience has shown that market forces alone will often lead to overexploitation, largely because many of the long-term costs associated with natural resource exploitation are not reflected in the market costs of natural resource production. Thus, current market mechanisms alone cannot drive conservation; conservation must be driven by a combination of international cooperation, effective government intervention, and greatly increased participation by local people.

In the case of freshwater turtles (as well as numerous other natural resources), serious problems in economic analysis remain. Approaches to assessing the economic values of natural processes and resources remain rudimentary at best, and the ethical, aesthetic, cultural, and scientific considerations that must be part of the economic equation are usually ignored (McNeely, 1988).

The threats to biological resources are complex and call for a wide range of responses across both private and public sectors. Since government policies are often responsible for depleting biological resources, it stands to reason that policy amendments are often a necessary first step toward conservation (McNeely et al., 1989).

One means to improve policy coordination is the preparation of a National Conservation Strategy (NCS)—a broad national environment management plan. An NCS defines policies and actions, including the conservation of biological resources, upon which sustainable development can be built. A Bangladesh NCS Draft Report, now under consideration by the government, includes a proposed management plan for the country's wildlife resources. The Draft Report recommends that the government impose a ban on the export of CITES Appendix I species (already an obligation for Bangladesh as a CITES signatory), strictly regulate and monitor local turtle trade, ban collection of adult freshwater turtles during their nesting seasons and cease the export of gravid females, and train wildlife and air customs personnel to correctly identify turtles and other endangered species.

Recently, the Government of Bangladesh revised the Bangladesh Wildlife Preservation Amendment Act 1974 (BWPA) to include all fauna in Schedule III, which prohibits capture, killing, or trade in wildlife species. Any exempt wildlife species is now announced by gazette. Presently, there are six chelonians included in Schedule III of the BWPA, including both *A. gangeticus* and *A. hurum*. Despite this protection, however, intentional misidentification of these species still facilitates their export.

The significant annual earnings in foreign currency from the export of these freshwater turtles gives the government a logical motivation to encourage their continued export. Moreover, it has been estimated that more than 15,000 people are involved in the collection, hunting, and trade of freshwater turtles in Bangladesh (Rashid and Swingland, 1990). However, the income and subsequent involvement of these people will eventually end if exploitation of these turtles remains at unsustainable levels. A study on the socio-economic condition of these people, which would lay the groundwork for alternative employment linked with conservation of stocks, would enhance the development of future conservation actions.

LITERATURE CITED

Ahamed, N. 1958. On edible turtles and tortoises of East Pakistan. East Pakistan Directorate of Fisheries, Dhaka. 18 pp.

Ahsan, M. F. 1997. The Bostami or black softshell turtle, *Aspideretes nigricans*: Problems and proposed conservation measures. In J. Van Abbema (ed), Proceedings: Conservation, Restoration, and Management of Tortoises and Turtles—An International Conference, pp 287–289. July 1993, State University of New York, Purchase. New York Turtle and Tortoise Society, New York.

Ahsan, M. F. and M. A. Saeed. 1989. The Bostami turtle, *Trionyx nigricans* Anderson: Population status, distribution, historical background and length-weight relationship. J. Bombay Nat. Hist. Soc. 86(1): 1–6.

Ahsan, M. F., M. N. Haque, and C. M. Fugler. 1991. Observations on *Aspideretes nigricans* (Anderson), a semi-domesticated endemic species of eastern Bangladesh. Amphibia-Reptilia 12:131–136.

Akonda, A. W. 1989. Introduction to wetlands in Bangladesh. In D. A. Scott (comp.), A Directory of Asian Wetlands, pp. 541–581. IUCN, Gland, Switzerland. I–xiv + 1181 pp. + maps.

Alam, K. 1988. Seasonal variation in the salinity in Sunderbans, Bangladesh. Bano Bignan Patrica (Journal of Bangladesh Forest Research Institute, Chittagong) 12(1):68–78.

Anderson, J. 1878–79. Anatomical and Zoological Researches and Zoological Results of the Yunnan Expeditions. Bernard Quaritch, London. 985 pp.

Annandale, N. 1906. Contributions to Indian herpetology—No. 4: Notes on the Indian Tortoises. J & P Asiatic Soc. Bengal (n.s.) 2: 183–202.

Annandale, N. and M. H. Shastri. 1914. Relics of the worship of mud-turtles in India and Burma. J. Asiatic Soc. Bengal 10(5):131–134.

Barua, G. and M. A. Islam. 1986. Status of the edible chelonian export from Bangladesh. Bangladesh J. of Fish 9(1–2):33–38.

Boulenger, G. A. 1890. Fauna of British India, including Ceylon and Burma. Reptilia and Batrachia. Taylor and Francis, London. 541 pp.

Chaudhuri, B. L. 1912. Aquatic tortoises of the middle Ganges and Brahmaputra. Rec. Indian Mus.7:212–214.

Daniel, J. C. 1983. The Book of Indian Reptiles. Bombay Natural History Society, Bombay. 141 pp.

Das, I. 1985. Indian Turtles: A Field Guide. World Wildlife Fund—India (Eastern Region). WWF, Calcutta. 119 pp.

Das, I. 1990. The trade in freshwater turtles from Bangladesh. Oryx 24(3):163–166.

Das, I. 1991. Colour Guide to the Turtles and Tortoises of the Indian Subcontinent. R&A Publishing Ltd., Portishead, UK. iv + 133 pp.

Davenport, J., T. M. Wong, and J. East. 1992. Feeding and digestion in the omnivorous estuarine turtle, *Batagur baska* (Gray). Herpetological Journal 2(4):133–139.

Deraniyagala, P. E. P. 1939. The Tetrapod Reptiles of Ceylon. Colombo Museum, Colombo. 412 pp.

Duda, P. L. and V. K. Gupta. 1981. Courtship and mating behaviour of the Indian softshell turtle, *Lissemys punctata punctata*. Proc. Indian Acad. Sci. (Anim. Sci.) 90:453–461.

Ernst, C. H., and R. W. Barbour. 1989. Turtles of the World. Smithsonian Inst. Press, Washington, D.C. i–xii + 313 pp.

Ewert, M. A. 1979. The embryo and its egg: Development and its natural history. In M. Harless and H. Morlock (eds.), Turtles: Perspectives and Research, pp. 333–413. John Wiley & Sons, New York.

Export Promotion Bureau. 1992. Trade records for Bangladesh 1980-1990. EPB, Govt. of Bangladesh, Dhaka. 45 pp.

Fugler, C. M. 1984. The commercially exploited chelonia of Bangladesh: Taxonomy, ecology, reproductive biology and ontogeny. Bangladesh Fisheries Information Bulletin 2(1):i–v, 1–52.

Gittins, S. P. 1980. A survey of the primates of Bangladesh. Project

Report, Fauna and Flora Preservation Trust, and Condor Conservation Trust, Cambridge, England. 64 pp.

Hart, D. 1983. Dietary and habitat shift with size of red-eared turtles (*Pseudemys scripta*) in a southern Louisiana population. Herpetologica 39(3):285–290.

Hossen, L. 1989. Ecology of freshwater turtles of Bangladesh. M.S. thesis, Department of Zoology, University of Dhaka, Dhaka.

Husain, K. Z. 1979. Bangladesher bonnyajontu swampada o tar sangraskhan (in Bangla). Bangla Academy Bignan Patrica 5(3):23–31.

Iverson, J. B. 1992. A Revised Checklist with Distribution Maps of Turtles of the World. Earlham College, privately printed, Richmond, Indiana. 363 pp.

Khan, M. A. R. 1982a. Chelonians of Bangladesh and their conservation. J. Bombay Nat. Hist. Soc. 79(1):110–116.

Khan, M. A. R. 1982b. Wildlife of Bangladesh—A Checklist. Dhaka University, Dhaka. 170 pp.

Khan, M. A. R. 1987. Bangladesher Bonnyaprani (in Bangla). Vol. 1. Amphibians and Reptiles. Bangla Academy, Dhaka.

Maxwell, F. 1911. Reports on inland and sea fisheries in the Thongwa, Myaungmya and Bassein Districts and turtle banks of the Irrawaddy Division. Government Printing Office, Rangoon. 57 pp.

McDowell, S. B. 1964. Partition of the Genus *Clemmys* and related problems in the taxonomy of the aquatic Testudinidae. Proc. Zool. Soc. London 143(2):239–279.

McNeely, J. A. 1988. Economics and Biological Diversity: Developing and Using Economic Incentives to Conserve Biological Diversity. IUCN, Gland, Switzerland. i–xv + 200 pp.

McNeely, J. A., K. R. Miller, W. V. C. Reid, and R. A. Mittermeier. 1989. Conserving The World's Biological Diversity. IUCN, WRI, WWF-US, Gland, Switzerland and Washington, D.C.

Meylan, P. A. 1987. The phylogenetic relationships of soft-shelled turtles (family Trionychidae). Bull. Amer. Mus. Nat. Hist. 186(1):1–101.

Minton, S. A. 1966. A contribution to the herpetology of West Pakistan. Bull. Amer. Mus. Nat. Hist. 134(2):27–184.

Moll, E. O. 1978. Drumming along the Perak. Natural History 87:36–43.

Moll, E. O. 1987. Survey of the Freshwater Turtles of India. Part II: The Genus *Kachuga*. J. Bombay Nat. Hist. Soc. 84(1):7–25.

Nutaphand, W. 1979. The Turtles of Thailand. Mitbhadung Press, Bangkok. 222 pp.

Olivier, R. C. D. 1979. Wildlife conservation and management in Bangladesh: Report to F.A.O. Food and Agriculture Organization of the United Nations, Rome. 148 pp.

Pritchard, P. C. H. 1979. Encyclopedia of Turtles. T.H.F. Publications, Inc., Neptune, New Jersey. 895 pp.

Rao, R. J. and L. A. K. Singh. 1987. Notes on comparative body size, reproductive effort, and areas of management priority for three species of *Kachuga* (Reptilia; Chelonia) in the National Chambal Sanctuary. J. Bombay Nat. Hist. Soc. 84(1):55–65.

Rashid, S. M. A. 1990. The *Aspideretes nigricans* mystery. British Herpetological Society Bulletin 34:42–43.

Rashid, S. M. A. 1991a. On the occurrence of common roof turtle, *Kachuga tecta*, in the saline water in southern Bangladesh. British Herpetological Society Bulletin 36:39.

Rashid, S. M. A. 1991b. On the ecology of some freshwater turtles in Bangladesh. M.Sc. thesis, Durrell Institute of Conservation & Ecology, University of Kent, Canterbury, U.K. 141 pp.

Rashid, S. M. A. and I. R. Swingland. 1990. Interim report on freshwater turtle trade in Bangladesh. Asiatic Herpetological Research 3:123–128.

Rashid, S. M. A., E. O. Moll, and I. R. Swingland. In prep. The status of the estuarine turtle, *Batagur baska*, in the Sunderbans, Bangladesh.

Romer, A. S. 1956. Osteology of Reptiles. University of Chicago Press, Chicago.

Sarker, S. U. and N. J. Sarker. 1988. Wildlife of Bangladesh: A Systematic List. Rico Printers, Dhaka. i–ix + 70 pp.

Shafi, M. and M. M. A. Quddus. 1977. Bangladesher matshya swampada. Part 4. Kasim, kaitta o samudrik kasim (in Bangla). Bangla Academy Bignan Patrica 3(2):14–36.

Smith, M. A. 1931. The Fauna of British India, Including Ceylon and Burma. Vol. 1. Loricata, Testudines. Taylor and Francis, London. 185 pp.

Swingland, I. R. 1979. The natural regulation of giant tortoise populations on Aldabra Atoll, Indian Ocean. Recruitment. Philos. Trans. R. Soc. London B: Biol. Sci. 286(1011):177–188.

Uddin, M. K. 1983. Freshwater turtles of several districts of Bangladesh. M.S. thesis, Department of Zoology, University of Dhaka, Dhaka.

Vijaya, J. 1982. *Kachuga tecta* hatchlings at the Snake Park. Hamadryad 7(3):14–15.

Webb, R. G. 1980. Identity of *Testudo punctata* (Testudines: Trionychidae). Bull. Mus. Nat. Hist. (Sect. A) Zool. Biol. Ecol. Anim. 2(2):547–558.

Whitaker, R. 1982. Bangladesh: A general survey. Hamadryad 7(3):4–9.

Measuring Declines and Natural Variation in Turtle Populations: Spatial Lessons from Long-Term Studies

— PLENARY LECTURE —

J. WHITFIELD GIBBONS

Savannah River Ecology Laboratory, Drawer E, Aiken, SC 29802, USA [e-mail: gibbons@srel.edu]

ABSTRACT: Turtles are among the species threatened by biodiversity losses on a global scale as a consequence of habitat destruction. However, the responsibility for providing evidence that turtle numbers and populations are declining rests upon the scientific community. To provide cogent and credible arguments for protection of species or habitats, turtle biologists must document that particular species or populations are on a decline trajectory that will result in extinction. Documenting such declines is possible but will not be easy. To be effective, turtle biologists must measure population responses to natural environmental variability through studies that document spatial and genetic characteristics of metapopulations. Turtle ecologists should be vigilant of suspected problems and provide convincing documentation. Overstatement of the threats to turtles and their habitats must be balanced against understatement or ignorance of potential or actual problems. Finally, encouragement should be given for support of long-term, spatially extensive research on as many species' populations as possible.

Few biologists would dispute that biodiversity is being lost on a global scale as a consequence of habitat destruction. Turtles are unquestionably among the losers from the perspective of habitat loss. Turtles can also be included among other vertebrate groups, such as snakes, lizards, and tropical birds, in which the losses are exacerbated because of the removal of individual animals from the wild for commercial profit.

If turtles are indeed declining in populations in many parts of the world, the burden rests upon the scientific community to document such losses. Credible demonstration that turtles are declining in number is necessary before certain segments of the general public and their political representatives will accept that there is need for concern. Turtle biologists therefore have a responsibility to document that particular species or populations are on a decline trajectory that could result in extinction. Documenting such declines may not be an easy task but will be necessary if a convincing case that a problem exists is to be made to environmental managers, politicians, and even some scientists.

Numerous instances can be given where natural habitats have been destroyed as a consequence of the human activities of agriculture, urbanization, and industrialization that have affected turtles. For example, in South Carolina the majority of the natural wetlands known as Carolina Bays has been destroyed or significantly degraded during the past century (Bennett and Nelson, 1991). Although most turtle species of the region probably still exist in small numbers in many of these habitats, it is intuitive that the numbers of individuals and the viability of some populations have been reduced. The problem with a situation like this is that no one can truly document that the number of turtle species, or even the size of populations of a particular species, has declined. This inability to document species numbers and population sizes exists because we may know nothing of the historical relationships between the turtles and the array of aquatic habitats in a region.

Although complete destruction of an aquatic habitat clearly eliminates its use by most turtles, establishing population trends of species in habitats on which the level of human impact is equivocal is even more difficult. For example, the construction of dams has undoubtedly affected *Graptemys* populations that are indigenous to large rivers. But in most instances we have no documentation for what the level of effect was because we had little information about population levels of *Graptemys* prior to the building of the dams. Likewise, the partial draining of wetlands, especially temporary aquatic habitats such as Carolina Bays, freshwater wetlands that are known to have a high productivity and diversity of turtle species, has had an effect that has also, for the most part, gone unmeasured.

Surveys of populations before and after habitat modification are necessary to determine how a species has been affected. Long-term population studies are required in most instances, but some data sets do not have to be long term to draw the unarguable conclusion that a population of turtles has declined significantly. Thus, if it can be documented that a species is absent from an area it once inhabited, a decline is substantiated. An example of such a situation is the case of mud turtles (*Kinosternon subrubrum*) at Sun Bay on the Savannah River Site in South Carolina. Sun Bay, a Carolina bay, supported populations of at least 13 species of amphibians as well as a healthy population of mud turtles in 1979, based on the numbers of juveniles and adults (Table 1). The numbers captured each year after 1979 were lower, presumably because of ditch construction that drained the habitat. In 1983 the population levels declined even more dramatically when the wetland habitat was completely eliminated during a construction project.

Drift fence and pitfall trap studies (Gibbons and Semlitsch, 1982) were continued at the Sun Bay site to determine what species and which marked individuals returned to the former wetland. By 1983 no *K. subrubrum* inhabited Sun Bay. As part of our study of this area, man-made refuge ponds were created in the proximity to determine whether these would become inhabited by any of the same individuals that had occupied Sun Bay. The results were that none returned to the original site and only two adult male *Kinosternon* were caught in the following seven years at the man-made refuge pond; presumably individuals in the population dispersed and possibly died, since no other suitable, nearby aquatic habitats are present in the region. With the complete destruction of a known turtle habitat such as Sun Bay, even without prior data on many aspects of the population, a convincing argument can be made that the turtle population declined.

One recommendation that has been given for easing the uncertainty of our assessment of a population's status is to have pre-impact surveys and long-term data sets. However, in many situations, especially in relatively natural habitats and even in some in which human impact is apparent, population trends are not so easily assessed because of the dynamic nature of aquatic turtle populations.

Our long-term studies in areas with protected research sites such as the Savannah River Site, which has been safeguarded against most forms of public disturbance for more than 40 years, have permitted us to assess annual population levels of several species of turtles in truly protected habitats. The results permit a view of natural fluctuations in populations that can occur in response to what are presumed to be normal extremes of environmental variation.

The studies also show some of the difficulties that herpetologists can face with interpretation, even when armed with long-term studies, by revealing the potential ambiguity that can occur in defining a population and in the assessment of whether there have been declines or increases. One example is based on a study of several species of turtles at Ellenton Bay that demonstrate collectively that the temporal and spatial extent of the study could influence one's interpretation of whether a decline in the population has occurred.

The studies have been in progress in one form or another for more than 26 years, and a variety of techniques (Gibbons, 1990) have been used to capture the animals, including aquatic trapping, hand capture, and terrestrial drift fences with pitfall traps (Gibbons and Semlitsch, 1982). The drift

TABLE 1
Original captures (25 males, 43 females, 66 juveniles) and recaptures of eastern mud turtles, *Kinosternon subrubrum*, at Sun Bay, a freshwater wetland on the Savannah River Site near Aiken, South Carolina.

Year	Males	Females	Juveniles
1979	19	37	58
1980	8	18	4
1981	5	15	3
1982	7	9	3
1983	0	0	0
TOTAL	39	79	68

fence has been particularly useful in documenting when individuals left or entered the population as well as in assessing the numbers present (Table 2). Drift fence captures were supplemented by an additional 5,795 captures and recaptures of the six most common species during the same time period (Table 2).

The number captured per year or other time intervals has varied immensely for two reasons—trapping effort varied as did the actual number of inhabitants. However, the number of turtles captured in any year is a reflection of the number of individuals of a particular species that inhabited the Ellenton Bay habitat in that year and excludes those that occupied other sites in the metapopulation during that year (Burke et al., 1995).

In a comparison of abundance of *Trachemys scripta* based on the number of individuals captured at Ellenton Bay over two-year intervals, one's conclusion about whether the population is on the increase or decline would depend upon which set of years the population had been studied (Table 3). For example, from a six-year study from 1967 through 1972, from 1979 through 1984, or from 1985 through 1990, one would have concluded that the numbers of slider turtles in Ellenton Bay had declined dramatically. Yet, had either study been continued for two to four more years, the population would have been observed to be increasing.

The turtles in Ellenton Bay are an example of how one could be misled about the abundance of species for both temporal and spatial reasons that are interactive. The temporal reason is that some species, such as slider turtles, respond to a natural drought by traveling to other aquatic sites peripheral to the primary one (Gibbons et al., 1983). Thus, a temporal extension in assessment of the abundance of slider turtles at Ellenton Bay following the period of a major but natural environmental impact, a drought, would result in a different conclusion about declining numbers from that when abundance was considered from only a six-year study through 1972, 1984, or 1990. Because of the long-term

TABLE 2

Number (all captures, recaptures, and hatchlings) of freshwater turtles captured per decade at Ellenton Bay on the Savannah River Site from 1968 through 1993 by terrestrial drift fences (DF) and by other capture (OC) techniques. Numbers given are for the six most abundant species at Ellenton Bay.

	1960s DF	1960s OC	1970s DF	1970s OC	1980s DF	1980s OC	1990s DF	1990s OC	TOTAL
K. subrubrum	203	39	4,398	365	3,372	209	1,146	65	9,797
T. scripta	92	522	2,038	980	1,261	306	278	56	5,533
D. reticularia	115	78	920	244	439	99	63	8	1,966
P. floridana	9	25	429	50	255	26	104	12	910
S. odoratus	15	44	261	80	116	54	33	7	610
C. serpentina	7	5	209	176	147	66	61	33	704
TOTAL	441	713	8,255	1,895	5,590	760	1,685	181	19,520

study of the system, however, we were able to unravel what apparently happened. Some individuals had traveled to other aquatic sites—places that still had water.

In our examination of peripheral areas around Ellenton Bay, we actually captured individuals that had dispersed to other habitats. Thus, the proximity of suitable habitats to the unsuitable habitat they are residing in can determine population abundance by serving as a refuge that allows individuals to emigrate from the unsuitable habitat during a drought.

This is of course a metapopulation phenomenon (Levins, 1970; Burke et al., 1995); the population was originally viewed as more provincial than further investigation showed it to be. Following the end of the low water levels in 1984, we have documented that many of the individual *T. scripta* that made up the original Ellenton Bay population have returned. Sixty of these were captured in Ellenton Bay during the interval from 1986 to 1987, and 15 more were found from 1991 to 1993. The return of these earlier emigrants indicates that not only is the *T. scripta* population in Ellenton Bay itself recovering, but that the new composition consists of many of the older animals that contributed to the apparent decline.

Therefore, as the study was extended in both time and space, the perceived population decline in certain species was not realized. The decline was not as severe as originally thought. This leads to a very important point, a paradoxical one. One interpretation could be that we do not need to worry about declines in some populations, even those resulting from human-caused habitat destruction, because the turtles can take advantage of other habitats in the region. Genetic studies give further evidence that the transfer of genetic material among turtles in freshwater habitats in a region can be extensive, up to 4 km overland (Scribner and Smith, 1990).

However, as indicated above the point is paradoxical, so we can look at this in another way; that is, in defining the population, we sometimes need to consider a broader spatial area than the local aquatic habitat where a freshwater species occurs.

TABLE 3

Abundance of *T. scripta* at Ellenton Bay at two-year intervals from 1967 to 1992. Numbers are based on total numbers of unique captures (or recaptures) of turtles in each of the two years. Each individual turtle captured in a year was counted only once, although the same individual may also have been counted the following year.

Years	Total of unique captures per year
1967–1968	463
1969–1970	102
1971–1972[a]	21
1973–1974[a]	5
1975–1976	465
1977–1978	367
1979–1980	254
1981–1982	428
1983–1984[a]	39
1985–1986	127
1987–1988	141
1989–1990[a]	0
1991–1992	155

[a] Years following droughts and with low water levels in Ellenton Bay.

In the metapopulation model some habitats are sources (the producer habitats), whereas others are sinks (Gilpin, 1987; Opdam, 1991). During the life of a long-lived individual in a turtle population, a habitat's designation as a source or a sink can vary. Thus, an alternate interpretation of the results is that all aquatic habitats in a region are important to the maintenance of some turtle populations, but none is used by every individual every year. In addition, the intervening terrestrial habitat may also be critical as a corridor between aquatic sites, or the contiguous terrestrial habitat may be important as nesting or hibernation sites (Burke et al., 1994).

The studies demonstrate that sometimes the data are insufficient to draw ironclad conclusions but can provide support for perceptions about certain species. Another approach to determining whether some turtle species were truly undergoing a decline toward local extirpation would be by spatial extension of the study. This involves searching in neighboring habitats for the particular species, an approach that must always be weighed in terms of level of investment and potential returns. The variation observed in turtle population size assessment among years at Ellenton Bay as a consequence of dispersal suggests that one might regard with caution historical records in which a site is revisited at a later time, and a species is absent from the exact locality but may be present at a nearby one.

Based on the widely supported assumption that turtle population declines are occurring on a worldwide scale, I offer the following recommendations to research ecologists:

• **Accept and measure natural variability.** We must accept that population fluctuations are a natural response to natural environmental variability, and measure them. This is the only way we can confirm that some declines are occurring as a result of human influence. Also, we must accept that rarity and clandestine behavior of some species make them intrinsically difficult to assess because of the inadequacy of sampling techniques. We must strive to improve the techniques.

• **Document with convincing examples.** One recommendation, as determined from long-term data sets, for easing the uncertainty of our assessment of a population's status, is to have wider-ranging studies that allow spatial and genetic characteristics of metapopulations to be determined. Some data sets do not have to be long term to provide important information on movement patterns of individuals and spatial relationships of populations in order to draw the unarguable conclusion that a population's survival is dependent on more than one habitat in a region.

• **Be vigilant of and investigate suspected problems.** Turtle ecologists as a group are responsible for providing evidence for any putative population declines among the world's turtle species. We must remain vigilant of suspected problems and document them with convincing examples.

• **Be cautious of overstatement and understatement.** To be politically effective, we must avoid overstatement of the threats to turtles and their habitats while being cautious about understatement of potential problems. The most prudent course for avoiding criticism of overreaction while providing persuasive arguments of impending problems is to have a thorough understanding of turtle population dynamics, including comparative assessments among years, before making declarations about a problem.

• **Encourage support of long-term, spatially extensive research.** We must encourage support not only for long-term studies but also for spatially extensive research on as many populations of as many turtle species as possible.

Acknowledgments

I thank Nat B. Frazer, Justin D. Congdon, Vincent Burke, and Jeff Lovich for discussions of the topic. I appreciate the help of Judith L. Greene in data analysis and thank Mark Mills, John R. Lee, and Kurt Buhlmann for reading the final manuscript. Research and manuscript preparation were supported by DOE contract DE-AC09-76SR00819 with the University of Georgia.

Literature Cited

Bennett, S. H. and J. B. Nelson. 1991. Distribution and status of Carolina bays in South Carolina. South Carolina Wildlife and Marine Resources Department Publication, Columbia, South Carolina.

Burke, V. J., J. W. Gibbons, and J. L. Greene. 1994. Prolonged nesting forays by common mud turtles (*Kinosternon subrubrum*). Am. Midl. Nat. 131:190–195.

Burke, V. J., J. L. Greene, and J. W. Gibbons. 1995. The effect of sample size and study duration on metapopulation estimates for slider turtles (*Trachemys scripta*). Herpetologica 51:451–456.

Gibbons, J. W. 1990. Turtle studies at SREL: A research perspective. *In* J. W. Gibbons (ed.), Life History and Ecology of the Slider Turtle, pp. 9–14. Smithsonian Institution Press, Washington, D.C.

Gibbons, J. W., J. L. Greene, and J. D. Congdon. 1983. Drought-related responses of aquatic turtle populations. J. Herpetol. 39(3):254–271.

Gibbons, J. W. and R. D. Semlitsch. 1982. Terrestrial drift fences with pitfall traps: An effective technique for quantitative sampling of animal populations. Brimleyana 1982 (7):1–16.

Gibbons, J. W. and R. D. Semlitsch. 1991. Guide to the Reptiles and Amphibians of the Savannah River Site. University of Georgia Press, Athens.

Gilpin, M. E. 1987. Spatial structure and population vulnerability. *In*: M. E. Soulé (ed.), Viable Populations for Conservation, pp. 125–139. Cambridge University Press, Cambridge, U.K.

Opdam, P. 1991. Metapopulational theory and habitat fragmentation: A review of holarctic breeding bird studies. Landscape Ecology 5:93–106.

Smith, M. H. and K. T. Scribner. 1990. *In* J. W. Gibbons (ed.), Life History and Ecology of the Slider Turtle, pp. 74–81. Smithsonian Institution Press, Washington, D.C.

Development of Predictive Models for Wetland-Dependent Turtles in New England

ALISON L. WHITLOCK AND JOSEPH S. LARSON

Department of Forestry and Wildlife Management, University of Massachusetts, Amherst, MA 01003, USA
[e-mail: whitlock@tei.umass.edu]

Abstract: Many turtle species are undergoing serious population declines throughout their ranges from habitat fragmentation and other anthropogenic effects. Government agencies have an increasing need to identify important habitat features for impact assessment, mitigation, and conservation initiatives. There has previously been no methodology to predict potential habitat for wetland-dependent turtles. Based on an extensive literature review, a summary of reported physical characteristics of habitat, and an analysis of the use of these features by turtles, we developed a methodology for use in the northeastern United States. Predictive models were produced for 11 turtle species, nine of which are listed as "Rare," "Threatened," or "Endangered" in at least one of the six New England states. Such models will enable regulatory agencies to make decisions based upon sound biological information early in land use planning.

In the United States, regulations governing wetlands, endangered species, and wildlife habitat often require evaluation of habitat on local, state, and federal levels. Current methodologies for evaluating wildlife habitat typically focus on fish and waterfowl, but none has heretofore focused on wetland habitats of aquatic reptile species. Given the current and projected threats to turtle populations, recognition of their wetland habitat requirements by regulatory agencies is critical to ensure long-term viability of populations. Unfortunately, most wildlife biologists involved with regulatory assessments are not familiar with the habits and habitats of these species, and the number of skilled herpetologists is not sufficient for the number of evaluations being conducted regionally. Further, because standard methodologies to qualify these species' habitats are lacking, federal and state agencies rarely address them in habitat assessments. Biologists wishing to include these species in assessments usually refer to field guides or natural history summaries. These sources have inherent drawbacks for use in assessment of specific sites because they (1) may not include all species present in New England wetlands, (2) require cumbersome species-by-species sorting of habitat information, (3) generally do not contain up-to-date research, and (4) are not keyed to specific site characteristics.

The need to develop a rapid assessment methodology for amphibians, reptiles, and mammals was identified by the New England Transportation Consortium in 1991. The Departments of Transportation of Maine, New Hampshire, Vermont, Massachusetts, and Rhode Island, in cooperation with the U.S. Fish and Wildlife Service, U.S. Environmental Protection Agency, and U.S. Army Corps of Engineers funded a research team at the University of Massachusetts to develop such a method. This paper introduces the objectives and methods by which the turtle component of this project was developed.

Objectives

The specific objectives of this study were to (1) provide a comprehensive summary of the literature on habitat for wetland-dependent turtles in New England, and (2) produce models to identify potential turtle habitat for regulatory purposes.

METHODS

"Wetland-dependent" species were defined as those that may use non-wetland habitats but occur in wetlands a preponderance of the year or have critical life requirements met by wetlands that are not provided by non-wetlands (Adamus et al., 1987). A species list (Table 1) of New England turtles that met this definition was compiled and sent to biologists in local, state, and regional agencies and academic institutions for comment. The red-eared slider, *Trachemys scripta elegans*, was not included because the few Massachusetts populations have resulted from released pets. The eastern box turtle, *Terrapene c. carolina*, was also excluded because it is largely terrestrial.

Habitat Characteristics Tables

Using the Wildlife Worldwide CD-ROM database (NISC DISC, National Information Services Corporation, 1993), a literature review was conducted to identify major peer-reviewed articles by species. All pertinent literature from these sources and those found in the University and in herpetologists' personal libraries were reviewed for habitat data. Categories of common habitat features were then created

TABLE 1
Turtle species in New England considered for wetland model development. Key: 1 = Present but not listed by the state for protection, 2 = Present and under consideration for listing, FE = Federally Endangered, E = Endangered, T = Threatened, R = Rare, SC = Special Concern, SI = Special Interest, UD = Undetermined, IS = Indeterminate Status, W = Watch, * = Introduced population. Status categories are based on July 1993 information.

Species	Maine	New Hampshire	Vermont	Massachusetts	Connecticut	Rhode Island
Apalone s. spinifera			T			
Chelydra s. serpentina	1	1	1	1	1	1
Chrysemys picta spp.	1	1	1	1	1	1
Clemmys guttata	T	W	T	SC	2	2
Clemmys insculpta	IS	W	R	SC	2	SI
Clemmys muhlenbergii				E	E	
Emydoidea blandingii	T	W		T		
Graptemys geographica			R			
Malaclemys t. terrapin				T	2	T
Pseudemys rubriventris				FE		
Sternotherus odoratus	1	1	R	1	1	1
Terrapene c. carolina	E	UD		SC	1	1
*Trachemys scripta (elegans)**				1		

TABLE 2
Data categories of habitat features used in development of Habitat Characteristics Tables.

I. Habitat Features
   - Wetland type
   - Juxtaposition (of cover types)
   - Wetland size (including home ranges)
   - Landform (topography)
   - Wetland vegetation
   - Upland vegetation
   - Water depth (and hydroperiod)
   - Water quality (and velocity)
   - Water and air temperature
   - Food items
   - Density and biomass
   - Distribution in New England
   - Co-existing wetland-dependent species
   - Predators

II. Characteristic of Feature
III. Use of Characteristic of Feature
IV. Citation
V. Data Type or Sample Size
VI. Location of Study
VII. Focus of Study

(Table 2). Information that provided observable indicators of habitat or guidance in field assessment was also noted. Once categorized, the data were organized in tabular form as "Habitat Characteristics Tables" for each species. These summarized all habitat features found in the literature in an easy-reference format. The tables also included the animal's use of the habitat feature, the sample size of observation if recorded, and the literature citation.

Habitat Prediction Models

Following completion of Habitat Characteristics Tables, Habitat Predicting Models were developed to identify potential habitat for individual species. The models consist of data from the Habitat Characteristics Tables that could be identified from a map or photograph, or be identified in a field inspection. Model conditions are written in the same sequence as they appear in the Habitat Characteristics Tables so the user can easily refer to the original citation. The models were designed for identification of potential habitat only; all model conditions must be met by an assessed site for it to receive a positive prediction of habitat. The following basic assumptions were made in the creation of the models: (1) the literature reviewed (and subsequently the models) contain all significant indicators of habitat, and (2) all indicators have equal importance in predicting habitat.

Habitat Characteristics Tables and Habitat Predicting Models were sent for review to biologists who had experience with these species and their habitats in New England.

The wetland must have the following characteristics for a positive determination of wood turtle habitat:

I. Wetland Type:

Palustrine or Riverine (upper perennial or lower perennial), as defined in Cowardin et al. (1979).

IF Palustrine, THEN Riverine wetland or moving water channel within or adjacent to Palustrine system that has all the characteristics below.

II. Juxtaposition:

Upland forest and open canopy meadow within 200 m of channel.
[*Optimal*: Areas are contiguous, with few to no roads between them, and meadows infrequently mowed.]

III. Wetland or Upland Vegetation:

Channel within forest,
OR border of at least 15 m width of shrubs or saplings along channel.
[*Optimal*: Both meadow and forest have dense herbaceous undergrowth.]

IV. Wetland Substrate:

Sand, mud, or organic substrate,
OR overhanging dirt banks.

V. Upland Substrate:

Area of open canopy with well-drained sandy or loam soil within 200 m of channel.

VI. Water Depth:

Channel depth 0.5–2.5 m where bordered by trees or shrubs.

VII. Water Quality:

Permanent,
AND flowing,
AND unpolluted,
AND with areas that do not freeze to the bottom in an average winter.

Figure 1. Sample of species Habitat Predicting Model: The wood turtle, *Clemmys insculpta*.

RESULTS

Final revisions of individual species models were made before the development of a composite model. In the composite model, all species models were integrated into a hierarchical format that will allow assessment of a site for all species simultaneously.

Habitat Characteristics Tables and Habitat Predicting Models for 12 individual species, along with a composite model for all New England wetland-dependent turtles, have been published (Whitlock, 1994) and are a major component of a multi-species assessment method ("WEThings," Whitlock et al., 1994). Both assessment methods consist of four levels of inquiry that require more detailed information at each level to generate an increasingly refined list of species that may inhabit a site. The first level allows the user to generate a species list based on geographic area, the second level requires a field evaluation using a corresponding field form, the third level directs the user to individual species models (e.g., Figure 1), and the fourth level requires the review of individual species' Habitat Characteristics Tables (e.g., Figure 2). In addition, "WEThings" (Wetland Indicators for NonGame Species, Whitlock et al., 1994) includes computer software that analyzes field data from level two of the method and generates a predictive species list for these turtle species as well as wetland-dependent amphibians and mammals in New England.

HABITAT CHARACTERISTICS FOR THE WOOD TURTLE
(Clemmys insculpta)
Page 3

STRUCTURAL FEATURE	CHARACTERISTICS	USE	CITATION	DATA n = # INDIVIDUALS
Juxtaposition, cont'd.				
	Remained within 40 m of channel	Juvenile movement	Brewster and Brewster, 1991	n = 8
	Within 30 m of water	General activity	Quinn and Tate, 1991	n = 178 of 244 observations
	Travelled 3.6 km to return to home range	Movement	Quinn and Tate, 1991	n = 1
	Within 300 m of creek, occasionally up to 600 m	Movement	Kaufmann, 1992	n > 95% observations
	Almost bare soil within 100 m of creek	Ideal nesting	Kaufmann, 1992	n = 100% of ? nests
	0.8 - 4.9 ha	Home range	Harding et al., 1993	Summary
	Always < 200 m from nearest large stream in meadow or forest or along streambank	Activity	Robakiewicz, 1993	n = 5
Wetland Size				
	30 - 50 m	Home range	Carroll and Ehrenfeld, 1978	n = 189
	Travelled 8 km upstream; 3.2 km upstream	Movement to return home	Harding and Bloomer, 1979	n = 1 ♀; n = 1 ♀
	447 ± 223 m elongate along streams	Home range	Strang, 1983	n = 10
	2 - 30 m width channel	Population site	Buech et al., 1990	n = 30
	$\bar{x}$ = 24.3 ha	Activity center	Quinn and Tate, 1991	n = 6
	< 1 - 115 ha	Home range	Quinn and Tate, 1991	n = 6
	Remained within 6 - 8 m^2 area	Winter activity	Graham and Forsberg, 1991	n = 8
	3 - 5 m width river channel	Population site	Brewster and Brewster, 1991	n = 8
	5 - 10 m wide creek	Population site	Kaufmann, 1992	n = 84

Figure 2. Sample page of species Habitat Characteristics Table: The wood turtle, *Clemmys insculpta*.

DISCUSSION

The predictive models developed for wetland-dependent turtles in New England are primarily qualitative because of the nature of the literature upon which they are based. Until more in-depth, quantitative analyses of habitat requirements are conducted and published, the models available for use in early identification of critical habitat cannot provide the level of detail that has been attained for other wildlife species. Given the urgent need to protect turtle habitat and the increasing regulatory interest in early identification of critical habitat, researchers should be encouraged to provide these types of data. In the meantime, the Habitat Characteristics Tables and Habitat Predicting Models will serve as an important foundation for early identification of turtle habitat.

LITERATURE CITED

Adamus, P. R., E. J. Clairain Jr., R. D. Smith, and R. E. Young. 1987. Wetland Evaluation Technique (WET). Volume II: Methodology. National Technical Information Service, Springfield, Virginia. 205 pp.

Brewster, K. N. and C. M. Brewster. 1991. Movement and microhabitat use by juvenile wood turtles introduced into a riparian habitat. J. Herpetol. 25(3):382–385.

Buech, R. R., M. D. Nelson, and B. J. Brecke. 1990. Wood turtle (*Clemmys insculpta*) habitat use on the Cloquet River. Fifty-second Midwest Fish and Wildlife Conference. (Abstract only.)

Carroll, T. E. and D. W. Ehrenfeld. 1978. Intermediate-range homing in the wood turtle. Copeia 1978(1):117–126.

Cowardin, L. M., V. Carter, F. C. Golet, and E. T. LaRoe. 1979. Classification of wetlands and deepwater habitats of the United States. U.S. Fish & Wildlife Service Publ. FWS/OBS-79/31. Washington, D.C. 103 pp.

Graham, T. E. and J. E. Forsberg. 1991. Aquatic oxygen uptake by naturally wintering wood turtles, *Clemmys insculpta*. Copeia 1991(3):837–838.

Harding, J. H., J. L. Behler, R. J. Brooks, and M. W. Klemens. In press. *Clemmys insculpta* (LeConte, 1830) wood turtle. *In* P. C. H. Pritchard and A. G. J. Rhodin (eds.), The Conservation Biology of Freshwater Turtles. Chelonian Research Monogr., Chelonian Research Foundation, Lunenburg, Massachusetts.

Harding, J. H. and T. J. Bloomer. 1979. The wood turtle, *Clemmys insculpta*: A natural history. Bull. New York Herpetol. Soc. 15(1):9–26.

Kaufmann, J. H. 1992. Habitat use by wood turtles in central Pennsylvania. J. Herpetol. 26(3):315–321.

Quinn, N. W. S. and D. P. Tate. 1991. Seasonal movements and habitat of wood turtles (*Clemmys insculpta*) in Algonquin Park, Canada. J. Herpetol. 25(2):217–220.

Robakiewicz, P. 1993. Radio telemetry of wood turtles in the Scantic River Floodplain: Habitat selection and life history monitoring. Unpubl. report prepared for Natural Heritage and Endangered Species Program, Massachusetts Division Fisheries and Wildlife, Westborough, Massachusetts. 19 pp.

Strang, C. A. 1983. Spatial and temporal activity patterns in two terrestrial turtles. J. Herpetol. 17(1):43–47.

Whitlock, A. L. 1994. Habitat parameters for wetland-dependent turtles in New England. M.S. thesis, University of Massachusetts, Amherst, Massachusetts. 238 pp.

Whitlock, A. L., N. M. Jarman, and J. S. Larson. 1994. WEThings: Wetland Habitat Indicators for Nongame Species. Environmental Institute, University of Massachusetts, Amherst, Massachusetts.

Patterns of Gopher Tortoise Demography in Florida

HENRY R. MUSHINSKY, EARL D. MCCOY, AND DAWN S. WILSON

Department of Biology, Center for Urban Ecology, University of South Florida, Tampa, FL 33620, USA
[e-mail: mushinsk@chuma.cas.usf.edu]

ABSTRACT: We surveyed over 50 populations of the gopher tortoise, *Gopherus polyphemus*, in Florida to evaluate how the apparent demographic "health" of each population is influenced by area reduction over time, vegetation structure, and geographic isolation. The influence of isolation was evaluated by comparing demographic profiles of populations on islands and on large mainland sites. A few of the populations studied had been surveyed previously by other researchers, and we were able to relate changes in tortoise demography to changes in vegetation structure. A long-term study on a single population gave us insight into how management practices can influence growth and time to sexual maturity of gopher tortoises.

For all gopher tortoise populations surveyed, the same basic methods were used. We used transects to locate burrows, from which population sizes of tortoises were estimated. Gopher tortoises spend most of their time inside their burrows, and the width of a burrow is known to correlate strongly with the carapace length of the resident gopher tortoise. Therefore, we assessed the condition of burrows and used measurements of burrow widths to estimate both population sizes and the size class distribution of each population. The extent of gopher tortoise habitat area was estimated from the positions of burrows, and amount of area reduction was estimated from a temporal series of aerial photographs. We determined the density of plant cover at ground level and in two levels of canopy.

Our findings indicate that gopher tortoises respond in both obvious and subtle ways to the quality of their habitat. Area reduction and habitat degradation force tortoises into ever-fewer patches of suitable habitat and narrow their choices of locations for burrows. The size distributions of tortoises illustrate the detrimental effects of area reduction and habitat degradation on tortoise demography. The demography of tortoise populations on habitat remnants, therefore, does not necessarily resemble the demography of tortoise populations on equal-sized subsamples of large areas. Gopher tortoises in relatively small but highly managed areas can maintain healthy populations. One key to successful management is periodic controlled burning of the habitat. Without intensive management, most small, remnant populations are doomed to extinction, but nevertheless may persist for substantial periods of time.

The gopher tortoise, *Gopherus polyphemus* (Daudin), is one of four tortoise species in North America and the only species found east of the Mississippi River. The range of the gopher tortoise extends from eastern Louisiana to southern South Carolina. Within its geographic range, the gopher tortoise is found almost exclusively on deep, sandy soils suitable for construction of extensive burrows (Hansen, 1963). Its dependence on sandy substrates places the gopher tortoise in direct conflict with humans who modify upland habitats for mining, agriculture, or other uses. Fragmentation and loss of lands with suitable substrate are probably the most important factors contributing to the decline of gopher tortoises (Auffenberg and Franz, 1982; Diemer, 1986).

Many of the remaining gopher tortoise populations in peninsular Florida are small in size and will not persist (Auffenberg and Franz, 1982). This situation has arisen because vast areas of gopher tortoise habitat have been altered, leaving only small, often short-lived "habitat islands." Statewide, Auffenberg and Franz (1982) calculated that an 80% reduction in the number of tortoises had occurred over the last 100 years, largely because of reduction of suitable habitat. They estimated that 70% of the remaining tortoise habitat would be lost by the year 2000 and that virtually all would be lost by the year 2025.

The life history of the gopher tortoise conforms to the following pattern: Males court and mate with females in the spring and fall of the year. Females deposit their eggs during May and June, often in the sandy soil mounds immediately outside their burrows. Following an incubation period of 95–105 days, eggs hatch from mid-August through September (Landers et al., 1980). Males achieve sexual maturity one to four years before females, which begin to reproduce when their carapace lengths are approximately 240 mm at an age of 9–18 years (Auffenberg and Iverson, 1979; Alford, 1980; Landers et al., 1982; Mushinsky et al., 1994). Each female may produce a single clutch per year averaging five to eight eggs (Iverson, 1980; Linley and Mushinsky, 1994). Gopher tortoises grow less rapidly after sexual maturity (Mushinsky et al., 1994) and may live more than 60 years (Landers et al., 1982).

During the past decade we surveyed more than 50 tortoise populations throughout Florida and collected data to (1) construct a demographic profile, (2) assess the extent of the area occupied, (3) evaluate the vegetation structure, and (4) determine the extent of habitat reduction, if any, for each population. Because many of our findings have been published elsewhere, only a synopsis of those studies is presented with references to the pertinent literature. Here, we focus on the following question: Does vegetation structure, reduction of available habitat, or isolation on an island influence gopher tortoise demography?

Some of the populations studied had been surveyed previously by other researchers. Thus, for a few populations we were able to retrospectively assess changes in gopher tortoise demography relative to vegetation structure. Also, one of our gopher tortoise populations, at the University of South Florida Ecological Research Area (ERA) in Hillsborough County, has been studied extensively for more than ten years on land that is burned periodically. From this long-term study, we have gained insight into the relationships between fire frequency, habitat structure, and growth and age at sexual maturity for individual gopher tortoises.

Materials and Methods

We surveyed each population by walking side by side on 10 m wide transects. All burrows located along a transect were measured and classified as active, inactive, or abandoned. Active burrows showed evidence of recent tortoise activity, such as footprints or plastral scrape marks. Inactive burrows lacked evidence of recent activity. Abandoned burrows could not be used by a tortoise without modification because the burrow mouths were damaged or overgrown with vegetation (McCoy and Mushinsky, 1992a; Mushinsky and Esman, 1994).

Burrow widths were measured to the nearest 0.5 cm with a pair of meter sticks fastened together at the 50 cm mark to form a connected pair of calipers. The meter sticks were placed into each burrow to a depth of 50 cm and spread open so that one stick touched each side of the burrow, allowing the width of the burrow to be measured across the opposite ends of the sticks. Because gopher tortoises spend most of their time inside their burrows and the width of a burrow is known to correlate strongly with the carapace lengths of the resident gopher tortoise (Alford, 1980; Martin and Layne, 1987; Wilson et al., 1991), we used burrow width measurements to estimate the size class distribution of tortoises for each population.

The extent of habitat area for each population was determined by the occurrence of tortoises, not by our subjective evaluation of habitat suitability. The method used to determine the area occupied by a gopher tortoise population depended upon the size and method used to survey a given site.

For sites <10 ha in area, the position of each burrow was marked with a vertical, 1.5 m long PVC pipe. The area occupied by tortoises was then measured by locating the approximate center of the occupied habitat and measuring the distance from the center along eight major compass directions to the edge of a polygon derived by laying straight lines between peripheral burrows.

For sites between 10 and 120 ha in area, we used 10 m wide belt transects of varying lengths to survey tortoise burrows. The position and lengths of transects with evidence of tortoises were plotted on aerial photographs of each site, and the area occupied by the tortoises was derived by connecting the peripheral transects.

For sites >120 ha in area, we used 10 × 150 m belt transects. To determine the extent of tortoise habitat, we plotted the location of each transect on a topographic map and then estimated the area of tortoise habitat by connecting only peripheral transects with evidence of tortoises. Some of these sites were so large that we were able to sample only small percentages of them, and our estimates of area occupied by tortoises are relatively crude compared to the estimates for the moderate or small sites.

To quantify the amount of area reduction, if any, that may have influenced the current resident population, we obtained a series of old (20–40 years) aerial photographs of each site. The photographs were used only to construct broad, arbitrary categories of area reduction. For example, an area reduction of <25% was considered moderate, while area reduction of >25% was considered severe. We note that prior to the 1950s, Florida had experienced limited growth and disturbance of natural habitats by humans. Area reduction that had occurred within the previous ten years was considered recent, while area reduction that had begun more than 20 years prior to our study was considered long-term (McCoy and Mushinsky, 1988).

We quantified the vegetation structure of sites with resident gopher tortoise populations by a method modified from James and Shugart (1970). The density of plant cover was estimated visually at three levels, (1) from the ground to 1 m above ground, (2) between 1 and 3 m above ground (low canopy), and (3) above 3 m above ground (high canopy). At the lowest level, we determined vegetation structure from a standing position as the percent of ground surface area occupied by (1) legumes, other herbs, and grasses (collectively called herbaceous vegetation); (2) leaf litter and woody vegetation (litter/wood); or (3) bare ground. Above 1 m, the simple presence or absence of vegetation was noted in each of the two levels. These visual estimates were made in a series of randomly placed 4 m² quadrats. At least 20 quadrats were sampled in each site that supported tortoises and more in sites where tortoise habitat was extensive. The mean percentages of herbaceous vegetation, litter/wood, and bare ground were used as estimates of the percentages of these cover types for an entire site, and the percentage of samples in which low and high canopy was present was used as an estimate of these canopy covers over the entire site. We focused on the relative amount of herbaceous vegetation at each site as an indicator of habitat quality for gopher tortoises because tortoises are known to eat a wide variety of these plants (Macdonald and Mushinsky, 1988), and because tortoise densities are related to the biomass and structural components of the herbaceous vegetation (Auffenberg and Iverson 1979; Diemer, 1986).

A demographic profile of each surveyed gopher tortoise population was constructed by dividing the distributions of burrow widths into the size classes of tortoises recognized by Alford (1980). To have some "standard" against which our real size distributions could be compared, we (McCoy and Mushinsky, 1988) constructed two stationary size distributions, one for a "favorable" habitat and the other for a "harsh" habitat (see Cox et al., 1987). By comparing the standard size class distributions of the populations of gopher tortoises we surveyed with the size class distributions of tortoises from favorable or harsh habitats, we were able to assess the relative "health" of each population.

Ten of the populations surveyed were on true islands near the coast of Florida. To evaluate the burrowing behavior of tortoises in isolated habitats, the ratio of inactive burrows to active burrows was computed on each island. To interpret these data, we computed a similar ratio for tortoises in ten mainland populations. The higher the ratio, the more individuals tend to construct new burrows (Mushinsky and McCoy, 1994).

The gopher tortoise population on the ERA has been studied since 1982. More than 400 tortoises were given individual marks when first captured and many have been recaptured over the years. Each time a tortoise was captured, a series of ten measurements (McRae et al., 1981) were taken. The age of all young tortoises (up to about 15 years) was estimated by counting plastral rings, and the sex was determined if possible. Because the upland portion of the ERA has been subjected to frequent periodic controlled burning since 1975, this site represents a near ideal habitat for gopher tortoises (Mushinsky and Gibson, 1991).

Results and Discussion

On sites that had experienced severe area reduction, that had >50% tree canopy, or were <2 ha in size, gopher tortoise populations tended to have truncated demographic profiles. A truncated profile suggests little recruitment of individuals into the population and abandonment of the site by mature individuals. In contrast, tortoise populations on sites with no or limited area reduction, on sites with <50% tree canopy, or on relatively large sites (>2 ha) tended to have a high proportion of mature individuals but also with evidence of recruitment of young into the population (McCoy and Mushinsky, 1988). The potential influence of past harvesting of large adult tortoises (for human consumption) is unknown; however, the collection of tortoises in Florida was banned in 1988.

Comparisons of tortoise populations on true islands with populations on the mainland suggests that tortoises do respond to relatively small, isolated habitats. Both island and mainland tortoise populations show a positive relationship between the number of active and inactive burrows and the area of habitat. Density of burrows, however, decreased as area increased on the mainland, but density of burrows was not related to area on the islands. Also, on the mainland, the ratio of inactive to active burrows (a measure of the tendency of individuals to construct new burrows) increased with area of habitat, and burrow density increased with increasing herbaceous vegetation, but neither of these relationships could be demonstrated on the islands. Collectively, these findings suggest that tortoises have a greater selection of habitats on the mainland than on islands. Tortoises on islands are confined and forced to live in less than ideal conditions. The implications of these findings are profound for tortoises living in small, fragmented "habitat islands" on the mainland, which also may be confronted with less than ideal conditions. In time, perhaps a few decades, as the quality of their habitat island is degraded, mature adults may be forced to abandon a site in search of better quality habitat. Such individuals, which may be forced to abandon isolated patches of habitat in areas surrounded by human dwellings, seem doomed to perish. Prior to our study (Mushinsky and McCoy, 1994), observing large numbers of active and inactive gopher tortoise burrows in a confined area probably would have been viewed as indicators of a "healthy" population. However, our findings suggest just the opposite. Rather than a signal of a healthy population, the presence of large numbers of active and inactive burrows alone relative to the actual number of tortoises may signal a stressed population.

Our retrospective study of gopher tortoise populations residing on federal lands in Florida suggests that tortoises can respond to the quality of their habitat in a relatively short time period. For example, one population surveyed on Cape Sable in Everglades National Park had a demographic profile that suggested a healthy population. We found an 11% increase in the number of active burrows compared to a survey (Kushlan and Mazzotti, 1984) conducted six years earlier. This population inhabits an isolated near-island with sparse canopy and large amounts of herbaceous vegetation, probably because the region is subject to natural fires, hurricanes, and periodic drought. In contrast, the J. N. "Ding" Darling National Wildlife Refuge on Sanibel Island supports dense, high and low tree canopies and sparse amounts of herbaceous vegetation. A 33% decrease in the number of active burrows was found between our survey and that of T. Logan (1978–1979, unpubl.), which suggests a substantial decline in the number of tortoises (McCoy and Mushinsky, 1992b). We found no evidence of recent recruitment into the population: No burrows that could accommodate juvenile or young tortoises were located on the Refuge during our survey. Responses of gopher tortoises to vegetation structure may be partly responsible for the demographic trends we have documented on these two federal lands.

Gopher tortoises are restricted to habitats that permit them to dig their extensive burrows, which average about 5 m in length and extend to a depth of 2 m (Hansen, 1963). Many of the populations we surveyed resided on sandhill habitat, which occurs on well-drained deep yellow sands (Myers, 1990). Sandhill is a pyrogenic habitat (Abrahamson, 1984); hence, the time interval between fires strongly influences canopy cover and the herbaceous and grassy ground cover. Campbell and Christman (1982) suggested that gopher tortoises are attracted to the "openness" of the habitat, and McCoy and Mushinsky (1992b) reported that tortoises abandon habitats that become overgrown. On average, sandhill burns about once a decade (Myers, 1990). In the absence of fire for several decades, the patchy tree canopy is replaced by a dense canopy of other plant associations (Myers, 1990; Veno, 1976).

Frequent prescribed burning of the sandhill habitat at the ERA maintains a relatively open habitat (Mushinsky, 1985, 1992). The upland portion of the ERA supports a lush ground cover of grasses (*Aristida* spp.) and herbs (especially Asteraceae and Poaceae), partially covered by a shrub layer of saw palmetto (*Serona repens*), under a patchy canopy of longleaf pine (*Pinus palustris*), turkey oak (*Quercus laevis*), and sand live oak (*Q. geminata*). Tortoises at this site are known to ingest a large variety of grasses and herbaceous plants, including 68 genera from 26 families (Macdonald and Mushinsky, 1988). This flora is rich in legumes, which are an important source of protein and calcium (Garner and Landers, 1981).

We found that female gopher tortoises on the ERA grew more rapidly and attained sexual maturity several years earlier than female tortoises from a less well-maintained site in the same county or from southern Georgia (Mushinsky et al., 1994). At the ERA, tortoises begin to reproduce at a relatively young age for females (9–11 years) and probably for males as well. Rapid growth of tortoises at the ERA is probably a response to the length of the growing season and the high-quality habitat, which is maintained by periodic controlled burning. The rapid growth of tortoises on this intensely managed site also diminishes the degree of sexual size dimorphism in this population relative to tortoises in other populations (e.g., Landers et al., 1982). Because female tortoises mature only a year or so after male tortoises at the ERA, morphological characteristics associated with body size differences between the sexes (e.g., body width and body thickness) do not have sufficient time to become distinct. We suggest that rapid growth and nearly simultaneous attainment of sexual maturity in males and females diminish sexual size dimorphism in our central Florida population.

Landers and Speake (1980) recognized that gopher tortoises can be maintained on small management areas, but they proposed that larger areas (up to several hundred hectares) would lessen the impact of emigration and mortality. Similarly, Cox et al. (1987) suggested that areas of 10–25 ha of favorable, managed habitat should be set aside for populations occupying lands slated for development. We recognize the importance of protecting large areas (tens to hundreds of hectares) of gopher tortoise habitat but wish to emphasize the value of the numerous small isolated populations that exist throughout the range of the tortoise. We can present at least three arguments that support the maintenance of small populations:

1. Gopher tortoises function as "keystone species" (Campbell and Christman, 1982; Jackson and Milstrey, 1989; Witz and Wilson, 1991), and because of their role in maintaining biodiversity, even in small patches of habitat, they merit special consideration in ranking conservation priorities (see Soulé and Simberloff, 1985; Soulé, 1987). As a keystone species, the gopher tortoise may facilitate the continued existence of other species on patches of habitat that may be too small for their long-term survival without the presence of the safe retreat, topographic complexity, and additional microhabitat offered by the tortoise burrows.

2. Small populations can function as banks of individuals and of genetic diversity. As fragmentation of gopher tortoise populations continues, relatively large, undisturbed tracts of habitat are becoming rare. Development patterns throughout peninsular Florida are such that it is difficult or impractical to set aside even 10 ha of land in many places. Viewing fragmented gopher tortoise populations as metapopulations suggests alternate conservation strategies. Small populations serve as banks for individuals and their genes and may function to bridge gaps for gene exchange between large populations. To compensate for the extreme fragmentation of gopher tortoise populations in Florida, human intervention may be needed to effect gene exchange between isolated populations.

3. Small areas of gopher tortoise habitat may present some advantages over large areas. Small populations may be isolated from diseases that spread throughout a large population. Conservation of large areas of land also has the

potential side effect of creating false security about the future of resident tortoises. Continuous management is critical to these populations, but tortoises occupying extant large conservation areas typically have not been so managed (McCoy and Mushinsky, 1992b; Shaffer, 1987). Populations of tortoises on single large areas of land are vulnerable to stochastic disturbances that may affect the well-being of an entire population. Of course, small populations also are vulnerable to stochastic disturbances, but having numerous separate populations decreases the likelihood of any disturbance influencing all individuals (see Ogle and Wilson, 1985).

The fragility of tortoise demography may make tortoise populations even more vulnerable to extinction from disturbance events than other long-lived vertebrates (see Iverson, 1982). We believe it unwise to place full emphasis upon the single-large-area notion of conservation. We propose that greater emphasis be placed on alternate conservation strategies for the gopher tortoise in Florida. A two-pronged approach seems appropriate. When possible, large areas of land should be secured, with the stipulation that rigorous management practices are employed to monitor and ensure the demographic health of the resident populations. One clear outcome of our research is the value of active habitat management (frequent periodic burning) to resident tortoises (Mushinsky et al., 1994) (although in suburban environments, there may be regulatory difficulties impeding such necessary management practices as controlled burns). Besides securing large areas, we see a need to secure numerous small areas.

We view tortoise habitat quality as a dynamic gradient. Area reduction and habitat degradation are two of the greatest threats to the future of tortoise populations: As either increases, the probability of extinction also increases. The combined effects of area reduction and habitat degradation may increase the probability synergistically. Hence, although tortoises on all remaining lands need continuous management, the need is especially great for small areas. Poaching, predation, intraspecific competition, and other such interactions may be especially severe for remnant tortoise populations.

Identifying the appropriate scale of examination to use when researching gopher tortoises is important (McCoy et al., 1993). Two examples illustrate the importance of scale.

First, "the dispersion of gopher tortoise burrows within available habitats . . . is poorly understood" (Cox et al., 1987, p. 13). We found that burrow dispersion changes with area and that burrows are placed preferentially in open portions of habitat, away from thick vegetation (McCoy and Mushinsky, 1992b; Mushinsky and McCoy, 1994). If large areas of mixed habitats are studied, burrows are generally clumped within certain habitats. If suitable individual habitats are studied instead, burrows are generally relatively widely spaced and randomly distributed. When the individual habitats become smaller and canopy cover increases, burrows tend to be clumped within the remaining patches of open habitat. If these patches are studied, burrows are generally relatively closely spaced and randomly distributed. Comparisons of large habitats and small patches potentially could yield similar results, but would reveal little about gopher tortoise biology. We suggest, therefore, that comparisons of burrow dispersions are useful only if the scale of examination is held constant.

Second, "more precise measures and definitions of habitat quality are . . . needed . . ." (Cox et al., 1987, p. 33). Cox et al. (1987) suggest that population density estimates can contribute to evaluation of habitat quality. Our results indicate clearly, however, that comparisons of burrow densities, just like comparisons of burrow dispersions, must employ a single scale of examination. To illustrate the point, consider a hypothetical situation in which each of two 20 ha plots of land contains 50 tortoises. The density of tortoises, then, is calculated as 2.5 tortoises/ha in both plots. If all 50 tortoises were found to be confined to a 10 ha portion of one of the plots but were evenly distributed over the entire 20 ha of the other plot, would the calculated density of the first plot need to be altered? If the density were altered to 5.0 tortoises/ha, should the plot with the higher density be considered better gopher tortoise habitat? Answers to these questions do not come easily unless scale of examination is held constant between comparisons. Few researchers state clearly how they determined the area occupied by a population to calculate its density. Closer attention must be paid to the problem of scale in the future.

Conclusions

1. Burrow density is related positively to the degree of habitat reduction and to the amount of bare ground present at a particular site (McCoy and Mushinsky, 1988).
2. Many sites with relatively high densities of burrows are remnants of formerly larger areas of habitat.
3. Area reduction and habitat degradation force tortoises into ever fewer patches of suitable habitat and narrow their choices of locations for burrows.
4. The influence of poaching, predation, intraspecific competition, and other such interactions may be especially severe for remnant tortoise populations.
5. Size distributions of burrows illustrate the detrimental effects of area reduction and habitat degradation on tortoise demography.
6. Reduction in the amount of suitable habitat, with its concomitant isolation of the resulting remnant(s), affects size distributions of burrows most strongly.
7. Because of the considerations listed above, the demography of tortoise populations on habitat remnants cannot be expected to resemble the demography of tortoises on equal-sized subsamples of large areas.

8. Gopher tortoises in relatively small but highly managed areas can maintain healthy populations. One key to successful management is periodic controlled burning of the habitat.

9. Without intensive management (i.e., fencing and control of canopy formation), most small remnant populations are doomed to extinction but still may persist for substantial periods of time (decades).

10. Remnant populations may function within a "metapopulation" framework as banks of individuals and of genetic diversity, and thus provide an alternate conservation strategy for gopher tortoises. Human intervention may be necessary to facilitate gene exchange between isolated populations.

11. Implementation of this alternate strategy would involve intensive management of tortoises, including translocations, and would necessitate coordination of all activities involving gopher tortoises.

ACKNOWLEDGMENTS

Our research was supported, in part, by research grants from the Nongame Wildlife Research Program of the Florida Game and Fresh Water Fish Commission, The Florida Department of Natural Resources, and The Nature Conservancy. Without their support, this research would not have been possible.

LITERATURE CITED

Abrahamson, W. G. 1984. Post-fire recovery of Florida Lake Wales Ridge vegetation. Amer. J. Bot. 71:9–12.

Alford, R. A. 1980. Population structure of *Gopherus polyphemus* in northern Florida. J. Herpetol. 14:177–182.

Auffenberg, W. and R. Franz. 1982. The status and distribution of the gopher tortoise (*Gopherus polyphemus*). In R. B. Bury (ed.), North American Tortoises: Conservation and Ecology, pp. 95–126. Wildlife Research Report 12, U.S. Fish and Wildlife Service, Washington, D.C.

Auffenberg, W. and J. B. Iverson. 1979. Demography of terrestrial turtles. In M. Harless and N. Morlock (eds.), Turtles: Perspectives and Research, pp. 541–569. Wiley-International, New York.

Campbell, H. W. and S. P. Christman. 1982. The herpetological components of Florida sandhill and sand pine scrub associations. In N. J. Scott, Jr. (ed.), Herpetological Communities, pp. 163–171. Wildlife Research Report 13, U.S. Fish and Wildlife Service, Washington, D.C.

Cox, J., D. Inkley, and R. Kautz. 1987. Ecology and habitat protection needs of gopher tortoise (*Gopherus polyphemus*) populations found on lands slated for large-scale development in Florida. Florida Game and Freshwater Fish Commission, Nongame Wildlife Program Technical Report 4, Tallahassee, Florida.

Diemer, J. E. 1986. The ecology and management of the gopher tortoise in the southeastern United States. Herpetologica 42:125–133.

Garner, J. A. and J. L. Landers. 1981. Foods and habitat of the gopher tortoise in southwestern Georgia. Proceedings of the Annual Conference of The Southeastern Association of Fish and Wildlife Agencies 35:120–134.

Hansen, K. L. 1963. The burrow of the gopher tortoise. Quarterly Journal of the Florida Academy of Sciences 26:353–360.

Iverson, J. B. 1980. The reproductive biology of *Gopherus polyphemus* (Chelonia: Testudinidae). Amer. Midl. Nat. 103:353–359.

Iverson, J. B. 1982. Biomass in turtle populations: A neglected subject. Oecologia 55:69–76.

Jackson, D. R. and E. G. Milstrey. 1989. The fauna of gopher tortoise burrows. In J. E. Diemer, D. R. Jackson, J. L. Landers, J. N. Layne, and D. A. Wood (eds.), Gopher Tortoise Relocation Symposium Proceedings, pp. 86–98. State of Florida Game and Freshwater Fish Commission, Nongame Wildlife Program Technical Report #5, Tallahassee, Florida.

James, F. C. and H. H. Shugart. 1970. A quantitative method of habitat description. Audubon Field Notes 24:727–736.

Kushlan, J. A. and F. J. Mazzotti. 1984. Environmental effects on a coastal population of gopher tortoises. J. Herpetol. 18:231–239.

Landers, J. L., J. A. Garner, and W. A. McRae. 1980. Reproduction of gopher tortoises (*Gopherus polyphemus*) in southwestern Georgia. Herpetologica 36:353–361.

Landers, J. L., W. A. McRae, and J. A. Garner. 1982. Growth and maturity of the gopher tortoise in southwestern Georgia. Bulletin of the Florida State Museum, Biological Science 27:81–110.

Landers, J. L. and D. W. Speake. 1980. Management needs of sandhill reptiles in southern Georgia. Proceedings of the Annual Conference of the Southeastern Association of Fish and Wildlife Agencies 34:515–529.

Linley, T. A. and H. R. Mushinsky. 1994. Organic composition and energy content of eggs and hatchlings of the gopher tortoise. In R. B. Bury and D. J. Germano (eds.), Biology of North American Tortoises, pp. 112–128. Fish and Wildlife Research 13, Technical Report Series, U.S. Department of the Interior, National Biological Survey, Washington, D.C.

Macdonald, L. A. and H. R. Mushinsky. 1988. Foraging ecology of the gopher tortoise, *Gopherus polyphemus*, in a central Florida sandhill. Herpetologica 44:345–353.

Martin, P. L. and J. N. Layne. 1987. Relationship of gopher tortoise body size to burrow size in a south-central population. Florida Scientist 50:264–267.

McRae, W. A., J. L. Landers, and G. D. Cleveland. 1981. Sexual dimorphism in the gopher tortoise (*Gopherus polyphemus*). Herpetologica 37:46–52.

McCoy, E. D. and H. R. Mushinsky. 1988. The demography of *Gopherus polyphemus* (Daudin) in relation to size of available habitat. Florida Game and Fresh Water Fish Commission, Final Report, Tallahassee.

McCoy, E. D. and H. R. Mushinsky. 1992a. Studying a species in decline: Gopher tortoises and the dilemma of "correction factors." Herpetologica 48:402–407.

McCoy, E. D. and H. R. Mushinsky. 1992b. Studying a species in decline: Changes in populations of the gopher tortoises on federal lands in Florida. Florida Scientist 55:116–125.

McCoy, E. D., H. R. Mushinsky, and D. S. Wilson. 1993. Patterns in the compass orientation of gopher tortoise burrows at different spatial scales. Global Ecology and Biogeography Letters:3:33–40.

Mushinsky, H. R. 1985. Fire and the Florida sandhill herpetofaunal community: With special attention to responses of *Cnemidophorus sexlineatus*. Herpetologica 41:333–342.

Mushinsky, H. R. 1992. Natural history and abundance of southeastern five-lined skinks, *Eumeces inexpectatus*, on a periodically burned sandhill in Florida. Herpetologica 48:307–312.

Mushinsky, H. R. and L. A. Esman. 1994. Perceptions of gopher

tortoise burrows over time. Florida Field Naturalist 22:1–7.
Mushinsky, H. R. and D. Gibson. 1991. The influence of fire on habitat structure. *In* S. S. Bell, E. D. McCoy, and H. R. Mushinsky (eds.), Habitat Structure: The Physical Arrangement of Objects in Space, pp. 235–259. Chapman and Hall, London.
Mushinsky, H. R. and E. D. McCoy. 1994. Comparison of gopher tortoise populations on islands and on the mainland in Florida. *In* R. B. Bury and D. J. Germano (eds.), Biology of North American Tortoises, pp. 39–47. Fish and Wildlife Research 13, Technical Report Series, U.S. Department of the Interior, National Biological Survey, Washington, D.C.
Mushinsky, H. R., D. S. Wilson, and E. D. McCoy. 1994. Growth and sexual dimorphism of *Gopherus polyphemus* in central Florida. Herpetologica: 50:119–128.
Myers, R. L. 1990. Scrub and high pine. *In* R. L. Myers and J. J. Ewel (eds.), Ecosystems of Florida, pp. 150–193. University of Central Florida Press, Orlando.
Ogle, C. C. and R. R. Wilson. 1985. Where have all the mistletoes gone? Forest and Bird 13:8–15.
Shaffer, M. L. 1987. Minimum viable populations: Coping with uncertainty. *In* M. E. Soulé (ed.), Viable Populations for Conservation. Cambridge University Press, Cambridge, UK.
Soulé, M. E. 1987. Introduction. *In* M. E. Soulé (ed.), Viable Populations for Conservation. Cambridge Univ. Press, Cambridge, UK.
Soulé, M. E. and D. Simberloff. 1986. What do genetics and ecology tell us about the design of nature reserves? Biol. Conserv. 35:19–40.
Veno, P. A. 1976. Successional relationships of five Florida plant communities. Ecology 57:498–508.
Wilson, D. S., H. R. Mushinsky, and E. D. McCoy. 1991. Relationship between gopher tortoise body size and burrow width. Herpetol. Rev. 22:122–124.
Witz, B. W. and D. S. Wilson. 1991. Distribution of *Gopherus polyphemus* and its vertebrate symbionts in three burrow categories. Amer. Midl. Nat. 126:152–158.

Genetic Methodologies as a Technique for Captive Management

— ABSTRACT OF PRESENTATION —

WALTER SACHSSE

FB 21/Biologie, Institut für Genetik, Arbeitsgruppe Cytogenetik, Postfach 3980, Saarstraße 21, 6500 Mainz 1, Germany

In view of growing human populations, methodologies for the captive management of fauna must be given higher priority. A hands-off policy will not improve chances of survival in the wild for species that will not reproduce in captivity. My own work started in the late 1960s at a time when it was the prevailing opinion that it would be impossible to breed chelonians in captivity. Since then captive reproduction at the Institut für Genetik has been achieved in 38 species, 22 of them repeatedly for a number of years. These include 16 kinosternid, nine emydid, eight testudinid, one trionychid, and five chelid turtles. There have also extensive observations on other species, including sea turtles.

The following turtle conservation aspects have been investigated: ecological specialization, which represents a degree of difficulty in captive management; comparisons between easily bred species and those so far impossible to breed; stimuli for mating; egg production and growth; deviations from natural development; threatening diseases; and reproductive strategies, especially with regard to genetics. DNA fingerprinting has been initiated to determine evolutionary distances between populations. The selection of species has always been undertaken with consideration as to whether the species could be properly cared for at the Institut, how the species is endangered, and with consideration for the genetic aspects of species conservation. Attempts have been made to include members of nearly all families.

Molecular Variation in the Bog Turtle, *Clemmys muhlenbergii*

GEORGE D. AMATO[1], JOHN L. BEHLER[1], BERN W. TRYON[2], AND DENNIS W. HERMAN[3]

[1]*Wildlife Conservation Society, 185th St. and Southern Blvd., Bronx, NY 10460, USA*
[Amato e-mail: gamato1@aol.com] [Behler e-mail: jbehler.wcs@mcimail.com]
[2]*Knoxville Zoological Gardens, P.O. Box 6040, Knoxville, TN 37914, USA*
[3]*North Carolina State Museum of Natural Sciences, P.O. Box 29555, Raleigh, NC 27626-0555, USA*

ABSTRACT: In this study, we preliminarily explored mitochondrial (mt) DNA variation in geographically separated populations of the bog turtle, *Clemmys muhlenbergii*. Portions of the 16S ribosomal mitochondrial gene were amplified by polymerase chain reaction (PCR) and directly sequenced for 20 individuals. The sequences were assessed for diagnostic characters that would support designation as separate conservation units for northern and southern populations. Additionally, the same region was sequenced in representatives of the three congenerics, *C. guttata*, *C. insculpta*, and *C. marmorata*, and two outgroup taxa, *Chrysemys picta* and *Chelydra serpentina*, to determine whether this genomic region contained phylogenetic information for closely related species.

The bog turtle, *Clemmys muhlenbergii*, is North America's smallest chelonian. It is very secretive and occurs in colonies (some of which are widely separated) in the eastern United States from southern Massachusetts to northern Georgia. These colonies inhabit a variety of wetland types, preferring herbaceous sedge meadows and fens with an open canopy. They are dependent on unfragmented dynamic riparian systems, which permit the creation of open marshes and meadows. In recent years these fragile ecosystems have been severely impacted by land-use changes, highway construction, fertilizer contamination, and exotic plant invasion. Many populations have been plundered for the pet trade. Consequently, the species is now listed as "Endangered" throughout most of its range.

A major hiatus exists between northern (New England to Maryland) and southern (southern Virginia to Georgia) populations. Early this century, the "southern morph" was considered to be distinct enough to warrant specific status, i.e., *Clemmys nuchalis* (Dunn, 1917). Although this taxon was subsequently synonymized, its legacy continues to provoke taxonomic questions about allopatric populations of *C. muhlenbergii*. Developing a consensus on these questions is important for species and population management prioritization. Additionally, diagnostic markers for specific populations would be useful to law enforcement officials for controlling the illegal trade in this species.

In this study, we preliminarily explored a region of mitochondrial DNA from individuals collected throughout their range. The 16S ribosomal gene was considered a logical starting place as this region has been shown to demonstrate fixed differences at the subspecific/specific interface for a variety of vertebrate taxa (Amato and Gatesy, 1994). Because different regions of an organism's genome reflect varying degrees of variation ranging from totally invariant to individual-specific, it was important to select a region likely to reflect attributes that are useful for answering a specific question (e.g., phylogeny, paternity, etc.). For determining units of conservation, we have followed a lower level systematics approach (Amato and Wharton, 1993) that attempts to uncover evolutionary patterns at the interface of phylogeny and tokogeny (Hennig, 1966). Specifically, we have attempted to use a modified phylogenetic species concept (Cracraft, 1989) to determine which populations are on a separate evolutionary trajectory and are not simply differentiated by allele frequencies or genetic distances that reflect reticulate patterns below the species level. While we advocate a total evidence approach to this analysis, including morphological, behavioral, genetic, and biogeographic characters, we have confined ourselves to molecular data in this preliminary study. However, the results are discussed in the context of systematic studies of this group employing other data sets as well as generalizations about molecular evolution in chelonians.

MATERIALS AND METHODS

Twenty bog turtles representing populations throughout the known range of the species (Georgia, North Carolina, Maryland, Delaware, Pennsylvania, and New York) were sequenced for 291 bases of 16S mitochondrial fragments. Blood samples were obtained without harm to the animals during ongoing population censusing. Samples were preserved in RT buffer (100 mM Tris, 100 mM EDTA, and 2% SDS) and stored at room temperature until analysis. Total genomic DNA was isolated for all of the blood samples by previously described standard phenol/chloroform isolation procedures (Caccone et al., 1987). A method employing a chelating resin (Chelex 100, BioRad) optimized for forensics samples (Walsh et al., 1991) was used to isolate DNA from a few samples of particularly small volume.

16S ribosomal mitochondrial gene fragments were PCR amplified with modified universal vertebrate primers (Kocher et al., 1989; Palumbi et al., 1990). PCR reactions were carried out in 100 μl reaction volumes with reagents from Perkin-Elmer Cetus Gene Amp Kit. Reactions were performed in a Perkin-Elmer Cetus DNA Thermal Cycler with approximately 250 ngs of template DNA and a magnesium concentration of 1.5 mM. Cycling conditions were 94°C for 1 min., 55°C for 1.5 min., and 72°C for 2 min. for 40 cycles. Most often, unbalanced primers were used to accomplish asymmetric PCR (Gyllensten and Erlich, 1988). Single stranded PCR products were cleaned and concentrated with Centricon-30 columns (Amicon) and directly sequenced by the dideoxy method with reagents and protocol from USB's Sequenase 2.0 sequencing kit (Gatesy and Amato, 1992). Some sequences were obtained using an automated sequencer (Applied Biosystems Model 373A) following the manufacturer's protocols. Both strands were sequenced to assure accuracy.

Sequences were assigned to "northern" populations (New York to Maryland) and "southern" populations (North Carolina to Georgia). Base substitutions were assessed as either characters or traits as defined by Davis and Nixon (1992). This method, population aggregation analysis (PAA), involves successive searches for fixed differences between aggregations of local populations. Characters are attributes that are not polymorphic and are unique within populations. Traits are attributes that may be polymorphic or are not unique to a population. An assessment of conservation units for bog turtles was considered in light of the population aggregation analysis.

Additionally, the same 16S mitochondrial fragment was sequenced for the three congeners, *C. guttata*, *C. insculpta*, and *C. marmorata*, as well as *Chrysemys picta* and *Chelydra serpentina* as outgroups, to determine whether this region contained phylogenetic information. An unweighted maximum parsimony cladogram was constructed using exact searches with the branch and bound setting of PAUP 3.1 for the Macintosh (Swofford, 1991).

RESULTS

Two mitochondrial haplotypes were recovered from the 20 individuals sampled. Nineteen individuals had identical sequences for this region, while a single individual (New York #5) varied by a single base change (Table 1). Because this polymorphism did not characterize the other "northern" individuals, it does not support differentiation based on a population aggregation analysis (Davis and Nixon, 1992).

A single most-parsimonious tree for the *Clemmys* species was obtained using an exact search with the branch and bound setting of PAUP 3.1 (Swofford, 1991) (Figure 1). The topology is in agreement with the conclusion of monophyly for the genus *Clemmys* obtained by Lovich et al. (1991) based on plastral morphology. We also find support for their sister taxon relationship between *C. guttata* and *C. marmorata*. This is in contrast with Merkle (1975), who placed *C. guttata* as the sister taxon to *C. muhlenbergii* based on a limited allozyme survey.

DISCUSSION

The limited molecular data resulting from this study is inconsistent with separate conservation unit designations for "northern" and "southern" bog turtles. At this point we are surveying other areas of the genome for the same samples rather than surveying the same area in a larger number of samples. While small sample sizes can easily lead to erroneous oversplitting, it is clear from this study that this region is essentially invariant throughout the range of bog turtles. Also, we are continuing to survey for more variable areas for population-specific markers that would be useful for forensics.

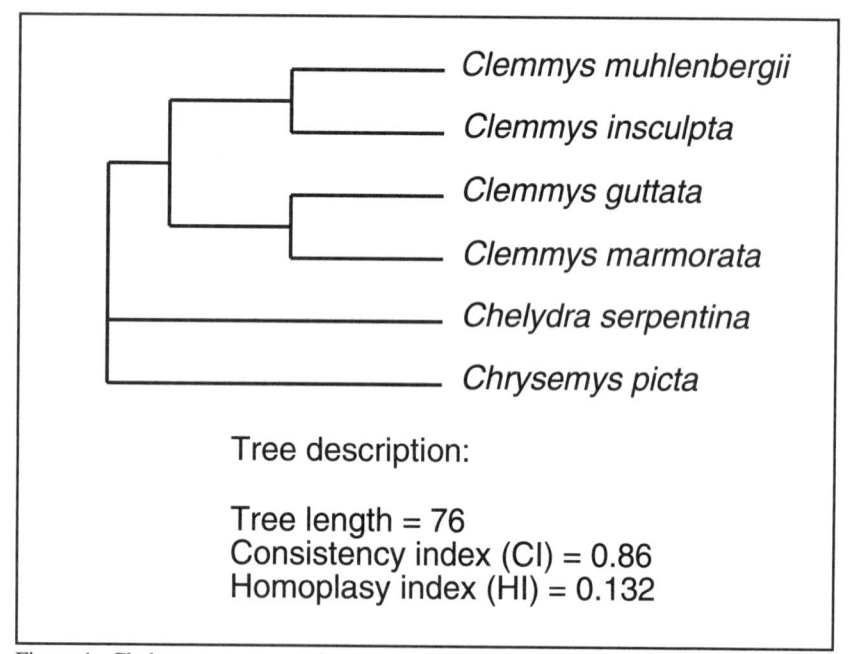

Figure 1. Cladogram constructed using exact searches with the branch and bound setting of PAUP 3.1 for the Macintosh (Swofford, 1991).

Tree description:

Tree length = 76
Consistency index (CI) = 0.86
Homoplasy index (HI) = 0.132

However, it is important to note that the data from this study reveal that the 16S ribosomal gene fragment contains phylogenetic information about the four species in the genus *Clemmys*. The phylogeny resulting from this data is in general agreement with the morphological data of Lovich et al. (1991), perhaps adding some greater resolution. While the results conflict with the electrophoretic studies of Merkle (1975), allozyme studies have frequently proved uninformative for systematics. We are currently employing a total evidence approach, using an expanded molecular data set in combination with published morphological characters to further explore these relationships (Amato and Behler, unpubl.).

Avise and colleagues (Avise et al., 1992; Bowen et al., 1989, 1991; Lamb and Avise, 1992) have suggested that mitochondrial evolution occurs at a slower rate in turtles, based primarily on studies of marine turtles. If this is accurate, mitochondrial DNA differences may not accumulate in isolated populations at a detectable rate over the same evolutionary time period as in some other vertebrates. However, this may not mean that mitochondrial DNA (especially ribosomal genes) is a poor marker for separating conservation units for turtles. Rather, it suggests that turtles are very conservative genetically and that for management purposes, we may not have to assume that every local population has unique suites of genetic characters.

Another hypothesis to explain the lack of detectable mitochondrial variation in North American turtles (Lamb and Avise, 1992; this study) involves the colonization patterns and glacial refugia of North American turtles. During the most recent advance of glacial ice sheets (20,000 years ago), turtles presumably were confined to southern refugia. Their current distribution reflects a recent dispersal over only the last 15,000 years. This may not be a sufficient time for the populations to have accumulated significant genetic variation from the refugia population. However, preliminary data on one species (*Pseudemys rubriventris*) clearly indicates subdivision based on 16S ribosomal and cytochrome b mitochondrial genes (Amato and Behler, in prep.).

While we continue to generate molecular data to address conservation unit questions in bog turtles, we cannot reject the null hypothesis: that there are no genetic characters separating the two purported subspecies. However, if the data continue to suggest that this species be considered a

TABLE 1

291 base fragment of 16S ribosomal mitochondrial gene. Reference sequence is *Clemmys muhlenbergii*. Periods signify identity with reference base. Dashes represent gaps (insertions/deletions) inserted for sequence alignment. Abbreviations are: Cl.mu. = *Clemmys muhlenbergii*, Cl.i. = *Clemmys insculpta*, Cl.g. = *Clemmys guttata*, Cl.ma. = *Clemmys marmorata*, Ch.s. = *Chelydra serpentina*, Ch.p. = *Chrysemys picta*.

```
Cl.mu.  gacattgtta aacggccgcg gtatcctaac cgtgcaaagg tagcgtaatc
Cl.mu.  .......... .......... .......... .......... ..........
Cl.i.   .......... .......... .......... .......... ..........
Cl.g.   .......... .......... .......... .......... ..........
Cl.ma.  .......... .......... .......... .......... ..........
Ch.s.   ....c..... .......... .......... .......... ..........
Ch.p.   .......... .......... .......... .......... ..........

Cl.mu.  acttgttttt taaataaaga ctagaatgaa tggccaaacg aggttctacc
Cl.mu.  .......... .......... .......... .......... ..........
Cl.i.   .......... .......... .......... .......... ..........
Cl.g.   .......... .......... .......... .......... ..........
Cl.ma.  .......... .......... .......... .......... ..........
Ch.s.   .......... .......... .......... .......... .....t....
Ch.p.   .........c c......... .......... .......... ..........

Cl.mu.  tgtctcttac agacaatcag tgaaattgat ctccccgtgc aaaagcgggg
Cl.mu.  .......... .......... .......... .......... ..........
Cl.i.   .......... .......... .......... .......... ..........
Cl.g.   ........t. ...t...... .......... .......... .......a..
Cl.ma.  ........t. ..gt...... .......... ..t....... .......a.a
Ch.s.   .........  .a.t...... .......... ..t....... ....t..a.a
Ch.p.   .......... ...t...... .......... .......... ..........

Cl.mu.  ataaccctat aagacgagaa gacctgtgg aactttaaat acagatcaac
Cl.mu.  .......... .......... .......... .......... ..........
Cl.i.   ......t... .......... .......... ...c...... ..........
Cl.g.   ......t... .......... .......... .......... ..........
Cl.ma.  .......... .......... .......... .......... ..........
Ch.s.   ..g..a.... .......... .......... .......... .ttt.....g
Ch.p.   .....a.... .......... .......... .c........ ...a......

Cl.mu.  tataatcaat atct--aact aaggacttat attcaattag ta---tttga
Cl.mu.  .......... ...c--.... .......... .......... ..---.....
Cl.i.   .......... ...c--.... .......... ...a...... ..---.....
Cl.g.   ...c..t-.c .c.c--.... .....t.... .c.t...... g.---.....
Cl.ma.  .........c ...c--t... .......... .c.t...... c---......
Ch.s.   ..ct.c.... t.a.--.c.. .g.....-..a .-c...c... ..cttc....
Ch.p.   ..cc..-... ..a.cc.... .....t.... .a...cc... .g---ca...

Cl.mu.  tccatatttt cggttggggc gactcggagt aaagaaactc g
Cl.mu.  .......... .......... .......... .......... .
Cl.i.   .......... .......t.. .......... .......... .
Cl.g.   .......... .......... .......... .......... .
Cl.ma.  ..t....... .......... .......... ...c...... .
Ch.s.   ..t.g..... .......... .........c ...c...... .
Ch.p.   ..t.gc.... .......... .........c ...c...... .
```

metapopulation, we will still be interested in using molecular techniques to provide important management information, such as reconstructing historical levels of gene flow for highly fragmented small populations of this unique taxa.

ACKNOWLEDGMENTS

This project was supported by conservation grants from the Institute of Museum Services; the Conservation Endowment Fund of the American Zoo and Aquarium Association; the Wildlife Conservation Society; the North Carolina Chapter—Nature Conservancy (1990), Endangered Nongame Wildlife Program, North Carolina Wildlife Resources Commission (91-SG-08; 92-SG-12); and Zoo Atlanta.

Permits were provided by the Delaware Department of Natural Resources Division of Fish and Wildlife; Georgia Department of Natural Resources, Wildlife Resources Division; Maryland Department of Natural Resources, Forest, Park, and Wildlife Service; North Carolina Wildlife Resources Commission; South Carolina Wildlife and Marine Resources Department; Tennessee Wildlife Resources Agency; and Virginia Department of Wildlife and Inland Fisheries.

Appreciation is extended to Dr. Rita McManamon and the veterinary staff (Zoo Atlanta) for assistance and supplies.

LITERATURE CITED

Amato, G. D. and J. Gatesy. 1994. PCR assays of variable nucleotide sites for identification of conservation units. *In* B. Schierwater, B. Streit, G. P. Wagner, and R. DeSalle (eds.), Molecular Ecology and Evolution: Approaches and Applications, pp. 215–226. Birkhauser, Basel, Switzerland.

Amato, G. D. and D. Wharton. 1993. A systematic approach to identifying units of conservation: Examples of progress and problems. Proceedings of American Zoo and Aquarium Association Annual Meeting, Omaha, Nebraska.

Avise, J. C., B. W. Bowen, T. Lamb, A.B. Meylan, and E. Bermingham. 1992. Mitochondrial DNA evolution at a turtle's pace: Evidence for low genetic variability and reduced microevolutionary rate in the Testudines. Mol. Biol. Evol. 9:457–473.

Bowen, B. W., A. B. Meylan, and J. C. Avise. 1989. An odyssey of the green turtle: Ascension Island revisited. Proc. Natl. Acad. Sci. USA 86:573–576.

Bowen, B. W., A. B. Meylan, and J. C. Avise. 1991. Evolutionary distinctiveness of the endangered Kemp's ridley sea turtle. Nature 352:709–711.

Caccone, A., G. D. Amato, and J. R. Powell. 1987. Intraspecific DNA divergence in *Drosophila*: A case study in parthenogenetic *D. mercatorum*. Mol. Biol. Evol. 4:343–350.

Cracraft, J. A. 1989. Speciation and ontology: The empirical consequences of alternative species concepts for understanding patterns and processes of differentiation. *In* D. Otte and J. A. Endler (eds.), Speciation and Its Consequences, pp. 28–59. Sinauer Associates, Sunderland, Massachusetts.

Davis, J. I. and K. C. Nixon. 1992. Populations, genetic variation, and the delimitation of phylogenetic species. Systematic Biology 41 (4):421–435.

Dunn, E. R. 1917. Reptile and amphibian collections from the North Carolina mountains, with special reference to salamanders. Bull. Amer. Mus. Nat. Hist. 37(23):593–634.

Gatesy, G. and G. D. Amato. 1992. Sequence similarity of 12S ribosomal segment of mitochondrial DNAs of gharial and false gharial. Copeia 1992:241–243.

Gyllensten, U. B. and H. A. Erlich. 1988. Generation of single-stranded DNA by the polymerase chain reaction and its application to direct sequencing of the HLA-DQA locus. Proc. Natl. Acad. Sci. USA 85:7652–7656.

Hennig, W. 1966. Phylogenetic Systematics. Univ. of Illinois Press, Urbana, Illinois.

Kocher, T. C., W. K. Thomas, A. Meyer, S. V. Edwards, S. Paabo, F. X. Villablanca, and A. C. Wilson. 1989. Dynamics of mitochondrial evolution in animals: Amplification and sequencing with conserved primers. Proc. Natl. Acad. Sci. USA 86:377–382.

Lamb, T. and J. C. Avise. 1992. Molecular and population genetics aspects of mitochondrial DNA variability in the diamondback terrapin, *Malaclemys terrapin*. J. Heredity 83:262–269.

Lovich, J. E., A. F. Laemmerzahl, C. H. Ernst, and J. F. McBreen. 1991. Relationships among turtles of the genus *Clemmys* (Reptilia, Testudines, Emydidae) as suggested by plastron scute morphology. Zool. Scripta. 20(4):425–429.

Merkle, D. A. 1975. A taxonomic analysis of the *Clemmys* complex (Reptilia: Testudines) utilizing starch gel electrophoresis. Herpetologica 31:162–166.

Swofford, D. L. 1991. Phylogenetic Analysis Using Parsimony, Version 3.1 (PAUP 3.1). Computer program, Illinois Natural History Survey, Champaign, Illinois.

Walsh, P. S., D. A. Metzger, and R. Higuchi. 1991. Chelex 100 as a medium for simple extraction of DNA for PCR-based typing from forensic material. BioTechniques 10(4):506–513.

Status Reports

Standing — Roger Wood (The Wetlands Institute, Stone Harbor, New Jersey), Ramon Mascort (Barcelona, Spain), Indraneil Das (Universiti Brunei Darussalam), and Marc Graff (California Turtle & Tortoise Club, Northridge, California). *Seated* — Md. Sohrab Uddin Sarker (University of Dhaka, Bangladesh), Olga Victoria Castaño-Mora (Universidad Nacional de Colombia, Bogotá, Colombia), and Peter Paul van Dijk (University College Galway, Ireland).

M. Farid Ahsan (University of Chittagong, Bangladesh).

Turtle Conservation in Myanmar: Past, Present, and Future

PETER PAUL VAN DIJK

Department of Biology, Faculty of Science, Chulalongkorn University, Bangkok 10330, Thailand
Department of Zoology, University College Galway, Galway, Ireland (correspondence) [email: Peter.vanDijk@UCG.IE]

ABSTRACT: Old, fragmentary observations are still the main source of information on occurrence and distribution of turtles in Myanmar. These old data and some recently collected status information indicate that populations of many turtle species have declined substantially. Several of these species are endemic to Myanmar. Causes of such decline include destruction of habitat, collection of eggs and adults for consumption, and incidental capture. To ensure survival of turtle populations will require collection and analysis of updated distribution and status information for the various species, upgraded legal protection, and immediate practical conservation projects for the priority species.

The Union of Myanmar, until recently named Burma, is traditionally considered one of the last frontiers in wildlife conservation, an unspoilt treasure chest of biological diversity and resources. It is a large country, covering 677,741 km², stretching over 2,000 km from north to south, with a diversity of habitats from coral reefs, mangroves, mighty rivers, and great expanses of forest to mountain peaks up to 5,881 m. The 41.5 million inhabitants live mainly on the plains along the Ayeyarwady (previously spelled Irrawaddy) and Sittang rivers and in the Salween estuary. Little explored before or even during British rule, the country's closure to the outside world after 1962 made it virtually impossible to obtain data on the status and conservation of its flora and fauna. As a result, our knowledge of the turtles inhabiting Myanmar is largely limited to the material collected and described between 1860 and 1940 by a handful of scientists such as John Anderson, William Theobald, Leonardo Fea, Nelson Annandale, and a few others. Myanmar (then Burma) was one of the first countries worldwide to establish a comprehensive legal framework for the exploitation of its turtle populations; the data on status and exploitation of economically important species, collected by Maxwell (1911) for a review of the Burma Fisheries Act of 1902, remains a valuable source of information. More recently, the United Nations Development Program (UNDP) and Food and Agriculture Organisation (FAO) conducted the Nature Conservation and National Parks Project from 1982 to 1984 to identify areas of conservation value and to assist in implementing an effective legal basis for wildlife conservation. The only recent turtle-oriented visit was by Frazier (1987), who concentrated his efforts on inspecting captive collections. Finally, there have been some studies and reviews of the turtle species that also occur in nearby countries; most widely known among these are Moll's work on *Batagur* (1980) and tortoises (1989) and Das' review (1991) of species shared with India and Bangladesh.

Figure 1. Preserved specimen of the Burmese star tortoise, *Geochelone platynota*, in the Yangon Natural History Museum. Adult female, carapace length approximately 27 cm.

From these sparse data, we know that at least 22 non-marine turtle species inhabit Myanmar. Among these are six endemic species: *Geochelone platynota* (Figure 1), *Morenia ocellata*, *Kachuga trivittata*, *Heosemys depressa*, *Nilssonia formosa* (Figure 3), and *Lissemys scutata*; the endemic subspecies *edeniana* of the widely distributed *Melanochelys trijuga*; and at least one undescribed species of *Mauremys* (IUCN/SSC TFTSG, 1989). Several more species may occur in areas bordering Bangladesh or Thailand, while some species alleged to occur in central Myanmar have never been confirmed. Conversely, a number of specimens alleged to originate from Burma-Myanmar, but coming from other places, and misidentified specimens from the country (e.g., the record for *Notochelys platynota*; see Theobald, 1874:82) have contributed to the confusion. The precise identities of the turtles of the *Kachuga* group and the large softshells remain unclear: *Kachuga kachuga, K. dhongoka, Callagur borneoensis*, and *Hardella thurjii* have all been reported without substantiation. Annandale (1912) alluded to the occurrence of *Chitra* in the Ayeyarwady system, but no specimens are known (Smith, 1931). For the species confirmed to occur in Myanmar, we have some general information where they occurred (Iverson, 1992), but this information generally dates from the last century and is far from complete.

In the past, Myanmar's turtle populations formed an important economic resource that was deemed worthy of careful regulation of its exploitation and conservation. Maxwell (1911) meticulously documented the numbers of turtle eggs, from marine turtles and *Batagur* and *Kachuga* terrapins, collected in the Ayeyarwady delta towards the turn of the century and detailed how licences to collect turtle eggs from particular beaches were auctioned. One of the conditions required the lessee to rebury a certain number of turtle eggs as a conservation measure. Maxwell also provided the prices of eggs and the amount of revenue collected by the government from the issue of licences; these figures indicate a considerable commercial value of the turtle resources in this area. They also indicate a considerable drop in *Batagur* and *Kachuga* numbers, an observation that was not lost on Maxwell who recommended improved conservation measures for these two species. Elsewhere, tortoises, freshwater turtles, and their eggs formed a supplemental source of protein for rural people.

The current conservation status of nearly all Myanmar turtle species is unknown. The limited data on population trends hardly inspire confidence: Maxwell (1911) calculated a total of 2,600 turtles (*Batagur baska* and *Kachuga trivittata* combined) nesting communally in the Ayeyarwady delta in 1890; by 1899 this was down to 820, a few were reported in 1982 by the UNDP survey of the area, and in recent years no terrapins were seen (Figure 2).

The number of sea turtles nesting in the Ayeyarwady delta region has also declined severely. At present, sea turtles are known to nest on only two islands located several kilometres off the mainland, Thamihla Kyun and Kadonlay Kyun (U Uga, pers comm., 1993); turtles no longer nest on any of the traditional nesting mainland beaches described by Maxwell (1911). Only green turtles, *Chelonia mydas*, nest on Thamihla Kyun, while the great majority of turtles nesting on Kadonlay Kyun appear to be olive ridleys, *Lepidochelys olivacea*. Traditionally uninhabited except for a few egg collectors during the nesting season, Kadonlay Kyun was permanently settled in 1987 when a village with about 700 inhabitants, primarily a fishing community, was established. During the 1991–1992 nesting season the total number of eggs laid on Kadonlay Kyun was only 36,240 in 594 nests (U Uga, pers. comm., 1993, 1994), about 3% of the number of eggs laid in this region at the turn of the century (Maxwell, 1911). On Thamihla Kyun (also known as Diamond Island), the number of turtle eggs collected in 1981–1982 (the last season for which data are available) was about 188,000 (FAO/UNDP, 1985), down from 1,700,000 in 1899 (Maxwell, 1911). The number of humans presently living on Thamihla Kyun is not available. At various times turtle eggs were collected by village cooperative associations, the private sector, the local Village Law and Order Restoration Councils, and currently by army soldiers stationed on the islands. Only a token number of eggs are reburied as a conservation measure. In addition, many adult turtles perish as incidental catch in fishing nets and on baited hooks (FAO/UNDP, 1985).

With assistance from the American Museum of Natural History-IUCN Turtle Recovery Program and on invitation from the Myanmar Ministry of Forests, I visited Myanmar in 1993 and again in 1994 to collect status information on the *Kachuga* and *Batagur* terrapins and other turtles. My first visit took me to Yangon and the Mandalay region (van Dijk, 1993), while my second visit was limited to Yangon and Shwe Settaw Wildlife Sanctuary. While obviously limited, they provided some recent data on the occurrence and abundance of turtles in these places.

In and around Yangon, I could fully confirm Frazier's (1987) observations of substantial numbers of *Morenia ocel-*

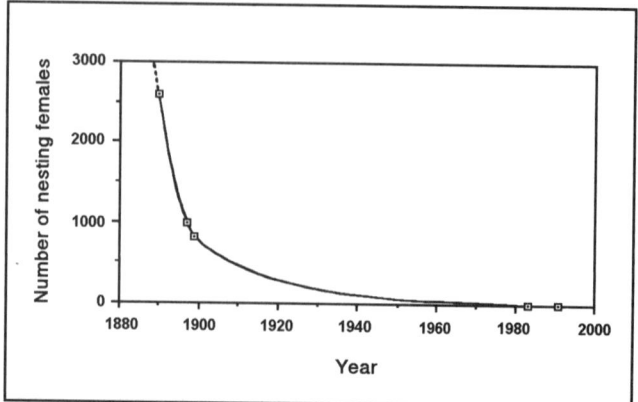

Figure 2. Number of *Batagur* and *Kachuga* females (combined) nesting in the Thaungkadun group of the Ayeyarwady delta, based on calculations from egg numbers reported by Maxwell (1911) with additional data from FAO/UNDP (1985) and the Myanmar Forest Department. Line drawn by computer interpolation.

lata and *Lissemys scutata* kept in temple ponds, with a few *Nilssonia formosa* softshells. In addition, the Yangon Zoo kept a few *Heosemys grandis*, *Platysternon megacephalum*, *Cyclemys dentata*, *Indotestudo elongata*, and *Manouria emys*. Of serious concern was the presence along with these native species of a few exotic red-eared sliders, *Trachemys scripta elegans*, indicating that this species is available in the country and could eventually establish populations in the wild.

In the zoo and temple ponds of Mandalay, no *Morenia* were evident, but several specimens of *Melanochelys trijuga edeniana*, some of enormous size, were basking in the midday sun. *Lissemys scutata*, *Nilssonia formosa* (Figure 3), and a single *Indotestudo elongata* were the other species seen.

According to local fishermen, only one or two small types of turtles, *Lissemys* and an unidentified type said to resemble a coconut, inhabit the middle Ayeyarwady in the Mandalay region. The river here is busy with regional boat traffic, while many of the extensive riverine sandbanks further upstream (Figure 4) are mined for Mandalay's booming construction industry. U Chin Khoke, head of the Fisheries Department for Upper Myanmar, told me that he observes very few turtles nowadays, in contrast to 20 years ago when turtles were often seen in the river.

Of great interest was a visit to Kywenah-pha Village on the Doke-tha-wady River, a clear-water river flowing from the Shan hills and joining the Ayeyarwady just below Mandalay. The inhabitants of Kywe-nah-pha and about a dozen similar villages further upstream depend considerably on fishing and hunting turtles in the river, as well as growing vegetable crops on the seasonally flooded riverbanks and adjacent plains (Figure 5).

The village headman claimed that the approximately 1,000 inhabitants of his village caught between 100 and 200 turtles per month, and while the village elders believe that tortoises were probably not as abundant as they were ten years ago, aquatic turtles were still easy to find and their numbers were believed to remain constant. In apparent contradiction to these statements, no live turtles were found in the village, and only after considerable searching were a small number of softshell carapaces and plastron fragments located; most of these were quite old.

The turtle fauna in and around the lower Doke-tha-wady River appears to be rich and deserves further investigation. The shell fragments that I examined came from *Lissemys scutata* and a much larger trionychine softshell, quite possibly *Chitra*. Various local sources indicate that *Melanochelys trijuga* and another hardshell inhabit the river's floodplains. Villagers said that they collect large, oval, flexible-shelled eggs from certain sandbanks in March, which points to the occurrence of a large *Kachuga* species. Further afield, tortoises are supposed to occur in the hills; based on recognition of photos, these are mainly *Indotestudo elongata*, but also a small number of *Geochelone platynota*. Nearby Mya Leik Thaung (whose name translates as "Emerald Turtle Mountain") forms a virtual tortoise sanctuary, because strong beliefs prevail that the mountain spirits will lead one astray on the steep slopes if one collects or harms a turtle there.

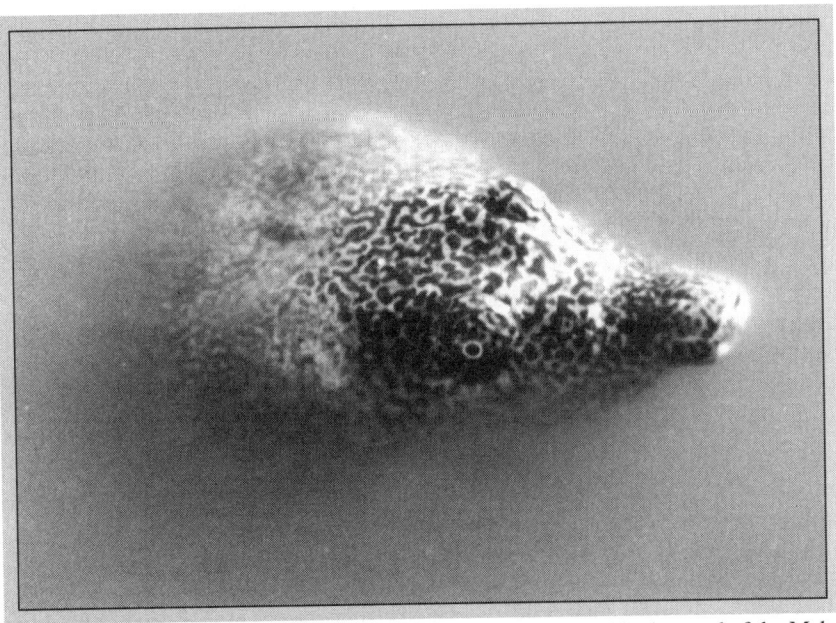

Figure 3. Head of adult *Nilssonia formosa* softshell, photographed in the pond of the Maha Myat Muni temple in Mandalay.

Shwe Settaw Wildlife Sanctuary was established in 1940 for the protection of Eld's deer. The sanctuary is located on the western edge of the central Myanmar dry vegetation zone and covers an area of 553 km² of deciduous forest. Most of this forest is considerably degraded by forest fires, agriculture, collection of wood and bamboo, cattle grazing, and other human activities. Despite virtually unregulated collection of forest produce, a few tortoises still occur as evidenced by shells of butchered specimens shown by villagers. Most of these were small *Indotestudo elongata*, but a single *Geochelone platynota* was collected in June 1990. There is a belief among Burmese people that tortoise flesh causes skin diseases; as a result it is not popular in this region, and tortoises are eaten only if no other food is available. If the incidence of forest fires could be checked, Shwe Settaw Wildlife Sanctuary would be a promising site for conservation of *G. platynota* and other tortoises. A program could be set up to buy tortoises from villagers for release

Figure 4. Ayeyarwady River between Mandalay and Sagaing, central Myanmar. Low water conditions, 26 January 1993.

into safe, relatively undisturbed sections of the sanctuary, where their progress could be followed by telemetry or other techniques. This extremely attractive species, endemic to the Central Myanmar dry zone, can be easily proposed as a flagship species for a more comprehensive habitat conservation and nature awareness program. At the same time, measures to prevent trade in this species should be strictly implemented.

The Man and Mon rivers border Shwe Settaw Wildlife Sanctuary at its southern and northern boundaries, respectively. These are rivers of small to medium size, with clear water and sandy to gravelly beds. Shells of three turtles collected in these rivers were identified as a juvenile *Melanochelys trijuga* and a half-grown *Chitra* or *Pelochelys* softshell. In addition, *Lissemys* is said to occur. All these tortoise and freshwater turtle species were perceived to be rare and possibly declining.

The legal protection status of turtles is obscure. The Forest Department is responsible for the management and protection of forests and wildlife, while the Fisheries Department has jurisdiction over all freshwater and many marine biological resources, and the Department of Marine Affairs is responsible for, among others, sea turtle nesting beaches. The only turtle conservation undertakings in recent decades have been some joint efforts to regulate collection of turtle eggs in the Ayeyarwady delta. The 1992 Forest Law prohibits commercial trade in wildlife, wildlife products, and logs, but every citizen of Myanmar retains the right to collect forest products for his or her own needs, and this right extends even inside wildlife sanctuaries. Officially, 15 wildlife sanctuaries and three national parks have been declared, together covering 7,147 km² or 1.07% of the total land area, and a number of additional protected areas have been proposed (Forest Department of Myanmar, 1990). However, until recently only some of these areas, totalling about 2,000 km², have been under effective control by the Forest Department, the others being located in or close to areas that were controlled by various insurgent groups. In these areas, logging, hunting, smuggling, gem mining, and other activities used to occur unchecked. Even the sanctuaries under active management by the Forest Department suffer from various pressures: cattle grazing and the collection of forest products, such as bamboo, fruits, firewood, and apparently also turtles are permitted, and agricultural encroachment is a problem. Forest fires, often deliberately set to encourage grass growth for subsequent cattle grazing, occur frequently. Logging operations in designated production forests are said to be selective and sustainable, but still have serious consequences for the ecosystem. Infrared satellite mapping indicates that Myanmar's deforestation problems are comparable to those of Thailand and India. Another threat comes from ambitious schemes to harness the great

Figure 5. Floodplain pond along the Doke-tha-wady, 25 January. In a few weeks this pond will be dried out. Such ponds are inhabited by *Lissemys scutata* and *Melanochelys trijuga*. Note the sparse vegetation on the hills in the background.

rivers for irrigation projects, power generation, or diversion of water for sale to neighbouring countries. Because of the severe lack of trained personnel and other resources, practical conservation work has progressed very slowly but is presently being given greater emphasis.

A realistic long-term conservation goal should be to preserve several viable populations of each species occurring in the country. This will be a great challenge with considerable biological and sociopolitical complications. Making all existing information about Myanmar's turtles available to conservation and other field workers is essential; this should include natural history, distribution, abundance, and exploitation data. Guidelines for identification of the various species can be issued to assist in local surveys and to clear up the confusion about species identity. Survey forms could be designed for district forest and fisheries officers to report back which species occur in their region and how abundant the various species are. From this, a comprehensive database of turtle species occurrence and abundance can be established. Subsequently, the severity of exploitation for food and traditional medicine should be assessed for each of the various species in every region and nationwide. This information can then be used to set priorities to conserve particular species or habitats that are recognised to be declining. Upgraded legal protection should be considered; this can take the shape of a complete ban on exploitation of certain species, declaring effective closed seasons for egg collection and restrictions on fishing activities near nesting areas.

But even the limited, often historical data we possess now clearly indicate priorities for turtle conservation. Top priority should be given to the species that are known to be declining, such as the endemic Burmese star tortoise (*Geochelone platynota*) and the Burmese river turtle (*Kachuga trivittata*). More widely distributed species that are particularly susceptible to exploitation and whose populations take a long period to recover form another priority group: *Batagur baska*, *Indotestudo elongata*, *Manouria impressa*, *M. emys*, and large softshells are all in this category. Other priority species are those that we know to suffer from intensive exploitation, such as the sea turtles and smaller softshells. The continuing survival and conservation requirements of species known from only a few specimens from a single location, such as *Heosemys depressa* and the undescribed *Mauremys* species, should be established urgently.

While a complete, nationwide turtle conservation program is still far away, small, specific conservation projects can have a great impact now. The potential to protect *Geochelone platynota* at Shwe Settaw Wildlife Sanctuary was noted previously. Nesting sites of *Batagur*, *Kachuga*, and the sea turtles at a small number of sites along the major

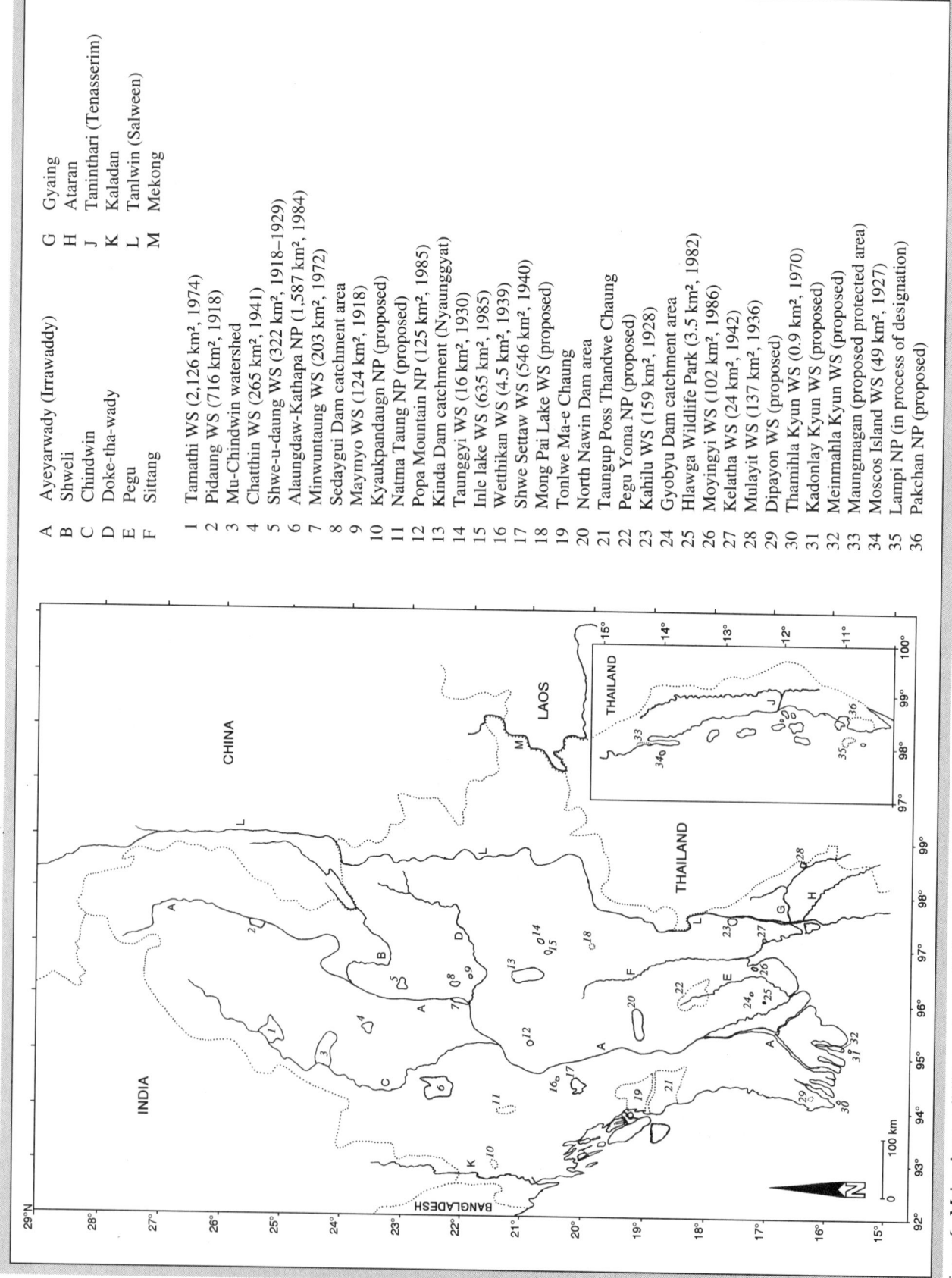

Figure 6. Major rivers, wildlife sanctuaries (WS) and national parks (NP) with area and year of designation, and other areas of conservation interest in Myanmar. Sources: Forest Department, Myanmar Ministry of Agriculture and Forests, Myanmar (1990); Scott (1989); and Nelles Maps.

A Ayeyarwady (Irrawaddy)
B Shweli
C Chindwin
D Doke-tha-wady
E Pegu
F Sittang
G Gyaing
H Ataran
J Taninthari (Tenasserim)
K Kaladan
L Tanlwin (Salween)
M Mekong

1 Tamathi WS (2,126 km², 1974)
2 Pidaung WS (716 km², 1918)
3 Mu-Chindwin watershed
4 Chatthin WS (265 km², 1941)
5 Shwe-u-daung WS (322 km², 1918–1929)
6 Alaungdaw-Kathapa NP (1,587 km², 1984)
7 Minwuntaung WS (203 km², 1972)
8 Sedaygui Dam catchment area
9 Maymyo WS (124 km², 1918)
10 Kyaukpandaugn NP (proposed)
11 Natma Taung NP (proposed)
12 Popa Mountain NP (125 km², 1985)
13 Kinda Dam catchment (Nyaunggyat)
14 Taunggyi WS (16 km², 1930)
15 Inle lake WS (635 km², 1985)
16 Wetthikan WS (4.5 km², 1939)
17 Shwe Settaw WS (546 km², 1940)
18 Mong Pai Lake WS (proposed)
19 Tonlwe Ma-e Chaung
20 North Nawin Dam area
21 Taungup Poss Thandwe Chaung
22 Pegu Yoma NP (proposed)
23 Kahilu WS (159 km², 1928)
24 Gyobyu Dam catchment area
25 Hlawga Wildlife Park (3.5 km², 1982)
26 Moyingyi WS (102 km², 1986)
27 Kelatha WS (24 km², 1942)
28 Mulayit WS (137 km², 1936)
29 Dipayon WS (proposed)
30 Thamihla Kyun WS (0.9 km², 1970)
31 Kadonlay Kyun WS (proposed)
32 Meinmahla Kyun WS (proposed)
33 Maungmagan (proposed protected area)
34 Moscos Island WS (49 km², 1927)
35 Lampi NP (in process of designation)
36 Pakchan NP (proposed)

rivers and on marine islands can be protected on a site-by-site basis. If managed well, several of these sites have potential for very carefully guided ecotourism, which can adequately compensate for the revenue lost when limiting egg collection. Any and all such projects should be set up in consultation and agreement with the local people so that the conservation action integrates with these peoples' needs, beliefs, and understanding.

However, for wildlife conservation to succeed completely, we have to look beyond turtles and aim to conserve the entire range of intact habitats. A number of forest and marine sanctuaries already exist in Myanmar, and the aim is to increase the area of protected lands from less than one to at least five percent of the country (Rabinowitz, 1995). It will be highly desirable to ensure that estuarine mangrove forests and large mid-level sections of major rivers, including their adjacent floodplains, are enclosed within the additional areas. Potential sites for a riverine sanctuary (which could be inspired by the National Chambal River Sanctuary in India) would be the middle Ayeyarwady along the monumental ancient capital of Pagan, along the lower Chindwin, or along the Shweli. Such sanctuaries should ideally be large enough that all the incoming and outflowing resources of their ecosystem are disturbed as little as possible. In this way, natural evolution—and not short-term human activities—will determine the fate not only of turtles but also of the birds, worms, orchids, and all other organisms inhabiting these areas.

ACKNOWLEDGEMENTS

Many people generously provided whatever information about Myanmar turtles they possessed, assisted in field work, or were helpful in other ways. I would like to take this opportunity to thank the staff of the Wildlife Conservation and Sanctuaries Division of the Forest Department of the Union of Myanmar, especially U Thein Lwin, U Aung Than, U Uga, U Aung Thin, U Shein Gay Ngai, and U Ye Htut; as well as U Myat Thinn, U Soe Kyi, U Tin Hla, and U Win Maw of the Myanmar Forest Department; U Chit Sein, U Than Aung, and U Pho Htung at Yatanabon Zoo, Mandalay; U Hla Win and U Chin Khoke of the Myanmar Fisheries Department; and especially U Tint Lwin Thaung. Mr. Corey Blanc, Dr. Jack Frazier, Dr. John B. Iverson, Dr. Gerald Kuchling, Dr. Edward O. Moll, and Mr. Jonathan Murray provided additional information. The Turtle Recovery Programme, a joint initiative of the American Museum of Natural History and the World Conservation Union/IUCN Tortoise and Freshwater Turtle Specialist Group, funded the field work and presentation of this project, while additional support came from University College Galway, Ireland, and Chulalongkorn University, Bangkok.

LITERATURE CITED

Annandale, N. 1912. The Indian mud-turtles (Trionychidae). Records of the Indian Museum, Vol. 7 (16): 151–180, Pls. 5–6.

Das, I. 1991. Colour Guide to the Turtles and Tortoises of the Indian Subcontinent. R & A Publishing Ltd., Avon, England. 133 pp.

van Dijk, P. P. 1993. Myanmar Turtles—report of a preliminary survey of the Testudines of the Ayeyarwady basin. Unpubl. report to The Turtle Recovery Program, AMNH, New York. 34 pp.

FAO/UNDP. 1985. Burma. Survey data and conservation priorities. Nature Conservation and National Parks Project FO:DP/BUR/80/006. Technical Report No. 1. United Nations Development Programme and Food and Agriculture Organization of the United Nations, Rome. 82 pp.

Forest Department, Ministry of Agriculture and Forests, Union of Myanmar. 1990. Wildlife conservation in Myanmar. Forest Department, Ministry of Agriculture and Forests, Yangon. 29 pp.

Frazier, J. G. 1987. [A biologist's visit to Rangoon]. United States Information Service, Rangoon. (Translation, orig. in Burmese.)

Iverson, J. B. 1992. A Revised Checklist with Distribution Maps of the Turtles of the World. Privately printed, Richmond, Indiana. 363 pp.

IUCN/SSC Tortoise and Freshwater Turtle Specialist Group. 1989. Tortoises and freshwater turtles: An action plan for their conservation (D. Stubbs, comp.). IUCN/SSC Tortoise and Freshwater Turtle Specialist Group, Gland, Switzerland. 47 pp.

Maxwell, F. D. 1911. Report on the turtle-banks of the Irrawaddy Division. In Reports on Inland and Sea Fisheries in the Thongwa, Myaungmya, and Bassein districts and the Turtle Banks of the Irrawaddy Division, pp. 1–57. Government Printing Office, Rangoon.

Moll, E. O. 1980. Natural History of the river terrapin *Batagur baska* (Gray) in Malaysia. (Testudines: Emydidae). Malaysian Journal of Science 6(A):23–62.

Moll, E. O. 1989. Tortoises of tropical Asia: Regional introduction; *Geochelone platynota*, Burmese star tortoise; *Indotestudo elongata*, elongated tortoise; *Manouria emys*, Asian brown tortoise; *Manouria impressa*, impressed tortoise. In I. R. Swingland and M. W. Klemens (eds.), The Conservation Biology of Tortoises, pp. 111–122. Occasional Papers of the IUCN Species Survival Commission (SSC) No. 5. IUCN, Gland, Switzerland.

Nelles Maps. Undated. Burma, 1:1,500,000. Nelles Verlag, München.

Rabinowitz, A. 1995. Myanmar's first marine park. Wildlife Conservation 98(6):8.

Scott, D. A. 1989. Myanmar. In A Directory of Asian Wetlands, pp. 635–666. IUCN, Gland, Switzerland.

Smith, M. A. 1931. The Fauna of British India, including Ceylon and Burma—Reptilia and Amphibia. Vol. 1.—Loricata, Testudines. Taylor & Francis Ltd. for the India Office, London. xxviii + 185 pp.

Theobald, W. 1874. Observations on some Indian and Burmese species of *Trionyx*. Proceedings of the Asiatic Society of Bengal, 1875:75–86, pls. 3–4.

The Turtles of Western Thailand—Pushed to the Edge by Progress

KUMTHORN THIRAKHUPT[1] AND PETER PAUL VAN DIJK[1,2]

[1]*Department of Biology, Faculty of Science, Chulalongkorn University,
Phya Thai Road, Bangkok 10330, Thailand [e-mail: kumthorn@mail.sc.chula.ac.th]*
[2]*Department of Zoology, University College Galway, Galway, Ireland [e-mail: Peter.vanDijk@UCG.IE]*

ABSTRACT: Turtles and other wildlife in Southeast Asia are under serious pressure from exploitation and habitat alteration. Our survey of turtles of western Thailand indicated that populations of several species, particularly the tortoises *Indotestudo elongata*, *Manouria emys*, and *M. impressa*, have been severely depleted in the last few decades. The construction of multipurpose reservoirs in the upper reaches of the Mae Klong River basin, their effects on downstream habitats, and other developments in and along the river have been detrimental to turtles that live in the river and nearby areas. Some turtle species not native to the river basin have been released into the reservoirs in efforts to increase their bioproductivity. Large areas of forest in western Thailand have been designated as sanctuaries for wildlife, and a great diversity of turtle species occurs there in relative safety. Forest fires and other factors still constitute a threat to the integrity of the ecosystem of these sanctuaries, and fire prevention is therefore the main priority for sanctuary management. A number of turtle species that do not or scarcely occur in protected areas, although legally protected from exploitation, are in a critical situation and need urgent conservation action. *Pelochelys cantorii* recently disappeared from the Mae Klong basin, and a local endemic species of *Chitra*, *C. chitra*, is highly endangered.

Natural habitats in tropical Asia are arguably under greater pressure than those anywhere else in the world. A combination of processes—from the growth of human population to the development of resources and industry to insurgencies and wars—has resulted in widespread alteration and destruction of natural habitats. In Thailand, which had one of the world's fastest rates of deforestation, the country's forest cover has been reduced from 53% of the land area in 1961 to about 28% in 1988 (ERD-TISTR, 1991). A logging ban was declared in 1989, and according to the Royal Forest Department, forest cover is currently 27%. To its credit, Thailand has designated many forested areas as National Parks, which are open to the public, and Wildlife Sanctuaries, which are primarily for the protection of wildlife and are not freely accessible to the general public. Together, these areas of moderate-to-good natural forest constituted 9.4% of the country in 1986 (Faculty of Forestry, Kasetsart University, 1987), and more has since been added with the total now standing at 11–12%. Almost all forests outside the protected areas are either severely degraded natural forest or commercial plantations of teak, rubber, and eucalyptus. Wildlife conservation laws were upgraded to prohibit all capture, possession, trade, and other forms of exploitation of most wildlife, including all turtle species with the single exception of the softshell *Amyda cartilaginea*.

Human activities threaten the survival of Southeast Asia's tortoises and freshwater turtles in several ways. Direct collection for food and the animal trade is still a major factor in the decline of many populations and species. The other main threat is habitat alteration, resulting from a variety of processes: agricultural expansion; pollution from domestic, agricultural, or industrial sources; logging; forest fires; mining and sand collection; human-induced erosion; and such infrastructure projects as roads, hydroelectric and irrigation reservoirs, and housing or recreational developments. Some species are able to adapt to living in human-altered habitats, and *A. cartilaginea* even appears to tolerate a moderate level of exploitation, but other species have been pushed back into the remnants of the once great forests mainly in the northern, western, and extreme southeastern border areas and in peninsular Thailand.

The primary geographical features of western Thailand are the Dawna chain of forest-clad mountains and hills that run essentially north to southeast, and the rivers and tributaries of the Mae Klong River system that flow in the valleys. This relatively small drainage basin (Figure 1) consists of the Khwae Yai (meaning "Large River" in western Thai dialect) and the more westerly Khwae Noi ("Small River"). These two rivers join at Kanchanaburi City to form the Mae Nam Mae Klong ("Mae Klong River" in central Thai language). Originally a swift-flowing river system with sandy beds and clear water, the character of the Mae Klong and its upper sections has been completely altered by the construction of Srinagarind and Khao Laem reservoirs. In the last few decades the lands of the region have also seen enormous changes with the disappearance of the great forests.

The composition and richness of the region's original flora and fauna are exceptional, a result of its location where the Indian, Malayan, and Eastern Palearctic biogeographical zones meet. The fish fauna of the Mae Klong system is

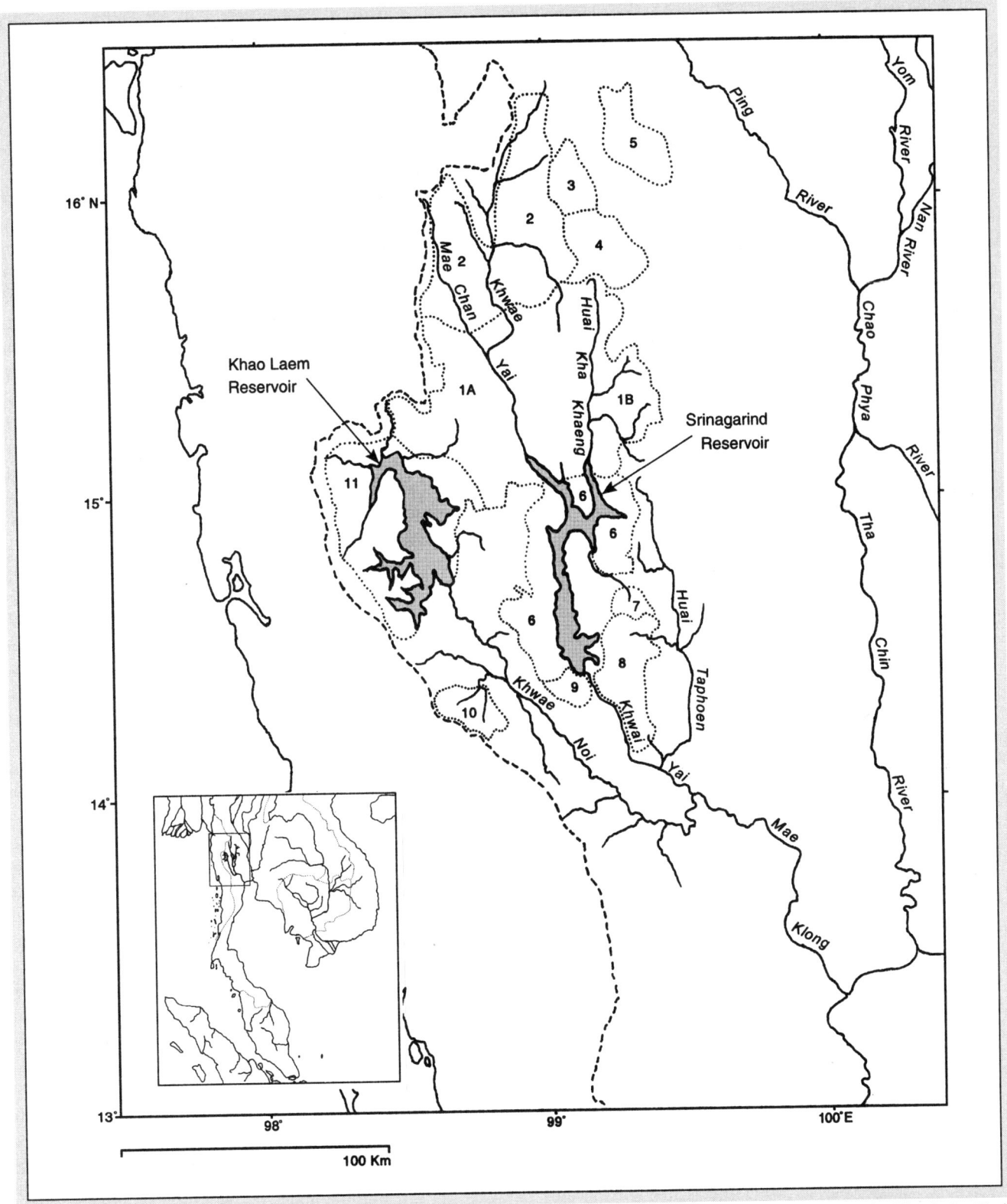

Figure 1. Locations of the rivers, reservoirs, wildlife sanctuaries (WS), and national parks (NP) in the study region. Dashed line is the Thai-Myanmar border; dotted lines indicate boundaries of protected areas. Legend to parks and sanctuaries: 1A = Thung Yai Naresuan WS; 1B = Huai Kha Khaeng WS; 2 = Umphang WS; 3 = Klong Larn NP; 4 = Mae Wong NP; 5 = Khao Sanam Prieng WS; 6 = Srinagarind NP; 7 = Chalerm Rattanakosin NP; 8 = Salak Pra WS; 9 = Erewan NP; 10 = Sai Yoke NP; 11 = Khao Laem NP. Inset is map of Southeast Asia showing general location of study region.

unique among Indo-Chinese rivers in showing a substantial affinity to the ichthyofauna of India and Burma (Kottelat, 1989).

The turtle fauna of the Mae Klong basin may be one of the most diverse assemblages in the world: Three tortoise species (*Indotestudo elongata*, *Manouria emys*, and *Manouria impressa*), six freshwater hardshells (*Cuora amboinensis*, *Cyclemys dentata*, *Heosemys grandis*, *Hieremys annandalii*, *Malayemys subtrijuga*, and *Siebenrockiella crassicollis*), the bigheaded turtle (*Platysternon megacephalum*), and four softshell species (*Amyda cartilaginea*, *Chitra chitra*, *Dogania subplana*, and *Pelochelys cantorii* [previously known as *P. bibroni*: see Webb, 1995]) are all confirmed to occur, while *Melanochelys trijuga* and *Lissemys scutata* could also inhabit this area (Nutaphand, 1979; Iverson, 1992; Thirakhupt and van Dijk, 1994). Several of these turtle species are of considerable conservation concern (IUCN, 1982; IUCN Tortoise and Freshwater Turtle Specialist Group, 1989).

During the past several years, we have studied the occurrence, abundance, and exploitation of turtles in the Mae Klong River basin. For this, we interviewed numerous people in dozens of towns, villages, roadside food shops, ferry crossings, and bus stops, including more than half of all settlements in the upper Mae Klong basin as well as a representative sample from the densely populated lower plains and estuaries. In addition, we carried out extensive field surveys and observations at 11 ranger stations in several of the wildlife sanctuaries and made observations in other parts of Thailand.

The findings of our survey were discouraging. We concluded that subsistence collection has severely depleted populations of most turtle species in all unprotected areas, an opinion shared by most local hunters. At present they consider it not worth their while to go out, even with their dogs, to try to find turtles, when all they will get is one tortoise after several days' searching. Capture of tortoises and other hard-shelled turtles now occurs only incidentally when tortoises wander into fields, across roads, or are found while people collect mushrooms, fruits, bamboo, or other forest products. Softshells are caught with traps and baited hooks set in the rivers or are speared when discovered in shallow water. In the course of this survey we collected shells and other remains of turtles that had been found and consumed by villagers living outside the protected areas. All together we collected remains of 67 turtles.* Rural folk usually keep these shells for possible later sale to wholesalers, who collect the plastra of tortoises for the manufacture of traditional medicine. Examination of such shells has provided a wealth of data about species occurrence, relative abundance, intensity of exploitation, average size at the time of capture, and sometimes even sex ratio and age structure of the exploited populations.

The population data thus collected in western Thailand give cause for grave concern, especially for all three tortoise species. Shells of *Indotestudo elongata* were collected in greater numbers than any other species. However, these considerable numbers do not indicate large populations still inhabiting the formerly extensive deciduous forests, but appear to be the last generation of tortoises inhabiting the area at the time that these forests were invaded and degraded by human settlement. The size of these tortoise shells is generally moderate to large, but really large specimens, as still found deep inside sanctuaries, are absent. Juveniles are lacking too, indicating a population that has not recruited significantly for a decade or more. The Asian giant tortoise, *Manouria emys*, seems restricted to a few areas of evergreen forest (which is itself now limited to protected areas) and even there it is rare. Populations of the impressed tortoise, *Manouria impressa*, appear to be strongly localised, occurring only in the cloudy evergreen forest of a few particular mountain slopes. Like its congener, *M. impressa* appears to be rare wherever it occurs.

Less information is available concerning the general abundance of freshwater turtle species. Specimens of the softshell *Amyda cartilaginea* were frequently seen for sale in the rural markets, and several carapaces were given to us. This species is much appreciated for consumption and is intensively hunted; populations appear to be in decline as hunters have to go ever farther afield to catch sufficient numbers. *Malayemys subtrijuga* was another species frequently offered in the markets, but this species is sold mainly for subsequent release for religious purposes rather than consumption. In recent years commercial trade in this species has almost disappeared. Specimens of *Heosemys grandis*, *Cyclemys dentata*, *Cuora amboinensis*, and an occasional *Dogania subplana* are captured and consumed or sold into the pet trade. The large *Chitra* and *Pelochelys* softshells are greatly sought and hunted whenever possible and their populations are now severely depleted. The bigheaded turtle, *Platysternon megacephalum*, seems to reach its most southerly distribution in a few localised areas of evergreen forest on high, often steep slopes where individuals are observed only rarely.

A look at any recent map of the habitats and vegetation of southeast Asia would indicate that the great area of relatively little-disturbed protected forest in western Thailand—with the combined Huai Kha Khaeng-Thung Yai Naresuan Wildlife sanctuaries at its core—could be of great importance to the survival of several southeast Asian turtle species. The results of our survey work confirmed this view beyond expectation. Huai Kha Khaeng-Thung Yai Naesuan together cover an area of 6,222 km² in the upper reaches of the Mae Klong River basin, encompassing nearly the com-

---

*Deposited mainly at the Reptile Collection, Museum of Natural History of Chulalongkorn University, Bangkok.

plete drainage basin above Srinagarind and Khao Laem reservoirs. Adjoining parks and sanctuaries cover an additional 6,534 km², making this one of the largest protected forest masses in Asia. Climatically, the area has a rainy season from May to October, a dry season from November to February, and a hot season with occasional showers from March to May. The topography ranges from forested mountain peaks to low rolling hills, with streams and rivers in all valleys during the wet season, most drying out as the dry and hot seasons progress. It is a region blanketed by a mosaic of different forest types: seasonal evergreen forests, mixed deciduous forests, and dipterocarp-dominated deciduous forests, with occasional areas of karst limestone vegetation, grass savannah, bamboo forest, and a few wetlands (Nakhasathien and Stewart-Cox, 1990). UNESCO declared the area a World Heritage Site in 1992.

At least eight turtle species are confirmed among the rich fauna of the sanctuary, and several more are presumed to occur (Thirakhupt and van Dijk, 1994). Yet during the many weeks of field surveys in western Thailand's protected areas we encountered only 18 live turtles of five species and examined photos and videotapes of several more. The only species we found to be moderately abundant are *Cyclemys dentata* and *Amyda cartilaginea*. Both occur in low densities, approximately one animal or less per kilometre of stream, but because the network of streams is very extensive, these species' overall populations are considerable. Moreover, we encountered several juveniles and young adults of these two species, indicating effective recruitment to the population. Yellow tortoises, *Indotestudo elongata*, (Figure 2) are not abundant in protected areas either, but a diverse population structure including some very large, old animals as well as juveniles exists, and this population seems relatively secure. The size of the protected populations of *Heosemys grandis*, *Dogania subplana*, *Manouria emys*, *M. impressa*, and *Cuora amboinensis* remains unknown, and the outlook for their continued survival in western Thailand is indeterminate.

Knowing that these species inhabit a protected area is no reason for complacency, however. Illegal incidental tree-cutting and encroachment of agricultural fields into the outer park regions continues to nibble away at the area of suitable wildlife habitat despite the Forest Department's conservation mandate and recent establishment of a 5 km buffer zone. Occasional capture of turtles still occurs. And even deep inside the sanctuary, far from human habitation, turtles are threatened by the effects of forest fires.

Forest fires in Thailand rarely have a natural cause. Most are intentionally started by humans to clear rice stubble in the dry fields adjoining the sanctuary or to get rid of refuse, or they may be accidentally started by collectors, poachers, tourists' campfires, or improperly extinguished cigarette butts. The fires subsequently get out of control and sweep into forested areas. The natural incidence of forest fires in

Figure 2. Adult female elongated tortoise or yellow tortoise, *Indotestudo elongata*, Thailand's most abundant tortoise species but in decline over most of its range. Animal was photographed in the safety of Huai Kha Khaeng Wildlife Sanctuary. (Photo by Peter Paul van Dijk.)

this seasonally dry region is about once in 20 years (Kanjanavanit, 1992), but in recent years most of the area has been burnt every year. For turtles the effects of forest fires include both direct mortality and increased detection by predators after all cover is burnt away. Fires also affect the availability of food by the short-term removal of all edible material and by the long-term effects on the forest. Trees in deciduous dipterocarp forests all belong to a small number of fire-resistant species, but the moister areas along streams are lined with evergreen species, and it is here that the effects of fire are at their worst. The evergreen forest consists of a great diversity of tall trees, including most of the valuable food providers like figs and other fruiting trees, and their dense foliage creates cool, humid valleys. The fig trees, which fruit at unpredictable times throughout the year, are an exceptionally important food source (Terborgh, 1986). Evergreen forests are less conducive to fires, but litter burns can sweep in from adjacent deciduous forest. While a single forest litter fire does not kill mature evergreen trees, regular annual fires damage the lower bark beyond recovery and eventually kill these important trees (J. Grogan, pers. comm., 1992, 1993). Saplings of evergreen trees are killed before they are large enough to survive occasional fires. Fire thus promotes the replacement of fire-sensitive evergreen trees with fire-resistant tree species (Stott, 1986), and within decades results in a dry deciduous dipterocarp forest, a severely impoverished forest type (Nakhasathien and Stewart-Cox, 1990). This further fragments the populations of those turtle species that are restricted to the humidity of evergreen forest and may be a major threat to *Manouria impressa* and *M. emys*. Yet occasional forest fires are not entirely without merit as they clear dried undergrowth and make nutrients available and so encourage the growth of new grass and herbs, with obvious benefits for grazing herbivores such as banteng, gaur, wild buffalo, and deer.

Management of parks and sanctuaries in Thailand is geared mainly towards protection of large mammals; turtles were never a priority group. Indeed, so little is known of their biology that specific conservation and management measures could not be effectively implemented even if one wanted to. In many cases, conservation and management decisions are based on only a fraction of the requisite scientific data, but urgency dictates that measures be taken now (Soulé, 1986). It is logical to suppose that the long-term survival of the various turtle species will depend upon the survival of viable populations inhabiting large areas of undisturbed habitat. For this to occur, an ecosystem-wide conservation strategy is required to balance the known requirements of particular groups of organisms with those demands we do not know. While the subject of forest fire management remains controversial, the control of fires and their elimination from lowland riparian areas should be the main management priority (see Rabinowitz, 1990).

The large-scale hydrological projects on the Khwae Yai and Khwae Noi have greatly affected the turtles originally inhabiting the rivers and surrounding areas. The creation of large, deep reservoirs forces tortoises out of their riverside forests and often concentrates them on islands where they are easily collected. Moreover, in contrast to the general belief that more water means more space for aquatic turtles, the habitat conditions in these reservoirs are such that turtles do not thrive. Indeed, our observations and interviews indicate that animals flee the reservoirs' cold water, low oxygen level, and lack of vegetation and associated invertebrate prey, moving into the tributary streams.

Large numbers of softshells and other turtles are regularly released by the authorities charged with the task to improve the reservoirs' bioproductivity. Turtles to be released are selected based on availability rather than their suitability for the habitat, and it is known that *Amyda cartilaginea*, *Batagur baska*, and *Callagur borneoensis* from a conservation-breeding project in peninsular Thailand have been introduced to the reservoirs in western Thailand and elsewhere. In other cases, private individuals have released surplus turtles from ponds in Bangkok into reservoirs, with no regard for species. The majority of turtles inhabiting Bangkok's ponds are red-eared sliders, *Trachemys scripta elegans*, an alien species whose imported hatchlings are widely sold as pets. The future release of turtles into reservoirs and other places should be carefully studied and monitored. The immediate need is to determine which if any turtle species adapt well to the highly unusual habitat conditions presented by a large reservoir; only such species should be released. Ideally, parental turtle stock should be collected from the same river basin where the captive-bred offspring will be released. The introduction and establishment of foreign exotic species, specifically the Chinese softshell, *Pelodiscus sinensis*, which is widely cultured for domestic and foreign consumption, and the red-eared slider, *Trachemys scripta elegans*, should be prevented at all cost.

The lower river sections have also been profoundly changed. The reservoirs cause a considerable drop in oxygen level and degrade other qualities of the discharged water. These effects continue to be felt more than 100 km further downstream (Tongkaseme and Torranin, 1990). Human settlement and agricultural expansion have resulted in increased pollution and erosion along the riverbanks. At the same time direct hunting increased as both the construction of the reservoirs and the demise of the communist insurgency opened the area for large-scale development. Regulation of the seasonal water flow cycle has brought many benefits for humans—among these, large irrigation projects and the prevention of flooding in the lowland regions—but this also means that rich seasonal feeding areas are no longer available to the riverine turtles. The extensive sandbanks that were exposed every dry season for turtles to nest no longer exist. Some were permanently flooded by the reservoirs; those downstream from the dams are flooded by the daily water release, even during the dry season. Moreover, the banks have been reduced because sand dredging for the construction industry rapidly removed the existing deposits, and most sand that is generated in the hills now settles out in the reservoirs.

Unfortunately, the altered and unprotected sections of the large rivers are the only known habitat of the population of giant *Chitra* softshells. Long assumed to be an outlying population of the Indian *Chitra indica*, it was recently described and validated as a distinct species, *Chitra chitra* (Nutphand, 1990). Its currently confirmed distribution is restricted to the larger stretches of the Mae Klong River system, generally below the reservoirs. Survival of this species may require a comprehensive program that will involve habitat protection, enforcement of the legal protection, possible relocation of some animals to river sections in protected areas, and/or captive breeding.

A species that has already lost the battle for survival in the Mae Klong basin is *Pelochelys cantorii*. In the past this species occurred throughout the large sections of the Mae Klong basin and was relatively abundant in the estuarine region, where it even occurred on the mudflats beyond the mangrove forest. Older fishermen who captured them at sea remembered *Pelochelys* to be "not rare" 20 years ago, yet none have been captured or seen since the mid-1980s, by which time most of the Mae Klong's estuarine mangrove forests had been cleared to make way for shrimp ponds.

Conclusion

We are only beginning to understand the role of turtles in the overall ecosystem of the forests, streams, rivers, and estuaries of Thailand. We have some appreciation of their role in the dispersal of plant seeds, but we still do not know how important turtles are as predators of such species as freshwater crustaceans, snails, fish, insects, and other creatures; as scavengers; and as prey themselves for larger predators. While studies of their natural history can contribute greatly to our understanding of turtle biology, research efforts should be focused on conservation-related aspects to develop effective strategies to safeguard species' survival. In the meantime species recognised to be in decline should receive immediate protection from exploitation. Conservation of the spectacular giant softshells *Chitra* and *Pelochelys* is Thailand's prime herpetological conservation challenge, closely followed by the tortoises with their slow growth, late maturity, and low recruitment and equally high exploitation pressures.

Turtle conservation cannot be seen in isolation from the wider, natural and social contexts. The only hope for the survival of most turtle species outside protected areas lies in the availability of sustainable sources of high-quality nutrition for rural people as well as increased environmental consciousness. Within protected areas, limiting direct mortality may be less important in the long run than preserving the ecosystem's structural integrity. As a focal point for research and conservation efforts, for individual turtle species and the overall seasonal forest ecosystem, the Huai Kha Khaeng-Thung Yai Naresuan Wildlife Sanctuary is of paramount importance.

Literature Cited

Ecological Research Department, TISTR. 1991. Endangered Species and Habitats of Thailand. Thailand Institute of Scientific and Technological Research. 243 pp.

Faculty of Forestry, Kasetsart University. 1987. Assessment of national parks, wildlife sanctuaries and other preserves development in Thailand. Final Report, prepared by Faculty of Forestry, Kasetsart University, Royal Forest Department and Office of the National Environment Board. 138 pp.

IUCN. 1982. The IUCN Amphibia-Reptilia Red Data Book. Part 1. Testudinidae, Crocodylia, Rhynchocephalia (B. Groombridge, comp.). IUCN, Gland, Switzerland. xiii + 426 pp.

IUCN/SSC Tortoise and Freshwater Turtle Specialist Group. 1989. Tortoises and freshwater turtles: An action plan for their conservation (D. Stubbs, comp.). IUCN/SSC, Gland, Switzerland. i–iv + 47 pp.

Iverson, J. B. 1992. A Revised Checklist with Distribution Maps of the Turtles of the World. Privately printed, Richmond, Indiana. 363 pp.

Kanjanavanit, S. 1992. Aspects of the temporal pattern of dry season fires in the dry diptocarp forests of Thailand. Unpubl. Ph.D. thesis, Dept. of Geography, School of Oriental and African Studies, University of London. 268 pp.

Kottelat, M. 1989. Zoogeography of fishes from Indochinese inland waters, with an annotated check-list. Bulletin Zoölogisch Museum-Universiteit van Amsterdam 12(1):1–55.

Nakhasathien, S. and B. Stewart-Cox. 1990. Nomination of the Thung Yai - Huai Kha Khaeng Wildlife Sanctuary to be a U.N.E.S.C.O. World Heritage Site. Document submitted to UNESCO by the Wildlife Conservation Division, Royal Forest Department, Bangkok, Thailand. 128 pp.

Nutaphand, W. 1979. The Turtles of Thailand. Siamfarm Zoological Garden, Bangkok. 222 pp.

Nutphand, W. 1990. Softshell turtles. Thai Zool. Mag. 5:93–114. (In Thai.)

Rabinowitz, A. 1990. Fire, dry dipterocarp forest, and the carnivore community in Huai Kha Khaeng Wildlife Sanctuary, Thailand. Natural History Bulletin of the Siam Society 38(2):99–115.

Soulé, M. E. 1986. Conservation Biology and the "Real World." *In* M. E. Soulé, (ed.), Conservation Biology: The Science of Scarcity and Diversity, pp. 1–12. Sinauer Associates, Sunderland, Massachusetts.

Stott, P. 1986. The spatial pattern of dry season fires in the savanna forests of Thailand. J. Biogeogr. 13:345–358.

Terborgh, J. 1986. Keystone plant Resources in the Tropical Forest. *In* M. E. Soulé, (ed.), Conservation Biology: The Science of Scarcity and Diversity, pp. 330–344. Sinauer Associates, Sunderland, Massachusetts.

Thirakhupt, K. and P. P. van Dijk. 1995. Species diversity and conservation of the turtles of western Thailand. Natural History Bulletin of the Siam Society 42:209–259.

Tongkasame, C. and P. Torranin (eds.) 1990. Post Environmental Evaluation of Khao Laem Dam Project—Final report. Vol. I, Summary Report, 78 pp.; Vol. II, Main Report, 459 pp.; Vol. III, Environmental Development Plan, 142 pp.; Vol. IV, Technical Appendices, 1404 pp. Pal Consultants, Aggie Consultants, and Thailand Institute of Scientific and Technological Research.

Webb. R. G. 1995. Redescription and neotype designation of *Pelochelys bibroni* from southern New Guinea (Testudines: Trionychidae). Chelon. Conserv. Biol. 1(4):301–310.

Status, Biology, Conservation, and Management of Tortoises and Turtles in the Himalayan Foothills of Nepal

TEJ KUMAR SHRESTHA

Central Department of Zoology, Tribhuvan University, Kirtipur Campus, Kathmandu, Nepal
[e-mail: k-mani@npl.healthnet.org]

ABSTRACT: The tortoises and turtles of Nepal have intrinsic biological, educational, religious, and inspirational value. They are deeply rooted in the Hindu and Buddhist cultures and traditional medicine. They are unique and are worthy of long-term conservation and management.

Up to the end of the nineteenth century, chelonians were widely distributed throughout the wetlands of the Terai lowlands and the Himalayan foothills of Nepal. However, populations in the floodplains of the Koshi, Gandaki, Karnali, and Mahakali rivers are now in steep decline as a result of habitat alteration (dam construction, deforestation, and draining of swamps), overfishing, pollution, and illegal hunting and trade.

The present status and distribution of *Aspideretes gangeticus*, *A. hurum*, *Chitra indica*, *Geoclemys hamiltonii*, *Hardella thurjii*, *Lissemys punctata*, *Melanochelys tricarinata*, *M. trijuga*, *Kachuga dhongoka*, *K. kachuga*, *K. smithii*, *K. tecta*, *K. tentoria*, and *Indotestudo elongata* are described. Various causes for population declines are examined, and recommendations are made for research and conservation action.

Several chelonian species inhabit the Terai lowlands and the Himalayan foothills of Nepal. During the nineteenth and twentieth centuries, the zoogeography of tortoises and turtles in southeast Asia, particularly the Indian sub-continent, was studied (Hodgson, 1836–1848; Gray, 1844; Waltner, 1873; Theobald, 1876; Chaudhuri, 1912; Smith, 1931; Hora, 1948; Ahmad, 1955; Minton, 1966; Moll and Vijaya, 1986). Baseline data on chelonian diversity has been compiled in the recent past (Swan and Leviton, 1962; Majupuria, 1981; Shrestha, 1981; Mitchell and Zug, 1985; Shrestha, 1990; Frazier, 1991), but these reports refer only to taxonomy.

Recent observations on the natural history, distribution, morphology, ecology, and exploitation of the freshwater and terrestrial chelonians of Nepal were presented by Mitchell and Rhodin (1996). The current work is intended to assess their ecology, behavior, and population status.

Study Area

The major rivers of Nepal are the Koshi in the east, the Gandaki in the centre, and the Karnali and Mahakali in the western part of the country. These riverine watersheds include diverse forests and wetlands of great biological importance, which support vast habitats for tortoises and turtles.

The floodplains of these four principal rivers range in altitude from 80 to 6,500 m. The watershed includes tropical, moist, and dry deciduous forest types, consisting mainly of sal (*Shorea robusta*), teak (*Tectonia grandis*), simal (*Salmalia malabricum*), and khair (*Acacia catechu*). Other dominant trees include *Kydia calycina*, *Sterculia vilosa*, *Lagerstroemia parviflora*, *Alstonia scholaris*, *Dilenia pentagyna*, and *Bombax cebia*. Tropical evergreen trees that provide shade and good canopy are *Schima wallichi*, *Ficus cunia*,

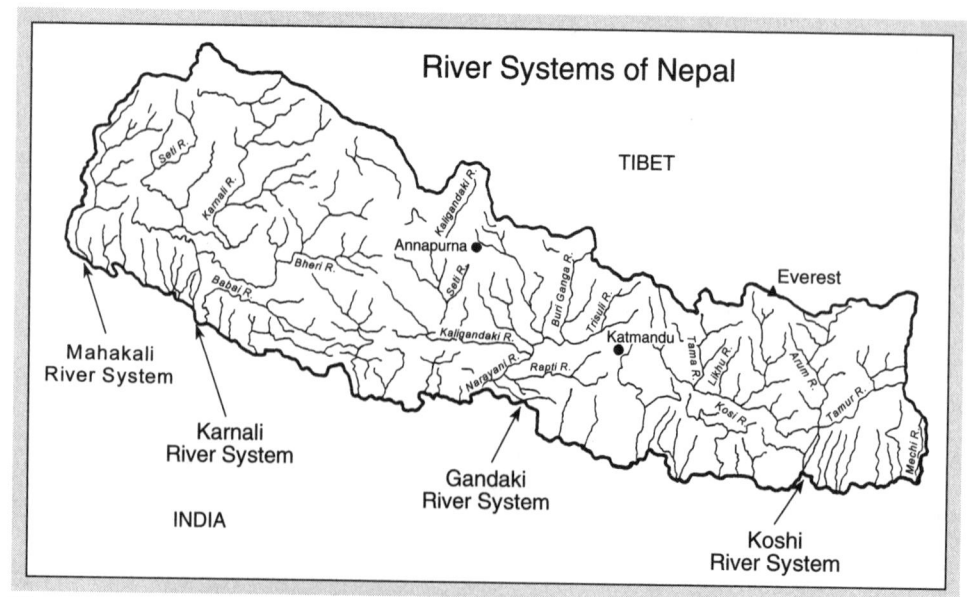

Figure 1. Map of Nepal showing major river systems.

Cordia myxa, and *Butea superba*. Aquatic plants of the families Nymphyaeceae, Lemaceae, Araceae, Eriocaulaceae, and Naiadaceae are common in the wetlands. In addition, the grasses *Typha elephantia*, *Arundo donax*, and *Phragmites communis* are also well represented.

There are three distinct seasons: pre-monsoon (March–April), monsoon (May–September), and retreating monsoon (late September–February). During the latter two seasons the water level of rivers, oxbows, and wetlands drops steadily until January when the lowest levels are recorded, and vast sand bars, reedy river embankments, lakes, and jheels (marshes) are exposed, leaving hibernating and den-making turtles and tortoises extremely vulnerable in these seasons.

METHODS

For the present study, the upper, middle, and lower reaches of the Gandaki, Koshi, Karnali, and Mahakali were visited regularly during the high-, low-, and mid-water phases of the rivers. Distribution and concentrations of the chelonian fauna in the main and feeder rivers were recorded using both direct observation (standardized surveys conducted by boat) and indirect surveys (recording the catch of anglers).

Turtle and tortoise habitats were divided into eight general habitat types: (1) small forested rivers and ephemeral creeks, (2) large intermittent creeks, (3) forest-clad hill streams with steep banks, (4) principal river channels meandering in the floodplain, (5) oxbow lakes, (6) marshes and swamps, (7) irrigation canals and reservoirs, and (8) fish ponds near villages. These are summarized in Table 2.

The River Systems

The major river systems of Nepal—the Mahakali, Karnali, Gandaki, and Koshi—are shown in Figure 1. These rivers support a diversity of chelonian species that have both esthetic and religious value to the local population. The rivers and holy shrines on their banks were visited at various times of the year to census chelonians. Physical data taken from the rivers (pH range, water temperature, and dissolved O_2) are shown in Table 1.

Mahakali River

The Mahakali is a perennial, torrential river at its upper headwater. The river originates from the Milan glacier near the Indian border. The river bed is rocky and sandy with sparse algal growth. The average depth at selected sites ranges from 5.0 to 13.0 m. The water is clear throughout the year except during the rainy season. Many small-scale water mills, industries, and power stations located near the lowland catchment area release pollutants into the river. The Sarada and Tanakpur dams are located in the lower reaches of Mahakali section, and the Suklaphanta Wildlife Reserve lies in the floodplain of this river. The river's watershed, which is not yet well explored, is rich in land tortoises.

Karnali River

The Karnali River is a perennial, torrential, and turbulent river in the Himalayas. It originates from the Mansarovar and Rakas lakes and receives water from snow-fed rivers such as the Mugu Karnali and Humla Karnali at the Himalayan belt. It has created a spectacular gorge near Chisapani, which contains diverse trans-Himalayan and sub-Himalayan chelonian species. The bottom of the Karnali River is largely boulder strewn at its upper reaches and sandy at its lower reaches. The water is clear except in the rainy season. Its depth ranges from 3 to 10 m, but in deep gorges varies from 50 to 100 m. This river carries a high sediment load. The upland watershed is sparsely populated with tortoises, but the river is rich in aquatic chelonians. The famous Chasapani Gorge is a nesting sanctuary for a variety of softshell turtles and tortoises. There is less human interference in the Karnali than in other Nepal river systems.

Koshi River

The Koshi is a perennial river arising from the Pei-Ko-Tso and Tso-Nu-Che lakes of Tibet, with seven tributaries: the Sun Koshi, Dudh Koshi, Tama Koshi, Likhu, Arun, Tamur, and Indrawati rivers. The bottom of the river is gravel and sand with rocks and boulders in some areas. Algal growth and aquatic plants are fairly dense in the downstream regions of the river. The feeder streams support the largest concentrations of several chelonian species of any river in

TABLE 1
Physical data from four major rivers during 1990–1991 season.

River	pH range	Temperature range (°C)	Dissolved O_2 range (ppm)
Mahakali	6.5–7.8	20.0–31.8	5.5–15.2
Karnali	7.0–8.5	22.8–31.5	7.0–13.8
Koshi (March–April)	6.0–7.5	13.0–28.5	6.0–12.0
Narayani (March–April)	6.7–7.5	18.0–28.5	7.8–13.8

Nepal; these include *Geoclemys hamiltonii, Kachuga smithii, K. tecta,* and *K. tentoria.* Extensive sandbar and basking promontories on the river banks provide ideal habitats for terrestrial and aquatic chelonians.

Narayani River

This perennial and torrential river originates on the southern slope of Himalayas. It has seven tributaries: the Kali Gandaki, Budi Gandaki, Trisuli, Marsyangdi, Made, and Seti rivers. The water now contains a high pollution load from household garbage and sewage as well as waste materials and biocides from paper mills and beer factories. Chelonian mortality was observed in June 1991 and January 1992. The algal growth and other aquatic flora in certain areas are profuse, possibly owing to the slow current and high nutrient load.

Biology of the Tortoises and Turtles

Aspideretes gangeticus (Cuvier)
Indian Softshell Turtle

This is a large turtle with an oval shell, the length of its carapace reaching up to 940 mm. It is characterized by a black-streaked head and an olive-green carapace with black reticulation or yellow vermiculation. The head is greenish with a black longitudinal line between the eyes and nape. It is difficult to distinguish this species from *A. hurum,* except when well-marked, relatively young specimens are in hand. The eggs are spherical and measure 2.5 cm in diameter. This omnivorous species feeds on the rotting flesh of animals in the river. It is distributed in the Koshi, Gandaki, and Karnali river systems. Nesting takes place in May and June or just afterward. Up to 35 eggs are laid in sand banks in a single nest. The species is primarily aquatic and is frequently seen with its head just above the water or basking on sand banks of the Karnali and Koshi rivers. It lives in oxbows, marshes, and irrigation channels and is subjected to intensive trapping by fishermen during the low-water phase of the river (March–May). In March and April indigenous people raid the nests and bring the eggs to local markets in Narayanghat, Biratnagar, and Mahendra Nagar.

Aspideretes hurum (Gray)
Indian Peacock Softshell Turtle

This is a large species with a carapace up to 600 mm or more. The head is large and the snout prominent and downturned. The carapace is olive green, reticulated with black, usually with four to five ocelli (each with three concentric yellow and black rings) that vanish with age. There is a variable pattern of yellow spots and black and greenish-yellow lines on the head and neck. The head is dark green with several yellow spots. The plastron of this species is ivory white. This is a purely aquatic turtle that has become rare due to habitat loss. It is found in the Gandaki, Koshi, Karnali, and Mahakali rivers, and is locally known as "Katakhiri."

Chitra indica (Gray)
Narrow-headed Softshell Turtle

One of the largest turtles in Nepal, it attains a carapace length exceeding 800 mm. It is distinguished by a long narrow head with eyes close to the comparatively short proboscis. The head has light-coloured streaks, and there is an inverted chevron on the neck in front of the carapace. The carapace is olive or grey, black-spotted in the young, and marked with yellow in the adult. The turtle is carnivorous. It lays approximately 100 eggs, and the hatchlings are extraordinarily small in contrast with the huge adult size, with a carapace length of approximately 30 mm.

Geoclemys hamiltonii (Gray)
Spotted Pond Turtle

A medium-size hard-shelled turtle, its carapace may attain a length of 300 mm. The head and carapace are dark brown to black with yellow spots on the head and (in younger turtles) on the carapace. The limbs have fully webbed digits and the forelimbs have transversely enlarged scales. The tail is quite short and is covered with small granular scales. The turtle is fully aquatic, living in shallow water with ample aquatic vegetation. Nothing is known about its breeding habits. This turtle has declined drastically from the clearing of aquatic vegetation.

Hardella thurjii (Gray)
Crowned River Turtle

This aquatic turtle displays pronounced sexual dimorphism, females attaining a length of 650 mm and males only 200 mm. The carapace is a dark brown or black with a yellow margin and a black midline keel. The plastron is pale

Figure 2. *Aspideretes gangeticus.*

yellow with dark blotches on each scute. The dark-brown to black head is large and pointed, with a small projecting snout that has a curved yellow stripe extending backward above the eye and curving downward on each side of the head. The limbs are brownish. This species is entirely herbivorous. Its eggs are oval. It is a most docile turtle often kept as a pet.

Kachuga dhongoka (Gray)
Three-striped Roofed Turtle

This medium-sized turtle of western Nepal is uncommon and is distinguished by a pointed second vertebral scute entering the third vertebral scute. The carapace is rather roughly textured, olive or brown with three black stripes. Females range up to 460 mm in length, males to 260 mm. The plastron is yellow. The forelimbs have five claws. Clutches of 30–35 elongated, oval eggs measure 55 × 33 mm and are buried in sandbanks. The meat of this species is eaten even by high-caste Hindu people. This and *K. kachuga* are commonly known as "Dodare" or "Dodari" in Nepal.

Kachuga kachuga (Gray)
Red-crowned Roofed Turtle

Also known as the "sail terrapin," it is the largest among this group of turtles. Males measure up to 290 mm, females to 560 mm. It occurs in eastern as well as western Nepal. Males have an olive or brown carapace with a yellow plastron; the central keel is prominent on the second and third vertebral shields. There is a red patch on top of the head and seven red stripes on the neck. Yellow stripes cross the blue-black ground colour on the sides of the neck. The colours are particularly bright during breeding season. Females are dark and drab with little or no pattern. The adult is approximately 15–25 kg and is distinguished from *K. dhongoka* by the absence of dark streaks along the carapace and larger size of the female. It breeds in March and April, laying eggs on sandbanks of the Koshi, Mahakali, and Narayani rivers. Digits are fully webbed.

Kachuga smithii (Gray)
Brown Roofed Turtle

A common turtle in the Terai, it measures up to 230 mm in length, is olive brown with a blackish keel along the midline, and the shell has a yellowish margin. There is a distinct reddish stripe on the neck extending from the mouth, and a reddish blotch behind the eye. The turtle has a yellowish upper beak and blue eyes. The limbs are webbed and bear enlarged scales; the forelimbs have five claws. It is found in the Narayani River near Tribeni Ghat.

Kachuga tecta (Gray)
Indian Roofed Turtle

This is a small turtle reaching about 230 mm in length. The male is smaller than the female. The blackish head is small and pointed with a red mark behind each eye, and fine parallel lines extend down the neck. The skin of the posterior part of the head is divided into large shields. The carapace is olive coloured with minute, dark spots and an orange vertebral stripe. The margin of the shell remains pink-yellow throughout adulthood. The plastron is yellow with dark spots. This turtle feeds chiefly on vegetable matter. There is little information about its breeding habits. These turtles are also kept as pets in temple ponds. The species has been reduced in numbers from trapping and overexploitation as food.

Kachuga tentoria (Gray)
Indian Tent Turtle

This turtle is paler than *K. tecta*. The males measure 139 mm and females 300 mm. It has a pale-olive carapace and a pale-red to yellow plastron. The head is dull olive; a series of reddish patches are located behind eyes, and there is a distinct marking behind the tympanum. The carapace is elevated and rounded in adults; a vertebral keel is prominent and forms a strong spiny process. It is a purely aquatic turtle and has been greatly affected by agricultural and industrial pollution as well as the destruction of nesting sites.

Lissemys punctata (Bonnaterre)
Indian Flapshell Turtle

This softshell turtle is distinguished by the presence of fleshy flaps on the plastron that can conceal the limbs and tail. The carapace is oval, measuring 175 mm in males, up to 275 mm in females, and is covered with smooth skin that is grey-green with yellow spots, which may appear plain in the young. The head is oval and terminates in tubular nostrils. It has rather prominent lateral eyes. The limbs are webbed with three claws on each foot. The tail is short.

Figure 3. *Lissemys punctata*.

TABLE 2
Habitat preference, conservation status, and distribution of tortoises and turtles in Nepal.

Family Name	Preferred habitat	Extralimital distribution	Cause of decline and economic uses	Status
Bataguridae				
Geoclemys hamiltonii (Gray) Spotted pond turtle	Shallow clear-water rivers. Favors weedy marshes, swamps, and oxbows connected to rivers. Feeds on snails, fish, and frogs. Distributed in Koshi, Gandaki, Karnali, and Mahakali rivers.	Ganga, Brahmaputra, and Sind; west Bengal as far as Siwalik hills. Fossils have been recorded from Siwalik hills.	Overfishing, pollution of habitat, eggs are taken as delicacy. Kept in cultural ponds as holy animal. Bones used in ethnic medicine.	Common
Hardella thurjii (Gray) Crowned River Turtle	Slow water or stagnant ponds, canals, oxbows of river. Avoids fast-flowing water.	Ganga, Brahmaputra, Indus rivers. Royal Chitwan National Park.	Habitat destruction and overexploitation. Brought into market and sold as food item.	Rare
Kachuga dhongoka (Gray) Three-striped roofed turtle	Riverine flood plain forested with sal (*Shorea*), marshes, and irrigation canals. Lives entirely on vegetable matter.	Indicator species of Ganga and Brahmaputra river systems.	Habitat changes because of dams and draining of swamps. Flesh esteemed as food.	Rare
Kachuga kachuga (Gray) Red-crowned roofed turtle	Shallow rivers, marshes, creeks. Prefers sand banks for nesting and basking sites. Occurs in Babai and Rapti rivers of Western Nepal.	Ganga River system.	Habitat modification because of dams and canalization, pollution, and overfishing.* Egg predation by humans.	Rare
Kachuga smithii (Gray) Brown roofed turtle	Slow moving river with sandy banks and weedy vegetation. Rapid swimmer. Deposits eggs in sand banks. Distributed in Koshi, Gandaki, Karnali, and Mahakali rivers.	Ganga, Brahmaputra, and Indus (Pakistan).	Habitat modification, overfishing,* and pollution. Young and adults used as pets; eggs eaten by hill tribes.	Indeterminate
Kachuga tecta (Gray) Indian roofed turtle	Rivers, lakes, marshes with weedy vegetation; less active in summer. Occurs in the Narayani and Koshi rivers.	Ganga, Brahmaputra, Indus (Pakistan). Fossils have been recovered from Pleistocene deposits.	Draining of wetlands and clearing of vegetation. Used as food and soup; collected for pets.	Rare
Kachuga tentoria (Gray) Indian tent turtle	Slow-running waters, backwaters, and still pools of large and small rivers. Active swimmer, lives only on vegetation. Found in the Koshi, Gandaki, Karnali, and Mahakali rivers.	Mahanadi, Godawari, and Krishna river systems.	Habitat modification, pesticides, DDT, and domestic pollution. Netting and trapping operations.	Rare

* Snaring, trapping, gill netting, drift netting, and dynamiting.

Family / Name	Preferred habitat	Extralimital distribution	Cause of decline and economic uses	Status
Melanochelys tricarinata (Blyth) Tricarnate hill turtle	Hill streams forested with dense subtropical vegetation. Purely terrestrial. Found in Narayani and Bagmati river watersheds.	Bihar, Assam, and Bangladesh.	Habitat modification, pollution, and draining of swamps. Eggs are taken by hill tribes.	Uncommon
Melanochelys trijuga Indian black turtle	Streambeds in sal forest near edge of Narayani River floodplain; Royal Chitwan National Park; Royal Bardia Wildlife Reserve.	Widespread in the Indian Subcontinent, except for arid northwest and northcentral regions. Sri Lanka, Bangladesh, Maldives, and Chagos Islands.	Similar to *M. tricarinata*. Taken for human consumption and commercial exploitation.	Common
Testudinidae				
Indotestudo elongata (Blyth) Elongated tortoise	A typical land tortoise of Siwalik hills. Inhabits sal (*Shorea robusta*) and teak (*Tectonia gramdis*) forests. A rare tortoise of the Bagmati and Narayani watershed.	Nepal, India, Bangladesh, Burma, Thailand, Malaysia, Indo-China, and China. Occurs in Utter Pradesh in India, particularly in Corbett National Park; possibly in Chitwan National Park, Suklaphanta Wildlife Reserve.	Flesh is considered medicinal and a delicacy. Reduction of dense sal forest has caused drastic decline of this tortoise.	Rare
Trionychidae				
Aspideretes gangeticus (Cuvier) Indian softshell turtle	Prefers deep, turbid, fast rivers. Uses sandy bank for nesting and basking sites. Rests in shallow water with head extending above water surface. Omnivorous scavenger.	Ganga, Mahanadi, Indus, Brahmaputra, and Narayani rivers.	Collection of sand and gravel from nesting areas, decline of fish populations from overfishing and dynamiting. Damming, channelization, and over-silting of river beds. Exploited as food.	Common
Aspideretes hurum (Gray) Indian peacock softshell turtle	Shallow muddy ditches, bogs, marshes. Feeds on frogs, shrimp, and small fishes. Aquatic and omnivorous. Occurs in Bhari and west Rapti rivers.	Ganga and Brahmaputra rivers.	Clearing of marshland and cultivation as rice paddies. Exploited as food.	Common
Chitra indica (Gray) Narrow headed softshell turtle	Shallow rivers with sandy bottom. Carnivorous. Feeds mainly on fish and gastropods.	Widely distributed in endogangetic plain up to Krishna and Godhari rivers.	Reduction of plant cover by deforestation and erosion in Siwalik mountains.	Common
Lissemys punctata (Bonnaterre) Flapshell turtle	Weedy, shallow-water river oxbows and reservoirs with muddy bottom.	Bangladesh, Burma, Andaman Islands, Sikkim, Sri Lanka, and Pakistan.	Extensive collection of sand and gravel from riverbanks. Development of irrigation and low irrigation power dam.	Common

Melanochelys tricarinata (Blyth)
Tricarnate Hill Turtle

This relatively small terrestrial turtle has a dark plum-coloured carapace up to 162 mm in length that is quite elongated and arched, with three rounded yellow keels. The plastron is yellowish brown. The head and limbs are dark plum coloured; a broad red stripe runs along each side of the head. The head is small. The digits of the forelimb are half webbed, whereas those of the rear limbs have only rudimentary webs. The tail is short. The turtle lays 3–6 eggs and is herbivorous. *M. tricarinata* is found along the Tribenighat section of the Narayani River and the Bagmati River. It is commonly called "Thotari."

Melanochelys trijuga indopeninsularis
Indian Black Turtle

This turtle has a dark-brown to black elongated carapace up to 342 mm; the plastron is brown with a yellow border. The head is olive-brown with a long spear-shaped mark on the forehead (Das, 1989). The species was reported from the Terai of central Nepal in the Royal Chitwan National Park and vicinity (Dinerstein et al., 1987). More recently Mitchell and Rhodin (1996) discovered three live juveniles in the western Chitwan in small, partially drying streambeds in sal forest near the edge of the Narayani River floodplain. They also collected five skeletons in western Nepal at the Royal Bardia Wildlife Reserve near Thakurdwara (on the Karnali River). Clutches of three and six eggs of this species were found by Dinerstein et al. (1987).

Indotestudo elongata (Blyth)
Elongated Tortoise

Commonly known as "Agri" in Nepal, it has a helmet-shaped carapace of 275–350 mm in length. Its carapace is yellowish with central dark blotches on the scutes. Males are usually larger than females. The head is a light-coloured cream yellow or yellowish green, and limbs are dark brown covered with yellow-brown scales. The plastron is yellowish and either plain or patterned with dark blotches. This species is herbivorous and weighs up to 3.5 kg; newly hatched young weigh 26 g. This tortoise prefers cool, humid areas of the Himalayan foothills but can tolerate temperatures up to 45°C. During the breeding season the skin around eyes and nostrils turns pink. One to five oblong eggs are laid per clutch, and incubation period varies from 95 to 142 days.

This is the most widespread tortoise in Asia. Smith (1931) first recorded this tortoise from Nepal, basing his description on a drawing made by Hodgson. Mitchell and Zug (1985) regarded this tortoise as apparently common in sal forests of Nepal. The tortoise is now rare in the Chitwan Valley, but a few populations still occur in western Nepal.

Conservation and Management

Basic Studies

For many species of chelonians in Nepal there are no basic data on the ecology, distribution, breeding habits, reproductive physiology, population dynamics, or status. Long-term studies should be initiated and management programs developed.

Threats to Habitat

Tortoises and turtles are heavily impacted by direct loss of habitat and pollution of aquatic habitat. Known and possible causes include:

- Deforestation and removal of sand and gravel from river banks;
- Destruction of nesting areas and collection of eggs;
- Extensive land use and the agricultural practice of draining swamps along the floodplains of rivers;
- Water development projects, e.g., dams and irrigation canals;
- Harmful fishing practices, e.g., gill netting, snaring, and poisoning; and
- Water pollution by direct release of industrial effluent and household sewage.

Conservation of riverine forest habitat components such as sandbanks and sandbars and the preservation of nesting sites is vital to the survival of both crocodiles and freshwater turtles.

Regulation and Enforcement

Turtle populations have declined drastically from various rivers as the result of illegal capture. There is a considerable turtle trade in the Terai, Narayanghat, Biratnagar as well as in Mahendra Nagar where freshwater turtles are taken to different parts of the Terai. Trade in tortoises and turtles is practiced by a relatively small percentage of the population, primarily the Tharu, Darahi, Raji, and Majhis, who sell both the meat and eggs. Higher castes, such as Brahmins, do not eat turtle meat because of religious considerations, but all lower castes are known to consume it. The turtles are often kept in temple ponds and their presence is considered a good omen.

Although laws have been enacted to protect the habitat of aquatic animals (including tortoises and turtles), they do not address the illegal exploitation of rare tortoises and turtles. Trapping of chelonians should be prohibited during breeding seasons, especially July–September.

Fishing should be banned along the waterfront near national park and wildlife reserves to prevent incidental turtle mortality in fishing gear. While the closure of large fishing areas cannot be justified (most of the people in Nepal depend upon the rivers for food), banning the use of drift nets and gill nets (3–7 cm mesh size) during the mass emergence of freshwater turtles in nesting periods should be given serious consideration. In the Royal Chitwan National Park, the Royal Bardic National Park, and the Royal Suklaphant Wildlife Reserve, nylon netting has been banned, and traditional methods of fishing have been reintroduced with permits being issued to local fishermen. Similar methods should be adopted in the Koshi-Tappu Wildlife Reserve to protect the tortoises and turtles. Core habitat and buffer zones should also be identified, and local fishermen should be allowed to fish (using traditional methods) in the buffer zones under the supervision of authorities.

In the Narayani River, the installation of fish ladders could help counterbalance the effect of the many small dams that have been constructed. River parks should be established, and habitat disrupted by dams and human activities should be restored. The Royal Chitwan National Park now protects significant segments of the Narayani River, including the habitat of the rare *Indotestudo elongata*. Tortoises are protected near the religious temple on the Narayani River bank near Deughat and Gajgraha.

Inadequate communication facilities make the monitoring of the wetland reserves more difficult than the terrestrial wildlife reserves. Proper monitoring of managed populations can be achieved if sufficient trained staff are appointed to the wildlife reserves.

Chelonian Ranching

Rehabilitation of chelonian populations by captive rearing and release of hatchlings, as in crocodile management programs, should be developed. Collecting eggs from the wild for hatching, rearing the juveniles in captivity for several years, and releasing them into protected wild habitats may help increase chances of survival. Wetland sanctuaries should be created for the ranched animals in Koshi-Tappu, Chitwan, Bardia, and Suklaphanta as well as in other wildlife reserves and protected areas. Trained field staff would be needed to regularly monitor these populations.

Enhancement of Chelonian Riverine Habitat

While the building of dams may prevent floods, facilitate irrigation and power production, and provide habitat to increase fish and chelonian reproduction, suitable water levels must be maintained in tailwater regions during chelonian breeding seasons (December–May and July–September). Scientific data on chelonian ecology and reproductive biology is essential in the management of these animals. Arti-

ficial breeding and rearing of rare chelonians will also help replenish natural stock removed by fisheries.

Economic development and watershed conservation must take into account both the conservation of turtle species and that of sympatric unrelated forms, including the endangered dolphin, *Platanista gangetica* (Shrestha, 1989). Due consideration should be given to partial compensation for this loss by constructing one or more artificial river parks at the tailwater release sites of the high dams and powerhouses. Diversion of dam or powerhouse water at suitable places would provide free-flowing, turbulent water, and habitats suitable for locally important food fish as well as for chelonians. River tributaries can be modified to construct wetland parks

Figure 4. Author praying in temple near Pachali Bhairab. Tortoises (*Indotestudo elongata*) are in foreground.

Figure 5. *Indotestudo elongata* (from photo above), venerated in Nepal, are kept in both Hindu temples and Buddhist monasteries. It is believed that incurable diseases can be cured if one touches tortoises kept in temples.

with small green forest belts and promontories that meet the basking and nesting requirements of chelonians. Such river parks, aquaria, and conservation centres will greatly enhance public awareness and further the long-term conservation of rare chelonians.

Public Awareness and Education

A public education program focused on wetland habitat conservation should be mounted. High priority should be given to the concerns of the people of the river communities, and efforts should be made to develop alternative food sources where possible.

DISCUSSION

Chelonians are restricted primarily to eastern, western, and central Nepal within the major drainage systems of the Himalayan foothills. Anthropogenic disturbances—principally gravel mining, sand removal, searching for gold along nesting areas, and over-siltation in the Koshi, Narayani, Karnali, and Mahakali river systems—have reduced or eliminated many fish, shrimp, and microinvertebrate communities necessary for the survival of tortoises and turtles. Other factors that limit chelonian numbers include agricultural runoff, domestic and industrial pollution, and low water levels during dry periods. These factors are reported to be of greater magnitude in the rivers of central and eastern Nepal, particularly the Narayani, Koshi, Kankai, and Mechi river systems.

Continued environmental degradation of the drainage systems in the Himalayan foothills could extirpate *Indotestudo elongata* with its rigid terrestrial habitat requirements. The reduced fish and invertebrate communities in the heavily impacted rivers and tributaries in central and eastern Nepal are further evidence of environmental degradation. Additional anthropogenic disturbances, such as overfishing by gill netting, drift netting, harpooning, and the dynamiting of pools, will very likely cause declines in populations of such aquatic species as *Chitra indica*, *Lissemys punctata*, and *Aspideretes gangeticus*.

Major national parks and wildlife reserves, strategically located in the Himalayan foothills or the Terai regions of Nepal, do provide some protection, but they do not include entire watersheds of the important rivers and tributaries. Control and management of the entire watershed of the major rivers are essential if chelonians are to survive in Nepal.

ACKNOWLEDGEMENTS

The author is thankful to Mr. K. B. Mathema, Vice Chancellor of Tribhuvan University, for his encouragement. Thanks are due to Dr. Ratna S. J. B. Rana, ex-Vice Chancellor of Royal Nepal Academy of Science and Technology, for endorsement and support while the author was affiliated with RONAST.

LITERATURE CITED

Ahmad, N. 1955. On Edible Tortoises and Turtles of East Pakistan. East Bengal Dir. Fish. 18 pp.

Chaudhuri, B. L. 1912. Aquatic tortoises of the Middle Ganges and Brahmaputra. Rec. Indian Mus. (Calcutta) 7:212–214.

Das, I. 1991. Colour Guide to the Turtles and Tortoises of the Indian Subcontinent. R & A Publishing, Ltd., Portishead, UK. 133 pp.

Dinerstein, E., G. R. Zug, and J. C. Mitchell. 1987. Notes on the biology of *Melanochelys* (Reptilia, Testudines, Emydidae) in the Terai of Nepal. J. Bombay Nat. Hist. Soc. 84(3):687–688.

Frazier, J. 1992. The land tortoise in Nepal. A review. J. Bombay Nat. Hist. Soc. 89(1) 45–54.

Gray, J. E. 1844. Catalogue of the Tortoises, Crocodiles, and Amphisbaenians in the Collection of British Museum. 80 pp.

Hodgson, B. H. 1836–1848. Drawings of reptiles, fishes, etc., presented by B. H. Hodgson. Original in the library of the British Museum (Natural History).

Hora, S. L. 1948. The distribution of crocodiles and chelonians in Ceylon, India, Burma and farther east. Proc. Nat. Inst. Sci. India. 14(6):285–310.

Majupuria, T. C. 1981–82. Wild Is Beautiful: Introduction to the Magnificent, Rich and Varied Fauna and Wildlife of Nepal. S. Devi, Lashkar, Gwalior, India.

Minton, S. A. 1966. A contribution to the herpetology of West Pakistan. Bull. Amer. Mus. Nat. Hist. 134(2):27–184.

Mitchell, J. C. and A. G. J. Rhodin. 1996. Observations on the natural history and exploitation of the turtles of Nepal, with life history notes on *Melanochelys trijuga*. Chelon. Conserv. Biol. 2(1):66–72.

Mitchell, J. C. and G. R. Zug. 1985. Guide to the amphibians and reptiles of the Royal Chitwan National Park. Unpubl. report, the King Mahendra Trust for Nature Conservation.

Moll, E. O. and J. Vijaya. 1986. Distributional records for some Indian turtles. J. Bombay Nat. Hist. Soc. 83:57–62.

Shrestha, T. K. 1981. Ecogeographic distribution of reptiles in Nepal. *In* T. C. Majupuria (ed.), Wild is Beautiful: Introduction to Fauna and Wildlife of Nepal, pp. 178–184. Lashkar, Gwalior, India.

Shrestha, T. K. 1989. Biology, status and conservation of Ganges River Dolphin, *Platanista gangetica*, in Nepal. *In* W. F. Perrin, R. L. Brownell, Jr., Zhou Kaiya, and Liu Jiankang, (eds.), Biology and Conservation of the River Dolphins: Proceedings of the Workshop on Biology and Conservation of the Platanistoid Dolphin, pp. 70–76. Wuhan, People's Republic of China, 28–30 October, 1986. IUCN Species Survival Commission, Gland, Switzerland.

Shrestha, T. K. 1990. Resource Ecology of Himalayan Waters. Curriculum Development Centre, Tribhuvan University, Kathmandu.

Shrestha, T. K. 1993. Fauna of wetlands in Nepal. National Workshop on Wetlands Management in Nepal. Organized by National planning Commission (HMG), IUCN, Department of National Parks and Wildlife Conservation, Kathmandu.

Smith, M. A. 1931. The Fauna of British India, including Ceylon and Burma. Reptilia and Amphibia. Vol. 1. Loricata, Testudines. Taylor and Francis, London. Reprinted 1973, Ralph Curtis Books, Miami; and 1974, Today & Tomorrow's Printers & Publishers, Faridabad.

Swan, L. W. and A. E. Leviton. 1962. The herpetology of Nepal: A history, checklist and zoogeographic analysis of the herpetofauna. Proc. Cal. Acad. Sci., Sr. 4.32(6):103–147. Republished 1966, J. Bengal. Nat. Hist. Soc. 34(2):88–144.

Theobald, W. 1876. Descriptive Catalogue of the Reptiles of British India. Thacher, Spink and Co., Calcutta. 238 pp.

Waltner, R. C. 1873. Geographical and altitudinal distribution of amphibians and reptiles in the Himalayas (Part IV). Cheetal 16(4):12–17.

The Bostami or Black Softshell Turtle, *Aspideretes nigricans*: Problems and Proposed Conservation Measures

M. FARID AHSAN

Department of Zoology, University of Chittagong, Chittagong 4331, Bangladesh
[e-mail: Abegum@dcci.agni.com or vc-cu@spct.com]

ABSTRACT: *Aspideretes nigricans*, a large freshwater turtle, is confined to a single pond attached to a Mohammedan shrine in Chittagong, Bangladesh. The total population is approximately 400 individuals and is dependant upon artificial food supplied by visitors and pilgrims. The very confined distribution, reduction of potential nesting grounds, and egg predation are major threats to its survival. Fungal infection is also suspected to be a further stress. These threats to the species' survival are discussed, and possible conservation measures are proposed.

Aspideretes nigricans (Anderson, 1875), the Bostami or black softshell turtle, is confined to a single pond near Chittagong, Bangladesh, and little is known about this species (Annandale, 1912; Annandale and Shastri, 1914; Smith, 1931; Khan, 1980; Ahsan, in press). The present paper discusses the problems related to the survival of the species and suggests possible conservation measures. The information is based on work done from 1983 to the present (Ahsan and Haque, 1987; Ahsan and Saeed, 1989, 1992; Ahsan et al., 1994; Ahsan, in press).

Population Status

In 1985 the total population was estimated at 320, of which 173 (54%) were adult males, 115 (36%) adult females, and 32 (10%) young, with an adult male-female ratio of 1.5:1 (Ahsan and Saeed, 1989). The author released 23 captive-hatched young in May 1987 and saw additional young in the pond in December 1990. The current population of *A. nigricans* in the Bostami pond is approximately 350–400 individuals (pers. obs.).

Anderson (1875) reported that *A. nigricans* inhabited a tract intermediate between the Brahmaputra river system and the Arakan streams (cf. Annandale, 1912). Its occurrence in the Chittagong pond was reported by Annandale and Shastri (1914), Khan (1980, 1982), and Ahsan and Saeed (1989). *A. nigricans* was shown to be distinct from *A. hurum* by Meylan (1987).

Habitat and Ecology

The species is restricted to an artificial, rectangular pond with concrete banks and access steps. It is located approximately 6.5 km northwest of Chittagong (approx. 22°25′ N, 91°49′ E) at the foot of a 50 m hill, the top of which is the "astana" (sitting place) of the shrine of Sultan

Figure 1. The Bostami pond and shrine of Sultan al-Arefin Hazrat Bayazid Bistami near Chittagong, Bangladesh. (Photos by Peter C. H. Pritchard.)

al-Arefin Hazrat Bayazid Bistami (popularly known as Bayazid Bostami). The general belief is that the famous Muslim saint was buried in this shrine, which in fact is not the case. His "mazar" (grave) is actually in Bistam, Iran (Arberry, 1963). Sultan Bayazid Bistami was born in 777 A.D. in Bistam and died in 874 A.D. (Ali, 1964). So, there is no mazar of the saint in the shrine, only an astana associated with the name of the great saint. It is possible that the 15th-century Bengal king named Shihab al-din Bayazid Shah is buried in the shrine, and his name may have been modified as Sultan Bayazid Bistami by some followers (see Huda, 1985 for details). Because of the strong religious belief about the attachment of the turtle to the shrine, the Bostami turtle has been named after the saint.

The Bostami pond was probably first excavated in the 17th century in front of the mosque. The pond has been excavated and expanded several times and is currently 94.5 × 61.3 m. The depth fluctuates seasonally from 2.5 m in the dry season to approximately 5 m during the monsoons. The primary source of water is rainfall, but seepage from the water table is a contributory factor. The water in the pond is clear (visibility is approx. 1 m) except during the monsoon season when turbidity is high. At the exposed steps of the platforms, the turtles come up to take food, offered on skewers, from the visitors and pilgrims upon whom these turtles depend. The old turtles are so tame they even accept food from the hand.

The main food offered to the turtles by visitors and pilgrims consists of bread, banana, and offal (mainly cattle lung), but occasionally puffed rice, chapati, etc. are also offered. The yearly expenditure for food was estimated to be about $10,500 in 1984 (Ahsan et al., 1994).

Gravid females either use the east bank of the pond for nesting or come on land to the west where a Mughal mosque and (more recently) a shrine office have been established. The east bank is now more suitable for nesting as a plant nursery was established there in 1985; human access is controlled, disturbance is minimal, and the soils are less compact. The western nesting ground is about 22.5 m away from the main platform of the pond. By passing through a narrow exit near the northwest corner of the mosque, gravid females can reach the elevated nesting area. The nesting area has been reduced in recent years by development projects such as factories and residences. Furthermore, it is partly inundated by rain water during breeding season. The northern and southern sides are no longer suitable for nesting not only because of obstruction but also because the soils on both sides are compact and too hard for nesting.

DISCUSSION

As the species is reported to have been confined to a single pond (Ahsan, in press), at least since its first description by Anderson (1875), there is a possibility of inbreeding depression, which may ultimately cause population collapse. Therefore, there is a need to study the genetic variability of the reproductively active adults and/or young individuals in the population, though remedies would be few even if inbreeding depression is found because no other population is known to exist anywhere in the world.

Figure 2. Turtles are fed by pilgrims and visitors to the Bostami shrine.

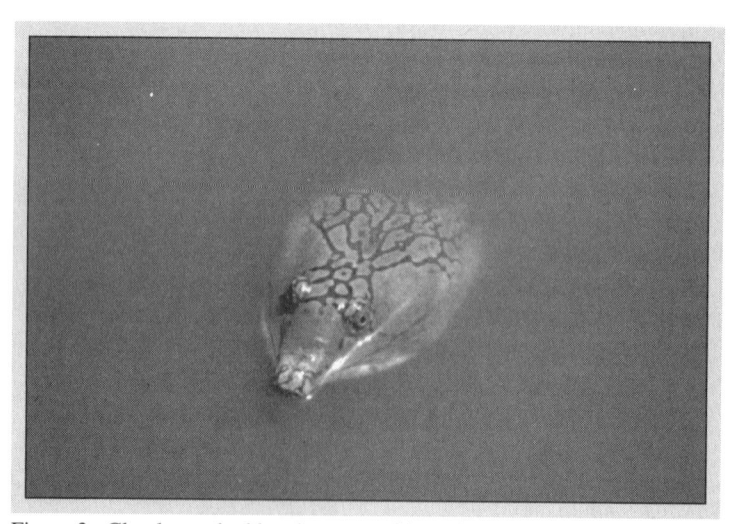

Figure 3. Clearly marked head pattern of juvenile *Aspideretes nigricans*.

Human encroachment on the nesting grounds and egg predation (Ahsan and Saeed, 1992) are other threats to its survival. Fungal infection has been noted, but whether it is a problem for survival needs further investigation. Without protection by local people (for religious reasons), this species would have been extinct by now. Preliminary research on egg incubation and rearing of young (Ahsan and Saeed, 1992) has been the only attempt at applied conservation for the species. Such work should be continued to build new populations to save the species from extinction by natural or anthropogenic factors. Studies on biological parameters

Threats to Survival

1. Very small absolute population size.
2. Physical confinement of the single known population.
3. Reduction of its nesting ground.
4. Possible egg predation.
5. Potential inbreeding depression.
6. Possible health risk from fungal infestation.

Conservation Measures Taken

1. *A. nigricans* is listed in *The IUCN Amphibia-Reptilia Red Data Book* (IUCN, 1982) as "Endangered."
2. It is listed on Appendix I of CITES (i.e., international commercial trade is prohibited).
3. It is listed under Action Plan Rating 2 of the IUCN/SSC Tortoise and Freshwater Turtle Specialist Group (i.e., little known and confined distribution).
4. It is protected under Schedule III of the Bangladesh Wildlife (Preservation) (Amendment) Act of 1974, which designated that the species not be hunted, killed, or captured.
5. It is actively protected by local people for religious reasons.
6. Preliminary research was conducted on egg incubation and rearing of young, which has provided some basic information on the species.

Conservation Measures Proposed

1. A detailed survey of the species should be conducted on its population status and distribution in Bangladesh.
2. Long term research and monitoring should be undertaken.
3. A captive breeding program should be initiated with a few breeding pairs. Probable suitable sites for the program would be Chittagong University Campus, Bangladesh Forest Research Institute, Chittagong Zoo, or government land, especially within the cantonment near the Bostami area.
4. A second captive colony should be established under controlled and monitored conditions in a suitable area in Bangladesh.
5. Fungal samples from the turtles should be tested to determine deleterious effects on the turtles and appropriate corrective measures taken.
6. Physical, chemical, and biological parameters of the Bostami pond water should be analysed to help understand the species' ecology.
7. The association between turtles and fish—the two major components of the pond's fauna—should be studied. The turtles do not eat the fish, but no one has determined whether the fish eat hatchling turtles.

of the pond water and the association between the turtles and fish in the pond may also provide additional information relevant to future conservation measures.

Acknowledgements

I am grateful to the Organising Committee of the International Conference on Conservation, Restoration, and Management of Tortoises and Turtles for inviting me to the conference, and for logistic support. I thank Mr. A. K. Gupta, Mr. A. D. Cuaron, and Dr. M. A. G. Khan for their helpful comments on the manuscript.

Literature Cited

Ahsan, M. F. In press. *Aspideretes nigricans* (Anderson, 1875), the black softshell turtle. *In* P. C. H. Pritchard and A. G. J. Rhodin (eds.), The Conservation Biology of Freshwater Turtles. Chelonian Research Monogr., Chelonian Research Foundation, Lunenburg, Massachusetts.

Ahsan, M. F. and M. N. Haque. 1987. Bostami kachim. Bangla Academy Bijjnan Potrika 13(2):15–39.

Ahsan, M. F., M. N. Haque, and C. M. Fugler. 1991. Observations on *Aspideretes nigricans* (Anderson), a semi-domesticated endemic species of eastern Bangladesh. Amphibia-Reptilia 12:131–136.

Ahsan, M. F., M. N. Haque, and M. A. Saeed. 1994. Notes on feeding habits and some morphological features of the Bostami turtle, *Aspideretes nigricans* (Anderson). J. Bombay Nat. Hist. Soc. 91(3): 45–461.

Ahsan, M. F. and M. A. Saeed. 1989. The Bostami turtle, *Trionyx nigricans* Anderson: Population status, distribution, historical background, and length-weight relationship. J. Bombay Nat. Hist. Soc. 86(1):1–6.

Ahsan, M. F. and M. A. Saeed. 1992. Some aspects of the breeding biology of the black softshell turtle, *Aspideretes nigricans*. Hamadryad 17:28–31.

Ali, M. 1964. History of Chittagong. Standard Publishers Ltd., Dacca. 178 pp.

Anderson, J. 1875. Description of some new Asiatic mammals and chelonia. Ann. & Mag. N. Hist. 16(4):282–285.

Annandale, N. 1912. The Indian mud-turtles (Trionychidae). Rec. Indian Mus. 7:151–179.

Annandale, N. and M. H. Shastri. 1914. Relics of the worship of mud-turtles in India and Burma. J. Asiatic Soc. Bengal 10(5):131–134.

Arberry, A. J. 1963. Sufism—An Account of the Mystics of Islam. George Allen and Unwin, London. 141 pp.

Huda, S. M. 1985. The saints and shrines of Chittagong. Ph.D. thesis, University of Chittagong, Bangladesh. 275 pp.

IUCN. 1982. The IUCN Amphibia-Reptilia Red Data Book. Part 1. Testudinidae, Crocodylia, Rhynchocephalia (B. Groombridge, comp.). IUCN, Gland, Switzerland. xiii + 426 pp.

Khan, M. A. R. 1980. A "holy" turtle of Bangladesh. Hornbill 4:7–11.

Khan, M. A. R. 1982. Chelonians of Bangladesh and their conservation. J. Bombay Nat. Hist. Soc. 79(1):110–116.

Meylan, P. A. 1987. The phylogenetic relationships of soft-shelled turtles (Family Trionychidae). Bull. Amer. Mus. Nat. Hist. 186(1): 1–101.

Smith, M. A. 1931. The Fauna of British India, including Ceylon and Burma. Reptilia and Amphibia. Vol. 1. Loricata, Testudines. Taylor and Francis, Ltd., London. 185 pp.

Population and Habitat Status of Freshwater Turtles and Tortoises of Bangladesh and Their Conservation Aspects

MD. SOHRAB UDDIN SARKER AND MD. LOKMAN HOSSAIN

Department of Zoology, University of Dhaka, Dhaka-1000, Bangladesh [e-mail: zooldu@citechco.net]

ABSTRACT: Twenty-eight species of turtles and tortoises are reported to occur in Bangladesh; 21 are freshwater, two are terrestrial, and the remaining five are marine. Bangladesh earns an average of U.S. $600,000 dollars per year from the export of freshwater turtles such as *Aspideretes hurum*, *A. gangeticus*, *Chitra indica*, *Lissemys punctata*, *Morenia petersi*, *Hardella thurjii*, and *Kachuga tecta*. Dried shells and turtle oil are also exported. Turtles are collected from their breeding grounds and exported, primarily during winter months when most of the females are gravid. Wild populations of these reptiles are in rapid decline from overexploitation, and habitats are being rapidly destroyed as a result of the increase in human population, urbanization, development of roads and highways, sand mining, expansion of agriculture, modern irrigation, widespread use of agrochemicals, drainage of wetlands, and deforestation.

The lack of educational programs to increase environmental awareness, limited research and conservation programs, and economic conditions also contribute to these declines. Both national and international cooperation are essential for conservation and management of these turtles.

This paper is based on the authors' experience with these animals both in the field and in captivity since 1982.

The total area of wetlands in Bangladesh has been variously estimated at seven to eight million hectares—approximately 50% of the total land surface of the country. This includes at least 480,000 ha of permanent rivers and streams, 610,000 ha of estuaries and mangrove swamps, 120,000–290,000 ha of "haors" (bowl-shaped depressions between the natural levees of rivers, flooding annually), "baors" (oxbow lakes), and "beels" (saucer-like depressions in which water may be retained throughout the year), over 90,000 ha of large water reservoirs, 150,000–180,000 ha of small pools and fish ponds, 90,000–115,000 ha of shrimp ponds, and approximately 770,000 ha of land that are seasonally inundated every year (Akonda and Scott, 1989; Scott and Poole, 1989).

The abundance of wetlands supports a wide variety of wildlife. Twenty-eight species of turtles and tortoises are known to occur in Bangladesh, of which 21 species are freshwater, two are terrestrial, and five are marine (Smith, 1931; Shafi and Quddus, 1976; Husain, 1979; Khan, 1982).

Turtles play an important role in maintaining ecological balance. By feeding on organic waste, dead animals, and on aquatic plants considered to be weeds in agricultural fields (such as water hyacinth, water cabbage, *Hydrilla*, and *Lemna* spp.), they help increase crop production (Sarker, 1992b). In the wild and in captivity *Chitra indica* is carnivorous; *Morenia petersi* is completely herbivorous; the two terrestrial species, *Geochelone elongata* and *Manouria emys*, are primarily herbivorous; and the remaining species are omnivorous (Moll, 1986; Hossain, 1989; Sarker, 1993b).

The elongated tortoise (*Indotestudo elongata*) and the Asian brown tortoise (*Manouria emys*) are completely terrestrial; the Indian flapshell turtle (*Lissemys punctata*) and the spotted pond turtle (*Geoclemys hamiltonii*) inhabit both terrestrial and aquatic habitats; all other species are aquatic.

Turtles in Bangladesh are threatened by a number of factors: Approximately 10–20% of both terrestrial and aquatic habitats have been destroyed, and the use of agrochemicals, industrial development, construction of roads and highways, and commercial exploitation have been responsible for the decline of turtle populations.

In addition, turtles are heavily exploited by commercial collectors. From the export of freshwater turtles, Bangladesh earns an average of Tk 24,118,200 per year (approx. U.S. $600,000). *Aspideretes hurum*, *A. gangeticus*, *Chitra indica*, *Lissemys punctata*, *Morenia petersi*, *Hardella thurjii*, and *Kachuga tecta* are exported to such countries as Japan, Hong Kong, China, Thailand, Malaysia, Singapore, Korea, and the UK (Export Promotion Bureau of Bangladesh, 1981–1982 to 1992–1993). These exports have continued even though many species are included on the appendices of the Convention on Trade in Endangered Species (CITES) and are "Endangered" or "Threatened." Turtles are collected from their breeding grounds and exported, primarily during winter months when most of the females are gravid (Sarker and Hossain, 1988).

Habitat

The terrestrial elongated tortoise (*Indotestudo elongata*) and the Asian brown tortoise (*Manouria emys*) occur only in the hilly forest habitats of greater Chittagong, Chittagong Hill-Tracts, Sylhet, and greater Mymensingh. In general, *I. elongata* and *M. emys* inhabit hilly, mixed or moist deciduous forest.

Scrub forests, woodland, jungles, bushes, bamboo thickets, pineapple and ginger gardens, water hyacinth, long grasses, and cultivated and fallow lands along or near bodies of water are appropriate habitats for the Indian flapshell turtle (*Lissemys punctata*) and the spotted pond turtle (*Geoclemys hamiltonii*). *L. punctata* utilises these habitats during cool weather. Toward the end of the flood season and at the beginning of winter season it migrates into this habitat and remains buried 5–10 cm below soft, semisolid, or muddy soil covered with secondary vegetation. Within 10–20 minutes it completely buries itself in the ground, making an air hole for respiration. Occasionally, this turtle buries itself under mud in shallow water.

The small Indian eyed turtle, *Morenia petersi*, usually frequents running bodies of water with floating vegetation (e.g., water hyacinth) as well as submerged and floating rooted vegetation such as *Hydrilla*, *Lemna*, and *Potamogeton* spp.

The crowned river turtle (*Hardella thurjii*), the Indian black turtle (*Melanochelys trijuga*), the brown roofed turtle (*Kachuga smithii*), and the Indian tent turtle (*Kachuga tentoria*) are found in riverine habitats, using the land along the banks and newly emerged river islands only for basking and nesting.

The common Indian roofed turtle, *Kachuga tecta*, usually utilises stagnant bodies of water such as ponds, "deghees" (reservoirs or large shallow lakes), canals, "tanks" (village or temple pools, usually long established), ditches, and other shallow water, but it is uncommon in the running water of rivers and streams. It also uses estuaries in coastal areas.

The river terrapin or common batagur, *Batagur baska*, is rare and lives only in estuarine and brackish water habitats in the Sundarbans. All other species of turtles live primarily in aquatic habitat.

Population Status

Lissemys punctata is fairly common and widely distributed throughout Bangladesh. *Kachuga tentoria*, *K. smithii*, *Hardella thurjii*, and *Morenia petersi* are also fairly common in all low-lying districts. *Aspideretes hurum* and *K. tecta* are common and widely distributed. Other species are more or less widely distributed but are less common (Table 1). Approximately 250–300 *A. nigricans*, originally said to have been released by a Muslim saint in the ninth century (Smith, 1931) are now endemic to the Bayazid Bostami Mazar pond in Chittagong (see also Ahsan, this volume).

Threats and Causes of Decline

Continued exploitation and loss of habitat of the softshell turtles *Lissemys punctata*, *A. hurum*, *A. gangeticus*, and *Chitra indica* as well as the hard-shelled turtles *Hardella thurjii* and *Melanochelys trijuga* will eventually lead to their extirpation; all other species are threatened by overexploitation for commercial export and domestic consumption.

Collection

In winter collectors probe for turtles primarily along the edges of shallow water with a 1–1.5 m bamboo stick equipped with a sharp spear 20–30 cm long. When the spear strikes the carapace of a turtle, the hunter pulls it from the water by hand and puts it in a jute sack fastened around his waist. Each hunter may collect 8–10 turtles a day.

Fishermen also collect turtles when they are encountered while fishing. The fishermen use "Hazari Barshi" (meaning a thousand hooks), an assembly of a large number of hooks that hang vertically by short threads from a long horizontal nylon line. The hooks remain just above or in the muddy bottoms of the rivers and pierce the carapace and legs of softshell turtles when they become entangled. They lodge in the mouth and throat when the baits are swallowed by both softshell and hard-shelled turtles. Whitaker (1982) reports that during the monsoon in the Sunderbans in Bangladesh about 200 katas (*Batagur baska*) are caught each year on hooks baited with keora fruit from the mangrove, *Sonneratia apetala*.

Turtles are also caught with harpoons as they float at the water's surface near the mouths of rivers, where they accumulate at the end of the flood season. Harpoons with long nylon lines are thrown obliquely from boats; they penetrate the carapace and the turtle is then taken on board. Spears attached to long bamboo poles are also used in deep water when turtles release air bubbles from the muddy bottom. Bamboo dams are also built across small rivers, canals, and streams, and turtles are captured when they try to cross the barriers.

In the Sundarbans, *Batagur baska* are caught by fishermen when they come onto riverbanks at night to nest. The eggs are also taken and consumed.

Loss and Alteration of Habitat

Human overpopulation (approx. 750 per km^2—nearly the highest density in the world) greatly increases pressure on various habitats of turtles and tortoises. Conversion of land for agriculture; agroforestry and commercial industry; urbanization; construction of roads and highways, airports, dams, barrages and embankments, and new settlements directly cause destruction or reduction of turtle and tortoise habitat.

Sedimentation alters aquatic habitats—muddy bottoms are exchanged for sandy bottoms; deep water habitats are

TABLE 1
Population status of freshwater turtles and tortoises of Bangladesh.

English name, scientific name	Status	Distribution
Family Trionychidae		
Indian flapshell turtle, *Lissemys punctata*	common	wide
Narrow-headed softshell turtle, *Chitra indica*	fairly common	Jamuna, Meghna, Sitalakha, and Padma rivers
Indian softshell turtle, *Aspideretes gangeticus*	fairly common	Jamuna, Meghna, Padma, and Ganga rivers
Indian peacock softshell turtle, *Aspideretes hurum*	common	wide
Black softshell turtle, *Aspideretes nigricans*	endemic	Bostami Mazar
Asian giant softshell turtle, *Pelochelys cantorii*	unknown	Meghna River
Family Testudinidae		
Elongated tortoise, *Indotestudo elongata*	few	Chittagong Hill Tracts, Sylhet
Asian brown tortoise, *Manouria emys*	fairly common	Chittagong Hill Tracts
Family Bataguridae		
Indian roofed turtle, *Kachuga tecta*	common	wide
Indian tent turtle, *Kachuga tentoria*	common	Jamuna
Assam roofed turtle, *Kachuga sylhetensis*	occasional	Sylhet
Brown roofed turtle, *Kachuga smithii*	few	Pabma and Jamuna rivers
Red-crowned roofed turtle, *Kachuga kachuga*	occasional	Padma R., Jamuna R., Chittagong Hill Tracts
Three-striped roof turtle, *Kachuga dhongoka*	few	unknown *
River terrapin, *Batagur baska*	few	Sunderbans
Malayan box turtle, *Cuora amboinensis*	occasional	Cox's Bazar
Crowned river turtle, *Hardella thurjii*	fairly common	Pabma River, Mymensingh
Spotted pond turtle, *Geoclemys hamiltonii*	fairly common	wide
Tricarinate hill turtle, *Melanochelys tricarinata*	unknown	Mymensingh, Chittagong
Indian black turtle, *Melanochelys trijuga*	few	wide
Indian eyed turtle, *Morenia petersi*	common	Noakhali, Jamuna River
Burmese eyed turtle, *Morenia ocellata*	few	Chittagong
Asian leaf turtle, *Cyclemys dentata*	few	unknown

*Khan (1982) reported a shell from Dacca.

converted to shallow water habitats. Embankments along rivers raise water levels above normal, which submerges small nesting islands and beaches. Commercial sand mining also destroys nesting sites for sand-nesting species (e.g., *Chitra indica*, *Kachuga tentoria*).

Deforestation by clear-cutting and by "jumming" (shifting cultivation) causes the loss of forest habitats. Moreover, annual fires eliminate the vegetation cover and food of terrestrial tortoises. In February and March local people burn vegetation cover to collect fire wood, which causes the death of the terrestrial tortoises, *Indotestudo elongata* and *Manouria emys*, as well as *Lissemys punctata* buried in aestivation. Grazing cattle also reduce vegetable cover.

The draining of ponds, canals, beels, jheels, haors, and ditches is responsible for the loss of the turtles that inhabit them. Modern systems of cultivation, irrigation, drainage, canalization, and barrages like Farakka, as well as siltation, erosion, and recreation are the main causes of reduction and destruction of aquatic habitats.

The discharge of heated water from river mills raises water temperatures, which may exceed optimum temperature ranges and the tolerance levels of turtles.

Repeated use of nylon fish nets may reduce floating and submerged vegetation, thereby threatening the food supply.

The hurricane and tidal bore of April 1991, resulting in sudden inundation by sea water, caused the death of *L. punctata* and other turtles in coastal zone habitats. In this case, the direct cause of death was kidney and respiratory failure and dehydration from saline water (Sarker, 1991).

Chemical Pollution

Random use of agrochemicals (insecticides, pesticides, herbicides, and rodenticides) may cause infertility, sterility, and the thinning of egg shells. The reproductive failure of adults and mortality of young are caused by the cumulative effects of agrochemicals over long periods through the contamination of food and water and subsequently the body tissues. The discharge of chemical wastes from industries, (e.g., Pakshi and Karnaphully paper mills) have contaminated the aquatic habitats of the Padma and Karnaphully rivers respectively, and turtles are no longer found in the downstream areas near the mills. Agrochemicals and fertilizer wastes from agricultural fields and other toxic chemicals from urban areas threaten nearby aquatic habitats.

Conservation Problems

Several problems affect the conservation and management of turtles and tortoises of Bangladesh; among them are illiteracy, poverty, human population density, and the lack of public awareness of the value of turtles and tortoises. Approximately 80–90% of the population live in rural areas and are devoid of even a primary level of education. Poverty is one of the most significant factors affecting the conservation of wild fauna. The dense population places a heavy demand on land areas; less than one percent (only 0.81%) of the land has been designated as protected reserve for wild fauna and flora.

Scientific information is limited for this group of reptiles. No national inventory has been undertaken, and no management plan has yet been created for the protection of turtles and tortoises. No wetland sanctuary exists in the country. A limited amount of work has been conducted by universities, the Wildlife Society, the Nature Conservation Movement (NACOM), and a few nongovernment organizations (Sarker, 1988, 1992a, 1992b, 1992c, 1993a, 1993b). Weak enforcement has prevented the proper implementation of the current wildlife preservation law.

Recommendations

For the conservation and management of turtles and tortoises of Bangladesh and their habitats, we make the following recommendations on a priority basis:

Public Education

Create public awareness of the value of turtles and tortoises in nature and their role in the ecosystem. Exhibitions, drawings, paintings, video and film shows, essay competitions, and debates for students are essential tools in this effort. In addition, posters and pamphlets, seminars and public speeches, news media, and radio and television could play an important role. Education on turtles and tortoises should be introduced in schools and colleges.

Enforcement

Commercial exploitation of endangered and threatened turtles and tortoises should be stopped through the strict application of existing laws. The export of these reptiles could be controlled through international organizations such as the Convention on International Trade in Endangered Species (CITES) and the Ramsar Convention.

Commercial Farming

A captive breeding programme could be initiated. Training and facilities could be provided to the professional hunters and collectors for the farming and culture of turtles as they are for fish and shrimp.

Research, Monitoring, and Establishment of a Sanctuary

A collaborative research project should be developed with international organizations for the monitoring of endangered and threatened turtles and for collecting scientific data related to their conservation and the restoration of their habitats. A wetland sanctuary should be established in a suitable area, and a management plan should be initiated.

Legislative Proposals

- Prohibit the random use of agrochemicals in turtle habitats. Water and soil contamination must be reduced and maintained below a standard level in aquatic and terrestrial habitats.

- Establish water quality standards for all wetlands.

- Require environmental impact assessments prior to any development project.

- Restrict the draining of wetlands.

- Prohibit the clear cutting and burning of forest habitats and control cultivation shifting (providing natural gas to people living in the area could reduce the burning of vegetation for domestic fuel in tortoise habitats).

- Designate a separate budget allocation for the conservation of turtles and tortoises in the annual national budget plan.

International cooperation in securing both technical expertise and financial support will be essential for the conservation, restoration, and management of tortoises and turtles of Bangladesh.

LITERATURE CITED

Ahsan, M. F. 1997. The Bostami or black softshell turtle, *Aspideretes nigricans*: Problems and proposed conservation measures. *In* J. van Abbema (ed.), Proceedings: Conservation, Restoration, and Management of Tortoises and Turtles—An International Conference, pp. 287–289. July 1993, State University of New York, Purchase. New York Turtle and Tortoise Society, New York.

Akonda, A. W. 1989. Introduction to wetlands in Bangladesh. *In* D. A. Scott (comp.), A Directory of Asian Wetlands, pp. 541–581. IUCN, Gland, Switzerland. i–xiv + 1181 pp. + maps.

Fuglar, C. M. 1984. The commercially exploited chelonia of Bangladesh: Taxonomy, ecology, reproductive biology and anatomy. Fisheries Information Bulletin 2(1):1–52.

Government of Bangladesh. 1981–82 to 1992–93. Export Promotion Bureau of Bangladesh.

Husain, K. Z. 1979. Wildlife wealth of Bangladesh and its preservation—Tortoise (in Bengali). Bangla Academy Biggan Patrika 5(3):23–31.

Hossain, L. 1989. Ecology of freshwater turtles of Bangladesh. M.S. thesis, University of Dhaka, Dhaka.

Khan, M. A. R. 1982. Chelonians of Bangladesh and their conservation. J. Bombay Nat. Hist. Soc. 79:110–116.

Moll, E. O. 1986. Survey of freshwater turtles of India. Part I: The genus *Kachuga*. J. Bombay Nat. Hist. Soc. 83:538–552.

Sarker, S. U. 1988. Management of wildlife of the Sundarbans. J. NOAMI 5(1-2):41–47.

Sarker, S. U. 1991. Cyclone, 1991. *In* Wildlife: An Environmental and Perceptional Study, pp. 9, 47–49. BCAS, Dhaka.

Sarker, S. U. 1992a. Ecology of wildlife. FAO/UNDP, Document No. 51, IFCU, Chittagong.

Sarker, S. U. 1992b. Environmental impact assessment study in the greater Dhaka City Flood Protection Plan. FAP. BA. Aqua. Consultant, JAICA, Japan.

Sarker, S. U. 1992c. Status and conservation problems of herpetological fauna of Bangladesh (abstract). Zoos' Print 7(11):2. Bhubaneswar, India.

Sarker, S. U. 1993a. Conservation of faunal resources of Hail Haor by involvement of local community. A.U.S.A.I.D.-funded consortium of WWF, The Nature Conservancy, and World Resources Institute, Washington, D.C.

Sarker, S. U. 1993b. Faunal diversity and their conservation in freshwater wetlands of Bangladesh. *In* Proc. Freshwater Wetlands in Bangladesh: Issues and Approaches for Management, pp. 105–122. BCAS, Dhaka.

Sarker, S. U. and L. Hossain. 1988. Ecological observation of freshwater turtles of Bangladesh (abstract). *In* 13th BAAS Annual Conf., May 1988, p. 19. Dhaka.

Sarker, S. U. and N. J. Sarker 1988. Wildlife of Bangladesh: A Systematic List. Rico Printers, Dhaka. i–ix + 70 pp.

Scott, D. A. and C. M. Poole. 1989. A Status Overview of Asian Wetlands. IWRB, Malaysia.

Shafi, M. and M. M. A. Quddus. 1976. Fish wealth of Bangladesh tortoises and marine turtles (in Bengali). Bangla Academy Biggan Patrika 3(2):14–36.

Smith, M. A. 1931. Fauna of British India. Reptilia and Amphibia. Vol. 1. Taylor Francis, London.

Whitaker, R. 1982. *Batagur baska*, alive and well in the Sundarbans? Hamadryad 7(3):7.

Conservation Problems of Tropical Asia's Most-Threatened Turtles

INDRANEIL DAS

Department of Biology, Universiti Brunei Darussalam, Gadong, Bandar Seri Begawan 2028, Brunei Darussalam
Current address: Centre for Herpetology, Madras Crocodile Bank Trust, Mamallapuram, Post Bag 4, Tamil Nadu 603 104, India

ABSTRACT: The ten most-threatened freshwater turtle and tortoise species of the Oriental region include *Aspideretes nigricans, Batagur baska, Chitra chitra, Geochelone platynota, Heosemys depressa, Heosemys leytensis, Kachuga kachuga, Kachuga sylhetensis, Manouria emys*, and *Manouria impressa*. The threatened status of these species (except for the recently described *Chitra chitra*) has been generally recognised, although the contributory factors are still poorly understood because data on the biology of most Oriental species is lacking. In general, large riverine species appear affected by overexploitation, although pollution of habitats and river development projects have also had significant effects on populations. On the other hand, many of the small- to medium-sized forest-dwelling turtles and tortoises appear to be declining from destruction and modifications of their forest habitats and from collection for food and the pet trade. Recommended conservation actions include the establishment of sanctuaries in areas that support viable turtle populations, public education about threatened turtle species at the regional level, and increased efforts to collect data on the biology of these species.

The Oriental region, including the Indian Subcontinent, the Indo-Malayan region, and the Sunda Islands, is one of the most species-rich for turtles on earth. Sixty-four species of freshwater turtles and land tortoises have been recorded from the region, with up to 17 species of freshwater turtles occurring in a single area, the lower reaches of the Ganges and adjacent regions (Iverson, 1992).

For the reptile fauna in general, the Indian Subcontintent shows both high species diversity and high levels of endemicity, indicating that the area is a centre of origin and diversification of many groups of reptiles; 39 genera and 404 species are endemic. After correcting for land area, more Indo-Malayan elements are present in the fauna of the Indian Subcontinent than vice versa. Turtle genera that are unique to the Indian Subcontinent include *Aspideretes, Geoclemys*, and *Hardella*, although a few genera of clearly Indian affinities extend their ranges with peripheral distributions, including *Lissemys, Kachuga*, and *Melanochelys*. More species of these three genera are found within the Indian Subcontinent (or in an adjacent region, e.g., *Lissemys scutata* and *Kachuga trivittata*) than outside the region. The endemic genera of the Indo-Malayan region include *Callagur, Heosemys, Hieremys, Notochelys*, and *Siebenrockiella*. Several species in the region are point-endemics, known from only one or a few sites. These include *Mauremys annamensis, Aspideretes nigricans, Chitra chitra*, and *Heosemys leytensis*. In most cases it is not known how much of the extant distribution has been influenced by human-induced changes of the environment. Thus, the Oriental region supports a highly distinctive turtle fauna, both at the generic and specific levels. A few genera are shared with the Eastern Palearctic, such as *Cuora* and *Pyxidea*.

In this paper, I have attempted to update the information on the conservation status of ten of Asia's most threatened non-marine turtle species and, using these and other threatened species as examples, have tried to determine what factors continue to impede conservation action.

The Most-Threatened Species

The IUCN/SSC Tortoise and Freshwater Turtle Specialist Group Action Plan (1991) lists 39 Oriental species as belonging to one of three threatened categories (Action Plan Ratings, or APR), based on information available at that time. This paper tries to update that list, taking into account new information available either through recent fieldwork undertaken personally, literature search, or unpublished information obtained from colleagues. The second half of the paper is devoted to suggestions I thought appropriate for threatened turtles of tropical Asia in general. The ten most-threatened species of freshwater turtle and land tortoise from the Oriental region include:

Black softshell turtle, *Aspideretes nigricans*. The sacred black softshell turtle is restricted to a single pond attached to a Mohammedan shrine near Chittagong, eastern Bangladesh. While in no immediate danger, this population needs to be monitored as disease could wipe out the entire population. All large individuals are infected with fungus on the head and limbs.

River terrapin, *Batagur baska*. The Oriental species that has rightly received most attention from conservation biologists is the river terrapin. Throughout its range, from India eastward to Sumatra, peninsular Malaysia, and Cambodia, river terrapin populations have shown great declines and no longer can support sustained exploitation. The biology and conservation of this turtle has been reviewed by Moll (1990).

Kanburi narrow-headed softshell turtle, *Chitra chitra*. The turtle is restricted to the Mae Klong basin of Thailand and was recognised only recently by Nutaphand (1990) as specifically distinct from populations in the Indian Subcontinent although more complete taxonomic papers on these softshell turtles are under preparation by Robert Webb. Not more than 16 individual animals may exist, and thus this large and attractive turtle may merit the status of one of the world's most endangered animal species.

Burmese star tortoise, *Geochelone platynota*. The rarity of this species was commented upon even by Edward Blyth who described it in the last century, writing that the Burmese were fond of eating the tortoise. This species is restricted to central Myanmar, although most members of its genus are distributed in the Afro-Madagascan region. Only its sister species, *G. elegans*, occurrs in the Oriental region. Remaining populations are reportedly intensively hunted with dogs, especially after the dry season fires in February and at the beginning of the rains (May–June) in the Kywenah-pha region, near Mandalay, Myanmar (van Dijk, 1993). Kuchling (pers. comm., 1993) found shells of the species in medicine shops in Yunnan in southern China.

Arakan forest turtle, *Heosemys depressa*. Until recently this turtle was known only from a few specimens collected in the last century from the Arakan hills near Sittwe (formerly Akyab), in Myanmar, the type locality of the species. Additional individuals have recently been forthcoming and a redescription is in Iverson and McCord (1997).

Philippine pond turtle, *Heosemys leytensis*. The Philippine pond turtle is known from just four specimens, three from near Cabalian, Leyte Island (Buskirk, 1989), and one from Taytay, Palawan Island (Timmerman and Auth, 1988), both in the Philippines. Unfortunately, two museum specimens were lost during World War II, and recent expeditions to southern Leyte have failed to find the species. None of the major museums of the Philippines has examples of this species.

Red-crowned roofed turtle, *Kachuga kachuga*. Fairly widespread in the River Ganga and its tributaries of northern India, this species is suspected to have suffered from both exploitation and from river pollution. This species is still exploited for food, but the status of wild populations outside of river sanctuaries is unknown.

Assam roofed turtle, *Kachuga sylhetensis*. Restricted to the hill streams of northeastern India and Bangladesh. The recent records of the species from protected areas do not assure its long-term survival since it is killed inside these reserves for food (Bhupathy et al., 1992). The clearing of primary forests and the resultant drying up of streams are factors that may further threaten the species.

Asian brown tortoise, *Manouria emys*. Widespread in southeast Asia, the two subspecies of this Asian giant tortoise have been recorded from northeastern India, Bangladesh, Myanmar, Thailand, southern China, Vietnam, Malaysia, and Indonesia (Kalimantan and Sumatra). Remains of the tortoise from the Shang ruins at Anyang, China (Wu, 1943) indicate it has been exploited by humans for a long time. The species has become rare in Thailand, where hunters claim that two or more weeks of searching may be needed to find one (Thirakhupt and van Dijk, 1993). In Bangladesh and India, this species is apparently restricted to forest reserves, but exploitation of the species has been reported from several sites. In the Chittagong Hill Tracts of Bangladesh, one to three animals were found in a year by a single Chakma tribesman in the late 1950s (Das, 1988). The shell and flesh of the species are utilised by these tribal peoples, and the tortoise commands a high price, especially during the *biju* festival (Khan, 1982). The shells are used in making cradles or doorsteps for thatched houses and as charms; the gall bladder is eaten to cure headache and stomach ache (Das, 1991).

Impressed tortoise, *Manouria impressa*. Less widespread than its sister species *M. emys*, the impressed tortoise has been recorded from eastern Myanmar, Thailand, peninsular Malaysia, Vietnam, Laos, Cambodia, and southern China. Isolated and often very old records exist for most of the aforementioned countries. To date we know of significant populations surviving only in a few protected areas in northern Thailand, which suffer extensively from forest fires. However, much of southeast Asia remains to be surveyed. In general, the species is threatened by collection for food and the pet trade, and it suffers from regular forest fires (Thirakhupt and van Dijk, 1993).

Problem Areas in Systematic Work

Pressing systematic problems that affect conservation decisions are:

- **The systematics of the *Geochelone elegans* group from the Indian Subcontinent.** Members of this complex show three highly disjunct ranges, each population morphologically distinct. In eastern Pakistan and adjacent northwestern India occurs a population whose adults are large and dull coloured. Animals from southeastern India are small but brightly coloured (Frazier, 1987; Das, 1991). The Sri Lankan adults are large and brightly coloured. Proponents of the Evolutionary Species Concept would claim species status for these forms (see Frost and Millis, 1990; Frost et al., 1992).
- **The status of *Cyclemys tcheponensis*.** While *C. tcheponensis* has been considered a variety of the highly variable and widespread *C. dentata* by some workers, the controversy has not been resolved.

- **The status of the various subspecies of *Melanochelys trijuga* in the Indian Subcontinent and southeast Asia.** The two eastern subspecies *M. t. wiroti* (see Obst, 1983, for comments on nomenclature) and *M. t. edeniana* appear inseparable in characteristics considered diagnostic.
- **The status of *Aspideretes nigricans*.** Juveniles and young adults are inseparable externally, including colouration, from *A. hurum*. New material is now available at Chittagong University and should permit detailed examination and reevaluation of the taxon.
- **The taxonomy of the turtles assigned to the genus *Pelochelys*.** Almost throughout its range, the turtle is dull coloured, but specimens from southern New Guinea are strikingly patterned (Whitaker et al., 1982). Webb (1995) showed that two species exist in New Guinea alone.
- **The taxonomy of the *Lissemys punctata* group in the Indian Subcontinent.** The taxonomy of this widespread species is still in flux.

Correlates of Threatened Status

Almost all large riverine species in the region appear affected by overexploitation for meat and eggs. Examples of species most affected by trade include *Batagur baska*, *Callagur borneoensis*, *Hardella thurjii*, *Kachuga kachuga*, *Chitra chitra*, and *C. indica*. Reliable population size data do not exist for either present or historic populations of any species except *B. baska* (summarised in Moll, 1990). Recent declines in trade levels in the Indian Subcontinent may be a reflection of the increasing rarity of animals in the wild, rather than tighter controls, although the enforcing authorities in India and Malaysia must be congratulated for their efforts to crack down on the mostly illegal trade in turtles. The effects of habitat modification and destruction are largely unknown. Significant river development projects have taken place in the region in recent years, leading to greater river traffic, damming of many small and large rivers, and mining of river sand. The effects these activities have had upon local turtle populations are largely unknown but are likely to be negative, although lacustrine turtles may benefit (at least over the short term) when rivers are converted into standing bodies of water.

Many upland forest species are threatened as logging continues under pressure from the timber industry in most southeast Asian countries. The few nations in the region that do not export timber (Bangladesh, Brunei, India, and Thailand) have already greatly depleted their primary rainforests (except for Brunei, which does not permit logging). Species linked to primary forests in the region are primarily tortoises or small- to medium-sized freshwater turtles, several of which have always been considered rare since their discovery (e.g., *Geochelone platynota*). In addition to local exploitation, suitable habitat for *G. platynota* and *H. leytensis* has become extremely limited because of deforestation in Myanmar and the Philippines, respectively.

Some species may be threatened by a host of factors: *Batagur baska* is threatened by exploitation for flesh and eggs and by river development projects, sand mining, and destruction of its mangrove habitats. This large, herbivorous estuarine turtle breeds on sandbanks and feeds on the leaves of the mangrove *Sonneratia* (Moll, 1990). The establishment of sanctuaries in areas supporting any remaining viable populations of each of the threatened species would be a recommended measure.

Suitable habitats may no longer exist in many localities where particular species were formerly recorded. Iverson's (1992) turtle distribution mapping project is the most detailed undertaken on a global scale. Efforts should be increased to collect data on the distribution of species listed in the IUCN/SSC/TFTSG Action Plan (1991) and in this paper (Table 1). These data can be collected as part of larger environmental projects so that sites with viable populations are protected along with the ecosystem.

Because significant numbers of turtles are exploited by the food and pet trades (see Das, 1990, for an account of the export of freshwater turtles from Bangladesh), trade should be closely monitored, and at least the commercial trade in threatened species should be controlled if not stopped.

Conservation Measures: Are They Working?

A conservation action plan must be drawn up and executed for each species. The creation of reserves does not automatically protect species. For example, in Bangladesh as well as the northeastern region of India, park guards and locals regularly consume turtles that are encountered within the reserves, and inventories of the turtle fauna have been made by verifying shells of turtles eaten at such sites (Bhupathy et al., 1992; Das, 1988, 1989, 1990a, 1990b). The situation is similar in northern Borneo and many other southeast and south Asian countries, where turtles, along with fish, are not considered "wildlife" and are therefore fair game, even within protected areas. For such long-lived, generally slow-maturing animals that occur in low densities in rainforest areas, the removal of even a small number of individuals may affect viability of local populations. In January 1992 at Batu Apoi, an otherwise undisturbed lowland dipterocarp forest on northwestern Borneo, in the Sultanate of Brunei Darussalam, a long-term field study programme was initiated on the community ecology of the local amphibian and reptile fauna. A year and a half later, only three individuals of three turtle species have been recorded. These include a single live animal (*Heosemys spinosa*) and two (*Notochelys platynota* and *Dogania subplana*) that were verified from photos taken by colleagues earlier. Hunting by the Iban tribesmen may be the reason for this low density.

Freshwater turtles and tortoises of the Oriental region (including the Indian and Indo-Malayan Subrealms): Their Action Plan Rating (APR), habitat, distribution, and presumed primary threats to wild populations. APR = Action Plan Rating from *Tortoises and Freshwater Turtles: An Action Plan for Their Conservation* (IUCN/SSC/TFTSG, 1991). Point-endemic = taxon known from three or less localities, or from a single small island. Restricted = taxon known from more than three localities but limited to two countries.

Species	APR	Habitat	Type of Distribution	Primary Threat
Family Bataguridae				
Batagur baska	1	Estuaries	Widespread	Exploitation, habitat loss
Callagur borneoensis	1	Estuaries	Widespread	Exploitation, habitat loss
Cuora galbinfrons	2	?	Restricted	?
Cuora pani	2	?	?	?
Cuora mccordi	2	?	?	?
Cuora yunnanensis	2	?	Restricted	?
Cyclemys dentata	3[a]	Hill streams	Widespread	Habitat loss
Geoclemys hamiltonii	3	Rivers, ponds	Widespread	Exploitation, habitat loss
Geoemyda silvatica	2	Forest floor	Restricted	Habitat loss
Geoemyda spengleri	3	Forest floor	Widespread	Habitat loss
Hardella thurjii	3	Rivers, ponds	Widespread	Exploitation, habitat destruction
Heosemys depressa	2	Forest floor	Point-endemic	Exploitation, habitat loss
Heosemys leytensis	2	?	Point-endemic	?
Heosemys spinosa	1	Forest floor	Widespread	Exploitation, habitat loss
Kachuga dhongoka	3[a]	Rivers	Widespread	Exploitation, habitat destruction
Kachuga kachuga	1	Rivers	Restricted	Exploitation, habitat destruction
Kachuga sylhetensis	1	Hill streams	Restricted	Habitat loss
Kachuga trivittata	1	Rivers, estuaries	Restricted	Exploitation, habitat loss
Malayemys subrijuga	3[a]	Ponds, rivers, swamps	Widespread	Exploitation
Mauremys annamensis	2	Lowland marshes, ponds	Point-endemic	?
Melanochelys tricarinata	3	Forest floor	Restricted	Habitat loss
Morenia occelata	3	Marshes, swamps	Restricted	Exploitation
Notochelys platynota	3[a]	Hill streams	Widespread	?
Ocadia philippeni	2	?	Point-endemic	?

TABLE 1 (continued)

Species	APR	Habitat	Type of Distribution	Primary Threat
Family Bataguridae (continued)				
Orlitia borneensis	3	Rivers, ponds	Widespread	?
Pyxidea mouhotii	3	Forest floor	Restricted	Habitat loss
Sacalia pseudocellata	2	?	Point-endemic	?
Family Platysternidae				
Platysternon megacephalum	3	Hill streams	Widespread	Habitat loss
Family Testudinidae				
Geochelone platynota	2	Forest floor	Restricted	Exploitation, habitat loss
Indotestudo elongata	1	Forest floor	Widespread	Exploitation, habitat loss
Indotestudo forstenii[b]	2	Forest floor	Restricted	Habitat loss
Manouria emys	3	Forest floor	Widespread	Habitat loss
Manouria impressa	1	Forest floor	Widespread	Habitat loss
Family Trionychidae				
Amyda cartilaginea	3[a]	Rivers, ponds	Widespread	Exploitation
Aspideretes nigricans[c]	2	Ponds	Point-endemic	?
Chitra chitra[d]	1	Rivers	Point-endemic	Exploitation, habitat destruction
Chitra indica	3	Rivers	Widespread	Exploitation, habitat destruction
Dogania subplana	3	Hill streams	Widespread	?
Nilssonia formosa	3	Rivers	Restricted	?
Pelochelys cantorii[e]	3	Rivers, estuaries	Widespread	Exploitation, habitat destruction

[a]Taxon may be more common than generally assumed. [b]Restricted to the Western Ghats, southwestern India. The populations on some of the islands in eastern Indonesia have been presumably introduced through human agencies. [c]Taxon restricted to a single pond attached to a religious shrine near Chittagong, Bangladesh. Threats to the population of the species are unknown. [d]Recently described by Nutphand (1990) and therefore not listed in the IUCN/SSC/TFTSG Action Plan. The APR of the taxon has been suggested by van Dijk and Thirakhupt (in press). [e]Now thought to be a species complex, members of which range from the west coast of India eastwards to the Philippines. Two species occur on New Guinea alone (Webb, 1995).

These settlers from adjacent Sarawak State of eastern Malaysia are efficient hunters, although they use traditional methods such as spears, dogs, and traps. A decree in 1962 banned firearms in Brunei. The low numbers of individual animals within the forest are contrasted by the high species diversity among the herpetofauna at the site (Das, 1996).

Thus, the existence of what appears to be pristine habitat within the known distribution of a species, even from a site where a species has been once recorded, does not necessarily assure its present existence in the area, or the continued persistence of a viable population in the future. To summarise, the populations of many species may be more threatened than is generally assumed. While reserve managers should be flexible in continuing to allow indigenous people to exercise traditional rights over land that has been theirs and to harvest its fruits for sustenance, I believe a totally inviolable core area should be created and maintained where non-subsistence hunting is not permitted. Few true subsistence hunters remain, even on Borneo, where technology such as outboard-powered longboats and chain saws have helped transform aboriginal communities into money- and market-based societies. More information on the forest resource exploitation patterns of human communities is therefore required before policies for land use by the local people are drawn up and implemented.

Another way in which species are lost within reserves is through fire management regimes. Much of the current theory and practice of forest management for wildlife conservation in the tropics centres around increasing the biomass of large ungulates such as deer and antelope in India. This is accomplished by decreasing cover (to enhance visibility), maintaining grassland habitats, and promoting growth of new grass and herbs. The effects of forest fires on non-target groups, such as amphibians, reptiles, and ground-dwelling birds and mammals, not to mention invertebrates and even herbaceous plant species, are largely unknown.

Thus, few conservation projects in tropical Asia have demonstrably benefitted turtles. Even for projects specifically directed towards turtles, because of lacking funds and political support, only a handful have proceeded beyond the survey stage. Pleas at the end of survey reports for improved legislation and controls on exploitation have had a less than desirable effect. Surveys do tend to generate publicity, which in turn generally increases public awareness, but much more intensive educational campaigns at the local level need to be conducted, especially in areas where threatened species occur.

In conclusion, unless efforts to publicise the fate of tropical Asia's threatened turtles are increased substantially through public education, especially at the regional level, little hope remains of saving this fauna.

ACKNOWLEDGEMENTS

For inviting me to this conference, I would like to thank the Conference organizers, in particular Michael Klemens of the American Museum of Natural History and Kristin Berry of the Bureau of Land Management. Various organisations supported my work on the turtles of Asia over the past several years, including the British Council, World Wide Fund for Nature, World Conservation Union, Madras Crocodile Bank Trust, Fauna and Flora Preservation Society, and Universiti Brunei Darussalam. Numerous colleagues provided data or aided in field work in many countries; a complete list is impossible but would include Farid Ahsan, Joseph Charles, Binod Choudhury, Peter Paul van Dijk, David Edwards, Richard Gemel, Bonani Kakkar, Gerald Kuchling, Edward Moll, Samhan bin Nyawa, Wolfgang Prieser, Peter Pritchard, Rogelio Sison, Kumthorn Thirakhupt, Robert Webb, and Romulus Whitaker.

LITERATURE CITED AND SELECTED BIBLIOGRAPHY

Bhupathy, S., B. C. Choudhury, and E. O. Moll. 1992. Conservation and management of freshwater turtles and land tortoises of India. Technical Report, May 1991–June 1992. Report submitted to the Wildlife Institute of India. Mimeo. 25 pp.

Bibby, C. J., N. J. Collar, M. J. Crosby, M. F. Heath, C. Imboden, T. H. Johnson, A. J. Long, A. J. Stattersfield, and S. J. Thirgood. 1992. Putting Biodiversity on the Map. International Council for Bird Preservation, Cambridge.

Buskirk, J. R. 1989. A third specimen and neotype of *Heosemys leytensis* (Chelonia: Emydidae). Copeia 1989: 224–227.

Das, I. 1988. A survey of land tortoises and freshwater turtles in north-eastern India. Report to the IUCN/SSC Tortoise and Freshwater Turtle Specialist Group, Gland. 25 pp + 5 maps + 8 pl.

Das, I. 1989. Turtle status scenario in Bangladesh. Turtles and Tortoises (Newsletter IUCN/SSC Tortoise and Freshwater Turtle Specialist Group) 4:12–16.

Das, I. 1990. The trade in freshwater turtles from Bangladesh. Oryx 24:163–166.

Das, I. 1990a. Notes on the land tortoises of Bangladesh. J. Bombay Nat. Hist. Soc. 87:155–156.

Das, I. 1990b. Noteworthy distributional records of chelonians from north-eastern India. J. Bombay Nat. Hist. Soc. 87:91–97.

Das, I. 1991. Colour Guide to the Turtles and Tortoises of the Indian Subcontinent. R & A Publishing Ltd., Portishead, UK. 133 pp.

Das, I. 1996. Spatio-temporal resource utilization by a Bornean rainforest herpetofauna. *In* Proceedings of the International Conference on Tropical Rainforest Research: Current Issues. Kluwer Academic Publishers, Dordrecht.

Das, I. 1996. Biogeography of the Reptiles of South Asia. Kreiger Publishing Co., Malabar, Florida. 86 pp. + 16 pl.

van Dijk, P. P. 1993. Myanmar turtles: Report on a preliminary survey of the Testudines of the Ayeyarwady Basin, Union of Myanmar, January 1993. Report submitted to the IUCN/SSC Turtle Recovery Program, American Museum of Natural History, New York. 48 pp.

van Dijk, P. P. and K. Thirakhupt. In press. *Chitra chitra. In* P. C. H. Pritchard and A. G. J. Rhodin (eds.), The Conservation Biology of

Freshwater Turtles. Chelonian Research Monogr., Chelonian Research Foundation, Lunenburg, Massachusetts.

Frazier, J. 1987. Biology and conservation of Indian turtles and tortoises. Interim report to the American Institute for Indian Studies. Mimeo. 64 pp.

Frost, D. R. and D. M. Hillis. 1990. Species in concept and practice: Herpetological applications. Herpetologica 46:87–104.

Frost, D. R., A. G. Kluge, and D. M. Hillis. 1992. Species in contemporary herpetology: Comments on phylogenetic inference and taxonomy. Herpetol. Rev. 23:46–54.

Iverson, J. B. 1992. Species richness maps of the freshwater and terrestrial turtles of the world. Smithsonian Herpetol. Inf. Serv. 88:1–18.

Iverson, J. B. 1992a. A Revised Checklist with Distribution Maps of the Turtles of the World. Privately printed, Richmond, Indiana. 363 pp.

Iverson, J. B. and W. P. McCord. 1997. A redescription of the Arakan forest turtle *Geoemyda depressa* Anderson 1875 (Testudines Bataguridae). Chelon. Conserv. Biol. 2(3):384–389

IUCN/SSC Tortoise and Freshwater Turtle Specialist Group. 1991. Tortoises and freshwater turtles: An action plan for their conservation, 2d ed. (D. Stubbs, comp.). IUCN/SSC Tortoise and Freshwater Turtle Specialist Group, Gland, Switzerland. i–iv + 47 pp.

Khan, M. A. R. 1982. Chelonians of Bangladesh and their conservation. J. Bombay Nat. Hist. Soc. 79:110–116.

Moll, E. O. 1990. Final report: WWF 3901/Asia—Status and management of the river terrapin (*Batagur baska*) in tropical Asia. Submitted to the WWF and IUCN. Mimeo. 37 pp. + 8 figs.

Nutaphand, W. 1990. Softshell turtles. Thai Zool. Mag. 5:93–114. (In Thai.)

Obst, F. J. 1983. Beitrag zur kenntnis der Landschildkröten-gattung *Manouria* Gray, 1852. Zool. Abh. Mus. Tierk. Dresden 38: 247–256.

Taylor, E. H. 1920. Philippine turtles. Philippine J. Sci. 16: 130–133.

Thirakhupt, K. and P. P. van Dijk. 1993. The turtles of western Thailand: Species diversity, population studies and conservation implications. A report to the Research Affairs Division of Chulalongkorn University for the Toray Science Foundation.

Timmerman, W. W. and D. L. Auth. 1988. *Heosemys leytensis* (Leyte pond turtle). Herpetol. Rev. 19:21.

Webb, R. G. 1995. Redescription and neotype designation of *Pelochelys bibroni* from southern New Guinea (Testudines: Trionychidae). Chelon. Conserv. Biol. 1(4):301–310.

Wu, H. W. 1943. Notes on the plastron of *Testudo emys* from the ruins of Shang Dynasty of Anyang. Sinensia, Nanking 14: 107–109.

Conservation and Management of Freshwater Turtles and Land Tortoises in India

— EXECUTIVE SUMMARY OF PUBLISHED REPORT* —

B. C. Choudhury,[1] S. Bhupathy,[1] and Edward O. Moll[2]

[1]*Wildlife Institute of India, Chandrabani, P.O. Box 18, Dehra Dun - 248 001, India*
[2]*Department of Zoology, Eastern Illinois University, Charleston, IL 61920-3099, USA*

A three-year study by the Wildlife Institute of India and the U.S. Fish and Wildlife Service collaborative on Conservation and Management of Freshwater Turtles and Land Tortoises in India was launched in May 1991. Major objectives of the project were (1) to determine the current status of tortoises, (2) to identify viable turtle populations and suitable habitats to establish Protected Areas, (3) to set up captive breeding units for endangered chelonians for the purpose of reintroduction, and (4) to provide scientific information and training to biologists and managers on turtle conservation and biology.

Data on the current status, exploitation, and captive breeding of turtles were collected by questionnaire and field surveys. A museum survey was conducted before initiating field surveys to determine the present distribution of little-known species. Sixty markets were surveyed covering most parts of the country to determine the exploitation pressure on turtles (see Choudhury and Bhupathy, 1993). Softshell turtles, namely *Lissemys punctata*, *Aspideretes gangeticus*, and *A. hurum*, are being exploited but in low quantity. An inventory of the captive stocks of turtles in Indian zoos was prepared, based on a questionnaire survey. Feedback was received from 35 zoos. Commonly exhibited species in zoos were *Lissemys punctata* and *Geochelone elegans*.

Sixty-two geographic localities (45 Protected Areas), covering all but two biogeographic zones, were surveyed during the present study, and information on the status of turtles was collected. Significant range extensions were recorded for several endangered species such as *Aspideretes hurum*, *Chitra indica*, *Cyclemys dentata*, *Melanochelys tricarinata*, *Geoemyda silvatica*, and *Indotestudo forstenii*. Detailed analyses were done on the status of chelonians at both biogeographic and state levels, and action plans are proposed. Also, a new status listing is suggested for turtles and tortoises to incorporate in the Indian Wildlife Protection Act (1972). A workshop on "Freshwater Turtle and Land Tortoise Conservation and Management" was conducted at Gwalior and National Chambal Sanctuary, Madhya Pradesh (10–13 March 1993) to disseminate information collected during the present study.

* Choudhury, B. C., S. Bhupathy, and E. O. Moll. 1994. Conservation and management of freshwater turtles and land tortoises of India. Final report: Turtle and Tortoise Conservation Project, a joint Indo-U.S. collaborative project of the Wildlife Institute of India and the U.S. Fish and Wildlife Service. Wildlife Inst. of India, Dehra Dun, India. 108 pp.

Choudhury, B. C. and S. Bhupathy. 1993. Turtle Trade in India: A Study of Tortoises and Freshwater Turtles. WWF-India (prepared by TRAFFIC-India), New Delhi.

Status of the Tortoises and Freshwater Turtles of Colombia

OLGA VICTORIA CASTAÑO-MORA

Instituto de Ciencias Naturales, Universidad Nacional de Colombia, Apartado 7495, Santafé de Bogotá, Colombia

ABSTRACT: This paper examines the 25 species of Colombian turtles (excluding marine species), their distribution, our knowledge of their natural history, their commercial exploitation, as well as some of their conservation-related problems. Updated information is used to propose changes in the legal conservation status of several species.

Colombia, with an area of 1,141,748 km², is the most biogeographically diverse country in South America and contains 25 species of tortoises and freshwater turtles, two of which have two recognized subspecies. The *IUCN Red Data Book* (IUCN, 1982) classification of Colombian turtles includes one endangered species (E), two vulnerable species (V), one rare species (R), two of indeterminate status (I), and four species that are insufficiently known (K), for a total of ten species of conservation concern.

However, the *Red Data Book* classifications were based largely on incomplete information, and the information presented here, which has been acquired mostly through fieldwork, indicates that the condition of Colombian turtles is much more serious (Table 1). It is clear that a greater exchange of information is needed, especially with biologists from neighboring countries that share some of our turtle species, to reclassify the conservation status of these species, to diagnose the common causes of their problems, and to arrive at joint solutions. This paper also reviews the status of our endemic turtles and targets the factors that threaten them. For each tortoise and freshwater turtle in Colombia a summary is presented that includes distribution and current status, factors that affect the species, and its proposed revised listing.

The illegal turtle trade has long been a conservation problem for Colombian turtles. Also, in recent years some turtle species, that due to their small adult size had not traditionally been hunted, are now being consumed because of the extreme poverty and exploding human populations of native and rural communities. Consumption of turtles frequently differs between indigenous peoples and more recent colonists of varied descents ("settlers"). Furthermore, the habitat of a significant number of our species is being transformed at an uncontrolled and accelerating rate. Thus, the status of many species may be expected to change soon if we do not take steps to protect them.

The current status of our endemic turtles is as follows:

Chelus fimbriatus

Inhabits the Orinoco and Amazonian drainages. While sometimes consumed by indigenous peoples, it is not always consumed by settlers because of its strange appearance. Although individuals are illegally exported for the pet trade, its wide distribution and cryptic habits have served to protect the species. Status: "Acceptable."

Chelydra serpentina acutirostris

Inhabits the Pacific coast, Departments of Quindío and Valle, and the Río Sinú drainage. It is consumed primarily by the natives of the Chocó and to a lesser extent by settlers. This species' ability to adapt well to habitat alteration and to survive in small tributaries with substantially contaminated waters is a survival advantage. Populations in the coffee regions (Quindío and Valle) are now under pressure from hunting because of economic problems there. Despite these factors, with its wide distribution and adaptability to habitat alteration, it does not yet appear to be in danger. Status: "Acceptable."

Geochelone carbonaria

Inhabits the Atlantic coast and the Magdalena and Orinoco lowlands. It is also abundant on Providencia Island. It is traditionally consumed by indigenous peoples and is also captured by settlers to keep as pets, to consume, or to trade, especially across the Venezuelan border. Populations are diminished and its status is "Endangered."

Geochelone denticulata

Inhabits the Orinoco and Amazonian drainages. It is highly prized by both indigenous people and settlers. It apparently has been extirpated in some areas where it had been previously reported, such as areas adjacent to the Sierra de la Macarena and in gallery forests in the eastern plains. Its actual status is not known, but is probably not good. Status: "Indeterminate."

TABLE 1

Current status of the tortoises and freshwater turtles of Colombia. Categories from the *IUCN Red Data Book* (IUCN, 1982): E = Endangered, V = Vulnerable, R = Rare, I = Insufficiently Known, K = Indeterminate. Proposed = proposals for Colombia based on the present study.

Scientific name	Distribution	IUCN	Proposed
Chelus fimbriatus	Amazonian drainage, Orinoco drainage	—	—
Chelydra serpentina acutirostris	Pacific lowlands, Quindío, Sinú drainage, Valle del Cauca	—	—
Geochelone carbonaria	Caribbean lowlands, Magdalena drainage, Orinoco drainage, Providencia Island	K	E
G. denticulata	Amazonian drainage	—	I
Kinosternon dunni	Chocó	R	R
K. leucostomum postinguinale	Caribbean lowlands, Magdalena drainage, Pacific lowlands	—	—
K. scorpioides albogulare	San Andrés Island	—	K
K. s. scorpioides	Caribbean lowlands, Amazonian drainage, Orinoco drainage	I	—
Phrynops dahli	Caribbean lowlands	—	V
P. geoffroanus	Amazonian drainage, Orinoco drainage	—	—
P. gibbus	Amazonian drainage, Orinoco drainage	—	K
P. raniceps	Amazonian drainage	K	K
P. rufipes	Amazonian drainage	—	—
Platemys platycephala	Amazonian drainage	—	K
Peltocephalus dumerilianus	Amazonian drainage, Orinoco drainage	K	V[a]
Podocnemis erythrocephala	Orinoco drainage	E	E[a]
P. expansa	Amazonian drainage, Orinoco drainage	I	E
P. lewyana	Magdalena drainage, Sinú drainage	K	K
P. sextuberculata	Amazonian drainage	V	V[a]
P. unifilis	Amazonian drainage, Orinoco drainage	—	K
P. vogli	Orinoco drainage	—	—
Rhinoclemmys annulata	Pacific lowlands	—	R
R. diademata	Maracaibo basin	—	—
R. melanosterna	Caribbean lowlands, Magdalena drainage, Pacific lowlands	—	—
R. nasuta	Pacific lowlands	—	—
Trachemys scripta callirostris	Caribbean lowlands, Magdalena drainage	V	V
T. s. venusta[b]	Chocó	—	V

[a] E and V: Threatened principally in the Orinoco populations (see text). [b] May be a distinct subspecies closely related to *venusta*.

Kinosternon dunni

It is confined to the central Chocó region. It is a Colombian endemic and is apparently quite scarce. In a 1990 field study we encountered 32 *K. leucostomum*, but only four *K. dunni*. It inhabits an area of extreme human poverty and although it is not actively hunted, people capture it opportunistically to eat or for pets. Very little is known about this species and its status should continue as "Rare."

Kinosternon leucostomum postinguinale

Inhabits the Pacific and Atlantic coasts and the Magdalena drainage. Its wide distribution, ability to survive in small bodies of water, and small size have traditionally helped to protect this species, although natives consume it. It is considered a delicacy in most of the Atlantic coast area. The turtle's status is "Acceptable."

Kinosternon scorpioides albogulare

Inhabits the island of San Andrés. It has been almost completely displaced from swamps and lakes by an introduced population of *Caiman crocodilus* and is now restricted to mangroves and sites with very contaminated water. In field surveys, a sex ratio of one male to 14 females was encountered and no juveniles or nests were found. Whether this observed ratio reflects an unidentified collecting bias is unknown. Status: "Insufficiently Known."

Kinosternon scorpioides scorpioides

Inhabits the Atlantic coast and Orinoco and Amazonian drainages. It has a wide distribution and is captured only occasionally. Status: "Acceptable."

Phrynops dahli

Endemic to the Atlantic coast of Colombia. It has a very localized distribution that is threatened by urbanization and habitat alteration from cattle ranching. We still know almost nothing about its natural history, but it is difficult to obtain funds in Colombia for studies given the species' lack of economic value. Status: "Vulnerable."

Phrynops geoffroanus

Inhabits highlands of the Orinoco and principally the periphery of the Amazon system. It is widely distributed in regions that still have relatively low human population densities. Its consumption is prohibited in some indigenous communities (Lamar and Medem, 1982), and its eggs or meat may produce allergies. Consequently, it is consumed only in some areas. Status: "Acceptable."

Phyrnops gibbus

Inhabits the Orinoco and Amazonian drainages. It has a wide distribution, small size, and foul odor, so it is not heavily exploited. Status: "Acceptable."

Phrynops raniceps

Inhabits the Amazonian drainage. Since 1975 we have not encountered a single specimen despite intensive searching. Whether it actually occurs in Colombia or its range ends in areas just adjacent to our borders is unknown. In past decades moderate numbers of this species were commercially exported from Leticia, Colombia to dealers in Florida. Status: "Insufficiently Known."

Phrynops rufipes

Inhabits the Amazonian drainage and ranges into Brazil. Its populations appear small and we have very limited knowledge of its biology. Natives are beginning to consume it, so studies of this species are urgently needed. Status: "Insufficiently Known."

Platemys platycephala

Inhabits the Amazonian drainage. Because of its small size and wide distribution in relatively uninhabited areas, it does not appear to be threatened. Status: "Acceptable."

Peltocephalus dumerilianus

Inhabits the upper Orinoco and Amazonian drainages. Because of its large size, it is exploited by indigenous people and settlers. In areas of sympatry with *Podocnemis erythrocephala* it is also heavily exploited. The impact of this is intensified by the fact that the turtle's populations are smaller and highly scattered (perhaps because of aggression between individuals within this species). The status of this species in the Llanos of eastern Colombia and adjacent Venezuela is unclear, but it appears not to be abundant. Status: "Insufficiently Known."

Podocnemis erythrocephala

Inhabits the Orinoco drainage and, as it is found in the Río Negro in neighboring Venezuela and Brazil, it is probable that it inhabits the Río Negro in Colombia as well. The turtle is confined to restricted areas, principally blackwater streams. Its distribution coincides with an area of numerous indigenous communities. Although small in size, this turtle is one of the principal sources of protein for natives during the dry season; it is consumed at large religious meetings and is traded to obtain goods from settlers. The situation is intensified by the practice of keeping juveniles as pets. Its status should be "Vulnerable."

Podocnemis expansa

Inhabits the Orinoco and Amazonian drainages. It is the largest in size and has the largest clutch of any non-marine turtle on the South American continent. Traditionally exploited for its meat and especially its eggs, *P. expansa* is considered by the IUCN to be "Endangered." Its habit of nesting in aggregations makes it very vulnerable. This turtle is in much greater danger in the Orinoco where populations have been greatly reduced. In the Amazon, it occurs in an area of low human density and benefits from a management program administered by a Colombian nongovernmental organization, and perhaps benefits also from recovery programs implemented in Brazil. The species should continue to be considered "Endangered."

Podocnemis lewyana

Endemic in Colombia to the Magdalena and Sinú drainages, although a single specimen is known from Lake Maracaibo, Venezuela (Pauler and Trebbau, 1995). Unfortunately, its distribution coincides with an area of extremely poor, subsistence fishing communities. Intensively exploited for its meat and eggs, its populations have declined dramatically. Studies and protective measures are urgently needed. Status: "Endangered."

Podocnemis sextuberculata

Restricted to the Amazonian drainage. It is very rare in Colombia, although it can be found in markets in Leticia. We know almost nothing about the species. Status: "Insufficiently Known."

Podocnemis unifilis

Inhabits the Orinoco and Amazonian drainages. It faces almost the same problems as *P. expansa*, although its more solitary nesting habits make this turtle less vulnerable, but also more difficult to protect. The Orinoco populations of this species are also more threatened. In the Amazon, results of recent studies (Páez and Bock, this volume) will hopefully lead to the implementation of a management program. The status of this species is at least "Vulnerable."

Podocnemis vogli

This small turtle inhabits the Orinoco drainage and is very common in the eastern plains. It has traditionally been consumed during the nesting season, when it is captured (sometimes with the use of dogs) while searching for a site to lay. The species may have problems. Status: "Insufficiently Known."

Rhinoclemmys annulata

Inhabits the Pacific coast. It does not occur in abundant populations but may be found scattered throughout its entire range. It is not valued for consumption because of its small size and because it is normally parasitized by ticks (Acaricidae: *Amblyomma*). Status: "Acceptable."

Rhinoclemmys diademata

Found only in the Catatumbo region, in a small enclave of the Maracaibo basin that is shared with Venezuela. For many years there have been no collections of or data obtained for this species in Colombia, but its natural history in Venezuela is reviewed by Pritchard and Trebbau (1984). The category of "Rare" is proposed.

Rhinoclemmys melanosterna

Inhabits the Pacific and Atlantic lowlands and Magdalena drainage. Although prized by indigenous people and settlers, it is very abundant in the remote parts of the Pacific lowlands. Elsewhere it seems to be declining. Its present status is considered "Acceptable."

Rhinoclemmys nasuta

Found in rivers of the Pacific lowlands, it is generally uncommon or localized but has a wide distribution. To date, it is only occasionally captured for consumption. Status: "Acceptable."

Trachemys scripta callirostris

Atlantic coast and Magdalena drainage. One of the most heavily exploited turtles in the country, it is a dietary requirement for many during Easter week, and a substantial volume of hatchlings are sold illegally as pets in the streets of most major cities. It is exploited over most of its range and shares many of the problems of *Podocnemis lewyana*. The fact that it is afforded local protection by some rural land owners may have protected the species from extirpation. It is considered "Vulnerable."

*Trachemys scripta venusta**

Inhabits the northern Chocó region. A small, very restricted population occurs in an area of ever-increasing development. Presently it is exploited intensively as an alternative to the rapidly disappearing, smaller *T. s. callirostris*. However, it appears that *T. s. venusta* may benefit from habitat disturbance at the expense of *Rhinoclemmys melanosterna*, which it replaces in low inundated areas as they are opened by deforestation. The status of "Vulnerable" is proposed.

CONCLUSIONS AND RECOMMENDATIONS

Our studies indicate that 16 species and one subspecies of Colombia's tortoises and freshwater turtles require conservation action. Given the unique circumstances of each turtle species and each region of Colombia, a single combined recommendation or proposal applicable to all the species is not possible. It is clear that the first step is to conduct studies on the basic biology of each threatened turtle species in order to provide a foundation for any protection measures. However, this has been done in only a few

---

* This may be a distinct subspecies closely related to *venusta*.

species. It is also important to bear in mind that the active participation and cooperation of local human communities will be vital for long-term conservation programs. For each of the major biogeographic regions (Figure 1), the following measures should be implemented:

• Chocó region: Enlarge the "Los Katios" Reserve or create a new one that includes important parts of the ranges of *Geochelone carbonaria* and *Trachemys scripta* (conservation priority zone 1 in Figure 1).

• Atlantic coast: Convince and help private landowners to protect and manage populations of *Geochelone carbonaria*, *Phrynops dahli*, and *Trachemys scripta callirostris* on their properties (conservation priority zone 2 in Figure 1).

• For *Podocnemis lewyana* in the north, and for *P. expansa*, *P. unifilis*, and *P. erythrocephala* in the east and south of the country, develop governmental programs for protection and management within the national parks and reserves. Because no funding has been available, we have yet to receive the necessary support from the governmental agencies in charge of protecting our natural resources (conservation priority zones indicated by 3 in Figure 1).

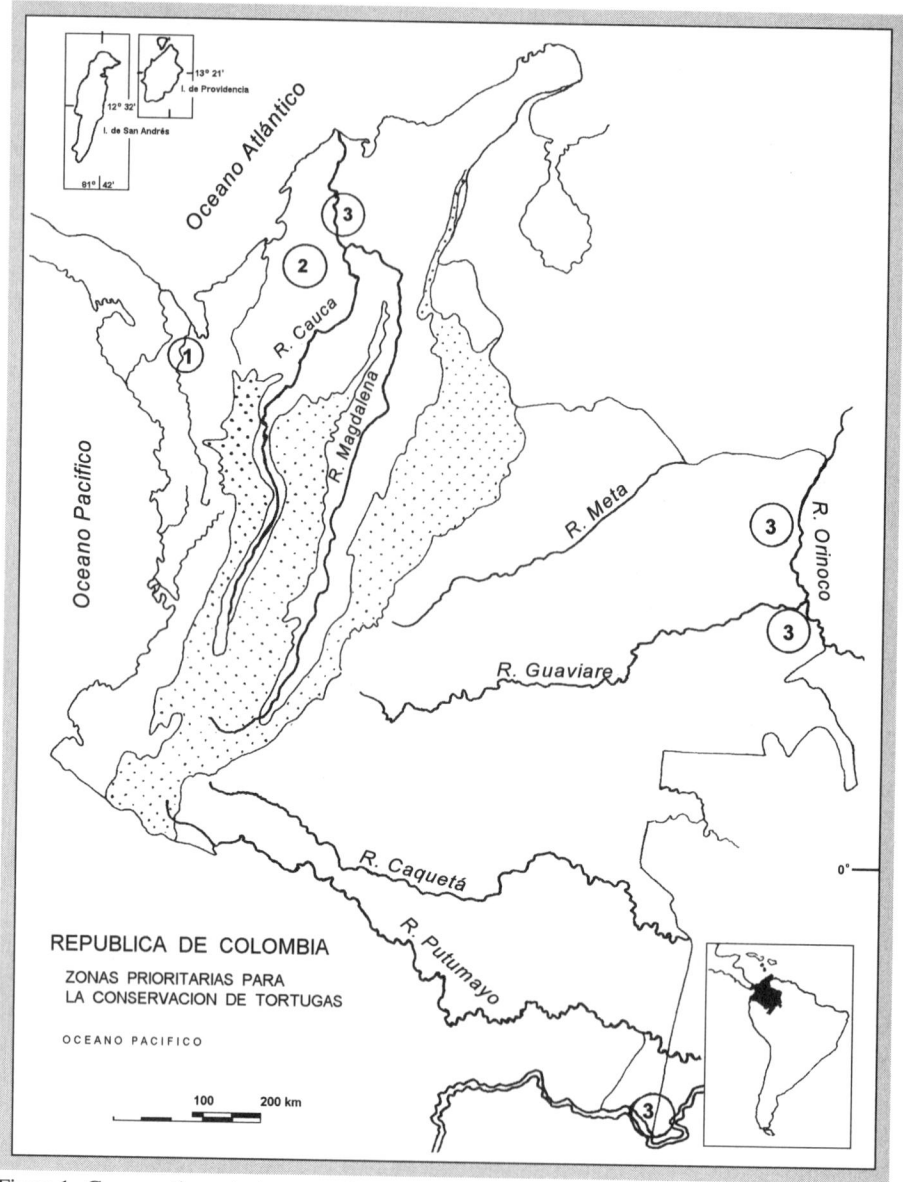

Figure 1. Conservation priority zones for turtles and tortoises in Colombia. Stipled areas = Andes Mountains.

ACKNOWLEDGMENTS

The information in this paper is the result of work on Colombian turtles initiated by Federico Medem and continued by the author. It was financed by the Universidad Nacional de Colombia—Colciencias. I would also like to thank Jaime Aguirre, Brian Bock, Michael Klemens, Vivian Patricia Páez, and Janis Roze for their support.

LITERATURE CITED

IUCN/SSC. 1982. The IUCN Amphibia-Reptilia Red Data Book. Part I. Testudines, Crocodylia, Rhyncocephalia (B. Groombridge, comp.). IUCN, Gland, Switzerland. 426 pp.

Lamar, W. W. and F. Medem. 1982. Notes on the chelid turtle *Phrynops rufipes* in Colombia (Reptilia: Testudines: Chelidae). Salamandra 18(3/4):305–321.

Páez, V. P. and B. C. Bock. 1997. Nesting ecology of the yellow-spotted river turtle in the Colombian Amazon. *In* J. Van Abbema (ed.), Proceedings: Conservation, Management, and Restoration of Tortoises and Turtles—An International Conference, pp. 219–224. July 1993, State University of New York, Purchase. New York Turtle and Tortoise Society, New York.

Pauler, I. and P. Trebbau. 1995. Erstnachweis von *Podocnemis lewyana* Duméril, 1852 (Testudines) in Venezuela. Salamandra 31(3): 181–186.

Pritchard, P. C. H. and P. Trebbau. 1994. The Turtles of Venezuela. Soc. Stud. Amph. Rept., Contrib. Herpetol. 403 pp.

Land Tortoises in Spain: Their Status and Conservation

Ramon Mascort

C.R.T. l'Albera, 17780 Garriguella, Girona, Spain [e-mail: rmascortb@mx3.redestb.es]

Abstract: Two species of tortoises occur in Spain, the spur-thighed tortoise (*Testudo graeca*) and Hermann's tortoise (*Testudo hermanni*). Although both species have received legal protection for over 20 years, their numbers continue to decline. The primary population of *T. graeca* in southeastern Spain is threatened by illegal collection and habitat fragmentation. A relatively stable population occurs in Doñana National Park and a reduced population is found in a small area in northwest Majorca. The endangered western race of Hermann's tortoise, *Testudo hermanni hermanni*, occurs in southeastern Majorca, some parts of Minorca, and in only one remaining locality on mainland Spain, in the northeastern corner of the country. Populations that occurred along the Mediterranean coast until the turn of the century have been extirpated in the last 50 years. The last indigenous population of Hermann's tortoise in Spain is of ecological and biogeographical interest as it is the westernmost population of the species, isolated from other populations such as those in southern France. Two *Testudo h. hermanni* reintroduction projects are being conducted within protected areas from which tortoises disappeared some decades ago.

Two species of land tortoises occur in Spain, the spur-thighed tortoise (*Testudo graeca*) and Hermann's tortoise (*Testudo hermanni*). The populations of *Testudo graeca* in Spain correspond to the nominate race, *Testudo graeca graeca*, which is found in North Africa (Morocco, Algeria, Tunisia, and Northeast Libya) and the Iberian Peninsula. Other populations reported in continental Italy and in Sardinia, Sicily, and Malta are considered to have been introduced (Bour, 1987; Stubbs, 1989; Ballsina, 1995) as is the population of *T. graeca* on Majorca. Highfield (1989, 1990) has revised the taxonomy of the genus *Testudo* in North Africa and, based on morphometric and osteological analysis, recognises species that differ from *T. graeca* and show high variability, even between adjacent populations. Variation also occurs amongst Spanish populations, although to a lesser extent.

There are still stable populations of the western subspecies of Hermann's tortoise, *T. hermanni hermanni*, in southeastern France as well as in western and southern Italy. In some regions of the country (Latium and Campania), tortoises from unknown origin were mixed with native animals, resulting in genetically mixed populations, but pure *T. h. hermanni* can still be found in Tuscany, Calabria, Puglia, and Basilicata (Ballasina, 1995). *T. h. hermanni* also occurs in Sardinia, Majorca, Minorca, and other small islands near the central western coast of Italy (Stubbs, 1989). The Spanish populations of *T. hermanni* and those in the south of France also correspond to the western subspecies. The Corsican populations present intermediate characteristics between the subspecies *T. h. hermanni* and *T. h. boettgeri* (Cheylan, 1992).

In 1973 both *T. graeca* and *T. hermanni* received legal

Figure 1. Distribution of tortoises in Spain.

protection in Spain in an effort to halt the tortoise trade that was endangering the existing populations. López-Jurado et al. (1979) reported that tortoises continued to be captured during the 1970s and estimated that 10,000–15,000 specimens were taken each year. Local tortoises were often kept as pets in the past, a practice that is less frequent today, but it is still possible to buy them on the black market in large cities or from travelling vendors in some southeastern towns.

Gradually, taxa such as Horsfield's tortoise, *T. horsfieldii*, or the eastern race of Hermann's tortoise, *T. h. hermanni*, were substituted for local tortoises in pet shops. American box turtles (*Terrapene* spp.) are currently imported and sold to fill the demand for tortoises, although few become acclimatized.

In general, the range and density of tortoises have decreased, and in some instances entire populations have been extirpated. Increased human pressure on tortoises inhabiting coastal areas has proved detrimental to their survival in these areas. However, nearly all remaining populations contain some areas of high density, which offers hope for their future. Recently, regional governments and nature conservation organisations have introduced programmes to save the last Spanish tortoises from extirpation.

Testudo graeca

Southeast Spain

This population, the largest both in number of tortoises and in geographical area, is most likely native. Bailón (1986, *in* Andreu, 1987) found Pleistocene fossil remains close to the species' present range that displayed characteristics similar to modern *T. graeca*.

T. graeca occupies approximately 2,700 km² in the southeast of the Iberian Peninsula along approximately 95 km of coastline (Sánchez et al., 1986) in the provinces of Murcia in the north and Almería in the south. Its range may be broadly delimited by a triangle, with Mazarrón in the north and Carboneras in the south as two of the vertices connected by the coastline. The third vertex, Valdeinfierno Reservoir, represents the tortoise's deepest inland record, approximately 50 km from the coast.

Within this zone, the proliferation of greenhouses has gradually reduced areas of native vegetation and has displaced tortoises from the floodplains. Tourism on the coast, commercial collection, and the expansion of agriculture continue to threaten the species, and *T. graeca* is now unevenly distributed throughout its original range. Populations are concentrated in the uppermost reaches of certain mountain ranges which, although not used for agriculture, are grazed by livestock. Some populations remain in hilly areas where xeric vegetation alternates with olive and almond groves. In an area of high density in the province of Murcia, Esteban and Pérez (1988) found 4.5 tortoises/ha, but densities were much lower in floodplains dominated by agriculture, near coastal tourist resorts, and around urban areas.

Eguía (1994), in a study conducted over more than 150 ha in three favourable sectors of the species' range within the province of Murcia, found average densities of 8.4 tortoises /ha, 6.2/ha, and 4.4/ha. In this same study, 37% of the animals captured were less than ten years old, suggesting active recruitment within the population.

In Murcia, a regional government wildlife recovery centre, the "Centro de Recuperación de Fauna Silvestre el Valle," has reintroduced tortoises near the northern limits of the range. Since 1970, 170 tortoises of an age-class structure similar to the wild population have been gradually released in two sectors selected as favourable habitat. The appearance of hatchlings and the good condition of the adults observed during recaptures attest to the success of these reintroductions (S. Eguía, pers. comm.).

Research has been conducted at this same centre on a potentially fatal respiratory tract disease that affects many tortoises. Unfortunately, the treatments tested have been only partially successful.

In 1994 the "Asociación de Naturalistas del Sudeste" (A.N.S.E.), a local nature conservancy, purchased 70 ha of *T. graeca* habitat that will be permanently protected. In the near future A.N.S.E. has plans to extend the reserve and to create additional ones.

Figure 2. Adult male spur-thighed tortoise, *Testudo graeca*, from southeastern Spain.

Several plans are currently being developed to establish protection for areas of optimal habitat in southeastern Spain. Unfortunately, regional jurisdictions prevent the application of a single, nationwide conservation plan.

Southwest Spain

This population is restricted entirely to Doñana National Park in the province of Huelva. The species formerly extended west over a much larger coastal area in the province of Huelva (González de la Vega, 1988), inhabiting the characteristic sand dunes and pine woodlands of the region. Its presence in the area was reported at least three times in the eighteenth century (Granados in Andreu, 1987). These reports suggest that this population is also native to the region, although Valverde (1967) mentioned the introduction of specimens from Morocco into the Park between 1949 and 1954. Andreu (1987), after examining park photographic records, concluded that no more than 100 African tortoises were released during those years.

The population's range is limited by quicksands to the west, the Guadalquivir River to the south, marshes to the east, and eucalyptus stands to the north. Andreu (1987) estimated that the population numbered between 5,000 and 6,000 individuals.

Tortoises live in stable sandy areas, occasionally in the sand dunes and adjacent areas (Braza et al., 1981), and on the edges of the marshes where high humidity promotes increased production of green undergrowth (Andreu, 1987). Braza et al. (1981) reported a density of 2 tortoises/ha in the 300 ha sector they studied. In an optimal 50 ha area, Andreu (1987) determined a density of 4 tortoises/ha in a ratio of almost two adults for each juvenile, although individuals from nearly all age classes were present.

Tortoises less than one year old suffered the highest mortality, representing 21.6% of the total deaths recorded. The park's high density of wildlife is probably responsible for the high numbers of young tortoises killed by predators. Exploitation for the pet trade and habitat degradation are not threats to this population, which appears to be stable and has a favourable prospect of remaining so.

Island of Majorca

The smallest and most endangered population of *T. graeca* in Spain occurs in the northwest corner of the island of Majorca, an area of approximately 80 km². This population was most likely introduced. According to Barceló (1876, in Mayol, 1985), the tortoise was "imported from Algeria, where they were abundant; it became acclimatized, many years ago, as an object of curiosity and adornment in some parks and gardens of Majorca, where it reproduces and attains the same size as in Africa." The present population, which now inhabits the hills near Palma de Mallorca, the principal city on the island, probably originated from escaped or released animals.

Twenty to thirty years ago tortoises were more abundant and could be found in coastal areas. However, except for their disappearance along the coast, their distribution appears to have remained the same since that time. Aguilar (1990) conducted a detailed study of the area in 1 km² transects, surveying farmers and local people and, according to their comments, classified each transect as low, medium, or high density. Forty-two percent (34 transects) of the area supported a medium or high density, and 58% (47 transects) were found with a low density or the mere presence of individuals. The central section of the area (approx. 2,000 ha) has the highest density, and virtually isolated from this central core are a few medium density subpopulations.

Although recurrent forest fires in summer 1993 reduced their numbers, the low areas most commonly frequented by tortoises in summer were least affected by these fires. The construction of new roads and highways threatens the survival of this fragile tortoise population, fragmenting its habitat and reducing genetic exchange between subpopulations.

A few tortoises kept at Son Reus, a regional government wildlife recovery centre, developed chronic rhinitis, apparently caused by an unidentified pathogen. It appears that the administration of broad-spectrum antibiotics and the addition of vitamin A to their diet provides temporary improvement. Approximately 3% of the tortoises in the wild also present symptoms of this disease (J. Aguilar, pers. comm.).

Small populations of *T. graeca* may have once existed on the islands of Ibiza and Formentera. Maluquer (1919) mentioned a few individuals on Formentera and Mayol (1985) reported a few on Ibiza, but the species can no longer be found on either of the two islands.

Testudo hermanni

Island of Majorca

Until a few decades ago *T. hermanni* was evenly distributed throughout the southeast of the island, which is characterized by scattered stands of pine with abundant Mediterranean undergrowth (e.g., *Pistacia lentiscus*, *Quercus coccifera*, *Cistus monspeliensis*, and *Cistus albidus*). Tortoises are currently abundant in only two sections, while isolated small patches of suitable habitat contain relict populations. Density in the two large sections is much higher than that found in the *T. graeca* population in the northwest of the island (Aguilar, 1990). In the southeast corner of the island, the tortoise occurs in uneven distribution near the coast and up to 15 km inland (it is reported to be absent from some hills close to the coast and in high density in other areas). The other principal population occurs in a smaller area (approx. 250 km²), where the distribution is more even (Aguilar, 1990).

Rivera and Arribas (1993) believe the species to have been introduced on the island, although the presence of *T. hermanni* on Majorca has been known for many years. Mayol (1985) notes that tortoise bones were found in the excavations of a 3,000-year-old settlement.

Illegal collecting is the most important threat to the species, and forest fires, which are fairly frequent on the island, pose an additional threat. The impact of fire on these populations depends upon a number of variables that can affect tortoise survival rate after a fire: structure of local vegetation, wind, slope of the land, time of day, and season (Aguilar, 1990).

The dramatic increase in human settlements over large areas along the coast and the growth of agriculture, including the construction of irrigation ditches, has forced the tortoises to recede into less-populated areas, fragmenting their population in the interior of the island. In general, the population tends to remain stable in those areas where tortoises are abundant, but the total range of the species on Majorca is clearly reduced.

The regional government of the Balearic Islands has a small centre on the island, which is conducting studies of tortoise biology. A recovery and captive breeding centre is planned, but it has not yet been built. There is also a small, privately owned reserve of approximately 20 hectares, where the species is well protected.

Individuals occasionally found on the island of Ibiza, southwest of Majorca, are most likely escaped pets and should not be considered vestiges of old populations.

Island of Minorca

Testudo hermanni is unevenly distributed throughout the island. Esteban et al. (1994) found tortoises in 31 of the 48, 5 km² transects into which the island had been divided. The tortoise's preferred habitat includes both dense bushes and the edges of fields, although it can also be found in open woodland and near dry creeks. It is absent from dense woodland areas or areas without bushes. Various visits to the same localities revealed a decrease in density or even a complete withdrawal from urbanized areas. However, a substantial increase was noted in some isolated sectors, confirming the recovery of some subpopulations after the massive commercial collection that continued until the 1970s.

On a five-hectare area in the south of the island, Esteban and Pérez (1988) reported a density of 9.4 tortoises/ha, similar to the 11/ha in southern France (Stubbs and Swingland, 1985) or the 11.7/ha in a sector of the plain of eastern Corsica (Cheylan, 1992). As on Majorca, the tortoise is believed to have been introduced, though in early times (Rivera and Arribas, 1993).

Northeast Spain

Until the middle of this century, several populations of *T. hermanni* inhabited coastal areas from the mouth of the River Ebro to the French border, scattered along more than 300 km of coastline. A few isolated tortoises may exist in a small sector south of the River Ebro, in what was the southern limit of the species' range. Seven references mentioning this population, dating from the sixteenth century to the mid-1950s, were reviewed by Bertolero and Marinez-Vilalta (1994).

These populations were gradually extirpated, and today only a single population remains in the northeastern corner of the Iberian Peninsula, in the l'Albera mountain range. This population was already known over 100 years ago, and

Figure 3. Young female Hermann's tortoise, *Testudo hermanni*, from northeastern Spain.

Companyó (1863, *in* Fèlix, 1984) reported the regular occurrence of the species in two nearby localities in southern France. Its present-day isolation from all other known localities in western Europe is of special ecological and biogeographical interest. Among other differences currently being studied, the black areas on the carapace of tortoises from northeastern Spain are larger than in tortoises from the Balearic Islands or southern France, which confers a darker overall appearance to the animal. Other differences include the slightly saddle-backed carapace of the islands form, which contrasts with the more domed carapace in the animals of mainland Spain, which are also slightly larger.

The species occurs in an area of approximately 90 km². Although tortoise densities are low in most of this area, recent samplings have shown that high densities of adults, and a considerable number of young and hatchlings can be found in certain localities. Fèlix et al. (1990) estimated a population of 10.95/ha in one locality before the 1986 forest fire, which burnt 25,000 ha of Mediterranean woodland and nearly all the tortoises' habitat. Following this disaster the same author recorded the loss of 30.4% of the tortoises in one valley. Considering that mortality from forest fires may have been even higher in other sectors of the area, as in southeastern France where 76% of the population was lost (Cheylan, 1981), recurrent forest fires could decimate the entire population within a few years.

Nearly all of the species' present-day range was established as a protected zone in 1986, but some small-scale collecting has been recorded, especially in recent years due to the increase in the number of visitors.

A few projects on behalf of the species have been undertaken. Open to the public since March 1994, a captive-breeding centre, the Centre de Reproducció de Tortugues de l'Albera (C.R.T. l'Albera), was established to release captive-bred tortoises into protected optimal habitat areas. A hermitage with an adjoining field was donated to the organisation that administers the centre. There, the tortoises' habitat has been reproduced and is currently occupied by 80 native tortoises, none of them taken directly from the wild. An educational programme for schools and the public has also been designed to raise awareness of the species and to teach the importance of its survival (Budó et al., 1995).

Two other projects have been undertaken. During 1987–1988, 53 *T. hermanni* were introduced into an 8.6 ha sector, which is isolated by the sea and connected to the mainland only by a sandbar (Bertolero, 1991). This population has been monitored continuously since 1991 and 222 juveniles had been marked up to 1995 (Bertolero et al., 1995). Reduced pressure from predators, which only occasionally enter the area, has allowed the survival of many juveniles and a rapid increase in the population to a density greater than other wild populations. This population would provide stock for future reintroductions of *T. hermanni* into areas where it has been extirpated.

Finally, a project to reintroduce the species in its former habitat is being conducted by government agencies and conservation organisations in a protected area near Barcelona. In April 1994 a forest fire burnt the entire area, and the release of tortoises had to be postponed. During 1995 six tortoises were released and radio-tracked, and they have adapted well to the new environment. This study led to the release of 65 individuals in July 1996, and up to 300 tortoises will be released in the near future (J. Fèlix, pers. comm.).

Literature Cited

Aguilar, J. S. 1990. La protecció de les tortugues terrestres i marines a les Balears. Documents Tècnics de Conservació. Govern Balear, Palma de Mallorca, Spain. 50 pp.

Andreu, A. C. 1987. Ecología y dinámica poblacional de la tortuga mora *Testudo graeca* L., en Doñana, Huelva. Ph.D. thesis, Universidad de Sevilla, Seville, Spain.

Ballasina, D. 1995. Conservation and reproduction techniques at the Carapax Centre, Italy. In Proc. International Congress of Chelonian Conservation, pp. 210–213. Tortoise Village, Gonfaron, France, 6–10 July 1995. Editions Soptom, Gonfaron, France.

Bertolero, A. 1991. La reintroducción de *Testudo hermanni hermanni* en el Parque Natural del delta del Ebro. Bull. Parc Nat. Delta de l'Ebre 6:22–25.

Bertolero, A. and A. Martinez-Vilalta. 1994. Presenciea histórica de *Testudo hermanni* en las comarcas del Baix Ebre y Montsià (Sur de Catalunya). Bol. Asoc. Herpetol. Esp. 5:2–3.

Bertolero, A., M. A. Carretero, G. A. Llorente, A. Martínez, and A. Montori. 1995. The importance of introductions in species conservation: The case of *Testudo hermanni* in the Ebro Delta Natural Park (NE Spain). In Proc. International Congress of Chelonian Conservation, pp. 187–191. Tortoise Village, Gonfaron, France, 6–10 July 1995. Editions Soptom, Gonfaron, France.

Bour, R. 1986. L'identité des tortues terrestres Européenes: Spécimens-types et localités-types. Revue Fr. Aquariol. 13:111–122.

Braza, R., M. Delibes, and J. Castroviejo. 1981. Estudio biométrico y biológico de la tortuga mora, *Testudo graeca*, en la reserva biológica de Doñana, Huelva. Doñana Acta Vert. 8:15–41.

Budó, J., X. Capalleras, J. Fèlix, and R. Mascort. 1995. The population status of *Testudo hermanni hermanni* in northeastern Spain and management by l'Albera Captive Breeding Center (C.R.T. l'Albera). In Proc. International Congress of Chelonian Conservation, pp. 196–197. Tortoise Village, Gonfaron, France, 6–10 July 1995. Editions Soptom, Gonfaron, France.

Cheylan, M. 1981. Biologie et Ecologie de la Tortue d'Hermann *Testudo hermanni hermanni* Gmelin, 1789. Contribution de l'Espèce à la Connaissance des Climats Quaternaires de la France. Mêm. Trav. Inst. num. 13. Montpellier, France. 383 pp.

Cheylan, M. 1992. La tortue d'Hermann *Testudo hermanni* Gmelin 1789. In M Delaugerre and M. Cheylan (eds.), Atlas de Répartition de Baraciens et Reptiles de Corse, pp. 42–46. Parc Naturel Regional de Corse & Ecole Practique des Hautes Etudes, Pampleune, Spain.

Eguía, S. 1994. Las poblaciones silvestres de tortuga mora, *Testudo graeca*, en Murcia. 1991–1994. Grupo ecologista acción verde, Murcia, Spain. 10 pp.

Esteban, I. and E. Pérez. 1988. Contribución al conocimiento de los testudínidos españoles. Ph.D. thesis, Universidad Complutense, Madrid, Spain.

Esteban, I., E. Filella, M. García-París, G. O. B. Menorca, C. Martín, V. Pérez-Mellado, and E. P. Zapirain. 1994. Atlas provisional de la distribución geográfica de la herpetofauna de Menorca (Islas Baleares, España). Rev. Esp. Herp. (1994)8:19–28.

Fèlix, J. 1984. Les tortugues continentals del Empordá. Proposició d'estació zoològica a la serra de la Balmeta. IAEDEN. Figueres, Spain. 40 pp.

Fèlix, J., J. Budó, X. Capalleras, and M. Farré. 1990. Conseqüéncies dels incendis forestals en una població mediterrànea (*Testudo hermanni hermanni* Gmelin, 1789) de l'Albera. Ann. Inst. Est. Empord. 23:13–36.

González de la Vega, J. P. 1988. Anfíbios y Reptiles de la Provinicia de Huelva. Ed. del autor, Huelva, Spain.

Highfield, A. C. 1989. A revision of the Testudines of north Africa, Asia and Europe, Genus *Testudo*. J. Chel. Herp. 1(1):1–12.

Highfield, A. C. 1990. Tortoises of north Africa; taxonomy, nomenclature, phylogeny and evolution with notes on field studies in Tunisia. J. Chel. Herp. 1(2):1–56.

López Jurado, L. F., P. A. Talavera, J. M. Ibáñez, J. A. MacIvor, and A. García. 1979. Las tortugas terrestres *Testudo graeca* y *Testudo hermanni* en España. Naturalia Hispánica num. 17:1–63. Icona, Madrid, Spain.

Maluquer, J. 1919. Les tortugues de Catalunya. Treb. Mus. Cien. Nat., pp. 93–159. Barcelona, Spain.

Mayol, J. 1985. Rèptils i Amfibis de les Balears. Manuals d'Introducció a la Naturalesa, 6 ed. Moll, Palma de Mallorca, Spain.

Rivera, J. and O. Arribas. 1993. Anfibios y reptiles introducidos de la fauna española. Quercus 84:12–16.

Sánchez, J. M., E. Crespillo, and J. Romero. 1986. La tortuga mora de la península ibérica. Vida Silvestre 59:170–187.

Stubbs, D. 1989. *Testudo graeca*: Spur-thighed tortoise. In I. R. Swingland and M. W. Klemens (eds.), The Conservation Biology of Tortoises, pp. 31–33. Occasional Papers of the IUCN Species Survival Commission (SSC) No. 5. IUCN, Gland, Switzerland.

Stubbs, D. and I. Swingland. 1985. The ecology of a Mediterranean tortoise (*Testudo hermanni*): A declining population. Can. J. Zool. 63:169–180.

Valverde, J. A. 1967. Estructura de una Comunidad Mediterránea de Vertebrados Terrestres. Mon. Estación Biol. Doñana, Madrid, Spain. 218 pp.

An Overview of a Threatened Population of the European Pond Turtle, *Emys orbicularis*

— SUMMARY REPORT —

RAMON MASCORT

C.R.T. l'Albera, 17780 Garriguella, Girona, Spain [e-mail: rmascortb@mx3.redestb.es]

The European pond turtle is widespread throughout rivers, ponds, marshes, and other wetlands of Europe, except for areas in the north and centre. It is also present in North Africa (Morocco, Algeria, and Tunisia), in western Asia as far east as the Aral Sea, and on some Mediterranean islands (Ernst and Barbour, 1989; Fritz, 1995).

Barbadillo (1987) reported this turtle to be extremely rare in Spain and continuing to decline. Relatively dense populations exist in only a few sites, and its numbers are falling rapidly in other locations from one year to the next. The species is in decline in Catalonia (northeast Spain), with several populations currently on the verge of extirpation. The stronghold of the species in this region was formerly the drainage basin of the River Ter, which served as a corridor connecting the scattered populations. Water pollution has caused the virtual disappearance of the species from this river as well as from other main rivers, and it now survives only in pools and in a few tributaries of these watercourses (Arribas, 1992). In the River Ebro delta, the largest wetland of the region, the species was known to be abundant until the 1960s, but now only isolated individuals are observed (A. Bertolero, pers. comm.).

A single healthy population remains in Catalonia as a result of protection of ponds, careful management, and close monitoring by a local conservation organisation. Turtle numbers have increased at this site from 40 individuals a decade ago to more than 300 in the 1995 census (E. Adroguer, pers. comm.). At another site, the northern-most locality of *E. orbicularis* in Catalonia, the release of several individuals in

Figure 1. European pond turtle, *Emys orbicularis*, hatchling.

a protected area has probably resulted in the creation of a new population, although no hatchlings have yet been observed.

A few turtles or only isolated individuals can be found at other sites, and very few animals now remain in areas where the species was formerly abundant. These turtles represent the remnants of old populations and are destined to disappear in the near future unless efforts are made to protect their habitat.

Status and Current Conservation Efforts in the Area

Pollution has greatly affected the population under study. It has now disappeared from the main channel of the Ter River near its mouth, and even from nearby irrigation ditches where it was present as recently as 15 years ago. According to local people, turtles could be observed more frequently and over a larger area until the mid-1950s. The extensive rice fields on the floodplain with their low water levels were particularly favoured by hatchlings.

Today, turtles remain in only two small groups of pools (former branches of the River Ter) through which water no longer flows but are now fed by ground water. The two groups of pools are 600 m apart and are surrounded by agricultural fields. An access road to an adjacent tourist area crosses between the two groups of ponds, which increases human pressure, including the occasional capture of individuals and the greater risk of roadkills. The pools located further inland are being filled in with various materials generated by the local farming practices: earth, tree trunks, and even wire and plastic sacks. Current plans to build summer residences over the other group of pools pose a further threat to the population.

The area was periodically surveyed during 1992 and 1993. Two adult males, four adult females, and two subadult females were captured, measured, and photographed. Two additional turtles were observed in irrigation ditches in 1994 and 1995, but only one additional adult was seen in the ponds inhabited by the turtles. No hatchlings or juveniles were detected, probably because nesting sites at the ponds' borders are destroyed each summer when the fields are ploughed. A captive breeding program was started in 1994 using the eight previously captured turtles; the first hatchlings emerged in 1995.

Contacts were made with local authorities and the landowner in an effort to conserve and restore the turtles' habitat. In addition, a private 1.5 ha reserve has been established 5 km from the ponds. The reserve, currently a dried-up marsh, will be restored and, if found to be suitable, will serve as a future release site for captive-bred turtles. The reintroduced population would be reinforced later with other captive-bred turtles, produced with breeding stock from the nearest known population, which is located in a neighbouring river drainage that was undoubtedly once connected to the study area by the River Ter. This second group of turtles would ensure genetic exchange necessary to maintain a healthy population. Because some dispersal of the newly released turtles must be expected (Servan, 1987; Gibbons et al., 1990; Naulleau, 1991), conservation of the entire area will be crucial to the survival of the population.

LITERATURE CITED

Arribas, O. 1991. Estatus y distribución del galápago europeo (*Emys orbicularis* L.) en Cataluña. VIII trobada de joves naturalistes. Ponencies i actes: 35–39. Depana, Barcelona, Spain.

Barbadillo, L. J. 1987. La Guía de Incafo de los Anfibios y Reptiles de la Península Ibérica, Islas Baleares y Canarias. Incafo, Madrid, Spain.

Ernst, C. H. and R. W. Barbour. 1989. Turtles of the World. Smithsonian Inst. Press, Washington, D.C. i–xii + 313 pp.

Fritz, U. 1995. Zur innerartlichen Variabilität von *Emys orbicularis* (Linnaeus, 1758). 5a. Taxonomie in Mittel-Westeuropa, auf Korsika, Sardinien, der Apenninen-Halbinsel un Sizilien un Unterartengruppen von *E. orbicularis* (Reptilia: Testudines: Emydidae). Zool. Abh. Mus. Tierkd. Dresden 48(13):185–242.

Gibbons, J. W., J. L. Greene, and J. D. Congdon. 1990. Temporal and spatial movement patterns of sliders and other turtles. *In* J. W. Gibbons (ed.), Life History and Ecology of the Slider Turtle, pp. 201–215. Smithsonian Inst. Press, Washington, D.C. i–xiv + 368 pp.

Naulleau, G. 1991. Adaptations écologiques d'une population de cistudes (*Emys orbicularis* L.) aux grandes variations de niveau d'eau et á l'assèchement naturel du milieu aquatique fréquenté. Bull. Soc. Herp. Fr. 58:11–19.

Servan, J. 1987. Use of radiotelemetry in an ecological study of *Emys orbicularis* in France. First results. *In* J. J. van Gelder, H. Strijbosch, and P. J. M. Bergers (eds.), Proc. Fourth Ord. Gen. Meet. S.E.H., pp. 357–360. Nijmegen, Holland.

Figure 2. Adult male European pond turtle, *Emys orbicularis*.

The Distribution and Status of Pancake Tortoises, *Malacochersus tornieri*, in Kenya

ROGER CONANT WOOD[1] AND ALEC MACKAY[2]

[1] *Faculty of Science and Mathematics, Richard Stockton College of New Jersey, Pomona, NJ 08240, USA*
[2] *Department of Reptiles and Amphibians, National Museums of Kenya, P.O. Box 40658, Nairobi, Kenya*

ABSTRACT: Pancake tortoises have a considerably greater geographic distribution in Kenya than previously realized. Although two of the three occurrences reported in the literature are probably erroneous, newly discovered localities confirm the widespread existence of this species within the country.

Our primary study site near Nguni, in the Kitui District of Kenya, has undergone significant habitat changes, with extensive clearing of indigenous thorn scrub for agricultural purposes. Pancake tortoises have a patchy distribution within this area, being found only in low, irregularly spaced, exfoliating rock outcrops. There appears to be a 1:1 adult sex ratio, with no notable sexual dimorphism except tail size and shape (those of males being longer and thicker). Tortoises were often found in male/female pairs.

In the 1960s and 1970s large numbers of pancake tortoises were exported from Kenya, a practice now prohibited. Local Kenyans who had formerly collected for the pet trade reported no overall decline in abundance since the 1970s. However, the current alteration of habitat may ultimately prove of greater consequence to Kenyan pancake tortoises than their former collection for the pet trade. While the tortoises spend most of their time in rock crevices, their essential life functions of feeding, nesting, etc. require intact vegetated habitat.

Of the approximately 270 extant chelonian species in the world, one of the most peculiar is unquestionably the aptly named pancake tortoise (or the equally appropriate Swahili, "kobe ya mawe," meaning "rock tortoise"), *Malacochersus tornieri*.

Little is known about this extraordinary species. Procter (1922) gave a detailed description based upon several dozen preserved specimens and captive individuals. Loveridge and Williams (1957) summarized information on the morphology and geographic distribution of this exotic tortoise, including Loveridge's firsthand observations of *Malacochersus* in the wild. More recently, Broadley (1989) published a brief review of the species based on museum records and a literature survey.

Our fieldwork that was focused specifically on pancake tortoises was conducted in Kenya in 1987 and is reported here for the first time. Shortly thereafter more extensive, ongoing field studies were initiated in Tanzania (Raphael et al., 1994; Klemens and Moll, 1995; Moll and Klemens, 1996).

The genus *Malacochersus* is monotypic; the single species is limited to certain parts of Tanzania and Kenya. The shell osteology is unique, being a fenestrated framework of thin, fragile bone overlain with normal epidermal scales (Procter, 1922). The shell structure of adult *Malacochersus* is essentially neotenic, with the characteristic fontanellization of a hatchling turtle. Moreover, instead of being moderately to highly domed as in most tortoises, the carapace is extremely flattened.

This distinctive shell configuration is an adaptation to the unusual habitat of pancake tortoises. *Malacochersus* is found only in areas where Precambrian gneissic rocks occur, and they spend much of the time deep in narrow rock fissures. The shell is flexible and can be expanded or depressed, thus permitting the tortoise to wedge itself, if threatened, firmly within its retreat (Klemens and Moll, 1995). Under such circumstances, a pancake tortoise can be extremely difficult to extract.

In the 1960s and 1970s large numbers of pancake tortoises were collected in Kenya and Tanzania for the international pet trade. Kenya prohibited exports of this species in 1981, and since 1992 the Tanzanian government has imposed a moratorium on further exports (Klemens and Moll, 1995). Conservationists and scientists have nonetheless been concerned that wild populations may have been seriously depleted. *Malacochersus* is now listed on Appendix II of the Convention on International Trade in Endangered Species (CITES) (USFWS, 1992). This increasing concern was reflected in East Africa by the depiction of a pancake tortoise as one of five animals on a set of endangered species postage stamps issued simultaneously by the governments of Kenya, Uganda, and Tanzania in 1977 (McKay, 1981).

The Study Area

Our fieldwork was centered on an area approximately three kilometers northeast of the village of Nguni, at a road junction known as Kalanga Corner, about midway along the main road between Thika and Garissa, Kitui District, Kenya (Figure 1). This region was chosen because it was the former center in Kenya for the collection of pancake tortoises for the pet trade.

This area was visited briefly on two separate occasions in 1987, once in late July (by RW) for two days and again in early September (by RW and AM together) for four days. Both field trips took place during the prolonged dry season. (This part of Kenya is characterized by two rainy seasons per year: short rains, typically in October and November, and long rains from April through June. Little or no rain falls at other times of the year.) The time of year fieldwork is conducted is apparently of considerable significance. Local residents informed us that pancake tortoises are much less retiring, and therefore easier to catch, during the rainy seasons.

We sampled an area approximately 37 km (along its north-south axis) by 17 km (on the east-west axis). Within this region we found, measured, marked, and released 33 live tortoises. We also collected partial or complete shells of six dead *Malacochersus*, all now in the collection of the Herpetology Department, National Museums of Kenya, Nairobi.

FIELD METHODS

We employed two professional reptile collectors (J. and R. Mutui, from the Nguni area) who had formerly participated in the commercial collection of pancake tortoises. The success of our field work was directly attributable to their skill in locating and extracting pancake tortoises from the rocks in which they were sheltering. No live tortoises were found in the open at any time.

Frequently, but not always, the presence of one or more pancake tortoises within a rock crevice was signaled by fecal material littering its entrance. Tortoises were extracted by using a pliable, hooked branch cut from nearby vegetation. Even when they were close to the entrance, an extractor stick had to be used because the fissures in the rock were too narrow to permit the insertion of one's arm. The deepest tortoise was nearly two meters in from the entrance. The tortoises usually retreated as deeply as the crevice would allow. All the live tortoises located were alert and active.

For each tortoise captured, standard data were recorded. These included locality, date and time of capture, sex, weight (using a 1000 g Pesola® scale calibrated in 10 g increments and read to the nearest 5 g), cloacal and air (shade) temperatures (using a Shultheis® rapid-reading thermometer), straight-line carapace length (SLCL), midline plastral length, and length over the curve of the carapace. In addition, growth annuli on the first right costal scute were routinely counted whenever possible. This scute was selected because, in most mature pancake tortoises, all the plastral scutes and many of the vertebral and costal scutes were abraded, with the annuli incomplete or lost.

The location of each tortoise was plotted on 1:50,000 scale topographic maps obtained from the Survey of Kenya (Nguni, sheet 137/4; Ngomeni, sheet 137/2; Nuu, sheet 151/2; and Engare Ondare, sheet 107/2).

Tortoises were marked with unique combinations of triangular notches filed in the periphery of the carapace.

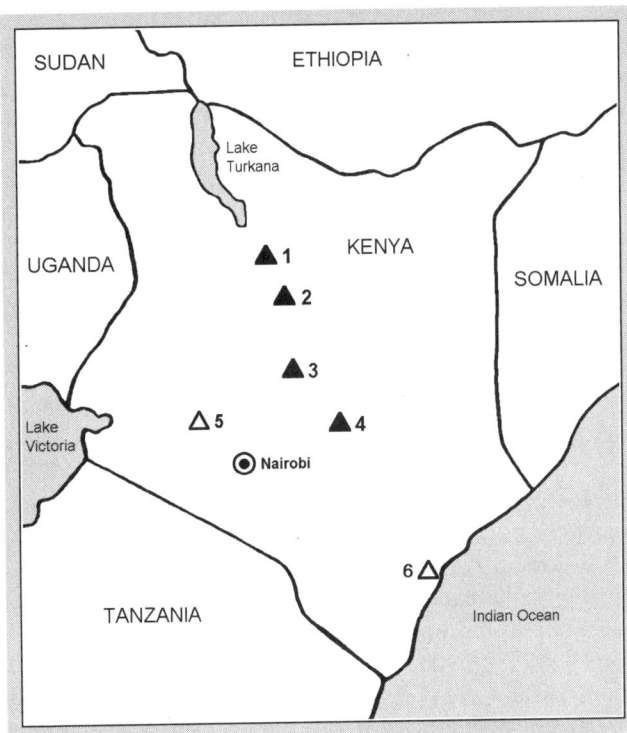

Figure 1. Map of Kenya showing distribution of pancake tortoises within the country. Symbols: ▲ = confirmed localities; △ = questionable localities reported in the literature. 1 = Tum, west flank of Mt. Nyiru; 2 = Milgris River, Mathews Range; 3 = Dalaban Hill, west of Isiolo; 4 = Nguni area; 5 = Njoro, southwest of Nakuru; 6 = Mida Creek, south of Malindi.

RESULTS

Geographic Distribution within Kenya

Only a few Kenyan localities for *Malacochersus* have been reported, all in the southern part of the country. The new sites documented here represent a significant northward range extension (Figure 1).

For many years large numbers of pancake tortoises were regularly collected for the pet trade from our study area in the vicinity of Nguni. However, the tortoises found during our two brief periods of field work indicate that a substantial population still survives here.

Northwest of Nguni, at Dalaban Hill (29 km by road west of Isiolo, Samburu District, Kenya), L. M. Hardy and J. L. Darling collected an adult female pancake tortoise in July 1987. This specimen is catalogued as KNM 9591 in the collections of the Herpetology Department, National Museums of Kenya, Nairobi.

Even farther to the north, two additional localities are represented by specimens now housed at the Los Angeles County Museum of Natural History. A single pancake tortoise (LACM 66160) was collected approximately 38 km northeast of Barsaloi, near the Milgris River, at the north end of the Mathews Range. (This confirms an anecdotal report from this area cited by Loveridge and Williams, 1957.) Three additional specimens (LACM 50620-22) were collected approximately 48 km from the southeast end of Lake Turkana in the vicinity of Tum, on the western flank of Mt. Nyiru (R. L. Bezy, pers. comm.).

Few pancake tortoise localities in Kenya have been reported in the literature. Loveridge (1936) cited the collection of a young specimen from the Sokoki Forest, adjacent to Mida Creek, approximately 15–20 km south of Malindi on the Indian Ocean coast. A second purported locality is Njoro, approximately 15 km southwest of Nakuru adjacent to the Mau Escarpment in the Rift Valley.

We question the validity of the Malindi and Njoro localities. Appropriate habitat does not, to our knowledge, occur at either of these places. If pancake tortoises were found there, they were probably released or escaped captives, but we have not personally checked either of these localities.

Based on these recent discoveries, and given what is known of the habitat requirements of *Malacochersus*, we suggest that this species may actually be far more widespread in Kenya than previously thought. A belt of appropriate metamorphic rocks (belonging to the Precambrian "basement complex") extends through arid terrain across Kenya for hundreds of miles from the region of Tsavo National Park in the southeast to the vicinity of South Horr in the northwest. Although their distribution is likely to be patchy, there may be scattered pancake tortoise populations throughout this area.

Habitat

The Nguni area is characterized by prominent Precambrian gneissic hills with lower, irregularly spaced and relatively small rock outcrops scattered about the intervening terrain. It is only in these latter types of outcrops that we have found pancake tortoises. The orientation of the rock crevices in which the tortoises hide is quite variable, ranging from essentially horizontal to nearly vertical.

Pancake tortoises often retreat more than a meter deep within the crevices. They were invariably difficult to spot and often equally difficult to extract. On several occasions tortoises could not be retrieved despite strenuous and prolonged efforts. Because of their highly cryptic behavior and the thick bush that often prevented visual location of all suitable rock outcrops, we undoubtedly failed to locate a substantial number of the tortoises. But we cannot estimate the proportion of the total population we overlooked.

The dense vegetation that typically surrounds and often envelops the gneissic outcrops in which *Malacochersus* is found is *Acacia/Commiphora* bush (known in the vernacular as thorn scrub). In addition to several species of *Commiphora*, which serve as the principal shade trees, other characteristic plants include *Lannia alata*, *Acacia senegal*, *Boscia coriacea*, and *Sterculia rhycocarpa*. Common climbers are *Entada leptostachys* and *Adenia venenata*. Some localities have almost pure stands of *Acacia senegal*, *Lannia alata*, and on a large rock outcrop near Nuu, *Albizia tanganyicensis adamsoniorum*. The Dolaban Hill locality west of Isiolo differs in vegetation only by the presence of *Euphorbia nyikae* on the lower slopes, intermixed with a sparse cover of *Commiphora*. The hilltop supports a dense *Acacia/Commiphora* thicket.

Our Nguni study area has undergone a number of significant habitat changes because of human activities. Most species of indigenous game animals have been largely, or in some cases entirely (e.g., rhinos and elephants) eliminated. However, the immense baobab trees, *Adansonia digitate*, which dominate the landscape, have for the most part been left standing. Kenya's dramatic human population explosion has resulted in increasingly intensive agricultural use (both farming and grazing) of the land. In several instances, outcrops harboring tortoises were entirely surrounded by farm land, and livestock trails everywhere penetrated the remaining bush. These trails, in fact, often provided the only access to outcrops. The impact of these human-related activities upon pancake tortoises cannot yet be accurately assessed. Certainly, however, there have been some marked changes in the habitat of our study area. In recent years Kenya has had one of the highest human birth rates of any country in the world, and comparable changes have undoubtedly occurred throughout much of the pancake tortoise's range in the country.

Population Characteristics

Because suitable rock habitats are irregularly scattered, *Malacochersus* has a patchy distribution within its range. Although the distance between the most southern and the most northern sites where tortoises were found in our Nguni study area is nearly 37 km, it seems reasonable to treat all 33 of the live tortoises we found as members of a single, even if composite, population.

The 33 tortoises varied from 8.4 to 16.5 cm in straight-line carapace length (SLCL) (Figure 2). The majority (27) were adults with a carapace length of 12 cm or more, and 21 were within 2.5 cm of the maximum length. This suggests a stable population characterized by relatively long-lived individuals with a low reproductive rate, typical of many turtle species. Indeed, because *Malacochersus* typically lays only a single egg (Shaw, 1970; Broadley, 1989), it may have an especially low reproductive potential.

Five of the six smallest tortoises could not be sexed with certainty. Discounting these, there were 13 males and 15 females (one subadult) in our sample. Our tentative conclusion, therefore, is that there is essentially a 1:1 adult sex ratio in the population.

We were able to count, with reasonable confidence, growth annuli on the first right costal scutes for 27 out of the 33 tortoises. In the remaining six individuals, all mature, the surface of the scutes was too worn to permit reliable counting. Figure 3 shows the results in terms of apparent (or relative) age. Based on the assumption that each annulus represents a year of growth, age estimates range from 4 to 17 years. All tortoises with eight or more annuli (except #27, a subadult with nine annuli and 11.3 cm SLCL) represent mature adults of 12.4 cm SLCL or more.

We are, however, uncertain whether each scute annulus actually represents an entire year's growth, or growth during a single wet season (two of which normally occur per year) when pancake tortoises are apparently most active (J. and R. Mutui, pers. comm.). Tanzanian tortoises provide evidence that the latter scenario may be more likely (Moll and Klemens, 1996), in which case the age estimates should be halved (to 2–8 years). In some years there may be only one rather than two rainy seasons or, in the worst case (a year of prolonged drought), the rains may fail completely. Unfortunately, reliable local weather data have not been compiled for our study area so that adjustments for irregular rains cannot be calculated.

Sexual dimorphism is not especially marked in *Malacochersus*. No significant difference in either shell length or body weight was discerned between the sexes. Young tortoises are difficult to sex with any degree of certainty, but mature individuals can be readily sexed on the basis of tail size. Adult females have relatively short, stumpy tails, whereas adult males have substantially thicker and longer tails. A less obvious but fairly consistent characteristic is the lateral profile of the carapace. Females have slightly more rotund shells than do males; the difference between the straight-line and over-the-curve measurements of carapace length tends to be slightly greater in females than in comparably sized males. With few exceptions, this difference appears to become more pronounced as carapace length increases. Presumably, the slightly more arched carapace of mature females is an adaptation that permits adequate space within the shell for egg development.

Body and air temperatures were recorded for 21 tortoises (8 males, 10 females, and 3 juveniles of undetermined sex) as soon as they were extracted from their crevices. Three of

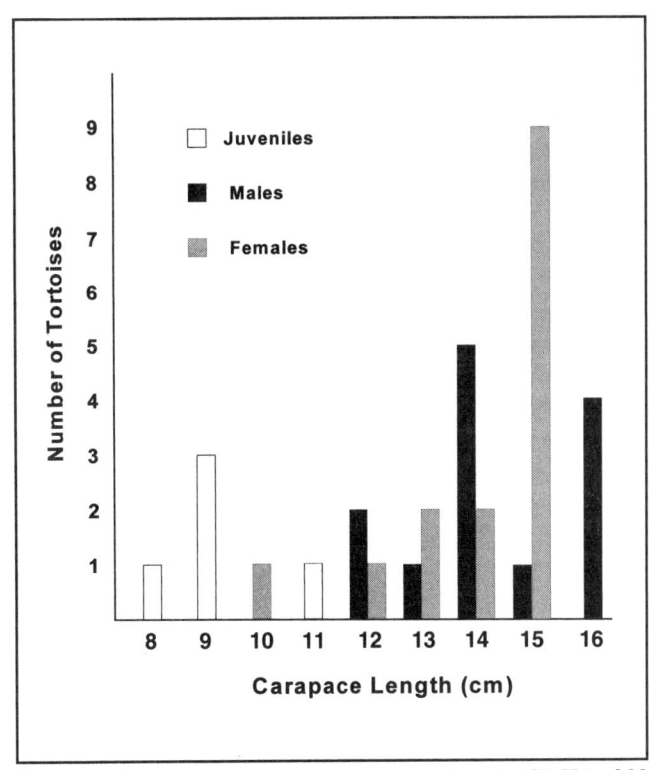

Figure 2. Size range in straight line carapace lengths (SLCL) of 33 pancake tortoises captured and released in the Nguni area. The smallest tortoise was 8.4 cm (SLCL); the largest was 16.5 cm (SLCL).

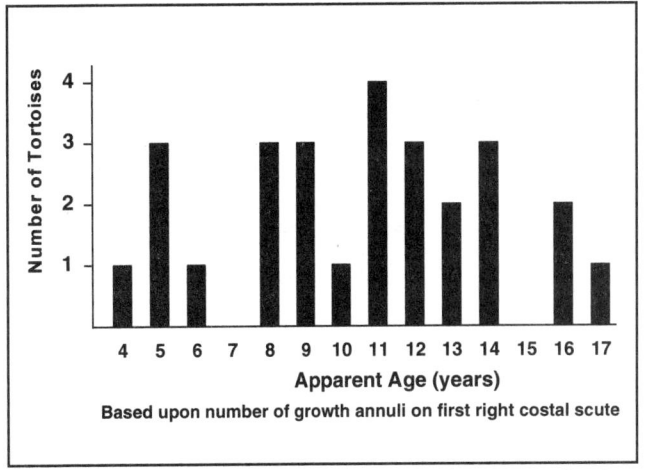

Figure 3. Age estimates of 27 live pancake tortoises captured and released in the Nguni area. Of the 33 tortoises found, six (all large adults) are not included because their scutes were worn too smooth to accurately count annuli. These individuals are #3 (14.2 cm ♂), #4 (15.9 cm ♂), #8 (15.4 cm ♀), #21 (15.1 cm ♂), #26 (15.3 cm ♀), and #28 (16.3 cm ♂).

the adults found in July were subsequently recaptured in September, providing a total of 24 sets of temperature data. The other 12 tortoises in our sample were brought into camp by local people long after they were initially found, so that body and air temperatures at the time of capture could not be obtained. Body (cloacal) temperatures ranged from 26.6 to 33.2°C (Table 1). Except for one exceptionally high temperature reading (33.2°C) for a single female, the range of temperatures for females (26.6–30.4°C) was essentially the same as for males. We could perceive no relationship between body temperature and either size or sex. There does, however, seem to be a correlation between body temperature and time of day (Table 2); cloacal temperatures tend to be higher (by as much as 3°C) in the afternoon than in the morning.

Cloacal temperatures invariably differed from air temperature (measured in shade) immediately outside the rock fissures from which tortoises were retrieved (Table 3). In most cases (21 out of 27 measurements), body temperatures were lower than air temperatures, from a fraction of a degree to over 6°C. Six cloacal readings were higher (up to 5.2°C) than corresponding air temperatures at the capture site. Five of these were early to mid-morning measurements (8:55–10:10 A.M.); the sixth was at noon. Undoubtedly, ambient air temperatures vary more than temperatures inside the fissures the tortoises occupy, so it is not surprising that body temperatures may be higher than air temperatures in the early part of the day. The differences between body and air temperatures in this sample of six tortoises decreased rapidly from 8:55 to 10:10 A.M.

Two adult tortoises of nearly identical size found together in the same rock fissure (#4, a male, and #5, a female) had essentially identical cloacal temperatures when first captured in July (28.0°C and 28.2°C, respectively) and then upon subsequent recapture in September (27.4°C and

TABLE 1
Range of variation in cloacal body temperatures (measured in °C) for 18 adult *Malacochersus tornieri* (8 males, 10 females) captured within the Nguni area.

	Males	Females
High	30.4	33.2
Low	27.0	26.6
Maximum difference	3.4	6.6

TABLE 2
Comparison of cloacal body temperature with the time of day for 18 adult *Malacochersus tornieri* (8 males, 10 females) and 3 juveniles of indeterminate sex. Within this sample, one male and two females were recaptured, thus providing nine temperature readings for the males and 12 for the females. No tortoises were found prior to 8 A.M. or after 4 P.M.

	Cloacal temperatures (°C)		
Time of day	Males	Females	Juveniles
8:00–8:59 A.M.	27.6	—	—
9:00–9:59 A.M.	—	—	—
10:00–10:59 A.M.	27.4	26.6	29.0
	30.2	27.6	—
11:00–11:59 A.M.	28.6	29.4	28.8
Noon–12:59 P.M.	27.0	27.4	—
	29.6	28.4	—
1:00–1:59 P.M.	28.2	27.6	—
	—	28.0	—
	—	30.0	—
2:00–2:59 P.M.	28.2	29.6	—
	30.4	29.9	—
3:00–3:59 P.M.	—	30.4	29.4
	—	33.2	—

TABLE 3
Correlation between pancake tortoise cloacal body temperatures and ambient air temperatures (°C). R = recaptured in September; NR = not recorded.

Time of day	Cloacal temp.	Air temp.	Difference (± °C)	Animal no.
8:55 A.M.	27.6	23.8	+3.8	10
9:00 A.M.	33.8	28.6	+5.2	1
9:00 A.M.	33.2	28.6	+4.6	2
10:00 A.M.	30.2	28.0	+2.2	3
10:10 A.M.	29.0	28.0	+1.0	32
10:45 A.M.	27.4	33.6	−6.2	4 R
10:45 A.M.	27.6	33.6	−6.0	5 R
10:50 A.M.	26.6	27.4	−0.8	33
11:15 A.M.	29.4	30.0	−0.6	6 R
11:20 A.M.	28.8	30.8	−2.0	11
11:45 A.M.	28.6	31.2	−2.6	23
12:10 P.M.	29.6	30.6	−1.0	12
12:15 P.M.	27.0	30.6	−3.6	24
12:15 P.M.	27.4	30.6	−3.2	25
12:30 P.M.	28.4	31.8	−3.4	13
1:05 P.M.	27.6	32.8	−5.2	26
1:20 P.M.	28.2	31.6	−3.4	4
1:20 P.M.	28.0	31.6	−3.6	5
1:45 P.M.	30.0	31.8	−1.8	14
2:05 P.M.	29.8	33.6	−3.8	6
2:30 P.M.	30.4	34.4	−4.0	15
2:30 P.M.	29.6	34.4	−4.8	16
2:30 P.M.	28.2	33.8	−5.6	28
3:00 P.M.	29.4	32.6	−3.2	29
3:20 P.M.	30.4	32.4	−2.0	30
3:40 P.M.	33.2	33.6	−0.4	31
NR	29.8	30.0	−0.2	27

27.6°C, respectively). Their initial capture took place in the early afternoon (1:20 P.M.) while their recapture, when body temperatures were both 0.6°C lower, occurred in mid-morning (10:45 A.M.). A third tortoise (#6) found nearby, also recaptured after the same time interval, likewise had a slightly higher temperature in the afternoon (29.8°C at 2:05 P.M.) than in the morning (29.4°C at 11:15 A.M.). These measurements are all consistent with the general tendency noted above for body temperatures to increase as the day progresses.

Morphology

Two marked changes related to increasing age are readily apparent in the shells of pancake tortoises. Growth rings are well defined on the epidermal scales of juveniles, but in adults these tend to become largely or entirely obliterated. Another obvious age-related change is decreasing contrast in shell coloration. The shells of young animals exhibit a bold, irregular pattern of deep brown and bright yellow colors, but with age both patterns and colors usually fade, ultimately becoming uniformly pale tan. Some adults, however, may be boldly marked.

Loveridge and Williams (1957) reported a plastral formula of AB>HU>FE. The remaining plastral scutes are quite variable in their relationship to one another (Table 4). The plastral formula of our Kenyan sample differs in part from Loveridge and Williams (AB>HU>PE> or <FE≥GU ≥AN). In our sample, the femoral is always greater than the pectoral, and the pectoral may be the shortest. It may be that the differences represent minor geographic variation, in that most (if not all) of the tortoises measured by Loveridge and Williams were probably from Tanzania rather than Kenya.

The shells of *Malacochersus* from Nguni tended to be remarkably free of scute abnormalities. However, in 11 of the 33 tortoises there was a 13th pair of marginals; in two others, a 13th marginal was present on one side only. The extra marginals appeared to result from either subdivision of the 11th pair of marginals or insertion of an extra element between the normal 11th and 12th marginals.

In a single individual (#28), the last vertebral scute was equally subdivided along the midline of the carapace.

Procter (1922) reported a number of scute abnormalities, including a striking example in which the fourth pair of costals met in the midline (the fourth vertebral scute being absent). Loveridge and Williams (1957) also noted numerous anomalies in Tanzanian specimens.

Behavior

We were struck by the high frequency with which we found an adult male/female pair under the same rock (Table 5). The data presented in Table 5 may actually underestimate the frequency of this occurrence. We suspect but cannot confirm that an adult male (#17) and an adult female (#18) captured by one of the Mutui brothers in the interval between our July and September visits to the Nguni area may represent still another instance. Moreover, when #33 (an adult female) was captured, there was a second adult deep within the same crevice that could not be retrieved and may have been a male. Thus, there were at least six and perhaps as many as eight male/female pairs of tortoises in our sample of 33, representing over one third—perhaps nearly one half—of all individuals found.

The frequent pairing of adult male and female pancake tortoises is not peculiar to the Nguni population. Klemens and Moll (1995) described similar occurrences in Tanzania. No male/male pairs were encountered in our field work in Kenya. Only one possible female/female pair was discovered; one (#6) was a small adult (12.4 cm SLCL), and the other, (#11) a juvenile (9.1 cm SLCL), was only tentatively identified as a female. In only one instance were more than two tortoises found together (#7, an adult male, 14.6 cm SLCL; #8, an adult female, 15.4 cm SLCL; and a juvenile female, 10.7 cm SLCL). Brought into camp by a farmer

TABLE 4

Variations in the plastral formula of *Malacochersus tornieri* from Nguni. Abbreviations for scutes: AB = abdominal; AN = anal; FE = femoral; GU = gular; HU = humeral; PE = pectoral. The number in parentheses indicates tortoises exhibiting each variation.

AB > HU > FE > AN ≥ PE ≥ GU	(11)
AB > HU > FE > AN ≥ GU ≥ PE	(4)
AB > HU > FE = AN > GU > PE	(1)
AB > HU > FE > PE > AN > GU	(7)
AB > HU > FE > PE ≥ GU > AN	(3)
AB > HU > FE > GU ≥ PE ≥ AN	(7)

TABLE 5

Localities of male/female pairs of pancake tortoises found together in the same rock crevice.

Locality	Male no.	Female no.
Kalanga Corner	1	2
Kalanga Corner	7	8
Kalanga Corner	20[a]	22[a]
Ivussya	4	5
Ivussya	15	16
Kathumula[b]	24	25

[a] These two adult tortoises were found with a juvenile in the same rock fissure. [b] Village on the west side of Mai Forest northeast of Nguni, not labeled on any map.

who found them on his property, all three tortoises were apparently captured at a single small rock outcrop, but whether or not all three were extracted from a single crevice could not be established. Every other tortoise in our study was found as an isolated individual.

The male/female pairings may represent temporary, seasonal, or even permanent monogamous associations between adults of the two sexes. These pairings may alternatively (or also) reflect territorial behavior. If adult pancake tortoises form lasting male/female relationships, this is a highly unusual behavior among chelonians. Only one other turtle species, a chelid (*Emydura* sp.) from the Macleay River, New South Wales, Australia, is known to exhibit comparable behavior (Cann, 1969).

Adult males and females may be territorial with respect to other members of their own sex but not to members of the opposite gender. Thus, a male may exclude all the other males and a female may do likewise with all other mature females. Such behavior may be a particularly effective strategy for dispersing populations in an environment with a limited number of suitable rock crevices (or a limited amount of food, which seems less likely in this case).

The three recaptured tortoises (numbers 4, 5, and 6) support our hypothesis that *Malacochersus* may remain within a well-defined home range. All three individuals were recaptured at the same small rock outcrops where they had first been discovered over a month earlier.

A member of our field crew (M. Cheptumo), who collected pancake tortoises for commercial purposes in the 1960s in the vicinity of Dodoma, Tanzania, reported that 20% of the pancake tortoises found shared their retreats with spitting cobras, *Naja nigricolis*. We did not find this in Kenya. Moreover, Klemens and Moll (1995) did not report the co-occurrence of snakes with pancake tortoises at any of their Tanzanian localities. However, they did note that the lizards *Agama* spp., *Gerrhosaurus flavigularis*, and *Hemidactylus* spp. are commonly found in the same rock crevices as pancake tortoises.

Mortality/Predation

We found partial and complete shells of six adult tortoises (all now in the KNM collection). The most complete specimen (missing only skull, neck, and forelimbs) was partially protruding from a rock crevice as if it had died there. The other shells were lying on exposed rock surfaces or on the ground. In view of their extreme fragility, these shells must represent tortoises that had recently died.

Whether these shells represented mortality from accidents, old age, or disease cannot be determined. None of the living tortoises we captured appeared to be diseased. Nor did we ever directly observe predation upon tortoises. A few (numbers 1, 4, 21, and 26) exhibited evidence of minor shell damage that had subsequently healed.

Commercial Exploitation

Commercial collections of pancake tortoises in the Nguni area were made by members of the Mutui family for only two exporters, a Mr. Whitehead, who died in the mid- to late 1960s, and J. Leakey, who ceased exporting pancake tortoises in the late 1970s.

Tortoises collected by the Mutuis were obtained locally (not farther south than Nuu and probably not farther north than Mai Forest, i.e., our study area). Pancake tortoises (according to J. and R. Mutui) now seem just as abundant in the Nguni area as they were when the Mutui family first started collecting large numbers for export in the late 1950s and early 1960s. As far as we have been able to determine, only a fraction of the Kenyan populations of *Malacochersus* (from the Nguni area) appears ever to have been commercially exploited, and apparently with no lasting detrimental effects.

People in the vicinity of Nguni had no gastronomic or any other kind of active interest in pancake tortoises. In this sense, the existing populations of *Malacochersus* are not obviously threatened. However, in our study area (and probably elsewhere within the Kenyan range of this species), land is being rapidly cleared and intensively used for agricultural purposes. Disruption or elimination of the indigenous thorn scrub vegetation characteristic of the region may prove to be hazardous to the continued survival of *Malacochersus* in Kenya.

CONCLUSIONS

- *Malacochersus* has a considerably greater geographic distribution within Kenya than has previously been realized.

- *Malacochersus* occurs in low-lying and often relatively small rock outcrops rather than on the slopes of the more massive rocky hillsides which are common and prominent features of the landscape in our study area.

- In many cases a single adult male and female were found in the same rock crevice. These occurrences may represent either a temporary or possibly even a longer-term monogamous association. Alternatively, adult males and females may both be territorial with respect to their own sexes but not to the opposite gender.

- At present, pancake tortoises in Kenya are not being exploited either for commercial purposes or as a food source by local people. But continuing and extensive human alteration of habitat may ultimately prove of greater consequence than the former collection of tortoises for the foreign pet trade. This collection ceased more than a decade before our fieldwork was undertaken, and the population known to be most heavily collected appears to have recovered.

Acknowledgments

We are greatly indebted to our companions in the field: Cmdr. and Mrs. William Ford (July 1987) and Michael Cheptumo, the brothers Jackson and Robert Mutui, and Joy and Ian McKay (September 1987). We are also much obliged to Dr. Richard E. Leakey, Director of the National Museums of Kenya at the time of our field work, for administrative support and encouragement. Dr. Laurence Hardy (Louisiana State University) and Dr. Robert Bezy (Los Angeles County Museum of Natural History) provided us with information about new pancake tortoise localities in Kenya, for which we are most appreciative. We are grateful to John Cann for information on "conjugal fidelity" in a population of *Emydura* from New South Wales, Australia. Roger Wood wishes to acknowledge the support of Richard Stockton College of New Jersey, which provided both a sabbatical leave during the fall of 1987 and also the financial support of a Distinguished Faculty Fellowship, which made his participation in this project possible.

Literature Cited

Broadley, D. G. 1989. *Malacochersus tornieri*: Pancake tortoise; soft-shelled tortoise. In I. R. Swingland and M. W. Klemens (eds.), The Conservation Biology of Tortoises, pp. 62–64. Occasional Papers of the IUCN Species Survival Commission (SSC) No. 5. IUCN, Gland, Switzerland.

Cann, J. 1969. Preliminary notes on some short-necked tortoises from eastern New South Wales. Vict. Nat. 86:191–193.

Klemens, M. W. and D. Moll. 1995. An assessment of the effects of commercial exploitation on the pancake tortoise, *Malacochersus tornieri*, in Tanzania. Chelon. Conserv. Biol. 1(3):197–206.

Loveridge, A. 1936. Scientific Results of an expedition to rain forest regions in Eastern Africa. V. Reptiles. Bull. Mus. Comp. Zoology 79(5):209–337.

Loveridge, A. and E. E. Williams. 1957. Revision of the African tortoises and turtles of the suborder Cryptodira. Bull. Mus. Comp. Zoology 115(6):163–557.

MacKay, J. A. 1981. The Story of Kenya and Its Stamps. Kenya Posts and Telecommunications Corp., Nairobi. 192 pp.

Moll, D. and M. W. Klemens. 1996. Ecological characteristics of the pancake tortoise, *Malacochersus tornieri* (Siebenrock), in Tanzania. Chelon. Conserv. Biol. (2)1:26–35.

Procter, J. B. 1922. A study of the remarkable tortoise, *Testudo loveridgii* Blgr., and the morphology of the chelonian carapace. Proc. Zool. Soc. London 34:483–526 + plates I–III.

Raphael, B., M. W. Klemens, P. Moehlman, E. Dierenfeld, and W. Karesh. 1994. Health profiles of free-ranging pancake tortoises (*Malacochersus tornieri*). J. Zoo and Wildl. Med. 25(1):63–67.

Shaw, C. E. 1970. The hardy (and prolific) soft shelled tortoise. Int. Turtle & Tortoise Soc. J. 4(1):6–13.

U.S. Fish and Wildlife Service. 1992. CITES: Appendices I, II, and III to the Convention on International Trade in Endangered Species of Wild Fauna and Flora. Title 50—Wildlife and Fisheries, Part 23, §23.23. Publication Unit, U.S. Fish and Wildlife Service, Washington, D.C.

Specific Threats to Tortoises in Israel

— ABSTRACT OF PRESENTATION —

ELI GEFFEN AND HEINRICH MENDELSSOHN

Department of Zoology, Tel Aviv University, Ramat Aviv, Tel Aviv 69978, Israel [e-mail: geffene@post.tau.ac.il]

The main threats to the continued survival of both tortoise species in Israel are agricultural and urban development, which are continually destroying natural habitats. The southern subspecies of *Testudo graeca* (*T. g. floweri**) has already disappeared, as its entire range is now being farmed or planted with eucalyptus trees. The future of the widespread *T. g. terrestris* is ensured by a number of nature reserves in the Mediterranean area. A large (220 km) nature reserve, Holot Agur, is planned for *Testudo kleinmanni* and for other psammophilous fauna, but it has yet to be finally approved, and developers are fiercely opposing the size of this reserve (Mendelssohn, 1982; Mendelssohn and Geffen, 1987; Stubbs, 1989a, 1989b). Trade in tortoises is completely forbidden in Israel, but *Testudo graeca* may be collected as personal pets. *Testudo kleinmanni* is completely protected.

Literature Cited

Mendelssohn, H. 1982. Egyptian tortoise. In B. Groombridge (ed.), The IUCN Reptilia-Amphibia Red Data Book, pp. 133–136. IUCN, Gland, Switzerland.

Mendelssohn, H. and E. Geffen. 1987. The Egyptian tortoise in Israel. Israel Land and Nature 12:153–157.

Stubbs, D. 1989a. *Testudo graeca*: spur-thighed tortoise. In I. R. Swingland and M. W. Klemens (eds.), The Conservation Biology of Tortoises, pp. 31–33. Occasional Papers of the IUCN Species Survival Commission (SSC) No. 5. IUCN, Gland, Switzerland.

Stubbs, D. 1989b. *Testudo kleinmanni*: Egyptian tortoise. In I. R. Swingland and M. W. Klemens (eds.), The Conservation Biology of Tortoises, pp. 39–40. Occasional Papers of the IUCN Species Survival Commission (SSC) No. 5. IUCN, Gland, Switzerland.

**T. g. floweri* has not been widely accepted as a subspecies.

Species Recovery and Management Strategies

Standing — Gerald Kuchling (University of Western Australia, Nedlands) and Gustavo Aguirre (Instituto de Ecología, Xalapa, Veracruz, Mexico). *Seated* — David Stubbs (Village des Tortues, Gonfaron, France) and Lora Smith (University of Florida, Gainesville).

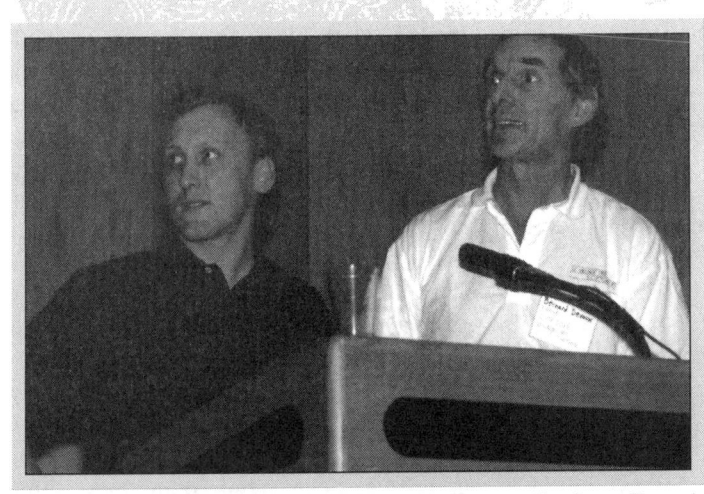

David Stubbs and Bernard Devaux (Village des Tortues, Gonfaron, France).

A Conservation Strategy for the Geometric Tortoise, *Psammobates geometricus*

ERNST H. W. BAARD

Cape Nature Conservation, Private Bag X5014, Stellenbosch 7599, South Africa [e-mail: baarde@cncjnk.wcape.gov.za]

ABSTRACT: The results of an investigation of biological aspects and the conservation status of the geometric tortoise, *Psammobates geometricus*, were used to compile a conservation strategy for this species. This strategy is firstly a synthesis of updated information on the species' distribution and biology; it discusses threats operating within the range of the species, provides information on reserves currently containing geometric tortoise populations, and suggests sites for additional reserves. Secondly, the proposed strategy provides guidelines for (1) the management of viable populations, (2) the consolidation of viable units, and (3) the compilation of reserve management plans. Thirdly, it discusses the role of fire in habitat upgrading, predator and alien vegetation control, and relocation of threatened populations. Privately owned sites supporting geometric tortoise populations are discussed in the fourth instance, and guidelines on communication with landowners, rehabilitation of old lands as buffer zones, and the sensitive development of infrastructure on properties are provided. Finally, the document proposes a cooperative programme for the medium- to long-term monitoring of the status of populations, with details on distribution surveys and methods (e.g., time scales, survey methods and design, and data collection).

The geometric tortoise, *Psammobates geometricus*, is South Africa's most threatened tortoise. Endemic to the southwestern Cape Province, it is also one of world's rarest. It is found only in an area of approximately 5,000 ha (±12,400 acres or ±20 mi²) of a low-lying, dwarf-shrub vegetation type, locally known as "renosterveld," with a prevailing Mediterranean climate. After concern had been expressed by the Cape Province's nature conservation authority about the status of the geometric tortoise, a project was launched in 1986 to investigate its endangered status and to study aspects of its biology.

The objectives of the above-mentioned study were (1) to establish the present distribution of *P. geometricus* and compare that to its 1977 distribution as reported by Greig and Boycott (1977), (2) to study certain biological aspects of the species, (3) to identify those aspects fundamental to its conservation and survival, and (4) to put forward ecologically based management proposals for its future conservation. These underlying objectives formed the basis for the overall aim of the project which was to compile a practical, ecologically based conservation strategy for the geometric tortoise in the southwestern Cape Province.

This paper presents a comprehensive summary of this strategy document (Baard, 1993a), which aims to put forward a practical strategy with regard to (1) the protection and management of all existing and newly discovered populations, and (2) the continued monitoring of the status of the species. The strategy was accepted and implementation started in autumn (April–May) of 1994.

The distribution of *P. geometricus* is characterized by small, isolated populations in low-lying renosterveld habitat—so named after the dominant shrub *Elythropappus rhinocerotis* ("rhinoceros bush") in the community—of the Cape lowlands, and the Worcester/Tulbagh and Ceres valleys (Figure 1; see also Baard, 1993b). Extensive agricultural development throughout its range (McDowell and Moll, 1992) has largely been responsible for the replacement of more than 97% of renosterveld with wheatlands, vineyards, orchards, and large, heavily grazed areas (Parker, 1982; McDowell and Moll, 1992). Geometric tortoises are presently known to occur at 31 localities (including one private and four provincial nature reserves) in the southwestern Cape Province. Other, as yet undiscovered, sites remain to be mapped. Updated information on geometric tortoise distribution, conservation status, and threats operating in its natural distribution range is provided by Baard (1993b).

Biological aspects, regarded as fundamental to a conservation strategy for *P. geometricus*, were identified and quantified (in terms of variance) as far as possible from results obtained during the course of the above-mentioned project (Baard, 1990) and subsequent research. It must be pointed out that this study addressed only main aspects of the biology of this species, and more research is required to present a comprehensive picture.

The mere listing of a species on a threatened list is no guarantee against extinction. Strategies to ensure the survival of endangered species are required and these should be aimed at the careful management of populations in a state where their vigour and viability are ensured. In other words, populations identified as vital nuclei of a species should be able to maintain themselves in their natural habitat, in order that an adequate level of population fitness can be maintained (Soulé, 1987).

A conservation strategy should have short-term conservation goals, addressing and identifying immediate problems, as well as a medium- to long-term predictive approach where, based on substantiating evidence, management proposals are created to identify, manage and maintain populations important to the survival of the species. The authority responsible for the management of such populations should base management decisions on research, ensuring that the populations would have the best chance to sustain themselves and minimizing the possibility of extinction. It is therefore important to understand the dynamics of the populations involved before predictions about their long-term survival are attempted. In supplying information about population dynamics and the minimum requirements for the long-term survival of species and populations, a basis is created for sound scientific management. This is emphasised by Soulé (1987), who points out that the formulation of management predictions are some of the most difficult problems in conservation biology because they require predictions based on an integration of biotic and abiotic factors in the spatial and temporal continuum.

The first step in the development of conservation programmes for particular species is the recognition of constraints that may impose detrimental effects on them (Dodd, 1986). Management should be geared towards the recognition of these constraints (see Baard, 1993a), and where possible, should be aimed at the prevention or elimination of these factors.

Another very important aspect of conservation strategies for threatened species is public interest. Without public concern, and especially that of the private landowner, towards threatened biota, conservation authorities can often do little to secure adequate natural habitat. Therefore, "research should provide the information—and public concern, the impetus—to insure that quality . . . habitat is available for the future" (Diemer, 1986).

Conservation biology aspects, such as minimum viable populations (MVPs), population viability analysis (PVA), and reserve system design should be addressed in any conservation strategy. Further, a conservation strategy should never be rigid and unwieldy. It should be flexible, practical, easy to implement, and should be evaluated and updated on a regular basis.

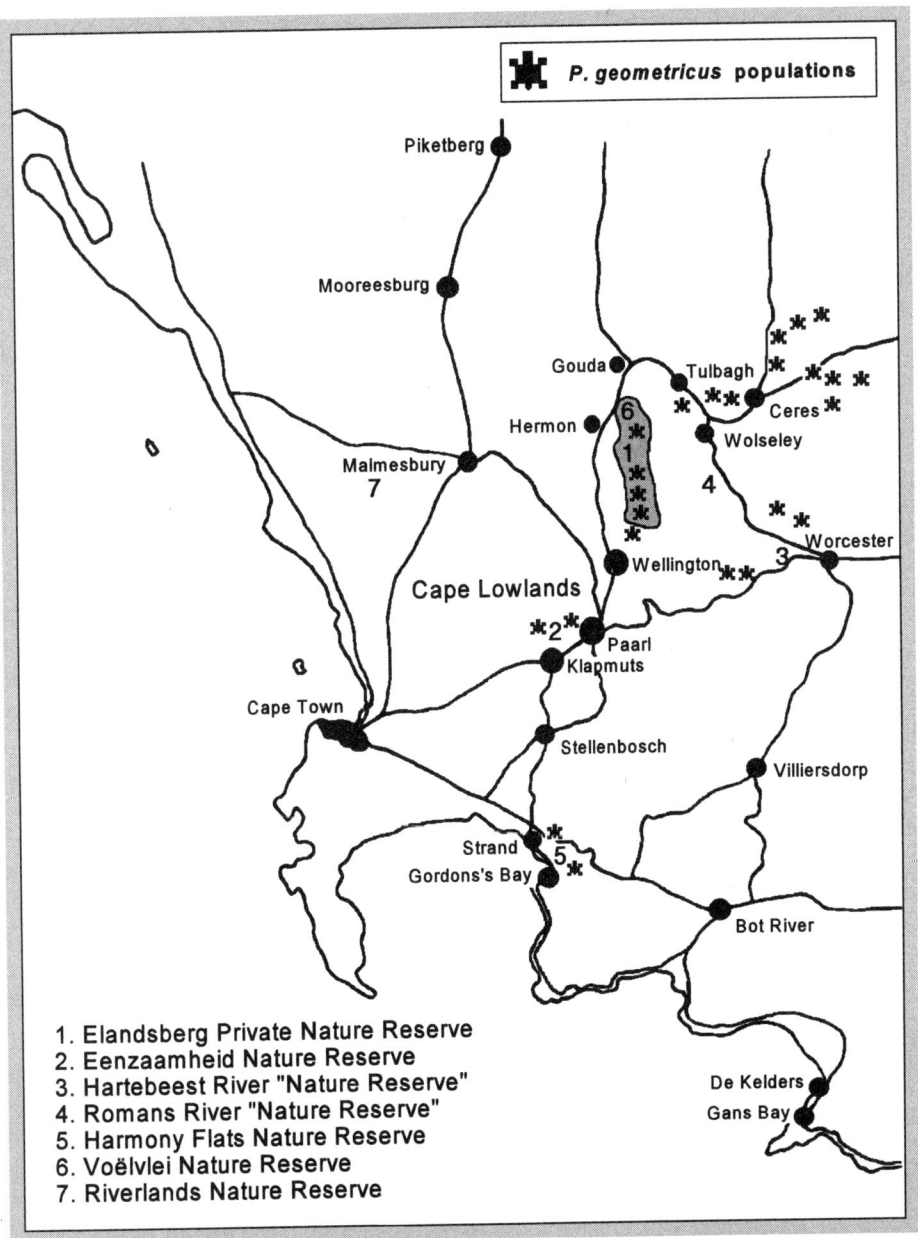

Figure 1. Map showing locations of nature reserves and geometric tortoise populations.

1. Elandsberg Private Nature Reserve
2. Eenzaamheid Nature Reserve
3. Hartebeest River "Nature Reserve"
4. Romans River "Nature Reserve"
5. Harmony Flats Nature Reserve
6. Voëlvlei Nature Reserve
7. Riverlands Nature Reserve

Preserved areas

Presently, geometric tortoise populations are contained in one private and four provincial nature reserves, namely Elandsberg Private Nature Reserve (3,603 ha with approx. 1,000 ha available habitat), Voëlvlei Nature Reserve (±360 ha), J. N. Briers-Louw Nature Reserve (±30 ha), Harmony Flats Nature Reserve (10 ha), and a relatively small portion (±100 ha) of the Riverlands Nature Reserve. Two other previously preserved areas (they have been deproclaimed), Hartebeest River (±44 ha) and Romans River (±35 ha) contain small populations as well. Severe, unforeseen habitat deterioration in the former, and private concern in the latter case, resulted in the deproclamation of the two nature reserves.

With the deproclamation of the two above-mentioned reserves, it has become necessary to initiate further steps to establish other preserved sites in this area. Two private landowners (Chelancé and Perdefontein) have indicated their willingness to have sites on their properties set aside and declared as preserves for geometric tortoises. These sites do not necessarily have to be proclaimed as provincial nature reserves but could be registered as either private nature reserves or sites of special interest, so-called "Natural Heritage Sites."

Apart from these two localities, it is suggested that the following properties be inspected to either initiate private nature reserves or to register them as Natural Heritage Sites: Krantzkop (±500 ha), Palmiet Valley (±150 ha), Lemietrivier (±150 ha, near Wellington), Die Oliene (±50 ha) and Skilpadrug (±60 ha, near Tulbagh), Onderplaas (±50 ha, near Worcester), and Elandsrivier (±500 ha, Prince Alfred Hamlet). With the rising cost of land purchase, Cape Nature Conservation will have to solicit the cooperation of these landowners to effectively conserve the geometric tortoise.

Guidelines for the Management of Geometric Tortoise Populations and Habitat

The remaining natural geometric tortoise populations must be maintained to ensure adequate genetic diversity of this species. The loss of marginal populations may reduce the survival potential of the species as a whole, and the loss of these populations should be prevented as far as possible. Incidentally, some of these marginal sites also contain threatened plants often found only at that particular site.

The recommendations that have been put forward for the future management of existing, and any new geometric tortoise populations and their habitats, are summarized and briefly explained below. Baard (1993a) provides more detailed information.

The following recommendations are made for existing reserves and viable populations:

1. Management plans should be compiled for all nature reserves containing geometric tortoise populations and should focus on the integrated management of viable populations. Condensed, minimum management plans for the Elandsberg Private Nature Reserve, Voëlvlei, J. N. Briers-Louw, and Harmony Flats Provincial Nature Reserves are presented in Appendix A of Baard's (1993a) conservation strategy document. These are based on the minimum management plan format as proposed in a working document of the British Nature Conservancy Council (British Nature Conservancy Council, 1988). These management plans incorporate the minimum information relevant to the conservation and management of *P. geometricus* on these reserves and are presented as a working guide to be incorporated in future management plans for the relevant reserves. In addition, probably the only long-term viable unit for the protection of *P. geometricus* as a species is a contiguous conservation area comprising the Voëlvlei Nature Reserve, the Cape Town City Council land next to Voëlvlei Dam, the Kasteelkloof Conservation Area, the Elandsberg Private Nature Reserve, the Krantzkop site, and parts of the two farms Palmiet Valley and Lemietrivier. Negotiations to consolidate the management of this area should be initiated as soon as possible. In most cases, the procurement of geometric tortoise preserves is dictated by economic constraints; the land is usually too expensive to be purchased by the conservation authority, and the latter has to rely on the cooperation of the landowner for leasing it or registering it as a site of high conservation value. It is therefore recommended that, as a short-term priority, the future of all present nature reserves for *P. geometricus* be secured in terms of either conservation authority ownership or a renewable, secure lease. In the medium- to long-term, future conservation sites should either be purchased, proclaimed as private nature reserves, or be registered under the auspices of the Department of Environment Affairs as Natural Heritage Sites.

2. It is desirable to establish (a) effective buffer zones around existing reserves to minimise detrimental effects from "outside" and (b) corridors between reserves to allow for gene flow and dispersal of individuals between the components of a reserve system. Private landowners should be encouraged to rehabilitate old, uncultivated agricultural lands as buffer areas around existing geometric tortoise sites (see below). Given the fragmented nature of geometric tortoise habitat and the present location of nature reserves, it is, however, impossible to establish corridors between reserves because the habitat no longer exists. Alternatively, manual interchange of genetic stock between populations could be considered. This aspect, however, requires more research before it is implemented.

3. With regard to a population's viability, a largest possible reproductive cohort should be preserved to ensure a high population survival probability. Franklin (1980) recommended a short-term effective (viable) population size (N_e) of 50 individuals, a "magic" or arbitrary number (see

Soulé and Simberloff, 1986) that is not widely accepted. Cox et al. (1987) define viable gopher tortoise populations as the size required to provide a 90% probability of surviving for at least 200 years and suggest a population of 40–50 animals to be the smallest population size generally considered for protection. The *Desert Tortoise Recovery Plan* (Berry, this volume) is designed for a 50% probability of survival for the desert tortoise for 500 years. This translates broadly into reserved areas ranging from 415 to 3,370 km² with target densities of 50,000 breeding adults.

The results presented by Cox et al. (1987) and the desert tortoise recovery plan cannot be unconditionally related to *P. geometricus* because the habitat requirements of these species, and especially their spatial attributes, differ completely. Preliminary results generated by VORTEX (Lacy and Kreeger, 1992) suggest a minimum threshold population of 250 breeding *P. geometricus* having a 95% chance of surviving for 200 years (stochastic events taken into account). It is, however, important that a positive trend in population growth be promoted and maintained, rather than maintaining a "magic" or arbitrary number indefinitely. Although reserves frequently must be established on a "preserve-what-is-left" basis, it is recommended that, for long-term preservation of viable geometric tortoise populations, the minimum size of reserves should not be less than approximately 80–100 ha to maintain a population of approximately 250 adult geometric tortoises. These figures of 80–100 ha or 250 tortoises (an average of approx. 3 tortoises/ha) are based on what are regarded as optimum densities of 2.0–3.4 tortoises/ha in the Elandsberg Private Nature Reserve and approximately 4.0/ha in the Eenzaamheid Nature Reserve (Greig, 1984). Two hundred and fifty reproductive adults at a sex ratio of approximately 1:1 should be able to maintain a medium- to long-term viable population, provided that management would strive to eliminate catastrophic events as far as possible. However, this generated model for the geometric tortoise should be approached with caution, and managers should not rely exclusively on it, as more research, especially on survivorship, fecundity, and longevity, is required to update these preliminary findings. Presently, these are the best data available. Population viability analysis is an important tool in conservation, but it should involve a long-term iterative process of modeling and research to continuously refine the parameters used to create the best possible model for the species, given the data available (Boyce, 1993).

The following recommendations are made for the management of populations and habitat:

1. Should fire be considered a tool in the management (and/or the upgrading) of renosterveld habitat, the following guidelines would be applicable:
   (a) A mosaic of differently aged habitat patches could be established at localities with degraded climax-stage renosterveld to promote its rehabilitation and enhance tortoise abundance. (However, should this option not be acceptable, manual removal of *E. rhinocerotis* shrubs has yielded promising results in rehabilitating degraded renosterveld habitat.)
   (b) Not more than 10% of the total reserve size should be burned at a time.
   (c) Burns should take place at intervals of not less than seven years to permit generations to reach sexual maturity (recommended frequency 11–12 years).
   (d) The burn period should be scheduled during March to early April as hatching of eggs takes place in late April to early May.
   (e) When possible, visible adult or juvenile tortoises may be "rescued" before a controlled burn to avoid fire mortality.

2. Increased human alteration of natural surroundings has created opportunities for the proliferation of potential predators of geometric tortoises. Although predation in healthy populations may enhance population resilience by statistical removal of less "fit" individuals, it may become necessary to initiate predator control where populations of truly endangered species are concerned. Therefore, should adequate evidence exist that any predators are threatening geometric tortoise populations, control measures should be considered.

3. The invasive potential of alien vegetation, especially in the southwestern Cape, is a threat to the last remnants of renosterveld. The prolific and "aggressive" dispersal potential of alien vegetation reduces the efficiency of eradication programmes, and continuous follow-up operations are called for. Eradication programmes should therefore be executed on a regular basis to reduce or stop the spread of invasive species, using all means of control deemed necessary, practical, and safe (e.g., manual, chemical, biological).

4. The feasibility of relocation of threatened populations to new sites is detailed by Berry (1986) and Diemer (1989). Tortoise relocation is a complex issue and it should be practised with great care. Important facets of relocation are, among others: habitat suitability of recipient sites, carrying capacities, size and shape of the area in relation to tortoise movements, season of translocation, disruption of recipient population dynamics, possible genetic contamination of local populations, social dysfunction, and translocation of diseases or vectors of diseases (e.g., upper respiratory tract disease and ticks, respectively). Tortoise relocation is also labour intensive, time consuming, and thus expensive. Diemer (1989) suggests that developers be required to contribute financially to the purchase of reserves, and to support relocations and follow-up surveys. In view of this, proposals for geometric tortoise relocations should be evaluated carefully and conservatively. Presently, too little is known about these aspects to make any firm recommendations, and every effort should be made to protect remaining populations *in situ*.

Privately Owned Sites Containing *P. geometricus* Populations

The attitude of landowners towards geometric tortoise conservation is of the utmost importance. Without their positive participation in the geometric tortoise conservation programme, there is little that Cape Nature Conservation can do to protect the remaining populations and habitat. Regular contact and feedback are two important aspects, and landowners should be contacted at least once every year to either relay information to them or perform a field evaluation of the status of the geometric tortoise population(s) on their properties.

Evidence from the Elandsberg Private Nature Reserve and other provincial nature reserves suggest that neighbouring, previously cultivated wheatlands, now left unplanted, can act as effective "browsing ranges" for geometric tortoises. They also act as effective barriers against unplanned fires. Although they were previously thought not to utilise these old lands, a surprising number of tortoises have been found there (pers. obs.), probably prompted to make use of the extensive ephemeral food plant component. In cases where the *E. rhinocerotis* shrub component at a geometric tortoise locality has become so dominant that it outcompetes the ephemeral component, adjacent, partially recovered old lands may play a significant role in supplying an additional food resource to the tortoises. The rehabilitation of unused lands adjacent to important geometric tortoise populations should therefore be encouraged. Overgrazing and extensive trampling by farm stock (cattle, sheep, and especially goats) should, however, be avoided.

Proposed development on these properties should always be undertaken bearing in mind the possibly detrimental effect of roads, new buildings, rubbish dumps, stock enclosures, stockpiling of soil or feed, alien vegetation, etc. on natural vegetation and its components. In many cases, natural habitat is regarded as "wasteland," being either too wet in winter, too rocky, or too steep to develop (or to plough). These sites are then often used as dumping sites for either garbage or builders' debris, are severely overutilised as grazing for stock, or are left to become infested with alien vegetation.

Private landowners with geometric tortoise populations on their properties should therefore be encouraged to (1) develop infrastructure on their properties with regard to the remaining natural habitat, (2) not use these habitats as dumping sites, (3) control grazing there, and (4) implement control programmes for alien vegetation at these sites.

Public Education

Public education programmes—including (1) the distribution of educational brochures, posters, pamphlets, and audio-visual material to members of the public; (2) visits to schools, farmers, farm workers, agricultural fairs; and (3) informing the public by means of the media (press, radio, and television)—are important to convey the plight of the geometric tortoise.

Reserves containing tortoise populations can also be utilised for educational visits by members of the public, e.g., wildlife clubs and school groups, under the supervision of managers who can assist in the interpretation of the plant and animal communities, with special emphasis on the geometric tortoise and its role in the environment. With guidance from managers, local communities can be involved in the day-to-day management of small reserves. Public interest groups may also assist in providing back-up for conservation authorities short of staff.

Monitoring of Geometric Tortoise Conservation Status

Probably the most important part of any conservation programme for endangered species should be the monitoring of the status of populations concerned. The aim of this is two-fold: (1) to act as an early warning system for declines in population sizes, and (2) to detect any effects that may lead to the extinction of populations (Beiswenger, 1986). The severe fragmentation of the southwestern Cape geometric tortoise "meta-population" calls for a cooperative effort to collate information about the status of remaining populations throughout its range.

Individual population status monitoring programmes have been initiated that involve visits once every year, or once every two or three years, to reserves and privately owned sites containing geometric tortoise populations. Standardised methods will be used and specific survey designs have been provided for individual sites. The data obtained in this manner will form the foundation of a comprehensive database on the geometric tortoise population status.

Recent Develepments

At the time of going to press, the number of sites where geometric tortoises are known has increased from 31 (see p. 324) to at least 42 properties, two private nature reserves on the farms Chelancé and Perdefontien were established, negotiations towards the establishment of a conservancy (a group of private properties with shared conservation objectives; see Figure 1) have started, and two reserved populations (J. N. Briers-Louw and Harmony Flats) have declined in status due to severe environmental impact. Habitat restoration measures in the form of a controlled burn of part of the reserve were initiated at the former.

Literature Cited

Baard, E. H. W. 1990. Biological aspects and conservation status of the geometric tortoise, *Psammobates geometricus* (Linnaeus, 1758) (Cryptodira: Testudinidae). Ph.D. dissertation, University of Stellenbosch, Stellenbosch, South Africa.

Baard, E. H. W. 1993a. A conservation strategy for the geometric tortoise, *Psammobates geometricus* in the southwestern Cape Province, South Africa. Chief Directorate Nature and Environmental Conservation (C.P.A.), Internal Report 11:1–64.

Baard, E. H. W. 1993b. Distribution and status of the geometric tortoise *Psammobates geometricus* in South Africa. Biol. Conserv. 63:235–239.

Beiswenger, R. E. 1986. An endangered species, the Wyoming toad *Bufo hemiophrys baxteri*—The importance of an early warning system. Biol. Conserv. 37:59–71.

Berry, K. H. 1986. Desert tortoise (*Gopherus agassizii*) relocation: Implications of social behavior and movements. Herpetologica 42(1):113–125.

Berry, K. H. 1997. The desert tortoise recovery plan: An ambitious effort to conserve biodiversity in the Mojave and Colorado deserts of the United States. *In* J. Van Abbema (ed.), Proceedings: Conservation, Restoration, and Management of Tortoises and Turtles—An International Conference, pp. 430–440. July 1993, State University of New York, Purchase. New York Turtle and Tortoise Society, New York.

Boyce, M. S. 1993. Population viability analysis: Adaptive management for threatened and endangered species. Trans. 58th N.A. Wildl. & Natur. Resour. Conf. (1993):520–527.

British Nature Conservancy Council. 1988. Site management plans for nature conservation—A working guide. Nature Conservancy Council, Great Britain.

Cox, J., D. Inkley, and R. Kautz. 1987. Ecology and habitat protection needs of gopher tortoise (*Gopherus polyphemus*) populations found on lands slated for large-scale development in Florida. Florida Game and Fresh Water Fish Commission Nongame Wildlife Program Technical Report 4:24–35.

Diemer, J. E. 1986. The ecology and management of the gopher tortoise in the southeastern United States. Herpetologica 42(1): 125–133.

Diemer, J. E. 1989. An overview of gopher tortoise relocation. *In* J. E. Diemer, D. R. Jackson, J. L. Landers, J. N. Layne, and D. A. Wood (eds.), Florida Game and Fresh Water Fish Commission, Nongame Wildlife Program Technical Report #5, pp. 1–6.

Dodd, C. K. 1986. Desert and gopher tortoises: Perspectives on conservation approaches. *In* D. R. Jackson and R. J. Bryant (eds.), The Gopher Tortoise and its Community, pp. 54–72. Proc. 5th Ann. Mtg. Gopher Tortoise Council.

Franklin, I. A. 1980. Evolutionary change in small populations. *In* M. E. Soulé and B. A. Wilcox (eds.), Conservation Biology: An Evolutionary-Ecological Perspective, pp. 135–149. Sinauer Associates, Sunderland, Massachusetts.

Greig, J. C. 1984. Conservation status of South African land tortoises, with special reference to the geometric tortoise (*Psammobates geometricus*). Amphibia-Reptilia 5:27–30.

Greig, J. C. and R. C. Boycott. 1977. The geometric tortoise (*Psammobates geometricus*)—Progress report 1977. *In* Cape Department of Nature and Environmental Conservation research report—Herpetology, 1977, pp. 56–66. Cape Department of Nature and Environmental Conservation, Cape Town, South Africa.

Lacy, R. C. and T. Kreeger (eds.). 1992. Vortex Users Manual. A Stochastic Simulation of the Extinction Process. IUCN/SSC/CBSG, Chicago Zoological Society, Brookfield, Illinois.

McDowell, C. and E. Moll. 1992. The influence of agriculture on the decline of West Coast renosterveld, south-western Cape, South Africa. J. Environ. Manage. 35:173–192.

Parker, D. 1982. The Western Cape Lowland fynbos: What is there left to conserve?! Veld & Flora 68(4): 98–101.

Soulé, M. E. (ed.). 1987. Viable Populations for Conservation. Cambridge University Press, Cambridge.

Soulé, M. E. and D. Simberloff. 1986. What do genetics and ecology tell us about the design of nature reserves? Biol. Conserv. 35: 19–40.

Species Recovery Programme for Hermann's Tortoise in Southern France

BERNARD DEVAUX AND DAVID STUBBS

*Station d'Observation et de Protection des Tortues des Maures (SOPTOM),
Village des Tortues, BP24, 83590 Gonfaron, France [Stubbs e-mail: ega.golf.ecology@dial.pipex.com]*

ABSTRACT: The conservation programme for Hermann's tortoise in southern France started as a traditional autecological research project in the early 1980s. The research findings prompted a locally based conservation initiative, which by the early 1990s had developed into an internationally acclaimed example of popular conservation in action.

The focus of the project is the Village des Tortues conservation/visitor centre, which annually attracts many tens of thousands of visitors both from the local area (including numerous school parties) and tourists from throughout Europe. The Village des Tortues provides the funding base for the direct conservation programme aimed at protecting and restoring wild tortoise populations in the Massif des Maures, Var.

The wide-ranging publicity derived from the project has helped spawn similar initiatives in other countries, notably Italy, and SOPTOM itself is currently promoting new Tortoise Villages in Corsica and Senegal. It is also "twinned" with the turtle centre at Les Hattes in French Guyana.

This paper reviews the development of the SOPTOM project, which combines the key elements of a strong local base within the target species' natural range and crucial support from national and international conservation organisations. The foundation of the project depended upon support from outside agencies. Now SOPTOM is itself able to export know-how and resources to aid other tortoise conservation programmes. Locally, the momentum of the tortoise conservation work has also contributed to safeguarding key habitats and other associated species that would otherwise not have received sufficient exposure and support to ensure their protection.

Wild populations of the nominate race of Hermann's tortoise, *Testudo hermanni hermanni*, are confined to a small number of scattered localities in the western Mediterranean region. One of the largest extant populations is that of the Massif des Maures, in the Department of Var, southern France. Hermann's tortoise is the only species of terrestrial chelonian in France and is one of the country's most endangered reptile species.

The tortoise is experiencing a long-term decline, the principal causes of which were highlighted by Stubbs and Swingland (1985) as (1) direct habitat loss and fragmentation caused by forest fires, urban and infrastructure development, and modern agriculture; and (2) as gradual habitat modifications caused by changes in agricultural practices and abandonment of traditional management regimes.

Since the end of the First World War there has been a shift away from a rural-based population, and large tracts of forest and hillside cultivations have been left untended. This has had a number of serious effects upon tortoises: first, a general reduction in habitat suitability; secondly, greater frequency of summer forest fires intensified by the tinder-dry brushwood accumulated in the neglected forest zones; and thirdly, a higher concentration of predators that are no longer actively controlled.

Suitable nest sites in forest clearings or small cultivations (e.g., olive groves) are much less available, and in those that do remain, up to 95% of nests are preyed upon by badgers (*Meles meles*) and beech martens (*Martes fouina*). Additional mortality results from casual collecting by visitors to the countryside and from road deaths.

The French Riviera attracts millions of tourists each year. It borders the Massif des Maures, and conservationists are faced with the problem of reconciling the protection of ancient fragile habitats and their flora and fauna with the excessive demands of a rapidly expanding regional economy. To conserve Hermann's tortoise within its remaining natural range in France, Devaux, Pouvreau, and Stubbs (1986) identified the following essential requirements:

- Protection of remaining natural range—bringing a conservation rationale to land use planning,
- Habitat management measures, and
- Restocking and reintroduction as complementary measures.

It is relatively simple to chart the decline of a species and to advocate conservation measures. Implementing them is the challenge and inevitably demands an amount of luck as well as hard work and commitment. Immediately following the initial research of the early 1980s (Stubbs and

Swingland, 1985), one of us (Devaux) established the project on the ground, in the heart of the tortoises' natural area. Locally based involvement has proved crucial to the project's success.

Chronology

1985   La Station d'Observation et de Protection des Tortues des Maures (SOPTOM) was founded. This is a nonprofit organisation dedicated to the study and protection of Hermann's tortoise in France and tortoise conservation in general.

1986   Species recovery programme was published (Devaux et al., 1986). This included proposals for a special conservation centre, and the recovery programme document served as a valuable fund-raising tool.

1987   The project developed gradually through concerted voluntary effort plus donations, subscriptions, small grants, and sale of local craft work. The main funding source was an "adopt-a-tortoise" scheme, in which individual wild tortoises (marked and recorded as part of the original research study) were sponsored by subscribers to the scheme.

1988   The new conservation centre, named the "Village des Tortues," was opened on 28 May at Gonfaron by the naturalist and writer Gerald Durrell. The Tortoise Village had cost Fr 150,000 (U.S. $25,000) to build—a heavily discounted cost due to extensive use of voluntary labour, including special project teams from the British Trust for Conservation Volunteers.

The Tortoise Village comprised a series of enclosed breeding and rearing pens, set in one hectare of semi-natural vegetation, and basic reception and educational facilities for the general public. During the first summer 25,000 paying visitors were received, including a large number of school parties.

1993   Over 65,000 visitors passed through the Tortoise Village, and SOPTOM realised a turnover of Fr 1.5 M (U.S. $250,000). The project is totally self-financed and receives no state aid.

1995   International Congress of Chelonian Conservation. From 6 through 10 July SOPTOM hosted and self-financed a truly international gathering of 230 participants from 36 countries. There were over 90 presentations covering chelonian conservation issues from all the continents where these creatures occur. The proceedings were published within three months of the congress (SOPTOM, 1995).

1996   The Tortoise Village expanded to two hectares and visitor numbers exceeded 100,000. The SOPTOM research programme is in full swing, and the first site purchase was completed.

Activities

The Tortoise Village is a facility that has expanded and developed since its original inception and now covers two hectares of land. Fundamentally, it supports the breeding and rearing of native French tortoises for release into the wild in specially selected release sites. In addition, the Education Programme includes an active display of conservation at work, single species focus, habitat and regional emphasis, guided visits, videos, lectures, booklets, and numerous school group visits as well as regular publicity at the local and national levels through press, radio, and TV.

Public Participation

All tortoises at the village are former "pets" donated by the public. These were all originally French wild tortoises, taken into captivity in the years before conservation became a public issue, and they had been subsisting in backyards for many years. Some people had small breeding colonies in their gardens and provided many young animals for the village. No wild animals other than recuperated injured individuals are accepted. On average, approximately 1,000 tortoises are received at the village each year, which, with the adoption scheme, provides a strong local public involvement in the project.

Research

The Tortoise Village serves as an important research base, both for in-house projects monitoring the situation in the wild and for visiting researchers. From 1987 to 1989 SOPTOM conducted a full census of wild populations and estimated that 85,000–100,000 animals remain in a total range area of 200,000 hectares. While representing less than half a tortoise per hectare overall, the best sites were found to support densities of up to 11 tortoises per hectare. This means there are vast areas either underpopulated or entirely empty—a very patchy, fragmented population dispersion. This study has been a vital factor in SOPTOM's conservation planning for the 1990s. Other technical research projects have included:

- Monitoring site fidelity and dispersal of released former captive tortoises by means of radio tracking;

- Comparison of two populations formerly linked but separated by an auto route construction since 1988;

- Dispersal of subadults (G. Guyot, 1996); and

- Village-based studies on nesting behaviour, feeding, pathology, epidemiology (B. Collins and E. Jacobson,

College of Veterinary Medicine, University of Florida, Gainesville, Florida, USA), and thermoregulation and genetics (Comité National pur la récherche scientifique, Institut d'Ecologie).

Conservation

Since 1988 over 6,000 Hermann's tortoises have been reintroduced at 15 different sites throughout the Massif des Maures. Release stock comprises a mixture of subadults (at least five years old) and male and female adults. Additional sites are being prospected and accompanying habitat management measures are envisaged to ensure that appropriate conditions are maintained.

The Tortoise Village has provided SOPTOM with considerable credibility and status at the local, regional, national, and international levels. This has enabled influence to be brought to bear on the French Government and the European Commission regarding the tortoise trade. The project was too young to stop the auto route construction, which damaged a prime site, but important mitigation measures were secured. More recently SOPTOM has successfully spearheaded a campaign to save the Maures Plain (a 1,500 ha area of lowland maquis) from development. The Maures Plain is of international conservation significance for several taxonomic groups (orchids, birds, reptiles, and invertebrates), but tortoises have been a strong focus in the presentation of the campaign.

On a broader level, SOPTOM has been lobbying for a general classification of the Massif des Maures as a Parc Naturel Régional, which is a long-term goal to secure political protection for the whole habitat block.

Overseas

Originally the SOPTOM project depended upon seed funding from organisations such as the Fauna and Flora Preservation Society. The difficulties in enabling new worthwhile projects to manage on their own is a major problem for conservation everywhere. This is why SOPTOM seeks to repay its original aid by helping in the establishment of new projects. This is accomplished primarily through the export of knowledge and expertise, but some financial aid is also granted where merited.

Overseas projects currently supported are:

- A second Tortoise Village (in Corsica);
- Sponsorship of the marine turtle sanctuary at Les Hattes, French Guyana;
- A conservation initiative for *Geochelone sulcata* in Senegal; and
- A conservation education programme on the Indian Ocean island of Réunion to stem the flow of large numbers of *Geochelone radiata* brought from Madagascar.

Conclusion

The SOPTOM programme is a successful implementation of one of the projects highlighted in the IUCN Tortoise and Freshwater Turtle Action Plan (IUCN/SSC, 1989). It owes its success to a combination of scientific and practical skills. The rationale for the project was based on original research and a technical conservation programme was devised, but making it happen required the participation of enthusiastic people who could offer a variety of creative and managerial skills.

Literature Cited

Devaux, B., J.-P. Pouvreau, and D. Stubbs. 1986. Programme de sauvegarde de la tortue d'Hermann. La Station d'Observation et de Protection des Tortues des Maures, France.

Guyot, G. 1996. Biologie de la conservation chez la Tortue d'Hermann Française. Ph.D. thesis, Université-Pierre et Curie, Paris.

IUCN/SSC Tortoise and Freshwater Turtle Specialist Group. 1989. Tortoises and freshwater turtles: An action plan for their conservation (D. Stubbs, comp.). IUCN/SSC Tortoise and Freshwater Turtle Specialist Group, Gland, Switzerland. 47 pp.

Station d'Observation et de Protection des Tortues des Maures (SOPTOM). 1995. Proceedings of the International Congress of Chelonian Conservation. Editions SOPTOM, Gonfaron, France.

Stubbs, D. and I. R. Swingland. 1985. The ecology of a Mediterranean tortoise, *Testudo hermanni*: A declining population. Can. J. Zool. 63:169–180.

Conservation Strategies for the Bolson Tortoise, *Gopherus flavomarginatus*, in the Chihuahuan Desert

GUSTAVO AGUIRRE,[1] DAVID J. MORAFKA,[2] AND GARY A. ADEST[3]

[1]*Instituto de Ecología, A. C., Km 2.5 Antigua Carretera a Coatepec,
Ap. Postal 63, 91000 Xalapa, Veracruz, Mexico [e-mail: aguirreg@sun.ieco.conacyt.mx]*
[2]*Department of Biology, California State University, Dominguez Hills, Carson, CA 90747-0005, USA*
[3]*P.O. Box 2155, Camp Nelson, CA 93208, USA*

ABSTRACT: Ecological studies of the Bolson tortoise, *Gopherus flavomarginatus*, were initiated by the Mexican Institute of Ecology in 1977 with the establishment of the MAB-UNESCO (Man and Biosphere-United Nations Educational, Scientific, and Cultural Organization) Mapimí Biosphere Reserve in the Chihuahuan Desert. The studies soon became a bi-national effort with the collaboration of U.S. researchers who developed a database and contributed to the formulation of conservation policies for the species.

The Bolson tortoise is endemic to the Mapimían subprovince of the Chihuahuan Desert. Its population decline and range contraction are a result of multiple factors, including climatic change and such increasing anthropogenic pressures as habitat modification and collection for food. During the last 15 years the Mapimí Reserve staff has developed a program to study and conserve this species, and significant knowledge of its biology has been accumulated. The program focused upon a wide array of topics to evaluate the status of the populations of this endangered reptile: the autocology of adult, juvenile, and neonatal classes; habitat use and spatial relationships; activity patterns; ecological distribution and tolerances; reproductive patterns and endocrinology; morphometry and sex dimorphism; diet and energetics; growth patterns; and thermal biology. Our primary concern has been the integration of these data into conservation, husbandry, and reintroduction programs.

Mapimí Reserve is successfully protecting tortoise populations within its boundaries. However, measures are needed to assure protection throughout the species' range. The World Wildlife Fund-U.S. and the Turtle Recovery Program have supported research in the Sierra del Diablo District (Chihuahua State) where healthy populations, comparable to those of Mapimí, still remain. A joint U.S.-Mexican plan to reintroduce the Bolson tortoise into the Big Bend region of southwest Texas has been explored. Efforts are underway to link the three biosphere reserves—Mapimí, Big Bend, and La Jornada—in a regional consortium to facilitate protection of natural biological corridors and to establish regional conservation strategies in the Chihuahuan Desert.

The program for the conservation of the Bolson tortoise, *Gopherus flavomarginatus*, in Mexico has been strongly influenced by the development of ecological conservation policies, begun in the mid-1970s, that emphasize the integration of tortoise management and human needs. In particular, the establishment of biosphere reserves as a part of the MAB-UNESCO program and their inclusion in Mexican environmental legislation has served as a framework for conservation and protection efforts on behalf of the Bolson tortoise. Since 1978 the Institute of Ecology (Mexico) has conducted the majority of the research on the biology of this species, concentrating its efforts in the Mapimí Biosphere Reserve (MBR), Durango, Mexico. In addition, tortoise populations living outside the boundaries of this reserve in the northernmost portion of the Bolsón de Mapimí have recently been evaluated (Morafka, 1977). The Institute of Ecology and U.S. scientists have collaborated since the inception of the program. By the time the MBR was founded, the first comprehensive study on the species' status and distribution had been completed by Morafka (1982), and this served as a basis to coordinate this bi-national effort to study the Bolson tortoise.

The Bolson tortoise is endemic to the Mapimían subprovince of the Chihuahuan Desert. Morafka (1977) reported that this species is severely affected by direct human predation and habitat loss, which provided evidence for its listing as "Endangered" under both the U.S. Endangered Species Act and the Mexican wildlife law issued by SEDESOL (as of May 1994). It has been placed on Appendix I of the Convention of International Trade in Endangered Species of Wild Fauna and Flora (CITES). Bolson tortoise populations continue to decline because of human activities;

Figure 1. Bolson tortoise, *Gopherus flavomarginatus*. (Photo by David Morafka.)

in some areas local residents still consume them. In other portions of its range, exploration for oil and gas in the 1980s created new roads that have fragmented tortoise habitat.

Distribution and Status

The Bolson tortoise was probably at its maximum geographic range in the Pliocene; its range may have contracted by as much as 90% during the Pliocene–Holocene transition as a result of orogeny, shifts in post-glacial climates, and gradual deterioration of habitat in the Mexican Plateau (Morafka, 1988). While the rates of decline are unknown, current population trends suggest that declines accelerated at the beginning of this century, coinciding with a gradual increase in the mechanization of agriculture, extension of railroad line, and the intensification of cattle raising in the arid grasslands of the Chihuahuan Desert.

The Bolson tortoise inhabits only specific portions of the Bolsón de Mapimí, a series of interconnected, closed drainage basins located in the Chihuahuan Desert. The present Bolson tortoise range has been fragmented into six discrete areas, suggesting that its range is deteriorating rapidly because of human influences. Bury et al. (1988) estimated the total area of tortoise occurrence to be nearly 6,000 km², a lower and more realistic figure compared to previous estimates of 50,000 km² (Morafka, 1982; Morafka et al., 1981). However, the actual area occupied by tortoises may not be larger than 1,000 km², supporting a maximum population of 10,000 adults.

Specific habitat requirements of the Bolson tortoise are a major distribution constraint. These requirements, which parallel those of the three other allopatric species of North American tortoises (*Gopherus agassizii*, *G. berlandieri*, and *G. polyphemus*), include suitable substrates for burrowing and nesting and sufficient plant cover for forage and shelter. Lieberman and Morafka (1988) characterized tortoise habitat by quantifying a series of key parameters and the range of environmental conditions at sites with known tortoise populations. Their analysis identified human-caused predation, topographic relief, and the presence of dry lake beds as the three most important variables that affect Bolson tortoise distribution. These variables are coupled with microdistributional factors that contribute to the patchy occurrence. The organization of tortoise populations into colonies (Aguirre et al., 1984) also contributes to an uneven distribution within a continuous area of suitable habitat.

Bolson Tortoise Research

The conservation research effort for *Gopherus flavomarginatus* at the MBR has investigated a variety of research areas and provided a database vital to understanding this species as a component of the Tobosa, *Hilaria mutica*, grassland environment. Previous research included species status reviews (Morafka, 1982; Aguirre, 1982; Morafka et al., 1989); home range, activity, and social interactions (Adest et al., 1988b; Aguirre et al., 1984; Morafka et al., 1981; Tom, 1988, 1994); historical biogeography (Morafka, 1988); geographical distribution (Bury et al., 1988; Morafka 1982; Morafka et al., 1981); ecological tolerances (Lieberman and Morafka, 1988; Morafka et al., 1981); demographics (Adest et al., 1989a); diet (Aguirre et al., 1979); reproduction (Adest et al., 1984; 1989a; Aguirre et al., 1987); thermal biology (Aguirre, 1978; Adest et al., 1984; 1989a); morphometrics and sex dimorphism (Lieberman et al., 1986); growth (Adest et al., 1989a); blood chemistry and hematology (Morafka et al., 1986); and life history as applied to conservation and husbandry (Adest et al., 1988a; 1989a, 1989b). Selected aspects of Bolson tortoise life history in comparison to North American tortoises have also been analyzed (Germano, 1989, 1994a). Studies of aspects of Bolson tortoise biology are under completion, including genetic variability and phylogenetics, endocrinology of the reproductive cycle, diet related to energetics, and age/growth patterns. Baseline information had been derived through field and laboratory techniques to establish a program for the husbandry and reintroduction of Bolson tortoises from 1984 through 1992. Reestablishment of this species will serve as a first step in the management of the tortoise as well as reinforcement of conservation strategies.

In spite of its present occurrence in an arid habitat, our studies suggest that this is not a desert specialist, either phylogenetically or ecologically, having spent more than 90% of its Quaternary evolutionary history in non-desert grasslands. We have found that the tortoise's thermal and metabolic requirements and its social behavior are more reflective of the burrow microhabitat than the Chihuahuan Desert surface environment (Aguirre et al., 1979, 1984; Adest et al., 1989a; Morafka, 1988). This apparent inability to cope physiologically with an arid environment has consequences for survival. Because of the tortoise's limited thermoregulatory capacity, the available time for social and reproductive interactions may be extremely reduced. Temperature-dependent environmental sex determination appears to be critical in this species, as it is in so many turtles. The skewed sex ratio, i.e., the preponderance of females in almost every population studied to date, may result from higher surficial temperatures found in the tortoise's currently over-grazed habitat (desert) compared to its historical habitat (grasslands). Eggs are often deposited just outside the burrow entrance in the burrow apron, where they are exposed to changes in plant cover, rather than being recessed deep within the burrow ramp.

Based upon direct and indirect census techniques, an evaluation of the population structure within one population in the MBR was made for the years 1980–1985 (Adest et al., 1989a). Changes in population structure occurred during this five-year period. Juveniles decreased from 31.4% to 14.3% of the total population, and subadults decreased from 14.3% to 4.8%. These decreases were related to maturation into higher categories only in low proportions (<25%); accordingly, emigration and mortality are suspected to be main factors causing this shift. In addition, surveys between 1983 and 1985 showed low percentages of juveniles (12.7%) and even lower percentages of subadults (6.3%), with adults comprising 81% of the population. A chaos process model is likely to operate on recruitment and dispersion of Bolson tortoise populations inhabiting an environment where precipitation is naturally low in amount, seasonal, or highly variable from one year to the next (Morafka, 1994).

Declining populations may assume a distribution in which there is a high proportion of large animals and a low proportion of small animals if growth rate is constant for all size animals. In this scenario, the greater numbers of large tortoises might have been the result of enhanced survivorship in small cohorts in the past. As recruitment declines, the less mortality-prone adults would persist. Furthermore, one could assume a slower growth rate as individuals increase in size. This has been observed in the sister species, *G. polyphemus* (Landers et al., 1982; Mushinsky et al., 1994) and is the case in *G. flavomarginatus* (Adest et al., 1989a; Germano 1994b). As individuals become adults, a blurring or overlap of size differences between members of different cohorts occurs, resulting in higher numbers of individuals in the adult class. If population size is declining, the mortality among hatchlings/juveniles is most likely to be responsible for the observed population structure. If population size is constant or increasing, juvenile secretiveness best explains census results.

The overall adult sex ratio in the entire Mapimi Reserve is 1(male):1.2(females). In addition, we have documented decreased proportions of reproductive adult males within our study areas in Mapimí. Field work revealed that only three out of seven males were responsible for all observed copulations. At the same time, reproduction is compromised by low hatching success. Nest predation and infertility, combined with prehatching and posthatching mortality, severely reduce recruitment. Radio-telemetric monitoring of hatchlings and one- to four-year old tortoises revealed that 67% of hatchlings and 69% of the older juveniles died within the first year of monitoring. We estimate that seven of eight clutches are destroyed before hatching by predation from a variety of mammalian, avian, and perhaps reptilian predators. Egg laying by wild female tortoises averages 1.4

clutches of 5.4 eggs per year. Consequently, a typical adult female may require six years of reproductive effort to produce one clutch that hatches.

The extent to which past reproductive success is responsible for the current adult-to-immature tortoise ratios is difficult to assess. Local residents throughout the Bolsón de Mapimí frequently note that tortoises were both far more abundant and larger in the past (approx. 30% greater body length and 50% greater mass). Disproportionately higher mortality in immature tortoises, coupled with decreased adult population sizes, may have resulted in the disproportionate immature-to-mature tortoise ratios observed in declining populations.

On the other hand, the consequences of habitat and population fragmentation are not yet fully understood. It is important to determine whether isolated clusters of Bolson tortoises still function as viable populations. We have found no evidence that recolonization of habitats (where populations were extirpated) is occurring. While mid- to long-range movements have been documented between established clusters (Aguirre et al., 1984) involving individuals from various size classes, none have been found in areas from which tortoises have been extirpated. Nor has there been any evidence of recruitment in the minuscule populations west of the Torreon-Chihuahua Highway (Mexico 49).

The Role of the Mapimí Biosphere Reserve

Scientific research in conjunction with the development of the MBR has made the design of a program for conservation of the endangered Bolson tortoise possible (Aguirre and Maury, 1988, 1990). Crucial to the overall success of this program have been the compliance of the reserve's human inhabitants in a voluntary abstention from tortoise hunting and cooperation with the reserve's policies. The protection and subsequent slow recovery of the Bolson tortoise population in the Mapimí Reserve is an example of successful participation by local residents in a conservation program (Kaus, 1993). It is critical to both tortoise conservation and the biosphere reserve to manage the habitat in a manner that is both economically feasible and acceptable to the local residents.

Protective measures for the Bolson tortoise, based on the assessment of its ecology, have been coupled with reintroduction of captive-bred individuals (Adest et al., 1989a, 1989b). As noted above, the limited geographical range of the tortoises, their limited surface activity, and their apparently low reproductive success indicated that a program of captive incubation and husbandry was a necessary first step in the management of the Bolson tortoise.

We have raised young tortoises for release to gather information on the biology of the first age classes. Our results on a hatchery and nursery operation in the MBR have been previously reported (Adest et al., 1989b), and the first data on microhabitat selection and behavior of free-ranging hatchlings tracked by radiotelemetry have been reported by Tom (1994). Several years of nursery operation have afforded advantages that include the opportunity for continuous monitoring of juveniles that are unavailable for study in the wild, veterinary management to optimize survivorship at early stages of development, and the exclusion of predation when it is most likely to be critical. Overall survival in the nursery is 65%. During the time the nursery has been operative, age-specific survival rates are 1 year, 80%; 2 years, 55%; 3 years, 50%. We have also initiated studies on the differential survivorship of laboratory-incubated age classes of young tortoises. Field data have confirmed the hypothesis of high hatchling mortality in the wild. High density vegetation coverage further contributes to the low numbers of young individuals in previous censuses, as their coloration and behavior makes them difficult to notice in the field. Bolson tortoise hatchlings spend more time under vegetation than in open areas (Tom, 1988, 1994), and most of their shelters are concealed under dense vegetation.

In addition to the established Bolson tortoise program in the Mapimí Reserve, significant efforts have been made in other sites to diversify our primary conservation strategy. These include the Research Ranch at Elgin, Arizona; Rancho Sombreretillo in the Mexican state of Chihuahua; and the Big Bend National Park (BBNP) and Biosphere Reserve in Texas.

The program at the Research Ranch in Elgin started virtually at the same time that the Mapimí Reserve was established. A captive group of adult tortoises from Mapimí was transferred to the Research Ranch in southern Arizona to be kept in an experimental enclosure (Appleton, 1978). In part, the purpose of starting this new colony was to determine how well the tortoises would adapt to this environment, which was once part of their range. The experiment soon developed into a captive breeding program that has allowed ecological research comparable to that of the MBR. The captive breeding program and the behavior and ecology of the reintroduced tortoises has been previously described (Appleton, 1978; Nathan, 1979; Tennesen, 1985). The captive group in Arizona represents the only group of Bolson tortoises thriving outside its current range.

Rancho Sombreretillo encompasses about 10,000 ha of isolated prime tortoise habitat in the extreme northern part of the current range of the Bolson tortoise. The area, situated 100 km north of Mapimí Reserve, represents one of the richest, most diverse, and relatively least disturbed tracts of Chihuahuan Desert grasslands. The ranch is staffed by a full-time caretaker and supports low-level and patchy cattle grazing. In contrast to our findings in the MBR, field work has confirmed the existence of robust tortoise populations living in well-developed perennial bunch grassland, with a wide range of age and size classes present. Life history data on the Sombreretillo population are needed to compare with the well-known population in Mapimí. The Turtle Recovery Program is currently funding a U.S.-Mexican team of biologists to survey and develop a management plan that may enable Rancho Sombreretillo to become an additional tortoise reserve. The management plan will guide the application of research as well as clarify both researchers' and land owner's responsibilities. As in Mapimí, the development of a rancher-researcher relationship will provide a conduit for environmental education and a basic starting point for allied efforts to protect tortoises and their habitat. This collaboration extends conservation management—including both local and institutional participation—into an area contiguous to the MBR.

The Big Bend National Park is a sister biosphere reserve to the Mapimí Reserve and shares similar conservation and research objectives to protect the Chihuahuan Desert environment. Recent MAB-sponsored meetings between cooperating units (Big Bend National Park, Mapimí Biosphere Reserve, and the La Jornada Experimental Station in New Mexico) have sought to develop stronger ties and to create a regional system. The objectives of this network are twofold: (1) to formally link scientists, educators, and land managers for the purpose of enhancing research, environmental education, and multi-purpose land management conducted in the Chihuahuan Desert of both countries; and (2) to develop an information management system that will promote sustainable use of the natural resources of the Chihuahuan Desert. Bolson tortoise conservation falls within the scope of the coordinated conservation efforts of the MBR and BBNP. While the tortoise does not presently occur in Big Bend, it inhabited the area during glaciopluvial times (Strain, 1966; Stevens et al., 1977; Van Devender, 1988) and now occupies a contiguous habitat only 280 km south of the park.

Our surveys at Big Bend indicate the tortoises' climatic, nutritional, and substrate needs would be met by a portion of the park's existing ecosystems. However, current National Park policy prohibits the reintroduction of taxa lost to pre-Columbian extinction. Adjacent Texas state parks and wildlife refuges may still qualify as optimal sites for reintroduction into the U.S. Reintroduction of tortoises into the Big Bend region would increase the species' range through the establishment of a triad of protected populations (Rancho Sombreretillo in the middle and the Mapimí Reserve in the southern extreme) and would substantially reduce the probability of extinction.

We believe that the most effective approach for the conservation of the Bolson tortoise is to link and extend some of the already viable populations, and that a mosaic of protected habitats within local systems of land management in the Chihuahuan Desert is a feasible means to ensure Bolson tortoise recovery in the long term. It is also a realistic approach, as the species has already been extirpated from a considerable portion of its post-Columbian distribution. This trend is unlikely to be reversed.

Implementation of the foregoing plans would eventually lead to the protection of regional yet international biological corridors, and to the establishment of regional conservation strategies in the Chihuahuan Desert. The ultimate goal is to broaden site-specific efforts by creating conservation initiatives for habitat protection that are compatible with the realities of human habitation in the Chihuahuan Desert.

LITERATURE CITED

Adest, G. A., J. V. Jarchow, and G. Aguirre. 1984. Reproduction of Bolson tortoises. Abstracts IX Desert Tortoise Council Symp: 5.

Adest, G. A., J. V. Jarchow, and B. Brydolf. 1988a. A method for manual ventilation of tranquilized tortoises. Herpetol. Rev. 19 (4):80.

Adest, G. A., M. A. Recht, and G. Aguirre. 1988b. Nocturnal activity in the Bolson tortoise (*Gopherus flavomarginatus*). Herpetol. Rev. 19(4):75.

Adest, G. A., G. Aguirre, D. J. Morafka, and J. V. Jarchow. 1989a. Bolson tortoise (*Gopherus flavomarginatus*) conservation. I. Life history. Vida Silvestre Neotropical 2(1):7–13.

Adest, G. A., G. Aguirre, D. J. Morafka, and J. V. Jarchow. 1989b. Bolson tortoise (*Gopherus flavomarginatus*) conservation. II. Husbandry and reintroduction. Vida Silvestre Neotropical 2(1):14–20.

Aguirre, G. 1978. Estudio preliminar de la tortuga del Bolsón de Mapimí, *Gopherus flavomarginatus* Legler en la Reserva de la Biosfera de Mapimí, Dgo. Memorias del II Congreso Nacional de Zoología, Vol. I: 233–247.

Aguirre, G. 1982. *Gopherus flavomarginatus* Legler 1959. *In* The IUCN Amphibia-Reptilia Red Data Book (B. Groombridge, comp.), pp. 103–107. IUCN, Gland, Switzerland.

Aguirre, G. and M. E. Maury. 1988. The Mapimí Biosphere Reserve, Durango, México. *In* E. Whitehead, C. F. Hutchinson, B. G. Timmermann, and R. G. Varaday (eds.), Arid Lands: Today and Tomorrow, pp. 223–231. Westview Press, Boulder, Colorado.

Aguirre, G. and M. E. Maury. 1990. Goals and objectives of research in the Mapimí Biosphere Reserve. *In* M. Powell, R. R. Hollander, J. C. Barlow, W. B. McGillivray, and D. J. Schmidly (eds.), Papers from the Third Symposium on Resources of the Chihuahuan Desert Region, pp. 35–42. Chihuahuan Desert Research Institute, Alpine, Texas.

Aguirre, G., G. A. Adest, M. Recht, and D. J. Morafka. 1979. Preliminary investigations of the movements, thermoregulation, population structure and diet of the Bolson Tortoise, (*Gopherus flavomarginatus*) in the Mapimí Biosphere Reserve, Durango, Mexico. Proc. Desert Tortoise Council Symp. 1979:149–165.

Aguirre, G., G. A. Adest, and D. J. Morafka. 1984. Home range and movement patterns of the Bolson Tortoise, *Gopherus flavomarginatus*. Acta Zool. Mex. Nueva Serie 1:1–28.

Aguirre, G., G. A. Adest, D. J. Morafka, and R. González. 1987. Características reproductivas de *Gopherus flavomarginatus*. Abstracts 1987 Annual Meeting SSAR-HL-Comité Herpetológico Nacional: 47.

Appleton, A. 1978. Bolson Tortoise (*Gopherus flavomarginatus*) at the Research Ranch. Proc. Desert Tortoise Council Symp. 1978: 164–174.

Bury, B., D. J. Morafka, and C. J. McCoy. 1988. Part I. Distribution, abundance and status of the Bolson tortoise. *In* D. J. Morafka and J. C. McCoy (eds.), The Ecogeography of the Mexican Bolson Tortoise (*Gopherus flavomarginatus*): Derivation of its Endangered Status and Recommendations for its Conservation. Annals Carnegie Mus. 57(1):5–30.

Germano, D. J. 1989. Growth and life histories of North American tortoises (genus *Gopherus*) with special emphasis on the desert tortoise (*G. agassizii*). Ph.D. dissertation, University of New Mexico, Albuquerque, New Mexico.

Germano, D. J. 1994a. Comparative life histories of North American tortoises. *In* R. B. Bury and D. J. Germano (eds.), Biology of North American Tortoises, pp. 174–185. Fish and Wildlife Research 13, Technical Report Series, U.S. Department of the Interior, National Biological Survey, Washington, D.C.

Germano, D. J. 1994b. Growth and age at maturity of North American tortoises in relation to regional climates. Can. J. Zool. 72:918–931.

Kaus, A. 1993. Environmental perceptions and social relationships in the Mapimí Biosphere Reserve. Conserv. Biol. 7(2):398–406.

Landers, J. L., W. A. McRae, and L. A. Garner. 1982. Growth and maturity of the gopher tortoise in southwestern Georgia. Herpetologica 36(4):353–361.

Lieberman, S. S. and D. J. Morafka. 1988. Part II. Ecological distribution of the Bolson tortoise. *In* D. J. Morafka and J. C. McCoy (eds.), The Ecogeography of the Mexican Bolson Tortoise (*Gopherus flavomarginatus*): Derivation of its Endangered Status and Recommendations for its Conservation. Annals Carnegie Mus. 57 (1):31–46.

Lieberman, S. S., D. J. Morafka, and G. Aguirre. 1986. Morphometrics of the Mexican Bolson Tortoise, *Gopherus flavomarginatus*. Abstracts, Annual Meeting Southern California Academy of Sciences: 13.

Morafka, D. J. 1977. A Biogeographical Analysis of the Chihuahuan Desert Through its Herpetofauna. Dr. W. Junk, B.V., Publishers, The Hague, Netherlands.

Morafka, D. J. 1982. The status and distribution of the Bolson Tortoise, *Gopherus flavomarginatus*. *In* R. B. Bury (ed.), North American Tortoises: Conservation and Ecology, pp. 71–94. Wildlife Research Report 12, U.S. Fish and Wildlife Service, Washington, D.C..

Morafka, D. J. 1988. Part III. Historical biogeography of the Bolson tortoise. *In* D. J. Morafka and J. C. McCoy (eds.), The Ecogeography of the Mexican Bolson Tortoise (*Gopherus flavomarginatus*): Derivation of its Endangered Status and Recommendations for its Conservation. Annals Carnegie Mus. 57(1):31–46.

Morafka, D. J. 1994. Neonates: Missing links in the life histories of North American tortoises. *In* R. B. Bury and D. J. Germano (eds.), Biology of North American Tortoises, pp. 161–173. Fish and Wildlife Research 13, Technical Report Series, U.S. Department of the Interior, National Biological Survey, Washington, D.C.

Morafka, D. J., G. A. Adest, G. Aguirre, and M. Recht. 1981. The ecology of the Bolson tortoise, *Gopherus flavomarginatus*. *In* R. Barbault and G. Halffter (eds.), Ecology of the Chihuahuan Desert. Organization of Some Vertebrate Communities, pp. 35–78. Publ. Instituto de Ecología No. 8, México, D.F.

Morafka, D. J., R. A. Yates, J. Jarchow, W. J. Rosskopf, G. A. Adest, and G. Aguirre. 1986. Preliminary results of microbial and physiological monitoring of the Bolson tortoise, *Gopherus flavomarginatus*. *In* Z. Rocek (ed.), Studies in Herpetology, pp. 657–652. Societas Herpetologica Europaea, Prague, Czechoslavakia.

Morafka, D. J., G. Aguirre, and G. A. Adest. 1989. *Gopherus flavomarginatus*: Bolson tortoise. *In* I. R. Swingland and M. W. Klemens (eds.), The Conservation Biology of Tortoises, pp. 10–13. Occasional Papers of the IUCN Species Survival Commission (SSC) No. 5. IUCN, Gland, Switzerland.

Mushinsky, H. R., D. S. Wilson, and E. D. McCoy. 1994. Growth and sexual dimorphism of *Gopherus polyphemus* in central Florida. Herpetologica 50:119–128.

Nathan, G. B. 1979. Behavior and ecology of *Gopherus flavomarginatus* in an experimental enclosure. M.S. thesis, University of Arizona, Tucson, Arizona.

Stevens, M. S., J. B. Stevens, and M. R. Dawson. 1977. Further study of Castolon local fauna (Early Miocene), Big Bend National Park, Brewster County, Texas. Pearce-Sellards Series, Texas Memorial Museum 28:1–69.

Strain, W. S. 1966. Blancan mammalian fauna and Pleistocene formation, Hudspeth County, Texas. Texas Memorial Museum Bull. 10:1–55.

Tennesen, M. 1985. Crawling out of limbo. International Wildlife 15(4):30–34.

Tom, J. 1988. The daily activity pattern, microhabitat, and home range of hatchling Bolson tortoises, *Gopherus flavomarginatus*. M.S. thesis, California State University, Los Angeles, California.

Tom, J. 1994. Microhabitats and use of burrows of Bolson tortoise hatchlings. *In* R. B. Bury and D. J. Germano (eds.), Biology of North American Tortoises, pp. 138–146. Fish and Wildlife Research 13, Technical Report Series, U.S. Department of the Interior, National Biological Survey, Washington, D.C.

Van Devender, T. R. 1988. Late Quaternary vegetation and climate of the Chihuahuan Desert, United States and Mexico. *In* J. L. Betancourt, T. R. Van Devender, and P. S. Martin (eds.), Packrat Middens: The Last 40,000 Years of Biotic Change, pp. 104–133. University of Arizona Press, Tucson, Arizona.

Managing the Last Survivors: Integration of *in situ* and *ex situ* Conservation of *Pseudemydura umbrina*

GERALD KUCHLING

Department of Zoology, The University of Western Australia, Nedlands, WA 6907, Australia
[e-mail: kuchling@cyllene.uwa.edu.au]

ABSTRACT: By 1987 the world population of *Pseudemydura umbrina*, a chelid freshwater turtle from the Perth region in Western Australia, numbered less than 50 individuals. Twenty to thirty animals survived in the wild in a single population on a small nature reserve, and 17 animals remained in captivity, only three of which were adult females. A rescue operation was started in 1987–1988, and by July 1993 the world population increased to over 130. A recovery programme, started in 1991, includes captive breeding, management and monitoring of the last wild population, integrated genetic management of the wild and the captive populations, improvements of marginal habitat, predator exclusion, acquisition and restoration of former habitat, and reintroduction. The integration of population management actions is discussed.

The first *Pseudemydura umbrina* known to science was brought to the Naturhistorisches Museum Wien (Vienna) in 1839, but it was not until 1901 that Siebenrock gave the specimen its scientific name. No further specimens were collected until 1953 when two were found in a swamp near Perth in Western Australia. During the 1950s some field data were gathered by researchers of the Western Australian Museum. In 1962 two small "Class A" nature reserves (as defined by the Western Australian Land Act; i.e., cannot be dissolved, reduced in area, or used for any other purpose unless by Act of Parliament) were created, which protected much of its remaining habitat of clay or sand over clay ephemeral swamps: Ellen Brook Nature Reserve (EBNR) (65 ha) and Twin Swamps Nature Reserve (TSNR) (155 ha). Research on the biology of the species by staff and students at the University of Western Australia was started in 1963 and was later continued by the state wildlife authority. In the mid-1960s more than 200 *P. umbrina* were estimated to live in the two reserves (Burbidge, 1967). Since then, numbers in the wild have steadily declined. At TSNR, numbers dropped from over 100 in the mid-1960s (Burbidge, 1967) to about 50 in the early 1970s (Burbidge, 1981) to near zero by 1985 (Burbidge et al., 1990). Over the same period the population at EBNR remained fairly static at around 20–30 animals.

A captive colony of 25 *P. umbrina* was established in 1959, and the 13 surviving captive animals were transferred

Figure 1. *Pseudemydura umbrina* hatching.

to Perth Zoo in 1964 (Kuchling et al., 1992). The first captive breeding was recorded in 1966, and 26 hatchlings were produced prior to 1978 (Spence et al., 1979), five of which survive today.

In 1979 the breeding stock from Perth Zoo and two females and one male of the TSNR population were transferred to the Western Australian Wildlife Research Centre of the Department of Conservation and Land Management to improve the captive population's reproductive output. Seventeen eggs were produced in 1979 and 1980, eight of which hatched. Seven hatchlings died during their first year and one in its second year. No further eggs were produced by the captive colony between 1981 and 1986. By 1987 the captive population comprised seven males and two females of the old captive founder group, five of the offspring hatched in Perth Zoo, and one male, one female, and one juvenile of the former TSNR population (Kuchling et al., 1992).

By 1987–1988 the wild population numbered 20–30 animals in a single population (EBNR). Only 17 animals remained in captivity, and only three were adult females. They had not produced eggs for six years. With a total world population of under 50 individuals and no success in captive breeding, *P. umbrina* was in a critical situation.

At this stage a rescue operation was undertaken, which initially concentrated on propagation of the species in captivity to increase the total population to a more secure level (Kuchling, 1988; Kuchling and DeJose, 1989). By 1990 the main procedural problems of captive breeding of *P. umbrina* had been solved (Kuchling et al., 1992; Kuchling and Bradshaw, 1993), and by July 1993 the world population had increased to over 130 individuals. In 1990 the Western Australian Department of Conservation and Land Management published a species management program for *P. umbrina* (Burbidge et al., 1990). Early in 1991 the last wild population of *P. umbrina* was protected against introduced predators, mainly the European red fox, by an electrified fence. During 1992–1993 a recovery program for *P. umbrina* was drafted that addressed the causes for the decline of the species and prescribed necessary conservation actions up to the year 2002 (Burbidge and Kuchling, 1994). A central part of that recovery program was the integrated management of the captive and the wild populations of *P. umbrina*.

Integrated Management

At present the total adult world population of *P. umbrina* numbers about 20 females and 20 males; more than two-thirds of all known individuals are in captivity. The low number demands integrated *in situ* and *ex situ* management to ensure the best survival prospects for the species. The management plan mandated the following tasks:

- Increase the total population to a more secure level.
- Ensure the viability of the last wild population.
- Preserve the genetic variability of the species.
- Establish a second wild population.
- Reduce the possibility of disease outbreaks.

Increase of the World Population through Captive Breeding

Captive breeding or headstarting operations are often a quick and cost-effective way to increase numbers of individuals in species that produce high numbers of offspring (or eggs) and that experience high natural losses of juvenile stages in the wild. Captive breeding therefore was considered a potential conservation tool for *P. umbrina* as soon as the critical situation of the species was recognised in the 1950s. Typically, *P. umbrina* females produce one clutch of three to five eggs per year, which is one of the lowest chelonian reproductive rates and which offered too few eggs to experimentally develop the optimal propagation techniques. Consequently, the captive breeding success at Perth Zoo during the 1960s and 1970s was rather low. Attempts by the Western Australian Conservation Authority to increase captive reproduction in the early 1980s were completely unsuccessful.

In that the problems of captive propagation of *P. umbrina* were solved in the late 1980s (Kuchling et al., 1992; Kuchling and Bradshaw, 1993), captive breeding is now clearly the quickest way to increase numbers of *P. umbrina*. Between 1988 and 1990 it was the policy to take wild adult females into temporary captivity to secure them from predation and to boost hatchling production. In early 1991, when the population at Ellen Brook Nature Reserve was secured by a fox-proof fence, all females collected there were repatriated. This short-term transfer of females into captivity, for periods of six months to three years, caused disruptions of the reproductive cycle in most of the females. Some did not ovulate and reabsorb follicles, and some did not initiate normal vitellogenic cycles (Kuchling and Bradshaw, 1993). The short-term transfer of wild females into captivity is therefore not a sound strategy to increase reproductive output.

Proponents of *in situ* conservation actions sometimes object to the removal of the last individuals of a critically endangered species from the wild for captive breeding. In the case of *P. umbrina*, it was fortunate for the species that the Conservation Authority did not authorise the removal of animals from the last wild population for captive breeding (except temporarily between 1988 and 1990, until the fence was built). During the 1970s and early 1980s the species fared much better at Ellen Brook Nature Reserve than in captivity. As long as a wild population seems to be stable, it is sensible not to remove animals. At the same time it was reasonable to take the last individuals of the disappearing population at Twin Swamps Nature Reserve into captivity.

During the last few years a few individuals of *P. umbrina* have been found outside the nature reserves on private land. Dispersed individuals on cleared and drained land may survive for years but are unlikely to reproduce successfully. It is the policy to take all these individuals into captivity to enlarge the captive breeding stock. They may be returned to the wild in the future if *P. umbrina* habitat is restored on the land where they were found.

Ex situ conservation of *P. umbrina* has three main purposes: to increase the total population, to produce animals for reintroduction into the wild, and to safeguard the species in the case of a catastrophe in the wild.

Management of the Last Wild Population

The last wild population lives in a fenced area of 29 ha at Ellen Brook Nature Reserve. Management strategies include predator control, fire management, regular patrols, monitoring of water quality, and habitat improvements (Burbidge and Kuchling, 1994). In this paper I will discuss only direct population management.

Over the last 30 years the number of animals has remained fairly static at 20–30 individuals (Burbidge and Kuchling, 1994). Because of favourable hydrological conditions (compared to Twin Swamps Nature Reserve), the wetland habitat is relatively secure during years with below-average rainfall, one of the stochastic environmental threats to *P. umbrina* populations.

Any considerations of population management have to be based on the conservation and biological importance of the last stable wild population of a species. Demographic theory implies that a population of 20–30 individuals is prone to extirpation through stochastic events. But *P. umbrina*, a long-lived species with low intrinsic rates of increase, may be less prone to extinction at such a low population number than the same number of a fast-growing, short-lived species (Pimm et al., 1988). On the other hand, individuals of the long-lived *Aldabrachelys elephantina* in high-density populations on Aldabra Atoll grow slower, stop growing at smaller body sizes, delay their sexual maturity, and decrease their fecundity compared with individuals in low-density populations (Swingland and Coe, 1978).

The carrying capacity of *P. umbrina* at Ellen Brook Nature Reserve is not known. Although an increase in the population at this reserve is a conservation goal, any interference with the demography of the population, e.g., through a restocking program, could also have destabilising effects. Population data of *P. umbrina* from the 1960s and 1970s show that growth and recruitment of hatchlings was lower, and age at maturity was higher, in the Ellen Brook population than in the population at Twin Swamps Nature Reserve (Burbidge, 1981).

The population management at Ellen Brook Nature Reserve is limited to the following procedures: Population size is estimated with mark-recapture techniques; reproductive success is assessed by radio tracking females; and nests, eggs, and hatchlings are monitored. In a policy that recognises the need to increase the total population of this species, about half the eggs from nests that are suspected to be prone to overheating or flooding are removed for artificial incubation. If the eggs that remain in the wild nest die, the captive hatchlings stay in captivity (or are used for reintroduction elsewhere). If the remaining wild eggs hatch, all of the captive hatchlings are released back into Ellen Brook Nature Reserve.

Insufficient time has passed since the fox-proof fence was built in 1991 to recognise changes in the population. A plan is under way to increase the area of *P. umbrina* habitat by acquiring privately owned land of former habitat adjacent to Ellen Brook Nature Reserve, re-creating the swamp habitat, and including it in the reserve. This should provide a possibility for expansion through natural recruitment from the Ellen Brook population.

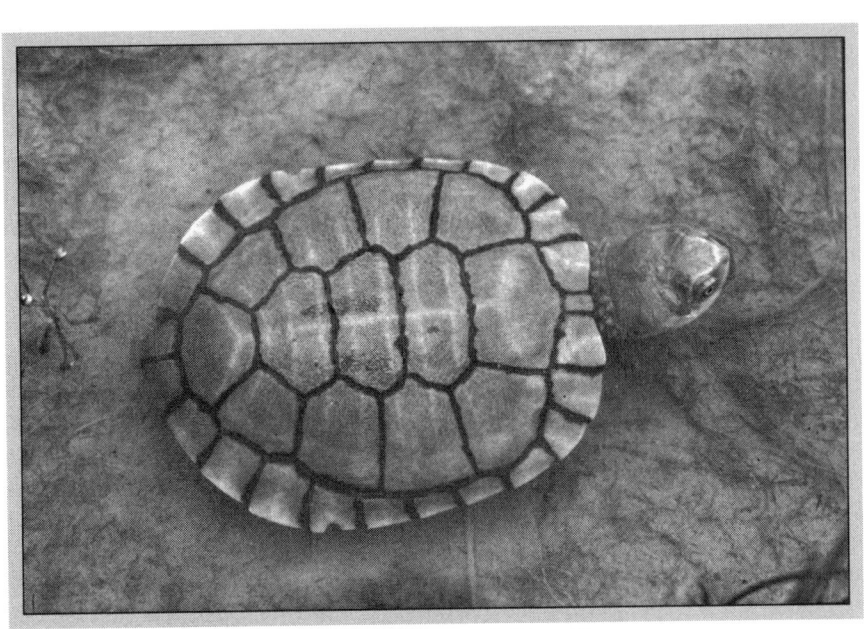

Figure 2. *Pseudemydura umbrina* at the Ellen Brook Nature Reserve.

Genetic Management

P. umbrina is in a severe genetic bottleneck. Loss of genetic variability can constrain the future evolutionary potential and therefore the long-term survival of the species. Conservation actions must take this into account and genetic management of the species is necessary so that genetic diversity is not lost. Another potential problem for small populations is inbreeding and its possible consequence of depressed fertility and vitality of the population.

Several aspects must be considered when choosing management options to preserve the genetic diversity of the small population of *P. umbrina*. Observations have shown that when animals are bred in captivity to reestablish wild populations, the usual methods of randomly selecting breeding pairs, choosing the best breeders, or managing mating pairs by allozyme data result in substantially reduced genetic diversity of the reintroduced population. Genetic management based on pedigree analysis (equalising founder contribution, maximising founder genome equivalents, or maximising allelic diversity) produces more genetically diverse release populations (Haig et al., 1990).

Figure 3. One of nine female *P. umbrina* left in the wild at Ellen Brook Nature Reserve. The Great Northern Highway of Western Australia in the background borders the reserve. A radio transmitter is attached to the turtle's back. A fox-proof fence (to control predation and to minimise losses of animals to road traffic) separates the reserve from the highway.

But the most important rule is: The less time (in generations) a species spends in captivity and the sooner reintroductions start, the better for its genetic status. The severe genetic bottleneck of *P. umbrina* is relatively recent (in generation times). Because of the longevity of *P. umbrina* (>50 years), many members of the surviving population are survivors from a time when the population was larger (i.e., 200–300 animals 30 years ago). The captive population still consists largely of wild-caught individuals. A continuation of the present captive breeding success should lead to a rapid population expansion. The use of F_1 offspring to reestablish populations in the wild will effectively prevent any potentially detrimental genetic drift during the time the species has to be bred in captivity.

Prior to 1988 all captive females were kept together with some of the males, which permitted random mating. Since 1988 males and females have been kept in separate enclosures and are individually introduced for mating purposes using a rotation scheme. Every female mates with a different male in consecutive years. All captive adults contribute their genes. This is an attempt to equalise founder contributions as much as possible without diminishing the breeding output of the best breeding females. As long as the world population is at such a low level, the breeding output has to be maximised.

It would be helpful for the genetic management of the species to assess the genetic variability of the captive as well as the wild population. The possible ability of females to store sperm over several years may be a complication. The reconstruction of patrilineages for captive-bred animals would be a helpful tool to assess the genetic contribution of males (which may be obscured by the ability of females to store sperm). Since 1988 chromosome banding, plasma enzyme gel electrophoresis, and DNA fingerprinting have been conducted, but only DNA fingerprinting was able to detect limited variability between individuals. All captive and most wild adults are now being DNA assayed. A serious constraint is the necessity to sample living tissues (blood or muscle biopsies) from tortoises that are small, rare, endangered, and difficult to breed. Since 1991 the allantoic sacs of the captive-bred hatchlings have been collected to provide DNA for fingerprinting (Hall et al., 1992).

In order to broaden the genetic basis of the captive stock and the animals produced for reintroduction, wild males of the Ellen Brook population may in the future be taken into captivity for a few weeks to mate with captive females. This has been done successfully in past years. If necessary for genetic management in the future, eggs may also be exchanged between the captive and the wild populations.

Reintroduction and the Establishment of a Second Population

Reintroduction of captive-bred *P. umbrina* into Twin Swamps Nature Reserve started in 1994 (Burbidge and Kuchling, 1994). The establishment of this second population in the wild is under way and will still be the emphasis of our conservation efforts for the next few years. Only three individuals of *P. umbrina* have been found at Twin Swamps since 1983, and two animals that were marked there in the 1970s were recaptured about one kilometer east of the reserve on private land in 1991 and 1992.

The causal factors for the species' near disappearance from the site seem to be (1) exotic predators, in particular the European red fox; (2) the loss of former drought refuges, the period of standing water being too short in below-average rainfall years; and (3) the threat of fire because *P. umbrina* at Twin Swamps Nature Reserve aestivate under leaf litter.

Remedial actions include the removal of exotic predators, the construction of a fox-proof fence and a well to pump groundwater into selected swamps to maintain and extend the wetland habitat in winters of average or below-average rainfall, and appropriate fire management (Burbidge and Kuchling, 1994).

Other options for reintroductions to establish additional populations may become available in the future if former habitats on private or public land can be secured and rehabilitated. These options will be considered in the recovery plan review and update for the period 1998–2002 because the success of the captive breeding operation is better than expected and will allow us to start establishing a third wild population during the second half of the ten-year phase of the recovery plan.

Health Management

Disease did not seem to play a role in the decline of *P. umbrina*. Health management of *P. umbrina* concentrates on preventing disease. When the rescue operation started in 1988 the captive population was divided and located at two sites 25 km apart to decrease the risk. This arrangement was suspended in 1991, mainly because of the associated costs and because no problems had emerged. Since then the whole captive colony is kept at one location about 30 km from Ellen Brook Nature Reserve.

The captive colony is kept isolated from all other reptiles at Perth Zoo. No tools or equipment are shared. In theory, the colony is kept under permanent quarantine from the other animal collections.

The separation of the wild and the captive colonies is less stringent. For example, wild males are sometimes introduced to captive females for mating purposes without quarantine procedures. The males are normally returned to the wild after two to four weeks, which is much less than the standard quarantine period of 90 days proposed by Jacobson (1993) for reptile collections. The difference between this and many other operations where animals are moved from the wild into captivity, or between captive collections, is that the transportation time is less than one hour, and the captive colony is kept in outdoor enclosures under climatic conditions similar to the wild population.

Figure 4. *P. umbrina* in natural habitat at the Ellen Brook Nature Reserve.

DISCUSSION

Since the late 1950s and 1960s a combination of *in situ* and *ex situ* strategies has been used in the conservation of *P. umbrina*. However, both approaches failed to stem the decline until a rescue operation started in 1988 and turned the tide for the species. Some of the lessons learned with *P. umbrina* may be of value in the conservation of other threatened chelonians.

The major problem for *P. umbrina* is that most of its habitat has been lost and that the preserved habitat is only of marginal quality. It would be difficult and expensive to alleviate this situation because of agricultural, industrial, and urban developments in the area of its distribution. Today the major efforts in conserving *P. umbrina* focus on predator control, habitat improvements and restoration, water supplementation and water quality, fire management, and captive propagation techniques (Burbidge and Kuchling, 1994). The integrated population management, as presented in this paper, is necessary to optimise the efficiency of all these conservation measures.

It is not always possible to optimise all individual aspects of population management simultaneously. Compromises are necessary. For example, survival of eggs and hatchlings may be better in captivity than in the wild, and the removal of eggs from the wild for artificial incubation and captive rearing of hatchlings may therefore increase the world number of *P. umbrina*, but at the same time decrease the viability of the wild population. Optimal strategies for genetic management may compromise health management, e.g., when animals are moved between the captive and the wild populations. The benefits of particular actions always have to be weighed against possible risks.

It is vital always to ask the goal of a particular action. This may seem trivial, but it is often overlooked when management actions, e.g., *ex situ* conservation or reintroductions, are proposed. Is a particular action proposed because it will decrease the risk of extinction, or simply because it is the easiest thing to do, or is it to serve some other purpose? Both *ex situ* and *in situ* strategies are necessary for the conservation of *P. umbrina*. This does not mean, however, that any such action per se necessarily decreases the risk of extinction of the species.

ACKNOWLEDGEMENTS

I thank the members of the Recovery Team—S. D. Bradshaw, A. A. Burbidge, J. P. DeJose, P. Fuller, D. Groth, D. Miller, L. Mutter, R. Nias, S. Stephens, and G. Wyre—for helping to establish and run the recovery program. I acknowledge funding from World Wide Fund for Nature Australia, Australian Nature Conservation Agency, Western Australian Department of Conservation and Land Management, Perth Zoo, Bundesverband für fachgerechten Natur und Artenschutz (Germany), Aherns Pty Ltd., AG Schildkroeten und Panzerechsen (DGHT), British Chelonia Group, California Turtle and Tortoise Club, Unidata Pty Ltd., East-West Veterinary Supplies, Minerva Air Conditioning, and the many individuals and companies that supported the project through financial contributions to some of the organisations mentioned above. I acknowledge contributions and help from staff of Perth Zoo, CALM, and the University of Western Australia.

LITERATURE CITED

Burbidge, A. A. 1967. The biology of south-western Australian tortoises. Ph.D. thesis, University of Western Australia, Perth.

Burbidge, A. A. 1981. The ecology of the western swamp tortoise, *Pseudemydura umbrina* (Testudines, Chelidae). Aust. Wildl. Res. 8:203–222.

Burbidge, A. A. and G. Kuchling. 1994. Western swamp tortoise recovery plan. Western Australia Wildlife Management, Program No. 11, Department of Conservation and Land Management, Perth, Australia.

Burbidge, A. A., G. Kuchling, P. J. Fuller, G. Graham, and D. Miller. 1990. The Western Swamp Tortoise. Western Australian Wildlife Management, Program No. 6., Department of Conservation and Land Management, Perth, Australia.

Haig, S. M., J. D. Ballou, and S. R. Derrickson. 1990. Management options for preserving genetic diversity: Reintroduction of Guam rails to the wild. Conserv. Biol. 4:290–300.

Hall, G., D. Groth, and J. Wetherall. 1992. Application of DNA profiling to the management of endangered species. Int. Zoo Yb. 31:103–108.

Jacobson, E. R. 1993. Implications of infectious diseases for captive propagation and introduction programs of threatened/endangered reptiles. J. Zoo Wildl. Med. 24:245–255.

Kuchling, G. 1988. Zur Fortpflanzung von *Pseudemydura umbrina* Siebenrock, 1901: Neue Untersuchungsmethoden für die Rettung einer vom Außterben bedrohten Schildkrötenart (Testudines: Chelidae). Herpetozoa 1:3–11.

Kuchling, G. and S. D. Bradshaw. 1993. Ovarian cycle and egg production of the western swamp tortoise *Pseudemydura umbrina* (Testudines: Chelidae) in the wild and in captivity. J. Zool. 229:405–419.

Kuchling, G. and J. P. DeJose. 1989. A captive breeding operation to rescue the critically endangered western swamp turtle *Pseudemydura umbrina* from extinction. Int. Zoo Yb. 28:103–109.

Kuchling, G., J. P. DeJose, A. A. Burbidge, and S. D. Bradshaw. 1992. Beyond captive breeding: The western swamp tortoise *Pseudemydura umbrina* recovery programme. Int. Zoo Yb. 31:37–41.

Pimm, S. L., H. L. Jones, and J. Diamond. 1988. On the risk of extinction. Am. Nat. 132:757–785.

Spence, T., R. Fairfax, and I. Loach. 1979. The Western Australian swamp tortoise *Pseudemydura umbrina* in captivity. Int. Zoo Yb. 19:58–60.

Swingland, I. R. and M. J. Coe. 1978. The natural regulation of giant tortoise populations on Aldabra Atoll: Reproduction. J. Zool. 186:285–310.

The Conservation Biology of the Angonoka, *Geochelone yniphora*, in Northwestern Madagascar: Progress Report

JAMES O. JUVIK,[1] A. ROSS KIESTER,[2] DON REID,[3] BRUCE COBLENTZ,[4] AND JEFFREY HOFFMAN[5]

[1] *Geography Department, University of Hawaii-Hilo, Hilo, HI 96720-4091, USA [e-mail: jjuvik@hawaii.edu]*
[2] *U.S. Forest Service, 3200 Southwest Jefferson Way, Corvallis, OR 97331, USA [e-mail: ross@krait.fsl.orst.edu]*
[3] *Jersey Wildlife Preservation Trust, WWF Aires Protegees, B.P. 738, Antananarivo 101, Madagascar*
[4] *Dept. of Fisheries & Wildlife, Oregon State University, Corvallis, OR 97331, USA*
[5] *NASA-Johnson Flight Center, Houston, TX 77058, USA*

ABSTRACT: The plowshare tortoise or angonoka, *Geochelone yniphora*, is one of the world's most-threatened reptile species with a surviving wild population estimated at only a few hundred animals. Remaining populations are restricted to fragmented and diminishing dry scrub forest habitat in the vicinity of Baly Bay, Madagascar. In addition to domestic cattle grazing, other alien species introductions (i.e., African bush pig) may also play a significant role in both habitat modification and direct predation on the angonoka. This paper reports on the results of recent (1992–1993) field research emphasizing (1) the establishment of a regional habitat database in a geographic information system (GIS) with the capability of providing high resolution identification and discrimination of actual and potential angonoka habitat, (2) continuing basic biological and ecological research on the best-known wild population (Cape Sada), which has been under active consideration for protected area status, and (3) monitoring of the introduced African bush pig and its impact on angonoka survival in the dry scrub forest ecosystems of northwestern Madagascar.

The angonoka, *Geochelone yniphora*, is a critically endangered land tortoise currently restricted in its distribution to small remnant patches of natural dry forest habitats surrounding Baly Bay on the northwest coast of Madagascar (Juvik et al., 1981). In the mid-1980s the Jersey Wildlife Presentation Trust (JWPT), in collaboration with the Malagasy Department of Waters and Forests, launched an integrated conservation initiative, Project Angonoka. A captive breeding facility stocked with 20 confiscated tortoises was established at Ampijoroa, in the Mahajanga Province, near the natural range of the species (Reid et al., 1989). More than 100 captive-bred offspring have been produced at this facility over the past six years. The project has also included basic ecological research and efforts to document the distribution and habitat preferences of the tortoise (Reid, 1990; Juvik et al., 1981).

In this paper we summarize field research undertaken during 1992, specifically:

1. The establishment of a regional habitat geographic information system (GIS) database with the capability of providing high resolution identification of actual and potential angonoka habitat. This research employed remote sensing imagery including satellite, space shuttle, and conventional aerial black-and-white, color, and color-infrared photography, along with ground verification surveys. In addition, because some of the remote sensing products were available from a 42-year period (1949–1991), we anticipated the possibility of evaluating changes in forest cover and fragmentation over time. Any changes would be important to future tortoise habitat conservation efforts.

2. Continuing basic biological and ecological research on the best-known wild population at Cape Sada, a site under consideration for "Protected Area" status.

3. Monitoring of the African bush pig, *Potamochoerus larvatus*, and its impact on angonoka survival and the dry forest ecosystems of northwestern Madagascar.

Computer analysis of satellite and space shuttle photography to identify habitat was conducted in the fall of 1991. In January 1992, during low-level overflights, color infrared photographs were taken of the Baly Bay area. We conducted ground surveys at Cape Sada and adjacent areas from 9 to 21 January 1992 (the height of the wet season); additional surveys for both tortoises and African bush pigs were conducted in the Baly Bay area from 5 to 26 July 1992 (during the dry season).

Remote Sensing Studies

During 1991 and 1992 we acquired five different sets of images of the Baly Bay area:

1. Low-level, black-and-white aerial photography (1949). Using Erdas image processing software (Erdas, Inc., 1994), we computer scanned these photos and digitally transformed the images to permit detailed spatial comparison with later satellite images.

2. Landsat Multispectral Scanner photography (1973). The photographs have sufficient resolution to determine forest/savanna boundaries for this date.

3. Landsat Thematic Mapper digital data (1990). This digital image became the major source of data pertinent to the assessment of potential angonoka habitat. Preliminary vegetation maps were prepared from the image (Figure 1) and taken into the field in January 1992 for verification.

4. Space shuttle photography (1990 and 1992). True-color photographs of the greater Baly Bay area were taken using a hand-held camera. These have proved extremely valuable in interpreting vegetation patterns from the satellite digital data (Kiester et al., 1993).

5. Low-level oblique-color and false-color aerial photography (1992). In a January 1992 overflight of the Baly Bay area, using a hand-held camera, nearly all potential tortoise habitat was photographed at a scale that often allowed identification of individual trees.

Preliminary Vegetation and Tortoise Habitat Map

Figure 1 illustrates our preliminary habitat discrimination map for the Cape Sada area, which was derived from the 1990 digital Landsat Thematic Mapper (LTM) images. This 4 km² area was chosen for initial analysis because actual vegetation patterns and tortoise distribution were reasonably well known from previous field work (Reid, 1990, 1993). Based on field verification in January 1992, the image adequately distinguished the main vegetation types in the area, including coastal mangroves, komanga forest (*Erythrophyleum couminga*), palm-savanna, bamboo thickets, and the open scrub forest habitat known to contain *G. yniphora*. The prime tortoise habitat on the central and southern portions of the Cape Sada Peninsula (area A in Figure 1) is characterized by a mosaic color pattern of green, black, yellow, and orange. The light yellow and orange colors signify high surface reflectivity associated with open rocky or sandy ground. Using LTM images we identified three additional small potential habitat patches (areas B, C, and D) with image signatures similar to area A. The new areas had not previously been searched for tortoises. During the January and July 1992 field work several unmarked tortoises were discovered in habitat fragments (areas B and D). A single tortoise scat was found in area C. We conclude that satellite image analysis can be used to direct ground searches to potential tortoise habitat in the Baly Bay area in the future.

Additional work is needed to determine whether the tortoise habitat identified on Cape Sada represents the only habitat type where tortoises occur. It is likely that further refinement of the spatial habitat model will be required if additional tortoise populations are discovered and associated vegetation types are determined. The January 1992 space shuttle overflight and our ongoing image analysis (Kiester and Juvik, in prep.) support historic data (Curl et al., 1985) that suitable habitat areas for *G. yniphora* occur to the west of Baly Bay (Belambo area), a region where tortoise populations are not yet well documented.

Cape Sada Biological and Ecological Research

Permanent Transects

To provide a geographic baseline on the Cape Sada Peninsula, permanent east-west and north-south transects were established. Following a constant compass bearing, vegetation was cleared for a 1 m wide foot trail along the transect. Aluminum tags were placed at 50 m intervals. The east-west transect (1,000 m long) crossed prime tortoise habitat in the middle of the Cape Sada Peninsula (Figure 2). The north-south transect (600 m long) intersected the midpoint of the east-west transect and extended to the south coast. Vegetation data collected along the transects will be used in the future to refine the satellite image interpretation.

1992 Tortoise Population Studies at Cape Sada

During three previous visits to Cape Sada, 1989–1991, 14 *G. yniphora* were marked (Reid, 1990) (an additional juvenile was found but not marked). Most of the tortoises were adults (straight-line carapace length >250 mm) and only two animals were male. During the January 1992 (wet season) field work, eight previously marked tortoises were recaptured in the central habitat area (A in Figure 1). In addition, two new adult tortoises and a hatchling were also found in this area. The habitat patch on the north coast (area B on Figure 1) was surveyed for the first time, and three new tortoises (including a juvenile and a hatchling) were discovered. In the July 1992 (dry season) resurvey, four previously marked tortoises were recaptured in the central Sada area, and one new tortoise was found in the north coast habitat fragment.

From the above data, it was possible to estimate the number of tortoises in the central Cape Sada population (area A). Using the Peterson index (Seber, 1973) and taking all pre-1992 data as one time period and all 1992 data as a second period, we estimate a total population of 18.75 adult tortoises. Given the small sample size and heterogeneity of the data in time, we conclude that there are at most 20–30 tortoises in the central population. The sex ratio in our sample was heavily skewed in favor of females (>80%). It is possible that our population may be significantly underestimated if males use a different habitat from that which was surveyed.

It is clear that the Cape Sada tortoise population is very small and vulnerable. However, the discovery of hatchling *G. yniphora* in both 1991 and 1992 field seasons and other juvenile and subadult tortoises confirms that successful reproduction (and some recruitment) is occurring. Cape Sada

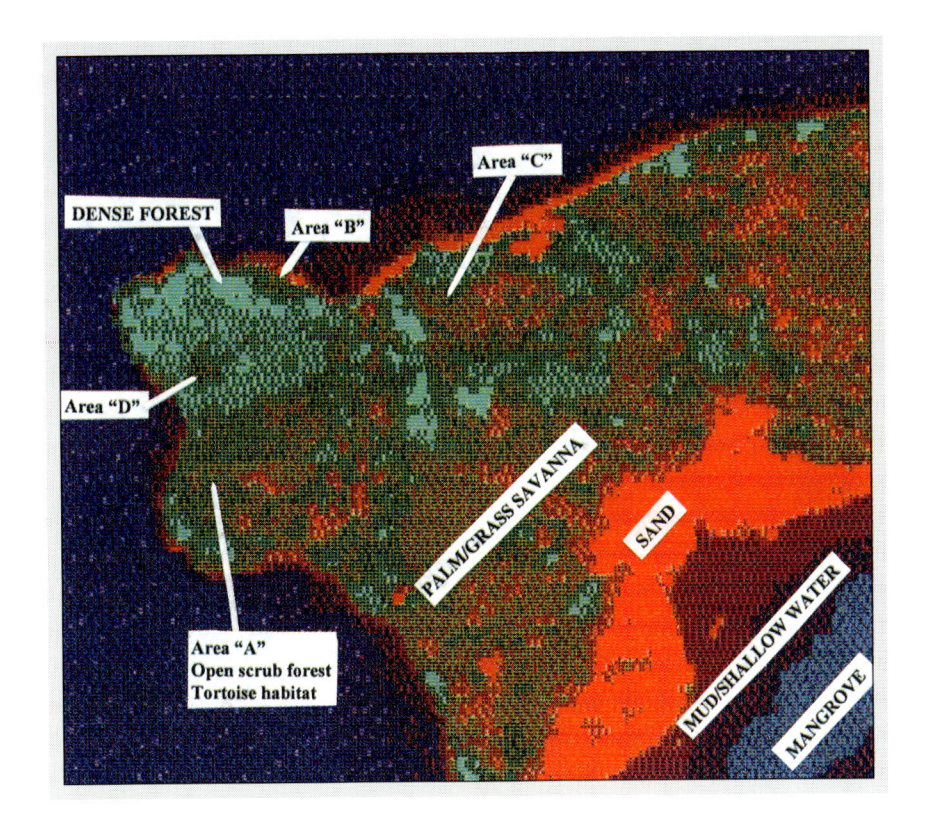

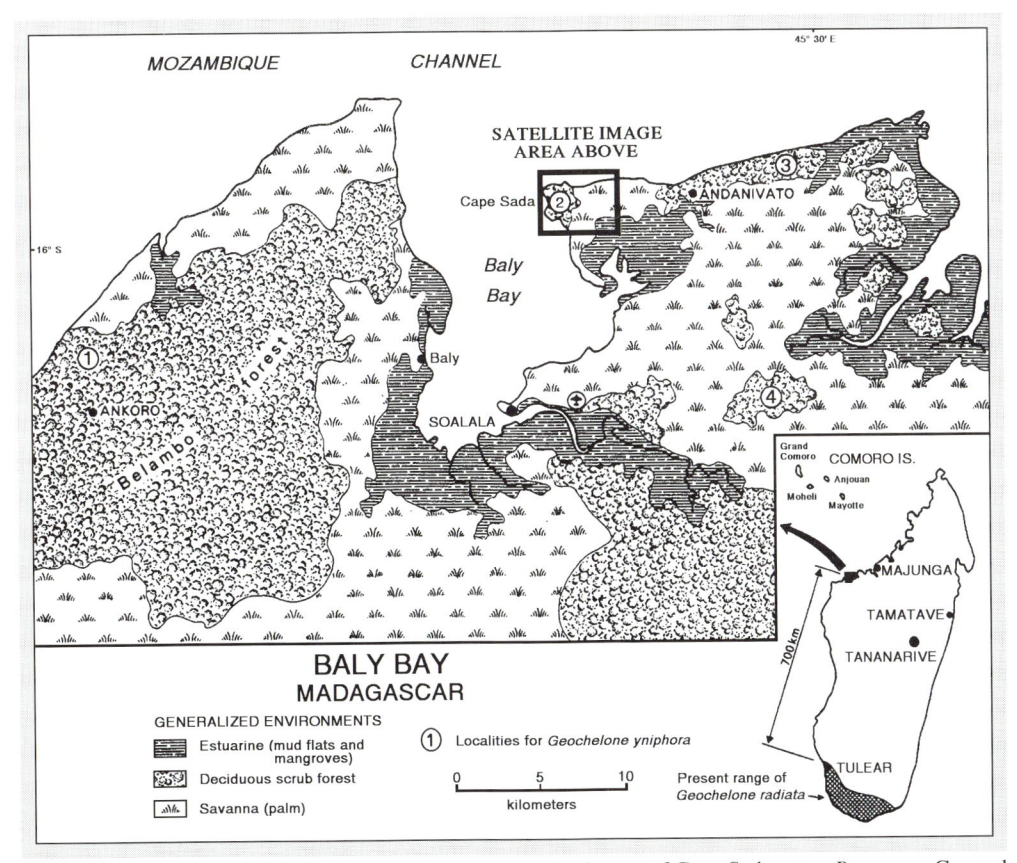

Figure 1. *Top* — Detailed 1990 Thematic Mapper Satellite image of Cape Sada area. *Bottom* — General study area, Baly Bay, Madagascar. See text for discussion of areas A–D.

is the only known site in the greater Baly Bay area where a reproducing population of *G. yniphora* has been confirmed.

Radio Telemetry

During the 1992 field period a total of 11 tortoises were fitted with radio transmitters (model SB2, AVM Instruments, Inc., Livermore, California) with one-year lithium batteries. Radio telemetry proved effective in locating tortoises (Reid, 1993). A two-year study of tortoise activity, population size, distribution, and movement patterns was initiated in 1993 (Smith, unpubl. report, 1994).

Status of the African Bush Pig (*Potamochoerus* sp.)

Evidence of pig rooting activity in the Baly Bay area was observed on previous field visits, and it has been presumed, but not documented, that this non-native predator may pose a significant threat to both eggs and young of *G. yniphora*. Accordingly, the first quantitative survey of pigs in *G. yniphora* habitat was conducted at Cape Sada and Beheta (a tortoise population 15 km east of Cape Sada) during the 1992 dry season (12–20 July). All pig scats observed at Cape Sada were old (none had been produced within the previous two weeks). Out of hundreds of scats examined in the field, none was less than 24 hours old. Therefore, the rate of deposition could not be evaluated, and we were unable to determine an index of pig numbers.

On a long-term basis bush pigs may have a major ecological impact in the Baly Bay region. However, during the 1992 survey it was evident that numbers were very much reduced, and the pigs were probably absent from Cape Sada during the visit. Factors that affect their numbers or how rapidly the pigs may respond to changing environmental conditions are unknown. Their numbers on Cape Sada could have decreased because of diminished food resources, either from reduced precipitation or increased domestic cattle grazing. In a later field visit (Reid, 1993), evidence of intensive cattle grazing at Cape Sada was much greater than in previous visits over the past five years, and pig activity had increased significantly, although not to pre-1992 levels.

At the Beheta tortoise habitat area we found considerably more evidence of pigs than at Sada; significantly more scats and rootings were observed, but only a single scat was identified as fresh. In addition, one live pig was seen in the area. A total of 579, 5 × 5 m sample plots were examined for pig scats in the Beheta area: 256 plots in presumed tortoise habitat (dry scrub forest) and 323 plots in nearby anthropogenic palm-savanna. Evidence of bush pig activity was observed in 39.5% of the tortoise habitat plots and 22.9% of the savanna plots. Scat was observed more frequently in the savanna habitat, while rooting activity was considerably more frequent in the dry forest tortoise habitat (under the woody shrub and bamboo canopy). These quantitative data, although limited, provide evidence of direct use of tortoise habitat by bush pigs, which suggests a significant threat of predation to tortoise eggs and young.

A number of alternatives for the control of pigs in the Baly Bay area have been considered, including snaring, live trapping, hunting, poisoning, and fencing. Until the ecology and population dynamics of the bush pig in the Baly Bay area are better understood, the costs and benefits of such control measures remain unknown, and it is an important topic for further field study.

CONCLUSIONS

With continued success of the captive breeding program for *G. yniphora* in Madagascar, increasing numbers of captive-bred tortoises will be reaching a suitable size (>200 mm carapace length) for possible reintroduction to the wild during the late 1990s. However, reintroduction as a conservation strategy is charged with questions and difficulties. Only a small percentage of reintroductions could be considered successful (Griffith et al., 1989), and the subject remains controversial among workers on reptiles and amphibians (see Dodd and Seigel, 1991; Burke, 1991; and Reinert, 1991). It has been suggested (Beck, MS) that no species should be reintroduced until the causes of the original decline are known and corrected, and that any introduction must be followed by careful monitoring of the introduced animals. We are only beginning to understand the causes of decline of *G. yniphora*. Radiotelemetry will be of great value in monitoring populations should reintroduction be undertaken. The current research on habitat delineation and habitat change over time will help identify potential reintroduction sites. Likewise, the future ecological research on the remaining wild populations of *G. yniphora* and the potential threats to its survival should provide information essential to long-term conservation of this species and its dry scrub-forest habitat in the Baly Bay area.

ACKNOWLEDGMENTS

This field work was undertaken as part of Project Angonoka under the leadership of its director, Dr. Lee Durrell, with the financial support of the Jersey Wildlife Preservation Trust. We would to thank Patrick Daniels and Rod Mast (Conservation International) for both financial and logistical support provided to this project in Madagascar. Project volunteers Drs. Liz and Mike Howe and University of Mahajanga students Marcel Chan-Kai and Mahatoly Joby were indefatigable contributors to the success of our 1992 field work. Additional thanks to Joanna Durbin, Dourette Razandrianakanirina, and our local guides, Adany and Remi.

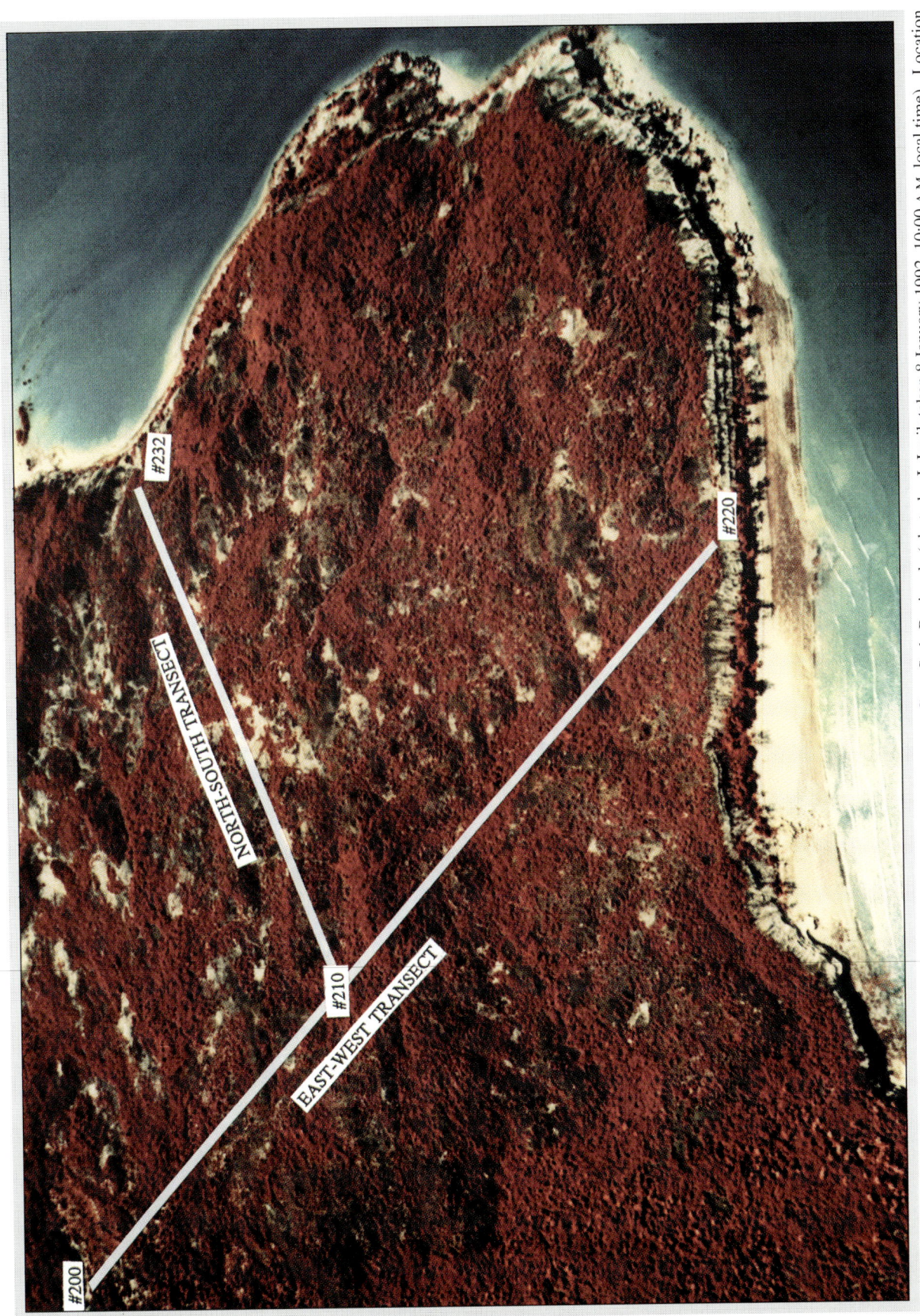

Figure 2. False-color infrared photograph of tortoise habitat on the southwestern Cape Sada Peninsula (photo by J. Juvik taken 8 January 1992, 10:00 A.M. local time). Location of the east-west (permanent tags #200–#220) and north-south (#210–#232) transects are indicated on the photo. The length of the east-west transect is 1,000 m. The east-west transect area between points #210–#220 corresponds to Area "A" tortoise habitat in the thematic mapper image (Figure 1).

LITERATURE CITED

Beck, B. B. (undated). Guidelines for reintroduction of captive-bred animals. Unpubl. MS, AAZPA Reintroduction Advisory Group.

Burke, R. L. 1991. Relocations, repatriations, and translocations of amphibians: Taking a broader view. Herpetologica 47(3):350–357.

Curl, D. A., I. C. Scoones, M. K. Guy, and G. Rakoarisoa. 1985. The Madagascar tortoise (*Geochelone yniphora*): Current status and distribution. Biol. Conserv. 34(1985):35–54.

Dodd, C. K., Jr., and R. A. Seigel. 1991. Relocation, repatriation, and translocation of amphibians and reptiles: Are they conservation strategies that work? Herpetologica 47(3):336–350.

ERDAS. 1994. ERDAS Field Guide, 3rd ed. ERDAS, Inc., Atlanta, Georgia.

Griffith, B., J. M. Scott, J. W. Carpenter, and C. Reed. 1989. Translocation as a species conservation tool: Status and strategy. Science 245:477–480.

Juvik, J., A. J. Andrianarivo, and C. P. Blanc. 1981. The ecology and status of *Geochelone yniphora*: A critically endangered tortoise in north-western Madagascar. Biol. Conserv. 19:297–316.

Juvik, J., D. E. Meier, and S. McKeown. 1992. Captive husbandry and conservation of the Madagascar ploughshare tortoise (*Geochelone yniphora*). *In* K. R. Beaman, F. Caporaso, S. McKeown, and M. Graff (eds.), Proceedings of the First International Symposium on Turtles & Tortoises: Conservation and Captive Husbandry, pp. 127–137. August 1990, Chapman University, Orange, California; California Turtle & Tortoise Club and Chapman University.

Kiester, A. R., J. O. Juvik, D. Reid, J. A. Hoffman, and B. E. Coblentz. 1993. Dry forest disturbance and boundary dynamics in western Madagascar: Implications for wildlife conservation. *In* Proceedings: 30th Annual Meeting, Association for Tropical Biology, pp. 99–100. San Juan Puerto Rico, June 1993.

Reid, D. 1990. Report on a field study of *Geochelone yniphora* in January 1990. Unpubl. MS, Jersey Wildlife Preservation Trust.

Reid, D. 1993. Report of a field study of wild angonoka *Geochelone yniphora* on Cape Sada in February 1993. Unpubl. MS, Jersey Wildlife Preservation Trust.

Reid, D., L. Durrell, and G. Rakotobearison. 1989. The captive breeding project for the angonoka *Geochelone yniphora* in Madagascar. Dodo (JWPT) 26:34–48.

Reinert, H. K. 1991. Translocation as a conservation strategy for amphibians and reptiles: Some comments, concerns, and observations. Herpetologica 47(3):357–363.

Seber, G. A. F. 1973. The Estimation of Animal Abundance. Griffin, London. 506 pp.

Reserves and Programs

BUFFER ZONES, RESERVE PLANNING, LANDSCAPE PRESERVATION, AND CONSERVATION PROGRAMS

Standing — Vitor Hugo Cantarelli (Centro Nacional dos Quelônios da Amazônia, Goiânia, Brazil), Thomas Herman (Center for Wildlife and Conservation Biology, Nova Scotia, Canada), Erik Kiviat (Hudsonia Ltd., Annandale, New York), Dennis Herman (North Carolina State Museum of Natural Sciences, Raleigh, North Carolina), Richard Buech (U.S.D.A. Forest Service, Grand Rapids, Minnesota), and Kurt Buhlmann (Savannah River Ecology Laboratory, Aiken, South Carolina). *Seated* — Roger Dale (The Natelson Company, Inc., Encino, California), Jun Lee (Nonprofit Counsel, Washington, D.C.), Devin Reese (U.S.A.I.D. Center for the Environment, Washington, D.C.), and Alison Whitlock (University of Massachusetts, Amherst, Massachusetts).

Use of Terrestrial Habitat by Western Pond Turtles, *Clemmys marmorata*: Implications for Management

DEVIN A. REESE[1,2] AND HARTWELL H. WELSH[1]

[1]*USDA Forest Service, PSW Redwood Science Laboratory, Arcata, CA 95521, USA*
[2]*Current Address: USAID/G/ENV, The Ronald Reagan Building, Room 308, Washington, D.C. 20523-1812*
[e-mail: dereese@usaid.gov]

ABSTRACT: Despite its extensive range, the western pond turtle, *Clemmys marmorata*, is currently a candidate for federal listing. Understanding its use of the landscape has become increasingly important to the development of appropriate management plans. Using radiotelemetry, we examined movements of turtles in a two-mile stretch of the Trinity River (Trinity County, California). We observed frequent and prolonged use of terrestrial habitat for both nesting and overwintering activities; the turtles travelled into upland areas as far as 500 m from the river. Males utilized terrestrial habitat in at least ten months of the year, and females were on land every month as a result of their additional terrestrial behavior while gravid. Hatchlings overwintered in the nest. These observations suggest that the terrestrial habitat is as important as the aquatic habitat to the viability of western pond turtle populations. The implications for management are significant, considering the variety of development pressures on lands adjacent to waterways.

The western pond turtle, *Clemmys marmorata*, is the only extant aquatic turtle native to California. Western pond turtles have an extensive range (western Washington to northwest Baja California; Stebbins, 1985) and appear to fill a variety of aquatic niches. They are found in ponds, rivers, vernal pools, streams, ephemeral creeks, reservoirs, agricultural ditches, sewage treatment ponds, and estuaries. Despite the fact that they are widespread habitat generalists, western pond turtles are declining (Holland, 1992). *C. marmorata* became a candidate for federal listing in 1991 (*Federal Register*, 1991). It has been given legal status as "Threatened" in Washington State, "Sensitive" in Oregon, and "Of Special Concern" in California.

All other members of the genus *Clemmys* are semi-terrestrial. *C. insculpta* feeds in alder thickets and corn fields (Kaufmann, 1992) and *C. guttata* aestivates in terrestrial habitats (Ward, 1976). *C. muhlenbergii* can be found in riparian vegetation (Chase et al., 1989). Preliminary observations of western pond turtles indicated that they may also have terrestrial affinities:

- They frequently cross roads in agricultural areas of California (Reese, pers. obs.).

- Their underwater numbers decrease appreciably in the main stem Trinity River as winter approaches (Reese and Welsh, 1992, unpubl. data), suggesting that they probably leave the river.

- They nest on land, a feature common to all but one known species of aquatic turtle. Nesting sites for *C. marmorata* can be as far as 400 m from water (Storer, 1930; Holland, 1991a, 1991c; Rathbun et al., 1992).

Figure 1. Ten-gram radio transmitter with whip antennae attached with epoxy cement. (Photo by Douglas Welsh.)

Understanding the function of terrestrial movements could be helpful in the interpretation of range-wide trends. It may also allow us to predict the extent and nature of terrestrial habitat use by turtles at poorly known sites. Movements of emydid turtles onto land for nesting are documented for numerous species (Burger, 1975; Congdon et al., 1983; Schwarzkopf and Brooks, 1987; Quinn and Tate, 1991). Terrestrial overwintering is less well understood (Bennett et al., 1970). Other potential triggers for land travel include movements to escape unsuitable conditions (Gibbons, 1986) or movements within a home range that includes multiple bodies of water.

The objective of this study was to investigate the role of the terrestrial environment in the life history of the western pond turtle. Although information exists on location of nest sites, there are few data regarding the frequency and duration of terrestrial movements. With the advent and refinement of radiotelemetry for small animals, collection of this data became possible. Our intent was to investigate overland movements associated with nesting as well as identify new terrestrial destinations, such as overwintering sites.

Study Area

The study area was a 2.8 km stretch of the main stem Trinity River (Trinity County, California). The stretch (Figure 2) runs between Douglas City and Junction City in a relatively unpopulated section of river. Surveys conducted previously (Lind et al., 1992) found high densities of western pond turtles along this stretch. The surrounding land is divided in ownership between the U.S. Bureau of Land Management, the U.S. Forest Service, and private owners. The dominant riparian tree canopy species are white alder (*Alnus rhombifolia*) and yellow willow (*Salix lasiandra*).

The adjacent upland habitat is characterized as montane hardwood-conifer and montane hardwood (Mayer and Laudenslayer, 1988). The former applies primarily to the north-facing slopes, which harbor a diverse mix of hardwood and conifer species. Conifers, including Douglas fir (*Pseudotsuga menziesii*) and Ponderosa pine (*Pinus ponderosa*) form a high canopy. The subcanopy consists of Pacific madrone (*Arbutus menziesii*), tan oak (*Lithocarpus densiflorus*), and California black oak (*Quercus kelloggii*). In contrast, south-facing slopes are dominated by hardwoods, including manzanita (*Arctostaphylos* sp.), Pacific madrone, several oak species, and gray pine (*Pinus sabiniana*).

Methods

This three-year, ongoing study of western pond turtle movements and habitat use was initiated in May 1992. Results presented here were generated from radiotelemetry data collected during the first year of study. Results from the remainder of the study are reported in Reese (1996). Our intent was to radio track 12 western pond turtles for the duration.

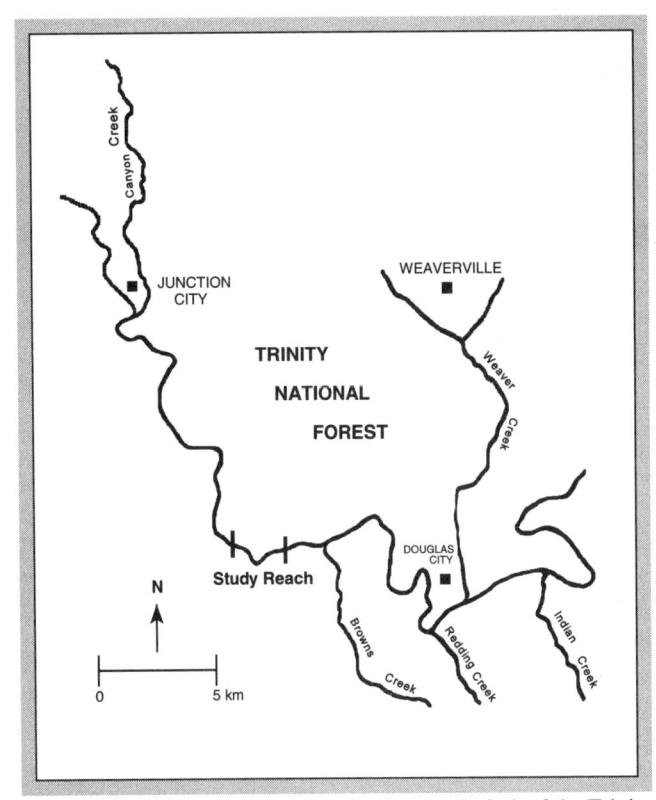

Figure 2. Location of study reach along the main fork of the Trinity River, Trinity County, California.

To minimize potential differences in observed behavior between males and females that may result from the location of capture rather than sex, we designated males and females found within 50 m of each other as pairs. We also required that pairs be separated by at least 300 m to minimize the degree of home range overlap, while keeping the study area to a manageable size for hiking to turtle locations. Juvenile turtles (<110 mm carapace length) were excluded.

Turtles were fitted with 160 MHz radios that have approximately a 2 km base range (AVM Electronics, Livermore, California). The 10 g radios (4.2 cm long, 3.3 cm wide, 1.0 cm thick) were affixed to the carapace using PC-7 overnight-drying epoxy cement (Protective Coating Company, Allentown, Pennsylvania) with the whip antennae attached to the marginals (Figure 1). The batteries were estimated to last approximately 12 months with a pulse rate of 85/min. The radio-equipped turtles were located weekly on a random day to avoid errors from systematic telemetry monitoring. (A systematic schedule could, for example, bias the results towards particular cyclical behaviors.) After a turtle was located its position and behavior were noted.

Turtles were disturbed only to the extent necessary to establish their locations on the ground. For terrestrial locations, this occasionally required manual searching through leaf and needle litter. For aquatic locations, triangulation was used to situate the turtle as precisely as possible. The following data were recorded for all terrestrial locations: shortest distance to the water, slope, aspect, canopy cover, and habitat type.

In addition to the 12 radio-tagged individuals, seven females were equipped with short-term radios to monitor nesting behavior. These females were checked every three hours from dawn to dusk while gravid. If they remained active after dusk, they were checked every three hours throughout the night. Monitoring continued for at least one week after nesting. For comparison, males were checked on a similar schedule during two weeks of the nesting season.

Active nests were covered with mesh cages to prevent predation of eggs or hatchlings (Holland, 1992), and this also ensured that we could ascertain the time of emergence.

Data Analysis

We calculated the proportion of turtles that spent time on land during each month from June 1992 to June 1993. A single location on land at least one meter from the water was considered sufficient to be designated a terrestrial sighting. This generated a conservative estimate of terrestrial behavior, considering that turtles may have made additional land trips during the week-long intervals between checks. We included the gravid females as well as females from the year-round set that were not gravid or of unknown reproductive status.

We calculated how many days gravid females spent on land during the weeks before and after nesting. The more intensive monitoring schedule (every 3 hours) during nesting season allowed us to generate these estimates. Analysis of radio-tracking data requires certain assumptions regarding the positions of individual turtles in the interim periods between successive locations. The following assumptions were chosen because they required the least conjecture and thereby seemed parsimonious:

1. If a turtle was in the same medium (river, land, or pond) at consecutive sightings, it was assumed to have remained there during the interim; and

2. If a turtle changed medium between consecutive sightings, the first location at the new medium was assumed to be the first time it was there.

RESULTS

Terrestrial movements were most common during the summer and winter (Figure 4). The result is best described as a bimodal distribution representing seasonal changes in level of terrestrial activity. The peak in June of each year represents movements of gravid females during nesting season. The winter peak represents movements of both sexes to overwintering sites. The graph shows a high level of terrestrial behavior; females spent time on land during every month of the year, whereas males spent time on land during all months except July and August. As described above, these are likely to be minimum estimates of the amount of actual terrestrial behavior in the monitored population.

Nesting

Although we observed only one female actually depositing its eggs, we were able to estimate the times the others nested, based on their behavior and reproductive status. Nesting occurred from mid-June to mid-July. Females were highly terrestrial while gravid, making multiple trips (rang-

Figure 3. *Clemmys marmorata* partially buried beneath leaf and needle litter. (Photo by Douglas Welsh.)

ing from 2 to 11) onto land, which were initiated as early as one month prior to nesting. While on land each female burrowed and was partially or completely concealed beneath leaf or needle litter (Figure 3). Females remained buried in single locations for as long as three days, occasionally changing orientation. The amount of time spent on land was greatest just before nesting and declined thereafter (Figure 5).

The female that was observed nesting had travelled at least 31 m from the river's edge, assuming that it had taken the shortest route. Located in a clearing surrounded by mixed hardwood, the nest was excavated in hard-packed silty soil on a slight, east-facing slope only a few meters from the riparian zone. Oviposition occurred in the evening and the female remained by the nest overnight before returning to the river. Hatchlings emerged from the nest the following March (eight months later). Hatchlings did not immediately leave the nest area after emerging, spending as many as nine days under leaves.

Overwintering

Following the high level of terrestrial activity associated with nesting in June, there was a lull during which few turtles were found on land (Figure 4). A second period of terrestrial behavior began in September, when all 12 radio-equipped turtles left the river. It was not possible to establish the exact departure dates, as the turtles were monitored weekly.

Between September and early December, turtles made as many as four changes in position on land. At each location, they were found completely buried under leaf or needle litter. The locations eventually occupied for the duration of the winter were all in upland habitat beyond the riparian zone at a mean distance of 203 m from the water. However, they varied with respect to microhabitat features (Table 1). Vegetation type included both hardwood-dominant and conifer-dominant woodlands. Two turtles overwintered in lentic bodies of water, whereas the other ten remained on land.

Return movements to the river from overwintering sites began in February 1993 and were not completed until as late as June. Turtles visited a variety of locations along the way; the average return time to the river was seven weeks. Although travel speed (meters travelled per day on average) was not related to distance of overwintering sites from the river, there was a significant correlation between travel speed and order of initiation of return movements ($P < .02$, Spearman rho, two-tailed). Specifically, turtles that initiated their return trips later travelled faster. The two individuals that overwintered in other bodies of water (slough and lake) were the last to initiate their return trips, and their movements overland were the fastest (Figure 6). The routes followed to overwintering sites were in some cases different from the return routes. For example, two individuals stopped for a few weeks at a vernal pool that had been dry in the fall during their outbound trip.

DISCUSSION

The western pond turtles we monitored exhibited considerable terrestrial activity. Females naturally travel onto land for nesting, but the large number of overland trips they made before actually ovipositing is noteworthy. Rathbun et al. (1992) also reported multiple trips by gravid females. It is possible that females gain a thermoregulatory advantage by spending time buried on

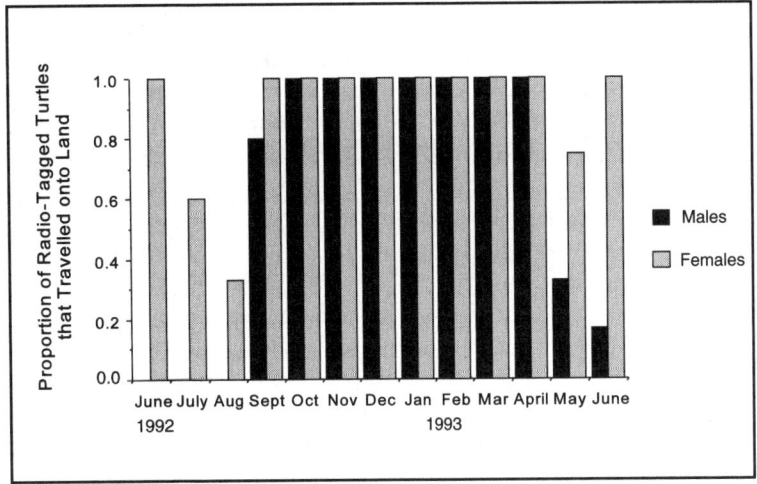

Figure 4. Proportion of radio-tagged turtles in the Trinity River study reach that travelled onto land during each month.

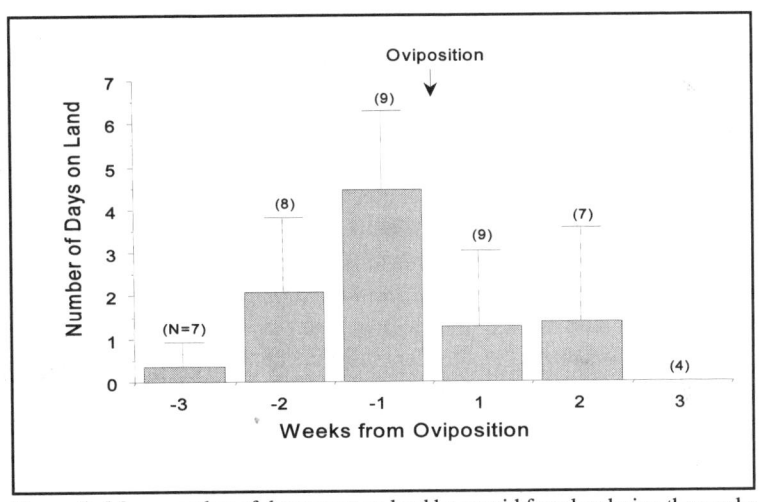

Figure 5. Mean number of days spent on land by gravid females during the weeks before and after oviposition.

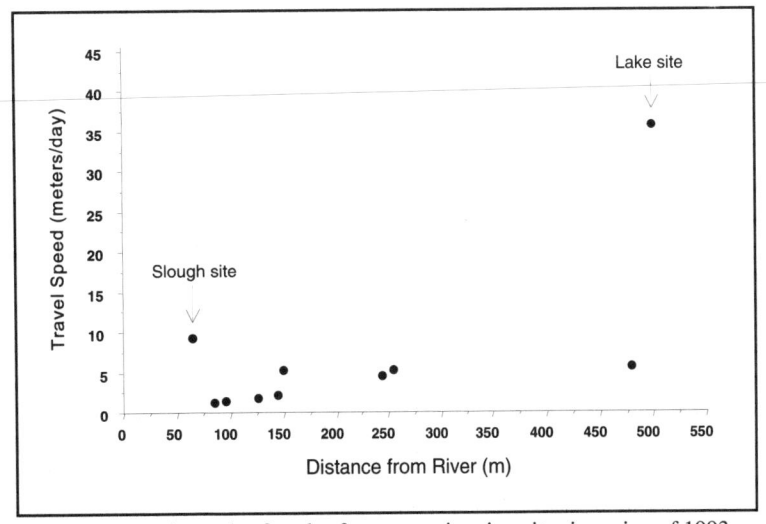

Figure 6. Travel speeds of turtles from overwintering sites in spring of 1993.

TABLE 1

Overwintering habitat of turtles on main stem Trinity River during 1992–1993. Douglas fir dominant = ≥75% Douglas firs; hardwood dominant = ≥75% hardwoods; conifer dominant = mix of conifers with none comprising more than 75%; mixed hardwood/conifer = neither comprising more than 75%; mixed alder/willow = neither comprising more than 75%.

Turtle/Sex	Slope aspect	Habitat type	Canopy cover (%)	Distance from shore (m)
698 ♀	25 NE	Douglas fir dominant	75	480
773 ♀	15 NE	Hardwood dominant	50	255
949 ♀	5 E	Hardwood dominant	50	75
749 ♀	None	Mixed hardwood/conifer	75	85
215 ♀	10 E	Mixed hardwood/conifer	90	126
868 ♀	5 N	Conifer dominant	75	215
678 ♂	None	Conifer dominant	80	245
725 ♂	20 E	Conifer dominant	15	95
528 ♂	None	Hardwood dominant	70	145
560 ♂	Lake	Hardwood dominant	0	500
377b ♂	14 NE	Mixed hardwood/conifer	50	65
335b ♂	Slough	Mixed alder/willow	59	65

land during preovipositional development of the embryo (e.g., *Podocnemis expansa*). The air on the Trinity River is consistently warmer than the water at this time of year (USFWS temperature records, Lewiston station). It is also possible that females are responding to our presence with preovipositional arrest, a mechanism that allows them to retain eggs until conditions are favorable (Ewert, 1985). In either case, their tendency to burrow under litter is consistent with known behavior of other species (e.g., *Kinosternon subrubrum* and *Clemmys insculpta*) during periods spent on land (Bennett, 1972; Kaufmann, 1992).

It is of interest that hatchlings did not emerge from the nest until spring. Hatchlings of other emydid species are known to remain in terrestrial nest cavities through their first winter (Hartweg, 1946; Gibbons and Nelson, 1978; Gibbons, 1990). Feldman (1982), who based his observations on captives, suggested that *C. marmorata* hatchlings may do the same. It is also possible that egg development was suspended and hatching delayed until just prior to the March emergence time. This phenomenon of embryonic diapause occurs in a number of turtle species (Ewert, 1985). Either strategy may be an adaptive response to unfavorable conditions on the Trinity River in the fall, such as high water levels or low temperatures. Gibbons and Nelson (1978) suggested that delayed emergence may provide the benefit of sanctuary during a period when the growth benefits gained from early emergence are likely to be outweighed by predation or by mortality from harsh environmental conditions.

All of the radio-equipped turtles spent seven months of the year away from the river at overwintering sites. These included both terrestrial refuges and lentic bodies of water as far as 500 m from the river. This overwintering strategy may be an adaptive response to winter flooding. However, reasons for the long distances the turtles travelled, well beyond the flood zone, are unknown. It is also of interest that most turtles overwintered on relatively cool north- and east-facing slopes rather than south- and west-facing slopes.

Microhabitat characteristics of the overwintering sites were variable. There did not appear to be an association with any single habitat type. The timing and duration of movements during the 1992–1993 winter varied with the individual turtles. The departure from the river was asynchronous and the spring return even more so. Turtles that left the river later travelled faster, which may be attributable to the warmer temperatures and consequently higher activity potential.

CONCLUSIONS

This study provides a preliminary framework for developing management programs for the long-term survival of this species. Western pond turtles travel onto land for a variety of reasons and consequently occur in the terrestrial environment during all times of the year. These findings prescribe a management strategy that provides protection for not only waterways but also adjacent lands. The upland area used by turtles at this study site far exceeds the size of traditionally protected buffer zones along rivers. Unfortunately, with our current knowledge we cannot predict specifically which portions of the terrestrial environment are critical for western pond turtles. They utilize a variety of upland habitats as well as the network of creeks, ponds, and ephemeral bodies of water associated with riverine systems.

The riparian habitat serves an integral role in the life history of the western pond turtle, and many other species may cross the uncertain boundary between river and land because of their specialized, seasonally varying requirements. We must therefore reevaluate our view of riparian habitat as "buffer zone," which connotes a supportive rather than primary role in the ecosystem. Terrestrial riverine habitat warrants consideration aside from its function of buffering the aquatic habitat from external impacts. Management strategies that address the functioning of entire watersheds are more likely to afford adequate protection for these vagile, semi-terrestrial species.

Acknowledgements

The U.S. Bureau of Reclamation Trinity River Restoration Project provided the majority of funding for this research. Additional funding was provided by the U.S. Forest Service Redwood Science Lab, Shasta-Trinity National Forest, and U.S. Forest Service Fish-Habitat Relationships program. We wish to acknowledge Amy J. Lind for her continuing role in providing logistical assistance as well as scientific expertise. Thanks to Harry W. Greene, Reginald H. Barrett, and Mary Power for their review of the manuscript. The following persons helped in the field: Jenny Glueck, Polly Taylor, Randy Wilson, Sarah Mook, Douglas Welsh, Logan Olds, and Amy Lind. We are grateful to all of them.

Literature Cited

Bennett, D. H. 1972. Notes on the terrestrial wintering of mud turtles (*Kinosternon subrubrum*). Herpetologica 28(3):245–247.

Bennett, D. H., J. W. Gibbons, and J. C. Franson. 1970. Terrestrial activity in aquatic turtles. Ecology 51:738–740.

Burger, J. and W. A. Montevecchi. 1975. Nest site selection in the terrapin *Malaclemys terrapin*. Copeia 1975:113–119.

Chase, J. D., K. R. Dixon, J. E. Gates, D. Jacobs, and G. J. Taylor. 1989. Habitat characteristics, population size, and home range of the bog turtle, *Clemmys muhlenbergii*, in Maryland. J. Herpetol. 23(4):356–362.

Congdon, J. D., D. W. Tinkle, G. L. Breitenbach, and R. C. van Loben Sels. 1983. Nesting ecology and hatching success in the turtle *Emydoidea blandingii*. Herpetologica 39:417–429.

Ewert, M. A. 1985. Embryology of turtles. *In* C. Gans, F. Billett, and P. F. A. Maderson (eds.), Biology of the Reptilia, Vol. 14, pp. 75–268. John Wiley and Sons, New York.

Feldman, M. 1982. Notes on reproduction in *Clemmys marmorata*. Herpetol. Rev. 13:10–11.

Gibbons, J. W. 1986. Movement patterns among turtle populations: Applicability to management of the desert tortoise. Herpetologica 42(1):104–113.

Gibbons, J. W. 1990. Life History and Ecology of the Slider Turtle. Smithsonian Institution Press, Washington, D.C. i–xiv + 368 pp.

Gibbons, J. W. and D. H. Nelson. 1978. The evolutionary significance of delayed emergence from the nest by hatchling turtles. Evolution 32(3) 297–303.

Hartweg, N. 1946. Confirmation of overwintering in painted turtle hatchlings. Copeia 1946:255.

Holland, D. C. 1991a. Status and reproductive dynamics of a population of western pond turtles (*Clemmys marmorata*) in Klickitat County, Washington in 1991. Report to the Washington Department of Wildlife.

Holland, D. C. 1991c. Distribution and current status of the western pond turtle (*Clemmys marmorata*) in Oregon. Report to the Oregon Department of Fish and Wildlife.

Holland, D. C. 1992. A synopsis of the ecology and current status of the western pond turtle (*Clemmys marmorata*). Report prepared for USDI Fish and Wildlife Service, San Simeon, California.

Kaufmann, J. H. 1992. Habitat use by wood turtles in central Pennsylvania. J. Herpetol. 26(3):315–321.

Lind, A. J., R. W. Wilson, and H. H. Welsh, Jr. 1992. Distribution and associations of the willow flycatcher, western pond turtle, and foothill yellow-legged frog on the main fork Trinity River. Interim report submitted to the Wildlife Task Group, Trinity River Restoration Project, USDI Fish and Wildlife Service, and Bureau of Reclamation, Weaverville, California.

Mayer, K. E. and W. F. Laudenslayer, Jr. (eds.). 1988. A Guide to Wildlife Habitats of California. California Department of Forestry and Fire Protection, Sacramento, California.

Quinn, N. W. A. and D. P. Tate. 1991. Seasonal movements and habitat of wood turtles (*Clemmys insculpta*) in Algonquin Park, Canada. J. Herpetol. 25:217–220.

Rathbun, G. B., N. Seipel, and D. Holland. 1992. Nesting behavior and movements of western pond turtles, *Clemmys marmorata*. Southwest. Nat. 37(3):319–324.

Reese, D. A. 1996. Comparative demography and habitat use of western pond turtles in northern California: The effects of damming and related alterations. Ph.D. dissertation, Unversity of California, Berkeley. 253 pp.

Schwarzkopf, L. and R. J. Brooks. 1987. Nest-site selection and offspring sex ratio in painted turtles, *Chrysemys picta*. Copeia 1987: 53–61.

Stebbins, R. C. 1985. Field Guide to Western Reptiles and Amphibians. Houghton Mifflin Co., Boston. 336 pp.

Storer, T. I. 1930. Notes on the range and life-history of the Pacific freshwater turtle, *Clemmys marmorata*. Univ. Calif. Publ. in Zool. 32:429–441.

Ward, F. P., C. J. Hohmann, J. F. Ulrich, and S. E. Hill. 1976. Seasonal microhabitat selections of spotted turtles (*Clemmys guttata*) in Maryland elucidated by radioisotope tracking. Herpetologica 32:60–64.

Evaluating Wetland Conservation Policies with GIS Models of Habitat Use by Aquatic Turtles

— ABSTRACT OF PRESENTATION* —

VINCENT J. BURKE[1,2] AND J. WHITFIELD GIBBONS[1]

[1] *Savannah River Ecology Laboratory, University of Georgia, Drawer E, Aiken, SC 29802, USA*
[2] *Current address: Univerity of Missouri, U.S. Geological Survey, Biological Resources Division, Midwest Science Center, 4200 New Haven Road, Columbia, MO 65201-9634, USA [e-mail: vincent_burke@nbs.gov]*

A variety of organisms depend upon freshwater wetlands for all or part of their life cycle. In the absence of wetlands, both upland and lowland ecosystems support vastly different and often less rich species assemblages. For these reasons, the loss of wetland acreage has become a primary concern in biological conservation. Current federal statutes in the United States protect many wetlands by deterring development within an officially delineated border between the aquatic and terrestrial habitats. We tested wetland boundaries by using a geographic information system model to define the land use activities of three species of freshwater turtles (*Kinosternon subrubrum*, *Pseudemys floridana*, and *Trachemys scripta*). Our results indicate that 100% of two critical life-cycle functions, nesting and terrestrial hibernation, occur exclusively beyond the federally delineated boundary. The most stringent state statute (i.e., Massachusetts) would have provided a 100 foot (30.49 m) buffer encompassing 44% of nest and hibernation sites (n = 93 nests, 24 hibernation sites). Total protection of the sites required a 275 m buffer beyond the federal wetland boundary. Excluding the most distal 10% of sites resulted in a buffer that extended 73 m beyond the federal delineated boundary. We suggest that without biologically based buffer zones, current and proposed wetland policies may postpone, but will not prevent, extirpation of turtles and other semi-aquatic wetland species.

*PUBLISHED PAPER:

Burke, V. J. and J. W. Gibbons. 1995. Terrestrial buffer zones and wetland conservation: A case study of freshwater turtles in a Carolina bay. Conserv. Biol. 9(6):1365–1369.

New Approaches for the Conservation of Bog Turtles, *Clemmys muhlenbergii*, in Virginia

KURT A. BUHLMANN,[1] JOSEPH C. MITCHELL,[2] AND MEGAN G. ROLLINS[3]

[1]*Savannah River Ecology Laboratory, University of Georgia, Drawer E, Aiken, SC 29802, USA*
[e-mail: buhlmann@srel.edu]
[2]*Department of Biology, University of Richmond, Richmond, VA 23173, USA*
[3]*Virginia Department of Conservation and Recreation, Division of Natural Heritage,*
1500 E. Main Street, Suite 312, Richmond, VA 23219, USA

ABSTRACT: The majority of research conducted on bog turtles, *Clemmys muhlenbergii*, over the past 20 years in Virginia has focused on distribution and identification of wetland habitats. Most populations inhabit small wetlands (1–2 ha) and consist of fewer than 20 adults. Many bog turtle habitats are not isolated wetlands but are distributed along low areas bordering stream drainages. Preservation of individual wetlands is unlikely to provide long-term protection due to small effective population sizes, lack of dispersal corridors to other wetlands, and the processes of natural succession. Inventory efforts have located 58 sites containing bog turtles in Virginia. We assigned each site to a U.S. Geological Survey hydrologic unit (drainage) and found that bog turtles occur within 13 of these drainages in Virginia. Five of the drainages contain 72% (42 of 58) of the known bog turtle sites. Long-term protection and viability of bog turtle populations in Virginia will require a bioreserve approach in which landowners, developers, county planners, conservation biologists, and state agency personnel are included in the formulation of management plans for each drainage. Computerized databases and mapping capabilities are available to assist in this planning process.

In Virginia, the long-term persistence of the bog turtle, *Clemmys muhlenbergii*, is considered by state resource management agencies and conservation biologists to be in jeopardy. The species has a fairly wide distribution in the eastern United States, occurring in appropriate wetland habitats in a disjunct range extending from New England to northern Georgia (Ernst and Barbour, 1972). Bog turtles have been placed on protected species lists in all states in which they occur, based primarily on their declining numbers from habitat destruction and collection for the pet trade. They were listed as "Endangered" by Virginia in 1987 (Mitchell et al., 1991). In most states protection is limited to restriction of the wildlife trade. Listing of a species as state "Threatened" or "Endangered" has not been effective at preventing the destruction of wetland habitats. For example, in Georgia the state Endangered Species Act protects listed species only if they are found on state-owned land (Buhlmann, 1993).

Various aspects of the bog turtle's ecology have been studied in many states in which it occurs: Connecticut and Massachusetts (Klemens, 1993a), Delaware (Arndt, 1977), Maryland (Nemuras, 1967), New Jersey (Bloomer and Bloomer, 1973; Arndt, 1986), New York (Eckler et al., 1990; Collins, 1990), North Carolina (Zappalorti and Johnson, 1981; Lovich et al., 1992), Pennsylvania (Ernst, 1977), and Tennessee (Tryon, 1990). Bury (1979) provided a review of the earlier bog turtle literature.

Although the bog turtle was first described from Pennsylvania in 1801 (Schoepff), it was not reported from Virginia until 1961 (Hutchison, 1963). During the 1980s and continuing into the 1990s, several individual investigators and organizations have conducted surveys of *Clemmys muhlenbergii* in Virginia (Herman, 1988; Mitchell and Buhlmann, 1991; Buhlmann, 1992). Through communication and exchange of information we have produced a refined range distribution of the bog turtle in Virginia. Therefore, the first step in setting conservation goals, which is the elucidation of the distribution of the species of concern, has been accomplished. In this paper, we discuss an approach that may help in formulating long-term, landscape-based, dynamic conservation strategies.

We want to stress that most populations of turtles exist as "metapopulations." According to Levins (1970), a metapopulation refers to a collection of populations that exist within a landscape matrix and are separated by areas of different or unsuitable habitat. However, for small populations to persist, some exchange of individuals between populations must occur (Gilpin, 1987; Primack, 1993).

Landscape fragmentation can be a major threat to the persistence of species with very specific habitat and area requirements (Wilcove et al., 1986). Protection of a site does not necessarily mean that the long-term persistence of the population is insured. We want to make clear the need for dynamic landscape conservation strategies. In studying bog turtles, we have learned that we cannot just put a fence around a natural area and expect the species to remain there as a viable permanent population.

TABLE 1
Common plants in natural vs. altered bog turtle habitat, Blue Ridge physiographic region, Virginia, USA.

Natural
- *Andropogon* sp. (blue stem)
- *Carex folliculata* (a sedge)
- *Carex lurida* (a sedge)
- *Carex stricta* (a sedge)
- *Chelone cuthbertii* (turtlehead)
- *Drosera* sp. (sundews)
- *Epilobium* sp. (willow herbs)
- *Polygonum* sp. (tearthumb)
- *Scirpus cyperinus* (marsh bulrush)
- *Scirpus expansus* (a sedge)
- *Sphagnum* sp.
- *Spiraea tomentosa* (steeplebush)
- *Spiranthes* sp. (ladies' tresses)

Grazed
- *Acorus calamus* (sweet flag)
- *Aster* sp. (asters)
- *Eupatorium* sp. (joe-pye-weed, boneset)
- *Solidago* sp. (goldenrods)
- *Vernonia* sp. (ironweeds)

TABLE 2
Bog turtle occurrences by hydrologic unit (HU) (USDA, 1991) and the number of definable metapopulations according to the criteria outlined by Klemens (1993b) in four counties in southwestern Virginia, USA.

River	HU[a]	Total sites	No. meta-populations	No. sites in each meta-population
New	A	10	2	3, 4
New	B	9	1	7
New	C	9	2	2, 4
New	D	8		
New	E	6		
New	F	5	1	3
New	G	3	1	2
New	H	1		
New	I	1		
Ararat	J	1		
Ararat	K	3		
Roanoke	L	1		
Roanoke	M	1		

[a] The HU names are not published to protect the locations of these sites.

RESULTS

Habitat

The majority of research conducted on *Clemmys muhlenbergii* over the past 20 years in Virginia has focused on distribution and identification of wetland habitats. The turtles inhabit small wetlands (1–2 ha), and populations consist of fewer than 20 adults. Most Virginia bog turtle habitats occur not as isolated wetlands but as patches within meadows and floodplains that border stream drainages.

On the Southern Blue Ridge Plateau in Virginia, *C. muhlenbergii* inhabits muddy seepage meadows adjacent to streams. Characteristic vegetation includes mosses (*Sphagnum* sp.), sedges (*Carex* sp.), and alder (*Alnus* sp.). The best bog turtle habitats have open canopies and contain large quantities of *Sphagnum*, rich black organic mud, and rivulets that meander through the habitat but have not cut deep trenches. Because rare plants are often associated with this habitat—including Cuthbert turtlehead (*Chelone cuthbertii*) and Gray's lily (*Lilium grayi*) (Ludwig, 1992)—conservation strategies that focus on bog turtles will protect other elements of biodiversity as well.

Many bog turtle habitats in Virginia are subjected to grazing, the benefits and disadvantages of which are controversial. Cattle help maintain an open habitat condition and are probably responsible for keeping alder and red maple, *Acer rubrum*, from closing the canopy. However, cattle also enrich the wetland with nutrients, decrease native plant diversity, and reduce *Sphagnum* which requires lower nutrient and pH conditions. We have found that *Sphagnum* provides important nesting habitat and is also utilized by hatchling turtles for hiding. Coarser vegetation, such as goldenrods (*Solidago* sp.) and ironweed (*Vernonia* sp.), tends to be more common in grazed habitats and are indicative of disturbance (Table 1). Cattle are not the natural regulator of succession in bog turtle habitat. However, at certain density levels they appear to have a positive effect, but at some undefined (unknown) higher density, they cease to be beneficial and actually degrade the habitat.

Bog turtle habitats on the Southern Blue Ridge Plateau in Virginia have probably always been ephemeral. As natural successional processes made sites unsuitable for bog turtles, other areas were created by the actions of beaver, *Castor canadensis*. However, certain hillside acidic seeps probably maintained their open canopy by the nature of the soils and plant communities.

Threats

Ditching destroys wetland habitat. This human activity, coupled with human efforts to prevent beaver from creating new wetlands, is probably an important reason for bog turtle declines and the small number of sites in certain stream drainages in Virginia. However, streams that flow through wet meadows eventually cut downward and drain the adjacent wet meadows. This erosion, although natural, is exacerbated by ditching, overgrazing, streambank trampling by cattle, and logging of adjacent forest cover. We speculate that the dams built by beaver were responsible for re-trapping sediments and setting back the successional stages. In the years immediately following abandonment by beavers, the wetland is probably most suitable as bog turtle habitat.

Because of the rapid natural succession of bog turtle habitats, small turtle population sizes, and lack of dispersal corridors to other wetlands, preservation of individual wetlands is unlikely to provide long-term protection.

Populations

Inventory efforts have located 58 sites in four counties containing bog turtles in Virginia. We assigned each site to a U.S. Geological Survey hydrologic unit (HU) (United States Department of Agriculture, 1991) and found that bog turtles occur within 13 of these drainages in Virginia. Five of the drainages (A, B, C, D, and E) contain 71% (42) of the known bog turtle sites (Table 2). Overall, 90% (52 sites) are found in drainages of the New River system, 7% (4 sites) are found in the Ararat River systems, and 3% (2 sites) are found in the Roanoke River system. However, all occurrences in the latter two river drainages, except one, are found in headwater drainages where a small geographic divide separates it from a New River drainage.

We suggest that overland (out-of-drainage) migrations by bog turtles have resulted in these colonizations. The collection of road-killed bog turtles by us and others, and observations of live road captures where no suitable habitat could be detected nearby, provide evidence that cross-drainage movements occur. Generally, most Virginia populations exist in headwater drainages. This may be the natural pattern, but more likely represents a recent relictual distribution since larger floodplain wetlands and meadows further downstream have been intensively farmed and altered while smaller wetlands along the headwaters were not as seriously impacted.

DISCUSSION

Metapopulation Concepts

A metapopulation has been defined as a collection of subpopulations of a species, each occupying a suitable patch of habitat in a landscape mosaic and separated by patches of unsuitable habitat (Levins, 1970; Meffe and Carroll, 1994). However, the metapopulation concept implies that individuals of the subpopulations are able to interact and exchange with other subpopulations. The degree to which this interaction occurs depends upon the proximity of adjacent subpopulations, availability of corridor habitats, and the ability and proclivity of individuals to disperse between suitable habitat patches.

Based on the analysis criteria presented by Klemens (1993b), the following characteristics are most important for determining whether or not a bog turtle site (subpopulation) can be considered part of a larger metapopulation. First, the sites must all be part of the same drainage basin. For Virginia, this was determined by using the Hydrologic Unit Atlas for the state (United States Department of Agriculture, 1991) and overlaying the drainage basin boundaries on maps with known bog turtle sites. The Biological and Conservation Data System (BCD), developed by The Nature Conservancy, is a database application that maintains site-specific and biological information on rare species and critical habitats. The Map and Image Processing System (MIPS), developed by MicroImages Corporation, is a geographical information system (GIS) application that interfaces with BCD to display the locations of rare species and other features, such as drainage basin boundaries, on computer-generated maps. Using these software programs at the Virginia Department of Conservation and Recreation's Division of Natural Heritage, we were able to assign the 58 bog turtle sites to 13 HUs. An example of the resulting product is represented by Figure 1.

Second, site quality analysis (Klemens, 1993b) specifies that no major impediments to movement between sites exist (e.g., fragmented wetland habitat, rocky streams, highways, large rivers). This implies that appropriate corridor habitat

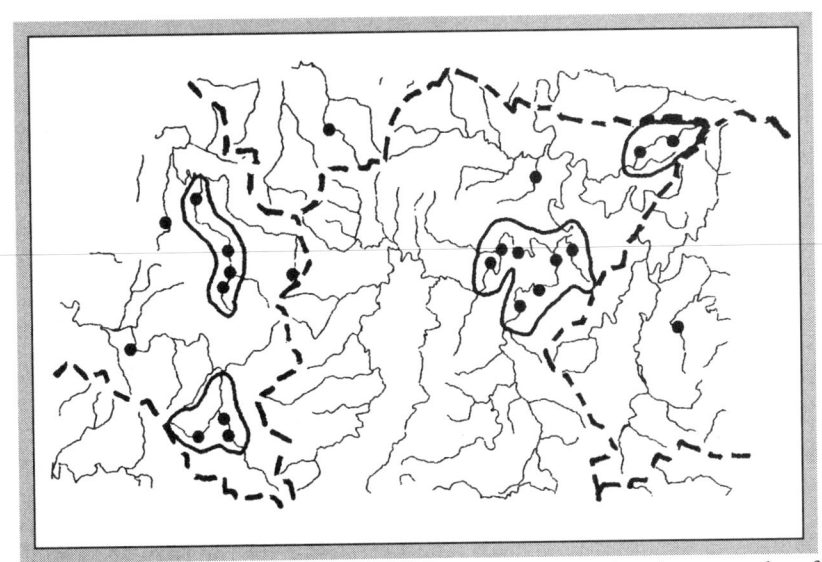

Figure 1. An example of a metapopulation analysis for bog turtles based on an overlay of hydrologic drainage units (USDA, 1991) on specific site locations obtained from BCD, analyzed based on the criteria in Klemens (1993b) and presented using MIPS. The sites are represented as solid dots, the HU boundaries are indicated with a heavy dotted line, and five hypothetical metapopulations are enclosed by heavy solid lines. Streams are illustrated with fine lines.

(possibly forested streams) exists and that distances between sites are not excessive. We found that all of our metapopulations that met the above criteria also tended to have their sites located less than 0.6 km (1 mile) from each other. We found that although HU drainages A, B, C, D, and E accounted for 71% of all sites, definable metapopulations (total = 7) existed in A, B, C, F, and G (Table 2).

Non-metapopulation sites, however, should not be ignored. In fact, some of the current highest quality sites do not fall into an identified metapopulation and should be protected with site-based conservation and management strategies. But, based on our knowledge of the ephemeral qualities of bog turtle sites, we believe that our chances of maintaining populations for the long term are best realized by managing for the metapopulation. Stochastic environmental events associated with isolated populations may reduce a population to a size from which it may not recover without the ability to be "recharged" through immigration (Gilpin and Soulé, 1986; Thomas, 1994).

Landscape Ecology

Landscape has been defined as a mosaic of habitat patches in which a particular patch (i.e., a "focal patch") is embedded (Dunning et al., 1992). Bog turtle habitats within Virginia fit this definition well and are embedded in a matrix of forests, pastures, and farms. The success of a landscape-based management plan, which is required if we are to protect metapopulations of bog turtles, must involve landowners, politicians, county planners, and conservation biologists.

Problems that need to be addressed and overcome in Virginia, as well as anywhere else in the world where this type of conservation is to be successfully implemented, include the following: First, there are the social and political problems of (1) multiple landowners, (2) diverse land use types (grazing, farming, development, road construction), (3) dissemination of locality information of rare species (which can lead to illegal collecting), and (4) negative landowner attitudes towards government regulation and support of the concept of landowner rights. Second, even in this era of increased environmental awareness, there is still an obvious lack of a satisfactory "land ethic," effective environmental education, and appreciation for non-consumptive wildlife (the "what-good-is-that-turtle-anyway" syndrome). Finally, despite improvements, greater participation in the public education system and public policy discussions must be encouraged among scientists and university faculty.

CONCLUSIONS AND FUTURE RESEARCH

Radio-tracking data based on short-term studies (e.g., Lovich et al., 1992) demonstrate that distances between recaptures of bog turtles in North Carolina ranged up to 87 m for males and up to 62 m for females. Ernst (1977) reported mean home ranges of bog turtles in Pennsylvania at 1.33 ha (males) and 1.26 ha (females). However, when we look at the data for a longer-term study, we find that some bog turtles can move up to 750 m over a four-year period (Eckler et al., 1990). In Virginia, 11 records of road crossings by bog turtles have been recorded. However, at three of these road-crossing sites, we were unable to find suitable bog turtle habitat nearby. Bog turtle sites were subsequently identified adjacent to each of four of the road crossings, while the remaining four were adjacent to suitable corridor habitat. Reasons given for terrestrial movements in turtles include nesting, emigration from unsuitable habitat, mate-searching, and food availability (Gibbons et al., 1990). Movements up to 9 km from the original capture site have been recorded for the slider turtle, *Trachemys scripta* (Gibbons et al., 1990). These observations help to underscore the point that all conservation plans need good biological data and that further research efforts should be included as part of any conservation plan.

Long-term protection and viability of bog turtle populations in Virginia will require a landscape/metapopulation approach in which landowners, developers, county planners, conservation biologists, and state agency personnel are included in the formulation of management plans for each drainage. Protection, through easement or acquisition of wetland habitats, is a goal of such conservation groups as The Nature Conservancy. At present, the only real protection afforded the bog turtle in Virginia is through the occurrence of several sites on federally owned land (National Park Service), where active management and law enforcement against illegal collectors are provided.

Databases such as BCD and GIS systems like MIPS are tools that can identify metapopulations for conservation action and can also produce visual educational products to help explain conservation concerns to land planners and the general public. Finally, conservation biologists must take an active role in educating the public and policy makers about the need for landscape ecology concepts to be incorporated into growth and development plans. At this time the best conservation-minded planners are sensitive to the present specific locations of endangered species. However, the bog turtle is a clear example of a species whose long-term needs will not be satisfied simply by site-specific protection.

ACKNOWLEDGMENTS

We thank Dennis Herman, James Warner, Bern Tryon, and Steven Roble for their companionship in the field and for providing us with their data, which facilitated this metapopulation analysis and prioritized conservation efforts. We also thank Randall Kendrick (National Park Service) and Ken Nemuras for supplying us with their records of bog turtle road-crossing observations and sites. Additional assistance in the field was provided by M. Klemens, J. Keith, L. Buhlmann, S. Martin, S. Smith, R. Reynolds, C. Hobson, and S. Bruenderman. This paper was enhanced through discussions with M. Klemens and J. Sciascia. J. W. Gibbons and A. L. Whitlock reviewed drafts of the manuscript. The National Park Service (Blue Ridge Parkway), the Virginia Department of Game and Inland Fisheries, and the Virginia Department of Conservation and Recreation's Division of Natural Heritage provided funding for portions of the fieldwork. We especially thank the landowners of southwestern Virginia who granted us access to their properties. Manuscript preparation was supported by contract number DE-AC09-76SR00819 between the United States Department of Energy and the University of Georgia's Savannah River Ecology Laboratory.

LITERATURE CITED

Arndt, R. G. 1977. Notes on the natural history of the bog turtle, *Clemmys muhlenbergii* (Schoepff), in Delaware. Chesapeake Sci. 18:67–76.

Arndt, R. G. 1986. Notes on the bog turtle, *Clemmys muhlenbergii*, in Warren County, New Jersey. Bull. Maryland Herp. Soc. 22: 56–61.

Bloomer, T. J. and D. M. Bloomer. 1973. New Jersey's bog turtle... destined to extinction? Bull. New York Herpetol. Soc. 9:8–12.

Buhlmann, K. A. 1992. An inventory of *Clemmys muhlenbergii* (bog turtle) in southwestern Virginia. Natural Heritage Technical Report # 92-20. Department of Conservation and Recreation, Division of Natural Heritage, Richmond, Virginia. 25 pp.

Buhlmann, K. A. 1993. Legislation and Conservation Alert. Herpetol. Review 24(4):125.

Bury, R. B. 1979. Review of the ecology and conservation of the bog turtle, *Clemmys muhlenbergii*. U.S. Fish and Wildlife Service Special Scientific Report No. 219, Washington, D.C.

Collins, D. E. 1990. Western New York bog turtles: Relicts of ephemeral islands or simply elusive? *In* R. S. Mitchell, C. J. Sheviak, and D. J. Leopold (eds.), Ecosystem Management: Rare Species and Significant Habitats, pp. 151–153. New York State Museum Bulletin 471, Albany, New York.

Dunning, J. B., B. J. Danielson, and H. R. Pulliam. 1992. Ecological processes that affect populations in complex landscapes. Oikos 65:169–175.

Eckler, J. T., A. R. Breisch, and J. L. Behler. 1990. Radio-telemetry techniques applied to the bog turtle (*Clemmys muhlenbergii* Schoepff 1801). *In* R. S. Mitchell, C. J. Sheviak, and D. J. Leopold (eds.), Ecosystem Management: Rare Species and Significant Habitats, pp. 69–70. New York State Museum Bulletin 471, Albany, New York.

Ernst, C. H. 1977. Biological notes on the bog turtle, *Clemmys muhlenbergii*. Herpetologica 33(2):241–246.

Ernst, C. H. and R. W. Barbour. 1972. Turtles of the United States. The University Press of Kentucky, Lexington. 347 pp.

Gibbons, J. W., J. L. Greene, and J. D. Congdon. 1990. Temporal and spatial movement patterns of sliders and other turtles. *In* J. W. Gibbons (ed.), Life History and Ecology of the Slider Turtle, pp. 201–215. Smithsonian Institution Press, Washington, D.C. i–xiv + 368 pp.

Gilpin, M. E. 1987. Spatial structure and population vulnerability. *In* M. E. Soulé (ed.), Viable Populations for Conservation, pp. 125–139. Cambridge Univ. Press, Cambridge, England.

Gilpin, M. E. and M. E. Soulé. 1986. Population vulnerability analysis. *In* M. E. Soulé (ed.), Conservation Biology: The Science of Scarcity and Diversity, pp. 19–34. Sinauer Associates, Inc., Sunderland, Massachusetts.

Herman, D. W. 1988. Status of the bog turtle, *Clemmys muhlenbergii* (Schoepff), in the southeastern United States. Unpubl. report to the Conservation and Research Committee, Friends of the Atlanta Zoo, Atlanta, Georgia. 11 pp.

Hutchison, V. H. 1963. Record of the bog turtle, *Clemmys muhlenbergii*, in southwestern Virginia. Copeia 1963:156–157.

Klemens, M. W. 1993a. The Amphibians and Reptiles of Connecticut and Adjacent Regions. State Geological and Natural History Survey of Connecticut, Hartford, Connecticut. 318 pp.

Klemens, M. W. 1993b. Standardized bog turtle site-quality analysis. Unpubl. report to the U.S. Fish and Wildlife Service. American Museum of Natural History, New York. 7 pp.

Levins, R. 1970. Extinction. *In* M. Gustenhaver (ed.), Some Mathematical Questions in Biology, Vol. II, pp. 77–108. American Mathematical Society, Providence, Rhode Island.

Lovich, J. E., D. W. Herman, and K. M. Fahey. 1992. Seasonal activity and movements of bog turtles (*Clemmys muhlenbergii*) in North Carolina. Copeia 1992:1107–1111.

Ludwig, J. C. 1992. Natural heritage resources of Virginia: Rare vascular plant list. Virginia Department of Conservation and Recreation, Division of Natural Heritage, Richmond, Virginia.

Meffe, G. K. and C. R. Carroll. 1994. Principles of Conservation Biology. Sinauer Associates, Inc., Sunderland, Massachusetts. 600 pp.

Mitchell, J. C. and K. A. Buhlmann. 1991. Distribution and status of the endangered bog turtle (*Clemmys muhlenbergii*) on the Blue Ridge Parkway in Virginia. Unpubl. report to the National Park Service, Asheville, North Carolina. 78 pp.

Mitchell, J. C., K. A. Buhlmann, and C. H. Ernst. 1991. Bog turtle *Clemmys muhlenbergii*. *In* Virginia's Endangered Species (K. Terwilleger, coord.), pp. 457–459. McDonald and Woodward Publ. Co., Blacksburg, Virginia.

Nemuras, K. T. 1967. Notes on the natural history of *Clemmys muhlenbergii*. Bull. Maryland Herpetol. Soc. 3:80–96.

Primack, R. B. 1993. Essentials of Conservation Biology. Sinauer Associates, Inc., Sunderland, Massachusetts. 564 pp.

Thomas, C. D. 1994. Extinction, colonization, and metapopulations: Environmental tracking by rare species. Conserv. Biol. 8:373–378.

Tryon, B. W. 1990. Bog turtles (*Clemmys muhlenbergii*) in the south —A question of survival. Bull. Chicago Herpetol. Soc. 25:57–66.

United States Department of Agriculture. 1991. Virginia Hydrologic Unit Atlas. Soil Conservation Service, Department of Agricultural Engineering, Virginia Tech., Blacksburg, Virginia.

Wilcove, D. S., C. H. McLellan, and A. P. Dobson. 1986. Habitat fragmentation in the temperate zone. *In* M.E. Soulé (ed.), Conservation Biology: The Science of Scarcity and Diversity, pp. 237–256. Sinauer Assoc., Inc., Sunderland, Massachusetts.

Zappalorti, R. T. and E. W. Johnson. 1981. The ecology of the bog turtle, *Clemmys muhlenbergii* (Schoepff), (Reptilia, Testudines, Emydidae) in western North Carolina. Unpubl. report to Highlands Biological Station, University of North Carolina. 24 pp.

Land Use, Development, and Natural Succession and Their Effects on Bog Turtle Habitat in the Southeastern United States

DENNIS W. HERMAN[1] AND BERN W. TRYON[2]

[1]Department of Herpetology, Zoo Atlanta, 800 Cherokee Ave. SE, Atlanta, GA 30315, USA
Current Address: North Carolina State Museum of Natural Sciences, P.O. Box 29555, Raleigh, NC 27626-0555, USA
[e-mail: Dennis_Herman@mail.ehnr.state.nc.us]
[2]Department of Herpetology, Knoxville Zoological Gardens, P.O. Box 6040, Knoxville, TN 37914, USA
[e-mail: btryon@knoxville-zoo.com]

ABSTRACT: The bog turtle, *Clemmys muhlenbergii* (Schoepff), has a very fragmented distribution along the Blue Ridge Plateau and Upper Piedmont in the southeastern United States. First reported from North Carolina in 1882, the bog turtle has had a long and varied history in the South. At least 164 occurrence records are known and a total of nearly 900 bog turtles have been reported or found in five states: Georgia, North Carolina, South Carolina, Tennessee, and Virginia. Southern bog turtle colonies are small (≤35 turtles per hectare), and individual sites are usually less than three hectares in size. Habitats supporting bog turtles have been described as southern Appalachian fen, southern Appalachian bog, swamp forest-bog complex, and hillside seepage bog natural communities. An additional community has been suggested, the meadow bog, a wetland type with many components of the previous types, but because of human land use practices (pasture and farmland), its natural integrity has been altered. The majority of bog turtle habitats fall into this latter classification. Small site size, fragmentation, and lengthy distances between sites indicate that dispersal and recruitment may occur infrequently or not at all in the South. Direct habitat threats include draining for pasture and farmland; development for business and recreation areas such as shopping centers, retirement villages, lakes, ponds, and golf courses; Department of Transportation projects, including new highway bypasses, road widening, and bridge construction; and natural successional processes from bog to climax forest. Management of sites, including restoration, selective cutting and pruning, cattle grazing, and education of landowners is recommended and necessary for the continued survival of the bog turtle in the southeastern United States.

North America's smallest chelonian, the bog turtle, *Clemmys muhlenbergii* (Schoepff), is a rare emydid species that is restricted to open herbaceous wetland ecosystems. Many aspects of its natural history and biology remain poorly understood, especially its status, distribution, and zoogeographic position in the southeastern United States. This species occurs in 12 eastern states, but a 400 km gap between central Maryland and southwestern Virginia separates the bog turtle's range into "northern" and "southern" populations. There is no evidence that these populations were contiguous in historic times, and the hiatus may be the result of the turtle's dispersal history during Pleistocene glacial episodes. Although this species was initially found in Pennsylvania (Lancaster County) in the late eighteenth century (Schoepff, 1801), first records for several states were reported only in the past 15 years, especially in the southeastern United States.

With the exception of North Carolina (Yarrow, 1882), the bog turtle is a recently discovered addition to several southern states' herpetofauna: Virginia (Hutchison, 1963), Georgia (Hale and Harris, 1980), South Carolina (Herman and Putnam, 1982), and Tennessee (Herman and Warner, 1986). Natural history studies and range extensions from this region have been published in recent years (Herman and Putnam, 1983; Herman, 1986; Herman and Weakley, 1986; Tryon, 1990; Tryon and Herman, 1990; Batson, 1991; Brown, 1992; Broaddus, 1992–1993; Herman et al., 1992; Lovich et al., 1992; Beane, 1993; Beane et al., 1993; Herman et al., 1993; and Herman et al., 1996).

The population status of *C. muhlenbergii* has been controversial for many years. Early accounts of the bog turtle included scattered distributional records and anecdotal observations. Most natural history studies (Arndt, 1977, 1978, 1986; Bloomer and Holub, 1977; Ernst, 1977; Case et al., 1989; and others) were from the mid-Atlantic and northeastern states where populations and available habitat appear to be greater than in other portions of the range (i.e., Maryland, New Jersey, Pennsylvania). Many of these studies were conducted in sites where the bog turtle was relatively common, so erroneous assumptions may have been made concerning the species' overall abundance. Even in these regions, researchers disagree on the bog turtle's status and its potential for continued viability because of rapid expansion of nearby metropolitan areas (see Bury, 1979; Ernst and Bury, 1977).

Tryon and Herman (1990) presented the results of a field study conducted over the last 15 years as the bog turtle was discovered in various states. Since the publication of that report, many new sites and county records in the Southeast have been located. This paper updates the bog turtle's status in the Southeast and includes estimates of population sizes, habitat availability, and site evaluations for five southern states. Conservation and management of the bog turtle are discussed with recommendations concerning its protection and continued viability in the South.

Status and Distribution in the Southeast

In the southeastern United States, bog turtles occur only in the Blue Ridge and upper Piedmont provinces from 214 m to 1,373 m elevation (Herman and Pharr, 1986). Most sites occur between 610 and 915 m and are reported from 12 major river systems in both the Atlantic and Ohio-Mississippi river drainages.

Bog turtle habitats may never have been expansive in the South, although they probably once covered larger areas. By 1963, 4,040 ha (10,000 acres) of bog turtle habitat in an east Tennessee valley were destroyed by the U.S. Army Corps of Engineers' stream channelization and drainage projects (Brown, 1992). Only 202 ha (500 acres) of mountain bog habitat may remain in North Carolina (A. S. Weakley, pers. comm.), but bog turtles have been reported from less than half of this area. We currently estimate that approximately 75 hectares (187 acres) of core bog turtle habitat remain in five southern states. Ongoing population studies indicate that a hectare of prime habitat may support 35–40 turtles (15–20 turtles per acre), making the total estimated population 2,800–3,800 bog turtles in the entire southeastern United States.

A total of 192 occurrence records are known from 31 southern counties. Many of these are literature records for which museum specimens are not available; site locations were unspecified or erroneous; or the site is currently a newly created subdivision, man-made lake, or golf course. Some were roadkills or live turtles found where suitable habitat was unavailable nearby. Other sites visited by us had become incapable of supporting a viable population because of some human alteration or through natural succession into a hardwood climax forest. A turtle sighting or a site inhabited by a few specimens does not necessarily indicate that a viable population is present. Bog turtles may live in excess of 50 years, so individual adults found in marginal sites may be holdovers from a remnant population, or they may have migrated to these areas when nearby wetlands were destroyed. An overview and evaluation of the bog turtle's status in five southern states is as follows:

Georgia—The bog turtle is known from seven occurrence records in three counties and from fewer than 50 specimens in Georgia. Only three of these records represent viable or potentially viable populations. The total area of these three sites covers only about 5.5 ha (14 acres). Georgia's bog turtle population is estimated at 200–280 turtles. At least 90% of the occupied bog turtle habitat occurs on privately owned land, which is not protected under conservation agreements or easements. The bog turtle was added to Georgia's protected species list in October 1992 as a "Threatened" species (Lenz, 1992–1993).

Figure 1. Range of the bog turtle in the southeastern United States.

South Carolina—There are three occurrence records known from two counties in South Carolina representing fewer than 15 individual turtles. Fontenot and Platt (1993) mentioned that several specimens from additional sites were found by one individual from 1980 to 1987, but these are undocumented and not included here. Only one population, having less than 4 ha (10 acres) of core habitat and an estimated population of 140–160 turtles, may be viable. Most of the occupied bog turtle habitat in South Carolina is suboptimal or marginal at best. All of the currently known sites are privately owned and unprotected. South Carolina lists the bog turtle as a "Threatened" species.

Tennessee—Only two occurrence records in a single county exist in Tennessee. These two sites are probably the best-studied sites in the southern portion of the turtle's range. A total of 79 bog turtles have been found in these two sites, 44 and 35 turtles, respectively. A mark-recapture study has been carried out by one of us (BWT) since their discovery in 1986. The estimated size of both populations, based on the Schnabel method (Smith, 1974), is 84 turtles. Though somewhat different in habitat makeup, both of these sites are considered capable of supporting viable bog turtle populations. Also purchased was an adjoining farm (64 acres), a portion of which was at one time wetland habitat before watershed channelization. An aggressive bog habitat restoration effort of the large section will be initiated in 1997. Ownership of the second site is private and involves two families and several landowners, all of whom are supportive of the project and protective of the turtles and their habitat. The total area of core habitat for both sites is currently 3 ha (8 acres). Tennessee upgraded the bog turtle from "In Need of Management" to "Threatened" status in 1991.

Virginia—Bog turtles are known from 64 occurrence records in four counties representing fewer than 500 individuals. An additional county has a questionable record (Tobey, 1985; Mitchell and Pague, 1987a) and is not considered here. Between 10 and 15 populations or metapopulations may be viable in Virginia, but little population work has been conducted. An estimated 26 ha (65 acres) of core habitat supports a total estimated population of 975–1300 turtles. At least 75% of the occupied bog turtle habitat is privately owned, while the remainder is federally owned (U.S. National Park Service Blue Ridge Parkway). The bog turtle was given "Endangered" status by Virginia in August 1987 (Hoffman, 1987).

North Carolina—North Carolina contains the majority (60%) of the bog turtle records in the southeastern United States. There are 116 occurrence records from 20 counties representing fewer than 1,000 total individuals. Tryon (1990) estimated the total North Carolina population at 1,500–2,000 turtles. Long-term population studies (mark-recapture) have been conducted in only five of the state's sites because most of the work has consisted of distributional surveys to determine the species' range. One site had an estimated population of 150–200 turtles in 1986, based on the Schnabel method; it is the largest known population in the South. Unfortunately, habitat loss and overcollecting have severely impacted this site. Three other sites had population estimates of 88, 46, and 35 bog turtles, respectively. Only 30 populations or metapopulations (35 sites) are considered viable or potentially viable. These cover approximately 36 ha (90 acres) of core habitat and, based on our present knowledge, support an estimated population of 1,350–1,800 turtles. Only 20% of the occupied bog turtle habitat is federally owned, while 60% is privately owned and not protected under conservation easements or agreements. Only 20% of the habitat is protected (13.6% private and 6.4% Nature Conservancy). The bog turtle was upgraded from "Species of Special Concern" to "Threatened" in 1990 and the state actively protects the species.

Bog Turtle Habitat Dynamics

The bog turtle is restricted to spring-fed wetlands that are organically rich but nutrient poor. Many bog turtle populations occupy natural communities with a diverse flora, in many cases typical of more northern communities. Viable bog turtle populations are dependent upon unfragmented riparian systems that permit natural creation of bogs, fens, marshes, and wet meadows. Unfortunately, few bog turtle populations fit into this ideal ecosystem in the southeastern United States. Several natural community wetlands that support bog turtles have been classified by Schafale and Weakley (1990) as: "southern Appalachian fen," "southern Appalachian bog" (northern and southern subtypes), "swamp forest-bog complex" (southern and typic subtypes), and "hillside seepage bogs." The "meadow bog" is an additional wetland community that has been proposed in North Carolina by Smith (1990) with which we are in agreement. The meadow bog is identical to the "wet meadow" as described by Kiviat (1978). In the southern part of the turtle's range, wet meadows (= meadow bogs) may show varying components of the southern Appalachian bog and other natural communities. In fact, many of the natural communities listed above usually become meadow bogs because of past alteration from human encroachment. Meadow bogs are either used for grazing or are in the vicinity of pastures, and turtle densities are likely to be higher there than in more natural communities that have a subcanopy of shrubbery. Meadow bogs are created and maintained by agriculture, cattle, beaver, deer, and possibly fire. The bog turtle's relationship to livestock is an interesting but inadequately studied subject. One of the authors (DWH) has received a grant from the U.S. Natural Resources Conservation Service for a two-year study (1997–1998) on the effects of grazing on bog turtle habitats.

Because meadow bogs are spring fed, they are technically fens, but with low nutrient levels. The groundwater flows constantly over a soft mud substrate as rivulets, forming small pools and pockets around sedge tussocks. The open canopy creates a sunny and rapidly warmed layer above the cool, saturated mud stratum where ground level humidity is high. While some bog turtle sites may lack many of these species, the plants listed in Table 1 are among the common components of bog turtle habitats.

Habitat development, formation, and maintenance were discussed in great detail by Kiviat (1978). Beaver activity and herbivore retardation of tall plant growth were major factors in the creation and continuity of bog turtle habitats prior to European colonization. This is still true to a limited extent, especially with respect to the effects of browsers (rabbits, deer, cows, horses, meadow voles, and muskrat) and seed predators (white-footed mice, golden mice, and southern bog lemmings). Beaver were nearly extirpated from the southern mountains by trappers and hunters, but they have recovered in many valleys in their former range. The effects they will have on existing bog turtle populations remains to be seen. Short-term flooding of sites has been observed in Georgia, North Carolina, South Carolina, and Virginia. The shallow wetlands created by beavers are dynamic and may undergo rapid vegetational changes over a period of a decade (Kiviat, 1978). Beaver activity and the effects of browsers or fire are important in preventing canopy closure, which is probably the most important factor limiting bog turtle habitat (Nemuras and Weaver, 1974).

Threats to the Bog Turtle and Its Habitat

In the southeastern United States bog turtle populations are threatened by agriculture (row crops, hay fields, pasture land), development (retirement villages and subdivisions, shopping centers, highway and bridge construction, golf courses, lakes, etc.), natural succession, and illegal collecting for the pet trade. Habitat loss has accelerated over the past 20 years because of human encroachment and natural succession.

Land Use

The transitional nature of meadow bogs and the turtle's limited power of dispersal have made the species especially vulnerable. Prior to European colonization in the 1700s, the dynamic wetlands used by bog turtles were a complex of habitat units and potential habitats interconnected by a mosaic of dispersal routes. This long-term, dynamic ecosystem could withstand the loss of a single habitat unit and still provide bog turtles with other usable habitats. The land use practices by early settlers and farmers may not have had a negative effect on the overall stability of this dynamic ecosystem. The felling of trees and the creation of mea-

TABLE 1
Common components of bog turtle habitats.

Sedges, *Carex, Eleocharis, Scirpus* spp.
Rushes, *Cyperus, Juncus, Rhynchospora* spp.
Ferns, *Dryopteris cristata, Osmunda cinnamomea, Osmunda regalis* var. *spectabilis, Thelypteris palustris, Woodwardia areolata*
Peat moss, *Sphagnum* spp.
Red maple, *Acer rubrum*
Sweet flag, *Acorus calamus*
Tag alder, *Alnus rugosa*
River birch, *Betula niger*
Holly, *Ilex* spp.
Sheep-kill, *Kalmia angustifolia* var. *caroliniana*
Mountain laurel, *Kalmia latifolia*
Arrow arum, *Peltandra virginica*
Pitch pine, *Pinus rigida*
Rosebay, *Rhododendron maximum*
Swamp rose, *Rosa palustris*
Silky willow, *Salix sericea*
Chokeberry, *Sorbus arbutifolia*
Hardhack, *Spiraea tomentosa*
Skunk cabbage, *Symplocarpus foetidus*
Poison sumac, *Toxicodendron vernix*

These habitats often support rare northern disjuncts or state and federally protected species such as:
Bog rose, *Arethusa bulbosa*
Tawny cottongrass, *Eriophorum virginicum*
Swamp pink, *Helonias bullata*
Gray's lily, *Lilium grayi*
Mountain sweet pitcherplant, *Sarracenia jonesii*
Cranberry, *Vaccinium macrocarpon*

The southern Appalachian fen and bog communities are considered critically imperiled ecosystems (Earley, 1989; Nicholls and Murdock, 1993).

dows may even have been beneficial, but the elimination of beaver populations and rapid human population growth quickly offset any benefits. With the advent of mechanized farm machinery, the loss of bog turtle wetlands accelerated. Ditching wet meadows and bogs for agricultural use was accomplished with hand tools until large earthmoving equipment came into use in this century.

Ditching of existing bog turtle habitats has been well documented over the past 20 years in North Carolina (Nemuras, 1974a; Herman, 1989; Tryon, 1990; Tryon and Herman, 1990), Virginia (Nemuras, 1974b; Mitchell and Pague, 1987b; Mitchell and Buhlmann, 1991; Mitchell et al., 1991; Buhlmann, 1992), and Tennessee (Tryon, 1988). The largest single example of habitat loss was the destruction of 4,040 ha in an east Tennessee valley by U.S. Army Corps of Engineers' stream channelization and ditching prior to 1963 (Brown, 1992). A few bogs remain in this valley, two of which support the only bog turtles known in the state. This valley may have been the home of the largest bog turtle population in the South prior to the draining regime. Land use practices are responsible for the loss of at least 28 sites since 1970.

Development

In recent years the southern mountains have become popular to both retirees and tourists. Retirement complexes have sprung up in the mountains from Virginia to Georgia. Golf courses have mushroomed throughout many mountain valleys to keep pace with the retiree population and vacationers that crowd the mountains during summer months. The type locality of the endangered pitcherplant, *Sarracenia jonesii*, for example, has been replaced by a large golf and country club in one North Carolina valley (N. Murdock, pers. comm.), and the two largest southern bog turtle populations are located nearby. Fertilizer and pesticide runoff from the golf courses increase the nutrient levels in the wetlands making them conducive to nutrient-loving invasive plant species (e.g., watercress). Shopping centers, apartment complexes, and subdivisions have been constructed either over previous habitats that were drained and filled or adjacent to existing sites, which has created proximal threats. Recreational farm ponds, lakes, and swimming pools have been built in poorly draining wetlands. Habitat fragmentation as a result of lakes and impoundments, golf courses, and crop land is widespread in the southeast. Department of Transportation projects (road construction, highway widening, bridge construction) have fragmented much of the available remaining bog turtle habitats. The building of U.S. Highway 64 and its bypasses during the early 1970s destroyed or adversely impacted several bog turtle colonies (Nemuras, 1974a; Herman, 1989). Migrating bog turtles cross highways to reach habitat units along dispersal corridors, but the current network of roads and highways make it virtually impossible for bog turtles to migrate safely. In North Carolina, 20 of 116 records (17%) are known from dead or living bog turtles found on roads (Herman, unpubl. data; North Carolina Natural Heritage Program, unpubl. data). Additional road records in the South have been documented from Virginia, especially on the Blue Ridge Parkway (Mitchell and Buhlmann, 1991; Mitchell et. al., 1991; R. Kendrick, pers. comm.). We have found eight bog turtles on roads since 1985; five had been crushed by vehicles. The loss of a single mature female bog turtle could have serious consequences to a population. Fragmentation and development have resulted in the loss of at least 18 sites since 1975.

Natural Succession

With the near extirpation of the beaver in the southern Appalachians prior to 1900, one of the integral components of bog creation and maintenance was eliminated. Lacking the periodic flooding and felling of trees by beavers, succession of bog turtle habitats into climax hardwood forests was dramatically increased. Periodic droughts, such as those experienced in the mid-1980s, accelerate the invasion of woody species like tag alder (*Alnus serrulata*), red maple (*Acer rubrum*), and tulip poplar (*Liriodendron tulipifera*). Natural succession, habitat fragmentation, and the previously discussed threats are responsible for making southern bog turtle populations so disjunct. Since 1975 we have witnessed the decline in several bog turtle populations as a direct result of natural succession in Georgia, North Carolina, and South Carolina.

Two Henderson County, North Carolina sites found in 1975 (Zappalorti, 1975; Zappalorti and Johnson, 1981) have been frequently visited by the authors since their discovery. The smaller site was a mature hardwood forest with a small canopy opening at the time of its discovery. Fewer than 10 bog turtles were captured from 1975 to 1982

TABLE 2
Habitat loss in five states. Qualifying sites = those capable of supporting viable or potentially viable populations.

	Georgia	North Carolina	South Carolina	Tennessee	Virginia	Total
Occurrence records	8	116	3	2	64	192
Actual sites	8	84	3	2	47	143
Estimated core habitat hectares (acres)	8 (20)	78 (194)	6 (14)	3 (8)	45 (112)	139 (348)
Number of qualifying sites	3	35	1	2	25	66
Estimated core habitat hectares (acres)	5.5 (14)	36 (90)	4 (10)	3 (8)	26 (65)	75 (187)
% Reduction in core habitat	31%	54%	33%	0%	42%	46%

(all old adults, among them the largest specimen from North Carolina). It was obvious that this was a dying population because of depressed reproduction and no recruitment. Attempts to find additional turtles at this site have been unsuccessful since 1984. The second site covered approximately 3 ha and was previously used for grazing a small herd of cattle. The cattle were removed in 1981 at the urging of botanists because pitcherplants grew there. From 1982 to 1989 at least 45 bog turtles were captured and marked. The removal of livestock and subsequent hydrological changes, nutrient runoff from nearby fields, and drought combined to accelerate succession. Red maples and woody shrubs now dominate the site. Only 10 bog turtles have been captured in the site since 1989. The North Carolina Chapter of the Nature Conservancy purchased the site in 1992 with plans to restore it to its former condition (Anon., 1992). The first bog turtles found in Georgia came from an area dominated by a mature hardwood forest with small open seepages along the creek. Eighty years prior to the turtles' discovery, the site had been a farm with open fields. Logging and placer mining altered the site over the years. Fewer than 10 old adult bog turtles have been found at the site since 1979 with no evidence of reproduction or recruitment (Fahey, 1992). Other examples of sites lost to natural succession are known from the southern states. Since 1975 at least 16 sites have been rendered incapable of supporting viable populations because of succession.

Other Threats

Commercial domestic and international trade in bog turtles is a major threat. Bog turtles are prized because of their rarity, and overcollecting has been a serious problem throughout the turtle's range. Evidence surfaced in 1987 that bog turtles were removed from several Virginia sites prompting the state to protect the species (Mitchell et al., 1991). An undetermined number of bog turtles, including marked individuals, were removed from two study sites in North Carolina in 1989 by unscrupulous collectors. The bog turtle commands the highest price of any native turtle species and is sought by international pet markets. Because of the black market trade in bog turtles, CITES upgraded the species from Appendix II to Appendix I in 1992 to restrict international trade. In 1993 the World Wildlife Fund placed the bog turtle on its top-ten list of the world's "most wanted" endangered species, alongside such charismatic species as the giant panda and black rhinoceros.

Effects of Habitat Loss

Over the past 15–20 years the effects of the previously discussed threats have been great in the southeastern United States. We have documented 192 occurrence records from Georgia, North Carolina, South Carolina, Tennessee, and Virginia based on our surveys, museum and literature records, state databases, and contacts with colleagues. One hundred forty-three of these records (74.5%) are actual localities where bog turtles have been captured. We have estimated that the core habitat of the 143 sites covers approximately 139 ha (348 acres). However, these figures are misleading because of the effects of the habitat threats previously discussed. The majority of the sites were visited at least once during the past eight years, some of them many times during population studies. Site evaluations were made, based on our observations of the extent and type of habitat loss or alteration and our knowledge of the census of previously captured turtles in each site. Once the evaluations were completed, we determined that 54% (77 of 143) of the sites are no longer capable of supporting viable populations, while the remaining 46% are still capable or are potentially capable with protection and management. The estimated core habitat of these sites covers 75 ha (187 acres), a 46% net reduction of habitat. A state-by-state analysis of the habitat loss since these sites were first identified as supporting bog turtles is shown in Table 2.

From our observations and evaluations, land use practices are responsible for the loss of at least 28 sites (45% reduction in sites), development another 18 sites (29% reduction), and natural succession 16 sites (26% reduction). We have not documented any extirpation of bog turtle populations from overcollecting, but there is no doubt that the decline in turtle numbers in some sites is attributable to this threat.

Management and Conservation

Management and conservation of mountain bogs and turtle populations have become necessary to ensure their long-term viability. The fluctuating nature of wetlands (i.e., water level, succession, herbivore populations, etc.) maintains their productivity and diversity. For this reason, simply stabilizing bog turtle habitat may be counterproductive. The concept of protecting entire metapopulations in bioreserves (suggested by Buhlmann et al., this volume) warrants consideration. Because these environments are dynamic, the mechanisms that create and maintain meadow bogs (i.e., beaver, herbivores, fire, etc.) and the dispersal corridors must remain intact. Unfortunately, many factors may make this concept impractical in the South. Very few of the existing bog turtle populations fit the criteria of the metapopulation-bioreserve concept. Multiple or hostile landowners along the stream corridors may be major obstacles to overcome. Kiviat (1978) suggested that preservation of habitat without management may be inadequate for many species, including the bog turtle. Management of bog turtle habitat should include, but not be limited to, the following strategies:

1. Retard woody vegetation development by browsing, selective cutting, or burning to prevent canopy closure.
2. Maintain potential and usable dispersal corridors that connect groups of habitat units and potential habitat.
3. Create new meadow bogs by artificial flow modifications (tapping into the aquifer where possible).
4. Encourage and protect beaver populations.
5. Control invasive and exotic plant species such as multiflora rose.
6. Manage predator and competitor populations (mainly raccoons).

Additional surveys are needed to best assess the status of the bog turtle in the southeastern United States (approx. 50% of the area has been adequately searched, as shortages of manpower and finances have hindered extensive surveys). Education of landowners, as well as their cooperation with wildlife and conservation personnel, is imperative. Purchase of habitat, conservation easements and agreements, and legislative action to reduce or eliminate property taxes for owners of protected habitat are important strategies that must be considered. A grant was recently received from the U.S. Fish and Wildlife Service for a two-year status survey (1996–1998) on the bog turtle in the southeastern U.S.

Acknowledgments

We are grateful for the support received from the administrative staffs of Zoo Atlanta and the Knoxville Zoological Gardens. For assistance in the field, for comments, advice, and other pertinent data we thank A. C. Boynton, A. L. Braswell, M. Lynch, N. Murdock, A. S. Weakley, P. Wyatt, P. Hamel, P. Somers, G. Roach, S. L. Alford, J. C. Beane, T. Bohannon, K. A. Buhlmann, J. R. Everhart, K. M. Fahey, G. A. George, J. F. Green, Sr., R. Kendrick, J. C. Mitchell, T. Morris, C. E. Putnam, Jr., A. B. Somers, T. Thorp, J. L. Warner, and J. Whitehead. Financial support was received through grants from the Nongame Wildlife Program, North Carolina Wildlife Resources Commission, Zoo Atlanta and Friends of Zoo Atlanta, and contracts with the North Carolina Natural Heritage Program and North Carolina Nature Conservancy, Knoxville Zoological Gardens, Tennessee Wildlife Resource Agency, and Tennessee Nature Conservancy. Voucher specimens and photographs from this study were deposited in the Clemson University collection, University of Georgia Museum of Natural History, and the North Carolina State Museum of Natural Sciences.

For permits applicable to our work we are indebted to the North Carolina Wildlife Resources Commission, the South Carolina Department of Natural Resources, the Tennessee Wildlife Resource Agency, the Virginia Department of Game and Inland Fisheries, and the National Park Service Blue Ridge Parkway.

Literature Cited

Anon. 1992. North Carolina Chapter protects mountain bog and its unique residents. The Nature Conservancy, North Carolina Chapter Newsl. 59:4.

Arndt, R. G. 1977. Notes on the natural history of the bog turtle, *Clemmys muhlenbergii* (Schoepff), in Delaware. Chesapeake Sci. 18:67–76.

Arndt, R. G. 1978. The bog turtle-an endangered species? Delaware Conserv. 22(2):18–21, 25.

Arndt, R. G. 1986. Notes on the bog turtle, *Clemmys muhlenbergii*, in Warren County, New Jersey. Bull. Md. Herpetol. Soc. 22: 56–61.

Batson, J. E. 1991. Geographic distribution: *Clemmys muhlenbergii*. Herpetol. Rev. 2(4):134.

Beane, J. C. 1993. A survey of bog turtle (*Clemmys muhlenbergii*) habitat in the western Piedmont of North Carolina. Bull. Chicago Herpetol. Soc. 28(11):240–242.

Beane, J. C., A. B. Somers, and J. R. Everhart. 1993. Geographic distribution: *Clemmys muhlenbergii*. Herpetol. Rev. 24(3):108.

Bloomer, T. J. and R. J. Holub. 1977. The bog turtle, *Clemmys muhlenbergii*: a natural history. Bull. New York Herpetol. Soc. 13(2): 9–23.

Broaddus, J. 1992/1993. North Georgia's bog turtle: A hidden treasure. Georgia Wildl. 2(4):46–48.

Brown, E. E. 1992. Notes on amphibians and reptiles of the western Piedmont of North Carolina. J. Elisha Mitchell Sci. Soc. 108(1): 38–54.

Brown, F. 1992. The berry of the Thanksgiving table had its beginnings in the bogs of east Tennessee. Knoxville News Sentinel: E1, Sunday, November 22, 1992.

Buhlmann, K. A. 1992. An inventory of *Clemmys muhlenbergii* (bog turtle) in southwestern Virginia. Nat. Heritage Technical Report #92-3. Dept. Conservation and Recreation, Div. Natural Resources. Richmond, Virginia. 24 pp.

Buhlmann, K. A., J. C. Mitchell, and M. G. Rollins. 1997. New approaches for the conservation of the bog turtle, *Clemmys muhlenbergii*, in Virginia. *In* J. Van Abbema (ed.), Proceedings: Conservation, Restoration, and Management of Tortoises and Turtles—An International Conference, pp. 359–363. July 1993, State University of New York, Purchase. New York Turtle and Tortoise Society, New York.

Bury, R. B. 1979. Review of the ecology and conservation of the bog turtle, *Clemmys muhlenbergii*. USDI/F'S Spec. Sci. Rep., Wildl. No. 219:1–9.

Case, J. D., K. R. Dixon, J. E. Gates, D. Jacob, and G. J. Taylor. 1989. Habitat characteristics, population size, and home range of the bog turtle, *Clemmys muhlenbergii*, in Maryland. J. Herpetol. 23(4):356–362.

Earley, L. S. 1989. Wetlands in the highlands. Wildlife in North Carolina 53(10):11–16.

Earley, L. S.. 1993. Black market wildlife. Wildlife in North Carolina 57(11):4–11.

Ernst, C. H. 1977. Biological notes on the bog turtle, *Clemmys muhlenbergii*. Herpetologica 33(2):241–246.

Ernst, C. H. and R. B. Bury. 1977. *Clemmys muhlenbergii*. Cat. Amer. Amphib. Rept. 204:1–2.

Fahey, K. M. 1992. Habitat survey and census of bog turtle, *Clemmys muhlenbergii* Schoepff, populations in Georgia—Final report for 1991–1992. Unpubl. report to Fish & Game Div., Georgia Dept. Nat. Resources. 14 pp.

Fontenot, L. W. and S. G. Platt. 1993. A survey of the distribution and abundance of the bog turtle, *Clemmys muhlenbergii*, in South Carolina. Unpubl. report submitted to South Carolina Wildl. and Marine Resources Dept., Heritage Trust Program. 47 pp.

Hale, P. E. and M. J. Harris. 1980. Geographic distribution: *Clemmys muhlenbergii*. Herpetol. Rev. 11(1):14.

Herman, D. W. 1986. Geographic distribution: *Clemmys muhlenbergii*. Herpetol. Rev. 17(2):50.

Herman, D. W. 1989. Tracking the rare bog turtle. Wildlife in North Carolina 53(10):17–19.

Herman, D. W. and R. D. Pharr. 1986. Life history notes: *Clemmys muhlenbergii*: elevation. Herpetol. Rev. 17(1):24.

Herman, D. W. and C. E. Putnam, Jr. 1982. Geographic distribution: *Clemmys muhlenbergii*. Herpetol. Rev. 13(2):52.

Herman, D. W. and C. E. Putnam, Jr. 1983. Two new records of the Bog turtle, *Clemmys muhlenbergii* Schoepff, in Georgia. Herpetol. Rev. 14(2):55.

Herman, D. W. and J. L. Warner. 1986. Geographic distribution: *Clemmys muhlenbergii*. Herpetol. Rev. 17(4):92.

Herman, D. W. and A. S. Weakley. 1986. Geographic distribution: *Clemmys muhlenbergii*. Herpetol. Rev. 17(2):50.

Herman, D. W., J. F. Green, Sr., and B. W. Tryon. 1992. Geographic distribution: *Clemmys muhlenbergii*. Herpetol. Rev. 23(4):122.

Herman, D. W., B. W. Tryon, and A. C. Boynton. 1993. Geographic distribution: *Clemmys muhlenbergii*. Herpetol. Rev. 24(4):154.

Herman, D. W., E. Hunter, and C. McGrath. 1996. Geographic distribution: *Clemmys muhlenbergii*. Herpetol. Rev. 27(4):210.

Hoffman, R. 1987. Four new species included on the Virginia "endangered" list. Catesbeiana 7(2):21.

Hutchison, V. 1963. Record of the bog turtle, *Clemmys muhlenbergii*, in southwestern Virginia. Copeia 1963:156–157.

Kiviat, E. 1978. Bog turtle habitat ecology. Bull. Chicago Herpetol. Soc. 13(2):29–42.

Lenz, S. J. 1992/1993. Guide to Georgia's newly protected species. Georgia Wildl. 2(4):56–61.

Lovich, J. E., D. W. Herman, and K. M. Fahey. 1992. Seasonal activity and movements of bog turtles (*Clemmys muhlenbergii*) in North Carolina. Copeia 1992(4):1107–1111.

Mitchell, J. C. and K. A. Buhlmann. 1991. Distribution and status of the endangered bog turtle (*Clemmys muhlenbergii*) on the Blue Ridge Parkway in Virginia. Report to Nat. Park Serv., Blue Ridge Parkway, Asheville, North Carolina. 46 pp. + attachments.

Mitchell, J. C., K. A. Buhlmann, and C. H. Ernst. 1991. Bog turtle. *In* Virginia's Endangered Species, K. Terwilliger (coord.), pp. 457–459. McDonald and Woodward Publ. Co., Inc., Blacksburg, Virginia.

Mitchell, J. C. and C. A. Pague. 1987a. "Virginia's amphibians and reptiles": Comments and corrections. Herpetol. Rev. 18(3):57, 59.

Mitchell, J. C. and C. A. Pague. 1987b. A review of reptiles of special concern in Virginia. Virginia J. Sci. 38(4):319–328.

Nemuras, K. T. 1974a. The bog turtle. Wildl. N.C. 38(2):13–15.

Nemuras, K. T. 1974b. The bog turtle—Profile of an endangered species. Virginia Wildl. 35(6):7–9.

Nemuras, K. T. and J. A. Weaver. 1974. The bog turtle: Synonym for extinction? Nat. Parks Conserv. Mag. 48(6):17–20.

Nicholls, J. and N. Murdock. 1993. Is the endangered species act endangered? Wildlife in North Carolina 57(8):18–23.

Schafale, M. P. and A. S. Weakley. 1990. Classification of natural communities in North Carolina, third approximation. North Carolina Natural Heritage report. 325 pp.

Schoepff, J. D. 1792–1801. Historia Testudinum Iconibus Illustrata. Ioannis Iacobe Palm., Erangae.

Smith, A. 1990. Inventory of high-quality wetlands natural communities in the North Carolina mountain region. North Carolina Natural Heritage report. 80 pp.

Smith, R. L. 1974. Ecology and Field Biology, 2nd Edition. Harper & Row, Publ., Inc., New York.

Toby, F. J. 1985. Viriginia's Amphibians and Reptiles, a Distributional Survey. Virginia Herpetol. Soc., Purcellville, Virginia. 114 pp.

Tryon, B. W. 1988. The rare little turtle of east Tennessee. Tennessee Wildl. 11(4):6–9.

Tryon, B. W. 1990. Bog turtles (*Clemmys muhlenbergii*) in the south—A question of survival. Bull. Chicago Herpetol. Soc. 25(4):57–66.

Tryon, B. W. and D. W. Herman. 1990. Status, conservation, and management of the bog turtle, *Clemmys muhlenbergii*, in the southeastern United States. *In* K. R. Beaman, F. Caporaso, S. McKeown, and M. Graff (eds.), Proceedings of the First International Symposium on Turtles & Tortoises: Conservation and Captive Husbandry, pp. 36–53. August 1990, Chapman University, Orange, California. California Turtle & Tortoise Club and Chapman University.

Yarrow, H. C. 1882. Checklist of North American reptiles and batrachia, with catalogue of specimens in U.S. National Museum. Bull. U.S. Nat. Mus. 24:36.

Zappalorti, R. T. 1975. The status of the bog turtle *Clemmys muhlenbergii* in North Carolina. Unpubl. report to Nat. Audubon Soc., New York. 22 pp.

Zappalorti, R. T. and E. W. Johnson. 1981. The ecology of the bog turtle, *Clemmys muhlenbergii* (Schoepff), (Reptilia, Testudines, Emydidae) in western North Carolina. Unpubl. report, The Highlands Biological Station, Univ. North Carolina. 24 pp.

Life on the Edge:
Managing Peripheral Populations in a Changing Landscape

THOMAS B. HERMAN

Centre for Wildlife and Conservation Biology, Acadia University, Wolfville, Nova Scotia B0P 1X0, Canada
[e-mail: tom.herman@acadiau.ca]

ABSTRACT: In Nova Scotia all four resident turtle species (*Chelydra serpentina, Clemmys insculpta, Emydoidea blandingii,* and *Chrysemys picta*) closely approach the northern limits of their geographic ranges. Two, *E. blandingii* and *C. insculpta*, are restricted in their distribution and are probably vulnerable to environmental changes associated with global warming and habitat fragmentation. Both are long-lived species with apparently strong site affinities. However, in Nova Scotia *E. blandingii* exists almost entirely within a protected landscape (Kejimkujik National Park), while *C. insculpta* occurs in scattered populations primarily within working landscapes (mostly managed forests and mixed agriculture). We are developing species-level and ecosystem-level management strategies for these two species, which recognize the differences in scale, jurisdiction, and intensity of management. Peripheral populations are often presumed to contain the adaptive solutions to problems posed by environmental change. However, depending on the speed and scale of that change, these same populations may also be highly vulnerable.

Herpetologically, Nova Scotia is species-poor because of its northern latitude and peninsular position. Although connected to the mainland by a narrow low-lying isthmus, Nova Scotia is an ecological island for most of its biota. Despite its small size (55,490 km²), the province has a latitudinal range exceeding 400 km and a complex geological and glacial history. Based on a recent analysis of landforms, chronosequences of vegetation and soils, microclimate, energy/material pathways, and disturbance regimes, 77 distinct landscape types have been described by the Parks Division, Nova Scotia Department of Natural Resources (Lynds and LeDuc, 1993).

Approximately 8% of the province is currently highly protected. Of that, 2.4% is contained in two national parks. Most of the remaining 92%, and even some of the designated protected areas, have been worked to varying degrees for the past 300 years, with most intensive development and modification along coasts and fertile river valleys. Approximately 70% of the land in the province is privately owned. Although most of the province is forested, less than 1% of its forests exceed 100 years of age (Lynds and LeDuc, 1993).

All four turtle species resident in the province (*Chelydra serpentina, Clemmys insculpta, Emydoidea blandingii,* and *Chrysemys picta*) are close to the northern limits of their range. In many species, such peripheral populations are patchy and fragmented because of the decreasing availability of suitable conditions near range limits. The additional isolation of Nova Scotia from mainland North America, as well as habitat fragmentation within Nova Scotia, may constrain the adaptability (at both individual and population levels) of its turtles. Two species, *Emydoidea blandingii* and *Clemmys insculpta*, are of special concern.

Emydoidea blandingii

Although the range of Blanding's turtle is centered in the Great Lakes region, numerous isolated populations exist along the periphery of the range, especially to the east. The most isolated of all peripheral populations occurs in southwestern Nova Scotia, where the species is restricted to an inland plateau characterised by relatively high summer temperatures (Gates, 1973) and is considered to be a relict of a warmer climatic period (Bleakney, 1958). Most individuals in this population occur within Kejimkujik National Park (44°24′ N, 65°15′ W).

Long-term monitoring and short-term intensive studies in the park have shown that turtles are concentrated primarily in three areas, all associated with darkly coloured waters and peaty soils along slow-flowing streams and adjacent shallow lake margins (Herman et al., 1995; Power et al., 1994). A fourth area in the park existed in the past at Grafton Lake, near the site at which the Nova Scotia population was first discovered in 1953 (Bleakney, 1958).

Generally, turtles move downstream in spring to the inflow of associated lakes, coincident with increasing water temperature. Most aquatic movements are restricted to shallow water (<1 m). Females nest primarily on cobble lakeshore beaches and occasionally on road shoulders and other gravel embankments. In late summer turtles move back upstream where they mate and hibernate.

Despite the presence of discrete activity centres, Blanding's turtles in Nova Scotia appear to be more vagile than populations elsewhere (Ross, 1989; Ross and Anderson, 1990; Rowe and Moll, 1991). Home ranges in this population frequently exceeded 1.5 km in at least one dimension (Power, 1989). Capture-mark-recapture and radio-tracking data show long-distance nesting migrations by females (up to 2.9 km straight-line distance) and range shifts involving long overland movements by some males (including three individuals moving minimum distances of 5, 8.5, and 11.5 km) (Herman et al., 1989). This vagility, in combination with observations of promiscuous mating, suggests the Nova Scotia population is panmictic.

The late discovery of the Nova Scotian population probably reflects the cryptic habits and low local density of the species. Based on a comparison of census data from three discrete marking intervals between 1969 and 1988, the adult population within the park is estimated to be 132 (95% Confidence Intervals: 99–179, Schnabel binomial estimate) (Herman et al., 1995). Despite searches in peripheral areas, the known range of the species remains restricted to parts of the Mersey River and Medway River watersheds (Powell, 1965; Dobson, 1971; Bleakney, 1976; Drysdale, 1983; Herman et al., 1989). Recent unconfirmed sightings have been reported from two additional adjacent watersheds (Herman et al., 1997).

Concerns and Actions

Age. Age structure in the sampled population is top-heavy; of 48 individuals aged recently, 31 exceeded 30 years (Herman et al., 1995). This suggests that longevity and reproductive life span are extended, but that recruitment is low. Sampling bias may account for the apparent absence of juveniles, which is commonly reported in *E. blandingii* populations elsewhere (Congdon et al., 1983; Gibbons, 1968; Graham and Doyle, 1977; Ross, 1989). However, the underrepresentation of age classes 16–20 and 21–25 (0% and 6.1% respectively) in that sample is troubling. Individuals in the latter age class are sexually mature, and females should be encountered only during routine surveys of nesting beaches. Intensive visual and trap sampling in spring 1995 encountered one individual in each of these age classes. The hatch years associated with these classes were not unusually inclement.

Reproduction. Reproductive potential and recruitment in Nova Scotia are apparently compromised by (1) the limited availability of suitable nesting areas (substrate, exposure, susceptibility to flooding), and (2) low egg and hatchling survivorship (from raccoon predation, flooding, and a short incubation season). Raccoons are the most important predators of eggs of Blanding's turtle in Nova Scotia (Power, 1989). Although accurate estimates of predation rates are unavailable, most protected nests show signs of attempted predation, and most unprotected nests are destroyed on the night of oviposition (Power, 1989). Nesting habitat of the Nova Scotia population is distributed along edges (beaches, roadsides), and nearly all nests occur on just a few beaches. Predation rates in such linear habitats can be relatively high (Temple, 1987). High raccoon populations in Kejimkujik National Park are sustained by campground and general park activities.

Habitat change and loss. The effects of habitat change throughout the population's range are largely unknown, although impoundments and diversions of waterways for power generation and aquatic habitat management (e.g., fish, waterfowl) may have altered availability of nesting, feeding, and hibernation sites and impeded seasonal movements.

Construction of a dam at Grafton Lake in the 1930s (within present park boundaries but before park establishment) submerged inflow and outflow brooks and probably altered nesting of females by blocking traditional routes to nesting beaches. The number of turtles in this part of the park has declined steadily since their discovery there in 1953. A recent decision by the park to remove the dam and restore the lake and inflows to original levels is designed in part to reestablish habitat for Blanding's turtles. Construction of roads, campgrounds, parking lots, and artificial beaches during the development of the park in the 1970s may also have influenced seasonal movements and availability of nesting sites.

Status. Blanding's turtle is federally protected (i.e., may not be collected or disturbed) in all National Parks where it occurs. In Nova Scotia the species has been protected since 1990 under the Nova Scotia Wildlife Act. In 1993 the Committee on the Status of Endangered Wildlife in Canada (COSEWIC) designated the Nova Scotia population of the Blanding's Turtle as "Threatened." As a result of this designation, a RENEW (Committee on the Recovery of Nationally Endangered Wildlife) Recovery Team for this population was established in fall 1993 and has submitted a recovery plan outlining essential research and management needs. Two projects were funded for summer 1994: one continuing the radio tracking of hatchlings and one examining microclimatic features of nest site selection. Both projects were continued, with funding, in 1995 and 1996. In addition, an intensive study of juvenile movements and distribution was initiated in the spring of 1995. Results of the latter suggest a pulse of recruitment coinciding with the initiation of nest predator exclosures in the late 1980s.

Outlook. Blanding's turtles mature later and live longer than most freshwater turtles. Sexual maturation occurs at about 14 years in most populations (Graham and Doyle, 1977; Petokas, 1986; Congdon and van Loben Sels, 1991). In northern populations, such as the one in Nova Scotia, it probably occurs even later. However, individuals frequently survive to 35 years (Gibbons, 1987; Herman et al., 1989; Congdon and van Loben Sels, 1991) and occasionally beyond 70 years (Brecke and Moriarty, 1989; Herman et al., 1989) with no evidence of reproductive senility.

Even though the reproductive life span of Blanding's turtle in Nova Scotia may commonly exceed 20 years, recruitment to the breeding population is low. This underlines the importance of high annual survivorship of breeding adults to the continued existence of this population. Fortunately, adults are relatively protected from predators and disturbance, although a few cases of road mortality and one of boat mortality within the park have been reported.

Among North American freshwater turtles, *Emydoidea blandingii* has one of the most latitudinally compressed ranges. This in addition to the fragmented distribution of existing populations suggests that the adaptability of the species to environmental change is limited. Substantial climatic warming, accompanied by changes in seasonal precipitation and moisture regimes, may occur within the lifetime of an individual turtle. Adaptive responses to such changes would thus have to be largely behavioural rather than genetic (Herman and Scott, 1992). Climatic changes, if they involve warming, could conceivably benefit the population, which at present is probably at the northern physiological limit of its range.

In Nova Scotia, Blanding's turtle serves as a symbol for Kejimkujik National Park, for "species at risk" programmes, and as a flagship species for conservation of the province's southwestern relict fauna and flora. Although the population is small, the majority of individuals occur in a highly protected landscape. The high public profile, availability of at least some funding for research and monitoring (because of the population's threatened status), and commitment of the park to long-term management, contribute positively to the future of the population.

Clemmys insculpta

In contrast to *E. blandingii*, which exists probably as a single panmictic population mostly within a protected landscape, *C. insculpta* in Nova Scotia occurs in scattered populations primarily within working landscapes, mostly managed forests and mixed agriculture. At least nine discrete populations are presently known from Nova Scotia, but none is centred in protected areas. Most occur in the central and northern mainland of the province, and at least seven may be declining, some sharply. It is believed that only two populations, St. Mary's River watershed (Antigonish County) and River Inhabitants watershed (Inverness and Richmond counties), contain more than 100 reproductively mature adults. These populations appear relatively undisturbed.

Although wood turtles in the province occur in a variety of geological formations, they tend to favour rich intervales with sandy-bottomed rivers and streams (Gilhen, 1984). Breeding activities and hibernacula tend to be concentrated on meandering sections. Most nesting occurs at natural sites on high sandy banks, well above normal flood levels.

Concerns and Actions

Information gaps. Nearly all recent data on wood turtle distribution and status in Nova Scotia are anecdotal. The last intensive work was carried out by Bleakney (1963) and Powell (1965). There is widespread concern that populations are declining but relatively little corroborating evidence. However, in contrast to the Nova Scotia Blanding's turtle population, juveniles appear to make up a substantial portion of some wood turtle populations, even the most highly disturbed ones. Extensive and intensive surveys of critical nesting sites, hibernacula, and juvenile activity centres are also needed.

Habitat change and loss. Unfortunately, the rich intervale habitats frequented by wood turtles are highly productive and are therefore also popular with farmers and foresters. Two agricultural practices threaten nesting habitat in particular. Stabilization of banks with rock cribbing is commonly practiced in agricultural areas along meandering sections of watercourses, especially where banks are high and unstable. These banks are often prime nesting sites, but once stabilized are unavailable to turtles. Allowing cattle free access to shorelines along watercourses also degrades nesting areas and may cause some mortality of developing eggs.

Extensive land clearing for agriculture fragments the landscape for turtles and may isolate subpopulations on individual watersheds or even single watercourses. There is virtually no information on daily or seasonal movements by adults or on the impact of land clearing on movements.

Collecting. Unfortunately, wood turtles are highly visible and easy to catch when basking along riverbanks. They are often collected as curiosities or for pets and as a result are often released or escape far from their home stream. In most cases these individuals are lost from the breeding population. Turtles are increasingly exposed to such "predation" as recreational activity along watercourses, especially canoeing, increases. The extent of such collecting in Nova Scotia is unknown. However, wood turtles are often picked up wandering along roads in developed residential areas far from any known turtle habitats, and occasionally live individuals are turned in to the Nova Scotia Museum and Department of Natural Resources. There is no current policy regarding reintroduction of these animals.

Status. At present the wood turtle is not explicitly protected under any federal or provincial legislation, although it is offered a modicum of protection under the Nova Scotia Wildlife Act. In 1996 it was designated by COSEWIC as "Vulnerable."

Outlook. Because this species occurs primarily in working landscapes, development of any realistic management models for it will require public education and local participation and stewardship, as well as active manipulation of turtle habitat and populations. To this end, "Turtlewatch," an informal group comprising individuals from the Acadia Centre for Wildlife and Conservation Biology, the Nova Scotia Museum, and private citizens, was formed in 1993 and began a public information campaign.

In spring 1994 an article on the species and its conservation, designed for a general audience, was published in *Nova Scotia Conservation*, a widely circulated publication of Nova Scotia Department of Natural Resources (Gilhen et al, 1994). Initial response to that article indicates a high level of interest among the public, particularly at the local level.

In summer 1994 a questionnaire, designed to identify individuals who may have long-term anecdotal data on wood turtle abundance at specific locations, as well as to locate unrecorded populations of turtles in the province, was circulated to members of local wildlife and naturalist groups, to interested private citizens, and to provincial regional wildlife biologists. Selected individuals, based on their questionnaire responses, were contacted for personal interviews, and field checks were made of some sites from which turtles were reported. These sites were plotted, described, and assessed for degree of fragmentation and disturbance, with special attention paid to location and characterization of suspected and confirmed nesting beaches (Adams, 1995). Although Adam's survey more than doubled the known range of the species in Nova Scotia, it reinforced the fear that most local populations are declining.

An understanding of movement patterns and site affinities of individual turtles and the response of turtles to displacement outside their home range is essential to predict the effects of fragmentation and inadvertent translocation, as well as to develop any restocking programmes where resident turtle populations have been reduced. In summer 1994 we used radio transmitters and thread-trailing to track individual turtles, first within their home range and then following displacement outside their home range. Displacement experiments involved reciprocal transplants of pairs of same-sex adult turtles from widely separated watersheds. Although sample sizes were small, transplanted turtles quickly adopted their new home ranges, shifting range size to that of the native (original) resident (McCurdy, 1995).

CONCLUSIONS

Wood and Blanding's turtles, like many chelonians, are declining in much of their range, primarily from habitat degradation and loss. Wood turtles are also susceptible to overcollection, especially of adults. Because of the longevity, delayed maturation, and high juvenile and egg mortality of both species, populations cannot sustain heavy adult mortality (Congdon et al., 1993), especially at the northern limits of their range (Galbraith et al., this volume). Site affinity of individuals may also constrain the response of populations to habitat changes because significant changes can occur within the life span of single individuals.

Although life histories of the two species are similar, the different nature of the landscapes in which the species occur in Nova Scotia demands different management strategies for the two. *E. blandingii* is well protected, both at the population and ecosystem levels. Funds for research and monitoring, although modest, are available and will probably continue to be for the foreseeable future as the population is centred in a national park. The apparent lack of adult recruitment for many years is troubling but can be addressed with intensive management.

C. insculpta, on the other hand, occurs almost exclusively in working landscapes and must rely largely on local stewardship programmes and volunteer management. Such programmes will be most effective if they focus on watershed management at the ecosystem level rather than on wood turtles alone. These models already exist in Nova Scotia (e.g., Clean Annapolis River Project) but take time to develop. In the interim, public education aimed especially at farming and forestry communities may help modify or eliminate some of the more damaging land use practices.

LITERATURE CITED

Adams, J. D. 1995. An evaluation of wood turtle (*Clemmys insculpta* LeConte) distribution in Nova Scotia through public surveys. B.S. Honours thesis, Acadia University, Wolfville, Nova Scotia.

Bleakney, J. S. 1958. A zoogeographical study of the amphibians and reptiles of eastern Canada. Bull. Natl. Mus. Canada 155: 1–119.

Bleakney, J. S. 1963. Notes on the distribution and life histories of turtles in Nova Scotia. Can. Field-Nat. 77:67–76.

Bleakney, J. S. 1976. Literature review related to the presence of Blanding's Turtle in Kejimkujik National Park. Unpubl., Kejimkujik National Park, RR 2 Caledonia, Queens Co., Nova Scotia. iv + 50 pp.

Brecke, B. and J. J. Moriarity. 1989. *Emydoidea blandingii* (Blanding's turtle) longevity. Herpetol. Rev. 20:53.

Congdon, J. D. and R. C. van Loben Sels. 1991. Growth and body size in Blanding's turtles (*Emydoidea blandingii*): Relationships to reproduction. Can. J. Zool. 69:239–245.

Congdon, J. D., D. W. Tinkle, G. L. Breitenbach, and R. C. van Loben Sels. 1983. Nesting ecology and hatching success in the turtle *Emydoidea blandingii*. Herpetologica 39:417–429.

Congdon, J. D., A. E. Dunham, and R. C. van Loben Sels. 1993. Delayed sexual maturity and demographics of Blanding's turtles (*Emydoidea blandingii*): implications for conservation and management of long-lived organisms. Conserv. Biol. 7:826–833.

Dobson, R. B. 1971. A range extension and basking observation of the Blanding's turtle in Nova Scotia. Can. Field-Nat. 85:255–256.

Drysdale, C. D. 1983. A resource analysis and management plan for the Blanding's turtle (*Emydoidea blandingii*) in Kejimkujik National Park. Parks Canada, Atlantic Regional Office Library, Halifax, Nova Scotia.

Galbraith, D. A., R. J. Brooks, and G. P. Brown. 1997. Can management intervention achieve sustainable exploitation of turtles? *In*

J. Van Abbema (ed.), Proceedings: Conservation, Restoration, and Management of Tortoises and Turtles—An International Conference, pp. 186–194. July 1993, Purchase, New York. The New York Turtle and Tortoises Society, New York.

Gates, A. D. 1973. The tourism and outdoor recreation climate of the Maritime Provinces. Environment Canada Atmospheric Environment Rec-3-73, Meteorological Applications Branch, Toronto. (Available from Information Canada.)

Gibbons, J. W. 1968. Observations on the ecology and population dynamics of the Blanding's turtle, *Emydoidea blandingii*. Can. J. Zool. 46:288–290.

Gibbons, J. W. 1987. Why do turtles live so long? BioScience 37: 262–269.

Gilhen, J. 1984. Amphibians and Reptiles of Nova Scotia. Nova Scotia Museum, Halifax. 162 pp.

Gilhen, J., T. Herman, and N. Meister. 1994. Wood turtles face an uncertain future. NS Conservation 18(1):5–7.

Graham, T. E. and T. S. Doyle. 1977. Growth and population characteristics of Blanding's turtle, *Emydoidea blandingii* in Massachusetts. Herpetologica 33:410–414.

Herman, T. B., T. D. Power, and B. R. Eaton. 1989. Population status and management of Blanding's turtle (*Emydoidea blandingii*) in Nova Scotia. Final report submitted to Environment Canada-Canadian Parks Service, Environment Canada-Canadian Wildlife Service, and World Wildlife Fund Canada and Canadian National Sportsmen's Shows. xix + 229 pp.

Herman, T. B. and F. W. Scott. 1992. Global change at the local level: Assessing the vulnerability of vertebrate species to climatic warming. *In* J. H. M. Willison, S. Bondrup-Nielsen, C. D. Drysdale, T. B. Herman, N. W. P. Munro, and T. L. Pollock (eds.), Science and Management of Protected Areas, pp. 353–367. Developments in Landscape Management and Urban Planning Series, Elsevier, Amsterdam.

Herman, T. B., T. D. Power, and B. R. Eaton. 1995. Population status of Blanding's turtle (*Emydoidea blandingii*) in Nova Scotia. Can. Field-Nat. 109:182–191.

Herman, T. B., I. P. Morrison, J. A. McNeil, and N. L. McMaster. 1997. Recovery of a threatened Blanding's turtle population: Linking conservation efforts in working and protected landscapes. Paper presented at SAMPA III—Third International Conference on Science and Management of Protected Areas, Calgary, Alberta, Canada, 12–16 May 1997.

Lynds, A. and J. M. LeDuc. 1993. Understanding and protecting biodiversity at the landscape level in Nova Scotia. *In* Protecting our Natural Heritage—Proceedings of a workshop on biodiversity and protected areas in Atlantic Canada, pp. 15–19. Atlantic Region Protected Areas Work Group, Environment Canada, Sackville, New Brunswick.

McCurdy, D. G. 1995. Orientation and movement patterns of reciprocally transplanted wood turtles (*Clemmys insculpta* Leconte) in northeastern Nova Scotia. B.S. Honour thesis, Acadia, University, Wolfville, Nova Scotia.

Petokas, P. J. 1986. Patterns of reproduction and growth in the freshwater turtle *Emydoidea blandingii*. Ph.D. dissertation, Graduate School of the University Center at Binghampton (SUNY). xi + 174 pp.

Powell, C. B. 1965. Zoogeography and related problems of turtles in Nova Scotia. M.S. thesis, Acadia University, Wolfville, Nova Scotia. 84 pp.

Power, T. D. 1989. Seasonal movements and nesting ecology of a relict population of Blanding's turtle (*Emydoidea blandingii* [Holbrook]) in Nova Scotia. M.S. thesis, Acadia University, Wolfville, Nova Scotia. 187 pp.

Power, T. D., T. B. Herman, and J. Kerekes. 1994. Water colour as a predictor of Blanding's turtle (*Emydoidea blandingii*) distribution in Nova Scotia. Can. Field-Nat. 108:17–21.

Ross, D. A. 1989. Population ecology of painted and Blanding's turtles (*Chrysemys picta* and *Emydoidea blandingi*) in central Wisconsin. Wis. Acad. Sci. Arts Lett. 77:77–84.

Ross, D. A. and R. K. Anderson. 1990. Habitat use, movements, and nesting of *Emydoidea blandingi* in central Wisconsin. J. Herpetol. 24:6–12.

Rowe, J. W. and E. O. Moll. 1991. A radiotelemetric study of activity and movements of the Blanding's turtle (*Emydoidea blandingi*) in northeastern Illinois. J. Herpetol. 25:178–185.

Temple, S. A. 1987. Predation on turtle nests increases near ecological edges. Copeia 1987:250–252.

Blanding's Turtle Habitat Requirements and Implications for Conservation in Dutchess County, New York

ERIK KIVIAT

Hudsonia Ltd., Bard College Field Station, Annandale, NY 12504, USA [e-mail: kiviat@bard.edu]

ABSTRACT: Blanding's turtle, *Emydoidea blandingii*, listed as "Threatened" in New York State, occurs in Dutchess County and one other region of the state. In Dutchess, at least 11 small populations (each 10–50+ adults) use complexes of several wetland units (0.03–7 ha). Primary wetland habitats usually include the following characteristics: permanent or intermittent hydroperiod with little through flow; high water depths of 25–120 cm; tree canopy open or absent; tree fringe present; and a dense cover of shrubs, forbs, lemnids or nymphaeids, with coarse and fine organic debris. A deeper permanent or spring-fed pond (used for drought refuge) and adjoining well-drained, gravelly soils are also believed to be important habitat components. Adults readily move 100–500+ m between pools, and females migrate up to 1,000 m overland to nest. There is evidence that existing small preserves are not large enough to contain nesting areas. Loss of habitat and loss of individuals to road and mowing-equipment mortality, to collecting, and to predation are believed to be significant threats.

Small reserves combined with statutory protection of wetlands were formerly thought adequate to conserve the species in Dutchess County, but the change from rural to suburban land use is overwhelming small-scale conservation efforts. Given this trend, effective conservation of Blanding's turtles requires that rural habitat complexes be conserved in large working landscapes of 5–10 km^2 that include parks, farms, and partially developed parcels. A buffer zone of 1,000 m around wetland habitats will be necessary for effective preserve design. I suggest habitat identification techniques and potential strategies that may balance the needs of Blanding's turtle with inevitable suburban development in Dutchess County.

The habitats of many vertebrates include multiple, spatially separated components used for different seasonal or life history activities. Classic examples include anadromous fish, migratory birds, and many species of amphibians and reptiles. The difficulties of conserving and managing animals with complex habitat requirements are well known. In this paper I summarize information on the spatial requirements of Blanding's turtle in Dutchess County and present techniques for predicting, assessing, and conserving the diverse habitat mosaic required by this species in a landscape that is rapidly evolving from rural to suburban.

Blanding's turtle, *Emydoidea blandingii*, occurs in 16 U.S. states and Canadian provinces, from Nebraska to Nova Scotia, with a discontinuous distribution east of Ohio (Conant and Collins, 1991). In New York State there are two centers of distribution: the St. Lawrence River and Lake Ontario (part of the continuous Great Lakes basin distribution) in the north, and a small disjunct population in the western half of Dutchess County in the southeastern corner of the state. The Dutchess population comprises 11 known subpopulations east of the Hudson River, 125 km north of New York City. Blanding's turtle is currently listed as "Threatened" by the New York State Department of Environmental Conservation (DEC).

Landscape

The soils are largely of glacial origin. The Hoosic terrain of western Dutchess County supports the glacial kettle shrub swamps, and the Nassau-Cardigan and Dutchess-Cardigan terrains support the intermittent woodland pools used by Blanding's turtles. The Hoosic soil series is characterized as deep, somewhat excessively drained, acidic, Typic Dystrochrepts on gravelly glacial outwash (Tornes, 1979); the Nassau, Dutchess, and Cardigan soils are shallow, rocky soils on glacial till. Hoosic soils are well suited to both agricultural and suburban uses; the Nassau soil complexes are often marginal for agriculture or residential construction but generally support (or formerly supported) both uses at lower intensities. Land use near Blanding's turtle sites varies from rural to suburban, and many farms have been converted to residential, commercial, industrial, or recreational use in the past 50 years. Upland vegetation includes young and mature hardwood forests, shrubby abandoned fields, hay, maize, cattle pasture, "waste grounds" such as abandoned gravel pits, and managed plant communities in residential yards, cemeteries, and parks. Historical information (ca. 1940 on) and recent records of turtles between extant populations suggest that Blanding's turtle sites in Dutchess County were formerly continuous and more extensive.

Habitat Requirements

Blanding's turtles use a habitat complex, which includes springtime pools, nesting areas with rehydration pools, and overwintering habitat. The habitat requirements of hatchlings and juveniles are undocumented. Substantial overland movement of adults occurs, particularly in spring and early summer. Distances between pools utilized within a site range from five meters to at least 300 meters. Inter-pool movements presumably allow the local population to find suitable microclimates, prey, and refuge from competition as biotic and physical parameters change differentially in individual pools. In the heat of mid-summer, drought refuges—usually spring-fed ponds or lakes (sometimes deeper portions of springtime habitats)—are also necessary habitat components. These refuges can be 250–900 m from the nearest springtime wetland habitats.

In late May and June gravid females migrate overland from the springtime habitat, in some cases traveling more than 1,000 m, to lay a single clutch of eggs in well-drained, loose, sunny soil. Nests have been found in a crevice of a rock outcrop, gardens, piles of cut vegetation, a powerline right-of-way, and other disturbed habitats near human habitation. The nest is located close to standing water (an artificial pond or a natural wetland) where females can rehydrate between their searches for nest areas. Two extant sites and one former site, each a park or reserve, were documented to have nesting areas outside the protected area boundaries. Terrestrial movement between pools and from pools to nesting areas increases the chance of mortality from collecting, highway vehicles and farm equipment, "pitfalls" (abandoned swimming pools, window wells, etc.), and predation by coyotes, dogs, and other mammals.

METHODS

Since 1979 I have observed, captured (by hand or baited trap), and marked Blanding's turtles in Dutchess County, mostly in May and early June when the turtles are active and conspicuous. Turtles were marked with serially numbered plastic tags glued with waterproof epoxy to a posterior marginal, pleural, or vertebral scute. These tags allowed easier reporting in cases when the recaptures were not made by the primary investigator. In 1994 radiotelemetry was used to document migration and nesting habitat. Additional telemetry and mark-and-recapture data for Blanding's turtles were available from Emrich (1991), Klemens et al. (1992), The Nature Conservancy Lower Hudson Chapter (unpubl. data), and the New York State DEC Endangered Species Unit (unpubl. data). I conducted habitat surveys of five sites between 1 July and 7 October 1993. In these surveys I identified vascular plants (and a few bryophytes) and visually estimated cover by each species and physiognomic class of plants in each pool known to be used by Blanding's turtles as springtime habitat. Plant species not readily identified in the field were collected and subsequently identified, and voucher specimens were deposited in the Bard College Field Station herbarium. The size of site and pool areas was estimated using a 1 ha grid overlay on U.S. Geological Survey 7.5 minute topographic maps. I consulted unpublished soil maps (U.S. Natural Resources Conservation Service, available from Dutchess County Soil and Water Conservation District, Millbrook, New York). Descriptive statistics were computed with Lotus 123 version 3.1 and Complete Statistical System (CSS) software. In some cases, additional soil sampling was undertaken in the field to confirm soil types.

RESULTS

Four of the five study sites had Hoosic soil on the site or within 1,000 m. Six other Blanding's turtle sites known in the county (not studied in 1993) also have Hoosic soils in varying amounts on or near the site. Nine of these 11 total sites are also associated with Nassau-Cardigan or Dutchess-Cardigan soils. Recapture data confirmed frequent adult overland movement between springtime pools involving distances of up to 500 m. I use the term "site envelope" to describe such a cluster of occupied pools within the landscape. Site envelopes support approximately 10–50 adult turtles. It was also necessary to categorize focal sites (many animals and consistent occupancy) and secondary sites (shallow wetlands only occasionally occupied by turtles) for the purpose of analysis. Telemetry data showed that nesting females may travel at least 1,000 m from spring pools to find suitable nesting sites.

Pools

Pools (n = 24) used by Blanding's turtles as focal springtime habitats were 0.1–7.2 ha in surface area (mean 1.3, median 0.7, interquartile range 0.3–1.3). Because pools within a site tended to be interconnected, the delimitation of pools for habitat analysis was somewhat arbitrary. Springtime habitats have hydroperiods of 8–12 months (at least late fall to early summer) with winter and springtime maximum water depths of 50–120 cm.

Springtime pools have organic substrates and are often dominated by shrubs, including buttonbush (*Cephalanthus occidentalis*), dogwood (*Cornus amomum*), winterberry (*Ilex verticillata*), highbush blueberry (*Vaccinium corymbosum*), and arrowwood (*Viburnum recognitum*) (Table 1). Dead trees, both standing and fallen, are usually present (Figure 1c). Besides a highly developed shrub component, other important vegetation characteristics include a fringe of trees comprised of red maple (*Acer rubrum*), red ash (*Fraxinus* sp.), and swamp white oak (*Quercus bicolor*). In some pools there was a moderate amount of purple loose strife (*Lythrum*

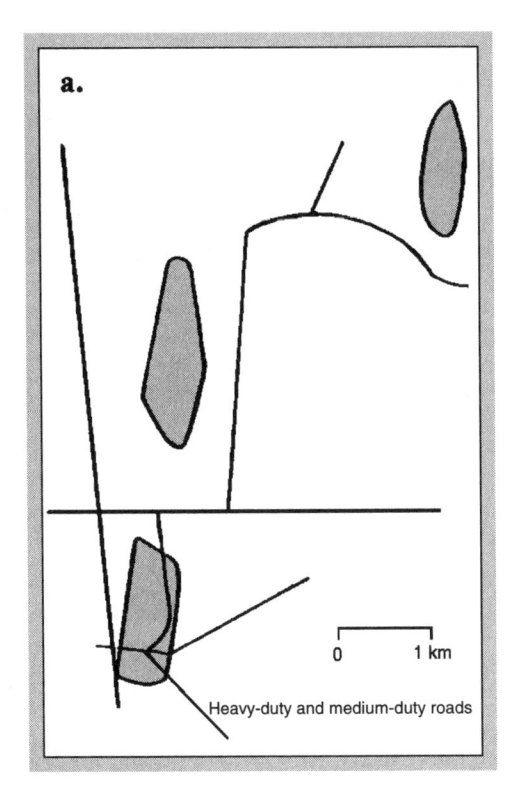

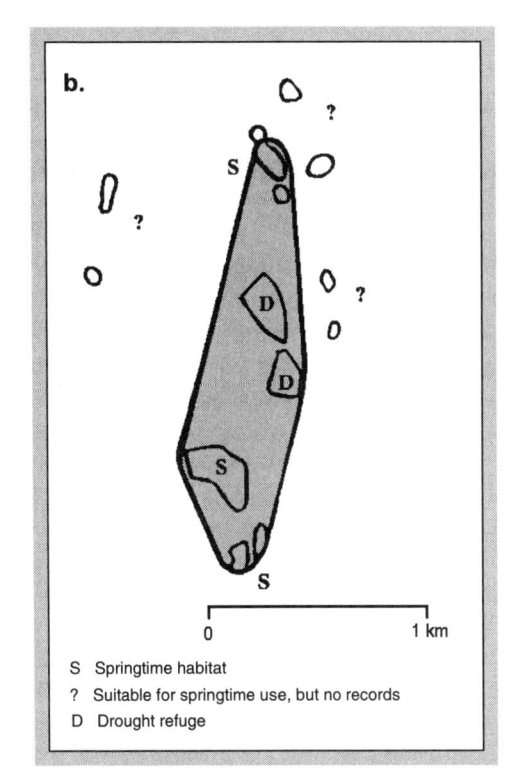

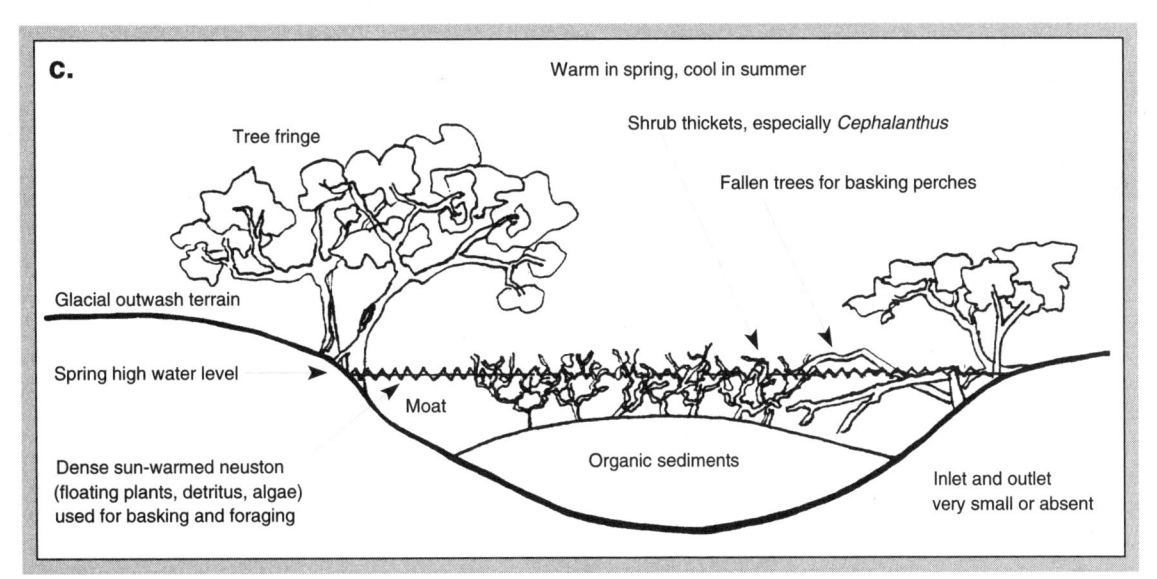

Figure 1. The landscape (**a**), site (**b**), and pool (**c**) environments of Blanding's turtle in Dutchess County, New York. The shaded areas in **a** and **b** are the site envelopes. (Drawings by Kathy Anne Schmidt.)

salicaria, a tall, shrub-like, exotic forb) with low forbs and lemnids. There was usually little cover of graminoids, submerged macrophytes, bryophytes, or floating filamentous algae.

Besides the deep and shrubby focal springtime pools, Blanding's turtles also used intermittent woodland pools and acidic bogs, especially if they were within several hundred meters of typical buttonbush pools. Such sites often have rather different vegetation and are considered to be secondary sites.

In the 24 pools studied during 1993 there were many alterations within the wetland boundary, occurring through the deposition of garbage (n = 11 cases), organic refuse (n = 6), or earth (n = 9); damming, berm construction, or unintentional blocking of drainage (n = 7); drainage or channelization (n = 18); and excavation or dredging (n = 8). Some

TABLE 1
Geometric cover classes of vegetation components in pools (n = 24) used by Blanding's turtles in springtime.

Component[b]	Cover classes[a]				
	Mean	Median	IQR[c]	OR[d]	Non-zero[e]
Tree fringe	3.8	4	4–4	0–4	23
Tree canopy	1.0	0	0–1.5	0–4	10
Transgressive	0.1	0	0–0	0–1	3
Shrub	2.9	3	2.0–4	1–4	24
Tall graminoid	0.0	0	0–0	0–0	0
Tussock sedge	0.04	0	0–0	0–1	1
Low graminoid	0.3	0	0–0	0–2	5
Purple loosestrife	1.2	0	0–2.0	0–4	11
Swamp loosestrife	0.1	0	0–0	0–2	1
Low forb	0.8	0	0–1.0	0–4	9
Nymphaeids	0.2	0	0–0	0–4	1
Lemnids	0.7	0	0–0	0–4	6
Floating filamentous algae	0.0	0	0–0	0–0	0
Submersed macrophytes	0.0	0	0–0	0–0	0
Sphagnum	0.3	0	0–0	0–4	1
Other bryophytes	0.4	0	0–0.5	0–2.0	7

[a] Classes are 0 = 0–6.25%, 1 = 6.25–12.5%, 2 = 12.5–25%, 3 = 25–50%, and 4 = 50–100% cover.

[b] The highest–ranking taxa in the components studied are trees (fringe, canopy, transgressives: *Acer rubrum, Fraxinus pennsylvanica, Quercus bicolor*); shrubs, approx. 1–4 m tall, (*Cephalanthus occidentalis, Cornus amomum, Ilex verticillatus, Rhododendron viscosum, Vaccinium corymbosum, Viburnum recognitum*); tall graminoids >1 m (*Scirpus cyperinus, Phalaris arundinacea*); tussock sedge (*Carex stricta*); low graminoids <1 m (*Carex* spp., *Eleocharis acicularis, E. obtusa*, Poaceae spp., *Sparganium americanum, S. chlorocarpum*); purple loosestrife (*Lythrum salicaria*); swamp loosestrife (*Decodon verticillatum*); low forbs and ferns <1 m (*Bidens connata, B. discoides, Galium tinctorium, G. trifidum, Lycopus uniflorus, Onoclea sensibilis, Osmunda regalis, Polygonum* spp., *Ranunculus flabellaris, Thelypteris palustris, Triadenum virginicum*); nymphaeids (*Nuphar luteum, Nymphaea odorata, Polygonum amphibium*, floating leaves of *Potamogeton*); lemnids (*Lemna minor, Spirodela polyrrhiza, Wolffia* spp., and the liverworts *Riccia fluitans, Ricciocarpus natans*); submersed macrophytes (*Ceratophyllum echinatum, Potamogeton* spp., Charophyta).

[c] IQR = interquartile range.

[d] OR = observed range.

[e] Non-zero = number of non-zero ranks, i.e., pools where the component is not rare.

hydrological alterations may have fortuitously improved habitat quality by raising or lowering former water levels. In some cases I was unable to determine whether a pool had a natural origin as a glacial kettle or it had originated from gravel mining.

During springtime the restricted flow of surface water, leafless buttonbush cover and tree fringe, open tree canopy, abundant neuston (from floating vegetation and detritus), and adjoining gravelly soils all promote rapid warming of the water surface. During summer the shady tree fringe, buttonbush thickets, neuston, and probable peripheral groundwater input combine to keep the deeper water layer cool. The tree fringe also contributes basking logs to the pools. The impermanence of standing water may reduce pool use by snapping turtles and painted turtles, both potential food competitors. Blanding's turtles are conspicuous and active when the water surface reaches 25–35°C in the sun. Turtles were observed as early as late March and as late as late October. The turtles often appear to bask and forage simultaneously, resting partly exposed in the neuston at the water surface with the head exploring below the surface.

Conservation

Ten years ago I assumed that Blanding's turtle could be protected in Dutchess County by creating small reserves encompassing a few pools and through the existing state regulation of freshwater wetlands and streams. Subsequently, however, residential subdivisions were built next to known or likely springtime habitats, pools were used for dumping, water levels were altered without knowledge of the effects on turtles, and one population in a park was extirpated (probably by mortality of turtles venturing outside the park). In some areas, the field delineation of wetlands under the state Freshwater Wetlands Act resulted in regulatory wetland boundaries smaller than the actual wetland boundaries.

Planners make decisions about the selection and configuration of development sites as well as the conservation of special habitats on or near them. Decisions are often made with incomplete information about the impacts of proposed land use on rare species. Planning procedures at the county and state level should incorporate the complex habitat requirements of the Blanding's turtle within the known historical or potential range of the species (Kiviat, 1993). Because it is likely that there are additional unknown site envelopes in the landscape, sites for proposed developments should first be assessed for this species. If one accepts a 1,000 m radius around a site envelope as a necessary conservation component (this may be conservative), then it follows that this same radial distance, when drawn around a proposed development site, would include all potential Blanding's wetlands possibly affected by the project. As known site envelopes contain 10–50+ adult turtles, the planning process should provide for corridors to enable genetic contact between them, possibly through use of existing landforms. To assess a proposed development site in western Dutchess County, I recommend the following procedures:

A. Locate all wetlands within 1,000 m of the proposed development if they occur near gravelly or sandy soils, especially those of the Hoosic series, by consulting soil maps (Dutchess County Soil and Water Conservation District, Millbrook, New York), topographic maps (U.S. Geological Survey, Reston, Virginia), National Wetland Inventory maps (U.S. Fish and Wildlife Service, Washington, D.C.), State Freshwater Wetlands maps (New York State Department of Environmental Conservation, New Paltz, New York), state bedrock and surficial geology maps (Fisher et al., 1970; Cadwell, 1989), and aerial photos. Field sampling may be necessary to confirm soil type.

B. Assess the suitability of potential Blanding's turtle habitats according to vegetation structure and other significant physical characteristics (under **Pools** section of this paper and Figure 1). These assessments can be made to some degree at any time of the year.

C. Confirm the presence of Blanding's turtles during the spring when they are most active (early May to mid-June). Binoculars are useful for visual inspection of ponds, and live trapping should be employed to capture adults. Trapping should occur for five continuous 24-hour periods during mild weather (when water surface or neuston reaches 26°C). Twenty-five or more baited commercial funnel-type turtle traps may be necessary to cover all suitable habitat within 1,000 m of the proposed site.

D. Plan to conserve and protect Blanding's turtles and their habitat within or near the proposed development. Techniques to achieve this goal include the following:

1. Maintain suitable hydrologic, chemical, and vegetational conditions of the wetlands.

2. Restrict road construction and employ other vehicle management within 1,000 m of known Blanding's turtle habitat and the migration corridors. Mitigating features of necessary roadways could include speed bumps and low speed limits, "Turtle Crossing" signs, a restriction of curbing, and the covering of open drains.

3. Eliminate or mitigate direct hazards or barriers to dispersal, such as abandoned swimming pools or foundations, soil pits and ditches, and stone walls.

4. Consider other planning and mitigation options as new information about nesting areas, drought refuges, and hatchling habitat becomes available.

5. Investigate the potential to create or improve wetland habitat for Blanding's turtles.

Known site envelopes (including all springtime habitats) range from 9 to 65 ha (mean = 34 ha) in size (Table 2). The addition of the 1,000 m radius believed necessary to accommodate most terrestrial activity of turtles results in an area requirement encompassing 4–8 km^2. Larger site envelopes may be defined as habitat information improves. If metapopulation dynamics and connecting corridors are considered, the landscape necessary to support the species could easily encompass 10–20 km^2.

CONCLUSION

Conservation of species and management strategies must increasingly consider the heterogeneity of habitat complexes in order to ensure viability of populations. Because it is now apparent that conservation of Blanding's turtle will require large preserves, appropriate planning should attempt to strike a balance between this need and the development projected for Dutchess County. It is important to recognize that the habitat analysis procedures and planning process outlined above will also identify areas where Blanding's turtles are not present. Known and potential Blanding's turtle habitat can be proactively mapped, and potential land buyers can be notified in advance that certain sites are habitat for a threatened species, which may have consequent land use conflicts. Compatible activities in a Blanding's reserve include some types of farming, forestry, hunting, fishing, and many other types of outdoor recreation. Land acquisition and use of conservation easements may be essential to protect key habitats and buffer areas, and various types of zoning could be employed to protect not only habitat features but also amenity values such as scenery, aquifer protection, and public open space.

ACKNOWLEDGMENTS

I gratefully acknowledge assistance from The Nature Conservancy; New York State Department of Environmental Conservation; New York State Office of Parks, Recreation and Historic Preservation; U.S. National Park Service; Bard College Library; land owners, persons reporting tagged turtles, assistants in the field and laboratory, and other field workers; and Gretchen Stevens, Jerry C. Jenkins, Michael W. Klemens, Al Breisch, Marla Emrich Briggs, Peter J. Petokas, Rebecca Miller, Peter Groffman, and Peter Keibel. Research was conducted under New York State Department of Environmental Conservation permits. Financial support came from individual donors; technical assistance clients; The Nature Conservancy; New York State Office of Parks, Recreation and Historic Preservation; the Norcross Wildlife Foundation; U.S. National Park Service; International Business Machines; and a 1993 Cary Summer Research Fellowship from the Institute of Ecosystem Studies. This paper is also Bard College Field Station—Hudsonia Contribution 63.

LITERATURE CITED

Cadwell, D. H. (ed.) 1989. Surficial geologic map of New York. New York State Museum, Map and Chart Series 40. 5 sheets, 1:250,000, 100 ft contour.

Conant, R. and J. T. Collins. 1991. A Field Guide to Reptiles and Amphibians: Eastern and Central North America. 3rd ed. Houghton Mifflin Co., Boston. 450 pp.

Emrich, M. E. 1991. Blanding's turtle (*Emydoidea blandingii*) nesting behavior and response to an artificial nest habitat. M.S. thesis, Bard College, Annandale, New York. 67 pp.

Fisher, D. W., Y. W. Isachsen, and L. V. Rickard. 1970. Geologic map of New York 1970. New York State Museum and Science Service, Map and Chart Series 15. 5 sheets, 1:250,000, 100 ft contour.

Kiviat, E. 1993. A tale of two turtles: Conservation of the Blanding's turtle and bog turtle. News from Hudsonia 9(3):1–6.

Klemens, M. W., R. P. Cook, and D. J. Hayes. 1992. Herpetofauna of Roosevelt-Vanderbilt National Historic Sites Hyde Park, New York, with emphasis on Blanding's turtle (*Emydoidea blandingii*). U.S. National Park Service Technical Report NPS/NAROSS/NRTR-92-08. 34 pp.

Tornes, L. A. 1979. Soil Survey of Ulster County, New York. U.S. Department of Agriculture, Soil Conservation Service. 273 pp. + maps.

TABLE 2
Characteristics of five Blanding's turtle sites in Dutchess County, New York, USA. ("Pools" refers to springtime habitat units.)

Site	Pool elevation (m)	Bedrock geology[a]	Surficial geology[a]	Site envelope area[b] (ha)	Length by width[b] (m)	Pools[b]	Site envelope + activity range[b,c] (km²)
A	98–101	shale, argillite, siltstone, chert	outwash	47	1900 × 300	5	8
B	72	sandstone, shale	bedrock, outwash	18	500 × 400	6	5
C	116	dolostone or limestone	outwash	9	300 × 350	4	4
D	117–125	shale?, quartzite	till[a]	31	1200 × 300	4	6
E	94–96	shale, argillite, siltstone	outwash	65	1600 × 550	5	7

[a] From Fisher et al. (1970), Cadwell (1989), and Kiviat (pers. obs.). Site D appears to be partly outwash though mapped as till. [b] Additional, apparently suitable pools present at all sites may be used by Blanding's turtles regularly or occasionally, but data are not available. Pool numbers, site envelopes, and activity ranges will be larger if the use of additional pools is confirmed. [c] Approximate extent of site envelope plus activity range (1,000 m extension of site envelope in all directions).

Identification of Wood Turtle Nesting Areas for Protection and Management

RICHARD R. BUECH,[1] LYNELLE G. HANSON,[2] AND MARK D. NELSON[3]

[1] USDA Forest Service, Forestry Sciences Lab, 183 Highway 169 East, Grand Rapids, MN 55744, USA
[e-mail: buech002@maroon.tc.umn.edu] [2] 710 High St., Duluth, MN 55805-1135, USA
[3] USDA, Forest Service, North Central Forest Experiment Station, 1992 Folwell Ave., St. Paul, Minnesota 55108, USA

ABSTRACT: The wood turtle, *Clemmys insculpta*, is a long-lived, semi-aquatic, riverine species that inhabits forested regions of the northcentral and northeastern United States and adjacent regions of Canada. Many states list the wood turtle as "Endangered" or "Threatened," and it is now listed on Appendix II of the Convention on International Trade in Endangered Species (CITES). In this paper, we examine the hypothesis that nesting areas are critical determinants of wood turtle occurrence in northern portions of its range. We measured six habitat variables at 334 nesting sites and used those data to develop criteria that define suitable nesting areas. Our study demonstrated that wood turtles in the Upper Great Lakes Region prefer nesting areas that are near water, very sandy, elevated, bare, and well exposed to solar radiation. Using a geographic information system (GIS), we designed a model that used sandy soil and stream spatial data to locate potential wood turtle nesting areas. The accuracy of the model was evaluated using three methods: aerial photographic interpretation, aerial survey, and ground survey. The ground survey confirmed that all wood turtles and nearly all potential nesting areas meeting the criteria were located near river reaches predicted by the GIS to have potential for producing nesting areas. Aerial photographic interpretation yielded unacceptably poor information, while the aerial survey was acceptable for identifying major nesting areas.

Geologic factors most likely determine the local distribution of wood turtles. In glaciated portions of their range, the historic distribution of wood turtles was probably correlated with the soils from glacial outwash plains. Because these soils occur in isolated patches, wood turtle populations have probably always occurred in disjunct segments. However, human activity has altered the availability of sand and gravel, which in turn may have altered the local distribution of wood turtles. Wood turtles are vulnerable to loss or degradation of their nesting areas from streambank stabilization, channelization, damming, and dredging programs. Thus, it is essential that resource managers identify and protect this element of critical habitat. Because nesting areas are a landscape feature, a partnership of private and public entities is required to effectively manage wood turtles in entire watersheds.

The wood turtle, *Clemmys insculpta*, is a long-lived, semi-aquatic, riverine species that inhabits forested regions of the northcentral and northeastern United States and adjacent regions in Canada. Many states list the wood turtle as "Endangered" or "Threatened," and it is now listed on Appendix II of the Convention on International Trade in Endangered Species (CITES). Numerous hypotheses have been offered to explain the apparent decline of wood turtles: loss of aquatic and riparian habitats through channelization, damming, dredging, streambank stabilization, and general urban and agricultural development; pollution and pesticides; mortality from vehicles; increase in density and/or expansion of the range of important predators such as raccoons (*Procyon lotor*), striped skunks (*Mephitis mephitis*), and opossums (*Didelphis marsupialis*); commercial collection for the pet trade, biological supply houses, and food; and recreationists shooting or taking them for pets (Harding and Bloomer, 1979; Buech et al., 1991; Harding, 1991; Buech, 1992; Kaufmann, 1992; Garber and Burger, this volume).

From a study of the habitat requirements and reproductive success of wood turtles in northeastern Minnesota (Buech et al., 1990, 1991, 1993; Buech, 1992), we obtained information suggesting that wood turtles have very specific nesting requirements: very sandy, elevated, bare sites that were well exposed to the sun. This suggested that we could develop a simple model using only soil and hydrologic factors to predict where suitable nesting areas might occur in a watershed. Physiographic conditions conducive to the creation of suitable nesting areas appear uncommon and unevenly distributed in our region. Appropriate nesting areas may therefore be critical determinants of the occurrence of wood turtles, which would make identification, protection, and management of such areas crucial.

In this paper, we examine the hypothesis that nesting areas are critical determinants of the occurrence of wood turtles in the northern portions of their range. Our objectives were to (1) develop a set of criteria that describes a suitable nesting area for wood turtles in the Upper Great Lakes

Region, (2) develop and test a model that predicts which stream reaches are conducive to creating suitable nesting areas, and (3) compare the efficacy of three methods for locating nesting areas.

METHODS

To describe a suitable wood turtle nesting area, we measured six habitat variables: soil substrate (gravel, sand, sandy loam, etc.), slope (degrees), aspect (16-point compass), elevation above water (meters), distance to water (meters), and vegetative cover (percent cover). We measured these habitat variables at all wood turtle nests encountered during the 1990, 1991, and 1993 nesting seasons on three major nesting areas: an abandoned sand and gravel operation (n = 146), a large cutbank (n = 95), and an abandoned railroad grade (n = 93). Some areas did not provide a full range of conditions for all habitat variables (see Table 1). But collectively, these large nesting areas provided a broad range of possible habitat conditions. Sample sizes for analyses of nest site attributes were always less than the total sample of 334 nest sites because some data were missing for each habitat variable.

To meet our second objective, we tested the nesting area hypothesis on a relatively little-known segment of the St. Louis River between Seven Beavers Lake and Cloquet, Minnesota, a distance of 253 km. Using a geographic information system (GIS), the model was constructed with two digital sources of information: a U.S. Geological Survey (1: 250,000) topographic map of the St. Louis River watershed and a draft geomorphology map of St. Louis County created by the U.S. Natural Resources Conservation Service. The hydrology component of the model was based on the following premise: We assumed that under historic conditions, wood turtles nested on sandy points on inside turns of streams or on cutbanks on outside turns. Such features are usually created and maintained during episodic flooding in medium-size or larger stream reaches. Thus, we considered only stream orders (Horton, 1945; Strahler, 1957) size 3 or larger as likely to have sufficient hydraulic force to create wood turtle nesting areas. We considered the following characteristics as desirable for the geomorphic component of the model: glacial outwash plain, high sand content, and some topographic relief. Based on these attributes, we classified "Big Rice Outwash Plain" and "Brimson Outwash Plain" as having high potential of producing wood turtle nesting areas; "Upper St. Louis Valley Outwash," "Leora Lake Outwash Plain," and "Upham Basin Till Plain" as medium; "Lake Upham Sands" as low; and the remaining geomorphic classes as having low to zero potential for producing suitable nesting areas. A simple overlay of these hydrology and geomorphology data layers produced a map that predicted the nesting potential of various reaches of the St. Louis River.

The next step was to field test the model predictions. If our hypothesis is correct, we should find both potential nesting areas and wood turtles themselves in direct relation to habitat quality class; the higher the class, the more nesting areas and wood turtles we could expect to find. To meet the third objective, we evaluated the model using three methods: aerial photographic interpretation, aerial survey, and ground survey.

Aerial Photographic Interpretation

This method used aerial photographic interpretation of black-and-white infrared photos (1:15,840) to identify potential nesting areas on the test segment of the St. Louis River. The interpreter searched stereoscopic photo pairs for potential nesting areas on cutbanks (outside bends), sandy points (inside bends), islands, road beds (both railroad and highway) and utility rights-of-way at crossings, and gravel or borrow pits. Each potential nesting area was labeled on a map and classified by type (bank, point, island, gravel pit, and highway, railroad, or utility rights-of-way) and size (small, medium, and large) classes. A small nesting area was defined as having an area of 5–50 m² (in aerial views, size appears to be between that of a car and a two-car garage), a medium nesting area was 51–200 m² (between that of a two-car garage and 1⅓ times the size of a standard 7.3 × 14.6 m ranch style home), and a large nesting area was >200 m² (size appears larger than 1⅓ times the size of a standard ranch style home).

Aerial Survey

In this method, a pilot, navigator, and observer in a fixed-wing plane identified potential nesting areas on the same test segment of the St. Louis River. The observer was responsible for spotting potential nesting areas, classifying those that met minimum standards by type and size (using the same definitions given above), and assigning them identification numbers. The navigator was responsible for locating and labeling potential nesting areas on a map. The aerial survey was conducted 16 October 1992, timed so that it occurred after leaf fall when water levels were normal, and during the period 9 A.M. to 3 P.M. so as to minimize strong shadows. The observer had not participated in the ground survey.

Ground Survey

The ground survey served as the control. Two-person crews canoed the test segment of the St. Louis River to locate potential nesting areas. Each area was assigned an identification number and classified using the same type and size classes as in the two aerial methods. We also recorded soil substrate (silt, fine sand, coarse sand, gravel), slope (nearest 10 degrees), aspect (16-point compass), minimum and maximum elevation above water (meters), vegetative cover (percent cover by class in 10% increments), and presence of wood turtle nests destroyed by predators.

Wood turtles occur in both aquatic and terrestrial habitats, depending on seasonal, diurnal, and weather-related factors (Harding and Bloomer, 1979; Farrel and Graham, 1991; Kaufman, 1992). We recorded the following data on any wood turtle captured: identification number, new or recapture, sex, age, location (in water or on land), and distance from shoreline (Table 2). We conducted a systematic search for wood turtles in both aquatic and terrestrial habitats. The search was conducted on the side of the river that seemed to have the better basking habitat (less tree cover, sunnier). One person searched terrestrial habitat between 0 and 20 m from the river's edge, for a distance of approximately 160 m. The second person searched aquatic habitat along the same 160 m of shoreline. The search was conducted at regular intervals: every 0.8 km in high- or medium-quality habitat and every 3.2 km in low-quality or unlikely habitat. To increase the chance of encountering turtles, we conducted the ground survey when wood turtle activity is concentrated in and along riverine habitat, from 16 September to 1 October (1991). Unfortunately, we encountered cold and cloudy weather while canoeing reaches predicted to have high or medium-quality wood turtle habitat. We therefore resurveyed the much longer, medium-quality habitat segment in spring (18–22 May 1992), when the chance of encountering wood turtles should be even greater than in fall.

TABLE 1
Range of habitat conditions found on three nesting areas of *Clemmys insculpta*. Six habitat variables were measured to define a suitable wood turtle nesting area. SM = an abandoned sand and gravel operation; CB = a large cutbank; RR = an abandoned railroad grade.

Habitat variable	Nesting areas SM n = 146	CB n = 95	RR n = 93
Substrate (gravel, sand, sandy loam)	All	All	All
Slope (degrees)	0–45	0–50	0–40
Aspect (16-point compass)	All	ESE-SW	All
Elevation above water (m)	0–9	0–6	0–5
Distance to water (m)	0–100+	0–9	0–100+
Vegetative cover (%)	0–100	0–100	0–100

TABLE 2
Wood turtles captured during ground surveys of the St. Louis River in northeastern Minnesota in fall 1991 and spring 1992. Wood turtles were found either during systematic searches (Yes), or while we were casually canoeing (No). Distance class to shore when the turtle was first seen in the water is given within parenthesis. Distance class to shore when the turtle was first seen on land is given without parenthesis.

Date	I.D. No.	Sex	Age (years)	Systematic search zone?	Location	Distance to shore (m)	Temperature Air °C	Water °C	Cloud cover (%)
F 91	127	F	20+	No	Water	(2–0)	15	16	81–100
F 91	*	?	?	Yes	Water	(2–0)	14	16	81–100
F 91	200	M	20+	Yes	Land	2–10	11	16	81–00
F 91	125	M	20+	Yes	Water	(2–0)	16	18	0–20
S 92	129	F	20+	Yes	Land	2–10	23	17	0–20
S 92	128	?	4	Yes	Land	0–2	24	16	0–20
S 92	130	?	4	Yes	Land	2–10	25	17	0–20
S 92	131	F	20+	Yes	Land	2–10	26	17	0–20
S 92	134	?	2	Yes	Land	2–10	26	19	0–20
S 92	133	?	3	No	Land	0–2	26	19	0–20

* This turtle avoided capture.

RESULTS

Criteria for Suitable Nesting Areas

The substrates of 331 nests were evenly distributed between sand and sandy gravel. A contour plot of the density distribution of 270 nest sites with respect to slope and aspect (excluding nests where slope and aspect were zero) revealed an interaction (Figure 1). Where slope was low, aspects were distributed in all compass directions. However, at slopes equal to or exceeding 20°, southerly aspects within the range ESE–SW dominated (150 of 164 nests on slopes ≥20°). The greatest slope we encountered at any nest site was 40°.

Elevation above water also seemed important (Figure 2). Of 329 nests, none was located less than 1 m above water, and few (7%) were located <2 m above water. Most nests (86%) were located 2–5 m above water at a point where bank-full water level was about 1 m above the base-flow level.

Distance from the main river channel for 247 nests was skewed to shorter distances (Figure 3). Half of the nests were located 0–10 m from the main channel, and approximately one fourth were located more than 40 m away. This pattern is further exaggerated if distance is measured simply to the nearest open water. Using this measure, we found that 84% of 330 nests were located 0–10 m from the nearest open water, while only 5% of nests were located 50 m or more away. We found only six nests 100 m or more from water—the most distant at 151 m. Nesting sites on the cutbank, created by natural processes, were available only within 10 m of water. Thus, we analyzed nest sites on human-created nesting areas separately to determine whether females actually preferred sites close to water (these areas provided a full range of distances from water). Still, 78% of 236 nest sites were located within 10 m of water (Figure 4). A contingency table analysis of the distribution of nest sites with respect to distance from water by 10 m categories yielded highly significant differences when compared to a uniform distribution. We obtained $X^2 = 493.5$, $P = <0.001$ for a 2 × 5 table and $X^2 = 71.6$, $P = <0.001$ for a 2 × 2 table, e.g., 0–10 vs. >10 m. These data strongly suggest that females prefer to nest close to water.

The distribution of nests with respect to vegetative cover was strongly skewed to the low-cover categories (Figure 5). Approximately 35% of 327 nests had no vegetative cover in the vicinity of the nest, 72% had 0–10% vegetative cover, and 93% had 0–20% vegetative cover. Only two nests had more than 50% vegetative cover. Combining the above information, we produced a minimum set of criteria for defining a suitable nesting area for wood turtles in the Upper Great Lakes Region (Figure 6).

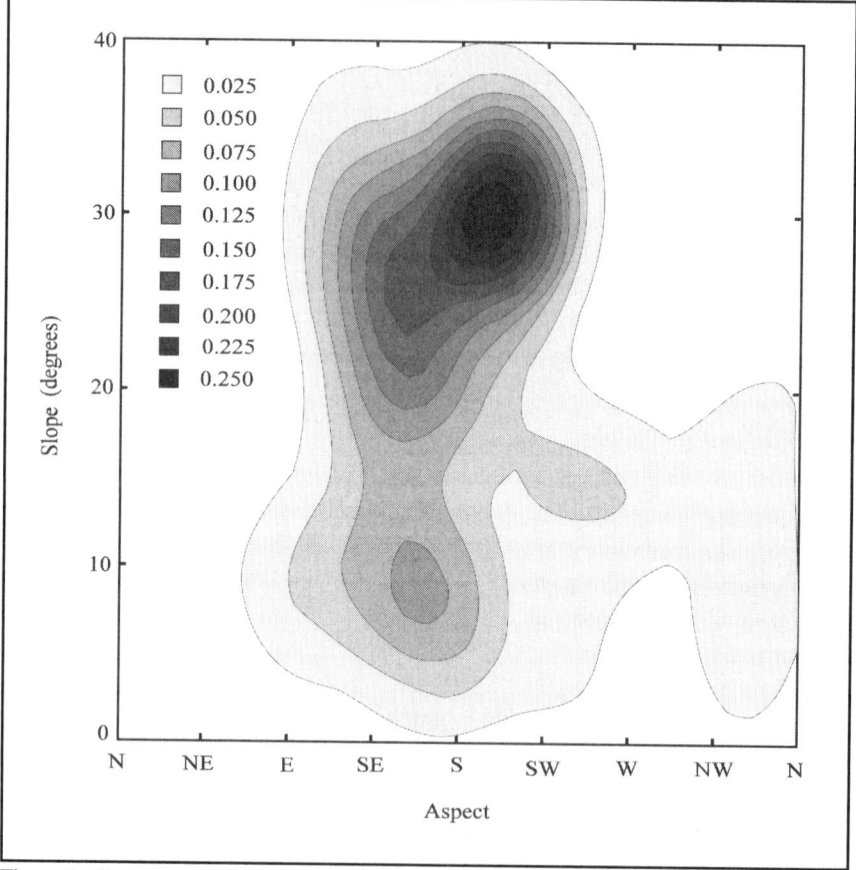

Figure 1. Contour plot of the density distribution of 270 wood turtle nest sites classified by slope and aspect. Nest sites with a slope and aspect of 0 were excluded. Density estimation used the bivariate nonparametric kernel (Silverman, 1986). Shading indicates nest site density; the darker the shading, the greater the proportion of total observations found in that nest site density class.

Evaluation of Nesting Area Model

The GIS model classified 3.2 km of the test segment of the St. Louis River as having high potential value for producing wood turtle nesting areas, 75.6 km as medium, and the remaining 173.8 km as having low or insignificant potential value. The ground survey identified 24 potential wood turtle nesting areas. About 90% of these nesting areas (21 of 24) were found in medium-quality habitat. A Fisher's Exact Test ($P < .0001$, df = 2, FI = 28.8) rejected the null hypothesis expectation that nesting areas would be distributed in proportion to the availability of habitat by class. The three nesting areas found in habitat classified as having unlikely potential were located about 5, 13, and 19 river km

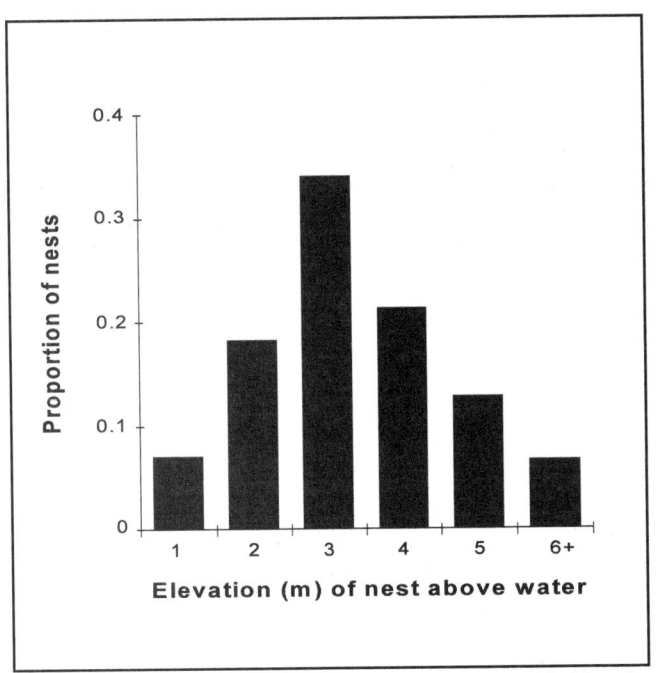

Figure 2. Distribution of 329 wood turtle nest sites classified by elevation above water in 1 m class intervals.

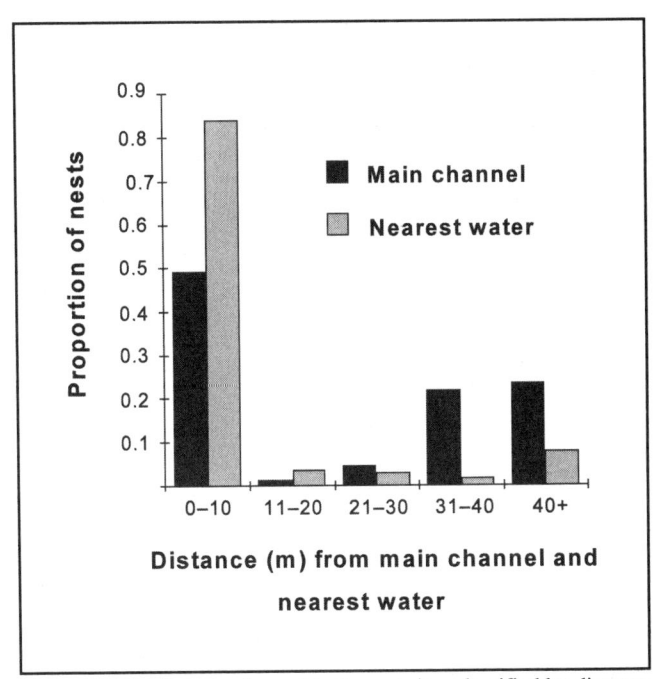

Figure 3. Distribution of wood turtle nest sites classified by distance to the main river channel (n = 247) and distance to the nearest water (n = 330), in 10 m class intervals.

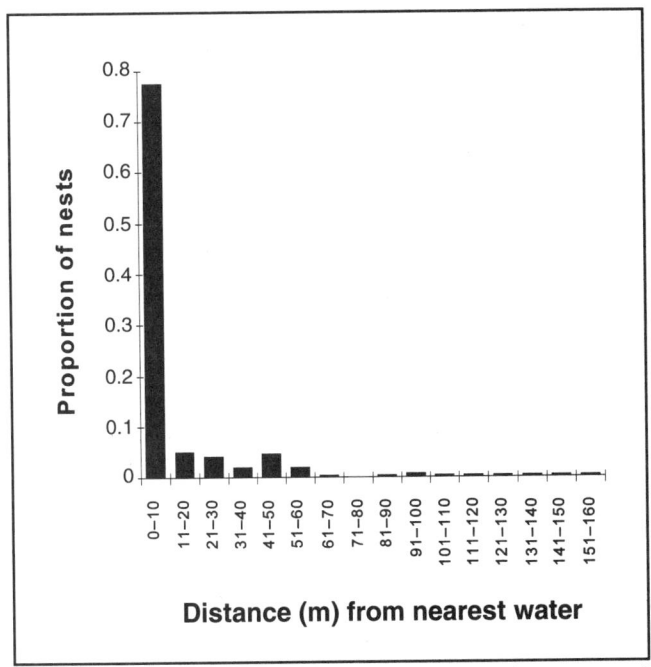

Figure 4. Distribution of 236 wood turtle nest sites on human-created nesting areas classified by distance to the nearest water in 10 m class intervals.

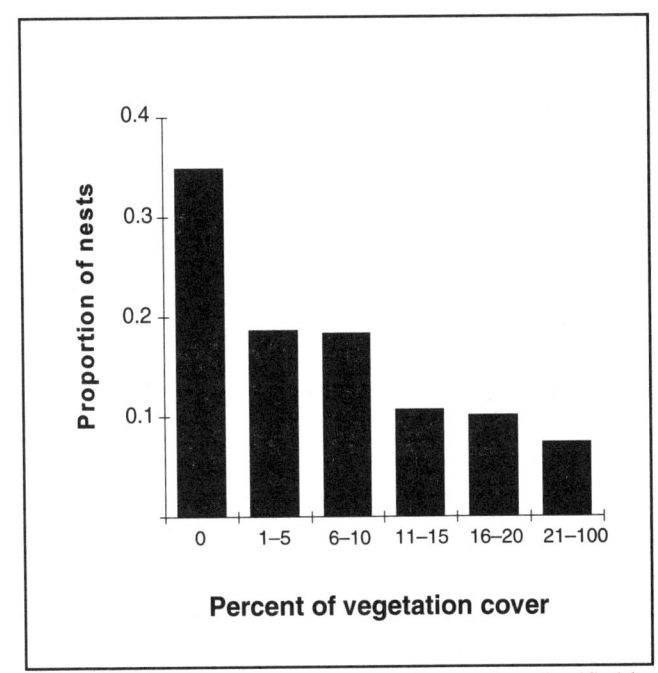

Figure 5. Distribution of 327 wood turtle nest sites classified by cover of vegetation in percent.

from the boundary of medium-potential habitat. However, on a straight-line basis, the 5 km nesting area was located only 1.1 km from the boundary, and the 13 and 19 km nesting areas were located 1.7 and 3.6 km, respectively, from nearby low-potential habitat.

Another measure of the adequacy of the model is the occurrence of wood turtles themselves. We found only four wood turtles during the fall ground survey; all were located in medium-quality habitat. A Fisher's Exact Test ($P < .02$, df = 2, FI = 8.9) rejected the null hypothesis expectation

TABLE 3
Number of potential wood turtle nesting areas classified by type and size using three methods: aerial photo interpretation, aerial survey, and ground survey.

Type and size class of potential nesting areas	Aerial Photo Interpretation – Number of nest areas	Aerial Photo Interpretation – Number correctly classified	Aerial Survey – Number of nest areas	Aerial Survey – Number correctly classified	Ground Survey – Number of nest areas	Ground Survey – Number not identified by other methods
Bank						
Large	11	0	4	1+2*	1	0
Medium	30	0	8	0	3	1
Small	1	0	4	1	2	1
Point						
Large	15	0	1	1	1	0
Medium	56	1*	9	2*	0	0
Small	9	0	6	4	16	9
Island or sand bar						
Large	5	0	0	0	0	0
Medium	12	0	2	0	0	0
Small	3	0	1	0	0	0
Highway right-of-way						
Large	2	0	0	0	0	0
Medium	15	1*	0	0	0	0
Small	0	0	1	1	1	0
Utility right-of-way						
Large	4	0	0	0	0	0
Medium	1	0	0	0	0	0
Small	0	0	0	0	0	0
Gravel pit						
Large	0	0	3	0	0	0
Medium	0	0	0	0	0	0
Small	0	0	0	0	0	0
Total	164	2	39	12	24	11

*Correctly classified by type of nesting area, but size misclassified one class too large.

that wood turtles would be distributed in proportion to the availability of habitat by class. The resurvey of habitat classified as medium the following spring occurred under much better weather conditions but still yielded only six wood turtles. Several points are worth noting about wood turtle observations (Table 2). Of the ten wood turtles found in both fall and spring, only two were found off the systematic search segments. In contrast to the results of the fall survey, four of the six captures in spring were very young turtles. Furthermore, weather in spring was clear and warm, which produced a high contrast in air and water temperatures. With one exception, we found wood turtles on land when the air temperature exceeded water temperature and in the water when the water temperature exceeded air temperature. Wood turtles found in water were all close to shore (0–2 m). Despite our search of terrestrial habitat between 0 and 20 m from the shoreline, all wood turtles found on land were found within 10 m of shore, and half of these were found within 2 m of water. On an area basis, including only habitat where we found wood turtles (0–2 m in water and 0–10 m on land), the capture density of wood turtles was 0.22 wood turtles per ha of habitat for fall 1991 and 0.33 wood turtles per ha for spring 1992.

sons in fall 1991. If we assume salaries of $10 per hour and a plane at $125 per hour, the costs are $175 for conducting the aerial photo interpretation, $725 for the aerial survey, and $3,200 for the ground survey. (No costs were incurred for the aerial photographs, which were borrowed for this project.)

CRITERIA FOR SUITABLE NESTING AREA

- **SUBSTRATE:** Sand or gravel
- **SLOPE:** < 40°
- **ASPECT:** If slope < 20°, any aspect is OK; If slope > 20°, aspect is ESE to WSW
- **ELEVATION:** > 1 meter above normal water level
- **VEGETATION COVER:** < 20% ground vegetation; height of woody vegetation < distance to southern edge of nesting area
- **DISTANCE TO WATER** Close
- **DISTURBANCE:** Low

Figure 6. Summary of criteria for defining a suitable wood turtle nesting area in the Upper Great Lakes Region.

Efficacy of the Three Methods

The number of wood turtle nesting areas correctly classified by aerial methods was low (Table 3). Aerial photographic interpretation identified 164 potential nesting areas, but only two were correctly classified as nesting areas and both of these were misclassified as one size too large. Thus, aerial photographic interpretation yielded a large number of false positives (n = 162) while only correctly identifying two of the 24 nesting areas that met minimum criteria. Accuracy of the aerial survey was better but still poor. It yielded fewer false positives (n = 27) and correctly identified 12 of the 24 nesting areas, but four of the 12 were misclassified as to size. Of the 11 nesting areas located in the ground survey that were not identified by aerial methods, 10 were small.

Cost of the three methods differed greatly. Aerial photo interpretation took 17.5 hours and the aerial survey took even less time: five hours of air time for two persons. The ground survey took the most time: two weeks for four per-

DISCUSSION

Criteria for Suitable Nesting Areas

Wood turtles have been reported to nest in a variety of habitats including meadows, hay and corn fields, open and sparsely vegetated fields, forest openings, elevated railroad beds, road embankments, and high banks on streams (Carroll and Ehrenfeld, 1978; Harding and Bloomer, 1979; Farrell and Graham, 1991; Harding, 1991; Kaufmann, 1992). In our study we observed wood turtles nesting on natural features such as sandbars, sandy points, and cutbanks along streams as well as areas of human origin including sand and gravel pits, railroad and road beds, and utility rights-of-way (Buech et al., 1991; Buech, 1992; Buech et al., 1993).

Despite the variety of habitats used by wood turtles for nesting, they have some characteristics in common. Characteristics of nesting areas noted in the literature include within 100–200 m of water; sandy loam, sand, sandy gravel, and gravel soils; well-drained workable soil not prone to flooding; areas exposed to direct sunlight; and almost bare soil (Carroll and Ehrenfeld, 1978; Harding and Bloomer, 1979; Tyning, 1990; Farrell and Graham, 1991; Harding, 1991; Kaufmann, 1992). The quantitative criteria we used to characterize wood turtle nesting areas (Figure 6) are consistent with the qualitative descriptions listed above. Our females clearly chose to nest exclusively on sites with sand or sandy gravel soils, with little or no vegetation, and exposed to direct sunlight. They showed a preference for the upper half of southerly aspects on slopes between 20° and 40°. They also chose sites close to water, but at least 1 m above water. In short, wood turtles prefer nesting areas that are generally very sandy, bare, well exposed to solar radiation, and close to water but elevated. These characteristics are consistent with areas likely to be created and maintained by natural disturbance processes operating with riverine habitat. However, well-exposed nest areas occur infrequently on the landscape. Thus, the distribution of wood turtles in northern regions is probably constrained by the availability of nesting areas.

Evaluation of Nesting Area Model

Virtually all areas meeting our criteria were either located on reaches of the St. Louis River classified as having medium potential for producing nesting areas or located near habitat classified as medium or low. Although we anticipated a degree of error, the three potential nesting areas located outside of expected regions appeared near the boundaries of appropriate geomorphic types. The fact that we captured wood turtles only within medium-potential habitat further supports our belief that the nesting area model performed well. Overall, the results for the nesting area model support our contention that in the Upper Great Lakes Region, the occurrence of wood turtles is dependent upon the occurrence of nesting areas, which is dependent upon the juxtaposition of very sandy soils with rivers of appropriate size.

Efficacy of the Three Methods

The least expensive method was aerial photographic interpretation, but it produced the least reliable information. The major problem was distinguishing between sand and grass. Numerous grass openings were falsely classified as potential nesting areas, although accuracy could be expected to improve with experience. Another problem with aerial photographs is uncertainty about water levels. Suitable nesting areas could be missed or rejected if photos were taken at high water levels. Conversely, unsuitable nesting areas could be classified suitable if photos were taken at low water levels. Ground surveys yield the best information, but are most expensive and labor intensive. Aerial surveys provide a compromise; they are intermediate in cost and quality of information (they tend to generate false positives, and to miss small nesting areas).

Management Applications

The performance of the nesting area model demonstrates the ultimate dependence of wood turtles on the occurrence of sand soils. It suggests that geologic factors limit the availability of nesting areas and thus the occurrence of wood turtles themselves. Furthermore, in the Upper Great Lakes Region, glaciation created heterogeneity in the spatial distribution of geomorphic types. Thus, we can expect the occurrence of wood turtles to be similarly distributed. Wood turtle populations in the Upper Great Lakes Region probably occur in short, disjunct river segments. This segmented distribution has implications not only for gene flow but also for our perception of the historic abundance of wood turtles. Because of their dependence on sand soils, wood turtles in the Upper Great Lakes Region were probably never uniformly distributed, but were locally abundant in patches of optimal habitat.

There is a caveat in using this model to predict the current distribution of wood turtles: Human activity has altered the availability of both sand and gravel throughout the region, and it has introduced new disturbance processes that can create or eliminate suitable nesting areas. Prior to human influence, nesting areas were probably created and maintained primarily during high water events on third-order or higher streams that intersected sandy soils. These events create and maintain bare cutbanks on outside turns and sand bars on inside points, some of which would be suitable for wood turtle nesting areas. In recent times, human activity has created additional nesting areas in the form of gravel road or railroad beds, utility rights-of-way, gravel pits, and agricultural fields near streams. However, human activity has also eliminated nesting areas through streambank restoration, dams, dredging, and channelization (Harding and Bloomer, 1979; Harding, 1991; Buech, 1992; Kaufmann, 1992; Buech et al., 1993). This activity has probably changed the current distribution of suitable nesting areas and, ultimately, may have affected the distribution of wood turtles throughout the region.

The relative scarcity of wood turtles and their specific nesting requirements strongly suggest a need to identify and protect their nesting areas. The performance of the nesting area model and the results of our study of the efficacy of aerial and ground survey methods open new opportunities for managing their nesting areas. First, we recommend that managers use soils and hydrology maps to identify stream reaches where wood turtle nesting areas may occur. Attention should be focused on stream reaches that meander, which are far more likely to possess nesting areas than straight reaches. Alternatively, third- or higher-order stream segments that intersect areas of red pine (*Pinus resinosa*) and especially jack pine (*Pinus banksiana*) are good indicators of the potential occurrence of wood turtle nesting areas in our region. Once such segments are identified, they should be checked by air, canoe, and/or ground survey (depending on how much area one has to cover) to confirm whether suitable nesting areas are present. Aerial surveys provide an economical way of rapidly locating reaches containing nesting areas, especially larger nesting areas. Ground surveys can then be used to confirm potential sites identified from the air. We used a fixed-wing plane; a helicopter can be used for greater accuracy but at additional cost.

In our fall and spring ground surveys, we found only two wood turtles in segments not systematically searched (25% and 17% of captures, respectively). This suggests that systematic (rather than casual) surveys are preferable in confirming the presence of wood turtles. The presence of wood turtles may also be confirmed by visiting potential nesting areas in spring, shortly (1–2 weeks) before the nesting season. Adult females tend to stage near nesting areas during that season. The chance of finding wood turtles is increased when surveys are conducted during the spring nesting season, and if done systematically over time, could form the basis of a wood turtle monitoring program.

Conservation of nesting areas begins by identifying their geographic location. We then need to ensure that human activity does not degrade existing nesting areas. Streambank stabilization, channelization, dams, and recreation programs are particularly troublesome because they can severely degrade or eliminate wood turtle nesting areas. Managers should therefore ensure that there is an administrative process to review such programs for potential impact on wood turtle nesting areas. Because nesting areas are a landscape feature, it will require a partnership of private and public entities to effectively manage wood turtles across entire watersheds.

The importance of maintaining suitable nesting areas for this long-lived species must be emphasized. Managers should not be lulled into thinking that because adults are present, the population is doing well. Wood turtles commonly live 30 years or longer. If recruitment is inadequate, many years could pass before attrition would become evident in the population. The viability of wood turtle populations is already a concern because of direct and indirect impacts of human activity. Loss of nesting areas would exacerbate the problem. Thus, nesting areas should be considered an essential element in any management plan for viable wood turtle populations.

LITERATURE CITED

Buech, R. R. 1992. Streambank stabilization can impact wood turtle nesting areas. 54th Midwest Fish and Wildlife Conference, Abstract 190, p. 260. 6–9 December 1992, Toronto, Ontario.

Buech, R. R., M. D. Nelson, and B. J. Brecke. 1990. Wood turtle habitat use on the Cloquet River watershed in Minnesota. 52nd Midwest Fish and Wildlife Conference, Abstract 256, p. 292. 2–5 December 1990, Minneapolis, Minnesota.

Buech, R. R., M. D. Nelson, B. J. Brecke, and L. G. Hanson. 1991. Wood turtle habitat research. 53rd Midwest Fish and Wildlife Conference, Abstract W19, p. 228. 30 November–4 December 1991, Des Moines, Iowa.

Buech, R. R, L. G. Hanson, and M. D. Nelson. 1993. Is streambank stabilization a restoration? 55th Midwest Fish and Wildlife Conference, Abstract 194, p. 274. 11–15 December 1993, St. Louis, Missouri.

Carroll, T. E. and D. W. Ehrenfeld. 1978. Intermediate-range homing in the wood turtle. Copeia 1978:117–126.

Farrell, R. F. and T. E. Graham. 1991. Ecological notes on the turtle *Clemmys insculpta* in northwestern New Jersey. J. Herpetol. 25: 1–9.

Garber, S. D. and J. Burger. 1997. A twenty-year study documenting the relationship between turtle decline and human recreation (poster abstract). *In* J. Van Abbema (ed.), Proceedings: Conservation, Restoration, and Management of Tortoises and Turtles—An International Conference, p. 477. July 1993, State University of New York, Purchase. New York Turtle and Tortoise Society, New York.

Harding, J. H. and T. J. Bloomer. 1979. The wood turtle (*Clemmys insculpta*): A natural history. Bull. New York Herpetol. Soc. 15 (1):9–26.

Harding, J. H. 1991. A twenty year wood turtle study in Michigan: Implications for conservation. *In* K. R. Beaman, F. Caporaso, S. McKeown, and M. Graff (eds.), Proceedings of the First International Symposium on Turtles & Tortoises: Conservation and Captive Husbandry, pp. 31–35. August 1990, Chapman University, Orange, California; California Turtle & Tortoise Club and Chapman University.

Horton, R. E. 1945. Erosional development of streams and their drainage basins: Hydrophysical approach to quantitative morphology. Bull. Geological Society of America 56:275–370.

Kaufmann, J. H. 1992. Habitat use by wood turtles in central Pennsylvania. J. Herpetol. 26:315–321.

Silverman, B. W. 1986. Density Estimation for Statistics and Data Analysis. Chapman and Hall, London.

Strahler, A. N. 1957. Quantitative analysis of watershed geomorphology. Trans. Amer. Geophysical Union 38:913–920.

Tyning, T. 1990. A Guide to Amphibians and Reptiles. Little, Brown, and Company, Boston.

Transportation Corridor Impact Assessment: A Regulatory Process and an Associated Analytical Tool

ROBERT S. DE SANTO

De Leuw, Cather & Company, 290 Roberts St., East Hartford, CT 06118, USA [e-mail: Robert_Desanto@parsons.com]

ABSTRACT: Turtle conservation in the United States may be influenced by the "environmental assessment process," a cornerstone of the National Environmental Policy Act (NEPA). If wetlands are affected, the Clean Water Act requires a federal permit, over which the U. S. Army Corps of Engineers (USACOE) has jurisdiction. Accordingly, USACOE has published a "Highway Methodology," authored by its New England Division, which now guides the preparation of assessments required as part of its permit process in New England.

In practice, the regulatory processes for environmental protection in the United States have revealed a genuine conflict between socioeconomic and cultural resource preservation and environmental conservation. Project alternatives that may be preferred for cultural (i.e., social) resource management and protection are frequently the least desirable from a natural resource preservation perspective. Conversely, alternatives preferred from an environmental conservation perspective are often undesirable for socioeconomic and cultural reasons.

Emphasizing the function and value of habitats, especially wetlands and water courses, the Highway Methodology has been adapted with computer-aided drafting and design (CAD) and geographic information systems (GIS) to help describe complex natural and human environments so that a consensus may be built among developers, regulators, and the public when searching for project alternatives.

The Highway Methodology described in this paper was designed to be unbiased; it has been used to clarify impacts associated with large transportation-related projects (i.e., major railroads and highways). Examples of resource mapping and the checklists and forms used to guide assessments of wetland function and value are provided.

Regulation of large transportation corridor projects in the United States requires the development of methodologies to quantify and qualify both social (cultural) and natural (ecological) resources. Such assessments are intended to help weigh potential benefits and impacts associated with large-scale development projects. Environmental protection depends upon the practical application of environmental management, which draws upon science, engineering, socioeconomics, and law (De Santo, 1976).

However, enforcement of laws and regulations that preserve natural resources are often viewed as conflicting with socioeconomic and cultural resource management objectives. Environmental law is focused on environmental protection and stewardship, where the impacts are clearly quantifiable. Socioeconomic issues, however, generally do not provide as clear a means of comparing the costs and benefits. A wide range of technical proficiency is required to analyze these important issues, as summarized and reviewed by De Santo (1978); Miller (1982, 1990); and Palmisano (1989).

Conflicts may arise when projects are assessed in light of a variety of functions: cultural, economic, recreational, and environmental management objectives. Resolution of these conflicts is possible when the consideration of alternatives begins by following a scientific methodology, defining resources objectively and with standardized methods. This approach has been used to define resource values and propose protection strategies for wood turtles (*Clemmys insculpta*) and Blanding's turtles (*Emydoidea blandingii*) in two major New England highway corridor projects. Alternative highway layouts to protect these rare turtles and their habitat mosaic were required as an integral part of the decision-making process to permit these projects, including receiving crucial U.S. Army Corps of Engineers (USACOE) and Environmental Protection Agency permission to construct within wetland boundaries.

For example, a Department of the Army permit is likely to be required for proposed highway or railroad projects in the United States. Discharges of dredged or fill material into waters of the United States, including wetlands, require permits under Section 404 of the Clean Water Act. Coastal and certain inland projects may also require permits under Section 10 of the Rivers and Harbors Act, and these are required in addition to state and local permits. In 1987 the New England Division of the U.S. Army Corps of Engineers published its "Highway Methodology" (USACOE, 1993) as a means to integrate highway or railroad planning and design with the requirements of the crops permit regulations and the

National Environmental Policy Act, and with the Federal Highway Administration's funding requirements.

The Highway Methodology applies the principles of geographic and land-use overlaying (McHarg, 1969). In that process, maps of such resources as wetlands, soil types, habbitats, structures, roads, and other features of the landscape are combined. The composite picture illustrates the geography of landscape features, which helps reviewers make objective judgments about those resources and the impacts and benefits caused by using (i.e., changing or removing) these diverse features as part of a proposed project. The Highway Methodology is one defined and tested procedure to assemble resource characteristics required for USACOE environmental permits. Its principles organize and prioritize resources so that project planning (1) avoids impacts, (2) minimizes unavoidable impacts, and (3) provides for compensation for any minimized, yet still residual, impacts.

This approach to environmental management is important to all objectives of good environmental stewardship—including the conservation, management, and restoration of turtles. It guides a primary governmental environmental permit process (i.e., the USACOE Section 404 wetlands permit) which affects habitats and species both directly and indirectly. The better the analytical tools upon which it is based, the better it will support environmental stewardship, and the better it can help conserve, manage, and restore turtle populations.

The Highway Methodology continues to be tested and modified. It advocates the use of tools and methods that qualify and, to the extent practical, quantify major categories of environmental assessment; these data may then be used by the regulatory branch of the USACOE to make its permit determination. Although a primary concern of the USACOE is conservation of the functions and values of wetlands, it is also charged with weighing societal and other environmental issues such as community cohesion, socioeconomics, and habitat fragmentation. For the purpose of this paper, however, only the procedure recently adopted by the New England Division of the USACOE will be addressed, which deals with functions and values of wetlands, including those used by freshwater turtles in this region.

Itemized Functions and Values of Wetlands

Because they are a prominent natural resource, wetlands are a major emphasis of the Highway Methodology, which makes it strongly relevant to turtle conservation. The focus of this paper is on non-tidal wetlands and is largely dependent on literature reviewed earlier by Mitsch and Gosselink, 1986. Because wetlands are critical to both water quality and quantity and to wildlife and habitat stability, and are important recreational resources, they are a critical component of the Clean Water Act Section 404 regulatory agenda. Accordingly, they have been placed at the center of the Highway Methodology assessment protocol. Wetlands serve as living filters that help restore storm water by "digesting" or adsorbing pollutants, sediments, and nutrients (Hammer, 1990). These attributes increase the importance of considering wetland functions and values in the protection of habitat.

While largely consistent with the science and methods of the Wetland Evaluation Technique II (WET II), developed by a combined effort of the Federal Highway Administration, the Department of Interior, and the USACOE (Adamus et al., 1987), the present Highway Methodology diverges from WET II because it does not place any weighting factors on the checklists that rate the relative "importance" of one factor over others. For example, one may weight recreational use of a wetland as being twice as important as its function in flood flow alteration. Such subjective weighting is not used in the Highway Methodology. The purpose of this particular USACOE assessment procedure is three fold: (1) to report the presence or absence of 13 generally accepted wetland functions, (2) to report which one or more of these 13 functions are predominant in each wetland studied, and (3) to provide descriptive information, including photographs, which helps reviewers decide if they should conduct their own direct field inspections.

Figure 1 illustrates a form that guides wetland functions and values assessments. The top portion of the form reports the physiographic characteristics of the wetland, including its size, type, location in the watershed, habitat characteristics, aquatic and vegetative diversity, and anticipated impacts. The lower portion of the form lists specific functional characteristics of the wetland, annotated by numbers in the "Rationale Why" column. These reference numbers are used as a shorthand to identify specific and important characteristics from the accompanying checklists. Comments may be added for special emphasis, and a column is provided for an "Army Corps of Engineers (ACOE) Confidence Level" because the Corps requires its own certification of a level of confidence in the reported findings.

The "Principal Function(s)" column is used to identify dominant valuable functions. Space is provided at the bottom of the form for a narrative of the wetland to record unusual or noteworthy conditions, or to add comments helpful in defining unique aspects of the wetland being studied.

Following these procedures each wetland is evaluated for 13 possible functions and values all of which are derived from the literature (Golet, 1976; Larson, 1976; Ammann et al., 1986; Adamus et al., 1987; Larson et al., 1989; Ammann and Stone, 1991). That literature provides documentation of the functions being evaluated, thus helping to insure uniformity and objectivity in guiding field inspections. Each wetland is inspected and photographed to illustrate potential impact areas, unusual aspects of the wetland, or other significant features. A generalized sketch of each wetland is also prepared to summarize shape, vegetative interspersion, cover type, interconnections, number and types of inlets and outlets, cross-sections, bank height, open water, vegetation zonation, and the location of each photograph. The dominant plant species and observed wildlife or wildlife signs are also recorded. This information is collected in data files, an example of which is shown in Figure 2. The 13 functions and values are as follows:

I. Groundwater Interchange (Recharge/Discharge) — This function considers the potential for a wetland to serve as a groundwater recharge and/or discharge area.

Considerations/Qualifiers
1. Public or private wells occur downstream of the wetland.
2. Potential exists for public or private wells downstream of the wetland.
3. Wetland is underlain by stratified drift.
4. Gravel or sandy soils present in/or adjacent to the wetland.
5. Fragipan (a dense, brittle, high-silt, low-porosity subsoil that restricts roots) does not occur in the wetland.
6. Fragipan, impervious soils, or bedrock occur in the wetland.
7. Wetland is associated with a perennial or intermittent watercourse.
8. Signs of groundwater recharge are present.
9. Wetland is associated with a watercourse, but lacks a defined outlet or contains a constricted outlet.
10. Wetland contains only an outlet.
11. Groundwater quality of stratified drift aquifer within or downstream of the wetland meets drinking water standards.
12. Quality of water associated with the wetland is high.
13. Signs of groundwater discharge are present.
14. Water temperature suggests it is a discharge site.
15. Wetland shows signs of variable water levels.

II. Flood Flow Alternation (Storage and Desynchronization) — This function considers the effectiveness of the wetland in reducing flood damage and water retention over long periods, adding to the stability of the wetland ecological system or its buffering characteristics to provide social or economic value relative to erosion and/or flood-prone areas.

Considerations/Qualifiers
1. Area of this wetland is large relative to its watershed.
2. Wetland occurs in the upper portions of its watershed.
3. Effective flood storage is small or non-existent upslope of or above the wetland.
4. Wetland watershed contains a high degree of impervious surfaces.
5. Wetland contains hydric soils that are able to absorb and detain water.
6. Wetland exists in a relatively flat area that has flood storage potential.
7. Wetland has an intermittent outlet, water in ponds, or signs are present of variable water level.
8. During flood events, this wetland can retain higher volumes of water than under normal or average rainfall conditions.
9. Wetland receives and retains overland or sheet flow runoff from surrounding uplands.
10. In the event of a large storm, this wetland may receive and detain excessive floodwater from a nearby watercourse.

STOP HERE IF THIS WETLAND IS NOT ASSOCIATED WITH A WATERCOURSE.

11. This wetland is associated with one or more watercourses.
12. This wetland watercourse is sinuous or diffuse.
13. This wetland outlet is constricted.
14. Channel flow velocity is affected by this wetland.
15. Land uses downstream are protected by this wetland.
16. This wetland contains a high density of vegetation.

III. Sediment/Shoreline Stabilization — This function considers the potential and effectiveness of this wetland in preventing stream bank or shoreline erosion.

Considerations/Qualifiers
1. Indications of erosion, siltation present.
2. Topographical gradient is present in wetland.
3. Potential sediment sources are present up-slope.

   STOP HERE IF THIS WETLAND IS NOT ASSOCIATED WITH A WATERCOURSE.
4. No distinct shoreline or bank is evident between the water body and the wetland or upland.
5. A distinct step between the open water body or stream and the adjacent land exists (i.e., sharp bank) with dense roots throughout.
6. Wide wetland (>10 feet) bordering watercourse, lake, or pond.
7. High flow velocities in the wetland.
8. Potential sediment sources present upstream.
9. The watershed is of sufficient size to produce channelized flow.
10. Open water fetch is present.
11. Boating activity is present.
12. Dense vegetation is bordering watercourse, lake, or pond.
13. High percentage of energy absorbing emergents and/or shrubs bordering watercourse, lake, or pond.
14. Vegetation comprised of large trees and shrubs that withstand major flood events or erosive incidents and stabilize the shoreline on a large scale (feet).
15. Vegetation comprised of dense, resilient herbaceous layer that stabilizes sediments and the shoreline on a small scale (inches) during minor flood events or potentially erosive events.

IV. Sediment/Toxicant Retention — This function considers the effectiveness of the wetland as a trap for sediment in runoff water from surrounding uplands or upstream eroding wetland areas.

Considerations/Qualifiers
1. Potential sources of excess sediment are in the watershed above the wetland.
2. Potential or known sources of toxicants are in the watershed above the wetland.
3. Opportunity for sediment trapping by slow moving water or deep-water habitat are present in this wetland.
4. Mineral, fine grained, or organic soils are present.
5. Long duration water retention time is present in this wetland.

   STOP HERE IF WETLAND IS NOT ASSOCIATED WITH A WATERCOURSE.
6. Wetland is associated with an intermittent or perennial stream or a lake.
7. Channelized flows have visible velocity decreases in the wetland.
8. Effective floodwater storage in wetland is occurring. Areas of impounded open water are present.
9. No indicators of erosive forces are present. No high water velocities are present.
10. Diffuse water flows are present in the wetland.
11. Wetland has a high degree of water and vegetation interspersion.
12. Dense vegetation provides opportunity for sediment trapping and/or signs of sediment accumulation are present beside dense vegetation.

V. Nutrient Removal/Retention/Transformation — This function considers the effectiveness of the wetland as a trap for nutrients in runoff water from surrounding uplands or contiguous wetlands, and the ability of the wetland to process these nutrients into other forms or trophic levels.

Considerations/Qualifiers
1. Wetland is large relative to the size of its watershed.
2. Deep water or open water habitat exists.
3. Overall potential for sediment trapping exists in the wetland.
4. Potential sources of excess nutrients present in the watershed above the wetland.
5. Wetland saturated for most of the season. Water in ponds is present in the wetland.
6. Deep organic/sediment deposits are present.
7. Slowly drained mineral, fine grained, or organic soils are present.

8. Dense vegetation is present.
9. Emergent vegetation and/or dense woody stems are dominant.
10. Aquatic diversity/abundance sufficient to utilize nutrients.
11. Opportunity for nutrient attenuation exists.
12. Vegetation diversity/abundance sufficient to utilize nutrients.

   STOP HERE IF WETLAND IS NOT ASSOCIATED WITH A WATERCOURSE.

13. Water flow through this wetland is diffuse.
14. Water retention/detention time in this wetland is increased by constricted outlet or thick vegetation.
15. Water moves slowly through this wetland.

VI. Production Export (Nutrient) — This function evaluates the suitability or ability of this wetland to produce food or usable products for man or other living organisms.

Considerations/Qualifiers
1. Wildlife food sources grow within this wetland.
2. Detritus development is present within this wetland
3. Economically or commercially used projects found in this wetland.
4. Evidence of wildlife use found within this wetland.
5. Higher trophic level consumers are utilizing this wetland.
6. Fish or shellfish are developing or occurring in this wetland.
7. High vegetation density is present.
8. Wetland exhibits high degree of plant community structure/species diversity.
9. High aquatic diversity/abundance is present.
10. Nutrients exported in wetland watercourses (permanent outlet present).
11. Flushing of relatively large amounts of organic plant material occurs from this wetland.
12. Wetland contains flowering plants that are used by nectar-gathering insects.
13. Indications of export are present.
14. High production levels occurring; however, no visible signs of export (assumes export is attenuated).

VII. Fish and Shellfish Habitat — This function considers the suitability of watercourses associated with the wetland in question for fish and shellfish habitat.

Considerations/Qualifiers
1. Forest land dominant in the watershed above this wetland.
2. Abundance of cover objects present.

   STOP HERE IF THIS WETLAND IS NOT ASSOCIATED WITH A WATERCOURSE

3. Size of this wetland is able to support large fish/shellfish populations.
4. Wetland is part of a larger, contiguous watercourse.
5. Wetland has sufficient size and depth in open water areas so as not to freeze solid and retains some open water during winter.
6. Stream width (bank to bank) is more than 50 feet.
7. Quality of the watercourse associated with this wetland is able to support healthy fish/shellfish populations.
8. Stream-side vegetation provides shade for the watercourse.
9. Spawning areas are present (submerged vegetation or gravel beds).
10. Food is available to fish/shellfish populations within this wetland.
11. Barrier(s) to anadromous fish (e.g., dams, beaver dams, water falls, and road crossings) are absent from the stream reach associated with this wetland.
12. Evidence or occurrence of fish sighted within this wetland.
13. Wetland is stocked with fish.
14. The watercourse is persistent.
15. Man-made streams are absent.
16. Water velocities are not too excessive for fish usage.
17. Defined stream channel is present.

VIII. Wildlife Habitat — This function considers the suitability of this wetland as habitat for those animals typically associated with wetlands and the wetland edge, as well as the use of the wetland as habitat for migrating species and species dependent upon the wetland at some time in their life cycles.

Considerations/Qualifiers
1. Wetland is not degraded by human activity.
2. Water quality of the watercourse, pond, or lake associated with this wetland meets or exceeds Class A or B standards (state water classification standards of purity).
3. Wetland is not fragmented by development.
4. Upland surrounding this wetland is undeveloped.
5. More than 40% of this wetland edge is bordered by upland wildlife habitat (i.e., brushland, woodland, active farmland, or idle land) at least 500 feet in width.
6. Wetland contiguous with other wetland systems via watercourse or lake.
7. Wildlife overland access to other wetlands is present.
8. Wildlife food sources are within this wetland or are nearby.
9. Wetland exhibits a high degree of interspersion of vegetation classes and/or open water.
10. Two or more islands or inclusions of upland with the wetland are present.
11. Dominant wetland class includes deep or shallow marsh or wooded swamp.
12. More than three acres of shallow permanent open water (<6.6 feet deep), including streams in or adjacent to wetland are present.
13. Density of the wetland vegetation is high.
14. Wetland exhibits a high degree of plant species diversity.
15. Wetland exhibits a high degree of diversity in plant community structure (e.g., trees, shrubs, vine, grasses, mosses, etc.).
16. Plant/animal indicator species present.
17. Animal signs observed (tracks, scats, nesting areas, etc.).
18. Seasonal uses vary for wildlife, wetland appears to support varied population diversity/abundance during different seasons.
19. Wetland contains or has potential to contain a high population of insects.
20. Wetland contains or has potential to contain large amphibian populations.
21. Wetland has a high avian utilization or its potential.
22. Indications of less disturbance-tolerant species present.
23. Signs of wildlife habitat enhancement present (birdhouses, nesting boxes, food sources, etc.).

IX. Endangered Species Habitat — This function considers the suitability of the wetland to support threatened or endangered species because of specialized habitat requirements.

Considerations/Qualifiers
1. Wetland contains or is known to contain threatened or endangered species.
2. Wetland contains critical habitat for a state or federally listed threatened or endangered species.
3. Wetland is a national natural landmark or recognized by a state natural heritage or similar agency noting the exemplary nature of the site in question.
4. Wetland has local significance because it has biological, geological, or other features that are locally rare or unique.
5. Wetland is known to be a study site for scientific research.
6. Little disturbance has occurred in and around the wetlands.
7. A large area of undeveloped land surrounds this wetland.

X. Visual Quality/Aesthetics — This function considers the visual and aesthetic quality or usefulness of the wetland.

Considerations/Qualifiers
1. Multiple wetland classes visible from primary viewing locations.
2. Emergent marsh and/or open water visible from primary viewing locations.
3. Diversity of vegetation species visible from primary viewing locations.
4. Wetland dominated by flowering plants or plants that turn vibrant colors in different seasons.

5. Surrounding land use visible from primary viewing locations undeveloped.
6. Visible surrounding land form contrasts with wetland.
7. Wetland views absent of trash, debris, and signs of disturbance.
8. Wetland is considered to be a valuable wildlife habitat.
9. Wetland is easily accessed.
10. Low noise level at primary viewing locations.
11. Unpleasant odors absent at primary viewing locations.
12. Relatively unobstructed sight line through wetland exists.

XI. Educational/Scientific Value — This function considers the suitability of the wetland as a site for an outdoor classroom or as a location for scientific study or research.

Considerations/Qualifiers
1. Wetland contains or is known to contain threatened, rare, or endangered species.
2. Little or no disturbance is occurring in this wetland.
3. Potential educational site contains a diversity of wetland classes that are accessible or potentially accessible.
4. Potential educational site undisturbed and natural.
5. Wetland is considered to be a valuable wildlife habitat.
6. Wetland is located within a nature preserve or wildlife management area.
7. Signs of wildlife habitat enhancement present (bird houses, nesting boxes, food sources, etc.).
8. Off-road parking at potential educational site suitable for school buses within or near wetland.
9. Potential educational site is within safe walking distance or a short drive to schools.
10. Potential educational site within safe walking distance to other plant communities.
11. Direct access to perennial stream at potential educational site available.
12. Direct access to pond or lake at potential educational site available.
13. No known safety hazards within the potential educational site.
14. Public access to the potential educational site is controlled.
15. Handicap accessibility is available.
16. Site is currently used for educational or scientific purposes.

XII. Recreation (Consumptive and Non-consumptive) — This function considers the suitability of the wetland and associated watercourses for canoeing, boating, fishing, hunting, and other active or passive recreational activities.

Considerations/Qualifiers
1. Wetland is part of a recreation area, park, forest, or refuge.
2. Fishing is available within or from the wetland.
3. Hunting is permitted in the wetland.
4. Hiking occurs or has potential to occur within the wetland.
5. Wetland is a valuable wildlife habitat.
6. The watercourse, pond, or lake associated with the wetland is unpolluted.
7. High visual/aesthetic quality of this potential recreation site.
8. Access to water is available at this potential recreation site for boating, canoeing, or fishing.
9. The watercourse associated with this wetland is wide and deep enough to accommodate canoeing and/or non-powered boating.
10. Off-road public parking available at the potential recreation site.
11. Accessibility and travel ease is present at this site.
12. The wetland is within a short drive or safe walk from highly populated public and private areas.

XIII. Uniqueness/Heritage — This function considers the wetland for certain special values such as archaeological sites, critical habitat for endangered species, its overall health and appearance, its role in the ecological system of the area, and its relative importance as a typical wetland class for this geographic location.

Considerations/Qualifiers
1. Upland surrounding wetland primarily urban.
2. Upland surrounding wetland developing rapidly.

3. More than three acres of shallow permanent open water occur in wetlands (<6.6 ft deep) including streams.
4. Three or more wetland classes present.
5. Deep and/or shallow marsh or wooded swamp dominate.
6. High degree of interspersion of vegetation and/or open water occurring in this wetland.
7. Well-vegetated stream corridor (15 ft on each side of the stream) occurs in this wetland.
8. Potential educational site is within a short drive or a safe walk from schools.
9. Off-road parking at potential educational site is suitable for school buses.
10. No known safety hazards exist within this potential educational site.
11. Direct access to perennial stream of lake at potential educational site.
12. Two or more wetland classes visible from primary viewing locations.
13. Low-growing wetlands (marshes, scrub-shrub, bogs, open water) visible from primary viewing locations.
14. Half an acre or open water of 200 feet of stream is visible from the primary viewing locations.
15. Large area of wetland is dominated by flowering plants or plants that turn vibrant colors in different seasons.
16. General appearance of the wetland visible from primary viewing locations is unpolluted and/or undisturbed.
17. Overall view of the wetland is available from the surrounding upland.
18. Quality of the water associated with the wetland is high.
19. Opportunities for wildlife observations are available.
20. Historical buildings occur within the wetland.
21. Presence of pond or pond site and remains of a dam occur within the wetland.
22. Wetland within 50 yards of the nearest perennial watercourse.
23. Visible stone or earthen foundations, berms, dams, standing structures, or associated features occur within the wetland.
24. Wetland contains critical habitat for a state or federally listed threatened or endangered species.
25. Wetland is known to be a study site for scientific research.
26. Wetland is a natural landmark or recognized by the state natural heritage inventory authority as an exemplary natural community.
27. Wetland has local significance because it serves several functional values.
28. Wetland has local significance because it has biological, geological, or other features that are locally rare or unique.
29. Wetland is known to contain an important archaeological site.
30. Wetland is hydrologically connected to a state or federally designated scenic river.
31. Wetland is located in an area experiencing a high wetland loss rate.

Graphical Representation

A graphical representation of the functions and values of each wetland involved in the overall assessment of a project provides both technical and lay reviewers with a visual perspective. Such a summary is the first step in recognizing interrelationships, indirect impacts, and the significance of alternative project plans. Figure 3a represents one graphical means of summarizing wetland functions and values. It contains all the basic characteristics of each wetland investigated, using symbols (i.e., icons) to represent complex ecological and sociological relationships. The specific and complete documentation of each such relationship is not needed for agencies to make initial choices between project alternatives to satisfy USACOE jurisdictional requirements. Refinement of that initial choice and the final issuance of a Section 404 permit to allow project construction requires that this initial information be augmented. The additional information includes detailed delineation of wetlands as well as construction specifications to insure the inclusion of contract stipulations that protect all defined resources and to ensure that their functions and values are recognized and conserved.

Once the characteristics of each wetland are identified by an icon box, a map is prepared to show the geographic relationship between each such wetland and the alternative locations of the proposed project. Figure 3b is a sample of such a map.

CONCLUSIONS

The Highway Methodology of assessing functions and values of wetlands is intended to avoid any hidden weighting of evaluation criteria. Yet, it permits such biasing to take place in open forum when review agencies or other interested parties can review and argue their individual perspectives. Those opportunities are intended to be open debates of the scientific methods and objectives of the assessment. They allow consideration and balancing of natural

Figure 1. This wetlands functions and values assessment protocol guides field inspectors to use descriptive categories that document useful characteristics when judging environmental impacts on wetland systems.

TRANSPORTATION CORRIDOR IMPACT ASSESSMENT

FUNCTION-VALUE ASSESSMENTS

WETLAND I.D. EF3A WP26

WETLANDS EVALUATION

LATITUDE 42 45'82" **LONGITUDE** 71 23'23" **Prepared by:** KLS,LDC,DMM **Date:** 91/10/10

TOTAL AREA OF WETLAND: NW 1.15 acres **SCS** None **MAN MADE?** No **IS WETLAND PART OF A WILDLIFE CORRIDOR?** Yes **OR A "HABITAT ISLAND"?** No

ADJACENT LAND USE Deciduous Forest **DISTANCE TO NEAREST ROADWAY OR OTHER DEVELOPMENT** 300+ ft

DOMINANT WETLAND SYSTEMS PRESENT PFO1E (Circle Impacted Types) **CONTIGUOUS UNDEVELOPED BUFFER ZONE PRESENT** No

IS THE WETLAND A SEPARATE HYDRAULIC SYSTEM? No **IF NOT, WHERE DOES THE WETLAND LIE IN THE DRAINAGE BASIN?** Upper

HOW MANY TRIBUTARIES CONTRIBUTE TO THE WETLAND? 1 **AQUATIC DIVERSITY/ABUNDANCE** Y/N **VEGETATIVE DIVERSITY/ABUNDANCE** Y/Y

WILDLIFE DIVERSITY/ABUNDANCE N/N **ANTICIPATED IMPACTS** Cut and fill will eliminate this wetland **WETLAND IMPACTED:** NWI 1.15 SCS None ACOE

FUNCTION	Occurrence Y / N	Rationale (Number)	Principal Function(s)	Comments
Groundwater Recharge/Discharge	x	1,2,6,7,11-13, 15 Discharge		Wetland is underlain by bedrock and till, and occurs along the base of a slope.
Floodflow Alteration	x	6-9,11,12,14,16		Wetland occurs in the upper watershed and protects the low density residential area downstream. Floodwater can be detained here.
Sediment/Shoreline Stabilization	x	1,4,6,8,9,12-15		Vegetation stabilizes soil in this wetland.
Sediment/Toxicant Retention	x	1-4,6,9-12	x	Receives runoff from roads and trailer park upstream.
Nutrient Removal (Retention/Transformation)	x	3,5-9,11,12,13		Sediment deposition evident in all wetland. Diffuse flow thru herbaceous layer enhances value.
Production Export (Nutrient)	x	1,2,5,7,8,10,14		Some export of nutrients in watercourse but system is primarily a nutrient sink.
Fish & Shellfish Habitat	x	1,2,3,7-10,14-17		Food source, protective cover/spawning areas. Small size/shallow limits fish. Interconnected with adjacent wetlands.
Wildlife Habitat	x	1-9,11,13-15,18,19		Vegetation well stratified. Small but well-buffered, likely a small corridor rather than a nesting or feeding source.
Endangered Species Habitat	x	6,7		No known occurrence here.
Visual Quality/Aesthetics	x	3-5,7,10,11		Visually homogeneous and inconspicuous.
Educational Scientific Value	x	2,4,9-11,13		Limited by small size and homogeneity.
Recreation (Non-Consumptive)	x	6-8,10,11,15,16,18,19,22		Hunting limited by proximity to houses. Hiking possible. Wildlife low population.
Uniqueness/Heritage	x	6-8,10,11,15,16,18,19,22		

NOTES: Located in upper reaches of an important stream. Consists of alternately diffuse and well defined channel. Flat, well saturated herbaceous floodplain. Wetland width varies with surrounding topography. Scattered windthrows create discontinuous tree canopy. Shrub layer is patchy. Clumps of dense shrubs interspersed with open herbaceous flat areas. Waterflow is alternately diffuse and confined to a distinct channel. Water received from surrounding roads and trailer park directly upstream. Siltation evident in wetland.

Figure 2a. This sample form was prepared as part of the field inspection conducted on 10 October 1991. Identified on the project plans as Wetland EF3A, its photographic record was labeled WP26 in the convention used during field inspections (See Figure 2c).

Species List   EF3A   WP26

Vegetative

Red Maple	*Acer rubrum*
Slippery Elm	*Ulmus rubra*
White pine	*Pinus strobus*
Ash	*Fraxinus* sp.
Yellow birch	*Betula lutea*
Grey birch	*Betula populifolia*
Speckled alder	*Alnus rugosa*
Poison sumac	*Rhus vernix*
Dogwood	*Cornus* sp.
Highbush blueberry	*Vaccinium corymbosum*
Maleberry	*Lyonia ligustrina*
Winterberry	*Ilex verticillata*
Sensitive fern	*Onoclea sensibilis*
Poison ivy	*Rhus radicans*
Skunk cabbage	*Symplocarpus foetidus*
Steeple bush	*Spiraea tomentosa*

Wildlife

Black capped chick-a-dee	*Parus atricapillus*
Blue jay	*Cyanocitta cristata*
Green frogs	*Rana clamitans melanota*
Grey squirrel	*Sciurus carolinensis*

* ENTIRE WETLAND LIES IN IMPACT ZONE

OPEN GRASSY & FERNS

CLUMPS OF ALDERS (DENSE)

PHOTO LOCATION

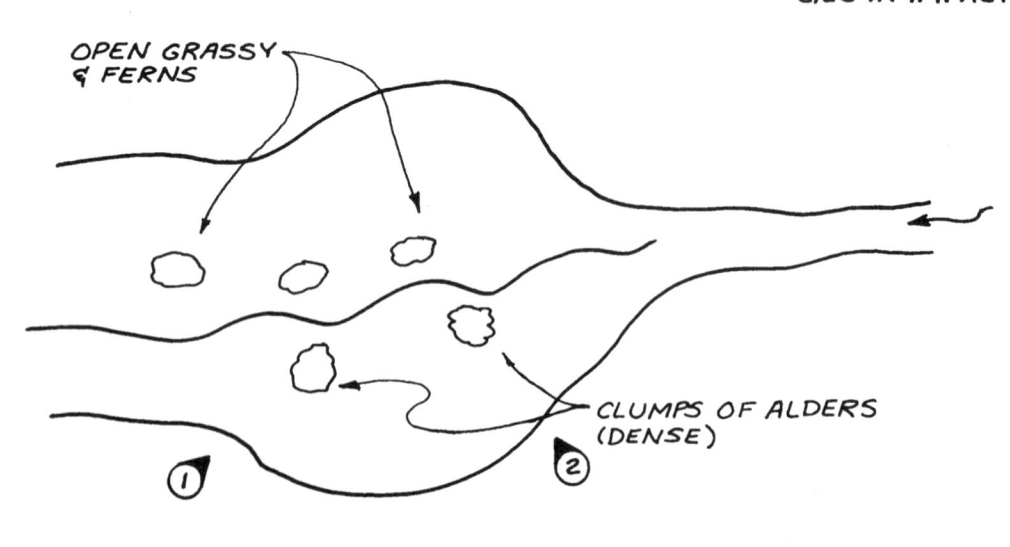

Figure 2b. The species list is based on observed species, or their signs, during site investigations.

Figure 2c. Photographs record each investigated wetland. The relative location of each photograph is indicated on the site sketch map (see Figure 2b).

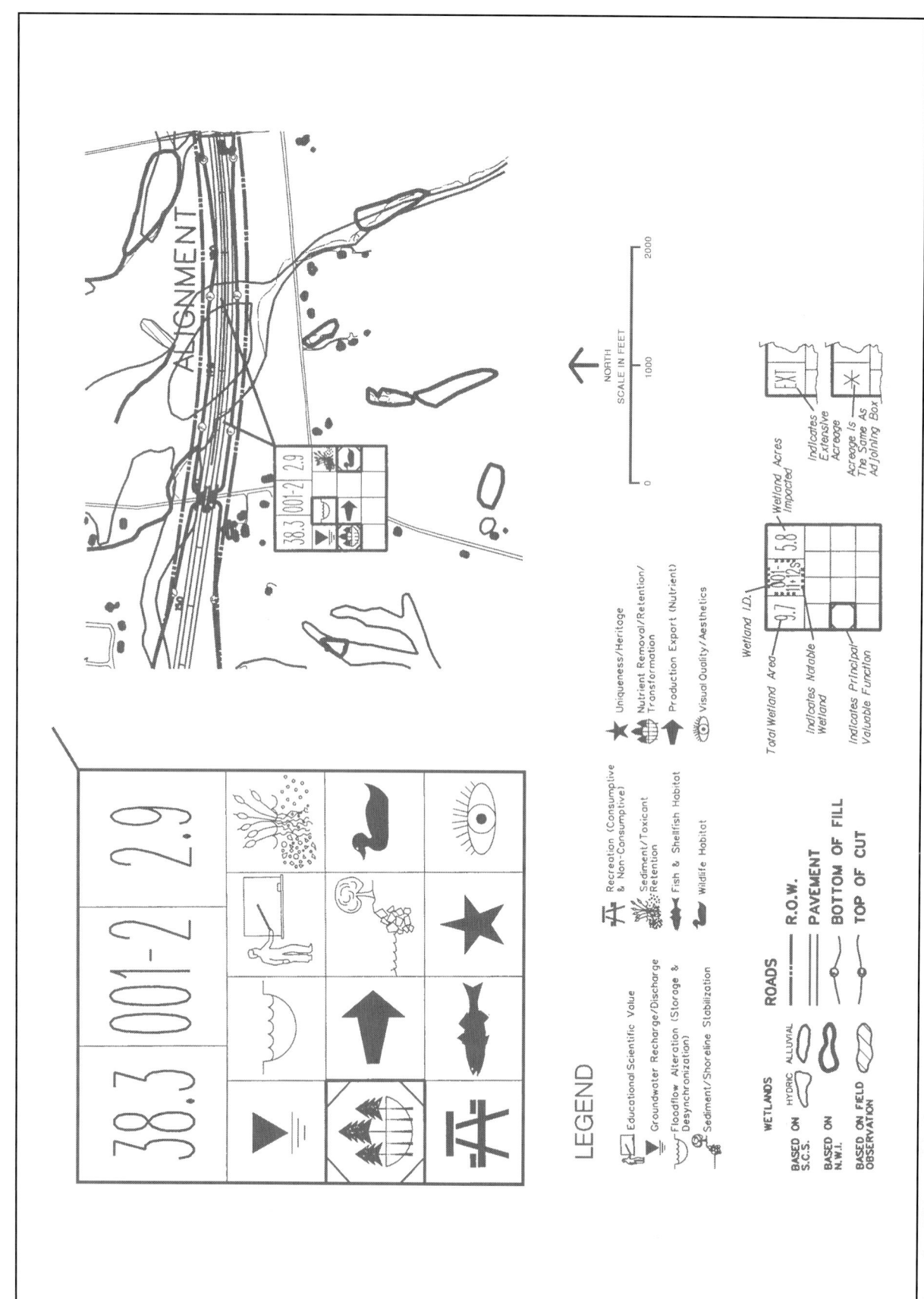

Figure 3a. This graphical summary of wetland characteristics was developed as a tool to help construct an annotated map of functions and values for linear projects such as highways and railroads. Based on findings reported on an assessment form (see Figures 1 and 2), an icon box is prepared for each wetland investigated. (The specific function of a wetland as Endangered Species Habitat is not illustrated by an icon so there are 12 icon possibilities shown here. Therefore, this method can represent 12 of the 12 functions and values itemized on the form shown in Figure 1 and Figure 2.)

TRANSPORTATION CORRIDOR IMPACT ASSESSMENT

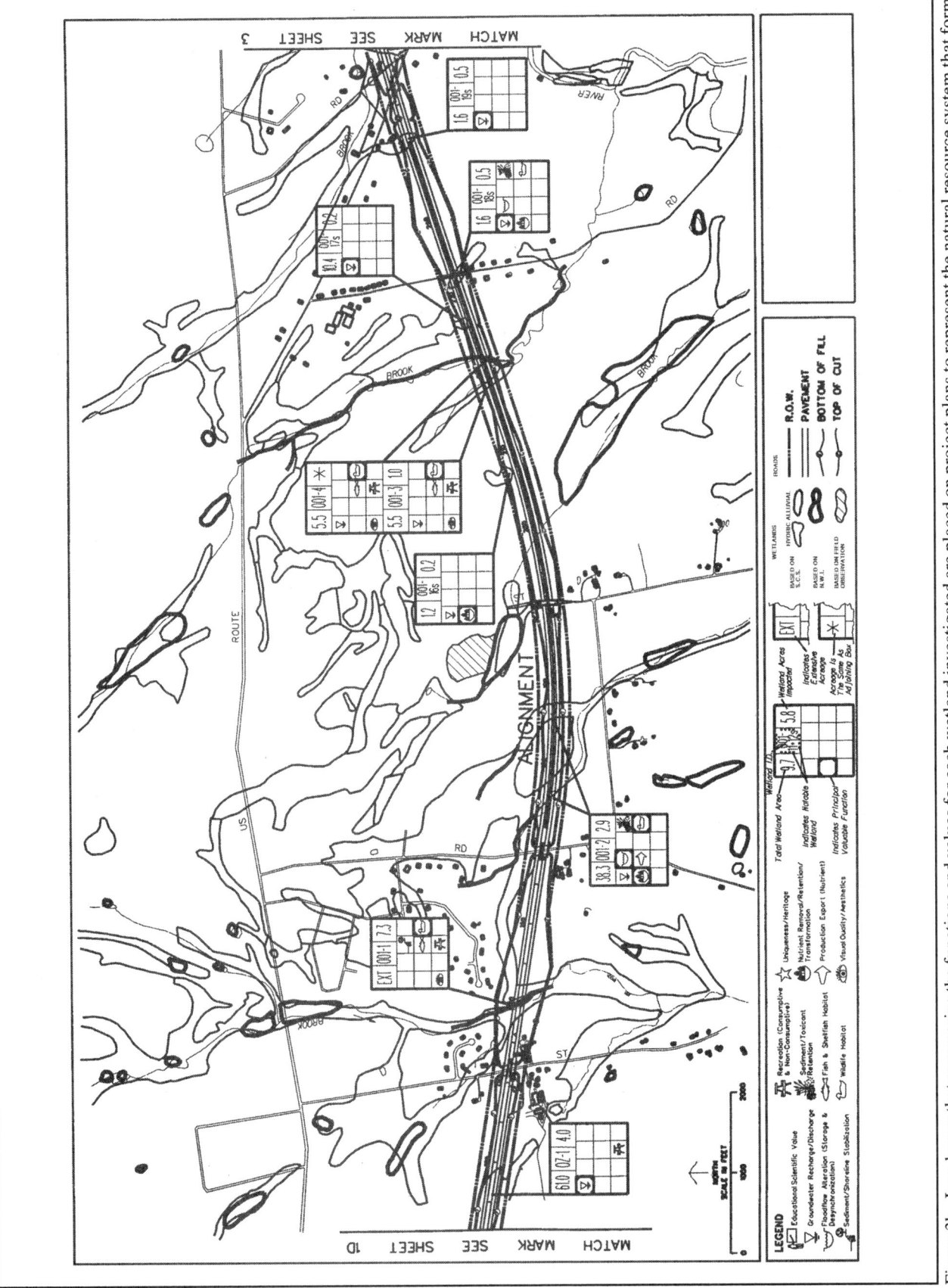

Figure 3b. Icon boxes that summarize the functions and values for each wetland investigated are placed on project plans to represent the natural resource system that forms the basis for primary agency reviews under the USACOE Section 4040 permit procedures.

resources and socioeconomic resources. Such considerations require choices that are imperfect because natural resources and socioeconomic resources are often mutually exclusive. Protection of one class of resources may require impact upon or removal of another class. The desired result of this process is a negotiated consensus or mediated choice that one imperfect project alternative is acceptable for the greater good, even though from one perspective or another no alternative is perfect. This goal can be achieved provided the jurisdictional parties can exercise and balance professional creativity and restraint to serve the environmental conservation process as good stewards.

Such good environmental stewardship requires the public to correct its false belief that environmental preservation can be achieved as our present-day standard of living is advanced. Preservation of the environment has a significant cost, as does management of a transportation system. It is an anthropogenic oversimplification, as well as a fatal flaw in philosophy, to proclaim that on the one hand Mother Nature will take care of and nurture herself and all her creatures, while on the other hand mankind can pursue unbridled population and technological growth.

Conservation proceeds by providing impartial scientific data to decision makers with the appropriate expertise to effectively use those data. One important step in revealing the data is to develop the tools to define functions and values of wetlands as described in this paper.

Acknowledgments

I am pleased to acknowledge the many significant contributions friends and colleagues have made over the past several years to the investigation of environmental impacts associated with transportation-related projects. In particular, I thank Kevin Slattery and Lynn Clements for their tireless efforts in assessing wetlands and in working to help perfect the data forms used in this method. I also thank Torger Erickson, whose skill with computer-aided drafting and design and geographic information systems was a vital contribution to the graphical representation and statistical application of this assessment technique. I am indebted to Bill Lawless, the chief of the regulatory branch of the U.S. Army Corps of Engineers, New England Division, and his staff, and I especially acknowledge Terresa Flieger, a project manager at the Corps for her help, encouragement, and remarkable patience and stamina while the tools needed to develop this techniques were evolving "on the job." I also gratefully acknowledge the administrative and technical staffs of the departments of transportation of New Hampshire and Connecticut for the opportunities they provided to develop the ideas and to acquire the experience that this work reflects.

Literature Cited

Adamus, P. R., E. J. Clairain, Jr., R. O. Smith, and R. E. Young. 1987. Wetland evaluation technique (WET); Volume II: Methodology. Operational Draft Technical Report FHWA-IP-88-029, U.S. Army Engineer Waterways Experiment Station, Vicksburg, Michigan. 279 pp.

Ammann, A. P. and A. L. Stone. 1991. Method for the comparative evaluation of nontidal wetlands in New Hampshire. New Hampshire Department of Environmental Services, NHDES-WRD-1991-3.

Ammann, A. P., R. W. Franzen, and J. L. Johnson. 1986. Method for the evaluation of inland wetlands in Connecticut. Bulletin No. 9, Connecticut Department of Environmental Protection.

De Santo, R. S. 1976. The journal's policy and objectives. Environ. Manage. 1(1):3.

De Santo, R. S. 1978. Concepts of Applied Ecology. Springer-Verlag, New York. 310 pp.

Golet, F. C. 1976. Wildlife wetland evaluation model. *In* J. S. Larson (ed.), Models for Assessment of Freshwater Wetlands, pp. 13–34. Publication No. 32, Water Resources Research Center, University of Massachusetts at Amherst. 91 pp.

Hammer, D. 1990. Constructed wetlands. Land and Water 34:4–7.

Larson, J. S. (ed.). 1976. Models for Assessment of Freshwater Wetlands. Publication 32, Water Resources Research Center, University of Massachusetts at Amherst. 91 pp.

Larson, J. S., P. R. Adamus, and E. J. Clairain. 1989. Functional Assessment of Freshwater Wetlands: A Manual and Training Outline. Publication No. 89-6, University of Massachusetts at Amherst. 62 pp.

McHarg, I. 1969. Design with Nature. Natural History Press. 198 pp.

Miller, A. 1982. Psychosocial factors in environmental problem solving. Environ. Manage. 6:535–541.

Miller, A. 1990. The competent environmental auditor. Environmental Auditor 1(4):191–203.

Mitsch, W. J. and J. G. Gosselink. 1986. Wetlands. Van Nostrand Reinhold, New York. 539 pp.

Palmisano, J. 1989. Environmental auditing: Past, present, and future. Environmental Auditor 1(1):7–12.

USACOE. 1993. The highway methodology workbook. U.S. Army Corps of Engineers, New England Division, NEDEP-360-1-30. 28 pp.

The Amazon Turtles—Conservation and Management in Brazil

VITOR HUGO CANTARELLI

CENAQUA/IBAMA Rua 229 N° 95, Setor Leste Universitário, Goiânia-GO 74.609-090, Brazil [e-mail: vcantar@ibama.gov.br]

ABSTRACT: This paper summarizes the turtle conservation and research undertaken by CENAQUA/IBAMA in the Brazilian Amazon, mainly with *Podocnemis expansa*. During 13 years of work more than 17,000,000 young turtles have been released into the rivers. From 1979 to 1991 the project oversaw a 1200% increase in number of eggs laid, with an average increase of approximately 25% per year. This paper describes some of the methodologies and achievements of management in the wild. The feasibility of captive breeding for commercial purposes is also discussed.

Throughout the centuries, Amazonian turtles have served as a significant source of protein for a great many communities that have been settled along the rivers of the Amazon basin. Freshwater turtles have represented an important means of livelihood for these people. However, the indiscriminate use of these resources has led to the depletion of many of the large populations of *Podocnemis expansa* in the Amazonian region. From 1860 to 1900 excessive exploitation of these animals destroyed a great number of females. The collecting of turtle eggs reached the incredible number of 48 million per year (Bates, 1864). In addition to exploitation for human consumption, large numbers of eggs as well as turtle fat, used in the manufacture of butter and oil, were exported to Europe. Other researchers (Pereira, 1940, 1967; Tocantins, 1961) noted the decline in Amazon turtle populations and urged the adoption of a management program to restore the natural population and to meet the demand for turtle consumption.

In the 1970s, Brazilian scientists warned that within ten years all the turtles might be extirpated if the level of destruction remained the same. In response to these warnings, Brazil has developed appropriate policy measures in an effort to bring about a sustainable balance in the human population vs. turtle resource equation.

Based upon data collected by Alfinito (1975), the Brazilian Government created the Projeto Quelônios da Amazônia (Amazonian Chelonia Project) in 1979. The Chelonia Project began to set up protection and management systems in the most important areas of nesting habitat—the Amazonian rivers and west central region of Brazil. During the past 13 years the project has identified existing nesting beaches and has created additional nesting areas. It has taken measures to increase the number of adult females and has undertaken a management program for hatchlings.

In 1990, to establish a permanent research facility, the Brazilian Institute for the Environment and Renewable Natural Resources (IBAMA) formed the National Center for the Amazonian Chelonia (CENAQUA). In turn, CENAQUA has established an experimental chelonian breeding program, seeking to improve captive breeding techniques, mainly with *Podocnemis expansa* (tartaruga-da-amazônia) and *Podocnemis unifilis* (tracajá). Over the years since it was founded, the Chelonia Project nesting beach protection program has produced more than 17,000,000 hatchling turtles, which have been returned to the wild.

CENAQUA and the Amazonian Chelonia Project have focused upon the following species: *Podocnemis expansa* (tartaruga-da-amazônia, tartaruga verdadeira, charapa, arrau, giant South American river turtle), *Podocnemis unifilis* (tracajá, taricaya, cupiso, yellow-spotted Amazon River turtle), *Podocnemis sextuberculata* (iaçá, pitiú, six-tubercled Amazon River turtle), *Podocnemis erythrocephala* (irapuca, red-headed Amazon River turtle), and *Peltocephalus dumerilianus* (cabeçudo, big-headed Amazon River turtle). *P. expansa* is the most widespread species in the Amazon region. It occurs in the Amazon River basin in the states of Amapá, Pará, Amazonas, Rondônia, Acre, Roraima, and Mato Grosso. These areas include both rainforest and scrub woodland ecosystems.

Implementing the technical programs of CENAQUA, the principal purpose of the Amazonian Chelonia Project is the management of the reproduction and feeding areas. The Project conducts its activities throughout the following rivers: Purus and Juruá (in Acre); Pauini, Purus, Juruá, and Uatumã (in Amazonas); Tapajós, Trombetas, and Xingu (in Pará); Branco (in Roraima); Guaporé (in Rondônia); Amazonas (in Amapá); Araguaia (in Goiás and Tocantins); das Mortes (in Mato Grosso).

METHODS AND MANAGEMENT

In the management of *Podocnemis expansa* reproduction, the Chelonia Project has adopted strategies that have allowed the recovery of natural stocks in the wild (Cantarelli, 1980). Briefly, our operation is outlined as follows:

Figure 1. Eggs are collected from a nest that could become flooded for transfer to an artificial nest.

Figure 2. Two team members work in the enclosed artificial nest area.

1. Enlistment and training of the personnel. The "Agentes de Praia," (beach guards) must be interested and committed to the work. They are trained in the practical application of our basic methods. Selected personnel must be physically fit and able to handle challenging situations. More than 100 nesting areas are covered by a group of 70 people.

2. Location and identification of the nesting areas. Almost all the nesting areas are in remote regions. Observations are made at each site of such physical conditions as the width and length of the beach, presence of vegetation, and distance to the nearest village. The beaches are searched to determine the positions of the "boiadouro" (the site where females normally gather before laying their eggs) and whether there is a possibility of flooding of the nests.

The proximity of human inhabitants and the level of human predation in the area are noted. Reports from the riverbank communities have helped us to locate turtle nesting sites and determine laying frequencies. The team's activities have been well received by the people of these communities, who understand that they are the beneficiaries of the increased turtle population.

3. Encampments and monitoring of the laying areas. Encampments are strategically located to permit the team a good view of the beaches and nesting sites. To prevent the nesting zone from becoming polluted or obstructed, the team sweeps the laying areas to remove all rubbish, refuse, and remains of vegetation. Large objects such as tree trunks are also removed. This action is very important as it allows freer access to the beaches by the turtles.

The vigil begins when the turtles come in groups to the beaches and begin to search the environment prior to nesting. Any kind of disturbance must be avoided at this time, otherwise the turtles shift nesting to unprotected beaches.

4. Nest identification, care, and protection. Every day the team searches the beaches for nests, which are marked to facilitate monitoring of hatchling emergence. In the search, nests are carefully probed with a stick that, when introduced into the soft sand, easily penetrates to the eggs without damaging them. The nests are then marked by placing a numbered picket next to each one.

When nesting occurs in a very low part of the beach that may become flooded, the team transfers the eggs from the natural nest to an artificial one. To reduce potential impact upon the eggs, this work is done during periods of mild temperatures without sun, rain, or wind.

Generally, the nesting areas, which are marked by flags, are under legal protection that forbids commercial fishing and other activities in the vicinity, and the team must monitor and facilitate the traffic of passing boats.

5. Management of hatchlings. When the hatchlings begin to emerge 45–60 days after nesting, the team opens the nest to remove the neonates. They are counted, classified, and placed in a nursery where they are kept for a period of up to 15 days while their carapaces harden. Afterwards, they are released into areas that have fewer predators to increase their probability of survival. A few of the hatchlings are retained to be added to the Chelonia Project's permanent captive breeding stock.

The hatchlings are counted and classified as "perfect" (normal umbilical scars), "defective" (any imperfection or deformity), or "dead." The number of unhatched eggs is also recorded. From these data the team can statistically monitor the efficiency of the adopted management procedures.

Figure 3. Thousands of hatchlings in a protected nesting beach area.

Figure 4. Fifteen-day-old hatchlings are released into an area that has few predators.

RESULTS

During 13 years of work the Amazonian Chelonia Project has returned more than 17,000,000 young turtles to the rivers. From 1979 to 1991 we had a 1200% increase in number of eggs laid; the average increase was approximately 25% per year. In 1991 we produced approximately 3 million hatchlings at a cost of Cr $74 (U.S. $.09) per hatchling.

CENAQUA has been working to set up experimental captive breeding centers. The first one was established in the city of Anápolis (state of Goiás). The next ones will be set up in Balbina (state of Amazonas) and Macapá (state of Amapá). Two others will be built in the states of Mato Grosso and Acre.

Captive Breeding for Commercial Purposes

Because of both the demand for turtles' high-quality meat and byproducts (mainly of the species *Podocnemis expansa*) and their integral role in nature, it is essential to pursue a wise and balanced use of these animals. Ten percent of the total number of hatchlings produced by the management program in each Amazonian state are made available to commercial turtle breeders whose proposed breeding projects have been approved by IBAMA. The turtle breeders must then proceed on their own.

With its high protein level, the meat of "tartaruga-da-amazônia" is preferred to that of most traditional domestic animals. Approximate protein levels are compared in Table 1.

TABLE 1
Comparisons of approximate protein levels of meat of traditional domestic animals and that of turtles. Based on Ferreira and Graça (1961), Leung and Flores (1961), and Morrisson (1955).

Domestic animal	Protein
Sus scrofa domestica (pig)	45%
Gallus gallus (chicken)	43–72%
Bos taurus (steer)	47%
Bos taurus (bull calf)	70%
Palinuros vulgaris (lobster)	86%
Turtles	85–88%

TABLE 2
Comparisons of approximate costs of fish, beef, and turtle in the Amazon ($U.S.).

Type of meat	Cost
1 kg of white meat (fish)	$1.00
1 kg of beef	$2.30
1 kg of turtle meat	$6.00

It should be noted that, given an equal amount of space in which to raise the animals, turtles may produce more than 100 times the meat produced by cattle. In the Amazon one bull requires 3–4 ha to produce 40 kg of meat per year. In one hectare of water it is possible to raise up to 4,500 turtles with a yield of about 1,800 kg of turtle meat per year. (This comparison assumes that space is the limiting factor; turtles raised in this density will require a major external food source.) Turtles can also be raised with fish.

In 1991 some individual turtles commanded a price of Cr $200,000 (U.S. $80) in the market of Manaus and Belém. One 25 kg turtle can supply 13 kg of meat and viscera. On the other hand, once captive-raised turtle meat becomes widely available, the price may well come down. Nevertheless, the captive breeding of turtles may soon become a profitable activity in the Amazon.

Conclusion

CENAQUA has sought a balance between the basic protection of the ecosystem and the careful intervention in the natural process of reproduction, and through its management programs has succeeded in reversing the decline of wild turtle stocks. And while it will not be possible to restore the turtle populations to the original levels of more than 400,000 nesting females, we are sure that we will achieve a significant number.

Created in 1990, CENAQUA has specific programs for the conservation of chelonians which include research, protection and management, captive breeding, and environmental education programs. We are seeking a rational alternative in the use of a renewable natural resource without damaging it. However, all this will be possible only with the cooperation of other national and international institutions (both public and private). In spite of its great effort, CENAQUA/IBAMA has faced a number of problems and is in need of financial support to carry out its activities. The budget from the environmental ministry is inadequate: in the last two years it has covered just 30% of our requirements. With greater financial support the Project could manage more than 500 beaches. If additional funding is not forthcoming, we may not be able to continue our programs, and some turtle species may need to be returned to the list of endangered species in Brazil.

Literature Cited

Alfinito, J. 1975. A preservação da Tartaruga-da-Amazônia. Revista Brasil Florestal 6(21):20–23.

Bates, H. W. 1864. The Naturalist on the River Amazons, a Record of Adventures, Habits of Animals, Sketches of Brazilian and Indian Life and Aspects of Nature Under the Equator During Eleven Years of Travel. John Murray, London. 466 pp.

Cantarelli, V. H. 1980. I° Encontro Técnico Administrativo sobre Quelônios da Amazônia. Unpubl. report.

Ferreira, F. A. G. and M. E. S. Graça. 1961. Tabela de Composição dos Alimentos Portugueses. Ministério Saúde e Assist. I. S. H. "Dr. Ricardo Jorge," Lisboa. 173 pp.

Leung, W. T. W. and M. Flores. 1961. Tabela de Composição de Alimentos para uso em América Latina. Nat. Inst. Health, Bethesda, Maryland, USA. 132 pp.

Morrisson, F. B. 1955. Alimentos e Alimentação dos Animais. Ed. Melhoramentos. 821 pp.

Pereira, J. R. 1940. Amazônia: Impressões de Viagem. Editora Civilização Brasileira, São Paulo.

Pereira, J. R. 1967. Moronguitá: Um Decameron Indígena. Editora Civilização Brasileira, Rio de Janeiro.

Smith, N. J. H. 1979. Destructive exploitation of the American river turtle. Chelonia Magazine (2)5:3–9 (Sept.–Oct.).

Tocantins, L. 1961. O Rio Comanda a Vida: Uma Interpretação da Amazônia. Editora Civilização Brasileira, Rio de Janeiro.

An Action Plan for Nonprofit Organizations in Turtle and Tortoise Conservation

ROGER DALE[1] AND JUN LEE[2]

[1]The Natelson Company, Inc., 16633 Ventura Blvd., Suite 1200, Encino, CA 91436, USA [e-mail: tnci@earthlink.com]
[2]Nonprofit Counsel, 1804 T Street, NW, Washington, DC 20009, USA [e-mail:jlee@nonprofit-counsel.com]

ABSTRACT: The recovery of the desert tortoise, *Gopherus (Xerobates) agassizii*, will require a comprehensive conservation strategy that integrates the resources of government and industry with those of the nonprofit sector. Accordingly, the Desert Tortoise Preserve Committee has developed an action plan to serve as a model for nonprofit organizations that includes three major categories of conservation programs: (1) habitat protection through land use regulation and/or direct acquisition; (2) habitat enhancement and stewardship, including establishment of management guidelines and monitoring procedures; and (3) programs designed to promote species recovery, including scientific research and public education. Specific steps and recommendations, including examples from the Committee's own experience, are outlined and discussed.

During its twenty-year history, the Desert Tortoise Preserve Committee, Inc. has successfully interacted with industry and various levels of government to foster protection of the desert tortoise, *Gopherus (Xerobates) agassizii*. Many of the conservation strategies utilized by the Preserve Committee are legally based in the Endangered Species Act of 1973 and are therefore somewhat unique to the United States. Nevertheless, the basic concepts represented by these strategies may be applicable in other nations with comparable legislation.

The Preserve Committee recognizes that the recovery of the desert tortoise will require a comprehensive conservation strategy that integrates the resources of government, industry, and the nonprofit sector. The optimal role of the nonprofit sector is to enhance the conservation programs of government and industry by filling the "gaps" created by the funding, bureaucratic, and political constraints faced by the other sectors. In order to maximize the effectiveness of their resources, nonprofit organizations must carefully identify the roles they can play without duplicating the efforts of the public sector. In some instances, the nonprofit sector acts as a "watchdog" over public agencies responsible for carrying out conservation policies.

Programs the Preserve Committee has successfully implemented include the following:
1. Land acquisition in cooperation with various government agencies;
2. Habitat stewardship through cooperative management agreements with state and federal agencies;
3. A pilot land bank program through which the Committee assists private firms to meet mitigation requirements and at the same time generates funds for land acquisition and management;
4. Various public education programs;
5. Advocacy efforts including litigation; and
6. Lobbying to obtain funds for government-operated conservation programs.

Based on the above experiences, the Preserve Committee has developed an action plan to serve as a model for other nonprofit organizations involved in turtle and tortoise conservation. The action plan encompasses three major categories of conservation programs:
1. Habitat protection through land use regulation and/or direct acquisition;
2. Habitat enhancement and stewardship, including establishment of management guidelines and monitoring procedures; and
3. Programs designed to promote species recovery, including scientific research and public education.

The Preserve Committee's recommends the following steps for nonprofit organizations:
1. Identify potential joint venture partners for conservation efforts;
2. Take inventory and determine limitations of existing conservation programs conducted by the potential joint venture partners;
3. Identify program areas where the nonprofit sector could provide supplemental support in conservation efforts for target species;
4. Enter into cooperative management agreements with joint venture partners; and
5. Develop an advocacy program for recovery of the target species.

Specific recommendations with respect to these action plan components, including examples from the Committee's own experience, are provided below. The recommendations are oriented towards threatened and endangered species and are based on two major presumptions:

1. The species in question is either currently or potentially subject to some form of legislation (e.g., the U.S. Endangered Species Act), which serves as the legal basis for protecting it.
2. The protective legislation carries with it a mandate or framework for the involvement of government agencies in developing conservation programs.

Thus, the action plan assumes that the nonprofit sector would not be acting alone in protecting target species, but would serve in a support role to fill the gaps left by government programs. It is probable that these gaps will tend to increase in the future as the increased demand for species protection outpaces available government funding. This situation further underlines the need for coordinated conservation programs that integrate both public and private resources.

Recommended Steps

1. Identify Potential Joint Venture Partners. The search for possible interested parties should be based on general criteria. Prospective joint venture partners for conservation programs should not necessarily be limited to environmental experts or concerns. Indeed, the broader the base of support a group can generate early in the formation of its program, the lower the likelihood of resistance as the conservation project develops. Possible factors that may attract a potential joint venture partner to a newly forming project may include land ownership, legal mandates, resource utilization, or an affinity for a particular issue. Certainly, such assets as technical expertise, organizational capacity, and the ability to influence public officials should be given the highest priority.

2. Inventory Existing Conservation Programs. It is important to assess the protection requirements of the target species and the existing programs that have been dedicated to the issue. To properly assess the conservation needs of the existing programs, one should (1) determine the total funding and staffing needed for ultimate success (apportioned in predefined time periods), (2) identify bureaucratic inefficiencies of the agencies responsible for managing programs, and (3) define any legal or political constraints that limit the ability of the agencies to make the programs as effective as possible. Ideally, a rigorous assessment of conservation requirements will reveal any gaps that occur in the existing programs, which may then be addressed.

3. Identify Partnership Opportunities. Once the nonprofit organization (NPO) has identified the limitations of the existing conservation programs for the target species, it may then take steps to either support an existing program to help make it more effective, or fill a need that is currently being neglected or overlooked. Two examples from the Preserve Committee's experience illustrate the role of an NPO in supporting government conservation programs.

The first example relates to joint funding of conservation efforts. By managing conservation programs through private/public partnerships, available funding is increased since government agencies typically do not have access to such private funding sources as foundation grants and individual contributions. In some instances, an NPO may even be able to utilize funds that *would* be available to a government agency more effectively. For example, the Preserve Committee believes that there is a tremendous opportunity for NPOs to take an active role in managing mitigation funds.

The Preserve Committee is currently taking such a role in the western Mojave Desert. Over the past five years we have taken the initial steps to develop a land bank using private mitigation funds. The pilot project for the Committee's land bank involved two churches that were constructing facilities in desert tortoise habitat. Pursuant to the provisions of the Endangered Species Act, the churches were required to mitigate for their impact on desert tortoise habitat by providing funds to acquire and manage "replacement" habitat elsewhere in the tortoise's range. Historically, most mitigation funds of this nature have been paid to a government agency, which was then responsible for acquiring appropriate land and providing long-term stewardship of the acquired habitat. The drawbacks of this arrangement are that it typically is more costly than necessary to the project proponent (i.e., the churches), and the acquired habitat does not consistently receive an adequate level of protective management.

In the case of the church mitigation project, the Preserve Committee acted as an intermediary between the churches and the government agencies responsible for granting the necessary construction permits. The required mitigation funds were paid directly from the churches to the Preserve Committee and were sufficient to acquire the replacement habitat and to establish an endowment fund for long-term management of the land. The Preserve Committee will be responsible for long-term stewardship of the acquired habitat and will periodically report to the government agencies that approved the project. Due to the Committee's long history of acquiring small parcels of land, it was able to act efficiently in locating and purchasing an appropriate replacement parcel for the church project, which in turn lowered the overall project cost to the churches. Moreover, the Committee's involvement in this mitigation agreement ensures that the land will be appropriately managed for the long-term benefit of the desert tortoise.

In the second example, the Preserve Committee supports the land acquisition program managed by the United States Bureau of Land Management (USBLM). This joint program has focused on the acquisition of private inholdings of land within the Desert Tortoise Natural Area in California. The USBLM's land acquisition program is funded by Land and Water Conservation Funds appropriated annually by the United States Congress. Whereas the USBLM typically focuses on the purchase of relatively large parcels of land, i.e., 40 acres (16.2 ha) or larger, it is less efficient at purchasing smaller parcels due to the labor intensive process of negotiating with a large number of land owners. The Preserve Committee has been able to effectively complement the USBLM's efforts by acquiring these smaller parcels and then reselling them to the USBLM in packages of 40 acres (16.2 ha) or more. This ensures that the USBLM is able to expend all funds available for land acquisition in each year, resulting in an overall increase in land that is protected annually. The USBLM's purchases of land from the Preserve Committee provide the Committee with a revolving source of revenue to support future land acquisitions.

4. Cooperative Management Agreements. Once the NPO has identified its joint venture partner(s) and has established what the partnership should accomplish, cooperative management agreements should set specific goals and should be formalized by memoranda of understanding (MOUs). MOUs should clearly define the unique roles of each partner and should set time frames for meeting the goals. Cooperative agreements should also include provisions for periodic revision, status reporting, and conflict resolution.

In entering into joint venture partnerships, the partners should recognize that their differing constituencies may be a basis for potential conflicts between the partners. In the event of conflicts, the MOU becomes an important tool in assuring that progress continues in common areas while disagreements are resolved.

5. Develop an Advocacy Program. A nonprofit agency can play a unique role as an intermediary between the public (government) and private sectors. Because the NPO is composed of private individuals, however, it is also able to articulate independent positions or those that may be considered the "public will." As an advocate for its constituents—defined as both members and such non-human entities as a river or an animal species—the NPO has a vital position in helping to define the priorities of its community. This leadership role may require such activities as lobbying, litigation, and community organizing.

An effective advocacy program should be designed with special attention toward potential disagreements and possible failure of joint efforts. Though most conflicts are addressed through legislative means or litigation, it should be noted that there is now a growing tradition of non-legal dispute resolution that has resulted in superior outcomes for programmatic and policy disputes. A nonprofit agency that utilizes alternative dispute resolution will usually find not only a means to resolve disputes, but also a potentially powerful vehicle to refocus fractious partners on shared goals.

Identifying Areas of High Herpetological Diversity in the Western Ghats, Southwestern India

INDRANEIL DAS

Department of Biology, Universiti Brunei Darussalam, Gadong, Bandar Seri Begawan 2028, Brunei Darussalam
Current address: Centre for Herpetology, Madras Crocodile Bank Trust, Mamallapuram, Post Bag 4, Tamil Nadu 603 104, India

ABSTRACT: The Western Ghat forests in southwestern India harbour the last intact tropical rainforest in peninsular India. Species diversity and endemicity are high and the region is biogeographically closer to Sri Lanka than to continental Asia. An analysis of the distribution pattern reveals that many species are localised; however, the distribution and diversity of the region's herpetofauna is highly heterogenous over the Western Ghats. Human pressures on these forests, including logging, agriculture, and settlements are considerable, and vast tracts of once-contiguous forest have been lost.

To detect areas of high diversity and endemicity within the Western Ghats, data are being collected from the literature, museum records, and by recent field work. Many key areas identified presently receive minimal legal protection, lying within Reserve Forests (the lowest category of forest-land protection in India) or even as fragments within tea, coffee, and cardamom estates. This paper presents a strategy for identifying the remaining pockets of high herpetological diversity within the Western Ghats and recommends measures for their protection.

India supports the fifth-largest area of rainforest in the world, with a closed tropical forest area estimated at 51,841,000 ha (Office of Technology Assessment, 1984), most of which is located in the northeastern region (Collins et al., 1991). However, significant areas of unlogged forest, known as the Western Ghats, run parallel to the Malabar (western) coast of peninsular India. These are composed of a series of hill ranges that may exceed 1,000 m, which are separated by low altitude gaps, and extend north to south for a distance of approximately 1,600 km between 8° and 21° north latitude. The highest peaks, which exceed 2,000 m, are found in the southern parts of the Ghats and include the Nilgiris, Palnis, and Annamalais. Because these hill ranges are ecologically distinct from the intervening 100–150 m flat savanna, they serve as "islands." Regional endemism on these often-isolated islands is suspected to be an important aspect of the high diversity of the region (Inger et al., 1987).

OBJECTIVES AND METHODS

While the extensive clear-cutting of primary forests for timber export, evident in much of southeast Asia, is not prevalent in the Western Ghats, fragmentation of the forests through "swidden" (slash-and-burn) agriculture, logging for firewood, establishment of dams and human settlements, grazing, and forest fires have greatly reduced both the extent and quality of the majestic dipterocarp forests.

The impact of these anthropogenic changes upon the fauna is largely unknown. However, a large number of species that are recognised as threatened dwell in these mesic forests. Among amphibians and reptiles are *Geoemyda silvatica*, *Indotestudo forstenii*, *Python molurus*, *Ophiophagus hannah*, *Crocodylus palustris*, *Pedostibes tuberculosus*, and *Melanobatrachus indicus*. In addition to the poikilothermous vertebrates, important populations of many large mammal and bird species that are listed as "Threatened" occur in these hill ranges. These include the Nilgiri tahr, Malabar civet, tiger, leopard, gaur, elephant, and the great pied hornbill. Of the ten physiographic zones within the Indian Subcontinent identified by Das (1994, 1996), the Western Ghats, apart from the northeast, is the only zone with endemic species of Testudines—*Geoemyda silvatica* and *Indotesduo forstenii*.

The Western Ghats fauna is unique with many endemic species. Because it is linked to the rapidly shrinking hill forests, the fauna is restricted to a few existing reserves and is threatened with extinction. Rodgers and Panwar (1988) have proposed a network of protected areas for the whole of India; the current mapping and analysis project will, it is hoped, contribute to that goal.

The working hypotheses here are as follows: Each area that is defined by non-historic events (e.g., mountains high enough to be refugia) is likely to support endemic species. Areas of high herpetological diversity outside existing protected areas will be recommended for protection. Since relatively more species are known to occur on larger "islands" than small ones, the former type of sites will be favoured in case of trade-offs for developmental and forestry requirements. Because extinction is area-dependent, larger parks will also support more species than smaller ones as well as

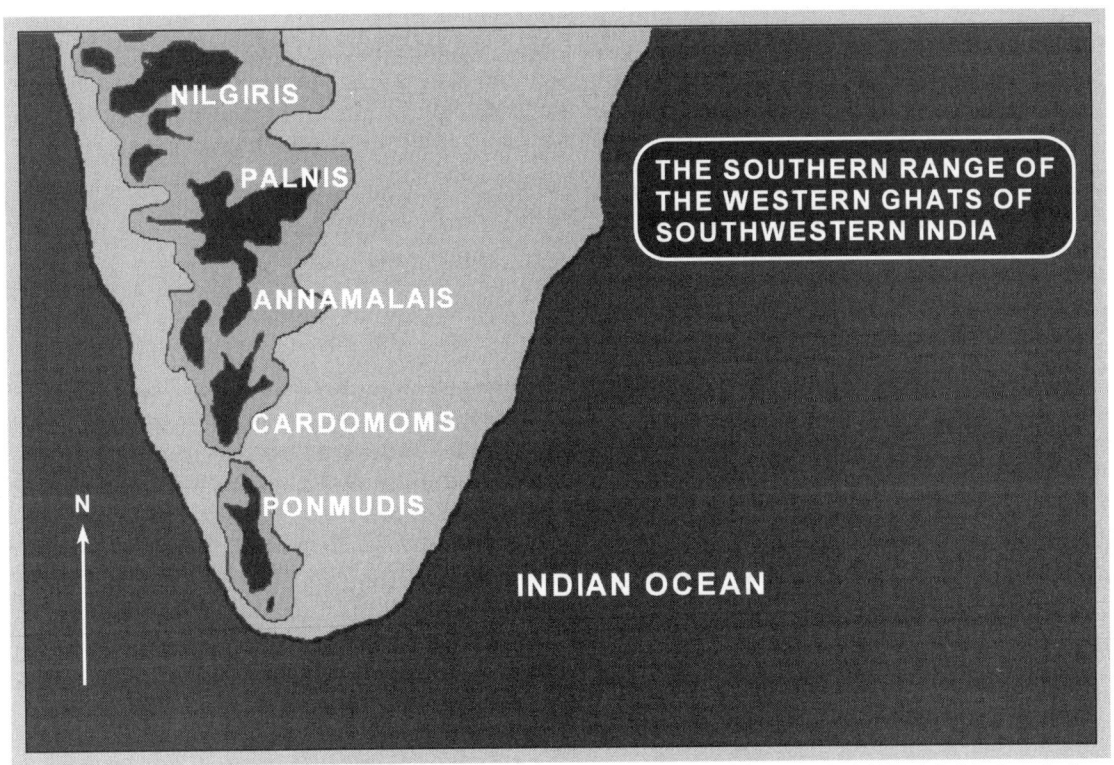

Figure 1. The Western Ghats of southwestern India (in dark grey), showing hill ranges (>1,000 m) in black and often-intervening lowlands (300–1000 m) in dark grey.

larger populations of each species, although habitat diversity and quality may be as important or more important than just size (MacArthur and Wilson, 1967). Given that a minimum area is maintained to satisfy the per capita area requirements to prevent inbreeding depression of the target species, several isolated subpopulations (where some migration between them is allowed) may be preferable to a single large one (see Simberloff, 1982). Preliminary data indicate that large numbers of sites of high diversity lie outside of protected areas and are thus vulnerable. Using the Geographical Information System (GIS) capabilities now widely available for microcomputers (Wills, 1996), the distribution of amphibians and reptiles will be collated and superimposed upon other data types, such as altitude, precipitation, and vegetation. Zones of high herpetological diversity that also have low human densities and relatively undisturbed vegetation will be identified and their protection recommended. The eventual goals are:

1. To identify and maintain functioning ecosystems in the Western Ghats where all plant and animal species are protected, with special attention given to the endemic amphibians and reptiles. Attention will be focussed on the identification of potential "mega-reserves" or areas of high species diversity outside existing protected areas. Preliminary studies indicate that many species-rich sites lie outside protected areas, within tea, coffee, and cardamom estates that are under private ownership. Some of these islands of vegetation are protected by the estates as part of local watershed protection schemes.

2. To utilize the Western Ghats' unique biological characteristics to their fullest, through education, tourism, and research.

3. To promote the socioeconomic development of the aboriginal people, such as the Kadars, of these hill ranges.

4. To identify and/or publicise secondary benefits of protection of the areas proposed, i.e, watershed management, prevention of floods as well as soil and nutrient erosion, ethnobiological studies and other research, education, outdoor recreation, and ecotourism.

Localities of amphibian and reptile species are being obtained from the literature (e.g., Inger, Marx, and Koshy, 1984; Inger, Shaffer, Koshy, and Bakde, 1984; Murthy, 1986, 1989; Pillai, 1986), museum specimens, as well as by recent field work (see Das and Pritchard, 1990; Das and Whitaker, 1990; Das, 1991; Brown et al., 1992). A Geographical Information System (such as ArcView) will be utilised to compile all data on localities and to superimpose climatic information (including altitude, precipitation, atmospheric humidity, and temperature data) as well as information on geology and vegetational diversity onto these records.

Each location will be classified on a standard vegetation classification system and an index of herpetofaunal diversity estimated after correction for land area. On a finer scale, in the second phase of the project, plot studies will be initiated.

A series of 8 × 8 m plots will be selected in all major hill ranges, and long-term sampling using similar techniques are to be conducted. Levels of human pressure, including population density, length of occupation, and human-forest interactions will be assessed. Each locality will be scored for human density, length of occupation, and degree of disturbance (e.g., logging, hunting, etc.).

The greater diversity of amphibians in the southern part of the Western Ghats (compared to the northern half and the higher hills) is linked to more widespread rainfall and less variable climatic conditions (Daniels, 1992, using data from Pascal, 1988). While rainfall along the Ghats undoubtedly increases along a north-south gradient, local conditions of exposure should also be noted. For instance, a site on the windward side in the north should receive more rainfall than a ridge in the south. The role of forest fragmentation on local microclimate is also largely unknown, as are the effects of environmental change on species and populations.

The herpetofauna of the Western Ghats is exceptionally rich, with 117 species of amphibians (Daniels, 1992) and 165 species of reptiles (Das, 1996). However, this fauna is also poorly known, and many undescribed species remain (see Whitaker and Dattatri, 1982; Das, 1991). Acceleration of efforts to understand and protect this fauna is thus critical in the face of increasing pressures to clear the last of the remaining tropical moist forests of southwestern India.

Acknowledgements

My work on the Western Ghats is supported by the Madras Crocodile Bank Trust. Thanks are due to Harry Andrews, Shekar Dattatri, and Romulus Whitaker for logistic support to conduct field work. The curators of many museums in Asia, Europe, and North America assisted in the study of material or with information such as printouts of their holdings (acknowledged in Das, 1996). Manuscript preparation was supported by Universiti Brunei Darussalam, and I thank David Edwards, then Head of Department of Biology, for facilities. Peter Paul van Dijk, Romulus Whitaker, and an anonymous reviewer read earlier drafts of the paper.

Literature Cited

Brown, S., J. Elster, and D. Pulverer. 1992. The Oxford University herpetological expedition to South India 1991. Unpublished report. 48 pp.

Collins, N. M., J. A. Sayer, and T. C. Whitmore (eds.). 1991. The Conservation Atlas of Tropical Forests: Asia and the Pacific. Macmillan Press, Ltd, London and Basingstroke.

Daniels, R. J. R. 1992. Geographical distribution patterns of amphibians in the Western Ghats, India. J. Biogeogr. 19:521–529.

Das, I. 1991. A new species of *Mabuya* (Reptilia: Squamata: Scincidae) from Tamil Nadu, South India. J. Herpetol. 25:342–344.

Das, I. 1994. The reptiles of south Asia: Checklist and distributional summary. Hamadryad 19:15–40.

Das, I. 1996. Biogeography of the Reptiles of South Asia. Krieger Publishing Co., Malabar, Florida. 16 pl + i–vii + 87 pp.

Das, I. and P. C. H. Pritchard. 1990. Intergradation between *Melanochelys trijuga trijuga* and *M. t. coronata* (Testudines: Emydidae: Bataguridae). Asiatic Herpetol. Res. 3:52–53.

Das, I. and R. Whitaker. 1990. Herpetological investigations in the Western Ghats, South India. Part I. The Vanjikadavu and Nadukani forests, Kerala State. Hamadryad 15:6–9.

Inger, R. F., H. Marx, and M. Koshy. 1984. An undescribed species of gekkonid lizard (*Cnemaspis*) from India with comments on the status of *C. tropidogaster*. Herpetologica 40:149–154.

Inger, R. F., H. B. Shaffer, M. Koshy, and R. Bakde. 1984. A report on a collection of amphibians and reptiles from the Ponmudi, Kerala, South India. J. Bombay Nat. Hist. Soc. 81:406–427; 551–570.

Inger, R. F., H. B. Shaffer, M. Koshy, and R. Bakde. 1987. Ecological structure of a herpetological assemblage in south India. Amphibia-Reptilia 8:189–202.

MacArthur, R. H. and E. O. Wilson. 1967. The theory of island biogeography. Princeton University Press, Princeton, New Jersey.

Murthy, T. S. N. 1986. Reptiles of Silent Valley. Rec. Zool. Surv. India 84:173–184.

Murthy, T. S. N. 1989. A collection of reptiles from the Kalakad Wildlife Sanctuary, Tamil Nadu, India. British Herpetol. Soc. Bull. (28):37–40.

Office of Technology Assessment. 1984. Technology to Sustain Tropical Forest Resources. Congress of the United States, Office of Technology Assessment, Washington, D.C. 344 pp.

Pascal, J. P. 1988. Wet evergreen forests of the Western Ghats of India. Inst. Fra. Pondichéry Tra. Sec. Sci. Tech. 20:1–345.

Pillai, R. S. 1986. Amphibian fauna of Silent Valley, Kerala, S. India. Rec. Zool. Surv. India 84:229–242.

Rodgers, W. A. and H. S. Panwar. 1988. Planning a Wildlife Protected Area Network in India. Wildlife Institute of India, Dehradun.

Simberloff, D. 1982. Big advantages of small refuges. Natural History 91(4):6–14.

Whitaker, R. and S. Dattatri. 1982. A new species of *Oligodon* from the Palni Hills, south India (Serpentes: Colubridae). J. Bombay Nat. Hist. Soc. 79:630–631.

Wills, J. T. 1996. The creation of a Geographical Information System for the Kuala Belalong Field Studies Centre. *In* Proceedings of the International Conference on Tropical Rainforest Research: Current Issues. Bandar Seri Begawan, 1993. Kluwer Academic Publishers, Dordrecht.

A Second Reserve for the Bolson Tortoise, *Gopherus flavomarginatus*, at Rancho Sombreretillo, Chihuahua, Mexico

EDDIE TREVIÑO,[1] DAVID J. MORAFKA,[1] AND GUSTAVO AGUIRRE[2]

[1]*Department of Biology, California State University, Dominguez Hills, Carson, CA 90747-0005, USA*
[2]*Instituto de Ecología, A. C., Km 2.5 Antigua Carretera a Coatepec, Ap. Postal 63, 91000 Xalapa, Veracruz, Mexico*

ABSTRACT: In 1992 a team of U.S. and Mexican scientists, funded by the American Museum of Natural History Turtle Recovery Program, assessed the distinctiveness of a population of Mexican Bolson tortoises, *Gopherus flavomarginatus*, occurring on Rancho Sombreretillo in the state of Chihuahua. Situated along the northern edge of the species' current range, the ranch contains several demes of these tortoises. Following the team's investigative surveys, Rancho Sombreretillo was determined to be suitable and appropriate as a reserve for this endangered tortoise.

Starch gel electrophoresis of frozen whole blood identified 18 isozymes (presumptive gene loci) through differential staining and mobility. No differences in allozymes were found between the northern (Sombreretillo) population and the better-studied southern population from the Mapimí Reserve in Durango. The close relationship of this species to the gopher tortoise, *G. polyphemus*, was confirmed, again by the absence of fixed allozyme differences.

Surveys confirmed that yellow pigments in the Sombreretillo tortoises are largely confined to the marginals, especially in subadult to adult individuals. Yellow pigment was more extensively distributed in juvenile carapaces than previously reported.

Since the late 1980s habitat quality at Rancho Sombreretillo had deteriorated as a result of increased cattle grazing. Cattle densities had increased, partly as a result of expanded pumping of underground water to local troughs and reservoirs. However, tortoise populations remained robust, with ample evidence of nests, hatchlings, and juvenile age size classes.

The process of establishing Rancho Sombreretillo as a Bolson tortoise reserve is reviewed in this paper. From the options of (1) purchase, (2) lease, (3) easement, and/or (4) cooperative agreement, the latter was chosen because it was the most acceptable to the landowner, would generate local community support, and involved less investment. Purchased land could also be more easily exploited by local poachers if subsequent patrolling proved inadequate.

The Bolson tortoise, *Gopherus flavomarginatus*, largest of the North American tortoises, was originally described by Legler (1959) and subsequently modified by Legler and Webb, 1961; Auffenberg and Franz, 1978b; Aguirre et al., 1979; Morafka, 1982; Bury et. al., 1988; and Lieberman and Morafka, 1988; Adest et al., 1989.

This massive, dark olive-brown tortoise is identified by the yellowish-green, lateral marginal scutes. Maximum carapace dimensions range 370–400 × 290–300 mm, and maximum weights range 35–50 kg (Legler and Webb, 1961). Native to the Bolson de Mapimí in north-central Mexico, its distribution is confined to southeastern Chihuahua, northeastern Durango, and western Coahuila.

In 1992 a team of U.S. and Mexican scientists, assembled and funded by the American Museum of Natural History Turtle Recovery Program, began an evaluation of the genetic differentiation of the Bolson tortoise in various regions of Chihuahua. Finding that the most robust population existed on Rancho Sombreretillo, a large privately owned cattle ranch, the Turtle Recovery Program commissioned a subsequent study to determine the feasibility and methods for protecting this area as a reserve.

The first phase was to assess the biological status of the Sombreretillo Bolson tortoise population by investigating its genetic differentiation and demographic vigor, and the stability and biodiversity of its local supporting ecosystem. Once these criteria were satisfied, we also assessed the socioeconomic and political practicalities of establishing a reserve. In the second phase (once it was determined to be a realistic objective), we undertook the formal establishment of the reserve. This included the formulation of agreements with land owners and the appointment of administrative and field staff. In the third phase (implementation and maintenance phase), the Instituto de Ecología is provided financial support through the Turtle Recovery Program to ensure the continued and effective operation of the reserve.

Phase One: Evaluation

Biological Assessments

Field trips were conducted primarily to perform the biological assessments, but secondarily to confirm the socioeconomic and political availability of the targeted site for future tortoise conservation. Joining the authors were IUCN member and tortoise conservationist Mrs. Ariel Appleton and Dr. David J. Germano, an expert in tortoise morphometrics.

Rancho Sombreretillo was found to support a large, dense tortoise population, which appears to recruit new generations, as evidenced by the presence of active nesting and intermediate age size classes. Tortoises occur throughout the ranch properties but appear to be concentrated on both the lower west and east slopes of the Cerros Emilio and south of Rancho Papalote. Another concentration of large individuals occurs in the southern portion of the ranch, bordering Rancho Esperanzas (Figure 1).

By 1992 (and since the last U.S. team visit in 1987), grassland had deteriorated dramatically in both density and diversity. Native perennial bunch grasses and annual gramas appeared to have suffered differentially. Underground water was now pumped to the surface both at the main ranch house and the small house at Rancho Papalote. The 10,000 ha ranch supports up to 1,800 head of cattle in the winter and spring months, with about 6% of that herd located on the 2,000 ha surrounding Cerros Emilio. Drought years encourage the bringing of additional cattle to this well-watered area, which further exacerbates the overgrazing problem.

The only conspicuous difference found between these tortoises and the better-studied population to the south in Mapimí, Durango, was the yellow coloration of the carapace. In the Mapimí population the intensity and distribution of yellow color vary widely, and yellow is often present on the vertebral and costal scutes. Surveys conducted in 1992, 1993, and 1994 confirmed that yellow pigments in the Sombreretillo tortoise are largely confined to the marginals, especially in subadult to adult individuals. Juvenile carapaces showed more extensively distributed yellow than previously reported. Shell measurements also determined differences in shell morphology between the two populations at Mapimí and Sombreretillo.

A blood-based survey of North American tortoises identified 13 enzyme systems including 18 presumptive gene loci. Bolson tortoises were distinctive and the closest extant relative, the gopher tortoise, were only separated by a single fixed locus difference. Both Benton (adjacent to Sombreretillo) and Mapimí Bolson tortoise samples revealed much lower gene polymorphism and overall heterozygosity than any of the other three species sampled. No differences in allozymes, fixed allozymes, or gene frequencies were found between the two Bolson tortoise samples (Morafka et al., 1994).

Sociopolitical Assessments

Rancho Sombreretillo tortoises were still highly vulnerable to poaching, evidenced by recently (<1 year old) excavated burrows. The resident Vega family was attempting to deflect or intercept intruders, but their efforts had been largely confined to horseback patrols.

The Chow family of Delicias, Chihuahua, which has owned Rancho Sombreretillo for nearly 100 years, is dedicated to tortoise protection and was found to be open to developing a cooperative protection program with the Turtle Recovery Program, Fundación de la Fauna, and the Instituto de Ecología.

The Chow family was offered four alternative arrangements for establishing a cooperative agreement for tortoise conservation. These were (1) outright purchase of their ranch, (2) an arrangement of land exchanges, in which conservationists would purchase an alternative cattle ranch for them elsewhere, (3) the formulation of a long-term (>20 years) lease or easement to the 2,000 ha surrounding Cerros Emilio to protect optimal tortoise habitat, and (4) a memorandum of understanding in which the consortium of conservationists would provide the ranch with technical assistance, including a patrol vehicle, improved radio/telephone communication, and a scientific advisor to monitor grassland recovery as well as a tortoise mark-and-recapture program at Cerros Emilio. Of these, options 1 and 2 were rejected and option 3 was viewed with limited potential but was not well received. Option 4 appeared to be the most cost-effective approach for the Turtle Recovery Program and the most acceptable to the Chow family.

Phase Two: Formal Establishment of the Reserve

In summer 1993 the team further investigated the official land title to the ranch and defined its boundaries using GPS and GIS technology (Figure 1). Legal counsel from the various Mexican government agencies such as SEDASOL, Fundación Chihuahuense de la Fauna, and the Registro Agrario Nacional were consulted to establish a Memorandum of Understanding (MOU) between the Chow family and scientists conducting research at the ranch. The Instituto de Ecología agreed to act as liaison between American scientists and the Chow family.

In September 1993 a MOU between the Chows and the researchers was completed and signed. The agreement, designed to develop a structured program of tortoise protection compatible with cattle ranching, called for rotational grazing to minimize the impacts of cattle upon young tortoises and to allow the complete growth cycle of the grasslands during the wet season (July–September). This agreement also provided the Mexican government incentive to grant reserve status to the ranch—a designation that enabled the Chows to receive the services of a game warden.

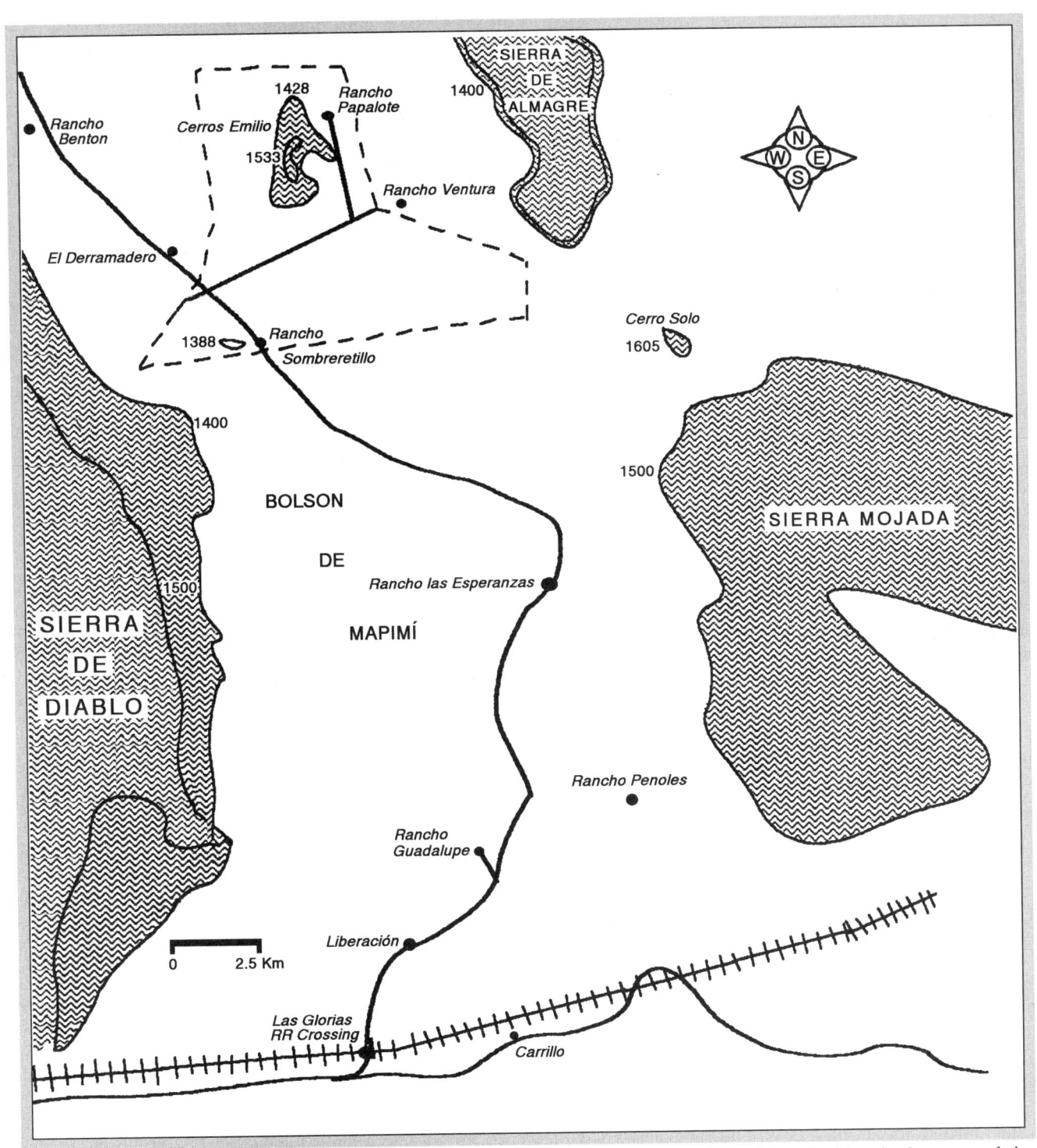

Figure 1. Map of the Bolson de Mapimí, in the state of Chihuahua. This area is approximately 230 km due north of the other known population (n <1,000) of Bolson tortoises located at the Laboratorio del Desierto, Durango, Mexico. The Rancho Sombreretillo tortoise reserve is shown within the dashed line. Patterned areas represent elevations above 1,400 m. The greatest density (n >1,000) of Bolson tortoises is located near Cerros Emilio. The reserve is actually made up of two ranches, Rancho Papalote at the north end of the Chow family properties (including Cerros Emilio), and Rancho Sombreretillo proper, to the south.

Phase Three: Implementation and Maintenance

With the advice and assistance of the Fundación Chihuahuense de la Fauna, a game warden/caretaker was chosen to manage the continued protection and maintenance of the tortoise population, thus releasing the Chow family from these duties. The Instituto de Ecología, experienced in addressing the socioeconomic issues involved in the establishment of a nature reserve (Halffter, 1977), is providing support in monitoring Rancho Sombreretillo, and the Turtle Recovery Program (now under the auspices of the Wildlife Conservation Society) is continuing to provide financial and technical support.

DISCUSSION

From the options of (1) purchase, (2) lease, (3) easement, and/or (4) cooperative agreement, the latter was chosen because it was most acceptable to the landowner, it would generate local community support, and it involved less investment. Purchased land could also be more easily exploited by local poachers if subsequent patrolling proved inadequate.

This fourth option also reinforced the current practice of sending calves to market between April and June. The resulting low density livestock in ranch pastures during the summer and fall wet season (when grasslands are most productive) decreases the impact upon tortoises during the time they are most active and reproductive. Any financial hardship for the ranch owners would also be minimized as most cattle production at Rancho Sombreretillo is already confined to growing calves during the fall and winter months, which are shipped to U.S. markets by summer.

ACKNOWLEDGMENTS

We wish to thank Michael Klemens and the Turtle Recovery Program for their support in establishing a reserve for the Bolson tortoise. To Kiko's family at the Laboratorio del Desierto, Instituto de Ecología, Mapimí, Durango, who provided a very warm and friendly atmosphere, we are very grateful. Their knowledge of the area was extremely helpful in our endeavors.

We also wish to thank all the Mexican officials from the various government and private agencies for their cooperation in this research project. To the Chow family and the residents at Rancho Sombreretillo, we extend our gratitude and thanks. Their hospitality, cooperation, and assistance was greatly appreciated by all of us.

And last, but not least, to all the families, friends, and colleagues, we appreciate your patience and understanding, which allowed our research efforts to succeed, and for this we are grateful.

LITERATURE CITED

Aguirre, G., G. Adest, M. Recht, and D. Morafka. 1979. Preliminary investigations of the movements, thermoregulation, and population structure and diet of the Bolson tortoise, *Gopherus flavomarginatus*, in the Mapimí Biosphere Reserve, Durango, Mexico. Proc. Desert Tortoise Council Symp. 1979:149–165.

Auffenberg, W. and R. Franz. 1978b. *Gopherus flavomarginatus*. Cat. Am. Amphib. Reptiles: 214.1–214.2.

Bury, R. B., D. J. Morafka, and C. J. McCoy. 1988. Part I. Distribution, abundance and status of the Bolson tortoise. Annals of the Carnegie Museum 57:5–30.

Halffter, G. 1977. Las Reservas de la Biosfera en la Estado de Durango: Una nueva politica de conservacion y estudio de los recursos bioticos. In G. Halffter, (ed.), Reservas de la Biosfera en el Estado de Durango, Publ. 4, pp. 12–45.

Legler, J. M. 1959. A new tortoise, genus *Gopherus*, from north central Mexico. Unv. Kans. Publ. Mus. Nat. Hist. 11:335–343.

Legler, J. M. and R. G. Webb. 1961. Remarks on a collection of Bolson tortoises, *Gopherus flavomarginatus*. Herpetologica 17:26–37.

Lieberman, S. S. and D. J. Morafka. 1988. Part II. Ecological distribution of the Bolson tortoise. In D. J. Morafka and C. J. McCoy (eds.), The Ecogeography of the Mexican Bolson Tortoise (*Gopherus flavomarginatus*): Derivation of its Endangered Status and Recommendations for its Conservation. Annals Carnegie Museum 57(1):37–46.

Morafka, D. J. 1982. The status and distribution of the Bolson tortoise (*Gopherus flavomarginatus*). In R. B. Bury (ed.), North American tortoises: Conservation and ecology, pp. 71–94. Wildlife Research Report 12, U.S. Fish and Wildlife Service, Washington, D.C..

Morafka, D. J., G. A. Adest, G. Aguirre, and M. Recht. 1981. The ecology of the Bolson tortoise, *Gopherus flavomarginatus*. In R. Barbault and G. Halffter (eds.), Ecology of the Chihuahuan Desert: Organization of Some Vertebrate Communities. Publication 8, Instituto de Ecología, A.C., Mexico, D.F.

Morafka, D. J., G. Aguirre, and R. W. Murphy. 1994. Allozyme differentiation among gopher tortoises (*Gopherus*): Conservation genetics and phylogenetic and taxonomic implications. Can. J. Zool. 72:1665–1671.

Integrated Management Strategies and Public Policy

Standing — John Polisar (University of Florida, Gainesville), Molly Olson (The Natural Step, Sausalito, California), John Frazier (Sección de Ecología Humana, Merida, Yucatan, Mexico), and Peter Pritchard (Florida Audubon Society, Winter Park, Florida). *Seated* — Kristin Berry (U.S. Geological Survey, Biological Resouces Division, Riverside, California), Suzi Oppenheimer (New York State Senator, Westchester County), and Suzanne Dohm (President, New York Turtle and Tortoise Society).

Jeffrey Lovich (U.S. Geological Survey, Biological Resources Division, Palm Springs Field Station, Palm Springs, California).

Turtle Conservation and Halfway Technology: What Is the Problem?

— PLENARY LECTURE —

NAT B. FRAZER

Savannah River Ecology Laboratory, University of Georgia, Drawer E, Aiken, SC 29802, USA [e-mail: frazer@srel.edu]

ABSTRACT: How we define a problem often will predetermine what we are willing to consider as a viable solution. Thus, when we define the impending extinction of a turtle species solely in terms of there being too few turtles, we seek solutions based solely on increasing the numbers of turtles. Hatcheries, headstarting, and captive breeding programs all may provide observable increases in turtle numbers while they are in our care. However, successful repatriation or augmentation programs are extremely unlikely unless the original causes for a population's decline have been addressed. Hence, some of our attempts to conserve turtles may involve "halfway technology" in that they do not address the causes of nor provide amelioration for the actual threats turtles face in their natural habitats. In the final analysis, turtles need clean and productive aquatic and terrestrial environments in which to thrive. Without a commitment to such long-term ecological and evolutionary goals, our efforts to protect and restore turtle populations will be futile. Instead of designing conservation programs that rely on perpetual crisis management, we must, as Stephen R. Covey admonishes us, "Begin with the end in mind." The end result of our conservation efforts must be to establish (or reestablish) self-sustaining turtle populations in healthy habitats.

Pritchard (1980) pointed out that, "Nearly all sea turtle biologists, sooner or later, become turtle conservationists, at least by sympathy, and frequently as a major part of their professional activities." Now, some 15 years later, his statement can be applied equally well to terrestrial and freshwater turtle biologists. Few of us can sit idly by as up to two thirds or more of the species we study become ever rarer due to habitat destruction or overexploitation. But in our zeal to protect or restore the turtle populations under our charge, we must resist the temptation to abandon our understanding of turtle biology and evolutionary ecology for the technological quick fix. Pritchard (1980) also wisely warned us that "... sea turtle conservation remains without a theoretical framework, and almost all techniques that have been used remain unproven and riddled with paradox." As freshwater and terrestrial turtle conservation approaches the urgency and high public profile previously associated only with marine turtles, we must insure the development of a theoretical framework in which our efforts rest upon a firm foundation of ecological and evolutionary principles. Otherwise, we have little to offer as biologists other than wishful thinking. For example, despite a recent suggestion that the headstart programs common in sea turtle conservation also be aggressively applied to terrestrial and freshwater turtle populations (Iverson, 1991a), only one sea turtle headstart program has ever demonstrated that its released turtles have survived to maturity in the wild (Woody, 1990; Shaver, 1996). On the other hand, programs at both national (Byles, 1993) and state (Huff, 1989) levels have been terminated in recent years as the practice has been increasingly questioned as a viable conservation technique for sea turtles (Mrosovsky, 1983; Woody, 1990, 1991). This is not to say that headstarting cannot or will not work as one component of the successful conservation of any freshwater or terrestrial turtle species. However, as it does not address any of the causes by which a species originally became endangered or threatened, headstarting alone is likely to have little effect in restoring a species to former levels of abundance, or of sustaining a viable population (Frazer, 1992). The same can be said for programs that center on hatcheries or captive breeding as the focal points for turtle conservation activity.

As I have argued elsewhere (Frazer, 1992), such approaches to conservation fall into the category of "halfway technology," a phrase coined by Lewis Thomas (1974) in an essay on the technology of medicine in his widely read book, *The Lives of a Cell*. Lewis defined the term in the context of medical practices, such as heart transplants, that neither offer a true cure for a disease nor greatly further our understanding of its etiology or prevention. Halfway technology is, at best, he maintained, a means of buying time until some real understanding of underlying causes can be achieved and a methodology of correcting those causes developed. The problem with halfway technology in conservation is that we continue to apply palliatives that do not address the underlying causes of population decline, even though we often already know what needs to be done to cure or prevent them—arresting the habitat destruction or stemming the overexploitation. Unfortunately, society may be unwilling to pay the true cost of having turtles in a healthy, natural environment, but may be willing for us to salve our collective conscience by rearing hatchlings or yearlings to supply a constant stream of input back into the environment in perpetual crisis management. This was certainly the case with sea turtles, where congressional friends of the shrimping industry introduced legislation to fund headstarting programs as an alternative to requiring turtle excluder devices in shrimp trawl nets to reduce the incidental take of sea turtles (Williams, 1993).

There are at least three major problems with headstarting and other attempts at halfway technological quick fixes in turtle conservation. First, turtle biologists and conservationists must not assume that protecting any one life stage can, by itself, "save" a turtle species from extinction. Archie Carr (1984) rightly claimed in *So Excellent a Fishe* that, "Protection of sea turtles is not a parochial problem. They cannot be saved in any one place, or by controlling any one phase of the life cycle." This claim has been strengthened by the first computer models of sea turtle population dynamics (Crouse et al., 1987). Although a sensitivity analysis of their models showed that protection of larger juveniles and adults (as with turtle excluder devices deployed on shrimp trawl nets) would have a more rapid effect on population recovery than would protecting eggs or hatchlings (as in hatcheries or headstarting projects), Crouse et al. (1987) were careful to state that conservation efforts must not neglect any life stages. More recently, Carr's position also has been echoed by the authors conducting sensitivity analyses on a demographic model of freshwater turtles (Congdon et al., 1993). They concluded that, "Successful management and conservation programs for long-lived organisms will be those that recognize that protection of all life stages is necessary."

Another concern that exacerbates management of long-lived, late-maturing species such as sea turtles and Blanding's turtles is that the best models we have to date indicate that our conservation efforts may have to be implemented for many decades (i.e., up to 70 years or more) before substantial increases are observed in the populations under our care (Congdon et al., 1993; Crowder et al., 1994). Currently, additional computer models are being constructed with demographic information for other freshwater turtles (S. Heppell and J. Iverson, pers. comm.). But even if further demographic models of terrestrial and freshwater turtle populations were to indicate that their life histories are more amenable to headstarting and captive breeding programs than are those of marine turtles and Blanding's turtles, we still must remember that concentrating our protection on any one life stage may not be sufficient to protect a local population from extinction. Consider, for example, the report by Brooks et al. (1991) of the devastating effect on a natural population of snapping turtles when faced with a sudden increase of adult mortality brought about by mammalian predators. This example of a sudden change in age-specific survival rates points out the second problem with basing conservation strategies on simply enumerating turtles.

Turtles do fit a general life history pattern of low egg and juvenile survival, followed by high adult survival rates (Iverson, 1991a). However, recently published results from long-term studies of freshwater turtles have shown that there may be much variance in these underlying survival patterns over time, even within a given population (e.g., Frazer et al., 1990, 1991a; Iverson, 1991b; Congdon et al., 1993). In addition to variability in age-specific survival rates, even growth rates and age at maturity may vary temporally in a given population (Zweifel, 1989; Frazer et al., 1991b, 1993). Thus, we must take care not to base our conservation programs on outdated assumptions concerning static life tables.

Third, with apologies to Gertrude Stein, even if "A rose is a rose is a rose," we cannot assume that a turtle is a turtle is a turtle. Although demographers and proponents of headstarting or captive rearing programs may tacitly assume that their turtles are equivalent to wild counterparts and will enjoy the same (or better!) survival and reproductive rates, this usually is taken on faith rather than determined experimentally (Frazer, 1989). And even where headstarted animals have been documented to survive in the wild, the demographic statistics may not tell the whole story. There still are genetic and behavioral considerations to take into account before assuming that captive-reared or headstarted turtles will be able to replace, rebuild, or augment an existing population successfully. For example, Reinert (1991) has pointed out that captive-reared fish and reptiles may behave quite inappropriately during courtship or other encounters with conspecifics. And the well-founded fear expressed by fish conservationists (Meffe, 1986, 1992), that captive breeding in hatcheries may select for reduced genetic variance between populations, has yet to be addressed in turtle conservation. Therefore, even if headstarted or captive-reared turtles do survive upon their release, there is no simple guarantee that they will rebuild healthy, self-sustaining populations in the wild.

As Stephen R. Covey, author of *The Seven Habits of Highly Effective People*, has put it, "How we *see* the problem *is* the problem" (Covey, 1989). If we define the impending extinction of a turtle species solely in terms of there being too few turtles, we may be tempted to consider anything that appears to increase the numbers of turtles, even temporarily, as a viable solution to the problem. But if we are to be successful as conservationists, we must be more careful as to how we define the problem of impending turtle extinction.

It's easy for the public to slip into accepting the numbers game in conservation. Members of an overmanaged, technological society that bases its tremendous manufacturing capability on mass production of interchangeable parts will not question whether captive-reared turtles are equivalent to their wild counterparts. Those who themselves have increasingly confined the majority of their lives to school and office buildings, shopping malls, gymnasia, and playing fields are not likely to ask whether captive rearing is an acceptable preparation for life in the wild. When one adds to this the fact that even the average college graduate has only the most rudimentary understanding of ecological and evolutionary principles, it does not seem surprising that the public would accept the perpetual crisis management of continued releases of headstarted turtles as adequate payment for those taken by continued habitat destruction or overexploitation.

But even well-trained biologists and wildlife managers are susceptible to the lure of turtle enumeration in conservation planning. Is this because no less a figure than Darwin (1859) reminded us that rarity is the precursor to extinction? Do we take his statement to mean that if we just can prevent the rarity, we can prevent the extinction? As one who spent the majority of his life providing the ecological and evolutionary context in which we, as modern biologists, should be conducting our affairs, Darwin certainly would not have fallen for such a simplistic argument. After having read *The Origin of Species* once a year for the past eight years, I cannot imagine Darwin advocating that the way to prevent extinction is merely to put more and more individuals of a particular species back out into a habitat in which their parents had already demonstrated their inability to survive.

We know that if habitat quality is low, the chances for successful introduction or reintroduction of a species is also low (Griffith et al., 1989). One of the most successful reintroduction stories that conservationists have is that of peregrine falcons and other birds of prey. However, an essential ingredient of that success was stopping the use of the pesticides, which were originally responsible for the local extinctions before reintroducing the birds (Cade, 1988). The environmental context in which species introductions or reintroductions takes place is undeniably important. But so is some understanding of the evolutionary development of a species' current pattern of life history traits.

So, how *do* we see the problem? We now have information from a sufficient number of long-term studies on turtles to begin assessing the general patterns of their life histories (Iverson, 1991a), elucidating trends in their life history evolution (Wilbur and Morin, 1988; Congdon and Gibbons, 1990), and determining the extent of variation and plasticity in key life history traits (e.g., Frazer et al., 1990, 1991a; Iverson, 1991b; Congdon et al., 1993). As we begin to understand the selective pressures that have shaped turtle life histories since the Permian and the resulting variability that characterizes their demographic statistics over shorter time periods (i.e., decades), we must not act as though our new understanding of ecological and evolutionary biology has little to do with the practice of conservation. The problem is not simply numbers of turtles, but whether or not they can continue to persist as integral parts of functional ecosystems. Our conservation efforts must address much more than just numbers of individual organisms. If the desired end of our conservation efforts is to conserve turtles as turtles, we must allow for the continued interplay of demography, genetics, and behavior in as natural a setting as we can provide.

Presently, most turtle species are characterized by low egg and juvenile survival and high adult survival rates (Iverson, 1991a). But hatcheries and headstarting projects attempt to reverse this 200 million year evolutionary trend by heightening juvenile survival to make up for increased human-induced mortality of adult turtles. Like it or not, if we base our conservation activities on sequestering and protecting early life stages in captivity, while continuing to impact adults and larger juveniles in the wild, we are shaping selective pressures that will redefine that which we call a turtle. Once we have so drastically altered that which we first set out to conserve, how then do we define our goal? That *is* a problem.

Acknowledgments

The ideas presented in this paper have developed over the past 15 years in conversations (and arguments) with over 200 students in my ecology and evolution classes at Mercer University and several colleagues from various other universities, governmental agencies, and conservation organizations. I am particularly indebted to Jim and Thelma Richardson, Whit Gibbons, and Justin Congdon for guidance in clarifying my position. Writing and manuscript preparation were supported by contract DE-AC09-76SROO-819 between the University of Georgia and the United States Department of Energy.

Literature Cited

Brooks, R. J., G. P. Brown, and D. A. Galbraith. 1991. Effects of a sudden increase in natural mortality on a population of the common snapping turtle (*Chelydra serpentina*). Can. J. Zool. 69:1314–1320.

Byles, R. 1993. Head-start experiment no longer rearing Kemp's ridleys. Marine Turtle Newsletter 63:1–3.

Cade, T. J. 1988. Using science and technology to reestablish species lost in nature. In E. O. Wilson (ed.), Biodiversity, pp. 279–288. National Academy Press, Washington, DC.

Carr, A. 1984. So Excellent a Fishe. University of Texas Press, Austin, Texas.

Congdon, J. D. and J. W. Gibbons. 1990. The evolution of turtle life histories. *In* J. W. Gibbons (ed.), Life History and Ecology of the Slider Turtle, pp. 45–54. Smithsonian Institution Press, Washington, D.C. i–xiv + 368 pp.

Congdon, J. D., A. E. Dunham, and R. C. van Loben Sels. 1993. Delayed sexual maturity and demographics of Blanding's turtles (*Emydoidea blandingii*): Implications for conservation and management of long-lived organisms. Conserv. Biol. 7:826–833.

Covey, S. R. 1989. The Seven Habits of Highly Effective People. Simon and Schuster, New York.

Crouse, D. T., L. B. Crowder, and H. Caswell. 1987. A stage-based population model for loggerhead sea turtles and implications for conservation. Ecology 68:1412–1423.

Crowder, L. B., D. T. Crouse, S. S. Heppell, and T. H. Martin. 1994. Predicting the impact of turtle excluder devices on loggerhead sea turtle populations. Ecol. Appl. 4:437–445.

Darwin, C. 1979 (1859). The Origin of Species by Means of Natural Selection: Or, the Preservation of Favourable Races in the Struggle for Life. Avenel Books, New York.

Frazer, N. B. 1989. A philosophical approach to population models. *In* L. Ogren, F. Berry, K. Bjorndal, H. Kumpf, R. Mast, G. Medina, H. Reichart, and R. Witham (eds.), Proceedings of the Second Western Atlantic Turtle Symposium, pp. 198–207. NOAA Technical Memorandum NMFS-SEFC-226. National Marine Fisheries Service, National Oceanic and Atmospheric Administration, U.S. Dept. Commerce, Panama City, Florida.

Frazer, N. B. 1992. Sea turtle conservation and halfway technology. Conserv. Biol. 6:179–184.

Frazer, N. B., J. W. Gibbons, and J. L. Greene. 1990. Life tables of a slider population. *In* J. W. Gibbons (ed.), Life History and Ecology of the Slider Turtle, pp. 183–200. Smithsonian Institution Press, Washington, DC. i–xiv + 368 pp.

Frazer, N. B., J. W. Gibbons, and J. L. Greene. 1991a. Life history and demography of the common mud turtle, *Kinosternon subrubrum*, in South Carolina, USA. Ecology 72:2218–2231.

Frazer, N. B., J. W. Gibbons, and J. L. Greene. 1991b. Growth, survivorship, and longevity of painted turtles, *Chrysemys picta*, in a southwestern Michigan marsh. Amer. Midl. Nat. 125:245–258.

Frazer, N. B., J. L. Greene, and J. W. Gibbons. 1993. Temporal variation in growth rates and age at maturity of male painted turtles, *Chrysemys picta*. Amer. Midl. Nat. 130:314–324.

Griffith, B., J. M. Scott, J. W. Carpenter, and C. Reed. 1989. Translocation as a species conservation tool: Status and strategy. Science 245:477–480.

Huff, J. A. 1989. Florida (USA) terminates "headstart" program. Marine Turtle Newsletter 46:1–2.

Iverson, J. B. 1991a. Patterns of survivorship in turtles (order Testudines). Can. J. Zool. 69:385–391.

Iverson, J. B. 1991b. Life history and demography of the yellow mud turtle, *Kinosternon flavescens*. Herpetologica 47:373–395.

Meffe, G. K. 1986. Conservation genetics and the management of endangered fish. Fisheries 11:14–23.

Meffe, G. K. 1992. Techno-arrogance and halfway technologies: Salmon hatcheries on the Pacific coast of North America. Conserv. Biol. 6:350–354.

Mrosovsky, N. 1983. Conserving Sea Turtles. British Herpetological Society, London.

Pritchard, P. C. H. 1980. The conservation of sea turtles: Practices and problems. Amer. Zool. 20:609–617.

Reinert, H. K. 1991. Translocation as a conservation strategy for amphibians and reptiles: Some comments, concerns, and observations. Herpetologica 47:357–363.

Thomas, L. 1974. The Lives of a Cell. The Viking Press, New York.

Shaver, D. J. 1996. Head-started Kemp's ridley turtles nest in Texas. Marine Turtle Newsletter 74(5):5–7.

Wilbur, H. M. and P. J. Morin. 1988. Life history evolution in turtles. *In* C. Gans and R. Huey (eds.), Biology of the Reptilia, Vol. 16B, pp. 387–439. Alan R. Liss, New York.

Williams, P. 1993. NMFS to concentrate on measuring survivorship, fecundity of head-started Kemp's ridleys in the wild. Marine Turtle Newsletter 63:3–4.

Woody, J. 1990. Guest editorial: Is "headstarting" a reasonable conservation measure? On the surface, "yes"; in reality, "no." Marine Turtle Newsletter 50:8–11.

Woody, J. 1991. Guest editorial: It's time to stop headstarting Kemp's ridleys. Marine Turtle Newsletter 55:7–8.

Zweifel, R. G. 1989. Long-term ecological studies on a population of painted turtles, *Chrysemys picta*, on Long Island, New York. American Museum Novitates 2952:1–55.

Conservation of Covert Species: Protecting Species We Don't Even Know

JEFFREY E. LOVICH[1] AND J. WHITFIELD GIBBONS[2]

[1]*United States Geological Survey, Biological Resources Division, Palm Springs Field Station, 63500 Garnet Ave., North Palm Springs, CA 92258-2000, USA [e-mail: jeffrey_lovich@nbs.gov]*
[2]*Savannah River Ecology Laboratory, Drawer E, Aiken, SC 29802, USA [e-mail: gibbons@srel.edu]*

ABSTRACT: Advances in molecular biology and morphometrics are resolving systematic relationships at an unprecedented rate. As new species are discovered or recognized, the conservation burden becomes greater, emphasizing the need for protecting biodiversity at the level of major landscapes and ecosystems that are obviously composed of many species, including those not recognized as present. "Covert" species are those that (1) are hidden by faulty taxonomy, (2) possess significant intraspecific genetic variation, (3) have sibling species with poorly known distributions, or (4) are undescribed. In at least one case, a reptile species almost became extinct because of faulty taxonomy. Some species of recently described turtles are facing significant threats to their long-term survival, but as yet have no legal conservation status. Sibling species and undescribed species present special challenges to conservation. We can no longer afford the luxury of single-species conservation programs, nor wait for unidentified species to be described formally. Regional conservation efforts emphasizing the protection of communities that encompass sensitive as well as non-endangered species, including covert species, provide a proactive alternative to the tradition of listing single species for protective status.

Before we can conserve turtles on a large spatial scale, we must understand turtle ecology on a large spatial scale.
—Vincent Burke, 1992

Taxonomy is the foundation of traditional conservation and the underlying basis for quantification of biodiversity (Daugherty et al., 1990). Not only do we need to know how to identify an organism before it can be effectively protected (King and Braziatis, 1971), we also need to know how many distinct organisms (taxa) are in a given area before we can calculate the most basic measure of biodiversity: the number of taxa present. As Avise (1989) noted, "taxonomic assignments inevitably shape perceptions of biotic diversity, including recognition of endangered species." In this essay we discuss the relationship between taxonomy and conservation, and the consequences of failing to recognize the association.

Advances in morphometrics and molecular biology are resolving systematic relationships at an unprecedented rate. New morphometric techniques such as the Procrustes method (Rohlf and Slice, 1990) and thin plate spline analysis (Bookstein, 1989) allow us to resolve subtle differences in morphology between taxa. The use of molecular genetic markers has also given us new insight into the relationships of various taxa, challenging some established relationships and identifying new species. However, as molecular techniques have allowed us to look at finer levels of resolution (e.g., hypervariable regions of the genome), every subunit of a species (local population, family unit, individual) may prove to be distinguishable from all others. Clearly, we need to evaluate new data carefully (Avise, 1989, 1994).

As new species are discovered or recognized, the overall conservation burden increases, emphasizing the need for protecting biodiversity at the level of major landscapes and ecosystems that are obviously composed of many species, whether we recognize them or not. Unfortunately, there will always be species that are cryptic, or covert, in the sense that they (1) are hidden by faulty taxonomy, (2) possess significant intraspecific genetic variation, (3) have sibling species with poorly known distributions, or (4) are undescribed for reasons of being undiscovered or because descriptions have not been published. These species present special conservation challenges that will be reviewed in this paper. Our main objective is to illustrate the problems generated by single-species-oriented, taxonomy-driven conservation programs, with an emphasis on turtle conservation. Finally, we offer our recommendations for solutions.

Changes in Turtle Taxonomy and Perceived Diversity

Although it is widely known that we live in an era of massive global extinctions (Gibbons, 1993), we also live in an era of incredible discovery, with many new species being cataloged daily (Erwin, 1988). The rate at which species are described can be illustrated even by using turtles—a small group of familiar organisms, often assumed to be well known—as an example. The order to which turtles belong includes approximately 260 species (Ernst and Barbour, 1989). However, our perception of turtle diversity has changed significantly over the last several decades. While the majority of turtle species were described during the last century (Figure 1), many discoveries have occurred recently. New turtle species are being described on a regular basis, and each has its own suite of problems related to survival.

In the United States and Canada, the number of recognized species of turtles has increased by 48% in less than 45 years (Figure 2). The number of subspecies has also increased. Changes in perceived global turtle diversity in just the period 1986–1993 included the naming of seven new genera, 14 new species, and 20 new subspecies (Iverson, 1992; including species described by Ernst and Lovich, 1990; Lovich and McCoy, 1992). Unfortunately, 25 of the 54 native turtle species (Ernst et al., 1994) in the United States are in need of conservation action (Lovich, 1995).

Problems Associated with Taxonomy-driven Conservation

Faulty taxonomy. One of the worst mistakes we can make in our efforts to protect biodiversity is to allow the extinction of species because of a faulty taxonomy. The following examples show how the success or failure of conservation strategies often rests on the need for a solid taxonomic foundation. While recognizing the importance of good taxonomic research, we argue that single-species-oriented conservation programs may fail to adequately protect biodiversity because of faulty or fluid taxonomies and the presence of unrecognized species. Yet we also acknowledge that the public may rally around large, "flagship" species, and thereby set aside large areas of habitat that will also protect many small or unknown species.

Perhaps one of the best examples is provided by tuataras. Tuataras are an ancient lineage of reptiles almost universally recognized as containing a single species, *Sphenodon punctatus*. Conservation measures aimed at protecting the tuatara were based on the existence of the single species. However, in the 1800s taxonomists named two living and one extinct species. Subsequent research in this century proposed that the species *S. punctatus* comprised two subspecies (*S. p. punctatus* and *S. p. reischeki*). All of these taxonomic proposals were largely ignored until Daugherty et al. (1990) demonstrated significant morphological and genetic differentiation among living populations of this unique reptile. Their analysis provided strong support for recognition of two different species, *S. punctatus* and *S. guntheri*, and provisional recognition of the new subspecies of *S. punctatus*. One species, *S. guntheri*, is currently limited to one island with fewer than 300 individuals, while the subspecies *S. p. reischeki*, recorded only from Hauturu Island in Whangarei Bay, has not been seen in over a decade and is probably extinct. The failure to recognize documented taxonomic diversity of tuataras resulted in a lack of effort to prevent the extinction of a subspecies and the near extinction of a full species—a tragic loss of biodiversity.

Another example of a failure to recognize significant

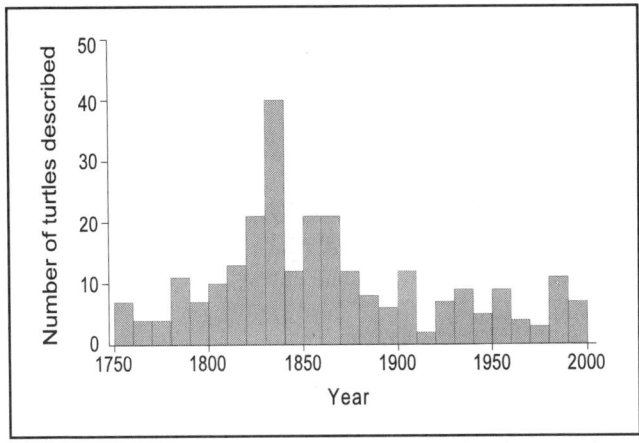

Figure 1. Number of turtle species described during five-year intervals. Dates for descriptions of taxa were taken from Iverson (1992) and updated with additional descriptions by Ernst and Lovich (1990) and Lovich and McCoy (1992).

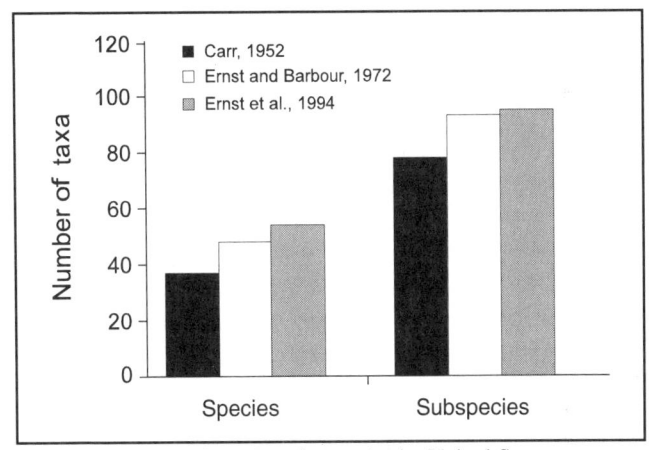

Figure 2. The number of turtle taxa in the United States as recognized in various references.

variation in what was originally described as a single wide-ranging species is shown by the Alabama map turtle, *Graptemys pulchra*. The species was originally described by Baur (1893) from specimens collected in the vicinity of Montgomery, Alabama. Subsequent workers extended the range of the species into several other drainage systems to the east and west of the Mobile Bay drainage system (Cagle, 1952). Detailed analysis of variation in *G. pulchra* (*sensu lato*) revealed that the "species" was actually composed of three taxa, *G. ernsti*, *G. gibbonsi*, and *G. pulchra*, that were separable on the basis of morphology, pattern, and mtDNA haplotypes (Lovich and McCoy, 1992). All three species are threatened by pollution and channelization (Lovich and McCoy, in press; McCoy and Lovich, in press a, in press b), and these threats are compounded by the restricted distributions of the individual taxa. As yet, no conservation plans exist for these species as they were formerly considered to be populations of a single widely distributed taxon.

It is important to note that faulty taxonomies can also

lead to the protection of populations that show little evolutionary differentiation. Avise (1989) reviewed the case of the colonial pocket gopher, *Geomys colonus*, which was described as a species distinct from nearby populations of its congener *G. pinetis*. The species *G. colonus* was subsequently listed as a state protected species in Georgia. Later, molecular genetic surveys failed to demonstrate any consistent distinctions between nearby populations of the two congeners. Avise concluded that either the original species description of *G. colonus* was unwarranted, or that an original colony of true *G. colonus* had become extinct and was replaced by immigrants of *G. pinetis*. In this case, a faulty taxonomy resulted in an unwarranted listing and a loss of funding and resources that might otherwise have been directed toward a valid conservation need. A similar case of mistaken identity involves the dusky seaside sparrow, and the reader is referred to Avise (1989) for details.

Unrecognized intraspecific variation. A related situation is the failure to recognize significant genetic diversity within a species. A recent example is shown by data for the federally protected ("Threatened") desert tortoise, *Gopherus (Xerobates) agassizii*. This wide-ranging species occurs from southwestern Utah southward into California, Nevada, and Arizona in the United States, and into Sonora and Sinaloa states in Mexico. Recent work with mtDNA analysis has identified significant phylogeographic variation in the species (Lamb et al., 1989). Three haplotypes have been identified (some with several genetic variants) with a major break occurring at the Colorado River. Effective conservation of biodiversity requires protection of genetic diversity below the level of species. In recognition of this, the Recovery Plan for the federally "Threatened" Mojave metapopulation requires protection of the full spectrum of genetic variants (U.S. Fish and Wildlife Service, 1994).

Sibling species. Some species are "covert" in the sense that they are difficult to distinguish from other species (sibling species) that are sympatric. The difficulty in differentiating taxa results in poorly known distributions. For example, discrimination of the eastern mud turtle (*Kinosternon subrubrum*) and the striped mud turtle (*K. baurii*) north of Florida was long complicated by extensive character overlap. New techniques for differentiating the two species resulted in a dramatic range extension for *K. baurii*, which was formerly thought to live primarily in peninsular Florida. Recognition that *K. baurii* occurs as far north as Virginia is illustrative of the need to ensure adequate protection over large areas to protect sibling species. Details of the history of misidentification between these two species are provided by Lamb and Lovich (1990).

Undescribed species. In addition to the problems discussed previously, there will always be undescribed species. The lack of formal species descriptions can result for two primary reasons. First, a valid and distinctive species has gone undiscovered by science, a situation which, in all likelihood, will diminish each year, even in the tropics, and is especially true for many temperate regions. Secondly, some new species are known by individual investigators who have not published the formal descriptions. An example of this is the two color morphs of the dwarf salamander, *Eurycea quadridigitata*, in South Carolina. Although the two morphs have been suggested as representing two genetically distinct species (Gibbons and Semlitsch, 1991), a formal description is still forthcoming.

The plight of undescribed species is particularly acute given that as long as they are unrecognized they will have few champions for their protection, although we concede that many described but uncharismatic species also have few champions. Megadiversity areas in the tropics doubtless place many undescribed taxa, including turtles (Lovich, 1994), at great risk because of habitat destruction (Wilson, 1992). One basic solution for remedying the problem is the dedication of higher levels of funding to support alpha taxonomy. Another is not to rely on species identifications as the sole rationale for developing conservation programs.

What Is the Alternative?

The flux in our understanding of turtle taxonomy, and consequently diversity, underscores the need to move away from traditional single-species oriented conservation efforts. We can no longer afford the expensive luxury of single-species conservation programs, or wait for unidentified species to be described formally. Regional conservation efforts emphasizing the protection of sensitive as well as non-endangered species and communities provide a proactive alternative to the tradition of listing single species for protective status. Methods such as GAP analysis provide an objective technique for identifying target areas (Scott et al., 1993).

The difficulty of using a taxonomically based system for conservation is exemplified by Vane-Wright et al. (1991), who advocated a cladistic approach, or taxic weighting, in an effort to provide a systematic approach for evaluating the conservation merit of a species. In the title of their article they posed the question "What to protect?: Systematics and the agony of choice." One answer to their question is "protect habitat." Because habitat loss is the greatest threat facing most species (Mittermeier et al., 1992), habitat protection is one of the greatest conservation priorities. One of the recurring themes of the International Conference, "Conservation, Restoration, and Management of Tortoises and Turtles," was a reliance on "headstarting" threatened and endangered turtles. In addition to the warnings offered by Frazer (1992) regarding headstarting, it is important to emphasize that if you pay to raise a hatchling turtle for later release, at most you generate a turtle that may or may not live to reproduce. However, if you buy a hectare of land, you effectively preserve all species capable of surviving on that parcel. As Odum (1994) noted, "Much of the concern for biodiversity has focused on the species level even though it is self-evident that preservation of habitats is the key to conserving a diversity of species."

Thus, the only way to effectively conserve covert species, as defined in this essay, is to protect habitat. However, documenting that covert species are predominant in many habitats is a worthwhile research effort that can provide justification for broad-scale habitat protection. Ironically, we must promote habitat preservation in order to insure the preservation of covert species and genetic variants while simultaneously demonstrating that the presence of covert species is a frequent phenomenon.

ACKNOWLEDGMENTS

Research was supported by contract number DE-ACO9-76SROO-819 between the United States Department of Energy and the University of Georgia, Savannah River Ecology Laboratory. Special thanks are extended to Hal Avery and Bill Boarman for their support and encouragement.

LITERATURE CITED

Avise, J. C. 1989. A role for molecular genetics in the recognition and conservation of endangered species. Trends in Ecol. Evol. 4:279–281.

Avise, J. C. 1994. Molecular Markers, Natural History and Evolution. Chapman and Hall, New York.

Baur, G. 1893. Two new species of North American Testudinata. Am. Nat. 27(319):675–677.

Bookstein, F. L. 1989. Principal warps: thin-plate splines and the decomposition of deformations. I.E.E.E. Trans. Pattern Anal. Mach. Intelligence 11:567–585.

Cagle, F. R. 1952. The status of the turtles *Graptemys pulchra* Baur and *Graptemys barbouri* Carr and Marchand, with notes on their natural history. Copeia 1952(4):223–234.

Carr, A. F. 1952. Handbook of Turtles. The Turtles of the United States, Canada, and Baja, California. Comstock Publishing Associates, Cornell University Press, Ithaca, New York.

Daugherty, C. H., A. Cree, J. M. Hay, and M. B. Thompson. 1990. Neglected taxonomy and continuing extinctions of tuatara (*Sphenodon*). Nature 347:177–179.

Ernst, C. H. and R. W. Barbour. 1972. Turtles of the United States. University Press Kentucky, Lexington.

Ernst, C. H. and R. W. Barbour. 1989. Turtles of the World. Smithsonian Inst. Press, Washington, D.C.

Ernst, C. H. and J. E. Lovich. 1990. A new species of *Cuora* (Reptilia: Testudines: Emydidae) from the Ryukyu Islands. Proc. Biol. Soc. Washington 103: 26-34.

Ernst, C. H., J. E. Lovich, and R. W. Barbour. 1994. Turtles of the United States and Canada. Smithsonian Inst. Press, Washington, D.C.

Erwin, T. I. 1988. The tropical forest canopy: The heart of biotic diversity. *In* E. O. Wilson and F. M. Peters (eds.), Biodiversity, pp. 123–129. National Academy Press.

Frazer, N. B. 1992. Sea turtle conservation and halfway technology. Conserv. Biol. 6:179–184.

Gibbons, J. W. 1993. Keeping All the Pieces: Perspectives on Natural History and the Environment. Smithsonian Inst. Press, Washington, D.C.

Gibbons, J. W. and R. D. Semlitsch. 1991. Guide to the Reptiles and Amphibians of the Savannah River Site. University of Georgia Press, Athens, Georgia.

Iverson, J. B. 1992. A Revised Checklist with Distribution Maps of the Turtles of the World. Privately Published, Richmond, Indiana.

King, F. W. and P. Braziatis. 1971. Species identification of commercial crocodilian skins. Zoologica 56:15–70.

Lamb, T. and J. E. Lovich. 1990. Morphometric validation of the striped mud turtle (*Kinosternon baurii*) in the Carolinas and Virginia. Copeia 1990:613-618.

Lamb, T., J. C. Avise, and J. W. Gibbons. 1989. Phylogeographic patterns in mitochondrial DNA of the desert tortoise (*Xerobates agassizii*), and evolutionary relationships among the North American gopher tortoises. Evolution 43:76–87.

Lovich, J. E. 1994. Biodiversity and zoogeography of non-marine turtles in Southeast Asia. *In* S. K. Majumdar, F. J. Brenner, J. E. Lovich, E. W. Miller, and J. F. Schalles (eds.), Biological Diversity: Problems and Challenges, pp. 380–391. Pennsylvania Acad. Sci., Easton, Pennsylvania.

Lovich, J. E. 1995. Turtles. *In* E. T. Laroe, C. E. Puckett, P. D. Doran, and M. J. Mac (eds.), Our Living Resources: A Report to the Nation on the Distribution, Abundance and Health of U.S. Plants, Animals and Ecosystems, pp. 118–121. National Biological Service, Washington, D.C.

Lovich, J. E. and C. J. McCoy. 1992. Review of the *Graptemys pulchra* group (Reptilia, Testudines, Emydidae), with descriptions of two new species. Ann. Carnegie Mus. 61:293–315.

Lovich, J. E. and C. J. McCoy. In press. *Graptemys pulchra*, Alabama map turtle. *In* P. C. H. Pritchard and A. G. J. Rhodin (eds.), The Conservation Biology of Freshwater Turtles. Chelonian Research Monogr., Chelonian Research Foundation, Lunenburg, Massachusetts.

McCoy, C. J. and J. E. Lovich. In press a. *Graptemys ernsti*, Escambia map turtle. *In* P. C. H. Pritchard and A. G. J. Rhodin (eds.), The Conservation Biology of Freshwater Turtles. Chelonian Research Monogr., Chelonian Research Foundation, Lunenburg, Massachusetts.

McCoy, C. J. and J. E. Lovich. In press b. *Graptemys gibbonsi*, Pascagoula map turtle. *In* P. C. H. Pritchard and A. Rhodin (eds.), Conservation of Freshwater Turtles. Chelonian Research Monogr., Chelonian Research Foundation, Lunenburg, Massachusetts.

Mittermeier, R. A., J. L. Carr, I. A. Swingland, T. B. Werner, and R. B. Mast. 1992. Conservation of amphibians and reptiles. *In* K. Adler (ed.), Herpetology: Current Research on the Biology of Amphibians and Reptiles. Proceedings of the First World Congress of Herpetology, pp. 59–80. Soc. Stud. Amphib. Rept., Oxford, Ohio.

Odum, E. P. 1994. Conservation of biodiversity. *In* S. K. Majumdar, F. J. Brenner, J. E. Lovich, E. W. Miller, and J. F. Schalles (eds.), Biological Diversity: Problems and Challenges, pp. 18–25. Pennsylvania Acad. Sci., Easton, Pennsylvania.

Rohlf, F. J. and D. Slice. 1990. Extensions of the Procrustes method for the optimal superimposition of landmarks. Syst. Zool. 39:40–59.

Scott, J. M., F. Davis, B. Csuti, R. Noss, B. Butterfield, C. Groves, H. Anderson, S. Caicco, F. D'Erchia, T. C. Edwards, Jr., J. Ulliman, and R. G. Wright. 1993. Gap analysis: A geographic approach to protection of biological diversity. Wildl. Monogr. 123:1–41.

U.S. Fish and Wildlife Service. 1994. Desert tortoise (Mojave population) recovery plan. U.S. Fish and Wildlife Service, Portland, Oregon. 73 pp. + append.

Vane-Wright, R. I., C. J. Humphries, and P. H. Williams. 1991. What to protect?: Systematics and the agony of choice. Biol. Conserv. 55: 235–254.

Wilson, E. O. 1992. The Diversity of Life. The Belnap Press of Harvard University Press, Cambridge, Massachusetts.

The Desert Tortoise Recovery Plan: An Ambitious Effort to Conserve Biodiversity in the Mojave and Colorado Deserts of the United States

KRISTIN H. BERRY

U.S. Department of the Interior, Bureau of Land Management, 6221 Box Springs Blvd., Riverside, CA 92507-0714, USA
Current Agency: U.S. Geological Survey, Biological Resources Division (same address) [e-mail: kristin_berry@nbs.gov]

ABSTRACT. In 1990 the U.S. Fish and Wildlife Service (USFWS) listed the desert tortoise, *Gopherus agassizii*, as "Threatened" over 30% of its geographic range and shortly thereafter selected a team to develop a plan for its recovery. The team developed a hypothesis-driven recovery plan, using population viability analyses and principles of reserve design. The *Desert Tortoise (Mojave Population) Recovery Plan* is designed to achieve a 50% probability of survival for the tortoise for 500 years.

Drawing from concepts outlined in the federal Endangered Species Act, the recovery team used a strategy of protecting evolutionarily significant population units and their associated ecosystems. The six population units, called "recovery units," were identified using published and unpublished data on genetic variability, morphology, and behavior patterns of populations as well as ecosystem types. Boundaries of the six units closely approximate major ecosystem boundaries in the Mojave and Colorado deserts. The goal is to reach a target (where possible) of 50,000 breeding adult tortoises for each recovery unit.

Within the recovery units, the recovery team recommended the establishment of 14 reserves or Desert Wildlife Management Areas (DWMAs), ranging from 415 to 3,367 km^2 (with one exception, the Virgin River DWMA, which was very small). The USFWS followed by designating 26,087 km^2 as federally protected "Critical Habitat" in 1994. Additional habitat is also protected within Joshua Tree National Park (est. 2,574 km^2) and within the existing boundaries of the Desert Tortoise Research Natural Area (est. 100 km^2).

The recovery team attributed declines in tortoise populations to the result of human activities. To reduce and ultimately eliminate many sources of mortality that are driving the desert tortoise toward extinction, they recommended prohibition of several activities in the reserves. Within each DWMA, they also recommended that <10% of habitat be designated as "experimental management areas," where intrusive and experimental research can occur.

Governments at the federal, state, county, and city levels have begun to implement the *Recovery Plan* through development of regional land-use plans (habitat conservation plans, coordinated resource plans, and multi-species plans). While tortoise recovery considerations are the driving force for land-use planning, agencies are taking a more comprehensive ecosystems approach. If implementation of the *Recovery Plan* and land-use plans are successful, the reserve system for the desert tortoise will not only conserve its genetic diversity, but also the biodiversity of several major ecosystems in the Mojave and Colorado deserts.

The U.S. Fish and Wildlife Service (USFWS) placed the desert tortoise, *Gopherus agassizii*, on the list* of "Threatened" species in 1990 (Figure 1; USFWS, 1990a) and shortly thereafter selected a recovery team to develop a plan for its recovery. This paper describes (1) the resulting *Desert Tortoise (Mojave Population) Recovery Plan* (hereafter called the *Recovery Plan*), (2) the system of reserves that are being established to protect the desert tortoise and the ecosystems in which it lives, (3) the threats facing desert ecosystems and measures being taken to reduce the threats, and (4) the government land-use plans that are being created to ensure long-term protection of the ecosystems.

---

* In the United States, Congress has delegated the authority to determine the status of species to the USFWS, a federal agency under the Department of the Interior. Species may be placed on federal lists as "Threatened" or "Endangered" under the Endangered Species Act of 1973, as amended, and the lists are published by the government in the *Federal Register*. The process is known as federal listing. Each state may also develop separate lists of "Rare," "Threatened," or "Endangered" species, using its own criteria and standards, and the lists are known as state lists. The term *listing* is used to refer to the lengthy process involved in candidacy for listing, proposals for listing, and the ultimate action—formal or legal listing as "Threatened" or "Endangered."

Early Efforts to Protect the Desert Tortoise

The desert tortoise, *Gopherus agassizii*, is a widespread species of the arid southwestern United States and northwestern Mexico. It occupies a wide variety of habitat types in the Mojave and Sonoran deserts (including the California subsection of the Sonoran Desert known as the Colorado Desert) and occurs in four states in the U.S. and two states in Mexico (Figure 1).

The organized effort to protect significant populations and habitat of the desert tortoise from numerous human and land uses in the U.S. has spanned more than 20 years. The U.S. Department of the Interior's Bureau of Land Management (USBLM), the agency that administers approximately 75% of the remaining high-quality desert tortoise habitat, identified the tortoise as a valued component of the deserts and as a sensitive species in the 1970s (see USBLM, 1980). At that time the USBLM and state fish and wildlife agencies selected the tortoise as one of several indicator species for long-term monitoring of environmental conditions using criteria similar to those later described by the National Research Council's Committee on the Applications of Ecological Theory to Environmental Problems (1986). The selection was based in part on the tortoise's longevity, low reproductive potential, and sensitivity to environmental perturbations.

In the early 1970s biologists realized that desert tortoise populations were declining in the U.S. (USFWS, 1994a). By 1980 very small segments of three populations had received substantial legal protection: the Beaver Dam Slope population in Utah (which occupied an est. 101 km²) was federally listed as "Threatened" under the Endangered Species Act (ESA) of 1973, as amended (USFWS, 1980); and parts of two populations were protected within small reserves, the Desert Tortoise Research Natural Area (est. 100 km²) and the Chuckwalla Bench Area of Critical Environmental Concern (213 km²) (USBLM, 1980). In 1984 three conservation organizations—Environmental Defense Fund, Natural Resources Defense Council, and Defenders of Wildlife—proposed federal listing for the remaining populations within the U.S. The USFWS (1985) responded by issuing a finding that federal listing was warranted but precluded by other, higher priority actions, thus briefly tabling conservation actions under the ESA.

Recognizing that tortoise populations were continuing to decline, the USBLM developed two plans to offset threats to tortoise populations and their habitats in 1988 (USBLM, 1988a, 1988b). One plan, *Desert Tortoise Habitat Management on the Public Lands: A Rangewide Plan*, contained a directive to ". . . manage tortoise habitats using an ecosystem management approach with emphasis on maintaining or restoring natural biological diversity" (USBLM, 1988a). The three aforementioned conservation groups also observed the continued population and habitat declines; they served notice of pending court action to the USFWS in mid-1989. Shortly thereafter (August 1989), the USFWS took emergency action to federally list approximately 30% of the tortoise populations within the geographic range (USFWS, 1989a, 1990a). Tortoise populations listed as "Threatened" occur in the Mojave and Colorado deserts; for administrative reasons, the USFWS refers to these populations as the *Mojave Population* (Figure 1).

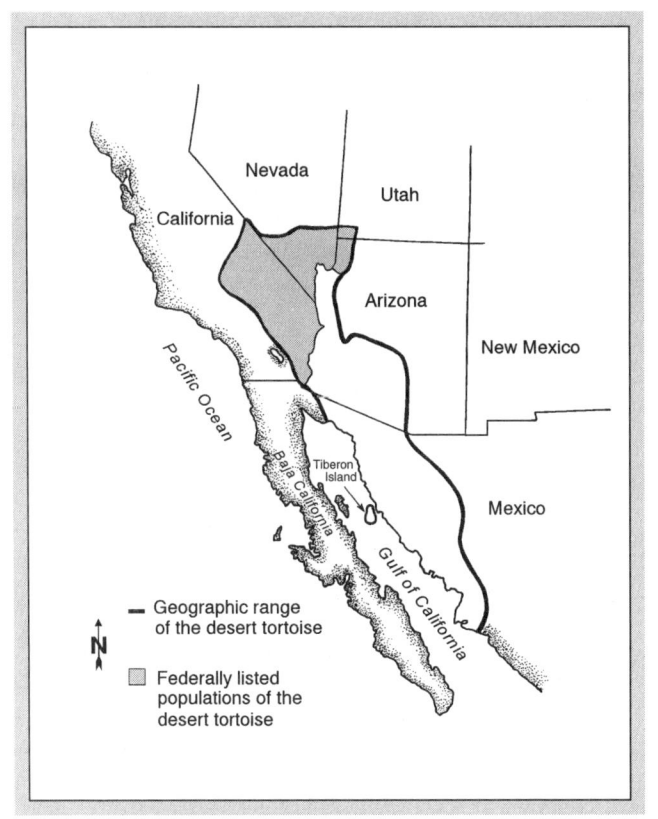

Figure 1. The geographic range of the desert tortoise, *Gopherus agassizii*, from Stebbins (1985). The portion of the geographic range where populations are federally listed is shaded.

Preparing the Desert Tortoise *Recovery Plan*

The Desert Tortoise Recovery Team

The USFWS has prepared several recovery plans for chelonians, such as the St. Croix population of the leatherback turtle (*Dermochelys coriacea*), the ringed sawback turtle (*Graptemys oculifera*), the Alabama red-bellied turtle (*Pseudemys alabamensis*), and the flattened musk turtle (*Sternotherus depressus*) (USFWS, 1981, 1988, 1989b, 1990b). In each of these cases, a single person prepared a short plan using traditional USFWS guidelines. In 1990 the USFWS took a different approach to draft a recovery plan for the desert tortoise, selecting a recovery team composed of nationally recognized scientists with expertise in genetics, plant and animal ecology, physiology, biogeography, veterinary medicine, and conservation biology. The recovery team, which was chaired by Peter F. Brussard, included Kristin H. Berry, Michael E. Gilpin, Elliott R. Jacobson, David J. Morafka, Cecil R. Schwalbe, C. Richard Tracy, and Frank C. Vasek. Judy Hohman of the USFWS was Executive Secretary. Six of the eight team members were academicians and two were government research scientists. The team met 17 times over a period of four years to develop the *Recovery Plan*.

The review process for the *Recovery Plan* was extensive. Comments received during the review process not only improved the *Recovery Plan* and associated documents, but also ultimately contributed to the acceptance of the concepts contained in the documents. Government agencies, the public, and the scientific community played important roles. Prior to release to the public, two drafts of the plan were prepared for government review, including review by a four-state, multi-government agency committee, the Desert Tortoise Management Oversight Group (MOG). The MOG, formed in 1989 after publication of the USBLM's *Desert Tortoise Habitat Management on the Public Lands: A Rangewide Plan* (USBLM, 1988a), coordinates research, management, conservation, and recovery efforts for the desert tortoise in the U.S. Government review of the *Recovery Plan* was followed by an official draft, published for a 90-day public comment period in 1993. Public hearings were held, and the USFWS received a total of 143 letters. The draft *Recovery Plan* was modified to reflect the additional information and criticisms, and the final *Recovery Plan* was distributed in 1994. During the same year, the government determined the boundaries of Critical Habitat and published the decision in the Federal Register (see footnote, page 430). The four-year time span* from the initial federal listing of the Mojave population as "Threatened" and selection of the recovery team to publication of the final *Recovery Plan* and determination of Critical Habitat is in large part a reflection of the complexity of the task, the disparate nature of the available data bases, and the large amounts of land involved. Much of what follows is taken directly or paraphrased from the *Recovery Plan* (USFWS, 1994a) and is, in part, an enlarged abstract of the plan.

The Approach: Using the Principles of Conservation Biology

The recovery team recognized that the tortoise is a widespread species and exhibits substantial variation in genetic, morphological, ecological, physiological, and behavioral characteristics throughout its geographic range (USFWS, 1994a). Drawing from the ESA and the works of Ryder (1986) and Waples (1991), the recovery team decided to use evolutionarily significant units, which they termed "population segments" or "recovery units," to encompass the genetic and environmental variation present in the species. Six recovery units were identified: Western Mojave, Eastern Mojave, and Northeastern Mojave; Northern Colorado and Eastern Colorado; and Upper Virgin River (Figure 2 and Table 1).

The six recovery units vary considerably in climate and vegetation (USFWS, 1994a). The mean number of freezing days annually (which affects length of tortoise burrows and amount of seasonal activity above ground) varies from as low as 2–16 days in the two Colorado Desert recovery units to 46–127 days in the Northeastern Mojave Desert recovery unit. The mean annual precipitation and distribution of precipitation within the year differ considerably from the western to the eastern portions of the geographic range and are important factors that affect amount and timing of vegetation available to tortoises for forage. The Western Mojave recovery unit, for example, is in a region where annual precipitation primarily occurs in winter and produces ephemeral vegetation in late winter and spring, but little precipitation (6–10%) and forage occur in summer. In contrast, the other five recovery units are in eastern or southern regions that receive two periods of precipitation per year, which in turn can result in two distinct seasonal floras that may be utilized for food.

Within each recovery unit, from one to four reserves or Desert Wildlife Management Areas (DWMAs) were identified as locations where desert tortoise populations could be managed to achieve recovery (USFWS, 1994a; Brussard et al., 1994). A total of 14 DWMAs were identified (Figure 2 and Table 1).

Genetic factors, minimum viable population size, sizes of reserves (DWMAs), and the probability of long-term persistence are critical elements in the strategy to recover the "Mojave Population" of desert tortoises (USFWS, 1994a). From a genetic standpoint, the recovery team concluded that a minimally viable population should probably contain at least 2,000–5,000 adult animals (USFWS, 1994a). Three population viability analyses were prepared, and predictions were developed based on the probabilities that tortoise populations would persist for 500 years. Using these analyses, the recovery team concluded that (1) tortoise populations at minimum densities (3.9 adults/km²) require reserves of at least 518–1,295 km² to be genetically viable; (2) where the discrete population growth rate (lambda) is slightly below 1.0 but varies over a range of approximately 25%, extremely large reserves (12,950 km² to support 50,000 adults at minimal density) are necessary to support populations that would be relatively resistant to extinction within the next half-century; and (3) if lambdas fall below 0.975 on average, no population size is sufficient to persist for 500 years.

---

* However, four years is considerably less than the average 9.4 years reported by Tear et al. (1995) for completion of recovery plans for threatened and endangered vertebrates in general.

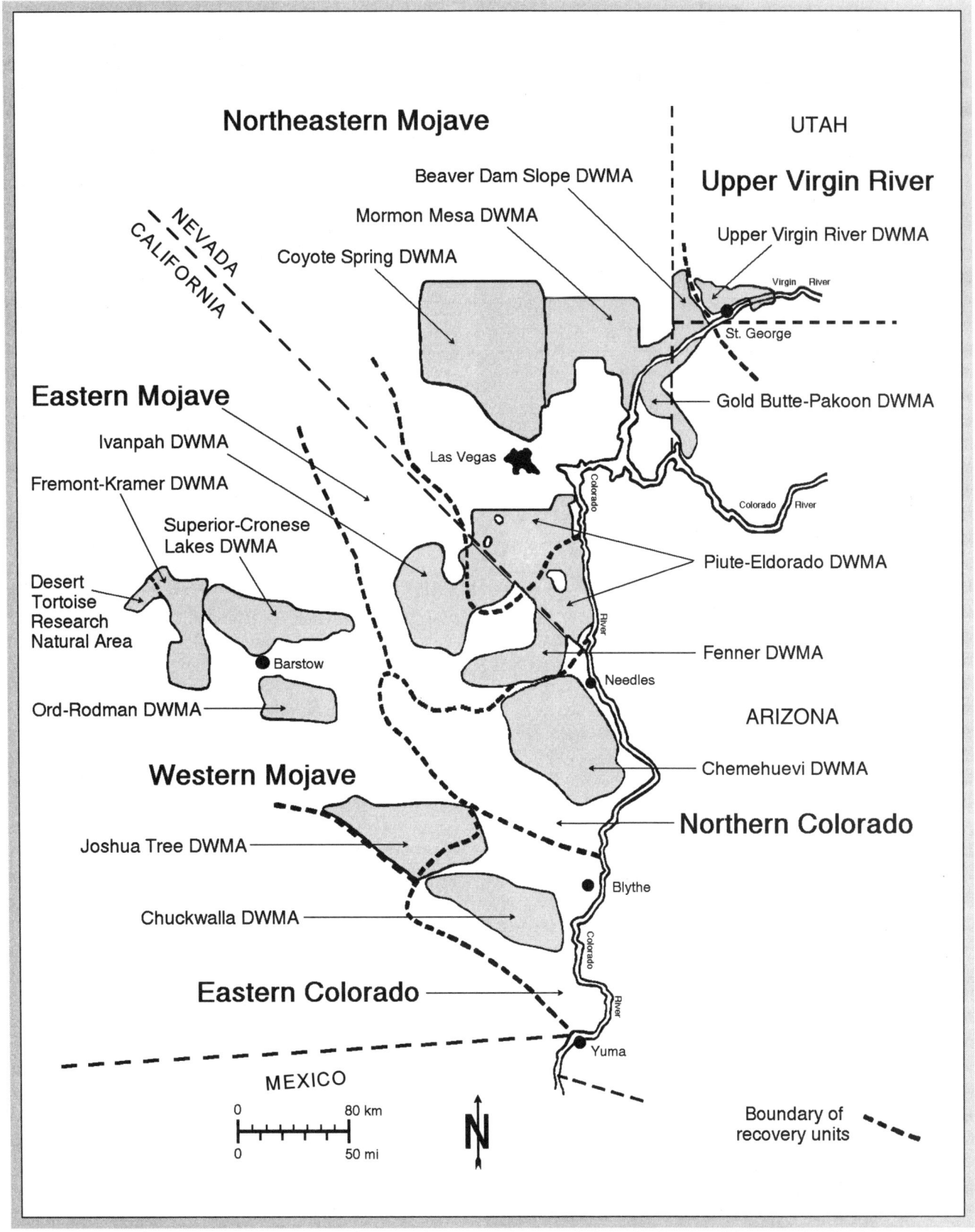

Figure 2. The portion of the desert tortoise population (Mojave population) that is federally listed as "Threatened." The six recovery units and 14 Desert Wildlife Management Areas (DWMAs) described in the *Desert Tortoise (Mojave Population) Recovery Plan* (USFWS, 1994a; Brussard et al., 1994) are shown.

The recovery team recommended a target size of >2,590 km² for DWMAs because reserves of this size would be likely to provide sufficient buffering from demographic stochasticity and genetic problems and would be sufficiently large to support recovered populations with a reasonable probability of persistence.

The shape and arrangement of DWMAs are essential to their success (USFWS, 1994a). The recovery team recommended the use of current theory and practice of reserve design (e.g., Thomas et al., 1990; Noss, 1991). Seven guidelines were followed in recommending DWMA boundaries (USFWS, 1994a):

TABLE 1

A comparison of sizes of Desert Wildlife Management Areas (DWMAs) recommended for protecting desert tortoises (Brussard et al., 1994) and the names and sizes of Critical Habitats ultimately designated by the federal government in February 1994 (USFWS, 1994b).

Recovery units DWMAs	Size (km²)	Names of corresponding Critical Habitat(s)	Size (km²)
Northern Colorado			
Chemehuevi	2,590.0–3,367.0	Chemehuevi	3,793.54
Eastern Colorado			
Chuckwalla	1,942.5–2,460.5	Chuckwalla [a]	4,130.24
Joshua Tree [a]	see Western Mojave	Pinto Mountains [a]	———
Western Mojave			
Fremont-Kramer	1,489.25–1,748.25	Fremont-Kramer	2,096.28
Ord-Rodman	1,165.5–1,424.5	Ord-Rodman	1,024.67
Superior-Cronese	2,331.0–2,849.0	Superior-Cronese	3,103.55
Joshua Tree [a]	2,136.75–2,913.75	Pinto Mountains	694.85
Eastern Mojave			
Fenner, California [b]	1,372.7–1,631.7	Piute-Eldorado, California	1,836.47
Piute-Eldorado, Nevada	1,740.16 [c]	Piute-Eldorado, Nevada	2,091.43
Northeastern Mojave			
Ivanpah Valley [d]	2,201.5–2,719.5	Ivanpah Valley	2,559.24
Coyote Spring	2,460.5–2,719.5	see Mormon Mesa	
Mormon Mesa	2,072.0–2,590.0	Mormon Mesa	1,731.66
Gold Butte-Pakoon	699.3–802.9	Gold Butte-Pakoon, Nevada	778.21
		Gold Butte-Pakoon, Arizona	1,197.88
Beaver Dam Slope in Utah, Nevada, Arizona	414.4–440.3	See below, by state	
		Beaver Dam Slope, Nevada	353.70
		Beaver Dam Slope, Arizona	172.80
		Beaver Dam Slope, Utah	301.49
Upper Virgin River			
Upper Virgin River	No number given	Upper Virgin River	220.96
Totals	22,615.56–27,407.06		26,086.97

[a] The Joshua Tree DWMA was located primarily in Joshua Tree National Park, with the vast majority of habitat in the Western Mojave recovery unit; only the southeastern part of the DWMA was in the Eastern Colorado recovery unit. When Critical Habitat was formally designated, the portions of the DWMA within the park were excluded. The northern part of the DWMA (in the Western Mojave recovery unit) became the Pinto Mountain Critical Habitat unit, and the southeastern portion of the DWMA outside the park was designated as part of the Chuckwalla unit of Critical Habitat.

[b] Located primarily in the Eastern Mojave recovery unit, with a small portion in the Northern Colorado recovery unit. When the habitat within the Fenner DWMA was designated as Critical Habitat, the name was changed to Piute-Eldorado, California.

[c] An estimate of the size, using 430,000 acres described in a proposed management plan (see Brussard et al., 1994).

[d] Located in both the Eastern Mojave and Northeastern Mojave recovery units.

1. Reserves that are well distributed across a species' native range will be more successful in preventing extinction than reserves confined to small portions of a species' range.

2. Large reserves (>2,590 km²) containing large populations of the target species are superior to small blocks of habitat containing small populations.

3. Blocks of habitat that are close together are better than blocks far apart.

4. Habitat that occurs in less fragmented, contiguous blocks is preferable to habitat that is fragmented.

5. Habitat patches that minimize edge-to-area ratios are superior to those that do not.

6. Interconnected blocks of habitat are better than isolated blocks, and linkages function better when the habitat within them is represented by protected preferred habitat for the target species.

7. Blocks of habitat that are roadless or otherwise inaccessible to humans are better than blocks containing roads and blocks easily accessible to humans.

The recovery team emphasized three related points: the desirability of redundancy, or more than one reserve per recovery unit, a strategy likely to increase the probability of recovery of populations within the recovery units; the importance of connecting small reserves with corridors containing functional habitat; and intensive management into perpetuity where small reserves are the only option. The recovery team also recognized the role of small, isolated populations, in the event that epidemic disease (such as upper respiratory tract disease) contributes to near extirpation in DWMAs.

The USFWS (1994b) used the guidelines to establish Critical Habitat in February 1994 (Table 2). Of the original 22,616–27,407 km² recommended for protection in 14 DWMAs (Brussard et al., 1994), the USFWS designated 26,087 km² as Critical Habitat (USFWS, 1994b). The USFWS (1994b) recognized that additional habitat was already adequately protected within Joshua Tree National Park (est. at 2,574 km², C. Collins, pers. comm.) and the Desert Tortoise Research Natural Area (est. 100 km²) and did not require designation as Critical Habitat. Thus, the overall total of protected habitats for the desert tortoise is 28,761 km².

Causes of Tortoise Population Declines and Recommended Regulations for DWMAs to Reduce Threats

Government agencies and the recovery team recognized that declines in desert tortoise populations as well as losses to their habitats were primarily due to human activities (USFWS, 1994a). The list of threats and factors contributing to declines is lengthy and is similar to the list of threats to tortoises worldwide (Swingland and Klemens, 1989). To reduce the factors contributing to tortoise mortalities and reverse population declines, the recovery team identified the human activities considered to be incompatible with recovery of the tortoise and recommended that the following activities be prohibited:

- all vehicle activity off of designated roads; all competitive and organized commercial and recreation events (associated with vehicles) on designated roads;

TABLE 2
Critical Habitat for the Mojave Population of the desert tortoise and ownership of land, as of February 1994 (USFWS, 1994b).

Land owner or administrator	Size (sq. km)	Percent
U.S. Dept. of the Interior, Bureau of Land Management	19,386.96 [a]	74.32 [a]
Dept. of Defense	980.15	3.76
U.S. Dept. of the Interior, National Park Service	595.70 [a]	2.28 [a]
State lands	672.59	2.58
Tribal lands	6.48	0.02
Private lands	4,445.09 [b]	17.04 [b]
Total	26,086.97	100.00

[a] On 31 October 1994 (eight months after designation of Critical Habitat), a substantial amount of public land under the jurisdiction of the Bureau of Land Management was transferred to the National Park Service for the Mojave National Preserve (California) and for additions to Joshua Tree National Park and Death Valley National Park (California). The transfer of land was part of the California Desert Protection Act of 1994, which was created by the 103rd Congress (Public Law 103-433, 108 STAT. 4471). Therefore, the figures shown in the above table are no longer accurate.

[b] A significant portion (no figures available) of private lands are owned by Catellus Corporation, formerly Southern Pacific Railroad lands.

TABLE 3
The relationships between desert tortoise recovery units and the existing and proposed multi-species, ecosystem, and bioregional plans.

Recovery units Name of management plan	Size of area (km²)	Proposed year of completion
Western Mojave *Draft West Mojave Coordinated Management Plan* (draft)[1]	37,969	est. 1997
Eastern Mojave California: *Northern and Eastern Mojave Desert Ecosystem/Coordinated Management Plan* (proposed[a])[2]	31,239	est. 1999
Nevada: *Short-term Habitat Conservation Plan for the Desert Tortoise in Las Vegas Valley, Clark County, Nevada*[3]	89,121	1991
Clark County Desert Conservation Plan[4] *and Final Environmental Impact Statement: Issuance of a Permit to Allow Incidental Take of Desert Tortoises, Clark County, Nevada*[5]	56	1995
Stateline Resource Management Plan (amendments and revisions)[6]	14,973	1992, 1994
Northeastern Mojave California: (same as Eastern Mojave recovery unit, combined into one plan[a])[2]	no data available	est. 1999
Nevada: (same as Eastern Mojave recovery unit, may be combined into one plan[a])[2] will also include parts of *Stateline Resource Management Plan and Caliente Resource Management Plan*[6]	no data available	est. 1997
Utah: *Dixie Resource Management Plan*[7]	no data available	no date
Arizona: *Arizona Strip Resource Management Plan*[8]	12,140	1992
Upper Virgin River *Proposed Habitat Conservation Plan, Washington County, Utah* (draft)[9]	226	June 1995
Northern Colorado *Northern and Eastern Colorado Desert Coordinated Management Plan*[10]	22,391	est. 1999
Eastern Colorado Planning effort combined with Northern Colorado recovery unit[10]	no data available	est. 1999

[a] May combine California and Nevada regions, crossing state jurisdictions.

References:
1. USBLM, 1995
2. U.S. National Park Service and USBLM (in prep.)
3. Regional Environmental Consultants, 1991
4. Clark County, Nevada, 1995
5. USFWS, 1995
6. USBLM, 1992a; supplement in 1994 (must be amended)
7. USBLM (in prep., 1985–1995; incomplete, may be amended)
8. USBLM, 1992b (must be amended)
9. Washington County Habitat Conservation Plan Steering Committee and SWCA, Inc., Environmental Consultants, 1995
10. USBLM and others (in prep.)

- habitat-destructive military maneuvers, clearing for agriculture, landfills, and other surface disturbances that diminish the capacity of the land to support desert tortoises, other wildlife, and native vegetation;

- domestic livestock grazing and grazing by feral burros and horses;

- vegetation harvest, except by permit (issued by the county for private land, by the USBLM for public land);

- collection of biological specimens, except by permit;

- dumping and littering;

- deposition of captive or displaced desert tortoises or other animals, except under authorized translocation research projects (guidelines established within the *Recovery Plan*);

- uncontrolled dogs out of vehicles; and

- discharge of firearms, except for hunting of big game or upland game birds from September through February.

The above recommendations will be a challenge to implement quickly and effectively because much of the habitat (Table 2) for the Mojave Population of desert tortoises is on federal land administered by the USBLM (74.3%), where there is a long history of multiple-use activities (USFWS, 1994b). Tortoise habitats on the Department of Defense facilities (3.8%) and National Park Service properties (2.9%) also receive intensive use in some areas and are likely to require adjustments to land-use practices in the immediate future.

The recovery team expected that people would visit the DWMAS (USFWS, 1994a). They identified some limited human activities that are compatible with desert tortoise recovery efforts, including:

- non-intrusive monitoring of desert tortoise population dynamics and habitat;

- limited-speed travel on designated, signed roads and maintenance of these roads;

- non-consumptive recreation (e.g., hiking, birdwatching, casual horseback riding, and photography);

- parking and camping in designated areas;

- fire suppression that minimizes surface disturbance;

- permitted or otherwise controlled maintenance of existing utilities;

- surface disturbances that enhance the quality of habitat for wildlife, enhance watershed protection, or improve opportunities for non-motorized recreation (includes construction of visitor centers, wildlife guzzlers or drinkers, camping facilities, etc. where appropriate);

- population enhancement of native wildlife species, such as desert bighorn, Gambel's quail, etc.;

- mining on a case-by-case basis, provided that the cumulative impacts of these activities do not significantly impact desert tortoise habitats or populations, that any potential effects on desert tortoise populations are carefully mitigated during the operation, and that the land is restored to its pre-disturbance condition; and

- non-manipulative and non-intrusive biological or geological research, by permit.

An important element in the recovery strategy was the division of DWMAs into core areas where human activities would be restricted, and experimental management zones (EMZs) where certain prohibited activities may be permitted on an experimental basis during the recovery period (USFWS, 1994a). As envisioned by the recovery team, the EMZs would be composed of no more than 10% of tortoise habitat within a DWMA and would be located at the DWMA periphery. The types of research recommended for the EMZs include research on effects of cattle grazing on tortoises and their habitats and intrusive research on the tortoises themselves (e.g., affixing radio transmitters to shells, monitoring health profiles by drawing blood, etc.). The recovery team recommended that experimental translocations occur outside of DWMAs and that no desert tortoises be introduced into DWMAs, at least until relocation is much better understood (Appendix B *in* USFWS, 1994a).

Hypothesis Testing and Long-Term Monitoring

Recovery of desert tortoise populations is likely to require decades, if not centuries (USFWS, 1994a). The recovery team based the *Recovery Plan* on a series of hypotheses and models that can be tested as new data are acquired. The effectiveness of the recovery strategies (e.g., establishing recovery units, 14 DWMAs, and removing or reducing perceived threats from DWMAs) can be most appropriately tested by comparing changes in desert tortoise population densities inside and outside of DWMAs. The key to such comparisons is a reliable and economical method for estimating population densities of large immature and adult tortoises (>140 mm in carapace length) on a regional scale. No single method has yet to be embraced by government and the scientific community as "scientifically credible," an essential part of delisting criterion 1 (see following).

Hypothesis testing should also be a part of long-term research programs to evaluate threats to desert tortoise populations and habitat using the EMZs. Several subjects requiring attention are described in the *Recovery Plan*, e.g., research on the effects of cattle grazing and road density, the effectiveness of tortoise-proof barriers along freeways and highways, and feasibility of restoration of habitat.

Criteria that Must be Met for Tortoise Populations to be Considered "Recovered"

An essential part of the *Recovery Plan* is a description of recovery objectives and "delisting criteria," the threshold at which populations can be considered "recovered" and can be removed from the list of federally "Threatened" species. The USFWS (1994a) determined that desert tortoise populations could be delisted by recovery unit and that the Mojave Population could be delisted when populations in all six recovery units were considered to be recovered. Five criteria must be met for recovery to occur within a unit:*

1. The population must exhibit a statistically significant upward trend or remain stationary for at least 25 years (one tortoise generation); trends must be measured using a scientifically credible monitoring plan, with population estimates taken at five-year intervals.

2. Sufficient habitat must be protected within a recovery unit (at least one DWMA of >2,590 km^2) or, in unusual circumstances, the tortoise populations must be managed intensively enough to ensure long-term population viability.

3. At each DWMA, population lambdas must be maintained at or above 1.0 into the future.

4. Regulatory mechanisms or land management commitments must be implemented to ensure long-term protection of tortoises and their habitats.

5. The population in the recovery unit should be unlikely to need protection under the ESA in the foreseeable future (as determined by detailed genetic, demographic, physiological, behavioral, and environmental analyses).

Implementing the *Recovery Plan*: The Use of Multi-Species, Ecosystem, and Bioregional Plans

The *Recovery Plan* (USFWS, 1994a) is being implemented through preparation of up to six bioregional, multi-species, or ecosystem plans (Table 3). The plans, most of which are regional in nature, are delimited in part by state boundaries. Three of the plans—the *Western Mojave Coordinated Management Plan*, the *Clark County Desert Conservation Plan*, and the *Proposed Habitat Conservation Plan, Washington County, Utah*—will probably be completed between 1995 and 1997, at least as draft plans, whereas the others are still in early stages. With one exception, the Beaver Dam Slope of Arizona, plans are underway or proposed for all DWMAs and recovery units.

One group of plans belongs to a special subset, "habitat conservation plans" (HCPs). Habitat conservation plans are an option described in the ESA, as amended, for protection and management of "Threatened" and "Endangered" species, while at the same time allowing for "incidental take" of individual animals and losses to their habitats. The best-known of the desert tortoise HCPs is the three-year or short-term HCP developed for Clark County, Nevada (Regional Environmental Consultants, 1991; Beatley, 1994), which has been followed by a long-term HCP (Clark County, 1994; USFWS, 1995).

These management plans, whether developed by federal, state, or county governments, are "desert tortoise driven": they would not have been identified and scheduled for preparation and implementation if the desert tortoise had not been federally listed and the *Recovery Plan* had not been prepared. The desert tortoise, because of its widespread distribution, public interest and support, scientific value, and charisma, is being used as an umbrella or "flagship" species to represent many different plants and animals and their ecosystems.

The management protections required to recover the desert tortoise necessitate major changes in existing land-use plans, some of which are 16 years old (e.g., USBLM, 1980), thereby stimulating new land-use planning efforts on a large scale. In all cases, preparers of the new plans are fully aware of the importance of using the multi-species and ecosystems approaches. They are following mandates in the ESA, which provides for protecting the ecosystems on which "Threatened" and "Endangered" species depend; agency directives in the USBLM's 1988 *Desert Tortoise Habitat Management on the Public Lands: A Rangewide Plan* (USBLM, 1988a); and current scientific thinking in conservation biology.

The draft *Western Mojave Coordinated Management Plan* (USBLM, 1995) provides an example of the scope and the numbers of at-risk species that will benefit. Twenty species of plants and animals within the planning region are already federally listed as "Threatened" or "Endangered" or are proposed for listing, and another 46 species are candidates for listing. The area covered by the plan is 37,969 km^2, of which 18% is designated Critical Habitat for the tortoise. When the protected habitats at the Desert Tortoise Research Natural Area and Joshua Tree National Park are added to Critical Habitat, 25.3% of the planning area would be managed for long-term recovery and survival of desert

---

* The *Recovery Plan* states: "These recovery criteria were designed to provide a basis for consideration of delisting, but not for automatic delisting. Before delisting may occur, the Fish and Wildlife Service must determine that the following five listing factors are no longer present or continue to adversely affect the listed species: (1) the present or threatened destruction, modification, or curtailment of the species' habitat or range; (2) overutilization for commercial, recreational, scientific, or educational purposes; (3) disease and predation; (4) inadequacy of existing regulatory mechanisms [e.g., laws, existing land use]; and (5) other human-made or natural factors affecting the continued existence of the species . . ."

tortoise populations. Additional areas will be protected for at least some of the other species, potentially raising the percentage even higher.

A key point about the desert tortoise is its federal status under the ESA as a "Threatened" species. Because the tortoise is classified as "Threatened" and is not considered endangered, the government may still allow some multiple use of the land, and some time is still permitted to allow ecosystems to recover naturally. With many endangered species, such opportunities have been lost. Because the remaining ecosystem remnants have reached such severe states of perturbation, draconian measures are necessary. Some endangered species, such as the California condor, remain extant primarily through breeding programs. It is hoped that the recovery measures for the tortoise can be quickly implemented, thereby reversing declining population trends. Recovery is expected to require centuries for some desert tortoise populations.

In summary, the *Recovery Plan* for the desert tortoise follows a recent trend of recovery plans, e.g., the grizzly bear (USFWS, 1993) and the spotted owl (Thomas et al., 1990), which are regional in scope, are designed to improve management of troubled ecosystems, and are potentially controversial. Recovery plans for single species—especially when the species are widespread, large, showy, charismatic or well-known to the public—may serve to stimulate public support for large-scale, bioregional or ecosystem land use plans. In the case of the tortoise, over 26,000 km^2 in the Mojave and Colorado deserts may receive new and significant management and conservation efforts. Single umbrella species such as the desert tortoise also can assist immeasurably in educating the government and the public about conservation biology, biodiversity, and the need for reserves.

Acknowledgments

I thank Frank Vasek, David J. Morafka, Peter Brussard, Larry Foreman, Peter C. H. Pritchard, Jim Van Abbema, Richard Crowe, Betty L. Burge, and E. Karen Spangenberg for useful and constructive comments on the manuscript. I am grateful to Keith Mann for providing GIS data, Marilet Zablan and Todd Esque for details on land-use plans for public and private land in Utah, and Tim Duck for information on the USBLM's management plans in the Arizona Strip District.

Literature Cited

Beatley, T. 1994. Preserving the desert tortoise: The Clark County habitat conservation plan. Chapter 10 *in* Habitat Conservation Planning: Endangered Species and Urban Growth, pp. 146–172. University of Texas Press, Austin.

Brussard, P. F., K. H. Berry, M. E. Gilpin, E. R. Jacobson, D. J. Morafka, C. R. Schwalbe, C. R. Tracy, F. C. Vasek, and J. Hohman. 1994. Proposed desert wildlife management areas for recovery of the Mojave population of the desert tortoise. U.S. Fish and Wildlife Service, Region 1-Lead Region, Portland, Oregon.

Clark County, Nevada. 1995. 1995 Clark County desert conservation plan. Clark County, Nevada.

Committee on the Applications of Ecological Theory to Environmental Problems, Commission on Life Sciences and National Research Council. 1986. Indicator species and biological monitoring. Chapter 7 *in* Ecological Knowledge and Environmental Problem-Solving: Concepts and Case Studies, pp. 81–87. National Academy Press, Washington, D. C.

Noss, R. F. 1991. Protecting habitat and biological diversity. Part I: Guidelines for regional reserve systems. Report to the National Audubon Society.

Regional Environmental Consultants (RECON). 1991. Short-term habitat conservation plan for the desert tortoise in Las Vegas Valley, Clark County, Nevada. Prepared for Clark County, Nevada, by RECON, San Diego, California.

Ryder, O. A. 1986. Species conservation and systematics: The dilemma of subspecies. Trends in Ecol. Evol. 1:9–10.

Stebbins, R. C. 1985. A Field Guide to Reptiles and Amphibians in the Western United States. Houghton-Mifflin Company, Boston.

Swingland, I. R. and M. W. Klemens (eds.). 1989. The Conservation Biology of Tortoises. Occasional Papers of the IUCN Species Survival Commission (SSC) No. 5. IUCN, Gland, Switzerland.

Tear, T. H., J. M. Scott, P. H. Hayward, and B. Griffith. 1995. Recovery plans and the Endangered Species Act: Are criticisms supported by data? Conserv. Biol. 9(1):182–195.

Thomas, J. W., (Chairman), E. D. Forsman, J. B. Lint, E. C. Meslow, B. R. Noon, and J. Verner. 1990. A conservation strategy for the northern spotted owl. Interagency Scientific Committee to Address the Conservation of the Northern Spotted Owl. U.S. Department of Agriculture, Forest Service; U.S. Department of the Interior: Bureau of Land Management, Fish and Wildlife Service, and National Park Service, Portland, Oregon. 427 pp.

U.S. Bureau of Land Management. 1980. The California Desert Conservation Area Plan, 1980. U.S. Department of the Interior, Bureau of Land Management, Riverside, California. 173 pp. + appendices.

U.S. Bureau of Land Management. 1988a. Desert tortoise habitat management on the public lands: A range-wide plan. U.S. Department of the Interior, Bureau of Land Management, Washington, D.C. 23 pp.

U.S. Bureau of Land Management. 1988b. Recommendations for management of the desert tortoise in the California Desert. U.S. Department of the Interior, Bureau of Land Management, Riverside, California. 54 pp. + appendices.

U.S. Bureau of Land Management. 1992a. Draft Stateline Resource Management Plan and Environmental Impact Statement. U.S. Department of the Interior, Bureau of Land Management, Las Vegas District Office, Las Vegas, Nevada. (Supplement to the Draft issued in May 1994. No final plan has yet been issued.)

U.S. Bureau of Land Management. 1992b. Arizona Strip Resource Management Plan. U.S. Department of the Interior, Bureau of Land Management, St. George, Utah.

U.S. Bureau of Land Management. 1995. Draft West Mojave coordinated management plan and environmental impact statement. May 1995 administrative review draft. U.S. Department of the Interior, Bureau of Land Management, Riverside, California.

U.S. Fish and Wildlife Service. 1980. Endangered and threatened wildlife and plants: Finding on desert tortoise petition. Federal Register 50:49868–49870.

U.S. Fish and Wildlife Service. 1981. Recovery plan for St. Croix population of the leatherback turtle (*Dermochelys coriacea*). Region 4, U.S. Fish and Wildlife Service, Fish and Wildlife Reference Service, Denver, Colorado. 20 pp.

U.S. Fish and Wildlife Service. 1985. Endangered and threatened wildlife and plants: Finding on desert tortoise petition. Federal Register 50:49868–498870.

U.S. Fish and Wildlife Service. 1988. A recovery plan for the ringed sawback turtle, *Graptemys oculifera*. Southeast Region, U.S. Fish and Wildlife Service, Atlanta, Georgia. 28 pp.

U.S. Fish and Wildlife Service. 1989a. Endangered and threatened wildlife and plants; Emergency determination of endangered status for the Mojave population of the desert tortoise. Federal Register 54(149):32326.

U.S. Fish and Wildlife Service. 1989b. Alabama red-bellied turtle recovery plan. U.S. Fish and Wildlife Service, Jackson, Mississippi. 17 pp.

U.S. Fish and Wildlife Service. 1990a. Endangered and threatened wildlife and plants; Determination of threatened status for the Mojave population of the desert tortoise. Federal Register 55(63): 12178–12191.

U.S. Fish and Wildlife Service. 1990b. Flattened musk turtle (*Sternotherus depressus*) recovery plan. U.S. Fish and Wildlife Service, Southeast Region, Jackson, Mississippi. 15 pp.

U.S. Fish and Wildlife Service. 1993. Grizzly bear recovery plan. Missoula, Montana. 181 pp.

U.S. Fish and Wildlife Service. 1994a. The desert tortoise (Mojave population) recovery plan. U.S. Fish and Wildlife Service, Region 1-Lead Region, Portland, Oregon. 73 pp. + appendices.

U.S. Fish and Wildlife Service. 1994b. Endangered and threatened wildlife and plants; Determination of critical habitat for the Mojave population of the desert tortoise. Federal Register 59(26): 5820–5866.

U.S. Fish and Wildlife Service. 1995. Final environmental impact statement: Issuance of a permit to allow incidental take of desert tortoises, Clark County, Nevada. Fish and Wildlife Service, Region 1, Portland, Oregon. 139 pp. + appendices.

Waples, R. S. 1991. Pacific salmon, *Oncorhynchus* spp., and the definition of "species" under the Endangered Species Act. Marine Fisheries Review 53(2):11–22.

Washington County Habitat Conservation Plan Steering Committee and SWCA, Inc., Environmental Consultants. 1995. Habitat conservation plan, Washington County, Utah. Submitted by the Washington County Commission, Utah to the U.S. Fish and Wildlife Service.

Effects of Exploitation on *Dermatemys mawii* Populations in Northern Belize and Conservation Strategies for Rural Riverside Villages

JOHN POLISAR

Florida Museum of Natural History, University of Florida, Gainesville, FL 32611, USA

ABSTRACT: *Dermatemys mawii* **is a large, highly aquatic, herbivorous freshwater turtle of the Gulf of Mexico and Caribbean drainages of southern Mexico, Belize, and Guatemala. Because** *Dermatemys* **lays its eggs in scattered locations during the high water periods of the late rainy season, exploitation of nesting females and their eggs is inconsequential. Exploitation is primarily for meat and is most intense during the latter part of the dry season. All three methods of capture in northern Belize are selective for large juveniles and adults. The effects of relentless hunting have been decreased densities and population structures skewed towards juveniles, with a marked reduction in the proportion of mature females.**

Dermatemys **nesting behavior makes headstarting programs impractical. Management recommendations have focused on increasing adult survivorship through reduction of large-scale commercial exploitation. In the absence of strong enforcement capabilities, and in an area of low human population density, legal restriction of commercial hunters' activities has proven a feasible initial strategy. By allowing continued small-scale removal by subsistence hunters, the support of that numerically larger constituency may be maintained.**

The Central American river turtle, *Dermatemys mawii*, is a large, highly aquatic, herbivorous freshwater turtle of the Gulf of Mexico and Caribbean drainages of southern Mexico, Belize, and Guatemala (Alvarez del Toro et al., 1979; Iverson and Mittermeier, 1980; Iverson, 1986). It is the sole living representative of the formerly widespread and diverse family Dermatemydidae, which dates from the Jurassic of Europe and the Cretaceous of North America, Europe, and East Asia (Romer, 1956; Iverson and Mittermeier, 1980; Hutchison and Bramble, 1981). Throughout its restricted range *Dermatemys* is heavily exploited for its meat (Holman, 1964; Lee, 1969; Mittermeier, 1970, 1971; Alvarez del Toro et al., 1979; Moll, 1986), which is consumed by rural people and sold in urban markets. Years of unrestrained exploitation have raised concern over the status of *Dermatemys*. It is listed on Appendix II of the Convention on International Trade in Endangered Species of Wild Flora and Fauna (CITES) (USFWS, 1992), as "Endangered" under the provisions of the U.S. Endangered Species Act (USFWS, 1994), and as the highest priority species (i.e., Action Plan Rating = 1) in the IUCN Species Survival Commission action plan for the conservation of tortoises and freshwater turtles (IUCN/SSC/TFTSG, 1991).

Hunting has virtually eliminated *Dermatemys* from much of its former range in southern Mexico (R. Vogt, pers. comm.), and the status of the species in Guatemala is unclear. As late as 1984 *Dermatemys* was common to abundant in sparsely populated areas of Belize, but declining where accessible to a harvesting public (Moll, 1986).

In 1986 Moll proposed that the remaining, relatively intact populations in Belize offered an opportunity to obtain the biological data needed to manage this species. That opportunity was seized when the leaders of seven villages of the Community Baboon Sanctuary, a grassroots wildlands management project that maintains riparian forest habitat for black howler monkeys, *Alouatta pigra* (Horwich, 1986, 1990; Horwich and Lyon, 1988), invited me to study *Dermatemys* in the 32 km section of the Belize River that bisects their sanctuary. The invitation stemmed from concern that local levels of harvest had become unsustainable. Field research began in late 1989 and expanded rapidly, eventually including an additional 54 km of the Belize River, 39 km of tributary systems, and an additional five villages. It also included urban market counts and fieldwork in the Río Bravo Conservation and Management Area and the Crooked Tree Wildlife Sanctuary, with focus on reproductive biology and exploitation patterns. Data on reproductive cycles, minimum sizes at maturity, nesting and mating seasons, incubation periods, methods of exploitation and marketing, and seasonality, scale, and effects of exploitation were collected. The high level of local cooperation contributed greatly to this research effort, and living in the villages during this study provided an understanding of local perspectives, needs, and customs.

In northern Belize, *Dermatemys* lays its eggs in scattered locations during the high water periods of the late rainy season (late September–December). As a result, exploitation of the difficult-to-locate nests has been inconsequential (Polisar, 1992). Exploitation for meat occurs year-round, but peaks during the last two months of the dry season (April and May), when low water levels facilitate capture. In northern Belize there has been a strong tradition of serving *Dermatemys* (locally known as "hickatee") for dinner at Easter.

The data showed that intensive hunting within an area resulted in decreased densities and lower proportions of adults, particularly adult females. All three methods of hunting—harpoons, nets, and freediving—were selective for larger size classes. When the small juveniles that had previously eluded capture matured, they too were collected, creating an illusion of continued abundance in populations that were probably already non-reproductive and in decline. These dynamics appeared less severe in lightly or intermittently exploited populations. The status of the central Belize River population in the vicinity of the Baboon Sanctuary, and that of other heavily exploited populations, indicated that the level of harvest was not sustainable.

The ultimate objective of the project was to develop pragmatic management recommendations that could be applied in a rural, undeveloped setting with minimal wildlife law enforcement. The formulation of these recommendations required gathering data over a wide range of topic areas—reproductive biology, exploitation and marketing patterns, cultural traditions, and legal and community conservation opportunities.

Headstarting was not a practical initial step in the conservation of *Dermatemys* because (1) nests were difficult to locate, (2) the flood season nesting pattern resulted in highly dispersed gravid females, making capture rates low, and (3) funding and infrastructure for captive breeding and care were lacking.

Because the cause of decline was the excessive removal of older turtles for human consumption, management needed to focus on increasing adult survivorship. A reduction in the overall scale of exploitation provided a practical way to begin that process, and restricting the activities of commercial hunters who removed large numbers for profit seemed feasible. Local subsistence hunters, though greater in number than the commercial hunters, removed fewer turtles. While a complete ban on turtle harvest would be ineffective in most locations due to opposition from the public and subsequent noncompliance, a harvest strategy that emphasized the reduction of large-scale removal for profit offered some opportunity for attracting public support. By allowing continued small-scale removals by subsistence hunters, the support of that numerically large constituency might be maintained. With strong public support, concerned villagers could initiate a legal means to curb market hunting.

It was also essential to recommend some completely closed zones which could provide insurance if harvest management should prove difficult to implement. Closed zones also had the potential to serve as natural restocking areas.

Some villages were interested in *Dermatemys* conservation, while others were not. One of the better-organized villages, Freetown Sibun, was interested in establishing legal restrictions for its section of the Sibun River. Residents

Figure 1. Atanacio "Taniko" Soler with typical adult female *Dermatemys*, lower Río Bravo, Belize.

were concerned about the decline of turtles in their area and were resentful that non-resident market hunters were removing turtles to sell elsewhere. Other villages expressed the same concerns, but were less well organized. Freetown Sibun subsequently submitted a request for local regulations to the Ministry of Natural Resources. That document was taken into consideration, as were my detailed recommendations for the remainder of northern Belize, when the Belize Fisheries Department drafted nationwide comprehensive legislation protecting and managing *Dermatemys mawii* in April 1993 (Statutory Instrument No. 55, 1993).

This new legislation includes year-round possession limits (which should eliminate large-scale removals without reducing small-scale use), a short closed season (1–31 May), a complete prohibition on the sale and purchase of *Derma-*

temys, and a series of protected zones in the major waterways of northern Belize, including the entire Río Bravo system, a section of the Belize River, a section of the New River Lagoon, Cox and Mucklehany lagoons, and the lower Sibun River. This includes large and small whitewater rivers, a large clearwater lagoon, darkwater lagoons, brackish lagoons, and an estuary.

Although the above describes the progress made, much remains to be accomplished. Management is a dynamic process that requires long-term commitment. Continued work with rural communities is required to increase appreciation of the uniqueness and vulnerability of *Dermatemys*, to assess compliance, and to identify need for further refinement of the regulations. Although it is essential to ensure compliance in urban meat markets, a substantial trade taking place outside those formal markets will also require monitoring. In some cases stricter regulations may be necessary. Freetown Sibun has recently expressed a desire for a complete ban on hunting of turtles in its area.

Field research on large, spatially dispersed, herbivorous turtles occupying large, deep aquatic habitats can be labor intensive and expensive, and is severely limited by funding constraints. A long-term study, comparing the population densities and structures of exploited and unexploited sections of rivers would provide a means of assessment of the efficacy of management measures, as well as information useful for the management of other turtles in other regions.

ACKNOWLEDGMENTS

Research was funded by the Wildlife Conservation Society, Chelonia Institute, Lincoln Park Zoo, Programme for Belize, IFAS International Programs and the Program for Studies in Tropical Conservation at the University of Florida, Manomet Bird Observatory, and Sigma Xi. Support for follow-through work came from the Chelonia Institute, Crystal Channel Foundation, Fossil Rim Foundation, and the Tropical Conservation and Development Program at the University of Florida. Logistical support is credited to the Community Baboon Sanctuary, Belize Audubon Society, Belize Center for Environmental Studies, Chau Hiix Lodge, Belize Meteorological Service and Hydrology Department, Lighthawk, and British Forces Belize. The Belize Forestry and Fisheries Department issued numerous research permits and assimilated the resulting information.

Dr. R. Horwich and F. Young were instrumental in the start-up of the project. P. C. H. Pritchard, A. Carr III, D. Collins, J. Behler, M. Klemens, the Chelonia Advisory Group of the American Zoo and Aquarium Association, and the Tortoise and Freshwater Turtle Specialist Group of the Species Survival Commission of IUCN-The World Conservation Union continued support. Scientific advice was provided by J. D. Congdon, M. W. Ewert, J. B. Iverson, K. Bjorndal, D. Moll, J. P. Ross, and R. C. Vogt. F. W. King, L. J. Guillette, Jr., J. F. Eisenberg, and F. Percival supervised the M.S. thesis (Polisar, 1992) associated with this project. Special gratitude is extended to over 75 residents of the villages of rural northern Belize. Although the significant contributors among them are too numerous to credit individually, the project would not have been possible without their assistance.

LITERATURE CITED

Alvarez del Toro, M., R. A. Mittermeier, and J. B. Iverson. 1979. River turtle in danger. Oryx 15:170–173.

Government of Belize. 1993. Statutory Instrument No. 55 of 1993. Fisheries (Amendment) Regulations. Belmopan, Belize. 4 pp.

Holman, A. J. 1964. Observations on dermatemydid and staurotypine turtles from Veracruz, Mexico. Herpetologica 19:277–279.

Horwich, R. 1986. A community baboon sanctuary in Belize. Primate Conservation 7(15):15.

Horwich, R. 1990. How to develop a community sanctuary: An experimental approach to the conservation of private lands. Oryx 24:95–102.

Horwich, R. and J. Lyon. 1988. An experimental technique for the conservation of private lands. J. Med. Primat. 17:169–176.

Hutchison, J. H. and D. M. Bramble. 1981. Homology of the plastral scales of the Kinosternidae and related turtles. Herpetologica 37:73–85.

Iverson, J. B. 1986. A Checklist with Distribution Maps of the Turtles of the World. Paust Printing, Richmond, Indiana. 283 pp.

Iverson, J. B. and R. A. Mittermeier. 1980. Dermatemydidae, *Dermatemys*. Cat. Amer. Amphib. Rept. 237:1–4.

IUCN/SSC Tortoise and Freshwater Turtle Specialist Group. 1991. Tortoises and freshwater turtles: An action plan for their conservation (D. Stubbs, comp.). IUCN/SSC Tortoise and Freshwater Turtle Specialist Group, Gland, Switzerland. i–iv + 47 pp.

Lee, R. C. 1969. Observing the tortuga blanca. Int. Turtle Tortoise Soc. J. 3(3):32–34.

Mittermeier, R. A. 1970. Turtles in Central American markets. Int. Turtle Tortoise Soc. J. 4(5):20–26.

Mittermeier, R. A. 1971. Status—the market in southeast Mexico. Int. Turtle Tortoise Soc. J. 5(3):15–19.

Moll, D. 1986. The distribution, status, and level of exploitation of the freshwater turtle *Dermatemys mawii* in Belize, Central America. Biol. Conserv. 35:87–96.

Polisar, J. 1992. Reproductive biology and exploitation of the Central American river turtle *Dermatemys mawii* in Belize. M.S. thesis, University of Florida, Gainesville. 179 pp.

Romer, A. S. 1956. Osteology of the Reptiles. University of Chicago Press, Chicago. 772 pp.

U.S. Fish and Wildlife Service. 1992. CITES: Appendices I, II, and III to the Convention on International Trade in Endangered Species of Wild Fauna and Flora. Title 50—Wildlife and Fisheries, Part 23, §23.23. Publication Unit, U.S. Fish and Wildlife Service, Washington, D.C.

U.S. Fish and Wildlife Service. 1994. Endangered and threatened wildlife and plants. 50 CFR 17.11 & 17.12. Title 50—Wildlife and Fisheries, Part 17, §17.11. Publication Unit, U.S. Fish and Wildlife Service, Washington, D.C.

Turtles as a Resource: Avoiding the "Tragedy of the Commons"

— SUMMARY REPORT —

PETER C. H. PRITCHARD

*Chelonia Institute, 401 South Central Ave., Oviedo, FL 32765, USA;
Florida Audubon Society, 1331 Palmetto, Suite 110, Winter Park, FL 32789, USA*

Gareth Hardin's epochal 1968 article "The Tragedy of the Commons" described how a shared resource, such as a community livestock grazing area or "commons," was doomed to overexploitation because there was no positive feedback to the individual who practiced restraint. Instead, excessive use was rewarded by a greater share of the "pie," even though the latter was diminishing overall.

Here I summarize the results of a three-decade campaign to reduce or eliminate the slaughter of sea turtles on their nesting beaches in Guyana, a classic example of a common resource overexploited by the actions of numerous competing individuals.

The turtle nesting area in Guyana includes one of the least developed parts of the entire South American coast —about 150 km of mangrove shoreline, with intermittent shell beaches, between the mouths of the Pomeroon and Waini rivers, in Northwestern Guyana. To date, environmental alteration of this area has been minimal. The rainforest is uncut; human habitations have been limited to isolated, temporary fishermen's huts; and agricultural development is limited to untended coconut palms and pawpaws. The coast is subject to drastic change even from year to year, as a result of erosion of both the shifting beaches and the façade of the mature mangrove forest.

The turtles nesting on these beaches are relatively few, but are of remarkable diversity. The green turtle is the first to nest each year, starting around mid-March, followed by the leatherback, and later the hawksbill and the olive ridley. Analysis of turtle carapaces and other remains on the beach during my first visits in 1964 and 1965 indicated that the green turtle, hawksbill, and olive ridley were all abundant—and heavily slaughtered—whereas the leatherback was very scarce.

Overtures were made to various government agencies to control the slaughter, and even high-level interventions between Buckingham Palace and the Prime Minister of Guyana took place, but to no avail. It gradually became clear to me that the standard "legislation plus enforcement" approach would not work. There was no great will to pass the legislation, and there was indeed reluctance to restrict the lifestyle of subsistence level Amerindian peoples, and the potential for enforcement was essentially zero. Then, as now, the Guyana wildlife department lacks funds for field operations.

The slaughter continued through the seventies and eighties, and various changes occurred. The traditional principal nesting beach, known as Shell Beach (actually a composite of Kamwatta and Three Pile beaches) became less suitable for nesting as the shell eroded away and extensive mud flats formed in the foreshore, and the center of nesting activity shifted to Almond Beach, close to Waini Point, about 30 km away. Moreover, the three cheloniid species became increasingly rare, whereas the leatherback increased

Figure 1. Hunters butcher a leatherback — a common practice amongst the Arawak people prior to our turtle conservation program.

significantly in abundance. The former was expected; the latter surprising—although hunters claim that this was never a preferred species. Nevertheless, my own observations in the mid-eighties indicated that all species were slaughtered and the leatherback, being the most abundant, was slaughtered most often.

The decision I finally reached was that control could only come with the support of the hunters themselves. Accordingly, I befriended the hunting community, composed of several dozen individuals primarily from the Santa Rosa Mission area of the Moruka River. I found general agreement that the turtle resource was becoming severely reduced, but that a social mechanism to act on this concern was lacking. I obtained funds to hire several of the principal hunters as "game wardens," to patrol the beach and to protect, tag, and monitor the turtles. This they have now done conscientiously for five five-month seasons. Our conservation and research camp has been kept deliberately low-tech, so as to avoid any concept of an alien presence. Rather, we have created a small Arawak village of eight or nine palm-thatched, mangrove-pole huts, we travel in dugout boats (with the compromise of small outboards rather than paddles for the 150 km sea journey), and our little community is complete with children, dogs, kittens, and even a parrot or two. Thus, fishermen, smugglers, and others visiting the area find a group of people with a familiar lifestyle but an unfamiliar mission—they are there to protect the turtles—and in this way we attempt to win them over by moral force and peer pressure rather than enforcement threats.

We have been successful to the extent that few if any turtles are now killed on the primary nesting beach, although small numbers continue to be killed on distant beaches where we have little control. We have consolidated our efforts in two additional ways: by means of an educational campaign, and also by providing capitalization for "alternative meat" production. We bring the Arawak youngsters to the beach in groups of 8–12, usually accompanied by at least one teacher or parent, and give them intensive daytime exposure to the environmental ethic by means of formal classes and informal discussions and activities, with nighttime patrols in search of nesting turtles. The alternative meat program devolved from a meeting with the former turtle hunters, asking them to identify which substitute for turtle meat would be acceptable to them. They identified pigs and chickens as acceptable alternatives, and we were able to obtain a grant from the Conservation, Food, and Health Foundation to provide core funding for loans or grants to individuals seeking to raise their own livestock, but who lacked the capital to do so.

All is not yet solved, and we are currently in the middle of a three-year period during which Guyana is under a mandate of United States law to promulgate turtle excluder devices on its large shrimp fleets, or lose access to the U.S. market for the product. But we have made sufficient progress with our approach of hands-on conservation combined with close involvement of local people and user communities to be convinced that this is the answer.

In the years to come, we hope to replicate the successful Arawak sea turtle conservation program amongst other tribes and communities, and with overexploited river turtles rather than sea turtles. In the deep interior of Guyana, in the Upper Essequibo and Rupununi River systems, two species of large river turtle, *Podocnemis expansa* and *Podocnemis unifilis*, have traditionally been exploited by the local Macusi and Wapisiana peoples. In the past the exploitation may have been tolerable, but in recent years, with the collapsing populations and increasing prices of these turtles in adjacent parts of Brazil, extensive smuggling of live turtles is taking place from Guyana to Roraima, Northern Brazil, and collapse of the unstudied and unquantified Guyana populations is a real danger.

Figure 2. Our first group of Arawak turtle conservation students.

Management of Tropical Chelonians: Dream or Nightmare? — Part 2

JOHN G. FRAZIER

Centro de Investigaciones y de Estudios Avanzados del IPN, Unidad Mérida, Apartado 73 "Cordemex," Mérida, Yucatán, México C. P. 97310 [e-mail: frazier@kin.cieamer.conacyt.mx]

ABSTRACT: In 1992 I evaluated the prospects for management of Indian tortoises. Although it was clear that management activity needed to be strengthened, basic biological information was lacking, and it was concluded that management plans for the majority of Asian tortoises must be put forth as both tentative and preliminary.

The purpose of the present paper is to reevaluate this issue by focusing on a single species. It emphasizes that a management plan must integrate diverse disciplines, take into account human attitudes and needs, and have a long-term vision. A management plan must be plainly understood to be an approximation, rather than a final product: management must not be a euphemism for manipulation. The periodic reexamination of the biological status of the species and habitats involved, as well as the social, economic, and political conditions impacting these species and habitats must be a non-negotiable feature of any management plan. Regular updating of the plan must be a priority.

This notion is especially important for the "Third World," with its acute social and political turmoil, as well as its extraordinary biological diversity. Habitat alteration in many parts of the tropics is so extensive and rapid that determination of the original geographic distributions of even the better-known chelonians is a major challenge. This, in turn, makes it next to impossible to understand such basic aspects as the habitat requirements of these species. The circumstances of one of the best-known tropical tortoises—the star tortoise, *Geochelone elegans*, illustrates these points, and details are presented here as a case study.

Wildlife Management: Terms and Concepts

The title of this conference begins with three key words: *conservation*, *restoration*, and *management*. Restoration is a specific form of management; both conservation and management—when referring to the rational use of natural resources—have the same objectives and essentially take on the same meaning. Thus, we can simplify our discussion by focusing on the issues of management. The term *management* is defined as the action of guiding, governing, controlling, taking charge, or taking care of.

There are many ways to define wildlife management; an endless polemic springs from the search for a universal definition (Bailey, 1984; Robinson and Bolen, 1984). However, one constant is that this discipline is not "pure" science but instead depends upon interactions between managers and other humans and their societies. To be successful, wildlife management, and its more recent incarnation, *biological conservation*, must integrate countless considerations and disciplines, some of which are outside the realm of pure science. At one level this involves dealing with biological units, be they species, habitats, or ecosystems. Clearly, this comprises tremendous inherent complexity—biological, spatial, and temporal. At another level, natural resource management must be integrated with human-dominated systems: economics, politics, culture, emotions, etc., which increase complexity in yet other dimensions, some of which may not be immediately obvious (e.g., Frazier, 1990; McShea et al., 1994).

Wildlife management actions are focused on target species, their habitats, or the ecosystems in which they live. Some of the better-known components include the use of quotas and seasons to regulate hunting, selective cropping, predator control, captive breeding, restocking, and habitat improvement. Traditionally, wildlife management has been centered on game animals—those species that people exploit directly for benefit (this concept is critical to the central tenets of wildlife management: to benefit people). It has also dealt with "problem" species that, for the benefit of humans, are "controlled." More recently, wildlife management has expanded to include certain non-game animals that are appreciated by people, but are not necessarily exploited or controlled. With few exceptions, this translates to conspicuous, attractive bird and mammal species (Schemnitz, 1980; Bailey, 1984; Robinson and Bolen, 1984; Sale and Berkmüller, 1988; Rodgers, 1991).

Only in the last few years have the "lower" vertebrates, including amphibians and reptiles, been considered relevant to wildlife managers, and it is only recently that herpetologists have begun to collaborate with wildlife managers in the conservation and management of herpetofauna (Scott and Seigel, 1992). As a result of this historic neglect, conservation protocols and management actions for amphibians and reptiles are generally scant and untested (e.g., Bury, 1988; Bury and Corn, 1988).

Given the extraordinary complexity of the issues involved in wildlife conservation, it is essential that managers select manageable units and attainable goals. Hence, management plans often address single species. However, there are growing concerns over this approach: funds, resources, and expertise are insufficient to provide for all the individual species that require attention. The problem of recently trained personnel is clearly demonstrated in India, which has approximately two dozen chelonian species: Only a half-dozen people in this vast territory have adequate experience, and in addition to attending to chelonians, they must deal with many other animals as well. In most other "Third World" countries, the situation is even more difficult.

Management activities that encompass a variety of species, as well as their interactions with habitats, are desirable because they are likely to be more cost-effective and, by conserving the tortoises' habitat and resource base, are more efficient at conserving the targeted species. It makes much more sense, both ecologically and economically, to protect entire systems rather than single species, and is more efficient in time, manpower, and resources over the long term. As biological conservation matures as a professional discipline, there is an ever-growing emphasis on ecosystem approaches, which make full use of biological principles. The focus and organization of this international conference are clear proof of the emergence of ecosystem conservation as an important tool to conserve chelonians.

The Case of the Star Tortoise in India

In 1987 authorities in the Indian government, concerned over the status of indigenous chelonians, requested information to develop a conservation program (Frazier, 1987a). In the same year, a symposium on "Tropical Ecosystems: Ecology and Management" was organized by the International Society for Tropical Ecology, an appropriate event at which to evaluate, on a broad basis, the prospects for management of chelonians in the Indian Region. Although it was clear that resource management activities needed to be strengthened, a warning was sounded: Because basic information (e.g., taxonomic status, geographic distributions, and basic biology and ecology) were lacking, management plans for the majority of Asian chelonians must be put forth as both tentative and preliminary (Frazier, 1992).

The purpose of the present paper is to reevaluate management prospects, this time by focusing on one species as a case study. *Geochelone elegans*, the star tortoise, is one of the best-known and the most-widespread chelonians on the Indian Subcontinent, and it is one of the most popular species among tortoise collectors in the western world. Most of the following biological information is drawn from an unpublished study on this species (Frazier, 1987b).

It is clear that this tortoise is under ever-increasing stress. Human population density in India is portentous, habitat alteration is intense, and direct exploitation of star tortoises for pets involves tens of thousands of animals a year (Frazier, 1987b). Rehabilitation and habitat management actions are clearly needed. By incorporating these actions into a system approach and by embracing conservation biology management concepts, one might assume that success would be assured. Unfortunately, it is not that simple; there are fundamental questions that remain unanswered, and in some cases even the appropriate questions are unknown.

Range

The geographic range of the star tortoise, *Geochelone elegans*, is usually reported to be Pakistan, India, and Sri Lanka. At least one author (Obst, 1985) has included the Burmese star tortoise as conspecific with the Indian species, but most other workers regard the separate population in Myanmar (formerly Burma) as a unique species, *G. platynota*. *G. elegans* is reported to have raised, cone-shaped scutes on the carapace and to have irregular scales on the top of the head (Smith, 1931). Neither of these characters has been quantified, and normal variation observed indicates that they are of little taxonomic use: 57% of the specimens from western India had only slightly raised carapacial scutes, and no star tortoise with less than four growth rings had noticeably raised scutes. The only consistent difference between the Burmese and Indian populations appears to be the conspicuous ischial spurs found only on the latter, but this character is rarely referred to in these animals.

Documentation of the historic range of *G. elegans* may be at least partly accomplished through the examination of available museum specimens. However, the holdings of the five museums that should have the most important collections of this species (as well as many sympatric chelonian species) provide inadequate information: The Indian Museum, Calcutta (administered by the Zoological Survey of India) has eight eggs and 30 shells; 15 of the shells are labeled "Ceylon" (the former name for Sri Lanka). In the heart of star tortoise country, the Zoological Survey of India's Desert Research Station in Jodhpur, Rajasthan has just three specimens; their Southeast Research Station in Madras, at the other extreme of the tortoise range, has but two specimens listed. The Bombay Natural History Society has 12 specimens, only eight with locality data. The definitive collections in the British Museum of Natural History (BMNH) have 30 specimens, seven without locality data, four with just "India," four with just "Ceylon," one with "Muscat, Oman," and so on; only seven specimens in the BMNH have useful locality data. Hence, the available museum collections are of little help in understanding the geographic distribution of this animal, and there is always the risk that the distribution pattern educed from museum specimens represents not where the organisms are (or were), but rather where the intensity of collection has been greatest.

We may also examine published records. The distribution

in Pakistan has been claimed to include the Hab Valley (Murray, 1884), or more generally "Sind" (Smith, 1931); the latter refers to the entire province and is a sizable territory. Yet, the only substantiated area of occurrence is Nagar Paker, approximately 2,000 km² at the extreme southeastern corner of Sind (Anderson and Minton, 1963; Minton, 1966). Whether the species ranges throughout Sind or has only a toehold in the province represents a dramatic difference from a conservation perspective.

This tortoise is well documented in Sri Lanka, including reports from the Northern, North-Western, North-Central, Eastern, and Southern provinces (Deraniyagala, 1939). Preliminary results of an ongoing field study being conducted near Andigama have recently been published (de Silva, 1996).

The distribution of *G. elegans* in India is commonly described as throughout central and southern India, extending west as far as Sind and south to Ceylon (Smith, 1931:139), peninsular India westward to Sind (Daniel, 1983), or central and southern India (Murthy, 1985). In fact, little precise information is available on localities, and upon close examination, a rather different pattern from the above emerges (Frazier, 1987b).

On the eastern side of peninsular India, there are records from central Orissa (approx. 20°N), south through Andhra Pradesh, extending into eastern Karnataka at Kolar District, and south through Tamil Nadu (except in the highlands). On the western side, this tortoise is reported from as far north as Seriska, south throughout most of the state of Rajasthan (except the extreme east and the Thar Desert in the west), throughout most of Gujarat, including Kutch and Saurashtra, but not The Dangs in the extreme south. Apparently, the tortoise's range extends into the western extreme of Madhya Pradesh, but it is otherwise absent from central India.

The northwestern and southeastern distributions are separated by the Deccan, or central plains—a distance of approximately 600 km. The two populations show morphological differences: those from the northwest are larger and the carapacial scutes are less raised. Genetic differences may also exist between the two populations (P. Kanan, pers. comm.). Despite usual descriptions (e.g., Smith, 1931; Pritchard, 1979; Daniel, 1983; Das, 1985; Ernst and Barbour, 1989) indicating one continuous range throughout most of India, at least two widely separated populations of the star tortoise inhabit the Subcontinent, and it is possible that we may be dealing with more than one species. If we add to this discussion the Burmese star tortoise, the problem becomes even more complex.

Finally, it is important to emphasize that even if the precise present-day range were known, we would have several major sources of uncertainty. Data are inadequate to derive historical geographic distributions, even at a gross level. During the past century there have been vast and intensive modifications of habitat throughout India. The most important of these may be deforestation, intensive grazing and agriculture, and declining ground water. Human population density is generally very high, and direct exploitation of chelonians is intense in some areas, which has surely resulted in the local extirpation of many species of chelonians over parts of their ranges. Although no systematic data exist, verbal accounts indicate that star tortoises have declined or even disappeared from some areas where they were formerly numerous (Frazier, 1987b).

Part of the decline is due to an estimated 10,000–15,000 star tortoises that have entered the pet trade yearly (Frazier, 1987b), and there is evidence that these animals have been transported great distances, to later be reported as occurring hundreds of kilometers from their original distribution. Furthermore, specimens such as those in the BMNH labeled "Muscat, Oman" make a clear case for the need for caution in evaluating the range of the species based on archival specimens rather than field data. It is highly probable that there have been major modifications to the natural range of this species, both from local extirpations and human-induced range alterations.

Status, Biology, and Ecology

For conservation and management purposes, it is necessary to know not only the distribution, but also the population status of the animal, population trends, preferred habitats, and other basic facts about its biology. These topics are summarized for the star tortoise as follows:

Majupuria (1973), Pritchard (1979), and Daniel (1983) report that females are larger than males. As in other tortoises, males have concave plastrons and longer tails. Males are distinguishable at 22 cm curved carapace length (CCL), and females appear to be reproductively active at 30 cm CCL. A. de Silva found 49 Sri Lanka females had a mean straight-line carapace length of 209 mm ±56.46 mm; 51 males had a mean SLCL of 169.35 ±47.55 mm. The largest Sri Lanka tortoise was 380 mm (J. Grigus to P. C. H. Pritchard, pers. comm.). In addition to being generally larger, females are relatively more highly domed, have longer claws on the hind feet, and have a wider gap between the anal and supracaudal scutes. Although the last three characters are easily observed and measured, they have not been previously described.

Daniel (1983) reported that star tortoises mature in two years. However, sexual dimorphism first becomes conspicuous in animals with seven or more growth rings; if these annuli are formed yearly, maturity may be reached after seven years. Females apparently grow rapidly for the first ten years. Longevity is not known; the most rings that could be counted on a wild animal was 17, but a half-century seems a reasonable estimate for the life span of a wild tortoise (Frazier, 1987b).

The development of the tortoise's distinctive starred pattern is poorly understood. Hatchlings emerge with beige or brownish blotches on the edges of the carapace scutes, and the star pattern is only discernible after the appearance of the first three growth rings. The star is actually formed by dark rays or polygons covering a yellow or horn-colored background (Smith, 1931), rather than radiating yellow streaks on a black background as stated by some authors (Pritchard, 1979; Daniel, 1983; Das, 1985). This is illustrated by the fact that carapaces that appear smooth from abrasion (presumably old specimens) have black spots and not lines. There is clear ontogenetic change—hatchlings and old individuals are light colored; immature tortoises are darkest. In general, there are at least eight arms per star, but each star is unique. The claim that there are more black lines in the northern specimens (see Frazier, 1987b) needs to be substantiated; the ontogenetic change may be responsible for the perceived difference. There is no known sexual difference in coloration. Annandale (1907) concluded that the color pattern is disruptive and cryptic, which was also noted by Pritchard (1979). It is amazing how fast a star tortoise in scrub habitat can disappear from view!

Information on habitat type is scanty. The few published detailed descriptions include rocky environments and foothill grasslands (Prakash, 1974) and sandy tracts of coastal scrublands (Daniel, 1983). Firsthand observations include arid or semiarid grasslands, scrublands (especially thorn scrub), agricultural lands, and deciduous woodlands. A source of midday shade seems to be crucial, whether occurring naturally or in artificial hedgerows (Frazier, 1987b).

No data on population density are in the literature. My own estimates in prime areas, e.g., Aravali Hills of Rajasthan and Zainabad of Gujarat, range from 4 to 12.5 individuals/ha. In other areas in western India and Andhra Pradesh, density is closer to 1/km². These tortoises apparently have the ability to return to a home site after having been displaced as far as 5 km, and individuals are likely to live within a home range.

Deraniyagala (1939) and Daniel (1983) report this tortoise to be nocturnal or crepuscular; little else is recorded. However, my observations show it to be diurnal, but on occasion remaining active shortly after sunset. (In Sri Lanka, 55% of the animals have been first observed between 16:30 and 17:30 [de Silva, 1995].) Shelter is usually sought during the heat of the day, but some animals may remain active all day in overcast or rainy weather. They have been active at 21–29°C during overcast conditions and at 24–28°C during sunny conditions. Star tortoises are inactive during dry seasons and cold weather, but scarcity of food and water may be as responsible for inactivity as extreme temperatures. Some persons interviewed during the study stated that these tortoises hibernate or aestivate, but I have no evidence to support these claims.

Although they live in arid conditions, these tortoises apparently need water at least every few days. They will eat animal matter, but they are essentially herbivores in nature. Food items may require six weeks to pass through the intestine of an immature tortoise (Frazier, 1987b).

Published details of reproductive biology are scant. Extensive interviews with zoo personnel, private collectors, and locals, mainly in western India, indicated that nesting occurs in nearly all months, but there seems to be more activity after the monsoons begin. Mating apparently occurs just before nesting. I know of three records of clutch size: 4, 4, and 5 (or 6). Incubation period is not known; there is a report of 223 days, evidently including incubation *and* emergence periods. It is likely that hatching and emergence from the nest is delayed to coincide with the monsoons and the availability of new plant growth (Frazier, 1987b).

Little is known about parasites and diseases. Ticks are carried, although not at high levels of infestation (Frazier and Keirans, 1990). Nematodes have also been observed. A curious condition, "exposed bone," was observed in 24% of the wild tortoises in western India. The vertebral and costal scutes, especially near sutures, were most often affected, showing an area as large as 10 × 10 cm of missing keratin with the underlying bone exposed. From the general appearance of the carapace, tortoises that had "exposed bone" did not show signs of scarring from fires (Frazier, 1987b).

DISCUSSION AND CONCLUSIONS

The star tortoise was chosen as an example because it is one of the most-widespread and better-known Indian chelonians. Yet, published information reveals little of the biology of the animal, and the geographic ranges given are inexact generalizations. Furthermore, most of the details in the above discussion are from an unpublished report (Frazier, 1987b), and even this is inadequate to describe the biology of the species.

Except for brief comments in the literature concerning the pet trade, no information covers the relationship between this animal and the approximately 900 million people inhabiting India. While the biological data are sparse and questionable, the information relevant to exploitation (e.g., for food or pets), impacts of (and on) agricultural crops, and attitudes and beliefs about the tortoises is virtually nil. Indeed, we have yet to formulate even the basic questions necessary to understand how people of various parts of the Subcontinent interact with the star tortoise.

If we define management as the guiding, governing, controlling, or the taking charge of a given situation, it is debatable whether "management" of star tortoises is feasible, given our present state of ignorance. In addition, any plan for biological conservation must address immense temporal and spatial variation as well as myriad biological and social variation. If this suite of fundamental problems characterizes one of the best-known species, only worse can be expected for lesser-known species. Surely, the prospects of managing an organism are bleak when information is lacking. Under the present circumstances, it is obvious that any plan to manage star tortoises would have to be revised rigorously and regularly to take into account new information, as well as any changes in the target species, its environment, and the human factors impacting it. Because basic information available on *any* species will always be incomplete and every biological system is dynamic, regular revision and updating of management plans must be a standard feature of these schemes. This must include not only biological information, but also social, economic, and political analyses.

As mentioned above, there are many strong arguments—not the least of which are ecological and financial—for adopting system approaches instead of concentrating on single species. If the goal is to manage individual species by managing the systems in which they occur, we must ask, Can we really "control" or "take charge" of an ecosystem? Have we the knowledge and techniques required?

Moreover, tropical systems—which include star tortoise habitat—present the greatest challenges, not only because the diversity of life forms (hence, biological complexity) is greatest (Groombridge, 1992), but also because the human situation is incredibly complicated. Tropical regions are characterized by the most intense pressure on wildlife and other natural resources; the least support for conservation activities and trained personnel; the highest rates of human population growth and poverty; the highest rates of habitat perturbation and transformation; and the greatest economic, social, and political instability (Tolba et al., 1992).

Serious concerns have been raised over our ability to manage single species, much less whole ecosystems (Hilborn and Ludwig, 1993; Ludwig et al., 1993), but the consequences may be devastating if we do not make an attempt. Diverse management activities have been employed with various chelonians. Ideally, these are carefully planned on the basis of ecological information and concepts, as well as specific social and political situations, and they can be essential to the survival of their target species. Management can be a very effective tool, and conservationists have embraced it widely for a variety of taxa, ecosystems, geographic areas, and sociopolitical systems (Groombridge, 1992; Tolba et al., 1992). However, the information on chelonians is generally dispersed, anecdotal, rarely current, and often lacking corroboration. A clear goal of this conference and its proceedings is to provide a compendium of up-to-date information and identify areas where research and conservation activities are needed.

Management and conservation actions must be tailored to the species, habitats, and human conditions in question. There are generalities that serve as guidelines, but one must be ever critical of those plans presented as panaceas. The wisdom that actions directed at single species are now old-fashioned and ineffective must be questioned; a system approach, although ideal, will not always be the option most likely to succeed. For example, a "flagship species" (i.e., a charismatic organism with vast and diverse environmental requirements) can be targeted for management in such a way that public support is mustered, and by providing for the needs of this one species, the requirements of numerous sympatric species are simultaneously fulfilled. In addition, an "indicator species" can be selected to assess the health of a system.

It is also imperative to keep in mind that any management plan or activity, no matter how complete or proficient, is but a tool—it must not become an objective in and of itself. It is no secret that in science and conservation, as in other human activities, there are fashions. The billowing plethora of terms and their associated acronyms—management plans, action plans, action strategies, Conservation Assessment and Management Plans (CAMPs), and Global Captive Action Plans (GCAPs), etc. is evidence enough. We must guard against using management activities as fashions rather than as tools. Management must not simply be a euphemism for that implacable human desire to tinker and control, to manipulate. Indeed, the effectiveness of management programs must be constantly evaluated by objective, external processes of appraisal—true management must be differentiated from manipulation.

Programs that involve captive rearing and reintroduction, as well as relocation, repatriation, and translocation serve as the clearest examples of this dilemma. There have been a few remarkable cases of success (e.g., *Astrochelys yniphora* [Reid, 1996], *Lepidochelys kempii* [Shaver, 1996], and *Geochelone nigra hoodensis* [Cayot, this volume]), but *in general*, despite vast amounts of effort, expert time, funds and other resources, and political appeal and popularity, there is little evidence that these activities successfully enhance wild reptile populations or save species (Dodd and Seigel, 1991; Beck et al., 1994; Wilson and Stanley Price, 1994).

One constant is that wildlife management, or biological conservation, is not "pure" science, but instead depends upon interactions with humans and their societies (Frazier 1990, 1994; Miller et al., 1994b). Perhaps it is because of the inclusion of this social, non-scientific component that wildlife managers have been spurned by pure-science ecologists. Curiously, with biological conservation now in vogue, ecologists and "hard" scientists, who were formerly highly critical of the social components of wildlife management, are now "discovering" that humans are an essential—but enigmatic—part of any formula for success in the management of natural resources (see Levin, 1993; Beck et al., 1994; Wilson and Stanley Price, 1994*)*. It is not surprising that applied ecology (another incarnation of wildlife management) is affirmed to be far more demanding than "rocket science" (Hilborn and Ludwig, 1993).

There is no single recipe. Integration of diverse disciplines and opinions is absolutely fundamental. When striving to integrate local people in conservation activities, it is essential to fully appreciate their attitudes and needs. During the past few years many major conservation agencies have learned, after countless failures, that users of natural resources must benefit from them and thus become interested in conserving and managing them. However, it is much too simplistic to reduce this to direct exploitation; incentives can and must be diverse (see Clark, 1991). Well-salaried people must not underrate the richness and generosity of the world's "poor"; despite an oppressive lack of material wealth and basic physical requirements for normal life, the poor have cultural and social values, as well as emotional and spiritual needs for which natural resources are fundamental (Shiva and Bandhyopadhyay, 1986; Durning, 1988; Roszak et al., 1995).

Other all-too-common pitfalls include equating levels of technology and budget size with success. Nothing could be more misleading and self-serving. Large budgets enable mediocre projects (including their managers and administrators) to persist despite failure (see Clark, 1991). If a relationship exists between budget size and success, it is often inverse (Frazier, 1990; Clark, 1991).

Collaboration is essential. Information and technology must be exchanged, and people must be trained and given follow-up support. These activities require investments in time and careful consideration. Unfortunately, the usual means of "helping" conservation is sending money; this is not only inadequate but irresponsible and dangerous in the long run. Resources (money, logistic support, information) must be carefully and effectively targeted, or the "help" may be counterproductive (Frazier, 1994).

Finally, it is essential to understand that biological conservation and wildlife management are *not* just biology nor even human ecology—in the end they are politics. The arguments for managing ecosystems have been presented, and less complex issues of single species management have been discussed; our ability to control or take care of ecosystems, or even single species, has been questioned. But the ultimate question remains, "Can we successfully manage ourselves?"

Acknowledgments

Field work in India was supported by the Indo-American Submission on Education and Culture, the University Grants Commission, and the U.S. Fish and Wildlife Service. Many organizations in India provided assistance: American Institute of Indian Studies; Bombay Natural History Society; Forest Departments of Andhra Pradesh, Gujarat, Karnataka,

General Recommendations

Management actions must be planned to
- provide necessary information, no matter how basic;
- address diverse biological issues, and integrate them into an ecosystem approach;
- address human attitudes and needs (further integrating them with the system approach); and
- incorporate various disciplines and integrate diverse groups of people—especially those who interact directly with the resources and environments to be managed.

Management actions must be carried out to
- target keystone or at least flagship species where this is feasible;
- run over the long term (preferably no less than the life cycle of the target organism);
- be revised and criticized vigorously, frequently, objectively, and constructively—by independent evaluators, free from personal and institutional self interest; and
- function as a tool for resource conservation, not as an end in themselves.

Rajasthan, and West Bengal; Hingolgadh Conservation Trust; Madras Crocodile Bank Trust; and Zoological Survey of India. In addition, many, many friends, colleagues, civil servants, and countless unknown persons in India provided generous and invaluable help. I am also grateful to the organizers of Conservation, Restoration, and Management of Tortoises and Turtles—An International Conference, and their sponsors, for the opportunity and support to participate in the conference. Drs. B. Faust, B. Miller, and I. Olmsted made valuable comments on earlier drafts of this paper.

Literature Cited

Anderson, J. A. and S. A. Minton Jr. 1963. Two noteworthy herpetological records from the Thar Parkar Desert, West Pakistan. Herpetologica 19(2):152.

Annandale, N. 1907. Notes on the fauna of a desert tract in Southern India. Part I. Batrachians and Reptiles, with remarks on the reptiles of the North-West Frontier. Mem. Asiatic Soc. Bengal 1:183–202.

Bailey, J. A. 1984. Principles of Wildlife Management. John Wiley & Sons, New York. i–x + 373 pp.

Beck, B. B., L. G. Rapaport, M. R. Stanley Price, and A. C. Wilson. 1994. Reintroduction of captive-born animals. In P. J. S. Olney, G. M. Mace, and A. T. C. Feistner (eds.), Creative Conservation: Interactive Management of Wild and Captive Animals, pp. 265–286. Chapman & Hall, New York.

Bury, R. B. 1988. Habitat relationships and ecological importance of amphibians and reptiles. In K. J. Raedeke (ed.), Streamside Management: Riparian Wildlife and Forestry Interactions, pp. 61–76. Institute of Forest Resources, University of Washington, Seattle, Washington.

Bury, R. B. and P. S. Corn. 1988. Douglas-fir forests in the Oregon and Washington Cascades: Abundance of terrestrial herpetofauna related to stand, age, and moisture. In Management of Amphibians,

Reptiles, and Small Mammals in North America (R. C. Szaro, K. E. Severson, and D. R. Patton tech. coords.), pp. 11–22. General Technical Report, RM-166, USDA Forest Service, Fort Collins, Colorado.

Clark, J. 1991. Democratizing Development: The Role of Voluntary Organizations. Kumarian Press, West Hartford, Connecticut. i–xii + 226 pp.

Daniel, J. C. 1983. The Book of Indian Reptiles. Bombay Natural History Society, Bombay. i–x + 141 pp. + 54 pls.

Das, I. 1985. Indian Turtles: A Field Guide. World Wildlife Fund India (Eastern Region), Calcutta. 119 pp.

Deraniyagala, P. E. P. 1939. Tetrapod Reptiles of Ceylon. Dulau & Co., London. i–xxxii + 412 pp. + 24 pls.

Dodd, C. K., Jr. and R. A. Seigel. 1991. Relocation, repatriation, and translocation of amphibians and reptiles: Are they conservation strategies that work? Herpetologica 47(3):336–350.

Durning, A. B. 1988. Action at the Grassroots: Fighting Poverty and Environmental Decline. Pap. 88. Worldwatch Institute, Washington, D.C. 70 pp.

Ernst, C. H. and R. W. Barbour. 1989. Turtles of the World. Smithsonian Inst. Press, Washington, D.C. and London. 313 pp.

Frazier, J. 1987a. The status of chelonians in India; and other reports to the Indian Government. Unpubl. reports, American Institute of Indian Studies, New Delhi.

Frazier, J. 1987b. The biology of the star tortoise, *Geochelone elegans* Schoepff. Unpubl. report, American Institute of Indian Studies, New Delhi. 98 pp. + 9 figs.

Frazier, J. 1990. International resource conservation: Thoughts on the challenge. *In* Transactions 55th North American Wildlife and Natural Resources Conference, pp. 384–395. Wildlife Management Inst., Washington, D.C.

Frazier, J. 1992. Management of tropical chelonians: Dream or nightmare? *In* K. P. Singh and J. S. Singh (eds.), Tropical Ecosystems: Ecology and Management, pp. 125–135. Wiley Eastern Ltd, New Delhi, India.

Frazier, J. 1994. Conserving sea turtles and other natural resources: What Ferdinand Marcos and Manuel Noriega can teach us. *In* Proceedings of the Thirteenth Annual Symposium on Sea Turtle Biology and Conservation, (B. A. Schroeder and B. E. Witherington, comps.), pp. 60–63. NOAA Technical Memorandum, NMFS-SEFSC-341, Miami, Florida.

Frazier, J. and J. E. Keirans. 1990. Ticks (Acari: Ixodidae) collected on chelonians (Reptilia) from India and Burma. J. Bombay. Nat. Hist. Soc. 87(2):247–249.

Groombridge, B. (ed.). 1992. Global Biodiversity: Status of the Earth's Living Resources. Chapman & Hall, New York. i–xix + 585 pp.

Hilborn, R. and D. Ludwig. 1993. The limits of applied ecological research. Ecol. Appl. 3(4):550–552.

Levin, S. A. (ed.). 1993. Forum: Perspectives on sustainability. Ecol. Appl. 3(4):545–589.

Ludwig, D., R. Hilborn, and C. Walters. 1993. Uncertainty, resource exploitation, and conservation: Lessons from history. Science 260: 17, 36.

Majupuria, T. C. 1973. Introduction to Chordates (for BSc. students of Indian Universities). 4th ed. S. Nagin & Co., Delhi. i–xvi + 1120 pp.

McShea, W. J., C. Wemmer, and M. Stüwe. 1994. Conflict of interest: A public hunt at the National Zoo's Conservation and Research Center. Wildlife Society Bulletin 21(4):492–497.

Miller, B., G. Ceballos, and R. Reading. 1994a. Prairie dogs, poison and biotic diversity. Conserv. Biol. 8(3):677–681.

Miller, B., R. Reading, C. Conway, J. A. Jackson, M Hutchins, N. Snyder, S. Forrest, J. Frazier, and S. Derrickson. 1994b. A model for improving endangered species recovery programs. Environ. Manage. 18 (3):637–645.

Minton, S. A. 1966. A contribution to the herpetology of West Pakistan. Bull. Amer. Mus. Nat. Hist. 134(2):27–184.

Murray, J. A. 1884. The Vertebrate Zoology of Sind. Richardson & Co., London. 421 pp. [Reprinted 1988, International Book Distributors, Dehra Dun.]

Murthy, T. S. N. 1985. Classification and distribution of the reptiles of India. The Snake 17(1):48–70.

Obst, F. J. 1985. Die Welt der Schildkröten. Edition Leipzig, Leipzig. 235 pp.

Prakash, I. 1974. Chapter XIII. The ecology of vertebrates of the Indian desert. *In* M S. Mani (ed.), Ecology and Biogeography in India, pp. 369–420. Junk, The Hague.

Pritchard, P. C. H. 1979. Encyclopedia of Turtles. T. F. H. Publications, Neptune, New Jersey. 895 pp.

Reid, D. 1995. Observations on hatchling and juvenile captive-bred Angonoka in Madagascar. Dodo, J. Wildl. Preserv. Trusts 31:112–119.

Robinson, W. L. and E. G. Bolen. 1984. Wildlife Ecology and Management. Macmillan, New York. i–xv + 478 pp.

Rodgers, W. A. 1991. Techniques for Wildlife Census in India: Field Manual. Wildlife Institute of India, Dehra Dun. i–vii + 82 pp.

Roszak, T., M. E. Gomes, and A. D. Kanner (eds.). 1995. Ecopsychology: Restoring the Earth, Healing the Mind. Sierra Club Books, San Francisco. xxiii + 338 pp.

Sale, J. B. and K. Berkmüller (eds.). 1988. Manual of Wildlife Techniques for India. Food & Agriculture Organization of the United Nations & Wildlife Institute of India, Dehra Dun (FO:IND/82/003).

Schemnitz, S. D. (ed.). 1980. Wildlife Management Techniques Manual (4th ed.). The Wildlife Society, Washington, D.C. i–vii + 686 pp.

Scott, N. J. and R. A. Seigel. 1992. The management of amphibian and reptile populations: Species priorities and methodological and theoretical constraints. *In* D. R. McCullough and R. H. Barrett (eds.), Wildlife 2001: Populations, pp. 343–368. Elsevier, New York.

Shaver, D. J. 1996. Head-started Kemp's ridley turtles nest in Texas. Marine Turtle Newsletter 74:5–7.

Shiva, V. and J. Bandhyopadhyay. 1986. Chipko: India's civilisational response to the forest crisis. The INTACH Environmental Series 5, Indian Trust for Art and Cultural Heritage, New Delhi. 23 pp.

de Silva, A. 1995. The status of *Geochelone elegans* in North Western Province of Sri Lanka: Preliminary findings. *In* Proceedings: International Congress of Chelonian Conservation, pp. 47–49. Tortoise Village, Gonfaron, France, 6–10 July 1995. Editions Soptom, Gonfaron, France.

Smith, M. A. 1931. The Fauna of British India, Including Ceylon and Burma. Reptilia and Amphibia. Vol. I: Loricata, Testudines. Taylor & Francis, London. [Reprinted Today and Tomorrow's Printers & Publishers, Faridabad.] i–xxviii + 185 pp. + 2 pls. + map.

Tolba, M. K., O. A. El-Kholy, E. El-Hinnawi, M. W. Holdgate, D. F. McMichael, and R. E. Munn. 1992. The World Environment 1972–1992: Two Decades of Challenge. UNEP, Chapman & Hall, New York. i–xi + 884 pp.

Wilson, A. C. and M. R. Stanley Price. 1994. Reintroduction as a reason for captive breeding. *In* P. J. S. Olney, G. M. Mace, and A. T. C. Feistner (eds.), Creative Conservation: Interactive Management of Wild and Captive Animals, pp. 243–264. Chapman & Hall, New York.

Global Conservation and the Sciences: People, Policy, and Pennies

— PLENARY LECTURE —

IAN R. SWINGLAND

The Durrell Institute of Conservation and Ecology (DICE), University of Kent, Canterbury, Kent CT2 7NX, United Kingdom
[e-mail: 106407.3135@compuserve.com]

Abstract: Conservation science is unprepared to fulfil the expectations of both the less-developed countries (the major centres of biodiversity) and the developed countries, which have depleted much of their natural resource base. Both want strategies and solutions to their environmental problems and reliable means of sustainably using their natural resources. Too often the debate over the world's remaining resources is polarised between *preservation* and *economic development*. Do the dwindling natural habitats contain resources and raw materials that can be tapped for greater economic development and welfare? Do we have the scientific and economic knowledge, and the evidence, to support the concept of sustainable use—the commercialisation of biodiversity assets that provides both political and economic reasons to conserve? How best can developing countries realise some of the value of their remaining resources, and what public policies and private actions are required? Do we have the necessary knowledge to insure success? Or is there a fundamental intellectual flaw in the concept that biodiversity resources can be simultaneously conserved and sustainably used?

Is it possible to reconcile the conservation of resources with economic development so that developing societies have an incentive to ensure the long-term management and survival of these resources? For example, clear evidence exists that single species conservation and the classical ecological paradigm are neither the only nor the best methods to ensure conservation. This paper will concentrate on the new strategic solutions to the current problems affecting conservation. I will address sustainable use and biodiversity management; using, valuing and commercialising biodiversity; appraising projects; policy appraisal and adjustment; institutional structures; surveys, inventories, and data bases; global information and dynamic models; expert systems; future scientific, economic, and policy goals; and a realistic agendum.

This paper concentrates on the hunt for the Holy Grail, the supreme prize of conserving biodiversity in perpetuity whilst sustainably using that biodiversity. Is it possible to reconcile conservation of natural resources with economic development to guarantee that society has an economic incentive to ensure their long-term survival? Or is there a fundamental intellectual flaw in the concept of sustainable use of biological resources?

The following terms are often confused and should be clearly defined: *Biodiversity*, or *biological diversity*, is the number, variety, and variability of living organisms and ecosystems. It can be defined in at least ten different ways—ways which predetermine policy, and it is used today both as a loose description to embrace the richness and variation of the living world, and politically for the purposes of national and international conventions and agreements within the context of economics and development. *Preservation* is unmanaged ecosystem protection. *Conservation, management, and restoration* is knowledgeable intervention in the environment with specific management objectives.

What is Biodiversity?

Biodiversity has three related components at different levels of organisation: genes, species, and ecosystems. Genetic diversity is the basis of biodiversity and, although the possible combinations of gene sequences will probably exceed the total number of atoms in the universe, only a small fraction (<1%) of genetic material in higher organisms is outwardly expressed in the form and function of the organism (Thomas, 1992).

Species diversity is the commonly considered measure of biodiversity. One million seven hundred thousand species have been described, although estimates for the total number of extant species range from five to forty million (even 100 million), consisting mainly of insects and microorganisms. However, such estimates, and the numbers of species already identified, depend upon how they were described as distinct by taxonomists and systematists—ecologically, morphologically, physiologically, genetically, mathematically. The need for commonly agreed names that define distinct species is essential (Rojas, 1992).

A tropical forest tree, supporting hundreds of invertebrate, botanical (epiphytic), and microorganism species, makes a significant contribution to biodiversity in absolute species richness compared to a temperate montane tree, which has many fewer dependent species. This, and the fact that tropical forests contain more threatened mammal species (for example) than any other habitat type (Thornback and Jenkins, 1982), explains why there is an international focus on tropical forests rather than on temperate habitats. It also explains why the concepts of "megadiversity" (Mittermeier and Werner, 1990) and species or taxa endemicity, built around the great species richness of a country or region (Myers, 1990; Vane-Wright et al., 1991), are being used to focus international funding support, even though the usefulness of species inventories alone is too limited for biodiversity.

In the last decade NGOs have wisely concentrated efforts on habitats (= ecosystems) rather than species, and the concept of ecosystem diversity has arisen (even though many nongovernmental conservation organizations raise most of their funds using charismatic flagship species).

It is imperative that an unequivocal and precise meaning of biodiversity and sustainability be established if we are to make informed decisions about the present and develop policy and programmes for the future. The definition of biodiversity affects objectives in management. One could easily promote a timber extraction, or a non-timber forest product programme, which conserves species richness (i.e., numbers of species) at the expense of genetic diversity. Indeed, work focussed on stimulating or increasing the range of harvested tropical tree species not currently in trade (to reduce pressure on the currently overexploited species) may be misguided. It may lead to increased genetic and species impoverishment when foresters expand the number of species they take, selecting only the best and most mature specimens, and thus removing the most productive and healthiest genetic stock.

I list below criteria that could be applied to determine which area, habitat, or ecosystem should be included, as a priority, in any protected area or biodiversity management programme. An area would qualify if it

1. has the highest level of endemicity or basal taxa (Myers, 1990; Vane-Wright et al., 1984);
2. has the highest number of species, i.e., species richness;
3. has the most significant ecosystem of its type, based upon general perceptions or criteria, and is an essential part of a national or international "portfolio" of habitats;
4. contains and supports flagship species upon which attention and funds can be focussed;
5. contains and supports keystone species upon which the ecosystem itself, and the ecological integrity of surrounding areas, depend;
6. contains a species, deemed important by some other criteria (e.g., a charismatic mammal which would attract funds, and/or is commercially important), where all indications point to extinction using viability modelling (population viability analysis) within a relatively short (and specified) period if no conservation measures are implemented; or if population analysis using comprehensive raw data (not estimates) indicates that the species is likely to enter a non-recoverable trend without management;
7. has a high potential to support long-term conservation because the local people can easily be integrated and involved in management, and benefit from such involvement (local integration);
8. contains species that can be *sustainably used*, e.g., for cropping, farming, ranching, or tourism; and/or
9. if there is political exigency.

Although the methods of conservation within the policy of a country may be driven by needs that are perceived to be pressing—family planning, education, politics, internal conflict, financial planning and investment, individual vested interests—the nine-point list above gives some ways in which current policy and decisions are being made. Each of the methods has drawbacks and while the list is not exhaustive, combinations of the various approaches are normally used.

Endemicity and species richness are useful starting points in defining priorities on the global level, but without information on the possibility of extinction using viability modelling or population analysis, the urgency of the position cannot be assessed. Moreover, with the increasing emphasis on the integration of local people into conservation programmes, the potential for small-scale, localised projects that attempt to sustainably use biological resources cannot be ignored. Since national or external funding will generally be involved in "pump-priming" most projects, it will become important for funds to be invested in a representative portfolio of ecosystems within, or even between, countries. The portfolio approach will be vital in this comparison between ecosystems. The presence of a flagship species may be a significant asset in raising such funds. Clearly, political exigencies or pure chance can enter the situation.

The differing approaches being advocated for biodiversity conservation are not just guided by the available methodologies but are symptomatic of the underlying philosophies. The evolution-based approach, predominantly the preserve of biologists, is concerned with the maintenance of diversity as an unqualified objective unaffected by economics; whereas the need for conservation and the uses of biodiversity—the resource-based argument—are used to "sell" the proposition to decision and policy makers. Where they come together is in the ideal of sustainability and the methods of achieving it.

Sustainable Use and Biodiversity Management

In examining biodiversity management and sustainable development, the three outstanding questions are
- Have we sufficient knowledge of ecosystem processes that control biodiversity?
- Have we been able to accurately define the parameters of use?
- And if so, can we develop appropriate, testable management objectives to sustainably use this biodiversity?

The classical view of stable, natural, closed, and self-regulating ecosystems is a poor foundation upon which to base conservation. Biologists now recognise that
- ecosystems are generally open and grade into each other;
- change is inevitable, constant, and often chaotic; and
- the role of humans, past and present, is a critical component.

Recognition of these complexities makes it very difficult to identify the goals of management regimes, although most conservationists would agree that the maintenance of certain vulnerable, endangered, or specialised creatures or ecological communities is an important criterion in determining management.

Conservation scientists, embracing both the natural and social sciences, would support this view but would further ask whether we know enough of the interaction of the biological system (including its human component), and whether we know what we are managing it for. Scientists do not know enough to answer the first question, although many projects are underway examining (for example) the interaction between local people and protected areas, and if the answer to the second question on objectives is "biodiversity management is for sustainability," then we must understand the parameters of sustainability and test this understanding against the facts from the field.

Economists have produced innumerable definitions of sustainable development (Pearce, 1989; Pezzey, 1989). However, biologists have been unsuccessful at coming to terms with this concept, possibly because many see a fundamental incompatibility between the majority of resource extraction programs and conservation. In a general sense, an economist's definition of sustainable development is that which leaves our total patrimony, including natural environmental assets, intact over a particular period of time. We should bequeath to future generations the same "capital," embodying opportunities for potential welfare, that we currently enjoy (Winpenny, 1991).

I would offer the hypothesis that sustainability, in the context of biodiversity management, is defined as any self-perpetuating system. But when we add the word *development*, cracks appear in the rationale and logic. Can we have sustainable development? Many believe that this is impossible (Robinson, 1993a, 1993b). The greatest biodiversity centres also have some of the largest and most rapidly growing human populations. For example, Indonesia now has 180 million people, which will increase to over 200 million by the next century. In a programme of transmigration, it moves people away from densely populated areas to forested areas, inhabited only by indigenous people, and establishes them as agriculture-based communities. Indonesia has vast biodiversity resources, but with the increasing population and its spread to other areas, biodiversity is being lost. In Thailand, the demand for agricultural land from 1962 to 1989 highlights the relationship between biodiversity loss and population increases (Phantumvanit and Panayotou, 1990). Forty percent of the increase in cultivated land in recent years has been achieved by conversion of forest land. The most important factor affecting the demand for cropland, and thus forest conversion, appears to be population growth. It is clear that species extinction, which could be a sustainability indicator, is predominantly due to anthropogenic factors.

Perhaps we must accept the need to choose which species live and which die. Economists might agree with this view (Swanson, 1992), but few biologists would.

Using, Valuing, and Commercialising Biodiversity

The use of biodiversity and its value to humans has been recognised for millions of years. Even Neanderthal man, a relatively recent ancestor, kept horses in stalls and began the process of domestication. Today, many examples exist of biodiversity utilisation and value. A crude estimate of the direct market value of all types of biodiversity is U.S. $410,810,000,000 per annum (Anon., 1995).

In valuing biodiversity we are attempting to trace the impact of changes in biodiversity on economic values. Information on the dynamics of ecosystems is needed to derive a model indicating how changes in the supply of a natural resource result in changes to the economic value of production. This "production function technique" can be successfully applied in developing countries where a large proportion of economic production comes from agriculture, fisheries, forests, etc. "Contingent valuation method" is a method of obtaining insights into people's preferences for environmental quality; how much they are willing to pay and what they are willing to accept in compensation for foregoing the benefits. Used mainly in the United States, it has not been applied to developing countries. "Hedonistic pricing" is another technique almost exclusively applied to developing countries that enables the valuing of non-marketed environmental services incorporated in the prices of marketed goods or services to be disentangled, e.g., soil fertility within the price of land. "Travel cost methods" are

TABLE 1
Nyaminyami Wildlife Management Trust revenue.*

Revenue	NWMT
Buffalo Range Safaris	148,349
Astra Wildlife	117,790
Mashonaland Hunters	6,048
Sub-total Safari Hunting	272,187
Cropping 1	11,554
Cropping 2	24,356
Sub-total Cropping	35,910
Meat and skins, Kapenta fishing	11,256
Total Revenue	319,353
Recurrent expenditure	
Cropping costs 1	−10,244
Cropping costs 2	−18,604
Wages and salaries	−16,378
Transport and equipment hire	−636
Vehicle maintenance/fuel/repair/insurance	−5,829
Wildlife compensation	−26,681
Kapenta licences	−2,400
Advertising, publications, printing	−4,341
Miscellaneous, bank charges	−1,469
Total Recurrent Expenditure	−86,582
Net Revenue	232,771
Zim Trust	20,093
Adjusted Net Revenue	252,864

SOURCE: Adapted from Jansen, 1990.
*In Zimbabwe $; Z$2.1 = U.S. $1 (in 1989).

applied to tourism derived from the environment. An indirect measure of what people are willing to pay for access to the site is obtained by aggregating tourist expenditure in getting to and from the site with the number of visitors.

With humans inexorably destroying biodiversity with their burgeoning populations, and because increasing productivity to feed and house these people will result in increasing homogeneity in production methods and processes (i.e., an increasingly narrower spectrum of species will meet all humankind's needs), biodiversity is doomed.

Current and future loss of biodiversity will be high for three reasons (Swanson, 1992): Biodiversity is too readily traded off for immediate gains in productivity; an increasing level of risk is attached to specialisation; and ecosystems are changing at an unprecedented rate, more rapidly than our knowledge of them advances.

Some examples of purported sustainable biodiversity use exist in community-based projects, ecotourism, non-timber forest products, medicine, pharmaceuticals, animal and plant genetics, and microbial (e.g., drugs) and macrobial (e.g., crops, traded plant and animal products) derivatives.

The Communal Area Management Programme for Indigenous Resources (CAMPFIRE) project in Zimbabwe is to administer the management of wildlife resources for the benefit of the local inhabitants (Table 1). You see in one District Council area that total revenues generated in 1989 was Z$319,353, net revenue was Z$232,771 and each household received Z$99 (20% of average annual household incomes). Although revenues must be channelled back to the community, less than 50% was returned to the districts. The main problems with this model are ensuring that it is financially self-sustaining, encouraging district councils to devolve genuine authority for wildlife management to wards and villages (particularly concerning revenue distribution), and changing the perceptions of policy makers and external donors who are prejudiced towards conventional systems (Barbier, 1993). Similarly, it is clear that tourism, or ecotourism (38.3% of tourists to South America, Table 2), does not contribute revenues that are re-invested in the touristic biodiversity resource (e.g., national park) that generates the revenue. For example, if expenditures at hotels and elsewhere are for the purchase of imported products, or are repatriated by foreign companies, developing countries can lose 55% of gross tourist revenues from such leakage (Boo, 1990). The Barawan people of Sarawak earn direct revenue from package tours and single tourists by providing food, accommodation, and boats, and by serving as guides into the Gunong Mulu National Park. Most of their income is disbursed internally as reinvestment in their local community to service their clients, particularly since their chief owns the local regional on-ground provider for international tour companies.

Non-timber forest products (mainly fruits and vegetable products, like rattan) are a possible source of sustainable utilisation of tropical forests when marketing co-operatives are formed by villages, but such arrangements still have structural and organisational problems. It is clear however that such co-operative local systems could be used for finding, identifying, and marketing natural medicines, cosmetics, and macrobial derivatives where local knowledge regarding location, use and propagation will be invaluable. Village-based or tribal systems possess the intellectual property rights and collect annual fees from a national Biodiversity and Marketing Institute (see below). Thailand exported U.S. $17 million of medical plants and spices in 1979 and consumed U.S. $20 million locally (Anon., 1981).

Without doubt, the existence value of biodiversity and its conservation are important to many people who value specific species (Table 3) and the organisations that conserve them (Table 4).

Values can be ascribed for the net benefit of a particular forest *in situ* (Table 5). Even floodplains can be valued using different discounted net rates over a particular time period (Table 6).

The importance of retaining the maximum biodiversity is vital for agriculture, horticulture, medicine, building materials, craft products, and a host of other anthropocentric reasons. The rosy periwinkle cures Hodgkin's disease and leukaemia; wild tomatoes and maize found in Central America improve cultivated types; and pygmy rice (which was nearly a lost variety) strengthens the stalks of high-yield cultivars. All demonstrate that genetic variations must be preserved. As modern screening techniques improve, new and unexpected characteristics will be uncovered (Table 7).

The dependency on rice (Table 8), the monoclonal nature of most of the world's livestock, and the genetic uniformity of other selected crops (Table 9) can bring crop catastrophes or epidemics (Table 10). Genetic diversity, on the other hand, not only makes a major contribution to desirable cultivar characteristics (Table 7) but also to yields (Table 11).

Pharmaceutical derivatives from higher plants are worth about U.S. $21 billion from U.S. sales alone and are based on only ≈40 species (Akerele et al., 1988). Such derivatives are either therapeutic agents, base materials for drug synthesis, or models for the synthesis of pharmacologically active compounds. Direct use values are limited to very few species and may be a way for developing countries to retain rights over medical products made from their own biodiversity (see below). However, in the last decade more new synthesised drugs have emerged from understanding the body's biochemical reactions and the use of biotechnology and genetic processes than from screening plants for active compounds. Valuing such biodiversity when its end use has so many indirect benefits (e.g., improved human health) is difficult.

Drug companies are increasingly interested in microorganisms rather than plants. Developing countries that have such organisms (and other sources of biodiversity) are concerned to obtain revenue and retain control over their development. Drug companies' development agreements with owner countries, even since the Rio Conference (June 1992) embraced the Biodiversity Convention, are skewed heavily in favour of the company on the basis that the development risks and costs are theirs, and the ownership of the particular organism is an act of God!

Institutional Structures: Surveys, Inventories, Information, Models, Databases, and Expert Systems

Many models are being put forward as exemplars of a National Biodiversity Institute with the capacity to collect, curate, store specimens and information, build biodiversity databases, educate, train, initiate public awareness, market, sell, and conserve the national biodiversity heritage. Many, such as InBio in Costa Rica, appear flawed since they rely heavily on foreign technical expertise. Clearly, the institutional structure and its strength are axiomatic for success in biodiversity management. A lack of substantive investment in and commitment to building national capacity to collect, manage, and analyse biodiversity data are the primary causes for the failure of these programmes.

TABLE 2
Reasons for selecting travel destinations in Latin America.

Reason	Respondents	%
Natural history	167	38.3
Sightseeing	161	36.9
Visiting friends and/or relatives	132	30.3
Sun, beaches, entertainment	130	29.8
Cultural/native history	102	23.4
Business/convention	87	20.0
Archaeology	63	14.4

SOURCE: Boo, 1990. NOTE: Total number surveyed = 436.

TABLE 3
Empirical measures of existence values: U.S. $ value per adult respondent in mid-1980s.

Natural Amenities	
Water quality (S Platte River Basin)	4
Visibility (Grand Canyon)	22
Additional park facilities (Australia)	6
Animal Species	
Bald eagle	11
Emerald shiner	4
Grizzly bear	15
Bighorn sheep	7
Whooping crane	1
Blue whale	8
Bottlenose dolphin	6
California sea otter	7
Northern elephant seal	7

SOURCES: Pearce, 1990; Majid et al., 1983.

TABLE 4
Gifts to surveyed environmental/wildlife organisations.

	U.S. $,000 1989	U.S. $,000 1990	Percent Change
TOTALS	**208,907**	**273,385**	**31**
Nature Conservancy	48,963	85,527	75
WWF and the Conservation Foundation	33,465	42,438	27
Ducks Unlimited, Inc.	25,501	29,674	16
Sierra Club	21,908	28,718	31
Natural Resources Defense Council	12,524	13,821	10
National Audubon Society	10,174	11,094	9
National Arbor Day Foundation	8,126	11,045	36
New York Zoological Society	17,073	9,531	-44
Sierra Club Legal Defense Fund	5,973	6,833	14
World Resources Institute	5,240	6,336	21
American Farmland Trust	2,716	5,195	91
International Fund for Animal Welfare	3,912	4,555	16
Resources for the Future	2,651	2,948	11
Animal Protection Institute	435	2,607	499
American Humane Association	1,992	1,903	-4
American Forestry Association	909	1,816	100
Clean Water Fund	719	1,607	124
Adirondack Council	1,178	1,542	31
American Rivers	1,728	1,502	-13
Trout Unlimited	1,180	1,309	11
Earth Island Alliance	1,007	1,026	2
Rainforest Alliance	254	798	214
Soil and Water Conservation Society	388	390	1
Farm Sanctuary, Inc.	165	346	110
Alliance for Environmental Education	19	186	879
Wildlife Habitat Enhancement Council	152	182	20
Lake Michigan Federation	133	165	24
Animal Rights Network, Inc.	200	118	-41
American Cave Conservation Association	87	108	24
Peace Garden Project	135	65	-52

TABLE 5
Cost-benefit analysis: The Korup Project.

Direct costs of conservation	−11,913
Opportunity costs	
Lost stumpage value	−706
Lost forest use	−2,620
Sub-total	−3,326
Direct benefits	
Sustained forest use	3,291
Replaced subsistence production	977
Tourism	1,360
Genetic value	481
Watershed protection of fisheries	3,776
Control of flood risk	1,578
Soil fertility maintenance	532
Sub-total	11,995
Induced benefits	
Agricultural productivity gain	905
Induced forestry	207
Induced cash crops	3,216
Sub-total	4,328
Net Benefit — Project	1,084
Adjustments	
External trade credit	7,246
Uncaptured genetic value	−433
Uncaptured watershed benefits	−351
Net Benefit — Cameroon	7,545

SOURCE: Ruitenbeek, 1989. NOTE: NPV £,000, 8% discount rate.

TABLE 6
Net present value of benefits from the Hadejia-Jama'are floodplain, Nigeria.

Base case	(8%, 50 years)	(8%, 30 years)	(12%, 50 years)	(12%, 30 years)
Total	1,360	1,251	922	895
Agriculture	921	848	625	607
Fishing	300	276	203	197
Fuel wood	139	127	94	91
Adjusted agriculture	838	773	574	558
Adjusted total	1,276	1,176	872	846

SOURCE: Barbier et al., 1991. NOTE: Values in Naire per hectare; N7.5 = U.S. $1 (1989–1990).

TABLE 7
Genetic diversity and agriculture: Specific contributions made by wild relatives of crops.

Crop	Found in	Effect on production
Wheat	Turkey	Genetic resistance to disease is valued at $50 million per year (Witt, 1985).
Rice	India	Wild strain proved resistant to the grassy stunt virus (World Conservation Monitoring Centre, 1992).
Barley	Ethiopia	Protects California's $160 million-per-year crop from yellow dwarf virus (Witt, 1985).
Hops		Added $15 million to British brewing industry in 1981 by improving bitterness (Witt, 1985).
Beans	Mexico	The International Center for Tropical Agriculture in Colombia used genes from the Mexican bean to beat the Mexican bean weevil which destroys as much as 25% of stored beans in Africa and 15% in South America (Rhoades, 1991).
Grapes	Texas	Texas rootstock (from land now covered by the Dallas-Fort Worth Airport) was used to revitalise the European wine industry in the 1860s after a louse infection (Rhoades, 1991).

TABLE 8
Area devoted to modern rice varieties in 11 Asian countries.

Country	Year	1000 ha	% of rice area
Bangladesh	1981	2,325	22
India	1980	18,495	47
Indonesia	1980	5,416	60
Korea, Rep.	1981	321	26
Malaysia, W.	1977	316	44
Myanmar	1980	1,502	29
Nepal	1981	326	26
Pakistan	1978	1,015	50
Philippines	1980	2,710	78
Sri Lanka	1980	612	71
Thailand	1979	80	09

SOURCE: Hazell, 1985.

TABLE 9
Extent of genetic uniformity in selected crops.

Crop	Country	Number of varieties/percent genetic uniformity
Rice	Sri Lanka	From 2,000 varieties in 1959 to 5 major varieties today (Rhoades, 1991); 75% of varieties descended from one maternal parent (Hargrove et al., 1988)
Rice	India	From 30,000 varieties (originally) to 75% of production from less than 10 varieties (Rhoades, 1991)
Rice	Bangladesh	62% of varieties descended from one maternal parent (Hargrove et al., 1988)
Rice	Indonesia	74% of varieties descended from one maternal parent (Hargrove et al., 1988)
Wheat	USA	9 varieties comprise 50% of crop (NAS, 1972)
Potato	USA	4 varieties comprise 75% of crop (NAS, 1972)
Cotton	USA	3 varieties comprise 50% of crop (NAS, 1972)
Soybeans	USA	6 varieties comprise 50% of crop (NAS, 1972)

TABLE 10
Past crop failures attributed to genetic uniformity.

Date	Location	Crop	Cause and result
900	Central America	Maize	Anthropologists speculate that the collapse of the Classic Mayan Civilization may have been a result of a maize virus (Rhoades, 1991).
1846	Ireland	Potato	Potato blight led to famine in which 1 million died and 1.5 million emigrated from their homeland (Hoyt, 1988).
late 1800s	Sri Lanka	Coffee	Fungus wiped out homogenous coffee plantations on the island (Rhoades, 1991).
1940s	USA		U.S. crops lost to insects have doubled since the 1940s (Plucknett and Smith, 1986).
1943	India	Rice	Brown spot disease aggravated by typhoon destroyed crop starting the Great Bengal Famine (Hoyt, 1988).
1953–54	USA	Wheat	Wheat stem rust affected most of hard wheat crop (Hoyt, 1988).
1960s	USA	Wheat	Stripe rust reached epidemic proportions in Pacific Northwest (Oldfield, 1984).
1970	USA	Maize	Decrease in yield 15%, $1 billion lost (NAS, 1972; Tatum, 1971).*
1970	Philippines/Indonesia	Rice	HYV rice attacked by leafhoppers spreading tungro virus (Hoyt, 1988).
1972	USSR	Wheat	Crop badly affected by weather (Plucknett et al., 1987).
1974–77	Indonesia	Rice	Grassy stunt virus destroyed over 3 million tonnes of rice. From the late 1960s to the late 1970s the virus plagued South and Southeast Asian rice production (Hoyt, 1988).
1984	Florida	Citrus	Bacterial disease caused 135 nurseries to destroy 18 million trees (Rhoades, 1991).

*Duvick (1986) reports that although the leaf blight attacked a widespread and uniform genotype, the problem was uniformity of cytoplasm introduced to eliminate the chore of detasseling—not the genetic material in the nucleus of the seed.

TABLE 11
Genetic diversity and agriculture: Genetic contributions of cultivars to crop yields.

Crop	Location	Period	Effect on production
All crops	USA	1980s	$1.0 billion/year (OTA, 1987, USDA est.)
Maize	USA	1930–80	≈ ½ of a fourfold increase in yields (OTA, 1987)
	USA	1930–80	89% of yield gain of 103 kg/ha/yr in commercials (Duvick, 1984)
	USA	1930–80	71% of yield gains in single cross hybrids (Duvick, 1984)
	USA	1985–89	Genetic gains to N. Dakota of $2.3 million/year (Frohberg, 1991)
Rice	Asia	GR	$1.5 billion/year
	USA	1930–80	≈ ½ of a doubling in yields (OTA, 1987)
Wheat	Asia	GR	$2.0 billion/year
	USA	1930–80	≈ ½ of a doubling in yields (OTA, 1987)
	USA	1958–80	0.74% genetic gain per year—½ of 32% yield gain (Schmidt, 1984)
	UK	1947–75	50% of an 84% gain in yields (Silvey, 1978)
	World	1970–83	43% of genetic gain totalling 46% (best data) (Kuhr et al., 1985)
			55% of genetic gain totalling 32% (all sites) (Kuhr et al., 1985)
Sorghum	USA	1930–80	≈ ½ of a fourfold increase in yields (OTA, 1987)
		1950–80	1–2% genetic gain per year from manipulating kernel numbers, plant weight, height and leaf area (Miller and Kebede, 1984)
Barley	USA	1930–80	≈ ½ of a doubling in yields (OTA, 1987)
Potato	USA	1930–80	≈ ½ of a fourfold increase in yields (OTA, 1987)
Soybeans	USA	1930–80	≈ ½ of a doubling in yields (OTA, 1987)
	USA	1902–77	79% of 23.7 kg/ha annual yield gains (Specht and Williams, 1984)
Pearl Millet	India	at present	genetic improvements worth $200 million annually (ICRISAT, 1990)
Cotton	USA	1930–80	≈ ½ of a doubling in yields (OTA, 1987)
	USA	1910–80	0.75% genetic gain per year (Meredith, Jr. and Bridge, 1984)
Sugar Cane	USA	1930–80	≈ ½ of a doubling in yields (OTA, 1987)
Tomato	USA	1930–80	≈ ½ of a threefold increase in yield (OTA, 1987)

Surveys and inventories are on everyone's mind today. Although they may serve to build a database, standardise nomenclature, and give a "picture" of what is in the "store cupboard," they alone cannot lead to biodiversity management or conservation. Databases must be value-added with other connected information (e.g., plant database with attached species-specific chemical information). Dynamic information about the ecology and conservation of species must be added. Global, geographic, and LANDSAT imagery systems must be combined to provide large-scale surveys to detect distributions and changes. Stochastic models that can be used to predict trends must be constructed. Finally, expert systems that allow non-technical decision and policy makers to interrogate the data sets (or databases) and to make educated judgments based upon sound natural and social science information will be the eventual target of all conservation scientists and biodiversity managers seeking appropriate tools for the future.

Future Scientific, Economic, and Policy Goals

After UNCED was held in 1992, natural and social scientists were caught unprepared for the ensuing demands for insights and action. Not only was there insufficient information about which species were where and what they were called, we also knew far too little about species population sizes and how they worked and behaved. Biologists were not the only ones wrong-footed. Economists and planners do not have adequate techniques or knowledge to advise on integrated protected area systems and local populations.

A Realistic Agendum

A realistic agendum must contrive to deal with current problems in the short term and invest in long-term institutional strengthening and information building that are relevant to biodiversity management for the future.

By recognising the use of biodiversity as the means of sustaining biodiversity, we must also embrace the concept that implies the North's obligation to pay for the maintenance of biodiversity in the South. Since development is occurring in areas of greatest diversity, we must create a clear link between development and diversity. Without it we will see the use of biodiversity as a once-and-for-all use. By having a policy that develops the investment potential of wild ecosystems, we will be able to conserve many of the wild places of the world.

ACKNOWLEDGEMENTS

I am grateful to the American Museum of Natural History for arranging this conference and to the compendium of reference material found in *Global Biodiversity* (1992) compiled by the World Conservation Monitoring Center and published by Chapman and Hall.

LITERATURE CITED

AAFRC Trust for Philanthropy. 1990. Annual Report 1990. Giving USA, New York.

Ackery, P. R. and R. I. Vane-Wright. 1984. Milkweed Butterflies. British Museum (Natural History), London.

Akerele, O., V. Heywood, and H. Synge (eds.). 1988. Global importance of medicinal plants. *In* The Conservation of Medicinal Plants. Proceedings of an International Consultation, 21–27 March 1988, Chlang Mal, Thailand. Cambridge University Press, Cambridge, UK.

Anon. 1981. Economics of Medicinal Plants. Mahidol University, Thailand.

Anon. 1995. Unpubl. report, ADB TA 1782-INO Project.

Barbier, E. B. 1993. Economics and Ecology. Chapman and Hall, London.

Barbier, E. B., W. M. Adams, and E. Kimmage. 1991. Economic valuation of wetland benefits: The Hadejia-Jama'are floodplain, Nigeria. LEEC Discussion Paper, IIED, London.

Boo, E. 1990. Ecotourism: The Potentials and Pitfalls. World Wildlife Fund, Washington, D.C.

Duvick, D. N. 1984. Genetic contributions to yield gains of U.S. hybrid maize, 1930–1980. *In* W. R. Fehr (ed.), Genetic Contributions to Yield Gains of Five Major Crop Plants, pp. 15–47. Crop Science Society of America, Special Publication 7, Madison, Wisconsin.

Frohberg, C. 1991. Natural Products Research and the Potential Role of the Pharmaceutical Industry in Tropical Rainforest Conservation. Rainforest Alliance, New York.

Hargrove, T. R., V. L. Cabanilla, and W. R. Coffman. 1988. Twenty years of rice breeding. BioScience 38:675–681.

Hazell, P. B. R. 1985. The impact of the Green Revolution and the prospects for the future. Food Reviews International 1(1).

Hoyt, E. 1988. Conserving the Wild Relatives of Crops. IPBGR, IUCN, WWF, Rome and Gland.

ICRISAT. 1990. ICRISAT's Contribution to Pearl Millet Production. ICRISAT, Cereals Program, Andhira Pradesh.

Jansen, D. J. 1990. Sustainable wildlife utilisation in the Zambezi Valley of Zimbabwe: Economic, ecological and political tradeoffs. Project Paper No. 10, WWF Multispecies Project, Harare.

Jenkins, M. 1992. Species extinction. *In* Global Biodiversity (World Conservation Monitoring Centre, Cambridge, comp.), pp. 192–205. Chapman and Hall, London.

Kuhr, S. L., V. A. Johnson, C. J. Peterson, and P. J. Mattern. 1985. Trends in winter wheat performances as measured in international trials. Crop Science 25:1045–1049.

Majid, I., J. A. Sinden, and A. Randall. 1983. Benefit evaluation increments to existing systems of public facilities. Land Economics 59:377–392.

Meredith, W. R., Jr. and R. R. Bridge. 1984. Genetic contribution to yield changes in upland cotton. *In* W. R. Fehr (ed.), Genetic Contributions to Yield Gains of Five Major Crop Plants, pp. 75–87. Crop Science Society of America, Special Publication 7, Madison, Wisconsin.

Miller, F. R. and Y. Kebede. 1984. Genetic contributions to yield gains in sorghum, 1950 to 1980. *In* W. R. Fehr (ed.), Genetic Contributions to Yield Gains of Five Major Crop Plants, pp. 1–13. Crop Science Society of America, Special Publication 7, Madison, Wisconsin.

Mittermeier, R. A. and T. B. Werner. 1990. Wealth of plants and animals unites "megadiversity" countries. Tropicus 4(1):1,4–5.

Myers, N. 1990. The biodiversity challenge: Expanded hot-spots analysis. The Environmentalist 10:243–256.

NAS. 1972. Genetic Vulnerability of Major Farm Crops. Committee on Genetic Vulnerability of Major Farm Crops, Agricultural Board, National Research Council, National Academy of Sciences, Washington, D.C.

Oldfield, M. L. 1984. The Value of Conserving Genetic Resources. Sinauer Associates, Sunderland, Massachusetts.

OTA. 1987. Technologies to Maintain Biological Diversity. OTA-F-330. U.S. Government Printing Office, Washington, D.C.

Pearce, D. W. 1989. Tourist Development. John Wiley, New York.

Pearce, D. W. 1990. An economic approach to saving the tropical forests. LEEC Paper DP 90-06. IIED, London.

Pezzey, J. 1989. Economic analysis of sustainable growth and sustainable development. Environment Department Working Paper No. 15, World Bank, Washington, D.C.

Phantumvanit, D. and W. Liengcharensit. 1989. Coming to terms with Bangkok's environmental problems. Environment and Urbanisation 1(1).

Plucknett, D. L. and N. J. H. Smith. 1986. Sustaining agricultural yields. BioScience 36:40–45.

Plucknett, D. L., N. H. J. Smith, J. T. Williams, and N. Murthi Anishetty. 1987. Gene Banks and the World's Food. Princeton University Press, Princeton.

Rhoades, R. E. 1991. The world's food supply at risk. National Geographic 179(4):74–103.

Robinson, J. 1993a. The limits to caring: Sustainable living and the loss of biodiversity. Conserv. Biol. 7(1):20–28.

Robinson, J. 1993b. Believing what you know ain't so: Response to Holdgate and Munroe. Conserv. Biol. 7(4):941–942.

Rojas. 1992. The species problem and conservation: What are we protecting? Conserv. Biol. 6:170–178.

Ruitenbeek, H. J. 1989. Social cost-benefit analysis of the Korup Project, Cameroon. Prepared for the World Wide Fund for Nature and the Republic of Cameroon, London.

Schmidt, J. W. 1984. Genetic contributions to yield gains in wheat. In W. R. Fehr (ed.), Genetic Contributions to Yield Gains of Five Major Crop Plants, pp. 89–101. Crop Science Society of America, Special Publication 7, Madison, Wisconsin.

Silvey, V. 1978. The contribution of new varieties to increasing cereal yield in England and Wales. Journal of the National Institute of Agricultural Botany 14:367–384.

Specht, J. W. and Williams, J. H. 1984. Contributions of genetic technology to soybean productivity—retrospect prospect. In W. R. Fehr (ed.), Genetic Contributions to Yield Gains of Five Major Crop Plants, pp. 48–73. Crop Science Society of America, Special Publication 7, Madison, Wisconsin.

Swanson, T. 1992. The economics of a biodiversity convention. Ambio Paper 92-02, Centre for Social and Economic Research in Global Environment, London.

Tatum, L. A. 1971. The southern corn leaf blight epidemic. Science 171:1113–1116.

Thomas, R. 1992. Biodiversity: An overview. In Global Biodiversity (World Conservation Monitoring Centre, Cambridge, comp.), pp. 1–6. Chapman and Hall, London.

Thornback, J. and M. Jenkins. 1982. The IUCN Mammal Red Data Book Part 1. IUCN, Gland, Switzerland and Cambridge, UK.

Vane-Wright, R. I., C. J. Humphries, and P. H. Williams. 1991. What to protect?: Systematics and the agony of choice. Biol. Conserv. 44:235–254.

Winpenney, J. T. 1991. Values for the environment. ODI. HMSO.

Witt, S. C. 1985. Biotechnology and Genetic Diversity. California Agricultural Land Project, San Francisco.

World Conservation Monitoring Centre (comp.). 1992. Global Biodiversity. Chapman and Hall, London.

International Conservation Partnerships: The BLM Perspective and Role

— TEXT OF PRESENTATION —

MOLLY H. OLSON

(FORMER) SPECIAL ASSISTANT TO THE DIRECTOR, U.S. BUREAU OF LAND MANAGEMENT

Current address: The Natural Step, 4000 Bridgeway, Ste. 102, Sousalito, CA 94965, USA [e-mail: mholson@naturalstep.org]

It is a real pleasure to be here today to represent the new team at the Department of Interior and the Bureau of Land Management at this important conference.

It is a personal pleasure too, because a decade ago, I had the rare privilege of working briefly with Archie and Tom Carr on my Master's thesis regarding the biology and conservation of hawksbill turtles in Mona Island, Puerto Rico.

Since that time, I have followed with distress the precipitous demise of herpetological fauna throughout the world. According to E. O. Wilson, there are approximately 6,300 described reptile species. He has estimated their present rate of extinction at 1,000–10,000 times the extinction rate before the intervention of humans.

This is a matter of grave urgency, and a matter that U.S. Secretary of the Interior Bruce Babbitt, Bureau of Land Management Director Jim Baca, and Fish and Wildlife Service Director Mollie Beattie understand is deadly serious. Their priorities for the Department are to make ecosystem management the guiding principle for public lands and all fish and wildlife management. In addition, Secretary Babbitt has established a National Biological Survey to avoid what I believe has been the monumental mismanagement of our endangered species in the past. Internationally, they recognize the importance of U.S. leadership in CITES and the Biological Diversity Treaty. The Secretary and the Director are committed to:

- Implementing effective recovery programs for endangered species,
- Greatly improving our scientific knowledge of the species we deal with,
- Using science and scientists to develop these recovery efforts, and
- Ensuring the long-term productivity of the public lands.

These lands, their resources, and our ability to sustain this diversity and productivity, are key in maintaining the Earth's quality of life.

The Bureau of Land Management is the Nation's steward for 270 million acres of public lands representing a variety of ecosystems, from the deserts of the arid Southwest to the forests of the Pacific Northwest to the tundra of Alaska. Under the leadership of the BLM's recently confirmed Director, Jim Baca of New Mexico, the BLM is now preparing to take a much more active role in the conservation of the resources that depend upon the public lands. It is our intention to use management practices that will address ecosystem and landscape-level issues to ensure more efficient management.

The BLM public lands provide habitat for a wide diversity of fish, wildlife, and plant communities. A significant part of these lands are in the arid regions of the southwest and provides habitat for approximately 70 percent of the remaining habitat of the desert tortoise—one of the most politically sensitive animals with which federal agencies are concerned.

More than 20 years ago the BLM became aware of desert tortoise population declines, and scientists were employed to evaluate populations and determine what management efforts would be required to reverse these declines. Since then, thanks to the tenacity of some of our employees, the BLM has conducted and funded extensive research, and our scientists have been recognized for these important efforts.

Research has involved many aspects of tortoise biology, habitat requirements, the effects of various land uses, and habitat management. The results of these research efforts were, in fact, the primary source of information used by the Fish and Wildlife Service to list the desert tortoise as "Threatened," providing the species protection under the Endangered Species Act.

During this conference you have heard reports on several of these research findings: Mary Christopher on health profiles, Hal Avery on the effects of cattle grazing on desert tortoises habitat, Bryan Jennings on implications of exotic vegetation, Bill Boarman on effects of roads on desert tortoises and on predation by subsidized predators, Elliot Jacobson on diseases in tortoises, Isabella Schumacher on serologic tests to monitor desert tortoise populations for disease, and Kristin Berry on demographic consequences of diseases in desert tortoise populations. These are but a few of the important contributions of our scientists.

Many of the problems associated with turtle and tortoise

conservation are common throughout the world. These problems cannot be addressed unilaterally. We need to cooperate in these efforts and make the best use of the available scientific resources and information. The BLM would like to make our scientific resources available to the other countries struggling to save populations of tortoises and turtles and establish international partnerships to enhance hemispheric conservation programs for these animals. However, we need all of you vigorously involved in public policy, in education, and in conservation—or it will never happen.

I know that the Secretary of the Interior and the directors of the BLM and the Fish and Wildlife Service are eager to develop international partnerships.

We can do this by facilitating and funding programs to (1) bring students/trainees to work with our scientists on tortoise and turtle research, and (2) make our scientists available to other countries to assist them in designing research and management prescriptions. We can assign scientists to help coordinate these efforts and to ensure that the latest research findings are available.

The BLM is ready to participate in the development of an international, interagency effort to further the exchange of scientists in order to develop and coordinate solutions to common problems. This commitment includes funding, personnel, training, scientific research, and the development of successful land management techniques.

If the turtles and tortoises of the world are to be saved from extinction, we must work together as partners, sharing the best information and scientists available. We must ensure that an aggressive program of training scientists and conducting research is continued.

Turtles have survived 200 million years on Earth; some of their species face possible extinction before the end of this century. The BLM challenges other agencies and countries to join this committed, cooperative venture to protect them.

Postscript

The greatest champion of endangered species was lost to all of us when Mollie Beattie succumbed to cancer last year. The Department of the Interior also lost the important contributions of Jim Baca when he returned to New Mexico. As a result of these developments, progress has been slow.

The question we must consider is, "Are we doing enough today to ensure the survival of these magnificent creatures?" Ultimately, it is not just the survival of endangered species, but our own that is in the balance.

—Molly Olson, June 1997

The Role of Policy Makers in the Development of Conservation Strategies

— SUMMARY OF PRESENTATION —

SUZI OPPENHEIMER
SENATOR, NEW YORK STATE

New York State Senate, L.O.B. Room 515, Albany, NY 12247, USA

New York State Senator Suzi Oppenheimer, ranking minority member of the Senate Committee on Environmental Conservation, emphasized to the members of the conference the importance of the role played by the scientific community in environmental policy decisions. Senator Oppenheimer stressed how scientific input into legislation and regulatory action is necessary to achieve real results. Existing New York State law on wetlands, water quality, planning, zoning, air quality, forestry, and many other issues affects the habitat of a variety of species. Without meaningful involvement of experts in species conservation, government policies that could protect habitats will be ineffective.

The Senator urged the conference attendees to take an assertive approach in participating in policy decisions—to lobby, work with elected officials and staff of government agencies, and join scientific associations. She reiterated the importance of monitoring government policies as they evolve, and working with broad-based citizen environmental organizations to achieve common goals.

Conservation Strategies—An Overview: Implications for Management

PETER C. H. PRITCHARD

Chelonia Institute, 401 South Central Avenue, Oviedo, FL 32765, USA
Florida Audubon Society, 1331 Palmetto, Suite 110, Winter Park, FL 32789, USA

Polite friends and relatives, making small talk, often ask me, "How are the turtles doing?" The focus of my professional life involves trying to find the answer to this question, but I assume that they do not really want several hours of commentary, and I generally give a brief and noncommittal reply. But the time has come that the question must be answered to whatever extent that is possible, and it may best be rephrased, "In a world where human impact reaches into almost every corner, how much punishment can turtle populations and turtle species take?"

The optimist would make certain observations, as follows:

• Apart from some giant tortoises on small islands (Pritchard, 1996), and perhaps one or two mud turtle subspecies in island-like refugia (namely isolated water holes in arid terrain, Iverson, 1981), we have not yet lost any taxa to extinction at the hand of man.

• Turtles logically *must* have some ultimate mechanism for responding to factors that cause population reduction or increase in such a way as to reduce the effect of those factors; otherwise, every natural population trend, upwards or downwards, would have continued either to infinity or extinction by now. Yet this has obviously not happened for any extant population.

• Many turtles are ecological generalists and can do well even in disturbed or unnatural habitat. Thus, red-eared sliders (*Trachemys scripta elegans*) can live almost anywhere; gopher tortoises (*Gopherus polyphemus*) do best in habitat that has been prevented from forming a closed canopy, by regular burning, hurricane action, etc.; and even the rare bog turtle (*Clemmys muhlenbergii*) may do well in habitat that has been influenced by such activities as cattle grazing.

• Tortoises (Testudinidae) are presumably amongst the slower breeding of chelonian species, yet even they have the capacity to reach spectacular concentrations within a few decades. We note the huge population of giant tortoises (*Aldabrachelys elephantina*) on Aldabra Atoll (over 130,000 animals), or the thousands of bowsprit tortoises (*Chersina angulata*) on Dassen Island, off eastern South Africa. The former population has expanded from an almost extinct natural population in 1890–1900 (Swingland, 1989), while Dassen Island, a speck of land only 222 hectares, has a population of tens of thousands of tortoises, reportedly derived from a founder stock of unknown but presumably small size introduced between 1896 and 1929 (Branch, 1991). This increase has occurred despite seemingly low reproductive potential (a single egg per clutch) and relatively severe predation on the juveniles by Kelp Gulls. Both situations attest to the power of geometric increase, once it gets under way in simple, closed ecosystems.

• The demonstrated "take" (capture or slaughter) that some turtle populations seem to have tolerated is sometimes impressive. Loggerhead sea turtles are gradually increasing in Florida despite tens of thousands of drowning mortalities annually, in recent years, by shrimp trawlers (National Research Council, 1990). The olive ridley colony in Oaxaca, Mexico was subjected to an annual take of many thousands of animals per year for over 20 years, yet in the year following the final closure of the legal take, arribadas of very large—and annually increasing—size were observed (Márquez et al., 1996). And, around the Mediterranean, where casual pickup of tortoises of the genus *Testudo* has occurred at least since Greek and Roman times, and continues to this day (whether for food, personal pets, commercial export, or manufacture of musical instruments), and where in recent decades a great deal of environmental destruction and highway mortality has occurred as well, tortoise populations continue to survive in most areas. Their documented retreat (e.g., in France, Devaux, 1988) is probably a result of both natural climatic shift and total conversion of habitat; the tortoises often survive well in areas of low-intensity viniculture, such as has been conducted near La Pardiguière (Guyot, 1995).

A tropical parallel would be the situation of the yellow-footed tortoise in forests of Amazonia and the Guianas. Throughout the range of this species, it is safe to say that virtually any time human eyes fall upon a specimen, it is collected for food (or, much more rarely, for the wildlife trade). Moreover, this has probably occurred for thousands of years. Yet the species remains abundant.

To these observations, the pessimist would make reply as follows:

• The extinctions that have occurred at the hand of *early* man have almost certainly been severe. Thus, the extinction of once-widespread giant tortoises in continental and continental-island ecosystems, including North America, the Caribbean, and Madagascar, almost certainly resulted from human predation (possibly in tandem with climate change).

Moreover, we are today in the midst of widespread, steady decline of most species, and we can anticipate numerous extinctions in the decades to come.

• Careful studies by Ron Brooks and his co-workers in Guelph (Galbraith et al., this volume) have demonstrated that an Ontario population of the common snapping turtle —the epitome of a robust species to most people—showed no density-dependent response or population recovery following a stochastic population-depletion event, and the conclusion was made that there was no possibility of sustained exploitation of mature turtles from populations at such latitudes.

• Not all turtles are ecological generalists. For example, map turtles (*Graptemys*) demonstrate specialization for pristine riverine conditions, and in circumstances where rivers have been heavily impacted by siltation, as has occurred in northeastern Arkansas, the map turtles may disappear and be replaced by the more tolerant *Trachemys*. Similarly, bog turtles, while tolerant of certain kinds of habitats with some degree of disturbance, have very precise "bog habitat" requirements, and their overall range thus shows trenchant discontinuities. The South African geometric tortoise, *Psammobates geometricus*, has demands for such a specialized habitat type ("renosterveld") that it cannot tolerate significant land alteration or even progressive, natural closure of the tree canopy (an event held at bay by fire, which ironically also kills many individuals of this non-burrowing species). The conversion of about 97% of its habitat to grape and wheat cultivation has reduced the range of the species by the same percentage (Baard, this volume).

• In isolated situations turtles may be able to increase geometrically to impressive population densities, but in most continental situations, informal observation by those whose interests or inclination causes them to notice turtles and tortoises indicates that, even in the absence of directed or obvious threats, populations progressively diminish from one year to the next. Witness, for example, the anecdotal but highly persuasive evidence for decreases in the "common" box turtle in many areas in the eastern United States in recent decades (Dodd and Franz, 1993), although on islands, even those with dense exotic vegetation, like Egmont Key Florida, impressively dense populations may build up (Dodd et al., 1994). In this case the population increase is fostered by a fortuitous combination: absence of mammalian predators, insignificant or absent human take, and a dense population of cockroaches that constitutes a crucial prey item.

• There are many reported situations that contrast sharply with the apparently large sustainable take of certain turtle populations. A number of these relate to species that are not evenly distributed over large tracts of land, but rather exist in microhabitats within a wide—or not-so-wide—overall range. Examples include the aforementioned bog turtle; Blanding's turtle (*Emydoidea blandingii*) in the northeastern United States (Congdon et al., 1993); the African pancake tortoise (*Malacochersus tornieri*) (Wood and MacKay, this volume); and probably other tortoise species, such as *Manouria impressa*, *Homopus boulengeri*, and *H. signatus*, which have very specialized habitat requirements. In cases like these, removal of just a few individuals from an individual deme may cause local extirpation and, because dispersal across alien habitat is chancy at best (and impossible at worst), recolonization may not occur within any practical time frame. But even in such cases, an isolated population may recover from an *episode* of collecting, if the harvest is not sustained—witness the reported recovery of a pancake tortoise population in Kenya within slightly over a decade after heavy exploitation (Wood and MacKay, this volume).

— oO0Oo —

The present volume is a goldmine of information on the population status, dynamics, and prospects of the tortoises and turtles of the world. When combined with the papers in the proceedings of the slightly more recent turtle conservation conference in Gonfaron, France (SOPTOM, 1995), it should be possible for us to come to some general conclusions to answer that naive but crucial question, "How are the turtles doing?"

The conclusions below are derived from my basically subjective evaluation of many scientific contributions from many parts of the world. I consider it entirely possible that a different commentator could arrive at significantly different conclusions, or at least present different emphases and propose different priorities.

• Species or populations that are naturally rare, or demes or populations of species existing near the latitudinal extremes of their natural range, are presumably rare for a reason. They are living under some kind of adverse circumstances that limit their success and their population increase. Reproduction or recruitment may fail entirely except in favorable years, and populations "hang on" mainly because of the longevity of adults. This being the case, the superimposition of sustained anthropogenic take or other stress upon these natural, limiting factors and hardships is likely to lead to progressive depletion and ultimately extirpation or extinction.

• Nonetheless, the generalization above should not be incautiously extended to populations living in more optimal habitat. In the various cases mentioned above in which abundant or robust turtle populations have survived heavy and protracted collection, it appears that some sort of enhanced recruitment or survival of juvenile year-classes, or even reduction of maturation time, may have occurred. A real-world example is offered by the two localities in Pacific Costa Rica where the olive ridley nests in great concentrations or *arribadas*. One of these sites, Playa Nancite, is constrained between rocky headlands about a kilometer apart and is totally protected from human interference by its national park status. Turtle populations progressively built up to such a level that the entire beach was overcrowded, the incubation medium became polluted by the remains of destroyed eggs, and hatching success dropped to about 1% (Cornelius, 1986). Now the adult population is starting to show a sharp decline. Meanwhile, on Ostional Beach to the south, a modest level of legal exploitation of the eggs has probably enhanced hatching success, which is significantly greater than that reported for Nancite, and the nesting population remains robust.

• In a stable, unexploited turtle population living in equilibrium within its ecosystem, it is indeed true that sexually mature individuals, especially females, are extraordinarily important. In most cases such animals should be protected at all costs. Nevertheless, some managers have extrapolated this rule to the indefensible corollary that, because adults are important, eggs are unimportant. While it is clear that a given breeding adult is more crucial than a given egg, the "real-world" question is nevertheless different from this, and harder to answer; it may be summarized as, "Is it better to take 100 kg of adult turtles or 100 kg of eggs?"

Oblivious of such subtleties, some managers have tolerated excessive levels of egg exploitation for human consumption, without having any idea how many eggs must be protected to maintain the overall population. This careless approach to eggs caused the collapse of the population of Kemp's ridley in the Gulf of Mexico and North Atlantic, and of the green turtle and leatherback populations in Malaysia (Talang Islands and Terengganu). Any wildlife manager will insist that animal populations can only be sustained if they are allowed to reproduce safely, yet some turtle biologists seem to have forgotten this fundamental principle. Nests and eggs *must* receive substantial protection; otherwise, although the population collapse may be delayed for many years, when it comes it will be irreversible.

• It is important not to be sidetracked by an excessively theoretical approach. One must have some hypothesis or theory to justify what one is doing, but the variables are so many that there is no substitute for careful monitoring to determine the *actual* outcome of a conservation program (as opposed to the *anticipated* outcome). Population biology and ecology have not yet reached the point where one can predict the outcome of any given manipulation of a reptile population in quantitative terms. I take respectful issue, for example, with the Desert Tortoise Recovery Team identifying its goal as giving the Mojave population a 50% chance of survival 500 years from now (Berry, this volume)—partly because the goal is too modest ("survival" means that at least a few individuals survive; thus, the chance of "recovery," a minor subset of the "survival" outcome, is actually far less than 50%)—and partly because one should, in the words of Margaret Thatcher, "never prophesy anything, especially about the future." It is now about 500 years since Columbus landed, and the absurdity of any prediction made in 1492 accurately reflecting the state of the nation or the world in the 1990s is obvious. Moreover, things are moving faster than ever these days; we don't even know what will happen a year from now, and the limitations on prediction offered by chaos theory and forces of contingency are now understood. About the only area of modern life where we look for prediction and expect any degree of success is in weather forecasting, and even there we restrict our expectations of accuracy to the next few days only.

• USDI and NMFS turtle recovery plans have often been utilized as excuses for decade-long delays in taking any conservation action. The mandate of the typical team—to ignore political considerations, to identify every single potential or actual stress upon a species or population, and to make sure that every agency represented on the team is allowed to protect its "turf"—has not been a recipe for quick action or success. Obvious, feasible, essential tasks are diluted by exhaustive inventories of theoretical, hopeless, or unnecessary recommended actions; the preparation of the average plan for listed vertebrate species takes 9.4 years (Tear et al., 1995). Sometimes only a single severe but easily identifiable stress may be holding a species back, and if this is corrected, the natural resilience of the species alone may allow it to tolerate other stresses.

In many cases, it would be far better for the whole job of preparing the recovery plan to be contracted out to a competent individual who knows the species, knows conservation biology, and knows his politics. Then one would have a result in three months, it would have a theme—even a vision—rather than a mere consensus, and it would be politically realistic without being politically compromised. A lot of conservation dollars, and a lot of time, would be saved.

• The general public, not to mention the herpetoculturist, is keenly aware of—and much dismayed by—the vulnerability of the hatchling stage of turtle life. Awkwardly straddling the philosophical fence between K- and r-selected reproductive strategies, turtle hatchlings are big enough to be cute and small enough to die in droves. Most hatchlings, even of species that are not particularly prolific, simply do not make it. It is a fortunate one that finds a safe retreat that is protected from climatic and humidity extremes and predators, which also offers adequate nutrition, for enough time, to allow the animal to grow and consolidate its bony shell until it can afford to be seen in public. Yet few professionals (apart from Mrosovsky, 1983) view this phase, during which the vast majority of individual turtles die of non-intrinsic causes (i.e., "bad luck" rather than genetic deficiency), as a conservation opportunity. In the case of Kemp's ridley, a binational, interagency, expensive, multi-year conservation effort finally yielded positive results for which the key factor may well have been headstarting (Pritchard, 1997). But the Recovery Plan (USFWS/NMFS, 1992) was conspicuously silent on the subject of headstarting. On the narrowly legalistic grounds that headstarting is an experiment, and experiments have no place in a recovery plan, no place was found for headstarting among the recommended actions. (It could be mentioned that virtually everything we do to enhance turtle populations is experimental, and the actual impact on the population of almost any manipulation remains speculative.)

Nat Frazer (this volume), who is one of the more brilliant theorists behind the science of turtle conservation biology, implies that manipulation of such juvenile stages to enhance survival or replace excessive take of post-hatchlings, juveniles, or adults is "half-way technology," which attacks symptoms rather than root causes. He is obviously right, but I prefer to emphasize that effective conservation plans, like good politics, represent "the art of the possible," and the correction of the fundamental wrongs of the world, while worth attempting (we are nothing if not optimists), may not be successful or may not yield results in time. In cases where root causes cannot be easily reversed and species or populations are disappearing, we have to do what Gerald Kuchling (this volume) has done in Western Australia with *Pseudemydura*, or Roger Wood (this volume) has done in New Jersey with diamondback terrapins (*Malaclemys*), and take matters in hand to ensure some recruitment where little or none would otherwise occur.

• Theoreticians and pessimists should note that there is now, at last, good evidence that headstarting does work, and headstarted turtles can contribute to breeding populations. It has happened with Kemp's ridley (Pritchard, 1997) and with the Hood Island Galápagos tortoise (Cayot and Morillo, this volume). Indeed, it may have saved both of those taxa.

Today, the heavy hand of man is extirpating whole populations, even whole species of rare or localized turtles in eastern and southeastern Asia, and is seriously depleting even widespread ones. A billion people in China, formerly constrained from regular consumption of luxury foods like turtle by lack of cash, are wielding new-found economic power. Ross Perot might describe the "giant sucking sound" of millions of turtles being wrenched from their habitats in Laos, Cambodia, Bangladesh, Vietnam, Malaysia, and Indonesia to meet the insatiable demand and high prices offered by Chinese markets. Even the newly described *Geoemyda yuwonoi*, whose natural range encompasses just a small area in northern Sulawesi, Indonesia (McCord et al., 1995), and represented in hardly any museums, is starting to appear in numbers in Chinese markets. And professional collectors report that several of the new taxa of Chinese box turtles described in recent years can no longer be found. They may or may not be biologically extinct, but they are apparently commercially extinct. Even the long-known and relatively widespread *Cuora trifasciata*, found in both China and Vietnam and formerly a common pet trade species, now fetches $1,000 per kilo on eastern markets.

I see no prospect of reversing these trends in any reasonable time frame by outside action. We are faced with the appalling choice of either doing nothing, or attempting to save at least a genetic remnant of the species in question by captive breeding. The latter option is not my first choice, and I am not capitulating to the lobbying pressure of herpetoculturists who are keen to acquire specimens without restrictions and who have advocated captive breeding as the method of choice all along. But there may be no other way.

This will require a new partnership between conservationists, zoological parks, government conservation agencies, and private breeders and hobbyists. Some of the latter may need a little redirection (away from preoccupation with designer snakes, albinos, and similar anomalies), but it is in this community that the husbandry expertise resides, not to mention the financial resources and interest. The majority of turtle species are actually relatively easy to maintain alive in captivity, and potentially to breed also, although there is a hard core of notoriously "difficult" forms—*Malayemys*, *Morenia*, *Manouria impressa*, *Notochelys platynota*, *Psammobates*, and *Homopus*—that rarely survive long in captivity, let alone breed. The softshells (Trionychidae) also, although kept for generations in often-filthy "tanks" in eastern temples, seem very susceptible to rapidly fatal skin eruptions in captivity.

Perhaps a widespread captive breeding program for depleted and endangered chelonian species would result in the happy dilemma faced by the average crocodilian headstarting, ranching, or captive-breeding program—after one crocodilian generation or so, the question of what on earth to do with all these fast-growing, hungry crocodiles (or caimans, or alligators) quickly becomes acute. In the case of turtles, creative minds could devise a formula for the percentage of offspring to be retained as breeding stock, how many to release into areas of local depletion or extirpation, how many to distribute to other institutions and individuals, and—most controversial of all—how many to sell on lucrative private markets in order to make the entire operation economically self-supporting, and perhaps even generate a surplus to allow for land acquisition or habitat management.

LITERATURE CITED

Baard, E. H. W. 1997. A conservation strategy for the geometric tortoise, *Psammobates geometricus*. *In* J. Van Abbema (ed.), Proceedings: Conservation, Restoration, and Management of Tortoises and Turtles—An International Conference, pp. 324–329. July 1993, State University of New York, Purchase. New York Turtle and Tortoise Society, New York.

Berry, K. H. 1997. The desert tortoise recovery plan: An ambitious effort to conserve biodiversity in the Mojave and Colorado deserts of the United States. *In* J. Van Abbema (ed.), Proceedings: Conservation, Restoration, and Management of Tortoises and Turtles—An International Conference, pp. 430–440. July 1993, State University of New York, Purchase. New York Turtle and Tortoise Society, New York.

Branch, W. R. 1991. The herpetofauna of the offshore islands of South Africa and Namibia. Annals Cape Prov. Mus., Nat. Hist. 18 (10):205–225.

Cayot, L. and G. Morillo. 1997. Rearing and repatriation of Galápagos tortoises: *Geochelone nigra hoodensis*, a case study. *In* J. Van Abbema (ed.), Proceedings: Conservation, Restoration, and Management of Tortoises and Turtles—An International Conference, pp. 178–183. July 1993, State University of New York, Purchase. New York Turtle and Tortoise Society, New York.

Congdon, J., A. E. Dunham, and R. C. van Loben Sels. 1993. Delayed sexual maturity and demographics of Blanding's turtles (*Emydoidea blandingii*): Implications for conservation and management of long-lived organisms. Conserv. Biol. 7 (4):826–833.

Cornelius, S. C. 1986. The sea turtles of Santa Rosa National Park. Fundación Parques Nacionales, Costa Rica.

Devaux, B. 1988. La Tortue Sauvage. Edit. Sang de la Terre, Paris.

Dodd, C. K. and R. Franz. 1993. The need for status information on common herpetofaunal species. Herpetol. Rev. 24:47–50.

Dodd, C. K., R. Franz, and L. L. Smith. 1994. Activity patterns and habitat use of box turtles (*Terrapene carolina bauri*) on a Florida Island, with recommendations for management. Chelon. Conserv. Biol. 1(2):97–106.

Frazer, N. B. 1997. Turtle conservation and halfway technology: What is the problem? *In* J. Van Abbema (ed.), Proceedings: Conservation, Restoration, and Management of Tortoises and Turtles—An International Conference, pp. 422–425. July 1993, State University of New York, Purchase. New York Turtle and Tortoise Society, New York.

Galbraith, D. A., R. J. Brooks, and G. P. Brown. 1997. Can management intervention achieve sustainable exploitation of turtles? *In* J. Van Abbema (ed.), Proceedings: Conservation, Restoration, and Management of Tortoises and Turtles—An International Conference, pp. 186–194. July 1993, State University of New York, Purchase. New York Turtle and Tortoise Society, New York.

Guyot, G. 1995. Status of Hermann's tortoise population after major disturbance of the area by the construction of a motorway. *In* Proceedings of the International Congress of Chelonian Conservation, pp. 184–186. Editions SOPTOM, Gonfaron, France.

Iverson, J. B. 1981. Biosystematics of the *Kinosternon hirtipes* complex (Testudines: Kinosternidae). Tulane Stud. Zool. Bot., New Orleans 23:1–74.

Kuchling, G. 1997. Managing the last survivors: Integration of *in situ* and *ex situ* conservation of *Pseudemydura umbrina*. *In* J. Van Abbema (ed.), Proceedings: Conservation, Restoration, and Management of Tortoises and Turtles—An International Conference, pp. 339–344. July 1993, State University of New York, Purchase. New York Turtle and Tortoise Society, New York.

Márquez, R., C. Peñaflores, and J. C. Vasconcelos. 1996. Olive ridley turtles (*Lepidochelys olivacea*) show signs of recovery at La Escobilla, Oaxaca. Marine Turtle Newsletter 73:5–7.

McCord, W. P., J. B. Iverson, and Boeadi. 1995. A new batagurid turtle from northern Sulawesi, Indonesia. Chelon. Conserv. Biol. 1(4):311–316.

Mrosovsky, N. 1983. Conserving Sea Turtles. British Herpetological Society, London.

National Research Council. 1990. Decline of the Sea Turtles: Causes and Prevention. National Academy Press, Washington, D.C.

Pritchard, P. C. H. 1996. The Galápagos tortoises. Nomenclatural and survival status. Chelonian Research Monogr. No. 1., Chelonian Research Foundation, Lunenburg, Massachusetts.

Pritchard, P. C. H. 1997. A new interpretation of Mexican ridley population trends. Marine Turtle Newsletter 76:14–17.

SOPTOM (ed.). 1995. Proceedings: International Congress of Chelonian Conservation. Tortoise Village, Gonfaron, France, 6–10 July 1995. Editions Soptom, Gonfaron, France.

Swingland, I. R. 1989. *Geochelone gigantea*: Aldabran giant tortoise. *In* I. R. Swingland and M. W. Klemens (eds.), The Conservation Biology of Tortoises. pp. 105–110. Occasional Papers of the IUCN Species Survival Commission (SSC) No. 5. IUCN, Gland, Switzerland.

Tear, T. H., J. M. Scott, P. H. Hayward, and B. Griffith. 1995. Recovery plans and the Endangered Species Act: Are criticisms supported by data? Conserv. Biol. 9(1):182–195.

USFWS and NMFS. 1992. Recovery Plan for the Kemp's ridley sea turtle, *Lepidochelys kempii*. National Marine Fisheries Service, St. Petersburg, Florida. 40 pp.

Wood, R. C. and R. Herlands. 1997. Turtles and tires: The impact of roadkills on northern diamondback terrapin, *Malaclemys terrapin terrapin*, populations on the Cape May Peninsula, southern New Jersey, USA. *In* J. Van Abbema (ed.), Proceedings: Conservation, Restoration, and Management of Tortoises and Turtles—An International Conference, pp. 46–53. July 1993, State University of New York, Purchase. New York Turtle and Tortoise Society, New York.

Wood, R. C. and A. MacKay. 1997. The distribution and status of pancake tortoises, *Malacochersus tornieri*, in Kenya. *In* J. Van Abbema (ed.), Proceedings: Conservation, Restoration, and Management of Tortoises and Turtles—An International Conference, pp. 314–321. July 1993, State University of New York, Purchase. New York Turtle and Tortoise Society, New York.

The Poster Session

HAROLD W. AVERY AND FRED CAPORASO, CO-CONVENERS

Indraneil Das (Universiti Brunei Darussalam) and B. C. Choudhury (Wildlife Institute of India, Dehra Dun). (Photo by Rita Devine.)

Eli Geffen (Tel Aviv University, Israel) with other Poster Session attendees. (Photo by Rita Devine.)

Karen von Seckendorf Hoff, Ron Marlow, and Todd Esque (University of Nevada, Reno), Anders Rhodin (Chelonian Research Foundation, Lunenberg, Massachussetts), Alison Whitlock (University of Massachusetts, Amherst), Hal Avery (U.S. Geological Survey, Biological Resources Division, Riverside, California), Tej Kumar Shrestha (Tribhuvan University, Kirtupur Kathmandu, Nepal), Bill Boarman (U.S. Geological Survey, Biological Resources Division, Riverside, California), Dick Buech (U.S. Dept. of Interior Forest Service, Grand Rapids, Minnesota), Joan Milan (University of Massachusetts, Amherst, Massachusetts), Steve Garber (Rutgers University, Piscataway, New Jersey), Bryan Jennings (University of Texas, Austin), and Rico Walder (Tennessee Aquarium, Chattanooga, Tennessee).

Poster Session: Ecology, Conservation, and Husbandry

HAROLD W. AVERY AND FRED CAPORASO
CO-CONVENERS

Tuesday, 13 July 1993

Abstracts of Presented Posters

Challenges to a Changing Plant Community: Food Selectivity and Digestive Performance of Desert Tortoises Fed Native vs. Exotic Forage Plants

HAROLD W. AVERY

U.S. Geological Survey, Biological Resources Division, 6221 Box Springs Blvd., Riverside, CA 92507, USA
[e-mail: hal_avery@usgs.gov]

The capacity of chelonians to grow, resist pathogens, and successfully reproduce depends upon their ability to acquire and process adequate amounts of foods that meet their nutritional requirements. The potential for nutritional constraints to affect herbivorous chelonians is magnified because many plant species are usually needed to meet all energy and nutrient requirements. Thus, nutritional constraints associated with food quality and abundance have important consequences for the management and conservation of herbivorous turtle and tortoise metapopulations inhabiting environments with modified plant communities.

Exotic annual and perennial plants have become major components of arid plant communities within the geographic range of the desert tortoise, *Gopherus agassizii*. Some hypothesized effects of exotic plant introductions on desert tortoise nutrition include: (1) reduction in food choice due to decline in species diversity of forage plants, and (2) nutrient imbalances due to the consumption of lower quality forage plants that do not meet minimum nutritional requirements. The objectives of this study were to: (1) compare the nutrient content of native and exotic annuals known to be consumed by free-living desert tortoises, and (2) determine the food preferences of tortoises fed exotic versus native plant species.

Fifteen desert tortoises were used in a selectivity trial in outdoor enclosures at The Living Desert, Palm Desert, California. The exotic annual species of filaree (*Erodium cicutarium*) and splitgrass (*Schismus barbatus*) were fed to one group of tortoises. The annual woody bottlewasher (*Camissonia boothii*) and the perennial shrub, wishbone bush (*Mirabilis bigelovii*) were fed to a second group of tortoises. A mix of all four plant species was provided to a third group of tortoises. Selectivity of forage plants was determined by measuring the consumption rates of each plant species by tortoises within morning feeding intervals.

For tortoises fed the two exotic annuals there were significant preferences for *Schismus* over *Erodium*. For tortoises fed native plants, there was no difference in preference for *Mirabilis* versus *Camissonia*. Tortoises fed a mix of native and exotic plants preferred *Schismus* over all other native and exotic plants. This finding was in direct contrast to field studies indicating that wild desert tortoises prefer native plants over exotic plants.

Nutrient contents for native and non-native plants were compared. Native plants were higher in crude protein than *Schismus*, but were similar to *Erodium*. Essential amino acids were greater in native plants versus non-native plants. Energy concentration was similar for all plants, and is not an adequate parameter for determining food quality. Dietary fiber, a nutritional challenge to all herbivorous vertebrates, was greater in exotic species than in native species. *Schismus* had a higher concentration of heavy metal ions than filaree or both native plant species.

Data on the food selectivity, nutritional quality, and digestive performance of tortoises fed native versus exotic plants are used to assess the potential for maintaining viable metapopulations of desert tortoises in habitats characterized by high relative abundances of exotic plants.

The Dynamics of Two Sympatric Tortoise Communities in a Stressful Environment

ERNST H. W. BAARD

Cape Nature Conservation, Private Bag X5014, Stellenbosch 7599, South Africa [e-mail: baarde@cncjnk.wcape.gov.za]

Geometric tortoises (*Psammobates geometricus*) and common parrot-beaked tortoises (*Homopus areolatus*) occur sympatrically in the isolated Harmony Flats nature reserve (10 ha) between the towns of Strand and Gordon's Bay, Western Cape Province, South Africa. The reserve is completely surrounded by urban development and isolated from any surrounding natural environments. Since its establishment in 1986, the reserve and tortoise populations have been under severe environmental stress in the form of frequent unnatural fires, alien vegetation encroachment, and lack of recruitment from surrounding areas. Despite efforts to inform local residents about the value of the reserve in terms of its floristic component and the endangered tortoises occurring there, lack of public concern for this reserve has resulted in at least three deliberately lit wildfires, each destroying a portion of the two tortoise communities. Close monitoring of population numbers indicated that *H. areolatus* has been able to successfully cope with these fires in terms of population numbers, whereas *P. geometricus* experienced an 88% drop in numbers over a period of seven years, with little recruitment from resident breeding pairs. Possible reasons for the decline of *P. geometricus* appear to be (1) its specialised habitat requirements, (2) low recruitment rates, (3) slow recovery after catastrophes (its inability to cope with frequently recurring fires), (4) competition with the more successful *H. areolatus*, and (5) the possibly negative impact of disease following relocation to this site.

A preliminary population viability analysis of the geometric tortoise population indicated that, should prevailing threats continue to operate, this most southern population of the species faced extinction before the end of this century. Steps to enhance its continued survival were initiated and by December 1993 the population appeared on its way to recovery. Population numbers were up, young were added to the population, and the habitat had recovered adequately. However, on New Year's Eve 1993 a deliberately lit wildfire wiped out approximately 80% of the recovered habitat and 78% of the remaining resident geometric tortoise population. The *H. areolatus* population was also reduced by approximately 51%. Steps to rescue remaining geometric tortoises from surrounding areas have been put into operation, but there is no guarantee that the same catastrophe will not recurr.

It is clear that the right areas (such as the Harmony Flats nature reserve) situated in the wrong places are often extremely vulnerable to non-stochastic, human-induced catastrophes and that the success of these areas as viable sites depends exclusively upon the ability of management authorities to eliminate or at least mitigate potential sources of threat.

Wood Turtle Habitat Research

RICHARD R. BUECH,[1] MARK D. NELSON,[2] LYNELLE G. HANSON,[3] AND BRUCE BRECKE[4]

[1] *USDA Forest Service, 1831 Highway 169 East, Grand Rapids, MN 55744, USA [e-mail: buech002@maroon.tc.umn.edu]*
[2] *USDA Forest Service, North Central Forest Experiment Station, 1992 Folwell Ave., St. Paul, MN 55108, USA*
[3] *710 High St., Duluth, MN 55805-1135, USA;* [4] *4131 Queen Ave. North, Minneapolis, MN 55412, USA*

The wood turtle, *Clemmys insculpta*, is found in the United States from the Midwest to the Northeast. Iowa, Minnesota, and Wisconsin list the wood turtle as either "Endangered" or "Threatened." We wanted to know why wood turtles are uncommon in the Eastern Great Lakes region. In cooperation with Minnesota Department of Natural Resources' Nongame Program, we studied wood turtles living on rivers in northeast Minnesota. We have studied their movements, habitat use, nesting behavior, and nesting success.

What have we learned?
The behavior of wood turtles has seasonal patterns. They are terrestrial in summer and aquatic in winter. Spring and fall are transitional periods, when they spend cool nights in the water and warm days on land. Wood turtles use a variety of habitats, most of which are common. However, nesting habitat is not abundant. Preferred nesting sites are bare sand

or gravel areas such as cutbanks and sand bars. Females traveled as far as 4.3 miles to nest, presumably because nesting areas are few. We found loss of nests to egg predators such as skunk and fox to be high. Furthermore, most wood turtles living on the Cloquet River are old; only 20% of turtles were <15 years old. We believe that the wood turtle population in the Great Lakes region is probably below historic levels because: (1) nesting areas are degrading and disappearing due to recreational disturbance and streambank restoration programs, (2) egg predators such as opossum, raccoon, and skunk are expanding their range, (3) adults are killed by vehicles when crossing roads, especially females seeking nesting areas in spring, and (4) in some regions, adults are collected and sold into the pet trade. We are most concerned about the lack of nesting areas and destruction of nests by egg predators.

What are we doing about these concerns?
• We are developing a set of standards and guides for managing riverine and riparian habitats to benefit wood turtle populations.
• We are informing fisheries and recreation managers of the potential negative impact of streambank restoration programs on wood turtle nesting areas and of potential disturbance from other sources.
• We are testing ideas for protecting nesting areas from egg predators. For example, we fenced part of an abandoned gravel pit. Whereas 70% of nests outside the fence were destroyed, all 18 nests inside the fence survived (we counted 190 hatchlings leaving the fenced area!).
• We are exploring ideas for creating new nesting areas; one has been created in the Superior National Forest, and others are planned. We will monitor their efficacy.
• We are testing ideas for enumerating and monitoring wood turtle populations at the watershed level so that managers can determine their status at will.

We recognize that it will take a partnership of numerous private and public entities to effectively manage wood turtles across entire watersheds. Our goal is to provide the knowledge that will allow this to happen.

Wetland Functions and Values: Documentation Methods and Tools that Give Landscape Perspectives

ROBERT S. DE SANTO

De Leuw, Cather & Company, 290 Roberts St., East Hartford, CT 06118, USA [e-mail: Robert_Desanto@parsons.com]

A study area of approximately 110 square miles is depicted, showing general land use and primary physiographic features, including gross habitat boundaries. Wetlands are delineated based on National Wetland Inventory maps and Soil Conservation Survey maps in conjunction with United States Geological Survey 7.5 minute quadrangle maps. Generated by Computer Aided Drafting and Design (CADD), the poster illustrates six proposed transportation corridors, each approximately 13 miles long, superimposed on the study area. Consistent with environmental assessment principles of overlaying resource maps (e.g., McHarg Techniques), the relationships between alternative transportation corridors and the study area can be assessed.

Based on field investigations, wetland functions and values associated with habitats intercepted by each corridor are annotated by using a new system of clustered icons in order to summarize characteristics of primary concern. In combination with navigation/positioning tools, the method assists environmental stewardship by providing confident field location of habitats and easily interpreted graphical summaries of habitat diversity and distribution. The methods are especially useful to regulatory agencies when making environmentally sensitive choices from various project alternative alignments. The poster is accompanied by explanatory text.

The Importance of Biological Research in the Habitat Conservation Planning Process

TODD C. ESQUE[1] AND R. A. FRIDELL[2]

[1]*U.S. Geological Survey, Biological Resources Division, Department of Biology,
University of Nevada–Reno, Reno, NV 89557-0015, USA [e-mail: todd_esque@nbs.gov or esque@unr.edu]*
[2]*Utah Division of Wildlife Resources, 122 North Main St., Cedar City, UT 84721, USA*

The Habitat Conservation Planning (HCP) process is a mechanism of the Endangered Species Act intended to reduce conflicts between economic development and endangered species conservation. Washington County is the fastest growing county in Utah and is inhabited by nine species listed under the United States Endangered Species Act and 41 candidate species. Many of these species' habitats are slated for urban growth. Therefore, in 1991 Washington County initiated the HCP process to receive a federal permit allowing incidental take of desert tortoises, *Gopherus agassizii*, and their habitat. Issuance of the permit is contingent upon the plan offsetting habitat losses by enhancing the prospects for long-term survival of impacted species. Mitigation actions being considered include: establishment of an ecological preserve; acquisition of habitat; withdrawal of livestock grazing; and funding of monitoring, research, and education programs. We present a case history of the Washington County HCP process and the biological considerations necessary for the successful development and implementation of a plan that insures the continued survival of federally protected species.

A Twenty-Year Study Documenting the Relationship between Turtle Decline and Human Recreation*

STEVEN D. GARBER AND JOANNA BURGER

Graduate Program in Ecology and Evolution, Rutgers University, Piscataway, NJ 08855-1059, USA

This study documents the detrimental effects of human recreation on the North American wood turtle, *Clemmys insculpta*, in Connecticut. We observed two North American wood turtle populations for 20 years, from 1974 through 1993. One hundred thirty-three different wood turtles were observed a total of 1,176 times. Human and wood turtle demographics were monitored throughout this period. The data support the following conclusions: (1) following a period of apparent stability two populations of wood turtles declined, (2) the declines were more or less synchronous in both populations, (3) the beginning of each decline corresponded to the opening of the habitat for recreation, (4) an increase in mean turtle age suggests a failure of recruitment, and (5) a simultaneous reduction in numbers of adult females suggests that the failure of recruitment alone is not sufficient to explain the declines.

Throughout our study the size of the forest remained the same, road building was restricted, and the quality of the air and water were constant. The wood turtle populations remained stable when people were denied access to the property. When the area was opened to human recreation (hiking, fishing), the two discrete wood turtle populations declined steadily; the total number of turtles in both populations declined by 100% in ten years. As wilderness areas become mixed-use recreation areas, wood turtle populations may suffer. We conclude that without proper management, the increasing recreational use of parks, reservoirs, and wildlife reserves will adversely affect the long-term survival of the North American wood turtle.

Key Words. *Clemmys insculpta* conservation; extinction; fishing forest; fragmentation forest management; hiking; horseback riding; human disturbance; human recreation; landscape ecology; long-term ecological study; long-term population monitoring; North American wood turtle; park management; population decline; population ecology; recreation; wildlife management.

Key Phrases. Effects of recreation on human-sensitive species; effects of recreation on turtle decline; turtle decline; turtle decline due to recreation; wood turtle decline.

*Garber, S. D. and J. Burger. 1995. A 20-yr study documenting the relationship between turtle decline and human recreation. Ecol. Appl. 5(4):1151–1162.

Eggs and Clutch Production of Captive *Graptemys*

MIKE GOODE

Columbus Zoo, 9990 Riverside Drive, Box 400, Powell, OH 43065, USA

Information is presented on egg production in five species of *Graptemys*.

G. flavimaculata: Twenty clutches were produced in six seasons (1982–1987) by a non-growing female (148 mm CL) of unknown age. Clutch size ranged from 2 to 5 with a mean of 3.40 and a mean clutch frequency (CF) of 3.33, egg mass ranged from 10.0 to 17.2 g with a mean of 14.49 g. Twenty-two additional clutches were produced by three young females in the years 1988–1992. These animals grew from a mean CL of 117 mm to 138 mm during that time and produced 22 clutches ranging from 1 to 5 eggs with a mean CS of 2.41 and egg mass ranging from 10.6 to 16.1 g with a mean of 13.25 g. Clutch frequency ranged from 1 to 5. Mean CF was not calculated as all females did not reproduce in each of the seasons. Nesting seasons (n = 10) ranged from 11 December through 28 June, with oviposition date of first clutch ranging from 11 December through 28 May with a mean date of 26 February, and date of last oviposition ranging from 11 April through 28 June with a mean date of 5 June. Mean length of the nesting season for the group was 98 days.

G. nigrinoda delticola: A group of 55 females of mean CL 141.8 mm, and in which growth was negligible, produced 91 clutches in the six seasons 1986–1992. Clutch frequency ranged from 1 to 5 with a mean of 3.57; CS ranged from 1 to 7 with a mean of 3.15; and egg mass ranged from 9.8 to 18.2 g with a mean of 14.2 g. Nesting seasons of the group had a mean length of 176 days, with date of oviposition of first clutch ranging from 2 October through 1 February with a mean of 31 November and dates of last clutch ranging from 15 April through 17 June with a mean of 29 May.

G. barbouri: In eight seasons, 25 clutches were produced with individual CF ranging from 1 to 4, CS ranged from 1 to 6 with a mean of 3.38 and egg mass ranged from 10.9 to 20.1 g with a mean of 15.13 g. Nesting seasons ranged from 13 March through 25 July.

G. pulchra: In five seasons, 13 clutches were produced with individual CF ranging from 1 to 2; CS ranged from 1 to 5 with a mean of 3.54 and egg mass ranged from 11.4 to 20.0 g with a mean of 16.38 g. Nesting seasons ranged from 21 December through 22 June.

G. versa: In five seasons, 19 clutches were produced. Individual CF ranged from 1 to 5, CS ranged from 1 to 6 with a mean of 4.63, and egg mass ranged from 8.0 to 14.0 g with a mean of 10.68 g. Nesting season ranged from 19 February through 28 June. Laying dates of first clutches of seasons were much more variable than laying date of last clutch of seasons (e.g., variance of those dates of *G. flavimaculata*: 63.76–17.72; variance of those dates of *G. n. delticola*: 60.5–10.94). In the series of the non-growing female *G. flavimaculata*, investment in egg production increased significantly through the first three seasons and remained high in subsequent seasons as represented by increased CF and egg mass and decreased CS (means for first three seasons: CF 2.33, CS 3.86, egg mass 13.96 g, mean annual clutch mass 125.5 g; those for subsequent seasons: CF 4.33, CS 3.15, egg mass 15.16 g, mean annual clutch mass 206.8 g). In the series of *G. n. delticola* clutches, investment in egg production was uniform in the first three as opposed to subsequent seasons as represented by higher CF and lower CS and egg mass (means for first three seasons: CF 3.40, CS 3.48, egg mass 14.66 g, mean annual clutch mass 179.4 g; those for subsequent seasons: CF 4.40, CS 2.79, egg mass 14.08 g, mean annual clutch mass 172.9 g).

Reproduction in Captive *Heosemys grandis*

MIKE GOODE

Columbus Zoo, 9990 Riverside Drive, Box 400, Powell, OH 43065, USA

Information is presented concerning egg production in a 15-season period (1978–1993) for a mature animal of unknown age ("old"), and of six progeny females, producing in an aggregate of 14 seasons. Clutch frequency (CF) for the old female was 2 in 13 seasons and 1 in the remaining two seasons. CF of progeny females, in their 5th through 12th year of age, was 2 in five seasons and 1 in nine seasons. Laying dates ranged from 25 October through 11 March in the entire series and did not differ significantly in the "old" and "progeny" series ($P > .2$ in each paired comparison of dates of CF1 and of 1st clutch or 2nd clutch of CF2). Mean date of clutches laid as CF1 and as 1st clutch of CF2 did not differ (23 December–10

December, $P > .1$), while dates of 1st and 2nd clutches of CF2 differed significantly (15 December–1 February, $P < .001$). Clutch size (CS) was larger in progeny females (mean 6.47–5.68). Mean size of clutches laid as CF1 were larger than those laid as CF2 in both series, and clutches laid as 2nd of CF2 were larger than those laid as 1st of CF2 in both series (mean for old and progeny: CF1 = 6.00, 6.77; CF2 = 5.65, 6.20; 1st of CF2 = 4.85, 5.80; 2nd of CF2 = 5.69, 6.60). None of these differences was significant at $P = .05$. Egg mass for the old female was consistent (with records kept only in the last ten seasons) and ranged from 32.8 to 58.3 g (mean 49.92 g, n = 69 eggs). Eggs laid as CF1 were significantly larger than those laid as CF2 (means 54.17 and 48.82 g, $P < .01$), and those laid as 1st of CF2 were larger than those laid as 2nd of CF2 (means 52.68 and 48.18 g, $P < .001$). Progeny females began egg production at similar sizes (276–291 mm CL) but at differing ages (5 years, 9 months–9 years, 8 months) with faster growing animals producing at younger ages. The first, second, and third reproductive seasons of progeny females was characterized by low CF, high CS, and small egg mass (1st year means CS 6.00, CF 1.17; egg mass 35.21; n = 7 clutches; 2nd + 3rd year means CS 7.20, CF 1.25; egg mass 35.59; n = 5 clutches). Mean annual clutch mass for these years was 246.5 g in the 1st year and 320.9 g in the 2nd + 3rd years. Mean annual clutch mass increased to 471.3 g in the fourth season (mean CS 7.20, CF 1.6; egg mass 39.29 g; n = 5 clutches). Egg production in the fifth season of the progeny females did not differ from that of the old female (progeny and old: mean CS 6.00, 5.68; CF 2.00, 1.86; egg mass 48.02, 49.92 g; annual clutch mass 576.2, 527.4 g; n = 2 clutches of progeny series).

A Methodology for Determining Tortoise Food Habits in Arid Regions

W. BRYAN JENNINGS

Department of Zoology, University of Texas at Austin, Austin, TX 78712, USA [e-mail: jennings@mail.utexas.edu]

Knowledge of tortoise food habits can provide insights into tortoise dietary and habitat requirements, and it is therefore important in management of tortoise populations. The purpose of this paper is to present a methodology that was successful in elucidating desert tortoise, *Gopherus agassizii*, food habits in the western Mojave Desert. These methods are also applicable to studies of other tortoise species living in arid regions.

The methodology is useful in estimating tortoise diet and plant abundance, both of which are needed to quantitatively assess whether tortoises are selective foragers. To determine whether tortoises are selective foragers, a null model incorporating diet and plant abundance (i.e., H_0 : plant abundance = food choice) can be statistically evaluated. Moreover, other questions can be addressed such as whether tortoises prefer succulent to dried forage, and whether tortoises prefer native to exotic plant species.

Diet is estimated by direct observation of tortoises while plant abundance is estimated by following a stratified random sampling methodology. Estimating plant abundance in deserts is complicated because the investigator must make many subjective choices when formulating a sampling scheme. One must choose the number of unique vegetational/topographical strata; sample size; allocation of samples among habitat strata; quadrant size, shape, and number; when and how often to sample; whether herbaceous perennials are considered annuals or perennials; etc. The approach to each of these choices to achieve a satisfactory sampling methodology is discussed and results are presented.

Management of Wild Tortoise Populations is Complicated by Escape or Release of Captives

RONALD W. MARLOW, KARIN VON SECKENDORFF HOFF, AND PETER BRUSSARD

Biology Department, University of Nevada, Reno, NV 89557, USA

From 1990 to 1992 extensive field survey and collection of tortoises in southern Nevada has documented a pattern of occurrence of desert tortoises symptomatic for Upper Respiratory Tract Disease (URTD). Symptomatic tortoises were found throughout southern Nevada, but the highest occurrence was in habitat adjacent to urbanized areas and adjacent to highways and roads. In a sample of 841 tortoises removed from land in the Las Vegas Valley scheduled for development, 7.8% were obviously escaped or released captives, and 14.5% were symptomatic for URTD. Outside the Las Vegas Valley, the distribution of symptomatic tortoises closely corresponded to proximity to major highway access from Las Vegas. It is well known that captive tortoises (including those symptomatic for URTD) escape and are purposely released into the wild and that the disease may be spread in this manner. It is hypothesized that the pattern of distribution of symptomatic tortoises can be explained by the escape and release of captive tortoises into the wild. Management of wild tortoise populations has probably already been compromised by the existence of a large captive tortoise population and can be significantly complicated by future uncontrolled adoption programs.

Spotted Turtle Population Ecology and Habitat Use in Central Massachusetts

JOAN C. MILAM AND S. MELVIN

Department of Wildlife and Fisheries Biology, University of Massachusetts, Amherst, MA 01003, USA

Historically the spotted turtle, *Clemmys guttata*, was considered the most abundant turtle in Massachusetts. In the past century spotted turtle populations have declined substantially. Presently the spotted turtle is listed as a "Species of Special Concern" by the Massachusetts Division of Fisheries and Wildlife because of its scarcity, habitat loss, habitat fragmentation, road mortality, and collection for the pet trade. Using radiotelemetry techniques, we are intensively studying the demographics and habitat use of spotted turtle populations in central Massachusetts. The goal of this study is to provide necessary ecological information for the establishment and management of reptile and amphibian reserves.

Establishment of the Chelonian Research Foundation, a Private Nonprofit Organization for Support and Publication of Turtle and Tortoise Research

ANDERS G. J. RHODIN

Chelonian Research Foundation, 168 Goodrich St., Lunenburg, MA 01462 USA
[Fax: 508-840-8184; e-mail: RhodinCRF@aol.com]

Chelonian Research Foundation (CRF) was established in May 1992 as a nonprofit 501(c)(3) tax-exempt private operating foundation organized for the production, publication, and support of worldwide turtle and tortoise research, with an emphasis on systematic relationships, geographic distribution, natural history, morphology, and the scientific basis of chelonian diversity and conservation biology. Our goal is the increased scientific understanding and conservation of the diverse species of turtles and tortoises of the world. We hope to accomplish these aims through a combination of CRF turtle research and scientific publications, as well as through donations of CRF support for a wide range of scientific and conservation-oriented turtle research projects by other investigators.

In our capacity as a nonprofit organization we solicit support from the public at large and interested individuals and organizations for the on-going expenses of carrying out our goals. We are especially grateful for donations to our special research endowment, The Linnaeus Fund, which grants annual awards for turtle research projects carried out by scientists around the world. In our first year of operation, The Linnaeus Fund provided partial support of $500 each to four separate turtle research projects on endangered, threatened, and rare turtle species. Two of these projects concerned native New England species: a study on the seasonal movements and habitat preferences of spotted turtles in Connecticut, and a study on the ecology and natural history of the wood turtle in New Hampshire. Other supported projects included a study on the molecular systematics and evolution of sex-determining mechanisms in American marsh turtles, and a study on the taxonomic relationships of the giant Asian softshell turtle. Our awards will continue to be made annually, hopefully with steadily increasing support through the growth of our endowment fund. Linnaeus Fund Awards for 1992 were $500 each, as follows:

- Frye, Sheila E. The ecology and natural history of the wood turtle (*Clemmys insculpta*) in southern New Hampshire. Concord, New Hampshire.
- Janzen, Fredric J. Molecular systematics and evolution of sex-determining mechanisms in marsh turtles (*Clemmys*). University of California, Davis, California.
- Perillo, Kathy. Seasonal movements and habitat preference of spotted turtles (*Clemmys guttata*) in southern New England. University of New Haven, New Haven, Connecticut.
- Webb, Robert G. Geographic variation in the giant softshell turtle, *Pelochelys bibroni* (Owen). University of Texas, El Paso, Texas.

Chelonian Research Foundation is also undertaking the publication of a new journal of turtle and tortoise studies entitled *Chelonian Conservation and Biology, Journal of the IUCN/SSC Tortoise and Freshwater Turtle Specialist Group and International Bulletin of Chelonian Research*. This journal is published by CRF with support from Conservation International (Washington, D.C.), Chelonia Institute (Arlington, Virginia), Wildlife Conservation Society (Bronx, New York), Florida Audubon Society (Casselberry, Florida), and IUCN (The World Conservation Union)—Species Survival Commission. The journal will be under the joint co-editorship of John L. Behler, Peter C. H. Pritchard, and Anders G. J. Rhodin, and will be a peer-reviewed professional scientific journal with an Editorial Board of world-renowned turtle biologists and conservationists, including Indraneil Das, C. Kenneth Dodd, Jr., Arthur Georges, J. Whitfield Gibbons, John B. Iverson, Michael W. Klemens, Jeffrey E. Lovich, Russell A. Mittermeier, Edward O. Moll, David J. Morafka, Ian R. Swingland, Bern W. Tryon, and George R. Zug. The first issue of the journal is scheduled for November, 1993. The journal will be available by subscription and will not be limited to Specialist Group members. In addition, Chelonian Research Foundation is planning to publish a Monograph Series (not yet named) for longer chelonian research contributions, with the first issues planned for sometime in the near future. Works already in progress are: (1) a synoptic bibliographic database of all scientific turtle literature ever published, currently totaling over 24,000 scientific references; (2) a monograph by Peter C. H. Pritchard on the Galapagos tortoises, with special reference to their nomenclature and conservation status; (3) a synoptic nomenclator of all scientific names used for turtles at all systematic levels, currently numbering over 4800 names; and (4) a database of vernacular and common turtle names from around the world.

Interested individuals and scientists around the world will be encouraged to consider the CRF journal *Chelonian Conservation and Biology* and the planned Monograph Series as potential publication outlets for their turtle research. Anyone interested in making a donation to CRF, subscribing to the journal, or receiving more information about any of our activities, including applications for turtle research funding through The Linnaeus Fund (annual application deadline November 15), or information about our publications, please contact us at the address above.

Addendum

Since the presentation of the above poster in July 1993, CRF has continued its programs of chelonian research support and scientific publications. Our grants program has made awards on an annual basis through both the Linnaeus Fund and general CRF support of other worthwhile turtle research and conservation projects, with 32 proposals receiving a total of $26,500. Our two research publications have met with resounding success. Our journal has expanded rapidly to fill a needed publication niche for all chelonian studies and our monograph series has been initiated.

Chelonian Conservation and Biology—International Journal of Turtle and Tortoise Research. This is the only international scientific peer-reviewed journal of cosmopolitan and broad-based coverage of all aspects of conservation and biology of all chelonians, including freshwater turtles, marine turtles, and tortoises. We have produced seven issues to date (April, 1997) publishing 126 scientific papers and over 800 pages of text. Since our initial issue in November 1993, our worldwide distribution has grown steadily, and we currently have a circulation of over 1,000 to more than 60 nations. The depth and breadth of our coverage of turtle research has also increased; included in the contents are the formal descriptions of three new genera and four new species of turtles, as well as articles on ecology, systematics, conservation, distribution, reproduction, sex determination, breeding and husbandry, pathology, physiology, morphology, and wildlife management. We publish about two issues a year with the subscription price a very modest $25 per volume of four issues (over two years) for individuals, and $50 for institutions.

Chelonian Research Monographs—Contributions in Turtle and Tortoise Research. The first issue in this series, *The Galapagos Tortoises: Nomenclatural and Survival Status*, by Peter C. H. Pritchard (85 pages, 53 color plates, hard or soft cover available), was published in July 1996. The second issue, a two-volume set, *The Conservation Biology of Freshwater Turtles*, is due out relatively soon.

In addition to these existing publications, CRF is also developing a series of more popular works on turtles entitled *Cheloniana—Miscellaneous Turtle and Tortoise Publications*. The first issue in this series should be available soon.

Turtle Conservation in Nepal: Maintaining Ecological Integrity of the Wetlands Habitat

TEJ KUMAR SHRESTHA

Central Department of Zoology, Tribhuvan University, Kirtipur Campus, Kathmandu, Nepal [e-mail: k-mani@npl.healthnet.org]

Nepal's extensive wetlands lie in a vast and varied riverine floodplain formed by the four major rivers (the Gandaki, the Koshi, the Karnali, and the Mahakali) that emerge from the Himalayas. This riverine floodplain is among the first few areas where both agriculture and human civilization had their beginning. Historically, the wetlands of the Koshi River in eastern Nepal were renowned for their abundance and diversity of turtles and fish, but it is now greatly impacted by human activity (damming, diversion, and channelization) and is the most highly vulnerable of the four river systems. Most of the river's upper reaches remain in a pristine condition, but the lower reaches have been altered by the Koshi Dam, which has blocked all migration of fish and turtles. Because of changes in the river channel and sediment management activities, restoration of turtle habitat represents a significant environmental challenge and substantial cost. Nevertheless, restoration of the Koshi River wetlands ecosystem is vital to the management of the many remaining turtle populations of such species as *Indotestudo elongata*, *Hardella thurjii*, and *Kachuga tecta*. The present exhibit provides an overview of the ecosystem, biota, and endangered flora and fauna in the wetland at the bend of the Koshi River, at the religious temple there, and of the surrounding area. A conservation and management plan is presented for the threatened species in the wetlands of Nepal.

Highways and Roads are Population Sinks for Desert Tortoises

KARIN VON SECKENDORFF HOFF AND RONALD W. MARLOW

Biology Department, University of Nevada, Reno, NV 89557, USA

Highway and road traffic have been associated with significant decreases in the density of tortoise populations. Those decreases are most noticeable immediately adjacent to the roadway, but have now been documented to extend beyond 3.5 km from the road. Tortoise movement patterns suggest that highway and road traffic removes tortoises from a population faster than new tortoises can be recruited from adjacent habitat. Recently a tortoise preserve of approximately 584 km² was established in Piute Valley, Nevada, as partial mitigation for the take of 88 km² of tortoise habitat in Las Vegas Valley. This "preserve" is bounded and transected by approximately 80 km of federal and state highways and county roads that experience moderate to heavy traffic. A detectable decrement in tortoise sign extends at least 3.5 km perpendicular to and in both directions from these roads, indicating that 498 km² or 85% of this preserve is negatively impacted by roads. Unlike many other causes of mortality, highway impacts can be effectively managed and virtually eliminated by constructing tortoise barriers along highway shoulders. In addition to direct mortality, highways and roads fragment habitat and populations, support inflated predator populations, and provide for human access. Despite the obvious negative impacts of highways and roads on tortoise populations, no management agency in Nevada has yet required that highway and road impacts be effectively mitigated either through their management plans or through the permitting procedures associated with new roads or road expansion.

AZA Chelonian Advisory Group Hispaniolan Slider, *Trachemys decorata*, Conservation Program

RICO WALDER

Tennessee Aquarium, One Broad St., Chattanooga, TN 37401, USA [e-mail: elw@tennis.org]

Captive Breeding Program

The *Trachemys decorata* captive breeding program was developed under the umbrella of the AZA's Chelonian Advisory Group by a consortium of eight zoological institutions, Beardsley Zoological Gardens, Bermuda Aquarium Museum and Zoo, Columbus Zoo, Institute for Herpetological Research, Jersey Wildlife Preservation Trust, Lowry Park Zoological Garden, Zoo Atlanta, and ZooDom (the National Zoo of the Dominican Republic). The breeding stock (founders) was collected in the southwestern region of the Dominican Republic in June 1991, as a cooperative effort between James Conyers of the Bermuda Aquarium Museum and Zoo and ZooDom staff. The project had a successful start the same year, and an informal studbook was maintained to effectively manage the captive population.

José Ottenwalder (National Coordinator, GEF-UNDP Dominican Republic Biodiversity Project, United Nations Development Program) has coordinated both field and education aspects of the program in the Dominican Republic and has provided information on translocation, monitoring, and wild status.

Translocation and Monitoring

Under a cooperative research and conservation effort, a reintroduction program for captive-bred *T. decorata* is being implemented by ZooDom with the financial support of the Columbus Zoo. In addition, both the Toledo Zoo and Cleveland Metroparks Zoo have contributed a Trovan™ reader, 245 transponders, 3 radio transmitters, and funds to monitor the reintroduced turtles. The protocol and methodology for the translocation have been drafted. Turtles hatched in 1992 and 1993 were released in fall 1994. An additional 20 turtles produced by U.S. institutions will be returned for release in May 1997. Released turtles will be monitored for at least 6–10 years. The reintroduction site is located within the boundaries of the Jaragua National Park, southwestern Dominican Republic. Jaragua is the largest protected area (1,400 km²) in the Dominican Republic and the insular Caribbean. The specific site, known as Laguana de los Chupaderos, was selected in January 1993 based on previous field experience, remoteness, and existing protective infrastructure. In May 1993 the site was surveyed in anticipation of the release. During this visit, areas of the habitat utilized by young turtles in the lagoon were located; several adult females were captured, marked, and released; and park wardens were briefed on the project.

Wild Status

Despite their full legal protection and threatened status, the species is heavily exploited for food in the Dominican Republic and Haiti. While illegal hunting for commercialization and subsistence use take place throughout the year, most animals are taken during the nesting season, directly reducing the fraction of the population with the highest reproductive value.

Captive Status

Currently there are 18.24.107 captive *T. decorata* distributed among seven institutions and two private parties. Overall, the population looks very good, with a healthy founder population that probably has a minimal inbreeding coefficient (based on capture records and personal observation of their habitat by J. Conyers). A formal studbook was approved for the species in February 1995 by the AZA Wildlife Conservation and Management Committee. Approval was based primarily on the following factors:
1. Habitat/range reduction is high.
2. Captive status is good.
3. Enthusiasm of cooperating institutions is high.
4. Conditions of breeding/loan agreement for founders (30% of all hatchlings produced will be used for the reintroduction program).

Index to Contributing Authors

(Bolded page number indicates senior author.)

Adest, Gary A., 333
Aguirre, Gustavo, **333**, 417
Ahsan, M. Farid, **287**
Amato, George D., **259**
Andrews, Harry V., 166
Avery, Harold W., **13**, **474**
Baard, Ernst H. W., **324**, **475**
Behler, John L., 259
Benitez, José-Luis Villarreal, 210
Berry, Kristin H., 76, **91**, 147, **430**
Bhupathy, S., 301
Boarman, William I., **54**, **103**
Bock, Brian C., 219
Bozhanskii, Anatolij T., 20
Brecke, Bruce, 475
Brooks, Ronald J., 186, 195, 203
Brown, Gregory P., 186
Brown, Mary B., 86
Brussard, Peter, 479
Buech, Richard R., **383**, **475**
Buhlmann, Kurt A., **359**
Burger, Joanna, 477
Burke, Vincent J., 358
Butler, Brian O., **59**
Cantarelli, Vitor Hugo, **407**
Castaño-Mora, Olga Victoria, **302**
Cayot, Linda J., **178**
Choudhury, B. C., **301**
Christopher, Mary M., **76**
Coblentz, Bruce, 345
Collins, Bobby R., 86
Curtin, Charles G., **31**
Dale, Roger, **411**
Das, Indraneil, **295**, **414**
De Santo, Robert S., **392**, **476**
Devaux, Bernard, **330**
van Dijk, Peter Paul, **265**, 272
Elguezabal, Xabier, 171
Escalona, Tibisay, 109
Esque, Todd C., **477**
Foscarini, Dina A., **203**
Frazer, Nat B., **422**
Frazier, John G., **446**
Fridell, R. A., 477
Galbraith, David A., **186**
Garber, Steven D., **477**

Geffen, Eli, **73**, **105**, **321**
Gibbons, J. Whitfield, **243**, 358, **426**
Goode, Mike, **478**
Graham, Terry E., 146
Griffin, Curtice R., 146
Hanson, Lynelle G., 383, 475
Haskell, Alison, **146**
Herlands, Rosalind, 46
Herman, Dennis W., 259, **364**
Herman, Thomas B., **372**
Hestbeck, Jay B., 146
Hoffman, Jeffrey, 345
Hossain, Md. Lokman, 290
Jacobson, Elliott R., 84, 86, **87**
Jennings, W. Bryan, **10**, **42**, 54, **479**
Juvik, James O., **345**
Karesh, William B., 83
Kiester, A. Ross, 345
Kiviat, Erik, **377**
Klaassen, James K., 76
Klein, Paul A., 86
Klemens, Michael W., **83**, 135
Krzysik, Anthony J., **61**
Kuchling, Gerald, **113**, **339**
Larson, Joseph S., 247
Lee, Jun, 411
Licata, Lina, **171**
Lovich, Jeffrey E, **426**.
Luiijf, Wil, **125**
MacKay, Alec, 314
Makeyev, Viktorij M., **20**
Marlow, Ronald W., 20, **479**, 482
Mascort, Ramon, **307**, **312**
McCoy, Earl D., 252
Melvin, S., 480
Mendelssohn, Heinrich, 73, 105, 321
Micucci, Patricio A., 2
Milam, Joan C., **480**
Mitchell, Joseph C., 359
Moehlman, Patricia D., 83
Molina, Flavio de Barros, **174**
Moll, Don, **135**
Moll, Edward O., **37**, 301
Moore, James, E., **28**
Morafka, David J., **147**, 333, 417
Morillo, Germán E., 178

Mullen, Edward B., **140**
Mushinsky, Henry R., **252**
Mwaya, Reginald T., 83
Nagy, Ken A., 76
Neibergs, Alexander G., 13
Nelson, Mark D., 383, 475
Olson, Molly H., **465**
Oppenheimer, Suzi, **466**
Páez, Vivian P., **219**
Passmore, Heather L., **195**
Pérez, Nayibe, 109
Polisar, John, **441**
Pritchard, Peter C. H., **444**, **467**
Raphael, Bonnie L., 83, **84**
Rashid, Sheik M. A., **225**
Reese, Devin A., **352**
Reid, Don, 345
Rhodin, Anders G. J., **480**
Rollins, Megan G., 359
Ross, Patrick, 140
Sachsse, Walter, **258**
Sarker, Md. Sohrab Uddin, **290**
Sazaki, Marc, 54
Schumacher, Isabella M., **86**
von Seckendorff Hoff, K., 20, 479, **482**
Shammakov, Sahat, 20
Shrestha, Tej Kumar, **278**, **482**
Smith, Lora L., **100**
Spangenberg, E. Karen, 147
Stubbs, David, 330
Swingland, Ian R., 225, **453**
Thirakhupt, Kumthorn, **272**
Thorbjarnarson, John B., **109**
Treviño, Eddie, **417**
Tryon, Bern W., 259, 364
Vogt, Richard C., **210**
Walder, Rico, **483**
Waller, Tomás, **2**, **118**
Wallis, Ian, 76
Welsh, Hartwell H., 352
Whitaker, Romulus, **106**, 166
Whitlock, Alison L., **247**
Wilson, Dawn S., 252
Wood, Roger C., **21**, **46**, **314**

Conference Directory

		LEGEND			
SA	Senior Author	WS	Workshop Participant	CS	Conference Staff Member
CA	Co-Author	V	Vendor	PS	Poster Session Participant

Hank Adams
Box 3 EMC
Las Cruces, NM 88003
USA
505-646-3000

Gustavo Aguirre (SA, WS)
Instituto de Ecología, A. C.
Km 2.5 Antigua Carretera a Coatepec
Ap. Postal 63
91000 Xalapa, Veracruz
MEXICO 34000
52-28-18-6000, ext. 4110 & 4111
fax 52-18-7809
e-mail: aguirreg@sun.ieco.conacyt.mx

M. Farid Ahsan (SA, WS)
Department of Zoology
University of Chittagong
Chittagong 4331
BANGLADESH
e-mail: Abegum@dcci.agni.com
vc-cu@spct.com

Walter Allen
10456 Calle Madero
Fountain Valley, CA 92708
USA
714-962-0612

George Amato (SA)
Science Resource Center
Wildlife Conservation Society
185th St. and Southern Blvd.
Bronx, NY 10460
USA
718-220-6826
e-mail: gamato1@aol.com

Hal Avery (SA, PS, PS–Co-convener)
U.S. Geological Survey
Biological Resources Division
6221 Box Springs Blvd.
Riverside, CA 92507
USA
909-697-5363/fax 909-697-5299
e-mail: hal_avery@usgs.gov

Ernst H. W. Baard (SA, WS)
Cape Nature Conservation
Private Bag X5014
Stellenbosch 7599
SOUTH AFRICA
27-21-887-0111/fax 27-21-887-1606
e-mail: baarde@cncjnk.wcape.gov.za

Alan Baker
4262 Wood Stock Way
Syracuse, NY 13215
USA
315-435-8511

Julie Bank (CS)
ASPCA
441 East 92nd St.
New York, NY 10128
USA
212-876-7700

Margaret M. Barker
49 Helen Ave.
Maple Shade, NJ 08052
USA
609-667-7627

Flavio de Barros Molina (SA, WS)
Fundação Parque Zoológico de São Paulo
Av. Miguel Stefano, 4241
Cep 04301-905
São Paulo, SP
BRAZIL
55-11-276-0811/fax 55-11-276-0564

Kent Beaman
11431 S. San Juan Drive
Loma Linda, CA 92354
USA
714-684-7081

John L. Behler (CA, WS)
Department of Herpetology
Wildlife Conservation Society
185th St. and Southern Blvd.
Bronx, NY 10460
USA
718-220-5157/fax 718-220-7114
e-mail: jbehler.wcs@mcimail.com

Scott C. Belfit
Aberdeen Proving Ground
Bel Air, MD
USA
410-671-1208

Steve Benigni (V)
AVID Marketing, Inc.
3179 Hammer Ave.
Norco, CA 91760
909-371-7505/fax 909-737-8967

Kristin H. Berry (SA, CS, WS)
U.S. Geological Survey
Biological Resources Division
6221 Box Springs Blvd.
Riverside, CA 92507-0714
USA
909-697-5360/fax 909-697-5299
e-mail: kristin_berry@nbs.gov

William I. Boarman (SA, PS, WS)
U.S. Geological Survey
Biological Resources Division
6221 Box Springs Blvd.
Riverside, CA 92507
USA
909-697-5360
e-mail: william_boarman@usgs.gov

Jeanne Boccongelli-Walsh
100 Ross Drive, Apt. 8
Boonton, NJ 07005
USA
201-263-4647

Brian Bock (CA)
Departamento de Ciencias Forestales
Facultad de Ciencias Agropecuarias
Universidad Nacional de Colombia - Sede Medellin
COLOMBIA
574-230-7079/fax 574-230-5489, 230-0420
e-mail: bbock@perseus.unalmed.edu.co

Jerry Boggs
NAVFAC
8959 Ildica St.
Spring Valley, CA 91977
USA
619-532-1166

Barbara B. Bonner
1 Grafton Road
Upton, MA 01568
USA
508-529-6811

Robert E. Brechtel
2520 S. E. 163rd St. Road
Summerfield, FL 34491
USA
352-245-1572

Margaret Breen (CS)
191 Maywood Drive
San Francisco, CA 94127
USA
415-953-2153

Ronald J. Brooks (CA)
Dept. of Zoology
University of Guelph
Guelph, ON N1G 2W1
CANADA
519-824-4120/fax 519-767-1656
e-mail: rjbrooks@uoguelph.ca

Richard R. Buech (SA, PS, WS)
USDA Forest Service
Forestry Sciences Lab
183 Highway 169 East
Grand Rapids, MN 55744
USA
218-326-7105/fax 218-326-2958
e-mail: buech002@maroon.tc.umn.edu

Kurt A. Buhlmann (SA)
Savannah River Ecology Lab
University of Georgia
Drawer E
Aiken, SC 29801
USA
803-725-3309
e-mail: buhlmann@srel.edu

Patrick M. Burchfield
Gladys Porter Zoo
500 Ringold St.
Brownsville, TX 78520
USA
210-546-7187

Marianne Burguiere
1227 Claxton Road
Richmond, VA 23233
USA
804-741-6687

Vincent J. Burke (SA)
University of Missouri
USGS, Biological Resources Division
Midwest Science Center
4200 New Haven Road
Columbia, MO 65201-9634
USA
573-875-5377
e-mail: vincent_burke@nbs.gov

Brian O. Butler (SA)
Oxbow Wetlands Associates
P.O. Box 553
Lunenburg, MA 01462
USA
508-582-9350
e-mail: bbutler@bicnet.net

Ray Butler
P.O. Box 3119
Truckee, CA 96160
USA
916-587-6797

Vitor Hugo Cantarelli (SA, WS)
CENAQUA/IBAMA
Rua 229 N° 95
Setor Leste Universitário
Goiânia-GO 74.609-090
BRAZIL
55-062-225-0194/fax 55-062-225-0722
e-mail: vcantar@ibama.gov.br

Fred Caporaso (PS–Co-convener, WS)
Director, Food Science Research Center
Chapman University
Orange, CA 92866
USA
714-997-6638, 6831/fax 714-532-6048
e-mail: caporaso@chapman.edu

Peter Carnochan
2712 Blaine Drive
Chevy Chase, MD 20815-3942
USA
301-589-8396

John L. Carr
Conservation International
1015 18th St. NW, Ste. 1000
Washington, DC 20036
USA
202-973-2213

Olga Victoria Castaño-Mora (SA)
Instituto de Ciencias Naturales
Universidad Nacional de Colombia
Apartado 7495
Santafé de Bogotá
COLOMBIA
57-1-268-43-36/fax 57-1-268-24-85

Linda J. Cayot (SA, WS)
Charles Darwin Research Station
Casilla 17-01-3891
Quito
ECUADOR
e-mail: lcayot@fcdarwin.org.ec

Douglas Chin (CS)
57 Oakley
South Brunswick, NJ 08824
USA
908-940-6322

B. C. Choudhury (SA)
Wildlife Institute of India
Chandrabani
P.O. Box 18, Dehra Dun–248 001
INDIA
91-135-82910/fax 91-135-82217, 135-28392

Mary M. Christopher (SA)
Department of Pathology,
Microbiology, and Immunology
Haring Hall, School of Veterinary Medicine
University of California–Davis
Davis, CA 95616
USA
916-752-7970/fax 916-752-3349
e-mail: mmchristopher@ucdavis.edu

John Coakley
151 Library St.
Mystic, CT 06355
USA
203-536-8589

Michael P. Coffeen
12235 Spruce Grove Place
San Diego, CA 92131
USA
619-532-2805

Dave Collins
Tennessee Aquarium
P.O. Box 11048
Chattanooga, TN 37401-2048
USA
423-265-0695

Michelle Conant
% Greenworking, 19 Marble Ave.
Pleasantville, NY 10570
USA
914-741-2088

Justin Congdon (WS)
Savannah River Ecology Lab
University of Georgia
Drawer E
Aiken, SC 29802
USA
803-725-2472

Robert P. Cook
National Park Service
Floyd Bennett Field
Brooklyn, NY 11234
USA
718-338-3730

Cassandra L. Costley
7 Sage Court, Apt. E
Baltimore, MD 21208
USA
410-396-5154

Lorri and Abby Cramer (CS)
750 Columbus Ave., Apt. 4W
New York, NY 10025
USA
212-663-2415

Charles G. Curtin (SA, WS)
Department of Biology
167 Castetter Hall
Albuquerque, NM 87131-1091
USA
505-277-9173
e-mail: ccurtin@unm.edu

Barbara Daddario (CS)
308 Chateau Rive
Peekskill, NY 10566
USA
914-737-1920

Roger A. Dale (SA)
The Natelson Company, Inc.
16633 Ventura Blvd., Ste. 1200
Encino, CA 91436
USA
818-501-5219/fax 818-784-3679
e-mail: tnci@earthlink.com

Anne F. Darlington
11319 Crescendo Place
Silver Spring, MD 20901
USA
301-593-8176

Indraneil Das (SA, WS)
Madras Crocodile Bank Trust
Mamallapuram, Post Bag 4
Tamil Nadu 603 104
INDIA
673-2-427001/fax 673-2-427003

Joe DeRenzis (CS)
120-10 Drieser Loop
Bronx, NY 10451
USA
718-671-5950

Robert De Santo (SA, PS, WS)
De Leuw, Cather & Company
290 Roberts St.
East Hartford, CT 06118
USA
203-282-4402/fax 203-282-4415
e-mail: Robert_Desanto@parsons.com

Bernard Devaux (SA, WS)
Station d'Observation et de Protection
des Tortues des Maures (SOPTOM)
Village des Tortues, BP24
83590 Gonfaron
FRANCE
33-94-78-26-41/fax 33-94-78-24-27

Rita K. Devine (CS)
53 St. Marks Place
New York, NY 10003
USA
212-790-8950

Peter Paul van Dijk (SA, CA,WS)
Department of Zoology
University College Galway
Galway
IRELAND
353-91-24411/fax 353-91-25700

% Kumthorn Thirakhupt
Dept. of Biology, Faculty of Science
Chulalongkorn University
Bangkok 10330
THAILAND
662-252-7077, 250-1811/fax 662-253-0337
e-mail: Peter.vanDijk@UCG.IE
ppvd@sc.chula.ac.th

Suzanne Dohm (CS, WS)
40-23 204th St.
Queens, NY 11361
USA
718-428-5709
e-mail: dansuzy@idt.net

Diane and Phil Drajeske
8012 Greenwood Ave.
Munster, IN 46321
USA
219-838-8032

Deanne Dufresne
380 E. 46th Ave.
Eugene, OR 97405
USA
503-346-1105

Xabier Elguezabal (CA, WS)
Ministerio del Ambiente y de los Recursos,
Naturales Renovables (MARNR)
Servicio Autonómo de Fauna
Nivel Mezzanina, Entrada Oeste
Centro Simón Bolivar, Caracas
VENEZUELA
58-2-408-1643/fax 58-2-545-3912
e-mail: profauna@conicit.ve

Todd C. Esque (PS)
U.S. Geological Survey
Biological Resources Division
Department of Biology
University of Nevada–Reno
Reno, NV 89557-0015
USA
702-784-1703
e-mail: todd_esque@nbs.gov
esque@unr.edu

Kenneth M. Fahey
Rte. 3, Box 648, 26 Pinewood Drive
Dahlonega, GA 30533
USA
404-887-8151

Raymond Farrell
31 Fayette Ave.
Staten Island, NY 10305
USA
908-246-6391

Dean Fausel
Greenburgh Nature Center
Dromore Road
Scarsdale, NY 10583
USA
914-723-3470

Joseph P. Flanagan
Route 4, Box 4064
Pearland, FL 77581
USA
713-520-3273

Charles R. Ford
3017 Valley View Drive
Powder Springs, GA 30073-1847
USA

Dina A. Foscarini (SA)
9710 104th St.
Morinville, Alberta T8R 1C8
CANADA
403-939-7214

Allen Foust (CS)
Turtle Back Zoo
560 Northfield Ave.
West Orange, NJ 07052
USA
201-731-5801

Wayne Frair
1131 Fellowship Road
Basking Ridge, NJ 07920-3900
USA
908-604-8377

Nat B. Frazer (SA)
Savannah River Ecology Laboratory
University of Georgia
Drawer E
Aiken, SC 29802
USA
803-725-2472/fax 803-725-3309
e-mail: frazer@srel.edu

John G. (Jack) Frazier (SA)
CINVESTAV
Apartado Postal 73 "Cordemex"
Yucatan, MEXICO, C.P. 97310
52-99-812-931, 812-960
fax 52-99-812-919, 812-917
e-mail: frazier@kin.cieamer.conacyt.mx

Darrel Frost
Department of Herpetology
American Museum of Natural History
Central Park West at 79th St.
New York, NY 10024
USA
212-769-5852

Joan Frumkies
3850 Hudson Manor Terrace
Riverdale, NY 10463
USA
718-548-9386

David A. Galbraith (SA)
Canadian Botanical Conservation Network
Royal Botanical Gardens
P.O. Box 399
Hamilton, Ontario L8N 3H8
CANADA
905-527-1158 ext. 309/fax 905-577-0375
e-mail: turtle@earthling.net

Steven D. Garber (PS)
205 West End Ave., 8H
New York, NY 10023
USA
212-757-1405

Andrea L. Gaski (WS)
WWF-TRAFFIC USA
1250 24th St., NW
Washington, DC 20037
USA
202-293-4800/fax 202-775-8287

Eli Geffen (SA, WS)
Department of Zoology
Tel Aviv University
Ramat Aviv, Tel Aviv 69978
ISRAEL
972-3-640-9812/fax 972-3-640-9403
e-mail: geffene@post.tau.ac.il

Kathi Gerety
Department of Herpetology
Wildlife Conservation Society
185th St. and Southern Blvd.
Bronx, NY 10460
USA
718-220-5042

J. Whitfield Gibbons (SA, CA)
Savannah River Ecology Laboratory
University of Georgia
Drawer E
Aiken, SC 29802
USA
803-725-2472/fax 803-725-3309
e-mail: gibbons@srel.edu

Marga Giesbergen
TRAFFIC-Europe
Barbaralaan 120
Bredha 4834 SM
NETHERLANDS
31-76-601901

Rosemarie Gnam
U.S. Fish & Wildlife Service
4401 N. Fairfax Drive, Rm. 551
Arlington, VA 22203
USA
703-358-1993

Mike Goode (PS)
Columbus Zoo
9990 Riverside Drive, Box 400
Powell, OH 43065
USA
614-645-3418/fax 614-645-3465

Gary Gordon
10 Holder Place, 3G
Forest Hills, NY 11375
USA
(718) 793-6085

Marc D. Graff (WS)
17259 Ballinger St.
Northridge, CA 91325-1929
USA
818-993-1551

Charles C. Green
Turtle Talks
41 Marlborough Road
Asheville, NC 28804-1444
USA
704-254-6435

Richard Gritman
USDI—Div. of Law Enforcement
U.S. Fish and Wildlife Service
Hemisphere Center, Routes 1 & 9 South
Newark, NJ 07114
201-645-5910/fax 201-341-5910

Albert Gubar (CS)
580 West 215th St., Apt. 3B
New York, NY 10034-1205
USA
212-942-6505

Michael Hano (CS)
715 West 170th St., Apt. 22
New York, NY 10032
USA
212-795-8972

Alison Haskell (SA, WS)
Dept. Federal Aid
U.S. Fish and Wildlife Service
300 Westgate Center Dr.
Hadley, MA 01035
USA
413-253-8505
e-mail: Alison_Haskell@mail.fws.gov

Ronnie E. Hatcher
Columbus Zoo
2577 Sandburg Blvd.
Columbus, OH 43235
USA
614-792-5281

George Heinrich
Gopher Tortoise Council
P.O. Box 61301
St. Petersburg, FL 33784-1301
USA
813-893-7326/fax 813-893-7720

Dennis W. Herman (SA, CA)
NC State Museum of Natural Sciences
P.O. Box 29555
Raleigh, NC 27626-0555
USA
919-733-7450 ext. 70/fax 919-733-1573
e-mail:
Dennis_Herman@mail.ehnr.state.nc.us

Thomas B. Herman (SA)
Biology Department
Acadia University
Wolfville, NS B0P 1X0
CANADA
902-542-2201 ext. 1469/fax 902-542-3466
e-mail: tom.herman@acadiau.ca

Aileen and Jay Holovacs (CS)
32 Franklin Ave.
South Bound Brook, NJ 08880
USA
908-356-3150

Ken Howell
California Academy of Science
Steinhart Aquarium
Golden Gate Park
San Francisco, CA 94118
USA
415-750-7247

Judith Hoyer
945 Oaks Drive
Franklin Square, NY 11010
USA
516-775-0159

Frank Indiviglio
Department of Herpetology
Wildlife Conservation Society
185th St. and Southern Blvd.
Bronx, NY 10460
USA
718-220-5042

Elliott R. Jacobson (SA, CA, WS)
College of Veterinary Medicine
University of Florida
P.O. Box 100126, HSC
Gainesville, Fl 32610-0126
USA
904-392-4700 ext. 4773
e-mail: ERJ@vetmed1.vetmed.ufl.edu

Dave Jenkins
New Jersey Division of Fish,
Game, and Wildlife
2201 County Rte. 631
Woodbine, NJ 08270
USA
609-628-2103

Bryan Jennings (SA, CA, PS)
Department of Zoology
University of Texas at Austin
Austin, TX 78712
USA
512-471-7131/fax 512-471-9651
e-mail: jennings@mail.utexas.edu

Elizabeth Johnson
35 8th St.
Frenchtown, NJ 08825-1144
USA
908-996-4056

James O. Juvik (SA)
Department of Geography
University of Hawaii–Hilo
Hilo, HI 96720-4091
USA
808-933-3547/fax 808-933-373
e-mail: jjuvik@hawaii.edu

Robert F. Kennedy, Jr.
(Banquet Speaker)
Pace Environmental Law Clinic
78 North Broadway
White Plains, NY 10603
USA
914-422-4343

Barbara Kermeen
2356 Research Drive
Livermore, CA 94550
USA
510-449-2286

A. Ross Kiester (CA)
U.S. Forest Service
PNW Research Station
3200 SW Jefferson Way
Corvallis, OR 97331
USA
541-750-7269/fax 541-750-7329
e-mail: ross@krait.fsl.orst.edu

Erik Kiviat (SA)
Hudsonia Ltd.
Bard College Field Station
Annandale, NY 12504
USA
914-758-1881
e-mail: kiviat@bard.edu

Michael Klemens
(SA, CA, WS, Conference Chair)
Wildlife Conservation Society
185th St. and Southern Blvd.
Bronx, NY 10460
USA
718-220-5885
e-mail: mklemens.wcs@mcimail.com

Anthony J. Krzysik (SA)
U.S. Army–CERL
P.O. Box 9005
Champaign, IL 61826-9005
USA
217-333-8296/fax 217-244-1785
e-mail: krzysik@gis.uiuc.edu

Gerald Kuchling (SA, WS)
Dept. of Zoology
University of Western Australia
Nedlands, WA 6907
AUSTRALIA
61-9-380-2243
e-mail: kuchling@cyllene.uwa.edu.au

David Künstler
NYC Dept. of Parks & Recreation
1 Bronx River Parkway
Bronx, NY 10462
USA
718-430-1891

William Lawyer
Greenburgh Nature Center
Dromore Road
Scarscale, NY 10583
USA
914-723-3470

Jun Lee (CA)
Nonprofit Counsel
1804 T St., NW
Washington, DC 20009
USA
202-319-9886/fax 202-319-9887
e-mail: jlee@nonprofit-counsel.com

Diane and Stan Levine
13508 Debell St.
Arleta, CA 91331
USA
818-896-6493

Lina Licata (SA)
Ministerio del Ambiente y de los Recursos,
Naturales Renovables (MARNR)
Servicio Autonómo de Fauna
Nivel Mezzanina, Entrada Oeste
Centro Simón Bolivar, Caracas
VENEZUELA
58-2-408-1643/fax 58-2-545-3912
e-mail: profauna@conicit.ve

Peter V. Lindeman
Dept. of Biological Sciences
and Related Technologies
Madisonville Community College
2000 College Drive
Madisonville, KY 42431
USA
502-821-2250

H. Stevan Logsdon (V)
Wildlife Jewelry & T-shirts
P.O. Box 4070
Silver City, NM 88062
USA
505-388-4263

Elisabet Lopez
Antoni Cusido, 91
Sabadell 08208
SPAIN
34-3-4158567

Diane Lopinto
188 8th Ave.
New York, NY 10011
USA
212-924-1926

Thomas Loud
17 Hopf Drive
Spring Valley, NY 10977
USA
914-352-9451

Jeffrey E. Lovich (SA, WS)
U.S. Geological Survey
Biological Resources Division
63500 Garnet Ave.
North Palm Springs, CA 92258-2000
USA
619-251-4823/fax 619-251-4899
e-mail: *jeffrey_lovich@nbs.gov*

Bruce Lowder
Greenburgh Nature Center
Dromore Road
Scarscale, NY 10583
USA
914-723-3470

Wil Luiijf (SA, WS)
TRAFFIC Europe Enforcement Project
Barbaralaan 120, 4834 SM
P.O. Box 4625, 4803 EP Breda
NETHERLANDS
31-76-601901/fax 31-76-601938
e-mail: *traffeur@antenna.nl*

Frank Maccarrone
P.O. Box 202
Rhinebeck, NY 12572
USA
914-373-8105

Ronald W. Marlow (CA, PS, WS)
Biology Department
University of Nevada
Reno, NV 89557
USA
702-791-7057, 895-3121
fax 702-893-7707

Ramon Mascort (SA)
C.R.T. l'Abera
17780 Garriguella
Girona,
SPAIN
34-3-3010777/fax 34-3-3021475
e-mail: *rmascortb@mx3.redestb.es*

Janice B. McClatchey
30 Yereance Ave.
Clifton, NJ 07011
USA
201-772-2286

William P. McCord
East Fishkill Animal Hospital
285 Route 82
Hopewell Junction, NY 12533
USA
914-221-0695

Earl D. McCoy (CA)
Biology Department
University of South Florida
Tampa, Fl 33620-5150
USA
813-974-2878

Beverly and Tom Mcfarland (V)
12664 Polktown Road
Waynesboro, PA 17268
USA
717-762-5975

David McKenzie (CS)
Rte. 7, Box 1711
Everhart Road
Rogersville, TN 37857
USA
423-235-9535

Robert H. Melton
United States Army–CERL
ENR Division
2902 Newmark Drive
Champaign, IL 61821
USA
217-398-5476

Joan Milam (PS)
Dept. of Wildlife and Fisheries Biology
University of Massachusetts
Amherst, MA 01003
USA
413-545-1315

Thomas A. Milos
47 Nichols Ave.
Stratford, CT 06497
USA
203-378-8276

Joseph C. Mitchell (CA)
Department of Biology
University of Richmond
Richmond, VA 23173
USA
804-289-8234/fax 804-289-8482

Donald Moll (SA, WS)
Biology Department
Southwest Missouri State University
Springfield, MO 65804
USA
417-836-5062/fax 417-836-6934
e-mail: *dlm505f@wpgate.smsu.edu*

Edward O. Moll (SA, CA)
Department of Zoology
Eastern Illinois University
Charleston, IL 61920-3099
USA
217-581-5410/fax 217-581-2722
e-mail: *cfeom@eiu.edu*

James E. Moore (SA)
The Nature Conservancy of Nevada
1771 East Flamingo, Ste. 111B
Las Vegas, NV 89119
USA
702-737-8744/fax 702-737-5787
e-mail: *nvfo@aol.com*

David J. Morafka (SA, CA, WS)
Dept. of Biology
California State University–Dominguez Hills
Carson, CA 90747-0005
USA
310-516-3407/fax 310-516-4268
e-mail: *papaherp@aol.com*

Edward B. Mullen (SA, WS)
Science Applications International Corp.
816 State St., Ste. 500
Santa Barbara, CA 93101
USA
805-966-0811/fax 805-965-6944
e-mail: *edward.b.mullen@cmpx.saic.com*

William Mullin
506 West Sunnybrook Road
Royal Oak, MI 48073
USA
313-435-8608

Henry R. Mushinsky (SA)
Dept. of Biology
University of South Florida
Tampa, FL 33620-5150
USA
813-974-5218/fax 813-974-3263
e-mail: *mushinsk@chuma.cas.usf.edu*

Stephen V. Nash (WS)
TRAFFIC–Southeast Asia
Locked Bag 911
Jlh. Sultan P.O.
46990 Petaling Jaya, Selangor
MALAYSIA
60-3-791-3195

Danny Novo (CS)
147 Maryland Ave., #1
Paterson, NJ 07503-1615
USA
201-523-4528

Nyoman S. Nuitja
Director of Amphibian & Reptile
Conservation & Development Program
Bogor Agricultural University
Bogor, West Java 16003
INDONESIA
0251-312635

Deborah F. Oeky
Conway Road, Route 116
South Deerfield, MA 01373
USA
413-665-3768

Kirsten Oleson
TRAFFIC, WWF
1250 24th St., NW
Washington, DC 20037
USA
202-778-9500

Molly Olson (SA, WS)
The Natural Step
4000 Bridgeway, Ste. 102
Sousalito, CA 94965
USA
415-332-9394
e-mail: mholson@naturalstep.org

NY State Senator Suzi Oppenheimer (SA, WS)
New York State Senate, L.O.B. Rm. 515
Albany, NY 12247
USA
914-921-0221/fax 914-921-0224

Michael and Joann O'Reilly
95 South Howells Point Road
Bellport, NY 11713
USA
516-862-3000

Steve Otis (WS)
Counsel and Chief of Staff for N.Y. State Senator Suzi Oppenheimer
222 Grace Church St.
Port Chester, NY 10573
USA
914-921-0221/fax 914-921-0224

Vivian Páez (SA)
Departmento de Biología
Universidad de Antioquia
Medellin
COLOMBIA
e-mail: vpaez@quimbaya.udea.edu.co

Robert Papa
76 Commonwealth Ave.
Massapequa, NY 11758
USA
718-262-1729

Heather Passmore (SA)
Dept. of Zoology
University of Guelph
Guelph, ON N1G 2W1
CANADA
519-824-4120

Ray Pawley
Brookfield Zoo
Brookfield, IL 60513
USA
708-485-0263

Danny Peled (CS)
1341 E. 64th St.
Brooklyn, NY 11234
USA
718-968-8517

Peter Petokas
Dept. of Biology, Penn State
Worthington Scranton Campus
120 Ridge View Drive
Dunmore, PA 18512
USA
717-963-4797

Pandora Pipiringos
1709 Brown Road
Las Cruces, NM 88005
USA
505-524-0153

John R. Polisar (SA)
Florida Museum of Natural History
University of Florida
Gainesville, FL 32611
USA
904-392-1721

Ross W. Popenoe (CS)
8630 N.E. 24th St.
Bellevue, WA 98004
USA
425-635-0812

Peter C. H. Pritchard (SA, WS)
Florida Audubon Society
1331 Palmetto, Ste. 110
Winter Park, FL 32789
USA
407-539-5700

Chelonia Institute
401 South Central Ave.
Oviedo, FL 32765
USA

Christopher Raithel (WS)
Rhode Island Division of Fish and Wildlife
Great Swamp Management Area
P.O. Box 218
West Kingston, RI 02892
USA
401-789-0281/fax 401-783-7490

Bonnie Raphael (SA, CA, WS)
Wildlife Health Center
Wildlife Conservation Society
185th St. and Southern Blvd.
Bronx, NY 10460
USA
718-220-7104/fax 718-220-7126

Sheik M. A. Rashid (SA)
Centre for Advanced Research in Natural
Resources & Management (CARINAM)
70 Kakrail
Dhaka-1000,
BANGLADESH
e-mail: carinam@citecho.net

Celestine Ravaoarinoromanga
Direction des Eau et Forets Nanisana
Antananarivo BP243
MADAGASCAR
261-2-406-10

Jacqueline Record
Great Swamp Natural Wildlife Refuge
RD #1, Box 148A
Basking Ridge, NJ 07920
USA
201-425-1222

Devin A. Reese (SA)
USAID/G/ENV
The Ronald Reagan Building, Rm. 308
Washington, D.C. 20523-3800
USA
703-875-4411
e-mail: dereese@usaid.gov

DIRECTORY OF CONFERENCE ATTENDEES AND PROCEEDINGS AUTHORS

Anders G. J. Rhodin (PS)
Chelonian Research Foundation
168 Goodrich St.
Lunenburg, MA 01462
USA
508-582-9668/fax 508-840-8184
e-mail: RhodinCRF@aol.com

Lee Robbins
RD 1, Box 31
Hartwick, NY 13348
USA
607-547-3981

Laura E. Rogers-Castro
34 Hampshire Road
Meriden, CT 06450
USA
203-237-6247

Reuben and Vicki Rosen (CS)
225 West 71st St., #71
New York, NY 10023-3756
USA
212-799-3514

Evan M. Rosenoff
1574 Central Ave.
Yonkers, NY 10710
USA
914-779-5000

Aileen Russo
698 Green St., #5
Cambridge, MA 02139
USA
617-491-2998

Andrew Sabin
140 Cedar St., Ste. 1906
New York, NY 10006
USA
212-349-4800

Walter Sachsse (SA)
FB 21/Biologie, Institut für Genetik
Arbeitsgruppe Cytogenetik
Postfach 3980, Saarstraße 21
6500 Mainz 1
GERMANY
49-6131-395725

Richard A. Sajdak
Milwaukee County Zoo
10001 Bluemound Road
Milwaukee, WI 53226
USA
414-771-3040

Allen and Anita Salzberg (CS)
67-87 Booth St., Apt. 5B
Queens, NY 11375
USA
718-275-3307
e-mail: ASalzberg@aol.com

Md. Sohrab U. Sarker (SA)
Dept. of Zoology
University of Dhaka
Dhaka-1000
BANGLADESH
880-2-506330
e-mail: zooldu@citechco.net

Mary Ellen Saunders (CS)
132 West 15th St., #3A
New York, NY 10011
USA
212-989-8512

Isabella M. Schumacher (SA, WS)
BEECS Immunological Analysis Core
University of Florida
Gainesville, FL 32610
USA
904-392-1634

Karin von Seckendorf Hoff (CA, PS)
Biology Department
University of Nevada
Reno, NV 89557
USA
702-791-7057, 895-3121
fax 702-893-7707

Roz Seelig
225 West 23rd St., Apt. 6M
New York, NY 10011
USA
212-627-2711

Tej Kumar Shrestha (SA. PS)
Central Dept. of Zoology
Tribhuvan University
Kirtipur, Kathmandu
NEPAL
977-1-221645/fax 977-1-279748
e-mail: k-mani@npl.healthnet.org

Louise Silverman
92 Filors Lane
Stony Point, NY 10980
USA
914-429-5260

Frank and Kate Slavens
P.O. Box 30744
Seattle, WA 98103
USA
206-684-4831

Lora Smith (SA, WS)
Dept. of Wildlife Ecology and Conservation
University of Florida
Gainesville, FL 32611
USA
904-372-2571
e-mail: angonoka@grove.ufl.edu

Carl Stalnaker
1081 Cathedral Ave.
Franklin Square, NY 11010
USA
516-627-3888

Brett C. Stearns (WS)
Institute for Herpetological Research
415 Laurel Ave.
Menlo Park, CA 94025
USA
415-750-7278

David Stubbs (CA)
16 Bailey Road, Westcott, Dorking
Surrey RH4 3QS
UNITED KINGDOM
44 306 888 933/fax 44 1306 742 496
e-mail: ega.golf.ecology@dial.pipex.com

Bruce Stutz
Natural History Magazine
American Museum of Natural History
Central Park West at 79th St.
New York, NY 10024
USA
212-769-5500

Ian R. Swingland (SA, CA, WS)
Durrell Institute of
Conservation and Ecology (DICE)
University of Kent
Canterbury, Kent CT2 7NX
UNITED KINGDOM
44-227-475-480/fax 44-227-475-481
e-mail: 106407.3135@compuserve.com

Kumthorn Thirakhupt (SA)
Dept. of Biology, Faculty of Science
Chulalongkorn University
Bangkok 10330
THAILAND
662-252-7077, 250-1811
fax 662-253-0337
e-mail: kumthorn@mail.sc.chula.ac.th

John Thorbjarnarson (SA, WS)
Wildlife Conservation Society
185th St. and Southern Blvd.
Bronx, NY 10460
USA
718-220-7158
e-mail: jcaiman@aol.com

Eddie Treviño (SA)
Dept. of Biology
California State University
–Dominguez Hills
Carson, CA 90747-0005
USA
310-516-3818

Bern W. Tryon (CA)
Knoxville Zoological Gardens
P.O. Box 6040
Knoxville, TN 37914
USA
413-523-4023
e-mail: btryon@knoxville-zoo.com

Tomas F. Tyning
Massachusetts Audubon Society
208 South Great Road
Lincoln, MA 01773
USA
617-259-9500
e-mail: tyning@shaysnet.com

Jim Utter
Department of Biology
SUNY Purchase
735 Anderson Hill Road
Purchase, NY 10577
USA

Jim Van Abbema
(CS, Proceedings Editor)
2750 Olinville Ave., 2F
Bronx, NY 10467
USA
718-654-5705
e-mail: jimvan@easyway.net

Rick Van Dyke
4708 Everglade
Austin, TX 78745
USA
512-447-0468

Joseph Ventura
U.S. Fish and Wildlife Service
370 Amapola Ave., Ste. 114
Torrance, CA 90501
USA
310-328-6307

Gerard Veraldi
Jan Doret 272
Curacao
NETHERLANDS ANTILLES
599-9-376581

Craig Vitamanti
(Conference Coordinator)
Department of Education
American Museum of Natural History
Central Park West at 79th St.
New York, NY 10024-5192
USA
212-769-5306

Richard C. Vogt (SA)
Estación de Biología Tropical
"Los Tuxtlas"
Instituto de Biología, U.N.A.M.
A.P. 91
San Andrés Tuxtla
Veracruz, C. P. 95700
MEXICO
fax 52-294-24367

Harold Wahlquist
U.S. Fish and Wildlife Service
1895 Century Building, Ste. 240
Atlanta, GA 30345
USA
404-679-4166/fax 404-679-4160

Suzanne Wahlquist
1346 Arlene Court
Lilburn, GA 30247
USA
404-331-5446

Rico Walder (PS)
Tennessee Aquarium
One Broad St.
P.O. Box 11048
Chattanooga, TN 37401-2048
USA
423-265-0695 ext. 4067
fax 423-267-3561
e-mail: elw@tennis.org

Tomás Waller (SA, WS)
Zavalia 2090–3.B.
1428 Buenos Aires
ARGENTINA
tel/fax 54-1-784-8555
e-mail: curiyu@interserver.com.ar

James L. Warner
7 Gaylord Drive
Wilton, CT 06897
USA
203-762-5511

John P. Whelan
173 Senator St.
Brooklyn, NY 11220-5116
USA
718-748-7542

Romulus Whitaker (SA, WS)
Centre for Herpetology
Madras Crocodile Bank Trust
Mamallapuram, Post Bag 4
Tamil Nadu 603 104
INDIA
91-04114-46332/fax 91-44-491-0910

Alison Whitlock (SA, PS)
Dept. of Forestry and Wildlife Management
University of Massachusetts
Amherst, MA 01003
USA
413-545-2865
e-mail: whitlock@tei.umass.edu

Allan N. Williams
Connecticut Dept. of
Environmental Protection
165 Capitol Ave., Rm. 553
Hartford, CT 06106
USA
203-424-3644/fax 203-566-7292

Dawn S. Wilson (CA)
Biology Dept.
University of South Florida
Tampa, FL 33620
USA
813-974-5218

Stephan Woltman (CS)
18 Myrtle Ave.
Demarest, NJ 37627
USA
201-768-3375

Connie Wood
261 Chestnut Hill Road
Norwalk, CT 06851-1412
USA
203-838-1694

Roger C. Wood (SA)
Wetlands Institute
1075 Stone Harbor Blvd.
Stone Harbor, NJ 08247
USA
609-368-1236/fax 609-368-3871

Alex Ypsilanti (CS)
824 Bronx River Road
Bronxville, NY 10709
USA
914-776-2910

Metric and U.S. Unit Equivalents

LENGTH

U.S. Customary Unit	U.S. Equivalents	Metric Equivalents
inch	0.083 foot	2.540 centimeters
foot	1/3 yard, 12 inches	0.305 meter
yard	3 feet, 36 inches	0.914 meter
rod	5½ yards, 16½ feet	5.029 meters
mile (statute, land)	1,760 yards, 5,280 feet	1.609 kilometers
mile (nautical, international)	1.151 statute miles	1.852 kilometers

Metric Unit	Number of Meters	Approximate U.S. Equivalent
myriameter	10,000	6.214 miles
kilometer	1,000	0.621 mile
hectometer	100	109.361 yards
decameter	10	32.808 feet
meter	1	39.370 inches
decimeter	0.1	3.937 inches
centimeter	0.01	0.394 inch
millimeter	0.001	0.039 inch

AREA

U.S. Customary Unit	U.S. Equivalents	Metric Equivalents
square inch	0.007 square foot	6.452 square centimeters
square foot	144 square inches	929.030 square centimeters
square yard	1,296 square inches, 9 square feet	0.836 square meters
acre	43,560 square feet, 4,840 square yards	4,047 square meters
square mile	640 acres	2.590 square kilometers

Metric Unit	Number of Square Meters	Approximate U.S. Equivalent
square kilometer	1,000,000	0.386 square mile
hectare	10,000	2.477 acres
are	100	119.599 square yards
deciare	10	11.960 square yards
centare	1	10.764 square feet
square centimeter	0.0001	0.155 square inch

VOLUME

Metric Unit	Number of Cubic Meters	Approximate U.S. Equivalent
decastere	10	13.079 cubic yards
stere	1	1.308 cubic yards
decistere	0.10	3.532 cubic feet
cubic centimeter	0.000001	0.061 cubic inch